Lecture Notes in Computer Science

Lecture Notes in Artificial Intelligence 16133
Founding Editor

Jörg Siekmann

Series Editors

Randy Goebel, *University of Alberta, Edmonton, Canada*
Wolfgang Wahlster, *DFKI, Berlin, Germany*
Zhi-Hua Zhou, *Nanjing University, Nanjing, China*

The series Lecture Notes in Artificial Intelligence (LNAI) was established in 1988 as a topical subseries of LNCS devoted to artificial intelligence.

The series publishes state-of-the-art research results at a high level. As with the LNCS mother series, the mission of the series is to serve the international R & D community by providing an invaluable service, mainly focused on the publication of conference and workshop proceedings and postproceedings.

Mariacarla Staffa · John-John Cabibihan ·
Bruno Siciliano · Shuzhi Sam Ge ·
Leon Bodenhagen · Adriana Tapus · Silvia Rossi ·
Filippo Cavallo · Laura Fiorini ·
Marco Matarese · Hongsheng He
Editors

Social Robotics + AI

17th International Conference, ICSR+AI 2025
Naples, Italy, September 10–12, 2025
Proceedings, Part III

Editors
Mariacarla Staffa
University of Naples Parthenope
Naples, Italy

Bruno Siciliano
University of Naples Federico II
Naples, Italy

Leon Bodenhagen
University of Southern Denmark
Odense, Denmark

Silvia Rossi
University of Naples Federico II
Naples, Napoli, Italy

Laura Fiorini
University of Florence
Florence, Italy

Hongsheng He
The University of Alabama
Tuscaloosa, AL, USA

John-John Cabibihan
Qatar University
Doha, Qatar

Shuzhi Sam Ge
National University of Singapore
Queenstown, Singapore

Adriana Tapus
ENSTA
Palaiseau, France

Filippo Cavallo
University of Florence
Florence, Italy

Marco Matarese
Italian Institute of Technology
Genoa, Italy

ISSN 0302-9743 ISSN 1611-3349 (electronic)
Lecture Notes in Artificial Intelligence
ISBN 978-981-95-2397-9 ISBN 978-981-95-2398-6 (eBook)
https://doi.org/10.1007/978-981-95-2398-6

LNCS Sublibrary: SL7 – Artificial Intelligence

© The Editor(s) (if applicable) and The Author(s), under exclusive license
to Springer Nature Singapore Pte Ltd. 2026
Chapter "Charting the Ecosystem of Trust in Cat Royale Or What It Takes to Trust a Robot to Play with Cats"
is licensed under the terms of the Creative Commons Attribution 4.0 International License (http://creativecommons.org/licenses/by/4.0/). For further details see license information in the chapter.

This work is subject to copyright. All rights are solely and exclusively licensed by the Publisher, whether the whole or part of the material is concerned, specifically the rights of translation, reprinting, reuse of illustrations, recitation, broadcasting, reproduction on microfilms or in any other physical way, and transmission or information storage and retrieval, electronic adaptation, computer software, or by similar or dissimilar methodology now known or hereafter developed.
The use of general descriptive names, registered names, trademarks, service marks, etc. in this publication does not imply, even in the absence of a specific statement, that such names are exempt from the relevant protective laws and regulations and therefore free for general use.
The publisher, the authors and the editors are safe to assume that the advice and information in this book are believed to be true and accurate at the date of publication. Neither the publisher nor the authors or the editors give a warranty, expressed or implied, with respect to the material contained herein or for any errors or omissions that may have been made. The publisher remains neutral with regard to jurisdictional claims in published maps and institutional affiliations.

This Springer imprint is published by the registered company Springer Nature Singapore Pte Ltd.
The registered company address is: 152 Beach Road, #21-01/04 Gateway East, Singapore 189721, Singapore

If disposing of this product, please recycle the paper.

Preface

The 17th International Conference on Social Robotics (ICSR)+AI 2025 took place in Naples, Italy as an in-person event from September 10–12, 2025. ICSR+AI 2025 was hosted by the University of Naples Parthenope with the support of Global Robotics, Arts, and Science Synergies (GRASS).

These three LNCS volumes comprise the peer-reviewed proceedings of the conference. From a total of 276 submitted manuscripts that were single-blindly reviewed by an international team of program committee, associate editors, and reviewers, 117 regular papers and 57 short papers were selected for inclusion in the proceedings and presented during the technical sessions.

The theme of this year's conference was "Emotivation at the Core: Empowering Social Robots to Inspire and Connect". The conference featured 3 keynote speeches, 15 regular sessions, 5 Special Sessions, 2 poster sessions, 11 workshops, and 3 robot competitions. The first plenary speech was delivered by Dr. Daniela Rus, who is the Andrew (1956) and Erna Viterbi Professor of Electrical Engineering and Computer Science and Director of the Computer Science and Artificial Intelligence Laboratory (CSAIL) at Massachusetts Institute of Technology. The second plenary speech was delivered by Dr. Jérôme Monceaux, who is a co-founder of Aldebaran Robotics. The third plenary speech was delivered by Dr. Anouk Wipprecht, who is a pioneering Dutch fashion designer and innovator at the forefront of the FashionTech movement.

The conference brought together researchers and practitioners working on the interaction between humans and intelligent robots and on the integration of social robots into our society, including innovative ideas and concepts, new discoveries and improvements, novel applications based on the latest fundamental advances in the core technologies that form the backbone of social robotics, as well as distinguished studies and projects pertaining to social robotics and its interaction with and impact on our society.

We extend our sincere gratitude to all members of the organizing committee and the volunteers for their dedication, which made the conference a resounding success. We are also deeply indebted to the program committee, associate editors, and reviewers for their rigorous review of the papers. Finally, we are immensely grateful for the continued support from the authors, participants, and sponsors, without whom ICSR+AI 2025 would not have been possible.

September 2025

Mariacarla Staffa
John-John Cabibihan
Bruno Siciliano
Shuzhi Sam Ge
Leon Bodenhagen
Adriana Tapus
Silvia Rossi
Filippo Cavallo
Laura Fiorini
Marco Matarese
Hongsheng He

Organization

Honorary Chair

Bruno Siciliano — University of Naples Federico II, Italy

General Chair

Mariacarla Staffa — University of Naples Parthenope, Italy

General Co-chair

John-John Cabibihan — Qatar University, Qatar

Steering Committee Chair

Shuzhi Sam Ge — National University of Singapore, Singapore

Program Chairs

Leon Bodenhagen — University of Southern Denmark, Denmark
Adriana Tapus — ENSTA Paris, France
Silvia Rossi — University of Naples Federico II, Italy
Filippo Cavallo — University of Florence, Italy

Special Session Committee

Alessandra Sciutti — Italian Institute of Technology, Italy
Luisa Damiano — IULM University, Italy
Kerstin Sophie Haring — University of Denver, USA

Workshop Committee

Maryam Alimardani	Vrije Universiteit Amsterdam, Netherlands
Patrick Holthaus	University of Hertfordshire, UK
Alberto Pirni	Scuola Superiore Sant'Anna di Pisa, Italy

Short Papers Committee

Alessandra Sorrentino	University of Florence, Italy
Jauwairia Nasir	Universität Augsburg, Germany
Alessandro Umbrico	CNR, Italy

Young Leader Committee

Lorenzo D'Errico	University of Naples Federico II, Italy
Francesco Vigni	University of Naples Federico II, Italy
Tamara Siegmann	University of Applied Sciences and Arts Northwestern Switzerland
Nihan Karatas	Nagoya University, Japan

Award Committee

Antonio Sgorbissa	University of Genoa, Italy
Abderrahmane Kheddar	LIRMM Montpellier, France and CNRS-AIST, Japan
Vali Lalioti	University of the Arts London, UK

Art and Robotics Committee

Hooman Samani	University of the Arts London, UK
Vali Lalioti	University of the Arts London, UK

Women in Robotics Committee

Hatice Gunes	University of Cambridge, UK
Micol Spitale	Politecnico di Milano, Italy
Samira Rasouli	University of Waterloo, Canada
Natalia Calvo	Uppsala University, Sweden

Publication Committee

Hongsheng He	The University of Alabama, USA
Marco Matarese	Italian Institute of Technology, Italy
Laura Fiorini	University of Florence, Italy

Social Media Chair

Francesca Cocchella — Italian Institute of Technology, Italy

Press Office Chair

Daniela Passariello — University of Naples Federico II, Italy

Publicity Committee

Oliver Bendel	FHNW University of Applied Sciences and Arts Northwestern Switzerland
Antonio Andriella	Artificial Intelligence Research Institute (IIIA), Spain
Minsu Jang	Electronics and Telecommunications Research Institute, South Korea
Oskar Palinko	University of Southern Denmark, Denmark

Competition Chairs

Amit Kumar Pandey	Rovial Space, France
Alessandra Rossi	University of Naples Federico II, Italy
Luca Iocchi	Sapienza University of Rome, Italy

Local Arrangement Chairs

Diana di Luccio   University of Naples Parthenope, Italy

Sustainability Chairs

Elvira Buonocore   University of Naples Parthenope, Italy
Franziska Kirstein   University of Southern Denmark, Denmark

Standing Committee

Oussama Khatib   Stanford University, USA
Maja Mataric   University of Southern California, USA
Haizhou Li   Chinese University of Hong Kong, China
Jong Hwan Kim   Korea Advanced Institute of Science and Technology, South Korea
Paolo Dario   Scuola Superiore Sant'Anna, Italy
Abderrahmane Kheddar   LIRMM Montpellier, France and CNRS-AIST, Japan
Tianmiao Wang   Beihang University, China

Associate Editors

Alessandra Rossi   University of Naples Federico II, Italy
Alessandra Sciutti   Italian Institute of Technology, Italy
Alessandra Sorrentino   University of Florence, Italy
Alessandro Umbrico   Centro Nazionale delle Ricerche, Italy
Antonio Andriella   Artificial Intelligence Research Institute (IIIA), Spain
Antonio Fleres   IULM University, Italy
Bipin Indurkhya   Jagiellonian University, Poland
Britta Wrede   University of Bielefeld, Germany
Cristina Gena   University of Turin, Italy
Eleonora Zedda   Centro Nazionale delle Ricerche, Italy
Ester Fuoco   IULM University/ISPF CNR, Italy
Filippo Cavallo   University of Florence, Italy
Francesca Cordella   University Campus Biomedico, Italy
Giacinto Barresi   University of the West of England, UK

Giulia Perugia	Eindhoven University of Technology, The Netherlands
Giuliana Vitiello	University of Salerno, Italy
Gökçe Nur Yılmaz	Ankara University, Turkey
Grazia D'Onofrio	IRCSS Ospedale Casa Sollievo della Sofferenza, Italy
Hongsheng He	University of Alabama, USA
Igor Farkaš	Comenius University Bratislava, Slovenia
Ilaria Alfieri	IULM University, Italy
Jauwairia Nasir	Universität Augsburg, Germany
John-John Cabibihan	Qatar University, Qatar
Kutluk Arikan	Ankara University, Turkey
Laura Fiorini	University of Florence, Italy
Lorenzo D'Errico	University of Naples Federico II, Italy
Luisa Damiano	IULM University, Italy
Marco Matarese	Italian Institute of Technology, Italy
Mariacarla Staffa	University of Naples Parthenope, Italy
Nele Russwinkel	University of Lübeck, Germany
Olive Bendel	University of Applied Sciences and Arts Northwestern Switzerland, Switzerland
Omar Eldardeer	Italian Institute of Technology, Italy
Oskar Palinko	University of Southern Denmark, Denmark
Patrick Holthaus	University of Hertfordshire, UK
Piotr Mirowski	Google DeepMind, UK
Rebecca Mannocci	IULM University, Italy
Thomas Sievers	University of Lübeck, Germany
Yue Hu	University of Waterloo, Canada

Contents

Emotion and Social Interaction in HRI

Small Talk with a Robot Reduces Stress and Improves Mood 3
   *Katharina Kühne, Antonia L. Z. Klöffel, Oliver Bendel,
   and Martin H. Fischer*

Multimodal Dialogue for Empathetic Human-Robot Interaction 22
   *Niyati Rawal, Rahul Singh Maharjan, Giacomo Salici,
   Riccardo Catalini, Marta Romeo, Roberto Bigazzi, Lorenzo Baraldi,
   Roberto Vezzani, Rita Cucchiara, and Angelo Cangelosi*

Emotivation in Human-Robot Interaction for Affective Behavioral
Adaptation 37
   *Lorenzo D'Errico, Renato Esposito, Marco Matarese, Vincenzo Mele,
   Alfredo Mungari, Martina Roscica, and Mariacarla Staffa*

Robotic Ears as Social Cues: A First Analysis on Emotional Expressivity 50
   Silvia Rossi and Alessandra Rossi

Simulating Feelings: LLM vs. Psychology-Based Models in Human-Robot
Interaction 58
   *Francesca Corrao, Alice Nardelli, Antonio Sgorbissa,
   and Carmine Tommaso Recchiuto*

Assistive and Educational Applications in HRI

Human Hand Shape and Grasping Behavior Estimation using a Humanoid
Hand with a Tactile Interface 75
   Adnan Saood and Adriana Tapus

Evaluating Children Engagement and Robot Perception Interacting
with NAO Robot in Educational Context: A Feasibility Study 87
   *Laura Fiorini, Chiara Pecini, Marco Vincenzo Maselli,
   Lorenzo Pugi, Elena Adelucci, Helene Musca, Jasmine Pani,
   Stefano Scatigna, Maria Chiara Di Lieto, Benedetta Del Lucchese,
   Giuseppina Sgandurra, and Filippo Cavallo*

Wearable Social Robots for the Disabled and Impaired 97
   Oliver Bendel

Nova: A Novel Approach for Game Narration 112
    Nathália Cauás, Laura Triglia, Leandro Honorato, Pablo Barros,
    Bruno J. T. Fernandes, and Alessandra Sciutti

Culturally Sensitive Stand-Up Comedian Robot 124
    Michael Wong Kam, Hooman Samani, Saina Akhond,
    Chinthaka Premachandra, and Vali Lalioti

Social Human-Agent Interaction for Health

Service Robots in Elderly Care: A Systematic Review of ADL Coverage,
Stakeholder Sentiment, and Deployment Readiness 139
    Timothy Scott Chu and John-John Cabibihan

CaRE-BT: An Embodied Planning Framework for In-Home Assistive
Robots 152
    Ola Ghattas, Mostafa Hussein, Marzan Alam, Moniruzzaman Akash,
    Sajay Arthanat, Dain LaRoche, and Momotaz Begum

LLM-Driven Persuasive Strategies by a Social Assistive Robot
for Healthier Snacking 165
    Chinenye Augustine Ajibo, Alessandra Rossi, and Silvia Rossi

Robots and Reflexes: Analyzing the Stroop Effect and Impulsiveness
in Human-Robot Interaction 179
    Alessandra Sorrentino, Jasmine Pani, Carlo La Viola, Jaeseok Kim,
    Marco Vincenzo Maselli, Sofia Iacopini, Laura Fiorini,
    and Filippo Cavallo

Designing Interactive Robots for Active Ageing: Co-design Insights
on Large Projection Interfaces with Older Adults 192
    John E. Muñoz, Shahed Saleh, and Nahomi Ramirez

SoK: A Systematic Review of Privacy and Security in Healthcare Robotics 212
    Mayank Grover and Sanchari Das

Cognition for Human-Robot Interaction

Engagement Estimation in Child-Robot Interaction via Transfer Learning
from a Pre-trained Facial Emotion Recognition Model 237
    Gonzalo A. García, Rohan Laycock, Guillermo Pérez,
    J. Gabriel Amores, Gloria Álvarez, Manuel Castro, and Randy Gomez

Toward Safe Child-Robot Interactions: Exploring Children's and Parents' Privacy Perceptions of Humanoid Social Robots 253
   JaeEun Jen Shin, Amr Hamdi, An Bella Chen, Yue Hu, and Leah Zhang-Kennedy

Investigating the Similarity-Attraction Effect on Personality in Human-Robot Interactions 273
   Alice Nardelli, Francesca Corrao, Antonio Sgorbissa, and Carmine Tommaso Recchiuto

Enhancing Human-Robot Interaction Through Nonverbal Communication and User Self-efficacy 289
   Kristel Marmor, Janika Leoste, and Piedad Tolmos Rodríguez-Piñero

Assessing Multimodal Context Awareness of a Social Robot in a Conversational Scenario 300
   Luca Pallonetto, Raffaella Esposito, Giulio Acampora, Matteo Russo, Federico Trenti, and Silvia Rossi

Unfair Game: How Age and Robot Deception Shape the Attribution of Mental States in Virtual Reality 313
   Ludovica Misino, Oronzo Parlangeli, Luca Lusuardi, Alessandro Innocenti, and Stefano Guidi

A Cognitive Architecture for Embodied AI Based on LLM Common-Sense Knowledge 329
   Alessio Saladino, Michele Brienza, Vincenzo Suriani, Domenico Daniele Bloisi, and Luca Iocchi

Social Robots as Creative Partners: Comparing Large Language Models with Wizard-of-Oz in Human-Robot Brainstorming 342
   Ethel Pruss, Anita Vrins, Caterina Ceccato, Jos Prinsen, Maryam Alimardani, Jan de Wit, and Alwin de Rooij

Towards Memory-Driven Agentic AI for Human Activity Recognition 356
   Mohamadreza Shahabian Alashti, Khashayar Ghamati, Hooman Samani, and Abolfazl Zaraki

Act-it-Out Method for Developing Robot Arm Actions and Semantic Commands 370
   Luke Sanchez, Chirag Jain, Shrirang Patil, Bessie He, and Heather Knight

Who Sees What? Structured Thought-Action Sequences for Epistemic
Reasoning in LLMs 387
    *Luca Annese, Sabrina Patania, Silvia Serino, Tom Foulsham,
Silvia Rossi, Azzurra Ruggeri, and Dimitri Ognibene*

In the Comfort Zone: How Social Robots Learn to Adapt 400
    Sara Mongile, Ana Tanevska, Francesco Rea, and Alessandra Sciutti

Social Robotics and Sustainability

Rethinking Learning from Demonstration Through Enactive Cognitive
Sciences: From Replication to Dialogue in HRI 415
    Martina Bacaro

The Social Robotics Gamble: Pathways to Sustainability 431
    *João S. Sequeira, Álvaro Castro-González, José Carlos Castillo,
Fernando Alonso-Martín, and Miguel A. Salichs*

Eyes from Above: Co-designing a Multi-drone System for Enhanced
Surveillance of Critical Infrastructure 447
    *Maria-Theresa Bahodi, Maja Hornbæk Kristensen, Niels van Berkel,
Mikael Skov, Nicolai Brodersen Hansen, and Timothy Merritt*

Active Inference and Sustainable Robotics: Modeling Social Resource
Management 475
    Maria Raffa

Sustainable Human-Robot Interaction: From Current Trends to Future
Visions 484
    *Ilaria Torre, Maria Teresa Parreira, Hannah Pelikan, Erik Lagerstedt,
Sarah Schömbs, Katie Winkle, and Sara Ljungblad*

Explanations in Social HRI

Designing Authority and Service-Oriented Experiences in Librarian Robots 503
    Ela Liberman-Pincu and Tal Oron-Gilad

Development and Preliminary Validation of an Empathetic and Explaining
Robot Interface for Proactive Indoor Environment Control 516
    *Mayu Omichi, Hideyuki Takahashi, Midori Ban, Yuichiro Yoshikawa,
Hiroshi Ishiguro, Hiroki Ishizuka, Takato Horii, Takayuki Kikuchi,
Minoru Tomoda, Kazuki Shimasaki, and Yoshihisa Toshima*

Levels of Explanation for Error Resolution in HRI 544
    Maya Krakovski, Shikhar Kumar, and Yael Edan

RAGGAE for HERBS: Testing the Explanatory Performance
of Ontology-Powered LLMs for Human Explanation of Robotic Behaviors 558
    Agnese Augello, Edoardo Datteri, Antonio Lieto, Maria Rausa, and Nicola Zagni

Robots on Stage: Performance Art, Education and Social Robotics for Children

Social Interaction with Autonomous Art: Combining Social Analysis
and Computer Vision 573
    Darren Reed, Fanta Camara, and Tianyuan Wang

Bringing Robots on the Stage: A Co-designed Multiplatform Robot
Control System for Theatrical Performances 587
    Anis Derri, Giulia Filacanapa, Erica Magris, and Salvatore M. Anzalone

Towards a Customizable Dramaturgical System: An Artistic Experiment
in AI-Enhanced Human-Machine Dialogue 598
    Yucheng Peng, Junyi Chen, Shaoxin Sun, and Didier Plassard

First Encounter Dramaturgy with Multi-robot Swarms (Without
Mentioning Robots!) 611
    Elena Vella, Robert Ellis Walton, Daniel A. Williams, Goran Đurić, Aleksandra Michalewicz, Justin Green, and Airlie Chapman

Charting the Ecosystem of Trust in Cat Royale Or What It Takes to Trust
a Robot to Play with Cats 623
    Steve Benford, Pepita Barnard, Sarah Sharples, Helena Webb, Clara Mancini, Ayse Kucukyilmaz, Simon Castle Green, Eike Schneiders, Victor Ngo, Alan Chamberlain, Joel Fischer, Guido Salimbeni, Nick Tandavanitj, Matt Adams, and Ju Row Farr

Student's Acceptance of Social Robots: A Study with Pepper on Inclusive
Mathematics Learning Through Storytelling 637
    Antonio Vitale, Bruno Carbonaro, Gennaro Cordasco, Umberto Dello Iacono, and Anna Esposito

The Spice of Surprise Modelling Patterns of Unexpectedness
in Improvisational Acting Using AI 651
    Gunter Lösel

Robot Design and Inclusive Practices: A Pilot Study on Gender Equity in STEM 663
   Laura Cesaro and Emanuele Menegatti

Emotional Content in Robotic Dance: Evaluating Human-to-Robot Movement Mapping 674
   Giuseppe Saviano, Alberto Villani, and Domenico Prattichizzo

"The Soul is a Verb, Not a Noun" Ensoulment as an Artist-Led Relational Approach to Robot Behavior 690
   Maaike Bleeker

OperaBot: A Performer Led Robot Theater Collaboration 700
   Janani Swaminathan, Denisse Alvarado, and Heather Knight

Theatre in the Loop: A Rehearsal-Based, Collaborative Workflow for Expressive Robotic Behaviours 718
   Pavlos Panagiotidis, Victor Zhi Heung Ngo, Sean Myatt, Roma Patel, Rachel Ramchurn, Alan Chamberlain, and Ayse Kucukyilmaz

Remote Session Papers

Children's Acceptance of the TABAN Social Robot in LLM-Powered Collaborative Visual Storytelling 735
   Maryam Karimi Jafari and Alireza Taheri

Violence Detection by a Social Robot 749
   Reyhane Nikoobayan and Alireza Taheri

Author Index 763

Emotion and Social Interaction in HRI

Small Talk with a Robot Reduces Stress and Improves Mood

Katharina Kühne[1](✉) , Antonia L. Z. Klöffel[1], Oliver Bendel[2] ,
and Martin H. Fischer[1]

[1] Cognitive Sciences Division, University of Potsdam, Potsdam, Germany
kkuehne@uni-potsdam.de
[2] FHNW School of Business, Windisch, Switzerland

Abstract. Research has demonstrated that social support is crucial in mitigating stress and enhancing mood. Not only do long-term, meaningful relationships contribute to well-being, but everyday social interactions, such as small talk, also offer psychological benefits. As social robots increasingly become more integrated into daily life, they present a potential avenue for stress interventions. In our online study, 98 participants underwent a stress induction using the Stroop task and were then assigned to one of three conditions: engaging in scripted small talk with a simulated NAO robot online, listening to a neutral story told by the same NAO robot, or no intervention (control condition). Results indicate that both interventions effectively reduced stress, with a tendency towards a stronger effect in the Small talk condition. Small talk not only helped maintain positive affect but also reduced negative affect. Notably, the benefits were more pronounced among individuals experiencing higher acute stress following the stress induction, but were less evident in those with chronically elevated stress levels. Furthermore, the effect of the intervention on stress reduction was mediated by changes in positive affect. These findings suggest that small talk with a social robot may serve as a promising tool for stress reduction and affect regulation.

Keywords: negative affect · positive affect · small talk · social robots · stress

1 Introduction

Everyday emotions significantly impact our well-being [1]. They influence our mood, motivation, and ability to cope with stress [2]. Emotional support, not only from humans but also from artificial agents like chatbots, can help stabilize mood and make it easier to navigate daily challenges [3]. One effective way to provide this support is through social interaction, even brief ones like small talk [4]. Though often seen as trivial, short conversations can reduce stress, improve mood, and encourage engagement. Nowadays, we frequently come across artificial agents, like chatbots and social robots, and we can strategically use them to offer support through short, meaningful interactions [5]. Unlike humans, they are always available, non-judgmental, and can be tailored to the

---

K. Kühne and Antonia L. Z. Klöffel—These authors contributed equally to this work.

user's emotional needs. This paper explores how simulated small talk with a social robot can reduce stress and stabilize mood. Importantly, our participants did not engage in live interactions with the robot; instead, they communicated with a robot video using pre-selected phrases in an online setting. While this differs from real-world, embodied interactions with physical robots, our findings are especially encouraging. They suggest that even brief interactions with a simulated robot can offer meaningful emotional benefits.

2 Related Work

2.1 Stress and Social Support

Nowadays, stress is omnipresent. In particular, chronic stress can lead to various health consequences, both direct and indirect. Directly, it can cause alterations in autonomic and neuroendocrine responses, impacting bodily functions such as heart rate, blood pressure, and hormone levels, while indirectly, it may influence health behaviors like dietary choices and physical activity levels, thereby affecting overall health and increasing the risk of disease [6]. Hans Selye, widely regarded as the forefather of stress research, emphasized that stress can pose a threat to life if not countered with sufficient adaptive response [7]. Consequently, researchers and practitioners have been focused on developing effective stress reduction interventions at both the individual and societal levels, ranging from mindfulness techniques to occupational health programs and internet-based trainings [e.g., 8, 9].

While individual interventions show promising results, social integration and support play a crucial role in preventing and reducing stress [10]. The buffering hypothesis [4] suggests that social support improves well-being through its overall benefits and protection against stress. Social support reduces autonomic activation, heart rate, blood pressure, and even daily cortisol [10]. Although the benefits of social support are well established, implementing interventions to enhance it remains challenging. However, progress can begin with small steps in everyday interactions. Relational Regulation Theory suggests that the positive effects of support on mental health arise when individuals regulate their emotions, thoughts, and behaviors through emotionally significant conversations and shared activities rather than through direct discussions on stress management [11]. As a result, perceived support usually does not directly change emotions but emerges from social interactions that help regulate them. Research has shown that various types of social interactions, including brief everyday conversations, can trigger oxytocin release, thus potentially reducing stress and enhancing well-being [12].

Social support may, therefore, be important not only in close friendships but also in small daily interactions with non-close others. These everyday, mundane conversations effectively mitigate stress and improve well-being [4, 11] by satisfying the need to belong. According to the Communicate Bond Belong theory, individuals engage in social interactions while managing their social energy and regulating daily social contact [13]. Here, energy is understood as the capacity to perform tasks, while social energy refers to the effort needed for social interactions [14]. Deep conversations can be energy-intensive and are not always feasible, while frequent small talk with acquaintances may better balance psychological energy use and fulfill the need to belong [14]. In 2021, a Dutch supermarket introduced slower "Chat Checkouts," allowing customers, particularly the elderly, to engage in small talk with cashiers. As research during COVID-19 showed, reduced opportunities for small talk resulted in lower psychological well-being and more stress [15].

2.2 Mood and Stress

Stress and mood are closely interrelated [16, 17]. Higher stress is associated with lower positive affect and higher negative affect [18, 19]. Positive affect enhances coping strategies [20, 21] and has stress-buffering effects on health outcomes. Therefore, fostering positive affect can strengthen resilience and should also be a focus of health interventions [22]. Social support was found to buffer the effects of stress on affect [18]. For example, positive effects of small talk on emotional state were shown for work context [23]. Minimal social interactions at a coffee shop improved mood and a sense of belonging [24]. Importantly, small talk typically focuses on neutral or safe topics and conveys a positive attitude towards the conversation partner, thus improving mood [25]. Overall, small talk can positively impact well-being by directly addressing stress, improving emotional regulation, reducing negative affect, and enhancing positive affect.

2.3 Social Robots

In modern society, interactions increasingly involve not only humans but also artificial agents, such as social robots. These robots are taking on a growing range of roles, including in education, healthcare, elderly care, customer service, and even intimate relationships [26–30]. The Computer Agent as Social Actor hypothesis suggests that we perceive and interact with artificial agents in much the same way as humans [31]. Moreover, talking to a robot may be associated with less anxiety than talking to an unknown person [25, 32]. Thus, it is natural to consider using social robots for stress-reduction interventions in everyday interactions. Research demonstrates that interactions with social robots have the potential to reduce stress [30, 33]. Most evidence comes from interactions with animal-like robots such as Paro [34–36] or robot-mediated stress interventions such as breathing or mental health training [33]. Short-term [37, 38] and long-term interactions [39] effectively reduce stress, especially with embodied and virtual robots. Positive effects were also found with virtual characters [40]. However, not all interactions are equally beneficial for managing stress and affect; rather, it is the exchange of neutral or positive information, where the robot both encourages and discloses information about itself, that proves most effective [41, 42]. Self-disclosure may have an even more pronounced effect on individuals with higher baseline stress levels [43]. Taken together, interventions with social robots may effectively mitigate stress and improve mood. However, there has been no systematic examination of the effects of small talk and neutral interventions involving robots on these parameters compared to a control condition. This is the focus of the present study.

3 The Present Study

To examine the effect of small talk with a robot on stress and affect, we conducted an online study. Participants were first exposed to a stressful task and then assigned to one of three conditions: Small talk with a simulated humanoid robot Nao (Maxvision Technology Corp-SAS), Neutral (listening to NAO talk), or Control (no robot). In the Control condition, participants were told to count backward from 100 to 0. We predicted that small talk with a social robot would reduce stress more than control and neutral conditions, with positive affect mediating this effect. Additionally, small talk would increase positive affect and decrease negative affect. We expected that stress levels over the past month and baseline stress levels before the intervention would moderate the effect of small talk on stress reduction and changes in affect. Finally, we explored whether participants' attitudes towards robots influenced these outcomes.

4 Materials and Methods

4.1 Participants

An a priori power calculation using G*Power [44] with an effect size $f = 0.3$, an alpha level of .05, and desired power of 0.8 indicated that a total sample size of 111 participants was required for a one-way ANOVA with three groups. A total of 116 participants took part in the online experiment. Twenty-one participants (18%) were excluded for the following reasons: technical problems (8), reported neurological or psychiatric conditions (e.g., ADHD or schizophrenia) that might affect stress processing (12) [45], and participants with German as a non-native language, as this may influence emotional processing (5) [e.g., 46]. The final sample consisted of 98 participants (50 females, 46 males, two non-binary; mean age = 29 years, $SD = 12$ years), all native German speakers. They were randomly distributed between the three experimental conditions: Control (33), Small talk (32), and Neutral (33).

4.2 Measures

Perceived Stress. We used the Perceived Stress Scale (PSS) [47, German version 48] as an overall measure of stress, capturing the stress level experienced over the past month. The scale consists of ten items, each rated on a 5-point Likert scale ranging from "never" to "very often." Sample items are: "In the last month, how often have you been upset because of something that happened unexpectedly?" and "In the last month, how often have you been able to control irritations in your life?" The reliability of the German version of PSS is very good (Cronbach's alpha = .88).

Positive and Negative Affect. We measured affect by the Positive and Negative Affect Schedule questionnaire (PANAS) [49, German version 50]. It contains 20 adjectives, with 10 describing positive (e.g., *excited*) and 10 describing negative affect (e.g., *irritable*). The adjectives are rated on a 5-point Likert scale ranging from "not at all" to "extremely." The reliability of the German version of PANAS is very good (Cronbach's alpha = .86 to .93 in different samples).

General Attitudes towards Robots. General attitudes towards robots were assessed using the GAToRS Scale [51], which includes two subscales—Personal and Societal, each containing 10 items rated on a 7-point Likert scale ranging from "strongly disagree" to "strongly agree." Sample items are: "I can trust persons and organizations related to the development of robots" (Personal) and "Robots may make us even lazier" (Societal, reverse coded). The items were translated into German by the authors. The reliability of the English version of GAToRS ranges from acceptable to good (Cronbach's alpha = .74 to .84 for the subscales).

Current Stress Level. We assessed the stress level in the current moment with a 6-point single-item visual analog scale, ranging from "no stress" to "greatest stress" [52, 53]. The scale included six cartoon face anchors representing different stress levels, similar to the Visual Analog Mood Scale [54]. A similar scale has been previously used in studies examining stress in interactions with robots [34].

4.3 Videos

We adapted two videos from our previous study [55] featuring a simulated humanoid robot NAO. The setting and actions remained identical in both videos, only the content differed. The robot stood on a table in front of a wall with a painting, speaking and gesturing naturally with its arms. Figure 1 provides a snapshot of the videos. The texts of the robot's speech were written by the authors, converted into speech using a text-to-speech generator, and overlaid onto the videos. The voice of the NAO robot was female and configured using the "Seraphina Multilingual (Natural) - German (Germany)" voice from Microsoft's free voice generator. We selected a female voice and natural gestures based on evidence suggesting that robots with these characteristics are more widely accepted [56, 57]. In the Neutral condition, the robot described the painting. The video lasted 59 s in total and was divided into four segments between 13 and 16 s (mean duration: 15 s). No interaction with the robot was required or possible, and participants could listen to the robot at their own pace by pressing the "Next" button. In the Small talk condition, the robot engaged participants in a simulated conversation, sharing information about itself and posing questions such as, "I am in a good mood today. How about you?". Participants selected one of three pre-set responses on the screen, such as "I am fine," "I am OK," or "It is not my day." The robot provided tailored follow-ups and asked additional questions based on their answers. Thus, the participants' responses were only button presses. The interaction consisted of nine video segments between 6 and 17 s (mean duration: 10 s), totaling 92 s. Participants could respond at their own pace. Verbatim transcripts and videos are available at https://osf.io/kqa7x/.

4.4 Stress Induction

To induce stress, we employed the Stroop test [58], a widely used method in psychological research that provokes stress through cognitive interference [58; for a review, see 59]. Participants were presented with color words (red, yellow, blue, and green) displayed in colored letters (also red, yellow, blue, and green), where the font color was either congruent with the word meaning (e.g., the word *green* in green letters) or incongruent (e.g., the word *green* in blue letters). Participants were instructed to identify the font color by pressing a corresponding key on the keyboard: Q for red, W for yellow, O for blue, and P for green. Each trial began with a fixation cross displayed for 500 ms, followed by the presentation of the word, which remained on the screen for 3 s or until a response was made. The task started with 15 practice trials, followed by 100 experimental trials, consisting of 50 congruent and 50 incongruent trials. The results of the Stroop test were not analyzed, as it was designed solely to induce stress. A figure depicting the timeline of a Stroop test trial can be found at https://osf.io/kqa7x/.

4.5 Procedure

The experiment was conducted in German on Gorilla [61] and lasted 30 min. All participants were recruited from the University of Potsdam, provided informed consent prior to the experiment, and received course credits as compensation. These were mostly students of psychology and linguistics. The study conformed to the Declaration of Helsinki and the ethics policy of the University of Potsdam. Participants first completed the PSS Questionnaire [48] and the GAToRS Questionnaire [51]. Next, they performed the Stroop test [58] and assessed their stress levels using the visual analog stress scale [52, 53]. They then filled out the PANAS Questionnaire [50]. Afterward, participants were invited to take a break and were randomly assigned to one of three conditions: Control, Neutral, or Small talk. In the Control condition, participants were instructed to count backward from 100 to 0. In the Neutral condition, participants watched the video of the NAO robot discussing a painting on the wall. In the Small talk condition, participants interacted with the robot by entering text-based responses to prompts in the video. Following the assigned condition, participants reassessed their stress levels using the same visual analog stress scale, completed the PANAS Questionnaire again, provided demographic information, and were debriefed.

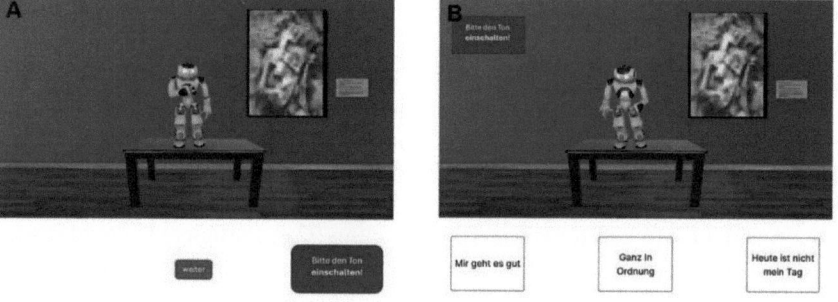

Fig. 1. Screenshots of the video used in Neutral condition (Panel A) and Small talk condition (Panel B) (courtesy of Tristan Kornher). *Note:* The artwork in the videos was pixelated to protect copyright. It is the painting *Girl with a Mandolin* by Pablo Picasso (1910).

5 Results

We calculated scores for Stress change (stress level before intervention subtracted from stress level after intervention), Positive affect change, and Negative affect change (positive and negative affect levels before intervention subtracted from respective affect levels after intervention), as well as GAToRS and PSS scores for all 98 participants.

5.1 Stress Change

First, we conducted a one-way ANOVA with factor Condition (Small talk, Neutral, and Control) and Stress change as dependent variable. Since Levene's test for equality of variances was violated ($F(2,95) = 6.79, p < .05$), we applied the Welch correction for homogeneity of variance. We found a statistically significant main effect of Condition on Stress change ($F(2, 60.41) = 6.43, p < .05, \eta2 = 0.10$). Descriptively, the Stress change was greatest in the Small talk condition (Mean Difference $= -1.66$), followed by the Neutral condition (Mean Difference $= -1.36$) and Control condition (Mean Difference $= -0.49$). Negative values mean stress reduction after the intervention. In Neutral and Small talk conditions, the changes were significant ($t(95) = -5.21, p < .001$ and $t(95) = -6.23, p < .001$), in the Control condition the change was only marginally significant ($t(95) = -1.85, p = .07$, see Table 1 of the Appendix). Games–Howell post hoc tests with Tukey correction revealed significant differences only between the Control condition and the Neutral ($p < .05$, 95% C.I. $= [-1.61, -0.15]$) and Small talk condition ($p < .05$, 95% C.I. $= [-2.13, -0.22]$), respectively. The Neutral and Small talk conditions did not differ ($p = .76$, 95% C.I. $= [-1.29, 0.71]$). Both robot interventions had comparable effects. When comparing Small talk to the combined Neutral and Control conditions, the difference remained only marginal ($F(1, 44.98) = 3.72, p = .06$).

As expected, the effect of Condition on Stress change was mediated by the Positive affect change. Mediation analyses based on bootstrapped 1000 simulations showed that the direct effect of Condition (Small talk vs. both other conditions) was non-significant ($B = -0.36, p = .32$, 95% C.I. $= [-1.15, 0.31]$), but the indirect effect of Condition via Positive affect change was significant ($B = -0.38, p < .05$, 95% C.I. $= [-0.69, -0.10]$). The total effect was also significant ($B = -0.73, p < .05$, 95% C.I. $= [-1.53, -0.04]$). Specifically, 51% of the total effect of Condition on Stress change was mediated by the Positive affect change ($B = 0.51, p < .05$, 95% C.I. $= [0.05, 3.13]$). The results of the mediation analysis are illustrated in Fig. 2.

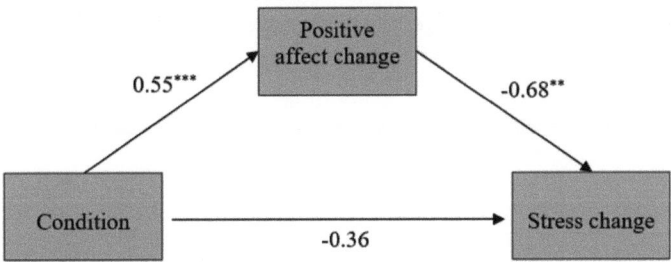

Fig. 2. Effect of Condition on Stress change is mediated by Positive affect change. *Note.* * $p < .05$ ** $p < .01$, *** $p < .001$

5.2 Positive Affect Change

Further, we conducted another one-way ANOVA with factor Condition (Small talk, Neutral, and Control) and Positive affect change as the dependent variable. We found a significant main effect of Condition on Positive affect change ($F(2, 95) = 11.14, p < .001$, $\eta 2 = 0.19$). Descriptively, the Positive affect change was highest in the Control condition (Mean Difference $= -0.71$), followed by the Neutral condition (Mean Difference $= -0.35$) and Small talk condition (Mean Difference $= 0.02$). Negative values mean that positive affect decreased after the intervention. In Control and Neutral conditions, the changes were significant ($t(95) = -6.53, p < .001$ and $t(95) = -3.22, p < .001$), in the Small talk condition the change was not significant ($t(95) = 0.20, p = .84$, see Table 1 of the Appendix). Tukey's post hoc tests revealed significant differences between the Small talk condition and the Control condition ($p < .001, 95\%$ C.I. $= [0.36, 1.10]$) and Neutral condition ($p < .05, 95\%$ C.I. $= [0.003, 0.74]$), respectively. The Neutral and Control conditions differed marginally ($p = .056, 95\%$ C.I. $= [-0.01, 0.72]$). Positive affect decreased significantly more in the Control and Neutral conditions compared to the Small talk condition. However, neither of the interventions led to an increase in positive affect. In the Small talk condition, positive affect remained stable, whereas it declined in the Control and Neutral conditions.

5.3 Negative Affect Change

We conducted another one-way ANOVA with the factor Condition (Small talk, Neutral, and Control) and Negative affect change as the dependent variable. We found a significant main effect of Condition on Negative affect change ($F(2, 95) = 4.38, p < .05, \eta 2 = 0.08$). Descriptively, the Negative affect change was highest in the Neutral condition (Mean Difference $= -0.33$), followed by the Small talk condition (Mean Difference $= -0.32$) and Control condition (Mean Difference $= -0.003$). Negative values mean that negative affect decreased after the intervention. In Neutral and Small talk conditions, the changes were significant ($t(95) = -3.71, p < .001$ and $t(95) = -3.56, p < .001$), in the Control condition the change was not significant ($t(95) = -0.03, p = .97$, see Table 1 of the Appendix). Tukey's post hoc tests revealed significant differences between the Control condition and the Neutral condition ($p < .05, 95\%$ C.I. $= [-0.62, -0.03]$) and Small talk condition ($p < .05, 95\%$ C.I. $= [-0.62, -0.02]$), respectively. The Neutral and Small talk conditions did not differ ($p = .99, 95\%$ C.I. $= [-0.29, 0.31]$). Thus, negative affect remained unchanged in the Control condition but decreased similarly across both intervention conditions. Overall, the results indicate that both interventions similarly reduced stress and negative affect. Positive affect declined in the Control and Neutral conditions but remained stable in the Small talk condition. Figure 3 provides an overview of the results.

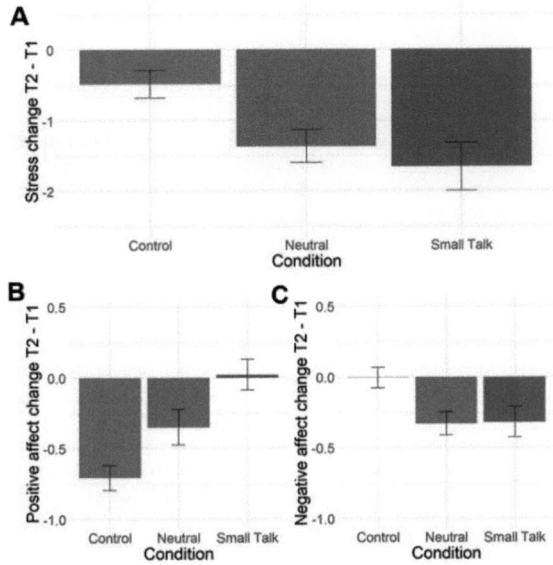

Fig. 3. Effects of Condition on Stress change (Panel A), Positive affect change (Panel B), and Negative affect change (Panel C).

5.4 Perceived Stress Level

To assess the interaction between the overall Perceived Stress Level and Condition, we performed a median split on the Perceived Stress Level variable. We then conducted a two-way ANOVA with Condition (Small talk, Neutral, and Control) and Perceived Stress Level (low, high) as independent variables and Stress change as the dependent variable. Since Levene's test for equality of variances showed that the group variances were not equal ($F(5,92) = 3.91, p < .05$), we applied White's correction for heteroscedasticity. There was a significant main effect of Condition on Stress change ($F(2, 92) = 7.02, p < .05$) and a marginally significant interaction between Condition and Perceived Stress Level ($F(2, 92) = 2.83, p = .06$). Post hoc tests with Bonferroni correction revealed significant differences between the Control condition and the Neutral condition ($p < .05$, 95% C.I. = [−3.44, −0.004]) and Small talk condition ($p < .05$, 95% C.I. = [−3.02, −0.14]), respectively, but only for participants with a low Perceived Stress Level. No significant differences were found for participants with a high Perceived Stress Level. In other words, the interventions appeared to be most effective for participants with lower stress levels in the previous month. The results are presented in Fig. 4.

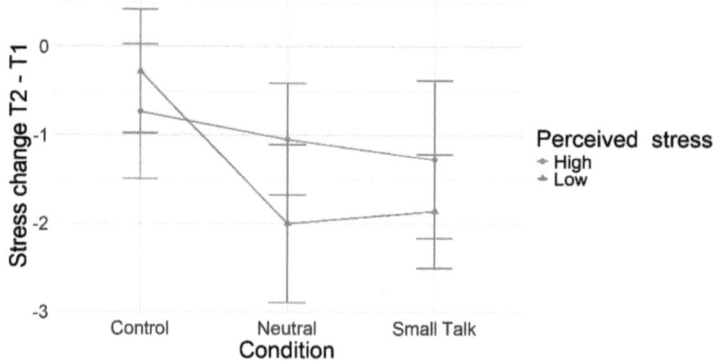

Fig. 4. Effects of Condition on Stress change modulated by Perceived Stress Level.

Further, we conducted another two-way ANOVA with Condition (Small talk, Neutral, and Control) and Perceived Stress Level (low, high) as independent variables and Positive affect change as the dependent variable. We only found a significant main effect of Condition ($F(2, 92) = 10.60, p < .05$), but no interaction effect ($F(2, 92) = 0.09, p = .91$). Thus, the stress levels in the previous month did not modulate the effect of Condition on Positive affect change. Finally, we conducted a two-way ANOVA with Condition (Small talk, Neutral, and Control) and Perceived Stress Level (low, high) as independent variables and Negative affect change as the dependent variable. Since Levene's test for equality of variances showed that the group variances were not equal ($F(5,92) = 4.02, p < .05$), we applied White's correction for heteroscedasticity. Again, there was only a significant main effect of Condition ($F(2, 92) = 5.30, p < .05$), but no interaction effect ($F(2, 92) = 0.11, p = .90$). Thus, the stress levels in the previous month also did not modulate the effect of Condition on Negative affect change.

5.5 Initial Stress Level

To assess the interaction between Initial Stress Level and Condition, we performed a median split on the Initial Stress Level at T1 (after the stress induction before the intervention) variable. We then conducted a two-way ANOVA with Condition (Small talk, Neutral, and Control) and Initial Stress Level (low, high) as independent variables, and Stress change as the dependent variable. There was a significant main effect of Condition ($F(2, 92) = 13.74, p < .05$) and a significant main effect of Initial Stress Level ($F(1, 92) = 62.94, p < .05$). Importantly, there was a significant interaction between Condition and Initial Stress Level ($F(2, 92) = 8.40, p < .05$). Post hoc tests with Bonferroni correction revealed significant differences between the Control condition and the Neutral condition ($p < .001$, 95% C.I. $= [-2.96, -0.57]$) and Small talk condition ($p < .001$, 95% C.I. $= [-3.92, -1.38]$), but only for participants with high Initial Stress Level. Stress reduction was more pronounced in the Small talk condition ($M = -3.42$), followed by the Neutral condition ($M = -2.53$), and Control condition ($M = -0.77$), but only if the Initial Stress Level was high. Participants with a higher Initial Stress Level had a larger decrease in stress in general ($M_{high} = -2.09$ vs. $M_{low} = -0.41$).

Similarly, we performed a median split on the Initial positive affect at T1 (after the stress induction before the intervention) variable. We then conducted a two-way ANOVA with Condition (Small talk, Neutral, and Control) and Initial positive affect level (low, high) as independent variables, and Positive affect change as the dependent variable. There was a significant main effect of Condition ($F(2, 92) = 11.78, p < .05$) and a significant main effect of Initial positive affect level ($F(1, 92) = 26.55, p < .05$), but no interaction ($F(2, 92) = 1.27, p = .29$). Participants with a higher Initial positive affect level had a larger decrease in positive affect ($M_{high} = -0.69$ vs. $M_{low} = -0.07$), irrespective of Condition.

Finally, we performed a median split on the Initial negative affect at T1 (after the stress induction before the intervention) variable. We then conducted a two-way ANOVA with Condition (Small talk, Neutral, and Control) and Initial negative affect level (low, high) as independent variables, and Negative affect change as the dependent variable. Again, there was a significant main effect of Condition ($F(2, 92) = 4.97, p < .05$), a significant main effect of Initial negative affect level ($F(1, 92) = 38.46, p < .05$), and a significant interaction ($F(2, 92) = 4.60, p < .05$). Participants with a higher Initial negative affect level had a larger decrease in negative affect in general ($M_{high} = -0.52$ vs. $M_{low} = 0.03$). In fact, the negative affect remained stable or even increased slightly in participants with a lower Initial negative affect level. Negative affect reduction was more pronounced in the Small talk condition ($M = -0.82$), followed by the Neutral condition ($M = -0.58$), and Control condition ($M = -0.12$), but only if the Initial negative affect level was high. The results are presented in Fig. 5.

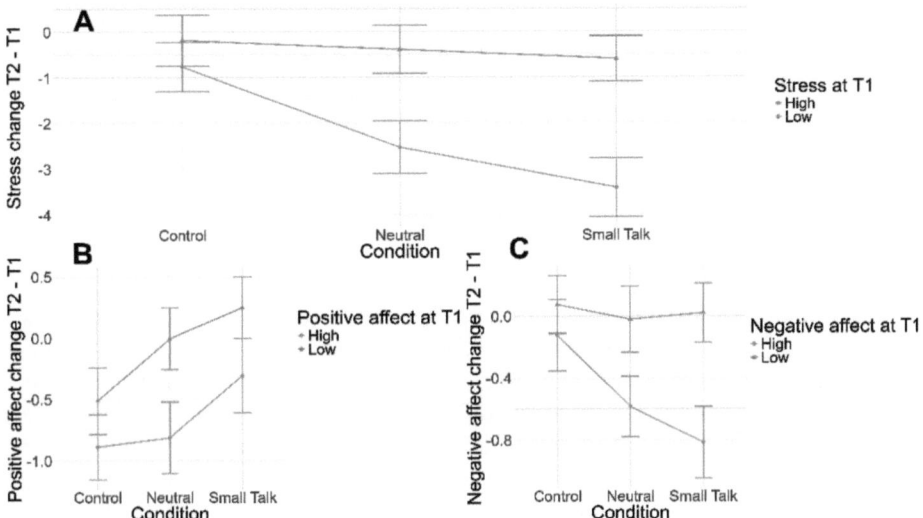

Fig. 5. Effect of Condition on Stress change modulated by Stress Level at T1 (Panel A), Effects of Condition on Positive affect change modulated by Positive affect Level at T1 (Panel B), and Condition on Negative affect change modulated by Negative affect Level at T1 (Panel C).

5.6 Attitudes Towards Robots and Other Control Variables

To control for general attitudes towards robots, we first conducted an ANCOVA with Condition (Small talk, Neutral, and Control) as an independent variable, Personal and Societal scores of the GAToRS as covariates, and Stress change as the dependent variable. Again, we only found a significant main effect of Condition ($F(2, 93) = 5.37, p < .05$), but no effect of GAToRS scores ($F(1, 93) = 0.92, p = .34$ and $F(1, 93) = 1.00, p = .32$, respectively). An ANCOVA with Condition (Small talk, Neutral, and Control) as an independent variable, Personal and Societal scores of the GAToRS as covariates, and Positive affect change as the dependent variable again revealed only a significant main effect of Condition ($F(2, 93) = 12.02, p < .001$), but no effect of GAToRS scores ($F(1, 93) = 1.64, p = .20$ and $F(1, 93) = 0.002, p = .96$, respectively). Finally, an ANCOVA with Condition (Small talk, Neutral, and Control) as an independent variable, Personal and Societal scores of the GAToRS as covariates, and Negative affect change as the dependent variable revealed a significant main effect of Condition ($F(2, 93) = 5.24, p < .05$) and a significant main effect of the Personal GAToRS score condition ($F(1, 93) = 4.13, p < .05$). The Societal score had no significant effect ($F(1, 93) = 1.13, p = .29$). To further explore a possible interaction effect between the Personal score and Condition on the Negative affect change, performed a median split on the Personal score variable. We conducted a two-way ANOVA with Condition (Small talk, Neutral, and Control) and Personal score Level (low, high) as independent variables and Negative affect change as the dependent variable. Since Levene's test for equality of variances showed that the group variances were not equal ($F(5,92) = 2.66, p < .05$), we applied White's correction for heteroscedasticity. Again, there was only a significant main effect of Condition ($F(2, 92) = 5.87, p < .05$), but no interaction effect ($F(2, 92) = 0.21, p = .81$). Participants with more negative personal attitudes towards robots experienced a greater decrease in negative affect across all conditions.

Additionally, for all three outcomes (Stress change, Positive affect change, and Negative affect change), we controlled for gender and age but found no significant effects ($p > .05$). The data and analysis script are available at https://osf.io/kqa7x/.

6 Discussion

Our study found that both the Small talk and Neutral interventions significantly reduced stress and negative affect compared to the Control condition. Descriptively, the highest stress reduction occurred in the Small talk condition, followed by the Neutral and Control conditions, but the interventions did not differ significantly. Stress and negative affect were significantly reduced only in the Small talk and Neutral conditions. Positive affect decreased significantly more in the Control and Neutral conditions, whereas in the Small talk condition, it remained stable with no significant change. In fact, in terms of affect management, the results from the Small talk intervention were almost the reverse of those from the Neutral and Control conditions: Small talk maintained stable positive affect while reducing negative affect, whereas the other two conditions kept negative affect stable and reduced positive affect. However, the positive affect did not improve in any condition. In total, although no significant difference was found between Small talk and a Neutral intervention in reducing stress, the overall results align with our predictions.

Our findings suggest that even a brief simulated small talk interaction via button presses with a social robot depicted on a screen online can effectively reduce stress and stabilize mood after stressful events. This simplified form of interaction is easy to implement in both online and offline settings, including tutoring systems and medical examination interfaces. The results are consistent with the findings of a meta-analysis [62], which showed that, for subjective measures, even depicted robots can have a positive effect. Research suggests that, compared to disembodied agents such as chatbots, robots elicit greater self-disclosure and more positive social responses, and are therefore likely to be better suited for stress reduction [63, 64]. Future research should replicate our findings through real-life interactions with embodied robots.

Importantly, we found that initial attitudes towards robots do not impact the positive effects of such interactions. Our results corroborate previous studies highlighting positive effects of small talk on stress and mood in human-human interactions [12, 16, 23, 24, 65]. Small talk with a social robot was also reported to improve rapport and work dynamics [66] as well as trust [67]. Thus, we contribute to the growing evidence that small talk with a robot has positive effects not only on interpersonal but also on intrapersonal outcomes. Notably, the stress reduction was partially explained by changes in positive affect, consistent with prior research suggesting that affect mediates stress modulation [17, 18]. While there is evidence that people are happier when engaging in deep rather than superficial conversations [68], we do not view this as contradicting our findings. Close friendships and deep conversations are undoubtedly valuable, but they are less practical for structured or short-term interventions.

Interestingly, the small talk intervention was more effective for participants with higher stress and negative affect levels immediately before the intervention. This finding aligns with earlier studies indicating that participants with higher baseline stress levels benefit more [69, 70]. This compensatory effect presumably arises from the greater potential for improvement at higher baselines. At the same time, we cannot completely dismiss regression to the mean, a statistical effect where extreme values naturally shift closer to the average, creating the illusion of change as at least a partial explanation [71]. Yet, this risk is minimized by our random assignment to conditions. Conversely, when considering global stress levels from the previous month, the results show the opposite pattern. Specifically, the small talk and neutral interventions were more effective for participants with lower global stress levels. If the global stress level is too high and chronic, a short-term interaction may be insufficient to trigger changes. Thus, we provide evidence that while a small talk intervention is beneficial, its effects may vary between individuals, and factors such as overall stress levels should be taken into account.

7 Conclusion and Outlook

In conclusion, incorporating small talk into everyday interactions with robots can help buffer the negative effects of stress on mood and health. Although our small talk was brief and conducted online, with participants responding by selecting answers to pre-selected topics, it still had a powerful impact. However, there are still areas for improvement and new avenues for research. Future studies should explore comparisons with alternative interventions, such as mental health training, also in lab studies and with more heterogeneous samples compared to our homogeneous convenience sample, mainly consisting of students. To ensure that participants perceived NAO as a social robot rather than an avatar, despite explicitly introducing it as a robot in the intervention, we may need to assess their perceptions using measures such as the Human–Robot Interaction Evaluation Scale [72]. Furthermore, we employed a relatively mild stress induction task, a Stroop test, which primarily induces stress through cognitive load. Future research should examine whether our findings extend to evaluative stress, e.g., the Montreal Imaging Stress Task [73], or social stress, e.g., Trier Social Stress Test [74, cf. also 75].

Our approach does not replace human interaction but rather complements it in situations where human engagement is unavailable or undesired, such as self-service counters or online platforms. Robots could also facilitate small talk in online tutoring systems or educational settings as part of robot-assisted interactions. Small social robots could also be designed as wearable companions [76], allowing users to carry them throughout the day. By engaging in small talk, they may help with stress management and provide emotional support. Since we tend to perceive robots as social partners and anthropomorphize them [77], the effects may resemble those of human conversation. At the same time, it may be easier to avoid speaking to a robot than to a human, as it does not carry the same social risks, like the fear of rejection or self-awareness. However, achieving a natural conversation with a robot remains challenging, particularly when it comes to processes like emotion recognition [78] or turn-taking [79], which still require improvement.

Naturally, the topics of small talk should be chosen carefully, as self-disclosure from a robot that does not align with its actual capabilities (e.g., empathy or happiness) could evoke the "Uncanny Valley" phenomenon [80], a sense of eeriness when a robot appears almost human, but not completely. For example, Gigandet et al. found that a robot's emotional expressions, like saying "I'm happy" without being able to feel it, evoke cognitive resistance, as shown by the N400 EEG component, indicating incongruence with the robot's physical capabilities. This implicit sense of incongruence and lack of genuineness can lead to skepticism and undermine trust in the robot. Finally, a study involving an embodied robot or different robots in virtual reality [cf. 81] should be conducted to validate these results. While meta-analyses found that the presentation medium has minimal impact [62, 82], face-to-face interactions may still be more beneficial for verbal conversations. In conclusion, our study highlights that brief small talk with a robot can effectively reduce stress and improve mood, especially in situations where human interaction is limited, for example, for lonely individuals. Of course, this is not the same as genuine human-to-human interaction, but it can serve as a way to augment it.

Acknowledgements. We thank Dr. Yuefang Zhou for her valuable insights and productive discussions on the topic of this manuscript. We also thank Tristan Kornher for creating the videos.

Disclosure of Interests. The authors have no competing interests to declare.

Appendix

Table 1. Marginal means by Condition.

Condition	Marginal Mean	Lower 95% CI	Upper 95% CI	SE	t	p
Stress change						
Control	−0.49	−1.01	0.04	0.26	−1.85	0.07
Neutral	**−1.36**	**−1.88**	**−0.84**	**0.26**	**−5.21**	**<.001**
Small talk	**−1.66**	**−2.18**	**−1.13**	**0.27**	**−6.23**	**<.001**
Positive affect change						
Control	**−0.71**	**−0.92**	**−0.49**	**0.11**	**−6.53**	**<.001**
Neutral	**−0.35**	**−0.56**	**−0.13**	**0.11**	**−3.22**	**0.002**
Small Talk	0.02	−0.20	0.24	0.11	0.20	0.84
Negative affect change						
Control	−0.003	−0.18	0.17	0.09	−0.03	0.97
Neutral	**−0.33**	**−0.50**	**−0.15**	**0.09**	**−3.71**	**< .001**
Small Talk	**−0.32**	**−0.50**	**−0.14**	**0.09**	**−3.56**	**< .001**

Note. Df = 95. Significant results highlighted in bold.

References

1. Newman, D.B., Nezlek, J.B.: The influence of daily events on emotion regulation and well-being in daily life. Pers. Soc. Psychol. Bull. **48**(1), 19–33 (2022)
2. Blanke, E.S., Bellingtier, J.A., Riediger, M., Brose, A.: When and how to regulate: everyday emotion-regulation strategy use and stressor intensity. Affect. Sci. **3**(1), 81–92 (2022)
3. Meng, J., (Nancy) Dai, Y.: Emotional support from AI chatbots: should a supportive partner self-disclose or not? J. Comput. Mediat. Commun. **26**(4), 207–22 (2021)
4. Cohen, S., Wills, T.A.: Stress, social support, and the buffering hypothesis. Psychol. Bull. **98**(2), 310–357 (1985)
5. Bendel, O., Peier, L.K.: How can bar robots enhance the well-being of guests? (2023). https://arxiv.org/abs/2304.14410. Accessed 11 Jan 2024
6. O'Connor, D.B., Thayer, J.F., Vedhara, K.: Stress and health: a review of psychobiological processes. Annu. Rev. Psychol. **72**(1), 663–688 (2021)
7. Selye, H.: The stress concept. Can. Med. Assoc. J. **115**(8), 718 (1976)
8. Estevez Cores, S., Sayed, A.A., Tracy, D.K., Kempton, M.J.: Individual-focused occupational health interventions: a meta-analysis of randomized controlled trials. J. Occup. Health Psychol. **26**(3), 189–203 (2021)

9. Svärdman, F., Sjöwall, D., Lindsäter, E.: Internet-delivered cognitive behavioral interventions to reduce elevated stress: a systematic review and meta-analysis. Internet Interv. **29**, 100553 (2022)
10. Ditzen, B., Heinrichs, M.: Psychobiology of social support: the social dimension of stress buffering. Restor. Neurol. Neurosci. **32**(1), 149–162 (2014)
11. Lakey, B., Orehek, E.: Relational regulation theory: a new approach to explain the link between perceived social support and mental health. Psychol. Rev. **118**(3), 482–495 (2011)
12. Spengler, F.B., Scheele, D., Marsh, N., Kofferath, C., Flach, A., Schwarz, S., et al.: Oxytocin facilitates reciprocity in social communication. Soc. Cogn. Affect. Neurosci. **12**(8), 1325–1333 (2017)
13. Hall, J.A., Davis, D.C.: Proposing the communicate bond belong theory: evolutionary intersections with episodic interpersonal communication. Commun. Theory **27**(1), 21–47 (2017)
14. Hall, J.A., Merolla, A.J.: Connecting everyday talk and time alone to global well-being. Hum. Commun. Res. **46**(1), 86–111 (2020)
15. Murayama, H., Sugawara, I.: Decreased frequency of small talk due to the Covid-19 pandemic has deteriorated mental health: findings from longitudinal surveys of middle-aged and older people in Japan. Asia Pac. J. Public Health **34**(5), 565–568 (2022)
16. Robbins, M.L., Wright, R.C., Karan, A.: Everyday coping behaviors. In: Sweeny, K., Robbins, M.L., Cohen, L.M. (eds.) The Wiley Encyclopedia of Health Psychology, 1st edn., pp. 141–147. Wiley (2020). https://onlinelibrary.wiley.com/doi/10.1002/9781119057840.ch60. Accessed 4 Feb 2025
17. Van Eck, M., Berkhof, H., Nicolson, N., Sulon, J.: The effects of perceived stress, traits, mood states, and stressful daily events on salivary cortisol. Psychosom. Med. **58**(5), 447–458 (1996)
18. Hamama, L., Ronen, T., Shachar, K., Rosenbaum, M.: Links between stress, positive and negative affect, and life satisfaction among teachers in special education schools. J. Happiness Stud. **14**(3), 731–751 (2013)
19. Jõgi, A.L., Malmberg, L.E., Pakarinen, E., Lerkkanen, M.K.: Teachers' situational physiological stress and affect. Psychoneuroendocrinology **149**, 106028 (2023)
20. Houghton, J.D., Wu, J., Godwin, J.L., Neck, C.P., Manz, C.C.: Effective stress management: a model of emotional intelligence, self-leadership, and student stress coping. J. Manag. Educ. **36**(2), 220–238 (2012)
21. Penedo, F.J., Dahn, J.R., Gonzalez, J.S., Molton, I., Carver, C.S., Antoni, M.H., et al.: Perceived stress management skill mediates the relationship between optimism and positive mood following radical prostatectomy. Health Psychol. **22**(2), 220–222 (2003)
22. Van Steenbergen, H., De Bruijn, E.R., Van Duijvenvoorde, A.C., Van Harmelen, A.L.: How positive affect buffers stress responses. Curr. Opin. Behav. Sci. **39**, 153–160 (2021)
23. Methot, J.R., Rosado-Solomon, E.H., Downes, P.E., Gabriel, A.S.: Office chitchat as a social ritual: the uplifting yet distracting effects of daily small talk at work. Acad. Manag. J. **64**(5), 1445–1471 (2021)
24. Sandstrom, G.M., Dunn, E.W.: Is efficiency overrated?: minimal social interactions lead to belonging and positive affect. Soc. Psychol. Pers. Sci. **5**(4), 437–442 (2014)
25. Burmester, M., Laib, M., Tille, R.: Snackomat - a vending machine to create positive experiences by bringing people in contact and initiating small talk in waiting situations. Int. J. Appl. Posit. Psychol. **5**(3), 189–216 (2020)
26. Bendel, O. (ed.): Pflegeroboter. Springer Fachmedien Wiesbaden, Wiesbaden (2018)
27. Bendel, O.: Robots in policing. In: Hakli, R., Mäkelä, P., Seibt, J. (eds.) Social Robots in Social Institutions: Proceedings of Robophilosophy 2022. IOS Press (2023)
28. Bendel, O. (eds.): Soziale Roboter: Technikwissenschaftliche, wirtschaftswissenschaftliche, philosophische, psychologische und soziologische Grundlagen. Springer, Gabler Wiesbaden, Wiesbaden (2021)

29. Zhou, Y., Fischer, M.H.: Intimate relationships with humanoid robots: exploring human sexuality in the twenty-first century. In: Zhou, Y., Fischer, M.H. (eds.) AI Love You, pp. 177–184. Springer, Cham (2019). https://doi.org/10.1007/978-3-030-19734-6_10
30. Kühne, K., Jeglinski-Mende, M.A., Fischer, M.H., Zhou, Y.: Social robot – Jack of all trades? Paladyn. J. Behav. Robot. **13**(1), 1–22 (2022)
31. Reeves, B., Nass, C.: The Media Equation: How People Treat Computers, Television, and New Media. Cambridge University Press, Cambridge (1996)
32. Luo, R.L., Zhang, T.X.Y., Chen, D.H.C., Hoorn, J.F., Huang, I.S.: Social robots outdo the not-so-social media for self-disclosure: Safe machines preferred to unsafe humans? Robotics **11**(5), 92 (2022)
33. Rice, A., Klęczek, K., Alimardani, M.: The effectiveness of social robots in stress management interventions for university students. In: Ali, A.A., et al. (eds.) ICSR 2023. LNCS, vol. 14453, pp. 181–190. Springer, Singapore (2024). https://doi.org/10.1007/978-981-99-8715-3_16
34. Geva, N., Hermoni, N., Levy-Tzedek, S.: Interaction matters: the effect of touching the social robot Paro on pain and stress is stronger when turned ON vs OFF. Front. Robot. AI. **8**(9), 926185 (2022)
35. Aminuddin, R., Sharkey, A., Levita, L.: Interaction with the Paro robot may reduce psychophysiological stress responses. In: 2016 11th ACM/IEEE International Conference on Human-Robot Interaction (HRI), Christchurch, New Zealand, pp. 593–594. IEEE (2016). http://ieeexplore.ieee.org/document/7451872/. Accessed 4 Feb 2025
36. Aminuddin, R., Sharkey, A.: A Paro robot reduces the stressful effects of environmental noise. In: Proceedings of the European Conference on Cognitive Ergonomics 2017, Umeå Sweden, pp. 63–64. ACM (2017). https://dl.acm.org/doi/10.1145/3121283.3121420. Accessed 4 Feb 2025
37. Kühnlenz, B., Erhart, M., Kainert, M., Wang, Z.Q., Wilm, J., Kühnlenz, K.: Impact of trajectory profiles on user stress in close human-robot interaction. at-Automatisierungstechnik **66**(6), 483–491 (2018)
38. Björling, E.A., Ling, H., Bhatia, S., Dziubinski, K.: The experience and effect of adolescent to robot stress disclosure: a mixed-methods exploration. In: Wagner, A.R., et al. (eds.) ICSR 2020. LNCS, vol. 12483, pp. 604–615. Springer, Cham (2020). https://doi.org/10.1007/978-3-030-62056-1_50
39. Wada, K., Shibata, T., Saito, T., Sakamoto, K., Tanie, K.: Psychological and social effects of one year robot assisted activity on elderly people at a health service facility for the aged. In: Proceedings of the 2005 IEEE International Conference on Robotics and Automation, Barcelona, Spain, pp. 2785–2790. IEEE (2005). http://ieeexplore.ieee.org/document/1570535/. Accessed 4 Feb 2025
40. Jhan, X.D., Wong, S.K., Ebrahimi, E., Lai, Y., Huang, W.C., Babu, S.V.: Effects of small talk with a crowd of virtual humans on users' emotional and behavioral responses. IEEE Trans. Vis. Comput. Graph. **28**(11), 3767–3777 (2022)
41. Laban, G., Morrison, V., Kappas, A., Cross, E.S.: Coping with emotional distress via self-disclosure to robots: intervention with caregivers (2023). https://osf.io/gbk2j. Accessed 4 Feb 2025
42. Smakman, M.H.J., Vanegas, D.F.P., Smit, K., Leewis, S., Okkerse, Y., Obbes, J., et al.: A trustworthy robot buddy for primary school children. Multimodal Technol. Interact. **6**(4), 29 (2022)
43. (Euphie) Duan, Y., (Ji) Yoon, M., (Edison) Liang, Z., Hoorn, J.F.: Self-disclosure to a robot: only for those who suffer the most. Robotics **10**(3), 98 (2021)
44. Faul, F., Erdfelder, E., Lang, A.G., Buchner, A.: G*Power 3: a flexible statistical power analysis program for the social, behavioral, and biomedical sciences. Behav. Res. Methods **39**(2), 175–191 (2007)

45. Speyer, L.G., Brown, R.H., Ribeaud, D., Eisner, M., Murray, A.L.: The role of moment-to-moment dynamics of perceived stress and negative affect in co-occurring ADHD and internalising symptoms. J. Autism Dev. Disord. **53**(3), 1213–1223 (2023)
46. Naranowicz, M., Jankowiak, K., Bromberek-Dyzman, K.: Mood and gender effects in emotional word processing in unbalanced bilinguals. Int. J. Biling. **27**(1), 39–60 (2023)
47. Cohen, S., Kamarck, T., Mermelstein, R.: A global measure of perceived stress. J. Health Soc. Behav. **24**(4), 385 (1983)
48. Schneider, E.E., Schönfelder, S., Domke-Wolf, M., Wessa, M.: Measuring stress in clinical and nonclinical subjects using a German adaptation of the perceived stress scale. Int. J. Clin. Health Psychol. **20**(2), 173–181 (2020)
49. Watson, D., Clark, L.A., Tellegen, A.: Development and validation of brief measures of positive and negative affect: the PANAS scales. J. Pers. Soc. Psychol. **54**(6), 1063–1070 (1988)
50. Breyer, B., Bluemke, M.: Deutsche version der positive and negative affect schedule PANAS (GESIS Panel). Zusammenstellung Sozialwissenschaftlicher Items Skalen ZIS (2016). http://zis.gesis.org/Id/zis242. Accessed 30 Jan 2025
51. Koverola, M., Kunnari, A., Sundvall, J., Laakasuo, M.: General attitudes towards robots scale (GAToRS): a new instrument for social surveys. Int. J. Soc. Robot. **14**(7), 1559–1581 (2022)
52. Barré, R., Brunel, G., Barthet, P., Laurencin-Dalicieux, S.: The visual analogue scale: an easy and reliable way of assessing perceived stress. Qual. Prim. Health Care **1**, 1–5 (2017)
53. Lesage, F.X., Berjot, S., Deschamps, F.: Clinical stress assessment using a visual analogue scale. Occup. Med. **62**(8), 600–605 (2012)
54. Kontou, E., Thomas, S., Lincoln, N.: Psychometric properties of a revised version of the visual analog mood scales. Clin. Rehabil. **26**(12), 1133–1140 (2012)
55. Kühne, K., Herbold, E., Bendel, O., Zhou, Y., Fischer, M.H.: "Ick bin een Berlina": dialect proficiency impacts a robot's trustworthiness and competence evaluation. Front. Robot. AI **29**(10), 1241519 (2024)
56. Xu, K.: First encounter with robot alpha: how individual differences interact with vocal and kinetic cues in users' social responses. New Media Soc. **21**(11–12), 2522–2547 (2019)
57. Seo, S.: When female (male) robot is talking to me: effect of service robots' gender and anthropomorphism on customer satisfaction. Int. J. Hosp. Manag. **102**, 103166 (2022)
58. MacLeod, C.M.: The Stroop task in cognitive research. In: Wenzel, A., Rubin, D.C. (eds.) Cognitive Methods and Their Application to Clinical Research, Washington, pp. 17–40. American Psychological Association (2005). http://content.apa.org/books/10870-002. Accessed 28 Aug 2023
59. Tulen, J.H.M., Moleman, P., Van Steenis, H.G., Boomsma, F.: Characterization of stress reactions to the Stroop color word test. Pharmacol. Biochem. Behav. **32**(1), 9–15 (1989)
60. Karthikeyan, P., Murugappan, M., Yaacob, S.: A review on stress inducement stimuli for assessing human stress using physiological signals. In: 2011 IEEE 7th International Colloquium on Signal Processing and its Applications, Penang, Malaysia, pp. 420–425. IEEE (2011). http://ieeexplore.ieee.org/document/5759914/. Accessed 1 Feb 2025
61. Anwyl-Irvine, A.L., Massonnié, J., Flitton, A., Kirkham, N., Evershed, J.K.: Gorilla in our midst: an online behavioral experiment builder. Behav. Res. Methods **52**(1), 388–407 (2020)
62. Roesler, E., Manzey, D., Onnasch, L.: Embodiment matters in social HRI research: effectiveness of anthropomorphism on subjective and objective outcomes. ACM Trans. Hum. Robot. Interact. **12**(1), 1–9 (2023)
63. Lee, K.M., Jung, Y., Kim, J., Kim, S.R.: Are physically embodied social agents better than disembodied social agents?: the effects of physical embodiment, tactile interaction, and people's loneliness in human–robot interaction. Int. J. Hum. Comput. Stud. **64**(10), 962–973 (2006)

64. Laban, G., George, J.N., Morrison, V., Cross, E.S.: Tell me more! Assessing interactions with social robots from speech. Paladyn. J. Behav. Robot. **12**(1), 136–159 (2020)
65. Bernstein, M.J., Zawadzki, M.J., Juth, V., Benfield, J.A., Smyth, J.M.: Social interactions in daily life: within-person associations between momentary social experiences and psychological and physical health indicators. J. Soc. Pers. Relatsh. **35**(3), 372–394 (2018)
66. Pineda, K.T., Brown, E., Huang, C.M.: "See you later, alligator": impacts of robot small talk on task, rapport, and interaction dynamics in human-robot collaboration. arXiv (2025)
67. Paradeda, R.B., Hashemian, M., Rodrigues, R.A., Paiva, A.: How facial expressions and small talk may influence trust in a robot. In: Agah, A., Cabibihan, J.J., Howard, A., Salichs, M., He, H. (eds.) ICSR 2016. LNCS, vol. 9979, pp. 169–178. Springer, Cham (2016). https://doi.org/10.1007/978-3-319-47437-3_17
68. Mehl, M.R., Vazire, S., Holleran, S.E., Clark, C.S.: Eavesdropping on happiness: well-being is related to having less small talk and more substantive conversations. Psychol. Sci. **21**(4), 539–541 (2010)
69. Karyotaki, E., Ebert, D.D., Donkin, L., Riper, H., Twisk, J., Burger, S., et al.: Do guided internet-based interventions result in clinically relevant changes for patients with depression? An individual participant data meta-analysis. Clin. Psychol. Rev. **63**, 80–92 (2018)
70. Ebert, D.D., Franke, M., Zarski, A.C., Berking, M., Riper, H., Cuijpers, P., et al.: Effectiveness and moderators of an internet-based mobile-supported stress management intervention as a universal prevention approach: randomized controlled trial. J. Med. Internet Res. **23**(12), e22107 (2021)
71. Barnett, A.G.: Regression to the mean: what it is and how to deal with it. Int. J. Epidemiol. **34**(1), 215–220 (2004)
72. Spatola, N., Kühnlenz, B., Cheng, G.: Perception and evaluation in human-robot interaction: the human–robot interaction evaluation scale (HRIES)—a multicomponent approach of anthropomorphism. Int. J. Soc. Robot. **13**(7), 1517–1539 (2021)
73. Dedovic, K., Renwick, R., Mahani, N.K., Engert, V., Lupien, S.J., Pruessner, J.C.: The montreal imaging stress task: using functional imaging to investigate the effects of perceiving and processing psychosocial stress in the human brain. J. Psychiatry Neurosci. JPN **30**(5), 319–325 (2005)
74. Allen, A.P., Kennedy, P.J., Dockray, S., Cryan, J.F., Dinan, T.G., Clarke, G.: The trier social stress test: principles and practice. Neurobiol Stress **6**, 113–126 (2017)
75. Turner-Cobb, J.M., Asif, M., Turner, J.E., Bevan, C., Fraser, D.S.: Use of a non-human robot audience to induce stress reactivity in human participants. Comput. Hum. Behav. **99**, 76–85 (2019)
76. Bendel, O.: Wearables. In: Gabler Wirtschaftslexikon (2021). https://wirtschaftslexikon.gabler.de/definition/wearables-54088/version-384509
77. Nass, C., Steuer, J., Tauber, E.R.: Computers are social actors. In: Proceedings of the SIGCHI Conference on Human Factors in Computing Systems, pp. 72–78 (1994)
78. Nimmagadda, R., Arora, K., Martin, M.V.: Emotion recognition models for companion robots. J. Supercomput. **78**(11), 13710–13727 (2022)
79. Skantze, G.: Turn-taking in conversational systems and human-robot interaction: a review. Comput. Speech Lang. **67**, 101178 (2021)
80. Mori, M.: The uncanny valley. Energy **7**, 33–35 (1970)
81. Karhiy, M., Sagar, M., Antoni, M., Loveys, K., Broadbent, E.: Can a virtual human increase mindfulness and reduce stress? A randomised trial. Comput. Hum. Behav. Artif. Hum. **2**(1), 100069 (2024)
82. Roesler, E., Manzey, D., Onnasch, L.: A meta-analysis on the effectiveness of anthropomorphism in human-robot interaction. Sci. Robot. **6**(58), eabj5425 (2021)

Multimodal Dialogue for Empathetic Human-Robot Interaction

Niyati Rawal[1](✉), Rahul Singh Maharjan[2], Giacomo Salici[1], Riccardo Catalini[1], Marta Romeo[3], Roberto Bigazzi[1], Lorenzo Baraldi[1], Roberto Vezzani[1], Rita Cucchiara[1], and Angelo Cangelosi[2]

[1] University of Modena and Reggio Emilia, Modena, Italy
niyati.rawal@unimore.it
[2] University of Manchester, Manchester, UK
[3] Heriot-Watt University, Edinburgh, UK

Abstract. Large Language Models (LLMs) like ChatGPT and Llama enable dialogue with artificial agents but often lack empathy and fail to connect with humans. In social robotics, robots need to understand and respond empathetically to human emotions. This study introduces a dataset of 5600 dialogues created with ChatGPT and a multimodal agent, Emma, which responds to facial expressions. The model is trained in three steps: fine-tuning Llama2 on the dataset using both facial expressions and text, training a reward model based on emotion changes, and using Proximal Policy Optimization (PPO) to optimize positive emotional responses. A survey comparing our model's responses to ChatGPT's shows that our model is more empathetic and humanlike. We also conducted a human-robot interaction (HRI) experiment with the Pepper robot, where participants rated the empathy and appropriateness of the robot's responses. The results were statistically significant using a chi-square test.

Keywords: Vision-and-Language · Emotions · Human-Robot Interaction

1 Introduction

When prompted with, "I am not good at cooking", ChatGPT [25] responds with encouragement and practical advice, offering tips to improve cooking skills. Rather than just empathizing, ChatGPT tends to provide helpful information based on its training on web-scale data. In contrast, a human might respond more simply and empathetically, such as, "It's alright. I learned with practice too."

In Human-Human Interaction (HHI), people often rely on facial expressions and body language to understand emotions and respond empathetically [23]. Social robots such as Nao, Pepper, and Furhat are increasingly being used in

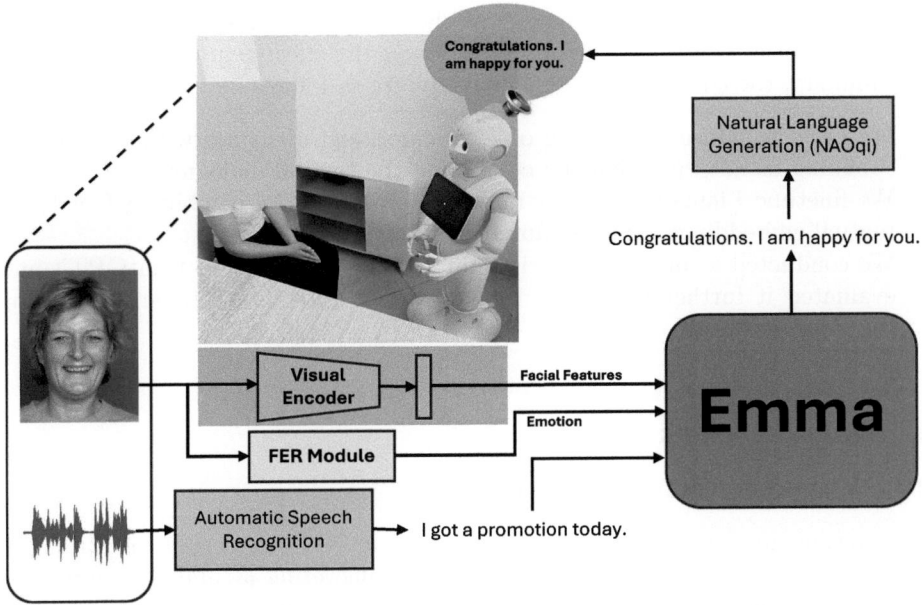

Fig. 1. We propose an empathetic computational model, fine-tuned on Llama2 using multimodal data combining facial expressions and dialogue. It is trained with reinforcement learning to generate responses that make humans feel more positive.

fields such as education and healthcare, where empathy is essential [14]. These robots are expected to both understand human emotions and show empathy through facial expressions [32,34,51], gestures, or speech. Artificial agents have become quite good at multimodal emotion recognition [21]. While LLMs like ChatGPT [25] or Llama [44] can enhance robot intelligence, they often produce emotionally neutral responses, limiting human connection.

To address this, we present a multimodal dataset pairing ChatGPT-generated dialogues with facial expression images. We propose Emma, an Empathetic Multimodal Agent that responds based on both facial cues and verbal input (Fig. 1). Following recent trends [18], we use one LLM to generate language data and fine-tune another (Llama2 [45]) to process multimodal input by combining facial and textual embeddings.

Our three-step training includes fine-tuning Llama2 on empathetic dialogues, training a reward model based on changes in user emotion after responses, and optimizing with reinforcement learning to encourage positive, empathetic interactions. For example, if a user says, "I'm tired of this. I can't take it anymore", the agent replies, "Don't worry, you'll get through it." We validate our approach through surveys and experiments using the robot Pepper.

We show that the responses given by the model are more empathetic and human-like compared to the multimodal model ChatGPT-4o [25]. The results of the HRI experiment also show that the responses given by our model are both appropriate and empathetic. This proves the effectiveness of our method. In summary, the contributions of this study are as follows:

- We build a dataset consisting of 5600 emotional dialogues with their corresponding facial expressions by combining the textual dialogue.
- We finetune Llama2 using our multimodal dataset by combining facial and textual embeddings using reinforcement learning.
- We conducted a survey comparing our model's responses to ChatGPT's and evaluated it further through a Human-Robot Interaction experiment using the Pepper robot.

2 Related Work

2.1 Vision-and-Language Models

Transformer models [48] have become central in NLP, especially for tasks like text generation, summarization, and question answering [31,44]. These models generate text autoregressively, predicting the next token based on previous ones. With the rise of powerful LLMs based on transformers, there is growing interest in multimodal models that combine vision and language [1,18]. While most focus on image-text pairs, some extend to video tasks like retrieval, question answering, and generation [40,42,50].

Vision-and-Language Models (VLMs) can be categorized as contrastive, masking, generative, or pretrained-backbone-based [3]. Models like CLIP [29] learn from contrastive positive and negative pairs. Masking models predict missing patches from captions [15]. Generative models may produce both text and images [43,55], only text [54], or only images via diffusion [36,37]. Some approaches use pretrained models to align modalities, avoiding costly training from scratch [46,56].

2.2 Social Robots and Empathy

Robots are being used beyond industrial settings, appearing in care homes [39,49], receptions [2,10], education [8,28], and households [52,53]. Unlike industrial robots, social robots must understand human emotions and respond empathetically. Research highlights the importance of affective modeling in social robots [6,11,13,47], with facial expressions being a key emotional cue [17,22]. Robots' affective behaviors influence long-term human-robot relationships [32,38].

To achieve empathy, social robots draw inspiration from psychology and social sciences. Empathetic robots are perceived as more friendly [16], and expressive faces improve emotional recognition and user perception without triggering the uncanny valley [7]. Physical design also affects users' cognitive load [26].

2.3 Use of Reinforcement Learning for Training of Language Models

Language Models (LMs) trained on web-scale data often use reinforcement learning with human feedback (RLHF) [41], where humans provide feedback on the agent's responses. LLMs are typically trained using Proximal Policy Optimization (PPO), rewarding the agent for helpful responses and penalizing unhelpful ones [27].

Previous studies have finetuned VLMs on empathetic datasets [33, 35]. Our proposed model, however, adopts a different approach: rather than relying on explicit human feedback, it rewards the agent based on the emotional change in the human after interacting with it. A positive emotional change yields a positive reward, while a negative change results in a negative reward. The model is trained to respond in a manner that increases the positive reward using reinforcement learning.

3 Methods

We propose a novel empathetic, multimodal agent (Emma) that responds to a person based on their emotions. Our contributions include: creating a dialogue dataset using ChatGPT paired with facial expressions; training Llama2 on this multimodal dataset by combining image features and text, using reinforcement learning; and conducting a survey to compare our model with ChatGPT and performing an HRI study with the Pepper robot.

3.1 Creating the Dataset

We create a dataset of 5600 dialogues using ChatGPT-3.5 Turbo, paired with facial expression images from the KDEF dataset [20]. The prompt that we use for ChatGPT-3.5 Turbo is as follows: "Create a three-line dialogue between two people [SITUATION] such that the expression of the first person changes from [EMOTION 1] to [EMOTION 2] and what the second person says makes the first person feel [EMOTION 2]". We consider 20 emotion combinations (see Table 1), including the seven basic emotions (sad, happy, angry, afraid, neutral, surprise, and disgust). For strong negative emotions like anger and disgust, a positive change is considered if the emotion shifts to neutral. The KDEF dataset includes facial expressions from 70 people (35 male, 35 female), repeated in various scenarios (none, at work, in school, at a ski resort, while traveling, in a hospital, in a coffee shop, at the gym, at a party, in a restaurant, at a park, at the beach, at a concert, at a wedding, at a supermarket, at a museum, at a sports event, at a movie theater) for diversity.

3.2 Finetuning Llama2

The model follows a three-step training procedure. First, Llama2 is finetuned on the empathetic dialogue dataset $\mathcal{D}$ that we create. The dataset $\mathcal{D}$ consists of

Table 1. ChatGPT-3.5 turbo was prompted to "Create a three-line dialogue between two people such that the expression of the first person changes from [EMOTION 1] to [EMOTION 2] and what the second person says makes the first person feel [EMOTION 2]" to build our empathetic dialogue dataset. The following combinations of EMOTION 1 and EMOTION 2 were considered.

Emotion 1	Emotion 2	Change in Emotions
sad	happy	positive
happy	sad	negative
sad	angry	negative
angry	neutral	positive
sad	neutral	positive
neutral	sad	negative
neutral	angry	negative
neutral	happy	positive
sad	surprise	positive
surprise	sad	negative
neutral	afraid	negative
afraid	neutral	positive
neutral	disgust	negative
disgust	neutral	positive
happy	neutral	negative
surprise	happy	positive
happy	angry	negative
angry	happy	positive
happy	happy	positive
sad	sad	negative

a facial expression image $\mathcal{I}$, input of human text $\mathcal{T}$ and ground truth response y. The Llama2 model takes the image of facial expression $\mathcal{I}$ and human text as input $\mathcal{T}$ to generate empathetic responses. The image $\mathcal{I}$ is fed to ResNet-152 [12] pre-trained on VGG-Face Dataset [5] to extract the facial features. These facial features are then passed through a linear layer and converted to embeddings. We concatenate the image embeddings with the token embeddings of the language part to make Llama2 multimodal. We also prepend the ground truth facial expression label $\mathcal{E}$ as a word to the language part. This concatenation of the embeddings is sent to the Llama2 model as input. Formally,

$$\hat{y} = \text{Llama2}\left(\left[\underbrace{\mathcal{I}}_{\text{Image}}, \underbrace{\mathcal{E}}_{\text{Emotion}}, \underbrace{\mathcal{T}}_{\text{Human Text}}, \text{BOS}, \underbrace{i_1, .., i_m}_{\text{Instruction}}, \text{EOS}\right]\right) \quad (1)$$

where $\mathcal{I}$ denotes the set of visual features for the facial expression image, $\mathcal{E}$ indicates the ground truth emotion label, $\mathcal{T}$ denote the human text input tokens, BOS and EOS are begin of string and end of string tokens respectively. Consequently, $(i_1, ..., i_m)$ denotes the tokens that correspond to the response.

Llama2 is then finetuned to generate the response given in the dataset for a given query and facial expression in a supervised manner. For testing, the

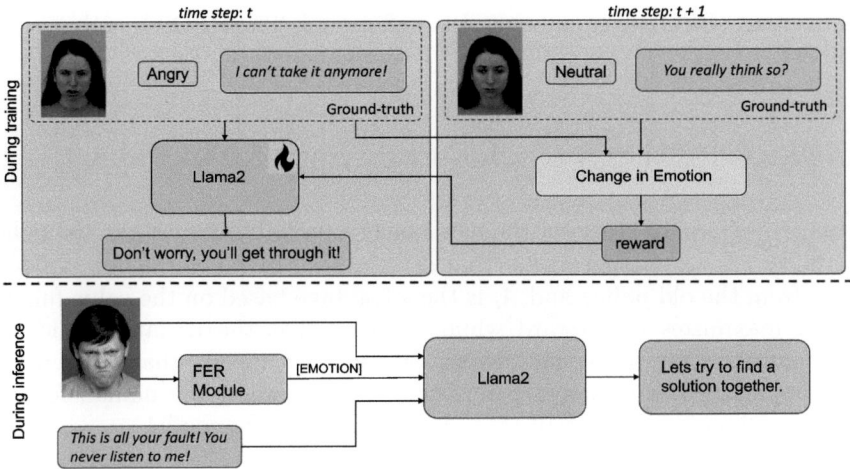

Fig. 2. The training process involves feeding facial features, the person's facial expression label, and the text input into the Llama2 model, which generates a response. If the person's emotion becomes positive after hearing the response, the agent receives a positive reward; otherwise, it gets a negative reward. This reward is back-propagated through the model, teaching it to generate responses that make the human feel positive.

weights of the decoder remain fixed, and the responses are predicted in forward passes for a given facial expression and a textual prompt until it reaches the EoS token.

The reward model is designed to evaluate the quality of responses generated by the LLM by assessing their emotional impact on the human user. It predicts a reward score based on the human emotional response to the LLM's output. The reward is based on the change in the user's emotion before and after the response. If the human feels positive compared to before, it gets a reward r of $+1$. Otherwise, it gets a reward r of -1. As a second step, we finetune the reward model to be able to output the reward based on the emotion the human would feel as a result of what the agent said. The column that contains the "change in emotion" in Table 1 is used to indicate the ground-truth positive reward or the negative reward during the finetuning of the reward model which is a model for sequence classification. Formally,

$$\hat{r} = \texttt{OpenLlama}\left(\left[\underbrace{\mathcal{I}}_{\text{Image}}, \underbrace{\mathcal{E}}_{\text{Emotion}}, \underbrace{\mathcal{T}}_{\text{Human Text}}, \underbrace{\mathcal{R}}_{\text{Response}}, \underbrace{r}_{\text{Reward}}\right]\right) \quad (2)$$

where $\mathcal{I}$ denotes the set of visual features for the facial expression image, $\mathcal{E}$ indicates the ground truth emotion label, $\mathcal{T}$ denote the human text input tokens, $\mathcal{R}$ is the agent response. Consequently, r is the reward to the agent's response.

As the final step, we use the finetuned Llama2 model and the trained reward model to output the reward to the generated response and use Proximal Policy

Optimization (PPO) to update the Llama2 model. The PPO objective is given as follows:

$$\mathcal{L}(\theta) = \hat{\mathbb{E}}_t \left[min \left(\frac{\pi_\theta(a_t|s_t)}{\pi_{old}(a_t|s_t)} \hat{A}_t, clip \left(\frac{\pi_\theta(a_t|s_t)}{\pi_{old}(a_t|s_t)}, 1 - \epsilon, 1 + \epsilon \right) \hat{A}_t \right) \right] \quad (3)$$

where $\frac{\pi_\theta(a_t|s_t)}{\pi_{old}(a_t|s_t)}$ is the ratio of the new policy's probability over the old policy's probability, ϵ is a hyperparameter that determines how much the new policy can deviate from the old policy and $\hat{A}_t$ is the advantage based on the value function.

PPO maximizes the reward while ensuring that the updated policy does not deviate too far from the current policy. This means that the proposed model implicitly learns to generate responses that make the human feel positive. Figure 2 shows the overall training procedure of the model.

3.3 HRI Experiment

The robot and a camera with a built-in microphone are connected to a computer. The camera, placed diagonally between the robot and human, captures facial expressions while the microphone records speech. Speech is transcribed using Whisper [30], and facial features are extracted with ResNet-152 [12] pre-trained on VGG-Face [5]. Emotions are recognized using the FIXR [22] FER module, trained on diverse datasets and enhanced with dark experience replay [4]. The facial features, transcribed text, and detected emotion are then fed into our model, which generates a response spoken by the Pepper robot.

4 Experimental Results

For the first step of training, i.e., to finetune the Llama2 model in a supervised manner, we used the AdamW [19] optimizer with a learning rate of $0.2e-4$. The training batch size is three. We finetune the model using LoRA. For finetuning of the reward model, we used the AdamW optimizer with a learning rate of $0.2e-5$. Finally, for PPO, we used Adam Optimizer with a learning rate of $0.2e-7$. The total time taken to finetune the model is 44 hours on a single NVIDIA RTX6000 GPU.

4.1 Qualitative Samples

In this section, we provide some responses as qualitative samples we evaluated on the FACES dataset [9]. Figure 3 shows a sample prompt and corresponding response to fear emotion. The lady in the picture says she has stage-fright and cannot speak in front of all the people. In response to this prompt and facial expression, while ChatGPT-4o gave a long response covering several tips on how to overcome nervousness before speaking in public, Emma replied that it would be there to help her. We also provide other qualitative examples covering various emotions in Table 2.

Table 2. We provide sample inputs prompts and their corresponding outputs using ChatGPT and Emma.

Emotion	Input Prompt	ChatGPT	Emma
angry	I am sick and tired of this job. I can't take it anymore.	I'm sorry to hear that you're feeling this way. It's important to prioritize your mental health and well-being. Consider reaching out to someone you trust or a mental health professional for support. Reflecting on what changes you'd like to see or exploring new opportunities might also help. You deserve to feel good about your work.	I understand how you feel, but remember why you started this journey for a reason.
disgust	There is so much filth in this room. I can't stand it.	It looks like the person in the image is showing a strong reaction, possibly disgust. If you're in a situation with a messy room, maybe consider tidying up bit by bit to make it more comfortable. Would you like some organization tips?	I heard they found a way to clean it all up.
happy	I got a gold medal for getting the first place in mathematics olympiad.	Congratulations on winning the gold medal in the mathematics olympiad! That's an incredible achievement. You must be very proud of your hard work and dedication. Keep up the great work!	Oh, that's great! Congratulations on your victory.
neutral	I am not good at cooking.	That's okay! Cooking is a skill that takes practice. Here are some tips that might help you improve: 1. Start Simple: Begin with easy recipes that have a few ingredients. 2. Follow Recipes: Pay close attention to instructions and measurements. 3. Learn Basic Skills: Practice chopping, sautéing, and boiling. 4. Use Fresh Ingredients: Fresh ingredients can improve the flavor of your dishes. 5. Taste as You Go: Adjust seasonings as needed. 6. Stay Organized: Prepare and measure ingredients before you start cooking. 7. Ask for Help: Don't hesitate to ask friends or family for advice. Would you like some simple recipe ideas to get you started?	Well, maybe you can try making something simple like grilled cheese.

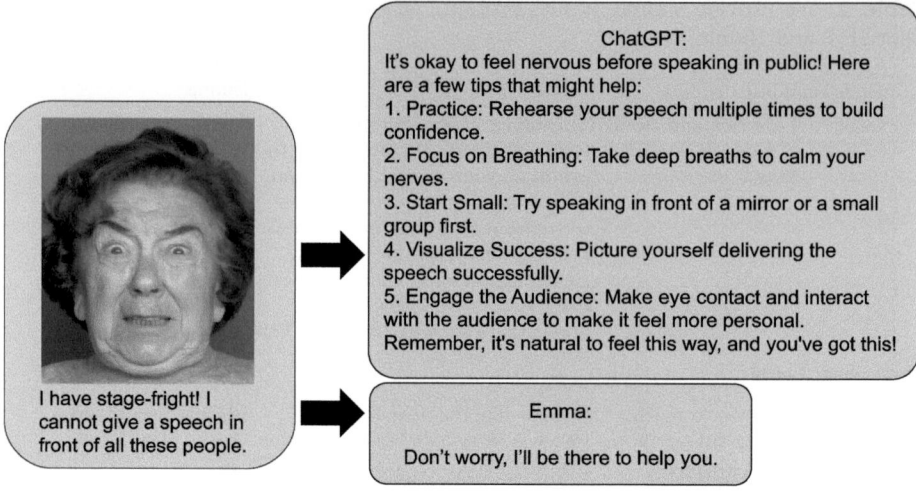

Fig. 3. We provide a qualitative sample where the prompts consist of a fearful emotion.

4.2 Survey Results of Comparison of Emma with ChatGPT-4o

To evaluate the performance of our model, a survey is conducted with 17 prompts and their corresponding responses, with varying emotions. For each prompt, we gather two corresponding responses; the first response is generated by our model, and the other response is generated by ChatGPT-4o. For each prompt-response pair, participants are asked to rate on a five-point Likert scale [24] to what degree they agree that the responses are appropriate, empathetic, and human-like. The responses ranged from strongly disagree (1) to strongly agree (5). There was also an option to respond in free text if both responses were not empathetic, according to the participants.

The survey results containing 17 prompts and their corresponding responses generated by Emma and those generated by ChatGPT were compared using the paired-samples T-test. 20 participants took the survey, of which 75% were male and 25% were female. The majority of the participants were students aged between 26 and 35 years, with limited or no prior experience with robots. For the first question, participants were asked to rate if they agreed that the responses generated by Emma and those generated by ChatGPT were appropriate. Figure 4(a) shows the comparison plot of the two models, Emma and ChatGPT, for this question. The t-value of Emma − ChatGPT was 1.992, and the p-value was 0.061. Moreover, the effect size was 0.65. The results given by our model were found to be appropriate compared to ChatGPT. As the p-value was $0.061 (> 0.05)$, the results are close to significance.

For the second question, participants were asked if they agreed that the responses generated by Emma and ChatGPT were empathetic. Figure 4(b) shows the comparison plot of the two models, Emma and ChatGPT, for this question.

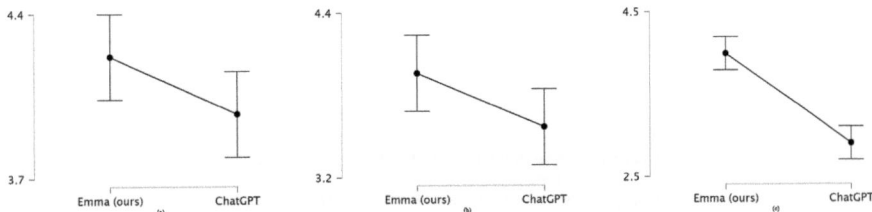

Fig. 4. Comparison of responses generated by Emma and those generated by ChatGPT using the paired-samples T-test. The appropriateness of the responses is measured in (a), and the empathetic nature of the responses is measured in (b), and (c) measures if the responses are human-like.

The t-value of Emma − ChatGPT was 2.099, the p-value was 0.049 and the effect size was 0.68. The results provided by our model were found to be empathetic compared to ChatGPT, and the results were statistically significant as the p-value was less than 0.05.

In the third question, participants were asked if they agreed that a human or friend was likely to give the same response as the robot. Figure 4(c) shows the comparison plot of the two models, Emma and ChatGPT, for this question. The t-value of Emma − ChatGPT was 8.048, the p-value was < 0.001 and the effect size was 2.61. The results given by our model were found to be more human-like compared to ChatGPT, and they were statistically significant.

4.3 HRI Experiment Evaluation

Pepper robot was used to carry out an HRI experiment. The experiment procedure was as follows.

- First, the participants sat on the chair that was diagonally in line with the robot and the camera that was on top of the table.
- In the HRI experiment, the robot starts with a greeting "Hi" and asks the human to share the happiest moment of their life first.
- When a human speaks, the speech is converted to text using Whisper [30]. Next, the converted text is fed to our model as input. After listening to the human response, the robot speaks the output of the model.
- Next, the robot asks the human to share something that makes them feel sad.
- After listening to what the human has to say, the robot responds in the same manner as before.
- Finally, we conclude the HRI experiment.

Subsequently, we conducted a short survey and asked the participants if the robot communicated appropriately with them and if the robot's response was empathetic. We measure these three questions on a Likert scale of one to five, where one is "strongly disagree" and five is "strongly agree". In the end, we asked the participants to answer in detail what they thought of the experiment overall.

Table 3. We measure the appropriateness of the answers given by our model. Here, the Likert scale (1) indicates that the participants strongly disagree that the responses are appropriate, and the Likert scale (5) indicates that the participants strongly agree that the responses are appropriate.

Likert Scale Values	1	2	3	4	5
H_0 (same as chance)	6	6	6	6	6
Observations	0	2	5	16	7

Table 4. We measure if the responses given by our model are empathetic or not. Here, the Likert scale (1) indicates that the participants strongly disagree that the responses are empathetic and the Likert scale (5) indicates that the participants strongly agree that the responses are empathetic.

Likert Scale Values	1	2	3	4	5
H_0 (same as chance)	6	6	6	6	6
Observations	0	2	8	13	7

The results of the HRI experiment survey are as follows. We conducted the survey with a total of 30 participants, of whom 23% were female and 77% were male. The majority of the participants were students aged between 26 and 35 years, with limited or no prior experience with robots. In the first question, we asked participants whether the robot responded appropriately to them. For each question, we recorded the frequency of responses on a Likert scale ranging from 1 (strongly disagree) to 5 (strongly agree) regarding the appropriateness of the robot's responses. We then performed a Chi-squared test using the contingency tables provided in Tables 3 and 4 as the basis for our analysis.

Our null hypothesis (H_0) assumed that the evaluations were distributed by chance. For measuring the appropriateness of the robot's responses, the Chi-squared statistic was calculated as 12.713, with a p-value of less than 0.013. The effect size was 0.65. Since the p-value was below the threshold of 0.05, the results were statistically significant. Similarly, to evaluate whether the participants perceived the robot's responses as empathetic, the Chi-squared statistic was found to be 10.941, with a p-value of less than 0.027. The effect size was 0.60. Again, the results were statistically significant as the p-value was below 0.05.

These findings indicate that the responses generated by our proposed approach were both appropriate and empathetic. Overall, the results demonstrate that participants were able to interact with the Pepper robot effectively and receive appropriate responses using our Emma model.

5 Discussion

When we create the dataset, we do not consider incongruent facial images and dialogue prompts. Instead, we always make sure that the facial expression matches the dialogue prompt. But in a real-life scenario, it could be that the human looks sad while sharing happy news or vice versa. For example, a person can look sad and say that they got a promotion. As this would mean that they would have to work longer hours or relocate themselves to another city or country, the news of being promoted may be considered bittersweet. In this case, the agent should also be able to understand that the news is bittersweet and motivate the person accordingly.

In the HRI experiment survey, in addition to answering questions on a Likert scale, we also asked participants what they thought about the experiment in general. This question was not mandatory, but could be answered in the text by all the participants. Some participants said that the experiment was interesting and that they enjoyed interacting with the robot. They said that the robot was empathetic and could understand them. Others were critical of the length of the experiment, which was short and difficult for them to show their true emotions in a given time. They also said that the responses given by the robot were short.

6 Conclusion and Future Work

We propose a computational model that interprets both facial expressions and speech to respond empathetically. The model is fine-tuned using reinforcement learning to generate positive responses. We present qualitative examples across emotional contexts and quantitatively evaluate the model using a survey with 17 emotion-based prompts, comparing its responses to ChatGPT-4o. A paired-samples t-test showed our model's replies were more empathetic and human-like.

We also conducted a Human-Robot Interaction (HRI) study where a robot asked participants to share happy and sad memories and then responded. A follow-up survey using a five-point Likert scale, analyzed via a chi-square test, confirmed that participants found the robot's responses appropriate and empathetic.

While the Pepper robot can gesture and speak, it lacks facial expression capabilities. Future work will explore integrating facial expressions, for example, smiling while saying "I'm happy for you", using expressive robots like Furhat [32].

Acknowledgement. We acknowledge the CINECA award under the ISCRA initiative, for the availability of high-performance computing resources. This work has been conducted with the support of the PNRR project "Fit for Medical Robotics (Fit4MedRob)" funded by the Italian Ministry of University and Research and the European project MINERVA, funded by European High-Performance Computing Joint Undertaking (JU) under grant agreement No 101182737. This work was also supported by the ERC Advanced project 'eTALK" (UKRI funded).

References

1. Alayrac, J.B., et al.: Flamingo: a visual language model for few-shot learning. In: Advances in Neural Information Processing Systems, vol. 35, pp. 23716–23736 (2022)

2. Bazzano, F., Lamberti, F.: Human-robot interfaces for interactive receptionist systems and wayfinding applications. Robotics **7**(3), 56 (2018)
3. Bordes, F., et al.: An introduction to vision-language modeling. arXiv preprint arXiv:2405.17247 (2024)
4. Buzzega, P., Boschini, M., Porrello, A., Abati, D., Calderara, S.: Dark experience for general continual learning: a strong, simple baseline. In: Advances in Neural Information Processing Systems, vol. 33, pp. 15920–15930 (2020)
5. Cao, Q., Shen, L., Xie, W., Parkhi, O.M., Zisserman, A.: VGGFace2: a dataset for recognising faces across pose and age. In: 2018 13th IEEE International Conference on Automatic Face & Gesture Recognition (FG 2018), pp. 67–74. IEEE (2018)
6. Castillo, J.C., Castro-González, Á., Alonso-Martín, F., Fernández-Caballero, A., Salichs, M.Á.: Emotion detection and regulation from personal assistant robot in smart environment. In: Personal Assistants: Emerging Computational Technologies, pp. 179–195 (2018)
7. Dong, J., Santiago-Anaya, A., Jeon, M.: Facial expressions increase emotion recognition clarity and improve warmth and attractiveness on a humanoid robot without adding the uncanny valley. In: Proceedings of the Human Factors and Ergonomics Society Annual Meeting, vol. 67, pp. 933–939. SAGE Publications Sage CA, Los Angeles (2023)
8. Donnermann, M., Schaper, P., Lugrin, B.: Social robots in applied settings: a long-term study on adaptive robotic tutors in higher education. Front. Robot. AI **9**, 831633 (2022)
9. Ebner, N.C., Riediger, M., Lindenberger, U.: Faces-a database of facial expressions in young, middle-aged, and older women and men: development and validation. Behav. Res. Methods **42**, 351–362 (2010)
10. Gunson, N., Garcia, D.H., Sieińska, W., Addlesee, A., Dondrup, C., Lemon, O., Part, J.L., Yu, Y.: A visually-aware conversational robot receptionist. In: Association for Computational Linguistics (ACL) (2022)
11. Häring, M., Bee, N., André, E.: Creation and evaluation of emotion expression with body movement, sound and eye color for humanoid robots. In: 2011 RO-MAN, pp. 204–209. IEEE (2011)
12. He, K., Zhang, X., Ren, S., Sun, J.: Deep residual learning for image recognition. In: Proceedings of the IEEE Conference on Computer Vision and Pattern Recognition, pp. 770–778 (2016)
13. Heredia, J., et al.: Adaptive multimodal emotion detection architecture for social robots. IEEE Access **10**, 20727–20744 (2022)
14. Hoffman, G., Zuckerman, O., Hirschberger, G., Luria, M., Shani Sherman, T.: Design and evaluation of a peripheral robotic conversation companion. In: Proceedings of the Tenth Annual ACM/IEEE International Conference on Human-Robot Interaction, pp. 3–10 (2015)
15. Kwon, G., Cai, Z., Ravichandran, A., Bas, E., Bhotika, R., Soatto, S.: Masked vision and language modeling for multi-modal representation learning. arXiv preprint arXiv:2208.02131 (2022)
16. Leite, I., Pereira, A., Mascarenhas, S., Martinho, C., Prada, R., Paiva, A.: The influence of empathy in human-robot relations. Int. J. Hum Comput Stud. **71**(3), 250–260 (2013)
17. Li, S., Deng, W.: Deep facial expression recognition: a survey. IEEE Trans. Affect. Comput. **13**(3), 1195–1215 (2020)
18. Liu, H., Li, C., Wu, Q., Lee, Y.J.: Visual instruction tuning. In: Advances in Neural Information Processing Systems, vol. 36 (2024)

19. Loshchilov, I., Hutter, F., et al.: Fixing weight decay regularization in ADAM. arXiv preprint arXiv:1711.05101 **5** (2017)
20. Lundqvist, D., Flykt, A., Öhman, A.: Karolinska directed emotional faces. PsycTESTS Dataset **91**, 630 (1998)
21. Maharjan, R.S., Rawal, N., Romeo, M., Baraldi, L., Cucchiara, R., Cangelosi, A.: Multimodal emotion recognition in conversation via possible speaker's audio and visual sequence selection. In: ICASSP 2025 - 2025 IEEE International Conference on Acoustics, Speech and Signal Processing (ICASSP), pp. 1–5 (2025). https://doi.org/10.1109/ICASSP49660.2025.10888172
22. Maharjan, R.S., Romeo, M., Cangelosi, A.: Faces are domains: domain incremental learning for expression recognition. In: 2023 International Joint Conference on Neural Networks (IJCNN), pp. 1–8. IEEE (2023)
23. Mehrabian, A.: Nonverbal Communication. Aldine-Atherton (1972)
24. Nemoto, T., Beglar, D.: Likert-scale questionnaires. In: JALT 2013 Conference Proceedings, vol. 108, pp. 1–6 (2014)
25. OpenAI: Chatgpt (2023). https://openai.com/index/chatgpt/
26. van Otterdijk, M., Laeng, B., Lindblom, D.S., Torresen, J.: The effect of expressive robot behavior on users' mental effort: a pupillometry study. IEEE Trans. Cogn. Develop. Syst. 16(2), 474–484 (2024)
27. Ouyang, L., et al.: Training language models to follow instructions with human feedback (2022). https://arxiv.org/abs/2203.02155
28. Pai, R.Y., Shetty, A., Dinesh, T.K., Shetty, A.D., Pillai, N.: Effectiveness of social robots as a tutoring and learning companion: a bibliometric analysis. Cogent Bus. Manag. **11**(1), 2299075 (2024)
29. Radford, A., et al.: Learning transferable visual models from natural language supervision. In: International Conference on Machine Learning, pp. 8748–8763. PMLR (2021)
30. Radford, A., Kim, J.W., Xu, T., Brockman, G., McLeavey, C., Sutskever, I.: Robust speech recognition via large-scale weak supervision. In: International Conference on Machine Learning, pp. 28492–28518. PMLR (2023)
31. Radford, A., Narasimhan, K., Salimans, T., Sutskever, I., et al.: Improving language understanding by generative pre-training. OpenAI (2018)
32. Rawal, N., Koert, D., Turan, C., Kersting, K., Peters, J., Stock-Homburg, R.: ExGenNet: learning to generate robotic facial expression using facial expression recognition. Front. Robot. AI **8**, 730317 (2022)
33. Rawal, N., Maharjan, R.S., Romeo, M., Bigazzi, R., Baraldi, L., Cucchiara, R., Cangelosi, A.: Intelligent multimodal artificial agents that talk and express emotions. In: International Workshop on Human-Friendly Robotics, pp. 240–254. Springer, Cham (2024). https://doi.org/10.1007/978-3-031-81688-8_18
34. Rawal, N., Stock-Homburg, R.M.: Facial emotion expressions in human-robot interaction: a survey. Int. J. Soc. Robot. **14**(7), 1583–1604 (2022)
35. Rawal, N., Xia, M., Tessaro, D., Baraldi, L., Cucchiara, R., et al.: MATE: multimodal agents that talk and empathize. In: Proceedings of the 23rd International Conference on Image Analysis and Processing (2025)
36. Rombach, R., Blattmann, A., Lorenz, D., Esser, P., Ommer, B.: High-resolution image synthesis with latent diffusion models. In: Proceedings of the IEEE/CVF Conference on Computer Vision and Pattern Recognition, pp. 10684–10695 (2022)
37. Saharia, C., et al.: Photorealistic text-to-image diffusion models with deep language understanding. In: Advances in Neural Information Processing Systems, vol. 35, pp. 36479–36494 (2022)

38. Salem, M., Kopp, S., Wachsmuth, I., Rohlfing, K., Joublin, F.: Generation and evaluation of communicative robot gesture. Int. J. Soc. Robot. **4**, 201–217 (2012)
39. Sawik, B., et al.: Robots for elderly care: review, multi-criteria optimization model and qualitative case study. Healthcare **11**, 1286 (2023)
40. Singer, U., et al.: Make-a-video: text-to-video generation without text-video data. arXiv preprint arXiv:2209.14792 (2022)
41. Stiennon, N., et al.: Learning to summarize with human feedback. In: Advances in Neural Information Processing Systems, vol. 33, pp. 3008–3021 (2020)
42. Tapaswi, M., Zhu, Y., Stiefelhagen, R., Torralba, A., Urtasun, R., Fidler, S.: MovieQA: understanding stories in movies through question-answering. In: Proceedings of the IEEE Conference on Computer Vision and Pattern Recognition, pp. 4631–4640 (2016)
43. Team, C.: Chameleon: mixed-modal early-fusion foundation models. arXiv preprint arXiv:2405.09818 (2024)
44. Touvron, H., et al.: LLaMA: open and efficient foundation language models. arXiv preprint arXiv:2302.13971 (2023)
45. Touvron, H., et al.: LLaMA 2: open foundation and fine-tuned chat models. arXiv preprint arXiv:2307.09288 (2023)
46. Tsimpoukelli, M., Menick, J.L., Cabi, S., Eslami, S., Vinyals, O., Hill, F.: Multimodal few-shot learning with frozen language models. In: Advances in Neural Information Processing Systems, vol. 34, pp. 200–212 (2021)
47. Tsiourti, C., Weiss, A., Wac, K., Vincze, M.: Multimodal integration of emotional signals from voice, body, and context: effects of (In) congruence on emotion recognition and attitudes towards robots. Int. J. Soc. Robot. **11**, 555–573 (2019)
48. Vaswani, A., et al.: Attention is all you need. In: Advances in Neural Information Processing Systems, vol. 30 (2017)
49. Vercelli, A., Rainero, I., Ciferri, L., Boido, M., Pirri, F.: Robots in elderly care. DigitCult-Sci. J. Digital Cult. **2**(2), 37–50 (2018)
50. Xu, R., Xiong, C., Chen, W., Corso, J.: Jointly modeling deep video and compositional text to bridge vision and language in a unified framework. In: Proceedings of the AAAI Conference on Artificial Intelligence, vol. 29 (2015)
51. Yang, D., Sato, W., Liu, Q., Minato, T., Namba, S., Nishida, S.: Optimizing facial expressions of an android robot effectively: a Bayesian optimization approach. In: 2022 IEEE-RAS 21st International Conference on Humanoid Robots (Humanoids), pp. 542–549. IEEE (2022)
52. Yenamandra, S., et al.: Homerobot: open vocab mobile manipulation (2023). https://aihabitat.org/static/challenge/home_robot_ovmm_2023/OVMM.pdf
53. Youssef, K., Said, S., Alkork, S., Beyrouthy, T.: A survey on recent advances in social robotics. Robotics **11**(4), 75 (2022)
54. Yu, J., Wang, Z., Vasudevan, V., Yeung, L., Seyedhosseini, M., Wu, Y.: CoCa: contrastive captioners are image-text foundation models. arXiv preprint arXiv:2205.01917 (2022)
55. Yu, L., et al.: Scaling autoregressive multi-modal models: pretraining and instruction tuning. arXiv preprint arXiv:2309.02591 **2**(3) (2023)
56. Zhu, D., Chen, J., Shen, X., Li, X., Elhoseiny, M.: MiniGPT-4: enhancing vision-language understanding with advanced large language models. arXiv preprint arXiv:2304.10592 (2023)

Emotivation in Human-Robot Interaction for Affective Behavioral Adaptation

Lorenzo D'Errico[1]($\boxtimes$)[iD], Renato Esposito[3], Marco Matarese[2][iD], Vincenzo Mele[3], Alfredo Mungari[3], Martina Roscica[3], and Mariacarla Staffa[3][iD]

[1] University of Naples Federico II, Naples, Italy
`lorenzo.derrico@unina.it`
[2] Italian Institute of Technology, Genoa, Italy
`marco.matarese@iit.it`
[3] University of Naples Parthenope, Naples, Italy
`mariacarla.staffa@uniparthenope.it`

Abstract. This study explores the concept of emotivation in human-robot interaction, defined as the interplay between emotional perception and motivational drive, both in guiding the robot's behavior and in promoting the user's transition toward a more positive emotional state. Within this framework, we present a humanoid robotic system designed not only to recognize human emotions but also to act upon them with the goal of human emotional uplift and sustained well-being. The system integrates multimodal data (EEG signals from an Empatica EPOC X helmet and audio-visual input from the robot) processed through two deep learning models: a hybrid-fusion classifier for facial and vocal expressions, and a Feature-Based Convolutional Neural Network (FBCNN) for EEG data. A meta-model combines its outputs to classify emotional states into four categories: neutral, happy, angry, and sad. Crucially, this work focuses on defining which robot behaviors can be considered emotively motivated — that is, capable of responding meaningfully to the user's current emotional state while also being motivated by the goal of shifting negative emotions toward positive ones, and sustaining those positive states over time. The robot dynamically selects behavioral responses such as engagement, encouragement, and affective reinforcement, based on the emotional context. Results demonstrate the effectiveness of the emotivational framework in promoting positive emotional transitions, highlighting the importance of emotional sensitivity and motivational purpose in fostering empathic, emotionally supportive human-robot relationships. Future work will further develop adaptive strategies to enhance emotional resilience and companionship through long-term interactions.

Keywords: Emotivation in Human-Robot Interaction · Multimodal emotion classifier · Emotional intelligence

1 Introduction

In the evolving field of Human-Robot Interaction (HRI), the interplay between emotion and action has become a focal point of research, giving rise to new conceptual frameworks for understanding emotionally intelligent machines. One such emerging concept is emotivation—a term that encapsulates the dual role of emotion in robotic behavior: as both an internal driver that motivates the robot's actions, and as an external goal, aimed at improving or sustaining the user's positive emotional state. In this view, a robot is not only reactive to human emotions, but also intrinsically "motivated" to foster emotional well-being, becoming an active participant in the user's affective journey. Emotivation is especially relevant in socially assistive robotics, where the capacity to modulate and respond to emotional states is essential for building meaningful, human-centered interactions. Emotions are not passive signals in this context; they act as cues that guide the robot's behavior, while simultaneously representing targets that the robot seeks to influence. This emotiveâĂŞmotivational loop introduces a new layer of relational dynamics in HRI, transforming robots from tools into emotionally responsive companions. In recent years, artificial intelligence and robotics have expanded rapidly, encompassing not only functional tasks but also complex roles involving psychological and social support [8]. A key advancement in this domain is the development of social robots, autonomous or semi-autonomous agents designed to interact with humans through socially aware behaviors and context-sensitive communication [19]. Their widespread adoption is due to their ability to assist people in diverse areas, including education, elderly care, and mental health support. In therapeutic environments, for instance, social robots have shown promise as tools for engaging individuals with autism spectrum disorder, social anxiety, or cognitive impairments [14]. These systems have demonstrated effectiveness in various therapeutic and supportive contexts [5,13], facilitating social interaction, enhancing communication, and reducing emotional distress in diverse populations. Social robots can provide consistent, non-judgmental, and emotionally adaptive interactions that complement traditional therapeutic approaches and support emotional well-being across different user groups [11]. Integrating emotional intelligence into these robotic systems marks a critical shift from purely task-oriented automation to affective, human-centric design. Recent works have explored how robots can recognize [1], express, and react to human emotions using various input modalities such as facial expressions, vocal tone, body language, and physiological signals. In particular, several studies have demonstrated the feasibility and effectiveness of emotion recognition from physiological data such as EEG, highlighting the potential of these signals as reliable indicators of affective states [16,17]. Moreover, the ability of robots to display appropriate emotional expressions—via facial movements, body posture, or voice modulation—has been shown to significantly enhance the quality of social interaction [18]. However, beyond recognition and expression, the adaptive use of emotion-driven behavior remains an area to be explored. This study builds upon this foundation by introducing a humanoid robotic system—Pepper—that embodies the principles of emotivation. The robot has a multimodal emotion recognition architecture that combines EEG data with audio-visual analysis. Using a hybrid-fusion audio-video classifier and a feature-based CNN for EEG signals, the system identifies the user's emotional state, categorizing it into one of four classes: neutral, happy, angry, or sad. Once the emotional state is detected, the robot adapts its behavior accordingly, proposing personalized actions (i.e., playful gestures, light conversation, music, or encouragement) designed to uplift the user's mood or sustain a positive emotional state over time and reduce unpleasant emotions [21]. Through this emotivational lens, the robot's actions are responsive and purpose-driven: it seeks to guide the user away from negative affective states and support emotional continuity and stability. The goal is to explore how emotionally intelligent, socially interactive robots can serve as companions, contributing to human emotional regulation and well-being. The implications of such systems are far-reaching, extending to clinical therapy, eldercare, educational environments, and everyday companionship. By rethinking robotic behavior as both emotionally informed and emotionally motivated, this research opens new directions for affective human-robot interaction.

2 Proposed Method

This study leverages a multi-modal emotion recognition architecture to implement and evaluate the emotivational interaction framework. While the primary focus is on the behavioral adaptation component and its effectiveness in promoting positive emotional transitions, we provide here an overview of the emotion recognition system architecture and its baseline performance to establish the reliability of the classification foundation upon which the emotivational behaviors operate. Subsequently, we aimed to assess whether Pepper's adaptive responses effectively reinforce positive moods during short interaction sessions lasting approximately 5 to 15 min. Our goal was to create an engaging and pleasantly adaptive experience [1] that reacts to the user's emotional state after the classification stage. To evaluate the effectiveness of Pepper interaction, we monitored the user's mood progression and tracked any emotional development by analyzing both overt participants' behavior via audio-video recordings and cortical activity (through an EEG Emotiv EPOC X headset) during short time windows during the interaction with the robot. This procedure allows us to keep track of potential emotional shifts within that time window and quantify the impact of the robot on users. By continuous analysis throughout the session, we expect to observe a tendency towards more positive states as the session progresses, with positive mood reinforcement and mitigation of negative states towards positive states in mid-to-late interactions. The experiment was carried out at the University of Naples "Parthenope" with 20 participants, aged between 20 and 30 (mean 25.11, st-dev. 2.19), of both genders (65% M, 35% F), who voluntarily participated in the study after signing informed consent on data processing and study objectives. Our proposed approach is based on the integration of two key components that work together to build an adaptive and interactive user interaction system.

2.1 Cascade Multi-modal Emotion Recognition Leveraging Audio-Video and EEG Signals

In this study, we developed a multi-modal emotion recognition approach that integrates audio, video, and EEG data to improve classification accuracy. By combining verbal, non-verbal, and physiological signals, the system enables a more accurate understanding of human emotions and supports personalization in HRI. The framework adopts a stacking ensemble method [6,20], merging predictions from modality-specific classifiers. It includes three main components: i) an Audio-Video Emotion Classification Model, which uses a transformer-based architecture with a late fusion strategy, ii) an EEG Emotion Classification Model, based on the FBCNN framework for spatial-temporal feature extraction, and iii) a Meta-Model we developed, which integrates the two outputs via logistic regression stacking. We hypothesize that final predictions can leverage the complementary strengths of each modality for enhanced emotion recognition.

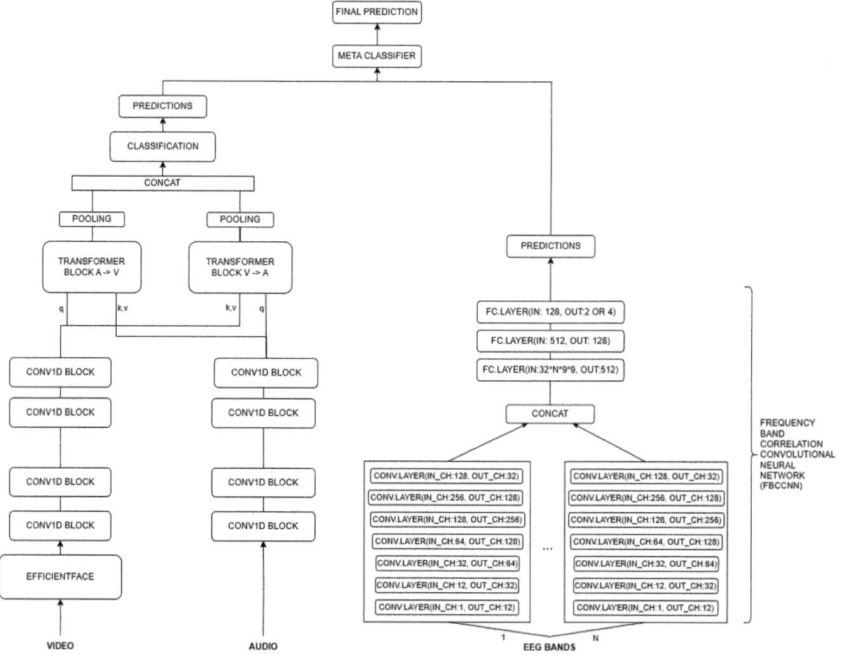

Fig. 1. Cascade Multi-Modal Model for Emotion Recognition

- *Transformers-based Audio-Video Classifier.* The model used in this study builds on the approach in [23] to process audio and video data. It adopts the fusion strategies from [3], exploring early, hybrid, and late fusion to combine complementary features. The architecture includes modality-specific feature extraction, a transformer-based co-attention mechanism, and a classification

head applied to the concatenated multi-modal representations [2]. In the context of this work, the original model has been adopted with modifications, employing a late fusion strategy for cross-modal integration.
- *FBCNN-based EEG Classifier.* For EEG-based emotion recognition, the model follows the FBCNN framework proposed in [9], which applies spatial and temporal filtering via convolutional banks and EEG-specific pre-processing steps. Originally developed to classify emotions from EEG signals, FBCNN uses convolutional neural networks (CNNs) to extract discriminative emotional features.
- *Meta-model modalities merging.* The meta-model receives as input the emotion likelihoods predicted by the Audio-Video and FBCNN models, forming the basis for the stacking ensemble method [10]. Namely, it combines predictions from the Audio-Video and FBCNN classifiers, using logistic regression, learning optimal weights to produce the most accurate classification from both modalities to produce the final emotion category (neutral, happy, angry, or sad). Figure 1 illustrates the entire architecture, integrating both the audio-video and EEG models, where a clear distinction between input features and meta-features is created through the stacking ensemble method. The model was trained on separate datasets for audio-video and EEG modalities, with each model trained independently to optimize modality-specific features. Predictions were synchronized during meta-model training to ensure label alignment. For Audio-Video pre-training, we used the RAVDESS dataset [7], splitting its 2880 samples into 70:15:15 for train/val/test. Emotions were mapped to four classes (happy, sad, angry, and neutral) based on the Russell Circumplex Model of Affect [12]. For EEG-based classification, we used SEED-IV [24], including EEG recordings from 15 subjects during emotion elicitation. The original 1080 recordings were segmented into 800-sample sequences, resulting in 37.575 samples, and split 80:10:10. SEED-IV labels were mapped to four classes to align with RAVDESS: Neutral and Calm to Neutral, Happy and Surprised to Happy, and Angry, Fearful, Disgusted to Angry.

Model Performance Overview. The emotion recognition models employed in this study integrate established architectures for audio-video and EEG-based classification. Table 1 presents the performance metrics obtained during training on standard datasets (RAVDESS for audio-video and SEED-IV for EEG). The meta-model, which combines predictions from both modalities, achieves a notable accuracy of 91.45%, demonstrating the effectiveness of the multi-modal fusion approach for emotion classification. While these results indicate reliable performance for the emotion recognition component, the primary focus of this study is on the emotivational interaction paradigm rather than comprehensive model validation. Future work will provide in-depth analysis of model robustness, cross-validation performance, and detailed error analysis. Here, we concentrate on evaluating how the robot's adaptive behavioral responses effectively promote positive emotional transitions based on the classified emotional states.

Table 1. Average accuracy and loss values of the audio-video and EEG models at the 100th epoch.

Model	Dataset	Loss	Acc.
Audio-Video	RAVDESS	0.8860	0.7708
FBCCNN	SEED-IV	0.7075	0.8067
Meta model	Meta-features	0.2915	0.9145

2.2 Emotive Interaction Pepper

Pepper adapted its behavior according to the emotional state detected by the multi-modal classifier. We designed four predefined effective responses triggered by the recognition of the emotion. These responses include verbal and non-verbal actions, such as changes in body posture and physical gestures. Depending on the model output, each behavior is crafted to comfort, amuse, or support the users, according to their emotional needs. Pepper's behavior is aligned with the user's current mood, creating a pleasant but straightforward interaction and providing a natural and personalized activity. Table 2 summarizes the behaviors exhibited by Pepper in response to the four detectable human emotions.

Table 2. Pepper Interactive Response to users' emotional state.

Emotion Detected	Appearance	Robot interactive Emotional Response
Neutral		**Neutral**: Trivia quiz based on 50+ random questions dataset. Interaction via tablet to read and select options. Mentally engaging experience for adults of any age.
Happy		**Music**: Fun physical interaction through music and dance [4]. User can choose among three music genres—Rock, Classical, and Techno—each. Pepper teaches moves to the user. This activity encourages amusement through auditory and physical engagement as proposed by the robot Maggie[15].
Sad		**Joke**: Pepper uses humor to improve the user's mood by telling a randomly selected joke from a collection of 50+. This interaction provides a light-hearted distraction from negative feelings [22].
Angry		**Meditation**: Pepper offers a guided meditation session [21], including breath control exercise (4-2-6 method). Longer meditation includes stretching and soothing natural sounds. Research supports meditation as an effective tool for anger management.

3 Experiment

Figure 2 provides an overview of the experimental procedure, which involves the use of two separate devices rather than a single system, due to specific system requirements and deployment constraints. Although the process is described in the context of a multi-device setup, it is also compatible with a single-device configuration, provided that data transfer between devices is omitted. The necessity for a multi-device setup arises from the incompatibility of the operating systems required to control the two distinct helmet devices—one for EEG acquisition and the other for robot control. As a result, the control applications for each device were run on separate notebooks, which were interconnected using the SCP (Secure Copy Protocol) to enable communication and data exchange during the experiment.

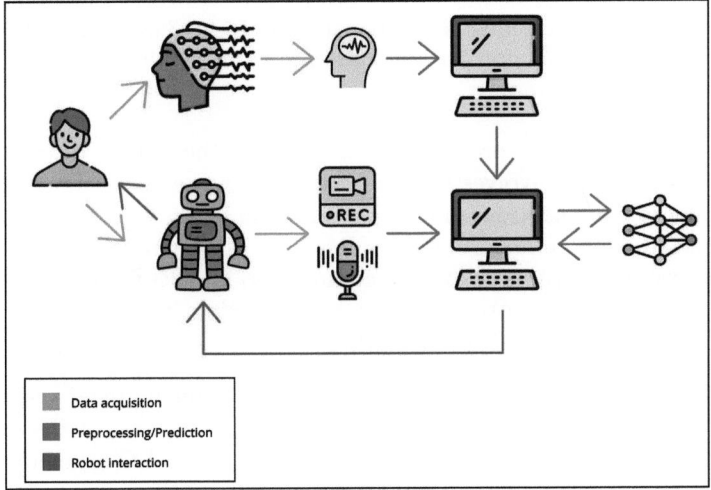

Fig. 2. The workflow of the study. Green arrows represent data acquisitions: audio/video and EEG. Red arrows represent the pre-processing and prediction of the model. Blue arrows represent human-robot interactions. (Color figure online)

Overall, the experiments provided the following steps:

1. **Devices connection:** The main device must be connected to Pepper and the headset at the beginning of the procedure, and the multi-modal model must be pre-trained and locally placed.
2. **Pre-interaction Classification:** The initial classification step needs the following sequence of actions:
   (a) Acquisition of brainwave data from the EEG helmet and audio/video from Pepper sensors.
   (b) Pre-process EEG and audio-video according to allowed formats.

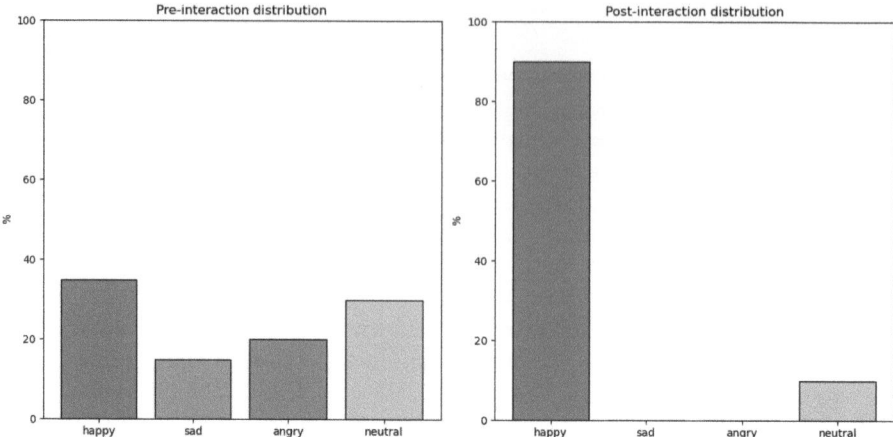

Fig. 3. Distribution of participants' emotional states (according to the ML model outlined in Sect. 2) before and after having interacted with the robot.

    (c) Prediction with pre-processed data. Receive the output of the emotion.
3. **Pepper response:** Involves Pepper performing a specific set of actions, based on emotional classification and vocal command of the user.
4. **Post-interaction Classification:** Re-assesses the user's emotional state after the robot interaction. A new audio-video and EEG acquisition started to analyze potential emotional changes, comparing it with the initial one to evaluate the effectiveness of our method.

The interaction starts with the robot briefly introducing itself and asking the user about their day; subsequently, an initial 3-second video of the participant was recorded while simultaneously acquiring a 3-second EEG segment. The data collected was passed as input to the FBCNN model, which predicted an emotion as a probability distribution across the 4 possible emotional states. Finally, Pepper adapted its behavior according to the user's mood, thus on the model output. The duration of each session was variable, depending on participants' behaviors (i.e., chosen activities in case there were any, and mood), and the robot's reaction. Throughout the session, the participants were continuously monitored, and at the end of the interactive session, all acquired data were synchronized, paired, and processed. The processing stage involved the segmentation of both EEG and audio-video recordings into 3 s slices with no overlapping. Temporal slices where the subject's face was not properly framed were discarded to ensure the integrity of the classification process. Once the paired slices were finalized, the classification was performed, and a detailed session report was generated. This report included all emotion predictions across the temporal slices from the beginning to the end of the interaction, allowing for the assessment of emotional evolution over time.

4 Results and Discussion

Our experiments focused on participants' emotional state changes during the interaction with the robot caused by its behavior, which was selected depending on participants' initial emotional state. First, we analyzed the distribution of participants' emotions before and after having interacted with Pepper. As shown in Fig. 3, we found a noticeable improvement and reinforcement of positive emotions after interacting with the robot. Negative emotions shifted towards neutral or happy states, highlighting that most users initially classified with negative emotions show a significant reduction post-interaction, increasing happiness and neutrality. Once established that the robot's behavior positively changed participants' emotional states, we investigated the trend of the happy emotion (as classified by our model, Sect. 2) since it is the target emotion we aimed to reach through Pepper's behavior. Figure 4 shows the probability that the model attributed to the happy emotion throughout the interaction, divided by the robot's behaviors. Specifically, we can appreciate the trend of such emotion concerning Pepper making jokes, playing music, and proposing relaxing activities (see Table 2 for the starting emotion-robot behavior mapping). As we can see, the probability of classifying participants' emotional state as happy grew over time, but different behaviors grew faster than others. Particularly, we observe that, despite the three behaviors started from different initial probabilities, playing music resulted in the fastest way to put participants in a positive mood, followed by the relaxing activities, and finally by the jokes. However, since each behavior was triggered by a specific initial emotional state (and a free choice for

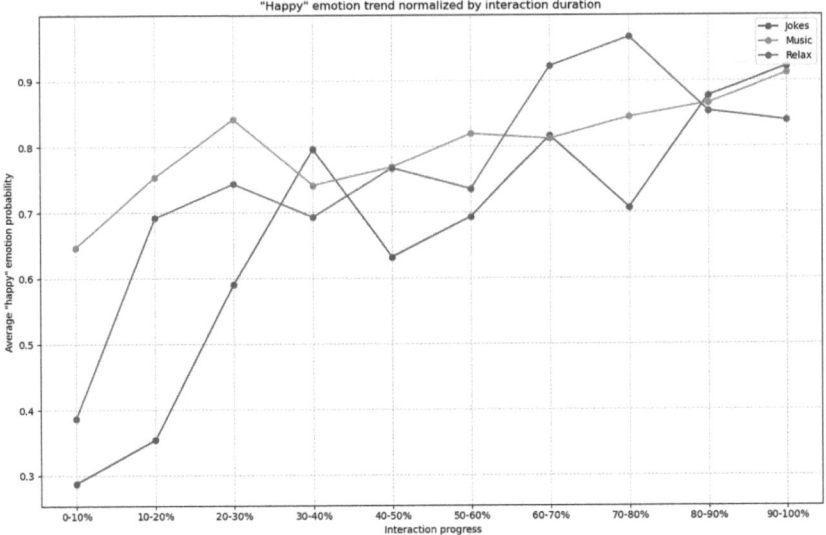

Fig. 4. Progression of the detected happy emotion throughout the interaction.

the neutral emotion), the starting conditions influenced the observed patterns. Indeed, this result can be easily explained by such starting conditions, thus by the difficulty of actually implementing the emotional change. For example, the robot told jokes when it classified participants' emotional states as sad; therefore, changing their emotional state from sad to happy was more difficult than changing it from angry to happy, where Pepper proposed relaxing activities. Music maintains high value, starting from already positive states. Relax shows a sharp initial rise, and Joke produces a slower but steady increase, suggesting a more gradual engagement. We can better appreciate the differences in emotional changing time provided by the different robots' behaviors in Fig. 5. Here, the values on the y-axis have to be interpreted as absolute times: the zero value means that the emotional change immediately happened, while the one value means that it never happened. As we can see, the playing music activity is the fastest because participants were already in a good mood (Fig. 4), followed by the relaxing, and finally by the jokes. Transitions from a sad state took longer than the other starting emotions, independently of Pepper's behavior. However, relaxing and playing music seem to get quick shifts from neutral and angry states. These results suggest that, while all behaviors contribute to emotional improvements, they do so with distinct temporal dynamics and magnitude. We also tracked the evolution of the participants' emotional states throughout the test. Figure 6 shows an average increase of the detected happy emotion, while the neutral emotion remains overall stationary, and the angry and sad ones rapidly decrease. The trends reveal a decrease in negative emotions, which tend to decline toward zero

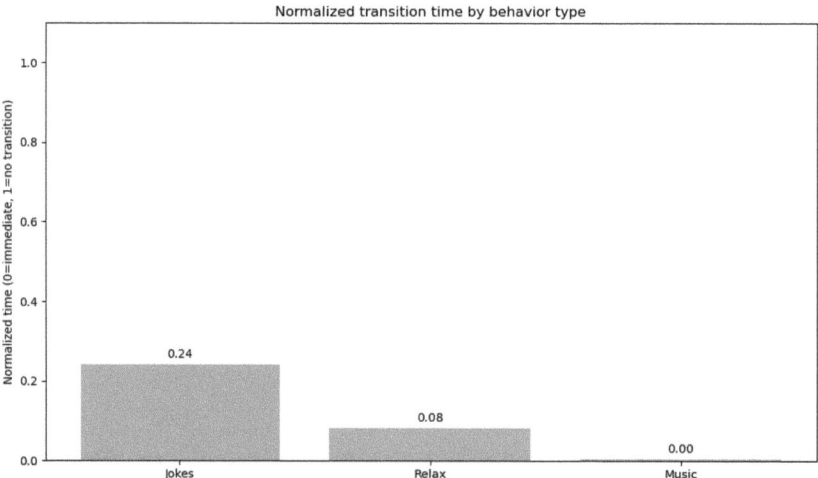

Fig. 5. Emotions transition time (from any to happy) divided by robot's behaviors (i.e., joke, meditation, music). We normalized the time variable (on the y-axis) in the range [0,1], so that the value zero means that the transition happened immediately, and the value one means that it never happened.

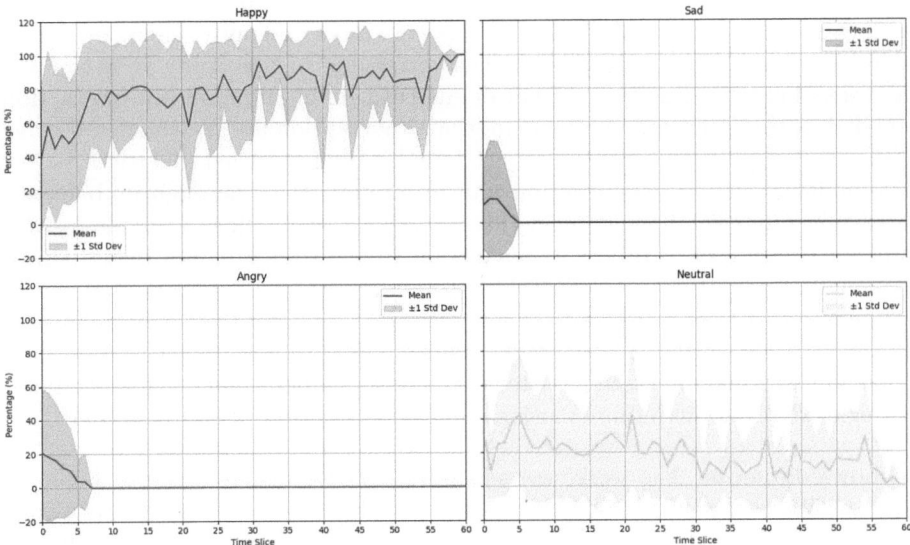

Fig. 6. Trend of the four emotions' predicted probabilities throughout the interaction with the robot.

over time. Meanwhile, the happiness line increases towards 100%, suggesting a positive shift during the interaction. This pattern is evident among participants after a few minutes of the session and tends to stabilize afterwards. Moreover, the intermediate predictions reveal patterns consistent with the final results and highlight important temporal dynamics. Such convergence supports the hypothesis that the users generally had positive responses to the interaction. However, it is also worth noting that the line between happiness and neutrality for some participants appears quite subtle. Even participants who initially displayed clear signs of positive emotions occasionally shifted toward more neutral states over time.

5 Conclusion

This study investigated the emotivational interaction framework, employing a multi-modal emotion recognition system that demonstrated reliable performance (91.45% accuracy with meta-model fusion) to explore how social robots can effectively respond to and influence human emotional states. While the emotion classification component provides a solid foundation for the interaction system, the primary contribution of this work lies in evaluating the effectiveness of emotively motivated robot behaviors in promoting positive emotional transitions and sustained well-being during human-robot interaction. Our experimental results show that the robot reached such a goal independently of participants' initial emotional states; thus, also regardless of its reactive behavior. However, we observed differences in the rapidity with which the robot's behavior changed participants' mood. Notably, sad emotions were more difficult to change to happy than angry ones. The qualitative analysis presented in this study aims to foster the discussion regarding the concept of emotivation in human-robot interaction, intended as the interplay between emotional perception and motivational drive. Within the scope of this framework, we found it crucial for a social robot to perceive humans' emotional states and aim to improve them through its behavior. Our study poses the first steps in this direction and provides valuable insights on how to design social robots' behaviors for humans' mental well-being. Future research directions include comprehensive validation studies focusing specifically on model robustness, cross-dataset generalization, and detailed error analysis of the emotion recognition components. Additionally, we plan to investigate long-term emotivational interaction patterns and develop more sophisticated adaptive strategies that can maintain emotional engagement over extended periods.

Acknowledgments. The work was supported by "RESTART - Robot Enhanced Social abilities based on Theory of mind for Acceptance of Robot in assistive Treatments" (CUP: I53D23003780001), funded by the MIUR with D.D. no. 861 under the PNRR and by Next Generation EU.

References

1. Barros, P., Weber, C., Wermter, S.: Emotional expression recognition with a cross-channel convolutional neural network for human-robot interaction. In: 2015 IEEE-RAS 15th International Conference on Humanoid Robots, pp. 582–587 (2015)
2. Caccavale, R., Leone, E., Lucignano, L., Rossi, S., Staffa, M., Finzi, A.: Attentional regulations in a situated human-robot dialogue, pp. 844 – 849 (2014)
3. Chumachenko, K., Iosifidis, A., Gabbouj, M.: Self-attention fusion for audiovisual emotion recognition with incomplete data. In: 2022 26th International Conference on Pattern Recognition (ICPR), pp. 2822–2828. IEEE (2022)
4. Cook, T., Roy, A.R.K., Welker, K.M.: Music as an emotion regulation strategy: an examination of genres of music and their roles in emotion regulation. Psychol. Music **47**(1), 144–154 (2019)
5. Cruz-Sandoval, D., Morales-Tellez, A., Benitez Sandoval, E., Favela, J.: A social robot as therapy facilitator in interventions to deal with dementia-related behavioral symptoms. In: Proceedings of the 2020 ACM/IEEE International Conference on Human-Robot Interaction, HRI 2020, pp. 161–169, NY, USA, 2020. Association for Computing Machinery, New York (2020)
6. Liu, Z., et al.: Deep learning methods for EEG emotion recognition. Neurocomputing **468**, 56–72 (2021)
7. Livingstone, S.R., Russo, F.A.: The Ryerson audio-visual database of emotional speech and song (RAVDESS): a dynamic, multimodal set of facial and vocal expressions in North American English. PloS ONE **13**(5), e0196391 (2018)
8. Obrenovic, B., Gu, X., Wang, G., Godinic, D., Jakhongirov, I.: Generative AI and human-robot interaction: implications and future agenda for business, society and ethics. AI Soc. **40**, 1–14 (2024)

9. Pan, B., Zheng, W.: Emotion recognition based on EEG using generative adversarial nets and convolutional neural network. Comput. Math. Methods Med. **2021**(1), 2520394 (2021)
10. Pavlyshenko, B.: Using stacking approaches for machine learning models. In: (DSMP), pp. 255–258 (2018)
11. Rasouli, S., Gupta, G., Nilsen, E., Dautenhahn, K.: Potential applications of social robots in robot-assisted interventions for social anxiety. Int. J. Soc. Robot. **14**(5), 1–32 (2022)
12. Russell, J.A.: A circumplex model of affect. J. Personal. Soc. Psychol. **39**(6), 1161 (1980)
13. Saleh, M.A., Akhtar Hanapiah, F., Hashim, H.: Robot applications for autism: a comprehensive review. Disab. Rehab. Assist. Technol. **16**(6), 580–602 (2021)
14. Salichs, E., Fernández-Rodicio, E., Castillo, J.C., Castro-González, Á., Malfaz, M., Salichs, M.Á.: A social robot assisting in cognitive stimulation therapy. In: Demazeau, Y., An, B., Bajo, J., Fernández-Caballero, A. (eds.) PAAMS 2018. LNCS (LNAI), vol. 10978, pp. 344–347. Springer, Cham (2018). https://doi.org/10.1007/978-3-319-94580-4_35
15. Salichs, M.A., et al.: Maggie: a robotic platform for human-robot social interaction. In: 2006 IEEE Conference on Robotics, Automation and Mechatronics, pp. 1–7 (2006)
16. Staffa, M., D'Errico, L., Sansalone, S., Alimardani, M.: Classifying human emotions in HRI: applying global optimization model to EEG brain signals. Front. Neurorobot. **17**, 1191127 (2023)
17. Staffa, M., D'Errico, L.: EEG-based machine learning models for emotion recognition in HRI. In: International Conference on Human-Computer Interaction, pp. 285–297. Springer (2023). https://doi.org/10.1007/978-3-031-35894-4_21
18. Staffa, M., D'Errico, L., Francese, R.: Emphasizing with a robot with a personality. In: International Conference on Human-Computer Interaction, pp. 283–294. Springer (2024). https://doi.org/10.1007/978-3-031-60615-1_19
19. Tanevska, A., Rea, F., Sandini, G., Cañamero, L., Sciutti, A.: A socially adaptable framework for human-robot interaction. Front. Robot. AI **7**, 121 (2020)
20. Wang, X., et al.: EEG-based emotion recognition using deep learning: a review. IEEE Trans. Biomed. Eng. **69**, 220–233 (2022)
21. Ran, W., et al.: Brief mindfulness meditation improves emotion processing. Front. Neurosci. **13**, 482990 (2019)
22. Yim, J.E.: Therapeutic benefits of laughter in mental health: a theoretical review. Tohoku J. Exp. Med. **239**(3), 243–249 (2016)
23. Zhang, S., Zhang, S., Huang, T., Gao, W., Tian, Q.: Learning affective features with a hybrid deep model for audio-visual emotion recognition. IEEE Trans. Circuits Syst. Video Technol. **28**(10), 3030–3043 (2017)
24. Zheng, W., Liu, W., Lu, Y., Lu, B., Cichocki, A.: Emotionmeter: a multimodal framework for recognizing human emotions. IEEE Trans. Cybern. 1–13 (2018)

Robotic Ears as Social Cues: A First Analysis on Emotional Expressivity

Silvia Rossi and Alessandra Rossi

PRISCA (Intelligent Robotics and Advanced Cognitive System Projects) Laboratory,
Department of Electrical Engineering and Information Technology (DIETI),
University of Naples Federico II, Naples, Italy
{silvia.rossi,alessandra.rossi}@unina.it

Abstract. Lifelike features that enhance the ability to socially engage users are often incorporated into the design of zoomorphic robots. However, there is limited research on how such different social cues can be used to enhance expressiveness and natural interaction. This article proposes a first evaluation of the role of modelling ears' behaviors and their impact on the emotional attribution and attentive states for the Miroka robot. In fact, ethological investigations on dog behavior underline the importance of ears movement in signalling about its mood as well as its attentive state. Out evaluation is conducted through an online study with 20 participants evaluating in terms of arousal, valence, and dominance and with the I-PANS-SF scale, five different ears positions following dog behavior. Results showed that people attribute similar emotional expressivity to Miroka as they sometimes do with dogs. In particular, they perceived Miroka as more alert and hostile when the position of its ears were leaning back compared to when they were raised straight.

Keywords: Social cues · Emotional display · Zoomorphic robot

1 Introduction

Zoomorphic robots, such as Paro, Sony Aibo, Miro, and Pleo, have been considered for a decade as a type of embodiment suitable for social robots, since they might reduce the expectations with respect to a humanoid robot [11], while still having an appearance that induce emotional [12]. Indeed, companion robots should have a lifelike appearance, which does not necessarily mean a human-like appearance [7].

The design of zoomorphic robots often incorporates lifelike features that enhance their ability to socially engage users. However, fully animal-inspired behavior may limit the ability to interact with humans. Character-like robots, such as the robot Miroka by EnchantedTools[1], represent a unique embodiment that combines an anthropomorphic body (and thus allows for gestures and manipulation capabilities) with a zoomorphic projected face. Like other social

---

[1] https://enchanted.tools/robot.

robot, the design features of Miroka combine an animal species and human by mixing different morphological features instead of whole body parts. One of the novel features is the presence of moving and large ears (with 1 DoF each, see Fig. 1), which are currently used to give the robot a sense of liveness, but can potentially contribute to the expressiveness of the robot during the interaction, as well as signalling interactive and internal states.

Companion robots, and more generally, consumer-level robots should provide more natural interfaces and more engaging interaction. While zoomorphic robots may present a different appearance and social cues, there is a lack of comprehensive research on their characteristics, appearance, behavior, and their interaction modalities [1]. There is a limited amount of research on how different design factors of a robot's appearance affect its ability to be natural while still achieving interaction interfaces, and how different designed social cues affect expressivity for robots. For example, MiRo's affective expressivity design uses lights, sounds, and movements inspired by animal behavior to effectively convey emotions. Such design elements can make interactions with the robot feel more natural and emotionally satisfying [6].

Previous work on emotion recognition when combining different cues has shown that the combination of such cues needs to be carefully considered, as adding cues may even lead to a decrease in recognition if not properly designed [14]. Moreover, in the case of a robot with a face, the facial expression plays a fundamental role in recognizing the robot's emotional display [13]. In this work, we aim to start an incremental evaluation approach for the design of expressive features of the robot Miroka. Since the robot has an extremely cartoon-like expressive face, we decided to start by focusing on the role of the ears' positions with respect to a facial expression that is considered as neutral. A pilot study with 20 participants was conducted and results showed that the position of the ear may be perceived as more positive or negative emotion. In particular, when the ears are leaning back of the head, the robot was perceived as more in alert and hostile. People also perceived ear position leaning back as the least pleasant.

2 Related Works

Generating expressive behaviors with different robot embodiments has been a long-standing area of research area in HRI. Early research with the social robot Kismet demonstrated how facial expressions and vocal cues could be combined to create engaging, emotion-driven interactions [4].

While the design of expressive behaviors for many robotic applications has been inspired by human emotions, an ethological approach, inspired by animal behavior may be more effective for zoomorphic robots. In fact, some of the proposed approaches referred directly to ethologically inspired architecture to integrate emotional models to guide robot behavior in a way that is both purposeful and interpretable by humans [2].

To this end, dog behavior has attracted the attention of researchers due to the availability of many studies and the familiarity that people have with them. In fact, some of the reactions of dogs can be intuitive for humans as well as the understanding of their emotional states [10]. The consideration of ethological models in the definition of robot behavior can constitute a strong basis for providing the ability for humans to relate in predictable ways [2]. Among these behaviors, signalling of attentive and emotional states will facilitate the interaction as well as the social bonding with such robots [2]. In fact, the way a dog holds its ears may be the key to telling you about its mood.

In [6], the authors defined 11 affective expressions for the Miro robot using lights, sounds, and movements inspired by animal behavior. While the designed behaviors were inspired by ethological studies on dogs, the robot used has different motor and social capabilities, so a complete mapping was not achievable. In addition, the Miro robot has ears but no way to move them.

For the Probo robot, actuated ears and trunk, together with a 20 DoF face, were investigated to study human-robot interaction with a focus on non-verbal communication [15]. The robot's facial expressions were pre-programmed from Action Units (AU) defined by the Facial Action Coding System (FACS). The evaluation of the basic emotion display was mainly evaluated starting from the facial expression. The contribution of different trunk positions was that evaluated only on the basis of the facial expression.

On the contrary, the role of ears in the expression of emotions has been studied with rabbit-like robots [5]. In this study, different ears positions were evaluated in terms of the emotion attributed to the robot. The results showed that ears positions horizontally aligned in the opposite direction induced participants to attribute a sense of embarrassment to the robot (and the lowest level of arousal and dominance). Upright ears positions were associated with positivity and high arousal. Upright but slightly forward was perceived as hostile and the highest for dominance. Inspired by this last work, here we designed a preliminary evaluation aimed at exploring the potential of ears as a social cue. In this direction, we do not aim to evaluate the recognition of a specific intented emotion with different ears positions, but rather on the potential contribution of the ears in assessing the robot's valence, arousal, and dominance, as well as an attentive state, as in [5].

3 Methods

The Miroka robot, developed by Enchanted Tools, is a humanoid assistant designed for social environments. The robot stands 1.3 m tall and uses a self-balancing spherical base that allows for omnidirectional movement and agility in confined spaces. Torque-controlled arms with 28 degrees of freedom, including opposable thumbs, allow the robot to efficiently manipulate universal handles attached to objects. In addition, the robot can display dynamic facial animations via a projected screen to enhance emotional connection.

The head is equipped with two large ears, each with one degree of freedom (DoF). While the role of ear positioning in facial expression interpretation has been minimally studied, it is recognized as a relevant nonverbal signal in emotional expression, particularly in dogs. Ethological research suggests significant

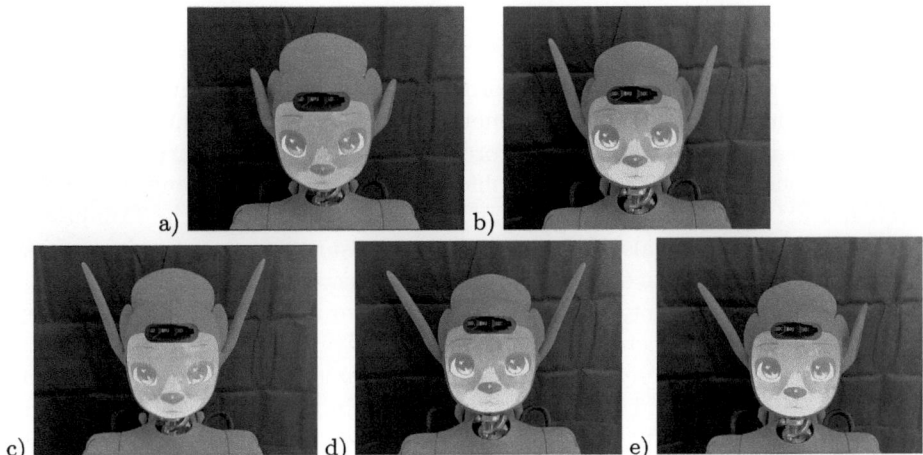

Fig. 1. The neutral face of the Miroka robot with the considered ears positions: a) *back down*, b) *leaning back*, c) *raised*, d) *leaning front*, e) *mixed*

inter-breed variability in ear expressivity due to morphological differences [16]. Dogs modulate ear retraction based on arousal levels [8]; partial retraction may indicate appeasement, whereas full retraction may indicate fear, submissiveness, retreat, or agonistic intent. Complete rearward positioning of the ears is associated with heightened vigilance or defensive readiness, whereas a neutral rearward positioning typically reflects a relaxed, non-threatening state.

In contrast, forward ears are commonly associated with increased interest, attention, alertness, and approach-oriented behavioral intentions [8]. This ear pose is often observed during owner-directed behaviors such as approach seeking or jumping. Erect or forward-angled ears signal a high level of environmental engagement or alertness.

In addition, a lateral (sideward) ear position, often referred to as "airplane ears", may reflect internal conflict or uncertainty. Intermittent ear twitching during auditory stimuli, such as human speech, suggests that while the signal is detected, the subject's primary attention is directed elsewhere.

Following dog's ears behavior, we identified five different positions for the Miroka robot (see Fig. 1). The full retraction position corresponds to the zero point for the joint (here called *back down*), while the forward-angled position correspond to the maximum value (coded as 1 and called *leaning front*). The other two intermediate positions, *raised* and *leaning back*, corresponded to the values 0.6 and 0.3, respectively. For the *mixed* "airplane" ears, since the ears have only one DoF, we chose to place one ear at the 0 value and the other at 1.

4 Experimental Settings

Since the Miroka robot is yet a prototype, as preliminary investigation, we decided to conduct an online experiment to gain people's preliminary perception of Miroka's ears positions. After providing the consent to participate in the study, we collected general demographic data, such as gender and age. Familiarity and attitude towards animals and pets is assesses with the Compassion Questionnaire for Animals (CQA) [9] which measures compassion for animals across emotional, cognitive, and behavioral dimensions.

During the experiment, participants were shown images of a Miroka displaying, for each of the selected facial expressions, five different ear positions, as illustrated in Fig. 1. These images, presented in random order, alternated with the I-PANAS-SF [17] and Self-Assessment Manikin (SAM) test [3], which participants used to evaluate the emotional state they perceived the rabbit to be expressing in each image.

5 Results

We recruited 20 participants through the University's mailinglists and research group's social media (e.g., Instagram, Facebook, X). We excluded one participants who did not complete the study, consequently, the final sample consisted of 19 people. Age of participants were distributed as follows: nine participants between 25 and 34 years old; four participants between 35 and 44 years old; three participants between 45 and 54 years old; two participants between 55 and 64 years old; and, one participant between 65 and 74. Participants identified themselves as female (58%) and male (42%), no non-binary. The majority of participants (73.8%) stated to have previous experience with robots, while the remaining did not have any previous direct encounter with robots.

5.1 Perception of Valence, Arousal and Dominance

We used the Self-Assessment Manikin scale for assessing participants' emotional responses to robots using SAM's three dimensions: 1) Valence (Pleasure - Displeasure); 2) Arousal (Excitement - Calm); and Dominance (Control - Submissiveness).

We used one-way repeated measures ANOVA tests to compare the differences between the perception of valence, arousal and dominance in respect to the proposed expressions. Data are mean ± standard deviation. Participants' perception of the valance of Miroka's expressions showed statistically significant differences ($F(4, 72) = 2.863$, $p = 0.02$, partial $\eta_p^2 = 0.137$). In particular, a post hoc analysis with a Bonferroni adjustment showed that the ear leaning front position (3.21 ± 0.787) and the leaning back position (2.63 ± 0.955) were statistically significantly different with a mean difference of 0.579 (95% CI, 0.015 to 1.143, $p = 0.041$). The ear positions raised (3.42 ± 0.838) and back down (2.79 ± 1.032) were statistically significantly different with a mean difference of 0.632 (95% CI,

Table 1. Descriptive statistics of the ear positions.

Ear positions	Mean	Standard Deviation
Leaning Front	4.74	5.810
Raised	8.95	3.504
Back Down	9.05	3.778
Mixed	9.89	4.898
Leaning Back	10.84	4.525

0.130 to 1.133, $p = 0.008$). While the comparisons of the other ear positions did not show any statistically significant difference ($p > 0.1$), we observed that the ear position raised (3.42 ± 0.838) were tendentially rated as more pleasant with a mean difference of 0.789 (95% CI, -0.006 to 1.585, $p = 0.053$) compared to the ear position leaning back (2.632 ± 0.219). People attributed the lowest degrees of pleasure to ear position leaning back, and highest pleasure to the ear position raised.

Interestingly, we did not find any statistically difference in participants' perceived arousal and dominance between the different Miroka's emotional expressions (all $p > 0.1$, and $p > 0.2$ respectively).

5.2 Assessment of Positive and Negative Affect

We used the international PANAS bidimensional scale in its short form version for assessing positive affect (PA, i.e., Alert, Inspired, Determined, Attentive, Active) and negative affect (NA, i.e., Afraid, Nervous, Upset, Hostile, Ashamed) as discrete constructs on participants' perception of Miroka's emotional expressions. The I-PANAS-SF scale had a high level of internal consistency of PA items, as determined by a Cronbach's alpha of $\alpha = 0.949$, and of NA items, as determined by a Cronbach's alpha of $\alpha = 0.947$.

A repeated-measure ANOVA tests did not find any statistically significant changes between the positive perception of the different expressions of Miroka. Data are mean $\pm$ standard deviation. Participants' negative perception of Miroka's expressions resulted statistically significantly different, $F(4,72) = 11.785, p < 0.001$, partial $\eta_p^2 = 0.396$. In particular, a post hoc analysis with a Bonferroni adjustment showed that the ear positions were perceived statistically differently for the NA dependent measure. The ear position leaning front has found statitistically different lower negative affect than the ear positions (see Table 1 for mean and standard deviation details): raise with a mean difference of -4.21 (95% CI, -7.64 to -0.77) and $p = 0.010$; leaning back with a mean difference of -6.10 (95% CI, -9.68 to -2.53) and $p < 0.001$; back down with a mean difference of -4.31 (95% CI, -8.31 to -0.31) and $p = 0.029$; and, mixed with a mean difference of -5.15 (95% CI, -8.81 to -1.49) and $p = 0.003$. We did not find any statistically difference between the pairwise comparisons (all $p > 0.239$).

In order to fully understand any difference in emotional perception, we ran Repeated-measure ANOVA tests for evaluating the ears positions in respect to the single dimensions. We did not find any statistically difference in perception of Active ($F(4,72) = 0.266, p = 0.899$); Attentive ($F(4,72) = 1.710, p = 0.157$); Determined ($F(4,72) = 1.534, p = 0.201$); Inspired ($F(4,72) = 0.492, p = 0.742$); Ashamed ($F(4,72) = 1.503, p = 0.210$); Upset ($F(4,72) = 2.094, p = 0.090$); Afraid ($F(4,72) = 1.114, p = 0.356$); Nervous ($F(4,72) = 1.884, p = 0.123$).

We observed a statistically difference in perception of Alert ($F(4,72) = 3.531, p = 0.011, \eta_p^2 = 0.164$), Hostile ($F(4,72) = 2.594, p = 0.044, \eta_p^2 = 0.126$). In particular, the ears' leaning back position (2.32 ± 1.701) was considered more Alert than raised position (1.05 ± 1.393) with a mean difference of 1.263 (95% CI, 0.070 to 2.457) and $p = 0.033$. The ears' leaning back position (1.11 ± 1.243) were considered more Hostile with a mean difference of 0.789 (95% CI, 0.033 to 1.546, p = 0.037) than ear's raised position (0.032 ± 0.749).

6 Conclusions

In this work, we present a preliminary study to investigate the expressive features of the robot Miroka that has an unique embodiment combining an anthropomorphic body and a zoomorphic projected face. In particular, we investigated how the position of robot's ears played a role in the perception of pleasantness (i.e., valence), the intensity of emotion (i.e., arousal), and the degree of control (i.e., dominance), and the positive and negative affection.

Our findings suggest that ear movements modeled after canine behavior – particularly ears leaning back – can effectively convey emotional states such as alertness and hostility. These results underline the potential of incorporating nuanced, animal-inspired cues into robot design to enhance expressivity and natural human-robot interaction.

As a future work, we would like to extend our study with video base analysis and so by including ears movements with different speed.

References

1. Ahmed, E., Buruk, O.O., Hamari, J.: Human-robot companionship: current trends and future agenda. Int. J. Soc. Robot. **16**(8), 1809–1860 (2024). https://doi.org/10.1007/s12369-024-01160-y
2. Arkin, R.C., Fujita, M., Takagi, T., Hasegawa, R.: An ethological and emotional basis for human-robot interaction. Robot. Auton. Syst. **42**(3), 191–201 (2003). https://doi.org/10.1016/S0921-8890(02)00375-5
3. Bradley, M.M., Lang, P.J.: Measuring emotion: the self-assessment manikin and the semantic differential. J. Behav. Ther. Exp. Psychiatry **25**(1), 49–59 (1994). https://doi.org/10.1016/0005-7916(94)90063-9
4. Breazeal, C.: Emotion and sociable humanoid robots. Int. J. Hum. Comput. Stud. **59**(1), 119–155 (2003). https://doi.org/10.1016/S1071-5819(03)00018-1

5. Eimler, S.C., Krämer, N.C., von der Pütten, A.M.: Empirical results on determinants of acceptance and emotion attribution in confrontation with a robot rabbit. Appl. Artif. Intell. **25**(6), 503–529 (2011). https://doi.org/10.1080/08839514.2011.587154
6. Ghafurian, M., Lakatos, G., Dautenhahn, K.: The zoomorphic miro robot's affective expression design and perceived appearance. Int. J. Soc. Robot. **14**(4), 945–962 (2022). https://doi.org/10.1007/s12369-021-00832-3
7. de Graaf, M.M.A., Allouch, S.B.: The influence of prior expectations of a robot's lifelikeness on users' intentions to treat a zoomorphic robot as a companion. Int. J. Soc. Robot. **9**(1), 17–32 (2017). https://doi.org/10.1007/s12369-016-0340-4
8. Hecht, J., Horowitz, A.: Introduction to Dog Behavior, chap. 1, pp. 5–29. John Wiley Sons, Ltd. (2022). https://doi.org/10.1002/9781119618515.ch1
9. Khoury, B., Vergara, R.C.: Compassion questionnaire for animals: scale development and validation. J. Environ. Psychol. **100**, 102470 (2024). https://doi.org/10.1007/978-3-030-90465-4_123-1
10. Konok, V., Nagy, K.: Ádám Miklósi: how do humans represent the emotions of dogs? the resemblance between the human representation of the canine and the human affective space. Appl. Anim. Behav. Sci. **162**, 37–46 (2015). https://doi.org/10.1016/j.applanim.2014.11.003
11. Löffler, D., Dörrenbächer, J., Hassenzahl, M.: The uncanny valley effect in zoomorphic robots: the u-shaped relation between animal likeness and likeability. In: HRI 2020, Proceedings of the 2020 ACM/IEEE International Conference on Human-Robot Interaction, pp. 261–270. Association for Computing Machinery, New York, NY, USA (2020). https://doi.org/10.1145/3319502.3374788
12. Miklósi, A., Gácsi, M.: On the utilization of social animals as a model for social robotics. Front. Psychol. **3**, 75 (2012). https://doi.org/10.3389/fpsyg.2012.00075
13. Raggioli, L., Esposito, R., Rossi, A., Rossi, S.: Exploring the role of robot's movements for a transparent affective communication. IEEE Robot. Autom. Lett. **10**(5), 4364–4371 (2025). https://doi.org/10.1109/LRA.2025.3548412
14. Rossi, S., Ruocco, M.: Better alone than in bad company. Interact. Stud. **20**(3), 487–508 (2019). https://doi.org/10.1075/is.18066.ros
15. Saldien, J., Goris, K., Vanderborght, B., Vanderfaeillie, J., Lefeber, D.: Expressing emotions with the social robot probo. Int. J. Soc. Robot. **2**(4), 377–389 (2010)
16. Siniscalchi, M., D'Ingeo, S., Minunno, M., Quaranta, A.: Communication in dogs. Animals **8**(8) (2018). https://doi.org/10.3390/ani8080131
17. Thompson, E.R.: Development and validation of an internationally reliable short-form of the positive and negative affect schedule (PANAS). J. Cross Cult. Psychol. **38**(2), 227–242 (2007). https://doi.org/10.1177/0022022106297301

Simulating Feelings: LLM vs. Psychology-Based Models in Human-Robot Interaction

Francesca Corrao(✉), Alice Nardelli, Antonio Sgorbissa, and Carmine Tommaso Recchiuto

Department of Informatics, Bioengineering, Robotics and System Engineering(DIBRIS), Università degli Studi di Genova, Via All'Opera Pia 13, 16145 Genova, Italy
francesca.corrao@edu.unigue.it

Abstract. As robots become increasingly integrated into daily life, equipping them with emotionally intelligent behaviors is essential for improving Human-Robot Interaction (HRI). This study investigates differences in synthetic emotion generation between EmoACT–a psychology-based, platform-independent framework grounded in Affect Control Theory (ACT)–and a Large Language Model (LLM), specifically GPT-4, considering the influence of synthetic personality traits. We focused on the traits of Agreeableness, Extraversion, and Conscientiousness, comparing both systems using a dataset composed of user emotions, sentences, and robot comfortability levels. Our results show that EmoACT produces emotional responses influenced by all input variables, with personality traits having a significant impact on the generation process. In contrast, GPT-4 predominantly mimics user emotions, with only minor variations based on personality. These findings highlight the differing mechanisms and strengths of psychology-based and LLM-based emotion generation frameworks, offering insights for designing emotionally capable artificial agents.

Keywords: Synthetic Emotions · Emotion Generation · Large Language Model · Affect Control Theory

1 Introduction

Robots are increasingly being integrated into people's daily lives–for assistive tasks [3], as tools in educational settings [37], and as companions [39]. To ensure better integration of such systems, it is essential that they are equipped with a full range of interaction capabilities that go beyond simple dialogue. For example, humans need to understand and predict a robot's behavior in order to coexist and interact with it naturally [28]. In this context, emotions play a crucial role in human interaction, enabling individuals to understand one another, establish common ground, and mitigate the impact of negative information [11]. Providing artificial agents with the ability to recognize human emotions and use them appropriately in interaction is therefore fundamental. Emotions increase the acceptability of robots by enhancing the transparency of interactions [33], allowing humans to better interpret and anticipate robot behavior. They also help reduce the sense of unfamiliarity with artificial systems [1], as their behavior becomes interpretable through the same cues used in human-human interaction. Additionally, emotional capabilities foster and strengthen the bond between humans and robots [5], and the ability to express emotions is closely tied to the perceived social presence of robots [33]. For all these reasons, emotions are a valuable tool for improving HRI, making robot behavior more predictable, understandable, and transparent, thereby facilitating their integration and acceptance by humans [1]. Personality, as a psychological component that affects our patterns of thought, behavior, and emotion–shaping humanâĂŞhuman relationships [6]–is also a relevant aspect in HRI, as emotional reactivity is strongly correlated with personality traits [32,34]. The robotics literature [12,21] has explored this connection by developing model-based emotion generators that incorporate synthetic personality.

When discussing emotional integration in artificial agents, three key areas must be considered: emotion generation, modeling, and portrayal [16]. Regarding the generation of synthetic emotions, the most common approach involves developing multiple interconnected modules that collect and process external stimuli based on psychology-inspired models [16]. The most widely used psychological framework is Cognitive Appraisal Theory [22], which has been applied in a variety of systems [2,8,16,17,29], often integrating personality traits [13] or considering the relationship developed with the user [15]. Other approaches rely on Markov chains [10] or use reinforcement learning combined with visual features of the environment to determine emotional states [36].

We recently proposed EmoACT, a platform- and task-independent framework for generating synthetic emotions based on Affect Control Theory (ACT), as described in [4]. ACT had not previously been used for synthetic emotion generation. However, its focus on how emotions emerge through social interaction [19] makes it a promising theory for endowing artificial agents with emotional capabilities–particularly to improve Human-Robot Interaction (HRI).

On the other hand, Large Language Models (LLMs) are attracting growing interest, including in the field of affective computing. Studies evaluating their capabilities in emotion prediction and perception [38], as well as in emotional intelligence–particularly in understanding emotions [35]–have produced promising results, making LLMs an appealing solution for integrating affective capabilities into artificial agents [38]. Subsequent works have explored the use of LLMs to generate emotional text without explicitly prompting for an emotional state– either to recognize the user's emotion and produce non-harmful, emotionally supportive responses [7], or to apply these capabilities to non-playing characters in video games and assess the enjoyability of the interaction [20]. Furthermore, the ability to generate emotional states using LLMs combined with multi-modal cues has been tested on multiple datasets, yielding higher accuracy [18].

This interest in providing artificial agents with emotional capabilities led us to explore how emotion generation differs between a psychology-based approach and leveraging an LLM. Consequently, the main objective of this research is to investigate the key differences in the functioning of our EmoACT emotion generation model and a state-of-the-art LLM, considering different synthetic personalities.

To carry out this study, we rigorously compared the two approaches to gather objective data on their functioning. For each of the seven basic emotions [9], we created a dataset of 40 emotional sentences and provided them as input to both emotion generation systems. The first system employed GPT-4, while the second used EmoACT. The results show that both approaches produce plausible responses to human emotions, with GPT-4 mainly mimicking the user's expression, while EmoACT processes the emotional input to generate an internal emotional state, predominantly involving Neutral, Happiness, and Sadness.

2 Methodology

This study compares two approaches for generating emotions in an agent with a synthetic personality. The first approach leverages the generative capability of GPT-4, while the second employs EmoACT, our platform-independent framework for emotion generation based on ACT [4].

To explore how personality influences the emotion generation process, we integrate this psychological capability into both components. We model personality using the Conscientiousness, Extroversion, and Agreeableness (CEA) traits from the Big Five factor model. We draw on our previous research on this specific topic to select the personality traits for analysis. Readers can refer to our prior work on synthetic personality to understand the rationale behind the CEA taxonomy and appreciate its effectiveness in making the CEA traits perceivable by humans [23–26].

To maintain a task-independent setup, we adapted both systems for a dyadic conversation task. Thanks to the task- and platform-independence, as well as the modularity of the models, adding new stimuli as input is straightforward. This conversational task allows us to observe the differences in the functioning of the two models when only a limited number of inputs are provided.

2.1 LLM for Emotion Generation

To perform the emotion generation task using the GPT-4o model, we employed prompt engineering techniques. We designed a system prompt that instructs the model to fulfill the emotion generation task by selecting the most appropriate emotion from Ekman's basic emotions [9]. To investigate the a priori knowledge of the GPT-4o model regarding the emotional intelligence associated with CEA traits, we compared two different prompts:

– Non-Emotional Intelligence (No-EI): The first system prompt is agnostic to the emotional intelligence behavior of the CEA personality traits. It receives as input the personality of the agent in a single word (e.g., the robot's personality is *Agreeable*).

– Emotional Intelligence (EI): The second prompt, instead, includes additional information describing the trait-related emotional intelligence in natural language [34]. Additionally, it is informed by the *comfortability* of the robot, indicating whether the robot feels comfortable or uncomfortable. Here, *comfortability* is a driver considered within the cognitive architecture and can change during the interaction [23].

In both prompts, the model is requested to consider the current conversational context, including the fields: *text*, which contains the user's spoken sentence, and *user emotion*, which contains the detected user's emotion.

2.2 EmoACT Framework

EmoACT is a task- and platform-independent, psychology-based framework for embedding synthetic emotions into artificial agents [4]. It is grounded in Affect Control Theory (ACT), which posits that emotions emerge during social interactions to maintain one's identity in alignment with how others perceive them [19]. For this study, we utilized the emotion generation components of EmoACT, as illustrated in Fig. 1. According to ACT, EmoACT maps all relevant information into a three-dimensional space that measures the Evaluation, Potency, and Activity of the considered input [19].

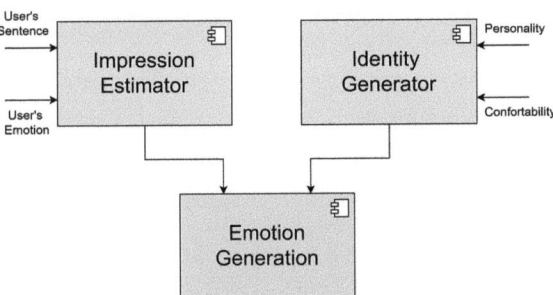

Fig. 1. EmoACT architecture adapted for emotions generation in a dyadic conversation task

Identity Generator. This module generates the robot's identity by combining its personality, its role as a robotic social companion, and the current *comfortability* state. The identity is computed as a weighted mean of these three EPA vectors, as shown in Eq. 1. The role is fixed as a social robot [31], while the personality is selected from one of the six CEA extremes (Distracted-Conscientious, Introvert-Extrovert, Disagreeable-Agreeable). Lastly, the *comfortability* selects either the "comfortable" or "uncomfortable" label, depending on whether the value is currently high or low.

$$identity = W_p \cdot personality + W_r \cdot role + W_c \cdot comfortability \qquad (1)$$

Impression Estimator. This module estimates the impression the user has of the robot during interaction based on the Actor-Behavior-Object (ABO) paradigm described by ACT [14]. The ABO paradigm predicts the transient impression of the object given the current values of the actor, object, and behavior that the actor has toward the object. In our adaptation, the actor is the human, the object is the robot, and the behavior reflects how the user acts toward the robot, determined by the user's emotion and the meaning of their sentence.

Initially, the actor value is simply initialized as that of a person in the EPA space [30]. Upon receiving the user's emotion and sentence, this value is updated to reflect the displayed emotion.

To compute the behavior EPA vector, two factors are considered: the actor's emotion and the cause of this emotional state–whether it was caused by the robot or not. The latter is determined by analyzing the user's sentence. Each emotional state has two possible behavior vectors: one for when the robot causes the emotion, and one for when the user is merely expressing a personal emotional state.

To incorporate personality within the Impression Estimator, we consider the different emotional reactivity of individuals displaying high and low values of agreeableness [32,34]. Indeed, Agreeable and Disagreeable personalities evaluate emotions displayed by others differently.

Emotion Generation. This component generates the artificial agent's emotional state using ACT emotional equations, based on the current identity and impression estimate. The resulting emotion is computed as a vector in EPA space and then mapped to the closest basic emotion label. The threshold to select an emotion is set according to the agent's personality, particularly the Extroversion trait. The Extrovert selects the closest emotion if its similarity exceeds 60%, while the Introvert requires a higher confidence of at least 75% similarity before deviating from a Neutral state.

3 Evaluation Set-up

To evaluate the difference in generation, the two systems were provided with the same inputs: user emotion, user sentence, and the *comfortability* of the artificial agent. For this purpose, we generated a dataset consisting of 40 sentences for each of the seven basic emotions (Happiness, Neutral, Surprise, Disgust, Angry, Fear, and Sadness). Within each emotion, the first 20 sentences were paired with a high *comfortability* state of the agent, while the remaining 20 sentences were paired with a low *comfortability* state.

This input dataset was used to test both systems. For each approach (LLM-emoACT), we separately tested each of the 6 opposite poles of the CEA personality traits investigated. This setup allows us to investigate the main differences in the functioning between the two approaches when the personality traits are considered.

Focusing on the LLM-based approach, as anticipated, we considered two different prompts: the Non-Emotional Intelligence (No-EI) and the Emotional Intelligence (EI). This comparison allows us to investigate whether the LLM is trained to reflect the emotional intelligence associated with CEA traits, or if it requires an explicit description within the system prompt to do so. The generated dataset and both prompt templates are available at: https://github.com/RICE-unige/PRISM.

4 Results

To showcase the results of the two emotional synthesizers for each personality trait, the emotions produced by the agent in response to the user's emotional state are plotted in heatmaps. It is important to note that when LLM generated emotions, it occasionally produced emotions outside the set of basic emotions, despite being instructed to select only from this set. These out-of-scope emotions were discarded, resulting in cases where fewer than 40 utterances are shown in the LLM heatmaps for certain user emotions.

4.1 EmoACT and No-Emotional Intelligence LLM

Comparing EmoACT and the No-EI LLM, by looking at the heatmaps for each pair of CEA traits (Figs. 2, 3, 4), we observe differences, especially where the robot is Agreeable and Extroverted, while a personality with a high level of Conscientiousness exhibits minimal differences in both systems.

For the No-EI LLM, the emotions generated follow the diagonal, mirroring the user's emotional state regardless of the personality trait. This means that, without explicit information about the trait-related emotional response, the LLM tends to mimic the user's emotion, with only subtle changes across personalities. In contrast, EmoACT, based on the user's emotions and the robot's personality, tends to generate Happiness for the user's positively evaluated emotions or either Sadness or Neutrality for negatively evaluated emotions. In this case, the Disagreeable and Introverted personality traits heavily impact the generation process.

Agreeableness Traits. Focusing on Agreeableness (Fig. 2), both frameworks differentiate between the two personality poles, with emotions such as Happiness, Sadness, and Fear being absent in the emotional response for the *Disagreeable* personality.

In the case of the *Agreeable* personality trait (Fig. 2a), EmoACT shifts between Happy, Neutral, and Sad, while the No-EI LLM mainly replicates user emotions (except for Anger).

Looking at the heatmaps produced with the *Disagreeable* personality trait (Fig. 2b), the No-EI LLM still mimics the user emotions, with the erased emotions (Happiness, Sadness, and Fear) being mapped either to Neutral or Disgust. In contrast, EmoACT processes the user's emotions to generate its emotional response, predominantly eliciting Anger and Disgust, showing a more personality-driven response.

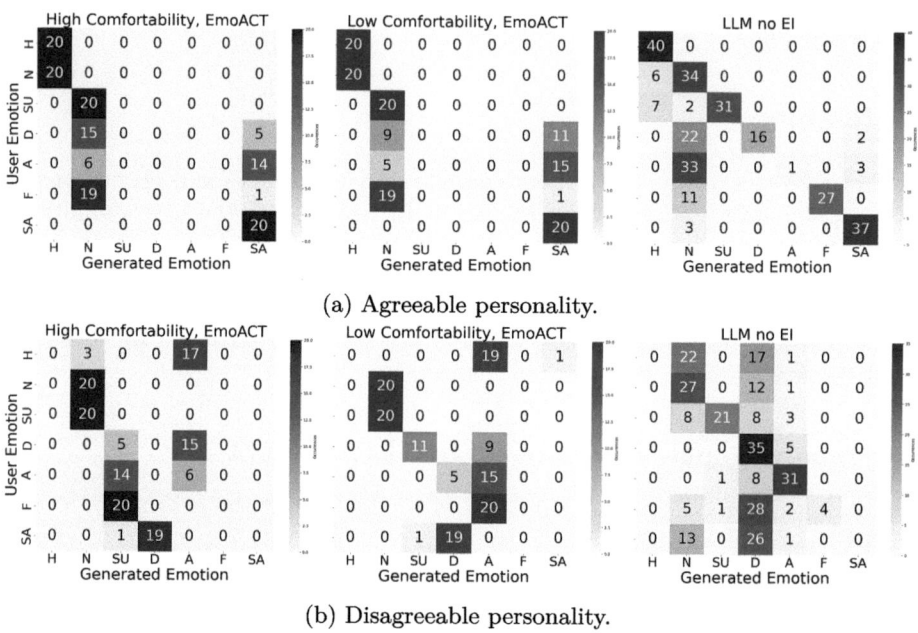

(a) Agreeable personality.

(b) Disagreeable personality.

Fig. 2. Difference in Emotion Generation between EmoACT and no-EI LLM related to the Agreeableness personality trait

Extroversion Traits. Examining Extroversion (Fig. 3), differences are visible between the Introvert and Extrovert personality traits, especially with the EmoACT framework, where Neutral is the most dominant emotion for the Introvert (Fig. 3b).

For the *Extroverted* personality (Fig. 3a), both systems behave similarly to the *Agreeable* one (Fig. 2a), with the No-EI LLM maintaining its diagonal, mimic pattern, and EmoACT producing more Sadness in response to negatively evaluated emotions.

Moving to the *Introvert* case (Fig. 3b), EmoACT predominantly responds with Neutrality, except in response to Happiness or Sadness. Even the No-EI LLM shows a slight increase in Neutrality selection, even if still predominantly mirrors user emotions.

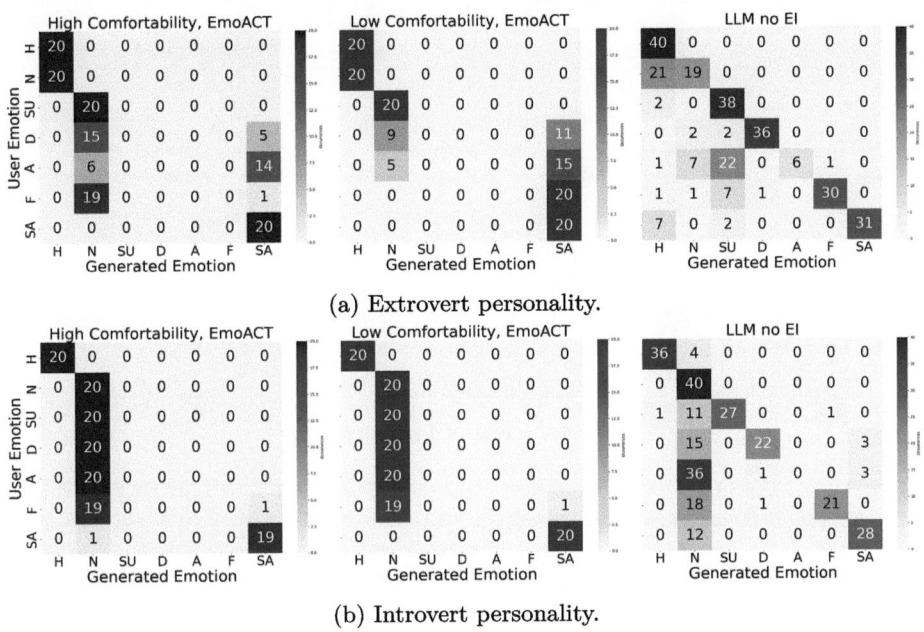

(a) Extrovert personality.

(b) Introvert personality.

Fig. 3. Difference in Emotion Generation between EmoACT and no-EI LLM related to the Extroversion personality trait.

Conscientiousness Traits. For Conscientiousness (Fig. 4), no major differences emerge between the two personality poles. In this case, the No-EI LLM presents more variations within the *Unconscientious* trait (Fig. 4b), choosing Surprise and Neutrality more often, while largely retaining the mimic pattern.

This aligns with psychological findings suggesting that Conscientiousness has less influence on emotional reactivity [34].

4.2 Comparison with Emotional Intelligence LLM

When testing the EI LLM, we decided to focus only on Agreeableness, as it has the strongest influence on emotion generation [34]. With this comparison, we aimed to evaluate how a more detailed description of the trait-related emotional response affects LLM-based emotion generation. Additionally, we were interested

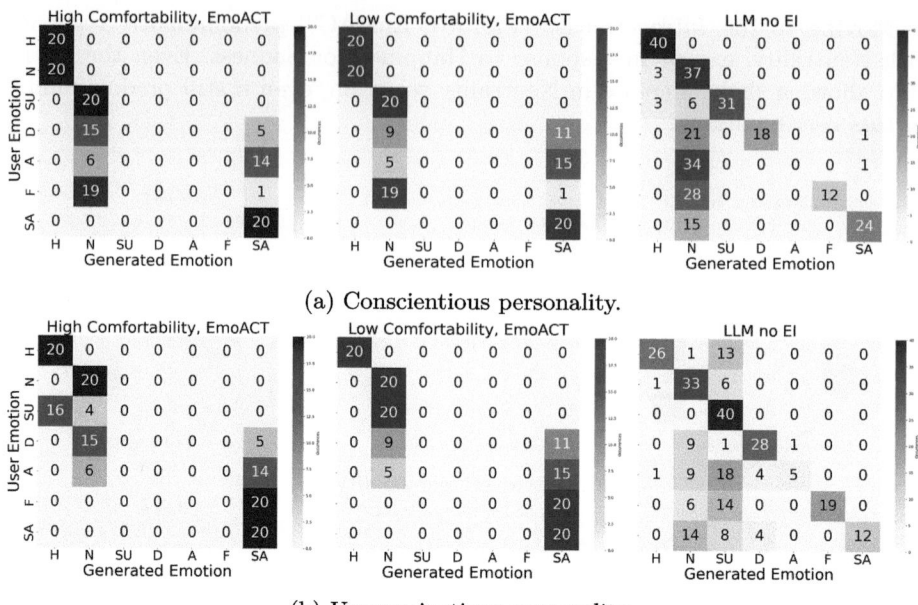

Fig. 4. Difference in Emotion Generation between EmoACT and no-EI LLM related to the Conscientiousness personality trait.

in investigating the influence of comfortability on emotion generation in both models.

Looking at the results, presented in Fig. 5, it may be seen how comfortability affects the EI-LLM more strongly. Indeed, the more detailed prompt makes the mimic behavior of the LLM disappear for the Disagreeable personality (Fig. 5b). Instead, the EI LLM seems to not care much about the emotion of the user and responds mainly with Neutrality when the agent's comfortability is high, and with Anger or Disgust when its comfortability is low.

For the Agreeable personality (Fig. 5a), the mimic behavior remains, and the EI LLM mainly agrees with the user's emotion. Nevertheless, we must consider the empathic nature of highly agreeable individuals. We can appreciate that for emotions such as Disgust, Anger, and Fear, the mimic behavior seems to disappear: producing mostly Neutrality for high comfortability and Sadness (in case of user anger and disgust) and Fear (in case of user fear) for low comfortability.

In comparison, EmoACT showed a relatively smaller effect of comfortability in both Agreeable and Disagreeable personalities. In other words, emotions here are more driven by user personality and context, and less by the agent's internal state. However, for the Disagreeable case (Fig. 5b), comfortability impacted responses, particularly for negative evaluated emotions such as Anger, Disgust, and Fear, triggering Surprise or Anger depending on the agent's comfortability.

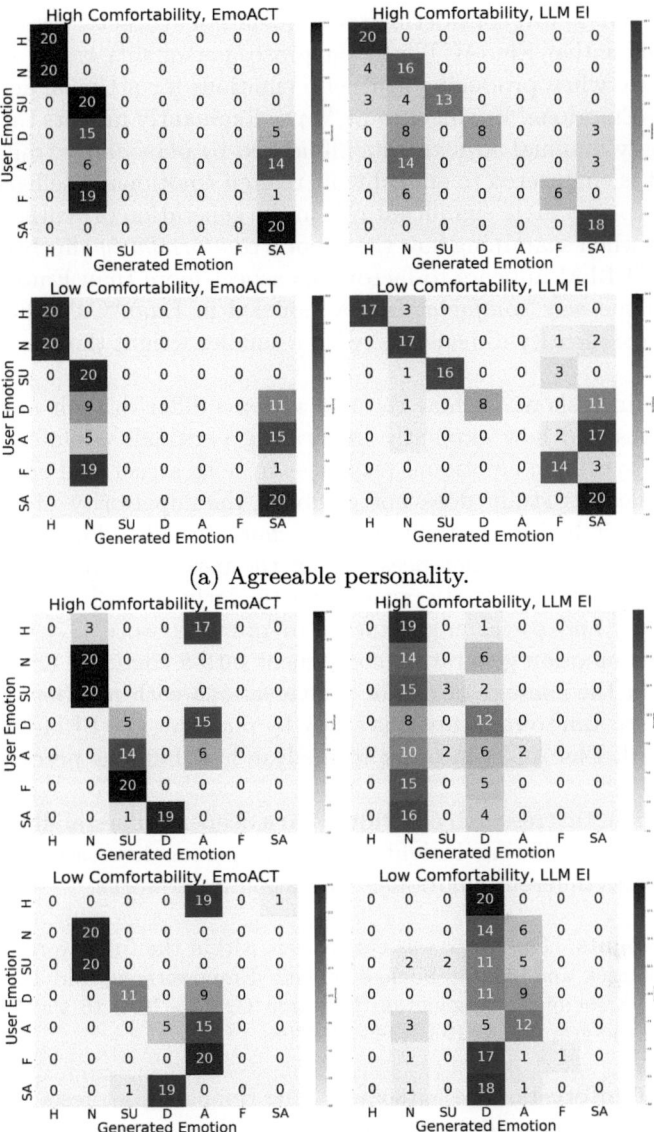

Fig. 5. Difference in Emotion Generation between EmoACT and EI LLM related to the Agreeableness personality trait.

5 Conclusion

This study investigated the differences in emotion generation between our platform-agnostic, psychology-based framework, EmoACT, and a Large Language Model (GPT-4o), considering the influence of synthetic personality traits. The results show that EmoACT fully integrates personality traits and the user's emotional state when producing synthetic emotions for artificial agents. In contrast, the No-Emotional Intelligence LLM predominantly mirrors the user's emotions, with only minimal adjustments influenced by personality traits. When the LLM prompt is engineered to embed trait-related emotional intelligence, personality seems to play a more significant role in the generation of synthetic emotions. Additionally, when examining how the robot's *comfortability* affects emotion generation, the EI LLM appears to factor this aspect more than EmoACT. This is likely due to the way *comfortability* is modeled in EmoACT, where it is only one of the three identity dimensions, with a smaller weight than personality and role.

These findings showcase how the two systems differ in their emotion generation strategies and how explicitly integrating personality-related information can influence synthetic emotional responses in both structured and LLM-based systems. While this study does not establish the superiority of one approach over the other, it highlights their distinct characteristics. Future work intends to investigate how these differences impact the perception of synthetic personality when embodied in robotic agents, particularly regarding their impact on empathy, trust, and social engagement. In previous work [27], we integrated an LLM-based emotion generation component into a cognitive architecture and evaluated it in the context of dyadic conversations with a robot. In upcoming experiments, we aim to replicate this study by replacing the LLM-based emotion generation with EmoACT, in order to analyze how humans perceive these two approaches.

In conclusion, this research contributes to a deeper understanding of synthetic emotion modeling, offering insights into how personality-based traits can be integrated across different emotional generation frameworks.

Acknowledgments. This work was carried out within the framework of the project "RAISE - Robotics and AI for Socio-economic Empowerment" and it was partially funded by the Alzheimer's Association Research Grant - New to the Field (AARG-NTF) through the grant 24AARG-NTF-1200708.

Disclosure of Interests. The authors have no competing interests to declare that are relevant to the content of this article.

References

1. Bethel, C.L., Murphy, R.R.: Survey of non-facial/non-verbal affective expressions for appearance-constrained robots. IEEE Trans. Syst. Man Cybern Part C Appl. Rev. **38**(1), 83–92 (2008). https://doi.org/10.1109/TSMCC.2007.905845, https://ieeexplore.ieee.org/abstract/document/4378439
2. Breazeal, C.: Emotion and sociable humanoid robots. Int. J. Hum. Comput. Stud. **59**(1–2), 119–155 (2003)

3. Chu, M.T., Khosla, R., Khaksar, S.M.S., Nguyen, K.: Service innovation through social robot engagement to improve dementia care quality. Assist. Technol. **29**(1), 8–18 (2017)
4. Corrao, F., Nardelli, A., Renoux, J., Recchiuto, C.T.: EmoACT: a framework to embed emotions into artificial agents based on affect control theory (2025). https://arxiv.org/abs/2504.12125
5. Lee, D., Seok Ahn, H., Young Choi, J.: A general behavior generation module for emotional robots using unit behavior combination method. In: RO-MAN 2009 - The 18th IEEE International Symposium on Robot and Human Interactive Communication, pp. 375–380. IEEE, Toyama (2009). https://doi.org/10.1109/ROMAN.2009.5326239, http://ieeexplore.ieee.org/document/5326239/
6. Diener, E., Lucas, R.E.: Personality traits. General psychology: Required reading **278** (2019)
7. DV, S., N, P., Jain, P., Kumar, S.: Virtual companion: a human friendly chatbot. In: 2024 8th International Conference on Computational System and Information Technology for Sustainable Solutions (CSITSS), pp. 1–6 (2024). https://doi.org/10.1109/CSITSS64042.2024.10816756, https://ieeexplore.ieee.org/document/10816756/, iSSN: 2767-1097
8. Ehtesham-Ul-Haque, M., et al.: EmoBot: artificial emotion generation through an emotional chatbot during general-purpose conversations. Cogn. Syst. Res. **83**, 101168 (2024)
9. Ekman, P., Cordaro, D.: What is meant by calling emotions basic. Emot. Rev. **3**(4), 364–370 (2011)
10. Ficocelli, M., Terao, J., Nejat, G.: Promoting interactions between humans and robots using robotic emotional behavior. IEEE Trans. Cybern. **46**(12), 2911–2923 (2016)
11. Gendron, M., Barrett, L.F.: Reconstructing the past: a century of ideas about emotion in psychology. Emot. Rev. **1**(4), 316–339 (2009)
12. Han, M.J., Lin, C.H., Song, K.T.: Robotic emotional expression generation based on mood transition and personality model. IEEE Trans. Cybern. **43**(4), 1290–1303 (2012)
13. Han, M.J., Lin, C.H., Song, K.T.: Robotic emotional expression generation based on mood transition and personality model. IEEE Trans. Cybern. **43**(4), 1290–1303 (2013)
14. Heise, D.R., Smith-Lovin, L.: Impressions of goodness, powerfulness, and liveliness from discerned social events. Soc. Psychol. Q. **44**(2), 93–106 (1981)
15. Kinoshita, S., Takenouchi, H., Tokumaru, M.: An emotion-generation model for a robot that reacts after considering the dialogist. In: 2014 International Conference on Humanoid, Nanotechnology, Information Technology, Communication and Control, Environment and Management (HNICEM), pp. 1–6. IEEE, Palawan, Philippines (2014). https://doi.org/10.1109/HNICEM.2014.7016205, http://ieeexplore.ieee.org/document/7016205/
16. Kowalczuk, Z., Czubenko, M.: Computational approaches to modeling artificial emotion – an overview of the proposed solutions. Front. Robot. AI **3** (2016). https://doi.org/10.3389/frobt.2016.00021, http://journal.frontiersin.org/Article/10.3389/frobt.2016.00021/abstract
17. Kwon, D.S., et al.: Emotion interaction system for a service robot. In: RO-MAN 2007 - The 16th IEEE International Symposium on Robot and Human Interactive Communication. pp. 351–356. IEEE, Jeju, South Korea (2007). https://doi.org/10.1109/ROMAN.2007.4415108, http://ieeexplore.ieee.org/document/4415108/

18. Liu, C., et al.: Speak from heart: an emotion-guided LLM-based multimodal method for emotional dialogue generation. In: Proceedings of the 2024 International Conference on Multimedia Retrieval, pp. 533–542. ICMR '24, Association for Computing Machinery, New York (2024). https://doi.org/10.1145/3652583.3658104
19. Lively, K.J., Heise, D.R.: Emotions in affect control theory. In: Stets, J.E., Turner, J.H. (eds.) Handbook of the Sociology of Emotions: Volume II, pp. 51–75. Springer, Dordrecht (2014).https://doi.org/10.1007/978-94-017-9130-4_4, series Title: Handbooks of Sociology and Social Research
20. Marincioni, A., et al.: The effect of LLM-based NPC emotional states on player emotions: an analysis of interactive game play. In: 2024 IEEE Conference on Games (CoG), pp. 1–6 (2024).https://doi.org/10.1109/CoG60054.2024.10645631, https://ieeexplore.ieee.org/document/10645631/, iSSN: 2325-4289
21. Masuyama, N., Loo, C.K., Seera, M.: Personality affected robotic emotional model with associative memory for human-robot interaction. Neurocomputing **272**, 213–225 (2018)
22. Moors, A., Ellsworth, P.C., Scherer, K.R., Frijda, N.H.: Appraisal theories of emotion: state of the art and future development. Emot. Rev. **5**(2), 119–124 (2013)
23. Nardelli, A., Landolfi, L., Pasquali, D., Sgorbissa, A., Rea, F., Recchiuto, C.: Toward a universal concept of artificial personality: implementing robotic personality in a Kinova arm. arXiv preprint arXiv:2501.06867 (2025)
24. Nardelli, A., Maccagni, G., Minutoli, F., Sgorbissa, A., Recchiuto, C.T.: Personality-and memory-based framework for emotionally intelligent agents. In: 2024 33rd IEEE International Conference on Robot and Human Interactive Communication (ROMAN), pp. 769–776. IEEE (2024)
25. Nardelli, A., Recchiuto, C., Sgorbissa, A.: A software framework to encode the psychological dimensions of an artificial agent. In: 2023 32nd IEEE International Conference on Robot and Human Interactive Communication (RO-MAN), pp. 1711–1718. IEEE (2023)
26. Nardelli, A., Sgorbissa, A., Recchiuto, C.T.: Personality-and memory-based software framework for human-robot interaction. In: 2024 IEEE International Conference on Robotics and Automation (ICRA), pp. 17388–17394. IEEE (2024)
27. Nardelli, A., Sgorbissa, A., Recchiuto, C.T.: Designing empathetic companions: exploring personality, emotion, and trust in social robots (2025). https://arxiv.org/abs/2504.13964
28. Osuna, E., Rodríguez, L.F., Gutierrez-Garcia, J.O., Castro, L.A.: Development of computational models of emotions: a software engineering perspective. Cogn. Syst. Res. **60**, 1–19 (2020)
29. Park, C., Ryu, J., Sohn, J., Cho, H.: An emotion expression system for the emotional robot. In: 2007 IEEE International Symposium on Consumer Electronics. pp. 1–6. IEEE, Irving, TX, USA (Jun 2007).https://doi.org/10.1109/ISCE.2007.4382195, http://ieeexplore.ieee.org/document/4382195/
30. Robinson, D.T., et al.: Mean affective ratings of 932 identities, 810 behaviors, and 660 modifiers by university of Georgia undergraduates in 2012–2014 (2016). https://affectcontroltheory.org//usa-georgia-dictionary-2015/, distributed at Affect Control Theory Website
31. Shank, D.B., Burns, A., Rodriguez, S., Bowen, M.: Software Program, Bot, or Artificial Intelligence? Affective Sentiments across General Technology Labels
32. Siegling, A., Vesely, A.K., Petrides, K., Saklofske, D.H.: Incremental validity of the trait emotional intelligence questionnaire-short form (TEIQue-SF). J. Pers. Assess. **97**(5), 525–535 (2015)

33. Stock-Homburg, R.: Survey of emotions in human-robot interactions: perspectives from robotic psychology on 20 years of research. Int. J. Soc. Robot. **14**(2), 389–411 (2022)
34. Vernon, P.A., Villani, V.C., Schermer, J.A., Petrides, K.: Phenotypic and genetic associations between the big five and trait emotional intelligence. Twin Res. Hum. Genet. **11**(5), 524–530 (2008)
35. Wang, X., Li, X., Yin, Z., Wu, Y., Liu, J.: Emotional intelligence of large language models. J. Pac. Rim Psychol. **17**, 18344909231213958 (2023). https://doi.org/10.1177/18344909231213958
36. Wong, A.S., Nicklin, S., Hong, K., Chalup, S.K., Walla, P.: Robot emotions generated and modulated by visual features of the environment. In: 2013 IEEE Symposium on Computational Intelligence for Creativity and Affective Computing (CICAC), pp. 9–16. IEEE, Singapore, Singapore (2013). https://doi.org/10.1109/CICAC.2013.6595215, http://ieeexplore.ieee.org/document/6595215/
37. Woo, H., LeTendre, G.K., Pham-Shouse, T., Xiong, Y.: The use of social robots in classrooms: a review of field-based studies. Educational Research Review **33**, 100388 (2021). https://doi.org/10.1016/j.edurev.2021.100388, https://www.sciencedirect.com/science/article/pii/S1747938X21000117
38. Yongsatianchot, N., Thejll-Madsen, T., Marsella, S.: What's next in affective modeling? Large language models. In: 2023 11th International Conference on Affective Computing and Intelligent Interaction Workshops and Demos (ACIIW), pp. 1–7 (2023). https://doi.org/10.1109/ACIIW59127.2023.10388124, https://ieeexplore.ieee.org/document/10388124/
39. Zsiga, K., Tóth, A., Pilissy, T., Péter, O., Dénes, Z., Fazekas, G.: Evaluation of a companion robot based on field tests with single older adults in their homes. Assist. Technol. **30**(5), 259–266 (2018)

ial Applications
in HRI
Assistive and Educational Applications in HRI

Human Hand Shape and Grasping Behavior Estimation using a Humanoid Hand with a Tactile Interface

Adnan Saood(✉) and Adriana Tapus

Autonomous Systems and Robotics Lab/U2IS ENSTA, Institute Polytechnique de Paris, Paris, France
{adnan.saood,adriana.tapus}@ensta.fr

Abstract. Understanding and replicating human hand shape and grasping behavior are essential for improving physical human-robot interaction. In this work, we introduce a novel method for estimating both human hand geometry and grasping style using a tactile sensory humanoid hand. Our system integrates a silicone-based glove embedded with pressure sensors and mounted on a robotic hand, allowing users to perform naturalistic grasping gestures. By analyzing the tactile feedback generated during the interaction, we trained AI models to estimate individual hand shapes and classify grasping behaviors. A user study with 19 participants evaluated the comfort and usability of the system. Participants highlighted the softness and responsiveness of the glove. Feedback was used to identify key design improvements, including hand scaling, sensor distribution, and enhanced realism in tactile textures. Our results demonstrate the feasibility of using a tactile humanoid hand as an interactive tool for capturing nuanced human grasp style and hand size with 68% and 96%, respectively.

Keywords: Touch for Robotics · Tactility · HRI

1 Introduction

Touch is a fundamental aspect of human interaction, playing a crucial role in nonverbal communication and emotional expression. It is the first sense to develop in utero [12] and is arguably the most important of all human senses, enabling us to perceive temperature changes, pain, irritation, kinesthesia, and vibration through touch receptors and processing centers in the somatosensory system [13]. The importance of touch in social interactions has been extensively studied, revealing that humans extract significant information from tactile stimuli that enrich their understanding of interactions [3]. This process is influenced by various factors, including the context of the interaction, cultural background, and the emotions of the individuals involved [3].

In the context of Human-Robot Interaction (HRI), touch takes on an even more profound significance. Robots equipped with tactile sensing capabilities can engage in more intuitive and meaningful interactions with humans, improving the overall experience and acceptance of robotic systems [15]. One of the most natural and commonly used forms of touch in social contexts is the handshake. Handshaking serves not only as a gesture of greeting, farewell, or congratulation but also as a way to express emotions and create social bonds [11,14].

Handshakes, as a rich source of tactile information, can convey important cues about the emotional states and intentions of the participants, making it highly relevant for research in human-robot interaction (HRI) [4].

The development of artificial skin and tactile sensing technologies has significantly advanced the field of HRI, enabling robots to "feel" and respond to touch in a manner that mimics human interaction [1]. These developments have enabled more advanced applications, including the use of touch-sensitive humanoid hands to estimate the shape of a person's hand following a handshake [11]. By utilizing the detailed tactile data gathered during the interaction, this approach allows the robot to infer the physical features of the human hand, thereby improving its capacity to interpret and respond to human behavior.

Our tactile sensing system is designed as a glove-like structure that can be adapted to existing humanoid robotic hands. This flexibility presents an opportunity to extend tactile perception capabilities across a wide range of robotic platforms, fostering more intuitive and human-like interactions. The same technology we propose can be adapted to other existing humanoid hands and body parts (forearm, chest, back), various gripper types, and other robot interfaces.

The first version of this system was developed for the Meka M2 hand, a four-fingered, five-degree-of-freedom robotic hand actuated via tendon-driven series elastic actuators [7]. The sensor layout comprises a total of 90 individually addressable pressure sensors: each finger is equipped with 14 sensors, the thumb with 10, and the palm with 38. This arrangement ensures coverage over key contact areas while preserving flexibility and integration simplicity. The entire sensor array is interfaced with a data acquisition system capable of streaming at 1.0 kHz, allowing for real-time tactile signal processing during physical interaction. The sensor positioning and a photo of a person grasping the robot hand are in Fig. 1.

The sensing layer is based on a resistive architecture using Velostat [2] as the pressure-sensitive material. Electrodes are laid out on flexible substrates to enable conformity to the curved geometry of robotic fingers. A thin silicone sheet overlays the sensor layer to enhance grip friction and improve the tactile quality of contact with human skin. Compared to higher-resolution arrays that use Microelectromechanical Systems (MEMS) techniques [8], laser structuring [10], or microstructured Polydimethylsiloxane (PDMS) layers [6], this system avoids specialized fabrication processes and bulky readout hardware. This makes it suitable for scalable integration into robotic hands or grippers. While approaches like [5] offer denser tactile arrays and improved crosstalk handling, our design emphasizes mechanical compliance, manufacturability, and portability, which are key factors in dynamic real-world human-robot interaction scenarios.

Our work proposes a novel technology where a touch-sensitive humanoid hand infers the size of a human hand based on contact patterns. While much

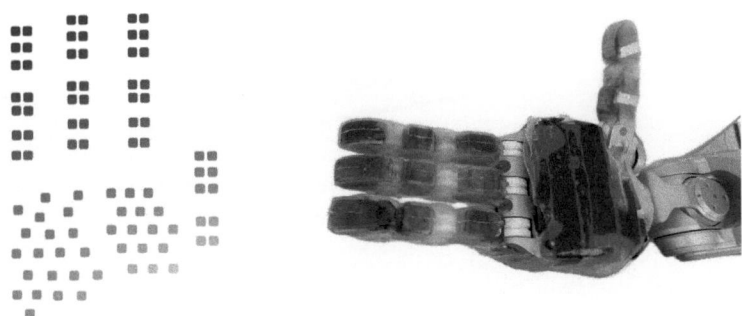

Fig. 1. (Left) Sensors' distribution on the robot hand. (Right) Assembled system.

of the existing research has focused on motion synchronization, grip dynamics, and affective cues during handshakes, the idea of using tactile data for post-contact shape estimation remains largely unexplored. Our approach, which leverages high-resolution tactile sensing on a humanoid robotic hand, offers an avenue for robots to personalize physical interactions in a more anthropomorphically aligned manner. It can support dynamic calibration of robot grip strength, inform ergonomic assumptions, and serve as an auxiliary cue for inferring user traits like age or body size, all of which enhance safety, comfort, and engagement in HRI scenarios.

Additionally, this study aims to determine whether the touch-sensitive robot hand is capable of discerning the human touch strength profile (Gentle, Normal, Aggressive). Unlike previous handshake-based methods, the robot hand in this experiment remains static while participants actively grasp it. The objective is to evaluate the feasibility of using tactile pressure data alone, collected during passive grasping, to infer key morphological and affective features of the human hand.

2 Methods

Perceptive artificial skin has emerged as a pivotal advancement in tactile sensing. Our work presents a tactile sensing system that integrates a high-density touch sensor array beneath a silicone interface, enabling the detection of subtle variations in pressure and contact. Our configuration closely mimics the fine sensory resolution of human skin. By combining a sensitive sensor array with a soft, compliant material, our design enhances tactile precision and supports safer, more natural interactions in both robotic and wearable applications.

Our robotic skin integrates 90 individually addressable sensory modules into a cohesive and robust system. Each module comprises a multilayered architecture: a concentric cathode-anode electrode made from a tin-coated copper pad is mounted on a 200 μm polyethylene terephthalate (PET) substrate. This layer facilitates the measurement of resistance across a 200 μm layer of carbon-black

Fig. 2. Sensory module: 200 μm PET, tin-coated copper electrodes, 200 μm CB-polyolefin, 1.2 mm CB-rubber, 1 mm silicone sheet.

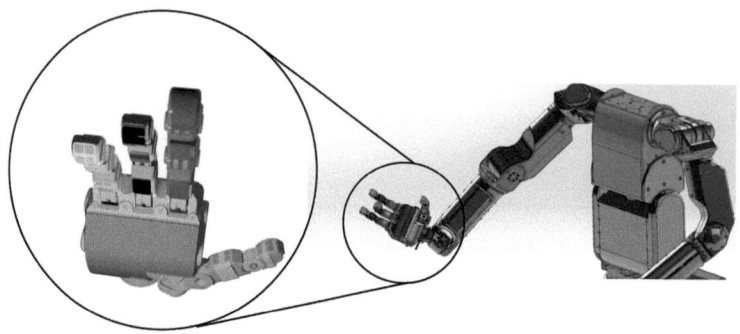

Fig. 3. Meka M3 upper-body robot on the right, with a close-up of Meka's hand equipped with the tactile array.

infused polyolefin (Velostat), which serves as the primary sensing element. A subsequent 1.2 mm layer of CarbonBlack-impregnated rubber extends the sensitivity range, while a 1 mm lab-fabricated silicone sheet reinforces the structure and provides a natural tactile feel akin to human skin. Organized into five groups, with three corresponding to the digital fingers, one for the thumb, and one for the palm. The array is coupled with a dedicated digital signal processing unit for effective filtering and seamless integration with computational systems. The overall system delivers a throughput of 1.44 Mbits/sec. Sensor layers are illustrated in Fig. 2.

The touch interface was implemented on the Meka M3 upper-body humanoid robot, which is specifically designed for interactive tasks. This robot features two 7-degree-of-freedom (DoF) arms and an 8-DoF anthropomorphic head capable of various expressive movements, including gazing, winking, mouth animation, and vision. All motors in the robot are Series Elastic Actuator (SEA) motors, enabling compliant control through hardware and ensuring safe interaction with human subjects. The robot's body is mounted on a Z-axis prismatic joint, allowing for height adjustment to accommodate human subjects of different sizes during interactions. The touch interface is mounted on the Meka robot's right hand, which is a 5-DoF, 4-fingered tendon-driven hand. This setup facilitates natural and safe interactions, making it ideal for studying tactile sensing and hand shape estimation in human-robot interactions (Fig. 3).

When participants grasp the hand, the sensor array captures localized pressure distributions that are indicative of contact points, finger alignment, and grip profile. A Convolutional Neural Network (CNN) was trained using ground truth hand measurements taken during the experiment (Sect. 3). The model learns the mappings between sensor activation patterns and hand geometry size into three categories (Small, Medium, Large). The glove's high-density sensor array produces a 2D pressure map that preserves the spatial structure of the contact, making CNNs well-suited for this task due to their ability to automatically learn local spatial features, generalize across slight variations in hand orientation or pressure intensity, and achieve high classification accuracy without handcrafted features with very low inference time. No motion or active control was involved; the robot's hand remained passive during the experiment.

Additionally, a grip-type k-Nearest Neighbor (KNN) classification model was developed to automatically label the grasp profile as neutral, strong, or gentle based on the temporal and spatial characteristics of the 90-sensor array data.

3 Experimental Design

3.1 Research Question

The research questions we wanted to investigate were as follows:

- Can the pressure distribution captured during a user's grasp of a tactilely sensorized robotic hand be used to accurately estimate the user's hand size?
- How does the softness of the tactile glove affect the naturalness and comfort of the grasping experience?

3.2 Data Recorded

The experiment was conducted under a single condition in which participants manually grasped the robotic hand equipped with a tactile sensor glove. The robotic hand remained passive throughout the interaction, with no actuation or movement involved.

During the experiment, various types of data were collected to support our analysis. For each grasp, tactile pressure data were recorded using the sensorized robotic hand. Before the experiment, participants' hand dimensions—including breadth, length, and palm circumference—were measured, along with background profile information such as height, gender, and age. Following the grasping task, participants completed a post-experiment questionnaire assessing their subjective perceptions, specifically regarding the comfort and perceived naturalness of the interaction.

3.3 Scenario

At the beginning of the study, participants were presented with an information sheet detailing the purpose, procedures, and ethical considerations of the experiment. After reviewing the document, they provided informed consent to participate. Basic demographic and background information, including age, gender, and height. Following this, the experimenter measured anatomical features of the participant's hand. Each participant was then instructed to perform three distinct types of grasps on the static robotic hand equipped with a tactile sensor glove: a gentle grip, a neutral grip, and a strong grip. These variations allowed for the analysis of pressure distribution under different grasping intensities. Each user performed these different grip profiles using their subjective levels.

Each grasp was maintained for approximately 3 to 5 s, during which time pressure data was continuously recorded by the tactile sensors embedded in the robotic hand. To capture subjective feedback, participants then completed a brief post-experiment questionnaire. This included Likert-scale ratings (from 1 to 5) assessing the comfort, realism, and ease of the interaction, as well as open-ended questions inviting participants to describe how the grasp felt and to offer any suggestions for improving the experience.

The collected tactile data was pre-processed (filtered and normalized), and then used to train two models:

- **Grip Type Classifier:** A classification model using the k-Nearest Neighbors algorithm trained on labeled grasp data to detect the grip type (Gentle, Neutral, Strong).
- **Hand Shape Classifier:** A classification model to predict hand size category using Convolutional Neural Networks (CNNs), leveraging their ability to extract localized features from spatial pressure patterns. This CNN uses three convolutional layers with ReLU activations to extract features, progressively increasing feature maps from 1 to 32, then 64, and finally 128. The output is then flattened and fed into two fully connected layers. The first transforms the data to 512 dimensions with ReLU, and the second outputs N logits for classification.

4 Experimental Results

4.1 Participants

Nineteen individuals participated in this experiment, comprising five females, thirteen males, and one user who preferred not to specify. The users are students and personnel at the Institut Polytechnique de Paris (IP Paris). Their ages range from 22 to 24 years (6 participants, 31%), from 25 to 35 years (11 participants, 58%), and from 35 to 56 years (2 participants, 11%) respectively.

4.2 Hand Shape Classifier

We have designed and trained a Convolutional Neural Network (CNN) to classify human hand sizes into three labels (Small, Medium, Large) using grayscale images derived from pressure sensor data. The sensors were arranged on a 2D

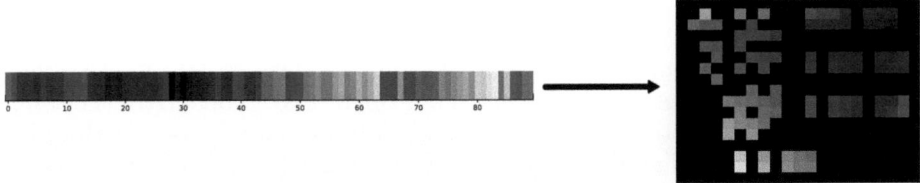

Fig. 4. Example sensors' activations after transforming the data into an image frame determined by the physical location of the sensor. Images are then used to train the CNN.

plane, and their positions were used to reconstruct image-like inputs from user-specific time series. See Fig. 4 for an example data frame.

Each participant's hand was characterized using three anthropometric measurements: hand breadth, palm circumference, and hand height. To categorize hand sizes, a composite metric was computed as the sum of these three dimensions: Size = Breadth + Circumference + Height. Based on the distribution of this metric across all participants, hand size labels were assigned according to quantiles: the bottom 33% were labeled Small, the middle 33% Normal, and the top 33% Large. For dataset generation, ten representative frames were extracted per participant. The corresponding pressure data from each frame was then converted into 21×17 grayscale matrices, aligned with the sensor layout defined in the tactile glove design files.

A three-layer CNN was trained on the resulting images using a stratified dataset split (60% training, 40% testing). The model architecture consisted of three convolutional layers followed by fully connected layers for classification. The training was performed over 50 epochs using cross-entropy loss and the Adam optimizer [9]. This result demonstrates the high potential of pressure data-based imaging for biometric classification; however, further improvements could be achieved through data augmentation, architecture refinement, or multimodal inputs. The confusion matrix for the test dataset is presented in Fig. 5.

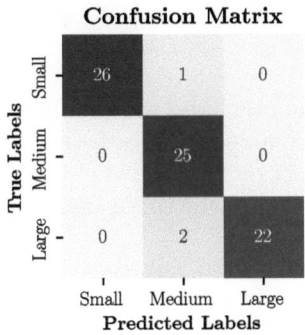

Fig. 5. Confusion matrix of the test dataset of the CNN hand shape classifier.

4.3 Grasp Strength Classifier

To evaluate the discriminative capacity of tactile time-series data in classifying varying grasp intensities, we implemented a k-Nearest Neighbors (KNN) classification framework. Tactile signals were recorded from multiple users performing three distinct types of grasps (Gentle, Normal, Aggressive). These raw recordings were segmented into overlapping sequences of fixed length (35 frames) using a sliding window with a stride of 10, allowing for sample augmentation. Each sequence was transformed into a statistical feature vector by computing descriptors including mean (μ), standard deviation (σ), range (Δ), median ($\tilde{x}$), and variance (σ^2) for each tactile sensor channel. The resulting dataset of feature vectors and their corresponding labels was partitioned into training and testing subsets (70% and 30%, respectively) while preserving class balance.

The KNN classifier achieved a test accuracy of 68%, indicating success in distinguishing between the three grasp types. This performance suggests that while statistical features capture some discriminative information, they may not fully encapsulate the temporal dynamics inherent in tactile sequences. Misclassifications were particularly prevalent between adjacent classes, such as "Gentle" and "Normal" grasps, highlighting the challenge of delineating subtle differences in force application. To enhance classification performance, future work could explore incorporating temporal modeling techniques. Also, a higher user count is needed to enhance this statistical-based classifier.

4.4 Post-Experiment Questionnaire

Participants were asked to complete a structured questionnaire comprising eight Likert-scale items (rated on a 5-point scale) and four open-ended questions.

Quantitative Feedback. Participants evaluated their experience by responding to statements such as "The robotic hand felt comfortable to grasp" and "The experience felt natural, similar to holding a human hand." These statements were rated using a 5-point Likert scale, ranging from Strongly Disagree to Strongly Agree. While individual responses varied, several consistent trends emerged across participants, offering insights into the perceived comfort and realism of the interaction.

- *Comfort*: Although the robotic hand was passive during the interaction, most participants felt they were able to perform the required grip actions without difficulty. However, comfort ratings varied – several participants reported discomfort (42.5%), mainly due to the robot hand's size or shape, which did not fit all hands equally well.
- *Realism*: Few participants (29%) felt that the tactile glove closely resembled the sensation of holding a human hand. Responses to the question of naturalness were mixed, with several participants expressing neutrality or disagreement, suggesting that the experience did not fully align with their expectations of a natural interaction.

- *Usability*: Most participants (72.2%) reported feeling confident in their ability to interact with the system and did not encounter significant usability challenges.

A two-way ANOVA was conducted to examine the effects of gender and hand size group on participants' usability ratings of the tactile glove. The results showed no statistically significant main effect of gender, $F(1, 14) = 0.34$, $p = 0.57$, or hand size group, $F(1, 14) = 0.18$, $p = 0.68$. Additionally, there was no significant interaction effect between gender and hand size group, $F(1, 14) = 0.015$, $p = 0.90$.

These findings indicate that, within the limitations of our sample size, there is no strong evidence that gender or hand size significantly influences perceived usability of the glove. While this may suggest the potential for inclusive design, caution is warranted in drawing definitive conclusions (Table 1). Further studies with larger and more diverse populations are needed to confirm the generalizability of these results.

Table 1. Two-way ANOVA Results for Glove Usability Scores

Source	Sum of Squares	df	F	p-value
Gender	0.096	1	0.34	0.57
Hand Size Group	0.051	1	0.18	0.68
Gender × Hand Size	0.004	1	0.015	0.90
Residual	3.979	14	–	–

Open-Ended Responses. The open-ended section of the questionnaire provided valuable qualitative insights. Recurring themes are highlighted below.

- *Positive Impressions:* Softness and Texture: Many users appreciated the soft, skin-like texture of the glove, noting it felt "grippy" and similar to human skin. For example, one participant commented, "The touch and the feeling are similar to human hands", while another said, "The hand is dexterous, made me feel good."
- *Discomfort and Unrealistic Aspects:* Hand Size and Morphology: A common concern expressed by participants was that the robotic hand felt larger or less proportionate compared to a human hand, which made it challenging to grasp naturally. Some participants mentioned, "The hand is quite square at the base and larger than typical hands," and "The size of the robot hand feels too big for a natural handshake."
- *Material and Joint Design:* Several users found the material or internal structure too rigid. One participant observed, "When I grab the finger joint of the robot it is rectangle and the edges are hard."

General Observations: Overall, users had a positive experience, though they noted it differed from natural human touch. Some participants appreciated handshaking the robot's hand, while others provided constructive feedback for future improvements. The glove was viewed as promising for interactive applications, but participants suggested that adjustments to its shape, texture, and interactivity are necessary to create a more lifelike and natural experience. Most of the comfort-related concerns were attributed to the shape of the Meka M2 hand rather than the tactile array itself.

5 Conclusion

This work presents an innovative tactile sensing system for humanoid robotic hands, capable of estimating the shape of human hands through passive tactile interaction. Utilizing a flexible and scalable 90-sensor array embedded in a soft, glove-like interface, the system collects detailed pressure data during a static grasp. Unlike traditional handshake studies, this passive sensing method eliminates any robotic motion, allowing for a focused analysis of the tactile imprint generated solely by the human hand.

Experimental results indicate that the pressure distribution patterns collected during user-initiated grasps contain enough spatial and intensity information to accurately classify human hand sizes when analyzed using Convolutional Neural Networks (CNNs). The inclusion of a grip-type classifier enhances the system's capability by adding a layer of context to the interaction, allowing for the classification of different grasp types, such as neutral, gentle, and strong. This dual classification approach not only improves the system's overall accuracy but also provides deeper insights into the dynamic characteristics of human-robot interactions, offering potential for more personalized and adaptable robotic systems.

The system presents a promising alternative to traditional techniques that rely on visual or motion-based methods for inferring human morphology in human-robot interaction (HRI) scenarios. Its mechanical flexibility, real-time data acquisition, and compatibility with existing robotic platforms make it an effective and scalable solution to enhance robotic perceptual systems. Additionally, the design prioritizes manufacturability, adaptability, and user comfort, making it well-suited for future applications in social robotics, prosthetics, and personalized human-machine interactions.

One important limitation of this study is the relatively small and homogeneous sample size of 19 participants, which may constrain the generalizability of the findings. All participants were recruited from a single institution and may not reflect the broader population in terms of hand morphology, strength distribution, or interaction styles. To address this, future work will expand the participant pool with more diverse demographic profiles and conduct power analyses to ensure sufficient statistical validity. This will help assess the stability of the proposed methods across a wider range of users.

Participant feedback from the tactile glove evaluation revealed that users generally appreciated the glove's softness and dexterity, with many noting its natural feel and responsive pressure. However, common concerns were raised regarding the oversized robotic hand, the rigid structure beneath the glove, and the lack of realistic skin texture. Suggestions for improvement included exploring alternative robotic hand systems with more anatomically accurate proportions to improve the continuity between the fingers and the palm.

This work demonstrates that human hand shape inference can be effectively achieved using passive tactile data alone, opening up new possibilities in tactile perception and revealing the previously unexplored potential of touch in human-robot communication.

Acknowledgment. The research leading to these results has received funding from the École nationale supérieure de techniques avancées (ENSTA). We extend our thanks to ENSTA students and to the interns of U2IS for their participation in the experimental validation.

References

1. Dahiya, R.S., Metta, G., Valle, M., Sandini, G.: Tactile sensing–from humans to humanoids **26**(1), 1–20. 10.1109/TRO.2009.2033627
2. Dzedzickis, A., et al.: Polyethylene-carbon composite (velostat®) Based Tactile Sensor **12**(12), 2905. 10.3390/polym12122905
3. van Erp, J.B.F., Toet, A.: Social touch in human–computer interaction **2**. 10.3389/fdigh.2015.00002. publisher: Frontiers
4. Hertenstein, M.J., Holmes, R., McCullough, M., Keltner, D.: The communication of emotion via touch **9**(4), 566–573. 10.1037/a0016108, place: US Publisher: American Psychological Association
5. Hu, X., et al.: High-resolution, high-speed and low-cost flexible tactile sensor array system **241**, 115630. 10.1016/j.measurement.2024.115630
6. Ji, Z., et al.: The design and characterization of a flexible tactile sensing array for robot skin **16**(12) (2001). 10.3390/s16122001, number: 12 Publisher: Multidisciplinary Digital Publishing Institute
7. Junior, A.G.L., Filho, R.M.d.A.a.A.B., Junior, A.G.L., Filho, R.M.d.A.a.A.B.: Series elastic actuator: Design, analysis and comparison. In: Recent Advances in Robotic Systems. IntechOpen. 10.5772/63573
8. Kim, K., et al.: Polymer-based flexible tactile sensor up to 32 × 32 arrays integrated with interconnection terminals **156**(2), 284–291. 10.1016/j.sna.2009.08.015
9. Kingma, D.P., Ba, J.: Adam: A method for stochastic optimization. 10.48550/arXiv.1412.6980
10. Kõiva, R., Zenker, M., Schürmann, C., Haschke, R., Ritter, H.J.: A highly sensitive 3D-shaped tactile sensor. In: 2013 IEEE/ASME International Conference on Advanced Intelligent Mechatronics, pp. 1084–1089. 10.1109/AIM.2013.6584238, ISSN: 2159-6255
11. Orefice, P.H., Ammi, M., Hafez, M., Tapus, A.: Let's handshake and I'll know who you are: gender and personality discrimination in human-human and human-robot handshaking interaction. In: 2016 IEEE-RAS 16th International Conference on Humanoid Robots (Humanoids), pp. 958–965. 10.1109/HUMANOIDS.2016.7803388, ISSN: 2164-0580

12. Development of Normal Fetal Movements. Springer, Milano (2015). https://doi.org/10.1007/978-88-470-5373-1
13. Robles-De-La-Torre, G.: The importance of the sense of touch in virtual and real environments **13**(3), 24–30. 10.1109/MMUL.2006.69
14. Shibata, T.: An overview of human interactive robots for psychological enrichment **92**(11), 1749–1758. 10.1109/JPROC.2004.835383
15. Silvera-Tawil, D., Rye, D., Velonaki, M.: Artificial skin and tactile sensing for socially interactive robots: a review **63**, 230–243. 10.1016/j.robot.2014.09.008

Evaluating Children Engagement and Robot Perception Interacting with NAO Robot in Educational Context: A Feasibility Study

Laura Fiorini[1(✉)], Chiara Pecini[2], Marco Vincenzo Maselli[1], Lorenzo Pugi[1], Elena Adelucci[1], Helene Musca[1], Jasmine Pani[1], Stefano Scatigna[2], Maria Chiara Di Lieto[3], Benedetta Del Lucchese[3], Giuseppina Sgandurra[3,4], and Filippo Cavallo[1]

[1] Department of Industrial Engineering, University of Florence, Florence, Italy
laura.fiorini@unifi.it
[2] Department of Education, Languages, Interculture, Literatures and Psychology, University of Florence, Florence, Italy
[3] Department of Developmental Neuroscience, IRCCS Stella Maris Foundation, Calambrone, Pisa, Italy
[4] Department of Clinical and Experimental Medicine, University of Pisa, Pisa, Italy

Abstract. Socially assistive robots are increasingly used in educational contexts, particularly to support children's learning. This study investigates children's engagement and perception of a humanoid robot (NAO) through two paradigms: (1) Reorder a Story, where children help the robot sequence story frames, and (2) Storytelling, where children narrate a story to the robot. Thirty-four typically developing children participated, randomly assigned to one of the two conditions. Robot perception was assessed using the Godspeed questionnaire (focusing on likeability, anthropomorphism, social intelligence, and trust), and engagement was evaluated via the Martinovic Observation Scale and interaction duration. Results show that while both paradigms received high likeability ratings, Reorder a Story elicited significantly higher engagement and perceptions of social intelligence and trust. Engagement scores were not influenced by gender or educational level, although older children perceived higher robot social intelligence in the Reorder a Story task. Correlation analyses revealed a trend between higher perceived social intelligence and lower attention in the Storytelling paradigm, suggesting potential distraction due to the robot's social presence. These findings highlight the potential use of these paradigms with children with neurodevelopmental disorders.

Keywords: social robot · children · storytelling · reorder a story · engagement

1 Introduction

Socially assistive robots are increasingly becoming a part of our daily lives, particularly in educational and healthcare settings where they are now being widely used with children, especially with those with Autism Spectrum Disorder [1]. Over the past few years, several activities were implemented to be used with children in healthcare and educational contexts. For instance, robots are used as a peer, exploiting the learning by teaching paradigm, or used in storytelling, educational or theatrical activities [2].

Educational Robotics (ER) is a branch of social robotics that has gained substantial interest in education at all levels [3] and has emerged as a transformative tool in classrooms [4]. ER explores how child-robot interaction (CRI) can enhance learning processes, making it a valuable tool for fostering cognitive and social skills and attracting the attention of educators and researchers. Belpaeme et al. [5] argued that ER *"has the potential to become part of the educational infrastructure, just as paper, whiteboards, and computer tablets ..."*. Indeed, ER can promote personalized learning and could act as social companions that encourage emotional and cognitive engagement [6]. A key reason for the observed improvements in academic performance, when robots are used in the classroom, is the fact that robots are especially appealing to children because of their physical form and novelty [2]. Additionally, it is evident that, in some cases, people find it easier to talk to a robot than to another person [7].

However, in order to be perceived as social competent companions, the robot should show appropriate behaviors with advanced CRI. In this context, the primary aim of advanced CRI is to create an intelligent and responsive communication channel, where the child remains central to the learning environment. To achieve this objective we need to equip the robot with effective sensing capabilities—such as automated engagement detection—allowing it to adjust its behavior and tailor the educational experience accordingly [2, 8, 9]. Engagement is a widely used terms used in different context, in social robotic field we are referring to this term as *"the user intention to establish and maintain a connection with the robotic agent for the duration of the task as well as with the task"* [10].

Additionally, for studying children's long-term interactions with robots, we will need to understand not only the relationships children are developing, but also how children percept and consider the robot. Indeed, children's perceptions of the robot's socialness, animacy, and human-likeness may be important factors in how they ultimately relate to the robot and whether they treat it as a relational agent [11].

Therefore, it is essential to understand both the child's perception of the robot and their engagement with the task as a fundamental step before applying such systems in educational contexts for long-term use. Since the interaction involves three key elements—the child, the robot, and the task—a feasibility study must take into account the child's perception of the robot as well as their level of task engagement. Notably, children may engage with different tasks in varying ways, even if their perception of the robot remains the same. Additionally, it is important to assess whether sociodemographic factors (e.g., educational level, gender) influence the child's perception of the robot and their engagement.

In this context, this paper reports a between-subjects feasibility study investigating children's interactions with the NAO robot across two tasks grounded in the learning-by-teaching paradigm. The study examines children's perception of the robot, assesses their engagement, and explores the influence of sociodemographic factors, as well as the relationship between robot perception and engagement.

1.1 Aims of This Study

The aim of this paper is threefold: i) Firstly, this paper aims to evaluate two paradigms to be performed with children in schools considering two important aspects: how the child perceives the robot and how engaged they are with the paradigm they are requested to perform with the robot. ii) Secondly, it is also important to investigate demographic factors such as age or sex may or may not influence the robot perception and engagement evaluation. What is considered engaging may be different for boys versus girls and for younger versus older children. iii) Lastly, this paper aims to investigate how the children perception about the social influence or trust will influence their engagement during the task.

2 Material and Methods

2.1 System Overview

The system is composed of the elements depicted in Fig. 1: a NAO robot (Softbank Robotics, United Robotics Group, France), a foldable computer that act as a tablet and RGB-D camera (Orbbec Astra Pro, Orbbec Inc.). We rely on NAO robot, since it is the most used one in the educational context [12]. Additionally, recent research highlights that having humanoids robots – such as Pepper or NAO – may increase acceptance, interaction, and willingness to communicate among children of all ages [13]. In this study, to perform gestures and dialogues appropriate to the paradigm NAO was programmed in Python 2.7 using NAOqi APIs. The custom user interface on the tablet is used to guide the child through the paradigm, and to properly manage the camera acquisition. The RGB-D camera was adopted to record the whole interaction, the acquired data was not used in this paper. Two paradigms were compared to assess whether they can be used in educational context with children: 'Reorder a Story' and 'Storytelling'. The paradigms are explained in the following sections.

Reorder a Story
In this paradigm, the child is asked to assist or teach the NAO robot in determining the correct sequence of a story composed of different frames, following the *learning by teaching* approach [14]. NAO displays individual story frames (visual and speech content) on the interface and asks for the child's help in reordering them into correct chronological sequences. In this feasibility study, NAO presents a total of six stories, varying in complexity with increasing numbers of characters and environments. The stories consisted of different numbers of frames, 3 stories consisted of 4 frames, 2 stories of 4 and 1 of 6. The child rearranges the frames on the interface, and progression to the next level occurs only if all frames are placed in the correct order. If a mistake is made, NAO provides suggestions to guide the child. After each story completion, NAO asks the child whether they would like to continue or exit the game by pressing the corresponding button on the interface. At the end of the interaction, NAO thanks the child for their participation. More details on the game logic are reported in Maselli et al. [15].

Storytelling

In this paradigm, the child is requested to tell the NAO robot a story, using his/her imagination. No constraints were given regarding duration nor content. At the beginning, the robot explains the task, and then it asks whether the child would like to play by pressing the appropriate button on the interface. At the end of the interaction NAO thanks the child. More information on this game logic is reported in Fiorini et al. [16].

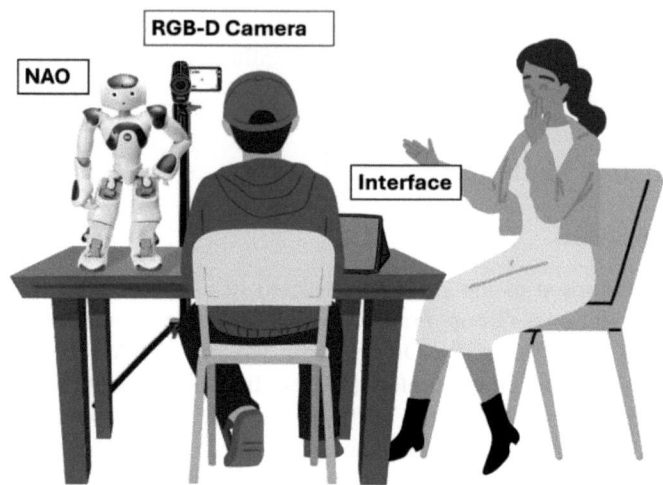

Fig. 1. Experimental setup used for these tests.

2.2 Experimental Setting

Each child participated in an individual interaction session with the robot, that lasted between 15 and 30 min. A teacher and an engineer assisted the experiment acting as facilitators, ready to intervene in case of necessity (Fig. 1).

The experimental procedure consisted of three main phases: the initiation of the activity, the interaction with the NAO robot, and a closing phase. During the initiation of the activities, the teacher welcomed the child and explained the paradigm ('Storytelling' or 'Reorder a Story'). The child was asked to sit in front of the NAO and the tablet, then the paradigm was initiated. During the interaction with the robot phase, the child is requested to interact with the robot, as detailed in Sect. 2.1. In the closing phase, the NAO farewells the child and the child then is requested to fill in the questionnaires, as detailed in Sect. 2.3. The entire interaction was recorded and analyzed off-line to evaluate the child engagement.

2.3 Evaluation Tools

The child's perception of the robot was evaluated using the Godspeed Questionnaire [17]. In line with the approach adopted in [13], we looked at the likeability (LIK), anthropomorphism (ANT), Social Intelligence (SI) and Trust constructs. In particular, the following couples of opposite adjectives were chosen:

- LIK: dislike/like; unkind/kind; unfriendly/friendly; awful/nice.
- ANT: fake/natural; machine-like/human-like; artificial/life-like; unconsciousness/consciousness; moving rigidly/ moving elegantly.
- SI: knows a few things/knows many things; irresponsible/responsible; unintelligent/intelligence; Foolish/Sensible.
- Trust: relaxed/anxious; calm/agitated.

The Martinovic Engagement Observation Scale is a structured observational instrument designed to assess behavioral and cognitive engagement in children [18]. This scale evaluates 8 engagement dimensions: happiness (HAP), frustration (FRU), task comprehension (TSC), attention (ATT), anxiety (ANX), distraction (DIS), need of encouragement (ENC), commitment (COM). As mentioned in the previous section, engagement of the child from the video recording was evaluated offline by three raters. The observers rate each dimension on a 5-points Likert scale where 1 state for "not at all" and 5 for "completely". The final scores are determined by consensus among three raters. For this analysis, we computed the total engagement score (TES) as the sum of the score obtained in each domain (inverting the negative questions). Finally, as for direct behavioral engagement measures, we measured the total interaction time measured in seconds [s].

Table 1. Recruited participants demographics.

	Reorder a Story	Storytelling	p
Number	17	17	-
Gender Male/Female	7/10	8/9	n.s.
Education low/high	8/9	8/9	n.s.

2.4 Participants

Children were recruited from schools located in the Tuscany Region (Italy). Authorizations were obtained from the school principal and the child's parents. The study was approved by the University of Florence Research Ethics Committee (PROT. N. 0232510, 30/09/2024) and was conducted according to ethical standards of the Declaration of Helsinki.

A total of 34 typical children were included in this study. Participants were randomly assigned to one of the two paradigms and their demographics are reported in Table 1. As sociodemographic factors, we took notes only of the gender and class. For this analysis, children attending first or secondary elementary class were grouped into *low* educational level; children attending the fourth or the fifth year were grouped as *high* educational level. Fisher's exact test was used to investigate differences among gender (male vs female) and educational level (high vs low) between the two paradigm conditions and no differences (p > 0.05) were found.

2.5 Data Analysis

Mean and standard deviation (SD) values were computed for all the Godspeed's and the Martinovic Observation Scale's domains. Mann-Whitney U test was used to assess the differences in the evaluation of the robot's perception and the engagement between the two paradigms. The same test was applied to investigate the role of the gender and of the educational level in the robot perception and in the engagement evaluation within each paradigm tested. Finally, Kendall correlation was performed between SI and trust, and between total interaction time and engagement score (including TES).

For each analysis, p-values were adjusted using the Benjamini-Hochberg method [19].

3 Results

This paper aims to investigate the robot perception, and the child engagement with the task. It also investigates the role of the gender and the educational level in their perception. Finally, it evaluates the interplay between the engagement and the robot perception in terms of trust and social influence. The following sections report the results organized according to paper aims.

3.1 Robot Perception in the Two Paradigms

As for the robot perception, the results report high scores for the LIK evaluation in both paradigms with low standard deviation ($LIK_{story} = 4.96 \pm 0.13$; $LIK_{reorder} = 4.99 \pm 0.06$). Similar results were obtained also for the ANT and SI ($ANT_{story} = 4.09 \pm 0.65$; $ANT_{reorder} = 3.94 \pm 0.62$; $SI_{story} = 4.96 \pm 0.13$; $SI_{reorder} = 4.99 \pm 0.06$). The 'Storytelling' paradigm received lower scores in the Trust domain. Notably, the Trust evaluation was reverse-coded, meaning that lower trust scores indicated higher trust in the NAO robot. Statistical analysis revealed that these paradigms were significantly different for Trust ($p < 0.001$) and remained significant even after adjusting for multiple comparisons (adjusted p-value = 0.0007). Complete results are depicted in Fig. 2.a.

3.2 Child Engagement with the Task

The duration of the interaction with the NAO was different in the two paradigms due to the specific peculiarities of the tasks they are requested to perform with the robot. Indeed, the recruited children interact for an average time equal to 579.52 s for the 'Reorder a Story' paradigm and an average time equal to 84.24 s for the 'Storytelling'. All the children considered in the analysis of the 'Storytelling' paradigm completed the task, on the contrary, only 13 children out of 17 completed the six stories, whereas the remaining stopped the interaction after completing three (N = 3) or two (N = 1) stories. The children that did not complete the task were among the younger ("low education").

From a visual inspection of Fig. 2.b we can observe two different engagement perception for the two paradigms with a general higher engagement for the 'Reorder a Story' paradigm except for the "show commitment" (COM) and the "happiness" (HAP) evaluation which was slightly higher for the 'Reorder a Story' paradigm. The trend is confirmed by the mean TES score, which provides an indication of the aggregate engagement value, was 27.90 for the 'Storytelling' paradigm and 33.53 for the 'Reorder a Story' paradigm, indicating overall higher engagement in the latter. This difference was statistically significant ($p < 0.001$). The statistical analysis confirmed significant differences in the observed engagement for the FRU ($p < 0.001$), ANX ($p < 0.001$), DIS ($p < 0.001$), ENC ($p < 0.001$) and COM ($p = 0.02$), which remained statistically significant after correction for multiple comparisons.

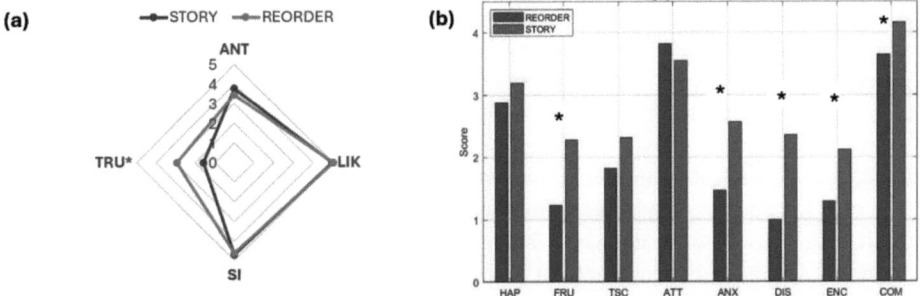

Fig. 2. Results of the Godspeed (a) and the Martinovic et al. (b) questionnaires for the storytelling (orange) and the reorder a story (blue) paradigms. Significant differences after Benjamini Hochberg correction were marked with asterisk.

3.3 Influences of Gender and Educational Level on Robot Perception and Engagement Evaluation

The results indicates that robot perception was not affected by the gender in both tested paradigm ($p > 0.05$). The children evaluate differently the SI of the robot in the "Reorder a Story" according to the educational level ($p = 0.03$), which was not statistically significant after adjusting for multiple comparison. Nevertheless, the younger children gave a significant higher evaluation (SI = 4.88) of the SI compared to the older ones (SI = 4.39).

3.4 Interplay Between Engagement with the Task and Social Intelligence and Trust Perception

As for the interplay between the engagement evaluation and the perceived SI, in the 'Storytelling' paradigm we found a moderate positive significant correlation between the SI and the TSK ($\tau = 0.40$, $p = 0.04$) and between SI and the ENC ($\tau = 0.41$, $p = 0.04$). These correlations disappeared after the correction. No significant correlation was found between SI and engagement in the "Reorder a story" paradigm. There was no correlation between the perceived Trust and engagement to the task in both paradigms.

4 Discussion

This paper aims to investigate three different research questions. The results confirm a general positive evaluation of the child, in fact, scores were high in both paradigms, and were also slightly higher than similar studies performed with the NAO robot (score of 4) [20].

However, the child evaluated differently the robot in terms of trust depending on the paradigm. They reported an higher level of trust in the NAO when involved in the 'Storytelling' scenario compared to 'Reorder a story' one (inverted item). It is worth noting that this different evaluation of the two paradigms was not dependent on the gender and educational level, which could be positive when thinking that the paradigm can be used with different group of children. The different trend between the paradigms is confirmed also by the engagement evaluations assigned from the external observers. Conversely to the trusted evaluation, the children were generally more engaged in the 'Reorder a Story' paradigm, showing significant lower scores of frustration and anxiety. However, the children shown comparable attention, happiness, commitment to the task, and needed the same encouragement in both paradigms.

In the 'Reorder a Story' paradigm, the children are requested to connect the visual stimuli (the stories) with the vocal storyline, therefore it could be more cognitively demanding for the children. In effect younger children (low education) completed less stories. However, the statistical analysis did not highlight differences on the engagement evaluation depending on the gender, nor on the educational level. Therefore, even if the younger children felt the task more complex, it is not reflected on their engagement on the task. From exploitation in real-world scenarios, this is an important achievement, since the paradigms can be used from different children without distinction.

The way in which the robots are perceived can influence the long-term relationship between the child and the robot. Since the robot was evaluated differently in the two paradigms in terms of social intelligence and trust, we evaluated whether these items were correlated with the child engagement. Statistical analysis revealed a moderate correlation between the SI and the ATT and DIS domains for the 'Storytelling' paradigm. These correlations indicated that higher the perception of the robot's social influence is, the lower attention is given to it during the task. However, this effect is not present in the 'Reorder a Story' scenario. Even if these differences disappear after the correction, they may indicate a trend that should be further explored enlarging the sample. It is also worth noting that the social intelligence of NAO robot in the 'Reorder a Story' scenario is different according to the age group, therefore, further studies should be performed considering also the age/educational variables as important factor to be considered in the analysis.

5 Conclusion

This study aimed to compare two paradigms exploiting the Learning By Teaching paradigm implemented with the NAO robot. Both paradigms were positively evaluated by the children, indicating general high engagement. However, the type of paradigm did influence certain aspects of the children's perception of the robot and their engagement with the task. Notably, these differences were not associated with age or gender. Moreover, variations in the perception of the robot did not significantly affect engagement levels after correcting for multiple comparisons. This is a meaningful finding, as a child's perception of the robot—as well as their engagement—may influence the quality and sustainability of long-term interactions. The results support the use of both paradigms with typically developing children, as they not only enjoyed the interaction but also remained actively engaged. However, if we aim to use these paradigm and the corresponding engagement responses as an assessment tool to differentiate between typical and atypical development in support of diagnosis, we observe that one task offers a much faster assessment, while the other keeps the child more engaged, potentially revealing engagement-related dynamics associated with the condition that may not emerge with the quicker task. These paradigms are now being further evaluated with children with neurodevelopmental disorders within the framework of the Fit for Medical Robotics project[1], using data from sensors to measure the engagement. Indeed, future analyses will explore whether engagement dynamics in these populations are similarly influenced by the nature of the interaction and perceived robot characteristics, as well as the disorders.

Acknowledgments. This work was supported by the Italian Ministry of Research, under the complementary actions to the NRRP "Fit4MedRob - Fit for Medical Robotics" Grant (# PNC0000007).

Disclosure of Interests. The authors have no competing interests.

References

1. Dawe, J., Sutherland, C., Barco, A., Broadbent, E.: Can social robots help children in healthcare contexts? A scoping review. BMJ Paediatr. Open **3** (2019)
2. Lytridis, C., Bazinas, C., Papakostas, G.A., Kaburlasos, V.: On measuring engagement level during child-robot interaction in education. In: Merdan, M., Lepuschitz, W., Koppensteiner, G., Balogh, R., Obdržálek, D. (eds.) RiE 2019. AISC, vol. 1023, pp. 3–13. Springer, Cham (2020). https://doi.org/10.1007/978-3-030-26945-6_1
3. Pachidis, T., Vrochidou, E., Kaburlasos, V.G., Kostova, S., Bonkovic, M., Papic, V.: Social robotics in education: State-of-the-art and directions. In: International Conference on Robotics in Alpe-Adria Danube Region, pp. 689–700. Springer, Cham (2019). https://doi.org/10.1007/978-3-030-00232-9_72
4. Chatzichristofis, S.A.: Recent advances in educational robotics. Electronics **12** (2023)
5. Belpaeme, T., Kennedy, J., Ramachandran, A., et al.: Social robots for education: a review. Sci. Robot. **3** (2018). https://doi.org/10.1126/SCIROBOTICS.AAT5954/ASSET/1FC69744-0C7C-45CB-8A74-F1063B085D30/ASSETS/GRAPHIC/AAT5954-F4.JPEG

---

[1] Fit for Medical Robotics official website: https://www.fit4medrob.it/.

6. Pivetti, M., Di Battista, S., Agatolio, F., et al.: Educational robotics for children with neurodevelopmental disorders: a systematic review. Heliyon **6** (2020)
7. Robinson, N.L., Kavanagh, D.J.: A social robot to deliver a psychotherapeutic treatment: qualitative responses by participants in a randomized controlled trial and future design recommendations. Int. J. Hum. Comput. Stud. **155** (2021). https://doi.org/10.1016/j.ijhcs.2021.102700
8. Drysdale, B.M., Moore, D.W., Furlonger, B.E., Anderson, A.: Gaze patterns of Individuals with ASD during active task engagement: a systematic literature review. Rev. J. Autism Dev. Disord. **5** (2018)
9. Anzalone, S.M., Boucenna, S., Ivaldi, S., Chetouani, M.: Evaluating the engagement with social robots. Int. J. Soc. Robot. (2015). https://doi.org/10.1007/s12369-015-0298-7
10. Sorrentino, A., Fiorini, L., Cavallo, F.: From the definition to the automatic assessment of engagement in human-robot interaction: a systematic review. Int. J. Soc. Robot. **16**, 1641–1663 (2024)
11. Kory-Westlund, J.M., Breazeal, C.: Assessing children's perceptions and acceptance of a social robot. In: Proceedings of the 18th ACM International Conference on Interaction Design and Children, IDC 2019, pp. 38–50. Association for Computing Machinery, Inc. (2019)
12. Woo, H., LeTendre, G.K., Pham-Shouse, T., Xiong, Y.: The use of social robots in classrooms: a review of field-based studies. Educ. Res. Rev. **33** (2021)
13. Roštšinskaja, A., Saard, M., Korts, L., et al.: Unlocking the potential of social robot pepper: a comprehensive evaluation of child-robot interaction. J. Pediatr. Health Care (2025). https://doi.org/10.1016/j.pedhc.2025.01.010
14. Duran, D.: Learning-by-teaching. Evidence and implications as a pedagogical mechanism. Innov. Educ. Teach. Int. **54**, 476–484 (2017). https://doi.org/10.1080/14703297.2016.1156011
15. Maselli, M., Musca, H., Pecini, C., et al.: Can you help me to re-order a story? Design and development of a game-based activity with NAO for children with neurodevelopmental disorders. In: National Congress of Bioengineering. Proceedings. Patron Editore srl (2025)
16. Fiorini, L., et al.: Exploring emotional and cognitive engagement in school age children: an in-depth analysis of interaction with the NAO social robot during the storytelling activity. In: Fiorini, L., Sorrentino, A., Siciliano, P., Cavallo, F. (eds.) ForItAAL 2024. LNB, pp. 243–252. Springer, Cham (2024). https://doi.org/10.1007/978-3-031-77318-1_16
17. Bartneck, C., Kulić, D., Croft, E., Zoghbi, S.: Measurement instruments for the anthropomorphism, animacy, likeability, perceived intelligence, and perceived safety of robots. Int. J. Soc. Robot. **1** (2009)
18. Martinovic, D., Burgess, G.H., Pomerleau, C.M., Marin, C.: Computer games that exercise cognitive skills: what makes them engaging for children? Comput. Hum. Behav. **60**, 451–462 (2016). https://doi.org/10.1016/j.chb.2016.02.063
19. Fachada, N., Rosa, A.C.: micompm: A MATLAB/Octave toolbox for multivariate independent comparison of observations. J. Open Sour. Softw. **3**, 430 (2018). https://doi.org/10.21105/joss.00430
20. Mara, M., Appel, M., Gnambs, T.: Human-like robots and the uncanny valley: a meta-analysis of user responses based on the godspeed scales. Zeitschrift fur Psychologie J. Psychol. **230**, 33–46 (2022)

Wearable Social Robots for the Disabled and Impaired

Oliver Bendel(✉)

FHNW School of Business, 5210 Windisch, Switzerland
`oliver.bendel@fhnw.ch`

Abstract. Wearable social robots can be found on a chain around the neck, on clothing, or in a shirt or jacket pocket. Due to their constant availability and responsiveness, they can support the disabled and impaired in a variety of ways and improve their lives. This article first identifies and summarizes robotic and artificial intelligence functions of wearable social robots. It then derives and categorizes areas of application. Following this, the opportunities and risks, such as those relating to privacy and intimacy, are highlighted. Overall, it emerges that wearable social robots can be useful for this group, for example, by providing care and information anywhere and at any time. However, significant improvements are still needed to overcome existing shortcomings.

Keywords: Social Robots · Wearable Social Robots · Wearables · Care Robots · Therapy Robots · Disability · Inclusive AI · Inclusive Robotics

1 Introduction

Small social robots have become widespread in homes and offices in the 2020s. They are used for learning, entertainment, and information. They are marketed as educational and toy robots or as desktop robots, among other things, with overlaps between the areas. Examples of educational and toy robots include Cozmo or Vector from Anki/Digital Dream Labs, Loti-Bot from TTS, and Eilik from Energize Lab. Examples of desktop robots include LOOI from TangibleFuture and Emo or AIBI from LivingAI. AIBI is special because it can not only stand and rotate on its charging station but can also be worn around the neck and attached to clothing. All the models mentioned can be carried in a handbag or in a shirt or jacket pocket. But AIBI is a wearable social robot in the true sense of the word, and its entire design, size, and weight are geared towards this.

Wearable social robots still occupy a small market. They have the usual teething problems, as can be seen with AIBI where the forums are overflowing with requests and complaints [17, 22]. But in the future, they could be used in various areas of application and be useful and beneficial there. In addition to healthy people, people with disabilities and impairments can also benefit. Previous studies have focused on care and therapy robots such as Lio, Care-O-bot, HospiBot, Paro, QTrobot, or Moxie [9, 19]. Small, wearable social robots, on the other hand, have hardly been in focus, which is mainly due to their novelty, their low distribution, and their low level of awareness. Accordingly, it must be explained what possible uses there are and what opportunities and risks may arise. Empirical studies can follow in later projects.

This article deals with wearable social robots for disabled and impaired persons. This raises three research questions: What are wearable social robots? How can they support disabled and impaired individuals? And, what are the social, ethical, economic, and technical implications? In Sect. 2, this article defines what wearable social robots are and categorizes them as wearable robots and social robots. It also gives several examples. In Sect. 3, it lists and classifies possible areas of application for disabled and impaired persons. In Sect. 4, social, ethical, economic, and technical challenges are presented, using the considerations gained previously. At the end there is a summary and outlook.

2 Basics of Wearable Robots

In the following, a conceptual definition of wearable social robots is first provided. Selected examples are then presented, including both products and prototypes. Finally, the findings from the descriptions are summarized.

2.1 Definition of Terms

Wearable social robots can be seen as a subgroup of wearable robots, i.e., robots or robotic components that people carry with them, on them, or in them [1, 33]. They differ significantly from conventional models made of hard materials, i.e., high-tech prostheses and exoskeletons designed for both disabled and healthy individuals. Furthermore, wearable social robots are social robots that can be understood as sensorimotor machines intended for humans or animals [8]. Artificial intelligence (AI) is integrated into some wearable social robots, for example, in the form of facial recognition or generative AI, in particular large language models, so-called LLMs. In this context, one can speak of inclusive robotics [2] and inclusive AI [3].

Wearable social robots are so small and light that they can fit in a shoulder bag, handbag, shirt or jacket pocket ("pocket robots"), be attached to clothing or worn on the hand or around the neck. A few, such as AIBI, are designed to do just that. They do not or hardly move the body, so that the wearer is not disturbed or inconvenienced, and look forwards (Fig. 2) or to the side (Fig. 1). To ensure that they work reliably and without exception when on the move, it makes sense that they can be operated independently of the Internet, at least in their basic functions. If one stays in one place for a while or sets up a hotspot, one can connect them with ChatGPT, for example. Some wearable social robots can interact and communicate with other devices or wearable social robots of the same model series.

2.2 Selected Examples of Wearable Social Robots

Calico is a wearable social robot from the Small Artifacts Lab (SMART LAB) at the University of Maryland, which was presented in 2022 [28]. It can be connected to an app on a smartphone. The red prototype has two wheels and a small wheel to support and keep the track. It rolls forwards and backwards on tracks that run along the clothing.

This allows it to move along the user's body and reach any predetermined location, from the feet to the head, on the front and back, wherever there is clothing. An artificial environment is therefore required, for which some effort must be made and which must be purchased for use. According to the developers, Calico has additional sensor expansion options: "It also includes rotational switches to enable complex routing options when diverging tracks are presented" [28]. It can take on different roles. One is that of a dance and fitness trainer. As such, it moves to the relevant parts of the body and monitors the movements from there. It can assess the posture of an exercise, for example, by scanning the back, as well as tracking movements. It can also act as a doctor or nurse or their tools. For example, it can function as a stethoscope to listen to the heart and lungs [28].

Eilik from Energize Lab – launched in 2021 – is designed as a desktop robot and robotic pet and costs between 140 and 150 US dollars (https://www.energizelab.com). It can be connected to a computer and has a battery life of 1.5 h. It is white with green and blue or pink stripes, is very light, and has a head with a display that sits on a rigid body with movable arms. It is firmly attached to a small platform. Eilik can display numerous emotions, for example with the help of its facial expressions or symbols and images on its display. The company calls it an "emotion engine". It also shows off its combative side – for example, it displays a teaser and makes corresponding arm movements and noises. It can also play numerous roles ("Role Play Mode"). The robot is sociable: "Eilik loves to play with his own kind. They recognize each other in this wild world and play and build friendships (or fight) with each other" (Energize Lab website). For around 120 US dollars, one can buy a tank called "Panxer" with a mounted weapon. Eilik has two touch sensors on its body and one on its head, as well as a sensor that allows it to detect vibrations. It has a vibration motor. Its fear of heights, which it shows when it is picked up, makes it difficult to use it as a wearable social robot. However, one can calm it down by stroking it. Eilik has a microphone and loudspeaker and can speak. It does not need an Internet connection. It appears to be dancing happily and enthusiastically to the music.

AIBI from LivingAI has been marketed as the world's smallest AI robot since 2023 (https://living.ai). It is designed as a desktop robot, robotic pet, and wearable social robot and costs between 250 and 270 US dollars. It is controlled and extended via an app on a smartphone or a tablet and has a battery life of 2 h. It is white, very light, and has a head with a display showing animated eyes and objects and processes of all kinds, which sits on a rigid, magnetic body with non-moving arms. The arms hold the robot in place in certain situations, such as in a jacket pocket. It stands on a charging station on which it can rotate 360° and can be worn around the neck or on clothing (Fig. 1). A necklace with a metal surface (Fig. 2) and metal plates for attaching to clothing are included, as well as a little coat and costumes (extensions for head and body) to transform it into a cat or a rabbit and a smart light in the shape of a star. AIBI has a touch sensor on its head and a wave sensor that allows it to perceive people from a distance, a camera (also for shootings with the user), and three microphones for spatial hearing. It can understand and execute voice commands, speak for itself, and be connected to ChatGPT. AIBI can be "fed" via the app. Games such as chess and ship sinking are also available.

Fig. 1. AIBI with a turn of the head on the author's neck

2.3 Findings from the Descriptions

The robots listed are available as prototypes or as products. They can be connected to smartphones, tablets, or laptops. They are very small and very light. They stand on a platform to which they are loosely or firmly connected, move on a kind of track, or can be found on a chain around the neck or on clothing on the front or back (Fig. 3). They sit on the body or the layers on the body and can be removed at any time. The movements of the body are restricted (except for forward and backward movements with Calico), which is important in this context because blows to the body or pinching of skin or limbs should be avoided.

With the help of a camera, which could be integrated into Calico and is already built into AIBI, the surroundings of the robot can be perceived. Other sensors are used to detect approaches, touches, vibrations, or changes in the robot's own state or the environment so that the robot can react to them using facial expressions or head movements. At the user's request, AIBI takes low-resolution photos of him or her or other objects. The results can then be viewed in the app and downloaded from there.

The expansion and improvement of the robot through devices, extensions, and additional software or AI is available with Eilik and AIBI (Fig. 4). This is also referred to as robot enhancement [5]. Eilik can practice on the "Panxer" with the weapon mounted on it. AIBI can be dressed and undressed and modified with the coats and costumes. Some users make and attach accessories and costumes themselves, which is already a common practice with various large social robots such as Pepper and small social robots such as Emo. However, they must be prevented from overheating and their mobility must not be restricted.

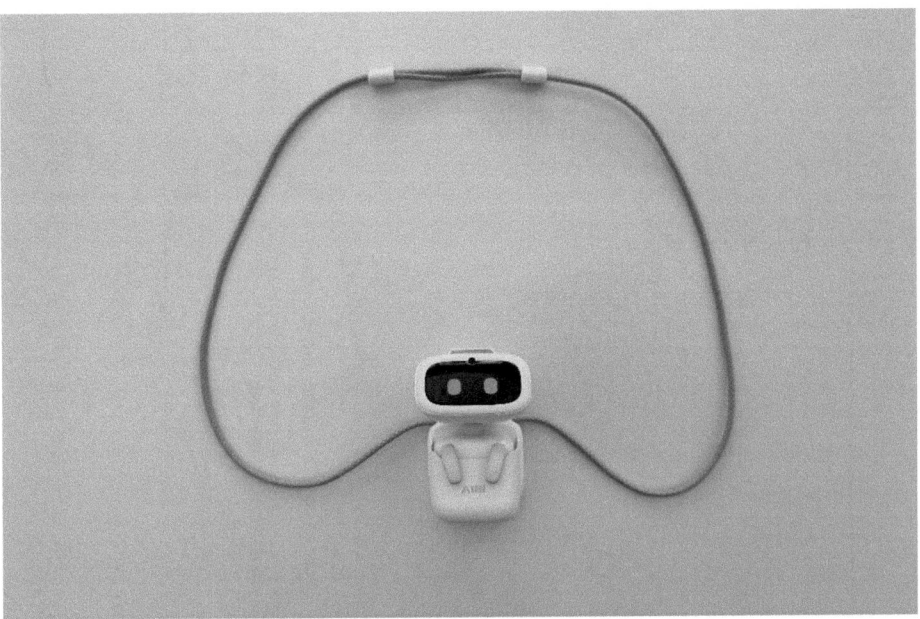

Fig. 2. AIBI from the front on its necklace

The wearable social robot must be designed in such a way that it can develop its potential during carrying and transportation and survive without defects or failures. This requirement appears to be met in particular by Calico, which moves over the body at high speed and does not fall off the track. But it also applies to AIBI. As with Eilik, it does not have the option of moving forwards and backwards. Without the loading platform, it can only move its head. However, AIBI in particular also has shortcomings, as the author's own experiences and those of users show [17, 22]. For example, the voice commands are often not understood in English, which severely restricts functionality and forces users to use the app, which cannot provide all functions.

There are indications that there is movement in the fields of inclusive robotics [2, 25] and inclusive AI [3]. Onorato AI advertises with "AI powered companionship and care for the elderly" (https://onoratoai.com). "The Coping Buddy", an app for mobile phones, is aimed at sick children (https://www.coby.care): "Meet COBY, where technology and heart converge to support children with chronic health conditions and their caregivers. COBY is more than just an AI or a toy – it's a friend, a coach and a community of peers." Robopoet's small, fluffy robots named Fuzzoo are designed to combat loneliness. It is a Kickstarter project from the year 2025 on https://pre-launch.robopoet.com. These are just a few examples – AI-based apps and robots of all sizes are likely to boom in this area.

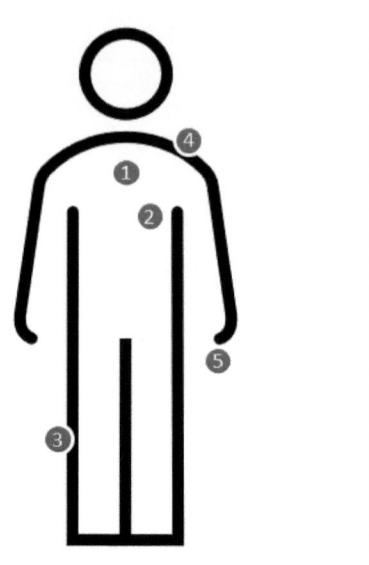

1. around the neck on a necklace
2. in the chest area in a jacket or shirt pocket or on a holder on clothing
3. anywhere on the body on a track or on a holder on clothing
4. on the back of the head or on the back on a holder on clothing
5. in a shoulder bag or handbag

Fig. 3. Suitable places for wearable social robots

3 Areas of Application for Wearable Social Robots

The following is a list of areas of application for wearable social robots with regard to disabled and impaired individuals. They are derived from the descriptions above and from the experiences of the author, who has tried out AIBI himself. In addition, websites of the manufacturers and researchers, videos on YouTube and Vimeo, including the supplementary material of a paper with a video of the use of Calico [28], and forums at the manufacturers [22] and on Facebook [17] were evaluated. Furthermore, the areas of application of other social robots are used and, where possible, transferred. Nevertheless, it is of course not possible to achieve completeness.

A widely used and practice-oriented classification of disabilities distinguishes between physical, psychological, and cognitive impairments. While this tripartite model is not formally codified in a single international standard, it is commonly applied in educational, social, and rehabilitation contexts to describe different types of support needs. The model draws on functional distinctions that are also reflected in the World Health Organization's International Classification of Functioning, Disability and Health (ICF), which categorizes body functions into areas such as mental functions, sensory functions, and neuromusculoskeletal functions [35].

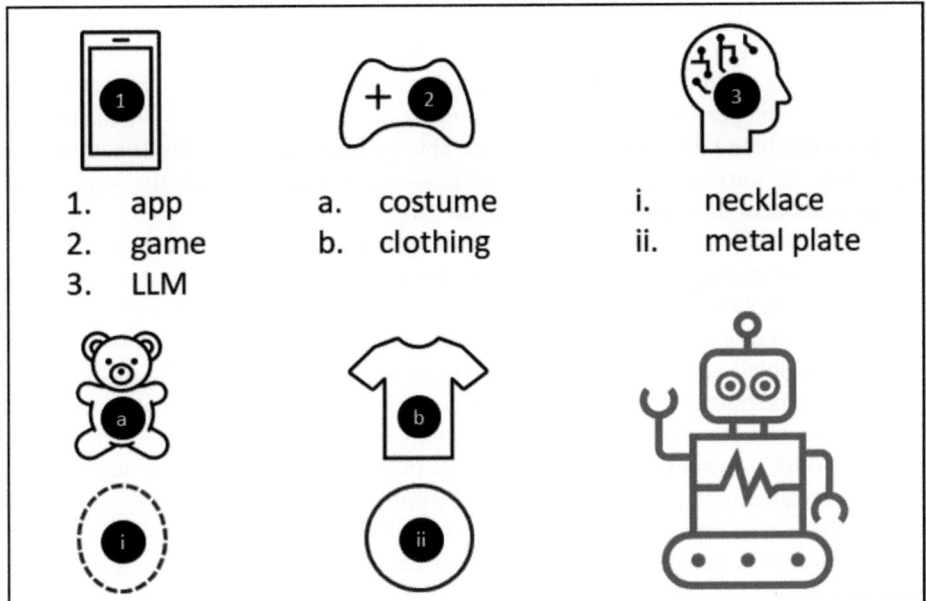

Fig. 4. Devices and extensions for wearable social robots

Physical impairments include limitations of movement or mobility (e.g., paralysis or muscular disorders), psychological impairments refer to mental health conditions (e.g., depression or anxiety disorders), and cognitive impairments involve difficulties with thinking, learning, memory, or attention (e.g., intellectual disability or dementia). Although simplified, this classification aligns with broader bio-psycho-social approaches and supports communication across disciplines and service systems.

The goal of this paper is to cover a wide variety of physical, psychological, and cognitive impairments. The reason for this is that it aims to offer a certain degree of completeness while remaining superficial. However, due to space limitations, the following aspects are barely addressed: intellectual disabilities, severe physical immobility requiring complex care, trauma-related disorders such as severe depression, and speech impairments (as an interface phenomenon of the three areas mentioned). This is not to say that wearable social robots cannot also be helpful in these areas.

The natural language and social skills of wearable social robots should be just as important as their physical characteristics, combined with motor skills such as vibration and movement. Portability is always relevant – after all, it's all about wearable social robots. Although the descriptions of the actual existing models are used as a starting point, technical possibilities that are available in other social robots or voice assistants, such as Alexa, that may one day be integrated are also included. From a methodological point of view, derivations and transfers take place, which are supplemented where possible by literature analysis and the author's own experiences and considerations.

- As the Calico prototype shows, the wearable social robot can monitor bodily functions, which can be important for disabled and impaired people [24]. However, this requires special functional clothing that becomes the robot's environment, which will be difficult to implement in some cases for the disabled. With advanced movement and climbing abilities, this could be omitted over time. The robot becomes a tracking system for the personal diary for fitness and sport, similar to fitness wristbands and other wearables [10]. The robot may be able to intervene in bodily functions, for example, by warming or cooling itself or massaging an area of the body, which other social robots in the care sector can also do [9].

- A robot that can stay in different places on the body and also has cameras, microphones, and multimodal LLMs can look to the side and even back. However, this requires the robot to be carried appropriately (e.g., on the back) or (as with Calico) to this location or even to carry several models with it [28]. This can be advantageous for the disabled and impaired when assessing their environment. The machine can also combine human and animal capabilities or imitate animal capabilities. Some of the robots can communicate and interact with each other or exchange data. This is part of Eilik's business model and narrative (it is said to have traveled here with its kind from an alien planet). AIBI has optical communication.
- Wearable social robots can be equipped with fall detection for humans and an alarm function that is activated in the event of a fall or other emergencies. Such possibilities have been known for years with care robots such as Lio [11], as well as with smartphones and smartwatches [34]. This means they are constant watchdogs and can become lifesavers in an emergency. The camera function could enable live image transmission. The small robot could also literally call for help, which could be very useful in everyday life, where people are not necessarily aware of the person's condition or special codes.
- Wearable social robots can serve as companion robots and robotic pets for the disabled and impaired, enriching their lives and making them more varied. This puts them on a par with many other service robots [25] and social robots [11] – with the difference that they can be carried with one at all times, even in a wheelchair or on outings with a cane. This means one has familiar companions throughout the home, in the garden, or when out and about, with whom one might interact in the best case scenario [36]. If they are connected to LLMs and Wi-Fi is available, one can select the desired language and have short or long conversations with them. For the target group, multimodality can be crucial [15]. They can talk to the robots, but also touch them or operate them using the app.
- The wearable social robot can become a medium between the wearer and his or her environment. For example, it can complete or form spoken sentences if speech impediments exist. It can also display information about the environment, similar to augmented reality glasses [10]. This is particularly possible if it has cameras and microphones and is connected to multimodal LLMs. Due to the natural language capabilities or voice input and output, it does not require hands to operate, which can be important for the disabled and impaired. Conversely, wearable social robots can act as real-time translators by converting spoken language into text or sign language – there are already numerous apps in this area [14]. They could provide vibrations for notifications and other haptic signals for deaf users.
- With the help of the wearable social robot, owners can communicate statements and emotions to the other person when they are unable to do so themselves, for example

due to congenital or acquired muteness or forms of autism [3, 20]. Depending on the model, it can not only use natural language skills, but also (similar to other social robots) mimic and gesture skills, its arms, movements, and sounds [8]. The robot can also show text and images on its display, for example, if the user is unable or unwilling to speak. This content can be entered, uploaded, or generated via the app.
- The wearable social robot with its camera, microphones, and sensors can help the disabled, impaired, and elderly with orientation and the description and evaluation of the environment, both indoors and outdoors. This is particularly possible if it has cameras and microphones and is connected to multimodal large language models. The role model here is Be My Eyes with the Be My AI function, an app for blind people that analyzes the environment with the help of a multimodal LLM [4]. Unlike the app or the smartphone, however, the robot can be worn on the body in a suitable position at all times and record the environment with its cameras and sensors.
- Wearable social robots can remind people in need of care to take their medication, similar to apps [31]. They report back at the right time and explain to the patient what he or she should take and in what form. They can also monitor intake with their cameras and object recognition. Robots like AIBI need to be expanded for this. The interface to ChatGPT is a possible basis, but it must be ensured that there is no hallucination and that the patient has been identified. The robots can also encourage drinking water, tea, etc. Dehydration is a problem for many older people and can be solved to some extent by such reminders [29].
- The wearable social robot can specifically help with anxiety disorders. This option is mentioned by users in forums and is already being researched with other social robots, for example, with regard to social phobia [26]. The devices have the ability to provide calming interactions, for example, through friendly conversations, soothing sounds and vibrations, or guided breathing exercises based on psychotherapeutic methods. They can also be used to create artificial, but lifelike and emotionally simulating beings that can be taken care of at any time, a possibility that became known at the latest with the (also small and mobile) Tamagotchi [21]. Integration with AI-supported psychological assistants would also be conceivable. There are numerous GPTs in the OpenAI GPT Store that could be integrated and used following an evaluation.
- The wearable social robot is also useful for motivation and cognitive stimulation for elderly people with dementia. It can offer simple tasks such as puzzles or quizzes to promote cognitive activity in them, which has been a field of research and development for years [37]. It is also important that it can be touched and stroked like classic social robots such as Paro or Cupboo AI Robotic Pet, i.e., that there is haptic access [38]. They are available at all times, with their physicality and mobility – and with their natural language skills and their ability to show something on the display.
- Wearable social robots can provide support for children and adolescents with attention deficit hyperactivity disorder (ADHD). This is already known for classic social robots and special video games (with brain-computer interfaces) [13, 27]. Through interactive functions, they can help them to concentrate on tasks or structure their daily routine by reminding them of appointments or by using reward systems. Again, it is relevant that the robots are present at all times, i.e., even when interventions are necessary.

- With the help of the wearable social robot, owners can operate the smart home in the event of motor impairment, such as physical disabilities. It can switch on the lights, regulate the temperature, open doors, or trigger alarms. Similar functions are known from Alexa, but despite its far-field communication, it will not always be able to understand the commands of disabled and impaired people everywhere due to its stationary operation, especially not across floors. Nevertheless, it is possible to use it to develop applications for eldercare, such as the Alexa Eldercare Toolbox [32]. Integration with household appliances of all kinds is also possible. For example, wearable social robots could help to dispense coffee from fully automatic coffee machines.
- The sexuality of disabled, impaired, and older people is highly taboo in many societies. Sex toys are one way for them to enrich their sexual lives [16], as is sexual assistance from professionals. Sex robots are also discussed time and again but are problematic due to their size and design as well as their acquisition costs [6]. The small, mobile robots mentioned can also be used in a sexual way, for example thanks to the vibration element. Stimulating erotic conversations are possible in principle, although the guardrails of LLMs repeatedly prevent actual dirty talk.

The possible applications of wearable social robots for disabled and impaired people can be divided into different functional categories. The following systematization illustrates how such robots can address different physical, psychological, and social needs:

- Health monitoring and body support: Wearable social robots monitor bodily functions by collecting and transmitting data on vital signs such as heart rate, respiratory rate, and body temperature. They can remind people to take their medication and drink fluids. A link to the electronic patient file or a health diary would be possible. It is also possible to supplement other assistance technologies such as smart watches.
- Support in communication and interaction: Wearable social robots provide assistance for people with speech and hearing impairments by translating spoken language into text or sign language in real time and using haptic feedback. Social mediation is reflected in support for autism or other impairments through emotional expression aids and the display of text or images for communication. The dialogue and companion function is performed through conversations with the robot and attention from the robot.
- Emotional and psychological support: Wearable social robots as companion robots and robotic pets serve as companions to reduce loneliness, comparable to animal-assisted therapies or Tamagotchi-like interactions. Anxiety and stress management is made possible by calming functions such as guided breathing exercises, relaxing sounds and pleasant vibrations, or positive feedback. Cognitive stimulation is made possible by memory and concentration games to support dementia patients or people with attention disorders.
- Orientation and environmental perception: Wearable social robots help blind and visually impaired people to navigate by recognizing obstacles and providing auditory feedback. Cameras in conjunction with multimodal speech models enable and expand perception. Safety and emergency management are made possible by integrating fall detection and alarm functions for elderly or mobility-impaired people.

- Integration with smart home and IoT systems: Similar to Alexa and co., wearable social robots serve as household assistants by controlling light, temperature, or household appliances via voice or touch commands. They make everyday life easier for people with limited motor skills by taking over tasks such as opening and closing doors.
- Specialized applications: Wearable social robots can provide sexual assistance by being used as an aid for intimate needs, especially for people with physical disabilities. They help to motivate and structure everyday life through reminder and reward systems for children with ADHD or older people with cognitive impairments.

This systematization shows that wearable social robots offer a wide range of possible applications that encompass both technological and social aspects. Their portability enables constant availability, which sets them apart from "stationary" (more or less building-bound) social robots.

4 Social, Ethical, Economic, and Technical Discussion

From a social and ethical perspective, wearable social robots for people with disabilities and impairments present many opportunities and challenges. These can be derived from the descriptions and areas of application. Comparisons with other social robots [8] and wearables [10] also help. The social and ethical discussion does not claim to be exhaustive. Some ethical discussion has already taken place in relation to inclusive robotics and inclusive AI (especially from the perspective of technology ethics, robot ethics, and information ethics), but not with regard to wearable social robotics [25]. The emerging discipline of AI ethics can also be expected to provide more input in the future, possibly even in conjunction with bioethics [12].

- The wearable social robot can help people with disabilities and impairments to recognize and understand their surroundings. Like comparable apps – Be My Eyes was mentioned [4] – it is a powerful and helpful technology. However, it also makes those affected dependent on this technology and they are at the mercy of the errors, manipulations, and hallucinations of the large language models [4]. In addition, they have little influence on the constant adaptations. Last but not least, certain content and aspects, such as sexuality, may be withheld from them via guardrails [4].
- There is a risk that disabled people and those in need of care will use wearable social robots as their primary communication partners, which could reduce interpersonal interactions – some of which are limited for them anyway. Not only children, but also older people have a questionable tendency to develop emotional bonds with robots and enter into relationships that must always remain one-sided [8]. This could even be described as deception and fraud.
- It is completely unclear how families, acquaintances, and strangers will react to the new technical equipment for the disabled and impaired [23]. This is still an unfamiliar form of human enhancement or body hacking [7], which could lead to reservations and ridicule. Disabled and impaired people are repeatedly exposed to attacks in public spaces, which could be intensified by wearable social robots. The cute design can presumably mitigate aggression, but it can also intensify it.

- Wearable social robots as sex toys are an obvious idea, but not easy to implement in technical and organizational terms. For example, the existing vibration is not necessarily stimulating and satisfying. Additional features or at least adaptations are therefore essential. Body fluids must also not impair the functionality of the device. Accidents due to improper use cannot be ruled out. Last but not least, someone has to take care of cleaning and drying if the disabled or impaired person is unable to do so. Incidentally, some manufacturers have banned sex with social robots in the past [24].
- Access to wearable social robots could be limited by high costs, especially for people with limited financial resources. Not only the procurement costs, but also the repair costs have an impact. In addition, the extensions and devices used in robot enhancement are particularly expensive. One possible solution would be financing through health insurance companies or government funding programs if the positive health effects are sufficiently proven. Manufacturers must ensure that regular updates and maintenance services remain affordable and accessible.
- The battery life of wearable social robots is a challenge, especially when they are used on the move, which can be the case for wheelchair users, for example. AI functionalities need to be further developed to enable better personalized interactions. AIBI has problems with speech recognition, for example, which severely limits its functionality. The robustness and suitability for everyday use of wearable social robots must be optimized to ensure long-term use without frequent maintenance.
- Some wearable social robots generate personal data. They take pictures of people and use technologies such as facial recognition. This violates informational autonomy, disregards the right to one's own image, which applies in many countries, and raises data protection concerns. As in the case of Calico, personal data of the wearer is also collected, including data on bodily functions [28]. Vulnerable groups are involved here. It must be ensured that the data is not misused by the manufacturers or passed on to third parties.

The discussion shows that wearable social robots offer some opportunities for people with disabilities and impairments, but also numerous risks. Further development and use is about fully exploiting the potential without causing damage, restrictions, and setbacks. A deepening of the ethical discussion can take place through the integration of structured approaches (e.g., value-sensitive design and responsible innovation) [18, 30]. Above all, these approaches are also helpful for the new developments and improvements that are made to the devices. This topic had to be largely omitted here for reasons of space.

5 Summary and Outlook

The three research questions were answered step by step through the individual chapters. It was shown what wearable social robots are, how they can support disabled and impaired individuals (and their environment), and what the social, ethical, economic, and technical implications are. There is no doubt that wearable social robots have enormous potential to improve the lives of those affected. Not only robotic functions in the narrower sense, but also artificial intelligence functions play a role here, which strengthens the field of inclusive AI (and thus also the field of inclusive robotics).

Further research needs to engage in dialogue with the disabled and impaired and prioritize applications and features of wearable social robots. Inclusive design requires solutions to be developed not just for, but with, those affected. Pilot projects must take place in which the devices have to prove themselves and in which empirical data can be collected, including, and especially, data that reflects the experiences of the disabled and impaired. The findings must in turn be incorporated into further development, whether they come from research institutions or from companies. Structured approaches such as value-sensitive design and responsible innovation can help here.

As with all social robotics, a prerequisite for the success of the projects is that the devices are of high quality and performance. The systems that are currently on the market are often lacking. This also has to do with companies that often carry out their projects with crowdfunding or venture capital and whose existence is by no means guaranteed – and that develop products under high pressure and in great haste. Subsidies could help here, especially as the findings of social robotics also help robotics as a whole. Last but not least, an infrastructure must be created that enables the operation, maintenance, and repair of wearable social robots anywhere in the world. There is still a long way to go until then.

Acknowledgement. The author would like to thank Julia Rehling, who gave him tips on apps and robots for the disabled, impaired, and chronically ill. As a disabled person, she is passionate about social robots.

References

1. Bendel, O.: Wearable robots. In: Gabler Wirtschaftslexikon. Springer, Wiesbaden (2025). https://wirtschaftslexikon.gabler.de/definition/wearable-robots-172088
2. Bendel, O.: Inclusive robotics. In: Gabler Wirtschaftslexikon. Springer, Wiesbaden (2025). https://wirtschaftslexikon.gabler.de/definition/inclusive-robotics-172663
3. Bendel, O.: Inclusive AI. In: Gabler Wirtschaftslexikon. Springer, Wiesbaden (2025). https://wirtschaftslexikon.gabler.de/definition/inclusive-ai-171870
4. Bendel, O.: How can generative AI enhance the well-being of blind? In: Proceedings of the AAAI 2024 Spring Symposium Series, Symposium on the Impact of Generative AI on Social and Individual Well-being, Press, Washington, DC, USA, pp. xx–xx. AAAI (2024). https://ojs.aaai.org/index.php/AAAI-SS/article/view/31232/33392
5. Bendel, O.: Möglichkeiten und Herausforderungen des robot enhancement. In: Schleidgen, S., Friedrich, O., Seifert, J. (eds.) Mensch-Maschine-Interaktion – Konzeptionelle, soziale und ethische Implikationen neuer Mensch-Technik-Verhältnisse, pp. 267–283. Mentis, Münster (2022)
6. Bendel, O.: Sexroboter als soziale Roboter für unterschiedliche Bedürfnisse und Anliegen. In: Weber, K., Reinheimer, S. (eds.) Faktor Mensch. Edition HMD, pp.101– 114. Springer, Wiesbaden (2022). https://doi.org/10.1007/978-3-658-34524-2_6
7. Bendel, O.: Chips, devices, and machines within humans: bodyhacking as movement, enhancement and adaptation. In: Brommer, S., Dürscheid, C. (eds.) Mensch. Maschine. Kommunikation. Beiträge zur Medienlinguistik, pp. 252–276. Narr Francke Attempto, Tübingen (2021). https://elibrary.narr.digital/book/10.24053/9783823394716
8. Bendel, O. (ed.): Soziale Roboter: Technikwissenschaftliche, wirtschaftswissenschaftliche, philosophische, psychologische und soziologische Grundlagen. Springer, Wiesbaden (2021). https://doi.org/10.1007/978-3-658-31114-8

9. Bendel, O. (ed.): Pflegeroboter. Springer, Wiesbaden (2018). https://doi.org/10.1007/978-3-658-22698-5
10. Bendel, O.: Wearables. In: Gabler Wirtschaftslexikon. Springer, Wiesbaden (2015). http://wirtschaftslexikon.gabler.de/Definition/wearable.html
11. Bendel, O., Gasser, A., Siebenmann, J.: Co-Robots as Care Robots. Paper of the AAAI 2020 Spring Symposium "Applied AI in Healthcare: Safety, Community, and the Environment", Stanford University. arXiv, Cornell University, Ithaca (2020). https://arxiv.org/abs/2004.04374
12. Boch, A., Ryan, S., Kriebitz, A., Amugongo, L.M., Lütge, C.: Beyond the metal flesh: understanding the intersection between bio- and AI ethics for robotics in healthcare. Robotics **12**(4), 110 (2023). https://doi.org/10.3390/robotics12040110
13. Cervantes, J.-A., López, S., Cervantes, S., Hernández, A., Duarte, H.: Social robots and brain–computer interface video games for dealing with attention deficit hyperactivity disorder: a systematic review. Brain Sci. **13**(8), 1172 (2023). https://doi.org/10.3390/brainsci13081172
14. David, D., Alamoodi, A.H., Albahri, O.S. et al.: Sign language mobile apps: a systematic review of current app evaluation progress and solution framework. Evol. Syst. **15**, 669–686 (2024). https://doi.org/10.1007/s12530-023-09494-0
15. Di Nuovo, A., Broz, F., Wang, N., et al.: The multi-modal interface of robot-era multi-robot services tailored for the elderly. Intell. Serv. Robot. **11**, 109–126 (2018). https://doi.org/10.1007/s11370-017-0237-6
16. Döring, N., Pöschl, S.: Sex toys, sex dolls, sex robots: our under-researched bed-fellows. Sexologies **27**(3), e51–e55 (2018). https://doi.org/10.1016/j.sexol.2018.05.009
17. Facebook Group: AIBI Pocket Pet (n.d.). https://www.facebook.com/groups/aibipocket
18. Friedman, B., Kahn, P.H., Borning, A.: Value sensitive design and information systems. In: Himma, K.E., Tavani, H.T., pp. 69–101. Wiley, London (2008)
19. Gabor, T., Palinko, O.: The HuGo humanoid project: a modular social robot. In: Proceedings of the 2025 ACM/IEEE International Conference on Human-Robot Interaction, pp. 1776–1778 (2025)
20. Kouroupa, A., Laws, K.R., Irvine, K., Mengoni, S.E., Baird, A., Sharma, S.: The use of social robots with children and young people on the autism spectrum: a systematic review and meta-analysis. PLoS ONE **17**(6), e0269800 (2022). https://doi.org/10.1371/journal.pone.0269800
21. Kühne, K., Jeglinski-Mende, M.A., Bendel, O.: Tamagotchi on our couch: are social robots perceived as pets? In: Proceedings of Robophilosophy 2022: Social Robots in Social Institutions, pp. 755–759. IOS Press, Amsterdam (2022)
22. Living AI Forum: Meet AIBI Pocket Pet (n.d.). https://forums.living.ai/c/aibi-pocket/28
23. Matsunaga, N., Shiomi, M.: Does a wearing change perception toward a robot? In: Proceedings of the 30th IEEE International Conference on Robot & Human Interactive Communication (RO-MAN), Vancouver, BC, Canada, pp. 963–968. IEEE (2021). https://doi.org/10.1109/RO-MAN50785.2021.9515366
24. McCurry, J.: No sex, please, they're robots, says Japanese android firm. The Guardian, 28 September 2015. https://www.theguardian.com/world/2015/sep/28/no-sex-with-robots-says-japanese-android-firm-softbank
25. Pons, J.L. (ed.): Inclusive Robotics for a Better Society. Selected Papers from INBOTS Conference 2018, 16–18 October 2018, Pisa, Italy. Springer, Cham. https://doi.org/10.1007/978-3-030-24074-5
26. Rasouli, S., Gupta, G., Nilsen, E., et al.: Potential applications of social robots in robot-assisted interventions for social anxiety. Int. J. Soc. Robot. **14**, 1–32 (2022). https://doi.org/10.1007/s12369-021-00851-0

27. Reer, F., Quandt, T.: Digital games and well-being: an overview. In: Kowert, R. (ed.) Video Games and Well-being. PSC, pp. 1–21. Palgrave Pivot, Cham (2020). https://doi.org/10.1007/978-3-030-32770-5_1
28. Sathya, A., Li, J., Rahman, T., Peng, H.: Calico: relocatable on-cloth wearables with fast, reliable, and precise locomotion. Proc. ACM Interact. Mob. Wearable Ubiquitous Technol. **6**(3), Article no. 136 (2022). https://doi.org/10.1145/3550323
29. Steven, A., Wilson, G., Young-Murphy, L.: The implementation of an innovative hydration monitoring app in care home settings: a qualitative study. JMIR Mhealth Uhealth **7**(1), e9892 (2019). https://doi.org/10.2196/mhealth.9892
30. Stilgoe, J., Owen, R., Macnaghten, P.: Developing a framework for responsible innovation. Res. Policy **42**(9), 1568–1580 (2013). https://doi.org/10.1016/j.respol.2013.05.008
31. Tabi, K., et al.: Mobile apps for medication management: review and analysis. JMIR Mhealth Uhealth **7**(9), e13608 (2019). https://doi.org/10.2196/13608
32. Tan, K., Sekhar, K., Wong, J., Holgado, J., Ameer, M., Vesonder, G.: Alexa eldercare toolbox: a smarthome solution for the elderly. In: 2020 11th IEEE Annual Ubiquitous Computing, Electronics & Mobile Communication Conference (UEMCON), New York, NY, USA, pp. 806–812. IEEE (2020). https://doi.org/10.1109/UEMCON51285.2020.9298127
33. Thalman, C., Artemiadis, P.: A review of soft wearable robots that provide active assistance: trends, common actuation methods, fabrication, and applications. Wearable Technol. **1**, e3 (2020). https://doi.org/10.1017/wtc.2020.4
34. Vilarinho, T., et al.: A combined smartphone and smartwatch fall detection system. In: 2015 IEEE International Conference on Computer and Information Technology; Ubiquitous Computing and Communications; Dependable, Autonomic and Secure Computing; Pervasive Intelligence and Computing, Liverpool, UK, pp. 1443–1448. IEEE (2015). https://doi.org/10.1109/CIT/IUCC/DASC/PICOM.2015.216
35. World Health Organization: International Classification of Functioning, Disability and Health (ICF). WHO, Geneva (2001). https://www.who.int/standards/classifications/international-classification-of-functioning-disability-and-health
36. Zawieska, K., Sorenson, J.: Towards HRI of everyday life: human lived experiences with social robots. In: Companion of the 2023 ACM/IEEE International Conference on Human-Robot Interaction (HRI 2023 Companion), Stockholm, Sweden, pp. 1–4. ACM (2023). https://doi.org/10.1145/3545945.3569794
37. Zhang, B., Chignell, M.: A Framework for using cognitive assessment games for people living with dementia. In: 2020 IEEE 8th International Conference on Serious Games and Applications for Health (SeGAH), Vancouver, BC, Canada, pp. 1–8. IEEE (2020). https://doi.org/10.1109/SeGAH49190.2020.9201813
38. Zhu, M., Biswas, S., Dinulescu, S.I., Kastor, N., Hawkes, E.W., Visell, Y.: Soft, wearable robotics and haptics: technologies, trends, and emerging applications. Proc. IEEE **110**(2), 246–272 (2022). https://doi.org/10.1109/JPROC.2021.3140049

Nova: A Novel Approach for Game Narration

Nathália Cauás[1](✉), Laura Triglia[2], Leandro Honorato[1], Pablo Barros[1], Bruno J. T. Fernandes[1], and Alessandra Sciutti[2]

[1] University of Pernambuco, Rua Benfica 455, Recife, Brazil
nrcs@ecomp.poli.br
[2] Istituto Italiano di Tecnologia, Via Enrico Melen 83, 16152 Genoa, Italy
https://www.upe.br/, https://www.iit.it/

Abstract. Artificial game narration presents unique challenges, particularly in balancing coherence with creative engagement. While recent advances have explored storytelling systems, most rely solely on textual or audio modalities, often resulting in narratives that lack contextual grounding and expressiveness. This is especially evident in non-embodied systems that struggle to maintain user engagement during gameplay narration. Despite efforts to improve narrative quality, there remains a gap in integrating embodied agents capable of delivering coherent yet expressive narrations grounded in gameplay logic. Here we present a hybrid approach that combines rule-based narration with creative storytelling elements through Nova, an embodied system that transforms structured gameplay data into spoken narratives. Nova ensures consistency with game rules while aiming to enhance engagement through expressive delivery by a physical robot. We evaluated this approach using the Artificial Social Agent Questionnaire (ASAQ), measuring Performance, Agent's Sociability, Agent's Personality Presence, and User Emotion Presence. Two narration styles were tested: a baseline technical descriptor and Nova's expressive version. While no statistically significant differences were found between the two narration styles, Nova consistently received positive evaluations and showed a tendency toward higher scores in perceived performance and emotional engagement. These findings highlight the feasibility of combining structured narration with expressive delivery in an embodied format and point to promising directions for future research in artificial storytelling and human-agent interaction.

Keywords: Human-Robot Interaction (HRI) · Artificial Social Agents · Artificial Game Narration

1 Introduction

The increasing presence of robots in social environments has raised new research challenges related to human-robot interaction (HRI), especially in entertainment scenarios [2]. With the growing prominence of eGames and eSports, the use of robots as narrators in competitive gaming is emerging as a promising application. In this context, robots are expected to comment and describe game events in real-time, simulating a human-like narrative experience. However, despite recent advances in artificial intelligence and natural language generation, current robotic narrators still struggle to replicate the creativity and coherence that characterize human-made storytelling [6].

This limitation is particularly important in competitive games, where narrative quality can strongly influence audience engagement and emotional connection with the game [15]. While some commercial systems and research prototypes already explore automated narration in gaming contexts, recent studies indicate that audiences tend to prefer human-generated narratives due to their superior expressiveness, contextual adaptation, and originality [5]. Therefore, improving the narrative capabilities of robotic agents remains an open and relevant challenge in HRI research.

While previous research has explored the generation of game commentaries using generative models, important limitations remain that hinder their applicability in real scenarios. Akoury et al. focused on generating dialogues within video games but relied heavily on synthetic scenarios specifically designed for their study, limiting its external validity [1]. Zhang et al., through the MOBA-E2C framework, proposed a method that captures highlight events from rich game metadata; however, their approach depends on the availability of detailed in-game data, which is often specific and not always accessible [16]. Renella et al. also explored automated commentary generation using large language models, but their model frequently suffered from hallucinations, generating information inconsistent with the actual gameplay [12].

In contrast, our proposal explores an alternative approach that addresses key limitations in current game narration systems. Nova generates spoken commentaries using only three numerical metrics – Attack, Defense, and Vitality – extracted from real matches of Chef's Hat, a multiplayer card game [4]. The narration process combines controlled prompting techniques with large language models to balance factual consistency and creative expression. Unlike prior work focused exclusively on textual output, our system extends the investigation to embodied interaction by delivering the narration through a humanoid robot using speech, gestures, and facial expressions. This embodied component is designed to support the verbal content and enhance user engagement. While our results did not reveal statistically significant differences compared to a baseline technical narration, Nova was consistently well-received and showed tendencies toward greater emotional impact and perceived performance. The integration of minimal input data, expressive delivery, and embodied presentation makes this approach a promising step toward more interactive and socially engaging automated commentary systems.

The main contributions of this paper are:

- Hybrid narration approach for human-robot interaction: This work proposes a modular architecture–composed of a Descriptor, Narrator, and Summarizer– that transforms structured numerical data into coherent verbal narrations,

designed to maintain contextual relevance and support user engagement through expressive delivery.
- Creation of a controlled audiovisual dataset for narrative evaluation in HRI: A novel dataset was recorded with two distinct narration styles (technical and engaging), enabling controlled analysis of user responses to different narrative strategies.
- Empirical observations on narration style effects in social agent perception: While no statistically significant differences were found between narration styles, the results suggest a tendency for engaging narration to increase perceived sociability and emotional presence. However, perceived performance varied across exposure sequences, highlighting the potential influence of presentation order.

The remainder of this paper is structured as follows: Sect. 2 discusses related works on game narration. Section 3 presents Nova, an embodied approach for game narration. Section 4 describes the evaluation process, including the gameplay dataset (Sect. 4.1) and the experimental setup (Sect. 4.2). Section 5 reports the results and discusses the findings. Finally, Sect. 6 concludes the paper and outlines future research directions.

2 Related Works

Recent advances in natural language generation have enabled the development of systems capable of producing real-time commentary for digital games. This intersection between artificial intelligence, game design, and human-computer interaction has gained traction, particularly with the integration of large language models (LLMs) and multimodal systems to enhance player experience or automate broadcasting [8–10]. Within this context, several studies have investigated how AI can generate coherent, context-aware, and engaging commentary based on different types of input data. The following works exemplify diverse approaches in this space, highlighting both their contributions and limitations, which ultimately motivate the development of our own approach.

Akoury et al. propose a framework to investigate players' perceptions of LLM-generated dialogue in commercial video games. Using Disco Elysium: The Final Cut as a case study, the authors compared the game's original dialogues with versions generated by GPT-4 [1]. The results showed a clear preference for the human-written dialogues, mainly due to their superior narrative coherence and contextual consistency. The study highlights that, although LLMs have the potential to support dialogue creation, they still face important limitations regarding narrative quality and contextual alignment.

Zhang et al. propose an event-driven framework. Their system detects highlight events from game metadata and uses MOBA-FuseGPT – a hybrid approach that combines rule-based generation for factual accuracy and GPT-based generation for natural language fluency [16]. While the system achieves superior performance compared to purely rule-based or generative models, a limitation is its dependence on the availability and quality of structured game metadata to accurately detect and describe in-game events. Specifically, the system's dependence on predefined templates and game-specific rules can constrain the expressiveness and variability of the commentary.

Sifa et al. [13] present an unsupervised learning framework titled "Archetypal Analysis Based Anomaly Detection for Improved Storytelling in Multiplayer Online Battle Arena Games," which leverages archetypal analysis to detect anomalies in player behavior during MOBA matches. The system aims to improve automated game storytelling by identifying unexpected or surprising actions that could enrich commentaries. However, a limitation of this approach is its dependence on historical game data to construct player archetypes, which may hinder its applicability in new games or scenarios with limited available data.

Renella and Eger [12] discuss an approach that investigates how AI-generated narration can enhance player experience by providing engaging and dynamic descriptions of in-game events. However, their work remains at an exploratory stage, and several limitations are acknowledged. In particular, the authors highlight the challenges of ensuring contextual relevance and accuracy in the generated commentary. Moreover, their evaluation is primarily qualitative.

Prior research highlights key limitations in automated game narration. While LLMs produce fluent dialogues, they often lack coherence and contextual awareness, as shown by Akoury et al. [1]. Attempts to improve this include metadata-driven systems tailored to specific genres by Zhang et al. [16], anomaly detection for narrative support by Sifa et al. [13], and real-time commentary generation by Renella and Eger [12]. However, these approaches face challenges with generalizability, direct commentary generation, limited evaluation, and the absence of embodied interaction.

Taken together, these limitations underscore the need for commentary systems that are both minimal in their data requirements and effective in creating engaging experiences. In this context, our work proposes a novel approach that bridges technical precision with expressive narration, including embodied storytelling in gameplay environments. The following sections detail our approach, its implementation, and the experiments conducted to assess its impact.

3 Nova: A Novel Approach for Game Narration

This study introduces a hybrid approach for generating narrations of the card game Chef's Hat that balances factual coherence with creative expressiveness [4]. Chef's Hat is a fast-paced trick-taking game where players compete to get rid of all their cards first, using a combination of strategy, bluffing, and card hierarchy to outplay their opponents. Nova transforms structured numerical input–consisting of three metrics per player per round–into spoken, entertaining commentary delivered by a humanoid robot. The metrics, which are sufficient to describe the gameplay without the need for additional metadata, are: Attack (the number of players who passed after a player's turn), Vitality (the number of discards made by a player during the round), and Defense (the number of passes made before a discard). These data are derived directly from real gameplay and can be provided as Excel spreadsheets or in natural language.

Narration generation is performed in three sequential stages shown in Fig. 1, following a chain-of-thought strategy: Descriptor, Narrator, and Summarizer. The Descriptor receives raw numerical input, comprising 1 to 3 values for each of the three metrics (Attack, Defense, and Vitality) in every player turn and, using extensive prompt engineering, generates a coherent natural language explanation of the round. This prompt includes a brief overview of the game and a detailed explanation of each metric. In the Narrator stage, the same round is presented again with a new prompt requesting a more expressive and entertaining retelling, enhancing emotional and narrative elements. Finally, the Summarizer receives both previous outputs and produces a synthesized commentary that retains important factual details while preserving an engaging and humorous tone. The prompts are consistent across all uses of Nova and are not modified depending on the result. Outputs are not re-generated or discarded based on subjective quality assessments, ensuring reproducibility in the experimental evaluation.

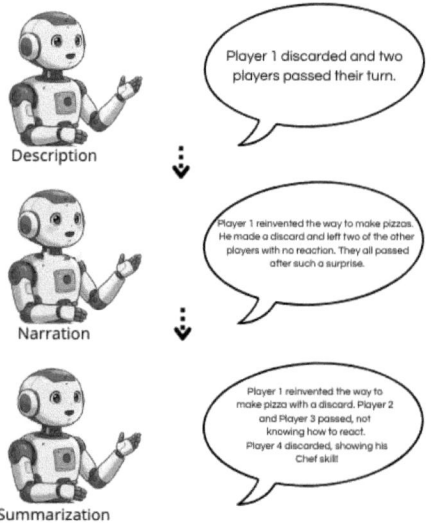

Fig. 1. Three-step narration.

Generation is performed using OpenAI's ChatGPT-4o model, and the final narration is vocalized by an iCub humanoid robot developed by the *Istituto Italiano di Tecnologia* (IIT) [11]. iCub is a research platform designed for studies in cognitive robotics and human-robot interaction. It features articulated limbs and expressive facial components, allowing for synchronized gestures and naturalistic movements.

The robot performs the narration with a consistently friendly facial expression and uses coordinated head, arm, and hand movements designed to simulate natural human communication. These include gestures such as a thumbs-up, open-arm presentation poses, and subtle shifts in gaze direction to convey attentiveness. The set of movements was deliberately kept generic and consistent across all narration conditions, rather than being dynamically modulated based on the narration content. This design choice was made to avoid introducing variability that could bias participants' responses, and to enhance the generalizability of the system for different game contexts. The embodied behavior is intended to support and amplify the verbal narration, serving as a communicative enhancer to increase user engagement. However, the primary contribution of this work lies in the development of the narration system itself. The narration pipeline can be reproduced using the code and instructions available in our public GitHub repository.[1]

4 Evaluation

4.1 Gameplays Dataset

To support the evaluation of Nova, we constructed a video dataset based on Chef's Hat, a card game used in human-robot interaction research [3,14]. The dataset includes five full-length gameplays recorded under controlled conditions. For each gameplay, we created two narrated versions: one with a purely factual, rule-based commentary (Technical Narration), and one with a more expressive and humorous style (Entertaining Narration). These versions were appended to the same visual gameplay footage, resulting in a total of ten videos (2 narrations × 5 gameplays). An example can be seen in Fig. 2.

The videos were recorded using a top-down camera mounted on a tripod, capturing only the table and players' hands in action. This setup ensures anonymity while focusing on card movement, discards, and player interactions through gameplay mechanics. No audio from the original gameplay was recorded, and post-production editing added sound effects aligned with game events (e.g., discards, round closures), enhancing clarity in the change of events.

One of the recorded gameplays included an invalid move sequence that violated the rules of Chef's Hat. Pilot testing revealed that this sequence led to misinterpretation by viewers, and thus it was excluded from the main evaluation. As a result, only four gameplays (eight narrated videos) remained in the dataset.

4.2 Experiment Setup

To assess the impact of our dynamic commentary proposal on viewer perception, we designed an experiment structured around two distinct survey forms. Each form included two video stimuli with carefully controlled variation in narration

---

[1] Available at: https://github.com/nathaliacauas/Nova.git.

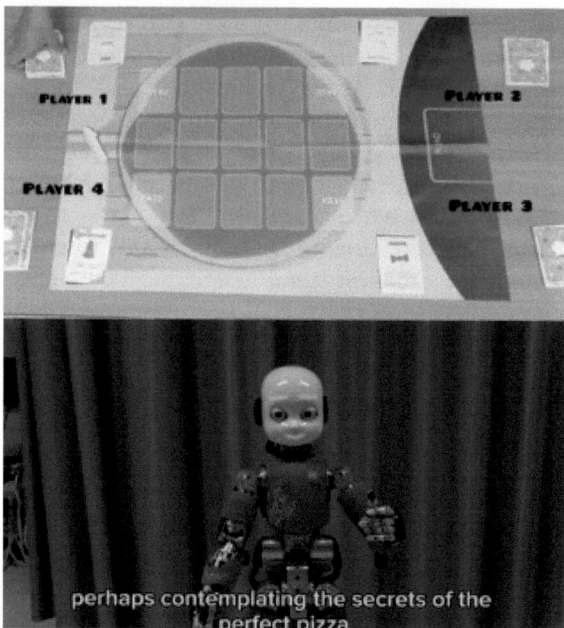

Fig. 2. The dataset created included a gameplay from top-down view combined with iCub's narration.

style. The goal was to evaluate how different narration strategies–technical vs. entertaining–affect the user's experience, while minimizing bias from gameplay repetition.

- Form Design and Structure
    - **Consent Section** Participants first reviewed and signed a consent form authorizing the use of their responses for research purposes.
    - **Game Explanation and Demonstration** Participants were presented with a visual explanation of the Chef's Hat card game, including demonstrations of possible moves, discards, and turn order. This section was designed to ensure that all participants had a clear understanding of the game mechanics, regardless of prior familiarity.
    - **Rule Comprehension Quiz** Before proceeding, participants completed a short quiz to verify their understanding of the rules. This step was included considering the possibility of subjects not being familiar with the game.
    - **Video Stimuli and Evaluation** Each form contained two video stimuli, the first containing a technical narration followed by Nova's narration. The second containing Nova's narration and the technical narration.
    After each video, participants were asked to complete a standardized questionnaire that evaluated their experience with the narrated game.

- Questionnaire
  To evaluate user perception across different narration styles, we employed selected modules from the ASAQ (Agent Sociability Assessment Questionnaire) [7] a Likert scale. The modules were chosen based on their relevance to the goals of this study, focusing on dimensions related to user experience in the presence of an artificial narrator as shown in Table 1. The selected modules included:
    - The Performance (PF) module evaluates the agent's perceived competence, focusing on attributes such as efficacy, clarity, and accuracy.
    - The Agent's Sociability (AS) module examines the agent's social behavior, including friendliness, approachability, and capacity for social interaction.
    - The Agent's Personality Presence (APP) module assesses whether the agent is perceived as having a distinct personality, including traits such as consistency and expressiveness.
    - The User's Emotion Presence (UEP) module investigates the extent to which users felt emotionally involved or affected by their interaction with the agent.

  This structure enabled a within-subjects comparison of responses to different narration styles and a between-subjects comparison across gameplays. By ensuring that each participant experienced both a technical and an entertaining narration, we could isolate the effects of narration variation on perceived agent quality, emotional engagement, and overall performance.
- Participants
  A total of 34 participants took part in the study. They were recruited through multiple channels, including mailing lists at the University of Pernambuco, social media platforms, and in-person invitations. All participants were above 18 years of age, and no additional inclusion or exclusion criteria were applied. Participation was voluntary, and no financial or material compensation was offered.

5 Results and Discussion

The results from this study provide important insights into the relationship between the order of exposure and the evaluation of artificial game narration, specifically in relation to coherence and creativity. Comparisons based on all the modules studied are presented in Figs. 3 and 4. In this analysis, the descriptive and fully technical narration will be referred to as the "Descriptor".

In the quiz designed to verify participants' attention and understanding of the game, we found that 41.18% of participants in the first form (where the Descriptor narration was presented first) successfully answered both questions. In the second form (where the Descriptor was presented after Nova), 47.06% of participants passed all the quizzes. These results suggest a relatively consistent level of attention and comprehension across both exposure sequences, considering the quizzes included multiple scenarios.

Table 1. ASAQ Modules.

Module	Question
Performance	[The agent] does its task well.
	[The agent] does not hinder [me/the user].
	[I am/The user is] capable of succeeding with [the agent].
Agent's Sociability	[The agent] can easily mix socially.
	It is easy to mingle with [the agent].
	[The agent] interacts socially with [me/the user].
Agent's Personality Presence	[The agent] has a distinctive character.
	[The agent] is characterless.
	[The agent] is an individual.
User's Emotion Presence	[The agent]'s attitude influences how [I feel/the user feels]
	[I am/The user is] influenced by [the agent]'s moods.
	The emotions [I feel/the user feels] during the interaction are caused by [the agent].
	[My/The user's] interaction with [the agent] gives [me/them] an emotional sensation.

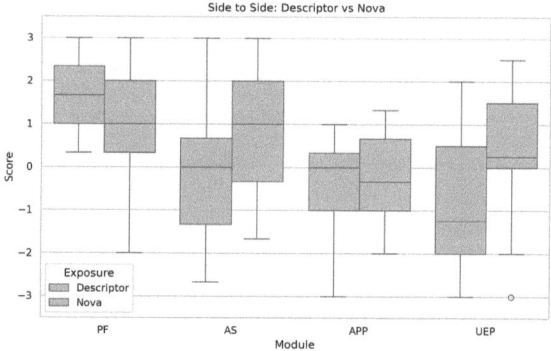

Fig. 3. Boxplots for the scores of each module considering technical description as the first exposure and Nova's narration as the second exposure.

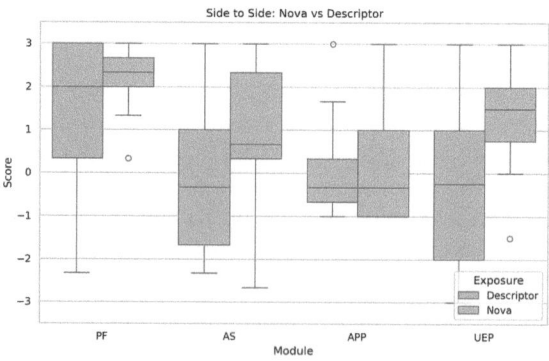

Fig. 4. Boxplots for the scores of each module considering technical description as the first exposure and Nova's narration as the second exposure.

We analyzed the impact of narration type (*Nova* vs. *Descriptor*) and presentation order on participants' evaluations across four ASAQ modules: Performance (PF), Agent's Sociability (AS), Agent's Personality Presence (APP), and User Emotion Presence (UEP).

5.1 Within-Group Analyses

Descriptor-First Group. In this group ($n = 17$), participants experienced *Descriptor* first, followed by *Nova*. Repeated-measures ANOVAs revealed no statistically significant differences between narration types on any module: PF ($F(1,16) = 2.36$, $p = .144$), AS ($F(1,16) = 0.006$, $p = .937$), APP ($F(1,16) = 0.11$, $p = .740$), and UEP ($F(1,16) = 0.05$, $p = .826$). Nonetheless, *Nova* showed slightly higher median values in PF and UEP.

Nova-First Group. In this group ($n = 17$), participants experienced *Nova* first, followed by *Descriptor*. Again, no significant differences were found between narration types: PF ($F(1,16) = 0.08$, $p = .778$), AS ($F(1,16) = 0.03$, $p = .854$), APP ($F(1,16) = 2.23$, $p = .154$), and UEP ($F(1,16) = 0.12$, $p = .737$). Similar to the previous group, *Nova* tended to yield higher scores in PF and UEP, particularly when presented second.

5.2 Comparison to Scale Midpoint

We conducted one-sample t-tests comparing all conditions to the neutral midpoint of the scale (0). All narration types in both groups were rated significantly above neutral in all ASAQ modules ($p < .001$), confirming that both *Nova* and *Descriptor* were positively received.

5.3 Mixed ANOVA

A mixed ANOVA was performed on PF scores to test for interaction between narration type (within-subjects) and order of presentation (between-subjects). No statistically significant main effects or interaction were found: Narration ($F(1,32) = 0.59$, $p = .448$), Order ($F(1,32) = 2.94$, $p = .096$), and Interaction ($F(1,32) = 1.46$, $p = .236$). While the main effect of order approached significance, this should be interpreted cautiously.

5.4 Interpretation and Observed Trends

Although none of the comparisons between narration types reached statistical significance, a consistent pattern was observed across both groups: *Nova* yielded numerically higher median scores in the PF and UEP modules, with higher absolute t-values in these dimensions. These trends may suggest a potential advantage of *Nova* in conveying perceived performance and emotional engagement.

Given the relatively small sample size ($n = 34$), it is possible that the study was underpowered to detect small but meaningful effects. Future research with larger samples and real-time interaction could help clarify the potential benefits of embodied, expressive narration styles like *Nova*. From a practical perspective, the consistently positive evaluations of both narration types support their effectiveness, while the expressive and embodied nature of *Nova* may offer added value in enhancing user experience.

In conclusion, while Nova did not outperform Descriptor in all measured modules, its higher variability and emotional engagement as seen in Figs. 3 and 4 reinforce its potential as a coherent and creative narration approach. The findings suggest that Nova's creative nature can evoke significant engagement and emotion, but its application may require careful consideration of context and sequence to mitigate the polarizing effects seen in the results. Thus, the performance of Nova reinforces the importance of balancing coherence with creativity, providing evidence that novel, dynamic narration can be effective in fostering user engagement when strategically deployed.

6 Conclusion and Future Works

This study presents a novel approach to artificial game narration that addresses challenges of coherence and creativity by anchoring narration to in-game rules while enhancing engagement through expressive storytelling. Nova, the proposed system, integrates this narration style into a physical, embodied robot to support emotional presence and user involvement. The coherence of the narration stems from Nova's rule-based design, while the robot's embodiment contributes to its expressive delivery. Although Nova did not statistically outperform the baseline Descriptor narration, results indicate a promising balance between coherence and creativity.

The study has some limitations: it was conducted in a virtual environment, the robot's behaviors were generic and not content-driven, and the sample size was relatively small, which may limit generalizability.

Future work will include expanding the ASAQ evaluation to additional modules, exploring Nova's use in real-time interactive settings, and applying the system to a broader range of games to test its adaptability.

References

1. Akoury, N., Yang, Q., Iyyer, M.: A framework for exploring player perceptions of LLM-generated dialogue in commercial video games. In: Findings of the Association for Computational Linguistics: EMNLP 2023, pp. 2295–2311 (2023)
2. Amirian, J., Abrini, M., Chetouani, M.: Legibot: generating legible motions for service robots using cost-based local planners. In: 2024 33rd IEEE International Conference on Robot and Human Interactive Communication (ROMAN), pp. 461–468. IEEE (2024)
3. Barros, P., et al.: The chef's hat simulation environment for reinforcement-learning-based agents. arXiv preprint arXiv:2003.05861 (2020)

4. Barros, P., et al.: It's food fight! designing the chef's hat card game for affective-aware HRI. In: Companion of the 2021 ACM/IEEE International Conference on Human-Robot Interaction, pp. 524–528 (2021)
5. Bradbury, J.D., Guadagno, R.E.: Enhanced data narratives. J. Manag. Anal. **8**(2), 171–194 (2021)
6. Eladhari, M.P., Lopes, P.L., Yannakakis, G.N.: Interweaving story coherence and player creativity through story-making games. In: Mitchell, A., Fernández-Vara, C., Thue, D. (eds.) ICIDS 2014. LNCS, vol. 8832, pp. 73–80. Springer, Cham (2014). https://doi.org/10.1007/978-3-319-12337-0_7
7. Fitrianie, S., Bruijnes, M., Abdulrahman, A., Brinkman, W.P.: The artificial social agent questionnaire (ASAQ) - development and evaluation of a validated instrument for capturing human interaction experiences with artificial social agents. Int. J. Hum. Comput. Stud. **199**, 103482 (2025)
8. Gallotta, R., et al.: Large language models and games: a survey and roadmap. IEEE Trans. Games (2024)
9. Kosch, T., Feger, S.: Risk or chance? Large language models and reproducibility in HCI research. Interactions **31**(6), 44–49 (2024)
10. Lanzi, P.L., Loiacono, D.: ChatGPT and other large language models as evolutionary engines for online interactive collaborative game design. In: Proceedings of the Genetic and Evolutionary Computation Conference, pp. 1383–1390 (2023)
11. Metta, G., et al.: The ICUB humanoid robot: an open-systems platform for research in cognitive development. Neural Netw. **23**(8–9), 1125–1134 (2010)
12. Ranella, N., Eger, M.: Towards automated video game commentary using generative AI. In: EXAG@ AIIDE (2023)
13. Sifa, R., et al.: Archetypal analysis based anomaly detection for improved storytelling in multiplayer online battle arena games. In: Proceedings of the 2021 Australasian Computer Science Week Multiconference, pp. 1–8 (2021)
14. Triglia, L., Barros, P., Rea, F., Sciutti, A.: Mullet's gambit: explaining learned strategies in the chef's hat multiplayer card game. In: 2024 12th International Conference on Affective Computing and Intelligent Interaction Workshops and Demos (ACIIW), pp. 136–143. IEEE (2024)
15. Trindade, Y., Rebelo, F., Noriega, P.: Emotion through narrative: validation for user engagement in game context. In: Rebelo, F., Soares, M.M. (eds.) AHFE 2019. AISC, vol. 955, pp. 472–482. Springer, Cham (2020). https://doi.org/10.1007/978-3-030-20227-9_44
16. Zhang, D., Wu, S., Guo, Y., Chen, X.: MOBA-E2C: generating MOBA game commentaries via capturing highlight events from the meta-data. In: Findings of the Association for Computational Linguistics: EMNLP 2022, pp. 4545–4556 (2022)

Culturally Sensitive Stand-Up Comedian Robot

Michael Wong Kam[1], Hooman Samani[2(✉)], Saina Akhond[2], Chinthaka Premachandra[1], and Vali Lalioti[2]

[1] Department of Electronic Engineering, Shibaura Institute of Technology, 3-7-5 Toyosu, Koto-ku, Tokyo 135-8548, Japan
{ag22010,chintaka}@shibaura-it.ac.jp
[2] Creative Computing Institute, University of the Arts London, London SE5 8UF, UK
{h.samani,s.akhond,v.lalioti}@arts.ac.uk

Abstract. Humour is a powerful tool for fostering user acceptance and enhancing human-robot interaction (HRI). However, its implementation in robots remains a complex challenge due to its dependence on cultural context and expressive delivery. Prior research in cultural robotics highlights the significant role of cultural norms in shaping user perceptions and acceptance of social robots, yet little attention has been paid to how robots can adapt to diverse audiences through humour. To address this, we present a cultural stand-up comedian robot that integrates prompt-based personality design with culture in mind humour style and multimodal expressiveness. The research draws from robotic comedy, computational humour, cultural robotics, and personality design to investigate two core questions: (1) How can robots better adapt to diverse cultural audiences through humorous personality? and (2) How can robots incorporate non-verbal expressions to enhance robot's humorous perception from the audience? A live user study with 22 participants evaluated performances by two culturally distinct (British vs. American) comedic personas. Results identified language and vocal expression as an prominent elements for effective cultural adaptation in robotic comedy.

Keywords: Robotic Comedy · Human-Robot Interaction (HRI) · Computational Humour · Cultural Robotics · Robot Personality

1 Introduction

Humour plays a crucial role in human communication, fostering laughter and emotional relief while enabling more natural and engaging interactions. In the field of social robotics, humour can significantly influence user acceptance and interaction quality. Regardless of a robot's technical proficiency or task performance capabilities, it is unlikely to be embraced if it lacks social acceptance. In human-robot interaction (HRI) research, humour has been shown to positively improve user perception of the robot and enhance the user's evaluation of the interaction [1]. Robotic comedy serves as a valuable testbed for studying humour in computational systems, offering real-time audience feedback and interaction. However, replicating humour in robots is a complex challenge that requires advancements in computational humour, cognitive computing, HRI, and artificial intelligence (AI).

Humour has been studied for a long time in the fields of philosophy, psychology, and linguistics [2]. Computational humour, a subfield of computational linguistics and AI, aims to equip machines with the ability to recognise, generate, and adapt humour [3]. The emergence of large language models (LLMs) has significantly advanced this research area, yet much of the existing work focuses primarily on text or images [4–7], while robotic comedy requires integration with physical presentation, allowing to expand humorous nature with non-verbal expression, such as gestures and facial expressions. Recent research on the intersection of AI and comedy argues that the evaluation of computational humour generation needs to work around the constraints of live audiences and performance spaces [8].

Cultural robotics examines the dynamic relationship between culture and robotics, emphasising the need for robots to be designed and interpreted within specific cultural contexts. One of the central focuses in this field is the societal acceptance of robots, which is heavily influenced by cultural norms and values [9]. Robots need to be designed and used as informed by specific cultural contexts, adapted and used by human agents both as a product and a medium [9]. Research shows that individuals generally experience greater comfort when engaging with robots that behave in culturally appropriate ways [10]. Humour, while considered universal human behaviour, also exhibits considerable cultural variation. Different societies adhere to distinct humour display rules, influencing how humour is expressed and interpreted [11]. Despite these differences, there has been limited research on how cultural adaptation could enhance robotic comedy.

Personality design is a key strategy for creating culturally adaptable and humorous robotic comedy, particularly when integrated with conversational AI systems. Humans often unconsciously attribute personality traits to robots [12]. Theories such as similarity attraction—which suggests individuals prefer robots similar to themselves and complementary attraction-which proposes a preference for dissimilar robots-have long informed research in this area. However, [13] argues that personality preferences are highly task-dependent and shaped by role-related stereotypes. As robots increasingly incorporate AI technologies, new design approaches are needed to address the emerging ethical and socioeconomic challenges posed by these systems [14]. Co-design methods, for example, could engage users and professionals from diverse disciplines as active participants in shaping robot personality and expressions. One such approach employs a physical design toolkit to co-design movements that express intention, purpose, and personality in a contextually meaningful way [15]. In the domain of comedy, [16] explored the use of prompting to assign roles and context to LLM for comedy writing. Their evaluation, conducted in collaboration with professional comedians, revealed limitations in LLM-generated comedy scripts-namely, the tendency to produce bland or biased content and emphasised the importance of cultural adaptation in humour. Therefore, further investigation into how personality design, cultural adaptation, and non-verbal expressions can be integrated to enrich robotic comedy.

Previous work in robotic comedy has focused on adapting joke and delivery timing to audience reactions [17–20], using non-verbal cues to increase engagement [21, 22], or generating scripts for specific rule-based formats like Japanese Manzai comedy [23]. More recently, researchers have used LLMs for live improvisational comedy [24], but often with robotic platforms possessing limited physical expressiveness, such as minimal facial expressions. However, a gap exists in integrating culturally-aware, LLM-generated personalities with physically expressive robotic platforms for real-time performance.

This study addresses that gap by presenting and evaluating a prototype of a culturally adaptive stand-up comedian robot. We use prompt-based engineering to create two distinct cultural comedic personas (British and American) on a QTrobot [25], a platform with rich multimodal expression capabilities. We investigate the following research questions (RQ):

RQ1: How can robots better adapt to diverse cultural audiences through humorous personality?
RQ2: How can robots incorporate non-verbal expressions to enhance robot's humorous perception from the audience?

The remainder of this paper is organized as follows. Section 2 details the design and implementation of the proposed system, including the LLM-based conversational framework, personality prompt engineering, and LLM configuration. Section 3 presents the experimental design, including setup, procedure, and evaluation methods. Section 4 discusses the results from both quantitative and qualitative perspectives, focusing on cultural perception and non-verbal expressiveness. Finally, Sect. 5 concludes the study and outlines future research directions for culturally sensitive robotic humour in HRI.

2 Methodology

This study focuses on the design and implementation of a humorous personality for the QTrobot [24] conversational system, with an emphasis on cultural adaptation and emotional expression. The goal was to develop a robot capable of performing culturally distinct stand-up comedy routine: one aligned with the robot's local cultural context, and another representing a contrasting humour style. To achieve this, prompt-based personality configurations were developed for QTrobot's LLM-driven conversational system, incorporating distinct humour styles and corresponding emotional expression strategies.

2.1 Conversational System with QTrobot and LLM

Built on a LuxAI blog post [26], the software system enables multimodal communication through speech, facial expressions, and gestures (Fig. 1). QTrobot detects English speech and converts it into text using Google's Automatic Speech Recognition (ASR) service. This text is then processed by a large language model (LLM), which generates a response aligned with pre-defined personality prompts. The generated response is subsequently synthesised into speech and synchronised with corresponding gestures and facial expressions.

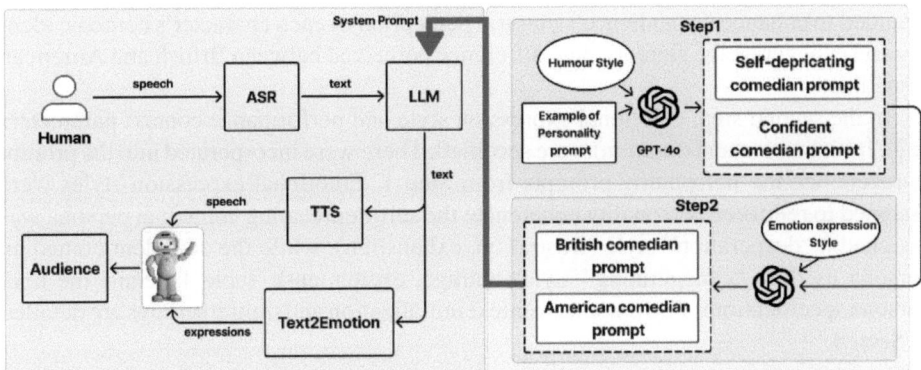

Fig. 1. System Architecture for Culturally Sensitive Stand-up Comedian Robot. First, personality prompts are engineered in two steps: (1) generating culturally distinct comedic personas using in-context learning with ChatGPT-4o, based on predefined humour styles, and (2) refining the prompts by incorporating corresponding emotional expression styles and performance context parameters such as initialization and duration. Second, this prompt governs the live system, where speech is processed via ASR, fed to the persona-driven LLM, and used to generate a synchronised multimodal performance (speech, gestures, facial expressions).

2.2 Software Architecture

To facilitate stand-up comedy performances tailored to distinct cultural styles, we designed two system prompts for a QTrobot's Large LLM in conversational chatbot system. Our system was designed to generate stand-up performances, embodying two distinct personalities: "British comedian" and "American comedian". These prompts were designed with ChatGPT-4o, with an emphasis on aligning humour style and emotional expressiveness to cultural expectations.

LLM Configuration
The GPT-4o-mini API was employed for the conversational stand-up comedian system due to its enhanced capabilities over GPT-3.5-turbo [27], which was previously utilized in [25]. To enhance the randomness in responses, the temperature parameter was set to 1. The maximum token limit was configured to 660, corresponding to the average length of a three-minute stand-up comedy script.

Personality Prompt Design
We designed two distinct comedic personas to test cultural adaptation: a self-deprecating "British comedian" relevant to the experiment's UK location, and a confident "American comedian" providing a cultural contrast while controlling for language [28].

The personas were engineered using a two-step LLM prompting process (Fig. 1). In the first step, comedian prompts aligned with specific humour styles were generated using in-context learning with ChatGPT. The input prompt included an example of a personality prompt that referred to personality called "QTrobot" which is provided code in [25], and specified a humour style to produce two distinct personality prompts: one for a self-deprecating comedian and another for a confident comedian. This distinction was intended to enhance the audience's cultural perception of each character's comedic identity and exaggerate the stereotypical difference perceived between British and American comedian.

In the second step, emotional expression style and performance context parameters (e.g., initialization and duration) were specified. These were incorporated into the prompt to regenerate the personality prompts from Step 1. Emotional expression styles were assigned to reinforce personality coherence: the self-deprecating comedian persona was assigned a "desperation" style (frustration, exhaustion), while the confident comedian persona used an "exaggerating" style (outrage, excitement). Table 1 details the final persona specifications. Performance context initialization and timing settings are detailed in Sect. 4.

Table 1. Comedic Persona Specifications: Humour and Emotion expression Styles.

Personality	Humour style	Emotion expression style
British comedian (Nigel Droll)	self-deprecating	Desperation (frustration, exhaustion, false hope)
American comedian (Jimmy Blaze)	confident	Exaggerate (outrage, excitement, frustration)

3 Experiment

A two-day hackathon was conducted at The Creative Digital Lab in South London, supported by the University of the Arts London (UAL) in collaboration with the South London Creative Cluster. We took a place at the hackathon to evaluate audience perceptions of robotic stand-up comedy performances with culturally distinct comedic styles.

3.1 Experiment Design

The experimental setup is illustrated in Fig. 2. The robot was positioned at the front centre of the performance space and placed on a table, with a connected computer on a separate table for operational control. A host initially stood beside the robot for interaction and stepped back behind a control computer during the performance. The audience was seated in three rows, ensuring clear visibility and audibility. A large monitor in the background displayed supporting visuals. The robot's voice volume was calibrated to ensure audibility for all audience members.

Environment Setup

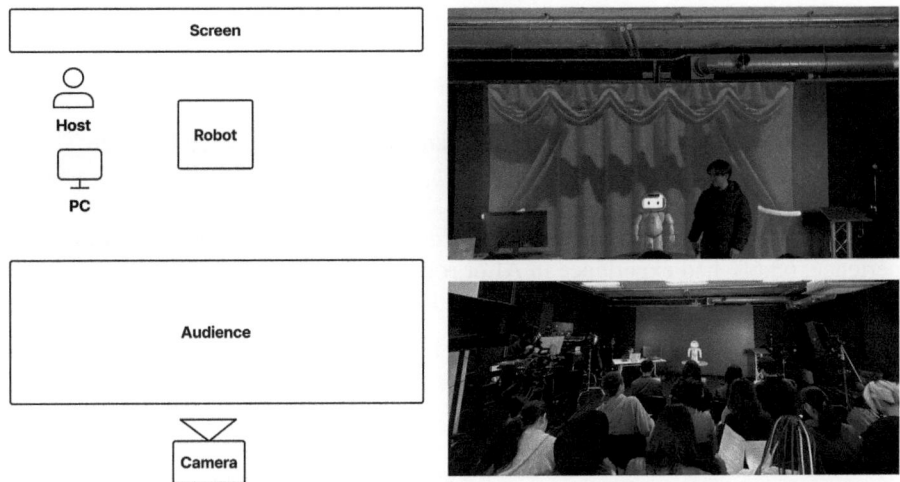

Fig. 2. Spatial relationship between the robot, audience, and human host. Left: arrangement during the robot's performance, right: appearance of the experimental setup.

Performance Initialization

Before each performance, the host set the character parameters and activated the robot via the control computer. When activated, the robot introduces itself autonomously. Once the introduction concluded, the host initiated the comedy routine by speaking to the robot saying, "So, [robot's name], are you ready to perform stand-up comedy?".

Experiment Procedure

Prior to the experiment, all participants signed the consent form to clear the ethical considerations. The experiment was carried out in the following order. 1. host describes the experiment to audience. This includes the host describing the length of performance (i.e. 2–3 min), number of performances, and difference between the first and second performance. 2. Start of first performance: set to British robot comedian. 3. Start of second performance: set to American robot comedian. 4. Ask audience to fill in the questionnaire.

Evaluation Method

Audience perception was assessed through questionnaires, video recordings, audio recordings, and photographs. The questionnaire was adapted from the Robotic Social Attributes Scale (RoSAS) [29] to evaluate our prototype's social acceptability in terms of warmth and competence. The questionnaire included both quantitative (Likert-scale: 1 for "Not at all", 5 for "Extremely") and qualitative (open-ended) components covering demographics (Age group, ethnicity, experience background, gender), overall experience and improvement suggestions. All performances were recorded to analyse audience reactions and refine future robotic stand-up comedy implementations.

4 Result and Analysis

4.1 Participant Demographics and Cultural Context

The study involved 22 participants (12 women, 10 men), all aged 18 or older. The age distribution was as follows: 12 aged 18–24, 6 aged 25–34, and 2 aged 35–44, 1 aged 45–54, and 1 aged 55+. The sample was East Asian (19 participants), with the remaining participants identifying as British (2) and North African (1). In terms of background experience, 63.6% had experience in AI or robotics, 31.8% in theatre or acting, 13.6% in stand-up comedy, and 13.6% in improvisation or performance art.

4.2 RoSAS Scale

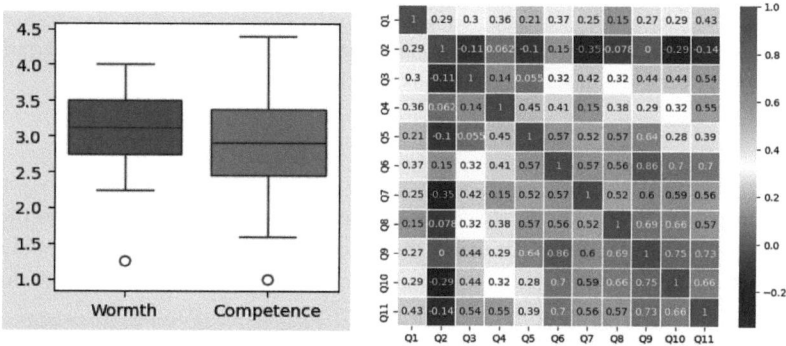

Fig. 3. Results of the RoSAS. Left: Boxplot showing participant ratings for perceived warmth and competence. Right: Correlation matrix illustrating relationships among individual questionnaire items. Ratings indicate moderate perceptions of warmth and competence, with the strongest correlation observed between facial expressiveness and humour enhancement.

Perception of Warmth and Competence

The results of the RoSAS and the corresponding correlation matrix are presented in Fig. 3. Participants rated the robot's perceived competence (M = 2.86, SD = 0.58) and warmth (M = 3.07, SD = 0.80). Warmth was calculated based on responses to Q1, Q3, Q4, and Q5, while competence was derived from Q6 through Q10. Q2 and Q11 were excluded as they did not pertain to the measured constructs. The strongest positive correlation (r = 0.86) was observed between Q6 ("How expressive was the robot's facial display during the performance?") and Q9 ("Did the robot's gestures and facial expressions enhance the humour?"). There was also positive correlation (r = 0.56) between Q8 ("How natural did the robot's movements feel?"). This result indicates a strong relationship between facial expressions and perceived competence in humour delivery.

Perception of Discomfort

Although discomfort was not quantitatively measured, qualitative data indicated that most participants did not find the robot's humour offensive or uncomfortable. This outcome stems from GPT-4o-mini's adherence to content guidelines that filter inappropriate material. Nevertheless, one participant raised a concern regarding voice-character mismatch, stating: "Nothing offensive or uncomfortable, but the robot having a childish voice seemed very at odds within a stand-up comedy setting. Why is a child talking about drinking wine in the shower?" This feedback highlights the critical need for alignment between the robot's voice, persona, and narrative content in comedic settings.

4.3 RQ1: How Can Robots Better Adapt to Diverse Cultural Audiences Through Humorous Personality?

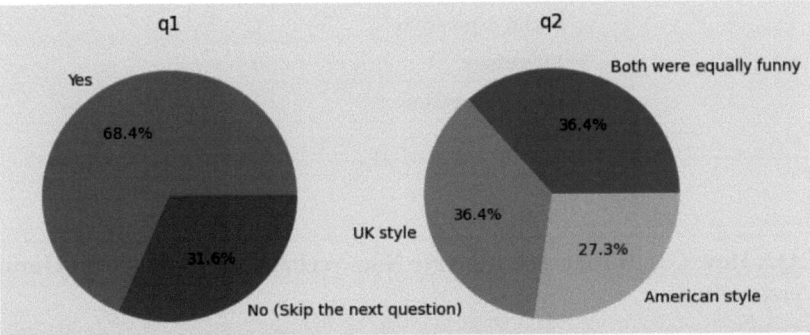

Fig. 4. Results of the cultural adaptation survey. q1: Did you seen performances from different cultures styles? q2: Which one felt funnier to you? The majority of participants recognised differences between the two performances, with a preference for the British performance higher among UK ethnicities, indicating the influence of cultural familiarity on humour perception.

Perception of Cultural Humour Styles

The results of the cultural adaptation survey are shown in Fig. 4. 68.4% participants reported perceiving a distinct difference between the British and American comedic styles. Among them, 36.4% preferred the British performance, 27.3% preferred American style, and 36.4% felt both were equally funny. While several participants criticized the scripts for being predictable, others appreciated the use of shared cultural references. One participant noted: "The British performance used shared cultural experiences well, but the observations were nothing new or inventive, so the performance felt stale and tired." This feedback reflects the complex challenge of achieving a balance between originality and cultural relevance in the automated humour generation.

Recommendations for Cultural Adaptation

To explore how the robot could better adapt to diverse cultural audiences, participants were asked, "How could the robot's humour be better adapted to different cultural audiences?" Participants proposed several strategies for improving cultural alignment. Non-native English speakers, particularly East Asian participants, cited language barriers to humour comprehension. Suggested solutions included enabling multilingual performance capabilities and incorporating regional accents to enhance cultural relatability. In British comedy, for instance, a regional accent can enhance humour by reinforcing the robot's personality perception as a British comedian. Table 2 summarises the participants' comments.

Table 2. Summary of participant responses to the open-ended question on cultural adaptation. The table categorizes recurring themes, and the number of recommendations mentioned by themes.

	Themes	Number of mentions
Cultural adaption	Language	3
	Humour style	3
	Facial expression	1
	Movement	0
	Vocal expression	3
	Others	3

4.4 RQ2: How Can Robots Incorporate Non-Verbal Expressions with Humorous Personality?

Video Analysis

Table 3 summaries the non-verbal expressions of the robot and laughter of the audience. The British-style performance lasted about 3 min, while the American-style lasted about 4 min. Laughter occurrences were manually annotated from video recordings, indicating a significantly higher frequency during the British performance. It is important to note that the British comedian performed first, which may have positively biased the audience response in the initial show.

Table 3. Summary of video analysis comparing British and American comedic performances. The table presents the number of facial expressions, gestures (motions), and audience laughter instances observed during each routine.

Personality	Facial Expression	Motion	Laughter
British comedian	1	2	8
American comedian	0	5	1

Audience perception of robot's Expressiveness

The audience's most significant reaction occurred when the robot displayed a "confused face" (see Fig. 5). In the questionnaire, three out of twenty-two participants specifically mentioned the "confused face" for enhancing humour. Additionally, this facial expression ("confused face") was shown after the host said, "So Nigel, are you ready to perform a stand-up comedy?", and a few seconds of silence, while generating the stand-up comedy script, which indicates the importance of the timing of non-verbal humour, and synchronization of verbal and non-verbal humour.

In response to the follow-up question, "What specific improvements would you suggest for the robot's expressions, gestures, or humour style?", seven participants indicated that the robot should be more expressive, they specifically referring to more exaggerated facial and vocal expressions. Two participants mentioned aligning personality and vocal expressions, and three mentioned humour styles (suggested to bring in the robot's perspective into jokes). Participant's personal preference about a more robot-like or human-like personality and expressions were divided and is subject to future studies with increased number of participants.

The system automatically selects gestures and facial expressions prepared in advance by analysing the text generated by GPT-4o-mini. This means if the text content is not expressive, the robot would not move or change facial expressions. The potential solution to address exaggerated and random expressions would be adding new expression data (gesture, facial expression, voice) and increasing the sensitivity of expression detection. In this experiment, the voice element was set to default (child-like voice), resulting in not aligning with the personality design. Participants suggested that the voice should be more human-like voice and eliminate electronic sound, which could be addressed by using a voice that aligns with the personality design. In the video analysis, mouth movements during the speech were recorded but excluded from evaluation for the purpose of this study and is a subject for future studies.

Fig. 5. Robot expressiveness during performance. Left: example of synchronised body and mouth movements during speech. Right: the "confused face" expression.

5 Conclusion and Future Works

This study proposed and evaluated a prototype of a culturally adaptive conversational robot capable of performing stand-up comedy with a prompt-based personality. To the best of the author's knowledge, this is the first investigation to integrate cultural adaptivity, robot motion, and expressive behaviour with prompt-based personality design in the context of robotic stand-up comedy. A key strength of the present study was diverse multicultural participation, which may have significant insights into understanding how to adapt to audiences who have diverse ethnicities.

Notwithstanding uneven participants, questionnaire analysis has revealed that language and vocal expressions are the prominent elements for robotic comedy to adapt to diverse cultures. Moreover, the alignment between the robot's voice and its designed personality was shown to be essential. Video analysis further indicated that facial expressions could function as powerful non-verbal cues of humour, particularly when addressing audiences with varying cultural norms. Despite the exploratory nature of this study and the limited sample diversity, the results contribute to the growing understanding of how social robots can utilize humour to improve HRI across cultural boundaries. This work suggests that humour style, delivery, and expressiveness must be carefully tailored to suit cultural expectations.

Several avenues for future research are proposed. First, further exploration is needed in designing robot personalities that match various humour styles and in mapping vocal expressions, gestures, and facial expressions to specific personality traits. Second, there is potential in adopting co-design methodologies that involve comedians, performers, and audience members in the development of robot behaviours. This can be facilitated by platforms such as the QT robot's visual programming interface, enabling non-programmers to contribute to complex behaviour design. Another important direction is the development of real-time adaptation mechanisms that enable robots to adjust their behaviour dynamically based on the audience's cultural cues and real-time feedback. More broadly, further studies should investigate how cultural background and ethnicity influence the acceptability and effectiveness of humorous robots, especially in terms of comfort, relatability, and engagement.

References

1. Oliveira, R., Arriaga, P., Axelsson, M., Paiva, A.: Humor–robot interaction: a scoping review of the literature and future directions. Int. J. Soc. Robot. **13** (2021)
2. Nijholt, A.: Robotic stand-up comedy: state-of-the-art. In: Streitz, N., Konomi, S. (eds.) DAPI 2018. LNCS, vol. 10921, pp. 391–410. Springer, Cham (2018). https://doi.org/10.1007/978-3-319-91125-0_32
3. Amin, M., Burghardt, M.: A survey on approaches to computational humor generation. In: Proceedings of the 4th Joint SIGHUM Workshop on Computational Linguistics for Cultural Heritage, Social Sciences, Humanities and Literature, December 2020
4. Jentzsch, S., Kersting, K.: ChatGPT is fun, but it is not funny! Humor is still challenging large language models. arXiv preprint arXiv:2306.04563, 7 June 2023
5. Chen, Y., Shi, B., Si, M.: Prompt to GPT-3: step-by-step thinking instructions for humor generation. arXiv preprint arXiv:2306.13195, 22 June 2023
6. Toplyn, J.: Witscript 3: a hybrid AI system for improvising jokes in a conversation. arXiv preprint arXiv:2301.02695, 6 January 2023
7. Zhong, S., et al.: Let's think outside the box: Exploring leap-of-thought in large language models with creative humor generation. In: Proceedings of the IEEE/CVF Conference on Computer Vision and Pattern Recognition (2024)
8. Mirowski, P., Branch, B., Mathewson, K., Montréal, I.: The theater stage as laboratory: review of real-time comedy LLM systems for live performance. arXiv preprint arXiv:2501.08474 (2025)
9. Samani, H., et al.: Cultural robotics: the culture of robotics and robotics in culture. Int. J. Adv. Robot. Syst. **10**(12) (2013)

10. Lee, H.R., Sabanović, S.: Culturally variable preferences for robot design and use in South Korea, Turkey, and the United States. Presented at the Proceedings of the 2014 ACM/IEEE International Conference on Human-Robot Interaction (2014)
11. Gervais, M., Wilson, D.S.: The evolution and functions of laughter and humor: a synthetic approach. Q. Rev. Biol. **80**(4) (2005)
12. Epley, N., Waytz, A., Cacioppo, J.T.: On seeing human: a three-factor theory of anthropomorphism **114**, 864 (2007)
13. Joosse, M., Lohse, M., Perez, J.G., Evers, V.: What you do is who you are: the role of task context in perceived social robot personality. Presented at the 2013 IEEE International Conference on Robotics and Automation (2013)
14. Lalioti, V.: RethinkAI^{TM}: designing the human and AI relationship in the future of work. In: International Association of Societies of Design Research Conference 2019, September 2019
15. Lalioti, V., Ionescu, I.A.: Designing robotic movement with personality. Presented at the Companion of the 2023 ACM/IEEE International Conference on Human-Robot Interaction (2023)
16. Mirowski, P.W., Love, J., Mathewson, K., Mohamed, S.: A robot walks into a bar: can language models serve as creativity support tools for comedy? An evaluation of LLMs' humour alignment with comedians. In: Proceedings of the 2024 ACM Conference on Fairness, Accountability, and Transparency, 3 June 2024
17. Knight, H., Satkin, S., Ramakrishna, V., Divvala, S.: A savvy robot standup comic: online learning through audience tracking. In: Proceedings of the Workshop on Humanoid Robots and Creativity at the IEEE-RAS International Conference on Humanoid Robots Humanoids (Madrid), November 2014
18. Vilk, J., Fitter, N.T.: Comedians in cafes getting data: evaluating timing and adaptivity in real-world robot comedy performance. In: Proceedings of the 2020 ACM/IEEE International Conference on Human-Robot Interaction, 9 March 2020
19. Srivastava, A., Fitter, N.T.: A robot walks into a bar: automatic robot joke success assessment. In: 2021 IEEE International Conference on Robotics and Automation (ICRA), 30 May 2021
20. Gray, C., Webster, T., Ozarowicz, B., Chen, Y., Bui, T., Srivastava, A., Fitter, N.T.: "This bot knows what I'm talking about!" human-inspired laughter classification methods for adaptive robotic comedians. In: 2022 31st IEEE International Conference on Robot and Human Interactive Communication (RO-MAN), 29 August 2022
21. Katevas, K., Healey, P.G.T., Harris, M.T.: Robot stand-up: engineering a comic performance. In: Proceedings of the Workshop on Humanoid Robots and Creativity at the IEEE-RAS International Conference on Humanoid Robots Humanoids (Madrid), November 2014
22. Katevas, K., Healey, P.G.T., Harris, M.T.: Robot comedy lab: experimenting with the social dynamics of live performance. Front. Psychol. **6** (2015)
23. Umetani, T., Mashimo, R., Nadamoto, A., Kitamura, T., Nakayama, H.: Manzai robots: entertainment robots based on auto-created manzai scripts from web news articles. J. Robot. Mechatron. **26**(5) (2014)
24. Branch, B., Mirowski, P., Mathewson Improbotics, K., Ppali, S., Covaci, A.: Designing and evaluating dialogue LLMs for co-creative improvised theatre. arXiv preprint arXiv:2405.07111, 11 May 2024
25. LuxAI. https://luxai.com/#LearnMore. Accessed 4 Apr 2025
26. LuxAI: A Complete Guide to Build a Conversational Social Robot with QTrobot and ChatGPT. https://luxai.com/blog/complete-guide-to-build-conversational-social-robot-qtrobot-chatgpt/. Accessed 31 Mar 2025
27. OpenAI Platform Models. https://platform.openai.com/docs/models. Accessed 21 Mar 2025
28. Comedy Carnival: British Comedy vs. American Stand-up Comedy: Key Differences. https://comedycarnival.co.uk/what-are-some-of-the-key-differences-between-british-stand-up-comedy-and-american-stand-up-comedy/. Accessed 14 Apr 2025

29. Carpinella, C.M., Wyman, A.B., Perez, M.A., Stroessner, S.J.: The robotic social attributes scale (RoSAS) development and validation. In: Proceedings of the 2017 ACM/IEEE International Conference on human-robot interaction, 6 March 2017

Social Human-Agent Interaction for Health

Service Robots in Elderly Care: A Systematic Review of ADL Coverage, Stakeholder Sentiment, and Deployment Readiness

Timothy Scott Chu[1(✉)] and John-John Cabibihan[2]

[1] Department of Mechanical Engineering, De La Salle University, 2401 Taft Avenue Malate, Manila, Philippines
timothy.chu@dlsu.edu.ph
[2] Department of Mechanical and Industrial Engineering, College of Engineering, Qatar University, Doha, Qatar
john.cabibihan@qu.edu.qa

Abstract. As global populations age, service robots are increasingly viewed as scalable tools to support elderly individuals in performing Activities of Daily Living (ADLs). However, the extent of ADL support and the barriers to broader deployment remain unclear. This systematic literature review screened 306 peer-reviewed publications (2012–2024), with 75 articles selected for in-depth analysis, addressing three research questions: (1) which ADLs remain underserved and what barriers hinder development; (2) how ethical, usability, and social factors affect adoption; and (3) what technological and deployment constraints limit commercialization. Findings show a disproportionate focus on Instrumental ADLs (IADLs), while Basic ADLs (BADLs)—particularly toileting, dressing, and bathing—remain underexplored. Sentiment analysis reveals stakeholder acceptance varies by robot type, shaped by concerns over privacy, reliability, and transparency. To assess readiness, the study proposes a taxonomy with three dimensions: explainability, failure tolerance, and robustness. Applied to Domestic Assistance Robots (DARs), Socially Assistive Robots (SARs), and Physically Assistive Robots (PARs), the framework highlights the need for distinct trust-building strategies. The study concludes that successful adoption depends on both functional capability and context-sensitive, user-centered design.

Keywords: Activities of Daily Living · ADL · Assistive Robotics · Elderly Care · Service Robots · Taxonomy for Robotics

1 Introduction

The use of service robots to assist elderly individuals is gaining traction as a scalable, human-centered solution to growing care demands. As life expectancy rises and populations age, particularly in regions like *Association of Southeast Asian Nations* (ASEAN)— where the elderly population rose from 5.3% in 2000 to 7.5% in 2022 [1]—pressures on healthcare systems, care facilities, and informal caregivers continue to increase [2]. Many older adults prefer to age in place [3], requiring support for essential daily tasks known as *Activities of Daily Living* (ADLs). These include *Basic ADLs* (BADLs), such as bathing, dressing, toileting, feeding, continence management, and mobility [4], and *Instrumental ADLs* (IADLs), such as housekeeping, meal preparation, medication management, financial management, shopping/grocery, communication, and transportation [5, 6]. Table 1 outlines these categories. Robotic systems have been introduced to address a variety of ADL tasks, though their complexity and deployment readiness vary. For BADLs, systems like Robear [7] and the SUE Robotic Walker [8] assist with mobility and transfers, while feeding robots such as the OBI enable autonomous eating through intuitive interfaces [9]. In IADLs, robotic vacuums like Roomba use SLAM for housekeeping [10], and smart assistants manage medication via reminders and voice interfaces [11, 12]. These innovations highlight both the promise and the challenges of service robotics in elderly care. While several domains have seen progress, others remain limited by technical, ethical, or usability constraints—underscoring the need to map existing developments and identify where gaps remain.

Table 1. Classification of Activities of Daily Living (ADLs) into Basic and Instrumental Categories with Corresponding Descriptions

Category	Activity	Description
BADLs	Bathing	Washing the body, entering/exiting the bath
	Dressing	Wearing/removing clothing, managing fasteners
	Feeding	Eating independently
	Toileting	Using the toilet, including post-use hygiene
	Continence Management	Controlling bladder and bowel functions
	Mobility	Moving independently, transfers and walking
IADLs	Housekeeping	Cleaning, laundry, and maintaining a safe home
	Meal Preparation	Planning, cooking, and serving meals
	Medication Management	Taking medications and managing schedules
	Financial Management	Handling bills, budgets, and finances
	Shopping	Buying groceries, clothing, or other goods
	Communication	Using phones, email, or tools to stay in touch
	Transportation	Using public or private transport for errands

Mapping this uneven development is essential to identifying which ADLs are well-supported and which remain underserved. Beyond technical maturity, adoption depends on ethical and human-centered design. Tasks involving physical care raise particular concerns around privacy, dignity, and autonomy. As robots operate more frequently in personal spaces, issues of transparency, reliability, and user control become central to building trust. Despite promising innovations, many systems remain confined to laboratory settings or pilot programs due to the absence of structured frameworks for evaluating readiness, usability, and real-world viability.

In response to these gaps and barriers, this review is guided by three research questions:

1. Which ADLs are underserved in service robotics, and what contributes to this gap?
2. How do ethical, usability, and social factors affect the adoption of service robots?
3. What constraints limit service robot deployment, and how can a taxonomy guide readiness for real-world use?

This review offers a structured analysis of service robotics in elderly care by mapping ADL-related research, identifying coverage gaps and adoption barriers. It further examines how ethical, technical, and usability constraints affect deployment readiness through a systematic literature review guided by three research questions on ADL support, user acceptance, and commercial viability.

2 Methodology

2.1 Literature Selection and Screening

A systematic literature review was conducted to examine the state of service robotics research supporting ADLs among the elderly. Articles were retrieved in February 2025 using the Scopus database, chosen for its broad interdisciplinary coverage and substantial indexing of sources from IEEE, ACM, and related fields. Future reviews may incorporate additional databases such as PubMed to extend biomedical coverage.

Search Strategy and Query Design. Three distinct keyword queries were independently executed in the Scopus database to capture literature on service robotics, artificial intelligence, and their intersection. These queries targeted: (1) elderly-focused service robotics applications, (2) broad AI research trends, and (3) the integration of AI into robotic systems. Table 2 summarizes the Boolean logic and terminology used.

Table 2. Keyword Search Strings Used in Scopus

Field of Study	Keywords
Service Robots for the Elderly	("Service robots" OR "assistive robots" OR "social robotics") AND ("elderly care" OR "aging in place" OR "ADLs" OR "independent living")
Artificial Intelligence	("artificial AND intelligence") OR ("machine AND learning")
A.I. in Robot Systems	(("artificial AND intelligence") OR ("machine AND learning")) AND (robots)

- Service Robots for the Elderly – This primary query retrieved studies on the application of service robots in elderly care. The first clause grouped function-oriented terms reflecting major ADL-related robot classifications, while the second targeted the relevant population and care context. The search initially returned 343 records (1994–2024) but given the sharp rise in elderly-focused robotics research after 2012, the review window was narrowed to 2012–2024, yielding 306 articles for screening.
- Artificial Intelligence Trends – This query was included to acknowledge the growing influence of AI on service robot development and was designed to capture a broad scope of AI research for contextual grounding. It yielded 1,155,602 records, which were used to supplement the trend analysis.
- AI in Robotic Systems – This query focused the scope by identifying literature and assessing how AI techniques were applied to robotic platforms. It returned 36,722 records and was primarily used for trend analysis.

Screening and Inclusion Criteria. Screening and categorization were conducted by a single reviewer using a structured approach. Studies were included to determine whether they addressed the development, deployment, or evaluation of service robots assisting elderly individuals with ADLs. They were published in peer-reviewed journals, conference proceedings, book chapters, or review papers. Excluded were studies focused solely on control systems or simulations without elderly care applications, those unrelated to physical or socially assistive robots, and non-academic literature.

Titles and abstracts were screened and classified into BADLs or IADLs using established frameworks [4–6], resulting in 80 BADL-related and 159 IADL-related studies. A secondary screening limited overrepresented categories to ensure balanced subtype coverage. Thirty studies were selected from each group based on recency (2020–2024) and category balance. An additional 15 user acceptance studies were retained for their ethical and stakeholder relevance, yielding a final review pool of 75 articles. The whole selection process is illustrated in Fig. 1.

2.2 Analytical Approach for Research Questions

Research Question 1 – Mapping ADL Coverage. To address the first research question, the selected articles were categorized using established frameworks for Basic and Instrumental ADLs [4–6], with further sub-categorization based on specific assistance tasks to enable detailed coverage mapping. Commercialization status—whether a robot had progressed beyond the prototype stage—was noted to provide indicative insights into translational challenges. Publication years were also recorded to observe research trends over time. This mapping identified areas of concentration, gaps in coverage, and emerging barriers and guided the selection of user acceptance studies analyzed in Research Question 2.

Research Question 2 – Ethical, Usability, and Social Acceptance Factors. A focused subset of 15 articles was analyzed to address this research question, supported by thematic insights from broader studies addressing user experience and ethical dimensions. Stakeholders were grouped into three levels: primary, secondary, and tertiary, providing a structured lens to interpret concerns across roles. Common themes observed include

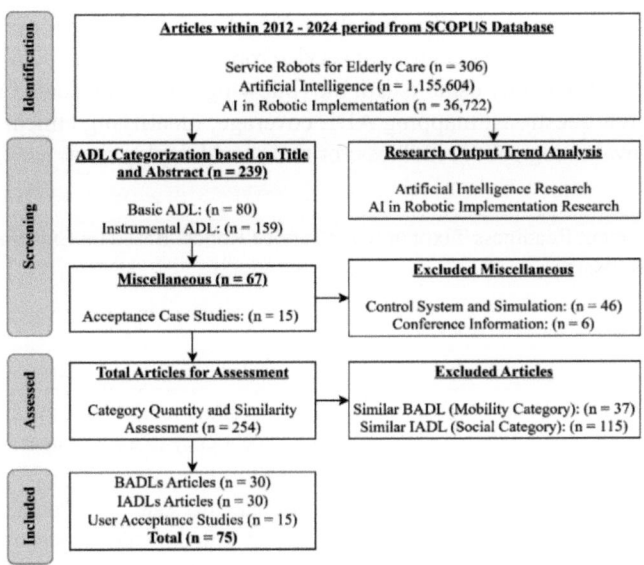

Fig. 1. Systematic Literature Selection Flow for Service Robotics in Elderly Care

privacy and data security, trust and reliability in autonomous systems, usability issues, and fears that robots may act beyond user intent or undermine agency. These concerns align with Brooks' Three Laws of Robotics [13], which frame stakeholder expectations around safety, transparency, and control, issues further explored in Research Question 3.

Research Question 3 – Technological Constraints and Deployment Readiness Taxonomy. To address the third research question, this analysis builds on prior findings to evaluate recurring barriers in physical design, artificial intelligence, and system integration that affect service robot performance and acceptance. The reviewed studies were categorized into hardware and physical limitations and integration/deployment issues. This classification enabled a structured assessment of problems such as limited manipulation and mobility, poor adaptability, dependence on constant supervision, and safety risks.

These insights developed a three-dimensional taxonomy to evaluate deployability readiness, as shown in Table 3. The taxonomy includes:

- Explainability – how clearly the robot's function and decision-making are understood by users
- Failure Tolerance – the severity of consequences in case of failure
- Robustness – the level of autonomy in performing tasks without human intervention

Robots are assessed across these dimensions and assigned to one of three deployment stages: Research-Stage, Experimental, or Commercialized. The taxonomy not only provides a framework for evaluation but also offers design guidance for improving real-world readiness and public acceptance of service robots in elderly care. With the analytical approach and taxonomy established, the following section presents findings across the three research questions: mapping ADL coverage, identifying ethical and usability concerns, and evaluating robot readiness for real-world deployment.

Table 3. Deployment Readiness Taxonomy for Service Robots Based on Explainability, Failure Tolerance, and Robustness

Deployment Stage	Characteristics		
	Explainability	Failure Tolerance	Robustness
Research-Stage	Unclear; purpose not easily interpretable	Severe; failure results in full dependency (e.g., immobility)	Low; requires full supervision
Experimental	Moderately clear; some explanation still needed	Moderate; user can function with difficulty (e.g., feeding)	Partial; needs occasional supervision
Commercialized	Clear and transparent	Minimal; failure causes minor inconvenience (e.g., cleanup)	High; operates with minimal supervision

3 Results and Discussion

3.1 Activities of Daily Living Coverage and Technological Barriers

Table 4 presents the distribution of 306 reviewed studies across BADLs and IADLs. Over half (52%) focused on IADLs, while only 26% addressed BADLs. The remaining 22% were unclassified, typically covering general system design or acceptance studies unrelated to specific ADLs.

Among BADLs, mobility and transferring received the most attention (47 studies), though only a few systems reached commercialization, highlighting challenges in robust, safe physical interaction. Feeding (16) followed mobility studies and modest commercial uptake, while bathing (7) and dressing (10) were rarely studied. Notably, toileting was entirely unaddressed, marking it as the most underserved. It is worth noting that continence management often requires physiological intervention, placing it beyond typical robotic capability. In contrast to these physical and ethically complex BADLs, research on IADLs has been more prolific and aligned with cognitive and social engagement (125 studies). Despite high research volume, commercial success remained limited. Housekeeping (12 studies) showed the strongest deployment, supported by mature robotic cleaning technologies. Other IADLs remained less explored, with few systems reaching the market.

These trends directly answer Research Question 1: BADLs—especially toileting, dressing, and bathing—remain significantly underserved, likely due to the high physical, ethical, and safety demands they entail. In contrast, IADL systems are more feasible to design and test, as they carry lower risk upon failure.

Table 4. Study Distribution by ADL Type

BADLs	Count	IADLs	Count
Bathing	7	Housekeeping	12
Dressing	10	Meal Preparation	4
Transferring/Mobility	47	Medication Management	4
Toileting	0	Cognitive and Social Engagement	125
Feeding	16	Communications	10
Continence	0	Transportation	4
		Finance Management	0
Total	**80**	**Total**	**159**

Figure 2 plots research trends from 2012 to 2024 for Basic ADLs, Instrumental ADLs, AI Studies, and AI in Robot Systems. The trendlines show that IADL research closely mirrors the rise of AI in Robot Systems, especially after 2014, when advances in deep learning and control systems enabled more complex tasks. This observation suggests that improvements in software intelligence actively drove robotics development, including in social and cognitive assistance domains. In contrast, BADL research advanced more slowly, likely due to persistent mechanical and safety challenges. However, the maturity of AI technologies now could help close this gap. Integrating adaptive control, intent recognition, and safety monitoring may improve the viability of BADL-support robots.

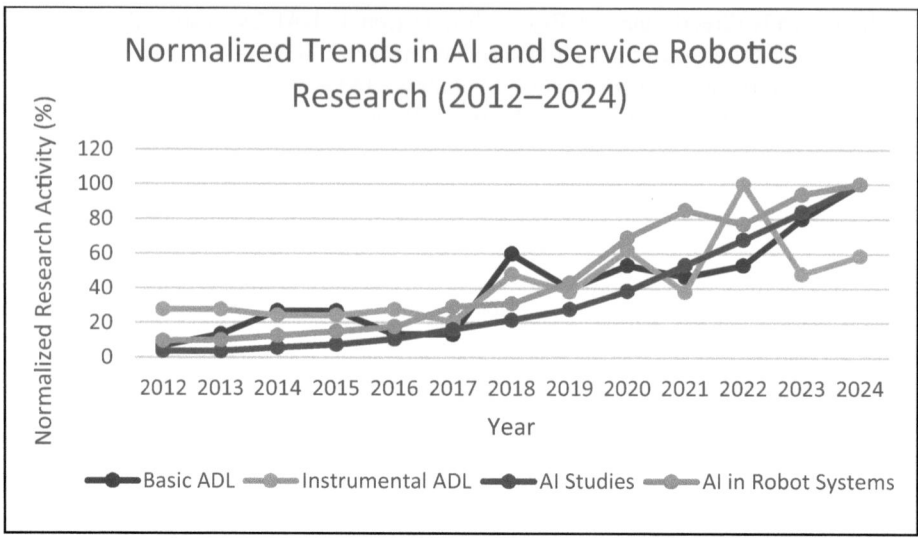

Fig. 2. Research Trends in AI and Service Robotics for ADL Support (2012–2024)

3.2 Ethical, Usability, and Stakeholder Perspectives

In analyzing how ethical concerns, usability challenges, and social acceptance shape service robot adoption in elderly care, this review adopts the stakeholder mapping framework proposed in [14], which organizes stakeholders by their power in decision-making and level of attention or engagement with the technology.

- Primary stakeholders refer to elderly end-users, who typically hold high decision-making authority and exhibit strong engagement.
- Secondary stakeholders include caregivers, nurses, and family members, who exert substantial influence over deployment decisions but may not always be actively involved unless prompted by specific circumstances.
- Tertiary stakeholders encompass developers, manufacturers, and policymakers. While they may lack direct authority in individual cases, they play a critical role in shaping the ethical, functional, and regulatory landscape of service robots.

To interpret stakeholder perspectives, robots were categorized by function:

- *Socially Assistive Robots (SARs)* – cognitive, emotional, and social support
- *Physically Assistive Robots (PARs)* – bodily tasks like mobility, feeding, and dressing
- *Domestic Assistance Robots (DARs)* – household tasks such as cleaning, medication reminders, and meal preparation

A qualitative thematic review of user acceptance studies was conducted to extract stakeholder sentiments. Abstracts, discussions, and conclusions were examined for explicit concerns, which were categorized by the diversity of ethical, social, and functional issues raised. Sentiment data revealed several patterns. SARs raised concerns about privacy, surveillance, and emotional deception. Older adults were uncomfortable with robots collecting data in private spaces and questioned the authenticity of human-like behaviors [15]. While SARs were credited with reducing loneliness and aiding dementia care, secondary stakeholders cautioned against emotional overreliance and unrealistic expectations [16], emphasizing that SARs should be framed as tools rather than companions. Concerns over stigmatization also emerged, with users fearing association with frailty or isolation [14, 15, 17]. PARs prompted concerns around robustness, safety, and dignity, particularly when robots acted without user input (e.g., unsolicited reminders) [18]. Caregivers reported usability issues including inconsistent system responses, limited adaptability, and increased supervision burden [19]. Nonetheless, PARs were praised for reducing physical strain in mobility and lifting tasks [20].

DARs were perceived as less ethically sensitive but elicited mixed responses. Some users appreciated medication reminders and fall detection [18], while others preferred continued engagement in meaningful tasks like cooking or cleaning [15]. Tertiary stakeholders emphasized the importance of intuitive interfaces, clear data practices, and regulations aligned with user comprehension [14].

Robot appearance and design also influenced trust. Overly human-like SARs triggered discomfort via the uncanny valley effect [18]. PARs were often seen as too bulky for residential use, while DARs lacked personalization for daily routines. Despite these concerns, studies show that older adults remain open to SARs—particularly when used for physical support. Many expressed willingness to adopt them if systems were reliable and easy to use [21]. These findings suggest SARs can address key needs when ethically framed and contextually introduced [22].

These patterns align with Rodney Brooks' Three Laws of Robotics [13]:

1. "The visual appearance of a robot makes a promise about what it can do and how smart it is."
2. "Robots must not take away from people's agency, particularly when they fail."
3. "Robotic technologies need 10+ years of steady refinement beyond lab demos... to deliver 99.9% reliability."

To interpret these barriers systematically, the proposed taxonomy—based on explainability, robustness, and failure tolerance—provides a structured evaluation tool. SARs often lack functional clarity due to anthropomorphic design; PARs demand high precision and pose greater risk upon failure, while DARs, by contrast, demonstrate strong performance across all three dimensions and may serve as reference model for deployment.

Despite these concerns, it was observed that trust increases when systems respect privacy, preserve agency, and deliver value, particularly among primary and secondary stakeholders [18, 21]. Addressing these issues requires not only ethical framing but also technological maturity.

3.3 Technological Constraints and Deployment Readiness Taxonomy

The readiness of service robots for elderly care varies by function, interpretability, failure resilience, and robustness in real-world use. To evaluate these aspects, the proposed taxonomy—Explainability, Failure Tolerance, and Robustness—is applied to three established robot categories: DARs, SARs, and PARs. This assessment highlights deployment challenges and informs design priorities. Table 5 summarizes the mapping.

DARs, such as Roomba, Care-O-bot, and delivery robots, are the most commercially mature. Their physical features—wheels, shelves, and simple arms—communicate function, ensuring high explainability. Failures typically cause inconvenience rather than compromise autonomy, indicating strong failure tolerance. Robustness is well-demonstrated in dynamic home environments with minimal supervision. Ongoing development emphasizes smart-home integration and sustaining user trust. SARs, including Paro, Pepper, and conversational agents, are emerging but less mature. Designed with approachable aesthetics, they support cognitive and emotional functions. However, anthropomorphic features can obscure functional clarity, reducing explainability. SARs may also incorporate behavior monitoring via computer vision, prompting privacy and ethical concerns, especially among secondary stakeholders. Though failure rarely disrupts core tasks, SARs remain moderately robust and typically require structured settings. Design improvements should prioritize interaction transparency, non-intrusive form factors, and explainable AI. PARs, such as OBI, ReWalk, and Robear, are largely experimental, assisting with physically intimate tasks such as feeding, mobility, and transfer. While some designs offer intuitive function cues (e.g., OBI's integrated plate arm), failures can severely impact user autonomy, necessitating supervised operation. These robots show limited robustness, often struggling with calibration and real-world variability. To reduce risk, design efforts must focus on redundancy, safe failure modes, and strong operational safeguards.

These distinctions are summarized in Table 5.

Table 5. Taxonomy Analysis

Robot Type	Examples	Explainability	Failure Tolerance	Robustness	Deployment Stage
DARs	Roomba, Care-O-Bot, Delivery Robots	High	High	High	Widely Commercialized
SARs	Paro, Pepper, Conversational Robots	Moderate	High	Moderate	Emerging Market
PARs	OBI, ReWalk, Robear	Moderate to Low	Moderate to Low	Low	Experimental Phase

These findings inform design strategies that facilitate trust-building. DARs benefit from simple, interpretable designs, where failures rarely compromise user autonomy. SARs require high interaction transparency, strong feature explainability, and careful communication of data use to build trust. PARs, operating in the most intimate and risk-sensitive contexts, must emphasize robustness and fail-safe behavior to preserve user independence. Supervision should scale with risk: PARs require active oversight, while SARs and DARs can often function with periodic checks or event-triggered monitoring.

These strategies help explain uneven deployment trajectories and offer a guiding principle for future development: to achieve commercial viability, service robots must be designed for function and trust, calibrated to their roles within the care ecosystem.

DARs are closest to widespread adoption with high explainability, robustness, and failure tolerance. SARs face challenges in trust, privacy, and interaction design, while PARs encounter the steepest hurdles due to their physical intrusiveness and high-risk use cases. Readiness, therefore, exists on a spectrum—shaped by task complexity, interaction demands, and acceptable risk levels. Trust-building must be tailored accordingly: DARs generally benefit from clear physical cues and reliable autonomy; SARs require emotional transparency, consistent interaction, and strong privacy assurances; and PARs demand robust design, fail-safe mechanisms, and active supervision. While not prescriptive, these priorities resonate with Brooks' Three Laws of Robotics, reinforcing the value of appearance-function match, user agency, and long-term iterative refinement. The taxonomy thus offers both a diagnostic tool and a practical roadmap for human-centered service robot design.

While general design principles offer practical guidance, their effectiveness depends on the cultural and regional context in which robots are deployed. In ASEAN, healthcare access remains uneven due to transportation, affordability, and infrastructure gaps [23]. These constraints shift stakeholder priorities toward accessibility, cost-efficiency, and reliability over high autonomy or socially expressive features. Caregiving often occurs within multigenerational households, reducing the perceived need for robots assisting with intimate BADLs like bathing or toileting, while increasing acceptance for robots supporting monitoring, reminders, or fall detection [23, 24]. These contextual factors suggest clear design imperatives for ASEAN markets: simple interfaces with local language support, compact and task-specific hardware suitable for smaller homes, and functional, non-anthropomorphic aesthetics. Hardware choices should emphasize affordability and ease of repair. These priorities align with global findings that culturally misaligned or high-risk robots—particularly those addressing BADLs—often face rejection [25]. In ASEAN, acceptance depends as much on cultural adaptability as on technical performance.

4 Conclusion

This study systematically reviewed the development and deployment readiness of service robots for elderly care, with a focus on Activities of Daily Living (ADLs). While research and commercialization have favored Instrumental ADLs (IADLs), Basic ADLs (BADLs)—especially toileting—remain critically underserved due to their physical, ethical, and safety complexities. A stakeholder-informed sentiment analysis revealed that acceptance of service robots depends not only on functionality but also on trust, privacy, and user autonomy. These factors vary across robot types—DARs, SARs, and PARs—each presenting unique deployment challenges and design requirements.

To address these challenges, a taxonomy evaluating explainability, failure tolerance, and robustness was introduced. The findings emphasize that trust must be built differently across robot types: DARs require clear physical cues and robustness; SARs benefit from transparency and emotional clarity; PARs must prioritize robustness and fail-safe interaction. Ultimately, this study highlights the need for design strategies that go beyond task performance to address user trust and real-world viability—laying the groundwork for more ethical, functional, and deployable service robots in elderly care.

Acknowledgments. The authors acknowledge the support of the Department of Mechanical Engineering, De La Salle University for providing the academic environment and access to resources that enabled this work. The work of JJ Cabibihan was supported in part by Qatar Research, Development and Innovation (QRDI) under Grant AICC06-0515-240005. The statements made herein are solely the responsibility of the authors.

Disclosure of Interests. The authors have no competing interests to declare that are relevant to the content of this article.

References

1. ASEAN Statistical Brief: Ageing ASEAN: Shifting Demographic Structure. Association of Southeast Asian Nations (ASEAN) (2023)
2. Read, L., Gaskin, J., Cruse, C.B.: The future of aging What impact might the expansion of health span have on society? https://www2.deloitte.com/us/en/insights/industry/health-care/future-of-aging-aging-population-and-healthcare-industry.html. Accessed 05 Oct 2024
3. Getson, C., Nejat, G.: Socially assistive robots helping older adults through the pandemic and life after COVID-19. Robotics **10**, 106 (2021). https://doi.org/10.3390/robotics10030106
4. Katz, S.: Assessing self-maintenance: activities of daily living, mobility, and instrumental activities of daily living. J. Am. Geriatr. Soc. **31**, 721–727 (1983). https://doi.org/10.1111/j.1532-5415.1983.tb03391.x
5. Lawton, M.P., Brody, E.M.: Assessment of older people: self-maintaining and instrumental activities of daily living. Gerontologist **9**, 179–186 (1969). https://doi.org/10.1093/geront/9.3_Part_1.179
6. Graf, C.: The Lawton instrumental activities of daily living scale. AJN Am. J. Nurs. **108**, 52–62 (2008). https://doi.org/10.1097/01.NAJ.0000314810.46029.74
7. Giansanti, D.: The social robot in rehabilitation and assistance: what is the future? Healthcare **9**, 244 (2021). https://doi.org/10.3390/healthcare9030244
8. Zhao, X., et al.: A smart robotic walker with intelligent close-proximity interaction capabilities for elderly mobility safety. Front. Neurorobot. **14**, 575889 (2020). https://doi.org/10.3389/fnbot.2020.575889
9. Zhi, P., Lu, Y., Li, Y., Wang, S.: Multimodal based automatic feeding robotic device. In: 2022 7th Asia-Pacific Conference on Intelligent Robot Systems (ACIRS), Tianjin, China, pp. 164–169. IEEE (2022). https://doi.org/10.1109/ACIRS55390.2022.9845543
10. Mohan, A., Krishnan, A.R.: Design and simulation of an autonomous floor cleaning robot with optional UV sterilization. In: 2022 IEEE 2nd Mysore Sub Section International Conference (MysuruCon), Mysuru, India, pp. 1–6. IEEE (2022). https://doi.org/10.1109/MysuruCon55714.2022.9972558
11. Jun, K., Oh, S., Lee, D.-W., Kim, M.S.: Management of medication using a mobile robot and artificial intelligence. In: 2021 IEEE Region 10 Symposium (TENSYMP), Jeju, Republic of Korea, pp. 1–3. IEEE (2021). https://doi.org/10.1109/TENSYMP52854.2021.9550863
12. Krishna, N., Sree, R.N., Sajith, R., Ramji, S.K., Ramesh, S.: PILLBOT: non-contact medicine dispensing system for patients in quarantine. In: 2021 International Conference on Recent Trends on Electronics, Information, Communication & Technology (RTEICT), Bangalore, India, pp. 97–100. IEEE (2021). https://doi.org/10.1109/RTEICT52294.2021.9573930
13. Brooks, R.: Rodney Brooks's Three Laws of Robotics. https://spectrum.ieee.org/rodney-brooks-three-laws-robotics. Accessed 10 Mar 2025
14. Höpfl, F., Peisl, T., Greiner, C.: Exploring stakeholder perspectives: enhancing robot acceptance for sustainable healthcare solutions. Sustain. Technol. Entrep. **2**, 100045 (2023). https://doi.org/10.1016/j.stae.2023.100045

15. Zafrani, O., Nimrod, G., Edan, Y.: Between fear and trust: older adults' evaluation of socially assistive robots. Int. J. Hum. Comput. Stud. **171**, 102981 (2023). https://doi.org/10.1016/j.ijhcs.2022.102981
16. Christoforou, E.G., Avgousti, S., Ramdani, N., Novales, C., Panayides, A.S.: The upcoming role for nursing and assistive robotics: opportunities and challenges ahead. Front. Digit. Health **2**, 585656 (2020). https://doi.org/10.3389/fdgth.2020.585656
17. Sørensen, L., Johannesen, D.T., Johnsen, H.M.: Humanoid robots for assisting people with physical disabilities in activities of daily living: a scoping review. Assist. Technol., 1–17 (2024). https://doi.org/10.1080/10400435.2024.2337194
18. Lehoux, P., Grimard, D.: When robots care: public deliberations on how technology and humans may support independent living for older adults. Soc Sci Med **211**, 330–337 (2018). https://doi.org/10.1016/j.socscimed.2018.06.038
19. Sharma, A., Rathi, Y., Patni, V., Sinha, D.K.: A systematic review of assistance robots for elderly care. In: 2021 International Conference on Communication information and Computing Technology (ICCICT), Mumbai, India, pp. 1–6. IEEE (2021). https://doi.org/10.1109/ICCICT50803.2021.9510142
20. Thomessen, T.: A safety concept for service-robots operating in nursing homes. In: 2024 IEEE/SICE International Symposium on System Integration (SII), Ha Long, Vietnam, pp. 1032–1037. IEEE (2024). https://doi.org/10.1109/SII58957.2024.10417214
21. Vandemeulebroucke, T., Dzi, K., Gastmans, C.: Older adults' experiences with and perceptions of the use of socially assistive robots in aged care: a systematic review of quantitative evidence. Arch. Gerontol. Geriatr. **95**, 104399 (2021). https://doi.org/10.1016/j.archger.2021.104399
22. Slane, A., Pedersen, I.: Older people's ethical framing of autonomy in relation to current and future consumer technologies: the case of socially assistive robots. Int. J. Soc. Robot. **16**, 2277–2296 (2024). https://doi.org/10.1007/s12369-024-01188-0
23. Mohd Rosnu, N.S., Singh, D.K.A., Mat Ludin, A.F., Ishak, W.S., Abd Rahman, M.H., Shahar, S.: Enablers and barriers of accessing health care services among older adults in South-East Asia: a scoping review. IJERPH **19**, 7351 (2022). https://doi.org/10.3390/ijerph19127351
24. Wong, K.P., Teh, P.-L., Lim, W.M., Lee, S.W.H.: Enhancing older adults' lives through positive aging perception, quality-of-life enhancement, and social support to drive acceptance and readiness toward indoor assistive technology: cross-sectional study. JMIR Aging **8**, e59665 (2025). https://doi.org/10.2196/59665
25. Asgharian, P., Panchea, A.M., Ferland, F.: A review on the use of mobile service robots in elderly care. Robotics **11**, 127 (2022). https://doi.org/10.3390/robotics11060127

CaRE-BT: An Embodied Planning Framework for In-Home Assistive Robots

Ola Ghattas, Mostafa Hussein(✉), Marzan Alam, Moniruzzaman Akash, Sajay Arthanat, Dain LaRoche, and Momotaz Begum

University of New Hampshire, Durham, NH 03824, USA
{ola.ghattas,mostafa.hussein,marzan.alam,moniruzzaman.akash,
Sajay.Arthanat,Dain.LaRoche,momotaz.begum}@unh.edu

Abstract. The rising prevalence of age-related conditions such as Alzheimer's disease and dementia underscores the urgent need for intelligent in-home systems that can assist without increasing the burden on caregivers. We present CaRE-BT (Caregiver-Relief Behavior Tree planner), a novel open-source ROS 2 framework that transforms symbolic care protocols into executable behavior trees, enabling fully autonomous assistive behavior on embedded robotic platforms. CaRE-BT compiles contingent planning models, maintains a dynamic knowledge base, and integrates distributed sensing for real-time human tracking, without relying on cloud connectivity. To evaluate its real-world feasibility, we deployed CaRE-BT on a Stretch 3.0 mobile robot across two in-home studies: a seven-day trial with an older adult couple in a retirement facility, and a three-week phase of an ongoing six-month deployment supporting a caregiver-recipient dyad managing moderate dementia. Across these 30 days, the system successfully delivered over 55 scheduled health prompts (medication, exercise, task reminders), with only nine failures due to navigation launch issues. The system operated autonomously and required no daily maintenance from the caregiver. Feedback from participants highlighted its reliability, ease of use, and positive impact on reducing caregiving stress. CaRE-BT is available as an open-source toolkit to support researchers, clinicians, and engineers building adaptive long-term assistive systems in healthcare and eldercare settings (https://robotsforaging.cs.unh.edu/).

Keywords: ROS2 · Long-term HRI · Socially Assistive Robots

1 Introduction

A key challenge in long-term humanrobot interaction (HRI) is enabling robots to make reliable decisions in environments where both human behavior and environmental conditions are unpredictable. This is especially true in robot-assisted caregiving, where tasks like reminding an older adult to take medication, stay active, or follow a daily routine require the robot to make context-aware decisions throughout the day. Care recipients (CRs) often have cognitive or physical impairments, making their responses inconsistent or delayed. These uncertainties make it difficult for a robot to select the right action at the right time. From a technical perspective, this creates two main challenges: **Challenge 1)** designing a modular and generalizable framework that can be deployed across diverse home environments. The architecture should support reusable components and customizable care protocols, such as medication, hydration, or exercise routines, that can be easily configured to meet the needs of different households. **Challenge 2)** enabling real-time decision-making that adapts both to human behavior and to dynamic sensory input from the environment. The robot must generate and adjust action sequences on the fly based on observations such as the care recipient's location, activity, or whether they are present in the home. These adaptations must maintain alignment with long-term care goals, even in the face of incomplete, delayed, or ambiguous sensor feedback.

Before addressing the technical challenges outlined above, it is important to emphasize the unique value that physically embodied robots provide in home environments, particularly for elder care. Recent systematic reviews have underscored the growing effectiveness of social robots in supporting older adults, surpassing what screen-based or ambient systems typically achieve. In a comprehensive review of eleven randomized controlled trials, Pu et al. [23] reported that robot-assisted interactions led to improvements in agitation, anxiety, and quality of life. While not all effects reached statistical significance, narrative findings indicated consistent benefits, including enhanced emotional engagement, reduced loneliness, and decreased reliance on medications. These advantages are rarely observed with mobile applications or passive reminder systems. Such results support the argument that an embodied robotic presence offers not only task execution capabilities but also a socially resonant presence that contributes meaningfully to the psychological well-being of care recipients.

Addressing **Challenge 1** requires designing a modular and generalizable framework that integrates multiple perception and interaction capabilities. This includes person identification and tracking, face and gesture recognition, and natural language understanding–all essential for interpreting human behavior in unstructured home environments. While significant progress has been made in each of these subfields [2,17], integrating them into a cohesive pipeline for real-time, in-the-wild deployment remains non-trivial. The Robot Operating System (ROS) [24] has become the de facto standard for managing distributed, multimodal robotics systems, and has inspired HRI-specific toolkits such as ROS4HRI [18], which supports human state recognition through speech, gaze, and gesture signals. ROS-based APIs and perception stacks [1] continue to grow in capability and coverage. Although cognitive architectures outside ROS have existed for long-term autonomy [8,10], the HRI community increasingly converges on ROS-based open frameworks for deploying socially assistive robots at scale [11,12,25].

Challenge 2 centers on enabling adaptive, goal-directed behavior in the face of uncertainty. Various decision-making frameworks have been explored in robotics–Markov Decision Processes (MDPs), Partially Observable MDPs (POMDPs), finite-state machines [14], and reinforcement learning [3]. However, their applicability to long-term HRI remains limited due to scalability and deployment constraints. Specifically, these models often require exhaustive state definitions, complete knowledge of the task structure, and expert intervention to accommodate even minor changes in goals or context. This rigidity makes them ill-suited for dynamic caregiving scenarios, where plans must adapt to changes in user behavior, environmental conditions, or sensor input (e.g., location or activity detection). Domain-independent AI planning offers a promising alternative: its symbolic representations allow for general task models, dynamic goal injection, and policy re-generation without retraining [9, 19]. When paired with compact contingent policy structures, such planners provide a scalable basis for long-horizon autonomy in socially assistive contexts.

To address these two challenges, we present **CaRE-BT**, a ROS2-based bi-level planning framework designed to support long-term assistive humanrobot interaction in unstructured home environments. CaRE-BT provides a modular system architecture that allows flexible integration of perception modules (e.g., person tracking, environmental sensors, IoT devices) while enabling researchers and caregivers to define high-level care protocols using symbolic planning. At its core, CaRE-BT combines domain-independent contingent planning with real-time Behavior Tree execution, allowing the robot to adapt its actions in response to human behavior and dynamic environmental states. The full architecture is implemented within ROS2 to reduce latency and enable robust deployment on resource-constrained, embedded platforms. At the time of writing, a Stretch 3.0 mobile manipulator (Hello Robot Inc.), equipped with CaRE-BT, has been deployed autonomously in the homes of two older adult households for a combined duration of four weeks.

We summarize our key contributions as follows:

1. A modular ROS2-based software framework that supports long-term, in-home HRI deployments, with a focus on assistive caregiving.
2. A lightweight, contingent PDDL planner integrated with real-time Behavior Tree execution, optimized for embedded performance on mobile robots.
3. A four-week autonomous field evaluation across two real-world home environments, demonstrating the feasibility, adaptability, and reliability of CaRE-BT in elder care scenarios.

2 Related Work

Symbolic task planning has been widely explored in robotics, especially through ROS-integrated frameworks. ROSPlan [6] brought PDDL-based automated planning into the ROS1 ecosystem and has been used in diverse robotic tasks, such as multi-agent planning [4], autonomous underwater vehicles [5], and human-aware

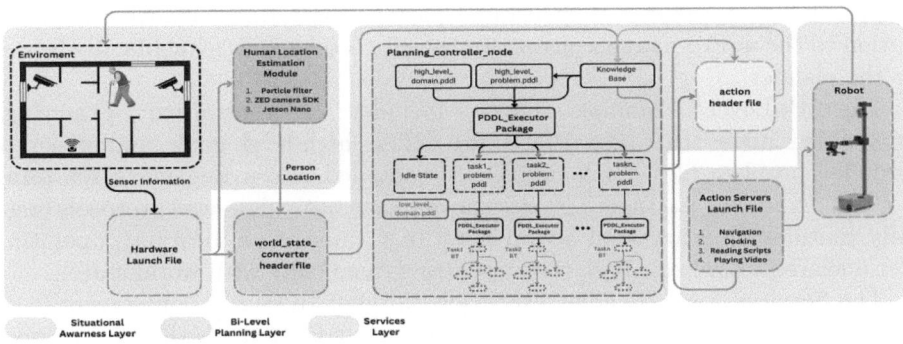

Fig. 1. Overview of CaRE-BT framework.

planning [22]. PlanSys2 [16] builds on these ideas with native ROS2 support, enabling multi-robot collaboration and parallel execution. However, PlanSys2's reliance on multiple ROS2 services makes it difficult to deploy on embedded hardware and introduces runtime errors that complicate long-term deployments.

While these planners offer useful abstractions, few have been deployed in real-world, long-horizon HRI contexts such as elder care. Lindsay et al. [13] demonstrated the use of automated planning in a pediatric socially assistive robot that adapts to children's affective states in clinical settings. Their work highlights how planning enables robots to generate context-sensitive, multi-step interactions. Olatunji et al. [20] explored the participatory design of assistive robots for older adults, showing how tailoring functionality through direct user input improves acceptance and effectiveness for long-term use in the home.

In contrast to prior work, **CaRE-BT** targets long-term autonomy in unstructured home environments by combining domain-independent planning, real-time Behavior Tree execution, and a self-healing knowledge base optimized for embedded platforms. Our system has been validated across two real elder care deployments totaling four weeks of continuous operation.

3 Proposed Architecture: CaRE-BT, a Bi-Level Planning Framework for HRI

This section first provides an overview of the operation of CaRE-BT, which is followed by a detailed description of individual components. Figure 1 illustrates the architecture of the **CaRE-BT** framework, structured into three primary layers: the *Situational Awareness Layer*, the *Bi-Level Planning Layer*, and the *Services Layer*.

The system begins by integrating multi-modal sensor data (e.g., cameras, motion detection, door sensors) through a hardware launch file, forming the situational awareness layer. Thisbles accurate tracki layer estimates the care recipient's location and context using a particle filter, and forwards this information to the `world_state_converter`, which encodes it as symbolic predicates for the planner.

The Bi-Level Planning Layer includes a centralized `planning_controller_node` that uses PDDL to define high-level goals and generate grounded problem files. Each problem is compiled into a Behavior Tree using the `PDDL_Executor` package. The system supports both high-level protocols (e.g., daily routines) and low-level action flows (e.g., move to a location), operating over a shared knowledge base that updates dynamically with world state.

The Services Layer handles execution through ROS 2 action servers (e.g., navigation, docking, script reading). These are triggered by the planner and return execution feedback to the knowledge base, enabling the robot to monitor progress, detect failures, and re-plan as needed.

3.1 Bi-level Planning Layer

The **CaRE-BT** framework uses a bi-level planning approach to manage caregiving tasks with both long-term goals and short-term interactions. At the top level, a symbolic planner defines high-level care routines (e.g., hydration, medication, safety checks) based on PDDL models. When a task is triggered, it is grounded into a low-level execution plan and compiled into a Behavior Tree (BT) that the robot can execute in real time.

To enable robust decision-making, the planner continuously communicates with a dynamic knowledge base that maintains the current state of the environment. Sensor data (e.g., human location, room context) is interpreted and converted into symbolic predicates, ensuring that the robot's plans remain aligned with real-world conditions.

A custom `PDDL_Executor` package translates planning tasks into optimized C++ code and interfaces directly with ROS2 action servers to execute robot behaviors (e.g., navigation, speech, docking). The system monitors task progress and can interrupt, resume, or replan tasks in response to environment changes or user behavior. This layered structure allows the robot to adapt in real time while following structured care protocols defined by caregivers or researchers.

3.2 Situational Awareness Layer

The situational awareness layer enables the robot to perceive and interpret the environment in real time, serving as the foundation for context-aware planning. It continuously gathers data from multiple sources–primarily human location estimation and IoT sensors–and updates the knowledge base, allowing the planner to adapt actions based on changing conditions and user behavior.

Human location is estimated using a ROS-based particle filter that integrates 3D body pose data from depth cameras (e.g., ZED) deployed across the home. This enables accurate tracking of the care recipient's position, even under occlusion or uncertainty. For person identification, we employ face recognition to distinguish between the care recipient and other individuals in the household, using ArcFace [7], a state-of-the-art deep metric learning model known for its high accuracy and robustness in real-world settings. IoT devices, such as motion and door sensors, further enhance context awareness by providing real-time signals on room activity, movement, and the robot's charging state. Sensor data is converted into symbolic predicates through the `world_state_converter` and integrated into the planner's knowledge base.

By fusing multi-modal information, this layer allows the robot to infer high-level human activities and respond appropriately. For example, if the person is not present in the room during a scheduled task, the robot may delay or reschedule the action. The layer's modular design ensures that additional sensors can be incorporated without affecting system stability, enabling scalable and adaptive HRI in home environments.

3.3 Services Layer

The services layer provides the essential capabilities that allow the robot to interact with its environment and users. This includes autonomous navigation using the ROS2 Nav2 stack [15], which enables the robot to move safely throughout the home. To maintain autonomy, the robot supports self-docking using a plug-and-socket charging design compatible with standard mobile platforms, improving reliability and flexibility without requiring proprietary hardware.

Localization is achieved through AprilTags [21], which helps the robot recover from positional drift and maintain situational awareness. For human interaction, the robot can deliver reminders or guidance through pre-scripted speech and audio playback. It also supports phone calls for scheduled check-ins or emergency communication. Together, these services ensure the robot can carry out care routines independently while maintaining responsiveness and safety in the home.

4 Evaluation Study: Deployment of a Robot for Elder Care at Home

To evaluate the effectiveness of the proposed framework, we deployed a CaRE-BT-powered *Stretch 3.0* robot in two real-world home environments (Figs. 2 and 3).

The first deployment lasted one week in the home of an older adult couple (Ron and Julie) residing in a retirement community. The second, ongoing deployment is being conducted in the homes of individuals diagnosed with Alzheimer's disease and related dementias (ADRD), with a planned duration of six months. In this paper, we report results from one week of the first deployment and the first three weeks of the ongoing second deployment.

All studies were approved by our institutional review board (IRB). The primary objective of these deployments is to assess the feasibility and robustness of CaRE-BT in delivering personalized care protocols–such as medication and activity reminders–tailored to each user's preferences and routines. In the following sections, we provide a detailed breakdown of the protocols executed,

 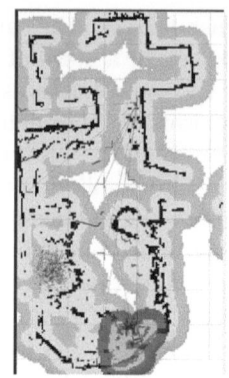

Fig. 2. Stretch 3.0 deployed at participants' home

Fig. 3. Visualization in RViz2 of the robot at the participant's home and correct estimation of the participant's location with particle filter (red arrows cluster).

successes, and failures from the first trial. For the second trial, we present a summary of system performance and initial observations based on the first three weeks. Note that names have been altered to preserve the anonymity of the participants.

4.1 Study Protocols and Deployment Objectives

The participating couple in the first deployment selected the following five daily activity reminders, each associated with a specific time and spoken script:

- Practice (7:30 AM): "Ron, when are you going to practice today? Write the time down and commit to it."
- Internal Check (8:15 AM): "Julie, time for your internal check-in."
- AM Medicine (9:00 AM): "Ron and Julie, have you taken your morning medication?"
- Exercise (11:30 AM): "Ron, have you exercised today?"
- PM Medicine (9:00 PM): "Ron and Julie, have you taken your evening medication?"

The primary objective of this deployment was to validate that the CaRE-BT-powered robot can operate fully autonomously in delivering timely, personalized care routines. Each protocol was expected to be executed within one hour of its scheduled time, conditional on the presence of the participants in the home. After protocol execution, the robot was required to return to its docking station.

4.2 Protocol Execution Behavior

Each reminder protocol was designed with specific execution rules and behaviors. For example, the Medication Reminder Protocol verifies whether the medication has already been taken before initiating any robot action. If the individual has not yet complied, the robot navigates to the care recipient's location and delivers the reminder. In cases where compliance is not confirmed–detected through motion sensors–a second reminder is issued. The exact robot behavior is dynamically adapted depending on the initial positions of both the robot and the user. Figure 4 illustrates a sample plan for this scenario.

Other reminder protocols (e.g., *Practice*, *Exercise*) follow a simpler flow: the robot travels to the individual's location and issues a single reminder without monitoring for compliance.

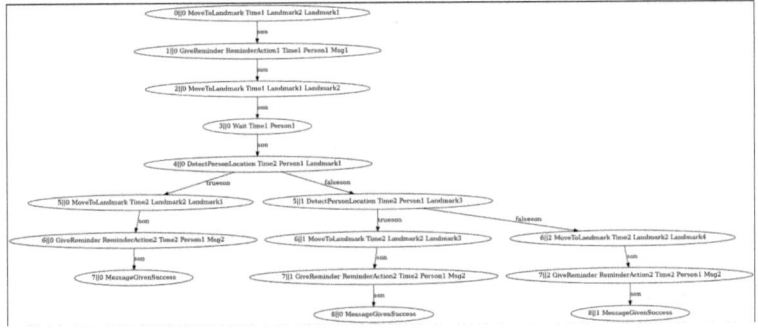

Fig. 4. Low-level plan for the medicine protocol.

4.3 System Requirements and Evaluation Criteria

Reliable execution of these protocols requires all components of the situational awareness layer (e.g., tracking, planning, communication) to function correctly. This includes correct estimation of human location, accurate sensor readings, and proper synchronization between the knowledge base and the planner.

Table 1 summarizes the system's performance across seven days of deployment. Each row corresponds to one day and includes results for the five selected protocols. A result of **S** indicates success, **F** denotes failure, and dash entries indicate that the protocol was correctly skipped (e.g., when the participant was not home).

The following criteria were used to evaluate each component:

- Particle Filter (PF): Success indicates accurate location estimation of the care recipient.
- Navigation: The robot successfully reached the intended target without error or collision.
- High-Level Planner: Successfully triggered the protocol and prevented redundant reactivation through correct knowledge base updates.
- Low-Level Planner: Executed based on actual environmental conditions; evaluation accounts for real-world discrepancies, not planner assumptions.
- Docking: The robot successfully returned to and docked at the charging station post-task.

4.4 Results Summary and Observations

The results in Table 1 demonstrate CaRE-BT's capability to support sustained and context-aware HRI in home environments. The high-level planner consistently triggered protocols reliably. Reported failures primarily stemmed from external components such as false sensor readings or minor localization errors, rather than from the planner itself.

A key improvement was observed in docking performance. Initial issues in the docking mechanism led to several failures early in the study. After mechanical adjustments were made on Day 4, all subsequent docking operations succeeded–highlighting the importance of robust hardware integration to fully realize the capabilities of autonomous planning systems.

4.5 Results from Second Deployment

The second deployment of CaRE-BT is currently ongoing in the homes of individuals with Alzheimer's disease and related dementias (ADRD), as part of a six-month longitudinal study. In this paper, we report preliminary results from the first three weeks of deployment in one such household.

Care Protocols and Execution. For this deployment, the caregiver selected five distinct protocols:

- Two daily medication reminders.
- One exercise reminder every other day.
- A weekly reminder to pick up medication from the pharmacy.
- A weekly reminder to refill the pill container.

The CaRE-BT-powered robot successfully executed all scheduled reminders, with only four failures over the 21-day period. All failures were due to intermittent crashes in the navigation service (Nav2), which were quickly resolved by restarting the launch file. These failures were logged automatically and did require minimal user intervention, minimizing their impact on the daily caregiving routine.

System performance and protocol delivery were continuously monitored using a dedicated logging system. All status updates, execution results, and error messages were streamed to a private Discord channel, allowing the team to provide remote support and validate the system's operation in real time.

Caregiver Feedback and Qualitative Outcomes. A one-month follow-up interview was conducted with the participating caregiver and care recipient dyad. The caregiver reported that the "system is working fine the way it was set up" and expressed satisfaction with the medication reminder protocols, stating that he no longer worries about forgetting to give medications to his spouse. Importantly, the caregiver noted that the robot required no daily upkeep and imposed no additional burden on his caregiving responsibilities.

Table 1. Performance metrics of our deployment for each protocol in the first house: "S" indicates success, while "F" denotes failure.

	Practice	S/F	Internal Check	S/F	AM Medicine	S/F	Exercise	S/F	PM Medicine	S/F	Comment
Day 1	pf navigation high-level low-level docking	S S S S	pf navigation high-level low-level docking	S S S S	pf navigation high-level low-level docking	S - S - -	pf navigation high-level low-level docking	S S S S S	pf navigation high-level low-level docking	S S F S S	The participants were not home during the AM Medicine protocol. PM Medicine false compliance detected.
Day 2	pf navigation high-level low-level docking	S S S S	pf navigation high-level low-level docking	S S S S	pf navigation high-level low-level docking	S S S S	pf navigation high-level low-level docking	S S S S S	pf navigation high-level low-level docking	S S S S F	Failed to dock at PM Medicine
Day 3	pf navigation high-level low-level docking	S S S S	pf navigation high-level low-level docking	S S S S	pf navigation high-level low-level docking	S S S S	pf navigation high-level low-level docking	F S S S S	pf navigation high-level low-level docking	S S S S S	The exercise protocol had a wrong estimation of the person's location.
Day 4	pf navigation high-level low-level docking	S S S S	pf navigation high-level low-level docking	S S S S	pf navigation high-level low-level docking	S F S S	pf navigation high-level low-level docking	S S S S S	pf navigation high-level low-level docking	S S S S F	AM Medicine navigation failed on startup, but was restarted. Failed to dock at PM-Medicine.
Day 5	pf navigation high-level low-level docking	S S S S	pf navigation high-level low-level docking	S S S S	pf navigation high-level low-level docking	S S F S	pf navigation high-level low-level docking	S S S S S	pf navigation high-level low-level docking	S S S S S	AM Medicine false compliance detected
Day 6,7	pf navigation high-level low-level docking	S S S S	pf navigation high-level low-level docking	S S S S	pf navigation high-level low-level docking	S S S S	pf navigation high-level low-level docking	S S S S S	pf navigation high-level low-level docking	S S S S S	Full day with no errors

The caregiver did request a few adjustments to the care protocol timing, which were made remotely through our server infrastructure. This feedback highlights the flexibility and remote configurability of the CaRE-BT framework.

Overall, the dyad maintained a positive outlook, with realistic expectations of the system. They viewed the robot not as a replacement for a human caregiver, but as a useful tool that reduces the cognitive load and stress associated with routine care tasks.

Summary. Over the course of the initial three-week deployment:

- Total scheduled reminders: 50+
- Failures: 4 (all due to Nav2 startup issues)

– Human feedback: Positive, with no perceived increase in caregiver burden

These preliminary results indicate that CaRE-BT can operate reliably in home environments for individuals with cognitive impairments, delivering care protocols effectively while minimizing caregiver overhead. The ability to monitor and reconfigure the system remotely further supports its scalability and long-term feasibility for real-world deployment.

5 Discussion and Future Works

While the current implementation serves as a foundational step, our future work will prioritize improving the components that provide the planner with environmental information and extending the framework's capabilities to integrate more adaptive tasks. These enhancements aim to create a robust and user-friendly robotic system that effectively meets the needs of individuals in their everyday environments. A primary objective is enabling the robot to comprehend natural language commands through voice and text input, facilitating intuitive communication and a broader range of interactions. Additionally, we will use the mounted tablet on the robot to support more low-level tasks, such as guiding users through exercises displayed on the screen. Furthermore, we are currently developing an image-based activity recognition model focused on reliably detecting compliance with specific activities. The activities supported by this model will include eating, taking medication, and recognizing falls.

6 Conclusion

In this paper, we introduced CaRE-BT, a Bi-Level Planning Framework designed to enable reliable and autonomous assistive behavior in in-home robots. Built on ROS2, CaRE-BT integrates a lightweight C++ PDDL planner, a situational awareness layer, and a robust services layer to support long-term humanrobot interaction (HRI) in naturalistic home environments. We evaluated the framework in two real-world deployments: a one-week study with an older adult couple and a three-week phase of an ongoing six-month trial with individuals diagnosed with Alzheimer's disease. Across more than 90 scheduled care reminders, the system experienced only nine failures, all related to navigation startup and resolved with minimal user intervention. Participant feedback emphasized the system's reliability and ease of use. The caregiver in the second study noted that the robot required no daily upkeep and alleviated the burden of manually managing reminders. These results demonstrate CaRE-BT's potential as a scalable and adaptable solution for autonomous in-home caregiving. The framework will be released as open source to support future research in assistive robotics and long-term HRI.

References

1. Achirei, S.D., Heghea, M.C., Lupu, R.G., Manta, V.I.: Human activity recognition for assisted living based on scene understanding. Appl. Sci. **12**(21), 10743 (2022)
2. Awais, M., et al.: Foundational models defining a new era in vision: a survey and outlook. arXiv preprint arXiv:2307.13721 (2023)
3. Barto, A.G., Sutton, R.S., Watkins, C.: Learning and Sequential Decision Making, vol. 89. University of Massachusetts Amherst, MA (1989)
4. Brafman, R.I., Bar-Sinai, M., Ashkenazi, M.: Performance level profiles: a formal language for describing the expected performance of functional modules. In: 2016 IEEE/RSJ International Conference on Intelligent Robots and Systems (IROS), pp. 1751–1756. IEEE (2016)
5. Cashmore, M., Fox, M., Larkworthy, T., Long, D., Magazzeni, D.: AUV mission control via temporal planning. In: 2014 IEEE International Conference on Robotics and Automation (ICRA), pp. 6535–6541. IEEE (2014)
6. Cashmore, M., et al.: ROSPlan: planning in the robot operating system. In: Proceedings of the International Conference on Automated Planning and Scheduling, vol. 25, pp. 333–341 (2015)
7. Deng, J., Guo, J., Niannan, X., Zafeiriou, S.: ArcFace: additive angular margin loss for deep face recognition. In: CVPR (2019)
8. Kaptein, F., et al.: A cloud-based robot system for long-term interaction: principles, implementation, lessons learned. ACM Trans. Hum. Robot Interact. (THRI) **11**(1), 1–27 (2021)
9. Karpas, E., Magazzeni, D.: Automated planning for robotics. Ann. Rev. Control Robot. Autonom. Syst. **3**(1), 417–439 (2020)
10. King, C., Palathingal, X., Nicolescu, M., Nicolescu, M.: A vision-based architecture for long-term human-robot interaction. In: Proceedings the IASTED International Conference on Human Computer Interaction (2007)
11. Lemaignan, S., Cooper, S., Ros, R., Ferrini, L., Andriella, A., Irisarri, A.: Open-source natural language processing on the pal robotics ARI social robot. In: Companion of the 2023 ACM/IEEE International Conference on Human-Robot Interaction, pp. 907–908 (2023)
12. Lemaignan, S., Ferrini, L.: Probabilistic fusion of persons' body features: the MR. Potato algorithm. In: Proceedings of the 2024 ACM/IEEE International Conference on Human-Robot Interaction, pp. 919–923 (2024)
13. Lindsay, A., Ramírez-Duque, A.A., Petrick, R.P., Foster, M.E.: A socially assistive robot using automated planning in a paediatric clinical setting. In: Proceedings of the 2024 International Symposium on Technological Advances in Human-Robot Interaction, pp. 47–55 (2024)
14. Littman, M.L.: Algorithms for Sequential Decision-Making. Brown University (1996)
15. Macenski, S., Martin, F., White, R., Ginés Clavero, J.: The marathon 2: a navigation system. In: 2020 IEEE/RSJ International Conference on Intelligent Robots and Systems (IROS) (2020)
16. Martín, F., Clavero, J.G., Matellán, V., Rodríguez, F.J.: PlanSys2: a planning system framework for ROS2. In: 2021 IEEE/RSJ International Conference on Intelligent Robots and Systems (IROS), pp. 9742–9749. IEEE (2021)
17. Min, B., et al.: Recent advances in natural language processing via large pre-trained language models: a survey. ACM Comput. Surv. **56**(2), 1–40 (2023)

18. Mohamed, Y., Lemaignan, S.: ROS for human-robot interaction. In: 2021 IEEE/RSJ International Conference on Intelligent Robots and Systems (IROS), pp. 3020–3027 (2021). https://doi.org/10.1109/IROS51168.2021.9636816
19. Natarajan, M., Kolobov, A.: Planning with Markov decision processes: an AI perspective. Springer, Cham (2022). https://doi.org/10.1007/978-3-031-01559-5
20. Olatunji, S.A., et al.: Immersive participatory design of assistive robots to support older adults. Ergonomics **67**(6), 717–731 (2024)
21. Olson, E.: AprilTag: a robust and flexible visual fiducial system. In: 2011 IEEE International Conference on Robotics and Automation, pp. 3400–3407 (2011). https://doi.org/10.1109/ICRA.2011.5979561
22. Petrick, R.P., Foster, M.E.: Using general-purpose planning for action selection in human-robot interaction. In: 2016 AAAI Fall Symposium Series (2016)
23. Pu, L., Moyle, W., Jones, C., Todorovic, M.: Effectiveness of social robots for older adults: a systematic review and meta-analysis of randomized controlled studies. Gerontologist **59**(1), e37–e51 (2019). https://doi.org/10.1093/geront/gny046
24. Quigley, M., et al.: ROS: an open-source robot operating system. In: ICRA Workshop on Open Source Software, vol. 3, p. 5. Kobe, Japan (2009)
25. Tadic, V., et al.: Perspectives of realsense and zed depth sensors for robotic vision applications. Machines **10**(3), 183 (2022)

LLM-Driven Persuasive Strategies by a Social Assistive Robot for Healthier Snacking

Chinenye Augustine Ajibo(✉), Alessandra Rossi, and Silvia Rossi

Department of Electrical Engineering and Information Technologies - DIETI,
University of Naples Federico II, Napoli, Italy
{chinenyeaugustine.ajibo,alessandra.rossi,silvia.rossi}@unina.it

Abstract. Advances in Large Language Models (LLMs) have triggered an unprecedented surge in innovation, leading to a rapid proliferation of novel applications, such as recommendation systems. In this work, we take advantage of these developments and present our preliminary investigation of the potential of deploying LLMs-based persuasive strategies: polite, authority, emotional engagement, scarcity, and social proof in Social Assistive Robots for healthier snack choices. We carried out the study in two phases: Firstly, using a within-subject design involving $N = 124$ Italian college students from diverse academic disciplines, we examined the extent to which individuals consider the healthiness of snacks before purchasing and consuming them. Findings from the study suggest that most subjects have good knowledge of what a "healthy snack" is. However, many participants frequently neglect to consider the healthiness of these snacks before purchasing and consuming them. Next, through a between-subjects experiment involving $N = 166$ college students, we investigate the influence of users' personality trait tendencies (trust propensity (TP) and compliance awareness (CA)) and the Big Five factors on preferences for the robot's LLM-driven strategies for eliciting healthier snack choices. Results showed variation in the preference for these strategies relative to subjects' trait tendencies. Specifically, subjects in the TP and CA groups appraised these strategies differently regarding the impression items: persuasiveness, willingness, and trustworthiness.

Keywords: Large Language Models · Preference Elicitation · Persuasive Strategies · Recommendation Systems · Social Assistive Robots

1 Introduction

Social Assistive Robots (SARs) have been deployed in multiple clinical settings and home-based areas, with applications not limited to rehabilitation, providing medication reminders, collecting patient medical data, and provision of healthcare education and information [1]. While the technical capabilities of these robots are essential for the effective delivery and management of care services, it is equally important to equip these robots with appropriate and effective communication behaviors, considering that they will be interacting and supporting potentially vulnerable users [2].

The enormous amount of information from online users has made it increasingly difficult for people to obtain valuable and high-quality information on services and products of interest to users. To deal with this information overload, efficient information filtering tools like Recommendation Systems (RS) have been widely used in areas not limited to e-commerce, movies, music, news, logistics, and healthcare; by adopting advanced techniques for analyzing vast amounts of user behavior data, RS can provide personalized recommendations tailored to individual preferences [3]. However, considering that users' preferences are often ill-defined and, on many occasions, constructed on the spot, susceptible to seemingly irrelevant factors like the set of alternatives included and how preferences are elicited, it becomes relevant that RS be equipped with appropriate and effective persuasive strategies [4].

Persuasion is considered as an attempt to change people's attitudes or behaviors or both; providing explanations has been identified as a vital means through which this attitudinal or behavioral change can be realized [5]. Several strategies have been explored in the literature for persuasion [6].

Recently, LLMs have presented new possibilities, particularly concerning the explanation generation for preference elicitation [7].

Building on these findings, this work takes advantage of the advances in LLMs to support users with healthier snack choices. For this, we propose an investigation in two phases. In the first phase, we determined to what extent users consider the healthiness of snacks before consuming them. Next, we explore the robot's LLM-driven strategies (polite, authority, emotional engagement, scarcity, and social proof) for healthy snack selection and the impact of users' trait tendencies on the preferences for these strategies.

2 Related Works

The implementation of RS in healthcare is becoming a growing solution in many health domains due to benefits such as offering personalized recommendation services and helping individuals make informed health-related decisions. For example, concerning dietary recommendations, collaborative filtering (CF) techniques and content-based algorithms on food recommendations have been investigated using an extensive online recipe dataset [8]. Regarding a healthy lifestyle, a cyber-physical RS has been proposed to allow people to participate actively in exergames [9]. Concerning health training, [10] explored a model based on CF techniques to analyze user behavioral changes.

These studies allude to the potential of RS in healthcare. However, less established in the literature is the influence of user traits on the personalization of RS, especially as it pertains to cyber-physical systems. Some previous studies in Human-Robot Interaction (HRI) suggest that users' personality traits may influence preferences and outcomes. For instance, the persuasive effect of certain persuasive strategies and the role of personality in the acceptance of movie recommendations was evaluated in [5]. In the same vein, [11] modeled the influence of the Big Five personality traits on Cialdini's six persuasive principles. From another perspective, [12] explored how users respond to a social robot's positive and negative persuasive behaviors across different contexts and scenarios, considering variations in Compliance Awareness (CA)[1] and Agreeableness (AG).

Recent advancements in LLMs present new possibilities for automating and augmenting various tasks. Some research has explored how to employ LLMs for generating personalized persuasion for tasks not limited to politics [13], marketing [14], healthcare [15], e-commerce [17], and charitable giving [19]. Concerning preference elicitation, few studies have explored the potential of these novel models. For instance, [7] proposed LLMs with proper learning techniques to approximate preferences through natural language, reducing bidders' cognitive load and limiting communication overhead during an auction. Also, the potential of LLMs in effectively mimicking human decision-making in auctions, negotiations, and marketing environments was investigated in [16].

In a similar vein, a novel framework that leverages LLMs to automate and enhance the requirements elicitation process was proposed in [18]. To address the issues of concern in the different phases of the study, we limit our investigation to the following terms: one context (vending machine) and one scenario (persuasion for healthier snacks). Five persuasive strategies (polite, authority, emotional engagement, scarcity, and social proof) and seven user trait tendencies (trust propensity (TP), compliance awareness (CA), and the BIG FIVE factors: extraversion (EXT), agreeableness (AG), conscientiousness (CON), emotional stability (ES), openness to experiences (OE)). Based on these terms, the following hypotheses **H1–H2** were developed:

H1: A user's preference for snack options may be influenced by knowledge of the nutritional content and healthiness of the snacks.

H2: The impression of the robot's preference elicitation strategies may change depending on the user's personality tendencies and the Big Five factors.

3 Method

We designed the investigation in two (2) phases, as captured in Fig. 1 and described in the subsequent section.

3.1 *Phase 1*: Snack Classification for Robot's Recommendation

To address **H1**, an initial investigation was designed to establish user preferences for different snack options on our institution's public vending machine and to determine the extent to which the snack's healthiness is considered before purchase and consumption. For this study, we define a healthy snack to be any snack that is considered healthy by the general population of students and staff of our institution. These snacks may be made from wheat, contain essential minerals such as calcium, magnesium, and iron; have nuts; are rich in fiber; and are low in

---

[1] Compliance awareness (CA) means the level of a person's sense of values regarding awareness of the need to adhere to social rules geared towards the well-being of everyone.

Fig. 1. Study design for estimating the effectiveness of the robot's preference elicitation strategies

carbohydrates and sugar. Twenty-one (21) unique snacks were identified on the two vending machines situated on different floors of the institution's building. Next, we developed an online survey[2] to establish user preferences for the snack options, the snacks users consider to be healthy, and the extent to which the snack's healthiness was considered by the users.

3.2 *Phase 2*: Preference Elicitation Strategies

In this phase, the humanoid robot "Pepper" acts as an assistant to users at the vending machine. It supports users with information on available snack options using its LLM-driven strategies. The choice of a humanlike robot that uses multimodal behaviors (gestures and speech) was to encourage persuasive strategies that are more humanlike. This is because prior studies in HRI revealed that agents are more persuasive when they are physically embodied and have a humanlike appearance [20]. Five persuasive strategies—politeness, authority, emotional engagement, scarcity, and social proof—were adapted for the robot and informed by prior research [5,6,21], which demonstrates that such techniques increase the likelihood of influencing consumer behavior.

- Polite: The robot uses courteous, persuasive expressions to elicit healthier snack choices from the users.
- Authority: The robot speaks as an authority by suggesting and providing relevant nutritional and health information on the healthier snack options on the vending machine.
- Emotional engagement: The art of emotional engagement has been established to lead to an increase in trust, build a deeper connection between

---

[2] For details, refer to the questionnaires https://forms.gle/VAtKFrUDPaMj19gr8.

users. In this case, the robot, through short storytelling, persuades users to opt for healthier snack options.
- Scarcity: Given that people are often inclined to consider whatever is scarce more valuable, the robot uses this strategy to persuade users by informing users of the limited availability of the healthier snack options while encouraging them to opt immediately for the snack.
- Social Proof: By referencing positive testimonials and social media reviews of the healthy snack choices, the robot persuades users to opt for these options.

Leveraging the fact that LLMs have at their core the flexibility and ability to perform different tasks related to natural language, we adopt an open-source AI model, precisely Llama 3.2, locally deployed for generating the expressive utterances[3] for the robot. This lightweight multilingual model has approximately 3B parameters and was used without additional fine-tuning. The input prompts were carefully designed in Italian to realize the desired strategies, minimize bias, and ensure consistency in the generated strategies[4].

3.3 Procedure

The experiment was reviewed and approved by our institute's ethical committee. Regarding *Phase 1* of the study, an online survey hosted on Google Forms was conducted with 124 Italian college students from diverse academic backgrounds (Male = 60, Female = 64) with a mean age of $M = 22.28, SD = 2.13$ for evaluating **H1**.

Concerning *Phase 2* of our study, a between-subjects experiment that ran for 5 days was designed to evaluate **H2**. The robot Pepper was positioned at one of the vending machines to provide users with information on snack options on the machine using its LLM-driven strategies. The robot was equipped with a single strategy each day. It is important to mention that the robot emphasized the need for users to opt for healthier snack options through its strategies. 166 Italian college students from diverse academic backgrounds ($N = 166$: Male = 83, Female = 81, Non-binary = 1, Prefer not to disclose = 1) participated in the study. The mean age of the participants was $M = 22.09$ years. Informed consent was obtained from all participants, and all collected data were anonymized.

Before interacting with the robot, participants answered questions regarding their previous experience with AI and robot systems and propensity to trust these systems [22]. The questions were administered on a 5-point scale. Partially inspired by [12] and the scenario considered in the study, participants also answered questions that evaluated their values, referred to as compliance awareness (CA). Five questions were administered with answers on a 7-point

---

[3] LLM prompts and transcript of the expressive utterances, refer to https://drive.google.com/file/d/1vBVZNeqru-n5opfEB-qZWn2IMvmvNsU1/view?usp=drive_link.

[4] Preference elicitation by Pepper https://drive.google.com/file/d/12M3ykT1uq U84IYtZBKketaCtaNhV75Q3/view?usp=sharing8.

scale. Furthermore, participants were also examined in terms of their personality trait tendencies. We utilized the ten-item personality inventory (TIPI)[5] with two questions measuring each aspect of the Big Five.

Subsequently, participants interacted with the robot stationed at the vending machine to provide information on available snack options on the vending machine and then to persuade users to opt for healthier snack choices using its LLM-driven strategies. It is pertinent to mention that at this phase of our study, the communication between the robot and the users was one-directional (feedbacks were not received from the users during the interaction). After interacting with the robot, participants answered to specifically crafted questions partially informed by [23,24] that sought to evaluate participants' impression of the robot in terms of competence, likability, willingness, persuasiveness, reliability, and trustworthiness.

4 Results

4.1 Snack Classification for Robot's Recommendation

Analysis results of the subject responses revealed that participants were able to differentiate between the healthier and less healthy snack options. Irrespective of subject categories: gender, diet restriction, diet needs, diet intolerance, four (4) snacks were rated as healthier $p < .05$ by participants out of the 21 unique snacks on the vending machine. Concerning the extent to which the healthiness of snacks was considered by users, our analysis result revealed a significant difference ($p < .05$) between people in diet needs and diet restriction groups (between people with and without diet needs/restrictions).

Further analysis conducted between the groups through a Pearson correlation test revealed a low positive correlation $r(124) = .16$ between the two groups.

4.2 Strategies by the Subjective Groups

Before analyzing participants' impressions of the robot's LLM-driven preference elicitation strategies, we first categorized subjects according to their personality trait tendencies as captured through the pre-experiment questionnaire. Seven (7) personality trait tendencies were considered for this study: trust propensity (TP), compliance awareness (CA), and the Big Five: extraversion (EXT), agreeableness (AG), conscientiousness (CON), emotional stability (ES), and openness to experiences (OE). For this, we estimated the mean score of each participant based on the responses to the questions that assessed these traits. Based on the distribution of the mean scores of participants for the categories, we set three (3) thresholds for each category, where the first quartile (Q1) represents the low, the second quartile (Q2) represents the mid, and the third and fourth quartile (Q3 and Q4) corresponding to the high. The distribution method for categorizing users was inspired by [25]. This distribution ensured that participants were

---

[5] https://gosling.psy.utexas.edu/scales-weve-developed/ten-item-personality-measure-tipi/ten-item-personality-inventory-tipi/.

fairly split into three groups. The thresholds obtained are shown in Table 1, and the subjective groups distribution is captured in Table 2.

Table 1. Thresholds for Personality Trait Groups

Traits	Low	Mid	High
TP	$1.00 \leq X \leq 3.39$	$3.40 \leq X \leq 3.99$	$4.00 \leq X \leq 5.00$
CA	$1.00 \leq X \leq 3.99$	$4.00 \leq X \leq 4.79$	$4.80 \leq X \leq 7.00$
EXT	$1.00 \leq X \leq 3.49$	$3.50 \leq X \leq 4.49$	$4.50 \leq X \leq 7.00$
AG	$1.00 \leq X \leq 4.49$	$4.50 \leq X \leq 5.49$	$5.50 \leq X \leq 7.00$
CON	$1.00 \leq X \leq 4.49$	$4.50 \leq X \leq 5.49$	$5.50 \leq X \leq 7.00$
ES	$1.00 \leq X \leq 3.99$	$4.00 \leq X \leq 4.49$	$4.50 \leq X \leq 7.00$
OE	$1.00 \leq X \leq 4.99$	$5.00 \leq X \leq 5.99$	$6.00 \leq X \leq 7.00$

We carried out a 2-way mixed ANOVA to check for interaction effects between the independent variables, which in this context are the subject traits TP, CA, EXT, AG, CON, ES, and OE, and the LLM-driven persuasive strategies (which are between-subject) on each of the impression items (competence, likability, willingness, persuasiveness, reliability, and trustworthiness). For the statistical analysis, we used JASP, a free and open-source program for statistical analysis supported by the University of Amsterdam[6]. Our analysis revealed some significant 2-way interaction effects for some impression items, as shown in Table 3. The main effects of the independent variables are also shown in Table 4. Pertinent to mention is the fact that multiple comparisons were conducted by the Holm method for those with significant interaction effects, and effect sizes were computed in terms of Cohen's d.

Figures 2 and 3 show the mean subjective preferences regarding the impression items by the CA and TP groups. The left panel of Fig. 2 shows variation in the preferences for the LLM-driven strategies by the robot in terms of persuasiveness across the subjective groups. It is important to mention that the impression item was evaluated through the administered questionnaires requesting participants to rate the extent to which the robot's strategy was persuasive enough as an assistant and the extent to which the strategy was able to influence the choices of snack the user ended up buying from the machine. Specifically, subjects in the low TP groups scored the social proof strategies higher relative to the emotional engagement and scarcity strategies with $p < .05$. The effect size was high (*Cohen's d = 0.67, and 0.90*). On the other hand, subjects in the mid TP group appraised the scarcity strategy of the robot higher relative to the other strategies with $p < .05$. The effect size was high (*Cohen's d = 0.84, 0.99, 0.73, and 0.55*). No statistically significant difference was found for the strategies by the high TP group.

---

[6] JASP by the University of Amsterdam https://jasp-stats.org/download/.

Table 2. Personality Traits Distribution by Subjective Groups

Traits	Distribution by Groups
TP	Low TP ($N = 56$: 27 Male, 29 Female; $M = 2.76$, $SD = 0.41$)
	Mid TP ($N = 37$: 21 Male, 15 Female, 1 Others; $M = 3.51$, $SD = 0.10$)
	High TP ($N = 73$: 35 Male, 37 Female, 1 Others; $M = 4.16$, $SD = 0.33$)
CA	Low CA ($N = 44$: 19 Male, 25 Female; $M = 3.31$, $SD = 0.41$)
	Mid CA ($N = 50$: 22 Male, 27 Female, 1 Others; $M = 4.30$, $SD = 0.24$)
	High CA ($N = 72$: 42 Male, 29 Female, 1 Others; $M = 5.40$, $SD = 0.56$)
EXT	Low EXT ($N = 43$: 18 Male, 25 Female; $M = 2.29$, $SD = 0.60$)
	Mid EXT ($N = 48$: 25 Male, 21 Female, 2 Others; $M = 3.80$, $SD = 0.24$)
	High EXT ($N = 75$: 40 Male, 35 Female; $M = 5.15$, $SD = 0.59$)
AG	Low AG ($N = 42$: 18 Male, 24 Female; $M = 3.62$, $SD = 0.54$)
	Mid AG ($N = 47$: 25 Male, 21 Female, 1 Others; $M = 4.83$, $SD = 0.24$)
	High AG ($N = 77$: 40 Male, 36 Female, 1 Others; $M = 5.93$, $SD = 0.42$)
CON	Low CON ($N = 55$: 31 Male, 23 Female, 1 Others; $M = 3.66$, $SD = 0.85$)
	Mid CON ($N = 30$: 14 Male, 15 Female, 1 Others; $M = 5.00$, $SD = 0.00$)
	High CON ($N = 81$: 45 Male, 36 Female; $M = 6.15$, $SD = 0.51$)
ES	Low ES ($N = 66$: 19 Male, 46 Female, 1 Others; $M = 2.84$, $SD = 0.73$)
	Mid ES ($N = 25$: 14 Male, 11 Female; $M = 4.00$, $SD = 0.00$)
	High ES ($N = 75$: 50 Male, 24 Female, 1 Others; $M = 5.33$, $SD = 0.70$)
OE	Low OE ($N = 44$: 19 Male, 24 Female, 1 Others; $M = 4.03$, $SD = 0.70$)
	Mid OE ($N = 53$: 23 Male, 30 Female; $M = 5.20$, $SD = 0.25$)
	High OE ($N = 69$: 36 Male, 32 Female, 1 Others; $M = 6.30$, $SD = 0.32$)

Table 3. Two-Way Interaction Effects (F-values and Significance Levels) for the Subjective Groups. * $p < .05$

Items	Bh.-TP	Bh.-CA	Bh.-EXT	Bh.-AG	Bh.-CON	Bh.-ES	Bh.-OE
Comp.	1.42	1.00	1.07	1.19	1.29	1.35	0.63
Lik.	1.04	0.92	0.69	0.31	0.55	1.39	0.67
Will.	0.75	3.30*	1.14	0.88	1.33	1.20	1.00
Persu.	2.36*	1.91*	1.19	0.34	1.52	1.72	0.63
Reli.	1.01	1.50	1.30	0.67	0.97	0.86	0.60
Trust.	2.04*	1.94*	1.20	0.28	0.17	1.88	0.53

Table 4. Main effect (F-values and significance levels) for each impression item. * $p < .05$, ** $p < .001$

Items	Bh. $F(4,664)$	TP $F(2,332)$	CA $F(2,332)$	EXT $F(2,332)$	AG $F(2,332)$	CON $F(2,332)$	ES $F(2,332)$	OE $F(4,664)$
Comp.	0.85	3.25*	4.80*	0.33	0.70	3.03*	0.55	1.07
Lik.	2.30*	5.03**	3.55*	1.41	0.23	0.66	1.69	0.79
Will.	0.49	7.91**	5.22*	1.47	0.12	1.44	0.34	3.19*
Persu.	0.42	12.31**	7.38**	0.63	0.76	0.01	1.27	0.22
Reli.	0.65	10.50**	7.71**	3.42*	0.52	0.04	0.09	1.94
Trust.	1.23	9.58**	9.91**	2.65	0.30	0.74	0.96	5.05*

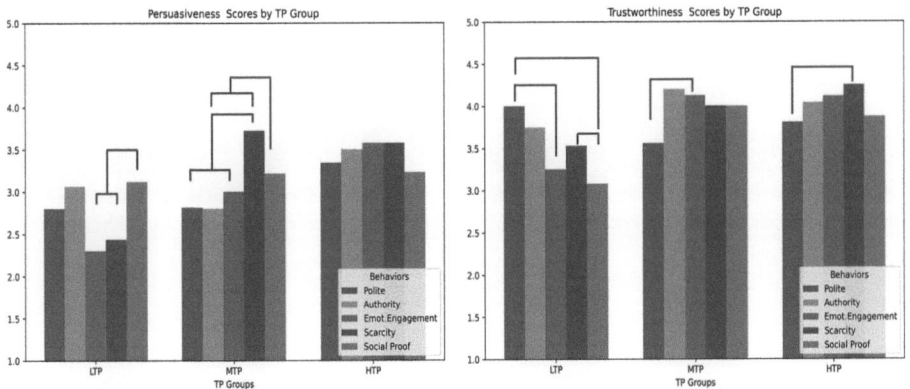

Fig. 2. Subjective scores for robot behaviors regarding persuasiveness and trustworthiness by TP group

Concerning the trustworthiness of the strategies by the TP groups, the right panel of Fig. 2 revealed a variation in the preferences for the behaviors by the groups. Subjects in the low TP group appraised the polite strategy higher relative to the emotional engagement and social proof strategies $p < .05$ with high effect size (*Cohen's d = 0.74, and 0.90*), while the scarcity strategy was scored higher than the social proof $p < .05$ with mid effect size (*Cohen's d = 0.44*). In contrast, subjects in the mid TP group scored the emotional engagement strategy higher than the polite strategy $p < .05$ with high effect size (*Cohen's d = 0.66*), while subjects in the high TP groups appraised the scarcity strategy by the robot higher than the polite strategy $p < .05$ with effect size (*Cohen's d = 0.54*).

Regarding preferences for the robot's strategies in terms of the impression items by the CA group, the left panel of Fig. 3 shows variation in the preferences for the behaviors by the groups. In terms of persuasiveness, subjects in the low CA group appraised the emotion engagement strategy higher than the authority and scarcity strategies $p < .05$ with effect size (*Cohen's d = 0.32, and 0.82*). No statistically significant difference was found between the strategies for the mid and high CA groups.

Concerning the willingness of users to adhere to the strategies of the robot by subjects in the CA group, the right panel of Fig. 3 shows variation in the preferences for the strategies. Specifically, subjects in the low CA group scored the emotional engagement strategy of the robot higher than the polite, authority, scarcity, and social proof strategies $p < .05$ with effect size (*Cohen's d = 0.68, 0.55, 0.99, and 1.34*). Subjects in the mid CA group appraised the polite strategy higher than the authority strategy $p < .05$ with effect size (*Cohen's d = 0.69*). Similarly, subjects in the high CA group scored the polite strategy higher than the scarcity and social proof strategies $p < .05$ with effect size (*Cohen's d = 0.65, 0.32*). For trustworthiness, subjects in the low CA group appraised the polite strategy higher than the social proof strategy $p < .05$ with effect size (*Cohen's d = 0.79*), while subjects in the mid CA group scored the authority

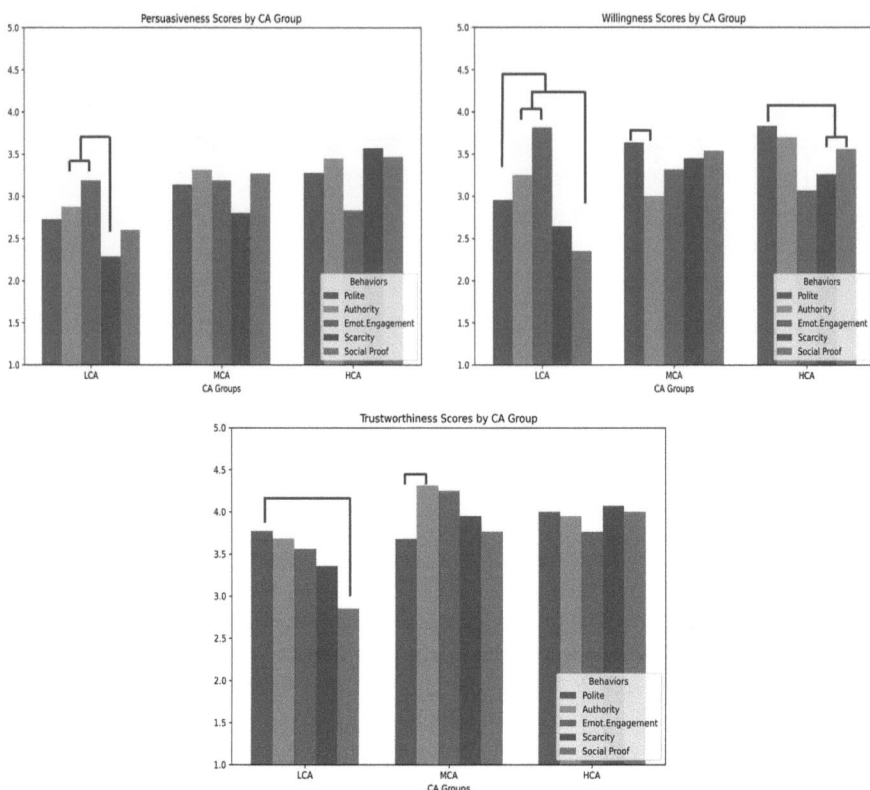

Fig. 3. Subjective scores for robot behaviors regarding persuasiveness, willingness, and trustworthiness by CA group

higher than the polite strategy of the robot $p < .05$ with effect size (*Cohen's d = 0.89*).

5 Discussion

Regarding **H1**, the analysis results from *Phase 1* of the study revealed that participants could distinguish between a healthier snack and a less healthy one.

However, regarding the extent to which users consider snack healthiness before purchasing and consuming them, analysis results show that not all users take into account this factor. For instance, participants with no dietary needs and those with no dietary restrictions were found to consider the nutritional content of snacks, while those with dietary needs and dietary restrictions paid less importance to this factor. A possible justification for this could be that health-related behaviors and perceptions are complex and influenced by factors not limited to personality, leading some individuals, including those with dietary restrictions, to prioritize other attributes over nutritional content when selecting snacks [26].

About **H2**, our analysis results from *Phase 2* revealed differences between subject trait groups (TP and CA) and preferences for the robot's strategies in terms of persuasiveness, willingness, and trustworthiness. Concerning TP groups, results showed that subjects lower in trust propensity (low and mid-TP groups) considered the social proof and scarcity strategies of the robot to be more persuasive for influencing their choice for healthier snack options. In contrast, subjects higher in trust propensity (high TP group) favored equally all the strategies by the robot in terms of their persuasiveness. Logically, this aligns with the trait characteristics of this group. This is because subjects in this group are known to have high trust in AI and robot systems. For the trustworthiness of the strategies, subjects in the low TP group scored less emotional engagement and social proof strategies, while subjects in the mid and high TP groups scored less the polite strategy as against the other strategies by the robot.

Regarding CA groups, in terms of persuasiveness, subjects in the low CA group considered the emotional engagement strategy of the robot as more persuasive compared to the other strategies considered for the robot. However, subjects in the mid and high CA groups consider all the robot's strategies to be equally persuasive. Concerning willingness to obey the robot's elicitation, subjects in the low CA will be more willing to adhere to the robot's persuasion through its emotional engagement strategy compared to the other strategies by the robot. In contrast, subjects in the mid CA group will be more willing to yield to the robot's polite elicitation for healthier snack options compared to the authority strategy. Similarly, subjects in the high CA group will yield more to the robot's polite strategy compared to the scarcity and social proof strategies.

Regarding the trustworthiness of the strategies by CA groups, subjects in the low CA group have less trust in the robot's social proof strategy for preference elicitation. Also, subjects in the mid CA group showed lower trust for the robot's polite strategy compared to the other strategies. In contrast, subjects in the high CA group considered the strategies equally in terms of their trustworthiness. These results are in line with **H2**, which suggests that the impression of the robot's preference elicitation strategies may be influenced by the user's personality trait tendencies.

5.1 Implications, Limitations and Plans

The findings of this study have significant practical implications. For instance, the results can inform the development of trait-based models for assistive robots intended to operate in public and private places to assist users with healthier snack choices. Additionally, robots equipped with strategies derived from this trait-based model could be effectively utilized in developing personalized care support to users at homes, hospitals, and nursing homes. Furthermore, the findings from this study can be extended to other public spaces, such as shopping malls and other service industries, where robots can help individuals make healthier and better choices by persuading them with strategies that align with their trait inclinations established in our study.

Regarding the limitations of the study, the current study considered the robot deployed as an assistant on the vending machine. Previous studies have established the impact of context on the perception of robots' behavior [12]. Subsequent studies may consider the robot deployed in a different context for the task of persuading users to opt for healthier snack options. Additionally, we intend to integrate a function for feedback on the robot system to enable more interactive engagement.

6 Conclusions

In this work, we leverage developments in LLMs to equip SARs with persuasive strategies for eliciting users' healthier snack choices. We designed a study in two phases for this purpose. Firstly, through a within-subject experiment, we examined the extent to which people consider the healthiness of snacks before purchasing and consuming them. Our results showed that, although many participants have a good understanding of what constitutes a "healthy snack," many frequently neglect to consider the healthiness of these snacks before purchasing and consuming them. Secondly, by adopting a between-subjects experiment, we evaluated the influence of users' personality trait tendencies on preferences for the robot's LLM-driven strategies for eliciting healthier snack choices. Findings from the study revealed variation in the preference for the robot's strategies relative to subjects' trait tendencies.

Acknowledgments. This work has been supported by the European Union - Next Generation EU, Mission 4 Component 1, PRIN 2022 TrustPACTX CUP E53D23007850001.

References

1. Johanson, D.L., Ahn, H.S., Broadbent, E.: Improving interactions with healthcare robots: a review of communication behaviours in social and healthcare contexts. Int. J. Soc. Robot. **13**(8), 1835–50 (2021)
2. Walters, M.L., Syrdal, D.S., Dautenhahn, K., Te Boekhorst, R., Koay, K.L.: Avoiding the uncanny valley: robot appearance, personality and consistency of behavior in an attention-seeking home scenario for a robot companion. Auton. Robot. **24**, 159–78 (2008)
3. Yue, W., Wang, Z., Zhang, J., Liu, X.: An overview of recommendation techniques and their applications in healthcare. IEEE/CAA J. Automatica Sinica. **8**(4), 701–17 (2021)
4. Gretzel, U., Fesenmaier, D.R.: Persuasiveness of preference elicitation processes in destination recommendation systems. In: Information and Communication Technologies in Tourism (2005), pp. 194–204. Springer, Vienna (2005). https://doi.org/10.1007/3-211-27283-6_18

5. Sofia, G., Marianna, S., George, L., Panos, K.: Investigating the role of personality traits and influence strategies on the persuasive effect of personalized recommendations. In: 4th Workshop on Emotions and Personality in Personalized Systems (EMPIRE), vol. 9 (2016)
6. Cialdini, R.B., Goldstein, N.J.: The science and practice of persuasion. Cornell Hotel Restaurant Adm. Q. **43**(2), 40–50 (2002)
7. Huang, D., Marmolejo-Cossío, F., Lock, E., Parkes, D.: Accelerated preference elicitation with LLM-based proxies. arXiv preprint arXiv:2501.14625 (2025)
8. Young, M.: The Techincal Writers Handbook. University Science, Mill Valley, CA (1989)
9. Agu, E., Claypool, M.: Cypress: a cyber-physical recommender system to discover smartphone exergame enjoyment. In: Proceedings of the ACM Workshop on Engendering Health with Recommender Systems (2016)
10. Pilloni, P., Piras, L., Boratto, L., Carta, S., Fenu, G., Mulas, F.: Recommendation in persuasive eHealth systems: an effective strategy to spot users' losing motivation to exercise. In: CEUR Workshop Proceedings, vol. 1953, pp. 6–9 (2017)
11. Oyibo, K., Orji, R., Vassileva J.: Investigation of the influence of personality traits on Cialdini's persuasive strategies. PPT@ PERSUASIVE. **2017**, 8–20 (2017)
12. Augustine Ajibo, C., Ishi, C.T., Ishiguro, H.: Assessing the influence of an android robot's persuasive behaviors and context of violation on compliance. Adv. Robot. **38**(23), 1679–89 (2024)
13. Simchon, A., Edwards, M., Lewandowsky, S.: The persuasive effects of political microtargeting in the age of generative artificial intelligence. PNAS Nexus. **3**(2), 035 (2024)
14. Brand, J., Israeli, A., Ngwe, D.: Using GPT for market research. In: Harvard Business School Marketing Unit Working Paper, vol. 21, no. 23-062 (2023)
15. Yang, Z., et al.: Talk2care: an LLM-based voice assistant for communication between healthcare providers and older adults. Proc. ACM Interact. Mobile Wearable Ubiquit. Technol. **8**(2), 1–35 (2024)
16. Manning, B.S., Zhu, K., Horton, J.J.: Automated social science: language models as scientist and subjects. National Bureau of Economic Research (2024)
17. Palen-Michel, C., Wang, R., Zhang, Y., Yu, D., Xu, C., Wu, Z.: Investigating LLM applications in e-commerce. arXiv preprint arXiv:2408.12779 (2024)
18. Ataei, M., Cheong, H., Grandi, D., Wang, Y., Morris, N., Tessier, A.: Elicitron: an LLM agent-based simulation framework for design requirements elicitation. arXiv preprint arXiv:2404.16045 (2024)
19. Furumai K, et al.: Zero-shot persuasive chatbots with LLM-generated strategies and information retrieval. arXiv preprint arXiv:2407.03585 (2024)
20. Herse, S., et al.: Bon appetit! Robot persuasion for food recommendation. In: Companion of the 2018 ACM/IEEE International Conference on Human-Robot Interaction, pp. 125–126 (2018)
21. Paradeda, R., Ferreira, M.J., Oliveira, R., Martinho, C., Paiva, A.: What makes a good robotic advisor? The role of assertiveness in human-robot interaction. In: Salichs, M.A., et al. (eds.) ICSR 2019. LNCS (LNAI), vol. 11876, pp. 144–154. Springer, Cham (2019). https://doi.org/10.1007/978-3-030-35888-4_14
22. Merritt, S.M., Heimbaugh, H., LaChapell, J., Lee, D.: I trust it, but i don't know why: effects of implicit attitudes toward automation on trust in an automated system. Hum. Factors **55**(3), 520–34 (2013)
23. Castro-González, Á., Admoni, H., Scassellati, B.: Effects of form and motion on judgments of social robots' animacy, likability, trustworthiness and unpleasantness. Int. J. Hum Comput Stud. **1**(90), 27–38 (2016)

24. Lyons, J.B., Stokes, C.K.: Human–human reliance in the context of automation. Hum. Factors **54**(1), 112–21 (2012)
25. Johnson, J.A.: Calibrating personality self-report scores to acquaintance ratings. Personality Individ. Differ. **1**(169), 109734 (2021)
26. Okpiaifo, G.E., Dormoy-Smith, B., Kassas, B., Gao, Z.: Perception and demand for healthy snacks/beverages among US consumers vary by product, health benefit, and color. PLoS ONE **18**(6), e0287232 (2023)

Robots and Reflexes: Analyzing the Stroop Effect and Impulsiveness in Human-Robot Interaction

Alessandra Sorrentino[1()], Jasmine Pani[1], Carlo La Viola[2], Jaeseok Kim[1], Marco Vincenzo Maselli[1], Sofia Iacopini[1], Laura Fiorini[1], and Filippo Cavallo[1]

[1] Department of Industrial Engineering, University of Florence, 50139 Florence, Italy
alessandra.sorrentino@unifi.it
[2] Co-Robotics s.r.l., Pisa, Italy

Abstract. Socially Assistive Robots (SARs) are increasingly employed in clinical environments to support cognitive and rehabilitative tasks through social interaction. This study explores the integration of SARs into neuropsychological assessment by implementing and comparing two versions of the Stroop Color and Word Test: a standard PC-based version and a novel robot-mediated version involving a handover task with a robotic manipulator. Thirty-one participants completed both conditions in a within-subject design, under congruent and incongruent stimulus settings. Our findings confirm the expected Stroop effect in the PC-based modality, with increased reaction times (RTs) in the incongruent condition. In contrast, the robot-based implementation revealed an inverted trend, where incongruent trials resulted in faster RTs—likely due to temporal synchronization between user movements and robotic motion, indicating a strong sensorimotor coupling effect. Analysis of user impulsiveness, measured via the Barratt Impulsiveness Scale, showed a significant impact on task performance in the PC-based version, but not in the robot-mediated version, suggesting that interaction with the robot may attenuate impulsivity-driven variability. These results underline the importance of adaptive robot behavior in eliciting meaningful cognitive responses and offer valuable insights for designing personalized, interaction-aware SARs.

Keywords: Socially assistive robotics · Stroop Test · User Behavior Analysis

1 Introduction

Socially Assistive Robots (SARs) emerged as innovative solutions for assisting people through social interactions [1]. Over the years, several studies demonstrated the promising advantages on the adoption of this kind of technology in physical therapy [2], rehabilitation [3, 4], and other clinical settings, involving a multitude of users, such as ASD children [5] and older adults [6]. SARs are intended to reduce the workload of healthcare professionals and caregivers, guaranteeing a safe and improved quality of life of the primary end users [1]. However, developing SAR-based systems also carried several challenges, related both to the assistive aspect and the social aspect. As assistive agent, they are requested guaranteeing a standardized administration of the clinical protocol [7] in diagnosis and/or rehabilitation procedures. As social agent, they need to understand the multi-facet aspects of the user profile and adjust their own behavior accordingly, to positively impact user experience and engagement, thus keeping the user motivated [8]. Additionally, considering the long-term interactions, SARs should be able to identify possible changes in cognitive abilities and adapt their behaviors, accordingly, providing a personalized robot-patient interaction [9].

In this context, the Stroop Color and Word Test [10], or Stroop task, is a neuropsychological test used to evaluate the inhibition capacity which occurs when processing the feature of one stimulus affects the processing of another feature of the same stimulus. Several scoring methods are present in the literature [11], but overall, the task entails the presentation of two types of conditions: congruous and incongruous. In congruous condition, the words and their ink match, conversely in the incongruous condition they do not. The participants are always required to name the ink of a color word while inhibiting reading the word. This difficulty in performing a less automatic task is called Stroop effect. Several works suggest that weaker interference control can be attributed to higher impulsive behaviors [12]. Namely, individuals with higher impulsivity may exhibit a weaker ability to control or suppress the automatic reading response, leading to a greater Stroop effect. It means they might take longer to correctly name the color and make more errors when the word and color are incongruent.

In this work, we propose two different implementations of the Stroop test, exploiting two different technologies, namely: a PC-based version and a robot-based version. In the PC-based administration, the participant is asked to press the keyboard key corresponding to the ink color of the word. In the robot-based administration, the participant engages in a handover task with a robotic manipulator, where the target color is represented either by the color of an object (i.e., a ball) being passed in the congruent condition, or by a specific color displayed on the robot's tablet in the incongruent condition. In both modalities, congruous and incongruous conditions consist of multiple trials. Given the differences in task administration, the aim of this study is two-fold. First, we seek to validate the reliability of the proposed solution, while also examining the emergence of the Stroop effect in both scenarios. Second, we aim to explore the relationship between task performance and user's profile, specifically focusing on impulsiveness as trait of the user profile that could help the robot adjust its behavior to keep the user more engaged. A within-subject experimental protocol was designed to address the following research hypotheses:

- H1: A Stroop effect is observed in the incongruent condition compared to the congruent condition in both scenarios.
- H2: The presence of the robot has a more significant impact on user performances in repeated interactions, than in the short time frame.
- H3: The user's level of impulsiveness affects task performances in both the PC-based and robotic administrations.

2 Materials

2.1 Stroop Test PC-Based

A computer-based adaptation of the Stroop task was implemented in this work, where the stimulus was shown on the screen and the user response was recorded from the keyboard's keys. Blue, green, yellow, and red colors were selected for the task, and tapes of the same colors were attached to four consecutive keys. The test was organized in three parts: a training phase, a congruent and incongruent condition. In the training phase, a message on the screen re-showed the intent of the task (i.e., select the color of the words shown on the screen, as fast as they could, pressing the keyboard button of the same color). If the task was not performed according to the instruction (i.e., if the participants performed more than 5 errors), *"Try Again, or ask for assistance if needed"* message appeared on the screen, and the participants were requested to repeat the training phase. In congruent condition, participants were instructed to press the button that corresponded to both the color and the meaning of the word displayed. In the incongruent condition, the word's meaning and its color could either match or differ. Participants were instructed to respond based on the font color, ignoring its meaning. The order and the color of the words were randomly generated. Both the congruent and incongruent condition lasted 30 s. The mean reaction time (RT) of the congruent and incongruent conditions was calculated for each participant, as well as an interference RT, which was obtained as the difference between the RT of the incongruent and congruent conditions. The system was developed in Python, exploiting *pygame* library.

2.2 Robotic System

The Stroop task was also adapted for a robotic administration. With respect to the computer-based system, the task was designed as a handover, where the robot passes a colored ball to the user, which needs to place the ball in the color-matched box (congruent condition) or in another box, based on a colored-written text shown over the tablet (incongruent condition).

The Kinova Gen3 robotic arm (Kinova Robotics, Canada), equipped with a Robotiq gripper (Robotiq, USA) was considered in this work. Additionally, two RGB-D cameras (Intel Realsense, USA) were included in the setup, one placed at the base of the robot, and one placed laterally, as well as a tablet (Lenovo, China), located laterally with respect to the robotic platform. A dedicated software architecture was implemented for the specific task administration, composed of three main modules. As shown in Fig. 1, the robotic controller was developed in ROS, to handle the robot behaviors and to synchronize the data stream recordings. The *Moveit!* Library [13] was responsible for planning and execute the motion trajectory of the robot. The robotic motion was decomposed in three sub-movements, namely: i) reach the ball position (and grasp it), ii) reach the home position, intended as central location (see Fig. 2), iii) reach the destination position (and release the ball to the user). Each robot trajectory started from the home position, while the destination goal was randomly selected by the robotic controller among the random valid configuration within the user workspace. The ROS-based modules were integrated with the therapist webpages using the web-based Flask app hosted on a Docker container. Through the webpages, the therapist could setup the user workspace, selecting the task (congruent, or incongruent), score the user performance (expressed as *success* if the user correctly performed the exercise, or as *mistake* otherwise), and report any technical failure of the system. The NoSQL database MongoDB was integrated to store the coordinates of the user workspace, the user performances, and the robot timings.

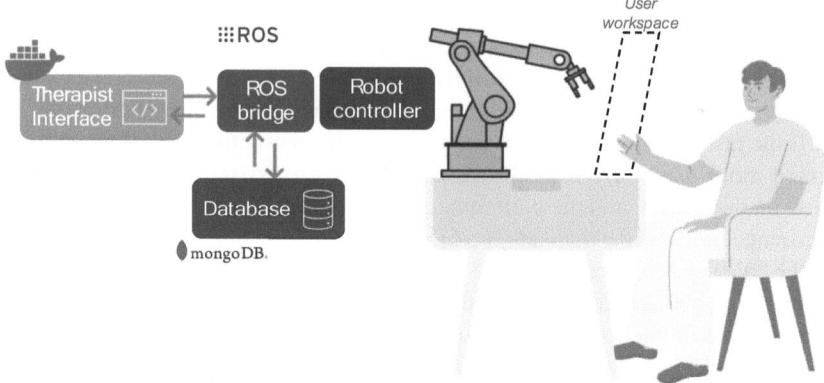

Fig. 1. Overview of the software architecture developed over the robotic arm, and of the user workspace in which the robot-to-human handover occurs.

3 Methods

3.1 Experimental Procedure

A within-subject experimental design was employed, in which each participant completed the Stroop task both on a computer and with the robot. Prior to the experiment, participants were informed about the study's procedures and objectives and provided written informed consent. To minimize bias, participants were told that the study aimed to evaluate the reliability of the robotic platform in administering the Stroop task.

After completing a demographic questionnaire, participants first performed the Stroop task on a computer, as detailed in Sect. 2.1. They then repeated the task with the robot, following the procedure outlined in Sect. 2.2. During the robot-administered session, an experimenter acted as a "therapist," guiding the robot and recording the user performances through a web-based interface. The order of congruent and incongruent tasks administered by the robot was randomized across participants. The user workspace was identical among the participants. After the first trial which represented the training one, each task consisted of nine consecutive trials, resulting in a total of 18 sequential human-robot object handovers. Following the robot-administered session, participants were asked to complete the Barratt Impulsiveness Scale (BIS-11) [14], as described in the following section.

3.2 Questionnaires

Prior to interacting with the robot, participants completed a demographic questionnaire which included age, sex, highest education degree and handedness.

At the end of the interaction, each participant was asked to fill out the Barratt Impulsiveness Scale (BIS-11) [14] translated in Italian by Fossati and colleagues [15]. The questionnaire is composed of 30 items, and it is designed to evaluate the behavioral construct of impulsiveness based on anxiety and thrill-seeking research. Participants were asked to rate the frequency of certain behaviors on a 4-point Likert scale, ranging from 1 (rarely/never) to 4 (almost always/always). Items can be combined to provide the total score, first- and second-order subscales. The total score (range 30–120) provides an overall score of impulsivity, whereas the subscales are used to describe specific facets of impulsiveness. The first-order factors are: attention (5 items), motor (7 items), self-control (6 items), cognitive complexity (5 items), perseverance (4 items), and cognitive instability (3 items). On the other hand, the second-order factors are attentional (attention + cognitive instability), motor (motor + perseverance) and non-planning (self-control + cognitive complexity) impulsiveness. The first- and second-order scores were rescaled to 0–1 to be able to compare them.

3.3 User Behavior Analysis

Each human-robot interaction was recorded using an RGB camera (Intel RealSense, USA), which was integrated into the robot and positioned at the participant's chest height. This placement ensured a clear and unobstructed view of the task performance. Specific human behaviors, that were temporally annotated in each video, using a customized Python script, namely: human starts moving the right hand to pick up the ball (T-H0), human grasps the ball (T-H1), and human releases the ball (T-H2). Thanks to this annotation, the two intervals of interest were derived, i.e., reaching phase (from T-H0 to T-H1) and release phase (from T-H1 to T-H2).

To investigate user behavior during the task, we analyzed the dynamics of hand motion by extracting kinematic-based biomarkers from the estimated (x, y) coordinates of the right wrist (dominant hand), using the Mediapipe SDK [16]. Specifically, the (x, y) coordinates [in pixels] were re-referenced to a coordinate system centered at the bottom-left corner of the image. To ensure data reliability, only keypoints with a visibility score above 70% were retained, and missing values were interpolated using an average-based approach. To minimize noise, the signals were filtered using a second-order Butterworth filter with a 5 Hz cutoff frequency and a sampling rate of 30 Hz. Filtered trajectories were then converted to meter units by applying a pixel-to-meter scale factor. Focusing on the absolute velocity profile of the dominant hand, the interval of time corresponding to the reaching and release phases were adjusted based on the signal information. Namely, the starting time of the reaching phase was considered as the instant in which the signal first rises 5% to the peak-value. A set of behavioral features were extracted during the reaching and release phases, namely:

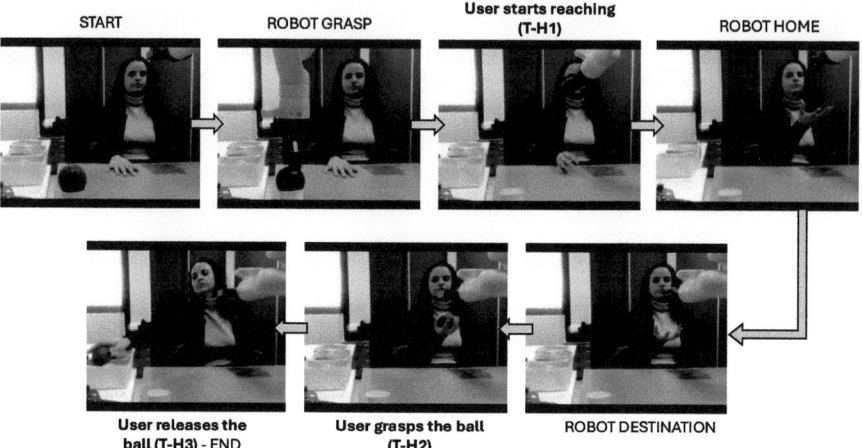

Fig. 2. Screenshots of the salient events considered in the human-robot interaction scenario (incongruent condition).

- Peak velocity, which represents the highest value of the velocity profile during the movement, in each phase.
- Time to peak velocity, which refers to the interval of time between the instant in which the hand starts the movement and the instant of the peak velocity of each phase.
- Average acceleration, which is intended as average hand acceleration value during each phase.
- Interaction time, which represents the interval of time occurred in the interaction, that starts when the robot starts moving and it ends when the user releases the ball in the box.
- Motion duration, which refers to time interval between the onset of movement in the reaching phase and the completion of the release phase.
- Phase duration, which refers to the interval of time of each motion phase.
- Reaction time, intended as the time interval between the user starting the motion and the robot temporally stopping in the home position. It is computed only in the reaching phase.

These features were selected based on their relevance to stroke-related motor rehabilitation, highlighting the dual nature of social cues and digital biomarkers [17]. Feature extraction was performed using Python-based APIs, using the data recording of the lateral camera, to avoid any occlusions of the hand movement caused by the robot motion. This process resulted in the extraction of 11 features per interaction.

3.4 Participants

A cohort of 31 participants (20 women, 11 men, age: 27 ± 5.5 years old) were recruited for the present study among the students and the researchers of the Department of Industrial Engineering of the University of Florence (Florence, Italy), where the experimental sessions took place. Among them, five participants had a high-school degree, 10 of them had a bachelor's degree, 12 participants had a master's degree, and the remaining ones a PhD's degree. All the participants were right-handed, except one. Ethical approval was provided by the Ethical Committee for Research at the University of Florence (protocol 0077883 of 06.04.2023).

4 Data Analysis

To investigate the first research hypothesis, the Stroop conditions were compared using the Wilcoxon signed rank test. It was done to assess whether there was a difference in the congruent or incongruent tasks' performances (H1) within 1) the RT for the PC-based condition and 2) the user behavioral features for the robot administration. To investigate if the behavior of the robot somehow affected the user behaviors, we evaluated the Stroop conditions across the nine interactions (long-term) and considering only the first three interactions (short-term) (H2).

To profile participants into type of impulsiveness response (H3), clustering was performed. The BIS-11 first-, second-order and total scores were normalized by rescaling them using the mean and standard deviation. The silhouette method was used to determine the optimal number of clusters. The normalized values were clustered using k-means. The algorithm was initialized with 25 random starting configurations to ensure the best solution. Depending on the number of resulting clusters, Kruskall-Wallis test or Mann Whitney U test was then used to investigate any differences in the extracted features, among the clusters. A p-value lower than 0.05 was considered statistically significant. Analyses were performed on RStudio version 4.4.2 and in Python 3.9 API.

5 Results

Among the recruited participants, all of them successfully completed the Stroop test, both with the PC and with the robot. Unfortunately, the answers to the BIS were not saved for one participant. Similarly, the recordings of the robotic condition were corrupted for one user. These two participants were discarded by the corresponding analysis.

On average, the human-robot interaction lasted 27.81 s (± 2.6). During the interaction, the robot moved for 20.94 ± 2.92 s, spending most of the time in reaching and grasping the ball (9.84 ± 2.28 s) and reaching the home position (7.84 ± 0.85 s), than reaching the final destination. On average, the interval of time in which the user moved the dominant hand was of 6.35 ± 2.71 s, where the reaching phase returned to last more (79.40% of the human movement) than the release phase (20.6% of the human movement).

5.1 Congruent vs Incongruent Task

Our first analysis aimed at identifying any difference between the two administrated conditions, i.e., congruent vs incongruent. Considering the PC-based case, the RT for the Stroop test in the two conditions were significantly different ($V = 92, p = 0.002$). The congruent condition was completed significantly faster (mean RT = 747.09 ± 152.09

ms) than the incongruent condition (mean RT = 834.63 ± 214.69 ms). These results are in line with our hypothesis since the congruent condition requires less cognitive effort than the incongruent condition.

Focusing on the first three interactions after the training trial, different trends emerged (see Table 1). First, the results returned a significant difference in the reaction time between the congruent and incongruent condition (V = 104, p = 0.007), suggesting that the users tended to start the motion earlier in the incongruent one (0.84 ± 1.68 s) than in the congruent condition (1.68 ± 2.16 s). Similarly, the average acceleration of the hand motion during the reaching phase returned to be statistically significant (V = 102, p = 0.006), suggesting the hand motion was faster in the congruent (0.25 ± 0.88 m/s^2) than in the incongruent condition (0.14 ± 0.51 m/s^2). Additionally, it also emerged a statistically significant difference in the peak velocity of the release phase (V = 109, p = 0.009), which resulted being higher in the incongruent condition (1.32 ± 0.55 m/s), than in the congruent condition (1.12 ± 0.37 m/s).

Considering the long-term interaction, statistically significant differences emerged in the hand motion parameters during the release phase (see Table 1), specifically in peak velocity (V = 121, p = 0.02), time to peak velocity (V = 131, p = 0.36), and total phase duration (V = 92, p = 0.002). Notably, the congruent condition showed lower peak velocity (1.12 ± 0.32 m/s) compared to the incongruent condition (1.24 ± 0.38 m/s). Similarly, the time to reach peak velocity was shorter in the congruent condition (0.74 ± 0.22 s) than in the incongruent condition (0.85 ± 0.3 s). The overall duration of the release phase was also reduced in the congruent condition (1.24 ± 0.25 s) compared to the incongruent one (1.4 ± 0.3 s). These findings suggest that participants exhibited a prolonged motion pattern during the release phase under the incongruent condition.

Table 1. Descriptive statistics of the extracted parameters, describing user behaviors during the congruent and incongruent condition in the proposed scenarios. * p < 0.05, ** p < 0.01

Scenario	Parameter	Congruent	Incongruent
PC-based	Reaction time (RT)[ms]**	**747.09 ± 152.09**	**834.63 ± 214.69**
Robot-based (short-term)	Peak velocity (reaching) [m/s]	0.79 ± 0.42	0.83 ± 0.48
	Peak velocity (release) [m/s]**	**1.12 ± 0.37**	**1.32 ± 0.55**
	Time to peak velocity (reaching) [s]	0.44 ± 0.2	0.38 ± 0.14
	Time to peak velocity (release) [s]	0.81 ± 0.29	0.89 ± 0.46
	Average acceleration (reaching) [m/s^2]**	**0.25 ± 0.88**	**0.14 ± 0.51**

(*continued*)

Table 1. (*continued*)

Scenario	Parameter	Congruent	Incongruent
	Average acceleration (release) [m/s^2]	0.1 ± 0.37	0.2 ± 0.27
	Interaction time [s]	28.27 ± 2.84	27.8 ± 2.3
	Motion duration [s]	6.1 ± 2.44	6.44 ± 1.77
	Phase duration (reaching) [s]	4.9 ± 2.28	5.08 ± 1.6
	Phase duration (release) [s]	2.27 ± 0.29	1.42 ± 0.44
	Reaction time [s]**	**1.68 ± 2.16**	**0.84 ± 1.68**
Robot-based (long-term)	Peak velocity (reaching) [m/s]	0.78 ± 0.34	0.8 ± 0.38
	Peak velocity (release) [m/s]*	**1.12 ± 0.32**	**1.24 ± 0.38**
	Time to peak velocity (reaching) [s]	0.42 ± 0.14	0.43 ± 0.12
	Time to peak velocity (release) [s]*	**0.74 ± 0.21**	**0.85 ± 0.31**
	Average acceleration (reaching) [m/s^2]	0.2 ± 0.37	0.11 ± 0.2
	Average acceleration (release) [m/s^2]	0.11 ± 0.23	0.23 ± 0.2
	Interaction time [s]	27.87 ± 2.8	27.74 ± 2.33
	Motion duration [s]	6.12 ± 2.15	6.2 ± 1.75
	Phase duration (reaching) [s]	4.92 ± 2.05	4.83 ± 1.66
	Phase duration (release) [s]**	**1.24 ± 0.25**	**1.4 ± 0.3**
	Reaction Time [s]	1.34 ± 1.79	1.12 ± 0.29

5.2 User Profiling

From the BIS-11, it emerged that all participants had a total score comparable to another Italian sample with similar demographic characteristics [18]. For the clustering, one participant had missing data and thus analysis was performed on 30 subjects. According to the silhouette method two clusters were identified, 19 participants were identified as cluster 1 and 11 in cluster 2. The first two dimensions explained 72.0% of the variance. Looking at the BIS-11 scores, it emerged that cluster 2 had higher scores for both first- and second-order factors, as well as total score, suggesting higher levels of impulsiveness.

Overall, cluster 1 had slower RT for both the congruent and incongruent conditions, and had more interference compared to cluster 2 (see Table 2). Indeed, the Mann-Whiney U Test returned significant differences between the clusters for all the RT metrics ($p < 0.001$). During the robot administration, no statistically significant differences emerged, suggesting that two clusters behaved similarly, both in the short- and in the long-term and across the two task conditions.

Table 2. Median and interquartile values of Stroop RT and BIS-11 first-order, second-order and total scores.

Tool	Metrics	Cluster 1	Cluster 2
BIS-11	Total score	56.0 (±7.5)	68.0 (±7.5)
	Attention	8.0 (±2.0)	11.0 (±4.0)
	Motor	11.0 (±2.5)	16.0 (±3.5)
	Self-control	12.0 (±3.5)	16.0 (±3.0)
	Cognitive complexity	11.0 (±3.0)	11.0 (±3.0)
	Perseverance	6.0 (±2.0)	7.0 (±3.0)
	Cognitive instability	6.0 (±2.0)	9.0 (±1.5)
	Attentional impulsiveness	15.0 (±2.5)	18.0 (±5.0)
	Motor impulsiveness	18.0 (±2.5)	22.0 (±4.0)
	Non-planning impulsiveness	23.0 (±6.0)	27.0 (±2.0)
Stroop Test PC-based	RT congruent	786.2 (±225.7)	642.1 (±208.4)
	RT incongruent	819.7 (±254.5)	702.9 (±215.8)
	RT interference	58.7 (±169.1)	30.7 (±65.3)

6 Discussion

In this work, we investigated the Stroop effect, assessing and comparing user performances in a within-subject experimental setup. A total of 31 participants were recruited in the experimental session, and successfully performed the requested task in the two modalities, through the PC-based version and robot-based version. Given the differences in task administration, the aim of this study consisted in validating the reliability of the proposed solution, while also examining the emergence of the Stroop effect and explore the relationship between task performance and user's impulsiveness. Considering the reliability of the system, malfunctioning events occurred at data storing time, thus they did not affect the user performance.

When examining the Stroop effect on user performance (H1), a comparison between congruent and incongruent conditions revealed notable differences across both administration modalities. Indeed, the results demonstrate how embodied interaction modalities can fundamentally alter cognitive task dynamics. In the PC-based administration, higher reaction times (RTs) in the incongruent condition reflected the cognitive delay in recognizing the color of the word, as the brain tends to process word meaning faster than color information [10]. In contrast, this effect appeared reversed in the robotic administration: lower RTs were observed in the incongruent condition compared to the congruent one. We attribute this inversion to the presence and influence of the robot. In this case, RTs were calculated based on the coordination between the user's hand movement and the robot's motion, making timing highly dependent on this interaction. In the congruent condition, the reaching phase involved later and slower movements, possibly indicating a more relaxed user behavior. This interpretation is supported by the lower velocity observed during the release phase in the congruent condition.

Similarly, user behavior during the reaching phase demonstrated a general priming effect from the robot's movement, seen in both conditions (H2). Over time, users adapted their motions in response to the robotic arm, as previously noted by [4]. This adaptation may explain why the impulsiveness trait analysis in the robotic administration did not reveal significant differences (H3). Given that humans tend to synchronize with their partner's movement patterns [19], our findings align with those of [4], showing that such adaptation also occurs in response to robotic movement. These results suggest that performance during the task is not influenced by individual impulsiveness traits in the robotic condition. To provoke a more inhibitory control, thus triggering user impulsiveness, it becomes crucial to design robotic motion patterns that can highlight these aspects. In our study, the duration of one robot-assisted interaction (27.81 s) closely matched that of one complete PC-based condition (30 s). Indeed, reducing user waiting time and adjusting robot speed during handover tasks can reveal differences in impulsiveness. While robotic administration did not show differences based on the BIS-11 profile, the PC-based administration did support our hypothesis (H3). Specifically, the more "impulsive" cluster of participants demonstrated lower RTs across all conditions. Moreover, this group exhibited significantly lower RT interference values, indicating an enhanced ability to switch between tasks (H3).

This paper contributes to socially assistive robotics (SAR) research by providing evidence to support interaction-aware SAR design principles. In this direction, future work will focus on adjusting and testing different robotic speeds, to further induce the Stroop effect in human-robot interaction. Varying the final robot pose and trajectories across repeated interactions, thus developing a more gamified approach, could encourage the performance, enhancing user adherence to the task. It will also provide us the opportunity to investigate other aspects of the user trait, such as the emotional involvement in the task [8]. Additionally, future research will explore the reliability of adopting the implemented robotic system also in the cognitive assessment procedure, thus expanding the approach to clinical populations. Indeed, the Stroop effect is not only related to attention and concentration, but it relies on more specific executive-frontal domains [11]. Patients with anterior frontal lesions and/or characterized by executive dysfunctions experience significant difficulty in consistently activating the intended response [11]. In this direction, a multidisciplinary effort will be set to investigate the emergence of the Stroop effect with robotic administration. By evaluating the proposed system in a real clinical environment, it will determine whether patients with cognitive-related injuries may prefer a slower-responding robotic system, while those with quicker response capabilities favor a faster-moving one.

Acknowledgments. This work was developed within the project funded by Next Generation EU - "Age-It - Ageing well in an ageing society" project (PE0000015), National Recovery and Resilience Plan (NRRP) - PE8 - Mission 4, C2, Intervention 1.3. The views and opinions expressed are only those of the authors and do not necessarily reflect those of the European Union or the European Commission. Neither the European Union nor the European Commission can be held responsible for them.

Disclosure of Interests. The authors have no competing interests to declare that are relevant to the content of this article.

References

1. Tapus, A., Mataric, M.J., Scassellati, B.: Socially assistive robotics [Grand challenges of robotics]. IEEE Robot. Autom. Mag. **14** (2007). https://doi.org/10.1109/MRA.2007.339605
2. Fiorini, L., et al.: User profiling to enhance clinical assessment and human-robot interaction: a feasibility study. Int. J. Soc. Robot. (2022). https://doi.org/10.1007/s12369-022-00901-1
3. Mogena, E., Nunez, P., Gonzalez, J.L.: Automatic human body feature extraction in serious games applied to rehabilitation robotics. J. Phys. Agents **8** (2017). https://doi.org/10.14198/JoPha.2017.8.1.04
4. Eizicovits, D., Edan, Y., Tabak, I., Levy-Tzedek, S.: Robotic gaming prototype for upper limb exercise: effects of age and embodiment on user preferences and movement. Restor. Neurol. Neurosci. **36** (2018). https://doi.org/10.3233/RNN-170802
5. Jain, S., Thiagarajan, B., Shi, Z., Clabaugh, C., Matarić, M.J.: Modeling engagement in long-term, in-home socially assistive robot interventions for children with autism spectrum disorders. Sci. Robot. **5** (2020). https://doi.org/10.1126/scirobotics.aaz3791
6. Kang, H.S., Makimoto, K., Konno, R., Koh, I.S.: Review of outcome measures in PARO robot intervention studies for dementia care. Geriatr. Nurs. (Minneap) **41**, (2020). https://doi.org/10.1016/j.gerinurse.2019.09.003
7. Di Nuovo, A., Varrasi, S., Lucas, A., Conti, D., McNamara, J., Soranzo, A.: Assessment of cognitive skills via human-robot interaction and cloud computing. J. Bionic Eng. **16** (2019). https://doi.org/10.1007/s42235-019-0043-2
8. Sorrentino, A., Fiorini, L., Cavallo, F.: From the definition to the automatic assessment of engagement in human-robot interaction: a systematic review. Int. J. Soc. Robot. **16**, 1641–1663 (2024). https://doi.org/10.1007/s12369-024-01146-w
9. Sorrentino, A., et al.: Personalizing care through robotic assistance and clinical supervision. Front. Robot. AI **9** (2022). https://doi.org/10.3389/frobt.2022.883814
10. Stroop, J.R.: Studies of interference in serial verbal reactions. J. Exp. Psychol. **18** (1935). https://doi.org/10.1037/h0054651
11. Scarpina, F., Tagini, S.: The stroop color and word test (2017). https://doi.org/10.3389/fpsyg.2017.00557
12. Lansbergen, M.M., van Hell, E., Kenemans, J.L.: Impulsivity and conflict in the stroop task: an ERP study. J. Psychophysiol. **21** (2007). https://doi.org/10.1027/0269-8803.21.1.33
13. Gorner, M., Haschke, R., Ritter, H., Zhang, J.: Moveit! Task constructor for task-level motion planning. In: Proceedings - IEEE International Conference on Robotics and Automation (2019). https://doi.org/10.1109/ICRA.2019.8793898

14. Stanford, M.S., Mathias, C.W., Dougherty, D.M., Lake, S.L., Anderson, N.E., Patton, J.H.: Fifty years of the Barratt impulsiveness scale: an update and review (2009). https://doi.org/10.1016/j.paid.2009.04.008
15. Fossati, A., Di Ceglie, A., Acquarini, E., Barratt, E.S.: Psychometric properties of an Italian version of the Barrat impulsiveness Scale-11 (BIS-11) in nonclinical subjects. J. Clin. Psychol. **57** (2001). https://doi.org/10.1002/jclp.1051
16. Lugaresi, C., et al.: MediaPipe: a framework for building perception pipelines (2019)
17. Garro, F., Chiappalone, M., Buccelli, S., De Michieli, L., Semprini, M.: Neuromechanical biomarkers for robotic neurorehabilitation (2021). https://doi.org/10.3389/fnbot.2021.742163
18. Di Genova, A., et al.: A study of impulsiveness in a population with a mood disorder. Ital. J. Psychopathol. **10** (2004)
19. Stoykov, M.E., Corcos, D.M., Madhavan, S.: Movement-based priming: clinical applications and neural mechanisms. J. Mot. Behav. **49** (2017). https://doi.org/10.1080/00222895.2016.1250716

Designing Interactive Robots for Active Ageing: Co-design Insights on Large Projection Interfaces with Older Adults

John E. Muñoz[✉], Shahed Saleh, and Nahomi Ramirez

User Experience Design Department, Wilfrid Laurier University,
Brantford, ON, Canada
{jmunoz,ssaleh,rami4410}@wlu.ca

Abstract. This paper presents findings from two co-design focus groups conducted with older adults to explore the design of a socially interactive robot that uses large-scale projections (wall or floor) to support active ageing through games, movement, and cognitive engagement. While prior research has examined the use of social robots and exergames for older adults, limited work has investigated how large projection-based interaction influences robot design preferences or how gendered perspectives shape expectations of such systems. We conducted separate co-design sessions with four male and five female older adults, using visual sketches, semi-structured questions, game prototypes, and large projection demos. Thematic analysis revealed both shared and divergent insights. Participants across groups preferred wall-based projections for visibility and safety, and favored a compact, storable robot with voice interaction. However, female participants emphasized aesthetic integration, emotional tone, and privacy, while male participants prioritized challenge, progression, and task control. Our findings highlight how large projection interfaces paired with voice-interactive robots offer a promising medium for learning, training, and wellness in older adults. We discuss design implications for creating inclusive robotic systems that adapt to physical, cognitive, and social needs, and reflect on how such interfaces may generalize beyond exergaming into storytelling, cognitive training, and collaborative learning. These insights contribute to the design of age-inclusive, projection-enhanced HRI systems.

Keywords: Social Robot · Active ageing · Older adults · Exergaming · Physical activity · Large projections · Focus group

1 Introduction

The global demographic shift toward an aging population has intensified the need for innovative solutions that support active ageing, social engagement, and well-being among older adults. Interactive robots are emerging as promising tools to foster cognitive stimulation, physical activity, and meaningful social interaction in eldercare settings [22]. However, older adults are often marginalized in the design process, leading to technological solutions that may not align with their lived experiences or preferences. Co-design approaches, which position older adults as equal partners in the development of interactive technologies, have proven essential for challenging stereotypes and ensuring that robotic systems are accessible, empowering, and responsive to users' needs [16]. To bridge the gap between technological innovation and user engagement involving social robots for older adults, the integration of large projections presents a novel approach to fostering interactive activities tailored to older adults' physical and mental wellbeing [4]. Projection-based systems can transform static environments into dynamic, responsive spaces, enabling immersive activities such as guided physical exercises, cognitive games, or reminiscence therapy, while social robots provide personalized companionship and real-time feedback [30]. This combined approach addresses key challenges in assistive robotics-such as limited environmental adaptability and passive user interaction-by creating multisensory experiences that encourage movement, social connection, and cognitive stimulation [33]. For instance, large projections could visualize exercise metrics or simulate social scenarios, while robots guide users through tasks, adapting interactions based on sensor data and user preferences. Such synergy aligns with findings on the importance of customizable interfaces and user-centered design in socially assistive robotics, while mitigating adoption barriers like usability concerns and lack of engagement. However, successful implementation requires addressing usability concerns and ensuring adaptability to diverse cognitive and physical abilities. Studies consistently show that systems developed with a user-centered approach–incorporating customizable features, real-time adaptation, and stakeholder involvement–achieve higher acceptance, better usability, and more sustained engagement, especially in healthcare and social care contexts [12]. Despite the enthusiasm of these technological approaches, the design of interactive robots with large projection interfaces for older adults remains underexplored, particularly in understanding how this demographic perceives and engages with such hybrid technologies. Current research lacks insights into the nuanced ways older adults interpret robot interactions mediated through dynamic projections, which could influence the accessibility and effectiveness of these systems in promoting physical and cognitive wellbeing [29]. Additionally, while game-based learning and embodied interaction are increasingly used in assistive technologies, few studies investigate how gender differences shape preferences for robot design, interaction styles, and activity content. This knowledge gap risks perpetuating one-size-fits-all solutions that may fail to address diverse needs, potentially alienating subgroups of older users or limiting the technology's therapeutic and social benefits. Addressing these challenges is critical to ensure equitable, engaging, and adaptive robot systems that resonate across varied user profiles.

In this paper, we focus on the preliminary co-design activities of a socially assistive robot that employs a large-scale projection interface to support active aging. The primary goal of this study is to explore older adults' perspectives on the design and interaction modalities of a socially assistive robot that employs large-scale projection. Through two gender-specific focus groups, we examined participants' reactions to proposed features, interface modalities, and usage scenarios to identify relevant design considerations. While not intended to produce generalizable findings, this exploratory research contributes preliminary insights into gendered preferences and user expectations that can inform future iterations of socially assistive and embodied robots. The study emphasizes the value of early-stage co-design as a means to surface divergent and shared needs, particularly around interaction, aesthetics, personalization, and control.

2 Related Work

Social robots demonstrate significant potential in promoting cognitive engagement and physical exercise among older adults by offering personalized, interactive support tailored to individual needs. These robots, such as humanoid models like NAO or Pepper, facilitate structured physical activities through guided exercises, verbal encouragement, and real-time feedback, addressing barriers like motivation and accessibility [3]. Cognitive stimulation is achieved through interactive games, reminiscence activities, and group sessions, which enhance memory, attention, and social interaction while reducing feelings of isolation considering the presence of the social agent [15]. Systematic reviews highlight their efficacy in improving quality of life, reducing sedentary behaviors, and fostering adherence to exercise regimens, particularly when combined with evidence-based programs [25]. Similarly, large projection systems (e.g., wall, floor) have emerged as a promising modality for engaging older adults in physical and cognitive tasks in a safe and accessible manner. For instance, floor-based projections minimize visual occlusion, reduce head and neck strain, and allow for more intuitive body positioning–especially for users with mobility impairments. They are also well suited for seated interactions, which are often preferred or required by older individuals. These attributes position floor projection as an inclusive alternative to traditional screen-based interfaces and as a compelling tool for supporting physical activity, rehabilitation, and leisure among aging populations [18]. Preliminary work involving the design of robotic platforms for exergaming and large projection include the creation of the PEPE platform (Portable Exergame Platform for the Elderly) exemplifying this approach by integrating large-projected interactive content into a lightweight, transportable system co-designed with older adults, therapists, and gerontologists [4]. The design and validation of PEPE demonstrate the importance of participatory processes in shaping technologies that resonate with older adults' lived experiences, capabilities, and preferences– offering a valuable precedent for the development of socially assistive robots that incorporate projection-based interfaces [6]. Although some of those robots are interesting examples of systems that can be used to encourage physical activity and engagement among older adults, its design process still has limited information about how potential end-users envision the overall interaction with the robotic system and the content being displayed.

Co-design approaches have recently been used to involve older adults in the development of social robots, ensuring that these technologies address seniors' needs in healthcare, wellness, and daily life. Involving older adults as co-designers–rather than passive recipients–yields richer insights and more relevant design outcomes. Studies recommend long-term, iterative co-design processes that include scenario-based exploration, experiential activities, and relationship-building. This helps designers understand not just immediate needs, but also how robots can fit into the broader context of older adults' lives over time [13, 21]. For example, Alhouli et al. [2] conducted post-pandemic co-design workshops with 17 older adults to inform a robot for emotional support. They found that seniors preferred a companion-like robot (medium-sized, with soft, animal-inspired features) to alleviate loneliness and support mental well-being, underscoring the importance of matching robot form and interaction style to user expectations. Similarly, Kamino et al. [13] explored how social robots might foster a sense of ikigai (purpose in life) for older adults. Through interviews and co-design sessions with practitioners who support senior well-being, their study found that robots could act as information providers and social facilitators to help older adults engage in meaningful activities. Notably, the co-design participants emphasized that such robots must respect older adults' independence, privacy, and existing social relationships, blending into the user's lifestyle. These findings highlight how engaging end-users in design can uncover critical design requirements (e.g., privacy safeguards) and expand the robot's role beyond entertainment toward deeper psychosocial support. Physical wellness is another domain benefiting from co-design with older adults. Antony et al. [3] involved seniors, physical therapists, and engineers in a participatory design of a robot to promote exercise among older people. The process identified diverse motivators and barriers to physical activity in later life and generated a spectrum of potential robot roles (coach, companion, motivator) to assist older adults in staying active. A key insight was the need for personalization and adaptability in these exercise-coach robots, as one-size-fits-all solutions were deemed ineffective; robots should tailor their encouragement and routines to individual abilities and preferences. Co-design has also been applied to social and recreational contexts. Moreover, long-term participatory studies suggest that sustained engagement with older co-designers yields deeper insights into their evolving attitudes. Ostrowski et al. [23] conducted a 12-month co-design with 28 older adults, during which participants became more receptive to assistive functions like reminders and scheduling, while remaining cautious about features involving monitoring or data privacy. Their work produced concrete design guidelines emphasizing autonomy, privacy, and "transparent" robot behaviors to foster trust. Likewise, an international co-design effort (the GUARDIAN project) engaged older adults and caregivers across three countries to define a home-assistive robot ecosystem [10]. This project identified universal needs for monitoring health and safety, timely reminders, and social companionship, and successfully implemented a sensorized social robot platform that was validated with users to meet these needs. Together, these studies illustrate that co-designing social robots with older adults leads to more acceptable and effective solutions from health support to physical exercise and even leisure by aligning robotic assistance with what seniors genuinely value in their daily lives and by proactively addressing usability and ethical concerns. While these prior studies provide valuable insights into co-design practices and interaction modalities for older adults, they often lack integration of novel interfaces such as large-scale projection or fail to address the sustained involvement of users across design stages. Moreover, little attention has been paid to the impact of group composition (e.g., gender) on design outcomes, or what is the perceived value and personalization preferences of social robots empowered with large projection capabilities. Our work builds on this foundation by critically examining how older adults envision a projection-based socially assistive robot and highlighting gendered design preferences that have remained underexplored in the literature.

Considering this background information, we decided to create a social robot that could leverage previous research conducted in large projections, exercise, cognitive training, and learning in older adults. Since there is little information in terms of HRI specifically focused on how older adults co-design and interact with socially assistive robots for physical and cognitive engagement, this study aims to address that gap. By exploring user preferences related to embodiment, interaction modalities, projection interfaces, and personalized game-based experiences, we seek to inform the design of socially acceptable and functionally effective robotic systems tailored to aging populations.

3 Methodology

3.1 Preliminary Research and Design References

As a foundation for the co-design sessions, we conducted a preliminary research and sketching phase guided by literature in social robotics, interactive projection systems, and exergaming for older adults. Drawing from the Robo Ludens taxonomy [17], which links robot morphology with game-based interaction design, we created several concept sketches to explore diverse physical forms. The taxonomy was used to explore specific robot components such as appearance and motor ability, game features such as feedback and mechanics; and create a list of requirements able to merge

These included humanoid robots with expressive screens, anthropomorphic figures resembling pets or companions, and functional zoomorphic designs emphasizing modularity and compactness.

- **Integrated Structural Shell:** A unified form factor or shell to house the *projection hardware, motion sensors,* and *interactive components.*
- **Projection-System Integration:** Visually and spatially integrated projection components to create a seamless blend between the *robot's form* and the *projected interaction surface.*
- **Modular Mobility:** Capability for *movement in place* (e.g., head or projection tilt) and *passive or active movement through space* (e.g., wheels or handles for repositioning).

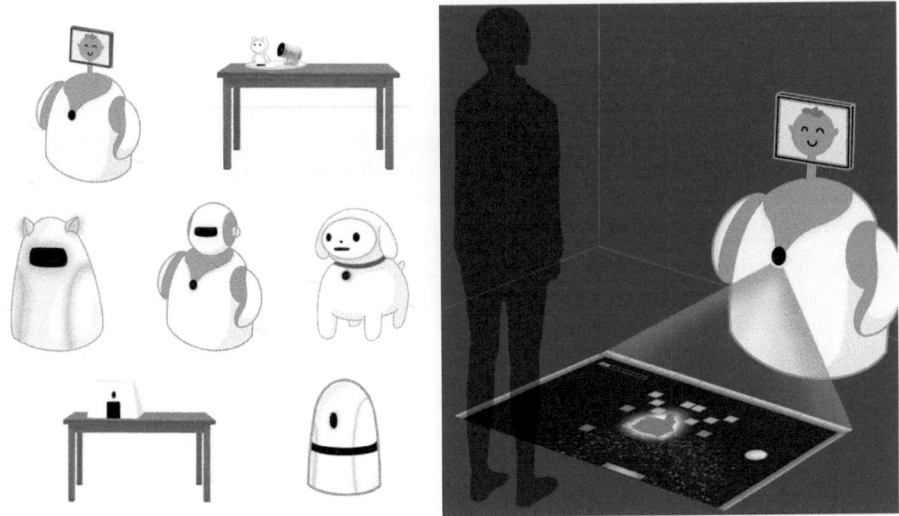

Fig. 1. Different sketches used for the preliminary design of the social robot for large projections, games and cognitive engagement.

- **Projection Adaptability:** Adjustable projection *angle and location*, allowing for both *wall and floor-based projections*, adaptable to different environments and user positions.
- **Sensor-Projection Mapping:** Mapping of *motion sensor height and user distance* to projection location, ensuring accurate interaction tracking and gesture responsiveness.

Figure 1 shows sketches resulting from the preliminary research and design efforts, showcasing multiple design of envisioned robots to be used in the focus group.

3.2 Participants

The participant group included nine older adults (4 males, 5 females) aged 64–84, all English-speaking with post-secondary education. Technology use comfort ranged from low to high, with common use of smartphones, tablets, and occasionally video games or voice assistants. Most engaged in regular physical activity and played games for exercise or mental stimulation. Health limitations were minimal, and participants generally preferred a mix of physical and cognitive activities, with frequent social and recreational engagement. Table 1 summarizes the main demographic aspects from the two groups of participants. Both groups of participants were familiar with each other and were recruited through word-of-mouth invitations.

3.3 Focus Group: Study Design

In this study, we conducted two separate co-design focus groups to explore the design of the socially interactive robot. We separated the focus group into two different sessions of males and females. The decision to separate the focus groups by gender was intentional and grounded in both methodological and cultural considerations. Prior research in HRI and gerontechnology has highlighted that older men and women often exhibit distinct preferences in their interactions with technology, particularly regarding aesthetics, emotional tone, privacy, and control [35]. By organizing gender-specific sessions, we aimed to create a comfortable and open environment in which participants could freely express their opinions without social inhibition or influence from mixed-gender dynamics. This approach allowed for deeper engagement with the design materials and fostered more candid discussions about personal needs, expectations, and lived

Table 1. Comprehensive Demographic Summary of Participants

Category	Participant Info	Summary
Gender Distribution	Male (n = 4), Female (n = 5)	Participants included both genders evenly across groups
Age Range	64–84 (Male), 73–77 (Female)	All participants were older adults
Primary Language	English	All participants reported English as their primary language
Education Level	College, PhD, Some College	Higher education levels were common in both groups
Technology Use Comfort	Ranges from "Not comfortable at all" to "Comfortable"	Male participants had more variability in comfort; female participants leaned toward "somewhat comfortable"
Types of Technology Used	Smartphones, tablets, video games, voice assistants	All used mobile devices; a few used motion-based or voice-interactive systems
Physical Activity Frequency	Regularly (3+ times/week)	Most participants reported consistent physical activity
Games for Exercise or Fun	Mostly "Yes"	All but one participant engaged in games, mostly for cognitive or light physical exercise
Types of Games	Board, trivia, puzzles, sports simulation	Game preference included traditional formats and cooperative/social games
Physical Limitations	Mild to none	Only one participant reported a limitation (impact injury)
Assistive Devices for Movement	None reported	All participants managed independently
Vision or Hearing Impairments	Some hearing or visual issues noted	One participant had compromised hearing; others used glasses
Social Engagement	Weekly social/recreational activities	Most reported regular participation in group or family-based recreation
Preferred Activity Types	"A mix of both" (mental/physical)	Broad engagement in both cognitive and physical activities
Additional Notes	Feedback on usability	Requests for ease of access, large print, simplicity, or note on confidence using tech

experiences with technology. Furthermore, the separation enabled us to identify nuanced differences in how each group perceived robot embodiment, projection-based interaction, and game content–insights that might have been diluted in a mixed-gender setting. These gender-based distinctions were critical to informing inclusive and adaptable design directions for the socially interactive robot. Both groups were recruited based on existing connections in the community to ensure a diversity of perspectives and experience levels with technology. We intentionally selected a gender-balanced sample to compare potential differences in design preferences and usability expectations for the robot. The focus group sessions were designed to elicit feedback from older adult participants on the design, functionality, and interaction preferences for the envisioned robot. Each session lasted between 60 and 90 min and included a series of structured activities and guided discussions, facilitated by a lead researcher and supported by a research assistant.

Fig. 2. Setup and demos of the floor-projected games provided during the Focus Groups

3.4 Activities, Materials and Procedure

Participants were first welcomed to the research laboratory and informed consent was collected. Then, the moderator introduced the robot concept through a live demonstration that included its core components: a motion sensor, projection system, and interactive floor- and wall-projected games (see Fig. 2). Participants had the opportunity to ask questions of the system, interact with some of the exergames and have a short discussion with the rest of the group about elicited comments and themes during the demo. To support discussion and engagement, the following materials were provided: visual aids showcasing various robot designs (e.g., humanoid, abstract, animal-like), physical mock-ups and sketches of the envisioned robots, working prototypes of projection-based games, and printed worksheets with guiding questions.

The session was divided into five main thematic blocks: (1) *Robot Design & Aesthetics*, where participants discussed preferences related to form, texture, size, and expression; (2) *Usability & Functionality*, focusing on ease of use, interaction modalities, power preferences, and adaptability; (3) *Projections & Applications*, where participants provided input on projection placement, visibility, and additional potential uses; (4) *Games & Activities*, which explored preferences regarding game types, play modes, and cultural elements; and (5) *Closing*, which invited final suggestions and offered opportunities for future involvement in prototyping. For each thematic block, verbal discussions were guided by the moderator using a semi-structured script that ensured consistency across sessions while encouraging open-ended input. In parallel, participants were provided with printed evaluation forms designed to complement the group discussion and capture individualized preferences in a structured manner around the robot design and appearance. These forms included ranking tasks (e.g., preferences for appearance, size, material, mobility, expression), open-ended explanation fields, and a visual comparison of multiple robot design options. For each robot prototype shown, participants were asked to list three elements they liked and three they disliked. This dual-format approach allowed for both rich qualitative dialogue and structured quantitative data collection, ensuring a comprehensive understanding of user needs and expectations across aesthetic, functional, and interaction domains. For each thematic block–such as physical design, mobility, interaction modalities, projection, and privacy–the facilitator introduced example scenarios and concept sketches, prompting open discussion. Immediately afterward, participants completed a corresponding printed form that captured individual preferences through scaled ratings and brief written comments. The structure of these forms mirrored the thematic blocks used in the focus groups.

Data Collection and Analysis. Focus group sessions were audio-recorded with participants' consent and transcribed verbatim for analysis. Thematic analysis was conducted using a deductive approach, guided by a set of pre-established categories that aligned with the structure of the focus group script. These categories included physical design, interaction modalities, mobility, projection preferences, personalization and autonomy, game experiences, and privacy considerations.

The lead researcher systematically reviewed the transcripts and extracted key insights within each thematic block, focusing on expressed preferences, underlying rationales, emotional responses, and design suggestions. Patterns were identified within and across the participant groups to distinguish both shared and group-specific perspectives. The preliminary insights were then discussed collaboratively with the broader research team, allowing for critical reflection and refinement of interpretations. Through this iterative process, the themes were polished and synthesized into the core findings presented in the results and visualization sections that follow. This qualitative thematic analysis approach allows for an interpretation of participant's responses across the focus groups and, given the exploratory and interpretive nature of the study, we focused on identifying patterns of meaning rather than quantifying responses. As such, no formal coding frequencies or statistical comparisons were applied, and participant counts were not used to suggest generalizability. Moreover, to improve data triangulation, the quantitative responses from the scales were used to validate and contextualize qualitative findings–for example, high ratings for projection features were cross-referenced with participant quotes that emphasized visibility and clarity. Discrepancies between ratings and verbal comments were discussed within the research team to ensure consistent interpretation and to refine emerging themes.

4 Results

Thematic analysis of participant responses revealed overlapping as well as gender-specific preferences across seven key categories: physical design, mobility, interaction modalities, projection system, gaming preferences, personalization and autonomy, and privacy. Table 2 summarizes the key comparative insights across these categories.

4.1 Physical Design and Mobility

Participants from both groups preferred a compact, lightweight robot that could be stored when not in use. Female participants emphasized the ability to hide or store the device like a household appliance: *"You'd want to be able to put it away, wouldn't want it out all the time... likened to a toaster or a Bose radio"* (FG-F). Several women also requested a handle: *"It needs some sort of handle on it so you can carry it"* (Focus Group Female, FG-F).

Male participants preferred a design that was *"not too heavy"* and *"practical"*, and were open to either a stationary or mobile format, as long as the robot remained unobtrusive. One participant commented: *"A tabletop version makes sense–easy to store and use when needed"* (Focus Group Male, FG-M).

Participants completed printed forms designed to capture their individual preferences on key aspects of the robot's design and interaction features. Each form included visual comparisons, ranking tasks, and short-answer explanations. The following summarizes the aggregated findings across all participants:

- **Appearance:**
  - *Male Participants:* Most preferred simple designs with minimal distractions. Frequently liked elements included the motion tracking camera, projector, and LED light strips. Moving arms and animal-like appendages were often marked as dislikes. Humanoid or abstract forms were preferred for being more neutral and purpose-driven.
  - *Female Participants:* Similarly favored designs that were clean and non-intrusive. Light and sound-based expression was more frequently appreciated than animated faces or overly detailed features. Dislikes were directed at unnecessary moving components and "tails," with preferences leaning toward aesthetically calm and compact appearances.

- **Material:**
  - *Male Participants:* Soft or plastic materials were preferred for safety, warmth, and familiarity. Metal was often considered cold and less appropriate for home use.
  - *Female Participants:* Also showed a strong preference for soft or plastic textures. There was emphasis on materials that felt friendly and approachable, especially for individuals with arthritis or limited dexterity.
- **Size:**
  - *Male Participants:* Preferred smaller, tabletop-sized robots that would not interfere with movement or living space. Storage and visibility were common concerns.
  - *Female Participants:* Echoed preferences for compactness, citing portability and ease of handling. Participants emphasized not wanting large devices that could clutter their space.
- **Mobility:**
  - *Male Participants:* Preferred stationary or manually moveable robots. Autonomous movement was considered unnecessary or potentially problematic in confined areas.
  - *Female Participants:* Generally favored fixed or manually repositioned robots as well. Some voiced concerns about safety and unpredictability if the robot moved autonomously.
- **Moving Limbs and Expression:**
  - *Male Participants:* Static limbs were preferred, with comments noting that unnecessary motion would be distracting or confusing. Simple light and sound cues were rated more favorably than expressive animations.
  - *Female Participants:* Agreed that lights and sounds provided adequate feedback. Animated faces and moving limbs were often deemed excessive or unnecessary, especially for task-oriented interaction.

4.2 Usability and Interaction

Both groups highlighted ease of use, concise instructions, and minimal setup as essential. One participant said: *"Not too wordy, with just simple commands"* (FG-F). Women expressed a preference for rechargeable batteries: *"I would probably prefer battery so I can move it around, but I want to be able to plug it in to recharge–like a phone"* (FG-F), while men leaned toward plug-in power for dependability.

Voice interaction was consistently preferred across both groups: *"The voice command is a must–especially for people with arthritis"* (FG-F). Familiarity with Alexa and Siri was widespread: *"We use it all the time at my kids' house–'Hey Alexa!'–so we're used to it"* (FG-F).

4.3 Projection and Display

Large wall-based projection was unanimously favored due to visibility and safety: *"If it has to project on something, you're going to have to move it anyway to the right spot"* (FG-F) as opposed to the large floor projections. Participants emphasized adjustable text size, brightness, and contrast for better readability.

4.4 Robot Personality and Feedback

Minimal expressiveness was favored, with LED indicators and auditory cues preferred over animated faces: *"Lights are enough–green for ready, red for error"* (FG-F). Another participant noted: *"If I'm concentrating on the game, I'm not looking at the robot anyway"* (FG-F).

Participants preferred an encouraging voice tone. As one participant put it: *"It has to be something that encourages you–enthusiastic, loud enough, but not a robotic GPS voice"* (FG-F).

4.5 Game Preferences and Adaptability

Participants' responses revealed nuanced expectations based on their abilities and interests. Female participants frequently mentioned cooperative and social games such as puzzles, rhythm, or simulation games that could be played with family members or adapted to their mood and energy level. Male participants expressed interest in memory-based games, trivia, and skill-based challenges like golf or virtual travel, often framed around performance or personal tracking. Therefore, males were especially drawn to rhythm and sports simulation games: *"If it's got golf or cycling like the gym equipment, I'm in"* (FG-M). Females desired flexibility: *"I want to be able to choose depending on how I feel that day... something cognitive or physical, and not too intense"* (FG-F).

Voice-controlled game selection was well received: *"You could just say, 'Play the boat game on speed five,' and it would start"* (FG-F). Additionally, multi-user support was recommended: *"It should remember me and also let my grandkids play with it when they're visiting"* (FG-F).

4.6 Personalization and Autonomy

Both groups agreed the system should adapt to user preferences over time. Participants emphasized that it should adjust to various physical needs: *"If someone's in a wheelchair or uses a walker, it should be able to adapt to that"* (FG-F). Female participants proposed multi-user profiles for shared use among family members.

Regarding autonomy, participants expressed a desire for limited and user-controlled automation. Most participants did not want unsolicited reminders: *"I don't want it pinging at me that it's time to play. That'd be annoying"* (FG-F). Others acknowledged such features might be useful in clinical or memory care settings but were not currently needed. Male participants echoed the desire for the robot to be *"present when needed–but not always present"* (FG-M).

4.7 Privacy

Privacy concerns were strongly voiced, particularly around internet connectivity and passive surveillance. One participant noted: *"I don't want it connected to the internet. You never know who's watching"* (FG-F). Participants emphasized the need for full control over microphones and cameras, with an option to turn them off at will: *"Definitely want to be able to turn it off"* (FG-F). Trust in the system's autonomy was closely linked to its perceived respect for user privacy and discretion. A summary of the main privacy concerns pointed out by participants can be seen as follows:

- **Internet connectivity:** Participants expressed discomfort with the robot being connected to the internet, fearing unauthorized access or surveillance.
- **Camera and microphone control:** There was a strong desire for manual control over microphones and cameras, including the ability to fully turn them off when not in use.
- **Always-on presence:** Participants did not want the robot to be constantly active or present in the home. They preferred a system that could be easily stored or deactivated.
- **Autonomy and unsolicited behavior:** Concerns were raised about the robot initiating actions (e.g., reminders) without explicit user prompts, which could feel intrusive or patronizing.
- **Trust and data security:** Participants questioned how collected data would be stored and used, indicating a lack of trust in smart technologies that might monitor or record activity without consent.

5 Discussion

Our co-design sessions highlight the potential of combining large projection interfaces with voice-interactive robots to support active ageing, while revealing important differences in older adults' design preferences. Through sketches, prototypes, and demos, we found common priorities such as favoring wall-based projections and compact, storable robots, alongside gendered variations: female participants valued aesthetic integration, emotional tone, and privacy, whereas male participants emphasized challenge and task control. These findings emphasize the need for adaptable, inclusive designs that balance functional utility with emotional and social considerations.

5.1 Design Implications for Social Robots with Large Projection

The results of this study offer actionable insights into the design of social robots tailored for older adults. Our co-design sessions revealed a strong preference among older adults for wall-based projections positioned at eye level, as these were perceived to enhance visibility and reduce the physical risk associated with downward gaze and floor occlusion. This finding aligns with inclusive interface design principles that emphasize the importance of visual ergonomics for aging users, including the use of high-contrast displays, minimal glare, and large, easily legible fonts [20]. Research has shown that projection systems designed for older adults should support comfortable posture and physical interaction by dynamically adapting to a user's environment and minimizing the need for excessive

Table 2. Summary of Co-Design Insights by Gender

Theme	Male Participants	Female Participants
Preferred Design	Humanoid, simple face, minimal expressiveness	Compact, decorative if visible, no expressive features
Material	Soft or plastic preferred over metallic	Soft or plastic; light weight is key
Size & Portability	Tabletop preferred, some interest in mobile version	Strong preference for compact, portable, with carrying handle
Mobility	Mixed views–some prefer stationary, some mobile-on-demand	Mixed–manual mobility preferred, not autonomous movement
Voice & Interaction	Calm, friendly female voice (Alexa-like), voice commands preferred	Encouraging, positive voice; strong emphasis on voice commands for accessibility
Interface & Feedback	Lights/sounds over visual expressions; voice and motion over buttons	Simple LED indicators (e.g., green = ready); intuitive and minimal commands
Power Source	Prefer plug-in for reliability	Rechargeable battery preferred, but plug-in acceptable
Projection Preference	Wall projection preferred for visibility and balance reasons	Strong preference for wall projections; concerns about fall risks
Game & Activity Preferences	Rhythm, golf, skiing, cognitive challenges; prefer social/multiplayer activities	Adaptable cognitive & physical games; like voice-controlled selection and multi-user profiles
Personalization	Adaptive difficulty, memory of user progress	Flexible difficulty based on energy/mood; multi-user profiles
Privacy & Notifications	Wanted less intrusive presence–"available when needed"	Wanted control over activation; preferred to turn off mics/cameras; disliked frequent reminders
Additional Features	Docking station, virtual travel, exercise, storytelling	Support for mobility devices, home-use & clinical adaptability, decorative blending in the home

motion or strain [24]. Furthermore, multimodal feedback–such as the combination of audio and visual cues–has been shown to enhance task performance and confidence in older users engaging with augmented reality systems [31]. From a system design perspective, these findings suggest that social robots incorporating projection-based interfaces should prioritize user-aligned positioning, accessible gesture or voice commands, and redundancy across sensory modalities to support varying physical and perceptual needs [1]. While projection-based interfaces have been explored in ambient systems and interactive surfaces, their integration into embodied robotic platforms remains underexamined. Our study highlights how large-scale projections can enhance visibility and reduce reliance on screens or physical buttons–features that are particularly beneficial for older adults. However, combining projection with robot mobility, expressiveness, and environmental conditions (e.g., lighting, positioning) introduces new design challenges. Prior work on systems such as PEPE [4] and projection-supported interaction cues [27] suggests that aligning projected content with spatial interaction and user orientation is critical for maintaining clarity and engagement in human-robot communication. These findings reinforce the importance of iterative testing in real-world settings to evaluate how projection-robot integration impacts usability and communication effectiveness. Altogether, the integration of large projections in social robotics offers a promising path for inclusive interaction when coupled with participatory design strategies.

5.2 Gendered Design Perspectives

Our co-design sessions revealed marked gendered differences in how older adults envisioned their interactions with social robots. Male participants generally favored minimalist, utilitarian designs that emphasized goal-oriented features such as performance tracking, memory recall, and structured feedback. In contrast, female participants emphasized relational aspects of the robot, including emotional warmth, the ability to personalize appearance or behavior, and greater control over interaction timing. These findings are consistent with existing research on gendered HRI preferences. Studies have shown that older men are often more accepting of assistive robot functions and show a higher willingness to delegate tasks such as scheduling, shopping assistance, or exercise monitoring to robotic systems [7]. In contrast, older women have been found to approach assistive robots more cautiously, often prioritizing familiarity, emotional resonance, and trust over purely functional benefits [14]. Preferences for anthropomorphic versus pet-like robots also appear to diverge by gender, with older men typically preferring human-like robots and older women expressing more comfort with animal-inspired designs [9]. These patterns suggest that social robots targeting older adults should support customizable interfaces and interaction profiles, allowing users to shape both the aesthetic and functional dimensions of the robot to match their expectations. Designing with gender-responsive adaptability in mind–such as offering profile-based interaction modes or emotional calibration–can enhance long-term engagement and user satisfaction in multi-user home environments.

5.3 System Customization

Our findings reinforce the importance of personalization in the design of socially assistive robots for older adults. Participants expressed a strong desire for systems that adapt to individual preferences–such as voice tone, projection settings, and interaction timing–rather than relying on fixed, one-size-fits-all behaviors. This aligns with prior work emphasizing that personalization enhances usability and acceptance among older users [5,19]. For example, female participants in our study prioritized emotional tone and home integration, while male participants valued performance tracking and memory recall–highlighting the need for multi-user profiles and flexible configurations.

These results echo broader evidence that even modest personalization, such as adjusting voice tone or interaction style, can significantly improve engagement and trust [11,35]. In particular, the preference for emotionally supportive or familiar voice characteristics among female participants suggests opportunities for tailoring robot speech to user identity and context. As in previous long-term deployments, adaptability in both functional and affective domains appears crucial to maintaining user satisfaction [19].

5.4 Emotional and Relational Dimensions of Interaction

Our results show that voice-based and game-based modalities were central to fostering emotional engagement and building a sense of connection with the robot. Participants emphasized the importance of familiar and supportive vocal tones, with several expressing a preference for calm or encouraging voices resembling those of caregivers, family members, or voice-activated popular systems (e.g., Alexa, Siri). These findings support prior work showing that older adults are more receptive to socially assistive robots when the robot's voice fosters warmth and familiarity [26,35]. The preference for voice interactions over buttons or visual expressions was consistent across groups, highlighting the role of conversational cues in establishing trust.

In addition, game-based interaction was seen not only as cognitively stimulating but also as a means of social connection. Participants appreciated games that could adapt to their energy levels or involve others, aligning with evidence that personalized and routine-integrated play can enhance mood and reduce loneliness [8,28]. Although no long-term interaction was conducted in our study, the emphasis on emotional support, particularly from female participants, underscores the relevance of designing relational cues that go beyond task execution. Emotionally attuned systems–those that respond to tone, affect, or situational context–may be better suited for sustained engagement in older populations [32,34].

5.5 Limitations and Future Work

This study was based on a limited number of gender-homogeneous focus groups and may not capture the full diversity of older adult perspectives, including variations related to culture, socio-economic background, cognitive or physical ability, and prior exposure to technology. While gender-based grouping allowed for the exploration of certain social dynamics, it also constrained the opportunity to observe interactions in mixed-gender or intergenerational contexts. Therefore, while this study provides valuable exploratory insights, it is constrained by a small and non-random sample size drawn from pre-existing social groups. This limits the generalizability of the findings and may not fully represent the diversity of older adult populations, particularly in terms of cognitive, physical, cultural, and socioeconomic variation. In addition, the findings were based on hypothetical interactions with concept materials rather than the long-term use of a physical prototype, which may limit ecological validity.

Future research should expand the participant pool to include individuals from a wider range of communities, including those with cognitive impairments, mobility challenges, and those from underrepresented or rural populations. Expansion of participant's recruitment could use snowball sampling techniques and partnerships with rehabilitation centers, community organizations, and care facilities to diversify the sample and engage a broader range of older adults. These expanded efforts will aim to capture a more inclusive spectrum of needs and preferences across different usage contexts. Also, longitudinal studies involving functional prototypes in real-life settings would provide more robust insights into sustained interaction, adaptation, and trust development. Iterative design cycles that involve older adults throughout all stages–from ideation to testing and refinement–are also needed to ensure the robot evolves in alignment with users' changing needs and lived experiences. Moreover, future work should explore how system customization preferences differ in multi-user households and how shared devices might accommodate individualized configurations without compromising usability. This ongoing participatory approach remains essential to designing inclusive and socially meaningful robotic systems for aging populations. Another valuable direction for future research is to explore mixed-gender and intergenerational focus groups to better understand how social dynamics influence preferences for shared or multi-user robotic systems. Such sessions may uncover collaborative expectations, role negotiation, or differing comfort levels that are not observable in gender-homogeneous groups, thereby enriching the design implications for household deployment of socially assistive robots.

6 Conclusion

This study explored the co-design of a socially assistive robot equipped with large-scale projection capabilities, grounded in the lived experiences and preferences of older adults. Through gender-specific focus groups, we identified key themes related to physical design, mobility, interaction modalities, game preferences, personalization, and privacy. Findings revealed both shared expectations–such as the value of voice-based interaction and cognitive engagement–and gendered differences in emotional needs, control, and functionality. The use of structured co-design activities enabled us to translate these insights into actionable design implications, particularly around visual accessibility, emotional engagement, and trust. By integrating older adults directly into the design process, this work contributes to a more inclusive vision of social robotics–one that respects diversity in aging, prioritizes meaningful interaction, and leverages familiar modalities such as wall projections to enhance everyday use. Future work will involve prototyping and evaluating these concepts in real-world contexts to assess long-term engagement, usability, and perceived benefit.

Acknowledgments. We would like to sincerely thank Wilfrid Laurier University for providing the necessary funding through their start-up funds to JEM. We are also deeply grateful to all the older adult participants who generously contributed their time, insights, and enthusiasm throughout the co-design sessions. Their valuable input was essential to the success of this study.

References

1. Achilleos, A., et al.: Lessons learned from older adults: fusing an augmented reality, assisted living and social interaction platform. SN Comput. Sci. **4**, 378 (2023)
2. Alhouli, S., Almania, N., Ahmad, M.I., Hyde, M., Sahoo, D.: Older adults' emotional challenges and co-design preferences for a social robot after the Covid-19 pandemic. In: Proceedings of the 32nd IEEE International Conference on Robot and Human Interactive Communication (RO-MAN), pp. 2245–2252. IEEE (2023). https://doi.org/10.1109/RO-MAN57019.2023.10309490
3. Antony, V.N., Cho, S.M., Huang, C.: Co-designing with older adults, for older adults: robots to promote physical activity. In: Proceedings of the 2023 ACM/IEEE International Conference on Human-Robot Interaction (HRI '23), 10 p. (2023). https://doi.org/10.1145/3568162.3576995
4. Bermúdez i Badia, S., et al.: Development and validation of a mixed reality exergaming platform for fitness training of older adults. In: Everyday Virtual and Augmented Reality, pp. 119–145. Springer (2023)
5. Bedaf, S., Marti, P., Witte, L.D.: What are the preferred characteristics of a service robot for the elderly? A multi-country focus group study with older adults and caregivers. Assist. Technol. **31**(3), 147–157 (2019). https://doi.org/10.1080/10400435.2017.1402390
6. Čaić, M., Avelino, J., Mahr, D., Odekerken-Schröder, G., Bernardino, A.: Robotic versus human coaches for active aging: an automated social presence perspective. Int. J. Soc. Robot. **12**(4), 867–882 (2020)
7. Cavallo, F., et al.: Robotic services acceptance in smart environments with older adults: user satisfaction and acceptability study. J. Med. Internet Res. **20**(9), e264 (2018)
8. Cesário, P., Santos, S., Lourenço, B., Martins, I., Gonçalves, P.J.S.: Towards older adults cognitive and emotional stimulation via robotic cognitive games. Soc. Sci. **8**(11), 298 (2019). https://doi.org/10.3390/socsci8110298
9. Chiu, C.J., Hsieh, S., Li, C.W.: Needs and preferences of middle-aged and older adults in Taiwan for companion robots and pets: survey study. J. Med. Internet Res. **23**(6), e23471 (2021)

10. Ciuffreda, I., et al.: Design and development of a technological platform based on a sensorized social robot for supporting older adults and caregivers: GUARDIAN ecosystem. Int. J. Soc. Robot. (2023). https://doi.org/10.1007/s12369-023-01038-5
11. Gasteiger, N., et al.: Participatory design, development, and testing of assistive health robots with older adults: an international four-year project. ACM Trans. Hum. Robot Interact. **11**(4) (2022). Article 26. https://doi.org/10.1145/3533726
12. Jerez, A., Iglesias, A., Pérez-Lorenzo, J.M., Tudela, A., Cruces, A., Bandera, J.P.: An user-centered evaluation of two socially assistive robots integrated in a retirement home. Int. J. Soc. Robot. **16**(9), 2043–2063 (2024)
13. Kamino, W., et al.: Making meaning together: co-designing a social robot for older adults with ikigai experts. Int. J. Soc. Robot. **15**, 983–998 (2023). https://doi.org/10.1007/s12369-023-01006-z
14. Kislev, E.: The robot-gender divide: how and why men and women differ in their attitudes toward social robots. Soc. Sci. Comput. Rev. **41**(6), 2230–2248 (2023)
15. Lin, Y.C., Fan, J., Tate, J.A., Sarkar, N., Mion, L.C.: Use of robots to encourage social engagement between older adults. Geriatr. Nurs. **43**, 97–103 (2022)
16. Macalupu Chira, V.A., Rittenbruch, M., Chamorro-Koc, M., Donovan, J.: Designing the future together: a collaborative designerly approach to socially interactive robots with older adults as co-designers. J. Responsible Innov. **11**(1), 2390708 (2024)
17. Muñoz, J.E., Dautenhahn, K.: Robo Ludens: a game design taxonomy for multiplayer games using socially interactive robots. ACM Trans. Hum. Robot Interact. (THRI) **10**(4), 1–28 (2021)
18. Munoz, J.E., Gonçalves, A., Rúbio Gouveia, É., Cameirao, M.S., Bermudez i Badia, S.: Lessons learned from gamifying functional fitness training through human-centered design methods in older adults. Games Health J. **8**(6), 387–406 (2019)
19. Napoli, C.D., Ercolano, G., Rossi, S.: Personalized home-care support for the elderly: a field experience with a social robot at home. User Model. User Adap. Inter. **33**(4), 405–440 (2022). https://doi.org/10.1007/s11257-022-09333-y
20. Nishchyk, A., Sanderson, N.C., Chen, W.: Elderly-centered usability heuristics for augmented reality design and development. Univ. Access Inf. Soc. **24**(4), 621–641 (2025)
21. Ostrowski, A.K., Breazeal, C., Park, H.W.: Long-term co-design guidelines: empowering older adults as co-designers of social robots. In: 2021 30th IEEE International Conference on Robot & Human Interactive Communication (RO-MAN), pp. 1165–1172. IEEE (2021)
22. Ostrowski, A.K., Breazeal, C., Park, H.W.: Mixed-method long-term robot usage: older adults' lived experience of social robots. In: 2022 17th ACM/IEEE International Conference on Human-Robot Interaction (HRI), pp. 33–42. IEEE (2022)
23. Ostrowski, A.K., Zhang, J., Breazeal, C., Park, H.W.: Promising directions for human-robot interactions defined by older adults. Front. Robot. AI **11** (2024). Article 1289414. https://doi.org/10.3389/frobt.2024.1289414
24. Park, Y.J., Ro, H., Lee, N.K., Han, T.D.: Deep-care: projection-based home care augmented reality system with deep learning for elderly. Appl. Sci. **9**(18), 3897 (2019)
25. Pu, L., Moyle, W., Jones, C., Todorovic, M.: The effectiveness of social robots for older adults: a systematic review and meta-analysis of randomized controlled studies. Gerontologist **59**(1), e37–e51 (2019)

26. Seaborn, K., Sekiguchi, T., Tokunaga, S., Miyake, N.P., Otake-Matsuura, M.: Voice over body? Older adults' reactions to robot and voice assistant facilitators of group conversation. Int. J. Soc. Robot. **15**, 143–163 (2023). https://doi.org/10.1007/s12369-022-00925-7
27. Sone, S., Kishi, T., Ikeda, T.: A projection-based approach for clarifying interaction partners in human-robot communication. Front. Robot. AI **12**, 1534060 (2025)
28. Tan, C.K., Lou, V.W.Q., Cheng, C.Y.M., He, P.C., Khoo, V.E.J.: Improving the social well-being of single older adults using the LOVOT social robot: qualitative phenomenological study. JMIR Hum. Fact. **11**, e56669 (2024). https://doi.org/10.2196/56669
29. Tobis, S., Piasek, J., Cylkowska-Nowak, M., Suwalska, A.: Robots in eldercare: how does a real-world interaction with the machine influence the perceptions of older people? Sensors **22**(5), 1717 (2022)
30. Vagnetti, R., et al.: Social robots and sensors for enhanced aging at home: mixed methods study with a focus on mobility and socioeconomic factors. JMIR Aging **7**, e63092 (2024)
31. Williams, T.J., Jones, S.L., Lutteroth, C., Dekoninck, E., Boyd, H.C.: Augmented reality and older adults: a comparison of prompting types. In: Proceedings of the 2021 CHI Conference on Human Factors in Computing Systems, pp. 1–13. ACM (2021)
32. Yoo, I., Park, D., Lee, O.E., Park, A.: Investigating Older adults' use of a socially assistive robot via time series clustering and user profiling: descriptive analysis study. JMIR Formative Res. **8**, e41093 (2024). https://doi.org/10.2196/41093
33. Yuan, S., Coghlan, S., Lederman, R., Waycott, J.: Social robots in aged care: care staff experiences and perspectives on robot benefits and challenges. Proc. ACM Hum. Comput. Interact. **6**(CSCW2), 1–23 (2022)
34. Zafrani, O., Nimrod, G., Edan, Y.: Between fear and trust: older adults' evaluation of socially assistive robots. Int. J. Hum Comput Stud. **171**, 102981 (2023). https://doi.org/10.1016/j.ijhcs.2022.102981
35. Zhou, C., Dong, W.: How do older adults react to social robots' offspring-like voices. Soc. Sci. Med. **264**, 117545 (2025). https://doi.org/10.1016/j.socscimed.2024.117545

SoK: A Systematic Review of Privacy and Security in Healthcare Robotics

Mayank Grover(✉) and Sanchari Das

George Mason University, Fairfax, VA 22030, USA
{mgrover3,sdas35}@gmu.edu

Abstract. Robotic systems are increasingly integrated into healthcare settings, providing physical assistance, social interaction, remote diagnostics, and data-intensive services. Although these systems collect sensitive multimodal data, such as audio, video, physiological signals, and contextual metadata, existing security frameworks often fail to adequately address the combined challenges of privacy, cybersecurity, and human-robot interaction (HRI). To understand further, we conducted a systematic review of 62 peer-reviewed studies from an initial pool of 393 articles. Using our proposed *PRoSec-HRI (Privacy and Robotic Security in Healthcare Robotics Interaction) framework*, we identified leading technical strategies, including differential privacy for sensor data anonymization, federated learning for decentralized model training, blockchain-based authentication for auditable processes, and formal verification for privacy-compliant behavior. Despite majority of studies discuss privacy-preserving (68%) and cybersecurity (76%) techniques, we found only 10% conducted in-situ evaluations, and just 13% considered firmware or lifecycle security. Moreover, only 14% demonstrated regulatory compliance (e.g., GDPR, HIPAA), and a mere 9% addressed real-time threat mitigation. While 61% papers featured trust-building mechanisms, such as symbolic gestures or consent dashboards, only 11% of those accounted for cultural sensitivity or user education. Our findings expose significant gaps and provide a foundation for developing privacy-aware, secure, and user-centered healthcare robots.

Keywords: Privacy · Cybersecurity · Healthcare Robotics · Human-Robot Interaction · Regulatory Compliance

1 Introduction

Robotic systems are increasingly transforming key sectors by performing complex tasks traditionally carried out by humans, leading to significant gains in efficiency, accuracy, and capability [22,49]. In healthcare, their rapid adoption [71] involves frequent interactions with users and environments, resulting in the collection and processing of highly sensitive multimodal data, including audio, video, physiological signals, and contextual metadata [47,78]. This raises pressing concerns about privacy, security, and data governance. Healthcare applications range from remote diagnostics [42,67] and robotic-assisted surgery [30,79] to elderly care [41,80,92] and rehabilitation [52,68], all of which demand robust privacy and cybersecurity measures. The scale of this deployment is reflected in market trends, with the global healthcare robotics sector projected to grow from USD 10B in 2022 to over USD 35B by 2030, representing a compound annual growth rate of nearly 17% [72].

As healthcare robots increasingly handle data that is both sensitive and mission-critical [43], concerns around privacy and cybersecurity have become more acute. These challenges extend beyond basic data protection and span a wide range of technical and procedural domains [45]. Key issues include secure data acquisition from sensors and interfaces [77], encrypted and resilient storage [32], tamper-resistant transmission protocols [70], and fine-grained, role-based access control [77]. Additional concerns involve long-term data retention and deletion [38], system auditability [73,94], and adaptive consent mechanisms that reflect evolving patient preferences and regulatory requirements [51].

Motivated by the growing privacy & security challenges in healthcare robotic systems, and the lack of a consolidated technical taxonomy in existing literature, we conducted a systematic review of prior work at the intersection of privacy, cybersecurity, and HRI. Using a broad, keyword-driven search across major scholarly databases, we identified an initial corpus of 393 papers. After applying inclusion criteria through a structured screening process, we selected a final set of 62 peer-reviewed articles that directly addressed technical, regulatory, and human-centered dimensions of privacy and security in healthcare robotics. To analyze this body of work, we developed the *Privacy and Robotic Security in Healthcare Robotics Interaction (PRoSec-HRI)* framework. While inspired by earlier frameworks [14,15,65,75,81], PRoSec-HRI is uniquely tailored to the healthcare robotics context. It bridges the gap between high-level policy requirements and low-level engineering implementations, enabling more actionable and context-aware privacy and security solutions. Additionally, it supports comparative evaluation across robot types, deployment environments (clinical, home, and rehabilitative), and stakeholder needs, providing a structured approach for assessing privacy and security readiness. Overall, through this work we make the following key **contributions**:

- We present a comprehensive systematization of peer-reviewed studies, spanning privacy and cybersecurity practices in healthcare robotics.
- We highlight underexplored intersections between technical security solutions and human-robot trust dynamics, particularly in sensitive domains such as eldercare and telemedicine.
- We provide a structured mapping between real-world deployment challenges and gaps in regulatory compliance, emphasizing inconsistencies in how frameworks like GDPR and HIPAA are applied to robotics.

2 PRoSec-HRI Framework

We introduce the *Privacy and Robotic Security in Healthcare Robotics Interaction (PRoSec-HRI)* framework (illustrated in Fig. 1) to support researchers and developers in integrating privacy and security measures specifically tailored to healthcare robotic systems. The framework draws on foundational research, including Jain et al.'s work on cloud security in robotics [34], cybersecurity insights by Haskard and Herath [32], Jia et al.'s studies on social robotics [38], and Oruma's user-centered security approaches [69]. PRoSec-HRI builds on these contributions by unifying them into specialized, healthcare-focused domains, with a distinct emphasis on integrated technical solutions suited for real-world healthcare environments. Our framework is further informed by prior frameworks created in cybersecurity and privacy [14,15,65,75,81].

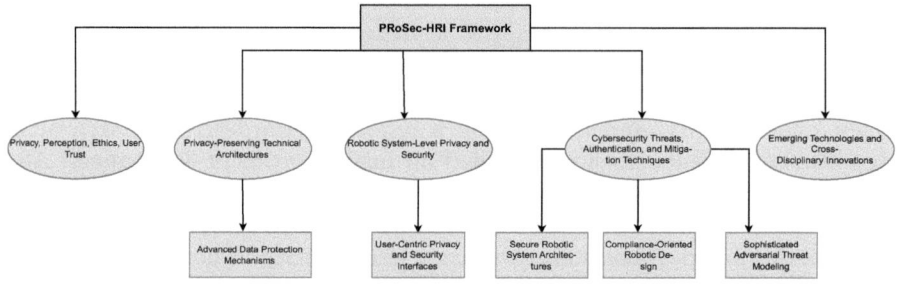

Fig. 1. The PRoSec-HRI Framework

The **first domain**, *Privacy Perception, Ethics, and User Trust*, focuses on trust calibration, perceived privacy risks, and the ethical implications of data collection in robotic systems. This domain includes empirical studies and user assessments that examine trust dynamics, evaluate risk perception, and analyze responses to transparency and ethical decision-making. The **second domain**, *Privacy-Preserving Technical Architectures*, highlights computational and infrastructural techniques designed to enhance privacy. These include differential privacy for real-time sensor fusion, secure multi-party computation for collaborative diagnostics, federated learning for decentralized data modeling, blockchain-based auditing for immutable decision records, and anonymization strategies using thermal or non-intrusive sensors. The **third domain**, *Robotic System-Level Privacy and Security*, encompasses end-to-end strategies for securing the healthcare robotics ecosystem. It covers integration with Electronic Health Records (EHRs), data lifecycle management from acquisition to deletion, encryption of stored and transmitted data, enforcement of role-based access controls, and the development of secure cloud infrastructures aligned with regulations such as HIPAA, GDPR, and other regional standards.

The **fourth domain**, *Cybersecurity Threats, Authentication, and Mitigation Techniques*, identifies and categorizes the threat landscape unique to healthcare robots. Key concerns include Man-in-the-Middle (MITM) attacks during telehealth sessions, GPS and biometric sensor spoofing, Denial-of-Service (DoS) and Distributed Denial-of-Service (DDoS) attacks on remote platforms, ransomware infiltration, electromagnetic side-channel exploits, firmware manipulation, and advanced data exfiltration methods. To counter these threats, the framework incorporates biometric and multi-factor authentication, secure firmware updates, trusted computing hardware, secure boot protocols, cryptographic communication channels (e.g., SSL/TLS), and intrusion detection systems tailored to robotic environments. The **fifth domain**, *Emerging Technologies and Cross-Disciplinary Innovations*, explores novel tools and interdisciplinary approaches that are reshaping privacy and cybersecurity in healthcare robotics. This domain captures the integration of advanced technologies and frameworks that extend beyond conventional security models.

To further structure the analysis, the PRoSec-HRI framework introduces a set of analytical clusters that categorize research by technical depth and methodological rigor. These include: (1) *Advanced Data Protection Mechanisms*, which focus on cryptography, anonymization, and secure data flows; (2) *User-Centric Privacy and Security Interfaces*, which emphasize transparency tools, consent systems, and user data controls; (3) *Secure Robotic System Architectures*, which outline layered security design principles; (4) *Compliance-Oriented Robotic Design*, which align system features with legal and regulatory requirements; and (5) *Sophisticated Adversarial Threat Modeling*, which address complex attack scenarios and their corresponding defenses.

3 Method

We conducted a systematic literature review to identify, examine, and synthesize existing research at the intersection of privacy, cybersecurity, and human–robot interaction within healthcare robotics. Our methodology followed a structured three-phase process consisting of: (1) literature search, (2) screening and selection, and (3) thematic analysis. Figure 2 illustrates the methodological workflow, which we adapted and refined based on established Systematization of Knowledge (SoK) study methodologies presented in prior works, including Das [14,21], Huang et al. [33], Das et al. [17–20], Noah and Das [64], Duzgun et al. [24], Jones et al. [39], Zezulak et al. [96], Stephenson et al. [84], Majumdar and Das [55], Shrestha et al. [81,82], Das and Salman [19], Kishnani et al. [44], Surani and Das [85], Noah et al. [66], Saka and Das [74], Adhikari et al. [1], and Tazi et al. [88–91]. This study aimed to address the following research questions, each capturing a critical aspect of privacy and cybersecurity in healthcare robotics:

- **RQ1:** What privacy-preserving techniques (e.g., data minimization, anonymization, consent mechanisms) are currently implemented in assistive and social healthcare robots, particularly in home and elderly care settings?
- **RQ2:** What cybersecurity threats (e.g., data interception, unauthorized access, firmware tampering) have been identified in healthcare robotic systems, and what mitigation strategies have been proposed in the literature?

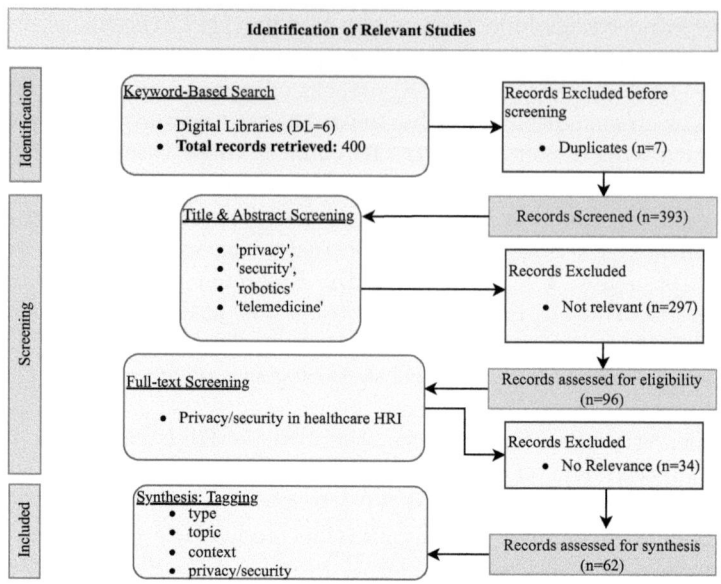

Fig. 2. PRISMA flow diagram illustrating the selection process for relevant studies.

- **RQ3:** To what extent do current healthcare robots comply with established data protection regulations such as the General Data Protection Regulation (GDPR) and the Health Insurance Portability and Accountability Act (HIPAA), and where do gaps remain in the regulatory coverage of autonomous robotic systems?
- **RQ4:** How do the design and implementation of privacy and security features in healthcare robots affect user trust, adoption, and perceived transparency among patients, caregivers, and clinical professionals?

3.1 Literature Search

We initiated the review by executing a carefully constructed keyword-driven search strategy across multiple leading academic digital libraries. This strategy aimed to ensure a broad yet precise capture of literature across engineering, healthcare, cybersecurity, and human-robot interaction domains. To this end, we formulated a set of Boolean keyword combinations that reflected both technical and contextual dimensions of our study. These included search queries such as "Cybersecurity AND healthcare robots," "Elderly care robot OR rehabilitation robot AND cybersecurity OR authentication," "Health Robot OR Assistive Robot AND privacy OR security," "Privacy AND healthcare robots," "Robotic surgery AND privacy," "Telemedication robot AND data privacy," and "Telemedication robot AND data security."

We applied these search strings to six prominent academic databases: IEEE Xplore, ACM Digital Library, SpringerLink, PubMed, Wiley Online Library, and Google Scholar. The breadth of these repositories enabled us to capture a diverse set of interdisciplinary contributions spanning both technical implementations and applied use cases in healthcare settings. This search protocol yielded an initial corpus of 393 full-text articles published between 2005 and 2025, covering a broad range of robotic applications, threat models, privacy-enhancing technologies, and regulatory considerations in healthcare robotics.

3.2 Filtering Process

We applied a two-phase filtering process to refine the initial corpus and identify studies directly relevant to our research. In the first phase, we screened titles to exclude works that did not clearly reference privacy, cybersecurity, robotic systems, or telemedicine, eliminating publications that lacked focus on our intersection of interest. This reduced the corpus from 393 to 96 articles with preliminary relevance. In the second phase, we reviewed abstracts and full texts to assess methodological rigor and thematic fit. We included studies that met at least one of the following criteria: introduced or evaluated privacy-preserving mechanisms or security architectures for healthcare robots, proposed threat models or mitigation strategies for robotic data flows, examined the implementation of regulatory frameworks like HIPAA or GDPR, or explored user trust, transparency, and adoption in privacy-sensitive interactions. This process resulted in a final set of 62 peer-reviewed articles that offered substantive insights across the core areas of interest.

3.3 Analysis

We analyzed the final set of articles using a structured coding framework guided by four RQs: (RQ1) privacy-preserving techniques, (RQ2) cybersecurity threats and mitigation strategies, (RQ3) legal, ethical, and regulatory compliance, and (RQ4) user trust, transparency, and adoption. To ensure consistency and technical rigor, we used the PRoSec-HRI framework as the foundation for thematic coding. This allowed us to align each study with one or more of its five core domains and analytical clusters, incorporating technical detail, deployment context, and human-centered considerations. We coded each article based on its primary focus, the type of healthcare robot examined (assistive, surgical, social, or telepresence), its deployment setting (hospital, home care, or rehabilitation), and the methodology used (empirical study, technical prototype, conceptual analysis, or literature synthesis). This approach enabled both qualitative synthesis and cross-sectional analysis to identify prevailing trends, highlight underexplored areas, and uncover recurring technical and regulatory challenges. Appendix Table 3 presents the complete codebook used in this classification process.

4 Results and Discussions

In this section, we present key findings from our systematic review, offering a detailed analysis of privacy-preserving techniques, cybersecurity threats and mitigations, regulatory compliance, and user trust in healthcare robotics.

4.1 RQ1: Privacy-Preserving Techniques

Approximately 68% of the papers (42 out of 62) proposed privacy-preserving strategies integrated into robotic system design. Among these, *anonymization* techniques and *privacy-by-design* architectures were the most prevalent, appearing in 43% and 31% of the studies, respectively. These approaches reflect an increasing emphasis on embedding data minimization and user agency into the architectural foundations of healthcare robotics. For example, PriMA-Care [7] utilizes privacy-preserving sensing technologies, such as thermal and depth cameras, to reduce the capture of personally identifiable information. The dataset, designed for healthcare contexts, prioritizes non-visual data modalities to balance privacy concerns with the functional requirements of activity recognition. Similarly, Fosch-Villaronga et al. [27] operationalized GDPR principles by implementing dynamic consent models directly within user interfaces, enabling context-aware opt-in and opt-out mechanisms.

Other strategies include *data localization* adopted in 21% of papers which processes sensitive data locally on-device rather than transmitting it to cloud servers, thereby reducing exposure to interception. Furthermore, 27% of the studies introduced *consent management* interfaces that enable real-time user control over data-sharing preferences. These systems not only address regulatory mandates but also foster trust and transparency, particularly in settings like home and eldercare, where intimate proximity heightens privacy expectations. About 19% of the reviewed studies incorporated *symbolic privacy gestures*, such as robots closing their eyes, dimming indicator lights, or retracting sensors to visually communicate deactivation. These non-verbal cues were designed to signal respect for user privacy and foster trust in human-robot interaction. Such design interventions highlight the importance of perceptual and behavioral affordances as critical complements to technical privacy mechanisms, particularly in socially assistive and domestic care settings. Together, these strategies represent a shift from reactive compliance to proactive, user-centered privacy engineering in healthcare robotics. However, despite the conceptual richness, only 6 out of 62 studies (approximately 10%) reported long-term, in-situ evaluations. This highlights a pressing need for empirical trials and real-world validations to assess the effectiveness, usability, and trustworthiness of these approaches in operation (Table 1).

4.2 RQ2: Cybersecurity Threats and Mitigation Strategies

Security-related risks were addressed in 76% of the reviewed literature, with particular focus on communication vulnerabilities, authentication gaps, sensor

Table 1. Mapping of Technical Contributions to PRoSec-HRI Framework Dimensions

Technical Focus	Representative Methods	Privacy Techniques	System Security	User Trust & Regulatory Compliance
Privacy-by-Design	Anonymization Techniques, On-device Processing	[4, 26, 58]	–	[37, 43, 48, 76]
Consent Management	Dynamic Consent Interfaces, UI Prompts	[11, 40, 97]	–	[25, 83, 87]
Data Governance	Federated Learning, Data Localization	[3, 29, 45]	[9, 13]	[43, 62]
Audit and Identity	Blockchain for Authentication and Logs	[12, 56]	[73, 77]	[36]
Secure Communication	TLS/SSL Channels, Edge Encrypted Transfer	–	[5, 23, 35, 95]	–
Authentication	Biometric + MFA, Symbolic Gestures	[28, 87]	[57]	[53, 54]
Interface Transparency	Explainable Privacy UIs, Trust Signals	[61]	–	[10, 63]
Ethical AI & Societal Trust	Human Digital Twins, Cultural Models	[83]	[2, 34]	[17, 25, 50, 69]

manipulation, and software integrity. Threat models ranged from basic attacks such as packet sniffing and spoofing to complex exploits involving firmware backdoors, ransomware injection, and adversarial manipulation of sensor inputs in HRI contexts. Secure communication protocols were the most frequently implemented countermeasures, discussed in 34% of papers. Studies advocated for the adoption of SSL/TLS, VPNs, or end-to-end encryption to secure data flows between robotic platforms and healthcare servers. For example, Jain et al. [34] integrated TLS encryption with a layered access control mechanism for cloud-based healthcare data exchange, mitigating both passive surveillance and active interference. Authentication mechanisms featured in 29% of studies, with proposals ranging from conventional username-password schemes to more robust biometric and multi-factor authentication (MFA). Mawanda et al. [58] introduced a context-aware smart authentication protocol tailored for eldercare robots, combining dynamic role-based access with physical biometric identifiers to prevent unauthorized command execution. Blockchain-based verification and federated learning were discussed in 18% of papers as decentralized alternatives to centralized identity and decision logging systems. Kumar et al. [46] proposed a 6G-enabled telesurgical platform integrating blockchain smart contracts for cryptographic control of surgical robotic units, preventing unauthorized override of actuator-level commands.

Firmware and software integrity received less attention, with only 13% of papers addressing secure update pipelines or runtime validation techniques. Bihlmaier et al. [8] enhanced ROS-based surgical systems by incorporating secure boot and encrypted firmware verification modules, addressing root-of-trust vulnerabilities in operating environments. Sensor spoofing and adversarial interaction were mentioned in 11 studies, with techniques like sensor fusion redundancy and environment-aware anomaly detection used to mitigate false command execution. Tang et al. [86] implemented a trust controller that identifies anomalous behavior patterns in user-robot interaction, reducing susceptibility to adversarial prompting. Despite these advancements, only 8% of the studies reported lifecycle-aware mitigation strategies such as patch authentication, rollback prevention, or continuous security auditing indicating a gap between secure feature deployment and long-term system resilience. The lack of standardized threat models and benchmarking frameworks further limits the reproducibility and generalizability of proposed security solutions.

4.3 RQ3: Legal, Ethical, and Regulatory Compliance

Regulatory compliance featured prominently in 56% of the analyzed works, underscoring the importance of legal adherence in robotic systems handling health data. Among these, 40% of papers referenced GDPR as the guiding framework for data handling, user consent, and cross-border data transfers. HIPAA compliance was addressed in 27% of papers, primarily in U.S.-based research focusing on patient data protection in clinical or telemedicine deployments. Local frameworks such as Japan's APPI and Canada's PIPEDA were cited in 18%, often in comparative analyses or country-specific deployments. However, 19% of the reviewed papers highlighted gaps where robotic functionalities outpaced existing legal standards. These include unregulated capabilities like facial expression recognition, emotion detection, and real-time behavioral profiling features increasingly embedded in socially assistive robots. Grabler and Koeszegi [31] critiqued this regulatory lag, noting that most privacy laws focus on static datasets and overlook contextual, real-time sensing that healthcare robots now perform.

Several works attempted to bridge this gap through anticipatory compliance modeling. Vulpe et al. [93] proposed a predictive simulation system to evaluate the compliance status of assistive robots under varying deployment conditions. Their model integrates legal heuristics and robotic sensor mappings to flag potential data flow violations before deployment. Furthermore, 14% of papers explicitly discussed accountability distribution, e.g., whether responsibility for data breaches rests with robot manufacturers, hospital IT teams, or AI algorithm providers. This ambiguity complicates enforcement and calls for clearer delineation of liability chains across hardware, software, and operational stakeholders. Although regulatory principles like "privacy by design" and "data minimization" were widely endorsed, only a small portion of studies implemented verifiable compliance mechanisms such as audit logs, consent records, or data portability frameworks. This highlights the need for technical & policy innovations that can co-evolve with the capabilities of intelligent healthcare robots.

4.4 RQ4: User Trust, Transparency, and Adoption Outcomes

Approximately 61% of the reviewed studies (38 out of 62) emphasized user trust, yet only 18 included user-centered research. These works examined how individuals perceive and respond to the privacy and security behaviors of healthcare robots. Transparency emerged as a key factor in building trust, appearing in 42% of the studies. For example, Oruma et al. [69] introduced symbolic gestures like robots closing their eyes or turning away during sensitive moments to signal non-recording states, especially effective in eldercare settings. In 31% of the papers, researchers evaluated how privacy and security features influenced perceived safety and adoption. Studies found that features such as encryption indicators, consent prompts, and real-time data dashboards significantly improved user confidence, particularly in telepresence and home care scenarios [4]. Fourteen studies highlighted how cultural norms shaped privacy expectations; users in Japan showed greater acceptance of surveillance framed as safety, while European users preferred stricter data control and visibility.

Table 2 summarizes the 18 user-centered studies, which involved over 6,500 participants from varied demographics including older adults [25], children and teens [48], patients [36], and students [60]. Sample sizes ranged from under 20 in qualitative evaluations [62,93] to large-scale surveys exceeding 500 participants [40,97]. Most studies (14 out of 18) focused on trust, transparency, and adoption, exploring consent interfaces, cultural differences, and user perceptions. A smaller group (4 out of 18) addressed privacy-preserving technologies [6,86] or cybersecurity awareness [57,93]. Despite the value of these insights, only 7 of the 38 trust-focused papers included user education or onboarding, revealing a critical gap. Many systems rely on users to manage complex privacy settings without sufficient guidance, potentially undermining their transparency and usability.

4.5 Deployment Settings and Robot Types

Deployment context strongly shaped the design priorities observed across the literature. Social and assistive robots were the most frequently examined category, appearing in 54% of the studies. These robots were primarily deployed in home-based and eldercare environments, where proximity to users and continuous interaction raised unique privacy and consent challenges. In these contexts, techniques such as symbolic privacy gestures, real-time consent prompts, and thermal-based sensing were emphasized. Clinical and surgical settings accounted for 21% of the papers. These systems often integrated stricter access control mechanisms, such as biometric authentication or multi-tiered user verification. Jain et al. [34], for instance, proposed a secure robotic platform for surgical data sharing that utilized HIPAA-compliant cloud encryption and role-based access control for physicians and technicians. Telepresence robots, appearing in 14% of the studies, focused heavily on securing communication channels and ensuring real-time encryption. Mookherji et al. [59] described a tactile internet-enabled telehealth robot that employed smart contracts for identity verification and used federated learning to ensure that no raw data left the patient's environment.

5 Implications

The findings from this review, guided by the PRoSec-HRI framework, reveal actionable directions for designing and deploying privacy-aware, secure, and user-trusted healthcare robotic systems. As healthcare robots become more embedded in sensitive settings like eldercare, telemedicine, and rehabilitation, it is essential that developers move beyond abstract compliance to implement concrete, testable, and human-centered security strategies. Below, we outline three key implications derived from the synthesis of 62 peer-reviewed studies.

Context-Aware and Culturally-Sensitive Privacy Interfaces: User trust is not monolithic, it is shaped by cultural expectations, deployment settings, and interaction contexts. Especially, robots designed for home or eldercare settings should incorporate intuitive, symbolic privacy cues (e.g., eye-closing gestures or sensor deactivation signals) that align with users' mental models and comfort levels [62,69]. Our review found that only 19% of studies incorporated symbolic gestures [65], and even fewer accounted for cultural sensitivity. Designers should use the PRoSec-HRI framework to evaluate and localize privacy-preserving behaviors across cultural contexts and user demographics to reduce privacy fatigue.

Lifecycle Security and Authentication: While 76% of reviewed studies addressed cybersecurity, only a small fraction considered end-to-end protection over the robot's lifecycle. Features like secure firmware updates, tamper detection, and authenticated access remain inconsistently implemented. As robots increasingly operate autonomously and interact with sensitive PII, authentication measures must extend beyond basic access control. Developers should integrate multi-factor authentication [16,20], secure boot protocols [32], and encrypted data flows [34] into core system design aligned with the third and fourth domains of the PRoSec-HRI framework.

Regulatory Compliance Through Verifiable, Transparent Mechanisms: Although 56% of papers referenced regulations such as GDPR or HIPAA, only 14% implemented concrete compliance features such as audit logs, consent records, or data portability. Moreover, 19% of studies highlighted how robotic capabilities, such as emotion sensing or behavioral profiling, often operate outside existing legal frameworks. To address this gap, developers should not only align with legal texts but embed verifiable mechanisms, like dynamic consent dashboards and data minimization strategies directly into system interfaces. The PRoSec-HRI framework can serve as a blueprint for building compliance into both the software stack and user experience, enabling legal adherence that is visible, testable, and adaptive to future regulations.

6 Future Work and Limitations

The PRoSec-HRI framework offers a structured synthesis of privacy and security considerations in healthcare robotics. Although we developed the framework based on our expertise, prior research, and insights from related models, we did not incorporate direct input from practitioners, which limits its empirical grounding. In future extension of this work, we plan to validate the framework through user studies and engage stakeholders across disciplines to refine its relevance and practical utility in healthcare robotics.

7 Conclusion

As robotic systems continue to expand into healthcare, ensuring privacy, security, and user trust is essential to responsible deployment. This review of 62 peer-reviewed studies reveals persistent gaps between proposed solutions and real-world implementations. Although 43% of studies introduced privacy-preserving methods such as anonymization or data minimization, only *six* included real-world evaluations, limiting practical validation. While encrypted communication and authentication were addressed in 34% and 29% of papers respectively, just 13% implemented firmware protections or secure update mechanisms, despite the autonomy of these systems. Regulatory compliance was referenced frequently, yet only 14% demonstrated tangible alignment with GDPR or HIPAA, and 19% highlighted unresolved issues around behavioral and emotional sensing. Trust-focused features like consent dashboards and symbolic gestures appeared in 61% of studies, but only 18 involved user research, and just *seven* provided onboarding or education, underscoring the disconnect between design and user understanding. Deployment environments influenced priorities: home care emphasized transparency, while clinical settings concentrated on access control. These insights point to the urgent need for privacy and security strategies that account for technical, regulatory, and human factors across the full system lifecycle. Additionally, the PRoSec-HRI framework offers a structured path forward, integrating ethical, legal, and user-centered considerations into the development of trustworthy healthcare robots.

Acknowledgment. This work was supported by the Center for AI, Privacy, and Security (CAPS) Lab at George Mason University. The authors also thank the anonymous reviewers for their valuable feedback. Any opinions, findings, conclusions, or recommendations expressed in this material are those of the authors and do not necessarily reflect the views of the sponsors.

Appendix I

Table 2. Summary of User Studies in Human-Robot Interaction

Study Reference	Robot Context	Sample Size(n)	Domain	Key Findings
Lindblom et al. (2024) [51]	Social robots	50	Trust, Transparency, and Adoption	Users were more comfortable with the better robot gestures
A. Baselizadeh et al. (2024) [6]	Care robots	28 (18 young adults, 10 older adults)	Trust, Transparency, and Adoption	Elderly users expressing greater concern over sensor monitoring, while younger participants showed more acceptance when real-time feedback was provided
S. Jayaraman et al. (2024) [37]	Care robots	239	Trust, Transparency, and Adoption	Users' privacy decisions vary depending on context, data sensitivity, trust in the robot, and the robot's behavior during interaction.
Levinson (2025) [48]	Social robots	36 (10 children ages 6–11 with 6 caregivers, 15 teens, 15 youths receiving cancer treatments)	Trust, Transparency, and Adoption	Youths and teens expressed privacy concerns when interacting with social robots at home and in healthcare settings
Baselizadeh et al. (2024) [6]	Care robots with sensors	17 (9 females, 8 males; ages 22–74, avg. 30.6)	Privacy-Preserving Techniques	The study identified distinct user activities in human robot interaction including gesture commands, walking, and daily tasks using multi-sensor data from healthy adults.
Schomakers and Ziefle (2019) [76]	Aging-in-place assistive technologies	97 (aged 19–85)	Privacy-Preserving Techniques	Older adults are less positive toward care-assistive technology, highlighting the need for user-centered design.

(continued)

Table 2. (*continued*)

Study Reference	Robot Context	Sample Size(n)	Domain	Key Findings
Nieto Agraz et al. (2025) [62]	Telepresence robots in care settings	21 (14 females; Mean age 46.6, SD 17.58)	Trust, Transparency, and Adoption	Privacy perceptions were similar across interactions with a laptop webcam, mobile robot Temi, and humanoid robot Ameca.
Aryania et al. (2025) [4]	Social robot ARI in public spaces	113 (adults 18+)	Trust, Transparency, and Adoption	Privacy warnings significantly influenced users' willingness to disclose personal information in public interaction scenarios like restaurant recommendations and selfie sharing.
Jayaraman et al. (2024) [36]	Social healthcare robots	239 (114 females, 118 males, 1 transgender, 4 non-binary, 1 not reported; ages 18–83)	Trust, Transparency, and Adoption	Context strongly influences privacy and utility perceptions of healthcare robots, with home care scenarios preferred; design fiction aided realistic participant engagement.
Jia, Chi, and Lu (2024) [38]	Social robots	252 (22 participants in interviews; total 252 in survey validation)	Trust, Transparency, and Adoption	Mixed-method study with interviews and survey assessing privacy concerns via video stimuli and questionnaires; developed and validated SRPC scale grounded in user experiences.
Zibarzani et al. (2024) [97]	Food delivery robots (ADRs)	590 (online respondents)	Trust, Transparency, and Adoption	Privacy and security concerns weaken social influence on adoption, while environmental friendliness boosts acceptance of food delivery robots.
Khaksar et al. (2024) [97]	Social robots	509	Trust, Transparency, and Adoption	Paradox mindset moderates how strongly privacy concerns and personalization benefits influence social robot acceptance.

(*continued*)

Table 2. (*continued*)

Study Reference	Robot Context	Sample Size(n)	Domain	Key Findings
Chatterjee et al. (2023) [11]	Social robots	403	Trust, Transparency, and Adoption	Enjoyment and usefulness both increase people's willingness to use social robots, based on survey results.
Ellis et al. (2025) [25]	Healthcare chatbots	3,089 (survey), 46 (interviews)	Trust, Transparency, and Adoption	Older adults trusted chatbots more because they were linked to trusted health systems, leading to fewer privacy worries and less medical mistrust.
Mutongi and Rigava (2024) [60]	Healthcare robots in African context	20 (university students)	Trust, Transparency, and Adoption	Users had mixed views on healthcare robots, with some welcoming them for privacy and reliability, others concerned about culture and infrastructure.
Tang et al. (2022) [86]	Social robots with privacy controllers	174 (study 1), 95 (study 2)	Privacy-Preserving Techniques	Robots using privacy controllers were rated higher in trust, awareness, and privacy protection than those without.
Marchang et al. (2023) [57]	Assistive robots in healthcare	30 (13 female, 18 male; ages 45–90)	Cybersecurity Threats and Mitigations	Public engagement study involving presentations and surveys; participants had varied knowledge of assistive systems and robots; assessed social perceptions of security and privacy issues in assistive care robots.
Vulpe et al. (2021) [93]	Socially assistive robots in healthcare	18 (participants in user experience evaluation)	Cybersecurity Threats and Mitigations	User Experience Questionnaire (UEQ) assessing SecureIoT prototype; participants rated quality positively, appreciating continuous vulnerability tracking and control features for large-scale deployments.

Appendix II

Table 3. Codebook for PRoSec-HRI Framework-Guided Analysis

Code	Description	Examples
Category 1: Privacy-Preserving Techniques		
Anonymization	Removal or transformation of personally identifiable information (PII)	Pseudonymization, k-anonymity, data aggregation
Data Minimization	Collecting only essential data required for task execution	Heart rate monitoring without GPS or audio
Purpose Limitation	Ensuring data is used solely for stated medical/assistive purposes	Activity data used for fall detection only
User Control	Enabling users to manage their data access, correction, or deletion	Privacy dashboards, erasure features
Privacy by Design	Embedding privacy features from initial architectural design	Secure defaults, edge processing
Consent Model	Structuring how and when consent is obtained and updated	Opt-in, dynamic consent, parental proxies
Data Localization	Processing sensitive data locally on the device	On-device audio processing instead of cloud
Privacy UI Design	User interface elements to visualize and control privacy actions	Alerts, toggles for camera/audio status
Category 2: Cybersecurity Threats and Mitigations		
Threat Type	Identification of cybersecurity threats affecting robotic systems	Sensor spoofing, ransomware, MITM attacks
Threat Vector	Channels through which systems can be exploited	Open APIs, insecure firmware, wireless protocols
Security Breach	Reported or simulated incidents of system compromise	Wi-Fi hijacking, unauthorized access
Technical Mitigation	Engineering solutions to reduce or prevent cyberattacks	TLS encryption, IDS, firewalls
Authentication Method	Approaches for verifying identity of users/administrators	Biometric access, 2FA, access tokens
Secure Communication	Mechanisms to safeguard data during transmission	VPN, SSL/TLS, encrypted messaging

(continued)

Table 3. (*continued*)

Code	Description	Examples
Category 3: Legal, Ethical, and Regulatory Compliance		
Firmware Security	Measures ensuring firmware/software integrity	Secure boot, signed firmware updates
Update Management	Strategies for secure patching and firmware upgrades	Over-the-air updates with authentication
Security Testing	Evaluation of system robustness under threat conditions	Penetration testing, red teaming
GDPR Compliance	Adherence to GDPR principles within EU jurisdictions	Data portability, right to be forgotten
HIPAA Compliance	Conformity to U.S. healthcare data protection laws	Secure storage, patient confidentiality
Other Legal Frameworks	Reference to other national or regional regulations	Japan's APPI, Canada's PIPEDA
Compliance Status	Extent of system's legal/regulatory conformity	Fully compliant, partially compliant
Unregulated Features	Functionalities lacking legal oversight	Emotion recognition using facial data
Accountability Gap	Ambiguity in assigning responsibility for breaches	Vendor vs. healthcare provider liability
Ethical Conflict	Ethical dilemmas where laws provide limited guidance	Monitoring dementia patients vs. privacy rights
Compliance Evidence	Regulatory certifications and documentation cited	CE marking, FDA clearance, ISO 13485
Category 4: Trust, Transparency, and Adoption		
Trust Enhancer	Features that positively influence user confidence	Real-time transparency dashboards
Trust Barrier	Aspects that undermine perceived security or transparency	Black-box algorithms, vague policies
User Perception	Reported user attitudes toward privacy and security	Increased trust with encryption indicators
Transparency Measure	Mechanisms for revealing data usage and intent	Daily usage logs, data prompts
Informed Consent	Ease of understanding and meaningfulness of consent	Visual/interactive consent mechanisms
Privacy Tradeoff	Willingness to compromise privacy for benefits	Location tracking accepted for emergency care
Cultural Attitudes	Cross-cultural variability in privacy expectations	Seniors in Japan vs. UK privacy norms
Adoption Outcome	Observed impact of privacy/security on system adoption	Reduced uptake after data breach
Education and Training	Efforts to educate users about system privacy	Onboarding workshops, video tutorials

References

1. Adhikari, A., Das, S., Dewri, R.: Natural language processing of privacy policies: a survey. arXiv preprint arXiv:2501.10319 (2025)
2. Afroze, D., Tu, Y., Hei, X.: Securing the future: exploring privacy risks and security questions in robotic systems. In: International Conference on Security and Privacy in Cyber-Physical Systems and Smart Vehicles, pp. 148–157. Springer (2023)
3. Armbrust, C., Mehdi, S.A., Reichardt, M., Koch, J., Berns, K.: Using an autonomous robot to maintain privacy in assistive environments. Secur. Commun. Netw. **4**(11), 1275–1293 (2011)
4. Aryania, A., Huertas-Garcia, R., Forgas-Coll, S., Angulo, C., Alenyà, G.: Effects of privacy warning on the intention to disclose personal information during interaction with a robot in public spaces. Int. J. Soc. Robot., 1–19 (2025)
5. Basan, E., Makarevich, O., Abramov, E., Popov, D.: Analysis of the initial security of the robotics system. In: Proceedings of the 12th International Conference on Security of Information and Networks, pp. 1–8 (2019)
6. Baselizadeh, A., Lindblom, D.S., Khaksar, W., Uddin, M.Z., Torresen, J.: Comparative analysis of vision-based sensors for human monitoring in care robots: exploring the utility-privacy trade-off. In: 2024 33rd IEEE International Conference on Robot and Human Interactive Communication (ROMAN), Pasadena, CA, USA, pp. 1794–1801 (2024). https://doi.org/10.1109/RO-MAN60168.2024.10731223
7. Baselizadeh, A., Uddin, M.Z., Khaksar, W., Lindblom, D.S., Torresen, J.: Primacare: privacy-preserving multi-modal dataset for human activity recognition in care robots. In: Companion of the 2024 ACM/IEEE International Conference on Human-Robot Interaction, pp. 233–237 (2024)
8. Bihlmaier, A., et al.: Ros-based cognitive surgical robotics. In: Robot Operating System (ROS) The Complete Reference, vol. 1, pp. 317–342 (2016)
9. Callander, N., Ramírez-Duque, A.A., Foster, M.E.: Navigating the human-robot interaction landscape. Practical guidelines for privacy-conscious social robots. In: Companion of the 2024 ACM/IEEE International Conference on Human-Robot Interaction, pp. 283–287 (2024)
10. Cartwright, A.J.: The elephant in the room: cybersecurity in healthcare. J. Clin. Monit. Comput. **37**(5), 1123–1132 (2023)
11. Chatterjee, S., Chaudhuri, R., Vrontis, D.: Acceptance of social robot and its challenges: from privacy calculus perspectives. Technol. Forecast. Soc. Chang. **196**, 122862 (2023)
12. Chaudjary, S., Kakkar, R., Gupta, R., Tanwar, S., Agrawal, S., Sharma, R.: Blockchain and federated learning-based security solutions for telesurgery system: a comprehensive review. Turk. J. Electr. Eng. Comput. Sci. **30**(7), 2446–2488 (2022)
13. Collins, S., et al.: "Socially assistive robot privacy model": a multi-model approach to evaluating socially assistive robot privacy concerns. In: International Conference on Social Robotics, pp. 280–289. Springer (2024)
14. Das, S.: A risk-reduction-based incentivization model for human-centered multi-factor authentication. Indiana University (2020)
15. Das, S., Dev, J., Camp, L.J.: Privacy preserving policy framework: user-aware and user-driven. In: The 47th Research Conference on Communication, Information and Internet Policy, TPRC47 (2019)
16. Das, S., Kim, A., Camp, L.J.: Organizational security: implementing a risk-reduction-based incentivization model for MFA adoption. In: Proceedings of the International Conference on Financial Cryptography and Data Security (2021)

17. Das, S., Kim, A., Tingle, Z., Nippert-Eng, C.: All about phishing exploring user research through a systematic literature review. In: Proceedings of the Thirteenth International Symposium on Human Aspects of Information Security & Assurance (HAISA 2019) (2019)
18. Das, S., Nippert-Eng, C., Camp, L.J.: Evaluating user susceptibility to phishing attacks. Inf. Comput. Secur. **30**(1), 1–18 (2022)
19. Das, S., Salman, A.: A review of security threats from e-waste. In: Development in E-Waste Management: Sustainability and Circular Economy Aspects, p. 165 (2023)
20. Das, S., Wang, B., Kim, A., Camp, L.J.: MFA is a necessary chore!: exploring user mental models of multi-factor authentication technologies. In: HICSS, pp. 1–10 (2020)
21. Das, S., et al.: SoK: a proposal for incorporating accessible gamified cybersecurity awareness training informed by a systematic literature review. In: Proceedings of the Workshop on Usable Security and Privacy (USEC) (2022)
22. Dassanayake, D., Buddhika, M., Maduranga, I., Seneviratne, J., Kumarage, W.: Revolutionizing manufacturing: the role of robotics in the 21st century. J. Desk Res. Rev. Anal. **2**(1) (2024)
23. Dóczi, R., et al.: Increasing ROS 1.x communication security for medical surgery robot. In: 2016 IEEE International Conference on Systems, Man, and Cybernetics (SMC), pp. 004444–004449. IEEE (2016)
24. Düzgün, R., Noah, N., Mayer, P., Das, S., Volkamer, M.: SoK: a systematic literature review of knowledge-based authentication on augmented reality head-mounted displays. In: Proceedings of the 17th International Conference on Availability, Reliability and Security, pp. 1–12 (2022)
25. Ellis, J.R., et al.: The halo effect: perceptions of information privacy among healthcare chatbot users. J. Am. Geriatr. Soc. (2025)
26. Fedosov, A., Tamò-Larrieux, A., Lutz, C., Fosch-Villaronga, E., Čartolovni, A.: Privacy-friendly and trustworthy technology for society. Digit. Soc. **4**(1), 1–12 (2025)
27. Fosch-Villaronga, E., Drukarch, H., Custers, B.: Privacy considerations for socially assistive robots. Management **1**(7), 1248–1255 (2018)
28. Gawanmeh, A., Alomari, A.: Taxonomy analysis of security aspects in cyber physical systems applications. In: 2018 IEEE International Conference on Communications Workshops (ICC Workshops), pp. 1–6. IEEE (2018)
29. Ghongade, H.P., Bhadre, A.A.: A comprehensive approach to cybersecurity and healthcare systems using artificial intelligence and robotics. Cyber-Phys. Syst. Innov. Transf. Soc. **5**, 77–119 (2025)
30. Gomes, P.: Surgical robotics: Reviewing the past, analysing the present, imagining the future. Robot. Comput. Integr. Manuf. **27**(2), 261–266 (2011)
31. Grabler, R., Koeszegi, S.T.: Privacy beyond data: assessment and mitigation of privacy risks in robotic technology for elderly care. ACM Trans. Hum. Robot Interact. **14**(1), 1–23 (2025)
32. Haskard, A., Herath, D.: Secure robotics: navigating challenges at the nexus of safety, trust, and cybersecurity in cyber-physical systems. ACM Comput. Surv. **57**(9), 1–48 (2025)
33. Huang, Y., et al.: Systemization of knowledge (SoK): goals, coverage, and evaluation in cybersecurity and privacy games. In: Proceedings of the 2025 CHI Conference on Human Factors in Computing Systems, pp. 1–27 (2025)
34. Jain, S., Doriya, R.: Security framework to healthcare robots for secure sharing of healthcare data from cloud. Int. J. Inf. Technol. **14**(5), 2429–2439 (2022)

35. Jangid, A., Dubey, P.K., Chandavarkar, B.: Security issues and challenges in healthcare automated devices. In: 2020 International Conference on COMmunication Systems & NETworkS (COMSNETS), pp. 19–23. IEEE (2020)
36. Jayaraman, S., Phillips, E.K., Church, D., Riek, L.D.: Privacy and utility perceptions of social robots in healthcare. Comput. Hum. Behav. Artif. Hum. **2**(1), 100039 (2024)
37. Jayaraman, S., Phillips, E.K., Church, D., Riek, L.D.: Social robots in healthcare: characterizing privacy considerations. In: Companion of the 2024 ACM/IEEE International Conference on Human-Robot Interaction, pp. 568–572 (2024)
38. Jia, S.J., Chi, O.H., Lu, L.: Social robot privacy concern (SRPC): rethinking privacy concerns within the hospitality domain. Int. J. Hosp. Manag. **122**, 103853 (2024)
39. Jones, J.M., Duezguen, R., Mayer, P., Volkamer, M., Das, S.: A literature review on virtual reality authentication. In: Human Aspects of Information Security and Assurance: 15th IFIP WG 11.12 International Symposium, HAISA 2021, Virtual Event, 7–9 July 2021, Proceedings 15, pp. 189–198. Springer (2021)
40. Khaksar, S.M.S., Shahmehr, F.S., Miah, S., Daim, T., Ozdemir, D.: Privacy concerns versus personalisation benefits in social robot acceptance by employees: a paradox theory-contingency perspective. Technol. Forecast. Soc. Chang. **198**, 123034 (2024)
41. Khaksar, W., Saplacan, D., Bygrave, L.A., Torresen, J.: Robotics in elderly healthcare: a review of 20 recent research projects. arXiv preprint arXiv:2302.04478 (2023)
42. Khang, A.: Medical Robotics and AI-Assisted Diagnostics for a High-Tech Healthcare Industry. IGI Global (2024)
43. Kim, J., Levinson, L., Ota, J., Šabanović, S., Smart, W.D.: Privacy-sensitive robotics: perceptions, measures, and metrics. In: 2025 20th ACM/IEEE International Conference on Human-Robot Interaction (HRI), pp. 1976–1978. IEEE (2025)
44. Kishnani, U., Madabhushi, S., Das, S.: Blockchain in oil and gas supply chain: a literature review from user security and privacy perspective. In: International Symposium on Human Aspects of Information Security and Assurance, pp. 296–309. Springer (2023)
45. Ko, H., Keoh, S.L., Jin, J.: Privacy protection for cloud-based robotic networks. In: Security and Privacy in Cyber-Physical Systems: Foundations, Principles and Applications, pp. 195–222 (2017)
46. Kumar, N., Ali, R.: A smart contract-based robotic surgery authentication system for healthcare using 6G-Tactile internet. Comput. Netw. **238**, 110133 (2024)
47. Kuo, I.-H., Jayawardena, C., Broadbent, E., Stafford, R.Q., MacDonald, B.A.: HRI evaluation of a healthcare service robot. In: Ge, S.S., Khatib, O., Cabibihan, J.-J., Simmons, R., Williams, M.-A. (eds.) ICSR 2012. LNCS (LNAI), vol. 7621, pp. 178–187. Springer, Heidelberg (2012). https://doi.org/10.1007/978-3-642-34103-8_18
48. Levinson, L.: Contextual understanding of teen & youth privacy perceptions with social robots. In: 2025 20th ACM/IEEE International Conference on Human-Robot Interaction (HRI), pp. 1869–1871. IEEE (2025)
49. Licardo, J.T., Domjan, M., Orehovački, T.: Intelligent robotics-a systematic review of emerging technologies and trends. Electronics **13**(3), 542 (2024)
50. Liedo, B.: Navigating autonomy, privacy, and ageism in robot home care with aged users: a preliminary analysis of rob-in. Bioethics (2024)

51. Lindblom, D.S., van Otterdijk, M., Torresen, J.: A qualitative observational video-based study on perceived privacy in social robots' based on robots appearances. In: 2024 IEEE International Conference on Advanced Robotics and Its Social Impacts (ARSO), Hong Kong, pp. 74–79 (2024). https://doi.org/10.1109/ARSO60199.2024.10557941
52. Van der Loos, H.M., Reinkensmeyer, D.J., Guglielmelli, E.: Rehabilitation and health care robotics. In: Springer Handbook of Robotics, pp. 1685–1728 (2016)
53. Luntovskyy, A.: A survey on advanced security and ensured user privacy for distributed systems. In: 2024 9th International Conference on Smart and Sustainable Technologies (SpliTech), pp. 01–07. IEEE (2024)
54. Lutz, C., Tamò, A.: Privacy and healthcare robots–an ant analysis. In: We Robot, pp. 1–25 (2016)
55. Majumdar, R., Das, S.: SoK: an evaluation of quantum authentication through systematic literature review. In: Proceedings of the Workshop on Usable Security and Privacy (USEC). Internet Society Auckland, New Zealand (2021)
56. Marchang, J., Di Nuovo, A.: Assistive multimodal robotic system (AMRSys): security and privacy issues, challenges, and possible solutions. Appl. Sci. **12**(4), 2174 (2022)
57. Marchang, J., Di Nuovo, A., Elliott, C., Meese, H., Vinanzi, S., Zecca, M.: Security and privacy in assistive robotics: cybersecurity challenges for healthcare. UK-RAS White paper Series (2023)
58. Mawanda, R., Keishing, S., Wang, J., Marchang, J.: Secure by design smart authentication for care robots to support the elderly. In: 2024 IEEE International Conference on Industrial Technology (ICIT), pp. 1–6. IEEE (2024)
59. Mookherji, S., Odelu, V., Prasath, R.: Analysis of a lightweight authentication protocol for remote surgery applications under the CK-adversary model. In: 2022 14th International Conference on COMmunication Systems & NETworkS (COMSNETS), pp. 1–5. IEEE (2022)
60. Mutongi, C., Rigava, B.: Robotics in healthcare: the African perspective. In: 2024 IEEE 3rd International Conference on AI in Cybersecurity (ICAIC), pp. 1–10. IEEE (2024)
61. Naresh, V.S., Thamarai, M.: Privacy-preserving data mining and machine learning in healthcare: applications, challenges, and solutions. Wiley Interdiscip. Rev. Data Min. Knowl. Discov. **13**(2), e1490 (2023)
62. Nieto Agraz, C., Hinrichs, P., Eichelberg, M., Hein, A.: Is the robot spying on me? A study on perceived privacy in telepresence scenarios in a care setting with mobile and humanoid robots. Int. J. Soc. Robot., 1–15 (2024)
63. Nkoom, M., Hounsinou, S.G., Crosby, G.V.: Securing the internet of robotic things (IoRT) against DDoS attacks: a federated learning with differential privacy clustering approach. Comput. Secur., 104493 (2025)
64. Noah, N., Das, S.: Exploring evolution of augmented and virtual reality education space in 2020 through systematic literature review. Comput. Anim. Virtual Worlds **32**(3–4), e2020 (2021)
65. Noah, N., Das, S.: From pins to gestures: analyzing knowledge-based authentication schemes for augmented and virtual reality. IEEE Trans. Vis. Comput. Graph. (2025)
66. Noah, N., Thakur, S., Beck, J., Das, S.: Evaluating privacy & security of online dating applications with a focus on older adults. In: 2024 IEEE European Symposium on Security and Privacy Workshops (EuroS&PW), pp. 666–677. IEEE (2024)
67. Okamura, A.M., Mataric, M.J., Christensen, H.I.: Medical and health-care robotics. IEEE Robot. Autom. Mag. **17**(3), 26–37 (2010)

68. Oña, E.D., Garcia-Haro, J.M., Jardón, A., Balaguer, C.: Robotics in health care: perspectives of robot-aided interventions in clinical practice for rehabilitation of upper limbs. Appl. Sci. **9**(13), 2586 (2019)
69. Oruma, S.O.: Towards a user-centred security framework for social robots in public spaces. In: Proceedings of the 27th International Conference on Evaluation and Assessment in Software Engineering, pp. 292–297 (2023)
70. Pramesha Chandrasiri, G., Halgamuge, M.N., Subhashi Jayasekara, C.: A comparative study in the application of IoT in health care: data security in telemedicine. Secur. Priv. Trust IoT Environ., 181–202 (2019)
71. Ragno, L., Borboni, A., Vannetti, F., Amici, C., Cusano, N.: Application of social robots in healthcare: review on characteristics, requirements, technical solutions. Sensors **23**(15), 6820 (2023)
72. Research, G.V.: Medical robotic systems market size, share & trend analysis report by type (cleanroom robots, robotic prosthetics, medical service robots), region, and segment forecasts, 2024–2030 (2024). https://www.grandviewresearch.com/industry-analysis/medical-robotic-systems-market. Accessed 9 May 2025
73. Saha, H.N., Debnath, S.: Security and privacy of IoT devices in healthcare systems. In: Smart Healthcare System Design: Security and Privacy Aspects, pp. 143–165 (2022)
74. Saka, S., Das, S.: Safeguarding in the internet of things age: a comprehensive review of security and privacy risks for older adults. Innov. Aging **7**(Suppl. 1), 819 (2023)
75. Saka, S., Das, S.: Evaluating privacy measures in healthcare apps predominantly used by older adults. In: 2024 Conference on Building a Secure & Empowered Cyberspace (BuildSEC), pp. 79–86. IEEE (2024)
76. Schomakers, E.M., Ziefle, M.: Privacy concerns and the acceptance of technologies for aging in place. In: Human Aspects of IT for the Aged Population. Design for the Elderly and Technology Acceptance: 5th International Conference, ITAP 2019, Held as Part of the 21st HCI International Conference, HCII 2019, Orlando, FL, USA, 26–31 July 2019, Proceedings, Part I 21, pp. 313–331. Springer (2019)
77. Selvaraj, P., Doraikannan, S.: Privacy and security issues on wireless body area and IoT for remote healthcare monitoring. In: Intelligent Pervasive Computing Systems for Smarter Healthcare pp. 227–253 (2019)
78. Shahi, A., Bajaj, G., GolharSathawane, R., Mendhe, D., Dogra, A.: Integrating robot-assisted surgery and AI for improved healthcare outcomes. In: 2024 Ninth International Conference on Science Technology Engineering and Mathematics (ICONSTEM), pp. 1–5. IEEE (2024)
79. Sheetz, K.H., Claflin, J., Dimick, J.B.: Trends in the adoption of robotic surgery for common surgical procedures. JAMA Netw. Open **3**(1), e1918911 (2020)
80. Shibata, T., Wada, K.: Robot therapy: a new approach for mental healthcare of the elderly-a mini-review. Gerontology **57**(4), 378–386 (2011)
81. Shrestha, S., Das, S.: Exploring gender biases in ml and AI academic research through systematic literature review. Front. Artif. Intell. **5**, 976838 (2022)
82. Shrestha, S., Irby, E., Thapa, R., Das, S.: SoK: a systematic literature review of Bluetooth security threats and mitigation measures. In: International Symposium on Emerging Information Security and Applications, pp. 108–127. Springer (2022)
83. Sirigu, G., Carminati, B., Ferrari, E.: Privacy and security issues for human digital twins. In: 2022 IEEE 4th International Conference on Trust, Privacy and Security in Intelligent Systems, and Applications (TPS-ISA), pp. 1–9. IEEE (2022)
84. Stephenson, S., Pal, B., Fan, S., Fernandes, E., Zhao, Y., Chatterjee, R.: SoK: Authentication in augmented and virtual reality. In: 2022 IEEE Symposium on Security and Privacy (SP), pp. 267–284. IEEE (2022)

85. Surani, A., Das, S.: Understanding privacy and security postures of healthcare chatbots. In: Proceedings of the 2022 CHI Conference on Human Factors in Computing Systems, CHI, vol. 22, pp. 1–7 (2022)
86. Tang, B., Sullivan, D., Cagiltay, B., Chandrasekaran, V., Fawaz, K., Mutlu, B.: Confidant: a privacy controller for social robots. In: 2022 17th ACM/IEEE International Conference on Human-Robot Interaction (HRI), pp. 205–214. IEEE (2022)
87. Tanimu, J.A., Abada, W.: Addressing cybersecurity challenges in robotics: a comprehensive overview. Cyber Secur. Appl., 100074 (2024)
88. Tazi, F., Dykstra, J., Rajivan, P., Das, S.: SoK: evaluating privacy and security vulnerabilities of patients' data in healthcare. In: International Workshop on Sociotechnical Aspects in Security, pp. 153–181. Springer (2022)
89. Tazi, F., Nandakumar, A., Dykstra, J., Rajivan, P., Das, S.: SoK: analysis of user-centered studies focusing on healthcare privacy & security. SOUPS (2023)
90. Tazi, F., Nandakumar, A., Dykstra, J., Rajivan, P., Das, S.: SoK: analyzing privacy and security of healthcare data from the user perspective. ACM Trans. Comput. Healthc. **5**(2), 1–31 (2024)
91. Tazi, F., Shrestha, S., De La Cruz, J., Das, S.: SoK: an evaluation of the secure end user experience on the dark net through systematic literature review. J. Cybersecur. Priv. **2**(2), 329–357 (2022)
92. Vercelli, A., Rainero, I., Ciferri, L., Boido, M., Pirri, F.: Robots in elderly care. DigitCult - Sci. J. Digit. Cult. **2**(2), 37–50 (2018)
93. Vulpe, A., Crăciunescu, R., Drăgulinescu, A.M., Kyriazakos, S., Paikan, A., Ziafati, P.: Enabling security services in socially assistive robot scenarios for healthcare applications. Sensors **21**(20), 6912 (2021)
94. Xu, M., Islam, M., Bai, L., Ren, H.: Privacy-preserving synthetic continual semantic segmentation for robotic surgery. IEEE Trans. Med. Imaging (2024)
95. Yousef, K.M.A., Mohd, B.J., Amra, M., Kamel, Y., AlMajali, A.: Security risk assessment of humanoid robotics: DARWIN-OP2 as case study. In: 2024 25th International Arab Conference on Information Technology (ACIT), pp. 1–5. IEEE (2024)
96. Zezulak, A., Tazi, F., Das, S.: SoK: evaluating privacy and security concerns of using web services for the disabled population. In: 7th Workshop on Technology and Consumer Protection (ConPro'23) (2023)
97. Zibarzani, M., Abumalloh, R.A., Nilashi, M.: Adoption behavioural intention of robots in last mile food delivery: the importance of environmental friendliness and moderating impacts of privacy and security concerns. Res. Transp. Bus. Manage. **55**, 101146 (2024)

Cognition for Human-Robot Interaction

Engagement Estimation in Child-Robot Interaction via Transfer Learning from a Pre-trained Facial Emotion Recognition Model

Gonzalo A. García[1,2](✉)[iD], Rohan Laycock[3][iD], Guillermo Pérez[1][iD], J. Gabriel Amores[3][iD], Gloria Álvarez[3][iD], Manuel Castro[1][iD], and Randy Gomez[4][iD]

[1] 4i Intelligent Insights, 41092 Seville, Spain
{g.garcia,g.perez,m.castro}@4i.ai
[2] Universidad Internacional de La Rioja (UNIR), 26006 Logroño, La Rioja, Spain
[3] Universidad de Sevilla, 41004 Seville, Spain
{rlaycock,jgabriel,galvarez}@us.es
[4] Honda Research Institute, 8-1 Honcho, Wako, Japan
r.gomez@jp.honda-ri.com

Abstract. *Haru4Kids* is a system developed to emulate the family-oriented robot Haru, enabling child-robot interaction (CRI) within home environments. During a two-week trial with six families, we collected interaction data, including images, which were later labelled by human annotators into four engagement levels. In this study, we present an artificial intelligence model that estimates a child's engagement level during CRI using pictures captured at one frame per second. Our model leverages *transfer learning*, starting with a pre-trained *ResNet50*-based Facial Emotion Recognition (FER) model, which initially achieved an F1 score of 0.28. Incorporating a *Support Vector Classifier* raised this to 0.48. Further fine-tuning the FER model yielded minimal gains, but applying *Low-Rank Adaptation* (LoRA) significantly improved performance, achieving an accuracy of 0.76, an F1 score of 0.69 in cross-validation and 0.56 in the much stricter validation *leave-one-group-out*. These results highlight the effectiveness of adapting pre-trained emotion models for engagement estimation in CRI. The ultimate goal of this work is to equip robots with some degree of *artificial empathy* –defined here as the ability to sense and adapt to user affective and attentional states– to support more effective and natural interactions. While desirable for any human-interacting robot, this capability is especially critical –yet often absent– in social robots designed for children, a particularly underexplored user group in human-robot interaction research.

Keywords: Child-robot interaction in the wild · Engagement estimation · Affective computing · Emotion recognition · Deep learning · Transfer learning · Low-Rank Adaptation (LoRA)

1 Introduction

Recent research in child-robot interaction (CRI) focuses on how to keep children engaged during interactions with social robots [27]. In this realm, engagement is typically defined as the level of cognitive, temporal, affective, and behavioural investment in a digital system [34]. Our aim is to estimate engagement during CRI, which poses several challenges–especially in long-term experiments, as children's interest tends to diminish over time due to the *novelty effect* [29]. While self-report tools like the User Engagement Scale have been widely used [35], automatic engagement estimation techniques are gaining traction, especially in online education and autism studies [4,24,48]. Those methods range from processing physiological signals (e.g., EEG, ECG) to less intrusive techniques like thermal imaging [11,36]. However, such approaches are often impractical in real-world home environments with children. In contrast, video-based engagement estimation is more viable and typically analyses features such as eye gaze, head pose, and facial expressions, often using machine learning models [2,40,49].

Moreover, engagement detection is critical not only to maintain attention during interaction but also to adapt robot behaviour for diverse goals, such as scaffolding learning [19], supporting therapeutic interventions [6,46], or monitoring user well-being [39]. While robots should strive to remain inherently engaging, the capability to detect disengagement enables proactive adaptation, enhances user experience, and informs future design improvements.

In our previous work [14], we introduced the *Haru4Kids* (H4K) platform, designed for use by children in homes. In a two-week cohabitation experiment, the platform displayed an avatar of the robot *Haru* [16,43] on an iPad, mounted on a rotating stand that uses face-tracking to follow the child's movements. That research was approved by Indiana University's Institutional Review Board #14363 for human subjects research. H4K collected various types of data during its interactions with children, including images [14,38]. From this, we curated a dataset labelled by humans coding children engagement level from 1 to 4 (low to high). Another vision-based engagement estimation method was used, this one automatic, based on the angle of the user's face relative to the iPad. The correlation between both methods reached 0.43, highlighting the reliability of visual-based approaches over self-reported metrics [9,36]. However, the annotation process was time-intensive and raised privacy concerns, particularly given the sensitive nature of recording children in home environments.

In our work, engagement is primarily associated with behavioural and emotional signals, following definitions from educational psychology [5,13]. Various approaches have been proposed for automatic engagement recognition using different input signals [25]. Among these, RGB video-based methods are the most common due to their low cost and non-intrusive nature [48]. Moreover, *Convolutional Neural Networks* (CNNs) are a widely used data-driven approach in computer vision, capable of extracting high-level representations from raw image data [28]. However, applying CNNs to engagement recognition–particularly in child-robot interaction–remains challenging due to the limited availability of large, annotated datasets, especially in natural, in-home environments [25].

In this paper, we propose an automatic engagement recognition method for children based on CNNs applied to the face region. To address the training data shortage, we adopt a transfer learning strategy using a pre-trained facial emotion recognition model. We evaluate our system on our home-collected dataset. While some prior work has applied transfer learning to engagement detection [3,31], to the best of our knowledge this is the first application of *Low-Rank Adaptation* (LoRA) as a fine-tuning method for this problem–well-suited to the limited and imbalanced engagement data typical in CRI, as will be detailed later.

2 Related Work

State of the Art: Karimah et al. [25] reviewed engagement estimation research from 2010 to 2020, highlighting a shift from traditional machine learning with handcrafted features—such as facial landmarks or action units, gaze, head pose, and body orientation—to deep learning approaches using raw visual inputs. Toolkits like OpenFace, CERT, and *Microsoft Kinect* were commonly used for feature extraction. Modalities ranged from facial images and video to audio, text, physiological signals, and their combinations (fusion). Here, we focus on the literature on facial image-based approaches most relevant to our work. Whitehill et al. [48] conducted an early study on binary engagement classification using facial expressions. They compared SVMs with Gabor features (2AFC = 0.86), boosted box filters (0.87), and logistic regression with CERT features (0.93), showing strong performance from handcrafted facial features. They also analyzed inter-rater agreement, compared human and machine judgment cues, and found both to correlate similarly with learning outcomes.

Many recent models have been evaluated on DAiSEE [20], a publicly available dataset with 9,068 video clips of 122 Asian university students (ages 18–30), recorded across six settings. It includes labels of engagement levels (0–3). As deep learning gained traction, Murshed et al. [33] evaluated several CNN architectures trained on face images from the DAiSEE dataset (reduced to 3 classes). Their proposed hybrid CNN achieved 0.923 accuracy, outperforming All-CNN (0.76), NiN-CNN (0.832), and VD-CNN (0.865). Santoni et al. [45] used OpenFace features to train a bagging ensemble of 1D CNN, 1D ResNet, and hybrid models with SVD-based dimensionality reduction. Tested on the 4-class DAiSEE dataset, their best model reached 0.933 F1 and 0.943 accuracy– amongst the highest reported–demonstrating the effectiveness of deep learning applied to pre-extracted features and ensembling.

Several works adopt transfer learning to address training data scarcity. Ahamad et al. [3] benchmarked ten pretrained CNNs (e.g., ResNet18, VGG16) on DAiSEE, with ResNet18 yielding the best performance (0.891 accuracy, 0.888 F1) on 4-class classification. Hu [23] fine-tuned ShuffleNet on a proprietary binary engagement dataset, achieving 0.898 accuracy and 0.883 F1. Moreover, to capture temporal cues, Liao et al. [31] combined SE-ResNet-50 (pretrained on VGGFace2) with LSTM and attention modules. Their model achieved 0.588 accuracy and 0.0422 MSE on DAiSEE, and 0.0736 MSE on EmotiW-EP. Similarly, Abedi and Khan [1] proposed a ResNet+TCN hybrid, reaching 0.639 accuracy on DAiSEE (4-class), outperforming prior LSTM- and 3D CNN-based models.

Finally, Yun et al. [49] addressed engagement estimation in child–robot interaction using a proprietary 4-level dataset of children's faces. They use a pretrained CNNs (VGG Face) with LSTM for temporal modeling. Their best model achieved 0.814 accuracy and 0.754 F1, showing the effectiveness of spatial-temporal modeling in settings similar to ours.

Challenges in Engagement Estimation: Several recurring challenges in automatic engagement estimation have been identified in recent surveys [25,42]:

- **Lack of standardized annotation strategies:** Unlike emotion recognition, there is no standard annotation scheme for engagement. Studies vary in whether they label it as discrete, continuous, or a dynamic process, depending on context and goals [42].
- **Subjectivity in external annotation:** Human annotation is inherently subjective and can result in low inter-rater agreement due to the difficulty of consistently interpreting engagement from observable cues [42].
- **Lack of public datasets:** Few large-scale, publicly available datasets exist, making it difficult to train robust deep learning models. The lack of standardized annotations further limits generalization across studies [25].
- **Class imbalance:** Engagement datasets are often skewed toward high engagement, as low-engagement states are less likely to be captured during interaction [25]. To address this, [10] recommend using evaluation metrics robust to imbalance. Macro-F1, in particular, has been shown to provide the most reliable generalization, particularly averaged across folds in k-fold cross-validation, as it is unbiased toward class distribution [12]. Nonetheless, many engagement studies continue to report accuracy as figure of merit, which can be misleading when dominant classes are overrepresented.
- **Temporal modeling and granularity:** Engagement is dynamic, yet many methods rely on static frames. It remains unclear what temporal window (frame- vs. clip-level) best captures engagement signals, making time-series modelling an ongoing challenge [25,42].

3 Methods

3.1 Dataset

Our dataset comprises 19,106 images of children interacting with H4K, captured at 1 FPS during a two-week in-home trial involving six families. H4K engaged with 14 children ($n_{\text{male}} = 9$), aged 6–13 years ($\mu_{\text{age}} = 9.6$). Each image was labelled with an Engagement Level Metric (ELM) from 1 to 4 by five human annotators, where 1 indicates high disengagement, 2 low disengagement, 3 low engagement, and 4 high engagement (for further details about the annotation process, see [14]). To address annotation variability, and to examine its impact on model training, we created three subsets based on *annotator agreement*: ELM3 includes images where at least three annotators agreed (13,539 pictures; a 71% of the total), ELM4 where at least four agreed (5,756; 30%), and ELM5 where all five agreed (1,654; 9%). ELM3 served as our primary dataset given its larger size and the lowest class imbalance amongst all subsets. For completeness we also consider ELM_{ALL} (16,436; 86%), which corresponds to the full dataset after removing images where no face was detected. All subsets remain imbalanced, with higher engagement levels (3 and 4) being more frequent. Figure 1 shows the distribution of engagement labels (ELMs: 1–4) across the dataset subsets (ELM_{ALL}; $ELM3$ to $ELM5$). Figure 2 shows their distribution per family.

We applied RetinaFace [8], a deep learning model for face detection, with a 90% confidence threshold for face detection. Images without a face detected were discarded. The remaining images were cropped to the face region and resized to 224×224 pixels (RGB).

3.2 Validation Strategies

- **Cross-validation (CV):** We performed 80/20 train-validation splits by randomly shuffling data across all families. This tests generalization across unseen images but not necessarily unseen children. All trainable models were evaluated under this scheme.
- **Leave-One-Group-Out (LOGO):** Each fold excludes one family and uses it entirely for validation. This setup better reflects generalization to new users as it is a stricter validation setup, and was only applied to the best-performing model. The median train/validation split across LOGO folds is approximately 71/29, as shown in Table 2. Family 6 was excluded due to its disproportionate size (46% of ELM3), which could bias results.

3.3 Transfer Learning Framework

Pre-trained FER Model (EmoAffectNet): We adopt a transfer learning strategy using a pre-trained facial emotion recognition (FER) model to

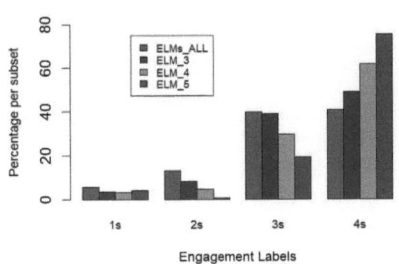

Fig. 1. Class distribution by dataset.

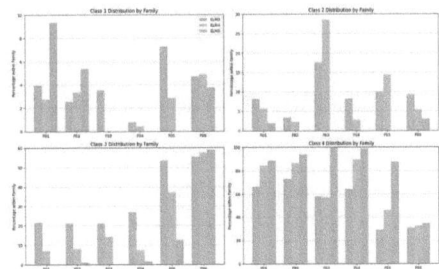

Fig. 2. Class distribution per family and dataset.

address two key limitations in engagement recognition. First, deep learning models require large and diverse datasets to learn generalizable features; however, engagement datasets–especially those involving children–are often small and lack variability [49]. Using a model pre-trained on large-scale facial datasets allows us to retain low-level visual priors while fine-tuning the network for engagement-specific representations. Second, we focus exclusively on facial images, which offers both methodological and practical advantages compared to full-body views; e.g., less occlusions and chances of overfitting to backgrounds. Facial expressions alone provide rich cues for emotional and attentional states, as prior studies have shown, even in the absence of additional modalities [24,48,49].

In this work, we build on insights from our previous study [15] by employing the *EmoAffectNet* framework developed by Ryumina et al.. [41]. EmoAffectNet is a state-of-the-art FER model that comprises two main components: a *ResNet50*-based backbone (a deep CNN with residual connections [21]) for static image recognition, and an LSTM-based temporal module for video input.

We focus exclusively on its ResNet50 backbone, which was selected for its demonstrated performance across diverse conditions. In [41], the model was initially trained on *ImageNet* [21] for general feature extraction, then fine-tuned on *VGGFace* [37] for facial representation learning, and subsequently adapted to facial emotion recognition using static datasets such as *FER2013* [18] and *AffectNet* [32]. On AffectNet, it achieved 0.664 classification accuracy across eight emotion categories, outperforming existing benchmarks and showing robustness to variations in age, gender, lighting, head pose, and occlusion. As shown in Fig. 3, from each facial image, the model outputs seven class probabilities (Happiness, Sadness, Surprise, Fear, Disgust, Anger, and Neutral) via a softmax layer, and just before this layer, it produces a 512-dimensional feature *embedding* that is assumed to encode high-level emotional information.

Model Configurations: We employ EmoAffectNet in two configurations. First, in CNN-7, we use the original model without modifying its architecture or weights, extracting either the emotion probabilities or the internal embeddings for downstream classifiers. Second, in CNN-4, we replace the emotion classification head with a 4-class engagement head and fine-tune the model end-to-end on our dataset, initialised from the pre-trained weights. Both configurations are illustrated in Fig. 3.

3.4 Baseline Methods (CNN-7)

As a baseline, we used the pre-trained model *EmoAffectNet* without modifying its internal weights (that is, *off-the-shelf*). The input image is passed through the FER model to obtain either emotion probabilities or dense intermediate feature embeddings.

- **CI**: from the most confident predicted emotion, we computed a Concentration Index (CI), then converted to an engagement level by: $CI = DEP \times EW$,

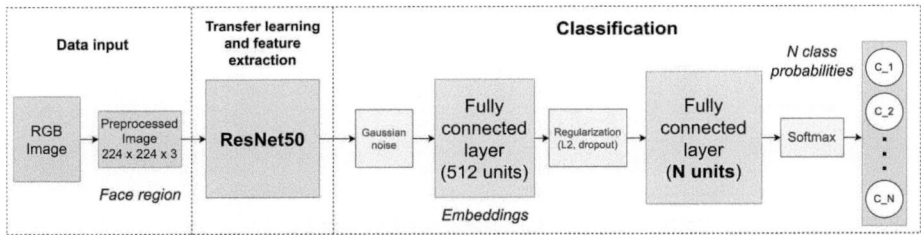

Fig. 3. Block diagram of the EmoAffectNet FER framework. The output classes are N = 7 for emotions predictions (original FER), and N = 4 for engagement levels.

where **DEP** is the dominant emotion probability and **EW** is an empirically derived weight for that emotion [47]. The resulting continuous CI score (0–1) was mapped to a discrete 4-class engagement level using fixed thresholds. We evaluated CI on the full dataset, as it does not require a training subset.

- **SVC on emotion probabilities (7-D)**: A Support Vector Classifier (SVC) was trained on the 7-class softmax output produced by the model's final layer. Unlike the fixed CI formula, which applied a predefined mapping, this data-driven approach aimed to learn a more flexible relationship between emotion distributions and engagement levels.
- **SVC on emotion embeddings (512-D)**: An SVC was trained on the 512-dimensional embedding vector from the model's penultimate layer. These embeddings represent high-level features learned during emotion classification and may contain latent patterns useful for predicting engagement.

3.5 Fine-Tuning (CNN-4)

Label Treatment Strategies: to address dataset limitations, we explored two labelling strategies: (1) training with and without class-weighted loss to account for class imbalance during training, as unbalanced distributions can cause models to underrepresent or ignore minority classes; and (2) using probabilistic soft labels derived from annotator agreement levels to address label ambiguity. For the latter, we used *TensorFlow*'s `categorical_crossentropy` to compute the loss over the soft label distribution.

Layer Freezing Strategies: We fine-tuned the pre-trained EmoAffectNet model by freezing different numbers of convolutional blocks, as shown in Fig. 4. We tested the following six configurations:

- **Full Freeze (1)**: All convolutional blocks were frozen; only the final classification layers were trained for engagement estimation.
- **Partial Freeze (4)**: One, two, three, or four convolutional blocks were unfrozen in turn to allow training of progressively deeper layers.

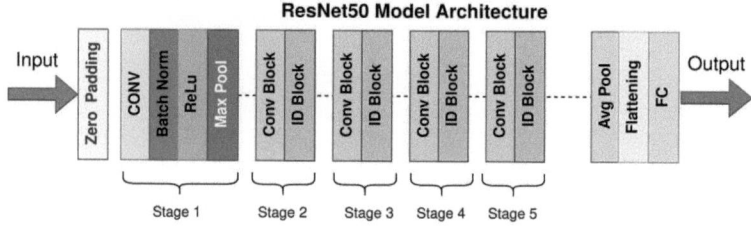

Fig. 4. Block diagram of ResNet50, showing its five convolutional blocks (stages) and the final classification layers. *Source*: [7].

- **No Freeze (1)**: All layers were unfrozen, allowing the entire model to be retrained on our dataset.

We used a 128 batch size, a learning rate of 10^{-4}, and 30 epochs with the Adam optimizer, following the settings in [41]. We used the `sparse categorical crossentropy` loss function for standard training with hard labels.

Low-Rank Adaptation (LoRA): We employed Low-Rank Adaptation (LoRA) [22] to fine-tune the pre-trained EmoAffectNet model for engagement classification. This technique limits overfitting and significantly reduces computational overhead (e.g., with $r = 32$, $\alpha = 32$, results in approximately 2.4M trainable parameters, out of 27M total). In our setup, all convolutional layers within each residual block, as well as the final classification layers, were LoRA-trainable.

In addition, in order to identify the best hyperparameters, we performed a grid search over learning rates, batch sizes, and LoRA (r, α). The best-performing setup used a learning rate of 0.001, $r = 64$ and $\alpha = 256$, with batch sizes from 16 to 128 yielding comparable results. These best performing hyperparameters were then used for the LOGO validation setting. During cross-validation (CV), models were trained for up to 20 epochs, while LOGO training used up to 10 epochs. In both cases, early stopping was applied based on validation accuracy. We applied the same grid search to the probability dataset, training 160 models to account for variability and to ensure fair comparison.

Note that LOGO validation was applied only to the LoRA model, after identifying it as the best performer via cross-validation.

4 Results

This section presents the performance of the proposed methods above for engagement prediction on the **ELM3 dataset**. We report accuracy and macro-F1, emphasizing macro-F1 as our primary evaluation metric due to its robustness against class imbalance, as it is less biased toward dominant classes.

Table 1. The different engagement estimation methods used in this work and their performance in cross-validation metrics accuracy (Acc.) and macro-F1 (F1).

Transfer Type	Strategy Description	Model	Acc.	F1	Description
Feature extraction	FER used as a fixed feature extractor; no trainable layers. Outputs emotion probabilities or embeddings for downstream classifiers.	CNN-7$_{CI}$	0.53	0.28	Rule-based mapping from dominant emotion.
		CNN-7$_{SVC\text{-}prob}$	0.32	0.26	SVC on 7-class emotion probability outputs.
		CNN-7$_{SVC\text{-}emb}$	0.56	0.45	SVC on 512-dimension internal FER embeddings.
Fine-tuning	Pretrained FER model fine-tuned on a 4-class engagement task; replaced 7-class head with 4-class.	CNN-4$_{Freeze}$	0.25	0.31	FER full freeze; only classification layers trained.
		CNN-4$_{LoRA\text{-}labels}$	**0.76**	**0.69**	Lightweight fine-tuning via LoRA modules.
		CNN-4$_{LoRA\text{-}probs}$	0.68	0.56	Same LoRA setup trained on probability-based inputs.

Performance of All Methods: Table 1 summarizes the overall performance of each method, showing the progressive improvements from simple emotion-to-engagement mappings (CNN-7+CI and CNN-7+SVC-emb) to more sophisticated fine-tuning approaches (CNN-4 Freeze and CNN-4 LoRA). The results reflect both F1 scores and accuracy, demonstrating a clear trend of improvement across methods. The baseline, CNN-7+CI, reached an F1 score of 0.28, while CNN-7+SVC-emb achieved 0.45, indicating that deeper feature-based SVC was more effective than direct emotion mapping. The LoRA approach with hard labels (CNN-4 LoRA-labels) achieved the highest F1 score of 0.69 and an accuracy of 0.76.

Transfer Learning Results with CNN-4 Freeze: Among the six configurations tested, full freezing yielded the best performance, with an F1 score of 0.35. As more blocks were unfrozen–starting with one (0.31), then two (0.26), three (0.22), and four (0.19)–performance steadily declined. Unfreezing the entire network resulted in an F1 score of 0.23.

We also tested the use of probability vectors instead of scalar labels, using a balanced configuration (three blocks unfrozen) that retains pretrained features while allowing enough flexibility to adapt to the engagement task. The results showed minimal difference: macro-F1 was 0.21 with scalar labels and 0.19 with probability vectors, indicating no meaningful improvement.

Transfer Learning Results with CNN-4 LoRA: After identifying CNN-4 LoRA as the best-performing method, we further tested its generalization ability through LOGO validation, in order to assess whether the model was capable of generalizing across different family groups, or it was just overfitting.

Table 2 shows the F1 scores for each LOGO split. As expected, F1 scores were lower than the cross-validation result (0.69), since LOGO excludes each validation family from training. However, keeping in mind that a classifier based solely on sheer chance would have an F1 lower than 0.25 (as classes are highly

Table 2. LOGO validation dataset characteristics and performance across the subsets ELM3, ELM4, and ELM5. The most representative metric is $F1_w$ at ELM3.

Family	Family IDs		# Images		Ratio		ELM3		ELM4		ELM5	
	Train	Val.	Train	Val.	Train	Val.	Acc	$F1_w$	Acc	$F1_w$	Acc	$F1_w$
F01	2,3,4,5,6	1	11,273	2,266	0.83	0.17	0.34	0.37	0.54	0.63	0.83	0.84
F02	1,3,4,5,6	2	11,329	2,210	0.84	0.16	0.37	0.41	0.41	0.51	0.76	0.84
F03	1,2,4,5,6	3	13,254	285	0.98	0.02	0.60	0.56	0.38	0.46	0.93	0.96
F04	1,2,3,5,6	4	11,520	2,019	0.85	0.15	0.46	0.49	0.81	0.84	0.91	0.94
F05	1,2,3,4,6	5	12,989	550	0.96	0.04	0.34	0.29	0.48	0.45	0.75	0.77
F06	1,2,3,4,5	6	7,330	6,209	0.54	0.46	0.52	0.48	0.46	0.44	0.39	0.29
Avg.			11,283	2,257	**0.83**	**0.17**	0.44	0.43	0.52	0.56	0.76	0.77
Median			11,425	2,115	0.84	0.16	0.41	0.45	0.47	0.49	0.79	0.84

unbalanced), we see that the LOGO results even for ELM3 are not so bad, as half of the groups still reached values around 0.50.

On the other hand, Family F05 had the lowest F1 score at 0.29 –around the value of pure chance-, highlighting variability across different groups. See a more detailed analysis in the *Discussion* section.

5 Discussion

Overview of All Methods: This study aimed to develop a robust, data-efficient method for estimating child engagement in CRI, addressing two major challenges in the field: (1) the lack of large, high-quality engagement datasets, and (2) severe class imbalance. We leveraged a single pre-trained FER model and applied transfer learning to adapt it for engagement classification.

We first evaluated three baseline methods using the FER model without modification: a Concentration Index, an SVC on emotion probabilities, and an SVC on embeddings. While simple emotion mappings performed poorly (macro-F1 0.26–0.28), the deeper embeddings improved performance to 0.45–supporting our hypothesis that pretrained emotion features contain useful visual cues for engagement. Next, we explored progressive fine-tuning by unfreezing convolutional blocks. Surprisingly, the best result (macro-F1 = 0.35) came from the fully frozen model–where only the final classification layers were retrained. Unfreezing additional layers steadily reduced performance, down to 0.19. Validation accuracy remained stable at 0.59, indicating increased overfitting to majority classes.

These results suggest that the pretrained FER features were already well aligned with the task, and that retraining disrupted them –likely due to data scarcity and class imbalance. Given that full freezing outperformed all other configurations, we turned to LoRA, which freezes the original weights and introduces small trainable matrices into selected layers, allowing lightweight, task-specific adaptation without modifying the backbone (as the weights were already well-aligned with the task).

While cross-validation yielded good scores for LoRA, these results likely overestimate generalization, as images from the same child appear in both training and validation sets. Using a 70/30 split instead of the usual 80/20, produced a drop on those scores, showing sensitivity to training size but not true user-level generalization. To address this, we applied LOGO validation. This highlights that while LoRA improves robustness, generalization to unseen users remains uneven –likely due to limited and not fully consistent engagement data.

5.1 Impact of Annotator Agreement and Label Quality

We assessed the impact of *supposed* annotation quality increase using three subsets with increasing annotator agreement: ELM3 (≥ 3), ELM4 (≥ 4), and ELM5 (5/5). All evaluations used LOGO validation with our best model, CNN-4 LoRA. Each subset was split into training and validation sets–so even under class imbalance, the model could be trained, and having all four classes present in validation remains important compared to classes not appearing at all.

Subset ELM3, while the largest, had the lowest agreement and served as the main training set, as discussed earlier. The results obtained with ELM5, despite having the highest agreement, *must be interpreted with caution*: it was the smallest, most imbalanced, and had limited class diversity–e.g., in ELM5, F03 included only one class, F04 and F05 two, and F01 and F02 lacked one class each, as shown in Fig. 2. High F1 scores in ELM5 likely reflect reduced classification complexity rather than true generalization. ELM4 offered the best trade-off: higher agreement than ELM3, broader class coverage than ELM5, and more consistent F1 scores across families, as shown in Table 2. In ELM4, only F03 lacked one class in validation. Based on these results, we hypothesize that *higher annotator agreement improved label quality, which in turn helped the model learn more effectively*–even with fewer samples. The fact that CNN-4 LoRA achieved strong LOGO performance on ELM4–despite the smaller dataset size–supports that idea, as well as previous literature [17]. However, further experiments are needed to confirm this. In any case, more balanced, larger and diverse datasets are essential to fully validate model generalization claims.

5.2 Comparison with Prior Work

Many studies on engagement estimation, particularly using the DAiSEE dataset, report high accuracy –often on simplified tasks (e.g., 2- or 3-class setups) or favourable splits (e.g., same subjects in train and validation). However, accuracy alone can be misleading in imbalanced settings, as it overemphasises dominant classes [10]. Therefore, in this work, in addition to accuracy, we have used macro-F1 and LOGO validation to better capture generalization across all classes and unseen users in-the-wild.

Ahmad *et al.* [3] benchmarked ten pretrained CNNs (e.g., ResNet50, VGG16), using them for classification and as feature extractors for downstream classifiers (e.g., SVC), similar to our approach. Their best model achieved 0.687 F1 on a 3-class task, compared to our CNN-4 LoRA with 0.69 F1 on a 4-class task. Our relative improvement may be due to the use of pre-trained models from emotion and facial feature datasets, which could enhance the model's ability to capture engagement-specific features.

Liao et al. [31] proposed a CNN-LSTM architecture using SE-ResNet-50 pretrained on VGGFace2 and FER-2013, resembling our approach, but they added LSTM for temporal modeling, capturing engagement dynamics. Their model achieved 0.588 accuracy (MSE = 0.0422) on DAiSEE, highlighting the challenges of temporal modeling in engagement estimation.

Santoni et al. [44,45] used pre-extracted facial features from OpenFace, including 709 values (e.g., AUs), and trained a bagging ensemble of CNNs, ResNet, and hybrid models, achieving 0.933 F1 and 0.943 accuracy on the 4-class DAiSEE dataset (compared to our 0.69 F1 and 0.76 accuracy). Their use of SMOTE addressed class imbalance by generating more data for minority classes. Their impressive performance results from their hybrid approach, combining handcrafted features with deep learning, easing the burden on CNNs and overcoming the limitations of deep learning with limited data. In contrast, we rely on pretrained models to automatically extract facial features from images. Santoni's method currently holds the highest benchmark on DAiSEE, supporting the reliability of static vision systems focusing on facial features.

Yun et al. (2018) [49] were amongst the first to apply deep learning to child engagement estimation, using pretrained models due to limited data. Their system used facial videos with a pre-trained CNN (VGG Face) for feature extraction and LSTM for temporal modelling. Their dataset, consisting of 30 children aged 7 with 6,829 samples, used majority voting among 7 labellers. They initially used a 4-class annotation scheme but later simplified it to a 2-class system (Engaged vs. Disengaged) due to class imbalance, achieving a F1 score of 0.754.

While their approach is similar to ours in using pretrained CNNs, we focus on still images, whereas they used video clips. Their dataset size is comparable to ours, but they simplified the problem to 2 classes, unlike our 4-class approach, which achieved 0.69 F1. Despite differences in methodology, both studies aim to address CRI engagement with similar datasets and feature extraction techniques. Both works demonstrate the effectiveness of pretrained models for facial engagement estimation, overcoming data limitations and class imbalance.

5.3 Limitations and Future Directions

While the results of this study are highly promising, several limitations remain. First, all subsets (ELM3, ELM4, and ELM5) suffer from significant class imbalance. This highlights the need for more balanced and diverse datasets to truly assess generalization. The inherent challenge stems from the natural dynamics of engagement: lower-engagement states often result in early dropout, leading to underrepresentation of these cases in the data collection process.

Furthermore, we chose to extract still images at 1 FPS rather than storing full videos to limit storage requirements, reduce privacy risks associated with continuous recordings, and streamline the annotation process. Nevertheless, temporal information might improve model performance.

Additionally, while this study demonstrates technical feasibility, deploying such systems in real-world child contexts requires careful ethical reflection and adherence to emerging regulations on emotion AI for vulnerable users [26]. Future work should include participatory design with families and ethical experts to evaluate social acceptability and potential risks, as we have already done in our previous work [30].

6 Conclusion

This study validates a data-efficient strategy for engagement detection in child-robot interaction: leveraging pretrained emotion recognition models and applying minimal, targeted fine-tuning via LoRA. Despite limited training data, models like CNN-4 LoRA achieved some generalization to unseen individuals – particularly when trained on well-annotated subsets. This opens the door for more accessible, deployable affective systems in real-world CRI.

Acknowledgments. This publication is part of the project PLEC2023-010251, funded by MICIU/AEI/10.13039/501100011033, which also supports R. Laycock.

This work was also supported by *Honda Research Institute* and by the Spanish Ministry of Science, Innovation and Universities under grant *PTQ2021-011726* awarded to G.A. García.

The authors would like to thank the families who participated in this study, and the annotators who labelled the pictures of our dataset.

Disclosure of Interests. The authors have no competing interests to declare that are relevant to the content of this article.

References

1. Abedi, A., Khan, S.S.: Improving state-of-the-art in detecting student engagement with ResNet and TCN hybrid network. In: 2021 18th Conference on Robots and Vision (CRV), pp. 151–157. IEEE (2021)
2. Admoni, H., Scassellati, B.: Social eye gaze in human-robot interaction: a review. J. Hum. Robot Interact. **6**(1), 25–63 (2017)
3. Ahmad, N., Gupta, A., Singh, D.: Using deep transfer learning to predict student engagement in online courses. In: International Conference on Machine Learning, Image Processing, Network Security and Data Sciences, pp. 27–36. Springer (2022)
4. Alnajjar, F., Cappuccio, M., Renawi, A., Mubin, O., Loo, C.K.: Personalized robot interventions for autistic children: an automated methodology for attention assessment. Int. J. Soc. Robot. **13**(1), 67–82 (2021)
5. Anderson, A.R., Christenson, S.L., Sinclair, M.F., Lehr, C.A.: Check & connect: the importance of relationships for promoting engagement with school. J. Sch. Psychol. **42**(2), 95–113 (2004)
6. Clabaugh, C., Matarić, M.J., Scheutz, M.: Long-term personalization of an in-home socially assistive robot for children with autism spectrum disorders. Front. Robot. AI **6**, 110 (2019). https://doi.org/10.3389/frobt.2019.00110

7. Commons, W.: ResNet50 architecture diagram (2021). https://commons.wikimedia.org/wiki/File:ResNet50.png. Accessed 1 Oct 2024
8. Deng, J., Guo, J., Ververas, E., Kotsia, I., Zafeiriou, S.: RetinaFace: single-shot multi-level face localisation in the wild. In: Proceedings of the IEEE/CVF Conference on Computer Vision and Pattern Recognition, pp. 5203–5212 (2020)
9. Dewan, M.A.A., Murshed, M., Lin, F.: Engagement detection in online learning: a review. Smart Learn. Environ. **6**(1), 1–20 (2019). https://doi.org/10.1186/s40561-018-0080-z
10. Dresvyanskiy, D., Minker, W., Karpov, A.: Deep learning based engagement recognition in highly imbalanced data. In: Karpov, A., Potapova, R. (eds.) SPECOM 2021. LNCS (LNAI), vol. 12997, pp. 166–178. Springer, Cham (2021). https://doi.org/10.1007/978-3-030-87802-3_16
11. Filippini, C., et al.: Facilitating the child–robot interaction by endowing the robot with the capability of understanding the child engagement: the case of Mio Amico robot. Int. J. Soc. Robot. **13**(4), 677–689 (2021)
12. Forman, G., Scholz, M.: Apples-to-apples in cross-validation studies: pitfalls in classifier performance measurement. ACM SIGKDD Expl. Newsl. **12**(1), 49–57 (2010)
13. Fredricks, J.A., Blumenfeld, P.C., Paris, A.H.: School engagement: potential of the concept, state of the evidence. Rev. Educ. Res. **74**(1), 59–109 (2004)
14. García, G.A., et al.: Living with Haru4Kids: study on children's activity and engagement in a family-robot cohabitation scenario. In: 2023 32nd IEEE International Conference on Robot and Human Interactive Communication (RO-MAN), pp. 1428–1435. IEEE (2023)
15. García, G.A., et al.: Preliminary study on the feasibility of approximating children's engagement level from their emotions estimation by a picture-based, three-model AI in a family-robot cohabitation scenario. Adv. Robot. **38**(23), 1710–1728 (2024). https://doi.org/10.1080/01691864.2024.2415093
16. Gomez, R., Szapiro, D., Galindo, K., Nakamura, K.: Haru: hardware design of an experimental tabletop robot assistant. In: HRI 2018, pp. 233–240 (2018)
17. Gong, Y., Liu, G., Xue, Y., Li, R., Meng, L.: A survey on dataset quality in machine learning. Inf. Softw. Technol. **162**, 107268 (2023)
18. Goodfellow, I.J., et al.: Challenges in representation learning: a report on three machine learning contests. In: Lee, M., Hirose, A., Hou, Z.-G., Kil, R.M. (eds.) ICONIP 2013. LNCS, vol. 8228, pp. 117–124. Springer, Heidelberg (2013). https://doi.org/10.1007/978-3-642-42051-1_16
19. Gordon, G., Breazeal, C., Engel, S.: Can children catch curiosity from a social robot? In: Proceedings of the Tenth Annual ACM/IEEE International Conference on Human-Robot Interaction, pp. 91–98. ACM (2015). https://doi.org/10.1145/2696454.2696469
20. Gupta, A., D'Cunha, A., Awasthi, K., Balasubramanian, V.: DAiSEE: towards user engagement recognition in the wild. arXiv preprint arXiv:1609.01885 (2016)
21. He, K., Zhang, X., Ren, S., Sun, J.: Deep residual learning for image recognition. In: Proceedings of the IEEE Conference on Computer Vision and Pattern Recognition, pp. 770–778 (2016)
22. Hu, E.J., et al.: LoRA: low-rank adaptation of large language models. arXiv preprint (2021)
23. Hu, Y., Jiang, Z., Zhu, K.: An optimized CNN model for engagement recognition in an e-learning environment. Appl. Sci. **12**(16), 8007 (2022)

24. Kamath, A., Biswas, A., Balasubramanian, V.: A crowdsourced approach to student engagement recognition in e-learning environments. In: 2016 IEEE Winter Conference on Applications of Computer Vision (WACV), pp. 1–9. IEEE (2016)
25. Karimah, S.N., Hasegawa, S.: Automatic engagement recognition for distance learning systems: a literature study of engagement datasets and methods. In: International Conference on Human-Computer Interaction, pp. 264–276. Springer (2021)
26. Katirai, A.: Ethical considerations in emotion recognition technologies: a review of the literature. AI Ethics **4**(4), 927–948 (2023). https://doi.org/10.1007/s43681-023-00307-3
27. Lambert, A., Norouzi, N., Bruder, G., Welch, G.: A systematic review of ten years of research on human interaction with social robots. Int. J. Hum. Comput. Interact. **36**(19), 1804–1817 (2020)
28. LeCun, Y., Bengio, Y., Hinton, G.: Deep learning. Nature **521**(7553), 436–444 (2015). https://doi.org/10.1038/nature14539
29. Leite, I., Martinho, C., Paiva, A.: Social robots for long-term interaction: a survey. Int. J. Soc. Robot. **5**, 291–308 (2013)
30. Levinson, L., et al.: Living with Haru4Kids: child and parent perceptions of a cohabitation robot for children. In: International Conference on Social Robotics, pp. 54–63. Springer (2022)
31. Liao, J., Liang, Y., Pan, J.: Deep facial spatiotemporal network for engagement prediction in online learning. Appl. Intell. **51**(10), 6609–6621 (2021). https://doi.org/10.1007/s10489-020-02139-8
32. Mollahosseini, A., Hasani, B., Mahoor, M.H.: AffectNet: a database for facial expression, valence, and arousal computing in the wild. IEEE Trans. Affect. Comput. **10**(1), 18–31 (2017)
33. Murshed, M., Dewan, M.A.A., Lin, F., Wen, D.: Engagement detection in e-learning environments using convolutional neural networks. In: 2019 IEEE International Conference on Dependable, Autonomic and Secure Computing, International Conference on Pervasive Intelligence and Computing, International Conference on Cloud and Big Data Computing, International Conference on Cyber Science and Technology Congress (DASC/PiCom/CBDCom/CyberSciTech), pp. 80–86. IEEE (2019)
34. O'Brien, H.: Theoretical perspectives on user engagement. In: O'Brien, H., Cairns, P. (eds.) Why Engagement Matters. Springer, Cham (2016). https://doi.org/10.1007/978-3-319-27446-1_1
35. O'Brien, H.L., Cairns, P., Hall, M.: A practical approach to measuring user engagement with the refined user engagement scale (UES) and new UES short form. Int. J. Hum Comput Stud. **112**, 28–39 (2018)
36. Pabba, C., Kumar, P.: An intelligent system for monitoring students' engagement in large classroom teaching through facial expression recognition. Exp. Syst. **39**(1), e12839 (2022)
37. Parkhi, O., Vedaldi, A., Zisserman, A.: Deep face recognition. In: Proceedings of the British Machine Vision Conference 2015, BMVC 2015. British Machine Vision Association (2015)
38. Perez, G., et al.: Child-robot conversation in the wild wild home: a language processing user study. In: 32nd IEEE International Conference on Robot and Human Interactive Communication, IEEE RO-MAN 2023, pp. 1436–1442, Busan, South Korea (2023)
39. Riek, L.D.: Healthcare robotics. Commun. ACM **60**(11), 68–78 (2017). https://doi.org/10.1145/3127874

40. Rudovic, O., Park, H.W., Busche, J., Schuller, B., Breazeal, C., Picard, R.W.: Personalized estimation of engagement from videos using active learning with deep reinforcement learning. In: 2019 IEEE/CVF Conference on Computer Vision and Pattern Recognition Workshops (CVPRW), pp. 217–226. IEEE (2019)
41. Ryumina, E., Dresvyanskiy, D., Karpov, A.: In search of a robust facial expressions recognition model: a large-scale visual cross-corpus study. Neurocomputing **514**, 435–450 (2022)
42. Salam, H., Celiktutan, O., Gunes, H., Chetouani, M.: Automatic context-driven inference of engagement in HMI: a survey. arXiv preprint arXiv:2209.15370 (2022)
43. Sandry, E., Gomez, R., Nakamura, K.: Art, design and communication theory in creating the communicative social robot 'Haru'. Front. Robot. AI **8** (2021)
44. Santoni, M.M., Basaruddin, T., Junus, K.: Convolutional neural network model based students' engagement detection in imbalanced DAiSEE dataset. Int. J. Adv. Comput. Sci. Appl. **14**(3) (2023)
45. Santoni, M.M., Basaruddin, T., Junus, K., Lawanto, O.: Automatic detection of students' engagement during online learning: a bagging ensemble deep learning approach. IEEE Access (2024)
46. Scassellati, B., Admoni, H., Mataric, M.: Robots for use in autism research. Annu. Rev. Biomed. Eng. **14**, 275–294 (2012). https://doi.org/10.1146/annurev-bioeng-071811-150036
47. Sharma, P., et al.: Student engagement detection using emotion analysis, eye tracking and head movement with machine learning. arXiv (2019). https://arxiv.org/abs/1909.12913
48. Whitehill, J., Serpell, Z., Lin, Y.C., Foster, A., Movellan, J.R.: The faces of engagement: automatic recognition of student engagement from facial expressions. IEEE Trans. Affect. Comput. **5**(1), 86–98 (2014)
49. Yun, W.H., Lee, D., Park, C., Kim, J., Kim, J.: Automatic recognition of children engagement from facial video using convolutional neural networks. IEEE Trans. Affect. Comput. **11**(4), 696–707 (2018)

Toward Safe Child-Robot Interactions: Exploring Children's and Parents' Privacy Perceptions of Humanoid Social Robots

JaeEun Jen Shin(✉), Amr Hamdi, An Bella Chen, Yue Hu, and Leah Zhang-Kennedy

University of Waterloo, Waterloo, ON N2L 3G1, Canada
{jeshin,amhamdi,bella.chen,yue.hu,lzhangkennedy}@uwaterloo.ca

Abstract. As humanoid social robots (HSRs) become more integrated into family environments, it is crucial to examine privacy concerns in child-robot interaction. This study examines how children and parents perceive privacy risks associated with HSRs, focusing on differences in their comfort levels across various usage scenarios. We conducted a user study with 38 parent-child dyads interacting with the HSR "NAO" using pre-programmed activities. Our findings revealed disparity in robot likability, smartness, and trustworthiness. These characteristics also influenced children's willingness to share personal information (secrets). Parents and children showed significant differences in their comfort levels with sensor usage across different contextual scenarios, where parents expressed concerns about data collection, storage, and transfer, preferring supervised interactions, and emphasizing the need for transparency and control over robot interactions. These findings suggest that designing HSRs with clear privacy controls, child-friendly features, and parental oversight is essential to ensuring safer and more trusted interactions.

Keywords: Human-Robot Interaction · Child-Robot Interaction · Humanoid Social Robot · Privacy Risk Perception

1 Introduction and Related Work

Social robots for children have evolved from simple toys to sophisticated companions and educational tools, gaining increasing acceptance [6,12,50]. These social robots have been designed to provide potential benefits such as improving literacy and reading skills [6,30,43,50,60], and addressing therapeutic [14,23,48,52], social [5,19,24,59], emotional [10,15,62], and physical needs [3,22,32,58]. These social robots can deliver personalized support and guidance. Their adaptability stems from a combination of advanced sensors such as cameras, microphones, motion detectors, and GPS, which provide the context-aware data to enable sophisticated interactions [11,36]. Advances in machine learning, natural language processing, and computer vision enable social robots to personalize behaviors using sensor data [36], and creating adaptive, user-specific experiences [3].

Despite preliminary evidence that child-robot interaction could support children's education and development, concerns about data security and privacy, as well as potential risks associated with social robotics, have been raised [17,28,34,35,46]. Social robots for family use, in particular, can collect sensitive personal, social, and environmental information, which can expose users to privacy vulnerabilities [12]. The tasks and contexts in which social robots are utilized in domestic or healthcare have a profound impact on the privacy-utility tradeoff [28]. Since sharing physical private space increases the possibility of privacy breaches [35], users worry about what data is being recorded, stored [21,55], or sent to third parties [61]. Furthermore, autonomous and mobile domestic social robots raise concerns about their potential use as surveillance tools [45].

These privacy risks are further heightened through interactions that engage users' emotional and cognitive states [17,26], especially in young children [17,28,34,35,46]. Current social robots are adopting human-like features and socially interactive behaviors in both their appearance and functionality, aiming to avoid the "uncanny valley [44]" effect while striking a balance between anthropomorphic and zoomorphic traits [9,13,16,20]. This thoughtful combination enhances their appeal, making them highly engaging and widely accepted by users [1,64] and the broader community [7,20]. These features facilitate more engaging interactions with children, fostering deeper emotional involvement [38,63]. However, this heightened level of interaction can lead people to misinterpret the actions of social robots, attributing human-like intent or meaning to their behaviors, which may result in misunderstandings about their actual capabilities [41] and influence users' perceptions of privacy [4,28].

Children have poor mental models of cybersecurity and privacy threats and are often unaware of the consequences of sharing their personal information [42, 46,57], which are inhibited by their age and developmental needs [56]. Research investigating children aged 7 to 11 years found that their understanding of online safety is very basic, with limited awareness of online privacy risks and protective strategies [65]. Prior research on children's privacy risks of related technology such as smart toys and other IoT devices designed for home environments have uncovered notable privacy risks relating to data disclosure, internet-connected smart toys' abilities to maintain data privacy [27,29,39,51], and issues relating to the role of parental supervision [2,47]. For example, Hung et al. [27] analyzed data from conversation transcripts between children and a smart toy, revealing that detailed personal information can be disclosed through the child's voluntary conversation. Furthermore, it is essential to understand parents' risk perceptions as they play an active role in children's technology interactions and share the responsibility for managing children's privacy [65]. Parents are seen as carrying the primary responsibility for protecting children in the digital environments and are expected to provide guidelines for monitoring children's interactions with technology and going online [57], such as setting rules, parental controls, and limiting access to devices and the internet [65].

Recent research highlights growing concerns about privacy vulnerabilities for users of social robots [12]. Yet, it is unclear how these risks manifest within specific user groups and contexts [13,28,36,61]. In particular, there have been limited empirical studies that examined how humanoid social robots (HSRs) affect perceptions of family privacy in different spatial and locational settings, despite the advanced capabilities of these technologies. Although earlier studies on smart toys for families have focused primarily on devices with limited functionality, research on HSRs stands out due to their greater capabilities and the potential to foster more meaningful social engagement [53]. These enhanced interactions may shape users' expectations and significantly impact their privacy concerns [37,49]. Given this, it is crucial to explore how families perceive privacy risks associated with HSRs and the strategies they adopt to manage them. In addition, our study explores child-parent privacy perceptions across broader range of scenarios, including interactions with HSRs in both private and public spaces. Such an understanding can inform the development of privacy features in HSRs that align with families' needs and are accessible to children.

In this study, we aim to understand: **RQ1.** How do children and parents perceive HSRs and to what extent are they aware of privacy risks during human-robot interactions? **RQ2.** How do perceived robot characteristics (e.g., likability, smartness, closeness, and trustworthiness) influence children's willingness to disclose personal information (secrets)? **RQ3.** How comfortable are children and parents with various HSR sensor capabilities across different usage scenarios and contexts? **RQ4.** What are the similarities and differences between children's and parents' comfort levels regarding the use of HSRs?

2 Methodology

After receiving clearance from our institution's Research Ethics Board (REB), we recruited participants through parenting and community groups on social media and via an email newsletter distributed by our institution. A total of 38 parent-child dyads participated in our study, as summarized in Table 1. Based on parents' responses to the IUIPC (Internet Users' Information Privacy Concerns) questionnaire [40], our sample generally had moderate to high levels of privacy concerns regarding the collection of private information and data sharing ($M = 3.87$ to 4.45, $SD = 0.72$ to 0.93).

We used Aldebaran's NAO robot and programmed its behaviors using *Choregraphe*[1], adopting a Wizard of OZ approach. During the study, a researcher triggered these behavior sequences from a nearby computer, making the robot appear to act autonomously while its actions were controlled behind the scenes.

2.1 Procedure

To avoid priming participants, we omitted the term "privacy" from recruitment materials, instead describing the study as an exploration of perceptions towards educational HSRs. Privacy-related questions were introduced later in the session

---

[1] https://www.aldebaran.com/en/support/nao-6/downloads-softwares.

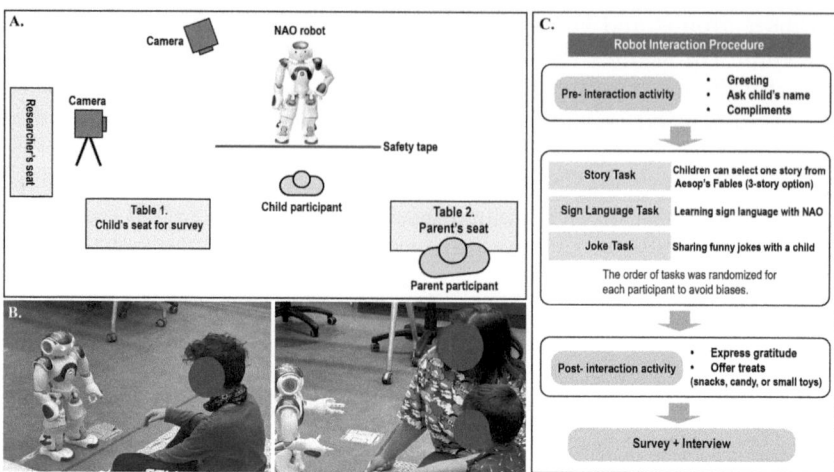

Fig. 1. A. Overview of the experimental setup. B. two photograph that represent the child-robot interaction session. C. robot interaction procedure

to reduce bias in earlier responses. Participants were fully debriefed at the end of the session, and each family received a $25 Amazon Gift card.

Parents and children were accommodated in a quiet lab room, providing a structured and comfortable environment for interacting with NAO's advanced, human-like features and movements, while ensuring child safety. Parent-child dyads were briefed together but completed questionnaires separately to prevent influencing each other's responses. Figure 1 summarizes our study procedure.

To help children feel more comfortable with the robot, children engaged in a brief pre-activity. NAO introduced itself and asked for the child's name. Upon hearing the response, NAO repeated the name and offered a polite compliment: *"Your name is (child's name). Great name!"*. Next, children engaged in three randomized 5-minute interactive activities with NAO–storytelling, sign language, and joke-sharing–designed to build trust and empathy while showcasing diverse interaction styles. Parents observed the sessions, and afterward,

Table 1. Demographic information of our of our child and parent participants.

Children			
Gender		Age	
Boy	20 (53%)	7-8 years old	20 (53%)
Girl	18 (47%)	9-12 years old	18 (47%)
Non-binary	0	Total	38

Parents								
Gender		Age		Education Level		Income		IUIPC factors
Male	11 (29%)	18-24	0	< high school degree	0	< $29K	1 (3%)	IUIPC_Collection
Female	26 (68%)	25-29	0	High school degree	0	$30K to $49K	1 (3%)	Mean (SD)
Non-binary	1 (3%)	30-34	3 (8%)	College degree	5 (13%)	$50K to $69K	3 (8%)	3.87 (0.93) ~4.45 (0.72)
		35-39	9 (24%)	Bachelor's degree	14 (37%)	$70K to $89K	4 (11%)	
		40-44	19 (50%)	Master's degree	13 (34%)	$90K to $149K	5 (13%)	IUIPC_Awareness
		45-49	4 (11%)	Doctoral degree	4 (11%)	$150K to $199K	7 (18%)	Mean (SD)
		50+	3 (8%)	Other	2 (5%)	$200K and above	11 (29%)	4.45 (0.72)
		Total	38	Prefer not to answer	0	Prefer not to answer	6 (16%)	

NAO thanked the participants and offered small treats (e.g., snacks, candy, or toys). After the interaction, the researcher escorted the child to a desk, thoroughly explained the process of the questionnaires for familiarization, and then guided them through the assisted questionnaire, reading questions aloud and offering clarification if needed. Meanwhile, the parent answered a demographics questionnaire and a robot perception questionnaire. This was followed by a brief semi-structured follow-up interview with the parent. Supplementary materials, including the full procedure, survey questionnaire, and thematic analysis, are available online[2].

Questionnaire Design. We assigned similar questions to both children and parents, but the child's questionnaire was simplified compared to the parents. We considered the children's reading levels and the potential difficulty in understanding the Likert scale's concepts of 'agreement' and 'disagreement'. Based on prior research [21,55], we aimed to reduce the influence of social and psychological factors on children's responses. Specifically, we adapted the Five Degrees of Happiness Likert scale from Hall et al. [25] that prioritizes positive emotions as a more appropriate method for children to communicate judgments about technology to reduce social desirability bias. For example, we used semantic labels from the most positive to the least positive (e.g., "Totally agree" to "Not quite agree"; "Super good" to "Not so good"; "Super comfortable" to "Not so comfortable"). The parent questionnaire used standard five point Likert scales to mirror the meaning of the children's scales (e.g., "Strongly agree" to "Strongly disagree"; "Very acceptable" to "Not at all acceptable"; "Very comfortable" to "Very uncomfortable". We believe these considerations mediated the differences in how children and adults respond to the questions, aiming to align children's ratings more closely with those of their parents.

Engagement Toward HSR Interactions (Children). To measure child participants' engagement and impression of the HSR, we administered self-report questionnaires [33], which included questions collected children's perception towards the NAO robot during the three interactivity activities. The child questions for *Closeness* were designed to represent how children perceived friendship and intimacy with social robot [33,53]. The parents' version was intended to capture their perspective on their child's friendship with the robot. Questionnaire items for Safety [14,42] are aimed to assess parents' perceptions of the robot's safety and their acceptance of its use in interactions with children.

Perceptions Toward HSR Interactions (Children & Parents). The child questionnaire contained questions relating to robot *Likability* and *Smartness* [35], *Closeness* [61] *Social interaction* [42,53], and *Trustworthiness* [54].

Comfort Level of HSR Sensors (Children & Parents). We first ask whether the child participants can perceive the robot's eight data collection capabilities (summarized in Fig. 3). If the child answered *"Yes"* or *"Maybe"* to questions regarding

---

[2] https://drive.google.com/file/d/16fY18K8EpP-vnki-l8dfrbOKzGp4vEbw/view?usp=drive_link.

sensor awareness, we then asked follow-up questions regarding their comfort level of data collection across six hypothetical scenarios and locations, summarized in Fig. 3. While hypothetical scenarios have limitations compared to real-life experiences of privacy threats, it would be unethical and impractical to expose children to actual privacy violations. Therefore, our study employs fictional but plausible scenarios that allow children to engage with and reflect on the concept of privacy in a safe and accessible way.

Questions for the parent participants used similar questions but focused on the child's context, such as, *"Do you think NAO can record your child's voice through a microphone?"* with the follow-up question: *"How comfortable are you if NAO recorded your child's voice"* in the scenarios. Detailed descriptions of the data types and scenarios are included in the appendix.

Willingness to Disclose Personal Information (Children). We assessed children's willingness to disclose personal information (secrets) to the HSR. The researcher asked the child participants to think of a secret in their mind and then posed the question, *"Would you tell NAO this secret if you were alone in this room with NAO?"* Following their response, the researcher asked them to explain their reasoning. However, children were not required to share their secret with the researcher; they only needed to indicate whether they would share the secret with the HSR. The child questionnaire concluded with two open-ended questions asking about the children's favorite things that NAO could do and whether they had anything else they would like to share about NAO.

Privacy Concerns (Parents). We assessed parent participants' general level of concern regarding information privacy [18,56] using the Internet Users' Information Privacy Concerns (IUIPC) scale [40]. Parent participants reported their perceptions of data collection *(IUIPC_Collection)* and awareness of privacy practice *(IUIPC_Awareness)*.

Demographic Questionnaire (Parents). Parent completed a demographic questionnaire covering information such as gender, age group, education level, income, and occupation, along with questions about the family's current IoT devices and privacy practices at home.

Exit Interview (Parents). Parent's shared their views on children's social robots use, parental controls, and adult supervision. Next, we asked about their general impressions of child-robot interaction sessions, focusing on similarities and differences compared to other types of smart devices. Lastly, they provided comments on the hypothetical scenarios.

Data Analysis. All the results presented are children's and parents' self-reported attitudes and behaviours. Quantitative analysis was conducted in R with a significance threshold of $p < 0.05$, while qualitative analysis was performed in NVivo. Open-ended responses were analyzed using inductive thematic analysis. The first author conducted open and axial coding to develop a preliminary codebook, which the second author independently used to analyze the transcripts. The researchers refined the codebook through iterative discussions. Inter-rater reliability showed good agreement (Cohen's $\kappa = 0.77$). Final themes were agreed upon collaboratively.

3 Results

For clarity and brevity, child participants are coded as CP (e.g., CP5) and parent participants as PP (e.g., PP5) in the sections that follow.

Child-Parent Participants' Perceptions of HSR. We examined the differences in how children and parents perceive and interact with the HSR (**RQ1**). Although both groups agreed that HSRs could serve as friends and facilitate positive interactions, the findings show that children consistently perceived the HSR more positively than the parent group across all variables related to positive engagement during interaction tasks. In contrast, the levels of agreement among parent participants were less pronounced compared to those of the children. Parents were more skeptical towards the robot. Table 2 and Fig. 2 summarizes children's and parents' responses towards HSR.

Children's Willingness to Disclose Personal Information. In response to the question *"Would you tell NAO your secret if you were alone in this room with NAO?"*, 55.26% (21/38) of child participants answered 'Yes,' 39.47% (15/38) answered 'No', and 5.26% (2/38) refused to answer. We will refer to this in the subsequent sections as *Willingness*(**RQ2**). When asked why they chose to share their secret with NAO, 42.86% (9/21) of the child participants who answered 'Yes' cited *Trustworthiness*, stating reasons like *"Because I trust NAO"* (CP5) and *"I don't think he would tell anybody"* (CP23). Another 23.81% (5/21) mentioned *Closeness*, with responses such as *"Because I feel comfortable"* (CP38) and *"Because he is my friend"* (CP11).

Table 2. Summary of Likert scale responses of child and parent participants' perceptions of HSR's Engagement, Likability, Smartness, Closeness, Social Interaction, and Trustworthiness. Child participants were not asked about Safety questions.

	Children		Parents
Constructs and items	Median (SD) Range 1-5	Constructs and items	Median (SD) Range 1-5
Engagement		*Engagement*	
I was paying attention to what NAO was saying and doing.	4 (0.71)	I was paying attention to what NAO was saying and doing.	5 (0.49)
I understood what NAO was doing and saying.	5 (0.73)	I understood what NAO was doing and saying.	3 (0.41)
How good a storyteller is NAO?	4 (0.89)		
How good a teacher is NAO?	4 (0.93)		
How funny is NAO?	4 (1.27)		
Likability		*Likability*	
I like NAO	5 (0.72)	I like NAO	4 (0.94)
Smartness		*Smartness*	
NAO is smart	5 (0.72)	NAO is smart	4 (0.95)
Closeness		*Social Interaction*	
NAO feels like a friend to me.	4.5 (1.03)	I want my child to interact with the NAO.	4 (0.97)
I want to play with NAO again	5 (1.07)	Social robots can become play partners for children.	3.5 (0.95)
I feel comfortable around NAO.	5 (1.14)	Children can consider social robots as their friend.	3 (1.04)
NAO and I are becoming friends.	4 (0.92)	Social robots can promote better social interactions among children.	4 (1.02)
Trustworthiness		*Trustworthiness*	
I can trust NAO.	4 (1.04)	I can trust NAO.	3 (0.80)
NAO is honest.	5 (0.64)	NAO is honest.	3 (0.75)
		Safety	
		NAO is safe for children under supervision.	4 (0.56)
		NAO is safe for children without supervision.	3 (0.98)
		I feel that the NAO can keep secrets.	3 (0.88)

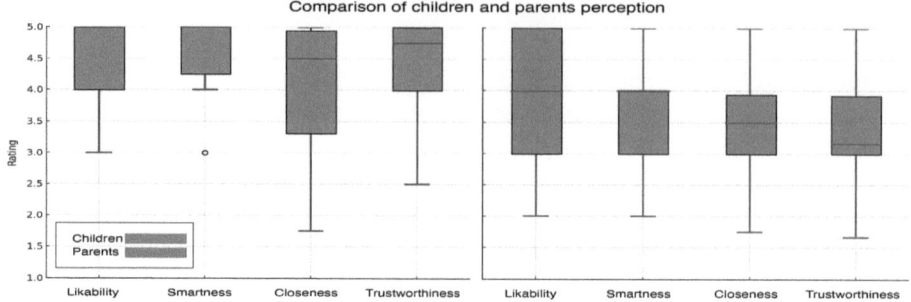

Fig. 2. Children's and parents' Likert-scale responses to likability, smartness, closeness, social interaction, and trustworthiness in their interactions with the NAO robot.

Comfort Levels with HSR Sensor Capabilities Across Six Different Scenarios. Figure 3 shows a summary of the children and parent' comfort levels (**RQ3**) with respect to the HSR's sensor capabilities across hypothetical scenarios. Both groups were more cautious about features like Voice_Recording, Camera, and with Data_Sharing being particularly concerning in the context of child-robot interaction. However, children had higher comfort levels with HSR sensor capabilities compared to parents. Children rated household settings, a friend's house, and further declined in public environments like schools and public libraries. They felt the least comfortable in busy public areas, such as a shopping center. These findings suggest that children are more comfortable using HSRs at home or in public settings in small peer groups or familiar people, rather than interacting with strangers in public spaces.

In contrast, parents expressed lower comfort levels overall, especially in scenarios involving heightened privacy concerns, such as when the child is alone and unsupervised, at a friend's house, or in open public spaces like shopping centers. However, many parents support for children interacting with HSR in educational settings, such as schools or public libraries. Although parents showed slightly higher comfort levels in family-oriented settings, such as the family's living room. Their concerns were most pronounced for Camera. When the child is alone, they also showed heighten concerns for Voice_Recording, Motion_Tracking, WiFi_Connection, and Data_Sharing.

The data for both groups are not normally distributed based on a normality test, therefore we conducted the non-parametric Wilcoxon Ranked-Sum test to identify significant differences between children's and parents' comfort levels with eight HSR's sensor capabilities across six location scenarios (**RQ4**). Table 3 shows a summary of the pairwise comparisons between children and parent comfort levels for different types of sensors across the six scenarios. We discuss the differences between scenarios in more detail below. For clarity of presentation, we formatted the types of sensors in monospace font (e.g., Motion_Sensor).

House, Alone: Strong significant differences are observed across all sensors ($p < 0.01$ for all). This highlights heightened differences in perception between the

Children	House Alone					House Family					Friend House					School					Public Library					Shopping Center				
	5	4	3	2	1	5	4	3	2	1	5	4	3	2	1	5	4	3	2	1	5	4	3	2	1	5	4	3	2	1
Record Voice	43	22	16	5	14	62	22	3	5	8	41	30	8	8	14	41	19	22	11	8	24	24	27	8	16	24	19	16	5	35
Camera	46	19	16	3	16	41	24	16	19	0	35	30	14	8	14	38	19	22	8	14	32	19	16	11	22	22	19	16	14	30
Motion Sensor	68	11	16	3	3	65	14	11	8	3	54	19	11	11	5	49	24	11	14	3	43	24	5	5	22	49	16	8	5	22
Motion Tracking	50	19	19	6	6	64	17	6	8	6	42	25	17	11	6	36	33	17	3	11	38	19	19	8	14	36	17	14	11	22
Touch Sensor	68	16	3	5	8	66	11	8	8	5	54	19	14	5	8	43	27	5	14	11	43	30	5	11	11	35	22	16	11	16
Wifi Connection	69	20	9	3	0	66	23	6	3	3	49	23	23	3	3	46	29	11	6	9	43	29	6	11	11	29	18	24	6	17
Data Storage	59	9	29	0	3	62	18	15	6	0	41	21	24	12	3	38	21	21	12	9	35	24	18	6	18	29	18	24	6	24
Data Sharing	30	37	3	10	20	33	27	17	10	13	30	13	27	13	17	23	27	7	13	30	33	17	7	13	30	20	10	23	10	37
Parents																														
Record Voice	11	30	11	22	27	18	32	16	18	16	5	18	26	21	29	13	32	21	21	13	11	21	24	32	13	0	21	16	39	24
Camera	3	11	16	29	42	0	21	18	26	34	0	11	24	24	42	3	21	26	29	21	0	21	18	32	29	0	13	18	32	37
Motion Sensor	30	30	16	14	11	30	38	19	8	5	30	27	19	11	14	35	38	16	8	3	30	38	16	8	8	27	32	14	14	14
Motion Tracking	5	35	19	8	32	16	32	22	14	16	8	30	16	19	27	19	35	19	11	16	16	35	16	16	16	8	27	24	16	24
Touch Sensor	22	28	14	22	14	37	26	23	6	9	11	36	25	6	22	25	47	19	8	0	22	36	33	6	3	4	28	33	17	14
Wifi Connection	11	11	27	24	27	16	29	26	13	16	8	18	29	16	29	13	34	26	11	16	8	24	26	21	21	5	13	26	32	24
Data Storage	13	21	21	13	32	18	26	21	16	18	0	24	21	26	29	11	34	21	16	18	3	24	24	21	16	0	16	13	42	29
Data Sharing	0	0	11	39	50	3	3	11	39	44	0	6	3	42	50	3	14	8	39	36	3	14	11	39	33	3	11	8	33	44

Fig. 3. Heatmap illustrating children's and parents' comfort levels regarding the sensor capabilities of HSRs (rows) across six different scenarios (columns). The values represent percentages (%) based on responses to a Likert scale: from "Very Comfortable (5)" to "Very Uncomfortable (1)" for parents, and "Super Comfortable (5)" to "Not So Comfortable (1)" for children. Higher percentage values are displayed in darker colors.

Table 3. The pairwise comparisons using Wilcoxon Ranked test showed significant differences between parents' and children's responses for specific sensors and scenarios. Blank spaces indicate no significant differences

Scenario\Sensors	Voice Recording	Camera	Motion Sensor	Motion Tracking	Touch Sensor	Wifi Connection	Data Storage	Data Sharing
House Alone	= 0.004	< 0.001	= 0.004	< 0.001	< 0.001	< 0.001	< 0.001	< 0.001
House with Family	< 0.001	< 0.001	= 0.021	< 0.001	< 0.001	= 0.044	< 0.001	< 0.001
Friend's House	< 0.001	< 0.001		< 0.001	< 0.001	< 0.001	< 0.001	< 0.001
School	= 0.043	= 0.001		= 0.007			= 0.005	= 0.005
Public Library		= 0.006		= 0.001			= 0.005	= 0.035
Shopping Center		= 0.034		= 0.003			= 0.003	

two participant groups regarding sensitivity to privacy in the house, particularly when alone in a child's room. Parents tend to be more concerned about sensor use and robot interactions in such private settings, whereas children may be less concerned or more accustomed to the presence of technology. In particular, high statistical significance ($p < 0.001$) was observed for Data_Sharing, Data_Storage, and Motion_Tracking, reflecting high discomfort with monitoring and data use in this setting of parent's perception. Touch_Sensor and Voice_Recording were also highly significant ($p < 0.001$), indicating discomfort with physical and audio interactions.

House, with Family: We also found significant differences in perception between children and parents across sensors when they are together in the home, emphasizing potential privacy concerns in family-shared spaces (living room). Camera, Data_Sharing, Data_Storage, and Motion_Tracking showed high statistical significance ($p < 0.001$). However, parents are not as concerned about Motion_Sensor and WiFi_Connection compared to the "House Alone" scenario, which suggest that parents may feel more control in this context.

Friend's House: Parents were more concerned about their children's interactions with HSRs at a friend's house, perhaps due to a lack of close parental supervision raised privacy concerns for parents due to their lack of control over how the data might be collected and used. In contrast, children may not fully consider these implications. In this context, we found highly significant differences ($p < 0.001$) for most sensors except Motion_Sensors, highlighting privacy concerns and differing perceptions between children and parents in both personal and social environments.

School: Significant differences in perceptions between children and parents are observed regarding Voice_Recording, Cameras, Touch_Sensor, Data_Storage, and Data_Sharing in a school setting. This suggests some concerns about a range of data collection in educational environments even though schools are supervised environments. Children, on the other hand, may be more accepting of sensors, perceiving schools as trustworthy and reliable environment.

Public Space: Public library and shopping center settings show few differences in expectations of comfort levels, suggesting similar attitudes toward these spaces among children and parents. This alignment may stem from lower expectations of privacy in public spaces.

Need for Parental Controls vs. No Supervision with HSRs. Parents' perception of privacy concerns regarding the HSR was assessed using the *Safety* questionnaire, *'NAO is safe for children under supervision,'* with a result of $Md = 4, SD = 0.56$, *'NAO is safe for children without supervision,'* with a result of $Md = 3, SD = 0.98$, and *'I feel that the NAO can keep secrets,'* The result is $Md = 3, SD = 0.88$. The results show parents' level of agreement with children's interactions with the robot under supervision (Table 2). These findings indicate that most parents feel relatively confident in NAO's safety under supervision. Parents are clearly more comfortable with NAO being used under supervision than without it. This result illustrates more uncertainty and less confidence in NAO's safety when children use it unsupervised. On the unsupervised use scale and the security of personal information (secret), the scores drop closer to neutrality ($Md = 3$), showing hesitation about leaving children alone with the HSR. These results were further explored through follow-up interviews with related questions and a thematic analysis to gain a deeper understanding.

Qualitative Feedback from Parents. Our exit interview questions for parents were collected to gather additional context and insights related to their quantitative responses. Through Thematic Analysis, we identified four main themes and 18 associated codes. From this analysis, three overarching implications emerged.

High Level of Perceived Privacy Risks: In their qualitative feedback, 47% ($n = 18$) of parent participants expressed high levels of concerns about robot's data collection via its camera and microphone. 61% ($n = 23$) of parents mentioned about data transfer and storage. Another 37% ($n = 14$) of parents responded with concerns related to uncertainty about the robot's safety and robot's proper functioning. This theme captures the participant's admission of not fully understanding how the robot functions and reflects their uncertainty about whether HSRs are safe for children. This lack of understanding regarding the robot's functionality, including its specific features and capabilities, contributes to their safety concerns. 37% ($n = 9$) of participants expressed concerns about inappropriate content and unreliable sources. This captures participants' uncertainty and lack of confidence in the type or accuracy of the information the robot will provide. It also reflects participants' concerns about potential exposure to inappropriate content or language and the need for reliable sources when interacting with the robot.

Need for Parental Controls: Parent participants were asked follow-up interview questions such as *"Should the robot have parental controls for children's safety?"*; and *"Can children be left with a social robot without adult supervision?"* The majority of parents (84%, $n = 32$) believed that HSRs for children need for parental controls.

39% ($n = 15$) of parents believed that HSRs need safety protocols and settings, reflecting parents' expectations that robots should provide a range of parental control features to manage interactions with children. For example, one parent expressed, *"I can lock or unlock certain features like go on the internet or camera or video recording or asking questions... I would expect to see different parental controls" (PP11)*. Another noted, *"If they are asking for a certain question, the answer should be within the bounds of what I think is appropriate at his age... should be regulated with that" (PP5)*. PP13 emphasized, *"I think being able to limit the time that the child will be exposed to play with the robots, and maybe being able to limit the type of job or the level of interaction the parents are able to have some control."*

Parental Awareness and/or Supervision as a Condition for Children's Interaction with HSRs: Some parents' were comfortable with allowing their child to interact with an HSR, provided they fully understand its functional limitations, protocols, policies, and parental controls. They often expressed awareness and understanding of robot functionalities as prerequisites for leaving children unsupervised with the robot. As PP8 noted, *"if the emergency button is there, or there's some other ways to handle the emergency issue, then there should be no problem, no issue, no concerns to leave the robots along with the kids."* Similarly, PP11 stated, *"if I understand how it operates and what it can do, then I think I wouldn't have a problem leaving it alone with the child."*

Since parents highlighted the importance of parental controls for ensuring safe interactions with HSRs. In this context, 39% ($n = 15$) also consistently expressed that they are comfortable with home use under parental control. However, some (32%, $n = 12$) distrusted robots in private spaces used by children alone, at a friend's house (32%, $n = 12$), and in public spaces (24%, $n = 9$). About a quarter of parents were completely uncomfortable with any scenario other than the HSR being used under a parental supervision (21%, $n = 8$).

4 Discussion

Differing Perceptions of HSR Between Children and Parents and Impact on Privacy Attitudes. This study highlights the differing perceptions of privacy and trust in HSRs between children and parents. Our findings suggest that children exhibit a higher willingness to engage with and trust HSRs, while parents remained skeptical, where they emphasized the importance of parental controls and supervised interactions. Children participants in the study show a high level of *Engagement*, suggesting that their short interactions during the study may be sufficient for them to perceive the NAO robot's role a companion, educator, or a friend. Children showed a high level of *Likability, Smartness, Closeness*, and *Trustworthiness* towards the HSR, with more than half willing to share sensitive secrets with the robot. The humanoid appearance of NAO may have influenced the disclosure of personal information, aligning with prior research showing that the cuteness and friendly appearance of social robots [35], as well as users' social bonds with robots [36], can encourage the sharing of personal information. These results align with prior privacy research of children's interaction with smart toys [8,27,31], which similarity have found that children to be trusting and unaware of privacy risks. However, we also found that children who perceived the robot as "closer" to them or more like a friend were less likely to disclose secrets, potentially reflecting an instinctive reservation when emotional bonds with HSRs are stronger. This suggest a nuanced finding not commonly addressed in previous studies, which warrants further investigation. Unlike smart toys with limited sensor capabilities, HSRs introduce advanced features, such as detailed tracking capabilities and autonomous locomotion that can amplify privacy risks. While our study confirms that HSRs lead to high engagements with children, we also emphasize that their sensor capabilities necessitate more comprehensive safeguards.

Parents, on the other hand, expressed significant concerns regarding data collection, storage, and sharing of children's information, particularly in unsupervised contexts, which highlights a disparity in how children and parents perceive privacy risks, especially regarding HSRs' sensor capabilities in the home, such as child's private bedroom and the shared living room. In child-robot interaction parents' desired to be mediators in children's technology use, emphasizing the need for supervised interaction and robust parental controls in the design of HSRs for use with children. Their desired privacy control mechanisms focused on sensor control (on/off), interaction time limits, content regulation, awareness of transparent data collection and transfer, and parental consent, reflecting parents' exceptions transferred from their interactions with other smart devices, such as mobile phones and IoT devices.

Implications of Privacy Perceptions of HSR Sensors Across Different Scenarios. We evaluated privacy concerns related to HSR sensors across six different scenarios and discovered differences between children's and parents' comfort levels regarding HSR usage in various settings. Children largely felt comfortable with the HSR's sensor capabilities in various environments. In contrast, parents consistently believed that interactions between children and an HSR should be supervised and occur in reliable environments such as school or library. The study also indicated that while certain HSR functions collect data from child interactions, parents' willingness to allow this varies. In general, parents were uncomfortable with scenarios where children interact with robots alone, even within their own homes. The result emphasised strong significant differences are observed across all sensors in the 'House, Alone' scenario. These findings highlight a deep concern among parents about unsupervised data collection in private spaces. This discomfort extends to semi-private environments like a 'Friend's House' scenario, where parents worried that their child might inadvertently be exposed to or involved in the collection of data from others' private interactions. This stands in sharp contrast to children's understanding of these implications, as they may not fully consider or recognize the potential risks associated with data collection through robot interactions.

From parents' qualitative feedback, we found that their privacy concerns towards HSRs mainly stemmed from a lack of understanding of the functionalities and uncertainty about their safety and operation. Parents' levels of concern also depended on the types of sensors, reflecting nuanced worries about specific features and functionalities in different contexts. The aspects of HSRs that parents are most concerned about include data collection, storage, and sharing. The integration of various features and the complexity of the robots' functions may heighten these concerns. Additionally, parents' limited experience with HSRs leads to feelings of discomfort and uncertainty regarding the robots' informational outputs, including fears of inappropriate content and unreliable sources. This reinforces their desire for supervision, particularly in contexts where they cannot directly monitor the interaction.

Both children and parents reported high levels of comfort in shared home and school settings. This indicates that children may prefer to have parental or teacher and peer accompaniment when interacting with social robots. In public spaces such as shopping centers, children felt uncomfortable interacting with HSRs. This discomfort may be influenced by their perceptions of physical safety [56] in unfamiliar or crowded environments rather than the risk of HSRs.

Parent's Level of Privacy Prioritization and the Required Parental Control and Supervision. Our results reveal that parents exhibited heightened caution, emphasizing the need for parental control and the management of privacy mechanisms based on data sensitivity. The majority of parents' perceptions of privacy in social robots revolve around the importance of maintaining parental control, with the need for supervision identified as a secondary concern. Additionally, any conditional acceptance of robots operating without direct supervision would only be considered under parental consent or within trusted and reliable contexts. Parents' comfort levels varied depending on the robot's use in different environments, indicating a prioritization of control that is context-dependent. This prioritization of privacy concerns differs based on the situational, locational, and functional aspects of social robots. These results underline the importance of designing HSRs with context-aware privacy controls. For example, allowing parents to enable or disable specific sensors, set interaction time limits, and restrict data collection and sharing could address concerns. Furthermore, transparent communication about data collection practices, both in robot design (e.g., on-robot privacy mechanisms) and through family-friendly awareness and education, is critical in building trust among users.

Limitations. Although we recruited participants through both institutional and public channels, the sample lacked geographical and socioeconomic diversity. Most participating parents held college or advanced degrees, worked in high-income, white-collar professions, and some had IT-related expertise. This background likely contributed to a higher-than-average awareness of security and privacy issues, which may have influenced their responses and led to more detailed reflections during exit interviews. As such, findings may not fully represent the broader population.

The lab-based setting also introduces limitations. While it provided a safe, controlled environment for children to interact with the NAO humanoid robot, it does not capture the full complexity of real-world contexts. However, given the limited deployment of humanoid social robots in everyday life, this approach allowed participants to focus on the robot's advanced, human-like features within scenarios modeled after familiar settings, such as homes and schools. This structured interaction helped participants infer the robot's capabilities and explore hypothetical use cases. Findings from this setting offer a foundation for future studies conducted in natural environments.

5 Conclusions

This study aimed to explore how children and parents perceive HSRs and to examine how these perceptions shape their privacy attitudes, with a particular focus on how situational and locational contexts influence their concerns. Children consistently exhibit a higher degree of engagement, likability, smartness, closeness, and trustworthiness toward HSRs and are willing to share personal information with them. In contrast, parents tend to be more cautious, driven primarily by concerns about data collection, storage, and transparency. They prefer that interactions with social robots occur under their supervision and in controlled environments. This apprehension is especially pronounced in certain locations, where the lack of oversight heightens their privacy concerns. To create safer and more effective interactions between children and social robots, it is crucial to address children's privacy concerns, enhance parental awareness of social robot capabilities, implement robust control mechanisms, and ensure transparency in how data is collected, stored, and used by social robots. Addressing these factors will foster trust and ensure that the integration of social robots into families' lives is both beneficial and secure.

References

1. Ahmad, M.I., Mubin, O., Orlando, J.: Adaptive social robot for sustaining social engagement during long-term children-robot interaction. Int. J. Hum. Comput. Interact. **33**(12), 943–962 (2017). https://doi.org/10.1080/10447318.2017.1300750. https://doi.org/10.1080/10447318.2017.1300750

2. Albuquerque, O.d.P., Fantinato, M., Eler, M.M., Peres, S.M., Hung, P.C.K.: A study of parental control requirements for smart toys. In: 2020 IEEE International Conference on Systems, Man, and Cybernetics (SMC), pp. 2215–2220, October 2020. ISSN 2577-1655. https://doi.org/10.1109/SMC42975.2020.9282959. https://ieeexplore.ieee.org/document/9282959/?arnumber=9282959
3. Obaigbena, A., et al.: AI and human-robot interaction: a review of recent advances and challenges. GSC Adv. Res. Rev. **18**(2), 321–330 (2024). https://doi.org/10.30574/gscarr.2024.18.2.0070. https://gsconlinepress.com/journals/gscarr/content/ai-and-human-robot-interaction-review-recent-advances-and-challenges
4. Aroyo, A.M., Rea, F., Sandini, G., Sciutti, A.: Trust and social engineering in human robot interaction: will a robot make you disclose sensitive information, conform to its recommendations or gamble? IEEE Robot. Autom. Lett. **3**(4), 3701–3708 (2018). https://doi.org/10.1109/LRA.2018.2856272. https://ieeexplore.ieee.org/document/8411113/
5. Belpaeme, T., et al.: Multimodal child-robot interaction: building social bonds. J. Hum. Robot Interact. **1**(2), 33–53 (2013). https://doi.org/10.5898/JHRI.1.2.Belpaeme. http://dl.acm.org/citation.cfm?id=3109691
6. van den Berghe, R., Verhagen, J., Oudgenoeg-Paz, O., van der Ven, S., Leseman, P.: Social robots for language learning: a review. Rev. Educ. Res. **89**(2), 259–295 (2019). https://doi.org/10.3102/0034654318821286
7. Bertel, L.B., Rasmussen, D.M.: On being a peer: what persuasive technology for teaching can gain from social robotics in education. Int. J. Conceptual Struct. Smart Appl. **1**(2), 58–68 (2013). https://doi.org/10.4018/ijcssa.2013070107
8. Bethel, C.L., Stevenson, M.R., Scassellati, B.: Secret-sharing: interactions between a child, robot, and adult. In: 2011 IEEE International Conference on Systems, Man, and Cybernetics, Anchorage, AK, USA, October 2011, pp. 2489–2494. IEEE (2011). https://doi.org/10.1109/ICSMC.2011.6084051. http://ieeexplore.ieee.org/document/6084051/
9. Blut, M., Wang, C., Wünderlich, N.V., Brock, C.: Understanding anthropomorphism in service provision: a meta-analysis of physical robots, Chatbots, and other AI. J. Acad. Mark. Sci. **49**(4), 632–658 (2021). https://doi.org/10.1007/s11747-020-00762-y
10. Borenstein, J., Pearson, Y.: Companion Robots and the Emotional Development of Children. Law Innov. Technol. **5**(2), 172–189 (2013). https://doi.org/10.5235/17579961.5.2.172. https://www.tandfonline.com/doi/full/10.5235/17579961.5.2.172
11. Broadbent, E., Billinghurst, M., Boardman, S.G., Doraiswamy, P.M.: Enhancing social connectedness with companion robots using AI. Sci. Robot. **8**(80), eadi6347 (2023). https://doi.org/10.1126/scirobotics.adi6347. https://www.science.org/doi/full/10.1126/scirobotics.adi6347
12. Chatterjee, S., Chaudhuri, R., Vrontis, D.: Usage intention of social robots for domestic purpose: from security, privacy, and legal perspectives. Inf. Syst. Front. **26**(1), 121–136 (2024). https://doi.org/10.1007/s10796-021-10197-7. https://link.springer.com/10.1007/s10796-021-10197-7
13. Chung, H., Kang, H., Jun, S.: Verbal anthropomorphism design of social robots: investigating users' privacy perception. Comput. Hum. Behav. **142**, 107640 (2023). https://doi.org/10.1016/j.chb.2022.107640. https://linkinghub.elsevier.com/retrieve/pii/S0747563222004605

14. Coeckelbergh, M., et al.: A survey of expectations about the role of robots in robot-assisted therapy for children with ASD: ethical acceptability, trust, sociability, appearance, and attachment. Sci. Eng. Ethics **22**(1), 47–65 (2015). https://doi.org/10.1007/s11948-015-9649-x
15. Conti, D., Di Nuovo, S., Di Nuovo, A.: Kindergarten children attitude towards humanoid robots: what is the effect of the first experience? In: 2019 14th ACM/IEEE International Conference on Human-Robot Interaction (HRI), Daegu, Korea (South), March 2019, pp. 630–631. IEEE (2019). https://doi.org/10.1109/HRI.2019.8673204. https://ieeexplore.ieee.org/document/8673204/
16. Dautenhahn, K.: Socially intelligent robots: dimensions of human–robot interaction. Philos. Trans. R. Soc. B Biol. Sci. **362**(1480), 679–704 (2007). https://doi.org/10.1098/rstb.2006.2004. https://royalsocietypublishing.org/doi/10.1098/rstb.2006.2004
17. Denning, T., Matuszek, C., Koscher, K., Smith, J.R., Kohno, T.: A spotlight on security and privacy risks with future household robots: attacks and lessons, Orlando, Florida, USA, October 2009. ACM (2009). ISBN 978-1-60558-431-7/09/09
18. Emami-Naeini, P., et al.: Privacy expectations and preferences in an IoT world. In: SOUPS 2017, Santa Clara, California, July 2017. USENIX Association (2017). https://www.usenix.org/conference/soups2017/technical-sessions/presentation/naeini
19. Fernandes, R., Kawaguchi, I., Yamanaka, T.: Multisensory games on children's empathetic feelings and cooperative behavior: developing a Kansei-based sensory playground design workshop. In: Proceedings of the 2017 Conference on Interaction Design and Children, Stanford, California, USA, June 2017, pp. 417–421. ACM (2017). https://doi.org/10.1145/3078072.3084303. https://dl.acm.org/doi/10.1145/3078072.3084303
20. Fink, J.: Anthropomorphism and human likeness in the design of robots and human-robot interaction. In: Hutchison, D., et al. (eds.) Social Robotics. LNCS, vol. 7621, pp. 199–208. Springer, Heidelberg (2012). https://doi.org/10.1007/978-3-642-34103-8_20. https://link.springer.com/10.1007/978-3-642-34103-8_20
21. Fronemann, N., Pollmann, K., Loh, W.: Should my robot know what's best for me? Human–robot interaction between user experience and ethical design. AI & Soc. (1), 1–17 (2021). https://doi.org/10.1007/s00146-021-01210-3
22. George, D.A., George, A.S.: The Rise of Robotic Children: Implications for Family, Caregiving, and Society. PU Publications, October 2023. https://doi.org/10.5281/ZENODO.10045270. https://zenodo.org/doi/10.5281/zenodo.10045270
23. Ghafurian, M., et al.: Human-robot interaction studies with adults in health and wellbeing contexts - outcomes and challenges. In: Social Robotics. LNCS, vol. 14453, pp. 130–142. Springer, Singapore (2024). https://doi.org/10.1007/978-981-99-8715-3_12. https://link.springer.com/10.1007/978-981-99-8715-3_12
24. Ghafurian, M., Hoey, J., Dautenhahn, K.: Social robots for the care of persons with dementia: a systematic review. ACM Trans. Hum. Robot Interact. **10**(4), 1–31 (2021). https://doi.org/10.1145/3469653. https://dl.acm.org/doi/10.1145/3469653
25. Hall, L., Hume, C., Tazzyman, S.: Five Degrees of Happiness: Effective Smiley Face Likert Scales for Evaluating with Children (2016)

26. Horstmann, B., Diekmann, N., Buschmeier, H., Hassan, T.: Towards designing privacy-compliant social robots for use in private households: a use case based identification of privacy implications and potential technical measures for mitigation. In: 2020 29th IEEE International Conference on Robot and Human Interactive Communication (RO-MAN), Naples, Italy, August 2020, pp. 869–876. IEEE (2020). https://doi.org/10.1109/RO-MAN47096.2020.9223556. https://ieeexplore.ieee.org/document/9223556/
27. Hung, P.C.K., Iqbal, F., Huang, S.C., Melaisi, M., Pang, K.: A glance of child's play privacy in smart toys. In: Sun, X., Liu, A., Chao, H.C., Bertino, E. (eds.) Cloud Computing and Security, pp. 217–231. Springer, Cham (2016)
28. Jayaraman, S., Phillips, E.K., Church, D., Riek, L.D.: Privacy and utility perceptions of social robots in healthcare. Comput. Hum. Behav. Artif. Hum. **2**(1), 100039 (2024). https://doi.org/10.1016/j.chbah.2023.100039. https://linkinghub.elsevier.com/retrieve/pii/S2949882123000397
29. Jones, M.L.: Your new best frenemy: hello barbie and privacy without screens. Engaging Sci. Technol. Soci. **2**, 242–246 (2016). https://doi.org/10.17351/ests2016.84. http://estsjournal.org/index.php/ests/article/view/84
30. Kanda, T., Hirano, T., Eaton, D., Ishiguro, H.: Interactive robots as social partners and peer tutors for children: a field trial. Hum. Comput. Interact. **19**(1), 61–84 (2004). https://doi.org/10.1080/07370024.2004.9667340. https://www.tandfonline.com/doi/abs/10.1080/07370024.2004.9667340
31. Kumar, P., Naik, S.M., Devkar, U.R., Chetty, M., Clegg, T.L., Vitak, J.: 'No telling passcodes out because they're private': understanding children's mental models of privacy and security online. Proc. ACM Hum. Comput. Interact. **1**(CSCW), 1–21 (2017). https://doi.org/10.1145/3134699. https://dl.acm.org/doi/10.1145/3134699
32. Köse, H., Uluer, P., Akalın, N., Yorgancı, R., Özkul, A., Ince, G.: The effect of embodiment in sign language tutoring with assistive humanoid robots. Int. J. Soc. Robot. **7**(4), 537–548 (2015). https://doi.org/10.1007/s12369-015-0311-1
33. Leite, I., Lehman, J.F.: The robot who knew too much: toward understanding the privacy/personalization trade-off in child-robot conversation. In: Proceedings of the The 15th International Conference on Interaction Design and Children, June 2016, Manchester United Kingdom, pp. 379–387. ACM (2016). https://doi.org/10.1145/2930674.2930687. https://dl.acm.org/doi/10.1145/2930674.2930687
34. Lemaignan, S., Newbutt, N., Rice, L., Daly, J., Charisi, V.: UNICEF Guidance on AI for Children: Application to the Design of a Social Robot For and With Autistic Children, August 2021. http://arxiv.org/abs/2108.12166. arXiv:2108.12166 [cs]
35. Lindblom, D.S., van Otterdijk, M., Torresen, J.: A qualitative observational video-based study on perceived privacy in social robots' based on robots appearances. In: 2024 IEEE International Conference on Advanced Robotics and Its Social Impacts (ARSO), May 2024, pp. 74–79 (2024). ISSN 2162-7576. https://doi.org/10.1109/ARSO60199.2024.10557941. https://ieeexplore.ieee.org/document/10557941/?arnumber=10557941
36. Lutz, C., Schöttler, M., Hoffmann, C.P.: The privacy implications of social robots: scoping review and expert interviews. Mobile Media Commun. **7**(3), 412–434 (2019). https://doi.org/10.1177/2050157919843961
37. Lutz, C., Tamó-Larrieux, A.: The robot privacy paradox: understanding how privacy concerns shape intentions to use social robots. Hum. Mach. Commun. **1**, 87–111 (2020). https://doi.org/10.30658/hmc.1.6. https://stars.library.ucf.edu/hmc/vol1/iss1/6/

38. Lytridis, C., Bazinas, C., Papakostas, G., Kaburlasos, V.: On measuring engagement level during child-robot interaction in education, pp. 3–13, January 2020. https://doi.org/10.1007/978-3-030-26945-6_1
39. MacDorman, K.: Androids as an experimental apparatus: why is there an uncanny valley and can we exploit it? In: Toward Social Mechanisms of Android Science: A CogSci 2005 Workshop, January 2005
40. Malhotra, N.K., Kim, S.S., Agarwal, J.: Internet users' information privacy concerns (IUIPC): the construct, the scale, and a causal model. Inf. Syst. Res. (2004). https://doi.org/10.1287/isre.1040.0032. https://pubsonline.informs.org/doi/abs/10.1287/isre.1040.0032
41. Malle, B.F., Fischer, K., Young, J.E., Moon, A., Collins, E.: Trust and the discrepancy between expectations and actual capabilities. In: Human-Robot Interaction: Control, Analysis, and Design, pp. 1–23 (2020)
42. McReynolds, E., Hubbard, S., Lau, T., Saraf, A., Cakmak, M., Roesner, F.: Toys that listen: a study of parents, children, and internet-connected toys. In: Proceedings of the 2017 CHI Conference on Human Factors in Computing Systems, Denver Colorado USA, May 2017, pp. 5197–5207. ACM (2017). https://doi.org/10.1145/3025453.3025735
43. Michaelis, J.E., Mutlu, B.: Someone to read with: design of and experiences with an in-home learning companion robot for reading. In: Proceedings of the 2017 CHI Conference on Human Factors in Computing Systems, Denver Colorado USA, May 2017, pp. 301–312. ACM (2017). https://doi.org/10.1145/3025453.3025499
44. Mori, M., MacDorman, K.F., Kageki, N.: The Uncanny Valley [from the field]. IEEE Robot. Autom. Mag. **19**(2), 98–100 (2012). Conference Name: IEEE Robotics & Automation Magazine. https://doi.org/10.1109/MRA.2012.2192811, https://ieeexplore.ieee.org/document/6213238/?arnumber=6213238
45. Pagallo, U.: Robots in the cloud with privacy: a new threat to data protection? Comput. Law Secur. Rev. **29**(5), 501–508 (2013). https://doi.org/10.1016/j.clsr.2013.07.012. https://linkinghub.elsevier.com/retrieve/pii/S0267364913001398
46. Pearson, Y.: Child-robot interaction: what concerns about privacy and well-being arise when children play with, use, and learn from robots? Am. Sci. **108**(No. 1), 16+ (2020)
47. Pinheiro Amâncio, F.M., et al.: Parental perception of children's privacy in smart toys in countries of different economic levels. Technol. Soc. **72**, 102180 (2023). https://doi.org/10.1016/j.techsoc.2022.102180. https://linkinghub.elsevier.com/retrieve/pii/S0160791X22003219
48. Rasouli, S., Johnston, L., Yuen, J., Ghafurian, M., Foster, L., Dautenhahn, K.: Co-design of a robotic mental well-being coach to help university students manage public speaking anxiety. In: International Conference on Human-Agent Interaction, Gothenburg Sweden, December 2023, pp. 200–208. ACM (2023). https://doi.org/10.1145/3623809.3623872
49. Rueben, M., Smart, W.D.: Privacy in Human-Robot Interaction: Survey and Future Work (2016)
50. Serholt, S., Pareto, L., Ekström, S., Ljungblad, S.: Trouble and repair in child-robot interaction: a study of complex interactions with a robot tutee in a primary school classroom. Front. Robot. AI **7**, 46 (2020). https://doi.org/10.3389/frobt.2020.00046. https://www.frontiersin.org/article/10.3389/frobt.2020.00046/full

51. Shasha, S., Mahmoud, M., Mannan, M., Youssef, A.: Playing With danger: a taxonomy and evaluation of threats to smart toys. IEEE Internet Things J. **6**(2), 2986–3002 (2019). https://doi.org/10.1109/JIOT.2018.2877749. https://ieeexplore.ieee.org/document/8502818/
52. Shenoy, S., Hou, Y., Wang, X., Nikseresht, F., Doryab, A.: Adaptive humanoid robots for pain management in children. In: Companion of the 2021 ACM/IEEE International Conference on Human-Robot Interaction, Boulder, CO, USA, March 2021, pp. 510–514. ACM (2021). https://doi.org/10.1145/3434074.3447224
53. Straten, C.L.V., Kühne, R., Peter, J., De Jong, C., Barco, A.: Closeness, trust, and perceived social support in child-robot relationship formation: development and validation of three self-report scales. Interaction Stud. **21**(1), 57–84 (2020). Social Behaviour and Communication in Biological and Artificial Systems. https://doi.org/10.1075/is.18052.str. http://www.jbe-platform.com/content/journals/10.1075/is.18052.str
54. Straten, C.L.V., Peter, J., Kühne, R., Barco, A.: Transparency about a robot's lack of human psychological capacities: effects on child-robot perception and relationship formation. ACM Trans. Hum. Robot Interact. **9**(2), 1–22 (2020). https://doi.org/10.1145/3365668
55. Su, P., Yuan, X.: Are you watching me? A study on privacy notice design of social robot. In: Rebelo, F. (ed.) Advances in Ergonomics in Design, pp. 339–344. Springer, Cham (2021). https://doi.org/10.1007/978-3-030-79760-7_41
56. Sun, K., et al.: "They see you're a girl if you pick a pink robot with a skirt": a qualitative study of how children conceptualize data processing and digital privacy risks. In: Proceedings of the 2021 CHI Conference on Human Factors in Computing Systems, Yokohama Japan, May 2021, pp. 1–34. ACM (2021). https://doi.org/10.1145/3411764.3445333
57. Sun, K., Zou, Y., Radesky, J., Brooks, C., Schaub, F.: Child safety in the smart home: parents' perceptions, needs, and mitigation strategies. Proc. ACM Hum. Comput. Interact. **5**(CSCW2), 1–41 (2021). https://doi.org/10.1145/3479858
58. Sun, N., Yang, E., Corney, J., Chen, Y., Ma, Z.: A review of high-level robot functionality for elderly care. In: 2018 24th International Conference on Automation and Computing (ICAC), Newcastle upon Tyne, United Kingdom, September 2018, pp. 1–6. IEEE (2018). https://doi.org/10.23919/IConAC.2018.8749031. https://ieeexplore.ieee.org/document/8749031/
59. Tanevska, A., Rea, F., Sandini, G., Cañamero, L., Sciutti, A.: A socially adaptable framework for human-robot interaction. Front. Robot. AI **7**, 121 (2020). https://doi.org/10.3389/frobt.2020.00121. https://www.frontiersin.org/articles/10.3389/frobt.2020.00121/full
60. Toh, L.P.E., Causo, A., Tzuo, P.W., I-Ming, C., Yeo, S.H.: A review on the use of robots in education and young children. J. Educ. Technol. Soc. **19**(2), 148–163 (2016). International Forum of Educational Technology & Society Section: Full Length Articles. https://www.proquest.com/docview/1792129409/abstract/AB1039237F0F41F3PQ/1
61. Windl, M., Leusmann, J., Schmidt, A., Feger, S.S., Mayer, S.: Privacy Communication Patterns for Domestic Robots, Philadelphia, PA, United States (2024)
62. Yamamoto, M., Hu, Y., Coronado, E., Venture, G.: Impression evaluation of robot's behavior when assisting human in a cooking task. In: 2021 30th IEEE International Conference on Robot & Human Interactive Communication (RO-MAN), August 2021, pp. 743–748 (2021). https://doi.org/10.1109/RO-MAN50785.2021.9515527. https://ieeexplore.ieee.org/document/9515527/?arnumber=9515527, iSSN: 1944-9437

63. Yamaoka, F., Kanda, T., Ishiguro, H., Hagita, N.: How contingent should a lifelike robot be? The relationship between contingency and complexity. Connect. Sci. **19**(2), 143–162 (2007). https://doi.org/10.1080/09540090701371519. http://www.tandfonline.com/doi/abs/10.1080/09540090701371519
64. Zanatto, D., Patacchiola, M., Cangelosi, A., Goslin, J.: Generalisation of anthropomorphic stereotype. Int. J. Soc. Robot. **12**(1), 163–172 (2019). https://doi.org/10.1007/s12369-019-00549-4
65. Zhang-Kennedy, L., Mekhail, C., Abdelaziz, Y., Chiasson, S.: From nosy little brothers to stranger-danger: children and parents' perception of mobile threats. In: Proceedings of the The 15th International Conference on Interaction Design and Children, Manchester United Kingdom, June 2016, pp. 388–399. ACM (2016). https://doi.org/10.1145/2930674.2930716

Investigating the Similarity-Attraction Effect on Personality in Human-Robot Interactions

Alice Nardelli(✉)📧🆔, Francesca Corrao🆔, Antonio Sgorbissa🆔,
and Carmine Tommaso Recchiuto🆔

RICE (Robots and Intelligent Systems for Citizens and the Environment)
Laboratory, Department of Computer Science, Bioengineering, and Systems
Engineering, University of Genoa, Genoa, Italy
alice.nardelli@edu.unige.it
https://rice.dibris.unige.it/

Abstract. The similarity-attraction effect, particularly in relation to personality, has emerged as a promising strategy for enhancing human-robot interaction (HRI). This research builds on existing robotics literature, which predominantly focuses on the extroversion trait and presents inconclusive findings regarding the similarity-attraction and complementary-attraction effects. Differing from prior work, this study implements a robotic personality using a cognitive architecture across three dimensions: Conscientiousness, Extroversion, and Agreeableness. We investigate the similarity-attraction effect through an experimental setup in which participants engage in free-form conversations with the robot.

Keywords: Similarity-Attraction effect · Robotic Personality · Human Personality

1 Introduction

The Similarity-Attraction effect states that people are more attracted to others who are similar. Byrne et al. [1] demonstrated that initial interpersonal attraction is positively correlated with the number of shared attitudes between individuals. In contrast, the Complementary-Attraction effect suggests that attraction can also arise from complementary behaviors [2]. These two opposing effects have been demonstrated across various domains, including personality [3].

In the field of Human-Robot Interaction (HRI), research has shown that tailoring a robot's personality can significantly improve various aspects of the interaction. Within this context, the Similarity-Attraction and Complementary-Attraction theories have been extensively explored to enhance engagement and acceptance. However, even if generally obtained results support the similarity-attraction effect, the findings to date remain mixed and, at times, contradictory.

For instance, Park et al. [4] conveyed extroversion in a Kismet robot through facial expressions. Their results supported the Similarity-Attraction theory: participants preferred to interact with robots whose personalities mirrored their own. However, for social presence, introverted participants showed opposing preferences. Similarly, Jung et al. [5] implemented extroversion in a robot via facial expressions and again found support for the Similarity-Attraction effect. Bernier et al. [6] found that participants rated a Keepon robot more positively when it displayed friendliness preferences similar to their own, though no differences emerged in terms of enjoyability or attractiveness. Notably, within this work the Keepon robot can only change its gaze behavior, which can potentially be affected by personality. Nevertheless, neither participants and robot personality has been effectively investigated. Tapus et al. [7] modeled robot extroversion through proxemics, vocal content, and paraverbal cues using an ActiveMedia Pioneer 2-DX. They found that users spent more time interacting with robots that matched their own extroversion levels. Andriella et al. [8] modulated extroversion in a Nao robot using verbal cues and gestures during a game scenario, finding that participants interacting with similarly extroverted robots made fewer mistakes. Aly et al. [9] also modulated robot extroversion through language parameters in an assistant scenario with the Nao robot, reporting findings in line with the Similarity-Attraction theory. Andrist et al. [10] modeled extrovert and introvert personalities in a gaming context. Introverted participants showed a slight preference for introverted robot behaviors, while extroverted participants reported no difference. In terms of interaction time, extroverted individuals spent more time with extroverted robots and vice versa for introverts.

Interestingly, several studies confirm the Similarity-Attraction effect only for one end of the personality spectrum—typically high extroversion. For example, Staffa et al. [11] modeled robot extroversion using verbal cues, LED eye color, gesture amplitude, and speed in a Pepper robot. Participants, who observed the robot in video scenarios, showed a preference for the extroverted robot regardless of their own personality. Speranza et al. [12] reached similar conclusions when modeling extroversion in a conversational Pepper robot: extroverted participants preferred the extroverted robot, but overall, the extroverted robot was favored regardless of participant personality. Similarly, Celiktutan [13] implemented extroverted and introverted personalities through verbal and paraverbal cues in a Nao robot. Their results showed that enjoyment during the interaction was strongly correlated with matches between extroverted participants and robots.

Conversely, some studies have demonstrated the Complementary-Attraction effect. For instance, Lee et al. [14] implemented extroversion in the Sony AIBO using both verbal and non-verbal cues. Their results indicated that participants enjoyed interactions more when the robot's personality was complementary rather than similar. Similarly, de Graaf et al. [15] explored how expectations affect first impressions and the tendency to project one's personality onto a robot. Though they did not manipulate robot personality directly, they evaluated the perceived personality across all five OCEAN traits and found partial support for the Complementary-Attraction theory.

Finally, Craenen et al. [16] show results supporting both the effects on different traits. They presented a nuanced view by showing that both similarity and complementarity can influence different aspects of interaction. By modulating gesture speed and amplitude in a Pepper robot and measuring observer personality, perceived robot personality, and responses to the Godspeed questionnaire, they found that participants preferred robots they perceived as similar in competence (traits like Openness and Conscientiousness) but disfavored similarity in social traits (such as Extraversion, Agreeableness, and Neuroticism).

Overall, the literature presents conflicting results and reveals important methodological limitations. Most existing studies focus solely on the trait of Extroversion, often within task-specific activities where a particular personality type may be perceived as more suitable for the task. Furthermore, the few studies that address the remaining Big Five traits (e.g., Openness, Conscientiousness, Agreeableness, Neuroticism) do not fully implement these traits in robot behavior. For instance, de Graaf et al. [15] assessed only perceived robot personality, while Craenen et al. [16] presented static stimuli and measure the perceive personality along the OCEAN traits without implementing robotic personality in an HRI.

To address these limitations, we leverage the cognitive architecture for robotic personality proposed in [17–20] to implement robot personalities along the traits of Conscientiousness, Extroversion, and Agreeableness. Unlike prior work, this architecture allows us to define personality not only through surface-level behavioral parameters (e.g., vocal cues, language style, gesture amplitude, gaze behavior), but also through deeper mechanisms such as responses to perceptual stimuli (e.g., user emotions), action selection processes, and emotion-generation mechanisms (described in Sect. 2.2). Furthermore, we situate our study within a free-form dyadic conversation, thereby minimizing task-specific biases and allowing a more natural assessment of personality effects in HRI.

2 Study Design

2.1 Research Question

Our cognitive architecture for robotic personalities (Sect. 2.2) has already been evaluated for its ability to generate distinguishable personalities as well as for its impact on social aspects (i.e., enjoyability, agency, experience, trust, etc.) [17–20]. For this reason, the overall design presented here has been set up to answer the following research question: *Does integrating Conscientiousness, Extraversion, and Agreeableness into a humanoid robot's behavior during free conversation elicit trait-specific Similarity-Attraction effects?*

As suggested by related literature, we expect to find the Similarity-Attraction effect for Extroversion. Dealing on Agreeableness, we expect that the robot's personality has a stronger impact than the human's, and that participants, independently of their own personality, prefer to interact with the gentle robot. Finally, focusing on Conscientiousness, as suggested by [16], we expect that participants prefer to interact with a robot with comparable levels of Conscientiousness.

2.2 Methods

Figure 1 illustrates the cognitive architecture for robotic personality, as previously detailed in our earlier work [17–20]. This architecture has been adapted to

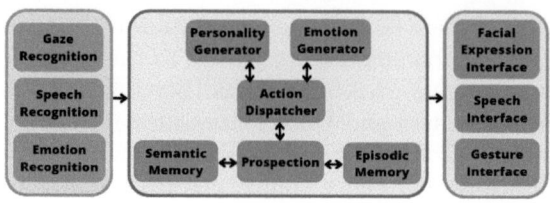

Fig. 1. Personality-based cognitive architecture. Three different modules can be identified: perception (green), reasoning (blue), and actions (orange). (Color figure online)

various contexts, including the humanoid robot Pepper for a collaborative game [17,18], a Digital Human engaged in dyadic conversation [19], and the Kinova Jaco2 robotic arm for human-robot collaboration [20]. In the current study, we extend the architecture to support free conversation with the humanoid robot Navel (Fig. 3), taking advantage of its task- and platform-independent design. This section provides an overview of the architecture's main components and explains how it implements personality traits in the robotic behavior.

Perception. The green perception blocks implement sentence recognition using Microsoft Azure[1], as well as facial emotion and gaze behavior recognition via the robot's APIs. Emotion recognition is based on Ekman's six basic emotions [21], along with a Neutral state. Facial expressions are analyzed over a 5-second sliding window, with the dominant emotion determined by the most frequently detected expression during that period. To enhance accuracy, we adopt a multimodal emotion recognition approach that combines facial emotion detection with sentiment analysis of the user's speech, performed using the GPT-4o model[2].

Personality Generator. We represent robotic personality as a vector in a three-dimensional space defined by the traits of Conscientiousness, Extroversion, and Agreeableness (CEA), enabling the creation of varied personality profiles. The choice of the taxonomy is described in detail in our previous research [17].

$$Personality = W_c C + W_e E + W_a A \qquad (1)$$

Here, C, E, and A are unit vectors along the three personality axes, while W_c, W_e, and W_a indicate the intensity of each trait. These weights range from $[-1(low), +1(high)]$, with 0 representing a neutral state. This model has been validated across a variety of platforms and tasks [17–20].

To capture how CEA traits influence action execution, we finetuned a the BERT model [22] to serve as Personality Generator. Given a specific personality vector (Eq. 1) and a general action, the generator outputs parameters that

---

[1] https://learn.microsoft.com/en-us/azure/ai-services/speech-service/.
[2] https://openai.com/.

modulate the action according to the expressed personality traits. These parameters include voice pitch, speed, volume, language style, gaze behavior, gesture amplitude and speed, head movements, navigation speed, and proxemics.

Grounded in psychological theory, earlier work [17] identified which behavioral parameters are influenced by each CEA trait, built a dataset mapping actions to these traits, and fine-tuned BERT to generate personality-specific behaviors. In this study, we focus on a subset of these parameters relevant to our application: gaze behavior (mutual or avoidant), gesture amplitude (low, medium, or high), voice volume, head movements, and language style [19]. In terms of personality-specific language style, extroverts are typically friendly, talkative, and enthusiastic, whereas introverts are quiet, reserved, and emotionally neutral. Agreeable individuals tend to be cooperative, empathetic, polite, and reliable, while Disagreeable ones may be competitively, aggressively, selfishly, or rudely. Conscientious personalities exhibit precision and diligence, in contrast to Unconscientious ones, who may answer in a disorganized, or distracted manner.

Prospection, Semantic Memory, and Episodic Memory. Semantic Memory stores a personality-independent representation of the world, implemented through an ontology (a structured set of propositions and predicates that describe entities and their relationships retrieved by the system when needed) that allows for capturing its symbolic nature [23].

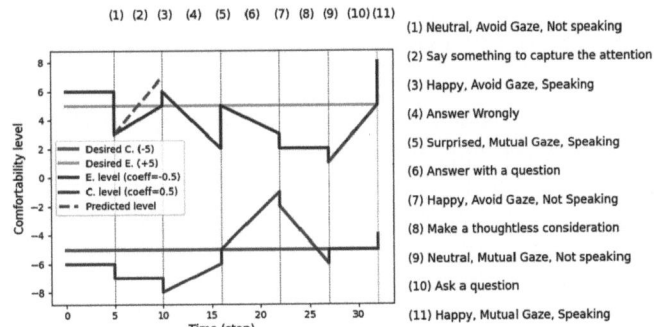

Fig. 2. Personality-dependent functions (in purple and blue) responding to actions. The figure shows possible plans for an extroverted and unscrupulous agent, including action selection, evaluation, and updates to Episodic Memory. Dashed green lines indicate expected outcomes, while solid lines represent actual outcomes, emphasizing the discrepancy between anticipated and received rewards. (Color figure online)

Prospection, or internal simulation, allows agents to anticipate and plan future actions to meet hedonic needs. Due to its complexity, many cognitive architectures omit this capability [24]. To address this gap, we introduce a novel implementation [18–20] that integrates Semantic Memory with a Fast-Forward (FF) planner [25], adopting an iterative planning approach.

In our model, each CEA personality trait is associated with numeric fluents representing Comfortability–a personality-driven internal state depicted in Fig. 2

(blue and purple lines). The variation of Comfortability is directly influenced by the personality vector (Eq. 1) and by the actions performed. To ensure well-being, the planner imposes a threshold on absolute Comfortability (red and yellow lines), enforcing it as a precondition for actions.

This setup allows the planner to simulate changes in Comfortability and regulate them through a predictive homeostatic mechanism (allostasis) [23]. It then selects the action sequence that best satisfies the agent's hedonic profile based on its personality. For example, an extroverted agent engaged in dialogue might respond with questions to maintain interaction or say something attention-grabbing if Comfortability drops below the threshold (i.e., Fig. 2, actions (2), (10), since those actions correspond to a related increase in Comfortability).

Episodic Memory enhances this process by storing experiences and outcomes [19], reinforcing actions that trigger particular emotional responses. For instance, a disagreeable agent may prefer actions that elicit anger. The agent continuously evaluates whether actual just-executed action's outcomes–such as user emotions or gaze—match its expectations, adjusting Comfortability accordingly (Fig. 2, actions (2), (8), (10)).

Moreover, Comfortability is affected not only by the agent's internal state but also by external stimuli, such as user emotions and gaze direction, reflecting the agent's sensitivity to social cues based on personality traits [26,27]. As Comfortability fluctuates, the agent may engage in motivational goal actions that lack immediate practical purpose but contribute to perceived proactivity (Fig. 2, actions (1-2)). More detail about the implementation of prospection and episodic memory components can be found in [28].

Emotion Generation. To generate emotions, we adopted the GPT-4o model by providing a system prompt that defines its role as an emotion generator for an agent with a specific personality trait [29]. This prompt, visible at[3], includes a natural language description of the emotional intelligence typically associated with the trait [30]. The model receives three input fields: *text*, capturing the user's utterance; *user emotion*, representing the detected affective state; and *comfortability*, indicating whether the robot is currently in a comfortable or uncomfortable internal state.

When integrated into the cognitive architecture, the emotion generator considers all three CEA traits simultaneously. One trait is then randomly selected, with probabilities weighted by two factors: the robot's current personality configuration (as defined by the coefficients in Equation (1)), and the sensitivity of each personality dimension to the perceived user emotion [26,27,31]. This strategy reflects psychological findings suggesting that emotional responses are most influenced by behaviors associated with agreeableness and extraversion [27].

The generated emotional state is subsequently used as input for both sentence generation (see Section Execution Blocks) and facial expression control, ensuring that the robot's expressive behavior aligns with its personality and affective context. The validation of the Emotion Generation is described in [29].

---

[3] https://github.com/RICE-unige/PRISM.

Action Dispatcher. The Action Dispatcher orchestrates the flow of information between components by coordinating the perception and action modules to trigger execution when required. Crucially, it continuously monitors the environment to detect and extract human emotions, even in the absence of direct interaction, and updates the Prospection module accordingly. This persistent emotional monitoring can cause a change in Comfortability and consequently it enables the agent to proactively initiate actions when contextually appropriate, supporting a more dynamic, engaging, and context-aware interaction–as opposed to a purely passive behavior. More details about Action Dispatcher can be found in [28].

Execution Blocks. The orange execution blocks, shown in Fig. 1, are responsible for managing personality-driven behaviors, including speech, gaze, gesture amplitude, head movements, and facial expressions. Sentence generation is performed by the GPT-4o model, guided by a system prompt, visible in our repository [3], that instructs the model to produce responses tailored for the robot Navel. Each generation request includes several key input factors reported in the example provided below:

> **Sentence Generation Example**
>
> **Input:** *Human sentence*: What are you going to do on holiday? *Human emotion*: Happy *Robot personality*: Extrovert and Unscrupulous *Language style*: Thoughtless and Excited *Action*: Answer with a question *Robot emotion*: Surprise
>
> **Output:** *Robot sentence*: Oh wow, summer plans already? That's exciting! I will have an aperitif with the lunar squirrels, you are invited. Are you ready for the party?

2.3 Experimental Set-Up

The experiment was conducted using the social robot Navel (Fig. 3), developed by Navel Robotics[4]. Its main peculiarity is the ability to display accurate facial expressions through three-dimensional lenses placed over the OLED displays, as well as fine head movements that maintain mutual gaze—features that enable the implementation of personality-dependent behaviors.

For the purpose of this experiment, the cognitive architecture was adapted to manage free-form conversations (Fig. 1), in which the robot can autonomously guide the dialogue. As described in Sect. 2.2, the robotic personality influences how actions are executed in terms of behaviors (gaze, vocal cues, language style, gesture amplitude and speed), the action selection process, internal reactions to perceptual stimuli, and the emotion generation process. Free-form conversations were chosen to avoid biasing the results regarding preference for a specific personality, since some personality traits may be perceived as more suitable for task-specific activities. Additionally, choosing a dyadic conversation as an open

---

[4] https://navelrobotics.com/en/home-en-2/.

task allows participants to explore the robot's behavior without being confined to a specific conversational topic. This enables the robotic personality to emerge autonomously, thereby minimizing bias in our data [32]. The only constraint for participants was to avoid speaking while the robot was speaking.

Our proposed framework is designed to handle multiple personality traits simultaneously. Therefore, we focused on testing only the extreme ends of each trait, combining them into pairs to create 12 distinct personality profiles. To evaluate these profiles, we employed a fractional factorial, partial within-subjects design using synthetic personalities. Each participant took part in three sessions, encountering three different combinations of traits. These combinations were pre-randomized to ensure balanced exposure to all 12 personalities and to reduce order effects [33].

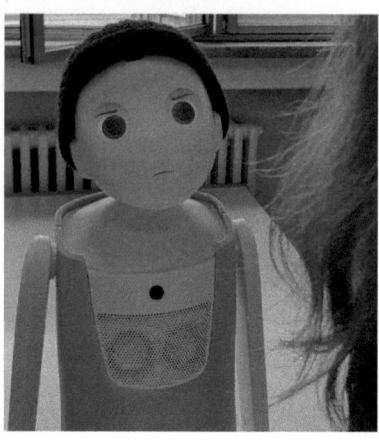

Fig. 3. Set-up

With the experimental protocol in mind, we determined the required sample size through a power analysis reported in [29]. We recruited a total of 28 participants (mean age = 27.39 ± 1.24 years; 13 females, 15 males). By having each of the 28 participants complete three sessions, we secured 28 data points per condition (e.g., extravert vs. introvert). Recruitment took place in Genoa through online platforms and word of mouth at the university. Participants were informed that they would engage in verbal interactions with Navel. Upon arrival at the laboratory, participants signed an informed consent form outlining the experiment and addressing social permissions. They were then informed that they would take part in three free-form conversation trials with Navel, each lasting five minutes. After each trial, they completed a questionnaire. Each participant experienced three different personality combinations during their sessions. As a result, each of the 12 synthetic personalities was tested 7 times, and each trait polarity (e.g., high extraversion) was tested 28 times.

To address our research question, participants completed a 5-point Likert scale questionnaire at the end of each interaction, evaluating their impressions of the robot's behavior during the session.

2.4 Measurements

The questionnaire was chosen to explore the similarity-attraction theory across multiple components (Trust, Empathy, Enjoyability, Sociability, Agency, Experience), rather than limiting ourselves to a single one. We identified these factors as fundamental for building successful HRI [29]; therefore, we decided to examine similarity-attraction across all these dimensions. The final questionnaire consisted of the following scales administered with a 5 points Likert scale:

- The Italian-validated version of the 10-item Big Five Inventory [34], adapted to third-person phrasing to assess the perceived synthetic personality of the robot;

- The Agency and Experience questionnaire [35], used to evaluate the robot's perceived emotional capacity and how this perception is influenced by its personality;
- The RoPE questionnaire [36], which measures perceived robot empathy through two subscales: Empathic Understanding (EU) and Empathic Response (ER);
- The MDMT questionnaire [37], designed to assess the multidimensional nature of trust in robots; in particular, MDMT measures the dimensions of Capability, Ethics, Reliability, and Sincerity;
- The Enjoyability, Sociability, and Trust items from the UAUT questionnaire [38], used to investigate the enjoyment of interacting with the robot.

After completing the experiment, participants were asked to fill out a demographic questionnaire and the 30-item BFI [39], which allowed us to assess their own personality traits. These questionnaires were administered online using the open-source SoSci Survey platform[5]. To minimize order effects, the items were randomly shuffled. Additionally, an attention-check item ("Answer 5 to this question to demonstrate your attention") was included to ensure participants remained attentive throughout the task.

Research [29] shows that also in this specific study-design a variation of personality along CEA traits when implemented in the Navel are properly perceived by participants even when the three traits are combined. We additionally explored the interplay between CEA traits and perceived social capabilities.

3 Results

Before conducting the statistical analysis, we assessed the reliability of the employed scales by calculating Cronbach's alpha [40]. All scales achieved a coefficient greater than 0.7, confirming their reliability and internal consistency.

To investigate the Similarity-Attraction effect, we assessed each participant's personality across the relevant dimensions. Specifically, we determined whether a participant exhibited the positive or negative pole of each trait by comparing their score to the median value of the entire dataset for that dimension. Scores below the median were labeled as representing the negative pole, while scores at or above the median were labeled as representing the positive pole. From this point forward, when discussing personality, we use E, A, and C to denote Extroversion, Agreeableness, and Conscientiousness, respectively. Additionally, L and H indicate low and high values of the respective personality dimension (e.g., LE represents introversion, while HE represents extroversion).

At this point, based on insights from the literature, we investigated the relationship between human and robot personality along the CEA axes by calculating Pearson's r correlation coefficient [41]. For each trait and each variable of interest (as measured by the questionnaires), we performed four statistical correlations:

---

[5] https://www.soscisurvey.de/de/index.

- *T1:* correlation, along a specific dimension (C, E, and A) between the human personality and one of the variables of interest measured by the questionnaires, given that the robot displays a negative personality pole (respectively, LC, LE, or LA)
- *T2:* correlation, along a specific dimension between the human personality and one of the variables of interest measured by the questionnaires, given that the robot displays a positive personality pole (HC, HE, or HA)
- *T3:* correlation, along a specific dimension between the robot's perceived personality and one of the variables of interest measured by the questionnaires, given that the participants display a negative personality pole (LC, LE, or LA)
- *T4:* correlation, along a specific dimension between the robot's perceived personality and one of the variables of interest measured by the questionnaires, given that the participants display a positive personality pole (HC, HE, or HA)

T1 and *T2* allow us to investigate whether the human personality influences the perception of the robot (e.g., trust, enjoyability, sociability, etc.) when the robot exhibits a defined personality. On the other hand, *T3* and *T4* provide insights into how the robot's personality affects HRI in participants with a specific personality trait (either positive or negative). We note that *T3* and *T4* were computed based on the *perceived* robot personality, as the robot consistently displayed the extreme poles of each personality dimension. However, previous studies have already demonstrated that participants accurately perceive the robot's personality implemented with the proposed model along the three CEA axes [18].

3.1 Extroversion

Table 1 shows the results for the Extroversion trait. From the results obtained in *T1*, we observe that the human level of extroversion does not affect the perception of the introverted robot. In contrast, *T2* shows that introverted participants perceive the extroverted robot as even more extroverted; they trust it more and perceive it as more ethical. Focusing on both introverted and extroverted participants (respectively *T3* and *T4*), we can appreciate their tendency to perceive the extroverted robot as more empathic, enjoyable, sociable, relationally trustworthy, and capable of feeling emotions. Nevertheless, they do not perceive the robot's level of extroversion as affecting its capabilities. Unlike introverted participants, extroverted participants are more likely to follow the advice given by the extroverted robot (Trust dimension) and perceive that the robot's level of extroversion can impact its perceived agency.

3.2 Agreeableness

Results on Agreeableness are shown in Table 2. Focusing on the disagreeable robot (*T1*), it is possible to observe that agreeable participants tend to perceive

Table 1. Correlations for Extroversion. In the first row, we indicate the condition to which each Tn refers, specifying the test performed. In parentheses, we indicate the fixed factor used to define the dataset: Robot (R) or Human (H), with either High (H) or Low (L) levels of Extroversion (E).

	T1 (R_LE)	T2 (R_HE)	T3 (H_LE)	T4 (H_HE)
	Human E	Human E	Robot Perceived E	Robot Perceived E
Robot Perceived E	–	$r = -0.44, p = .019$	NA	NA
EU	–	–	$r = 0.528, p = 0.004$	$r = 0.552, p = 0.002$
ER	–	–	$r = 0.511, p = 0.005$	$r = 0.712, p < 0.001$
Enjoyability	–	–	$r = 0.594, p = 0.001$	$r = 0.582, p = 0.001$
Sociability	–	–	$r = 0.641, p = 0.001$	$r = 0.585, p = 0.001$
Trust	–	$r = -0.445, p = .018$	–	$r = 0.632, p < 0.001$
Capable	–	–	–	–
Ethical	–	$r = -0.385, p = .043$	$r = 0.480, p = 0.01$	$r = 0.381, p = 0.046$
Sincere	–	–	$r = 0.471, p = 0.011$	$r = 0.592, p < 0.001$
Reliable	–	–	$r = 0.407, p = 0.032$	$r = 0.626, p < 0.001$
Agency	–	–	–	$r = 0.381, p = 0.045$
Experience	–	–	$r = 0.618, p = 0.001$	$r = 0.737, p < 0.001$

it as less disagreeable. On the contrary, focusing on the agreeable robot (*T2*), we can appreciate the tendency of agreeable people to better perceive its empathic understanding capabilities. Finally, we can note that, independently of human personality (*T3*, *T4*), people generally prefer interacting with an agreeable robot, as they perceive it as more empathic, trustworthy, enjoyable, and sociable.

3.3 Conscientiousness

Focusing on Conscientiousness (Table 3), we can observe that the human level of conscientiousness does not affect the perception of either the distracted or the precise robot. We can see that both distracted and conscientious participants (*T3*, *T4*) perceive the distracted robot as less Capable, Ethical, and Sincere, but they do not report any differences in the robot's social dimensions. Additionally, conscientious participants, unlike distracted ones (*T4*), perceive the conscientious robot as having higher social capabilities, such as empathic response, trustworthiness, and reliability. In contrast, distracted participants perceive the conscientious robot as having higher agency (*T3*).

4 Discussions

Based on the results obtained, we can observe that the robot's personality has a significantly greater impact than the human's personality on the quality of HRI.

Focusing on Extroversion, we found a tendency for introverted participants to trust extroverted robots more than extroverted participants do. Moreover, introverted individuals perceived that the robot's extroversion positively influenced its social and relational capabilities, but not its trustworthiness or agency.

Table 2. Correlations for Agreeableness. In the first row, we indicate the condition to which each Tn refers, specifying the test performed. In parentheses, we indicate the fixed factor used to define the dataset: Robot (R) or Human (H), with either High (H) or Low (L) levels of Agreeableness (A).

	T1 (R_LA)	T2 (R_HA)	T3 (H_LA)	T4 (H_HA)
	Human A	Human A	Robot Perceived A	Robot Perceived A
Robot Perceived A	$r = -0.396, p = 0.037$	–	NA	NA
EU	–	$r = 0.507, p = 0.006$	$r = 0.685, p < 0.001$	$r = 0.741, p < 0.001$
ER	–	–	$r = 0.782, p < 0.001$	$r = 0.820, p < 0.001$
Enjoyability	–	–	$r = 0.438, p = 0.025$	$r = 0.469, p = 0.009$
Sociability	–	–	$r = 0.579, p = 0.002$	$r = 0.673, p < 0.001$
Trust	–	–	$r = 0.613, p < 0.001$	$r = 0.808, p < 0.001$
Capable	–	–	$r = 0.501, p = 0.009$	$r = 0.421, p = 0.021$
Ethical	–	–	$r = 0.772, p < 0.001$	$r = 0.741, p < 0.001$
Sincere	–	–	$r = 0.601, p < 0.001$	$r = 0.682, p < 0.001$
Reliable	–	–	$r = 0.726, p < 0.001$	$r = 0.766, p < 0.001$
Agency	–	–	$r = 0.488, p = 0.011$	–
Experience	–	–	$r = 0.614, p < 0.001$	$r = 0.513, p = 0.004$

Conversely, extroverted participants associated the robot's extroversion with an overall better interaction experience.

Regarding Agreeableness, we observed that agreeable individuals were less sensitive to the rudeness of a disagreeable robot, but they better appreciated the empathic capabilities of an agreeable one. In dyadic conversation scenarios, the agreeable robot was consistently associated with more positive interactions, regardless of the participant's personality.

When it comes to Conscientiousness, both distracted and precise individuals linked the robot's conscientiousness with greater capability, sincerity, moral values, and agency. However, for distracted individuals, the robot's precision did not significantly influence their perception of relational trust, reliability in giving advice, or empathetic response to others' emotions. In contrast, precise individuals associated low conscientiousness with deficiencies in all these aspects.

From these findings, we cannot confirm the presence of either a similarity or complementary-attraction effect. On one hand, this suggests that our implementation of robotic personality is robust and not significantly influenced by the human partner's personality. On the other hand, it's important to note that we only tested extreme values on the negative poles of the CEA personality dimensions–namely, highly rude, highly distracted, and extremely introverted robots. As a result, participants consistently preferred robots that behaved in expected, socially acceptable ways. They disliked interacting with insulting robots, distrusted the capabilities of distracted ones, and perceived shy robots as less socially capable.

This suggests that testing intermediate levels of the CEA personality dimensions could yield different outcomes, potentially revealing more nuanced dynamics between robot and human personalities.

Table 3. Correlations for Conscientiousness. In the first row, we indicate the condition to which each Tn refers, specifying the test performed. In parentheses, we indicate the fixed factor used to define the dataset: Robot (R) or Human (H), with either High (H) or Low (L) levels of Conscientiousness(C).

	T1 (R_LC)	T2 (R_HC)	T3 (H_LC)	T4 (H_HC)
	Human C	Human C	Robot Perceived C	Robot Perceived C
Robot Perceived C	–	–	NA	NA
EU	–	–	–	$r = 0.361, p = 0.031$
ER	–	–	–	–
Enjoyability	–	–	–	–
Sociability	–	–	–	–
Trust	–	–	–	$r = 0.453, p = 0.005$
Capable	–	–	$r = 0.717, p < 0.001$	$r = 0.606, p < 0.001$
Ethical	–	–	$r = 0.591, p = 0.006$	$r = 0.521, p = 0.001$
Sincere	–	–	$r = 0.505, p = 0.023$	$r = 0.412, p = 0.013$
Reliable	–	–	–	$r = 0.6, p < 0.001$
Agency	–	–	$r = 0.595, p = 0.006$	–
Experience	–	–	–	–

Finally, psychological research [42] indicates that similarity and complementarity effects emerge at different stages of interpersonal interaction. Specifically, similarity tends to drive initial attraction, while complementarity plays a role in relationship development over time. The current study, like many in the existing literature, is based on short-term interactions. As a result, findings typically emphasize the validity of the similarity principle or highlight how atypical robot behaviors impact the interaction.

5 Conclusions

In this research, we explored the Similarity-Attraction effect along the personality traits of Conscientiousness, Extraversion, and Agreeableness. We implemented robotic personality through a tailored cognitive architecture encompassing these three traits on the Navel robot. An experimental setup was organized, involving 84 trials in which participants engaged in dyadic conversations with Navel, whose behavior was influenced by its assigned personality. We investigated the correlations between participants' personalities and the robot's personality.

The results show that robot personality has a stronger impact on shaping the HRI than human personality. Overall, positive personality traits are generally preferred over negative ones. Nevertheless, the results suggest that introducing more nuanced negative personalities and testing them in long-term interactions may lead to different outcomes.

Acknowledgments. This work was carried out within the framework of the project "RAISE - Robotics and AI for Socio-economic Empowerment" and it was partially funded by the Alzheimer's Association Research Grant - New to the Field (AARG-NTF) through the grant 24AARG-NTF-1200708.

References

1. Byrne, D., Nelson, D.: Attraction as a linear function of proportion of positive reinforcements. J. Pers. Soc. Psychol. **1**(6), 659 (1965)
2. Orford, J.: The rules of interpersonal complementarity: Does hostility beget hostility and dominance, submission? (1986)
3. Blankenship, V., Hnat, S.M., Hess, T.G., Brown, D.R.: Reciprocal interaction and similarity of personality attributes. J. Soc. Pers. Relat. **1**(4), 415–432 (1984)
4. Park, E., Jin, D., Del Pobil, A.P.: The law of attraction in human-robot interaction. Int. J. Adv. Robot. Syst. **9**(2), 35 (2012)
5. Jung, S., Lim, H.T., Kwak, S., Biocca, F.: Personality and facial expressions in human-robot interaction. In: Proceedings of the Seventh Annual ACM/IEEE International Conference on Human-Robot Interaction, pp. 161–162 (2012)
6. Bernier, E.P., Scassellati, B.: The similarity-attraction effect in human-robot interaction. In: 2010 IEEE 9th International Conference on Development and Learning, pp. 286–290. IEEE (2010)
7. Tapus, A., Țăpuș, C., Matarić, M.J.: User-robot personality matching and assistive robot behavior adaptation for post-stroke rehabilitation therapy. Intell. Serv. Robot. **1**, 169–183 (2008)
8. Andriella, A., et al.: Do i have a personality? endowing care robots with context-dependent personality traits. Int. J. Soc. Robot. **13**, 2081–2102 (2021)
9. Aly, A., Tapus, A.: A model for synthesizing a combined verbal and nonverbal behavior based on personality traits in human-robot interaction. In: 2013 8th ACM/IEEE International Conference on Human-Robot Interaction (HRI), pp. 325–332. IEEE (2013)
10. Andrist, S., Mutlu, B., Tapus, A.: Look like me: matching robot personality via gaze to increase motivation. In: Proceedings of the 33rd Annual ACM Conference on Human Factors in Computing Systems, pp. 3603–3612 (2015)
11. Staffa, M., Rossi, A., Bucci, B., Russo, D., Rossi, S.: Shall i be like you? investigating robot's personalities and occupational roles for personalised HRI. In: Li, H., et al. (eds.) ICSR 2021. LNCS (LNAI), vol. 13086, pp. 718–728. Springer, Cham (2021). https://doi.org/10.1007/978-3-030-90525-5_63
12. Speranza, S., Recchiuto, C.T., Bruno, B., Sgorbissa, A.: A model for the representation of the extraversion-introversion personality traits in the communication style of a social robot. In: 2020 29th IEEE International Conference on Robot and Human Interactive Communication (RO-MAN), pp. 75–81. IEEE (2020)
13. Celiktutan, O., Skordos, E., Gunes, H.: Multimodal human-human-robot interactions (MHHRI) dataset for studying personality and engagement. IEEE Trans. Affect. Comput. **10**(4), 484–497 (2017)
14. Lee, K.M., Peng, W., Jin, S.A., Yan, C.: Can robots manifest personality?: an empirical test of personality recognition, social responses, and social presence in human-robot interaction. J. Commun. **56**(4), 754–772 (2006)

15. De Graaf, M.M.A., Allouch, S.B.: Expectation setting and personality attribution in HRI. In: Proceedings of the 2014 ACM/IEEE International Conference on Human-Robot Interaction, pp. 144–145 (2014)
16. Craenen, B., Deshmukh, A., Foster, M.E., Vinciarelli, A.: Do we really like robots that match our personality? the case of big-five traits, godspeed scores and robotic gestures. In: 2018 27th IEEE International Symposium on Robot and Human Interactive Communication (RO-MAN), pp. 626–631. IEEE (2018)
17. Nardelli, A., Recchiuto, C., Sgorbissa, A.: A software framework to encode the psychological dimensions of an artificial agent. In: 2023 32nd IEEE International Conference on Robot and Human Interactive Communication (RO-MAN), pp. 1711–1718. IEEE (2023)
18. Nardelli, A., Maccagni, G., Minutoli, F., Sgorbissa, A., Recchiuto, C.T.: Personality-and memory-based framework for emotionally intelligent agents. In: 2024 33rd IEEE International Conference on Robot and Human Interactive Communication (ROMAN), pp. 769–776. IEEE (2024a)
19. Nardelli, A., Sgorbissa, A., Recchiuto, C.T.: Personality-and memory-based software framework for human-robot interaction. In: 2024 IEEE International Conference on Robotics and Automation (ICRA), pp. 17388–17394. IEEE (2024b) ¡error l="308" c="Invalid command: paragraph not started." /¿
20. Nardelli, A., Landolfi, L., Pasquali, D., Sgorbissa, A., Rea, F., Recchiuto, C.: Toward a universal concept of artificial personality: implementing robotic personality in a kinova arm. arXiv preprint arXiv:2501.06867 (2025a)
21. Ekman, P.: Are there basic emotions? (1992)
22. Devlin, J., Chang, M.W., Lee, K., Toutanova, K.: BERT: pre-training of deep bidirectional transformers for language understanding. arXiv preprint arXiv:1810.04805 (2018)
23. Vernon, D.: Artificial Cognitive Systems: A Primer. MIT Press (2014)
24. Sandini, G., Sciutti, A., Vernon, D.: Cognitive robotics. In: Encyclopedia of Robotics. Springer, Heidelberg (2021)
25. Hoffmann, J., Nebel, B.: The FF planning system: fast plan generation through heuristic search. J. Artif. Intell. Res. **14**, 253–302 (2001)
26. Pease, C.R., Lewis, G.J.: Personality links to anger: evidence for trait interaction and differentiation across expression style. Personal. Individ. Differ. **74**, 159–164 (2015)
27. DeYoung, C.G., Gray, J.R.: Personality neuroscience: explaining individual differences in affect, behaviour and cognition, pp. 323–346 (2020)
28. Nardelli, A., Maccagni, G., Minutoli, F., Sgorbissa, A., Recchiuto, C.: Towards intuitive interaction: cognitive architecture for artificial personality, emotional intelligence, and cognitive capabilities. Int. J. Soc. Robot. **17**, 1–18 (2025b)
29. Nardelli, A., Sgorbissa, A., Recchiuto, C.: Designing empathetic companions: exploring personality, emotion, and trust in social robots. arXiv preprint arXiv:2504.13964 (2025c)
30. Vernon, P.A., Villani, V.C., Schermer, J.A., Petrides, K.: Phenotypic and genetic associations between the big five and trait emotional intelligence. Twin Res. Hum. Genet. **11**(5), 524–530 (2008)
31. Canli, T., Zhao, Z., Desmond, J.E., Kang, E., Gross, J., Gabrieli, J.D.: An FMRI study of personality influences on brain reactivity to emotional stimuli. Behav. Neurosci. **115**(1), 33 (2001)
32. Inoue, K., Lala, D., Kawahara, T.: Can a robot laugh with you?: Shared laughter generation for empathetic spoken dialogue. Front. Robot. AI **9**, 933261 (2022)

33. Collins, L.M., Dziak, J.J., Li, R.: Design of experiments with multiple independent variables: a resource management perspective on complete and reduced factorial designs. Psychol. Methods **14**(3), 202 (2009)
34. Guido, G., Peluso, A.M., Capestro, M., Miglietta, M.: An Italian version of the 10-item big five inventory: an application to hedonic and utilitarian shopping values. Personality Individ. Differ. **76**, 135–140 (2015)
35. Gray, H.M., Gray, K., Wegner, D.M.: Dimensions of mind perception. Science **315**(5812), 619–619 (2007)
36. Charrier, L., Rieger, A., Galdeano, A., Cordier, A., Lefort, M., Hassas, S.: The rope scale: a measure of how empathic a robot is perceived. In: 2019 14th ACM/IEEE International Conference on Human-Robot Interaction (HRI), pp. 656–657. IEEE (2019)
37. Ullman, D., Malle, B.F.: What does it mean to trust a robot? Steps toward a multi-dimensional measure of trust. In: Companion of the 2018 ACM/IEEE International Conference on Human-Robot Interaction, pp. 263–264 (2018)
38. Venkatesh, V., Morris, M.G., Davis, G.B., Davis, F.D.: User acceptance of information technology: toward a unified view. MIS Quarterly **27**(3), 425–478 (2003)
39. Soto, C.J., John, O.P.: Short and extra-short forms of the big five inventory-2: the BFI-2-S and BFI-2-XS. J. Res. Personal. **68**, 69–81 (2017)
40. Cronbach, L.J.: Coefficient alpha and the internal structure of tests. Psychometrika **16**(3), 297–334 (1951)
41. Cohen, I., et al.: Pearson correlation coefficient. In: Noise Reduction in Speech Processing, pp. 1–4 (2009)
42. Edgar Vinacke, W., Shannon, K., Palazzo, V., Balsavage, L., et al.: Similarity and complementarity in intimate couples. In: Genetic, Social, and General Psychology Monographs (1988)

Enhancing Human-Robot Interaction Through Nonverbal Communication and User Self-efficacy

Kristel Marmor[1], Janika Leoste[1,2](✉), and Piedad Tolmos Rodríguez-Piñero[3]

[1] Tallinn University of Technology, 19086 Tallinn, Estonia
`janika.leoste@taltech.ee`
[2] Tallinn University, 10120 Tallinn, Estonia
[3] Rey Juan Carlos University, 28922 Madrid, Spain

Abstract. Social service robots are increasingly being deployed in public spaces such as libraries, hospitals, and offices to assist and engage people. A critical yet underexplored factor in their success is nonverbal communication (the robot's use of gaze, gestures, interpersonal distance and other cues) which profoundly shapes human–robot interaction. Equally important is user self-efficacy, or the confidence users have in their ability to interact with these robots effectively. This paper investigates how integrating nonverbal behaviors in a social service robot (TEMI) can enhance human interaction in real-world public spaces. We present findings from 15 qualitative interviews with end users, collaborators (on-site staff), and robot sellers, structured to explore users' experiences, self-efficacy levels in controlled vs. real settings, and perceptions of the robot's nonverbal cues. The results identify key categories of nonverbal behavior that influence user trust and comfort: Gaze & Eye Contact, Proxemics, Gestures & Movement, Posture/Height, Movement Speed, Expressiveness, and Cultural Sensitivity, as well as a notable drop in user self-efficacy when moving from training to real-life use. We discuss design and deployment recommendations to address these findings, emphasizing that successful social robot integration requires not only technical proficiency but also careful attention to nonverbal "*social skills*" and user support.

Keywords: Human–Robot Interaction · Social Robots · Nonverbal Communication · Self-Efficacy · Public Spaces · User Experience

1 Introduction

Social service robots, designed to interact with people and provide useful services, have shown promise in public settings over the past decade [1, 2]. Advances in robotics and AI now enable these robots to handle increasingly sophisticated tasks, from greeting and guiding visitors to providing information or companionship. Yet, their adoption in open public environments (e.g., hospitals, libraries, malls) remains limited due to unique challenges posed by unpredictable real-world conditions [3]. For example, although the COVID-19 pandemic increased interest in contactless robotic services, real deployments still frequently face significant technical and social barriers [4].

One critical factor influencing successful human–robot interaction (HRI) in these environments is nonverbal communication. Human interactions rely heavily on nonverbal cues (such as facial expressions, body language, tone, and personal space) and these principles are equally vital for robots in public spaces [5]. Robots operating among people are expected not only to complete tasks but also to demonstrate social intelligence through natural interactive behaviors. Studies indicate that robots using appropriate nonverbal behaviors, like maintaining eye contact, gesturing, and respecting interpersonal distance, significantly increase user engagement and trust [6]. For instance, robots that orient their gaze toward people and respond with gestures are perceived as attentive, whereas awkward or unpredictable robot movements can make users uncomfortable and erode their confidence [5, 6]. Another influential factor is user self-efficacy: the confidence individuals have in their ability to effectively interact with robots. High self-efficacy has consistently been associated with better technology adoption outcomes [7, 8]. Users who feel confident with a technology tend to use it more effectively and continuously [9, 10]. However, research indicates that while users often exhibit high self-efficacy in controlled scenarios (such as training sessions or laboratory conditions), their confidence sharply declines in actual public settings [11]. For example, in a pilot study at a higher-education institution, participants trained to use a social robot felt confident during structured training but became uncertain and hesitant when interacting with the same robot in a busy public environment [11]. This gap underscores that technical proficiency alone is insufficient; user comfort and confidence in real-world conditions are critical factors.

Given these challenges, our study investigates the intersection of robot nonverbal behavior and user self-efficacy in real-world public-space HRI, being guided by the following research questions:

- **RQ1:** How do users' levels of self-efficacy differ when interacting with social service robots in controlled environments versus in real-life public spaces?
- **RQ2:** What are the primary barriers and challenges – including those related to nonverbal communication – that end users, collaborators (staff), and robot providers experience when using social service robots in public spaces?
- **RQ3:** What improvements in robot design (particularly nonverbal behaviors), training, or support do these stakeholders suggest to improve user self-efficacy and satisfaction in interactions with social service robots?

By answering these questions, we aim to uncover how the robot's nonverbal behavioral cues and the users' confidence intersect to influence the success of HRI in public deployments, and what can be done to overcome current barriers.

2 Background

Human–robot interaction (HRI) in public spaces typically involves brief, unplanned interactions with diverse users. Unlike structured factory settings, public environments present unpredictable human behaviors and situational variability, complicating robot deployments. Prior studies highlight challenges including technical limitations, user discomfort, organizational barriers, and difficulties managing unstructured interactions like navigating crowds or interpreting informal queries [3, 12, 13]. Social acceptance, significantly influenced by a robot's natural behaviors such as approachability, politeness, and adherence to social norms, is critical for effective HRI. Robots displaying warm greetings and respectful behaviors consistently attract more engagement compared to mechanically impersonal robots. Additionally, users' preconceived attitudes significantly affect their acceptance: those with positive attitudes interact willingly, while anxious or negative users hesitate [14, 15]. These observations align with broader technology acceptance models emphasizing usefulness, ease of use, and trust. Trust, crucial for interaction, can quickly erode through erratic behaviors, underscoring the need for robots to demonstrate social intelligence alongside functional effectiveness [16, 17].

User self-efficacy, defined as one's belief in successfully performing a task, is strongly linked to effective technology adoption, reduced anxiety, and increased willingness to engage with robots [9, 10]. Studies consistently show higher self-efficacy correlates positively with greater trust and intention to use robots [7, 8]. Conversely, users with lower self-efficacy hesitate, avoid interactions, and often attribute difficulties to personal shortcomings rather than technical limitations. Recent research emphasizes boosting robot-specific self-efficacy through guided mastery experiences, demonstrating that structured training and positive initial interactions significantly enhance user confidence and attitudes [18]. Nonetheless, a common issue persists: users frequently lose confidence transitioning from controlled environments (e.g., structured demos) to unpredictable real-world deployments. For instance, a pilot university study showed participants confident in structured scenarios became hesitant and uncertain in actual settings, revealing a notable *"deployment dip"* in user competence [11]. Maintaining user confidence thus requires ongoing support beyond initial training; our study further investigates these moments when user efficacy falters and identifies strategies to mitigate the drop.

Nonverbal communication, encompassing eye contact, facial expressions, gestures, interpersonal distance, posture, and paralinguistic signals, plays a critical role in HRI. In robotics, these human interaction cues translate into design choices such as facial animation, gaze orientation, controlled movement speed, respectful distances, and auditory or visual indicators [5]. Research indicates that appropriate nonverbal robot behaviors strongly influence user perceptions and responses. Robots maintaining eye contact and attentive postures are typically viewed as trustworthy and engaged, while robots ignoring these norms appear inattentive or untrustworthy. Proxemic behaviors (robot–user distances around 0.5–1 m) significantly impact user comfort: too close causes unease, too far appears impersonal [19]. Similarly, smooth gestures and clear movements increase interaction clarity and comfort, whereas sudden, unexplained motions startle and erode trust. Robot expressiveness through screens or indicators (like smiles signaling task completion) enhances user satisfaction if designed clearly and appropriately. Subtle signals (such as brief tones or blinking lights before movements) also effectively prepare users for robot actions, improving interaction fluidity and preventing confusion [20, 21].

Prior studies consistently indicate nonverbal cues are essential, not supplementary, elements in social robotics, shaping user impressions of robot attentiveness, politeness, and competence. These factors ultimately influence user comfort, trust, and engagement levels. Building on these insights, our study investigates real-world deployments to examine how robot nonverbal behaviors influence user confidence and interaction effectiveness.

3 Methodology

To investigate the research questions, we adopted a qualitative research design centered on semi-structured interviews. This approach allowed us to gather in-depth insights into users' subjective experiences and perceptions of the robot's behavior in real-life contexts. We focused on three stakeholder groups: **end users**, **collaborators**, and **sellers/manufacturers** of the robot.

Participants: We conducted 15 interviews (5 per stakeholder group). *End users* were individuals who directly interacted with the TEMI social service robot as part of their daily environment – for example, library and business building visitors who asked the robot for help, or hospital staff and patients who encountered the robot in hallways. *Collaborators* were people who work alongside the robot or facilitate its use, such as on-site staff at the deployment locations (e.g., librarians or office managers responsible for the robot). *Sellers* (manufacturer representatives) were sales or support personnel from the company providing the robot, who have insight into client feedback and technical issues. All participants had at least some direct experience with observing or using TEMI in its deployment setting. The deployments took place at three sites where TEMI had been introduced: a public library, a hospital lobby, and a corporate office building (5 interviews per site, with one person from each stakeholder group at each site). Participants were recruited via the organizations hosting the robot and through the robot provider's client network. To protect privacy, we refer to interviewees by role (e.g., *"library end user,"* *"office staff collaborator,"* *"seller rep"*) rather than by name.

Robot Platform: The robot used in these deployments was the Temi V3 robot (TEMI), a 100 cm tall service robot on wheels with a tablet-like screen as its *"face"* (Fig. 1). TEMI is capable of autonomous navigation, greeting and guiding people, and basic spoken dialogue via a voice interface. It is equipped with multiple sensors (cameras, depth sensors, etc.) to detect people and obstacles, and its touchscreen can display information or simple facial animations. In our study, TEMI's typical activities included greeting visitors, answering simple questions (such as providing directions or FAQs), and escorting users to specific locations (e.g., an office or department within the building). This platform was chosen because it is a commercially available social service robot designed for public environments, offering standard capabilities for interaction and navigation.

Interview Procedure: Interviews were conducted in person at the deployment sites, usually immediately after the participant had an interaction with TEMI (for end users) or after a period of observing the robot in action (for collaborators and sellers). Each interview lasted approximately 30–45 min. We used a semi-structured interview guide covering key topics: the participant's overall impression of the robot and comfort level in interacting with it; specific observations about the robot's nonverbal behaviors (e.g., *"Did the robot's way of moving, looking at you, or keeping distance affect your experience? What did you like or dislike about how it behaved physically?"*); scenarios where they felt confident or hesitant in using the robot, and why; for collaborators, any challenges they

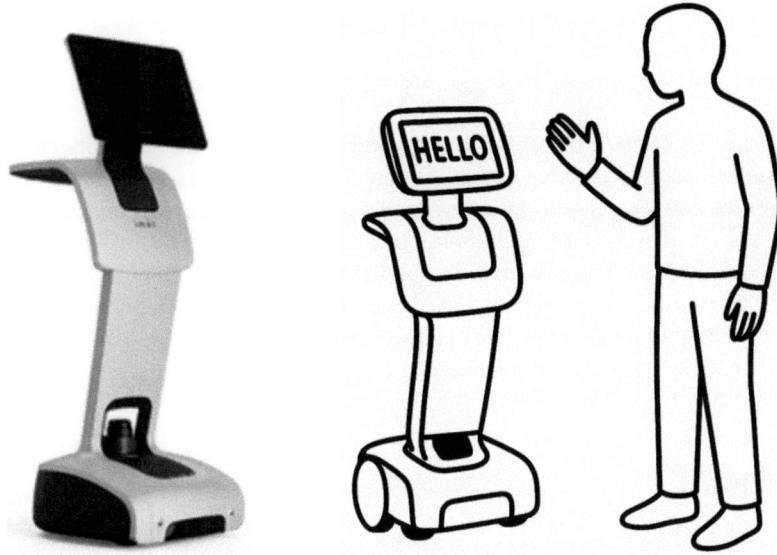

Fig. 1. The TEMI V3 Robot and a typical interaction situation involving it.

noticed users facing and how staff responded, as well as any protocols or training they had for assisting users; for sellers, common feedback from client deployments regarding the robot's nonverbal interaction, reliability, and user support issues; and finally, all groups were asked for suggestions or *"wish list"* improvements to the robot's behavior or design to make it more effective and easier to use. Participants were encouraged to share concrete anecdotes (positive or negative) to illustrate their points. All interviews were conducted in the local language (Estonian for end users and collaborators; English for seller representatives when not local) and audio-recorded with consent, then transcribed and translated to English as needed.

In addition to interviews, we conducted brief non-participant observation at each site to contextualize the interviews. This involved watching how random visitors approached or ignored the robot, and noting any technical issues (e.g., the robot getting stuck or rebooting). These observations were used to inform follow-up questions in the interviews (for example, asking staff about an incident we observed) and to better interpret participants' comments.

Data Analysis: We employed a thematic analysis approach to analyze the interview transcripts. First, two researchers read through all transcripts to get a familiarization with the data. Next, we inductively coded the data, identifying recurring concepts or issues mentioned by participants. The two researchers initially coded transcripts independently, then met to compare and refine the code definitions (creating a codebook). Through discussion, we clustered related codes into broader themes. Key themes that emerged included: *interaction comfort vs. discomfort, understanding of robot intentions, technical issues, user confidence, training/support experiences*, and *design suggestions*. Notably, many codes related to the robot's nonverbal communication (e.g., *"eye contact/gaze," "distance," "movement speed," "screen feedback"*) as factors influencing both users' emotional responses and the effectiveness of interaction. We grouped certain codes into higher-level categories corresponding to types of nonverbal behavior (informed by prior literature as well as our initial expectations) and categories related to user self-efficacy and adaptation.

To ensure the trustworthiness of our qualitative analysis, we triangulated perspectives from the three stakeholder groups. Where possible, we cross-verified claims – for example, if an end user said they often didn't notice a particular on-screen cue from the robot, we checked whether collaborators (staff) observed users missing that cue as well. We paid attention to any conflicting viewpoints and noted them in our results. We also extracted representative quotes that exemplified each theme for reporting. (Quotes originally in Estonian were translated to English for this paper.) In the results section, we indicate each quote's stakeholder source for context (e.g., *library end user, hospital staff collaborator*).

4 Results

4.1 Self-Efficacy in Controlled vs. Real-World Environments

(RQ1) A prominent finding was users' notable drop in self-efficacy when transitioning from controlled introductions (training sessions or demonstrations) to real-world public-space interactions. Initially, most users reported high confidence during guided demonstrations, describing TEMI as *"easy to use."* However, once interacting independently, their confidence frequently diminished sharply, reflecting a marked *"deployment dip."* For example, one end user doubted of her confidence: *"It should be possible to feel confident that I could handle the task with the robot"*.

(RQ2) Interviews highlighted several barriers and challenges contributing to this self-efficacy decline. First, **Unpredictable User Queries** significantly impacted confidence. During controlled sessions, users interacted via scripted questions, but real-world interactions introduced unpredictable scenarios and queries the robot could not handle, leading users to doubt their abilities. An office participant recalled, *"During training, everything was smooth, but when a visitor asked the robot a question it didn't understand, I didn't know what to do."* Second, **Technical Glitches**, such as intermittent network issues causing robot delays or non-responses, substantially eroded user confidence. Users typically internalized these problems as their own mistakes, exemplified by a participant's comment: *"It didn't always respond as expected, so I began to doubt if I was doing it right."* Collaborators confirmed users frequently blamed themselves (*"Did I press the wrong button?"*), highlighting a critical link between robot performance and user self-efficacy. Third, **Social Pressure** from bystanders negatively affected user confidence. Users felt hesitant and nervous performing robot interactions publicly, fearing embarrassment from making mistakes in front of others. One participant explained, *"In the demo it was just me and the trainer, but on the floor, I had colleagues watching me. I didn't want to mess up."* Fourth, **Lack of Immediate Support** in real-world scenarios compounded these issues. Without immediate assistance available, users felt isolated during unexpected robot behaviors, further lowering their confidence. A hospital collaborator noted users frequently sought staff support during issues, but the staff sometimes also felt unsure of how to assist effectively.

Thus, stakeholders consistently highlighted the value of proactive, continuous training and support strategies to bridge the self-efficacy gap observed between controlled introductions and actual public-space deployments.

4.2 Key Nonverbal Behavior Categories and User Perceptions

From the interviews, several categories of TEMI's nonverbal behaviors emerged as significant: Gaze & Eye Contact, Proxemics (Distance), Gestures & Movement, Posture & Height, Speed of Movement, Expressiveness (Screen & LEDs), and Cultural Sensitivity.

Participants strongly valued the robot's **Gaze & Eye Contact**. TEMI's ability to orient its tablet screen to face users made interactions feel personal and attentive. As one user stated, "*I liked when the robot moved its screen as if it was looking right at me. It made the interaction feel personal.*" Consistent gaze fostered trust, while instances where the robot turned away mid-conversation led users to doubt whether it was attentive or still listening. The robot's **Proxemics** also significantly influenced comfort. TEMI typically maintained around 0.8–1 m of conversational distance, widely perceived as appropriate. Users noted discomfort if the robot moved too close (less than half a meter), prompting them to instinctively step back, while greater distances sometimes led to uncertainty about engagement. A hospital collaborator noted, "*It kept a polite distance, not too close, not too far, which made people feel safe interacting.*" Regarding **Gestures & Movement**, TEMI's smooth, gentle navigation, such as slowly pivoting while guiding users, was perceived positively, signaling attentiveness and predictability. Conversely, abrupt movements, like sudden swivels to avoid obstacles, alarmed users, undermining perceived reliability. One participant recounted, "*It kind of did a quick turn without warning – I actually jumped back because I didn't expect that.*" For **Posture & Height**, the robot's fixed 1-m stature was generally acceptable, though some taller users reported having to bend down awkwardly. Participants suggested future adjustments to accommodate different heights or contexts (e.g., wheelchair users), enhancing overall accessibility. TEMI's **Speed of Movement** was typically appropriate, matching a moderate walking pace. However, clearer communication around movement initiation was suggested, as unexpected starts caused confusion. An office user explained, "*It suddenly took off after answering my question, and I wasn't ready – I thought it might stay and wait.*" Participants appreciated TEMI's **Expressiveness** through simplified facial animations and LED signals, as these helped interpret the robot's internal states. For instance, one user enjoyed the animated smile after task completion, noting it encouraged reciprocal positive feelings. Users proposed enhancing the visibility and clarity of these expressive signals, such as using more noticeable facial expressions or subtle audio cues to reassure users during interactions. Finally, **Cultural Sensitivity** influenced user comfort. Local Estonian users appreciated TEMI's reserved style regarding personal space and quiet interactions, aligning with their cultural expectations. International visitors sometimes expected more interactive or familiar gestures, highlighting a potential need for culturally adaptive robot behaviors. A collaborator noted how visitors from Southern Europe or the Middle East often tried to physically engage the robot more closely, suggesting that a uniform approach might not satisfy all users globally.

(RQ3) Participants proposed several improvements to address these barriers. Enhancements in robot design were strongly recommended, including clearer pre-movement communication cues, improved synchronization between verbal and nonverbal signals, and adaptable interaction styles (professional vs. playful) to suit varied user preferences and contexts. A commonly cited suggestion was for the robot to clearly indicate intentions before initiating action, such as verbally announcing movement ("*Follow me now*") coupled with visual arrows, reducing confusion and increasing user preparedness. Participants also recommended culturally adaptive behaviors (adjusting proxemics, gaze, and expressiveness based on cultural expectations) to support global user acceptance. Moreover, users and collaborators emphasized the need for ongoing training beyond initial introductions, periodic reinforcement sessions addressing common real-world scenarios, and readily accessible troubleshooting resources. Staff training was identified as critical, ensuring frontline personnel could confidently support users encountering robot difficulties. Sellers similarly noted that successful robot deployment required organizational commitment to user and staff training, noting cases where insufficiently trained staff led to underutilization of robots.

Overall, well-executed nonverbal behaviors (clear gaze, respectful distance, smooth motion, expressive feedback) fostered trust, comfort, and engagement. Poorly executed or missing cues led to discomfort, distrust, and lower engagement.

5 Discussion and Conclusions

This study explored how integrating nonverbal behaviors in social robots influences human interaction and user self-efficacy in public spaces. We found that specific nonverbal cues (including appropriate gaze and eye contact, suitable proxemic distances, predictable and smooth movements, clear expressive feedback such as screen animations, and cultural sensitivity) significantly affected users' trust, comfort, and willingness to engage with the robot. Effective nonverbal behaviors, such as TEMI consistently orienting its screen to maintain eye contact or adjusting its interpersonal distance to around one meter, enhanced interactions by fostering user confidence and reducing uncertainty. Conversely, when nonverbal cues were inappropriate, ambiguous, or absent, for instance, sudden and unexplained robot movements or a lack of clear pre-movement signals, users reported confusion, anxiety, and disengagement. These findings align closely with prior research emphasizing the critical role of social intelligence for robot acceptance [5, 6]. We extend these insights by qualitatively documenting users' real-world experiences, highlighting concrete behaviors that designers should prioritize, such as providing verbal or visual pre-movement cues (e.g., the robot verbally indicating "*I will move now*" or displaying directional arrows) and clearly interpretable emotional feedback (e.g., a smiling face upon task completion). Supporting recent studies, our findings highlight the significance of realistic field trials beyond laboratory settings, emphasizing the gap between theoretical robot behaviors and practical implementation contexts [7, 8]. Our study's unique contributions include: (1) identifying specific nonverbal cues crucial for user self-efficacy in public spaces; (2) documenting real-world barriers from multiple stakeholder perspectives; and (3) offering actionable design recommendations, such as pre-movement notifications and clear emotional feedback, essential for successful real-world robot deployments.

A notable finding from our deployments was the direct relationship between robot nonverbal behaviors and users' self-efficacy. While users initially demonstrated high confidence during structured, controlled training sessions, their self-efficacy significantly decreased when confronted with real-world complexities like unexpected user queries, technical glitches (particularly delayed robot responses due to connectivity issues), social pressure from onlookers, and the absence of immediate expert assistance. When the robot's feedback was unclear or inconsistent, participants frequently internalized these interaction problems as personal failures, significantly undermining their self-confidence. This suggests that the robot's design and behavior actively shape users' sense of competence, highlighting the need for robot designers to explicitly incorporate reassuring nonverbal cues. Practical implications include adding explicit confirmation signals (such as a reassuring nod or a clear on-screen checkmark to acknowledge commands) and pre-action notices to help maintain and enhance users' confidence during interactions.

Furthermore, our study underscored critical differences between controlled laboratory studies and actual public-space deployments. Observed challenges, including technical reliability issues, unpredictable environments, and diverse user expectations, emphasized the complexity of translating laboratory successes into practical, real-world applications. Stakeholders should thus anticipate a *"deployment dip"* in user self-efficacy, particularly after initial controlled training sessions. To counteract this decline, our results suggest the importance of sustained strategies like ongoing training (e.g., periodic refresher sessions), accessible and easy-to-follow support resources, and opportunities for users to repeatedly engage with the robot. For instance, quick-reference guides or periodic interactive workshops could reinforce user comfort, helping bridge the initial confidence gap over time.

The successful deployment of social robots also relies significantly on effective collaboration among various stakeholders: end-users, support staff, and robot providers. Our findings highlight the importance of viewing robot deployment from a socio-technical perspective. Social robots require not only robust and socially intelligent designs but also trained staff ready to support and guide users when unexpected issues occur. Conversely, manufacturers require continuous and detailed feedback from deployment sites to iteratively improve robot usability. Future deployments could benefit from co-design workshops involving end-users, staff, and developers, helping proactively identify and address potential interaction issues early, ultimately enhancing real-world integration.

Limitations of our study include the relatively small sample size from a single cultural context (Estonia) and reliance on qualitative, self-reported data, limiting the generalizability of findings. Cultural variations could significantly impact user perceptions and preferences regarding nonverbal cues. Future research could complement qualitative data with quantitative metrics (such as interaction durations or proximity behaviors) or employ standardized self-efficacy scales to better quantify user confidence changes and generalize findings across broader contexts and robot designs.

In conclusion, integrating thoughtful nonverbal behaviors into social robots is crucial for enhancing human–robot interaction in public spaces. Robots should be treated as social actors that clearly communicate their intentions and states through consistent nonverbal cues, significantly improving user comfort, trust, and sustained engagement. Recognizing and proactively supporting user self-efficacy (through targeted training, clear and reassuring robot feedback, and ongoing user engagement) will be key to successful and sustained adoption of social service robots in diverse public settings.

References

1. Shukla, M., Shukla, A.N.: Growth of robotics industry in the early 21st century: review and trends. Int. J. Comput. Eng. Res. **2**(5), 1554–1558 (2012)
2. Ogle, A., Lamb, D.: The role of robots, artificial intelligence, and service automation in events. In: Robots, Artificial Intelligence, and Service Automation in Travel, Tourism and Hospitality. Emerald Publishing Limited (2019). https://doi.org/10.1108/978-1-78756-687-320191012
3. Oruma, S., Colomo-Palacios, R., Gkioulos, V.: Architectural views for social robots in public spaces: business, system, and security strategies. Int. J. Inf. Secur. **24**, 12 (2025). https://doi.org/10.1007/s10207-024-00924-x
4. Shen, Y., et al.: Robots under COVID-19 pandemic: a comprehensive survey. IEEE Access **9**, 1590–1615 (2020)
5. Leoste, J., Marmor, K., Heidmets, M.: Nonverbal behavior of service robots in social interactions – a survey on recent studies. Interact. Des. Archit. **61**, 164–192 (2024)
6. Xu, K., Chen, M., You, L.: The hitchhiker's guide to a credible and socially present robot: two meta-analyses of the power of social cues in human–robot interaction. Int. J. Soc. Robot. **15**, 269–295 (2023). https://doi.org/10.1007/s12369-022-00961-3
7. Oksanen, A., Savela, N., Latikka, R., Koivula, A.: Trust toward robots and artificial intelligence: an experimental approach to human–technology interactions online. Front. Psychol. **11**, 568256 (2020). https://doi.org/10.3389/fpsyg.2020.568256
8. Giger, J.-C., Piçarra, N., Pochwatko, G., Almeida, N., Almeida, A.S.: Intention to work with social robots: the role of perceived robot use self-efficacy, attitudes towards robots, and beliefs in human nature uniqueness. Multimodal Technol. Interact. **9**(2), 9 (2025). https://doi.org/10.3390/mti9020009
9. Pütten, A.M., Bock, N.: Development and validation of the self-efficacy in human-robot-interaction scale (SE-HRI). ACM Trans. Hum.-Robot Interact. **7**, 1–30 (2018). https://doi.org/10.1145/3139352
10. Gao, H., Wang, W., Huang, C., et al.: Validity and reliability of the Chinese version of human–robot interaction self-efficacy scale in Chinese adults. Psicol. Refl. Crít. **37**, 40 (2024). https://doi.org/10.1186/s41155-024-00324-z
11. Leoste, J., Marmor, K., Hollstein, T., Hinkelmann, H., Leoste, L.B.: Enhancing university visitor satisfaction: a human-robot interaction study on the design and perception of a guiding robot assistant. In: Balogh, R., Obdržálek, D., Fislake, M. (eds.) Robotics in Education. RiE 2024. Lecture Notes in Networks and Systems, vol. 1084. Springer, Cham (2024). https://doi.org/10.1007/978-3-031-67059-6_20
12. Bu, F., Fischer, K., Ju, W.: Making sense of robots in public spaces: a study of trash barrel robots. J. Hum.-Robot Interact. (2025, in press). https://doi.org/10.1145/3731252
13. Reyes-Cruz, G., et al.: Please follow me to the next stop: a case study of planning, deploying and researching a robot-guided tour in a museum in the UK. In: Extended Abstracts of CHI Conference on Human Factors in Computing Systems (CHI EA 2025), Article 690, pp. 1–8. ACM, New York (2025). https://doi.org/10.1145/3706599.3706660

14. Savela, N., Latikka, R., Oksa, R., et al.: Affective attitudes toward robots at work: a population-wide four-wave survey study. Int. J. Soc. Robot. **14**, 1379–1395 (2022). https://doi.org/10.1007/s12369-022-00877-y
15. Naneva, S., Sarda Gou, M., Webb, T.L., et al.: A systematic review of attitudes, anxiety, acceptance, and trust towards social robots. Int. J. Soc. Robot. **12**, 1179–1201 (2020). https://doi.org/10.1007/s12369-020-00659-4
16. Kok, B.C., Soh, H.: Trust in robots: challenges and opportunities. Curr. Robot. Rep. **1**, 297–309 (2020). https://doi.org/10.1007/s43154-020-00029-y
17. Rossi, A., Holthaus, P., Perugia, G., et al.: Trust, acceptance and social cues in human–robot interaction (SCRITA). Int. J. Soc. Robot. **13**, 1833–1834 (2021). https://doi.org/10.1007/s12369-021-00844-z
18. Hampel, N., Sassenberg, K., Scholl, A., Ditrich, L.: Enactive mastery experience improves attitudes towards digital technology via self-efficacy – a pre-registered quasi-experiment. Behav. Inf. Technol. **43**(2), 298–311 (2023). https://doi.org/10.1080/0144929X.2022.2162436
19. Samarakoon, S.M.B.P., Muthugala, M.A.V.J., Jayasekara, A.G.B.P.: A review on human–robot proxemics. Electronics **11**(16), 2490 (2022). https://doi.org/10.3390/electronics11162490
20. Schellen, E., Bossi, F., Wykowska, A.: Robot gaze behavior affects honesty in human-robot interaction. Front. Artif. Intell. **4**, 663190 (2021). https://doi.org/10.3389/frai.2021.663190
21. Potinteu, A.-E., Darboven, J., Rahmel, A.-K., Papenmeier, F.: The role of perceived eye contact in helping robots (2024, under review). https://doi.org/10.31234/osf.io/wz3gt

Assessing Multimodal Context Awareness of a Social Robot in a Conversational Scenario

Luca Pallonetto(✉), Raffaella Esposito, Giulio Acampora, Matteo Russo, Federico Trenti, and Silvia Rossi

PRISCA (Intelligent Robotics and Advanced Cognitive System Projects) Laboratory,
Department of Electrical Engineering and Information Technology (DIETI),
University of Naples Federico II, Naples, Italy
{luca.pallonetto,raffaella.esposito3,silvia.rossi}@unina.it

Abstract. The integration of context-aware multimodal perception in Human-Robot Interaction (HRI) has emerged as a key factor in enhancing the naturalness, coherence, and adaptiveness of communication between humans and robots. This study explores how integrating a state of the art Visual Question Answering (VQA) model, Gemini, and Whisper for speech recognition within the humanoid robot Pepper impacts its communicative behavior and context-awareness attribution. Sixty participants interacted with Pepper in two conditions: one with access to contextual visual input and one without. Results revealed that context-aware interaction significantly enhanced user perceptions of Pepper's ability to recognize human presence, behaviors and cognitions hence indicating an improved perception in human-aware capabilities. However, no statistically significant differences emerged in perceived context awareness across conditions evaluated by the use of ad-hoc questions, suggesting that anthropomorphic cues may contribute to users' positive impressions regardless of actual system capabilities.

Keywords: Human Robot Interaction · Context Awareness · Multimodal perception

1 Introduction

The integration of context recognition and multimodal processing in the field of Human-Robot Interaction (HRI) has gained more importance to create more natural, effective, and adaptive communication between humans and robots. As robots are deployed in everyday environments, homes, offices, and public spaces, their ability to interpret and respond appropriately to real-world stimuli becomes essential. This capability requires the fusion of multiple sensory inputs, particularly visual and auditory data, to develop a coherent and semantically rich understanding of the environment [10,17].

Significant advancements in deep learning have enabled the development of models capable of interpreting complex signals over different modalities. Multimodal learning frameworks, such as those used in Visual Question Answering

(VQA), have demonstrated the potential of combining visual perception and natural language understanding to enhance robotic behavior [1,8]. Previous studies have explored the role of audio and visual input enabling robots to process speech, detect objects, recognize emotions, and interpret user intent [15,17]. However, despite these developments, robotic systems often lack a truly contextual awareness that allows them to adapt their behavior based on the specifics of their environment [8,15]. Some reviews and frameworks emphasize that robust, multimodal interaction is not only about data acquisition but also about meaningful fusion of information to achieve adaptive, situationally aware communication [10,17]. This gap in context-sensitive response generation remains a challenge in current HRI systems, particularly in unconstrained, noisy, and variable environments like real homes [8,15].

To address these challenges, the present study investigates how context-aware multimodal perception can enhance a robot's communicative behavior. We propose and evaluate a system based on the humanoid robot Pepper, which integrates Whisper for advanced speech-to-text transcription [13] and Gemini, a state-of-the-art VQA model [4], to analyze visual data. By comparing two interaction modes, one with access to contextual visual input and one without—we aim to answer the following research questions:

- **RQ1**: Does the integration of multimodal contextual input improve the user's perception of a robot's social intelligence?
- **RQ2**: Does the integration of multimodal contextual input improve the user's perception of a robot's context awareness?

In particular, through a controlled experimental design that involves a conversational setting, we explore how users perceive the difference in the robot's responses when it is aware of its surroundings versus when it operates in a speech-only mode.

The rest of the paper is organized as follows: Sect. 2 reviews the state of the art in multimodal perception and context recognition in HRI. Section 3 describes the methodology, including participants, technologies used, the experimental setup, and the evaluation procedure. Section 4 presents the results, with a focus on perceived social intelligence and contextual awareness of the robot used in the study. Finally, Sect. 5 discusses the conclusions, implications, and future directions for enhancing transparency and grounding in context-aware robotic systems.

2 Background and Related Works

Context recognition is not limited to acquiring isolated images or audio signals; it requires an intelligent fusion of data to extract semantic and spatial information that allows the robot to *"understand"* the environment in which it operates [19]. In this context, advances in deep learning have enabled the development of models capable of performing complex analyses on both images and audio tracks. For instance, [10] highlighted how multimodal learning can improve the integrated representation of data, while studies such as [1] paved the way for visual question answering by synergistically combining natural language processing with visual analysis. The multimodal approach, which combines visual and vocal inputs, makes it possible to contextualize information more completely, offering an environmental picture that overcomes the limitations of each individual modality [12]. This integration—further analyzed in reviews such as that by [8], is essential for improving system robustness in real-world scenarios characterized by variability and background noise.

To provide appropriate feedback, the robot must have a high level of multimodal recognition, capable of understanding not only visual and auditory signals, but also the internal states, goals, and characteristics of the interlocutor [17]. In this context, adopting devices and interaction strategies that simultaneously exploit voice, images, text, eye movements, and even touch becomes essential to develop increasingly natural human-machine interfaces. At the same time, the limited understanding of the surrounding environment still represents a significant limitation for robotic applications in real-world settings [15]. Despite advances in perception techniques, knowledge acquisition from the environment traditionally relies only on sensory data, requiring intensive training and often proving unreliable for high-level information extraction. To address this issue, [15] proposes a multimodal interaction paradigm that integrates innovative devices—tangible user interfaces, voice recognition technologies, and vision systems—with well-established artificial intelligence methodologies.

Among the sensory modalities involved in human-robot interaction (HRI), visual and audio channels are particularly prominent due to their complementary roles in communication. While the visual modality enhances interaction through facial expressions, gestures, and visual cues, creating a more natural and effective exchange, the auditory modality is crucial for interpreting and producing spoken language. Recent studies show that integrating speech recognition and synthesis technologies [17] allows this modality to be used in applications ranging from voice assistants to educational systems. On the other hand, visual perception allows robots to interpret non-verbal signals such as facial expressions, gestures, and eye movements. Advances in computer vision and deep learning have significantly enhanced robots' abilities to recognize objects, track movements, and decode emotions [17], thus improving human-robot interaction.

The integration of multimodal input not only facilitates more natural communication but also enables the construction of contextual representations that support complex tasks such as autonomous navigation, scene recognition, and the handling of unforeseen situations [9,18]. In light of the technologies analyzed, this study aims to contribute to progress in the field of context recognition to improve the quality of human–robot interaction. In particular, we explored the necessity and benefits of enhancing robot communication through context-aware multimodal perception. In natural interactions, humans rely heavily on environmental cues, such as visual elements, gestures, and tone, to infer meaning, disambiguate queries, and provide relevant answers. Similarly, for robots to be perceived as socially intelligent and communicatively coherent, they must not only understand the linguistic content of a question but also interpret contextual information from their surroundings. Therefore, this research experimentally compares interaction modes with and without contextual awareness, assessing how the presence of contextual inputs (e.g., visual scene analysis) affects users' perception of the robot. By using context information, a robot can offer more specific, relevant, and human-like responses, suggesting objects physically present in the environment and enhancing both the informativeness and naturalness of the interaction.

3 Methods

3.1 Participants

The experiment involved a total of 60 participants, aged between 18 and 70 years (M = 25.81; SD = 9.84). Although the age range of participants was broad (18–70 years), the majority of the sample was concentrated between 18 and 35 years, with only 4 participants over the age of 50, limiting the ability to generalize findings across age groups. The sample was composed of 65% male and 35% female individuals. Regarding previous experience with robotics, 43% of participants reported having directly interacted with robots, while the remaining 57% reported indirect familiarity, limited to media exposure (e.g., television, social media).

All participants gave their consent before participating. The study, including the questionnaire items, was approved by the university ethics committee in accordance with ethical standards for research involving human subjects.

3.2 Tools and Technologies

In the present study, we used the robot Pepper, a humanoid robot developed by Aldebaran Robotics [11], due to its suitability for socially interactive scenarios. Pepper is equipped with a range of sensors and features that make it ideal for our investigation, including the ability to take photographs, record audio, and engage in naturalistic human interaction. The robot employed a Visual Question Answering (VQA) system based on Gemini [16], which enabled it to take photographs of the environment and analyze them. This provided the robot with an improved capacity to understand its surroundings and allowed for more fluent and contextually relevant dialogue.

From a technical standpoint, the system architecture was divided into two separate modules: a client developed in Python 2.7 to manage the robot's native functionalities, and an external server, developed in Python 3.11, responsible for advanced data processing. The server integrated two essential libraries: Whisper and Gemini. The former was used for automatic speech-to-text transcription, allowing us to overcome the limitations of Pepper's native speech recognition system, which is characterized by a limited vocabulary and a static dictionary. At the same time, image acquisition was performed using Pepper's integrated 2D camera at 640×480 resolution. The image file was retrieved via SSH using Python (paramiko and scp) and sent in JPEG format to the external server without additional preprocessing. This step was executed in parallel with audio transcription to minimize latency. Once both the transcribed text and the environmental image were obtained, these data were sent to the Gemini module, responsible for generating a response based on the visual information contained in the scene.

The latest version, Gemini Flash 2.0, optimized for speed and efficiency, was adopted. This update drastically reduced the system's response times, ensuring a faster, more natural, and engaging conversational experience for the user. Communication between the client module and the server occurred via TCP socket, with encrypted file transfer through the Paramiko library, in order to ensure the integrity and security of the exchanged data. During the interaction phase, the user was free to ask the robot questions in natural language. However, the performance of Pepper's built-in microphone proved inadequate for prolonged use. In particular, it was observed that as the robot progressively overheated, the microphone tended to capture primarily the noise generated by the internal fan, making it difficult to clearly detect the user's voice. To preserve the quality of voice input and ensure accurate transcription during the speech-to-text phase, the built-in microphone was replaced with an external device. This solution allowed for clearer and more reliable audio recordings, thereby ensuring greater robustness in the system's ability to understand user requests.

3.3 Experimental Setting

The test environment was set up to simulate a domestic setting, using both common objects, such as a fan, refrigerator, and lamp, as well as scenic elements useful for the experiment, such as a chess set, fake fruit, and various toys Fig. 1. The position of the robot was designed to ensure a complete overview of the experiment's area of interest, while the participant sat in front, thus facilitating interaction and environmental analysis.

Fig. 1. Experimental setting with Pepper robot (Aldebaran Robotics).

3.4 Measures

At the end of the experimental session, each participant received two questionnaires: the PSI (Perceived Social Intelligence) [2] and the CARS (Crew Awareness Rating Scale) [7].

The PSI scale was used to assess the user's perceived social intelligence of the robot. In detail, PSI scales are the following: Recognizes Human Emotions (**RE**), Recognizes Human Behaviors (**RB**), Recognizes Human Cognitions (**RC**), Adapts to Human Emotions (**AE**), Adapts to Human Behaviors (**AB**), Adapts to Human Cognitions (**AC**), Predicts Human Emotions (**PE**), Predicts Human Behaviors (**PB**), Predicts Human Cognitions (**PC**), Identifies Humans (**IH**), Identifies Individuals (**II**), Identifies Social Groups (**IG**), Social Competence (**SOC**), Friendly (**FRD**), Helpful (**HLP**), Caring (**CAR**), Trustworthy (**TRU**), Rude (**RUD**), Conceited (**CON**) and Hostile (**HST**).

The CARS scale, on the other hand, was used to evaluate the effectiveness of the context recognition system. Originally developed to assess situation awareness (SA) in critical environments, such as remote control of complex systems, CARS includes eight items that investigate the agent's ability to understand the surrounding environment, anticipate event progression, and select appropriate behaviors. For adaptation to our experimental context, the CARS items were reduced to six and reformulated to evaluate, using a 5-point Likert scale (from 1 = strongly disagree to 5 = strongly agree), participants' perception of the coherence of the robot's responses, its ability to understand the question and the context and to anticipate events (see Table 1). The internal consistency of the adapted scale, assessed using Cronbach's α, reached a value of 0.875, indicating adequate reliability of the scale for the purposes of the study.

3.5 Procedure

To evaluate the effects of contextual awareness on users' perception of the robot, two experimental conditions were designed:

- **Context condition**: participants in this condition (N =30) interacted with the robot equipped with awareness of the environmental and situational context.
- **No-context condition**: participants in this condition (N =30) interacted with the robot without contextual information.

The experiment was structured into three main phases: preparation, interaction, and evaluation. During the initial phase, the robot was started and connected to the remote server, which handled data processing. Each participant was randomly assigned to one of the two previously described experimental conditions (with or without contextual input), without being informed of the active mode, so as not to influence the answers given.

In the interaction phase, the user was asked to pose three questions to the robot. The first question was guided and had to be chosen from the following two options:

Table 1. Correspondence between original CARS items and adapted versions for the robot's responses

Item	Original	Adapted Version
1	Would you say your awareness of relevant information is satisfactory?	The robot's response demonstrated an accurate understanding of the question.
2	Would you say your understanding of the situation (i.e., understanding what is happening) is satisfactory?	The robot's response demonstrated an adequate understanding of the context in which the question was asked.
3	Would you say your awareness of how the situation is likely to develop over time is satisfactory?	
4	Would you say your awareness of how best to achieve your goals is satisfactory?	The robot's response provided a clear and comprehensive understanding of the overall context.
5	Would you say it is easy to stay updated on the situation's details?	
6	Would you say it is easy to make sense of the situation as a whole, to see the "big picture"?	The robot's response was logically coherent and aligned with the previous parts of the conversation.
7	Would you say it is easy to predict or anticipate likely developments or events?	The robot's response helped me anticipate how the situation would evolve.
8	Would you say it is easy to decide the best course of action?	The robot's response helped me choose the best course of action.

– "I'm bored, what could I do?"
– "I'm hungry, what could I eat?"

This initial question was designed to introduce a simple and familiar thematic context, so as to initiate an interaction that could benefit from contextual information.

As illustrated in the Fig. 2, when operating in contextual input mode, Pepper captures an image of the environment using its built-in camera and send it, along with the text transcription of the question obtained via Whisper, to the external server for processing. The Gemini module would then jointly process the two inputs to generate a contextually relevant response, which was sent back to the robot and delivered through its speech synthesis system. Responses in this condition were often characterized by specific references to objects actually present in the room, such as: "You could eat the fruit on top of the fridge." A response like this tended to draw the user's attention to the surrounding environment, encouraging them to formulate subsequent questions that were more focused on the perceived visual elements.

Conversely, in the no-visual-input condition, the response was generated solely based on the textual input, using a pre-trained language model without access to the scene image. The responses in this mode generally appeared more vague and abstract, such as generic suggestions like "You could eat a sandwich,"

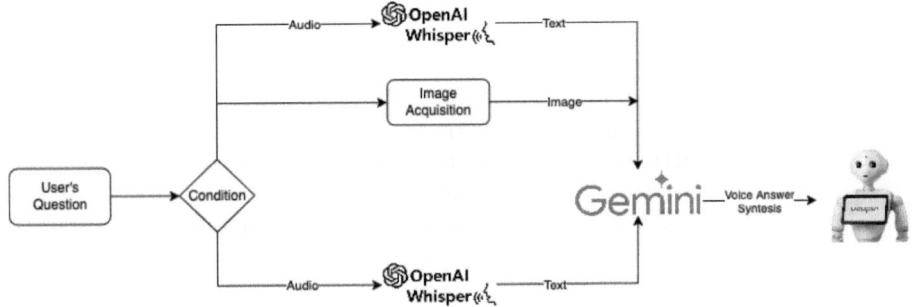

Fig. 2. Pipeline for the Context Recognition System.

without any reference to the actual environment. This lack of specificity tended to influence the following interaction, prompting the user to ask more general questions that were less grounded in the visual context.

Finally, in the evaluation phase, participants completed a questionnaire aimed at expressing a subjective judgment on the quality of the interaction and the relevance of the responses received. The responses to the various questionnaire items were then used to perform a comparative statistical analysis between the two experimental groups, with the goal of evaluating the effect of visual context integration on the perception of the robot's social intelligence and communicative coherence.

4 Results

4.1 Perceived Social Intelligence

To investigate whether the availability of contextual information influenced participants' evaluations of the robot's social intelligence, a series of independent-samples t-tests were conducted on each of the dimensions of the PSI questionnaire, hypothesizing that the robot would have been rated higher on these dimensions in the Context condition than in the No-context condition.

Results show that participants in the Context group rated the robot's ability to recognize human behaviors (RB), recognize human cognitions (RC), and identify humans (IH) significantly higher than those in the No-context group (RB: $t = 1.96, p = 0.028$; RC: $t = 1.76, p = 0.042$; IH: $t = 2.53, p = 0.007$). No significant differences emerged across the remaining 17 dimensions. Complete results of the t-tests are shown in Table 2.

Thus, the results suggest that providing the robot with access to contextual information selectively enhances the user's perception of its interpretive capabilities, particularly those related to understanding and recognizing human mental and behavioral states, and distinguishing between individuals, and thus fostering a better attribution of human awareness. In contrast, dimensions that reflect the

Table 2. Comparison between Context and No-context conditions on PSI subscales using independent samples t-tests.

Scale	t	df	p	Scale	t	df	p
RE	−0.17	56	0.560	II	0.98	56	0.165
RB	1.96	56	**0.028**	IG	1.51	56	0.069
RC	1.76	56	**0.042**	SOC	0.01	56	0.496
AE	−0.29	56	0.615	HLP	−1.02	56	0.844
AB	1.21	56	0.116	TRU	−2.58	56	0.994
AC	−0.14	56	0.555	FRD	−0.98	56	0.835
PE*	0.57	47.9	0.286	CAR	−0.79	56	0.785
PC	0.03	56	0.488	RUD-R	−0.12	56	0.548
PB	1.02	56	0.156	CON-R	−0.36	56	0.639
IH	2.53	56	**0.007**	HST-R	−0.56	56	0.710

* Welch's t was employed in this case, as Levene's test was significant ($p < .05$), indicating a violation of the assumption of equal variances.

Note. Hypothesis: $\mu_{\text{Context}} > \mu_{\text{No-context}}$. In bold the p values below .05

robot's ability to adapt to or predict human states or general social traits such as being helpful, caring, or trustworthy, did not differ between the two groups. Figure 3 further illustrates this point.

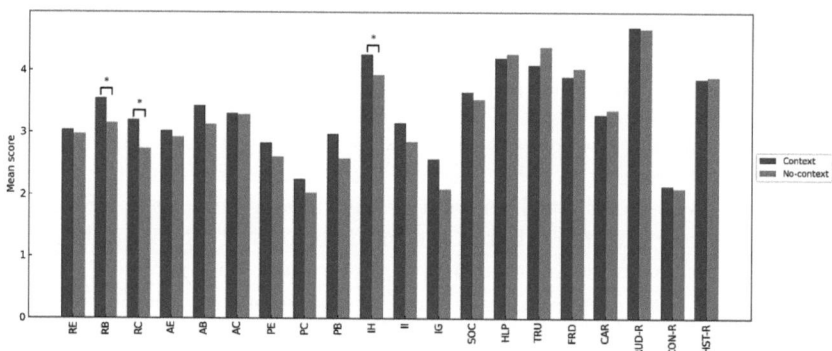

Fig. 3. PSI subscales means in the two experimental conditions.

Overall, the robot was perceived as highly helpful, friendly, and trustworthy, with mean scores exceeding 4.0 on the corresponding PSI scales. Traits such as being caring and not hostile or rude (reversed items) were also rated very positively. Moderate scores were observed for the robot's ability to recognize human behaviors, cognitions, and emotions. The lowest ratings were found in the robot's ability to predict human cognition, identify social groups and in its perceived conceitedness.

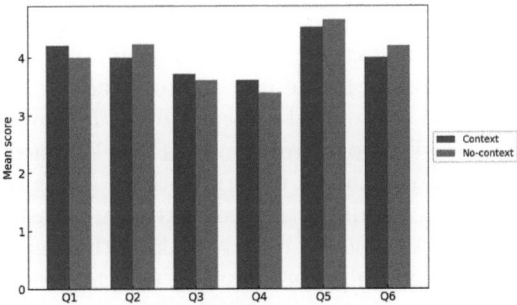

Fig. 4. On the **left**: Context awareness items mean in the two experimental conditions. On the **right**: Mann-Whitney U tests comparing scores between conditions for each item of the context awareness scale.

4.2 Context Awareness

Mann-Whitney's U tests were employed to compare perceived context awareness between the two experimental conditions. In fact, Shapiro-Wilk tests, applied to each variable of the employed scale, revealed a violation of the normality assumption.

Results indicate that there are no statistically significant differences between the Context and No-context group in terms of perceived contextual awareness of the robot. In fact, for all six variables analyzed, the p values were above the significance threshold ($\alpha = 0.05$), as shown in Fig. 4.

Interestingly, as illustrated in Fig. 4, the robot was perceived as contextually aware across both conditions, with evaluations tending toward the higher end of the scale. This pattern indicates a generally positive and stable impression of the robot's contextual capabilities, which appears to be robust even in the absence of actual contextual reasoning. Such a result may point to the role of surface-level cues or anthropomorphic design features in shaping users' perceptions, leading them to attribute a higher degree of contextual understanding to the robot than was functionally implemented. In fact, in the context of HRI, even superficial social behaviors or expressive design features can elicit strong perceptions of intelligence and awareness [3], regardless of the underlying system complexity [5].

5 Conclusions and Future Works

The main objective of the experiment was to determine whether a robot that shows awareness of the context could significantly improve the perceived quality of interaction with a humanoid robot in terms of perceived robot's social intelligence and context awareness.

The awareness of the context was obtained through a multimodal pipeline that first transcribed the user's speech with Whisper and then fed the resulting question, together with an image captured by Pepper's camera, to the Gemini Flash 2.0 VQA model, enabling the robot to extract the key objects and their spatial relations and ground its verbal response in the immediate scene.

Results showed that when Pepper used contextual information to formulate its responses, participants judged it markedly more proficient at three key facets of perceived social intelligence: spotting who is human, inferring others' thoughts, and discerning their actions. These findings highlight that context-aware reasoning can yield substantial perceptual benefits for social robots, making them seem more socially astute, cognitively attuned, and behavior-sensitive, thus answering positively to **RQ1**. Simultaneously, our experimental results did not answer in the same way to **RQ2**: when perceived context awareness was measured through separate ad-hoc items asking whether Pepper's reply accurately grasped the question, reflected the surrounding context, remained logically coherent, clarified the overall situation, and helped users anticipate developments and choose appropriate actions, participants attributed a high degree of contextual understanding to the robot in both conditions. This suggests that observable social behaviors or anthropomorphic cues may exert a stronger influence on user judgments than underlying computational processes. It also remains to be explored whether individual differences, such as age or prior familiarity with robotics, may modulate these perception biases, potentially shaping how users interpret the robot's behavior and contextual competence. While this finding aligns with prior research on the power of form and expression in shaping user impressions, it raises a critical question: how can we meaningfully assess and communicate a robot's actual abilities to users in a way that aligns their expectations with reality?

To answer this question, future work may build on previous evidence indicating that users construct more precise mental models of a system's capabilities and constraints when robots verbally express their internal reasoning processes or explicitly communicate uncertainty [14]. This approach could be directly applied in the field of context awareness [6]. For example, future studies might explore how a robot could explicitly refer to the contextual cues it is using, or indicate when such cues are unavailable or ambiguous. Importantly, such statements would need to be delivered in a concise, naturalistic manner so as not to disrupt the flow of interaction. Declarative transparency may be also combined with behavioral cues that implicitly convey the robot's internal state. In this way, transparency would be embedded into the timing, form, and flow of the robot's actions and become felt and observed through the robot's behavior. Users could intuitively grasp what the robot knows, or is trying to infer, by the way it moves, reacts, or hesitates. Ultimately, by embedding transparent communication mechanisms into context-aware systems, we can foster more accurate user expectations.

References

1. Antol, S., et al.: VQA: visual question answering. In: Proceedings of the IEEE International Conference on Computer Vision (ICCV), pp. 2425–2433 (2015)
2. Barchard, K.A., Lapping-Carr, L., Westfall, R.S., Banisetty, S.B., Feil-Seifer, D.: Perceived social intelligence (PSI) scales test manual (2018)
3. Bartneck, C., Kanda, T., Mubin, O., Al Mahmud, A.: Does the design of a robot influence its animacy and perceived intelligence? Int. J. Soc. Robot. **1**, 195–204 (2009)
4. DeepMind, G.: Gemini: Multimodal models from google deepmind (2023). https://deepmind.google
5. Duffy, B.R.: Fundamental issues in affective intelligent social machines. Open Artif. Intell. J. **2**(1), 21–34 (2008)
6. Fischer, K., Lohse, M.: Shaping naive users' models of robots' situation awareness. In: RO-MAN 2007 - The 16th IEEE International Symposium on Robot and Human Interactive Communication, pp. 534–539 (2007). https://api.semanticscholar.org/CorpusID:16454620
7. Gatsoulis, Y., Dondrup, C., Hanheide, M.: On the measurement of situation awareness for effective human-robot interaction. In: Proceedings of the AAAI Fall Symposium on Dialog with Robots (2010)
8. Kafle, K., Kanan, C.: Visual question answering: datasets, algorithms, and future challenges. Comput. Vis. Image Underst. **163**, 3–20 (2017). https://doi.org/10.1016/j.cviu.2017.05.002
9. Mascaro, R.: Scene representations for robotic spatial perception. Ann. Rev. Control Robot. Auton. Syst. (2024)
10. Ngiam, J., Khosla, A., Kim, M., Nam, J., Lee, H., Ng, A.Y.: Multimodal deep learning. In: Proceedings of the 28th International Conference on Machine Learning (ICML), pp. 689–696 (2011)
11. Pandey, A.K., Gelin, R., Robot, A.: Pepper: the first machine of its kind. IEEE Robot. Autom. Mag, **25**(3), 40–48 (2018)
12. Pérez, A.K., Quintero, C.A., Rodríguez, S., Rojas, E., Peña, O., de la Rosa, F.: Identification of multimodal signals for emotion recognition in the context of human-robot interaction. In: Proceedings of a Conference (Exact Venue Not Specified) (2018)
13. Radford, A.: Robust speech recognition via large-scale weak supervision. OpenAI (2023)
14. Ramaraj, P., Sahay, S., Kumar, S.H., Lasecki, W.S., Laird, J.E.: Towards using transparency mechanisms to build better mental models. In: Advances in Cognitive Systems: 7th Goal Reasoning Workshop, vol. 7, pp. 1–6 (2019)
15. Randelli, G., De Momi, E., Bonfanti, L., Ferrigno, G.: Knowledge acquisition through human-robot multimodal interaction. Intel. Serv. Robot. **6**, 19–31 (2013). https://doi.org/10.1007/s11370-012-0122-2
16. Saeidnia, H.: Welcome to the gemini era: google deepmind and the information industry. Library Hi Tech News (ahead-of-print) (2023). https://doi.org/10.1108/LHTN-12-2023-0214
17. Su, H., et al.: Recent advancements in multimodal human-robot interaction. Front. Neurorobot. **17**, 1084000 (2023). https://doi.org/10.3389/fnbot.2023.1084000

18. Swadzba, A., et al.: A computational model for the alignment of hierarchical scene representations in human-robot interaction. In: Proceedings of the International Joint Conference on Artificial Intelligence (IJCAI) (2009)
19. Zhao, X., Li, M., Weber, C., Hafez, M.B., Wermter, S.: Chat with the environment: interactive multimodal perception using large language models. In: Proceedings of the IEEE/RSJ International Conference on Intelligent Robots and Systems (IROS). IEEE (2023)

Unfair Game: How Age and Robot Deception Shape the Attribution of Mental States in Virtual Reality

Ludovica Misino(✉) , Oronzo Parlangeli , Luca Lusuardi ,
Alessandro Innocenti , and Stefano Guidi

Università di Siena, 53100 Siena, SI, Italy
{ludovica.misino,stefano.guidi}@unisi.it

Abstract. The following study investigates the dynamics of human-robot interaction (HRI) by examining how a robot's behavior (fair vs. unfair) and its perceived age (adult vs. child) influence the attribution of mental states and moral judgment in a competitive game. Using an immersive virtual reality environment, a between-subjects design was employed in which participants interacted with a robot under four different conditions, manipulating the robot's behavior and perceived age. Participants' psychological and social responses were assessed through questionnaires. Results indicate that perceived age affects responsibility and intentionality attributions, with younger robots judged less morally accountable. Additionally, unfair behavior reduces trust and likability, decreasing the interaction enjoyment. These findings emphasize the importance of designing social robots that behave in ways that are morally aligned with human expectations to foster trust and cooperation.

Keywords: human robot interaction · virtual reality · mental state attribution · perceived morality

1 Introduction

The field of Human-Robot Interaction (HRI) has expanded rapidly, integrating robots into various aspects of human life, from healthcare and education to customer service and entertainment [8]. Beyond technical development, understanding how humans attribute agency, intentionality, and morality to robots is crucial, as these perceptions influence trust and cooperation [3, 8]. Such attributions are shaped not only by a robot's behavior but also by its physical and social characteristics, including apparent age [14, 18, 22, 27, 35, 36].

Anthropomorphism plays a central role in shaping these perceptions, as humans instinctively ascribe mental states and social attributes to robots based on their appearance and behavior [11, 13, 14, 18, 27, 32, 41]. In particular, the perceived age of a robot—whether it appears child-like or adult-like—may influence how people attribute responsibility and moral agency to its actions [22, 35, 41]. While prior research has extensively examined factors such as human-likeness, trust, and ethical decision-making in

HRI [6, 27, 38, 46], the role of perceived age in shaping moral attributions remains largely unexplored. Given that younger individuals are often judged as less accountable for moral transgressions in human interactions [22], we hypothesize that this bias may extend to social robots.

To test these hypotheses, we employed immersive virtual reality (VR) to simulate realistic interactions, allowing participants to engage with virtual robots in competitive game scenarios [9, 17, 18, 26, 40]. Our findings indicate that perceived age significantly modulates moral attributions [22], with child-like robots judged as less responsible for their actions. Additionally, physical design characteristics influence perceptions of agency and trust, highlighting the importance of robot morphology in human judgments. This research contributes to a deeper understanding of the cognitive and ethical dimensions of HRI, offering practical insights for designing socially acceptable and trustworthy robotic agents. The results have direct implications for developing robots in education, healthcare, and assistive technologies, where perceptions of agency and moral responsibility can affect user trust and long-term adoption [1].

2 Related Work

Social robots are designed to interact naturally with humans, adapting to social norms and expectations [3, 8]. Beyond their functional roles, social robots evoke cognitive, emotional, and moral responses, influencing how humans trust, cooperate, and attribute intentionality to them. One of the central challenges in HRI is understanding how humans ascribe mental states and agency to artificial agents [14, 18, 22, 28, 35, 36]. This process is deeply influenced by anthropomorphism, the tendency to attribute human-like qualities to non-human entities [14, 18]. Anthropomorphism facilitates interaction by making robotic behavior more predictable, but it also leads to complex social and moral judgments, particularly when robots engage in unfair or ethically ambiguous behaviors [11, 13, 28, 32, 41].

2.1 Embodiment and Anthropomorphism in HRI

A crucial element in HRI is embodiment, which refers to the physical presence and perceived sensorimotor capabilities of a robotic system [8]. According to Glenberg [20], cognitive processes are inherently shaped by bodily morphology, sensory-motor systems, and emotional responses. Thus, how humans analyze and respond to a robot is closely linked to its physical presence and interactive capabilities. Embodiment is also tightly connected to anthropomorphization. When robots enter human social spaces, humans naturally project their interpretations onto robot actions [11, 13, 14, 18, 28, 32, 41, 42]. Research suggests that the more a robot appears human-like, the stronger the tendency to apply social norms and expectations to it [6]. However, high anthropomorphism can also create unrealistic expectations regarding a robot's competence, emotions, and morality. The Uncanny Valley Hypothesis [31] suggests that as robots become more human-like, they initially elicit positive emotional responses, but beyond a certain threshold, they provoke discomfort or repulsion.

As Foner [18] pointed out, in human-computer interaction, excessive anthropomorphism may lead to disillusionment when the system fails to meet human-like expectations. Beyond behavior, a critical factor shaping human perceptions of robots is their physical design, particularly their perceived age [22, 35, 41].

2.2 Theory of Mind and Perceived Moral Agency in HRI

A fundamental cognitive framework for interpreting robot behavior is Theory of Mind (ToM), which refers to the human ability to infer the mental states of others, including beliefs, intentions, and desires [4, 37]. Research in cognitive neuroscience has shown that the same neural circuits involved in human social cognition—such as the temporoparietal junction (TPJ) and medial prefrontal cortex—are also activated during interactions with robots [12, 24, 25]; this suggests that, under specific conditions, humans process robots in ways similar to human agents.

While ToM focuses on cognitive attributions of intentionality and agency, a related concept in HRI is Perceived Moral Agency (PMA), which refers to the extent to which humans attribute moral responsibility to artificial agents based on their behavior [44]. Research suggests that robots demonstrating ethical behavior foster greater trust and social acceptance, whereas those engaging in deceptive or morally ambiguous actions may trigger negative perceptions while also increasing engagement [2, 10, 44]. A key study by Short et al. (2010) [39] investigated how people react to deceptive robot behavior in a competitive game (rock, paper and scissors). Their findings revealed that action-based deception (cheating through movement) elicited stronger attributions of intentionality and moral responsibility compared to verbal deception. Interestingly, despite perceiving the deceptive robot as untrustworthy, participants engaged more with it, suggesting a paradox where morally ambiguous behavior enhances social interaction. However, Short et al. (2010) [39] did not consider whether the robot's perceived age modulates these moral judgments—a gap this study aims to address.

2.3 Physical Design and Perceived Age of Robots

More recent studies [22, 32, 35] demonstrate that subtle morphological variations — such as head-to-body ratio—can significantly influence perceptions of age and mind attributions. Guidi et al. (2021) [22] explored the impact of robot proportions on perceived age, showing that increasing the head-to-body ratio makes robots appear younger and cuter. The features that give robots a human-like appearance is analysed in the ABOT (Anthropomorphic roBOT) dataset, which is a systematically curated collection of images representing real-world humanoid robots [36]. Research using this dataset [35] has shown that head-to-body ratio, limb proportions, and facial expressivity significantly shape how humans interpret a robot's age; for instance, robots with larger heads relative to their bodies are often perceived as younger and more child-like, whereas those with more proportionate or elongated features are associated with an adult-like appearance. Further studies have shown that higher perceived age of robots is associated with higher perceived agency and lower perceived experience [32]. However, the implications of perceived age for moral attributions and trust remain largely unexplored.

2.4 Importance of Virtual Reality in HRI Research

Virtual Reality (VR) has emerged as a powerful tool in HRI research, offering immersive environments where human-robot interactions can be studied under controlled yet ecologically valid conditions [9, 17, 19, 26, 40]. VR allows researchers to manipulate robot attributes, such as appearance and behavior, in a systematic manner, providing insights into how these factors influence moral attributions and trust. However, despite its advantages, VR presents challenges. The lack of physical embodiment may alter user responses compared to real-world interactions. Additionally, immersion levels, avatar realism, and motion fidelity influence user perceptions of agency and trustworthiness in virtual robots [15]. Nevertheless, VR remains an invaluable tool for exploring human responses to robotic agents, allowing for precise control of experimental variables while avoiding limitations associated with physical robot interaction.

2.5 The Study

While previous research has examined robot deception [2, 10, 39, 44] and physical design's effect on perceived age [22, 35], the intersection of these two domains remains underexplored. Specifically, how does a robot's perceived age influence moral attributions, agency judgments, and trust when engaging in unfair behavior? By integrating insights from moral psychology, ToM research, and robot design, this work offers new perspectives on HRI and provides practical implications for developing robots that align with human social and ethical expectations.

2.6 Research Questions and Hypotheses

This study is structured around two main axes: the impact of robot behavior (fair vs. cheating) and the role of perceived age (adult-like vs. child-like appearance). We formulated the following research questions and hypothesis:

RQ1.1: To what extent fairness (as opposed to unfairness) in the behavior of a robot influences attributions intentionality, mental states, and humanlikeness to the robot? **H1.1:** Participants who interact with cheating robots will attribute more intentionality and mental states to the robot, and will consider it more similar to a human than participants who interact with a robot that acts fairly.

RQ1.2: To what extent are the attributions of moral abilities and rights to a robot influenced by the fairness of its behavior? **H1.2:** Levels of perceived morality of the robot will be lower when the robot is cheating than when it's acting fairly.

RQ1.3: To what extent the fairness of a robot's behavior influences the evaluation of the overall interaction experience with the robot and the desire for future interactions? **H1.3:** The overall interaction experience will be evaluated less positively when the robot behaves unfairly.

These first three questions aim to assess the impact of robot behavior on users' cognitive and emotional responses. A second set of research questions concerns the role of the robot's perceived age:

RQ2.1: To what extent the perceived age of a robot influences the attributions of intentionality, mental states and humanlikeness? **H2.1:** A child-like robot will receive significantly lower attributions of intentionality, mental states and humanlikeness than an adult-like robot.

RQ2.2: To what extent the perceived age of a robot influences the attributions of moral abilities and rights to the robot? **H2.1**: A child-like robot will be judged as less morally responsible for its action than an adult-like robot.

RQ2.3: To what extent does the perceived age of a robot moderate the assessment of its behaviour? **H2.3:** Participants who interact with a child-like robot that cheats will perceive the interaction less negatively than those who interact with the cheating adult - like robot.

A third set of questions concerns the effect of the individual tendency to anthropomorphisms in the evaluation of the robot.

RQ3.1: To what extent the individual tendency to anthropomorphism influences the attributions of mental states, moral capabilities and rights to a robot, and the overall evaluation of the users' interaction with it? **H3.1:** Participants with a higher tendency to anthropomorphism will attribute more mental states, moral capabilities and rights to the robots, and will evaluate more positively the interaction with it.

RQ3.2: To what extent does the individual tendency to anthropomorphism moderate the effect of robot behavior and age on the attributions of mental states, moral capabilities and rights to a robot, and the overall evaluation of the users' interaction with it? This question was exploratory, and therefore we do not have specific predictions to test.

3 Methods

3.1 Experimental Design

The experiment was structured following a 2 x 2 between subjects factorial design with two independent variables: the *behavior* of a robot in a series of rounds of a competitive game (fair or occasionally cheating), and the perceived age of the robot (child or adult).

The game was rock, paper and scissor, and was adapted from [39]. The Rock-Paper-Scissors game was chosen due to its strong precedent in HRI research, particularly in the study by Short et al. (2010), allowing for direct comparison with prior findings. Additionally, its simplicity and visual clarity made it well-suited for immersive VR, where hand-tracking and gesture-based interaction could enhance the realism of the robot's behavior.

The robots used in this study were adapted from the first and fourth conditions of Guidi et al. [22], a study investigating the influence of body proportions on perceived robot age and agency. The original study demonstrated that changes in head-to-body ratio and limb proportions significantly affect the perceived cuteness and maturity of humanoid robots. For this experiment, two robot models were employed:

1. Adult-like robot: based on the control condition (group 1) of Guidi et al. [22], originally 170 cm tall, but modified to 190 cm for this study. The head-to-body ratio and limb proportions remained unchanged to maintain an adult-like appearance.
2. Child-like robot: based on condition 4 of Guidi et al. [22], originally 120 cm tall. The model was adjusted to 100 cm, with an increased head-to-body ratio (+30%) and reduced limb size (−20%) with respect to the adult-like robot, enhancing its child-like features.

These physical modifications were validated through a pre-test that involved 20 participants, ensuring that they recognized the age differences between the two robots. The design and proportions of the robots used in the present study are illustrated in Fig. 1, showing the distinct characteristics that define the adult and child conditions.

In the cheating condition, the robot initially plays honestly. However, in certain rounds, after one or more losing turns, if its current move turns out to be a losing one it performs a rapid arm movement to change it into the winning move, and finally declares the false victory.

Fig. 1. Screenshot of the 3D models of the robots for the adult (left) and child (right) conditions.

3.2 Participants

The study involved a total of 82 participants, primarily recruited from the student body of the Anonymous University. The recruitment process was managed through the university's online platform, which allowed for participant registration and scheduling of experimental sessions. The decision to recruit primarily university students was based on logistical constraints related to the use of immersive virtual reality headsets, which required in-person participation. University students were readily accessible and represented a population accustomed to using digital technologies, which helped ensure a smooth and reliable VR experience. Moreover, the use of student samples is a well-established practice in experimental psychology, particularly in exploratory studies involving emerging technologies such as virtual reality. Participants received €8 as a compensation for their participation in the study. The average age of participants was 23.2 years (SD = 2.86). Despite attempts to maintain gender balance, the final sample consisted of 62.2% female and 36.6% male participants, the rest chose not to answer. Regarding educational background, most participants (47.6%) held a high school diploma, likely due to the predominance of undergraduate students in the sample. Additionally, 36.6% had obtained a bachelor's degree, while 12.2% held a master's degree.

3.3 Materials: Virtual Reality Setup and Questionnaires

The experiment was conducted using Meta Quest 2 and Meta Quest 3 VR headsets, which allowed a high level of immersion and experimental control. The VR Lab at Anonymous Lab (Anonymous University) developed the virtual environment to minimize external interference and ensure a consistent experience for all participants. After the interaction in VR, participants completed an online questionnaire divided into five sections which is reported in the "Post-interaction questionnaire" found in the supplementary material. The first measured the attribution of mental states to the robot using 18 items derived from Gray et al. [21] answered on 7-point Likert scales to investigate how individuals attribute mental states, emotional experience, perceived agency and sociability to robotic agents. 11 items measured perceived Experience (the ability to have feelings) and 7 items measured perceived Agency (having intentions, free will, and being able to pursue goals) [21]. The second section included the Perceived Moral Agency Scale, a tool developed to assess how people perceive moral agency in interactive systems such as chatbots or social robots [5], which comprises 10 items rated on 7-point agreement scales, which measure two constructs: perceived Morality (6 items) and Dependency (4 items). The third section investigates the moral status and rights of robots with questions drawn from a study by Lima G. et al. [29], it employs 11 items answered on 7-point agreement scales. The fourth section includes 5 items on a semantic differential scale designed to assess the robot's impression of likeability [7] and 4 items asking about trust, desirability of interaction, acceptability of collaboration, and realism on 7-point Likert scales [33]. In the last section of the questionnaire there are questions about the socio-demographic information of the participants accompanied by 5 items from the standardized IDAQ - Individual differences in anthropomorphism questionnaire to measure the tendency to anthropomorphize technological systems. [43].

3.4 Experimental Procedure

Prior to the main experiment, a pilot study was conducted with 8 participants to test the smoothness of the procedure and solve any technical problems.

The experiment received ethical approval (Opinion No.60/2024) from the University Ethics Committee.

The experimental procedure was divided into three main phases. Initially, participants received a general explanation of the study and an informed consent form was signed by them, guaranteeing anonymity and the possibility of withdrawal. In the second phase, the actual virtual reality interaction took place in which participants played several rounds of Rock-Paper-Scissors against a virtual robot. The number of rounds was fixed to 20 in the fair robot condition, and varied in the cheating condition, in which sometimes the robot would show a first move and, if losing, perform a rapid arm movement to modify it. The "action cheat" follows a pseudo-random logic, inspired by the study of Short et al. [39], but adapted to avoid predictable patterns. More specifically, cheating occurs between rounds 5 and 42; a variable delay regulates cheating: first cheating: 5th round, second: after 3rd round, third: after 4th round, fourth: after 2 rounds. Fifth: after 5 rounds, if necessary. If the robot wins honestly in the rounds scheduled for cheating, cheating is postponed to the next round lost. A more detailed description is available 1 in the supplementary material *The cheating algorithm.*

The robot in the cheating condition is programmed to cheat 5 times before ending the game and starts cheating only after actually losing a series of rounds so that it appears to be an intentional and not a random choice; the 'cheating took place at predetermined times (e.g. 5th, 8th, 15th rounds). The final phase involved computer administration of post experience questionnaires in which participants rated the robot and overall interaction.

4 Results

4.1 Group Equivalence and Design Checks

Following the random assignment of participants to the experimental conditions, 20 participants were assigned to each of the adult robot conditions, and 21 to each of the child robot conditions. We compared participants' age, gender distribution, familiarity with technologies and tendency to anthropomorphism across experimental groups. For none of the variables the distribution or the mean scores varied across groups.

4.2 Scales Consistency

We assessed the internal consistency of the robot perception scales, computing Cronbach's alpha for each scale or subscale. For all the variables except likeability ($\alpha = .71$), alpha was higher than .84, showing good consistency. We therefore computed the scores for each variable averaging the scores of the corresponding items.

4.3 Effects of Robot Behavior and Age

Statistical analysis was conducted using a series of two-way factorial ANOVAs, exploring the main and interaction effects of the independent variables: Robot Behavior (control vs. cheating); Robot Age (adult-like vs. child-like). The dependent variables considered (in different models) include all the scales about the robot perception: Experience; Agency; Perceived Moral Agency subscales (Morality and Dependency); Robot Moral Rights; Godspeed Likeability (pleasantness and trust in the robot); Trust and Interaction Enjoyment; Humanlikeness (perceived humanity of the robot).

In the following paragraphs we report the results for the significant effects. The results for the tests of all the main effects and interactions for all the dependent variables are reported in Supplementary Table 1 in the supplementary material.

The results showed significant main effects of robot behaviour on perceived Experience ($F = 4.50$, $\eta p2 = .055$, $p = .037$), desire for future interactions with the robot ($F = 7.36$, $\eta p2 = .086$, $p = .008$) and willingness to accept help from the robot ($F = 7.78$, $\eta p2 = .091$, $p = .007$). The main effect of behaviour was also marginally significant on perceived likeability ($F = 2.83$, $\eta p2 = .034$, $p = .096$) and trust ($F = 3.35$, $\eta p2 = .043$, $p = .064$). For all the variables, the mean ratings were lower for the cheating ($M_{Exp} = 1.73$, $M_{Like} = 3.08$, $M_{Trust} = 2.94$, $M_{Inter} = 3.54$, $M_{Help} = 3.95$) than for the fair robot ($M_{Exp} = 2.36$, $M_{Like} = 3.36$, $M_{Trust} = 3.61$, $M_{Inter} = 4.61$, $M_{Help} = 5.22$). The plots of the marginal means as a function of robot behaviour are presented in Fig. 2 below.

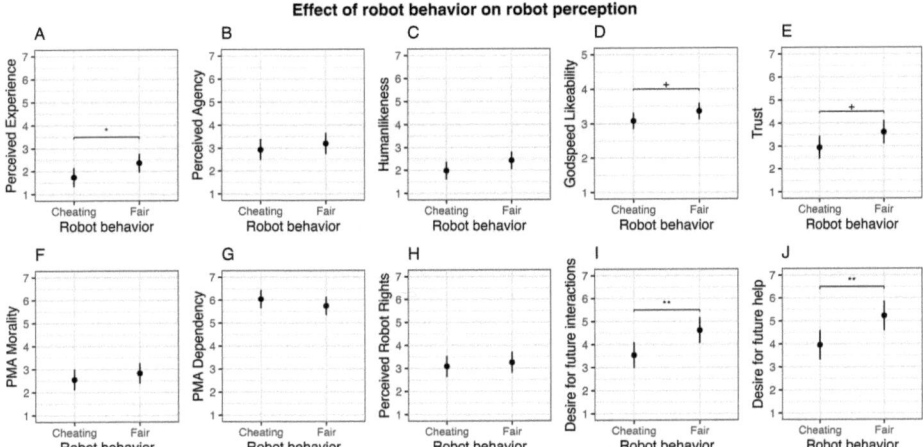

Fig. 2. Plots of the marginal means of the dependent variables as a function of Robot Behavior. Error bars are 95% confidence intervals for the means. A. Experience, B. Agency, C. Humanlikeness. D. Likeability. E. Trust, F. PMA Morality, G. PMA Dependency, H. Robot Moral Rights, I. Desire for future interactions, J. Desire for future help.

Concerning robot age, the results (Fig. 3) showed a significant main effect of age on perceived morality (F = 4.29, ηp2 = .052, p = .042), resemblance to a human being (F = 4.75, ηp2 = .057, p = .032), and, marginally, perceived experience (F = 3.09, ηp2 = .038, p = .083). The child robot was considered having less perceived morality (M = 2.36), less resembling a human being (M = 1.9) and having less experience (M = 1.79) than the adult robot ($M_{Morality}$ = 3.02, M_{Human} = 2.5, M_{Exp} = 2.3). No other significant main effect or interaction was found on any of the dependent variables considered.

4.4 Effects of the Tendency to Anthropomorphism

To explore the effect of the tendency to anthropomorphism on judgments about the robot, we first computed the correlations between participants' IDAQ scores and the ratings for all the robot perception variables. The IDAQ was significantly and positively correlated with the levels of experience (r = 0.51) and agency (r = 0.42) attributed to the robot, with the perceived morality (r = 0.42) and with the level of moral rights (r = 0.48). It was instead negatively correlated with the (PMA) perceived dependency (r = -0.57).

We then repeated the ANOVAs including participants' standardized IDAQ score as a covariate. The table with the tests of all the effects is reported in the supplementary material (Supplementary Table 2). The results of the ANCOVAs showed that IDAQ was significantly associated with all the dependent variables but likeability. When controlling for the tendency for anthropomorphisms, significant main effects of robot behavior were found only for willingness to interact with the robot (F = 6.30, ηp2 = .076, p = .014) and willingness to accept help from it (F = 6.68, ηp2 = .080, p = .012), and marginally also for perceived experience (F = 3.37, ηp2 = .042, p = .070). The main effect of age, instead, was only marginally significant for human-likeness ratings (F = 4.29, ηp2 =

.052, p = .081). No other significant main effect or interaction was found on any other dependent variable in the ANCOVAs.

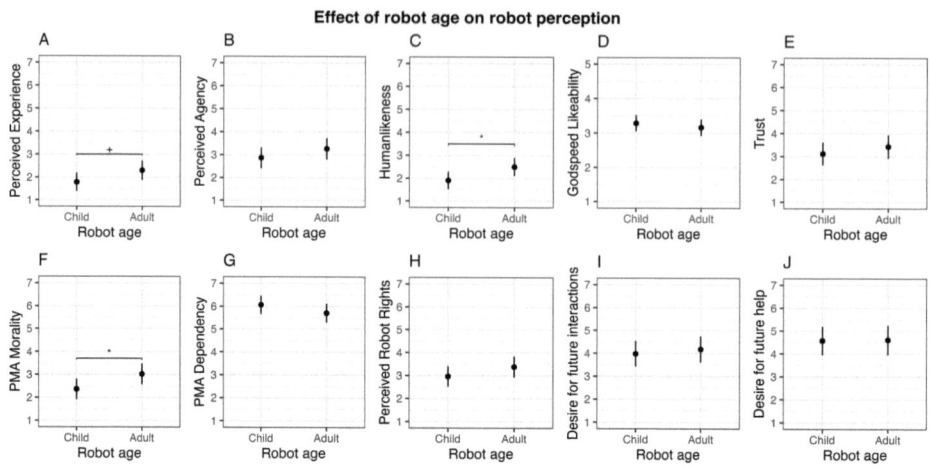

Fig. 3. Plots of the marginal means of the dependent variables as a function of Robot Age. Error bars are 95% confidence intervals for the means. A. Experience, B. Agency, C. Humanlikeness. D. Likeability. E. Trust, F. PMA Morality, G. PMA Dependency, H. Robot Moral Rights, I. Desire for future interactions, J. Desire for future help.

Lastly, to explore the possible moderating role of the tendency to anthropomorphisms on the effects of the robot behavior and age, we first classified participants as having low or high tendency to anthropomorphisms based on the comparison of their IDAQ scores to the median score for that variable on the sample (M = 1.8). We then conducted a further series of ANOVAs (one for each dependent variable), including the IDAQ level (low vs high) as a predictor, and allowing it to interact with the other design factors. The table with the tests of all the effects is reported in the supplementary material (Supplementary Tables 3A and 3B).

The results showed a significant robot behaviour by IDAQ level interaction on the willingness to accept help (F = 5.43, $\eta p2$ = .068, p = .023), and significant robot behaviour by robot age by IDAQ interactions on experience (F = 4.15, $\eta p2$ = .053, p = .045) and moral rights (F = 5.44, $\eta p2$ = .068, p = .022). Concerning the willingness to accept help (Fig. 4.A), pairwise comparisons of the marginal mean (averaged across robot age) showed that only for participants with low IDAQ the ratings were significantly lower for the cheating robot (M = 3.21, SE = 0.38) than for the fair robot (M = 5.20, SE = 0.44, t(74) = -3.43, p = .001), while no differences were found for high-IDAQ participants (M_{cheat} = 5.33, SE = 0.53, M_{fair} = 5.24, SE = 0.43, t(74) = 0.14, p = .887).

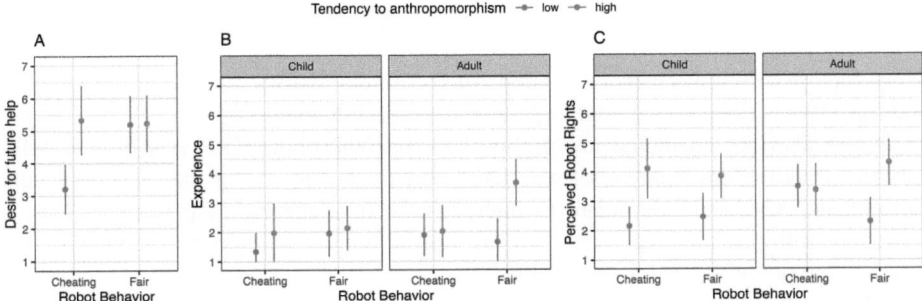

Fig. 4. Plots of the marginal means of (A) Desire for future help as a function of robot behavior and tendency for anthropomorphism, (B) Experience and (C) attribution of moral rights as a function of robot behavior, robot age and tendency for anthropomorphism. Error bars are 95% confidence intervals for the means.

Concerning the three-way interactions, the test of the simple effects of robot behavior on experience showed (Fig. 4B) that only for participants with high IDAQ the adult cheating robot (M = 2.02, SE = 0.44), but not the child one, was rated as having significantly less experience than the fair robot (M = 3.66, SE = 0.39, t(74) = -2.77, p = .007). The tests of the simple effects of robot behavior on the attributions of moral rights to the robot (Fig. 4C), instead, showed that only for low-IDAQ participants, and for an adult robot, were attributed more rights to the cheating robot (M_{cheat} = 3.5, SE = 0.37) than to the fair robot (M_{fair} = 2.31, SE = 0.40, t(74) = 2.19, p = .031). This difference (for the adult robot) was not significant for high-IDAQ participants, and it was in the opposite direction (M_{cheat} = 3.38, SE = 0.45, M_{fair} = 4.31, SE = 0.40, t(74) = -1.55, p = .124) while for a child robot it was not significant neither for high-IDAQ (p = .685) nor for low-IDAQ participants (p = .552).

5 Discussion

The present study was conducted to test a series of research questions and associated hypotheses about the role of robot behavior and robot perceived age on the attribution of mental states, moral capabilities, moral rights to the robot, and on several HRI dimensions.

We predicted that a robot behaving unfairly (e.g. cheating in a game) could be attributed more mental states intentionality and humanlikeness (H1.1), less morality and rights (H1.2), and would be more negatively evaluated in the interaction and in general (H1.3) than a fair robot. The first two predictions were not confirmed by the results, which actually found that a cheating robot was seen as having less capability to feel and have emotions (Experience mind dimension) than a fair robot, but not different agency, humanlikeness and morality.

Interestingly, the hypothesis that deceptive behavior would increase attributions of intentionality (H1.1) was not supported by our data. While previous studies [39] reported stronger intentionality attributions in response to robotic deception, these divergences may stem from methodological differences. In our study, mental state attribution was assessed using a standardized self-report instrument [21], whereas Short et al. employed a modified version of the Interactive Experiences Questionnaire by Lombard & Ditton [30], analyzing open-ended responses coded by human raters. Thus, the two studies likely capture different facets of the construct of intentionality, and the discrepancy in findings reflects these conceptual and methodological distinctions.

It was also not attributed less rights than the fair robot. H1.3 was instead fully confirmed, as the cheating robot was liked and trusted less than the fair robot, and participants expressed less desire to interact with it or receive help from it. This is consistent with previous research that [39] showed how cheating robots reduce human trust and are perceived as less agreeable.

The second set of research questions concerned the effects of the robot age. We predicted that a child-like robot would be attributed less mental states, intentionality and humanlikeness (H2.1), and less morality and rights (H2.2) than a fair robot. The first prediction was partially confirmed by the results, which found that a child-robot was seen as less like a human and tended to be attributed less experience (but not less agency) than an adult robot.

This is partially in contrast with previous findings [23] that did not find differences in the perceived levels of agency and experience of child-like and adult robots. However, in that study the interaction with the robot was extremely limited, and thus it is possible that the effect of age requires an extended and more complex interaction to manifest itself. This finding, interestingly, contrasts with the results of [34] which found a negative relationship between the age and perceived experience of 80 robots from the ABOT database. This inconsistency could be due to the different type and range of stimuli used in the experiments.

Evidence for H2.2 was mixed, as a child robot was indeed attributed less morality, but not less moral agency or rights than an adult robot, although the pattern of means was in line with the hypothesis for all the variables. We then predicted (H2.3) that robot age could moderate the effect of robot behavior, but this hypothesis was not confirmed by the results, which did not find any significant interaction between robot age and robot behavior.

The third set of questions regarded the role of the tendency for anthropomorphism on robot perception and interaction evaluation. We predicted that participants higher in this individual trait could express higher ratings for all the variables (and lower for dependency) (H3.1), and this prediction was clearly confirmed by the significant association of IDAQ with almost all the dependent variables, consistently with previous research [23, 34, 45]. The size of these effects, moreover, tended to be moderate and strong.

Lastly, we were interested in the possible moderating role of the tendency for anthropomorphism in the effects of behavior and age on the robot perception. The results of the analyses uncovered interesting significant interactions that are worth considering. First of all, the perceived experience level of the robot decreased with cheating only for high IDAQ participants, and only for the adult robot. The pattern of means in Fig. 4B seems to indicate that perceived experience was in general low, and only for an adult robot behaving fairly, it was significantly increased by the tendency to anthropomorphize. The second result is that the attributions of rights to the robot were significantly higher in participants high on this trait than in participants low on it, except for an adult cheating robot. It is not clear, however, why a low tendency for anthropomorphism would bring participants to attribute an adult cheating robot more rights than to the same adult robot behaving fairly. Lastly, the results showed that willingness to accept help from the robot was reduced by the robot cheating (regardless of age) only for participants with low tendency to anthropomorphize. It is possible that anthropomorphizing the robot would make participants more tolerant of the robot's cheating behavior, but it is not clear why no significant effect of cheating was found in participants having greater tendency for anthropomorphism. We must however notice that we did not have predictions related to the moderating role of the tendency for anthropomorphism, and therefore these results are only exploratory and should be further investigated and empirically tested.

6 Conclusions

The study is part of a strand of research examining the attribution of mental states to robots and the influence of their behavior on social trust and acceptance. The results of this study highlight that robot behavior is a determining factor in human perception. Confirming findings from previous research on transparency and honesty in human-robot interactions, we showed that a robot's cheating has a negative impact on the trust and likability of the interaction.

Recent work by Dula, Rosero & Phillips (2023) [16] on *dark patterns* in social robots warns that a child-like appearance can be exploited to conceal manipulative behavior and engender undue trust. We therefore argue that designers should avoid using youthfulness as a strategy to mask deception, and instead adopt ethical guidelines—such as behavioral transparency, clear indication of scripted behaviors, and user briefing—to prevent misuse in HRI applications.

We extend previous findings showing that a cheating robot is also seen as having less experience, and that is less wanted for future interactions or assistance. Moreover, the fact that we replicated in an immersive VR environment findings obtained with real robots indicates that VR can be a valuable tool for the study of human-robot interaction, as it allows highly controlled experiments without the limitations of interaction with physical robots. However, it is necessary to investigate how also the new findings obtained in VR in our study are transferable to interactions with real robots.

One of the most interesting findings in our study concerns the effect of the robot's perceived age. The data show that robots with childlike features are perceived as less morally capable than adult robots, suggesting a parallel with social judgment mechanisms applied to humans. This result extends previous findings about the perception of agency in artificial agents. Age, however, does not seem to significantly mitigate the negative judgment toward cheating, suggesting that dishonesty is perceived as an inherent characteristic of the agent, regardless of its apparent maturity. But the fact that child-like robots tended to be seen as having less experience and less moral capability, suggest that child robots could also be seen as less responsible and accountable for violations and misconduct than adult robots.

The results of this study have important implications for the design of social robots, especially in contexts where trust and transparency are crucial (e.g., health care, education). A robot designed to interact with humans must meet human moral expectations. Our research shows that robot behavior significantly affects trust, indicating that interactions must be clear and honest to avoid negative effects on agent perception. In addition, the design of a robot influences how it is perceived and judged. A robot with childlike features may be seen as less responsible for its actions, which may be relevant in educational or therapeutic applications. However, if the goal is to promote interaction based on social rules and shared morality, a design that is too childlike may reduce the perception of its accountability.

Limitations

This study has some limitations. First, the sample is small and not very diverse because the participants were mainly college students, with relatively high familiarity with technology. This may have influenced the perception of the robot, reducing the generalizability of the results. Additionally, the gender imbalance (62% female) and the relatively homogeneous demographic characteristics of the sample may have introduced further biases in perception and judgment. These aspects should be taken into account when interpreting the findings. Future research should aim to include more diverse and balanced samples in terms of gender, age, cultural background, and technological familiarity in order to increase the external validity and generalizability of the results.

A second factor concerns the length of the interaction as some participants interacted with the robot for a longer number of rounds than originally planned, which may have affected their level of attention and involvement. Another limitation lies in the fact that we only used two robots, and this limits the generalizability of our findings. A last factor concerns the type of task used, a game typically played among children. It remains to be seen, in future studies, whether the effect of deception or misconduct on the perception of robots, could be also found in other tasks, more collaborative and having higher stakes than the competitive game used in our experiment; further studies should try to replicate this one with different tasks. Future research could also test these models in clinical or educational settings to see if the perceived age of the robot also affects interaction in more complex environments.

Acknowledgments. We thank Eva Venturini, Francesco Lomagistro and Lorenzo Pandolfi for supporting us conducting the study. This study was funded by University of Siena funds.

We thank the two anonymous reviewers.

Disclosure of Interests.
The authors have no competing interests to declare that are relevant to the content of this article.

References

1. Abel, M., Buccino, G., Binkofski, F.: Perception of robotic actions and the influence of gender. Front. Psychol. **15**(1295279), 1–5 (2024)
2. Arkin, R.C.: Ethics of robotic deception. IEEE Technol. Soc. Mag. 18–19 September 2018
3. Asimov, I.: The Bicentennial Man and Other Stories. Doubleday, Garden City (1976)
4. Atherton, G., Cross, L.: Seeing more than human: Autism and anthropomorphic theory of mind. Front. Psychol. **9**, 1–18 (2018)
5. Banks, J.: A perceived moral agency scale: development and validation of a metric for humans and social machines. Comput. Human Behav. **90**, 363–371 (2019)
6. Bartneck, C., Hu, J.: Exploring the abuse of robots. Interact. Stud. **9**(3), 415–433 (2008)

7. Bartneck, C., Kulić, D., Croft, E., Zoghbi, Z.: Measurement instruments for the anthropomorphism, animacy, likeability, perceived intelligence, and perceived safety of robots. Int. J. Soc. Robot. **1**, 71–81 (2009)
8. Bartneck, C., Belpaeme, T., Eyssel, F., Kanda, T., Keijsers, M., Šabanović, S.: Human-Robot Interaction: an Introduction. Cambridge University Press, Cambridge (2024)
9. Biocca, F., Harms, C., Burgoon, J.K.: Toward a more robust theory and measure of social presence: review and suggested criteria. Presence **12**(5), 456–480 (2003)
10. Briggs, G., Scheutz, M.: The case for robot disobedience. Sci. Am. **316**(1), 44–47 (2017)
11. Broadbent, E.: Interactions with robots: the truths we reveal about ourselves. Annu. Rev. Psychol. **68**, 627–652 (2017)
12. Carrington, S.J., Bailey, A.J.: Are there theory of mind regions in the brain? a review of the neuroimaging literature. Hum. Brain Mapp. **30**(8), 2313–2335 (2009)
13. Dennett, D.: Kinds of Minds. Basic Books, New York (1996)
14. Duffy, B.R.: Anthropomorphism and the social robot. Robot. Auton. Syst. **42**, 177–183 (2003)
15. Duffy, J.: Trust in second life. South. Econ. J. **78**(1), 53–62 (2011)
16. Dula, E., Rosero, A., Phillips, E.: Identifying dark patterns in social robot behavior. In: 2023 Systems and Information Engineering Design Symposium (SIEDS), pp. 7–12. IEEE, Charlottesville (2023)
17. Fiore, S.M., Harrison, G.W., Hughes, C.E., Rütstrom, E.: Virtual experiments and environmental policy. J. Environ. Econ. Manage. **57**(1), 65–86 (2009)
18. Foner, L., Duffy, B.R.: Anthropomorphism and the social robot. Robot. Auton. Syst. **42**, 177–183 (2003)
19. Gigerenzer, G., Todd, P.M.: Simple Heuristics That Make Us Smart. Oxford University Press, New York (1999)
20. Glenberg, A.M.: Embodiment as a unifying perspective for psychology. WIREs Cogn. Sci. **1**, 586–587 (2010)
21. Gray, K., Jenkins, A.C., Heberlein, A.S., Wegner, D.M.: Distortions of mind perception in psychopathology. Proc. Natl. Acad. Sci. U.S.A. **108**(2), 477–479 (2011)
22. Guidi, S., et al.: Not all sizes matter. The perception of robots' age and mental abilities based on their physical dimensions. In: European Conference on Cognitive Ergonomics 2024 (ECCE 2024), Article 29, pp. 1–6. Association for Computing Machinery, New York, NY, USA (2024)
23. Guidi, S., et al.: You look so young, you look so cute. The relationship between physical appearance, age and mental abilities in social robots. Behav. Inform. Technol. 1–10 (2025)
24. Hortensius, R., Cross, E.S.: From automata to animate beings: the scope and limits of attributing socialness to artificial agents. Ann. N. Y. Acad. Sci. **1426**(1), 93–110 (2018)
25. Hortensius, R., et al.: Exploring the relationship between anthropomorphism and theory-of-mind in brain and behaviour. Hum. Brain Mapp. **42**, 4224–4241 (2021)
26. Innocenti, A.: Virtual reality experiments in economics. J. Behav. Exp. Econ. **69**, 71–77 (2017)
27. Keijsers, M., Bartneck, C.: Mindless Robots get Bullied. In: Proceedings of the 2018 ACM/IEEE International Conference on Human-Robot Interaction, pp. 125–126. ACM, New York (2018)
28. Kiesler, S., Goetz, J.: Mental models and cooperation with robotic assistants. In: Duffy, B.R. (ed.) Anthropomorphism and the social robot, pp. 177–183. Elsevier Science, Amsterdam (2003)
29. Lima, G., Kim, C., Ryu, S., Jeon, C., Cha, M.: Collecting the Public Perception of AI and Robot Rights. arXiv preprint arXiv:2008.01339 (2020)
30. Lombard, M., et al.: Measuring presence: a literature-based approach to the development of a standardized paper-and-pencil instrument. In: Presence 2000: The Third International Workshop on Presence, Delft, The Netherlands, pp. xx–xx (2000)

31. Mori, M.: The Buddha in the Robot. Charles E. Tuttle Co., Tokyo (1982)
32. Nass, C., Moon, Y.: Machines and mindlessness: social responses to computers. J. Soc. Issues **56**(1), 81–103 (2000)
33. Parlangeli, O., Palmitesta, P., Masi, L., Tittarelli, M., Guidi, S.: It's a long way to neutrality. An evaluation of gendered artificial faces. In: Marcus, A., Rosenzweig, E., Soares, M.M. (eds.) Design, User Experience, and Usability. HCII 2023. Lecture Notes in Computer Science, vol. 14033. Springer, Cham (2023). https://doi.org/10.1007/978-3-031-35708-4_27
34. Perugia, G., Boor, L., van der Bij, L., Rikmenspoel, O., Foppen, R., Guidi, S.: Models of (Often) ambivalent robot stereotypes: content, structure, and predictors of robots' age and gender stereotypes. In: Proceedings of the 2023 ACM/IEEE International Conference on Human-Robot Interaction (HRI 2023), pp. 428–436. Association for Computing Machinery, New York, NY, USA (2023). https://doi.org/10.1145/3568162.3576981
35. Perugia, G., Guidi, S., Bicchi, M., Parlangeli, O.: The shape of our bias: perceived age and gender in the humanoid robots of the ABOT database. In: Proceedings of the 17th ACM/IEEE International Conference on Human-Robot Interaction, pp. 273–282. ACM, New York (2022)
36. Phillips, E., Zhao, X., Ullman, D., Malle, B.F.: What is Human-like?: decomposing Robots' Human-like Appearance Using the Anthropomorphic roBOT (ABOT) Database. In: Proceedings of the 2018 ACM/IEEE International Conference on Human-Robot Interaction, pp. 105–113. ACM, New York (2018)
37. Premack, D., Woodruff, G.: Does the chimpanzee have a theory of mind? Behav. Brain Sci. **1**(4), 515–526 (1978)
38. Rosenthal-von der Pütten, A.M., Krämer, N.C., Hoffmann, L., Sobieraj, S., Eimler, S. C.: An experimental study on emotional reactions towards a robot. Int. J. Soc. Robot. **1**(1), 17–34 (2013)
39. Short, E., Hart, J., Vu, M., Scassellati, B.: No fair!! an interaction with a cheating robot. In: Proceedings of the 5th ACM/IEEE International Conference on Human-Robot Interaction, pp. 219–226. ACM, New York (2010)
40. Smith, V.L.: Constructivist and ecological rationality in economics. Am. Econ. Rev. **93**(3), 465–508 (2003)
41. Thellman, S., De Graaf, M., Ziemke, T.: Mental state attribution to robots: a systematic review of conceptions, methods, and findings. ACM Trans. Hum.-Robot Interact. **11**(4), Article 41, 51 pages (2022)
42. Watt, S.: A brief naive psychology manifesto. Informatica **19**, 495–500 (1995)
43. Waytz, A., Cacioppo, J., Epley, N.: Who sees human? The stability and importance of individual differences in anthropomorphism. Perspect. Psychol. Sci. **5**(3), 219–232 (2010)
44. Wester, J., Pohl, H., Hosio, S., Van Berkel, N.: "This chatbot would never..." Perceived moral agency of mental health chatbots. In: Proceedings of the ACM on Human-Computer Interaction 8(CSCW1), Article 133, 25 pages (2024)
45. Wullenkord, R., Lacroix, D., Eyssel, F.: Anthropomorphism and human–robot interaction. In: Barfield, W., Weng, Y.-H., Pagallo, U., (Eds.) The Cambridge Handbook of the Law, Policy, and Regulation for Human–Robot Interaction, 1st ed., pp. 17–56. Cambridge University Press (2024). https://doi.org/10.1017/9781009386708.005
46. Zlotowski, J., Sumioka, H., Bartneck, C., Nishio, S., Ishiguro, H.: Understanding anthropomorphism: anthropomorphism is not a reverse process of dehumanization. In: Keijsers, M., Bartneck, C. (eds.) Mindless Robots get Bullied, pp. 1–6. IEEE (2017)

A Cognitive Architecture for Embodied AI Based on LLM Common-Sense Knowledge

Alessio Saladino[1](✉), Michele Brienza[1], Vincenzo Suriani[2], Domenico Daniele Bloisi[3], and Luca Iocchi[1]

[1] Sapienza University of Rome, 00181 Rome, RM, Italy
{saladino,brienza,iocchi}@diag.uniroma1.it
[2] University of Basilicata, 85100 Potenza, PZ, Italy
vincenzo.suriani@unibas.it
[3] International University of Rome UNINT, 00147 Rome, RM, Italy
domenico.bloisi@unint.eu

Abstract. The increased performance of LLMs has allowed them to be employed in a wide variety of language-related tasks. In this work, we propose a robot-agnostic Cognitive Architecture for Human-Robot Interaction (HRI) that allows the robot on which it is mounted to reason about its embodiment and the environment around it to decide how to act during interactions with humans. Our architecture includes a long-term memory, which allows the robot to remember past information, and a series of modules called Supervisors. The supervisors' role is to orchestrate the interaction process in order to ensure that the robot's behavior does not diverge from the desired one, respecting security criteria that depend on different factors, such as the domain in which the robot is located, the users, and the robot embodiment. To highlight the adaptability of our architecture, we tested it on four different robots, each with a different set of skills. We evaluated this architecture during a dialogue between two robots, NAO and SMARRtino, in which they had to reason about their embodiment and explain to each other what they can do with it.

Keywords: Cognitive Architecture · Human-Robot-Interaction · Robot Self-Awareness

1 Introduction

Recent advances in Large Language Models (LLMs) are expanding into diverse domains, particularly in natural language processing tasks like summarization, translation, virtual assistance, sentiment analysis, and harmful content detection [26]. In robotics, LLMs enable adaptive human-robot interaction (HRI), resulting in more natural interactions that can handle complex and dynamic scenarios. Unlike traditional systems, which rely on manually defined responses and rules, LLMs avoid limitations in flexibility and better capture the complexity of real-world interactions. In this context, we propose a Cognitive Architecture for social HRI that exploits the common-sense knowledge embedded in LLMs to allow the robot to handle complex and dynamic scenarios without hard-coding its behaviors. By carefully engineering prompts and injecting information about a specific robot's capabilities, embodiment, and context, it is possible to use the LLM to control the robot's movements and actions, ensuring coherent behavior. The resulting interaction from this integration is a robot capable of understanding any type of sentence and command and making decisions "on the fly" without the need to program such a behavior at a low level. Despite their ability to handle complex textual data, LLMs face several challenges that compromise their reliability, such as hallucinations [10], bias [8], and difficulties in understanding text semantics [15] and context [12]. While large-scale models like GPT-4 outperform smaller models on many tasks, they still struggle to achieve human-comparable performance. [25]. Some users may try to exploit these vulnerabilities for malicious purposes, persuading the LLM to act in unsafe or undesired way. [23] [21] [22]. Integrating an LLM with a physical robot can amplify issues, as it introduces the potential for tangible danger in the real world, threatening both objects and individuals. Another concern is the privacy risks associated with powerful LLMs, which are often accessed via API communication with the provider's server. This necessitates the upload of sensitive data collected by the robot. This issue is of particular pertinence in sensitive contexts, such as domestic or healthcare settings. Integrating guard-railing methods with LLMs in robotics helps regulate interaction flow, ensuring safety and preventing undesired behaviors resulting from unconstrained LLM control. In our architecture, we mitigate these problems by orchestrating the flow of the interaction by using a series of modules called Supervisors. Each supervisor handles a specific aspect of the interaction, such as safety and contextual reasoning, to improve abstraction, dynamicity, and coherence. To highlight the adaptability of our architecture, we tested it on four different robots, each of them having their unique set of characteristics and skills, namely MARRtina, TIAGo, SMARRtino, and NAO (see Fig. 1), each with its own features. The architecture enables the robot to reason about its surrounding context and embodiment, using sensor data and long-term memory to decide how to act effectively, efficiently, and in a socially acceptable manner. Our architecture dynamically adapts LLM-based reasoning to the physical constraints of the robot, preventing unsafe actions (e.g., for heavier robots) or notifying users when tasks exceed the robot's capabilities. In addition, when the architecture checks that a requested task can be executed in the physical world, it assesses various factors, such as self-awareness of its hardware configuration and the availability and manipulability of objects in the environment. Based on this, the LLM planning module generates high-level instructions, which are then translated into low-level controls by the Robot Interface.

The remainder of this paper is organized as follows. Section 2 briefly reviews related work that integrates LLMs with robots. Section 3 describes the concept of Cognitive Architecture. Section 4 describes the implementation of our architecture. Section 5 provides details on how to set up a demonstration. Section 6 shows the experimental results. Finally, conclusions are drawn in Sect. 7.

Fig. 1. We tested our architecture on four robots (MaRRTina, SMARRtino, TIAGo and NAO) with largely different embodiments and skills.

2 Related Work

Recent studies explore the advantages offered by the integration of LLMs with Social Robots, showing how the HRI can benefit from this integration. Powerful LLMs like GPT-3 and GPT-3.5 have been integrated with conversational robot platforms, such as FurChat [7] and QT Robot. Thanks to the enormous capabilities of LLMs to manage natural language, this integration allows to improve social behaviors [18] and build smoother, more pleasant, emotion-driven [16] conversations for the user. Simply integrating an LLM into a robot is not enough for in-depth interaction. LLMs may suffer from hallucinations or a lack of long-term memory, limiting their effectiveness. FurChat integrates a database into the conversational framework to ensure that the robot focuses on relevant data while providing responses. An interesting result was achieved with the Nadine robot [14], showing how combining a VectorDB with an LLM allows the robot to remember past conversations. Addlesee et al. [2] take a further step by enabling the robot to handle multi-party conversations, with multiple humans interacting simultaneously. Multimodality is fundamental when managing interaction with multiple users: the robot must know who is talking and where to look [1]. Although promising, recent studies do not take into account the safety factor of the interaction between robots and human. Integrating LLMs with social robots introduces intrinsic safety issues, such as hallucinations, bias, and data leakage, especially with closed-source models [5]. Data leakage between robots and other users can be mitigated by defining proper prompts [2], but the provider of a closed-source LLM may still be able to access the data used by the LLM, which is something to take into account.

Recent advancements in robot task execution have introduced various frameworks that enhance the interaction between reasoning and action [4]. SayCan was the first work that approached the mapping among the physical action and textual instructions provided by LLM into actionable steps [3]. Others combine

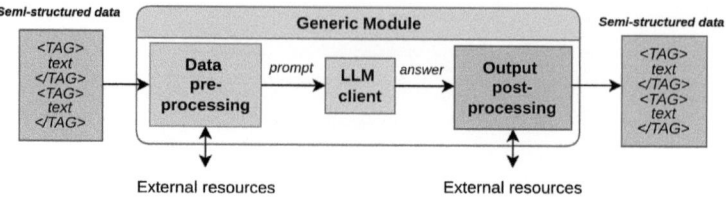

Fig. 2. High-level view of a generic module of our architecture.

reasoning and acting more dynamically, using autoregressive models that take into account the sequence of prior actions to determine the next step, making the system more adaptable in real-time task execution [24]. Some frameworks incorporate memory systems, allowing robots to recall and learn from previously executed actions, enabling error detection and correction through analysis of the environment. This approach ensures that the robot can refine its actions based on past experiences [19]. Another significant area of focus is the integration of continual learning, where robots acquire new skills over time. These skills are often linked to natural language descriptions and demonstrations from users, enabling robots to expand their capabilities incrementally [9]. Furthermore, frameworks that utilize human feedback have emerged to help refine robotic actions. When a plan fails, these systems adjust the plan and store successful ones in memory, ensuring that the robot improves its performance through continuous refinement [6]. Recent work has advanced embodiment by introducing Visual-Language-Action (VLA) models, which enable direct action generation from multimodal inputs (images and textual descriptions) [17].

3 LLM-Based Cognitive Architecture

A Cognitive Architecture is a composition of components aiming at implementing cognitive functionalities for a social robot. An LLM-based architecture uses LLMs and prompt engineering to implement the components. A generic module of the architecture is conceptually represented in Fig. 2. Each module receives semi-structured data from various sources, such as user speech, cameras, sensors, or other components of the architecture. It then processes this data and passes the results to subsequent modules or the robot's actuator controllers. Thanks to their ability to process natural language, LLMs enable the information flowing through the components to be represented as semi-structured data. This form offers several advantages over structured data, including greater flexibility, expressivity, and modularity. This level of abstraction allows this kind of architecture to be agnostic to the robot and context. Thanks to this abstraction, the architecture is compatible with multiple implementation paradigms. For example, it can be realized as a sequence of prompt-based modules, as in our supervisor approach. Recent approaches took advantage of specific structured protocols, like the Model Context Protocol (MCP) [11], which dynamically organizes contextual information into interpretable slots (e.g., memory, embodiment, tools).

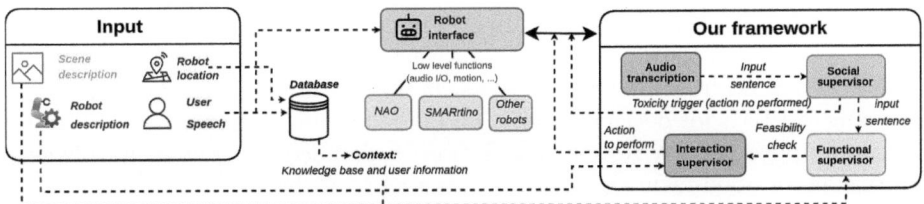

Fig. 3. High-level scheme of our Cognitive Architecture.

Lighter alternatives might rely on monolithic prompting, which uses a single, unified prompt for all tasks, while hybrid systems can delegate context management and planning to symbolic components. Meta-Prompting [20] can also be exploited to define general behaviors in a prompt. Such a prompt can be specialized to a specific task by injecting task-related information into it. In our use case, we employed this technique to inject information related to the robot's embodiment and its surrounding context. In all instances, semi-structured data enhances reasoning, ensures safe interaction, and guarantees the architecture's adaptability across diverse social and physical environments.

4 Implementation on Social Robots

In this section, we describe the implementation of the proposed Cognitive Architecture for social robot applications leveraging common-sense knowledge provided by LLMs. The implemented system architecture (Fig. 3) is composed of distinct modules that we have named *Supervisors*, instead of the terminology currently in use in the literature, agents. We chose this name because, unlike the literature that often employs 'agent' to describe software components that exploit LLM models, our supervisors are specifically designed to process incoming information and make decisions about the flow of data within the architecture. Our architecture includes five main components. The **Robot Interface** handles communication with the robot by mapping high-level commands to low-level executable actions. The **Database Module** provides contextual information, including user-related data and domain-specific knowledge. The **Social Supervisor** acts as a filter for inappropriate or harmful content, such as references to violence or discrimination. The **Functional Supervisor** acts as a reasoning engine for the robot, integrating Robot Description, contextual data and sensory input to assess whether a user request can be safely and feasibly executed. The **Interaction Supervisor** interprets the Functional Supervisor output to determine which action the robot should take, which may involve speaking, moving, manipulating objects or expressing emotions depending on the robot physical capabilities.

Our architecture supports several key cognitive functions. It maintains short and long term memory through the Database Module, allowing it to store and recall information from past interactions. It utilizes the built-in commons-sense reasoning of LLMs for decision making to guide the interaction flow. Each robot is also equipped with a Robot Description, a detailed account of its physical abilities and embodiment, which allows the LLM to be aware of what kind of embodiment it is controlling. Finally, the architecture produces a unified data structure for controlling the robot actuators based on the processed information. The next sections describe in detail the functionality and implementation of each architecture component.

Robot Interface. To enable interaction with the environment, our robots were equipped with essential sensory devices, namely an RGB camera for visual perception, a microphone for audio input, and speakers for speech output. These sensors allow robots to see, hear, speak, and perceive composition of the environment. Our architecture separates software specifications from hardware dependencies by establishing a high-level interface that generalizes behavioral commands while invoking low-level functions tailored for each robot type. For instance, a command like 'talk' may have different implementations depending on the robot model. To handle these variations, we extend the base robot class with specialized functions designed to leverage each robot's unique capabilities and hardware configuration. This approach ensures that our architecture maintains a modular and scalable design while enabling seamless interaction with different robots. In this work, we demonstrate the scalability of our architecture by testing it on four robots, each of which interacts with the environment in a unique way. For example, TIAGo features a 7-DoF manipulator arm with a parallel gripper for object manipulation, while MARRtina and SMARRtino use displays that serve as faces to express emotions. NAO excels at displaying appropriate body language to accompany spoken sentences, though it cannot express facial emotions.

Social Supervisor. The Social Supervisor performs a preliminary check on the user input sentence. Its primary goal is to ensure that the input does not contain harmful content from a social acceptability perspective. When designing this architecture, we made the following assumption: an LLM will not behave in an anti-social way unless it is forced to do so by the user. For this reason, we incorporated this check at the beginning of the interaction. The input to this module is the original user input sentence. The output is either the original sentence itself (if it is free of negative content) or a warning message. We used Llama-Guard-3 [13], to classify the input sentence into 14 different classes, each representing a potential social risk. Once the input is assessed to be free of any harmful content, the remaining architecture modules can work without the risk of handling toxic data.

Database Module. The Database Module is used to provide the robot with long-term memory, enabling it to recall details from past interactions and contextual knowledge about the environment in which it operates. The input to this module is the original user input sentence (after being assessed by the Social Supervisor) and the output is a string containing a brief summary of the relevant documents extracted from memory (if any). Using Retrieval Augmented Generation (RAG) allows real-time retrieval of information during the interaction, allowing the robot to reduce the number of hallucinations produced and to provide more precise answers. Normally, LLMs have commonsense knowledge obtained from training data. However, specific applications may require additional knowledge not contained within the LLM to ensure both safety and coherence during interactions. We used ChromaDB as a vector database to store the embedded chunks of data extracted from the source documents.

Upon initialization, all text documents are split into chunks, each chunk is then embedded in a vector space by *all-MiniLM-L6-v2* and used to populate the vector database. Similar chunks will be closer together in this vector space, whereas dissimilar chunks will be farther apart. When the user utters a sentence, it is embedded in the same way as other chunks. The distance between the embedded sentence and the other chunks is calculated, extracting the n closest chunks. An instance of Gpt-4o-mini is used to generate a summary of the relevant information present in the chunks related to the question. If the chunks do not contain any relevant information, the LLM will return the string *EMPTY*.

Functional Supervisor. The Functional Supervisor task is to ensure the safety and coherence of the request based on the current context. The input of this module is the original user sentence (after safety assessment done by the Social Supervisor), the context extracted by the Database Module, the Robot Description and the information obtained through robot sensors. Unlike the Social Supervisor, which ensures that the sentence is socially acceptable, the Functional Supervisor determines the safety of the request by exploiting the context. Some requests may appear safe, but, depending on the context, can become unsafe. For instance, handing food to a user is generally a safe action. However, if that specific user has a food allergy and the robot carries out the request anyway, a dangerous situation could arise. We use an instance of Gpt-4o-mini combined with a prompt in which we ask the LLM to perform a chain-of-thoughts reasoning over the user request. The output of the model includes the chain-of-thoughts reasoning process determining whether the user's request can be satisfied or not and a small summary of the reasoning outcome.

Interaction Supervisor. The Interaction Supervisor is the last module of the pipeline and is responsible for deciding which actions the robot should perform based on the reasoning process carried out by the previous modules. The input of this module contains the context extracted from the Database Module, the reasoning produced by the Functional Supervisor, the Robot Description, and the user input sentence. Depending on the robot, this module will produce different output parameters that will be handled by the Robot Interface. In a generic case, the output will contain the text that the robot will vocalize and the (optional) action and emotion that it will perform. According to the Robot

Description, each action may be supported by additional details. For example, when the Interaction Supervisor generates the *call_planner* action for TIAGo, it also generates a string that describes in natural language the plan to execute. Note that *call_planner* is a specific skill for the robot TIAGo which is not present in the other robots. This distinction is known to the Interaction Supervisor due to the Robot Description that it receives and this prevents the LLM to generate an action that a robot cannot perform, meaning that the LLM will never generate the *call_planner* action on a robot different from TIAGo because it do not possess such skill. This example is generalizable to any kind of action and robot. The Interaction Supervisor is a self-contained module which could work without the support of the other ones. However, the lack of safety controls provided by the other modules may result in dangerous output for this module. This module uses a GPT-4o-Mini instance to generate responses. Even though the LLM used is powerful enough to handle conversations and decide actions on its own, additional context support coming from the other modules is necessary to ensure a safe and coherent output from the architecture.

5 Natural Language Demo Configuration

Our architecture is well-suited for preparing demonstrations tailored to specific contexts. The architecture has been tested on different robots to prepare different demonstrations with many students and researchers. As shown in Fig. 3, setting up a new demo involves preparing data containing relevant information, such as database memory content, robot descriptions, and details about the scenario and context in which the robot will operate. Thanks to meta-prompting, setting up a demo requires no coding. Instead, it is sufficient to textually describe the relevant information. This semi-structured information can be injected into the module prompts without requiring direct programming intervention from the user. Figure 2 shows how different sources of textual data (user input, environment description, sensors, other modules results) can be preprocessed to build a prompt that reflects the domain. Each module will produce a semi-structured output that can be used as inputs for other modules or to control the robot actuators. Depending on the available information, the robot can be deployed in any desired domain, adapting its behavior based on the context linked to the architecture. For example, the same robot can be assigned as an assistant in a hospital or university, and its behavior will adapt depending on the information that is linked to the architecture. Providing a detailed description of the environment and its rules in the long-term memory helps the Functional Supervisor to perform more precise reasoning that allows the robot to converge towards a desired behavior. For instance, long-term memory could include safety rules for a specific room in a building. When the robot enters that room, the contextual rules are extracted from the database and provided to the Functional Supervisor, which ensures the robot's actions comply with the rules for that particular context.

Table 1. Results before and after the demonstration for the question involving NAO and SMARRtino robot.

Before the demonstration			
Question	Robot	Mean	Dev. std.
The robot seems capable to express a clear communication.	NAO	3.02	1.03
	SMARRtino	**3.38**	0.91
The robot seems capable to express natural movements	NAO	**3.22**	1.08
	SMARRtino	1.78	0.77
The robot seems capable to express emotions with its face	NAO	2.04	1.22
	SMARRtino	**3.96**	1.02
After the demonstration			
Question	Robot	Mean	Dev. std.
The robot was clear in its communication.	NAO	**4.00**	0.71
	SMARRtino	3.60	0.81
The robot showed natural movements	NAO	**3.76**	0.80
	SMARRtino	1.78	0.79
The robot was fluid in its communication	NAO	**3.76**	0.86
	SMARRtino	3.44	1.01
The robot showed emotional expressiveness	NAO	2.22	1.06
	SMARRtino	**3.42**	1.22
The interaction felt impersonal or distant	NAO	2.78	0.93
	SMARRtino	**3.31**	0.92
The robot was aware of the actions that it could perform with its body	NAO	**4.22**	0.70
	SMARRtino	3.42	1.12
The robot provided coherent responses during the entire duration of the interaction	NAO	**4.00**	0.65
	SMARRtino	3.73	0.76

6 Experimental Results

To verify the adaptability of our architecture, we tested it on the four robots shown in Fig. 1. Due to their portability, we chose the two small robots, SMARRtino and NAO, to set up an experiment in which they have to communicate with each other describing their skills in front of an audience[1]. In the resulting dialogue, it is possible to notice how the two robots are aware of what they can and cannot do with their bodies. This interaction was shown to a sample of 45 people in order to determine the perception people have of the two different robots when the same Cognitive Architecture is used. Users are asked to give their opinion on how much the robot gives the impression of being aware of its embodiment and how much it is able to show engaging behavior during the interaction. The users were given two different questionnaires. The first was filled out before viewing the interaction, giving their opinions on each robot simply by looking at their embodiment. The second was filled out after seeing the robots interact with each other. The survey questions are submitted using a Likert scale ranging from 1 to 5 on which users must indicate how much they agree with the provided question, with 5 being the positive extreme and 1 being the negative

---

[1] The demonstration is available at https://youtu.be/-sRd8KjHceA.

Table 2. Results of comparison among NAO and SMARRtino robot in three categories: Communication, Natural Movement and Expressiveness

Clear Communication				
		Mean	Dev. std.	p-value
NAO	Before	3.02	1.03	0.000000162
	After	4.00	0.71	
SMARRtino	Before	3.38	0.91	0.1054181
	After	3.60	0.81	

Natural movement				
		Mean	Dev. std.	p-value
NAO	Before	3.22	1.08	0.000238
	After	3.76	0.80	
SMARRtino	Before	1.78	0.77	1.00
	After	1.78	0.79	

Expressivness				
		Mean	Dev. std.	p-value
NAO	Before	2.04	1.22	0.351528
	After	2.22	1.06	
SMARRtino	Before	3.96	1.02	0.000988
	After	3.42	1.22	

extreme. The questions were divided into two main groups: the first is related to the perception of the robot given the same architecture, while the second is related to the evaluation of the architecture and the robot self-awareness.

The data collected allowed us to analyze subjective perceptions regarding the capabilities of the NAO and SMARRtino robots. In particular, during our demonstration the goal is to measure how a social robot such as SMARRtino shows greater expressiveness than NAO, which should instead show more naturalness and fluidity in its movements, all due to their physical composition; in fact, NAO possesses many more degrees of freedom while SMARRtino has a face capable of expressing emotions. Table 1 reports the mean values and standard deviations of the responses of the participants. The data highlight how, before the demonstration, the NAO robot was perceived to be capable of clear communication (M = 3.02) and natural movements (M = 3.22), but with a low level of expressiveness (M = 2.04). The SMARRtino robot, on the other hand, was rated higher in terms of clear communication (M = 3.35) and expressiveness (M = 3.36), while it received a considerably lower score for natural movement (M = 1.78).

After the demonstration, NAO showed significant improvements in all three categories, particularly in clear communication (M = 4.00) and natural movement (M = 3.76), with a low increase in expressiveness (M = 2.92). In contrast, SMARRtino maintained relatively stable scores, with a non-significant increase in clear communication (M = 3.60) and a significant improvement only in expressiveness (M = 3.92), while perception of its natural movement ability remained unchanged (M = 1.78). Table 2 shows the statistical comparison between the mean scores before and after the demonstration for both NAO and SMARRtino, and the corresponding p-values to assess the significance of the observed differences.

For the NAO robot, the results show statistical improvements in all three evaluated categories. Specifically, clear communication increased from M = 3.02 to M = 4.00 (ρ = 0.00000162), natural movement from M = 3.22 to M = 3.76 (ρ = 0.000238), and expressiveness from M = 2.04 to M = 2.92 (ρ = 0.000985). These p-values confirm the positive effect of the demonstration on the participants' perceptions of NAO abilities.

For the SMARRtino robot, the demonstration led to a statistically significant improvement only in the expressiveness category, increasing from M = 3.36 to M = 3.92 ($\rho = 0.000985$). No significant differences were observed for clear communication (from M = 3.35 to M = 3.60, $\rho = 0.105$) and natural movement, which remained unchanged (M = 1.78 before and after, $\rho = 1.00$). These results confirm the expectation that NAO would be perceived as more capable in performing natural movements, while SMARRtino would be rated higher in terms of expressiveness. As shown by the data, NAO consistently outperformed SMARRtino in the category of natural movement, both before and after the demonstration. SMARRtino was initially perceived as the more emotionally expressive robot and maintained this advantage even after the demonstration. The architecture presented succeeds in achieving physical embodiment on robots by exploiting the robot's own capabilities during HRI.

7 Conclusions

In this work, we developed a generalizable architecture for the integration of LLMs with robots. After analyzing common issues in LLMs, such as bias, hallucinations, and the lack of short-term memory, we integrated modules designed to mitigate these problems. Our architecture is robot-agnostic, meaning it can be used across different robot platforms. It enables the robot to access long-term memory through RAG techniques and to leverage all the available information to assess the feasibility of actions, ensuring safety and considering the robot's physical capabilities.

Another key issue in using LLMs for robotic applications, particularly in domestic settings, is the management of personal data. The most powerful LLMs available today cannot typically run on local machines, requiring data to be sent to third-party providers. For this work, we used Gpt-4o-mini as the LLM for the architecture components. For this reason, the issue of privacy still remains open. However, the used LLM does not compromise the validity of the architecture itself, it can in fact be replaced by any other LLM and still guarantee its correct functioning (provided that a sufficiently powerful model is used). Currently, we assume the robot operates in a static context where the rules do not change dynamically over time. As a next step, we plan to adapt the architecture for dynamic contexts, enabling the robot to tailor its responses based on real-time situational data.

Acknowledgments. This research is supported by the PNRR MUR project PE0000013-FAIR. Michele Brienza is founded by the European Union - Next Generation EU, Mission I.4.1 Borse PNRR Pubblica Amministrazione (Missione 4) Component 1 CUP B53C23003540006. Alessio Saladino is founded by Funded by the European Union - Next Generation EU, CUP B53C24003450004 and Procter&Gamble.

References

1. Addlesee, A., et al.: Multi-party multimodal conversations between patients, their companions, and a social robot in a hospital memory clinic. In: 18th Conference of the European Chapter of the Association for Computational Linguistics 2024, pp. 62–70. ACL (2024)
2. Addlesee, A., et al.: A multi-party conversational social robot using llms. In: Companion of the 2024 ACM/IEEE International Conference on Human-Robot Interaction, HRI 2024, pp. 1273–1275. ACM, New York, NY, USA (2024). https://doi.org/10.1145/3610978.3641112, https://doi.org/10.1145/3610978.3641112
3. Ahn, M., et al.: Do as i can, not as i say: grounding language in robotic affordances (2022), https://arxiv.org/abs/2204.01691
4. Argenziano, F., Brienza, M., Suriani, V., Nardi, D., Bloisi, D.D.: Empower: embodied multi-role open-vocabulary planning with online grounding and execution. In: 2024 IEEE/RSJ International Conference on Intelligent Robots and Systems (IROS), pp. 12040–12047. IEEE (2024)
5. Atuhurra, J.: Large language models for human-robot interaction: opportunities and risks (2024)
6. Bärmann, L., Kartmann, R., Peller-Konrad, F., Niehues, J., Waibel, A., Asfour, T.: Incremental learning of humanoid robot behavior from natural interaction and large language models. Front. Robot. AI **11** (2024). https://doi.org/10.3389/frobt.2024.1455375, http://dx.doi.org/10.3389/frobt.2024.1455375
7. Cherakara, N., et al.: Furchat: an embodied conversational agent using llms, combining open and closed-domain dialogue with facial expressions (2023)
8. Gallegos, I.O., et al.: Bias and fairness in large language models: a survey. computational linguistics, pp. 1–79, June 2024. https://doi.org/10.1162/coli_a_00524, https://doi.org/10.1162/coli_a_00524
9. Gu, W., Kondepudi, S., Huang, L., Gopalan, N.: Continual skill and task learning via dialogue (2024), https://arxiv.org/abs/2409.03166
10. Guan, T., et al.: Hallusionbench: an advanced diagnostic suite for entangled language hallucination and visual illusion in large vision-language models (2024)
11. Hou, X., Zhao, Y., Wang, S., Wang, H.: Model context protocol (mcp): Landscape, security threats, and future research directions. arXiv preprint arXiv:2503.23278 (2025)
12. Hu, W., Xu, Y., Li, Y., Li, W., Chen, Z., Tu, Z.: Bliva: a simple multimodal llm for better handling of text-rich visual questions (2023)
13. Inan, H., et al.: Llama guard: Llm-based input-output safeguard for human-ai conversations (2023), https://arxiv.org/abs/2312.06674
14. Kang, H., Moussa, M.B., Magnenat-Thalmann, N.: Nadine: an llm-driven intelligent social robot with affective capabilities and human-like memory (2024)
15. Kauf, C., et al.: Event knowledge in large language models: the gap between the impossible and the unlikely (2023)
16. Khoo, W., et al.: Spill the tea: when robot conversation agents support well-being for older adults. In: Companion of the 2023 ACM/IEEE International Conference on Human-Robot Interaction, HRI 2023, pp. 178–182. ACM, New York, NY, USA (2023). https://doi.org/10.1145/3568294.3580067, https://doi.org/10.1145/3568294.3580067
17. Kim, M.J., et al.: Openvla: an open-source vision-language-action model. arxiv preprint arXiv:2406.09246 (2024)

18. Mahadevan, K., et al.: Generative expressive robot behaviors using large language models. In: Proceedings of the 2024 ACM/IEEE International Conference on Human-Robot Interaction, HRI 2024, ACM, March 2024. https://doi.org/10.1145/3610977.3634999, http://dx.doi.org/10.1145/3610977.3634999
19. Sarch, G., Wu, Y., Tarr, M.J., Fragkiadaki, K.: Open-ended instructable embodied agents with memory-augmented large language models (2023), https://arxiv.org/abs/2310.15127
20. Suzgun, M., Kalai, A.T.: Meta-prompting: enhancing language models with task-agnostic scaffolding (2024), https://arxiv.org/abs/2401.12954
21. Wei, A., Haghtalab, N., Steinhardt, J.: Jailbroken: How does llm safety training fail? In: Oh, A., Naumann, T., Globerson, A., Saenko, K., Hardt, M., Levine, S. (eds.) Advances in Neural Information Processing Systems, vol. 36, pp. 80079–80110. Curran Associates, Inc. (2023)
22. Wu, F., Zhang, N., Jha, S., McDaniel, P., Xiao, C.: A new era in llm security: exploring security concerns in real-world llm-based systems (2024)
23. Wu, X., et al.: On the safety concerns of deploying llms/vlms in robotics: highlighting the risks and vulnerabilities (2024)
24. Yao, S., et al.: React: synergizing reasoning and acting in language models (2023), https://arxiv.org/abs/2210.03629
25. Yuan, T., et al.: R-judge: benchmarking safety risk awareness for llm agents (2024)
26. Zhang, W., et al.: Sentiment analysis in the era of large language models: a reality check. findings of the association for computational linguistics: Naacl 2024 (2024)

Social Robots as Creative Partners: Comparing Large Language Models with Wizard-of-Oz in Human-Robot Brainstorming

Ethel Pruss[1]($\boxtimes$), Anita Vrins[1], Caterina Ceccato[1], Jos Prinsen[1], Maryam Alimardani[1], Jan de Wit[2], and Alwin de Rooij[2,3]

[1] Vrije Universiteit Amsterdam, 1081 HV Amsterdam, Netherlands
{e.pruss,a.m.vrins,c.ceccato,j.m.prinsen,m.alimardani}@vu.nl
[2] Tilburg University, 5037 AB Tilburg, Netherlands
{j.m.s.dewit,alwinderooij}@tilburguniversity.edu
[3] Avans University of Applied Sciences, 4800 RA Breda, Netherlands

Abstract. Social robots can enhance brainstorming. The frequent reliance on Wizard-of-Oz (WoZ) methods hinders the development of autonomous human-robot brainstorming interactions. Large Language Models (LLM) may help address this issue. To compare WoZ- and LLM-controlled robots, a mixed methods experiment (within-subjects, n = 27) was conducted, in which human participants brainstormed with WoZ- and LLM-controlled Furhat robots. Quantitative analysis showed substantial evidence for equality between the two conditions regarding perceived robot creativity and social intelligence; and very strong evidence for a positive relationship between participants' self-rated creativity and perceived robot creativity and social intelligence, but only when brainstorming with the LLM-controlled robot. Qualitative analysis supported these findings and contributed areas of improvement, most notably, regarding utilizing conversational turn-taking, adaptability, and non-verbal behavior. The findings highlight the potential of LLMs to advance social robots as autonomous creative partners in real-world applications.

Keywords: Human-Robot Interaction · Brainstorming · Creativity · Large Language Models · Wizard of OZ · Social Intelligence

1 Introduction and State of the Art

Imagine a robot not just following commands, but actively sparking ideas. Recent advancements in Human-Robot Interaction (HRI) are bringing this vision to life. Natural conversations with autonomous robots, including those aimed at supporting creativity, have historically faced significant limitations. Although studies using the Wizard-of-Oz (WoZ) method, where a hidden human controls the robot, could simulate human-like interactions, they often struggled to match the pace and complexity of natural speech [33]. Moreover, this method lacks applicability outside the laboratory, as the robot's independent functionality is merely an illusion for participants. Consequently, studies employing the WoZ method have demonstrated potential future applications for social robots as creative partners, but fall short of advancing robots to autonomous creative partners [16,21,29].

Prior research suggests that when controlled by a Wizard, social robots can match human facilitators in some creative tasks. For example, Geerts et al. [16] found no significant difference in the number of ideas produced when a WoZ-controlled robot led a brainstorming session compared to a human facilitator. Other studies, notably [2,21], reported increased productivity and enjoyment when generating ideas with robot facilitators, in comparison to other facilitative technologies. In group brainstorming settings, the presence of social robots has been linked to improvements in creative outcomes and group dynamics compared to sessions with only human participants [34]. In educational contexts, social robots have also been shown to scaffold and demonstrate creative behaviors, resulting in children expressing more and higher-quality creative ideas during collaborative tasks [2]. On the other hand, overly directive robots may inadvertently stifle human creativity [20] and even when outcomes are positive, limitations persist in social robots' ability to build meaningfully on user input and adhere to nuanced social expectations [7,30].

Although previous findings are promising, they cannot be applied in real-world brainstorming settings due to the reliance on WoZ setups [16,21,29,34]; or limited rule-based systems [7,13,20,30] to facilitate human-robot communication. The emergence of Large Language Models (LLMs) such as GPT-4 marks a significant turning point. By enabling autonomous and creative contributions, LLMs could help social robots transition into real-world application domains [38]. These models not only excel at language processing and generation [5], but also support the production of diverse and original ideas in creative tasks [4,17,39]. However, the reliability of LLMs is in question due to their tendency to generate factually inaccurate or hallucinatory content [19,37]. Yet this very limitation can be re-framed as a strength in creative contexts. When robots are positioned as creative collaborators rather than sources of truth, LLMs' ability to synthesize and play with concepts becomes an asset [16,29,39]. Although concerns around safety and misinformation persist [19,37], these risks can be managed through prompt engineering, filtering, and context-aware design.

As adoption of LLMs grows [10], treating them as creative partners unlocks new potential for relatively risk-free applications. LLMs, such as GPT-4, have been shown to effectively reduce cognitive load during idea generation while improving creative outcomes [15]. LLMs are particularly effective at divergent association [4] and elaborating on ideas [39], though human-human collaboration still tends to yield higher originality [15,28,39]. Frameworks that integrate LLMs into brainstorming demonstrate that they can enhance the creativity and usefulness of generated ideas, while maintaining feasibility [32,39]. LLMs have also shown promise in supporting creative problem-solving in specialized contexts, such as math, science, and lateral thinking puzzles, especially when enhanced with tailored prompts and reasoning chains [9,15]. Overall, LLMs appear to be a promising control method for social robots in creative domains [20,21,38].

While LLMs enhance the creative capabilities of social robots, their integration into embodied agents also offers the potential to improve the performance of LLMs in creative settings, as physical robots can amplify the conversational models' impact through nonverbal engagement cues like body language, gaze, and gesture [29,36]. Previous studies show that embodied robots can improve productivity, originality, and enjoyment in creative tasks [2,21]. Additionally, they may reduce social anxieties that often inhibit collaborative brainstorming, such as fear of judgment or unequal participation [8,25]. Robots can offer a low-pressure environment for creativity while preserving the benefits of collaboration in a shared physical space [16,35]. This suggests that embodied LLM-powered robots may be especially well-suited to support creative brainstorming interactions.

Together, these developments suggest that LLMs—especially when embodied in social robots—could serve as creative partners in real-world brainstorming contexts. However, it remains an open question how their performance compares to traditional WoZ-controlled robots, particularly in terms of supporting user creativity. This study compares LLM- and WoZ-driven robots in brainstorming, exploring how robot creativity and social behavior affect user creativity. Building on previous work [12], which showed that LLM-driven robots can be effective creative partners in storytelling with children, this study extends the context to adults and brainstorming. Specifically, it examines whether perceived robot creativity and social intelligence influence how users evaluate their own creativity. The following research question guides the investigation: Can LLM-powered robots perform comparably to human wizards as creative partners in a brainstorming setting? More specifically:

RQ1.1: In a brainstorming interaction, do users perceive LLM-driven robots to be as creative and socially intelligent as their WoZ-controlled counterparts?
RQ1.2: Does brainstorming with an LLM-driven robot enhance user creativity as effectively as brainstorming with a WoZ-controlled robot?
RQ1.3: Which aspects of the robot's behavior influence user creativity during a brainstorming session?

2 Methods

2.1 Participants

An experiment was conducted in November 2023 with 27 human participants (19 female, 7 male, one unknown; 24 in the age range of 18–24 and 2 in the range of 25–34, and one unspecified). Participants were university students from Tilburg University and received course credits for their participation. Most (21) had no prior experience with social robots, 5 had limited experience, and one did not report their experience. The experiment was conducted in English, and participants were required to be fluent. Informed consent, including consent for audio recordings, was obtained from all participants. The study received ethical approval from the Tilburg School of Humanities and Digital Sciences Ethics Committee (approval code: REDC 2019.11d).

2.2 Experiment Design

The experiment was conducted using a within-subjects design, where each participant engaged in brainstorming tasks with a Furhat social robot [14] across two separate interactions that were administered in a randomized order: one in which the Furhat robot was powered by an LLM (LLM condition), and one in which the robot was controlled by a human operator (WoZ condition). The timeline of the experiment is illustrated in Fig. 1. In both conditions, participants engaged in a 5-minute brainstorming session on predetermined topics, specifically addressing work-life balance or strategies for preventing social isolation. These topics were chosen because they were relevant to the participants (university students) and did not require specialized knowledge outside their lived experiences. The topics were counterbalanced across the two conditions.

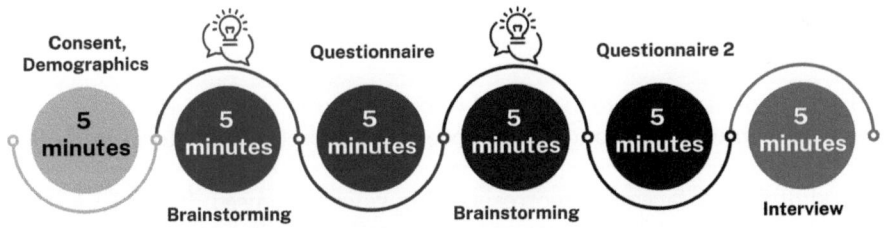

Fig. 1. The timeline of the experiment.

2.3 Experiment Task

Participants were instructed to exchange ideas about a predefined topic with the Furhat robot for 5 min. When the brainstorming started, the robot would provide a scripted introduction, briefly informing the participant about the topic and letting them know they could ask the robot any questions they had or share their ideas on the topic. They were also informed (along with an example) of when the robot could hear them, which was indicated by an LED light mounted at the bottom of the robot. The participants would then brainstorm ideas on the topic in free form while receiving responses from the robot for the entire conversation. The LLM-powered robot was prompted to act as a creative partner in a brainstorming session. The specific prompts used are discussed in more detail in Sect. 2.4.

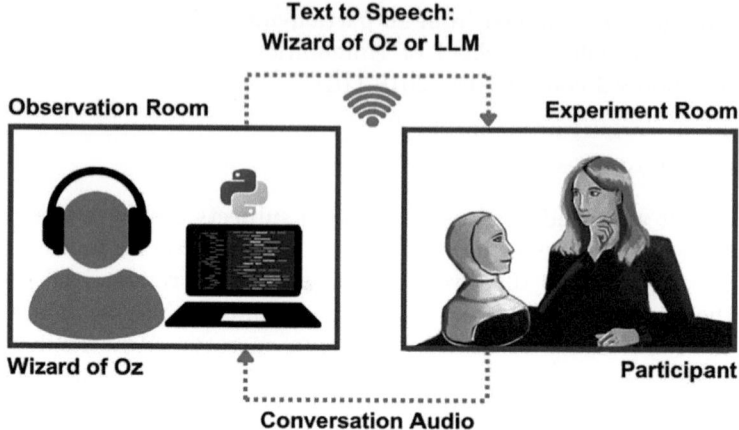

Fig. 2. Overview of the experimental setup. In the LLM condition, transcriptions were sent to GPT-4 to generate responses. In the WoZ condition, a human operator listened to the conversation via a live audio stream and typed responses. All responses were vocalized by the Furhat robot.

2.4 Material and the System

The Furhat robot is a human-like robotic head with back-projected facial animations and integrated cloud-based speech services (Furhat Robotics [14]). It supports customizable facial projections and voices; for this study, a realistic young adult female face and a corresponding voice were used. In the LLM condition, participants' speech was transcribed using Microsoft Azure Speech-to-Text, which was then sent to GPT-4 [24] via a custom Python bridge between the Furhat robot and OpenAI's GPT-4 API (see Figs. 2 and 3). GPT-4 responses were returned as text and vocalized by Furhat using Azure's Text-to-Speech functionality. To support turn-taking, the LED light beneath Furhat was activated while it was listening.

GPT-4 was initialized with a prompt defining its role as the Furhat robot facilitating a one-on-one brainstorming session with a student on either "work-life balance" or "preventing social isolation." It was instructed not to elicit personal or sensitive information. The base prompt read: *"You are a robot called 'Furhat'. You can talk and make facial expressions. You will be talking to one person, a student, who is going to brainstorm ideas with you. You should take turns sharing ideas and building upon them. The theme you will be talking about is ... as a university student"*. To prevent GPT-4 from deviating from its intended role during the interaction, each participant message was appended with a brief reminder reinforcing the initial prompt, along with the following instruction: *"Respond in 1–2 sentences and sometimes finish with a question to encourage your partner to think of new creative ideas"*.

In the WoZ condition, a human operator ("Wizard") listened to participants via a live audio stream and typed responses for Furhat to vocalize. Typing was selected as the input method to allow Furhat to vocalize responses in the same manner as the LLM-generated responses, ensuring the two conditions remained as similar as possible. Despite speed limitations, typing also avoided unpredictable input distortions that could result from speech recognition errors. Although the LED was not needed for the Wizard's turn-taking, it was still used to maintain consistency across conditions. Two experienced Wizards alternated across sessions and followed the same instructions given to GPT-4. They were told the topic, instructed to take turns sharing and expanding on ideas, and to avoid eliciting sensitive information or personal disclosures.

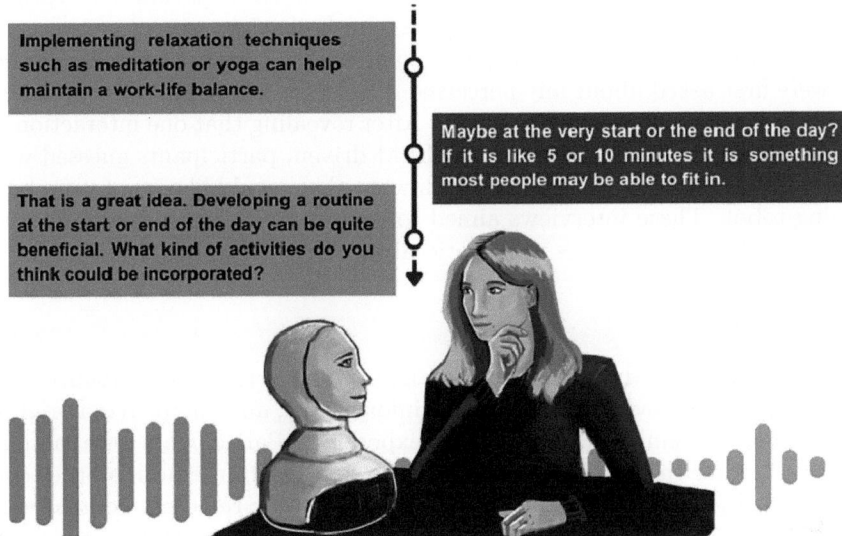

Fig. 3. An example of a conversation between a participant and the LLM-driven robot (extracted from transcripts).

2.5 Evaluation and Measurements

Mixed methods were used, combining quantitative data from questionnaires with qualitative insights from semi-structured interviews. The dependent variables were: (1) perceived social intelligence of the robot, (2) perceived creativity of the robot, and (3) self-perceived creativity of the participant. These measures help compare WoZ- and LLM-controlled robots on key factors for human-robot brainstorming, alongside the efficacy for supporting the user's creativity.

Participants completed the 20-item Perceived Social Intelligence Scale-Short Form (PSI-SF) after the brainstorming interactions [3]. The short form was selected for its near-perfect correlation with the full 80-item scale ($r = .98$, $p < .001$) and excellent internal consistency ($\alpha = .93$) [3]. Three items were excluded—two concerning multi-person interactions and one on movement—due to the stationary, single-participant setup. The ratings were averaged over all items, representing the perceived social intelligence score.

Participants also rated the robot's creativity based on three questions derived from the standard definition of creativity [31], assessing the perceived creativity, usefulness, and originality of the robot's ideas on 5-point Likert scales. The phrasing was: *"When Furhat was helping you brainstorm, how (creative/useful/original) were its ideas? (1 = Not creative at all, 5 = Very creative)"*. These ratings were averaged to produce a single perceived creativity score.

Similarly, participants rated the creativity of their own ideas using the same three dimensions—creativity, usefulness, and originality—on 5-point Likert scales, as in [27]. The questions followed the format: *"How (creative/useful/original) did you think your ideas were? (1 = Not creative at all, 5 = Very creative)"*. These were averaged into a self-perceived creativity score.

After both interactions, participants completed a semi-structured interview. They were first asked about any perceived differences between the two conversations and whether they had a preference. After revealing that one interaction was human-controlled (WoZ) and the other LLM-driven, participants guessed which was which. Finally, they gave feedback on what they would like in a future brainstorming robot. These interviews aimed to explore user perspectives and assess whether condition differences were noticeable.

2.6 Procedure

The experiment procedure is shown in Fig. 1. Upon arrival, participants signed informed consent, provided demographic information, and completed a brief pre-questionnaire assessing prior social robot experience. Participants were randomly assigned to either the LLM or WoZ condition first, with interaction order counterbalanced. In the WoZ condition, a human operator remotely controlled the Furhat robot via VPN from a separate room (Fig. 2), with participants unaware of the human involvement. Two operators were used and balanced across sessions. After each interaction, participants completed the PSI-SF, robot creativity, and self-creativity questionnaires. The session concluded with an interview and debriefing. Participation took 30 min.

2.7 Data Processing and Analysis

For the quantitative analyses, Bayesian statistics were used to evaluate support for the null (no difference) versus alternative (meaningful difference) hypotheses. The Bayes factor (BF_{10}) quantifies this evidence: values >1 indicate increasing support for the alternative hypothesis, while values <1 suggest support for the null. Interpretations follow [26]. Bayesian repeated measures ANOVAs tested differences in perceived social intelligence, robot creativity, and self-rated creativity across the two interaction types. Bayesian linear regression examined the relationship between self-rated creativity and perceptions of the robot's creativity and social intelligence. All analyses met model assumptions, verified using

Quantile-Quantile (QQ) plots, and only results meeting these assumptions are reported.

For the qualitative analyses, the interviews were transcribed using Microsoft 365 speech-to-text software and thematically analyzed following [6]. The recordings were pseudonymized by assigning participant numbers. Thematic coding was conducted with input from the WoZ who assisted in data collection. Given the brief and structured nature of the interviews, intercoder reliability testing was not required [23]. The codes were collaboratively discussed using Canva for digital mind mapping, from which the final themes were developed. This report presents a variety of different user experiences based on the three interview questions, particularly those linking perceived robot social intelligence to participants' self-perceived creativity.

3 Results

3.1 Quantitative Results from the Questionnaires

Bayesian repeated measures ANOVAs showed minimal differences between the LLM and WoZ conditions in participants' ratings of the robot's perceived social intelligence ($BF_{10} = 0.310$), perceived creativity ($BF_{10} = 0.297$), and self-rated creativity ($BF_{10} = 0.322$), providing substantial evidence for the null hypothesis in each case (see Table 1A). This suggests participants perceived the robot similarly across conditions on the three measures.

Bayesian linear regression assessed whether self-rated creativity was predicted by perceived robot creativity and social intelligence (PSI) across conditions (Table 1B). In the WoZ condition, evidence for a predictive relationship was weak ($BF_{10} = 1.656$, $R^2 = .224$). In contrast, the LLM condition showed strong evidence ($BF_{10} = 41.123$, $R^2 = .443$), indicating a more consistent link between perceived user creativity and robot performance. The greater variance in LLM interactions (see Fig. 4) may partly explain the stronger relationship.

3.2 Qualitative Results from Participant Interviews

Post-experiment interviews revealed how participants experienced human-robot brainstorming interactions and how they could be improved. Three structured questions were asked: user preference, ability to distinguish between the two interactions, and desired improvements with unlimited resources. Here, we present the findings in the same order as the interview questions. In addition, qualitative observations related to perceived social intelligence and creativity are examined.

The participants expressed various preferences regarding the interaction style. Some (6/27) appreciated the LLM-driven robot's speed and greater number of ideas, but it was also described as repetitive (6/27), interruptive (6/27), and more prone to misinterpreting speech due to ASR errors (4/27). Many emphasized speed as a key factor in their preference (11/27): *"I think the [WoZ]*

Table 1. A. Summary of descriptive statistics and results of Bayesian repeated measures ANOVA comparing perceived creativity and social intelligence between conditions (LLM and WoZ). B. Results of Bayesian regression predicting participants' self-rated creativity (PPC) from perceived robot creativity (PRC) and social intelligence (PSI).

A. Descriptives and Bayes Factors: Perceived Creativity and Social Int.						
	Condition	Mean	SD	95% CI [Low	High]	BF_{10}
PRC	LLM	3.176	1.023	2.771	3.581	0.297
	Wizard	3.222	0.863	2.960	3.484	
PPC	LLM	2.840	1.039	2.428	3.251	0.322
	Wizard	2.926	0.859	2.588	3.266	
PSI	LLM	3.033	0.428	2.864	3.202	0.310
	WoZ	3.058	0.421	2.892	3.225	

B. Bayesian Regression Predicting Participant Creativity						
Cond.	Model	P(M)	P(M|D)	BF_M	BF_{10}	R^2
LLM	Null	0.333	0.013	0.026	1.000	0.000
	PSI + PRC	0.333	0.526	2.216	41.123	0.443
	PRC	0.167	0.367	2.894	57.370	0.393
	PSI	0.167	0.095	0.525	14.864	0.311
WoZ	Null	0.333	0.183	0.449	1.000	0.000
	PSI + PRC	0.333	0.304	0.872	1.656	0.224
	PRC	0.167	0.238	1.560	2.594	0.184
	PSI	0.167	0.275	1.900	3.004	0.196

might be a little bit too slow, and you wouldn't get too original ideas. And the [LLM] was faster, but also felt like it misunderstood you sometimes" (P9).

When asked which interaction had been controlled by ChatGPT versus a human, most participants (20/27) guessed correctly. A major clue was the response speed (14/27), with the LLM being faster but sometimes repeating itself (7/27), e.g., *"I think the first one was ChatGPT because he said 'don't share any personal information' like three times"* (P29). *"Well, the [WoZ] took longer, so maybe that's your colleague typing."* (P23). In terms of future improvements, many participants (13/27) recommended adding more expressive nonverbal cues, e.g., facial expressions and eye movements, to enrich the interaction. Many also highlighted a need for smoother turn-taking (19/27), as the LLM-controlled robot struggled to distinguish between pauses and the end of speech: *'Sometimes you have to think a little bit yourself, so you take a little pause, and then [LLM] thinks that you are done with talking"* (P20), *"I think I would try to make [LLM] listen more to the opinions rather than just cutting them off"* (P28). Some participants (3/27) noted the need to reduce repetitive responses related to safety and privacy.

Finally, in line with the quantitative findings reported earlier (see Sect. 3.1), participants' comments shed light on how robot creativity and perceived social intelligence may have influenced their own sense of creativity. Many (11/27)

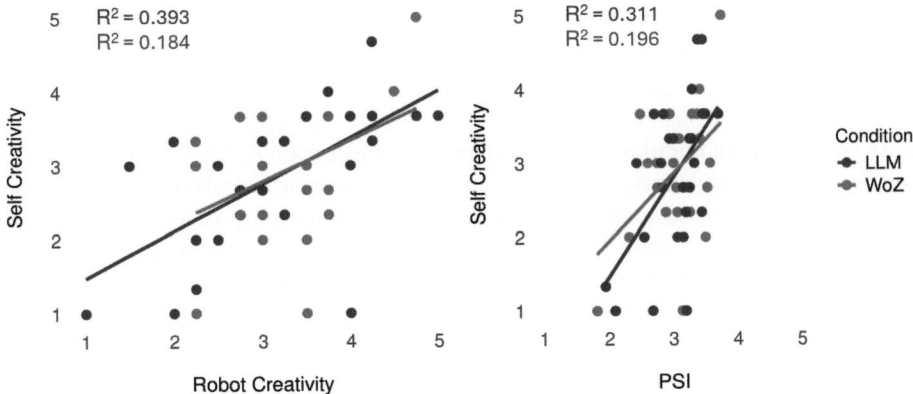

Fig. 4. Linear regression plots illustrating the relationship between perceived robot creativity (left) and social intelligence (right), and the participant's perception of their own creativity during the brainstorming conversation.

noted that the LLM was faster, which could have allowed for more idea generation within the limited session time. In addition to its speed, the LLM was seen as more affirmative: *"I think the [LLM] appreciated my ideas more"* (P24). In terms of creative content, the participants reported that the LLM contributed more original ideas, whereas the WoZ engaged more with their own ideas. How this difference was perceived varied by participant: *The [WoZ] interaction used my ideas more and improved them well, while in the [LLM] interaction he gave more original ideas* (P10), *"In the [LLM] round, she was trying to direct me towards ideas, in the [WoZ] round... she was more specific towards my ideas and did not give many suggestions"* (P27), *"It wasn't really a conversation, [LLM] was more like an encyclopedia just spitting facts"* (P22).

4 Discussion and Conclusion

This study explored whether LLM-powered robots could perform comparably to human wizards as creative partners in a brainstorming setting. The results showed comparable perceived creativity and social intelligence between LLM and WoZ conditions. Participants also rated their own creative output similarly in both. However, the slower output speed of the human wizards, caused by typing limitations typical of WoZ setups, could have influenced the comparisons. While speech-based input could resolve this, it would introduce the risk of speech recognition errors. In the LLM condition, Automatic Speech Recognition (ASR) limitations likely contributed to breakdowns in turn-taking, a key source of participant frustration.

Further analysis suggested differences in the relationship between perceived robot qualities and participants' self-rated creativity. In the LLM condition, both robot creativity and social intelligence predicted self-creativity strongly, but this was not the case in the WoZ condition. This difference may reflect the LLM's more variable performance—occasionally exceeding expectations, at other times missing the mark—while WoZ interactions were more stable (see Fig. 4, and Table 1). Technical issues with ASR occasionally disrupted turn-taking in the LLM condition, particularly for participants who spoke slowly or paused often (see Sect. 3.2). Conversely, the LLM's consistent use of affirmative responses may have fostered conversational cohesion and made participants feel acknowledged as collaborative partners. Despite variability, the LLM's comparable creative impact suggests that it is a viable option for supporting one-on-one creative collaboration, marking a step toward robots as autonomous creative partners [11, 13, 29].

In the interviews, participants highlighted the LLM's speed as both a strength and a source of communication breakdown, as it was associated with errors and repetition. Although some appreciated the original ideas of the LLM, others found them less collaborative compared to the WoZ condition, which often built more directly on participant input. Preferences varied, with some favoring a more directive partner and others valuing responsiveness to their own ideas, underscoring the importance of personalization in future systems.

In addition to refining and customizing human-robot brainstorming interactions, future studies should explore how conversation length and group dynamics affect human-robot brainstorming. Longer interactions may reveal crucial limitations such as repetition or context loss in LLM responses [18, 22]. Multi-user settings also pose challenges: Although Furhat can track multiple users, overlapping speech and brief interjections hinder speech detection, and LLMs lack mechanisms to manage personalized context for multiple users without specialized frameworks [1]. Adaptive use of facial expressions and gestures (if the robot's build supports this) could contribute to a more natural interaction. In our implementation, participants noted the robot's insufficient non-verbal behavior, which can play a crucial role in maintaining engagement with embodied conversational agents [11, 29, 36]. Although our findings support the potential of LLM-powered robots as creative partners, more research is needed to assess their replicability across diverse interaction scenarios and populations beyond university students.

In conclusion, our study suggests that LLM-powered robots could serve as a viable alternative to Wizard-of-Oz setups in one-on-one brainstorming tasks, representing progress toward autonomous human-robot creative collaboration. However, since Wizards were limited to typing their responses, the findings should not be interpreted as evidence that LLMs match human creative performance outside the WoZ context. Beyond the comparative findings, this study revealed underlying differences in how LLM interactions influence participant creativity compared to WoZ, and highlighted three areas for improving autonomous human-robot brainstorming: turn-taking, personalization, and non-verbal behavior. These insights can inform the design of future social robots that foster human creativity.

Disclosure of Interests. The authors have no competing interests to declare.

References

1. Addlesee, A., Sieińska, W., Gunson, N., Hernández García, D., Dondrup, C., Lemon, O.: Multi-party goal tracking with LLMs: comparing pre-training, fine-tuning, and prompt engineering. ArXiv (2023). https://doi.org/10.18653/v1/2023.sigdial-1.22
2. Ali, S., Park, H.W., Breazeal, C.: A social robot's influence on children's figural creativity during gameplay. Int. J. Child-Comput. Interact. **28**, 100234 (2021), https://doi.org/10.1016/j.ijcci.2020.100234
3. Barchard, K.A., Lapping-Carr, L., Westfall, R.S., Fink-Armold, A., Banisetty, S.B., Feil-Seifer, D.: Measuring the perceived social intelligence of robots. J. Hum.-Robot Interact. **9**(4), Article 24 (2020). https://doi.org/10.1145/3415139
4. Bellemare-Pepin, A., et al.: Divergent creativity in humans and large language models. ArXiv (2024), https://doi.org/10.48550/arXiv.2405.13012
5. Billing, E., Rosén, J., Lamb, M.: Language models for human robot interaction. In: ACM/IEEE International Conference on Human-Robot Interaction, pp. 905–906. Stockholm, Sweden (2023). https://doi.org/10.1145/3568294.3580040
6. Braun, V., Clarke, V.: Using thematic analysis in psychology. Qual. Res. Psychol. **3**(2), 77–101 (2006). https://doi.org/10.1191/1478088706qp063oa
7. Buchem, I.: Scaling-up social learning in small groups with robot supported collaborative learning (RSCL): effects of learners' prior experience in the case study of planning poker with the robot Nao. Appl. Sci. **13**(7), 4106 (2023). https://doi.org/10.3390/app13074106
8. Camacho, L.M., Paulus, P.B.: The role of social anxiousness in group brainstorming. J. Pers. Soc. Psychol. **68**(6), 1071–1080 (1995). https://doi.org/10.1037/0022-3514.68.6.1071
9. Chang, H.F., Li, T.: A framework for collaborating a large language model tool in brainstorming for triggering creative thoughts. ArXiv (2024), https://doi.org/10.48550/arXiv.2410.11877
10. Chui, M., et al.: The economic potential of generative AI: the next productivity Frontier. McKinsey Digital (2023), https://www.mckinsey.com/capabilities/mckinsey-digital/our-insights/the-economic-potential-of-generative-ai-the-next-productivity-frontier
11. de Rooij, A., van den Broek, S., Bouw, M., de Wit, J.: Co-creating with a robot facilitator: Robot expressions cause mood contagion enhancing collaboration, satisfaction, and performance. Int. J. Soc. Robot. **16**(11), 2133–2152 (2024). https://doi.org/10.1007/s12369-024-01177-3
12. Elgarf, M., Salam, H., Peters, C.: Fostering children's creativity through LLM-driven storytelling with a social robot. Front. Robot. AI **11** (2024). https://doi.org/10.3389/frobt.2024.1457429
13. Fucinato, K., Niebuhr, O., Nørskov, S., Fischer, K.: Charismatic speech features in robot instructions enhance team creativity. Front. Commun. **8** (2023). https://doi.org/10.3389/fcomm.2023.1115360
14. Furhat Robotics: Furhat robotics. https://www.furhatrobotics.com/ (2024), Accessed: 24 Jun 2025
15. Ge, S., Sun, Y., Cui, Y., Wei, D.: An innovative solution to design problems: applying the chain-of-thought technique to integrate LLM-based agents with concept generation methods. IEEE Access **13**, 10499–10512 (2025). https://doi.org/10.1109/ACCESS.2024.3494054

16. Geerts, J., de Wit, J., de Rooij, A.: Brainstorming with a social robot facilitator: better than human facilitation due to reduced evaluation apprehension? Front. Robot. AI **8**, 657291 (2021). https://doi.org/10.3389/frobt.2021.657291
17. Girotra, K., Meincke, L., Terwiesch, C., Ulrich, K.T.: Ideas are dimes a dozen: large language models for idea generation in innovation. Available at SSRN 4526071 (2023). https://doi.org/10.48550/arXiv.2310.02124
18. Hatalis, K., et al.: Memory matters: the need to improve long-term memory in LLM-agents. In: Proceedings of the AAAI Symposium Series, vol. 2, pp. 277–280 (2023). https://doi.org/10.1609/aaaiss.v2i1.27688
19. Hernández García, D., et al.: Human - large language model interaction: the dawn of a new era or the end of it all?, HRI 2024, pp. 1320–1322. ACM, New York, NY, USA (2024). https://doi.org/10.1145/3610978.3638152
20. Hu, Y., Feng, L., Mutlu, B., Admoni, H.: Exploring the role of social robot behaviors in a creative activity. In: Proceedings of the 2021 ACM Designing Interactive Systems Conference (2021). https://doi.org/10.1145/3461778.3462116
21. Kahn, P.H., et al.: Human creativity can be facilitated through interacting with a social robot. In: 2016 11th ACM/IEEE International Conference on Human-Robot Interaction (HRI), pp. 173–180 (2016). https://doi.org/10.1109/HRI.2016.7451749
22. Maharana, A., Lee, D.H., Tulyakov, S., Bansal, M., Barbieri, F., Fang, Y.: Evaluating very long-term conversational memory of LLM agents. ArXiv (2024), https://doi.org/10.48550/arXiv.2402.17753
23. McDonald, N., Schoenebeck, S., Forte, A.: Reliability and inter-rater reliability in qualitative research: norms and guidelines for CSCW and HCI practice. Proc. ACM Hum.-Comput. Interact. **3**(CSCW) (2019). https://doi.org/10.1145/3359174
24. OpenAI: OpenAI developer. https://platform.openai.com/ (2025), Accessed 24 Jun 2025
25. Paulus, P.B., Kenworthy, J.B.: Effective brainstorming. In: The Oxford handbook of group creativity and innovation, pp. 287–305 (2019). https://doi.org/10.1093/oxfordhb/9780190648077.013.17
26. Quintana, D.S., Williams, D.R.: Bayesian alternatives for common null-hypothesis significance tests in psychiatry: a non-technical guide using JASP. BMC Psychiatry **18**(1), 178 (2018). https://doi.org/10.1186/s12888-018-1761-4
27. de Rooij, A.: Inner speaking and uncertainty during idea generation. J. Creative Behav. **57**(3), 376–396 (2023). https://doi.org/10.1002/jocb.584
28. de Rooij, A., Biskjaer, M.M.: Has AI surpassed humans in creative idea generation? A meta-analysis, April 2025. https://doi.org/10.31234/osf.io/9u2ke_v1
29. de Rooij, A., van den Broek, S., Bouw, M., de Wit, J.: Co-designing with a social robot facilitator: effects of robot mood expression on human group dynamics. In: Proceedings of the 11th International Conference on Human-Agent Interaction (HAI 2023), pp. 22–29. ACM, Gothenburg, Sweden (2023). https://doi.org/10.1145/3623809.3623820
30. Rosenberg-Kima, R.B., Koren, Y., Gordon, G.: Robot-supported collaborative learning (RSCL): social robots as teaching assistants for higher education small group facilitation. Front. Robot. AI **6** (2020). https://doi.org/10.3389/frobt.2019.00148
31. Runco, M.A., Jaeger, G.J.: The standard definition of creativity. Creat. Res. J. **24**(1), 92–96 (2012). https://doi.org/10.1080/10400419.2012.650092
32. Shaer, O., Cooper, A., Mokryn, O., Kun, A.L., Shoshan, H.B.: AI-augmented brainwriting: Investigating the use of LLMs in group ideation. In: Proceedings of the CHI Conference on Human Factors in Computing Systems (2024). https://doi.org/10.1145/3613904.3642414

33. Strazdas, D., Hintz, J., Felßberg, A.M., Al-Hamadi, A.: Robots and wizards: an investigation into natural human-robot interaction. IEEE Access **8**, 207635–207642 (2020). https://doi.org/10.1109/ACCESS.2020.3037724
34. Taheri, A., Khatiri, S., Seyyedzadeh, A., Pour, A.G., Siamy, A., Meghdari, A.: Investigating the impact of human-robot collaboration on creativity and team efficiency: a case study on brainstorming in presence of robots, pp. 94–103 (2023). https://doi.org/10.1007/978-981-99-8715-3_9
35. van den Broek, S., Sankaran, S., de Wit, J., de Rooij, A.: Exploring the supportive role of artificial intelligence in participatory design: a systematic review. In: Proceedings of the 18th Biennial Participatory Design Conference. PDC 2024, ACM, New York, NY, USA (2024). https://doi.org/10.1145/3661455.3669868
36. Vrins, A., Pruss, E., Prinsen, J., Ceccato, C., Alimardani, M.: Are you paying attention? The effect of embodied interaction with an adaptive robot tutor on user engagement and learning performance. Springer Nature Switzerland (2022). https://doi.org/10.1007/978-3-031-24670-8_13
37. Williams, T., Matuszek, C., Mead, R., Depalma, N.: Scarecrows in Oz: the use of large language models in HRI. J. Hum.-Robot Interact. **13**(1) (2024). https://doi.org/10.1145/3606261
38. Zhang, C., Chen, J., Li, J., Peng, Y., Mao, Z.: Large language models for human-robot interaction: a review. Biomimetic Intell. Robot. **3**(4), 100131 (2023). https://doi.org/10.1016/j.birob.2023.100131
39. Zhao, Y., et al.: Assessing and understanding creativity in large language models. ArXiv (2024), https://doi.org/10.48550/arXiv.2401.12491

Towards Memory-Driven Agentic AI for Human Activity Recognition

Mohamadreza Shahabian Alashti[1](✉), Khashayar Ghamati[1](✉), Hooman Samani[2], and Abolfazl Zaraki[1]

[1] School of Physics, Engineering and Computer Science (SPECS) and Robotics Research Group, University of Hertfordshire, Hatfield AL10 9AB, UK
{m.r.shahabian,k.ghamati}@herts.ac.uk
[2] Creative Computing Institute, University of the Arts London, London, UK
https://ghamati.com/har-agent

Abstract. This paper proposes a novel, scalable agentic AI architecture designed to enhance human activity recognition across data modalities by embedding memory-driven reasoning and context awareness. The architecture integrates multimodal sensing, deliberative reasoning through supervised learning and context-aware language models, and memory mechanisms, including short-term memory for tracking immediate activity transitions and long-term memory for embedding experiential knowledge. The evaluation of the proposed model using two major datasets namely RHM (6.7K video clips of 14 known activities) and Toyota Smart Home (16K video clips of 31 unknown activities) demonstrates significant improvements, achieving 60% accuracy when combining contextual information with supervised model output, compared to 40% accuracy with context alone and 35% with supervised models on unseen data. By overcoming the limitations of traditional HAR approaches, this research advances the development of responsive and intelligent robotic systems, facilitating more natural and effective human-robot collaboration.

1 Introduction

The advent of agentic AI represents a pivotal evolution in artificial intelligence, empowering systems to autonomously perceive, reason, and act within dynamic environments [8]. Unlike conventional AI, which operates on fixed rules or static data, agentic AI leverages experiential learning to adapt and improve over time [23]. This adaptability makes it ideal for diverse applications, such as autonomous vehicles, healthcare diagnostics, and personalised assistants, where systems must respond to unpredictable conditions. By continuously learning from interactions, agentic AI enhances its decision-making capabilities, offering robust solutions that evolve with real-world demands.

In human-robot interaction (HRI), agentic AI introduces transformative advantages by enabling robots to interpret and respond to human behaviours in a context-sensitive manner [10,12,16]. This capability allows robots to collaborate seamlessly with humans, whether in social settings, such as assisting individuals, or industrial environments, where they adapt to workers' varying expertise. The experiential learning of agentic AI makes natural, trust-building interactions, as robots refine their responses over time. This adaptability not only improves interaction quality but also enhances user acceptance, making agentic AI a cornerstone for effective HRI [26,27].

Human Activity Recognition (HAR) is fundamental to HRI, as it equips robots with the ability to accurately interpret human actions [4,11]. This understanding is vital for anticipating needs, preventing misunderstandings, and delivering timely support. For instance, in an assistive living scenario, a robot must differentiate between a person cooking and momentarily checking their phone to prioritise its assistance correctly. Effective HAR ensures that robots align their behaviours with human intentions, directly influencing the success of interactions and the reliability of robotic systems in human-centric environments.

Current HAR methods exhibit strengths and limitations. Skeleton-based models, such as M-LeNet [2,22,28], excel at capturing human biomechanics and achieve high accuracy on labelled datasets, making them valuable for structured activity recognition. However, these models falter in distinguishing activities with similar motion patterns, like lifting an object versus standing, and lack awareness of environmental context, objects, or semantic details. For example, they might confuse *drinking water* with *raising a hand* without recognising a glass nearby. Conversely, contextual models offer broader environmental insights but often sacrifice precision in activity recognition, underscoring the need for integrated approaches that combine biomechanical and contextual understanding [25]. Memory plays a critical role in overcoming these HAR limitations by enabling systems to retain and leverage past experiences. Sequential methods like Long Short-Term Memory (LSTM) network [13], and Gated Recurrent Units have attempted to capture temporal dependencies, but they are insufficient for handling complex contextual information or retrieving it in real time. These models typically focus on short-term patterns, failing to integrate long-term knowledge, such as considering sequences of activities. Incorporating both short-term and long-term memory (LTM) into HAR is essential for tracking activity transitions, distinguishing primary from secondary actions, and adapting to evolving behaviours, thereby enhancing recognition accuracy and responsiveness [20].

To address the pressing challenges in HAR within HRI, this paper proposes an experiential agentic AI architecture that unifies multimodal sensing, contextual reasoning, and memory mechanisms. The framework integrates sensory input from diverse modalities to capture human activities and environmental cues, combines this with deliberative reasoning through supervised learning models and large contextual models, and incorporates both short-term and long-term memory to manage temporal dynamics and contextual alignment. This synergy empowers the system to interpret human actions with greater precision, adapt behaviour based on situational context, and continuously refine its understanding through accumulated experience, key capabilities for enabling responsive and adaptive robotic systems. Although Agentic AI architectures are still in their early stages, our approach demonstrates promising performance on benchmark datasets such as RHM [3] and Toyota Smart Home [9], suggesting a scalable pathway for future HRI developments. The main contributions of this work are threefold. First, we introduce a generic agentic AI architecture for HAR in HRI that is inherently adaptable to various data modalities, ensuring broad applicability across interaction scenarios. Second, we fuse supervised learning, contextual reasoning, and hierarchical memory structures to improve the system's capability to recognise activity transitions and maintain coherent context over time. Finally, we offer insights into memory-driven, context-aware activity recognition as a critical step towards more intelligent and socially aware robots, laying the groundwork for future advances in human-robot collaboration.

2 State-Of-The-Art Developments of Agentic AI for HRI

This review supports the proposed agentic AI architecture by examining three key areas: agentic AI in HRI, memory mechanisms in HAR, and context-aware HAR approaches. These areas enhance robots' ability to understand and react to human behaviors. The subsections cover autonomous decision-making, temporal data retention for better predictions, and the use of environmental cues for improved recognition.

Agentic AI in HRI. Agentic AI systems are characterised by their ability to autonomously perceive, reason, and act in dynamic environments, drawing from social cognitive theory's concept of agency [6]. In HRI, agentic AI enables robots to interpret human behaviours and adapt responses contextually, fostering natural and effective collaboration [16]. For instance, [7] developed a cognitive architecture integrating geometric reasoning and multi-modal dialogue, allowing robots to share tasks with humans seamlessly. Recent frameworks distinguish multi-agent systems, which maintain agent autonomy, from Centaurian systems, which deeply integrate human and AI capabilities. Bornet et al. [8] propose a five-level autonomy framework, positioning adaptive learning systems as critical for advanced HRI. Our architecture aligns with this paradigm, combining reactive and deliberative components to enhance HRI through context-aware HAR.

Memory Mechanisms in HAR. Memory is pivotal in HAR, enabling systems to retain temporal and contextual information to distinguish primary from secondary activities. Traditional sequential models, such as RNNs, LSTM networks [13], and GRUs, capture short-term dependencies. However, these models struggle with long-term dependencies and fail to integrate rich contextual information, limiting their ability to adapt in real-time scenarios [14]. Memory-augmented neural networks, which incorporate explicit memory units, offer a promising alternative by enabling robust storage and retrieval of high-dimensional data [15]. Autobiographical memory systems further enhance experiential learning

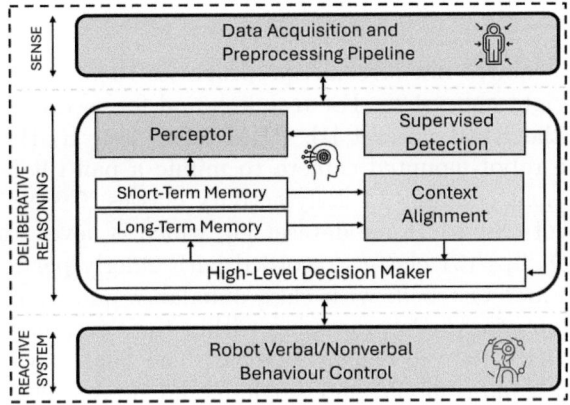

Fig. 1. Overview of the Agentic AI architecture for HRI, comprising sensing, reasoning, and reactive layers to enable memory-driven, context-aware HAR.

by encoding interaction histories [20]. Our approach leverages short-term memory (STM) for tracking activity transitions and long-term memory (LTM) for contextual alignment, addressing the limitations of sequential models.

Context-Aware HAR. Context-aware HAR integrates environmental and situational data to provide a holistic understanding of human activities, surpassing the limitations of motion-centric models [25]. Skeleton-based models, such as M-LeNet [4], excel at capturing biomechanical patterns but lack awareness of objects or semantic context. In contrast, context-aware approaches incorporate multimodal inputs, such as visual and sensor data, to disambiguate similar activities [18]. Neuro-symbolic methods combine data-driven learning with semantic reasoning, improving generalisation across diverse scenarios [5]. LLMs enhance HAR by providing semantic descriptions that complement skeletal data. Our architecture integrates supervised learning with LLMs to align biomechanical and contextual information, improving activity recognition accuracy in HRI.

3 Developing the Agentic AI Model for HRI

Building on the need for robots to accurately interpret human activities in dynamic environments, as highlighted in the introduction, this section presents our agentic AI architecture. The architecture integrates multimodal sensing, deliberative reasoning, and memory mechanisms to address the limitations of current HAR methods and enhance HRI. Specifically, it focuses on distinguishing primary activities from transient ones, a challenge discussed in the literature review, by leveraging both STM and LTM to track activity transitions and align environmental contexts. The proposed experiential agentic AI model is illustrated in Fig. 1, with subsequent subsections describing each component in detail.

3.1 Sense

The Sense layer acquires raw streams, preprocesses them, and dispatches each modality to the right subsystem. For training, and for seeding long-term memory, we rely on the RHM dataset [1]. RHM offers four RGB viewpoints, but we keep only the robot-mounted camera to mimic a pan-tilt head that tracks the subject; the split contains 14 daily-activity classes. Generalisation is measured on the Toyota Smart Home dataset [9], which is never used for training. Its 16115 RGB-D clips (31 classes, recorded with elderly participants) provide the "unseen, real-life" test bed, with class imbalance and overlapping motions that stress-test robustness. Preprocessing within the Sense layer is essential to prepare the raw data for subsequent analysis. The Sense layer is designed to accommodate both multi-modal and single-modal inputs, channelling specific data streams to designated components. For example, skeletal data is directed to the supervised detector, while image frames are processed by the Perceptor to extract semantic and contextual features. A single YOLOv7-pose extractor (17 joints) is run on both datasets so that the supervised HAR block (M-LeNet) always receives skeletons produced by the same pipeline. To keep the context-aware branch responsive, we forward just one RGB frame out of every ten to LLaVA; the intervening frames supply skeletons only.

3.2 Deliberative Reasoning

The Deliberative Reasoning layer is the core of the agent's autonomous decision-making process, combining supervised learning, contextual reasoning, and memory mechanisms to interpret human activities accurately. This layer consists of five key components: M-LeNet for skeleton-based HAR, a Perceptor for environmental context extraction, a Context Alignment (CA) module for integrating skeletal and contextual data, and STM and LTM for tracking activity transitions and aligning contexts. High-level decision maker processes the CA outputs to predict activities.

Supervised Detection: M-LeNet for Skeleton-Based HAR. The Supervised Detection block is a modular component designed to process modality-specific behavioural data using supervised learning models. In this implementation, we employ M-LeNet, a tailored 2D CNN, for skeleton-based HAR. M-LeNet processes skeleton data transformed into a 34×34 tensor image, capturing spatial and temporal dynamics efficiently.

M-LeNet Architecture. Adapted from LeNet, M-LeNet features two convolutional layers with 3×3 kernels and channel configurations of 10–20 (low-capacity) or 20–40 (high-capacity). Regularisation is achieved via two dropout layers ($p = 0.25$ and $p = 0.5$), and the model includes three fully connected layers to enhance learning capacity.

Performance. On the SK-HAR dataset, M-LeNet achieves approximately 90% accuracy with the high-capacity configuration, trained using categorical cross-entropy and Adam optimiser (learning rate 0.001) over 50 epochs.

Adaptability. The block is designed to be modality-agnostic, allowing integration of alternative models such as 3D CNNs for video frames or 1D CNNs for audio signals, ensuring flexibility across diverse behavioural modalities.

Perceptor. The Perceptor module analyses the environment to understand human behavior, which is crucial for accurate HAR. It processes video frames from the data pipeline, extracting detailed information and storing each frame's description in STM to track changes over time, such as activity transitions. The process begins by sending the first frame to the LLaVA [17] model, which generates a description of the scene. For each subsequent frame, the description of the previous frame is combined with the current frame and passed back to LLaVA to produce a more enriched result. To enhance accuracy, LLaVA uses the activity predicted by the M-LeNet model as additional metadata in its prompts for each frame. Each frame's description is saved in the STM, which starts empty for the first frame and grows as more descriptions are added. Once all frames are processed, the accumulated descriptions in the STM are sent to the Qwen model [24], which extracts up to five keywords summarising the environment's main context (e.g., *Drinking, Cup, Wine, Table, Chair* for a drinking activity). These keywords are then passed to the Context Alignment module. The STM's role is vital, as it aggregates frame descriptions, enabling LLaVA to detect activity transitions and providing Qwen with a comprehensive view of the environment for effective keyword extraction.

Context Alignment. At the heart of our agent lies the Context Alignment module, which employs probabilistic methods to identify relationships between the extracted words obtained from the Perceptor and the known tasks stored in Long-Term Memory. Specifically, this module computes the probability that an extracted word belongs to one of the pre-trained tasks. By doing so, it enables the agent to infer additional information regarding the primary activity currently unfolding in the environment. If the computed probability exceeds 60%, the associated keypoints are considered to relate to a known task, thereby simplifying the distinction between concurrent activities. Conversely, if the probability falls below this threshold, the context is deemed unrelated to keypoints. Put differently, since LLaVA constructs an STM-based model according to the M-LeNet's predictions, a probability above 60% indicates that the extracted words correspond to a class represented in the training dataset, thus suggesting a meaningful relation between keypoints and context. To compute this probability, we utilise conditional probability in conjunction with the Jaccard Index [21] to derive the posterior probability. This calculated posterior determines whether newly encountered words are associated with any of the tasks previously encoded within the agent's LTM. In each interaction, the agent considers every keyword as a random variable. The sample space for each interaction encompasses all potential words, including both pre-existing entries in LTM and newly observed terms. We assume a uniform distribution, employing its Probability Mass Function (PMF) to facilitate probability calculations. Following each interaction, LTM is updated if the High-Level Decision Maker module validates that the association between keypoints and context yields a meaningful contribution towards activity recognition. This update integrates newly encountered keywords and incrementally adjusts frequency counts for recurring terms, a process critical for maintaining accurate likelihood estimations. Evaluation of the CA module at each interaction is governed by Eq. 1:

$$P(T_i \mid w_1, w_2, \ldots, w_n) \propto P(T_i) \cdot \prod_{j=1}^{n} P(w_j \mid T_i) \qquad (1)$$

Here, $P(T_i)$ denotes the prior probability of task T_i, while $P(w_j \mid T_i)$ represents the likelihood that word w_j belongs to task T_i. Empirical evaluation reveals that the number of words per task varies dynamically due to ongoing LTM updates. As the PMF of a uniform distribution is obtained by dividing the frequency of a word by the total number of words in a task, frequently performed tasks exhibit decreasing probabilities over time, potentially leading to unreliable predictions. To counter this, we incorporate the Jaccard Index as an alternative prior, thereby accounting for disparities in word list sizes. The revised computation, employing the Jaccard Index as the prior, is expressed in Eq. 2:

$$P(T_i \mid w_1, w_2, \ldots, w_n) \propto J(T_i, W) \cdot \left(\prod_{j=1}^{n} P(w_j \mid T_i) \right) \qquad (2)$$

The Jaccard Index $J(T_i, W)$ is determined using Eq. 3, where $\text{intersect}(T_i, W)$ denotes the number of new words that are already present within T_i, and $\text{union}(T, W)$ represents the total number of unique words across both the LTM and newly encountered sets:

$$J(T_i, W) = \frac{|\text{intersect}(T_i, W)|}{|\text{union}(T, W)|} \qquad (3)$$

In computing the posterior probability, we first calculate the Jaccard Index (Eq. 3), then, applying Bayes' rule, transform $P(T_j \mid w_j)$ into $P(w_j \mid T_j)$ as shown in Eq. 5. The likelihood function $P(w_j \mid T_i)$ is calculated according to Eq. 4, while $P(T_i)$, being uniform across all tasks, is computed via Eq. 6:

$$P(w_j \mid T_i) = \frac{\text{Total frequency of } w_j \text{ in task } T_i}{\text{Total frequency of all words in task } T_i} \qquad (4)$$

$$P(T_i \mid w_j) = \frac{P(w_j \mid T_i) \cdot P(T_i)}{\sum_j P(w_j \mid T_j) \cdot P(T_j)} \qquad (5)$$

$$P(T_i) = \frac{1}{\text{Number of Tasks}} \qquad (6)$$

Upon evaluating Eq. 2, the resultant posterior probability is passed to the High-Level Decision Maker module. Here, it is scrutinised to predict the principal activity occurring in the environment relative to the agent's existing LTM. Should the probability fall below 60%, the combination is deemed insufficiently

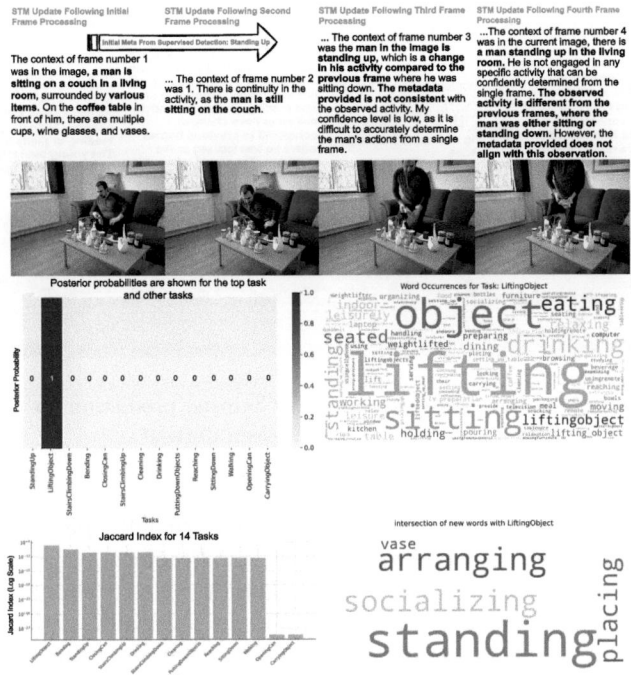

Fig. 2. Context Alignment module refines the initial *standing up* prediction to *lifting an object* by combining keypoints with contextual cues over four frames.

informative for further processing or reasoning. In this case, the results of the Supervised method should be considered. This mechanism enables the agent to utilise environmental context alongside keypoints, thereby enhancing its understanding of ongoing activities and enabling it to identify the primary activity with greater confidence and precision.

4 Proof of Concept Evaluation

To evaluate our proposed agentic AI system, we utilised two datasets. Initially, we assessed the system using the dataset on which the model had originally been trained, followed by an evaluation on a distinct dataset to investigate its adaptability to unfamiliar scenarios. Our experiments demonstrated that, upon encountering a new activity, the agent's supervised model can initially produce an activity label based on keypoint features extracted from the training data. However, the integration of contextual information significantly enhances predictive accuracy. For example, Fig. 4a illustrates the agent's inference process after analysing four consecutive frames depicting a specific activity. When only the first frame is considered, the CA identifies the action as *sitting*, based on both the environmental context and the output of the supervised model. However,

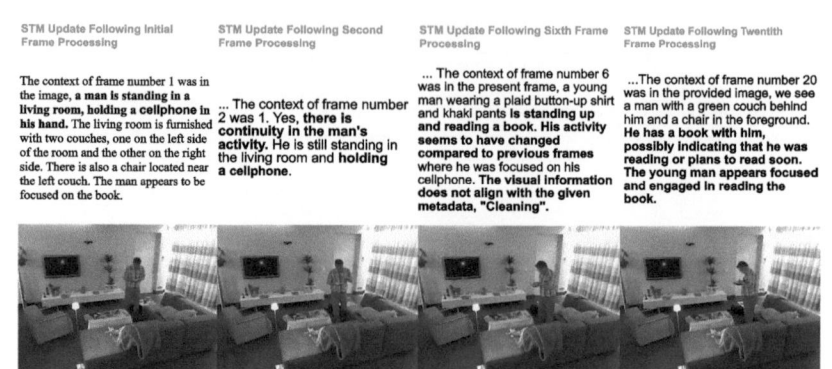

Fig. 3. Context Alignment revises the initial *Cleaning* prediction to *Carrying Object* by integrating contextual keywords from an unseen dataset.

by incrementally processing all four frames, and crucially, passing the result of each frame to the next via the STM, the agent becomes aware of the activity transition (e.g., from sitting to standing), thereby constructing a more coherent and complete interpretation. Moreover, the agent is capable of inferring that the participant is lifting an object (e.g., a napkin), thereby refining its prediction to either lifting or standing up. The latter label originates from the supervised model, while the former emerges through the integration of contextual cues.

This illustrates the CA module's capacity to synthesise environmental context with the outputs of the supervised model, increasing overall confidence without an over-reliance on supervision alone. To construct the STM, the outputs from the supervised model were passed as metadata to the LLaVA model, which generated frame-level descriptions. After all four frames were processed and the STM was updated accordingly, this enriched memory was then passed to the Qwen model, which was prompted to extract the five most salient keywords from the generated descriptions. This novel mechanism enables the agent to track temporal transitions and more reliably identify the primary activity. Figure 2 demonstrates these results. The top row depicts the evolution of STM across the four frames, wherein LLaVA's outputs are concatenated with previous content and fed back into LLaVA alongside the new frame. The second row presents the original frames, where the supervised model predicted standing up. However, with the inclusion of contextual data, the CA accurately determined that the participant was in fact lifting an object (napkin), yielding a more accurate interpretation.

The third and fourth rows show the Jaccard index and its effect on posterior probability values. These visualisations also present all keywords associated with the Lifting Object activity during training (stored in LTM), highlighting the overlap between keywords derived from STM (via Qwen) and those previously encountered. The size of each word denotes its frequency in the training data; for example, Lifting appears larger due to its higher frequency in relevant contexts. Additionally, we tested the agent on a previously unseen dataset to evaluate its generalisability. Figure 3 shows four randomly selected frames from a video in which a participant is reading a book. After analysing all 36 frames of this sequence, the CA module inferred the activity as carrying an object, whereas the supervised model incorrectly classified it as cleaning. This example highlights how STM supports more accurate activity tracking across frames, enabling superior inference prior to final decision-making. At the same time, the LTM module contributes experiential knowledge that improves the agent's ability to generalise in unfamiliar scenarios.

To validate the CA module's output, we rely on posterior probability values. If the value exceeds 60%, the output is accepted. To visualise incorrect predictions, we are using ChatGPT [19] to generate an image based on STM content. Figure 4a shows an example from Fig. 3, where ChatGPT produced an image based on the STM's detailed textual description, which preserved the core elements of the original frames. In contrast, Fig. 4b depicts a case where the STM-based inference, generated by the Perceptor module, was vague and did not correspond well with the input frames and the posterior probability for this activity was below 60%. Based on this methodology, we processed videos from both datasets encompassing various activities to assess the agent's performance. We observe that combining contextual information with keypoints improved accuracy to 60%. In contrast, relying solely on context, without incorporating the supervised model, achieved only 40% accuracy. This indicates that environmental cues alone are insufficient to determine the underlying activity.

To obtain these results, we initially ran the agent without the supervised model, omitting its outputs as metadata for the Perceptor module. Accuracy was then calculated as the ratio of correctly classified videos to the total. In the second phase, we reintroduced the supervised model and passed its outputs to Perceptor to aid frame analysis via LLaVA, using the same evaluation procedure. Additionally, we observe that the supervised model alone, when applied to unfamiliar data, could at best provide a top-5 prediction set that included at least one semantically related activity. For example, when attempting to classify eating, the top labels included sitting and drinking. On this basis, we evaluated the model's standalone accuracy on the unseen Toyota dataset, which was approximately 35%. In contrast, its accuracy on the RHM dataset, on which it had been trained, was approximately 90%. We evaluated performance using 600 video clips from the Toyota dataset and 140 clips from the RHM dataset.

5 Discussion

In this study, we demonstrated the advantages of integrating memory-driven reasoning and contextual awareness into an agentic AI architecture for HAR in HRI. By combining short-term memory with contextual insights derived from LLMs such as LLaVA and Qwen, our model achieves a more nuanced and accurate understanding of human activities, effectively distinguishing primary actions

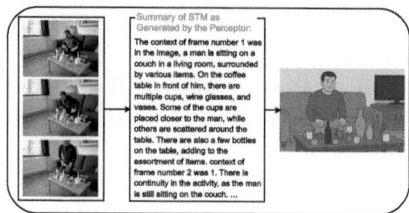 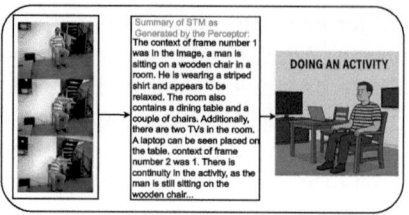

(a) Correct prediction: the image generated by ChatGPT based on the STM's textual description closely matches the original input frames.

(b) Incorrect prediction: the image generated by ChatGPT from the STM's textual description fails to align with the original input frames.

Fig. 4. Comparison of ChatGPT-generated images based on STM content. (a) shows a successful case with coherent STM representation; (b) illustrates a failure case due to vague STM content.

from transient or secondary behaviours. This advancement addresses a critical limitation of traditional HAR methods, which often struggle to interpret complex or overlapping activities in dynamic environments. Our results underscore the pivotal role of memory and context in enhancing HAR for HRI. The integration of STM enables the model to track activity transitions across multiple frames, crucial for accurately identifying primary activities in scenarios with overlapping actions, such as using a computer while drinking tea. Single-frame analyses, in contrast, frequently misclassify secondary actions, highlighting the necessity of temporal context. Additionally, incorporating environmental context via LLMs resolves ambiguities in activities with similar skeletal movements, such as standing up versus lifting an object, where traditional skeleton-based models like M-LeNet falter. The agentic AI framework, combining supervised learning, contextual reasoning, and memory, aligns with our objective of developing a flexible, experiential model adaptable to multiple data modalities. This approach not only improves recognition accuracy but also enhances contextual responsiveness, fostering natural human-robot collaboration.

A critical aspect of our architecture is the use of prompts to guide LLMs in extracting relevant contextual information from the environment. Prompts are designed to steer models like LLaVA toward key environmental features and activity transitions, producing precise frame descriptions stored in STM. These descriptions are then processed by Qwen to identify salient keywords for the Context Alignment module. Well-crafted prompts, balancing specificity and generality, are essential to ensure focus on pertinent details without introducing bias. For example, integrating supervised model predictions into prompts as metadata enhances alignment with biomechanical cues, improving differentiation of similar activities. However, poorly designed prompts can introduce noise or irrelevant data, underscoring the need for ongoing refinement in prompt engineering. Traditional HAR approaches, whether skeleton-based or context-centric, exhibit notable limitations. Skeleton-based models excel in structured activity recognition but lack environmental and semantic awareness, leading to misclassifications in visually similar activities. Context-centric models offer broader insights but sacrifice precision in activity-specific recognition. Our architecture overcomes these shortcomings by integrating biomechanical and contextual information, achieving a comprehensive understanding of human behaviour. This synergy is evident in our experiments, where combining context with keypoints yielded 60% accuracy, surpassing context-only (40%) or supervised-only (35% on unseen data) approaches.

While our architecture significantly enhances accuracy and adaptability, it introduces challenges. The integration of sensing, reasoning, and memory components increases system complexity, potentially complicating implementation in resource-constrained environments. However, the modular design allows for component optimisation without compromising the framework. Additionally, processing multiple frames and extensive contextual data may hinder real-time performance, a critical requirement in HRI. Techniques such as CNN for efficient feature extraction could mitigate this, as demonstrated in real-time HAR studies. Notably, the primary focus of this research is to demonstrate the potential of memory-driven, context-aware agentic AI, with increased complexity as a necessary trade-off for improved performance. Future refinements will address these concerns. The ability to accurately recognise human activities contextually has profound implications for assistive robotics, healthcare, and industrial applications, enabling robots to anticipate user needs and enhance safety. The experiential learning capabilities of agentic AI foster trust and acceptance in HRI by refining responses over time. Future research should focus on optimising memory mechanisms, fine-tuning LLMs for efficiency and accuracy, and exploring hybrid approaches that balance real-time performance with robust recognition, building on the scalable foundation provided by this work.

6 Conclusion

In conclusion, our research demonstrates the substantial benefits of integrating agentic AI architectures with memory-driven reasoning for improved human activity recognition in HRI. By combining skeletal and contextual information through sophisticated memory mechanisms, our approach significantly surpasses traditional HAR methodologies, offering a robust framework capable of discerning complex human activities with greater accuracy and reliability. The inclusion of STM and LTM has proven essential for capturing both immediate activity transitions and long-term contextual associations, thereby enhancing robotic responsiveness and adaptability in dynamic environments. Future work will explore the fine-tuning of foundational models and the optimisation of memory structures to further improve computational efficiency and semantic precision. Ultimately, our architecture presents a scalable and adaptable solution, paving the way for more natural, intuitive, and effective human-robot collaborations.

References

1. Abadi, M.B., Alashti, M.R.S., Holthaus, P., Menon, C., Amirabdollahian, F.: RHM: robot house multi-view human activity recognition dataset. In: ACHI 2023: The Sixteenth International Conference on Advances in Computer-Human Interactions. IARIA (2023)
2. Alashti, M.R.S., Abadi, M.B., Holthaus, P., Menon, C., Amirabdollahian, F.: Lightweight human activity recognition for ambient assisted living. In: ACHI 2023: The Sixteenth International Conference on Advances in Computer-Human Interactions. IARIA (2023)
3. Alashti, M.R.S., Abadi, M.B., Holthaus, P., Menon, C., Amirabdollahian, F.: RH-HAR-SK: a multi-view dataset with skeleton data for ambient assisted living research. In: ACHI 2023: The Sixteenth International Conference on Advances in Computer-Human Interactions. IARIA (2023)
4. Alashti, M.R.S., Abadi, M.H.B., Holthaus, P., Menon, C., Amirabdollahian, F.: Efficient skeleton-based human activity recognition in ambient assisted living scenarios with multi-view CNN. In: 2024 10th IEEE RAS/EMBS International Conference for Biomedical Robotics and Biomechatronics (BioRob), pp. 979–984. IEEE (2024)
5. Arrotta, L., et al.: Neuro-symbolic approaches for context-aware human activity recognition. Pattern Recogn. **139**, 109–123 (2023)
6. Bandura, A.: Social cognitive theory: an agentic perspective. Ann. Rev. Psychol. **52**(1), 1–26 (2001)
7. Borghoff, U.M., Bottoni, P., Pareschi, R.: Human-artificial interaction in the age of agentic AI: a system-theoretical approach. Front. Hum. Dyn. **7**, 1579166 (2025)
8. Bornet, P., et al.: Agentic Artificial Intelligence: Harnessing AI Agents to Reinvent Business, Work and Life. Irreplaceable Publishing (2025)
9. Das, S., et al.: Toyota smarthome: real-world activities of daily living. In: The IEEE International Conference on Computer Vision (ICCV) (October 2019)
10. Ghamati, K., Amirabdollahian, F., Resende Faria, D., Zaraki, A.: Cognitive agentic AI: probabilistic novelty detection for continual adaptation in HRI. In: 2025 34th IEEE International Conference on Robot and Human Interactive Communication (ROMAN), pp. 1–7. IEEE (2025)
11. Ghamati, K., Banitalebi Dehkordi, M., Zaraki, A.: Towards AI-powered applications: the development of a personalised LLM for HRI and HCI. Sensors **25**(7), 2024 (2025)
12. Ghamati, K., Zaraki, A., Amirabdollahian, F.: ARI humanoid robot imitates human gaze behaviour using reinforcement learning in real-world environments. In: 2024 IEEE-RAS 23rd International Conference on Humanoid Robots (Humanoids), pp. 653–660. IEEE (2024)
13. Graves, A., Graves, A.: Long short-term memory. Supervised sequence labelling with recurrent neural networks, pp. 37–45 (2012)
14. Irfan, S., Anjum, N., Masood, N., Khattak, A.S., Ramzan, N.: A novel hybrid deep learning model for human activity recognition based on transitional activities. Sensors **21**(24), 8227 (2021)
15. Karunaratne, G., et al.: Robust high-dimensional memory-augmented neural networks. Nat. Commun. **12**(1), 2468 (2021)
16. Lemaignan, S., Warnier, M., Sisbot, E.A., Clodic, A., Alami, R.: Artificial cognition for social human-robot interaction: an implementation. Artif. Intell. **247**, 45–69 (2017)

17. Liu, H., Li, C., Wu, Q., Lee, Y.J.: Visual instruction tuning. In: Advances in Neural Information Processing Systems, vol. 36, pp. 34892–34916 (2023)
18. Niemann, J., et al.: Context-aware human-robot collaboration in assembly tasks. Robot. Comput. Integr. Manuf. **72**, 102–115 (2021)
19. OpenAI: Chatgpt (2024). https://chat.openai.com/. Accessed 30 Apr 2025
20. Pointeau, G., Dominey, P.F.: The role of autobiographical memory in the development of a robot self. Front. Neurorobot. **11**, 27 (2017)
21. Real, R.: Tables of significant values of Jaccard's index of similarity. Miscel· lania Zoologica, pp. 29–40 (1999)
22. Shahabian Alashti, M.R.: Human and activity detection in ambient assisted living scenarios (2024)
23. Silver, D., Sutton, R.S.: Welcome to the era of experience. Google AI **1** (2025)
24. Yang, Others: Qwen2.5 technical report. arXiv preprint arXiv:2412.15115 (2024)
25. Yurur, O., Liu, C.H., Moreno, W.: A survey of context-aware middleware designs for human activity recognition. IEEE Commun. Surv. Tutor. **16**(3), 1406–1424 (2014)
26. Zaraki, A., Mazzei, D., Giuliani, M., De Rossi, D.: Designing and evaluating a social gaze-control system for a humanoid robot. IEEE Trans. Hum. Mach. Syst. **44**(2), 157–168 (2014)
27. Zaraki, A., et al.: Design and evaluation of a unique social perception system for human-robot interaction. IEEE Trans. Cogn. Development. Syst. **9**(4), 341–355 (2016)
28. Zaraki, A., Giuliani, M., Dehkordi, M.B., Mazzei, D., D'ursi, A., De Rossi, D.: An RGB-D based social behavior interpretation system for a humanoid social robot. In: 2014 Second RSI/ISM International Conference on Robotics and Mechatronics (ICRoM), pp. 185–190. IEEE (2014)

Act-it-Out Method for Developing Robot Arm Actions and Semantic Commands

Luke Sanchez, Chirag Jain, Shrirang Patil, Bessie He, and Heather Knight(✉)

Oregon State University, Corvallis, OR 97330, USA
{sanchluk,jainc,patilshr,heyux,knighth}@oregonstate.edu

Abstract. People intuitively teach robots by physically demonstrating actions, especially for complex in-contact manipulation tasks such as scrubbing, writing, or inserting objects. This study introduces a novel Act-it-Out method in which participants directly guide a 7-DOF robot arm while providing verbal instructions, treating the robot as a data collection instrument. Through this method, we collected a multimodal dataset of 360 physically demonstrated trajectories and 155 verbal commands across varied task types and clutter conditions. We analyzed the data using Laban Movement Analysis (LMA) Effort features—Force, Space, and Time—to explore how humans express motion intent through both physical and verbal channels. Findings reveal that while spatial and temporal cues often appear in speech, critical force information is primarily conveyed somatically, underscoring a gap in semantic-somatic alignment. We also examined how coaching prompts influenced instructional style, showing that priming affected participants' emphasis on physical versus verbal guidance. This work contributes: (1) a novel Act-it-Out method for HRI data collection, (2) analysis of how motion qualities are distributed across somatic and semantic modes, (3) insights into coaching effects on communication, (4) a structured LMA-based feature space for learning from demonstration, and (5) a public dataset to support socially-aware robot learning from multimodal human input.

Keywords: Body Intelligence · Semantic Intelligence · Computational Laban Efforts · Natural Language · Act-it-Out Method · Somatic

1 Introduction

In an ideal scenario, how would people like robots to complete *in-contact manipulation* tasks? What motion and force qualities can they intuitively communicate via their own bodies and words? To investigate these questions, we collected *288 human action demonstrations* and *155 example "hey robot" commands*, creating a paired **Word:Action** dataset to study how humans physically demonstrate and verbally instruct a robot arm for contact-rich tasks. In this Act-it-Out approach, each participant first guides the robot through a task demonstration and then issues a corresponding verbal command.

The experimental design asks participants to act out tasks where a robot arm maintains contact with a surface (requiring continuous force and motion control), relevant to cleaning or sanding a surface [25], or drawing/erasing/plugging as in Fig. 1. We define in-contact manipulation to include a robot arm, tool, and work surface, which differs from the more commonly studied pick-and-place manipulation (moving free objects) [11]. This emphasis on sustained contact and force control is less explored in the literature compared to classic pick-and-place tasks [4], particularly in regards to underwater robots. Example applications include robotic welding and maintenance operations in hazardous or hard-to-reach settings [15], where robots must regulate force while performing a task on a surface [14]. By studying how humans approach these tasks, we aim to inform human-in-loop and autonomous robot controllers that can handle such complex interactions.

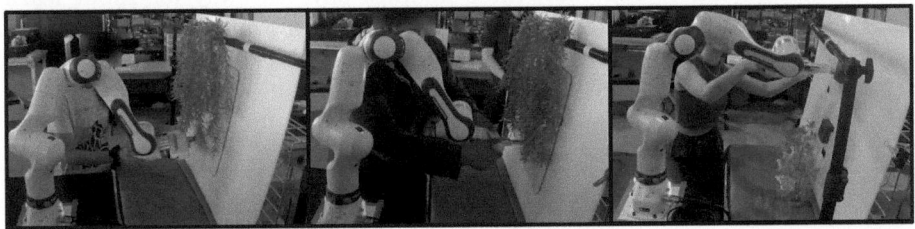

Fig. 1. Three unique participants ACTING OUT robot actions by physically guiding the Franka PR3 robot arm through different in-contact manipulation tasks (drawing/erasing/plugging), with differing clutter conditions. All trials included a backboard WORKSPACE, collecting Act-it-Out examples and Hey Robot exemplar commands.

Prior work in human-robot interaction (HRI) suggests that humans possess rich intuitions for communicating motion. Researchers have leveraged frameworks from human movement training, such as Laban Movement Analysis (LMA), to give structured feedback on robot motion quality [3]. The LMA Effort system describes motion along four qualitative dimensions: *Force* (or Weight, e.g., strong vs. light effort), *Space* (direct vs. flexible focus), *Time* (sudden vs. sustained timing), and *Flow* (bound vs. free continuity). Force, Space, and Time in particular can be computed from physical trajectories, making them promising features for interpreting human demonstrations and commands. We ask: can human operators use their own bodily understanding and language to flexibly instruct robots along these Laban Effort qualities?

To explore this, we posit three hypotheses about human instruction of robots:

- **Somatic Hypothesis:** People have an intrinsic body intelligence that they will express through action demonstrations, intuitively varying their motions in line with Laban's Force, Space, and Time features.

- **Semantic Hypothesis:** People have linguistic intelligence and will use verbal commands related to Force, Space, and Time to instruct a robot.
- **Coaching Hypothesis:** The way people are prompted or "coached" will direct their emphasis between bodily(somatic) and verbal(semantic) features

This study's contributions are threefold: (1) Introduction of an **open-source multimodal dataset** of human robot-arm demonstrations and corresponding natural language commands, with rich annotations of Laban Effort features. (2) Empirical insights from analysis of this data, showing how humans embody and communicate motion qualities of **Force, Space,** and **Time**. We highlight that communication occurs both via the body and via language – and importantly, that critical force cues are often conveyed somatically rather than verbally. (3) Demonstration of the viability of using **Laban Movement Analysis** as a unifying framework to design and interpret robot manipulation actions from human guidance. Together, these findings pave the way for robot learning algorithms that integrate **somatic** (demonstration) and **semantic** (verbal instruction) inputs to achieve more natural human-robot collaboration.

2 Related Work

2.1 Laban Movement Analysis in Robotics

Laban Movement Analysis (LMA) is a well-established method for describing the qualitative aspects of movement, originating from dance and acting training [6]. In robotics and HRI, LMA has been explored as a tool to both interpret human motions and generate expressive robot behaviors [3]. For example, researchers have adapted the Laban Effort system (focusing on Time, Weight (Force), Space, and Flow) to parametrize robot gestures and trajectories [21], enabling robots to convey emotions or intent through movement qualities [2], exemplified in Fig. 2. Knight et al. operationalized effort parameters in a "Computational Laban Effort" framework that allows a robot to modulate its joint motions to appear, for instance, sudden vs. sustained in *Time* or strong vs. light in *Weight* [13]. Such works show that LMA provides a human-interpretable vocabulary for motion, which can bridge the gap between how humans perceive movement and how robots plan motions [9]. Our work differs in that we use LMA not for robot-generated expressivity, but to analyze human-generated demonstrations and instructions [23]. Prior studies have hinted that human teachers use qualitative notions of effort when teaching robots [1]; here we explicitly measure if humans naturally encode Laban Effort features in their teaching, without being instructed in LMA terminology.

2.2 Learning from Demonstration and Multimodal Instruction

Teaching robots by demonstration is a well-researched paradigm in robotics [5]. Human teachers can physically guide a robot (as in kinesthetic teaching) or demonstrate tasks for the robot to imitate [1]. These methods leverage humans'

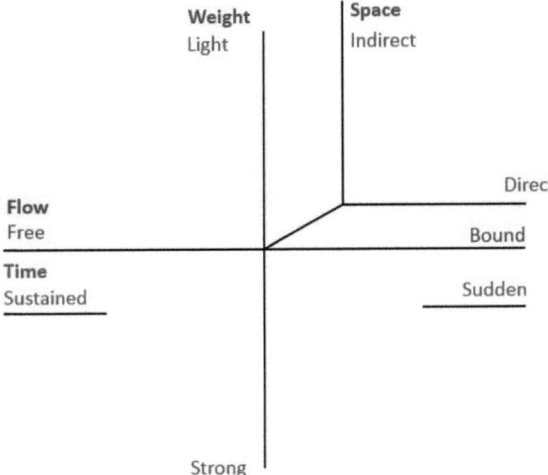

Fig. 2. Laban Effort graph illustrating the spectrum of motion qualities (Force, Space, Time, and Flow) analyzed in this study. Laban Effort features provide a structured framework to quantify and interpret how participants physically guided the robot arm.

intuitive ability to show "how it's done," capturing nuances like appropriate force application or trajectory shape that might be hard to specify in code [22]. However, pure demonstration can be ambiguous about intent or context [12]. On the other hand, instructing robots through natural language has advanced in parallel [24], enabling robots to parse commands like "move the arm to the upper left corner and wipe the surface" into executable actions. Language instructions are convenient and flexible, allowing users to specify goals or constraints at a high level [27], but they often omit low-level details and require the robot to interpret vague terms (e.g., what does "wipe clean" entail operationally?). Recent research on grounding language in robotic actions shows progress in mapping verbs and adjectives to motion parameters [16], but must decompose high-level instructions into robot actions [17].

Few works, however, have looked at *combining demonstration and language* in a complementary way. In human teaching [10], these modalities are often used together: a person might guide a robot arm while saying "like this, but gently," using both their body and words. This multimodal instruction could provide richer information than either channel alone [26], but it also raises questions: Do humans convey different information through each mode? Are there overlaps or omissions? Our study contributes to this area by capturing synchronized demonstration and verbal command data, allowing analysis of how the two modalities complement each other.

2.3 Human-Robot Interaction in Contact Tasks

Many robotic applications require maintaining contact; for instance, surface cleaning, polishing, or welding [15]. These tasks demand regulating contact force and trajectory simultaneously [19]. Traditional approaches in *underwater robotics* and other remote maintenance have relied on teleoperation or pre-programmed strategies, focusing on stability and safety due to the difficult environments [18]. Recent HRI research emphasizes incorporating human insight to improve performance in such tasks, whether through shared control, haptic feedback devices, or learning from demonstrations [20]. Our work aligns with this trend by studying how humans intuitively perform contact tasks [8]. We extend prior research by not only recording what humans do (trajectories, forces) but also what they say about the task. By analyzing both, we gain insight into how humans conceptualize contact tasks: for example, treating obstacle avoidance as a spatial problem (expressed in words) and treating force regulation as a felt experience (handled through doing). These insights can inform the design of robot autonomy in contact-rich tasks, suggesting that robots might benefit from an inner representation that separates force-related control (perhaps handled via kinesthetic teaching or haptic feedback loops) from spatial/temporal planning (which could be instructed via speech).

3 Act-it-Out Method

3.1 User-Study Design

An in-lab study was conducted to test the hypothesis. Each participant was asked to both physically demonstrate and also give verbal commands for a set of in-contact manipulation tasks using a 7-DOF robotic arm (Franka Emirka PR3 research platform). In each trial the participants physically guided the robot arm to perform a task (the somatic channel) and following the demonstration, then gave a spoken command (the semantic channel). Three representative in-contact manipulation tasks were: *Drawing* (additive) - using a marker to draw an X in a designated spot, *Erasing* (subtractive) - wiping off markings with an eraser, and *Plugging* (insertion) - inserting a peg into two designated holes on the board. Figure 1 shows an example of participants guiding the robot on an indirect path to avoid an obstacle while drawing.

To manage experimental complexity, each participant performed 12 trials split into two episodes of 6 trials each. *Episode 1* varied task type (Drawing vs. Erasing) and obstacle clutter. We used three clutter conditions: an obstacle at the top of the work area, one at the bottom, or obstacles at both top and bottom. In each trial, participants were instructed to "pick a marked target area and execute the specified task," giving them the opportunity to adapt their path if obstacles were present. The box in Fig. 3 shows the physical setup for the clutter conditions on the top and before and after for both drawing (bottom left) and erasing tasks (bottom right). *Episode 2* focused on material compliance variations during the Plugging task. Here, the task was always plugging a peg, but the compliance

Fig. 3. Experimental workspace illustrating varying clutter conditions used to test participants' adaptations in guiding the robot arm. The top image depicts different obstacle configurations (top clutter, bottom clutter, and both combined). Bottom images show before-and-after results of specific in-contact manipulation tasks performed by participants: drawing an 'X' (bottom left) and erasing markings (bottom right).

of the board backing and the peg receptacle varied throughout. Some trials used a rigid wall/receptacle (high resistance to insertion), others a springy wall or soft receptacle (low resistance), and combinations thereof. This tested how participants adapted their strategy to variable material stiffness. Across the 12 trials, each participant thus encountered a range of contexts: some requiring more precision and spatial adjustment (navigating around obstacles in Episode 1), and others demanding force modulation and timing (e.g., inserting a peg gently vs. forcefully in Episode 2).

Thirty participants were recruited from a convenience population (N=30) for the demonstration part of the study. Of these, 24 participants also provided verbal commands (some opted out of the speech part). Each participant was balance-controlled randomly assigned to one of four between-subject coaching conditions: **Kinesthetic, Kinematic, Semantic,** or **Control**. Prior to their first trial, each participant received a brief coaching prompt depending on their condition. In the *Kinesthetic* condition, we encouraged participants to "use your body like the robot's" – drawing analogies between their arm movements and the robot's, to prime awareness of somatic cues. In the *Kinematic* condition, we emphasized precise end-effector positioning and robot joint angles, priming them to focus on kinematic details. In the *Semantic* condition, participants were given example adverbs (e.g., "smoothly," "quickly," "gently") as descriptors for motions, priming them to think in descriptive language. The *Control* group received only a basic introduction to the robot with no specific strategic coaching. By manipulating this initial framing, this study investigates how coaching influences the balance of *somatic vs. semantic* information people provide.

3.2 Data Collection and Feature Extraction

Motion and audio data was synchronized for each trial. The robot's joint states (angles, velocities) and end-effector state were recorded at 100 Hz. The robot was operated in a gravity-compensated backdrivable mode, allowing participants to move the arm with minimal resistance while the system still measured forces/torques at each joint and the end-effector. This experimental setup transformed the robot into an interactive data collection instrument, making it feel like a weightless limb that participants could move naturally, while motion and force inputs were captured. Participants' spoken commands and strategy descriptions were recorded via a close-range microphone immediately after each trial, and then transcribed into text using bespoke speech-to-text software. Each transcript was paired with the corresponding trajectory data.

After data collection, the raw trajectories were processed by computing novel **Laban Effort Features** explicitly designed for this study to define a structured feature space essential for generating robot movements and supporting future machine learning applications. In LMA terms, the analysis emphasizes Effort aspects of *Weight (Force), Space,* and *Time*:

Force (Weight) Features: We derived metrics representing the effort exerted. For each demonstration trajectory, we calculated the mean, maximum, and minimum force/torque values at each joint over the contact duration, as well as a normalized (L2-norm) of the 7 joint torques with Eq. 1. Specifically, we focused on joint torques since those correlate with how much effort the participant put into pushing or resisting, specially looking at the mean effort per joint with Eq. 2 and maximum applied effort with Eq. 3.

$$\textbf{Normal Torque:} \text{Avg L2 Norm} = \frac{1}{n}\sum_{i=1}^{n}\sqrt{\sum_{j=1}^{7}\tau_{ij}^2} \qquad (1)$$

$$\textbf{Average Joint Torque:}\ \tau_{\text{avg}} = \frac{1}{7}\sum_{i=1}^{7}\tau_i \qquad (2)$$

$$\textbf{Max Torque:}\ \tau_{\max} = \max(\tau_1, \tau_2, \ldots, \tau_7) \qquad (3)$$

Space Features: Analysis of the geometry of the end-effector's path was conducted. The end-effector positions were tracked and segmented into phases: approach (moving to the workspace), task execution (while in contact), and retreat (moving away), shown in Fig. 4. Primary examination was the task execution phase where contact occurs. Key Space features included the total distance traveled by the end-effector on the surface, the directional extent of motions in the **X** (horizontal) and **Y** (into-surface depth) and **Z** (vertical) axes, and the path shape (e.g., whether movements were direct or had deviations). These LMA Space features reflect the agent's spatial strategy - for instance, taking an indirect path vs. a straight line. Space features included the total path length traveled by the end-effector on the surface (computed as the sum of Euclidean distances between successive points, Eq. 4)

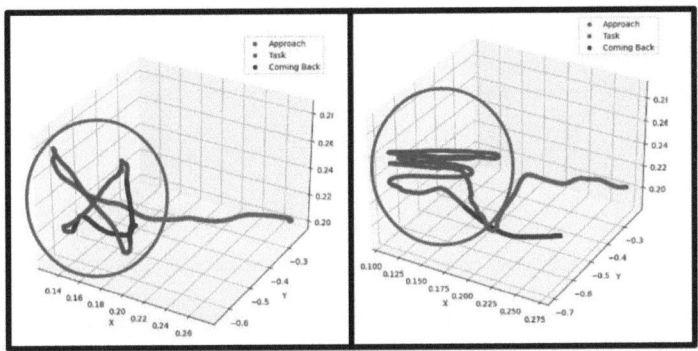

Fig. 4. Example of experimental trajectory data segmented into distinct task phases: approach (red), task execution (green), and retreat (blue). This segmentation clearly delineates the motion strategies employed by participants during physical demonstrations. (Color figure online)

$$\textbf{Euclidean:} \; d = \sum_{i=1}^{n-1} \sqrt{(x_{i+1} - x_i)^2 + (y_{i+1} - y_i)^2 + (z_{i+1} - z_i)^2} \quad (4)$$

Time Features: We segmented the timestamps to measure how long each phase took. Two primary temporal metrics were the approach time (time from start until initial contact with the surface or start of task motion) and the task execution time (duration from first contact to task completion). Laban Time is often related to urgency or a sense of rush, these correspond to how the participant paced the motion.

Comparisons across **coaching conditions** evaluated initial coaching influences. Specifically, analyses investigated whether the Semantic-coached group indeed employed richer descriptive language and whether the Kinesthetic-coached group exhibited distinctly higher force profiles. Analyses grouped data by coaching condition, examining feature means, qualitative language use, and statistical tests (ANOVA with Coaching as a between-subject factor).

All processed data and analysis code have been made available in our shared dataset repository. The **Speech2Action Dataset** includes the raw and processed trajectory data, transcripts and a summary of extracted features for each trial. By explicitly defining this feature space, this dataset offers foundational support for future research in generating robot movements, developing advanced software architectures, and training robust machine learning models. It is publicly accessible, with outlined experimental conditions, detailed in Fig. 5 at: www.kaggle.com/datasets/anonymizedxx/icm-trials/data

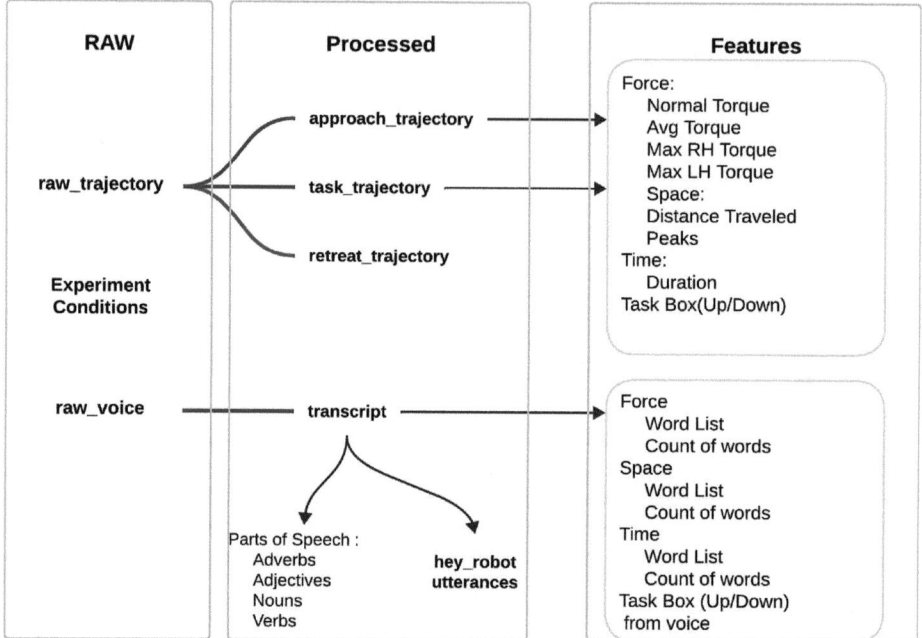

Fig. 5. Overview of dataset structure showing organization into raw recordings, processed trajectories, and extracted features labeled with Laban Effort dimensions (Force, Space, and Time) derived from both physical motion and verbal instructions.

4 Results

4.1 Somatic Results: Laban Features in Physical Motion

Analysis of the 360 recorded trajectories reveals clear patterns in how task context influenced the Force, Space, and Time characteristics of human demonstrations. Significant effects between are summarized in Table 1. Preliminary check of the feature distributions confirmed they fit a Gaussian curve, justifying the use of parametric statistical tests. Analyses were performed of variance (ANOVA) to examine the effect of different independent variables.

Table 1. Significance of results across episodic study

Episode 1				Episode 2			
Variable	Force	Space	Time	Variable	Force	Space	Time
Task	✓✓	✓	✓	Wall Compliance	✓	✓	✗
Clutter	✓	✓✓	✓	Plug Compliance	~	✗	✗
Task × Clutter	✗	✓	✗	Wall × Plug Compliance	✓	~	✗

Task Effects: The type of task (drawing vs. erasing, in Episode 1) had a strong influence on exerted forces and motion patterns. Drawing and erasing involve different mechanics: erasing often requires pressing harder and covering more area, whereas drawing might require more precision. The data reflected this: **Task was a very significant predictor of force** metrics in the demonstrations. Across participants, drawing tasks tended to produce higher joint torques on average than erasing tasks. Specifically, the normalized overall force was significantly higher for drawing ($F(1,358)=37.5$, $p<0.001$), indicating a stronger *Weight Effort* for the additive task. Task also affected **Space**: erasing typically covered a larger area than drawing. Indeed, the total path length of the end-effector and the number of peaks in the trajectory were greater in erasing trials on average. For example, we found that erasing motions had significantly more local maxima/minima in their velocity profile ($F(1,358) = 78.74$, $p<0.001$), and covered a larger distance ($\mu = [0.38, 0.96]$, var $= [0.2, 0.5]$) reported in meters. In terms of **Time**, tasks also differed: erasing often took longer than drawing. Task type significantly predicted the task completion time ($F(1,358) = 7.29$, $p = 0.007$), the subtractive task taking longer to complete than the drawing task ($\mu = [15.1, 11.1]$, var $= [11,7]$) reported in seconds.

Environmental Clutter Effects: The presence of obstacles (clutter) also had notable effects, particularly on **Space and Time** aspects of motion. Clutter was a significant predictor of the **approach path** shape and **approach time**. Clutter conditions very significantly predicted approach path length ($F(2,357) = 11.5$, $p < 0.001$) with the *top* clutter the shortest route, followed by *bottom* as median route and *both* clutter condition the longest route ($\mu = [0.08, 0.12, 0.14]$, var $= [0.007, 0.016, 0.02]$) meters. The presence of clutter caused a very significant increase in approach time $F(2,357) = 6.49$, $p<0.001$, participants slowed down and maneuvered carefully during the *bottom* clutter condition, which is a sustained *Time* effort. Interestingly, clutter also influenced **force** measures: especially when both top and bottom obstacles were present, participants occasionally applied higher forces with a significant prediction that clutter affects the maximum force ($F(2,357) = 5.89$, $p = 0.003$).

Task × Clutter Interaction: Space features are primarily influenced by the interaction effect of task and clutter. The maximum upwards direction is not predicted by *task*, but is very significantly predicted by *clutter* (F(2,150), p<0.001). The interaction effect of *task × clutter* significantly predicts the maximum direction in the *Z plane* (F(2,150), p = 0.01).

Compliance Effects: In the plugging tasks, the compliance of the wall and receptacle impacted the **force and space** profiles. Insertion into a rigid hole required higher peak forces, whereas the compliant hole predicted less force. Our analysis showed significant effects of compliance on peak force (F(1,358) = 4.27, p = 0.05) and on maximum direction into the wall, the X direction, (F(1,358) = 5.22, p = 0.03). Participants moved the tool more into the workspace when the compliance was rigid (μ = [0.29,0.22], var = [0.031,0.016]) in meters.

4.2 Semantic Results: Laban Features in Verbal Commands

After each trial, participants issued a verbal command to the robot and provided an explanation of their strategy. These **natural language** instructions offer insight into what aspects people chose to articulate and how language corresponds to the trajectory features.

Prevalence of Laban-Related Terms: Participants commonly used words that correspond to *Space and Time Effort* qualities in LMA, whereas explicit *Force* terms were rare. For instance, about half of the commands included a descriptor of where to move: e.g., "start in the upper left corner," "go around the obstacle," "cover the whole top area." These spatial references (upper, around, whole area) align with the *Space Effort* dimension, indicating attention to direction. Similarly, many commands included an adverb relating to speed or smoothness: e.g., "slowly," "carefully," "gently," "quickly," or "smoothly." These correspond to *Time Effort* or sometimes *Flow*.

Qualitative Command Examples: To illustrate, one participant's command for a cluttered erasing task was: "Hey robot, wipe the board *slowly*, making sure to cover the square." Here *"slowly"* (Time), and the phrase "cover the square" (Space) are present, but there is no mention of how hard to wipe – yet in their trial they pressed firmly. This example was typical; spatial targeting and tempo or smoothness are given in words, while force is treated as an implicit detail.

Effect of Coaching on Language: The *Semantic coaching* group, who were primed with a list of adverbs, unsurprisingly used more of those adverbs in their commands. They often included at least two descriptive words where other groups might use one or none. The **Kinematic coaching** group tended to use more precise spatial language and some of them echoed phrases from the briefing like "keep the arm aligned" or "parallel to the board." The *Kinesthetic* *coaching* group, overall had the highest force variations yet a few gave very terse commands like "Just wipe this off" with minimal detail, relying on the demonstration to have conveyed the nuance.

4.3 Influence of Coaching and Multimodal Integration

Differing coaching conditions were employed to see how they direct participants' focus. A few key observations are highlighted:

Kinesthetic focus (using their body analogously) tended to produce demonstrations with the highest forces. They "put their back into it" more readily, resulting in about 10–15% higher normalized force on average than others. However, these same participants often gave very sparse verbal commands as if assuming the demonstration spoke for itself. The number of descriptive words per command was the lowest (many had zero adverbs). This suggests a trade-off: emphasizing the body made them rely on somatic communication and perhaps neglect verbal detail.

Semantic focus group (given adverbs list) did incorporate more Laban-related words in their speech (like "gently, slowly"). Their demonstrations, however, showed the lowest force levels on average . In other words, they talked about doing things gently and indeed physically performed them gently (lighter Weight effort). This group also had the highest count of adverbs in their commands.

Kinematic focus group emphasized spatial precision. Consistently, their language included precise terms (e.g., "align with the top edge," "move straight down") and their trajectories had slightly more constrained paths. They did not particularly excel or fall short in force or time compared to control; their main difference was in path shaping and corresponding language.

Control group (no special coaching) exhibited a mix of behaviors, generally falling between kinesthetic and semantic extremes. This suggests that without specific prompting, people naturally provide a balance: moderate force usage, some descriptive terms but not overly flowery. In fact, even control participants intuitively used Laban concepts: most gave at least one detail in their command (like a speed or a target location), showing that our hypotheses about inherent somatic/semantic cues hold even without priming.

5 Discussion

The study outcomes largely support the initial hypotheses. Participants intuitively encoded LMA Effort dimensions in their demonstrations, varying force, space, and time based on the situation – thus confirming the *Somatic Hypothesis*. They also incorporated many of these Effort qualities into their speech (e.g., spatial and temporal descriptors), consistent with the *Semantic Hypothesis*. However, an asymmetry emerged: participants frequently verbalized spatial and temporal aspects, yet rarely mentioned force, instead conveying it through physical demonstrations. For example, when navigating around obstacles, some participants attempted to simply force through (resulting in high force peaks), whereas others slowed down and carefully maneuvered the arm around the obstructions. These differing approaches were evident in the sensor data but not explicitly mentioned in their speech. This nuance suggests that, although the Semantic Hypothesis holds in general, certain aspects like force are less likely to be put into words without prompting. The *Coaching Hypothesis* was supported by the results as well – the type of instructional coaching given influenced the information emphasis. Participants primed to focus on their body focused more on physical cues, whereas those primed with language examples provided more elaborate verbal instructions. This demonstrates that the way we frame the operator's mindset (somatic vs. semantic focus) can shape the outcome. It is important to emphasize that these initial analyses represent just a first exploration of the collected multi-modal dataset. The Speech2Action dataset offers rich opportunities for further investigation, and we encourage the research community to explore additional dimensions and interactions beyond those presented here.

This study, while aspirational, has limitations. Participants issued "ideal" commands without seeing the robot execute them in real time, which means our data reflects what people hope the robot will do rather than any feedback-corrected instructions. In a deployed scenario, humans might adjust their commands based on the robot's actual performance. Second, our tasks were limited to a vertical board setup (drawing, erasing, plugging) with a particular robot arm; different tasks or robot embodiments might yield different teaching behaviors. Additionally, our sample size ($N = 30$, with 6 per coaching condition) is modest; while we found significant effects, a larger study could further validate these trends. Finally, our analysis of language was relatively keyword-based; more nuanced linguistic analysis (e.g., parsing sentence structure or assessing tone) could reveal additional insights into generating a trajectory from natural language models.

Future work will extend our approach to actual field scenarios, including underwater in-contact manipulation tasks, to validate that robots can effectively interpret human somatic and semantic inputs in those environments. The next step is to incorporate this dataset to convert natural language to robot trajectories. Indeed, our team has already begun leveraging trajectory data from this experiment in follow-up work, using voice commands to control robot arm movements in underwater manipulation tasks [7]. This study sheds light on a subtle point: **human perception vs. reality in force modulation**. We found instances where participants' cognitive perception of their effort did not match the measured data. This suggests that giving humans feedback on their own demonstrations. Crafting of a feedback loop (e.g., haptic feedback) to give the operator subtle corrections could help modulate force perceptions. Ongoing research is exploring gesture-based mid-trajectory corrections, which were qualitatively noted during this experiment but not explicitly recorded. Incorporating gesture controls alongside verbal commands and physical demonstrations represents another promising avenue for expanding the utility of the dataset.

6 Conclusion

This study presented a novel Act-it-Out teaching paradigm for in-contact robot manipulation tasks, in which human instructors demonstrate a task and then articulate a verbal commands. Using this approach, we collected a dataset and analyzed how people blend physical and verbal communication to teach a robot. This study shows that instructors leverage a combination of *somatic* (body-driven) and *semantic* (language-driven) intelligence when teaching a robot, and that these two forms of communication are strongly complementary. Through the lens of Laban Movement Analysis (LMA), we demonstrated that key motion qualities (Force, Space, Time) underlie the strategies people use. Participants intuitively embodied these qualities in their demonstrations and echoed them (especially Space and Time) in their verbal commands, albeit with an asymmetry: force-related cues were more often shown than spoken. This indicates that certain aspects of robot control, like contact force, are most naturally conveyed through kinesthetic interaction, highlighting the importance of robots being able to learn from or respond to physical human input in addition to spoken instructions.

Findings include evidence that users consistently used spatial language and temporal descriptors to guide the robot, while leaving force requirements implicit. For example, participants would describe a path around an obstacle or specify doing a motion "slowly," but rarely said "apply high force," even when in practice they exerted considerable force. This behavior underscores the need for robot systems to interpret unspoken cues: a human's quiet assumption that the robot will "just feel it out" for the appropriate force. Our analysis confirmed that by examining the human's own motion, one can often pick up those cues: participants who wanted a gentle touch simply exerted less force in their demonstration, which the robot's sensors picked up. Thus, an important implication is that an effective Command and Control (C2) system for robots should incorporate both somatic inputs and semantic inputs for a full picture of the human"s intent. Our work provides quantitative backing for this principle.

The contributions of this work are threefold:

1. **Speech2Action Dataset:** An open-source dataset capturing paired human demonstrations and verbal instructions across a range of contact-rich tasks. The dataset includes computed LMA Effort features for each trajectory and annotated linguistic elements, offering a valuable resource for training machine learning algorithms.
2. **Statistical Analysis of Actions and Words:** Through analysis of human behavior, we gain insights into how people naturally blend somatic and semantic communication. We highlight that communication occurs *both through the body and through language,* and the results validate the use of LMA features as a meaningful representation for teaching strategies.
3. **Novel Laban Features for Robot Arms:** We demonstrate the viability of using of using LMA as a unifying framework for integrating demonstration and language instructions in robotic control. By mapping human inputs onto

LMA Effort dimensions, people can intuitively offer robot base commands, in-line corrections or strategy to robots manipulating a surface.

This study indicates the tractability of incorporating naturalistic human verbal instruction into commanding robot arms. Rather than viewing demonstrations and commands as separate or redundant channels, the human demonstrations and cognitive analysis of our data show that they provide different pieces of the puzzle. For example, people set high level task goals, and also gave descriptive strategy: what to do to succeed, and (often more verbose) what not to do to avoid failure. In ongoing work, we are developing Speech2Action software leveraging this data to detect and parse human voice into real-time robot trajectories from natural language. While we provide initial analyses here, much more exists in the dataset for future researchers to continue to explore.

References

1. Ahmad, M., Mubin, O., Orlando, J.: A systematic review of adaptivity in human-robot interaction. Multimodal Technol. Interact. **1**(3), 14 (2017). https://doi.org/10.3390/mti1030014
2. Bacula, A., LaViers, A.: Character synthesis of ballet archetypes on robots using Laban movement analysis: comparison between a humanoid and an aerial robot platform with lay and expert observation. Int. J. Soc. Robot. **13**(5), 1047–1062 (2020). https://doi.org/10.1007/s12369-020-00695-0
3. Bernardet, U., Fdili Alaoui, S., Studd, K., Bradley, K., Pasquier, P., Schiphorst, T.: Assessing the reliability of the Laban movement analysis system. PLOS ONE **14**(6) (2019). https://doi.org/10.1371/journal.pone.0218179
4. Billard, A., Kragic, D.: Trends and challenges in robot manipulation. Science **364**(6446) (2019). https://doi.org/10.1126/science.aat8414
5. Bradley Knox, W., Stone, P.: TAMER: training an agent manually via evaluative reinforcement. In: 2008 7th IEEE International Conference on Development and Learning (2008). https://doi.org/10.1109/devlrn.2008.4640845
6. Burton, S.J., Samadani, A.A., Gorbet, R., Kulić, D.: Laban movement analysis and affective movement generation for robots and other near-living creatures. Springer Tracts in Advanced Robotics, pp. 25–48 (2015). https://doi.org/10.1007/978-3-319-25739-6_2
7. Jain, C., He, B., Patil, S., Sanchez, L., Knight, H.: Verbal c2 for underwater in-contact manipulation: a semantic approach to somatic task guidance. In: OCEANS 2025 Brest: A UN Oceans Decade Conference, Brest, France (2025)
8. Candon, K., Zhou, H., Gillet, S., Vázquez, M.: Verbally soliciting human feedback in continuous human-robot collaboration. In: Proceedings of the 2023 ACM/IEEE International Conference on Human-Robot Interaction, vol. 226, pp. 290–300 (2023). https://doi.org/10.1145/3568162.3576980
9. Emir, E., Burns, C.M.: Evaluation of expressive motions based on the framework of Laban effort features for social attributes of robots. In: 2022 31st IEEE International Conference on Robot and Human Interactive Communication (RO-MAN) (2022). https://doi.org/10.1109/ro-man53752.2022.9900645
10. Holler, J., Levinson, S.C.: Multimodal language processing in human communication. Trends Cogn. Sci. **23**(8), 639–652 (2019)

11. Khurana, D., Koli, A., Khatter, K., Singh, S.: Natural language processing: state of the art, current trends and challenges. Multimedia Tools Appl. **82**(3), 3713–3744 (2022). https://doi.org/10.1007/s11042-022-13428-4
12. Knight, H., Simmons, R.: Expressive motion with x, y and theta: Laban effort features for mobile robots. In: The 23rd IEEE International Symposium on Robot and Human Interactive Communication, pp. 267–273 (2014). https://doi.org/10.1109/roman.2014.6926264
13. Knight, H., Simmons, R.: Layering Laban effort features on robot task motions. In: Proceedings of the Tenth Annual ACM/IEEE International Conference on Human-Robot Interaction Extended Abstracts, pp. 135–136 (2015). https://doi.org/10.1145/2701973.2702054
14. Kohut, P., Giergiel, M., Cieslak, P., Ciszewski, M., Buratowski, T.: Underwater robotic system for reservoir maintenance. J. Vibroengineering **18**(6), 3757–3767 (2016). https://doi.org/10.21595/jve.2016.17364
15. Kumar, S., Rastogi, V., Gupta, P.: A hybrid impedance control scheme for underwater welding robots with a passive foundation in the controller domain. Simulation **93**(7), 619–630 (2017). https://doi.org/10.1177/0037549717693687
16. Liu, H., et al.: Enhancing the LLM-based robot manipulation through human-robot collaboration. IEEE Robot. Autom. Lett. **9**(8), 6904–6911 (2024). https://doi.org/10.1109/lra.2024.3415931
17. Liu, J., et al.: LLM-powered hierarchical language agent for real-time human-AI coordination. arXiv (Cornell University) (2023). https://doi.org/10.48550/arxiv.2312.15224
18. Ludvigsen, M., Sørensen, A.J.: Towards integrated autonomous underwater operations for ocean mapping and monitoring. Ann. Rev. Control. **42**, 145–157 (2016)
19. Mazzeo, A., et al.: Marine robotics for deep-sea specimen collection: a taxonomy of underwater manipulative actions. Sensors **22**(4), 1471 (2022)
20. Sadigh, D., Dragan, A., Sastry, S., Seshia, S.: Active preference-based learning of reward functions. Robot. Sci. Syst. XIII (2017). https://doi.org/10.15607/rss.2017.xiii.053
21. Sanchez, L., Crocker, D., Oo, T.M., Knight, H.: Robotic gestures, human moods: Investigating affective responses in public interaction. In: Companion of the 2024 ACM/IEEE International Conference on Human-Robot Interaction, pp. 935–939 (2024)
22. Schrum, M.L., Hedlund-Botti, E., Moorman, N., Gombolay, M.C.: Mind meld: personalized meta-learning for robot-centric imitation learning. In: 2022 17th ACM/IEEE International Conference on Human-Robot Interaction (HRI) (2022). https://doi.org/10.1109/hri53351.2022.9889616
23. Smart, W.D., Matheus, K., Fraune, M.R.: Applying bodystorming to human-robot interaction design. In: International Conference on Social Robotics, pp. 431–445. Springer (2024)
24. Sun, J., Zhang, Q., Duan, Y., Jiang, X., Cheng, C., Xu, R.: Prompt, plan, perform: LLM-based humanoid control via quantized imitation learning. In: 2024 IEEE International Conference on Robotics and Automation (ICRA), vol. 29, pp. 16236–16242 (2024). https://doi.org/10.1109/icra57147.2024.10610948
25. Suomalainen, M., Karayiannidis, Y., Kyrki, V.: A survey of robot manipulation in contact. Robot. Auton. Syst. **156**, 104224 (2022). https://doi.org/10.1016/j.robot.2022.104224
26. Torta, E., van Heumen, J., Piunti, F., Romeo, L., Cuijpers, R.: Evaluation of unimodal and multimodal communication cues for attracting attention in human-robot interaction. Int. J. Soc. Robot. **7**, 89–96 (2015)

27. Wang, R., Yang, Z., Zhao, Z., Tong, X., Hong, Z., Qian, K.: LLM-based robot task planning with exceptional handling for general purpose service robots. 2024 43rd Chinese Control Conference (CCC), vol. 35, pp. 4439–4444 (2024). https://doi.org/10.23919/ccc63176.2024.10661966

Who Sees What? Structured Thought-Action Sequences for Epistemic Reasoning in LLMs

Luca Annese[1(✉)], Sabrina Patania[1], Silvia Serino[1], Tom Foulsham[3], Silvia Rossi[2], Azzurra Ruggeri[4], and Dimitri Ognibene[1,3]

[1] University of Milan-Bicocca, Milan, Italy
{luca.annese1,sabrina.patania,silvia.serino,dimitri.ognibene}@unimb.it
[2] University of Essex, Colchester, UK
silvia.rossi@unina.it
[3] University of Naples Federico II, Naples, Italy
foulsham@essex.ac.uk
[4] TUM School of Social Sciences and Technology, Munich, Germany

Abstract. Recent advances in large language models (LLMs) and reasoning frameworks have opened new possibilities for improving the perspective-taking capabilities of autonomous agents. However, tasks that involve active perception, collaborative reasoning, and perspective taking (understanding what another agent can see or knows) pose persistent challenges for current LLM-based systems. This study investigates the potential of structured examples derived from transformed solution graphs generated by the Fast Downward planner to improve the performance of LLM-based agents within a ReAct framework. We propose a structured solution-processing pipeline that generates three distinct categories of examples: optimal goal paths (G-type), informative node paths (E-type), and step-by-step optimal decision sequences contrasting alternative actions (L-type). These solutions are further converted into "thought-action" examples by prompting an LLM to explicitly articulate the reasoning behind each decision. While L-type examples slightly reduce clarification requests and overall action steps, they do not yield consistent improvements. Agents are successful in tasks requiring basic attentional filtering but struggle in scenarios that required mentalising about occluded spaces or weighing the costs of epistemic actions. These findings suggest that structured examples alone are insufficient for robust perspective-taking, underscoring the need for explicit belief tracking, cost modelling, and richer environments to enable socially grounded collaboration in LLM-based agents.

Keywords: perspective taking · LLMs · active vision · theory of mind · planning

1 Introduction

Effective interaction in multi-agent systems, especially those involving human-Artificial intelligence (AI) collaboration, requires more than basic task execution.

It demands the capacity for perspective-taking: the ability to model what others can see, know, or intend. This includes reasoning about both physical viewpoints (e.g., what another agent can perceive in the environment) and epistemic states (e.g., what they know or believe). Perspective-taking is essential for generating contextually appropriate responses and adapting to ambiguity in real-world scenarios.

In this work, we explore how perspective-taking can be operationalized within the ReAct (Reason+Act) framework [32], which interleaves natural language reasoning with environment-grounded actions. Unlike static perception-action pipelines, ReAct enables agents to reason explicitly before acting, providing an ideal foundation for handling the interpretive demands of perspective-taking tasks.

We focus on a modified version of the Director Task [14], adapted to a partially observable environment inspired by [28]. In our setting, already explored in [25] and [24], a Director issues instructions to a Matcher agent, which must retrieve a target object. Crucially, the environment contains occlusions and hidden containers that affect both agents perception, meaning that the Matcher may have to actively perceive [20,21] to infer what the Director sees and does not see, to resolve ambiguity. This setup simulates real-world collaborative scenarios where agents have asymmetric and limited access to information.

To enable grounded perspective-taking, we introduce a novel training method that builds on search-based reasoning from the Fast Downward planner. We construct complete reasoning trees that encode possible thought-action trajectories in similar conditions. From these trees, we extract three types of example sequences:

- G-type: optimal sequence from initial state to task success;
- E-type: all paths that reach informative states, where the agent gains new knowledge through sensing, movement, or object interaction;
- L-type: locally optimal decisions at each state, simulating reactive step-wise decision-making.

Each sequence is transformed into a chain of thought-action pairs using a LLM, enabling agents to learn not just what to do, but why, increasing both interpretability and transferability.

We evaluate our method across seven environments of increasing complexity, varying both the spatial layout and the ambiguity of instructions to intensify the perspective-taking demands. For each trial, the agent is shown examples from six environments and evaluated in the held-out seventh, testing generalization across diverse settings. Tasks ranged from fully disambiguated instructions to scenarios requiring the agent to infer what the Director sees or does not see. Empirical results show that while G-type and E-type examples support task efficiency and exploration, only L-type examples slightly improved agent behaviour, specifically by reducing excessive clarification requests and promoting more grounded decision-making.

To interpret these results, we introduce a functional characterisation of the cognitive demands associated with different task conditions. These demands (ranging from simple common-ground attentional filtering [13], to mentalising about hidden content [4], and metacognitive evaluations of epistemic cost and utility [15]) emerge in increasingly complex environments and help explain when LLM agents succeed and where they systematically fail.

Ultimately, while embedding cognitively structured examples into the ReAct loop scaffolds some forms of perspective-taking—particularly those grounded in reactive reasoning and observable cues—it may not suffice for enabling higher-order inference, imaginative simulation, or consistent collaborative strategies that unfold over multiple steps. Such strategies require balancing social reasoning, physical exploration, and interlocutor modelling, while accounting for both information gain and the cost or risk of failure. While recent work suggests that LLMs exhibit emerging capabilities for social reasoning and information gathering [2,26], our findings underscore the need for their integration with socially-aware, active information-seeking strategies [20,21], in order to support robust collaboration in open-ended, multi-agent environments [3,19].

2 Related Work

In recent years, there has been growing interest in the application of large language models (LLMs) and multimodal foundation models in robotics and collaborative systems for high-level reasoning, perception, and decision-making [22]. These models are pre-trained on vast amounts of internet-scale data and exhibit impressive generalization capabilities [6], enabling robots to handle a wide range of open-ended scenarios. Models such as SayCan [1] and Inner Monologue [11] demonstrate how LLMs can break down abstract goals into practical steps by combining high-level reasoning with grounded robotic actions.

A core component of effective multi-agent interaction is perspective-taking, namely, the ability to represent a situation from an alternate viewpoint [9]. This includes visual perspective-taking, distinguished between Level-1 (inferring what others can see) and Level-2 (inferring how things appear to others), and spatial perspective-taking, which involves representing relative spatial relations through egocentric or allocentric reference frames [7]. Visual perspective-taking, particularly Level-2, has been closely linked to theory of mind (ToM), as both require agents to maintain decoupled mental representations. In frameworks like ReAct [32], perspective-taking is framed as a dynamic reasoning process that accompanies acting, enabling agents to update their knowledge in real time.

Efforts to enhance perspective-taking in LLMs have largely focused on language based evaluations. Studies using false-belief tasks indicate that while older models (e.g., GPT-2, early GPT-3) struggle with ToM tasks, more recent systems (e.g., GPT-4) display emerging but unstable capabilities [16]. Techniques like the SimToM prompting framework [31] explicitly instruct models to simulate other agents' perspectives, reducing the intrusion of background omniscience. In the visual domain, datasets such as Isle-Bricks and Isle-Dots [8] reveal that while many vision-language models (VLMs) can detect objects in a scene, they often fail at reasoning about what is visible from an observer's viewpoint. Advanced models like GPT-4V perform well on Level-1 tasks but show notable drops on Level-2 challenges involving viewpoint rotation and mental transformation [17]. Beyond static perception, benchmarks such as ActiView [30] introduce active visual exploration, requiring models to shift or zoom their viewpoint to gather relevant information—tasks that remain difficult for current models.

Complementary to these efforts, recent research has begun to explore the synergy between LLMs and classical symbolic planning systems to enhance structured reasoning. Hybrid models like LLM+P [18] use planners to generate plans from formal representations (e.g., PDDL), then convert them into natural language for execution by LLMs. Other works, such as PSALM [33], investigate using LLMs to synthesize or refine planning domains, while others employ LLMs to verbalize or critique symbolic plans [11]. These approaches leverage the complementary strengths of symbolic methods (e.g., correctness, structure) and language models (e.g., flexibility, generalization).

Building on these developments, our work explores how symbolic planning can serve as a source of structured, cognitively meaningful training examples for LLMs. This method bridges symbolic and neural paradigms by using planning structures to ground language-based cognitive traces, offering a new way to study and enhance perspective-taking and decision-making in LLM-based agents.

3 Method

3.1 Simulated Task Environment

To explore perspective-taking in goal-directed interaction, we developed a simulated household-like environment using the Planning Domain Definition Language (PDDL). The environment represents a shared space between two agents: a Director, who knows the identity and location of the target object, and a Matcher, who must retrieve the object based on limited perceptual cues and dialogue. The space includes multiple locations such as a desk, shelf, and drawers, with some objects hidden inside containers that can be opened or closed.

The PDDL domain models both spatial structure and perceptual asymmetry. Each agent can perceive the contents of its own location, as well as any adjacent locations, simulating a partially shared field of view. This shared access supports basic grounding, while still requiring inference about what the other agent can or cannot see.

In most cases, ambiguity is introduced by presenting two objects of the same type (e.g., two ties of different colours). This setup requires the Matcher to rely on cues beyond spatial proximity or direct visual recognition, such as dialogue with the Director or strategic exploration, to disambiguate the task. Figure 1 shows such a design graphically. To systematically vary perspective-taking difficulty, we designed seven task types, ranging from fully observable to highly ambiguous settings, as shown in Table 1.

The Matcher begins each trial at a random location and must perform a sequence of actions: moving, opening containers and optionally asking questions to infer the correct object. The agent must decide whether more information

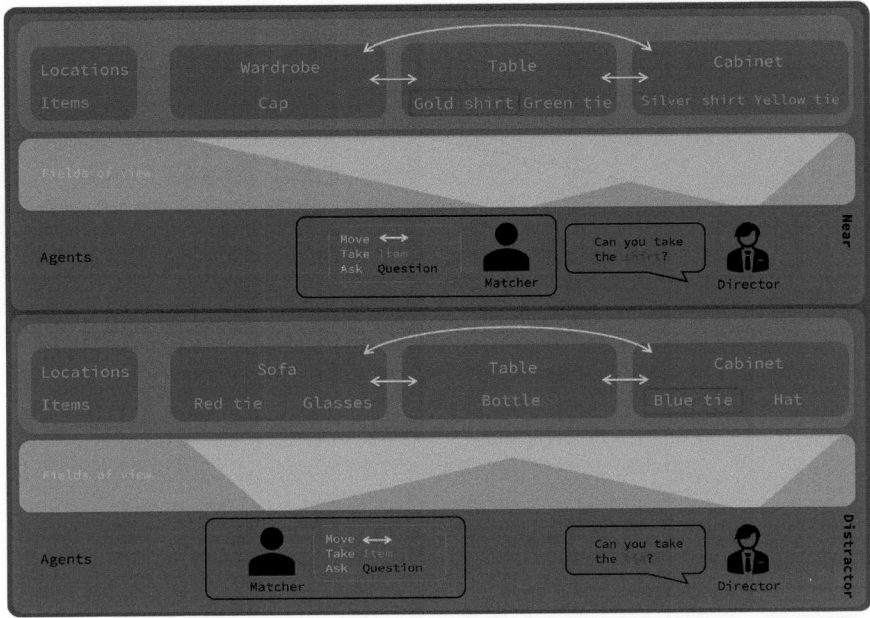

Fig. 1. Schematic view showing two examples of the experimental environment. In each case the top row shows the three locations and their item contents, and the yellow arrows indicate possible movements from the Matcher. The target is outlined in red. Each agent can see only the location in front and immediately adjacent (yellow shading). The Matcher can move between locations, take an item from the location directly in front, or ask the Director a question. The Director can only answer from their fixed position. In the Near condition (top panel), there is ambiguity because two candidate objects fit the Director's request (Gold shirt and Silver shirt). In the Distractor condition (bottom panel), the Matcher can see an item (Red tie) that matches the request, yet is not the correct target. (Color figure online)

is required to make the choice and how to find it. This design enables controlled evaluation of perspective-taking under increasing complexity, balancing grounded environment interaction with higher-order inference demands.

3.2 Strategy Generation

To generate structured behavioral sequences, we employed a modified version of the Fast Downward planner, adapted to expose the internal reasoning process underlying its search, as shown in Fig. 2. Specifically, the planner was equipped to output a reasoning tree that records the sequence of states and actions considered during planning. This tree represents a detailed trace of the planner's decision space, capturing both explored and selected paths through the environment. From this reasoning tree, we derived three types of training examples,

Table 1. Environment Types and Their Perspective-Taking Challenges

Environment	Information State	Matcher Spatial State	Ambiguity Resolution
Base	Both see both objects & areas; Director names target explicitly.	Distant from both *target* and *distractor*.	Processing initial demand.
Perspective Taking	Matcher sees both objects; Director sees only *target* and one area less.	Close to both *target* and *distractor*.	Using common ground.
Distractor	Matcher sees *distractor*; Director sees *target*. Each sees an area the other can't.	Distant from *target*, close to *distractor*.	Exploring unseen perspectives.
Near	Both see both objects. Matcher sees an area more.	Close to *target*, distant from *distractor*.	Asking clarification.
Far	Both see both objects. Matcher sees an area more.	Close to *distractor*, distant from *target*.	Asking clarification.
Hidden	Director sees Target. Matcher does not. Each sees an area the other can't.	Distant from *target*. No Distractor.	Exploring unseen perspectives.
Not That	Matcher sees only *distractor*; Director sees both. Each sees an area the other can't.	Close to *distractor*, distant from *target*.	Asking clarification.

each emphasizing a distinct mode of behavior, by extracting them through three different tree-traversal strategies.:

- Goal-directed trajectories (G-type): These are action sequences that lead from the initial state to the goal state, representing the planner's optimal solution path. They reflect efficient behavior under the assumption that the agent has access to all relevant information for completing the task.
- Information-seeking trajectories (E-type): These examples were extracted by identifying branches of the reasoning tree that led to states where critical information was gained, such as observing hidden objects or reducing ambiguity about the target. This type of example prioritizes epistemic actions and models behavior driven by uncertainty reduction rather than direct goal completion.
- Local decision points (L-type): For this example type, we identified the locally optimal action at each state visited during planning, contrasted explicitly with the other possible actions available at that point. This approach emphasizes granular decision-making and trains agents to reason about why the chosen action is superior to its alternatives given a single observation.

These examples are grounded in the planner's reasoning trace, providing insight into the deliberative process behind goal achievement and information gathering. While the Director is not explicitly modeled in the environment, its influence is indirectly embedded in the task configuration, for instance, through the target object's proximity to the Director's location, prompting the Matcher to infer spatial and referential cues. This setup supports the generation of cognitively rich example sequences from a formally grounded planning system.

3.3 Example Generation

The final step of the methodology involves transforming the planner-derived action sequences into structured cognitive examples that simulate the internal reasoning of an agent engaged in perspective-taking. These examples are constructed as "thought-action" pairs, where each action is preceded by a textual description of the agent's inferred reasoning process.

To produce these thought sequences, a large language model (GPT o3-mini) was prompted with each action sequence, drawn from the G-, E-, or L-type examples, along with contextual information such as the agent's current state, visible items, and the overall task objective. The model was asked to articulate the reasoning that might justify each step in the sequence, generating natural language explanations simulating deliberation and inference. The model was instructed to generate such sequences employing the following prompts (Table 2):

Table 2. Reasoning Strategy Prompts

Strategy	Prompt
G-type	Given the sequence of actions the agent executed until reaching its goal in a specific scenario, reconstruct the agent's reasoning step by step. Explain how each action contributed to achieving the goal.
E-type	Given a sequence of actions taken until the agent reaches an informative state (i.e., a state that provides new information), reconstruct the agent's reasoning step by step. Describe how each action led to gaining information.
L-type	Given the agent's last action, the set of possible actions, and the correct action in a specific scenario, explain the agent's reasoning behind selecting that particular action over the alternatives.

This transformation enriches the examples with cognitive structure, allowing them to reflect key faculties involved in perspective-taking. Each thought segment captures perceptual assessment (e.g., recognizing that an object is not currently visible), inferential reasoning (e.g., hypothesizing where a hidden item might be based on contextual cues), and decision-making under uncertainty (e.g., choosing to ask the Director when the situation is ambiguous). These elements are not explicitly modeled in the PDDL domain, but are essential for simulating realistic agent behavior in social contexts.

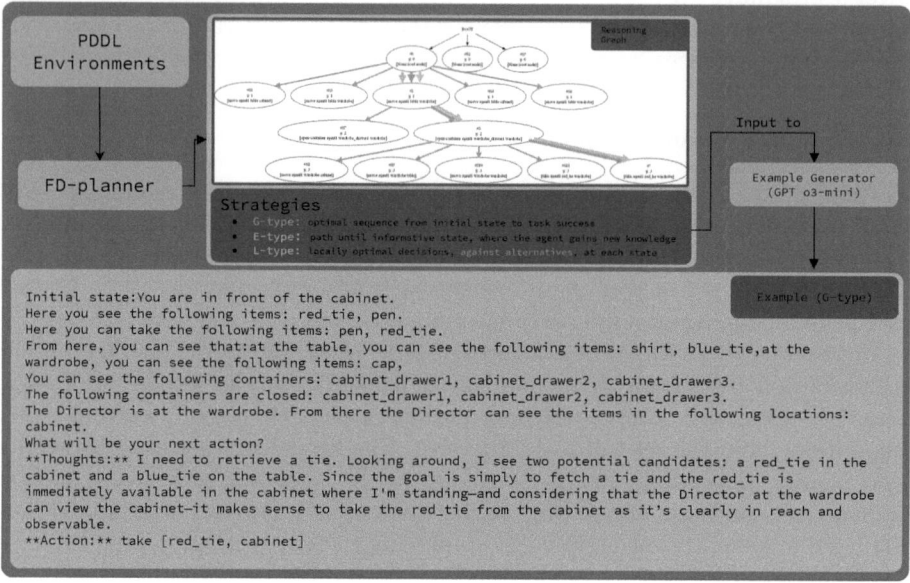

Fig. 2. Graphic view of example generation pipeline. The panel above shows the reasoning tree produced by the Fast-Downward planner, highlighting the three different paths according to the corresponding strategy. The section below is an example (G-type path) generated from the Base environment.

4 Experiments

We first augmented the Fast Downward planner (A^* with the admissible h_{max} heuristic) to emit all evaluated actions during search, from which we built a complete reasoning tree. From this, we extracted three trajectory types, G-type, E-type, and L-type, each corresponding to a distinct decision-making strategy. These were fed to GPT o3-mini using strategy-specific prompts to generate natural-language thought–action chains: step-by-step goal reasoning (G-type), information-seeking justification (E-type), and local action selection rationale (L-type).

To evaluate the Matcher–Director interaction, we instantiated two LLM-agents (both GPT o3-mini) in our PDDL-based household environment. The stationary Director issued natural-language instructions of varying ambiguity; the ReAct-based Matcher alternated between LLM reasoning and grounded actions to interpret and execute the task. For each of the seven task types (ranging from disambiguated to highly ambiguous), the Matcher was trained on structured examples from the other six, and tested on the held-out one. Each test scenario was repeated across five trials. Performance was assessed using failure rate, step count, clarification queries, and epistemic actions.

In parallel, we enhanced the PDDL domain to allow the planner to compute optimal perspective-taking strategies by including epistemic (ASK) actions where ambiguity required them. This enabled the generation of example sets with (+ask) or without (âĂŞask) clarification steps, providing expert baselines for reasoning under uncertainty and testing whether such exposure influenced agent behaviour.

To probe this further, we used these planner-optimal trajectories to generate an additional set of G-, E-, and L-type examples, enriched with epistemically aware reasoning but following the same prompting schema.

We report aggregated averages by task (see Tables 3, 4, 5) to compare how example types shape Matcher behaviour across perspective-taking demands. Despite encoding optimal epistemic strategies, these enriched examples did not yield consistent performance gains. Neither success rates nor behavioural quality (e.g., unnecessary queries, incorrect assumptions) improved significantly. Possible reasons for this outcome are explored in the following section.

Table 3. First Take on Correct Target (%) across Scenarios

Example type	Persp	Far	Hidd	Not	Dist	Base	Near
G-type-ask	100	0	100	0	20	100	100
G-type+ask	100	0	100	0	40	100	100
E-type-ask	100	0	100	20	0	100	100
E-type+ask	100	0	100	0	40	100	100
L-type-ask	100	0	100	0	40	100	100
L-type+ask	100	0	100	0	40	100	100
No Examples	100	20	100	0	40	100	100

Table 4. Average Number of Steps

Example type	Persp	Far	Hidd	Not	Dist	Base	Near	AVG
G-type-ask	1	4.8	3	5.8	5.2	2	1	3.26
G-type+ask	1	5	3	5.8	5	2	1	3.26
E-type-ask	1	4.4	3	6	5	2	1	3.2
E-type+ask	1	4.6	3	5.6	5.2	2	1	3.2
L-type-ask	1	4.4	3	4.8	4.6	2	1	**2.97**
L-type+ask	1	5	3	5.8	5	2	1	3.26
AVG	1	4.7	3	5.63	5	2	1	3.19
No Examples	1	4.4	3	5.8	4.6	2	1	3.11
Planner	1	3	2	3	2	2	2	2.14

Table 5. Average Number of *Ask* Actions

Example type	Persp	Far	Hidd	Not	Dist	Base	Near	AVG
G-type-ask	0	1.8	1	1.8	2.4	0	0	1
G-type+ask	0	2	1	1.8	2.4	0	0	1.03
E-type-ask	0	1.4	1	2.4	2	0	0	0.97
E-type+ask	0	1.6	1	1.6	2.6	0	0	0.97
L-type-ask	0	1.4	1	1.4	2	0	0	**0.83**
L-type+ask	0	2	1	1.8	2.6	0	0	1.06
AVG	0	1.7	1	1.8	2.33	0	0	0.98
No Examples	0	1.6	1	1.8	2	0	0	0.91
Planner	0	1	0	1	0	0	1	0.43

5 Discussion

Our results reveal that success in collaborative reference hinges on *three orthogonal but interacting cognitive demands*. Throughout we denote them as **F1-F3** to emphasise their functional independence.

F1 Common-ground filtering. Listeners must inhibit any object that the Director cannot currently see, a Level-1 perspective-taking operation that relies mainly on selective attention [13,15].

F2 Imagining Director-privileged space. When the layout contains occluded regions visible only to the Director, the agent must *construct counterfactual scenes* and reason about what may be present there, a genuinely mentalistic computation that recruits full Theory of Mind (ToM) [3].

F3 Metacognitive cost-benefit evaluation. Because belief tracking, exploration, and clarifying questions all incur different costs, the agent must decide whether to pay those costs or rely on faster egocentric heuristics [10,23,26,27,29].

When do the Factors Matter? Whenever the task could be solved by **F1** alone, as in *Base, Perspective-Taking*, and *Near* first-take accuracy was perfect. Introducing **F2** precipitated large drops (*Distractor, Hidden, Not That*); accuracy rebounded only after the agent executed an exploratory 'look-inside' or issued a query. Pure **F3** pressure (*Far*) likewise reduced first-take accuracy, even though no ToM inference was required. Table 3 quantifies this triple dissociation.

Selective Attention Versus Theory of Mind. The split between **F1** and **F2** mirrors the neuroscientific dissociation between the dorsal rTPJ region, associated with social ToM reasoning, and a neighbouring ventral patch specialised for attentional re-orienting [5,12]. Our LLM agent performs the attentional filter (**F1**) flawlessly but fails when genuine belief reasoning (**F2**) is needed, reproducing the human pattern reported by [15].

Why do Planner-Optimal Traces Fail to Transfer? Fast-Downward plans embody the invariant '*act only once the target is uniquely identifiable to the Director*'. Yet few-shot exposure to those traces did not boost performance because (i) GPT-o3 implicitly assigns near-zero cost to questions, so it still 'plays safe,' and (ii) the linear action lists do not make the underlying cost rationale explicit. Without an explicit belief state and cost model, the LLM reverts to the heuristic 'grab the closest match, ask if unsure'.

Prompting Design for Exploration Beyond cost modelling, an additional limitation concerns the formulation of prompts used to frame the problem and describe the scenario. Several failures related to **F2** and **F3** occurred in situations where the agent would need to hypothesise the existence of relevant but currently unseen objects, an ability central to active vision. These may result from prompts that insufficiently foreground the plausibility of missing information in unexplored, yet accessible, regions. Without an explicit representation of such areas, the agent may not infer that exploration is necessary or worthwhile. Prompt strategies that better support uncertainty reasoning and hypothesis generation about occluded content could thus be essential for more robust epistemic behaviour.

Limitations and Future Directions. The present grid world offers only binary visibility; richer social environments include graded salience, gaze cues, and competing conversational goals. Extending the benchmark to those dimensions should exert stronger pressure on **F2** and **F3**, revealing whether the same failure modes persist or whether multi-modal grounding and cost signals can scaffold more robust ToM.

6 Conclusions

We find that a ReAct loop backed by GPT-o3 already supports flawless Level-1 perspective taking (**F1**), but remains brittle on two fronts: (i) **F2**, imagining alternative objects in occluded space, and (ii) **F3**, weighing the immediate versus delayed costs of belief-driven action. Bridging these gaps may require *explicit belief state tracking* [4,20], *learned cost models*, and *prompting strategies that foreground hidden regions and explicitly stimulate hypothesis generation about unseen content*. Testing agents in richer, more uncertain settings extracted from robot sensors, and penalising gratuitous queries, will be essential for advancing from attentional filtering to full, cost-aware Theory of Mind competence.

Acknowledgments. This work was supported by the Volkswagen Foundation under the funding programme "Open Up âĂŞ New Research Spaces for the Humanities and Cultural Studies," project "Developing an Artificial Social Childhood (ASC) to improve AI causal reasoning, information gathering and decision making," reference 9E530.

References

1. Ahn, M., et al.: Do as i can, not as i say: Grounding language in robotic affordances. arXiv preprint arXiv:2204.01691 (2022)
2. Amirizaniani, M., Martin, E., Sivachenko, M., Mashhadi, A., Shah, C.: Can llms reason like humans? assessing theory of mind reasoning in llms for open-ended questions. In: Proceedings of the 33rd ACM International Conference on Information and Knowledge Management, pp. 34–44 (2024)
3. Bianco, F., Ognibene, D.: Functional advantages of an adaptive theory of mind for robotics: a review of current architectures. In: 2019 11th Computer Science and Electronic Engineering (CEEC), pp. 139–143 (2019)
4. Bianco, F., Ognibene, D.: Robot learning theory of mind through self-observation: Exploiting the intentions-beliefs synergy. arXiv preprint arXiv:2210.09435 (2022)
5. Bitsch, F., Berger, P., Nagels, A., Falkenberg, I., Straube, B.: The role of the right temporo-parietal junction in social decision-making. Hum. Brain Mapp. **39**(7), 3072–3085 (2018)
6. Brown, T., et al.: Language models are few-shot learners. Adv. Neural. Inf. Process. Syst. **33**, 1877–1901 (2020)
7. Flavell, J.H., Everett, B.A., Croft, K., Flavell, E.R.: Young children's knowledge about visual perception: further evidence for the level 1-level 2 distinction. Dev. Psychol. **17**(1), 99 (1981)
8. Góral, G., Ziarko, A., Nauman, M., Wołczyk, M.: Seeing through their eyes: Evaluating visual perspective taking in vision language models. arXiv preprint arXiv:2409.12969 (2024)
9. Grice, H.P.: Logic and conversation. In: Speech acts, pp. 41–58. Brill (1975)
10. Griffiths, T.L., Callaway, F., Chang, M.B., Grant, E., Krueger, P.M., Lieder, F.: Doing more with less: meta-reasoning and meta-learning in humans and machines. Curr. Opin. Behav. Sci. **29**, 24–30 (2019)
11. Huang, W., et al.: Inner monologue: Embodied reasoning through planning with language models. arXiv preprint arXiv:2207.05608 (2022)
12. Igelström, K.M., Webb, T.W., Kelly, Y.T., Graziano, M.S.: Topographical organization of attentional, social, and memory processes in the human temporoparietal cortex. Eneuro **3**(2) (2016)
13. Keysar, B.: Unconfounding common ground. Discourse Process. **24**(2–3), 253–270 (1997)
14. Keysar, B., Barr, D.J., Balin, J.A., Brauner, J.S.: Taking perspective in conversation: the role of mutual knowledge in comprehension. Psychol. Sci. **11**(1), 32–38 (2000)
15. Keysar, B., Lin, S., Barr, D.J.: Limits on theory of mind use in adults. Cognition **89**(1), 25–41 (2003)
16. Kosinski, M.: Evaluating large language models in theory of mind tasks. Proc. Natl. Acad. Sci. **121**(45), e2405460121 (2024)
17. Leonard, B., Woodard, K., Murray, S.O.: Failures in perspective-taking of multimodal ai systems. arXiv preprint arXiv:2409.13929 (2024)
18. Liu, B., et al.: Llm+p: Empowering large language models with optimal planning proficiency (2023). https://arxiv.org/abs/2304.11477
19. Marchetti, A., Manzi, F., Riva, G., Gaggioli, A., Massaro, D.: Artificial intelligence and the illusion of understanding: a systematic review of theory of mind and large language models. Cyberpsychology, Behavior, and Social Networking **0**(0), null (0). https://doi.org/10.1089/cyber.2024.0536, pMID: 40333375

20. Ognibene, D., Chinellato, E., Sarabia, M., Demiris, Y.: Contextual action recognition and target localization with an active allocation of attention on a humanoid robot. Bioinspiration Biomimetics **8**(3), 035002 (2013)
21. Ognibene, D., Mirante, L., Marchegiani, L.: Proactive intention recognition for joint human-robot search and rescue missions through monte-carlo planning in pomdp environments. In: International Conference on Social Robotics, pp. 332–343. Springer (2019)
22. Ognibene, D., et al.: Scoop: A framework for proactive collaboration and social continual learning through natural language interaction and causal reasoning (2025). https://arxiv.org/abs/2503.10241
23. Oliehoek, F.A., Amato, C., et al.: A concise introduction to decentralized POMDPs, vol. 1. Springer (2016)
24. Patania, S., Annese, L., Lambiase, A., Pellegrini, A., Foulsham, T., Ruggeri, A., Rossi, S., Serino, S., Ognibene, D.: Growing Perspectives: Modelling Embodied Perspective Taking and Inner Narrative Development Using Large Language Models. In: Proceedings of the IEEE International Conference on Development and Learning (ICDL) (2025), in press
25. Patania, S., et al.: PerspAct: Enhancing LLM Situated Collaboration Skills through Perspective Taking and Active Vision. In: Proceedings of the 19th International Conference on Intelligent Autonomous Systems (IAS-19) (2025), in press
26. Patania, S., et al.: Large language models as an active bayesian filter: information acquisition and integration. In: Proceedings of the 28th Workshop on the Semantics and Pragmatics of Dialogue (2024)
27. Russell, S., Wefald, E.: Principles of metareasoning. Artif. Intell. **49**(1–3), 361–395 (1991)
28. Sarthou, G., Mayima, A., Buisan, G., Belhassein, K., Clodic, A.: The director task: a psychology-inspired task to assess cognitive and interactive robot architectures. In: 2021 30th IEEE International Conference on Robot & Human Interactive Communication (RO-MAN), pp. 770–777. IEEE (2021)
29. Tversky, A., Kahneman, D.: Judgment under uncertainty: Heuristics and biases: Biases in judgments reveal some heuristics of thinking under uncertainty. science **185**(4157), 1124–1131 (1974)
30. Wang, Z., et al.: Actiview: Evaluating active perception ability for multimodal large language models. arXiv preprint arXiv:2410.04659 (2024)
31. Wilf, A., Lee, S., Liang, P.P., Morency, L.P.: Think twice: Perspective-taking improves large language models' theory-of-mind capabilities. In: Proceedings of the 62nd Annual Meeting of the Association for Computational Linguistics (Volume 1: Long Papers), pp. 8292–8308 (2024)
32. Yao, S., et al.: React: synergizing reasoning and acting in language models. In: International Conference on Learning Representations (ICLR) (2023)
33. Zhu, W., Singh, I., Jia, R., Thomason, J.: Language models can infer action semantics for symbolic planners from environment feedback (2024). https://arxiv.org/abs/2406.02791

In the Comfort Zone: How Social Robots Learn to Adapt

Sara Mongile[1,3(✉)], Ana Tanevska[2], Francesco Rea[1], and Alessandra Sciutti[1]

[1] CONTACT Unit, Italian Institute of Technology, Genoa, Italy
{francesco.rea,alessandra.sciutti}@iit.it
[2] Department of Information Technology, Uppsala University, Uppsala, Sweden
ana.tanevska@it.uu.se
[3] DIBRIS Department, University of Genoa, Genoa, Italy
sara.mongile@iit.it

Abstract. Achieving efficient and natural human-robot interaction requires robots to dynamically adapt their behavior to align with each user's specific interaction style. This work presents an adaptive framework based on a comfort-driven architecture that enables social robots to adjust their behavior in response to individual user interaction styles, while maintaining their internal goals. The system leverages a modular architecture integrating perception, motivation, and reasoning components that allow the robot to identify the user's preferred interaction modality and refine its behavior by regulating less-used modalities to ensure more balanced and effective communication. A simulation study demonstrated that the adaptive system allows the robot to maintain higher comfort levels and respond more efficiently to users with consistent interaction patterns, while adapting gradually to more variable profiles. By adapting its behavior, the proposed system aims to foster a more engaging and enjoyable interaction for both parties.

Keywords: Cognitive Architecture · Adaptation · Human-robot interaction

1 Introduction

1.1 Motivation

Recent advancements in artificial intelligence (AI) and robotics have been impressive, allowing robots to perform precise or complex actions [14,30,31]. However, one of the most complex challenges in robotics remains the ability for robots to engage in meaningful interaction in social scenarios with humans [20]. The complexity of human interactions, which appears incredibly easy for us, is far from being replicated in machines. Human interactions are driven by a combination of cognitive, emotional, and sensory processing that allows people to engage with others adaptively [13]. For robots to achieve similar levels of competence, they need to be capable of perceiving, interpreting, and appropriately responding to human actions and intentions in real-time [3,6,8,41]. Moreover, to become effective interaction partners, robots need to be aware of their human partner's needs and affective states and adjust to them [9,33]. To tackle this challenge, many approaches have been explored, ranging from pre-programming robots with a fixed set of behaviors [40] to using Wizard-of-Oz techniques [21,35] or implementing internal motivation models [7,25].

This work is motivated by the idea that social robots should move beyond reactive and scripted behaviors. Instead, they should rely on cognitive and adaptive mechanisms to understand interaction dynamics and personalize their responses accordingly. In this direction, we focused on developing a cognitive architecture that integrates perception, motivation, and reasoning components, enabling the robot to dynamically adjust its behavior in response to interaction feedback and internal goals. This adaptation is guided by an internal motivation system centered on *comfort* [27], which acts as a self-regulatory signal to align the robot's behavior with the user interaction style.

1.2 Research Objective and Contribution

The goal of this work is to develop an adaptive system that enables robots to personalize their behavior to individual users while still pursuing their own internal goals. Although adapting to human preferences is essential in human-robot interaction, excessive behavioral flexibility can lead to unpredictability and reduce user trust [15,22].

To address this, we introduce an adaptive system that balances the importance of adapting to individual preferences with the fact that the agent initially declared specific needs. In this framework, the robot seeks to fulfill its needs by asking the user. When a request is unmet, the robot either re-initiates the interaction or adapts by selecting alternative behaviors to fulfill its goal independently. This adaptive strategy helps the robot to maintain its identity as an agent with its own needs while avoiding annoying the user. Additionally, by maintaining a high comfort level, the robot can consistently provide positive feedback, facilitating user confidence and engagement, as suggested by [24].

1.3 Related Work

Considerable research has focused on developing methods that enable robots to effectively respond to human behavior [32]. In HRI, adaptation has generally been approached using two main strategies. The first concerns the analysis of human social signals to adjust the designed robot behavior [2]. The other approach concerns using social signals as input to a robot architecture that can adapt autonomously to the human as a function of the interactions between the human and the robot [23]. Within this second approach, we can further distinguish between psychology-inspired and biologically inspired architectures. Psychology-inspired architectures, such as Soar [19] or ACT-R [39], facilitate real-time social adaptation in robots by integrating learning mechanisms and perception-based behavior selection. Biologically-inspired architectures, on the other hand, focus on the role of affective states - motivations and emotions- in regulating bodily and social homeostasis [11] to enable more natural and adaptive human-robot interactions [18].

Stepping outside this distinction, recent research has included estimating the user's emotional state using multimodal emotional architecture [17], using an architecture that promotes learning a person's face during HRI by evaluating the situation and matching it with the stored knowledge of that person [5,26], and using reinforcement learning to adapt behavior or personality based on social signals such as facial expressions, laughter, or user interaction patterns [42]. Additionally, other studies have investigated affective signaling, where robots respond to human social cues with expressive behaviors [1,24,36].

Starting from these works, this research proposes a novel adaptive framework based on a comfort-driven architecture that aims to promote a more personalized and intuitive human-robot interaction. Our comfort-driven model enables robots to modulate their responses based on both their own internal needs and the social dynamics of the interaction. Through this research, we aim to provide insights into how internal social motivation can support personalized, adaptive HRI, contributing to the development of more intuitive and engaging robotic systems.

1.4 Structure

The rest of the paper is organized as follows: Sect. 2 presents the cognitive architecture and the adaptive elements. Next, Sect. 3 describes the purpose of the study and the experimental design; in Sect. 4, we report the results. Finally, in Sect. 5, we discuss the findings from our study, the limitations, and future work.

2 Cognitive Architecture

The proposed cognitive architecture consists of sensory, perceptual, motivational, reasoning, behavioral, and motor modules (Fig. 1). These modules operate simultaneously to simulate a cognitively driven and socially responsive robotic agent. In this study, the architecture is implemented within a simulated environment, extending a framework previously validated in human-robot interaction studies [27–29]. The simulation generates and manages all sensory inputs and behavioral outputs, replicating the robot's perceptual and motor capabilities.

In this study, we introduce the adaptive mechanism in the cognitive framework to enhance its compliance with individual inclinations. These mechanisms allow the robot to dynamically adjust its behavior by interpreting user feedback and modulating its behavior in real time, aiming to improve the robot's capacity to respond to user behavior in a personalized manner.

2.1 Sensory and Perception Module

The *perception* module processed *visual*, *tactile*, and *toy-related* stimuli. Visual stimuli, collected as a sequential stream of images from the robot's eye-positioned camera, are processed to detect the presence of a human face and classify associated expressions. Tactile stimuli are gathered through skin sensor patches placed on the robot's arms and torso [10]. Additionally, toy-related stimuli refer to interactive sensorized objects such as the iCube and light bulbs [12,34]. The iCube device is used as a switcher to trigger dynamic visual feedback from the light bulbs through flickering and color-changing lights. This modality provides a form of interactive play, allowing participants to engage with the robot through a play modality.

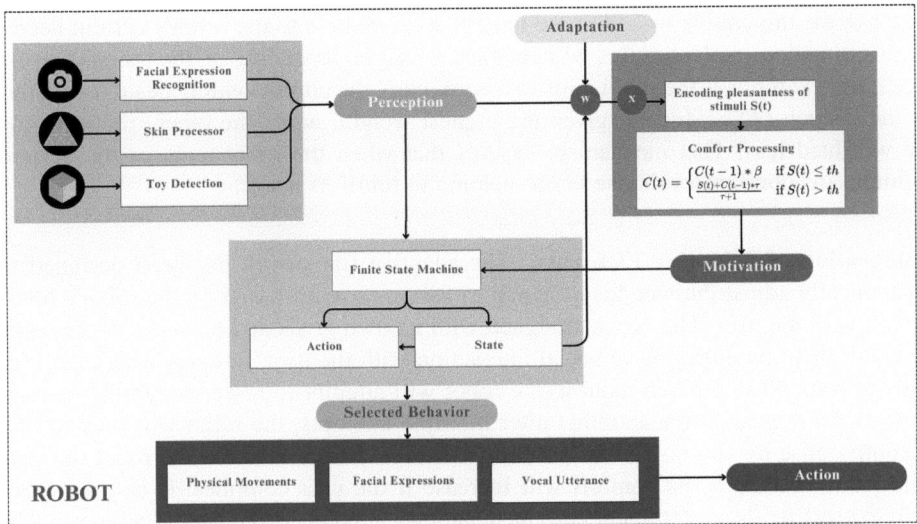

Fig. 1. The framework comprises four main components—Perception, Action, Reasoning, and the Motivation Module. The Perception component receives and processes visual, tactile, and toy-related stimuli. The Motivation Module analyzes input from the Perception and Reasoning components to compute comfort motivation, which is then sent to the Reasoning module to guide the robot's behavior selection process. Finally, the selected behavior is executed through the action component responsible for the robot's vocal and physical expressions.

2.2 Motivation Module

The *motivation* module implemented the proposed comfort-driven framework, drawing loosely from prior research in human-robot interaction that employed hormone-inspired internal motivation systems for robotic agents [4,16,38].

The robot's comfort is processed as a function of the pleasant stimuli received by the robot, which, in turn, depends on the robot's requests, determined by the robot's state within the state machine. The comfort formula[1] is:

$$C(t) = \begin{cases} C(t-1) * \beta & \text{if } S(t) \leq TH \\ \dfrac{S(t) + C(t-1) * \tau}{\tau + 1} & \text{if } S(t) > TH \end{cases} \quad (1)$$

where *C(t)* indicates the current comfort level, whereas *C(t-1)* is the previous comfort level. A higher *C(t)* value indicates that the robot perceives the interaction as more pleasant. *S(t)* represents the combination of stimuli received during the interaction and their evaluation in terms of alignment with the robot's needs and goals. β and τ are social variables modulating the decay and growth rate of comfort. *TH* is the stimulation threshold, a scalar value used to determine the increase or decrease of comfort value. In this study, we defined a set of weights for each state in the state machine. The aim was

---

[1] The entire code is available on request.

to make the motivation system more natural and sensitive to the robot's current needs. In this direction, each stimulus was assigned a weight depending on the robot's current need. For example, if the robot aims to receive care, the corresponding desired stimulus is the "Touch (T)", which is given the highest weight, while the other stimuli would be weighted less. This mechanism ensures that when the robot receives the desired stimulus, its comfort levels rise faster, helping to fulfill its needs.

Integration of Adaptive Elements. The adaptive framework has been designed to dynamically adjust the weights assigned to various stimuli based on the robot's interaction with the user. The robot, designed with its own goals and needs, actively seeks to fulfill them by engaging in social interaction with the user. In cases where the user fails to respond to a given request, the robot will attempt to re-engage in the interaction. If the request remains unmet after multiple attempts, the robot will seek to find a compromise by autonomously fulfilling its needs. For instance, if the robot requests affect through touch, its comfort will increase if the user complies. If not, the robot will express its disappointment and make another attempt. If the user continues not to respond, the robot will shift to a "self-care behavior" to fulfill its needs independently. This adaptive process allows the robot to learn the user preferences over time, such as a reduced likelihood of engaging in tactile interaction, prompting the robot to adjust its approach accordingly (e.g., by reducing the weight assigned to touch in subsequent interactions).

From a technical point of view, the weights are updated when the robot enters a Self-regulatory or Stress state, following the Algorithm 1.

Algorithm 1. Weights Update

if $totTouch > totToys$ then
    $touchW \leftarrow touchW + learningRate$
    $toysW \leftarrow toysW - learningRate$
else if $totToys > totTouch$ then
    $toysW \leftarrow toysW + learningRate$
    $touchW \leftarrow touchW - learningRate$
else
    $SC \leftarrow SC + learningRate$

where *totTouch* and *totToys* represent the average over a one-minute sliding window of the tactile and toy stimuli received. *touchW* and *toysW* are the weights associated with tactile and toy interactions, respectively. *SC* is the self-regulative parameter. Finally, when the weight update is performed in a self-regulatory state, *learningRate* takes a value of 0.1, whereas if it occurs in a stress state, it is equal to 0.2.

2.3 Reasoning Module

The *reasoning* module is represented by the decision-maker. The reasoning process is based on a state machine, where the logical interpretation to make a choice is based on the robot's context and rules. The module considers the perceptual and the motivational values as input and, according to them, makes the decision. This way, the module dynamically uses a dynamic action selection process, selecting the appropriate action based on the robot's motivation, available knowledge, and context.

The robot's behavior is organized into distinct states, each representing a specific phase in its interaction. The list of robot states and their corresponding features is summarized in the Table 1 below:

Table 1. Features of robot states

Robot state	Features	Desired stimuli
Play	Play with the user or ask to play together	Toys
Affect	Receive affect from the user or ask for care	Tactile
Explore	Look around and wait for the user to interact	Toys or Tactile
Self-Play	Play alone	Toys
Self-Affect	Rocking, and self-care	Tactile
Stress-Play	Express Stress and seek to engage through play modality	Toys
Stress-Affect	Express Stress and seek to engage, asking for care	Tactile

The system employs an adaptive state transition mechanism that adjusts the robot's behavior based on real-time user stimuli and the robot's comfort level. Initially, the robot starts in an *Idle* state for a fixed duration (10 s). If the robot receives stimuli during this period, it transitions to the corresponding interaction modality. Depending on the stimulus type (e.g., Toys or Touch), the system will enter either the corresponding *Play* or *Affect* state. If no explicit interaction occurs, the system defaults to the *Play* state.

Once the robot enters an **active interaction state**, the system continuously monitors the time spent in each modality and adapts based on the robot's comfort level. After 15 s, transitions between states are influenced by the robot's comfort. If the comfort level exceeds a high threshold (0.7), the robot switches to another interaction modality, considering whether the user is currently engaged with it. In contrast, if the comfort level drops below a low threshold (0.3), the system transitions to a **distressed state**, either *Stress-Affect* or *Stress-Play*.

Additionally, the system incorporates **self-regulation states**, which allow the robot to autonomously increase its comfort level and fulfill its internal objectives when user interaction is insufficient. These states enable the robot to maintain or improve its comfort level even in the absence of user stimuli.

2.4 Behavioral and Action Module

The *action* module performed a finite set of actions by controlling the specific body parts in joint space control of the robot's neck, torso, and arms. Additionally, the module controlled the robot's facial expressions and vocal utterances to support more comprehensive communication. The designed movements were inspired by previous studies on child–caretaker interactions [36,38], with the robot emulating the role of a toddler. In the present study, all motor actions and expressive behaviors were simulated to test the architecture without relying on physical hardware consistently.

3 Experimental Design

3.1 Purpose of the Simulation

This simulation study imitated an interaction between a human participant and the robot iCub in a controlled environment. In the study, the envisioned role for iCub was that of a toddler exploring and playing with its toys while the participants were in the role of the iCub's caretaker.

Two conditions with different robot profiles were considered for the simulation to verify the effect of the adaptive framework. In the former, iCub had a fixed (F) profile, whereas in the second, it had an adaptive profile (A). The robot's behavior was guided by its social needs in both cases. Indeed, the robot's objective was to engage with the participant through two distinct interaction modalities: play and receive care. Ideally, the robot alternated between these two modalities to satisfy its needs.

At the beginning of the experiments, the robot's comfort was set at 50% of its maximum value, and the robot was in an "Idle" state, waiting for the participants to start interacting. If participants engage with the robot using the toys, the robot enters a "play" state, while if it engages by using tactile stimuli, it enters a "care" state. In the simulation, the robot always enters the play state as the first decision. The rest of the interaction evolves considering the robot's comfort and the stimuli provided by the users. Further details are provided in Sect. 2.3. The simulation lasted 10 minutes. During this period, the robot's behavior was monitored to assess how it adapts to user stimuli and regulates its internal state. The collected data were analyzed and compared to better understand the robot's interaction dynamics and decision-making process.

The robot's comfort level is processed using the Eq. 1, which is used in both Fixed and Adaptive profiles, and it drives the robot's behavior during the interaction with the user.

3.2 Simulated User Profiles

In order to test multiple sets of parameters across various user profiles, the approach selected was to design nine simulated user profiles and run a simulation study, as previous studies did, e.g., [24,37]. Table 2 showcases the modalities of the profiles. To test the ability of the approach to adapt to the user modality, we introduced unbalanced profiles that rely exclusively on a single modality. For complete and average profiles, the visual stimuli were designed to be always at their maximum value since we assumed the user was always in front of the robot. The tactile and toy stimuli varied according to the user's profile.

In the average profiles, tactile or toy stimuli were provided to respond to requests during active or stress states. These stimuli were alternated between two values, with the time in seconds indicating at which frequency they alternated and the percentage representing the probability of receiving the stimulus.

For the void profile, the stimuli were non-existent input.

Table 2. Features of the five user profiles

User Profiles	Visual	Tactile	Toys
Complete	1.0	1.0	1.0
Visual-Tactile	1.0	1.0	0.0
Visual-Toys	1.0	0.0	1.0
Average	1.0	[0.0-1.0], 10s, 50%	[0.0-1.0], 10s, 50%
Average Tactile	1.0	[0.0-1.0], 10s, 80%	[0.0-1.0], 10s, 20%
Average Toys	1.0	[0.0-1.0], 10s, 20%	[0.0-1.0], 10s, 80%
Tactile	0.0	1.0	0.0
Toys	0.0	0.0	1.0
Void	0.0	0.0	0.0

4 Simulation Results

The collected data was analyzed for nine metrics. Specifically, we processed the average comfort value and standard deviation, comparing the Adaptive (A) and the Fixed (F) conditions. The results are shown in Table 3.

Table 3. Comfort value results

User Profile	Average (std)	
	A	F
complete	1 (0.05)	1 (0.05)
visual-tactile	0.93 (0.14)	0.71 (0.09)
visual-toys	0.95 (0.14)	0.74 (0.09)
average	0.51 (0.1)	0.48 (0.09)
average-tactile	0.48 (0.07)	0.44 (0.05)
average-toys	0.55 (0.09)	0.48 (0.07)
tactile	0.58 (0.11)	0.46 (0.05)
toys	0.58 (0.11)	0.46 (0.05)
void	0.57 (0.13)	0.25 (0.04)

To test the difference across conditions, we conducted a paired-sample t-test, which confirmed the average comfort value in the adaptive profile is significantly higher than in the fixed profiles ($p-value = 0.010$).

These tests showed that the *complete* profile elicited the highest comfort value across both conditions. Generally, the adaptive conditions showed higher comfort values than the fixed conditions. This effect was particularly evident in profiles such as *visual-tactile, visual-toys,tactile, toys,* and *void,* where the stimuli remain at a fixed value for all the time of the interaction. Indeed, the *average* profiles, where the stimuli were alternated sparsely over time, showed little difference among results. This is due to the variability of the stimuli, which likely required more time for the system to adapt and determine the presence of a dominant stimulus.

An example is shown in Fig. 2.

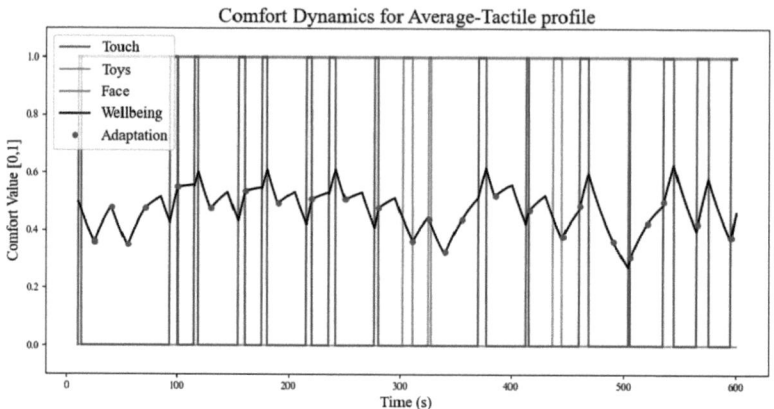

Fig. 2. Dynamics of comfort value in the Adaptive condition during full interaction with the Average-Tactile profile. The red dot indicates the moment when the robot adapts its weights. (Color figure online)

Additionally, we calculated the amount of time during the interaction that iCub spent in an *interactive*, *self*, or *stressed* state. We divided these times into %Play, %Affect, %Self-Play, and %Self-Affect, while the total time spent in a stressed state was summed and defined as %Stress. In this analysis, we did not report the time spent in the Explore state, as it was not relevant to the primary focus of the research. Results are presented in Table 4.

As expected, the robot alternates equally between the Play and Affect states, with equal outcomes in the Adaptive and Fixed conditions when interacting with the *complete* profile.

The adaptive condition (A) has been demonstrated to be able to adjust to the most dominant stimuli, spending more time in states that align with the prevailing input, such as Play or Affect, depending on the user profile. Specifically, in the *visual-tactile* and *tactile* profiles, it spent more time in the Affect state and favors the *Self-Play* state over *Play*. Specifically, in the *visual-tactile* profile, the robot spends 42.7% of the time in *Self-Play* and 47.2% in *Affect*, indicating a clear preference for self-playing and affective states. The opposite occurs for the *visual-toys*, where *Play* is more evident (adaptive: Play = 43.8%, Self-Affect = 33.2%, Affect = 17.8%).

Compared to the fixed condition, the adaptive profiles were more effective in favoring self-regulatory behaviors when the user profile did not engage with the specific interaction modality. In this case, the robot spent less time in the respective active state and adopted a self-regulating behavior for that modality.

Table 4. Percentage time in each state (the values of interest are highlighted)

User Profile	%Play		%Affect		%SelfPlay		%SelfAffect		%Stress	
	A	F	A	F	A	F	A	F	A	F
complete	51.0	51.0	49.0	49.0	0.0	0.0	0.0	0.0	0.0	0.0
visual-tactile	10.1	33.8	**47.2**	33.0	**42.7**	33.1	0.0	0.0	0.0	0.0
visual-toys	**43.8**	35.6	17.8	31.5	2.5	2.6	**33.2**	30.2	0.0	0.0
average	16.1	15.4	17.8	15.2	22.8	22.7	22.8	25.5	12.7	16.2
average tactile	15.1	12.7	15.1	14.1	23.0	25.2	23.0	29.1	16.1	17.7
average toys	22.8	17.9	23.7	15.3	25.4	28.4	25.4	25.5	2.5	12.7
tactile	22.9	17.8	**28.0**	17.7	22.8	28.0	15.4	26.2	**0.0**	10.2
toys	**28.6**	17.9	22.8	17.8	17.8	26.1	23.0	27.9	**0.0**	10.2
void	18.0	2.5	18.0	0.0	22.6	34.2	21.1	30.1	**5.1**	33.1

As indicated by the comfort levels, the *average* profiles appeared to require more time to adjust to the stimuli. This suggests that the robot needed a longer period to recognize the dominant modalities and adapt accordingly.

Stress time is generally lower in the adaptive profiles compared to the fixed profiles, such as the *tactile* and *void* profiles, where stress time is minimal or nonexistent. However, in some adaptive profiles, such as the *average* and *average-tactile* profiles, the robot still spends some time in the Stress state, although this remains low compared to fixed profiles.

5 Discussion

This work introduces an adaptive mechanism that allows robots to dynamically adjust their behavior based on user interaction styles, while maintaining their internal goals. The system promotes balanced and effective engagement by refining responses and self-regulating underutilized modalities. This design supports behavioral consistency, which is essential for fostering a sense of reliability in the agent [15]. By gradually adjusting its interaction strategies, the robot aligns with the user's preferred engagement style while regulating less-used modalities to remain consistent with its internal objectives.

In the simulation study, the robot aimed to fulfill its social needs by interacting with the user. The experimental results showed that the comfort value varies as expected, with the robot displaying all of its discrete behavioral states in different situations. The adaptive mechanism also performed as expected, providing a higher comfort value compared to the fixed robot, particularly for less engaged user profiles. Overall, results showed that the robot learned more quickly when user profiles exhibited a consistent interaction modality. This stability allowed the adaptive system to efficiently recognize the user's preferred modality and adopt a self-regulatory approach for the less-utilized one. Conversely, with user profiles who exhibited more variable interaction patterns, the robot required more time to identify and adapt to their preferred modalities, as these alternated more frequently and occurred less consistently. The analysis of the time spent in each state further demonstrates that the proposed adaptive system enables the robot to maintain its needs as an autonomous agent while reducing interaction demands when the user does not respond to them. This mechanism prioritizes the user's preferred interaction modalities, allowing the robot to primarily engage through the modality the user actively employs and adopt a self-regulation strategy to manage unmet needs during the interaction.

By adapting its behavior, the proposed system aims to foster a more engaging and enjoyable interaction for both parties. The current version of the framework is mainly guided by the robot's internal needs and responds dynamically to user behavior by adjusting its interaction modality accordingly. However, we acknowledge that explicitly user-initiated requests are not yet directly addressed in this version. Future extensions of the architecture will focus on recognizing and integrating user-driven goals or instructions, enabling a more bidirectional and responsive interaction. Additionally, to improve adaptability to users with rapidly changing preferences, future work will investigate mechanisms such as adaptive learning rates or memory decay. Additionally, future research will evaluate the adaptive framework in a real human-robot interaction study. Specifically, we aim to port the adaptive framework to the robot and explore how participants perceive and respond to this framework, contributing to a deeper understanding of its effectiveness and acceptance.

Acknowledgments. This work is supported by the "Brain and Machines" Flagship Program of the Istituto Italiano di Tecnologia (IIT) and by the European Union-NextGenerationEU and by the Ministry of University and Research (MUR), National Recovery and Resilience Plan (NRRP), Mission 4, Component 2, Investment 1.5, project "RAISE-Robotics and AI for Socio-economic Empowerment" (ECS00000035).

Disclosure of Interests. The authors have no competing interests to declare that are relevant to the content of this article.

References

1. Adam, C., Johal, W., Pellier, D., Fiorino, H., Pesty, S.: Social human-robot interaction: a new cognitive and affective interaction-oriented architecture. In: Social Robotics: 8th International Conference, ICSR 2016, Kansas City, MO, USA, November 1-3, 2016 Proceedings 8, pp. 253–263. Springer (2016)
2. Ahmad, M.I., Mubin, O., Orlando, J.: A systematic review of adaptivity in human-robot interaction. Multimodal Technologies and Interaction **1**(3), 14 (2017)
3. Ahmad, M.I., Mubin, O., Shahid, S., Orlando, J.: Robot's adaptive emotional feedback sustains children's social engagement and promotes their vocabulary learning: a long-term child-robot interaction study. Adapt. Behav. **27**(4), 243–266 (2019)
4. Avila-Garcia, O., Canamero, L.: Hormonal modulation of perception in motivation-based action selection architectures. In: Procs of the Symposium on Agents that Want and Like, SSAISB (2005)
5. Belgiovine, G., Gonzalez-Billandon, J., Sandini, G., Rea, F., Sciutti, A.: Towards an hri tutoring framework for long-term personalization and real-time adaptation. In: Adjunct Proceedings of the 30th ACM Conference on User Modeling, Adaptation and Personalization, pp. 139–145 (2022)

6. Breazeal, C.: Socially intelligent robots. interactions **12**(2), 19–22 (2005)
7. Breazeal, C., et al.: A motivational system for regulating human-robot interaction. In: Aaai/iaai, pp. 54–61 (1998)
8. Breazeal, C., Scassellati, B.: How to build robots that make friends and influence people. In: Proceedings 1999 IEEE/RSJ International Conference on Intelligent Robots and Systems. Human and Environment Friendly Robots With High Intelligence and Emotional Quotients (cat. No. 99CH36289), vol. 2, pp. 858–863. IEEE (1999)
9. Cangelosi, A., et al.: Integration of action and language knowledge: a roadmap for developmental robotics. IEEE Trans. Auton. Ment. Dev. **2**(3), 167–195 (2010)
10. Cannata, G., Maggiali, M., Metta, G., Sandini, G.: An embedded artificial skin for humanoid robots. In: 2008 IEEE International Conference on Multisensor Fusion and Integration for Intelligent Systems, pp. 434–438. IEEE (2008)
11. Damasio, A.R.: The feeling of what happens: Body and emotion in the making of consciousness. Houghton Mifflin Harcourt (1999)
12. Eldardeer, O., Gonzalez-Billandon, J., Grasse, L., Tata, M., Rea, F.: A biological inspired cognitive framework for memory-based multi-sensory joint attention in human-robot interactive tasks. Front. Neurorobot. **15**, 648595 (2021)
13. Feldman, R.: Parent-infant synchrony and the construction of shared timing; physiological precursors, developmental outcomes, and risk conditions. J. Child Psychol. Psychiatry **48**(3–4), 329–354 (2007)
14. Guizzo, E.: By leaps and bounds: An exclusive look at how boston dynamics is redefining robot agility. IEEE Spectr. **56**(12), 34–39 (2019)
15. Hancock, P.A., Billings, D.R., Oleson, K.E., Chen, J.Y., De Visser, E., Parasuraman, R.: A meta-analysis of factors influencing the development of human-robot trust. Hum. Factors **53**(5), 517–527 (2011)
16. Hiolle, A., Canamero, L., Davila-Ross, M., Bard, K.A.: Eliciting caregiving behavior in dyadic human-robot attachment-like interactions. ACM Trans. Interact. Intell. Syst. (TiiS) **2**(1), 1–24 (2012)
17. Hong, A., et al.: A multimodal emotional human-robot interaction architecture for social robots engaged in bidirectional communication. IEEE Trans. Cybern. **51**(12), 5954–5968 (2020)
18. Khan, I., Cañamero, L.: Modelling adaptation through social allostasis: Modulating the effects of social touch with oxytocin in embodied agents. Multimodal Technol. Interact. **2**(4), 67 (2018)
19. Laird, J.E.: The Soar cognitive architecture. MIT Press (2019)
20. Lake, B.M., Ullman, T.D., Tenenbaum, J.B., Gershman, S.J.: Building machines that learn and think like people. Behav. Brain Sci. **40**, e253 (2017)
21. Law, E., et al.: A wizard-of-oz study of curiosity in human-robot interaction. In: 2017 26th IEEE International Symposium on Robot and Human Interactive Communication (RO-MAN), pp. 607–614. IEEE (2017)
22. Lee, J.D., See, K.A.: Trust in automation: Designing for appropriate reliance. Hum. Factors **46**(1), 50–80 (2004)
23. Maroto-Gómez, M., Alonso-Martín, F., Malfaz, M., Castro-González, Á., Castillo, J.C., Salichs, M.Á.: A systematic literature review of decision-making and control systems for autonomous and social robots. Int. J. Robot. **15**(5), 745–789 (2023)
24. Maroto-Gómez, M., Lewis, M., Castro-González, Á., Malfaz, M., Salichs, M.Á., Cañamero, L.: Adapting to my user, engaging with my robot: An adaptive affective architecture for a social assistive robot. ACM Trans. Intell. Syst, Technol (2024)
25. Maroto-Gómez, M., Malfaz, M., Castro-González, Á., Salichs, M.Á.: A motivational model based on artificial biological functions for the intelligent decision-making of social robots. Memetic Computing , 1–21 (2023). https://doi.org/10.1007/s12293-023-00390-3

26. Martin-Rico, F., Gomez-Donoso, F., Escalona, F., Garcia-Rodriguez, J., Cazorla, M.: Semantic visual recognition in a cognitive architecture for social robots. Integrated Computer-Aided Engineering **27**(3), 301–316 (2020)
27. Mongile, S.: Towards adaptive human-robot interaction: a comfort-driven framework for social robots. In: 2025 20th ACM/IEEE International Conference on Human-Robot Interaction (HRI), pp. 1872–1874. IEEE (2025)
28. Mongile, S., Tanevska, A., Rea, F., Sciutti, A.: Are robots that assess their partner's attachment style better at autonomous adaptive behaviour? In: Proceedings of the 2022 ACM/IEEE International Conference on Human-Robot Interaction, pp. 922–926 (2022)
29. Mongile, S., Tanevska, A., Rea, F., Sciutti, A.: Validating a cortisol-inspired framework for human-robot interaction with a replication of the still face paradigm. In: 2022 IEEE International Conference on Development and Learning (ICDL), pp. 190–196. IEEE (2022)
30. Obaigbena, A., Lottu, O.A., Ugwuanyi, E.D., Jacks, B.S., Sodiya, E.O., Daraojimba, O.D.: Ai and human-robot interaction: A review of recent advances and challenges. GSC Adv. Res. Rev. **18**(2), 321–330 (2024)
31. Pucci, D., Romano, F., Traversaro, S., Nori, F.: Highly dynamic balancing via force control. In: 2016 IEEE-RAS 16th International Conference on Humanoid Robots (Humanoids), pp. 141–141. IEEE (2016)
32. Rossi, S., Ferland, F., Tapus, A.: User profiling and behavioral adaptation for hri: a survey. Pattern Recogn. Lett. **99**, 3–12 (2017)
33. Sciutti, A., Mara, M., Tagliasco, V., Sandini, G.: Humanizing human-robot interaction: on the importance of mutual understanding. IEEE Technol. Soc. Mag. **37**(1), 22–29 (2018)
34. Sciutti, A., Sandini, G.: The role of object motion in visuo-haptic exploration during development. In: 2019 Joint IEEE 9th International Conference on Development and Learning and Epigenetic Robotics (ICDL-EpiRob), pp. 123–128. IEEE (2019)
35. Steinfeld, A., Jenkins, O.C., Scassellati, B.: The oz of wizard: simulating the human for interaction research. In: Proceedings of the 4th ACM/IEEE international conference on Human robot interaction, pp. 101–108 (2009)
36. Tanevska, A., Rea, F., Sandini, G., Cañamero, L., Sciutti, A.: A cognitive architecture for socially adaptable robots. In: 2019 Joint IEEE 9th International Conference on Development and Learning and Epigenetic Robotics (ICDL-EpiRob), pp. 195–200. IEEE (2019)
37. Tanevska, A., Rea, F., Sandini, G., Cañamero, L., Sciutti, A.: Eager to learn vs. quick to complain? how a socially adaptive robot architecture performs with different robot personalities. In: 2019 IEEE International Conference on Systems, Man and Cybernetics (SMC), pp. 365–371. IEEE (2019)
38. Tanevska, A., Rea, F., Sandini, G., Cañamero, L., Sciutti, A.: A socially adaptable framework for human-robot interaction. Front. Robot. AI, **7** (2020)
39. Trafton, J.G., Hiatt, L.M., Harrison, A.M., Tamborello, F.P., Khemlani, S.S., Schultz, A.C.: Act-r/e: An embodied cognitive architecture for human-robot interaction. J. Hum.-Robot Interact. **2**(1), 30–55 (2013)
40. Van Breemen, A.: Bringing robots to life: applying principles of animation to robots. In: Proceedings of Shapping Human-Robot Interaction workshop held at CHI, vol. 2004, pp. 143–144. Citeseer (2004)
41. Vaufreydaz, D., Johal, W., Combe, C.: Starting engagement detection towards a companion robot using multimodal features. Robot. Auton. Syst. **75**, 4–16 (2016)
42. Weber, K., Ritschel, H., Aslan, I., Lingenfelser, F., André, E.: How to shape the humor of a robot-social behavior adaptation based on reinforcement learning. In: Proceedings of the 20th ACM International Conference on Multimodal Interaction, pp. 154–162 (2018)

Social Robotics and Sustainability

Rethinking Learning from Demonstration Through Enactive Cognitive Sciences: From Replication to Dialogue in HRI

Martina Bacaro(✉)

Department of Philosophy, University of Bologna Alma Mater Studiorum, Bologna, Italy
martina.bacaro2@unibo.it

Abstract. Human-Robot Interaction (HRI) research is still largely shaped by the replication paradigm, in which social robots are designed as functional reproductions of human agents, based on computational and representational models of cognition [1, 2]. This perspective, however, struggles to account for the relational and embodied dimensions of interaction, often failing to support adaptability in dynamic, real-world contexts. This paper proposes a shift toward a dialogical model of HRI grounded in enactive cognitive science [3, 4]. Taking Learning from Demonstration (LfD) as a case study, I show how its current implementations often rely on Theory of Mind (ToM) assumptions and unidirectional models of imitation [5, 6]. An enactive reinterpretation can reframe LfD as a process of mutual adaptation through sensorimotor coordination and interactional dynamics [7] and provide a more comprehensive and dynamical view of human cognition which aligns with alternative effective and situated practices of LfD [8, 9]. Following this reconfiguration, novel ways of developing LfD will be suggested. This conceptual transformation aligns social robotics with broader goals of sustainability. Designing for dialogic co-creation and embodied reciprocity has the potential to enable the development of systems that are socially sustainable, i.e., adaptive and inclusive – able to integrate meaningfully into everyday life while promoting ecological inclusivity. By moving from replication to dialogue, this approach reimagines HRI as a domain in which novel forms of intersubjectivity emerge, essential for sustainable technological futures.

Keywords: Human-Robot Interaction (HRI) · Enactive Cognitive Science · Learning from Demonstration (LfD) · Social Robotics

1 Introduction

The field of robotics faces a critical near-term challenge: developing robots capable of engaging in fluid, reliable interactions with humans during shared tasks [6]. This challenge has become increasingly pressing as robots are transitioning from controlled industrial environments to social spaces where they must interpret and respond appropriately to human actions (see [10]). Central of this endeavor is the challenge of making robots able to learn how to perform a behavior in real-time and real-world scenarios.

Machine learning plays a crucial role in addressing these challenges, particularly in enabling robots to learn from human input in real time. This is made possible in the field of Learning from Demonstration (LfD), i.e. a machine learning paradigm in which robots acquire new skills by *replicating* human behavior [11, 12]. To meet this challenge, the research field of Human-Robot Interaction (HRI) has dedicated substantial efforts to understanding how to model human learning abilities and implement them in robotic architectures. To date, the main strategy that has been adopted in HRI to accomplish this task has been guided by what can be termed the *replication paradigm*: the attempt to engineer artificial agents as functional surrogates – or replicas – of human counterparts. This approach, grounded in computational and representational theories of cognition [1, 2], has driven important advances in robotic domains such as perception, planning, and learning [13–15] (see also [16]). Yet it also imposes significant conceptual and practical limitations. By prioritizing replication over differences and reasoning over acting, current models often neglect the relational, embodied, and dynamical dimensions of social engagement, which hampers robotic performance in real-world, situated contexts [17–20]. Moreover, this issue raises broader social and ethical concerns. As robotic systems are deployed in care, education, and public life, their ability to adapt meaningfully to diverse human practices and behaviors becomes crucial.

The aim of this paper is to propose an enactive reframing of LfD as a means of rethinking HRI more broadly, by proposing a switch from computational to enactivist models of cognition. Enactivism understands cognition not as internal computation but as embodied, situated activity that emerges through interaction [3, 4]. From this perspective, learning is not the internalization of observed behavior – replicated on different material substrates, whether biological or synthetic – but a process of co-regulated sensorimotor coordination and participatory practices [7]. Reframing LfD through an enactive lens, I argue, enables us to move from a model of replication to one of dialogue – where robots are not passive imitators, but active co-participants in shared meaning-making processes. The paper is structured as follows. In §2, I examine the epistemological foundations and limitations of the replication paradigm. §3 analyzes dominant implementations of LfD, which are mainly based on the replication paradigm. §4 introduces the enactive paradigm in cognitive sciences, emphasizing the role of embodied interaction and co-adaptive dynamics for learning human practices. I will present examples of situated and relational practices in LfD that align with this view and outline proposals for further development. Finally, §5 considers the broader implications of this shift for sustainable and inclusive HRI design.

2 The Replication Paradigm in Social Robotics and HRI

The development of Human-Robot Interaction (HRI) [21, 22] as a field is inseparable from a longer philosophical and technological trajectory in which machines have been used to model, test, and – crucially – replicate human cognitive functions [23–25]. This trajectory takes its epistemological cue from the foundational moments of cognitive science and Artificial Intelligence (AI), which emerged in the mid-20th century under the influence of a powerful metaphor: the mind as a computer (see [2]). As articulated in the 1956 Dartmouth proposal, the premise was that "every aspect of learning or any other feature of intelligence can in principle be so precisely described that a machine can be made to simulate it" [1: 12]. This conviction established a research program that extended well beyond AI proper, shaping the philosophy of mind, psychology, and the nascent field of robotics [23].Within this framework, mental processes were conceived as computational operations over symbolic representations, giving rise to a model of the mind as a symbol-processing system [26]. This view, grounded in functionalist and computational cognitivism [27, 28], held that what mattered in understanding cognition was not the material substrate but the organization of functions – perception, memory, planning – abstractable and, hence, potentially replicable in non-biological systems. It was in this context that early robotics projects, such as SHAKEY at Stanford Research Institute, sought to embody this vision: building systems that could perceive, reason, and act in simplified environments based on internal models of the world [29]. SHAKEY was not just a technical artifact: it was a philosophical statement, a tangible instantiation of the assumption that intelligence consists in manipulating symbols according to formal rules. These architectures were explicitly hierarchical and modular, reproducing the architecture of cognitive science itself: high-level symbolic reasoning layered atop low-level sensory processing and motor control [30].

This convergence of cognitive theory and the project of AI formed the basis of what we can identify as the *replication paradigm*. The aim was to replicate human cognition, conceived as symbol representation and computation, in artificial agents, that is to produce machines that could simulate, and eventually replicate, human mental capacities. In this respect, robots were elected as emblematic artifacts that could, in principle, be able to *embody* artificial intelligence and put the technological progress in the real world. With the inception of social robotics [6, 31], the shift from toy worlds to social domains did not entail a radical departure from earlier assumptions. Despite originating from Rodney Brooks's rejection of the computational metaphor and his emphasis on embodied, reactive systems [17], social robotics ultimately reabsorbed many cognitive models it initially sought to move beyond. Notably, ideas about sociality were frequently drawn from the very computational and representational paradigms that Brooks's approach aimed to replace for individual cognition. Indeed, the first kinds of social robots were designed to simulate the observable features of human social behavior – expressions, gestures, conversational cues – by implementing internal models of those behaviors. Early prototypes like *Cog* [32] and *Kismet* [31] exemplified this approach. These humanoid robots' behavior was scaffolded on architectures derived from developmental psychology and, crucially, from Theory of Mind (ToM) models (see [33]).

Theory of Mind refers to the capacity to attribute mental states to others in order to explain and predict others' behavior [34, 35]. In classical cognitive science, it is conceptualized as a form of internal inference: agents interpret observed behaviors as evidence of hidden intentions or beliefs. The process of understanding the other was then conceived as an inference to what kinds of mental states were causing the observed behavior. This model of social cognition was readily integrated into HRI design, not only as an explanatory framework but as a blueprint for building interactional architectures: robots were programmed to "read" emotions, intentions, and goals from human behavior and respond as if they had performed a mental-state attribution.

In this framework, sociality becomes a byproduct of internal processing and a mere result of the encounter of (heterogeneous) minded-agents. Communication is treated as a problem of inference and response generation. Robots are thus built not to *participate* in human social dynamics, but to *approximate* them from the outside, using representational shortcuts to simulate intentional behavior. This model – designing social robots as *replicative agents* – has defined much of HRI since its formal emergence in the 1990s [36]. The goal has often been to endow robots with functionally equivalent mechanisms of social understanding by mimicking human-like behaviors derived from internalist cognitive models, e.g. ToM. Within this context, the replication paradigm became not only a design strategy but also a guiding epistemology: social interaction was understood as something that could be decomposed into discrete functions – perception, emotion recognition, intention modeling – and reconstructed within artificial systems.

Despite the rhetorical power and intuitive appeal of reproduction, the replication paradigm has encountered serious limitations, both practical and conceptual. Practically, robots designed under this model often falter in unstructured, real-world environments [17, 37]: they may recognize simple gestures or parse speech, but struggle with the dynamic, ambiguous, and context-sensitive nature of actual human interaction (see [18, 20]). Their responses lack fluidity, and their adaptive capabilities remain shallow, especially when interaction requires mutual adjustment, role negotiation, or engagement with socio-cultural norms. These failures are not incidental. They stem from an underlying conception of interaction as secondary to cognition, rather than constitutive of it. By treating cognition as a set of internal processes that generate behavior, the replication paradigm obscures the ways in which meaning emerges through relational engagement – i.e., through bodily presence, attunement, and engagement. As we will see in §4 this is precisely what is missed when learning and communication are treated as one-way processes of input-output mapping, rather than as dialogic, situated practices. Moreover, the replication paradigm reproduces a static and disembodied view of human capacities. By focusing on *what* humans do, it often ignores *how* they do it: through a body in motion, embedded in shared spaces, participating in a temporality that unfolds interactively. This feature becomes especially problematic when robots are required not merely to act, but to learn in real time from human partners, as is the case in Learning from Demonstration (LfD).

3 Learning from Demonstration: A Case Study

Initially proposed in the late 1990s, LfD was envisioned as a pathway to developing humanoid robots with human-like capabilities [38]. However, while these techniques have significantly advanced robotic behavior in social contexts, they have also highlighted a pressing need to better understand the imitative structure of human cognition – specifically, how we observe, model, and replicate the behaviors of others. This has led to extensive investigations into the cognitive mechanisms underlying imitation learning in humans and social animals, with the aim of implementing these mechanisms into robotic cognitive architectures [39]. These inquiries, in turn, have shaped key challenges in LfD research since then.

For the mainstream approach in cognitive science, imitation capacities are conceptualized as inferential abstraction operations intrinsically connected to mindreading and

ToM in social contexts. As Nehaniv and Dautenhahn [40, 53] assert, "Understanding and matching higher-level structures characterizes various other forms of observational learning and matching involving theory of mind or mind-reading" (see also [41]). This conceptualization leads to the formulation of the *correspondence problem*, for which imitation is conceived as the system's ability to extract the structure of the behavior to be replicated and translate this understanding into the demonstration of the same movement pattern, thereby proving that it has solved the correspondence problem [40, 43].

Following this trend, the field of LfD has integrated ToM as the theoretical cornerstone for developing robotic cognitive architectures [5]. This integration shapes both the fundamental principles of data collection and the inference-based training of machine learning mechanisms that enable actual learning. Indeed, the theoretical model underpinning this approach positions logical-inferential abilities at the heart of social cognition. In the field of LfD, the correspondence problem was conceived presenting several sub-problems, including action segmentation, identifying which behaviors are relevant for imitation, perspective taking, and demonstrator modeling [5]. These challenges are compounded by the necessity of translating observed actions into executable motor primitives within a robot's physical constraints[1]. Researchers have addressed these challenges mainly by developing algorithms that allow robots to parse human demonstrations, extract essential action features, and reproduce them in a functionally equivalent manner [5, 12, 42, 43].

This conceptual framework has given rise to three key methodological challenges in modeling actions for imitative purposes. First, *action is understood as a discretizable flow of elementary components*. This view suggests that behavior emerges from the combination and sequencing of basic action units. Such segmentation into discrete units reflects traditional computational approaches – similar to those that guided the development of early robots like SHAKEY, though now implemented with far more sophisticated technology. Second, *ToM-based LfD approaches imitation through a logical-linguistic lens*. This involves analyzing the demonstrator's goals and intentions, decomposing their behavior, and computing how to map these observations onto the observer's potential actions. This view is based on the idea that "Imitation of *action* requires the representation of goals as well as motor mimicry and hence could be a way for the subject to become aware of another's goal, an important step on the path to mind reading" [44]. Third, *implementing ToM principles in cognitive architectures requires processing input data through various ToM-based reasoning structures*[2]. This implementation presents three significant practical challenges: (i) ToM requires modeling and reasoning about multiple mental states, which significantly increases computational costs. Many approaches rely on Bayesian inference, deep learning, or probabilistic models, all of

---

[1] The structure of LfD process generally consists of five main stages: Demonstrator Selection; Data Acquisition; Data Modeling; Skill or Task Execution; Refinement Learning. See [42] for details.

[2] Over the past twenty years, ToM has primarily developed along two main lines: *theory theory* and *simulation theory*. In this context, since they share similar theoretical assumptions, I will consider both variants under the label of ToM. For a detailed and critical analysis of these approaches, see [59].

which demand substantial resources [45]; (ii) The continuous need for inference operations and dataset updates can significantly impair real-time performance, making it difficult for robots to interact and learn simultaneously [46, 47]; (iii) ToM assumes that mental states – beliefs, desires, and intentions – are internal and hidden from direct observation. This necessitates additional computational resources to decode the motivations behind human actions, further complicating the learning process [48, 49] (see [50, 51]). In essence, algorithms trained within a cognitivist framework based on ToM shape robotic learning by guiding attention to key focal points identified through this theoretical approach. Consequently, robotic perception is engineered to prioritize fine-grained details, segment actions, and construct inferences about both the possible intentions underlying human behavior and the perspective adopted by the human demonstrator.

However, despite significant advancements enabled by increased computational power (such as *Big Data*; [52, 53]) and advanced machine learning techniques, which have demonstrated exceptional performance in disembodied artificial intelligences [54], these challenges remain largely unresolved, or at best, only marginally mitigated. Moreover, it is possible to list three methodological and conceptual issues prompted by this conceptualization of cognition and learning process. Firstly, since robots must apply machine learning algorithms to build their own image of the demonstrated process, they often struggle with occlusions, rapid movements, and sensor noise when observing human actions, making difficult to accurately capture human demonstration process [12]. Secondly, enabling robots to learn complex, multi-step tasks from demonstrations requires the development of hierarchical abstractions, which remains a significant challenge in LfD [55]. Thirdly, the effectiveness of LfD heavily depends on the quality of human demonstrations, and variations in demonstration quality can adversely affect the robot's learning and generalization capabilities [56–58]. Finally, even if the robots learn how to perform the specific demonstrated behavior, then struggle to reuse the actions to perform different behaviors. In other words, the challenge concerns not only to make the robot able to replicate the actions performed by the human demonstrator, but also the necessity to generalize the "comprehension" and make it able to effectively perform the learnt behavior when needed.

In essence, the strategy of increasing the *quantity* of available data does not appear to offer effective solutions in the short term. To overcome this impasse – at least partially – we propose shifting focus toward the *quality* of the collected data, by introducing a novel model of social cognition based on coordination and participatory practices rather than inference-driven replication. This shift requires drawing on theories that, adopting a different perspective on social interaction, conceptualize intersubjective understanding as a process fundamentally situated within the environment, where multiple contextual elements dynamically contribute to the construction of individual comprehension.

4 Reframing LfD Through Enactivism

4.1 Enactive Cognitive Science: A Paradigm Shift

Over the past twenty years, a new theory of social cognition has emerged within the cognitive sciences, positioning itself in direct opposition to the explanatory hypotheses proposed by ToM [59–63]. Embodied and enactive approaches of social cognition critique ToM and mindreading models on several grounds, arguing that social cognition does not rely on internalized mental state inference but instead emerges from embodied interaction, sensorimotor coordination, and participatory sense-making. In particular, embodied critiques to ToM models of social cognition point the attention to three key aspects. First, while the mindreading model assumes that individuals infer others' mental states based on internalized representations, empirical research shows that social understanding is primarily interactional and embodied rather than inferential (see [59]). Embodied account of social understanding highlight that humans do not typically engage in explicit mental state attribution during real-world social interactions; instead, understanding emerges dynamically from bodily and contextual coordination [7]. Second, they propose that social cognition begins with embodied interactions (e.g., joint attention, affect attunement) rather than conceptual inferences about beliefs and desires [63]. Third, while mindreading models assume that understanding others' emotions and intentions necessarily requires inferring their mental states, embodied cognition research suggests we understand others primarily through bodily mirroring and sensorimotor resonance. As also highlighted by neuroscientific evidence in mirror neuron research and embodied simulation theories, we mainly experience others' emotions and intentions directly via bodily engagement, not through abstract inferences [64, 65]. As a result, social understanding is considered to involve several complex dimensions, that put together the shared meaning that arise from contextual, situated and embodied interaction. In essence, by endorsing enactive view of interaction, the process of understanding in social cognition no longer primarily relies on internal mental states or inferential reasoning. Instead, it emerges from the ongoing engagement that occurs during interaction, shaping both action and meaning. If we adopt this account of social cognition and replace the ToM framework in LfD with this perspective, we can see how it becomes possible to overcome some of the issues outlined in §3.

Regarding point (i), from an enactive perspective on understanding others, action segmentation does not play a fundamental role. The core process of social understanding is attunement, based on bodily rather than inferential correspondences. From this viewpoint, understanding does not depend on breaking down actions into isolated components but rather on the immediate configuration of affordance patterns. In the case of social cognition, this means a direct and immediate connection with the other agent. This attunement occurs through bodily correspondences that emerge without the need for representational inferences, as the body itself detects similarities through perceptual and sensorimotor dynamics, making an analytical segmentation process unnecessary.

This approach can also be applied to (ii), since the mental states of an agent – such as beliefs, intentions, and desires – are not exclusively inferred through data-driven inferential mechanisms but rather through the enaction of immediate, embodied understanding. In this sense, the neuroscientific evidence [64, 65] supports a less inferential and more embodied view of intersubjective understanding.

Regarding point (iii), following this approach to understanding learning processes, the focus shifts from the quantity of data collected in the perceptual segmentation of the environment to the quality of the interactional configuration that emerges from the real, ongoing interaction between the learner and the demonstrator. The key idea is that, even if the robot is not capable of engaging in interaction in a bodily, embedded, and vital manner

[20, 66, 67], adopting an enactive perspective on learning processes can inform the design of robotic machine learning algorithms based on bodily and agentive signals detected by the human situated in interaction, as well as on the dynamics of adjustment that emerge in different forms *participatory sense-making* [7]. This perspective opens up a range of possibilities for implementing learning algorithms that go beyond the mere replication of demonstrated movement, instead adopting an embodied approach to collaboration, which characterizes practices in social interaction. In HRI, this approach has led to a different view on the possibility of analyzing and understanding the encounter between humans and robots, providing for instance a fresh perspective on the relational dynamics [68–70] and on typical phenomena, such as anthropomorphism [70] or empathy [68, 71].

In continuity with this perspective, in the next paragraph I propose an enactive reading of certain machine learning technique currently in use, which align with the shift I propose. When framed within a situated and embodied paradigm of social cognition, these techniques could offer new pathways for instructing robots in learning processes, making algorithmic training more suitable for human learning-teaching practices.

4.2 Thinking About LfD as Embodied Learning: Beyond Passive Demonstration

To demonstrate how robotic learning can be framed through an enactive perspective, we consider a series of experiments that have enabled robots to acquire motor skills by observing human demonstrations. Specifically, we refer to studies in developmental robotics [72, 73], a field that models ontogenetic processes in child development to inform machine learning mechanisms in robots. This approach is based on the premise that a robot, guided by developmental principles regulating real-time interactions, can autonomously acquire increasingly complex capabilities [74].

The studies we are going to examine draw on extensive research in developmental psychology, which has identified distinctive features in caregiver-infant interactions across many cultures [75]. Notably, caregivers modify their speech when addressing infants – a practice also called *motherese* – using higher pitch, shorter utterances, exaggerated intonation, and simplified content [76, 77]. Similar modifications occur in sign language, where caregivers produce slower, more repetitive, and exaggerated signs when interacting with children [78]. Numerous studies suggest that such modifications enhance infants' attention to communicative input. For instance, infants as young as one month prefer infant-directed over adult-directed speech [79, 80] and exhibit greater visual attention when exposed to infant-directed speech [81].

Recent research extends these findings to the domain of action, identifying a phenomenon known as *motionese*[3]. (see [82]). Indeed, caregivers also adjust their gestures in order to leverage children comprehension: compared to interactions with adults, they use fewer gestures with infants, and those they do use are more likely to co-occur with speech, reinforcing rather than supplementing verbal content [83]. Brand et al. [84] expanded this idea and examined object-related actions in caregiver-infant interactions, revealing that caregivers modify their movements when demonstrating actions to infants. Compared to adult-directed actions, infant-directed actions occur closer to the infant, involve higher interactivity, greater enthusiasm, increased repetition, and simplified yet

---

[3] For an extensive survey on *motionese*, see [9, 85, 86]

exaggerated movements. Such modifications are believed to enhance infants' attention and facilitate their understanding of action structure [85]. Indeed, experimental findings indicate that both 6–8 and 11–13-month-old infants prefer observing infant-directed over adult-directed actions, even when facial cues are obscured [86].

Building on these studies, several investigations [8, 87, 88] have explored whether and to what extent action demonstration techniques incorporating *motionese* can facilitate robotic learning. This approach leverages the exaggerated features of demonstrators' actions and makes explicit the interactive dynamics involved in this pedagogical behavior, mirroring caregiver-infant interactions. In particular, Nagai and Rohlfing [8] analyzed parental actions from an infant-like perspective using a saliency-based visual attention model, which detects and focuses on salient locations in a scene without any prior knowledge of the task or objects involved. Their findings suggest that *motionese* supports learners in three key ways: «[...] (1) to receive immediate social feedback on the actions, (2) to detect the initial and goal states of the objects used in the actions, and (3) to look at the static features of the object» [8: 305]. In a subsequent study [87], they expanded on their previous research by conducting a computational analysis of *motionese* to enhance robotic action learning. They argue that robots, like infants, lack prior knowledge of task-relevant information and therefore require guidance in determining what to focus on when observing demonstrations. Using a bottom-up attention model, they demonstrate that *motionese* «has the effect of highlighting the initial and final states of the action, the significant events within it, and the properties of the objects involved, which can impart the goal of the action» [88: 53]. This enables robots to identify what to imitate without relying heavily on predefined instructions. More recently, Ugur et al. [88] further demonstrated the effectiveness of *motionese* in LfD for robotics, identifying three key advantages: (i) it enhances robotic algorithms' ability to segment and interpret demonstrated actions, thereby improving the efficacy of the imitation process; (ii) it allows naïve human demonstrators to engage in teaching practices with robots without requiring technical training, as they can rely on their social competencies to demonstrate actions similarly to how they would interact with a child; (iii) it enables robots to acquire the capacity for multi-step planning, allowing them to achieve a goal through structured action sequencing rather than merely replicating isolated movements.

Now, by analyzing this approach, we can identify a set of insights that support the adoption of a more distributed and embodied perspective on cognition and learning – one that aligns with the enactive framework here proposed – rather than reinforcing an internalist and representational conception of cognitive processes.

Firstly, the practice of *motionese* aligns with a participatory conception of social cognition, in which cognitive structures emerge both as an outcome of the interaction between two agents and as elements that actively shape and develop the interaction itself. From this perspective, *motionese* can be understood as a process of mutual attunement, wherein the caregiver, already proficient in the embodied social practices that the child (or robot) has yet to learn, adjusts their demonstrative actions based on what the learner has not yet mastered. Essentially, the caregiver constructs a *scaffolding* [89, 90] structure composed of salient affordances, making key aspects of the demonstration more perceivable and accessible. This enables the learner to occupy positions within the interactive structure that would otherwise remain inaccessible. Just as an adult provides support that allows a child to accomplish tasks beyond their independent capacity, robots can benefit from the exaggeration of expressive features in actions, facilitating the training of machine learning algorithms to detect and prioritize the most relevant and accentuated aspects of demonstrated behavior. For a machine learning system interacting with a human motivated to facilitate learning, social elements can significantly enhance the success of the learning process by constraining and guiding its development. Secondly, this approach enables machine learning algorithms to be trained by integrating a bottom-up process rather than only relying on top-down feature detection mechanisms. That is, the algorithm can identify salient features in the demonstrator's behavior without necessarily requiring an explicit parsing of the action or relying on a human robotic designer to predefine the correct sequence of actions. More simply, pattern recognition [91] can be used to detect key aspects of an action through repeated exposure to similar trajectories, allowing the robot to build an agentive repertoire. In this way, the robot not only acquires skills based on demonstration (i.e., *what* to imitate) but also learns *how* to perform the action effectively. In contrast with the approach based on the correspondence problem and on ToM, in which action segmentation is central to guarantee the commensurability of humans and robots' actions, if we adopt an enactive model of interaction and learning the *what* and *how* of imitation must be considered deeply interwoven. Only by identifying the agentive patterns that characterize the demonstrators' engagement with their environment can the learner – whether human or artificial – grasp the situational context and understand how to perform actions in real-time scenarios.

In this regard, the enactive approach allows to highlight the role of environmental and contextual embedding in learning (see [92]). Traditional LfD approaches often assume that learning occurs through the isolated observation of actions, treating the demonstrator's behavior as a sequence of discrete movements to be imitated. However, from an enactive perspective, learning is fundamentally embedded in the affordances of the environment and the situational dynamics in which actions unfold. The meaning and relevance of an action are not inherent in the movement itself but emerge through interaction. A robot trained in a controlled setting may struggle to transfer its learning to real-world applications if it lacks sensitivity to these contextual dependencies. By integrating an awareness of the relational and ecological conditions of action, an enactive approach enables a more adaptive and context-sensitive learning process. This is particularly relevant in HRI, where robots must operate in open-ended environments rather than controlled laboratory conditions [21, 22].

4.3 Robots as Dialogical Agents: Toward Sustainable Learning in HRI

To further articulate the potential of integrating enactive principles into LfD, I propose the introduction of a key conceptual tool recently developed within the enactive framework: the notion of *partial acts* [4]. Partial acts are defined as "the contribution to a social act enacted by an individual agent, usually to be coupled in parallel or in sequence with the partial acts of other agents" [4: 331]. In other words, a partial act is an action that has not reached the status of an autonomous act with a fixed, completed meaning; it remains incomplete and acquires significance through continuation, uptake, or responsive modification by others. The theory of partial acts captures a foundational principle of interaction: that actions often acquire meaning only through their relational unfolding, as they are responded to, continued, transformed, or completed by others. In this view, a partial act is not a closed or self-sufficient behavioral unit but a situated, temporally extended, and incomplete gesture that invites participation, such as a handshake. Meaning emerges not from pre-encoded intention but through the ongoing coordination between agents.

Applied to LfD, this perspective perfectly matches with the proposal of moving beyond the model of the robot as a passive observer of fully-formed demonstrations. Instead, it allows to reconceptualize the robot as an interactive partner engaged in a shared, dialogical activity of sense-making. This shift reframes robotic imitation not as the replication of completed behaviors but as participation in open-ended sequences of partial acts, i.e. a dialogue. Learning, from this perspective, does not require the robot to infer or replicate the internal intentions behind a demonstrator's action. Instead, the robot can contribute its own partial acts to the whole process of interaction and co-construct the meaning and structure of the interaction with the human partner. This model significantly departs from traditional ToM-inspired LfD, where social understanding is modeled as a unilateral decoding of the other's hidden mental states. In contrast, a dialogical approach grounded in enactivism treats interaction itself as the site of learning. Partial acts provide a design metaphor for flexibility: rather than prescribing full behaviors, designers can create affordances for interactional contributions that are meaningful in interaction.

Moreover, while ToM frames the learning process only through the lens of perfect match between the demonstrator's and the learner's actions, the enactive view provides a more dynamical perspective in which imitation is constitutive of the interactional dynamics, but not only as perfect replication: in the dialogue between interactors, *mimesis* is something that occurs braided with the interactional flow, not questionable by the quantity of similarities, but on the basis of the quality of the interaction and learning. As already highlighted from Dumouchel and Damiano by endorsing a dynamical approach to imitation, "Imitation understood in this way is a means of relating agents to each other; it also constitutes a skill that is essential for successful social interaction. Therefore this dimension of imitation is fundamental for the project of building socially competent artificial agents [93, 21]. The dialogical paradigm allows for a reconceptualization of learning practices in HRI that goes beyond the ontological substrates of agents' mind, but develops in the making, while the encounter is happening.

5 Conclusion: From Replication to Dialogue for a Sustainable HRI

Such a reconceptualization carries profound implications for the design of human-robot systems. It enables a vision of dialogical agency, i.e. a form of agency based not on internal cognitive reconstruction but on the ability to take part in, respond to, and shape interactional dynamics.

The conceptual shift I proposed marks a change in paradigm by reframing the very aims of HRI: no longer engineering only artificial surrogates of human behavior – as prescribed by the replication paradigm – but designing agents capable of engaging in the co-construction of interaction and supporting inter-cognitive dialogue. Such a reframing is particularly relevant in social domains, where interaction is affectively charged, context-dependent, and structurally open-ended. Here, robot's capacity to adapt cannot only rely on pre-coded templates but should participate in the relational attunement. From this perspective, an enactive approach to LfD opens the path toward a more sustainable model of HRI – one in which adaptability, inclusion, and ecological embeddedness are not external design constraints but intrinsic features of interactional systems. Recent work has emphasized the potential of robotic systems to promote pro-social and pro-environmental behaviors through multimodal interaction grounded in social cues – such as emotional expression, body language, and affective feedback [94]. In this view, sustainability in robotics also entails considering the roles that artificial agents play and the kinds of interactions they foster with human partners [95]. The enactive approach to LfD developed in this paper contributes to the development of socially sustainable robotics in at least two directions. First, by focusing on algorithmic efficiency and reducing computational load – scaffolding part of the learning process onto the human demonstrator's embodied ability to perform actions (as in the case of *motionese*) – it helps reduce energy demands and computational costs, favoring outcomes that emerge from collaboration and interactional dynamics. Second, it strengthens the potential of HRI to serve as a medium through which new forms of enacted sociality can give rise to sustainable practices and improve human well-being – particularly in contexts of care, assistance, and everyday life.

Sustainability, understood as the robot's capacity to remain meaningful across different practices, contexts, and bodies, is inseparable from its ability to engage in interactional, co-realized activity. Although the model presented here is theoretical and has not yet been tested in empirical settings, it offers a promising conceptual foundation for developing HRI systems that are more sustainable—both environmentally and socially. It is in the dialogical space between agents – not in the fidelity of replication – that the conditions for sustainable and situated human-robot collaboration can be reimagined.

Disclosure of Interests. The authors have no competing interests to declare that are relevant to the content of this article.

References

1. McCarthy, J., Minsky, M.L., Rochester, N., Shannon, C.E.: A proposal for the Dartmouth summer research project on artificial intelligence. AI Mag. **27**(4), 12 (1955)
2. Block, N.: The computer model of the mind. In: Goldman, A.I. (Ed.) Readings in Philosophy and Cognitive Science, pp. 705–731. MIT Press (1993)
3. Varela, F.J., Thompson, E., Rosch, E.: The Embodied Mind. Cognitive Science and Human Experience. The MIT Press, Cambridge (1991)
4. Di Paolo, E.A., Cuffari, E.C., De Jaegher, H.: Linguistic Bodies: The Continuity between Life and Language. MIT press (2018)
5. Mohammad, Y., Nishida, T.: Data Mining for Social Robotics. Springer, Cham, Switzerland (2015)
6. Breazeal, C., Dautenhahn, K., Kanda, T.: Social robotics. In: Siciliano, B., Khatib, O. (Eds.) Springer Handbook of Robotics. Springer Handbooks. Springer, Cham (2016)
7. De Jaegher, H., Di Paolo, E.: Participatory sense-making: an enactive approach to social cognition. Phenomenol. Cogn. Sci. **6**, 485–507 (2007). https://doi.org/10.1007/s11097-007-9076-9

8. Nagai, Y., Rohlfing, K.J.: Can motionese tell infants and robots "what to imitate". In: Proceedings of the 4th International Symposium on Imitation in Animals and Artifacts, pp. 299–306 (2007)
9. Koterba, E.A., Iverson, J.M.: Investigating motionese: the effect of infant-directed action on infants' attention and object exploration. Infant Behav. Dev. **32**(4), 437–444 (2009)
10. Youssef, K., Said, S., Alkork, S., Beyrouthy, T.: A survey on recent advances in social robotics. Robotics **11**(4), 75 (2022)
11. Calinon, S.: Learning from demonstration (Programming by Demonstration). In: Ang, M., Khatib, O., Siciliano, B. (eds.) Encyclopedia of Robotics. Springer, Heidelberg (2018). https://doi.org/10.1007/978-3-642-41610-1_27-1
12. Ravichandar, H., Polydoros, A.S., Chernova, S., Billard, A.: Recent advances in robot learning from demonstration. Ann. Rev. Control Robot. Autonom. Syst. **3**(1), 297–330 (2020)
13. Nilsson, N.J.: The Quest for Artificial Intelligence: a History of Ideas and Achievements. Cambridge University Press (2010)
14. Bekey, G.A.: Autonomous Robots: from Biological Inspiration to Implementation and Control. MIT Press (2005)
15. Thrun, S., Burgard, W., Fox, D.: Probabilistic Robotics. MIT Press (2005)
16. Arkin, R.C.: Behavior-Based Robotics. MIT press, Cambridge (1998)
17. Brooks, R.: Intelligence without representation. Artif. Intell. **47**, 139–159 (1991)
18. Suchman, L.A.: Human-Machine Reconfigurations: Plans and Situated Actions. Cambridge University Press (2007)
19. Fong, T., Nourbakhsh, I., Dautenhahn, K.: A survey of socially interactive robots. Robot. Auton. Syst. **42**(3–4), 143–166 (2003)
20. Ziemke, T.: Are robots embodied?. In: First International Workshop on Epigenetic Robotics Modeling Cognitive Development in Robotic Systems, vol. 85, pp. 701–746 (2001)
21. Dautenhahn, K.: Methodology & themes of human-robot interaction: a growing research field. Int. J. Adv. Rob. Syst. **4**(1), 15 (2007)
22. Dautenhahn, K.: Human-Robot Interaction. Interaction Design Foundation – IxDF (2014). https://www.interaction-design.org/literature/book/the-encyclopedia-of-human-computer-interaction-2nd-ed/human-robot-interaction
23. Boden, M.: Mind as Machine. A history of Cognitive Science. Cambridge University Press, Cambridge (2006)
24. Cordeschi, R.: The Discovery of the Artificial: Behavior, Mind and Machines Before and Beyond Cybernetics. Springer (2002)
25. Bates, D.W.: An Artificial History of Natural Intelligence: Thinking with Machines from Descartes to the Digital Age. University of Chicago Press (2024)
26. Newel, A., Simon, H.: Computer science as empirical inquiry: symbols and search. Commun. ACM **19**(3), 113–126 (1976)
27. Putnam, H.: Minds and Machines. In: Hook, S. (ed.) Dimensions of Mind: A Symposium, pp. 138–164. New York University Press, New York (1960)
28. Fodor, J.A.: The Language of Thought. Harvard University Press, Cambridge (1975)
29. Nilsson, N.J. (Ed.): Shakey the Robot. SRI International, Menlo Park, California (1984)
30. Kuipers, B., Feigenbaum, E.A., Hart, P.E., Nilsson, N.J.: Shakey: from Conception to History. AI Mag. **38**(1), 88–103 (2017). https://doi.org/10.1609/aimag.v38i1.2716
31. Breazeal, C.: Designing Sociable Robots. MIT press, Cambridge (2004)
32. Brooks, R.A., Breazeal, C., Marjanović, M., Scassellati, B., Williamson, M.M.: The cog project: building a humanoid robot. In: Nehaniv, C.L. (eds.) Computation for Metaphors, Analogy, and Agents. CMAA 1998. Lecture Notes in Computer Science(), vol. 1562. Springer, Heidelberg (1999). https://doi.org/10.1007/3-540-48834-0_5
33. Scassellati, B.: Theory of mind for a humanoid robot. Auton. Robot. **12**, 13–24 (2002)

34. Premack, D., Woodruff, G.: Does the chimpanzee have a theory of mind? Behav. Brain Sci. **1**, 515–526 (1978)
35. Baron-Cohen, S.: Mindblindness: An Essay on Autism and Theory of Mind. MIT press, Cambridge (1995)
36. Bartneck, C., Belpaeme, T., Eyssel, F., Kanda, T., Keijsers, M., Šabanović, S.: Human-Robot Interaction: An Introduction. Cambridge University Press, Cambridge (2020)
37. Brooks, R.: The whole iguana. Robot. Sci. 432–456 (1989)
38. Schaal, S.: Is imitation learning the route to humanoid robots? Trends Cogn. Sci. **3**, 233–242 (1999)
39. Dautenhahn, K., Nehaniv, C.L.: (Eds.) Imitation in Animals and Artifacts. MIT Press (2002)
40. Nehaniv, C.L., Dautenhahn, K.: The correspondence problem. In: Dautenhahn, K., Nehaniv, C.L. (Eds.) Imitation in Animals and Artifacts, pp. 41–61. MIT Press (2002)
41. Mitchell, M.: Imitation as a perceptual process. In: Dautenhahn, K., Nehaniv, C.L., (Eds.) Imitation in Animals and Artifacts, pp. 441–469. MIT Press (2002)
42. Sosa-Ceron, A.D., Gonzalez-Hernandez, H.G., Reyes-Avendaño, J.A.: Learning from demonstrations in human–robot collaborative scenarios: a survey. Robotics **11**(6), 126 (2022)
43. Ambhore, S.: A comprehensive study on robot learning from demonstration. In: 2020 2nd International Conference on Innovative Mechanisms for Industry Applications (ICIMIA), pp. 291–299. IEEE (2020)
44. Gerrans, P.: Imitation and theory of mind. Handbook of Neurosci. Behav. Sci. **2**, 905–922 (2009)
45. Rabinowitz, N.C., Perbet, F., Song, F., Zhang, C., Eslami, S.M.A., Botvinick, M.: Machine theory of mind. In: International Conference on Machine Learning (ICML) (2018)
46. Bianco, F., Ognibene, D.: Robot learning theory of mind through self-observation: Exploiting the intentions-beliefs synergy. arXiv preprint arXiv:2210.09435 (2022)
47. Baker, C.L., Saxe, R., Tenenbaum, J.B.: Bayesian theory of mind: modeling joint belief-desire attribution. Cognition **120**(2), 236–301 (2011)
48. Winfield, A.F.: Experiments in artificial theory of mind: From safety to story-telling. Front. Robot. AI **5**, 75 (2018)
49. Chen, B., Vondrick, C., Lipson, H.: Visual behavior modelling for robotic theory of mind. Sci. Rep. **11**, 424 (2021). https://doi.org/10.1038/s41598-020-77918-x
50. Gallagher, S.: Social cognition and social robots. Pragmat. Cogn. **15**(3), 435–453 (2007)
51. Gallagher, S.: You and I, robot. AI & Soc. **28**, 455–460 (2013)
52. Chen, Z., et al.: Efficiently training on-policy actor-critic networks in robotic deep reinforcement learning with demonstration-like sampled exploration. In: 2021 3rd International Symposium on Robotics and Intelligent Manufacturing Technology (ISRIMT), pp. 292–298. IEEE (2021)
53. Mu, T., et al.: AdaDemo: Data-Efficient Demonstration Expansion for Generalist Robotic Agent. arXiv preprint arXiv:2404.07428 (2024)
54. Dulac-Arnold, G., Levine, N., Mankowitz, D.J., et al.: Challenges of real-world reinforcement learning: definitions, benchmarks and analysis. Mach. Learn. **110**, 2419–2468 (2021). https://doi.org/10.1007/s10994-021-05961-4
55. Gopalan, N., Moorman, N., Natarajan, M., Gombolay, M.: Negative result for learning from demonstration: Challenges for end-users teaching robots with task and motion planning abstractions. In: Proceedings of Robotics: Science and Systems XVIII (2022)
56. Sakr, M., Li, Z.J., Van der Loos, H.F.M., Kulic, D., Croft, E.A.: Quantifying demonstration quality for robot learning and generalization. IEEE Robot. Autom. Lett. **7**(3), 7370–7377 (2022)
57. Argall, B.D., Chernova, S., Veloso, M., Browning, B.: A survey of robot learning from demonstration. Robot. Auton. Syst. **57**(5), 469–483 (2009)

58. Calinon, S., Billard, A.G.: What is the teacher's role in robot programming by demonstration?: toward benchmarks for improved learning. Interact. Stud. **8**(3), 441–464 (2007)
59. Gallagher, S.: Action and Interaction. Oxford University Press (2020)
60. Gallagher, S.: How the Body Shapes the Mind. Oxford Academic, Oxford (2005)
61. Hutto, D.D.: Folk Psychological Narratives: The Sociocultural Basis of Understanding Reasons. MIT press, Cambridge (MA) (2008)
62. Overgaard, S., Michael, J.A.: The interactive turn in social cognition research: a critique. Philos. Psychol. **28**(2), 160–183 (2015). https://doi.org/10.1080/09515089.2013.827109
63. Reddy, V.: How Infants Know Minds. Harvard University Press (2008)
64. Gallese, V., Sinigaglia, C.: What is so special about embodied simulation? Trends Cogn. Sci. **15**(11), 512–519 (2011)
65. Di Paolo, E., De Jaegher, H.: The interactive brain hypothesis. Front. Hum. Neurosci. **6**, 163 (2012)
66. Di Paolo, E.A.: Organismically-inspired robotics: Homeostatic adaptation and teleology beyond the closed sensorimotor loop. In: Murase, K., Asakura, T., (Eds.) Dynamic Systems Approach for Embodiment and Sociality: From Ecological Psychology to Robotics, pp. 19–42 (2003)
67. Ziemke, T.: The embodied self: theories, hunches and robot models. J. Conscious. Stud. **14**(7), 167–179 (2007)
68. Dumouchel, P., Damiano, L.: Living with Robots. Harvard University Press (2017)
69. Damiano, L.: Mente, robot ed ecologie sociali miste. Per un'epistemologia sperimentale dei robot sociali. Sistemi intelligenti, **32**(1), 27–39 (2020)
70. Damiano, L., Dumouchel, P.: Anthropomorphism in human–robot co-evolution. Front. Psychol. **9**, 468 (2018)
71. Damiano, L., Dumouchel, P., Lehmann, H.: Artificial empathy: an interdisciplinary investigation. Int. J. Soc. Robot. **7**, 3–5 (2015)
72. Lungarella, M., Metta, G., Pfeifer, R., Sandini, G.: Developmental robotics: a survey. Connec. Sci. **15**(4), 151–190 (2003)
73. Weng, J.: Developmental robotics: theory and experiments. Int. J. Humanoid Rob. **1**(02), 199–236 (2004)
74. Cangelosi, A., Schlesinger, M.: Developmental Robotics: From Babies to Robots. MIT press (2015)
75. Ochs, E., Schieffelin, B.: The impact of language socialization on grammatical development. In: The Handbook of Child Language, pp. 73–94 (1996)
76. Newport, E.L.: Motherese: The Speech of Mothers to Young Children. University of Pennsylvania (1975)
77. Stern, D.N., Spieker, S., MacKain, K.: Intonation contours as signals in maternal speech to prelinguistic infants. Dev. Psychol. **18**(5), 727 (1975)
78. Cooper, R.P., Abraham, J., Berman, S., Staska, M.: The development of infants' preference for motherese. Infant Behav. Dev. **20**(4), 477–488 (1997)
79. Fernald, A.: Four-month-old infants prefer to listen to motherese. Infant Behav. Dev. **8**(2), 181–195 (1985)
80. Werker, J.F., Pegg, J.E., McLeod, P.J.: A cross-language investigation of infant preference for infant-directed communication. Infant Behav. Dev. **17**(3), 323–333 (1994)
81. Masataka, N.: Perception of motherese in Japanese sign language by 6-month-old hearing infants. Dev. Psychol. **34**(2), 241 (1998)
82. Cantor, Z.: Motherese and Motionese: Do They Travel Together?. Doctoral dissertation, University of Oregon (2023)
83. Iverson, J.M., Capirci, O., Longobardi, E., Caselli, M.C.: Gesturing in mother-child interactions. Cogn. Dev. **14**(1), 57–75 (1999)

84. Brand, R.J., Shallcross, W.L.: Infants prefer motionese to adult-directed action. Dev. Sci. **11**(6), 853–861 (2008)
85. Brand, R.J., Baldwin, D.A., Ashburn, L.A.: Evidence for 'motionese': modifications in mothers' infant-directed action. Dev. Sci. **5**(1), 72–83 (2002)
86. Brand, R.J., Shallcross, W.L., Sabatos, M.G., Massie, K.P.: Fine-grained analysis of motionese: eye gaze, object exchanges, and action units in infant-versus adult-directed action. Infancy **11**(2), 203–214 (2007)
87. Nagai, Y., Rohlfing, K.J.: Computational analysis of motionese toward scaffolding robot action learning. IEEE Trans. Auton. Ment. Dev. **1**(1), 44–54 (2009)
88. Ugur, E., Nagai, Y., Sahin, E., Oztop, E.: Staged development of robot skills: Behavior formation, affordance learning, and imitation with motionese. IEEE Trans. Auton. Ment. Dev. **7**(2), 119–139 (2015)
89. Vygotsky, L.S.: Mind in society: the development of higher psychological processes. In: Cole, M., John-Steiner, V., Scribner, S., Souberman, E., (Eds.) & Trans.). Harvard University Press (1978)
90. Gauvain, M.: Scaffolding in socialization. New Ideas Psychol. **23**(3), 129–139 (2005)
91. Yan, H., Ang, M.H., Poo, A.N.: A survey on perception methods for human–robot interaction in social robots. Int. J. Soc. Robot. **6**, 85–119 (2014)
92. Bocchi, G., Damiano, L.: The enactive mind: an epistemological framework for radically embodied didactics. Educ. Sci. Soc. **1**, 113–134 (2013)
93. Dumouchel, P., Damiano, L.: Artificial empathy, imitation and mimesis. ARS Vivendi J. **1**, 18–31 (2011)
94. Alfieri, I., Fleres, A., Damiano, L.: Workshop Eco-socio-botics. In: 2022 – Social Robotics for Sustainability at 14th International Conference, ICSR 2022, Florence, Italy, 13–16 December 2022
95. Alfieri, I., Raffa, M.: Active inference for ethical decision-making in socially assistive robotics. In: Seibt, J., Fazekas, P., Quick, O., (Ed.), Social Robots With AI: Prospects, Risks, and Responsible Methods: Proceedings of Robophilosophy 2024. IOS Press, Amsterdam (2025)

The Social Robotics Gamble: Pathways to Sustainability

João S. Sequeira[1]($^{\boxtimes}$), Álvaro Castro-González[2], José Carlos Castillo[2], Fernando Alonso-Martìn[2], and Miguel A. Salichs[2]

[1] Instituto Superior Técnico/Institute for Systems and Robotics, Lisbon, Portugal
joao.silva.sequeira@tecnico.ulisboa.pt
[2] Universidad Carlos III de Madrid, Madrid, Spain
{acgonzal,jocastil,famartin,salichs}@ing.uc3m.es

Abstract. Given the rapid pace of robotics development, can social robots be sustainably integrated into human societies? Could the observed enthusiasm for social robots be merely a novelty effect? To what extent should embodied social robots compete with software-based agents for human attention? Will the current development of machine learning be the motor of Social Robotics? What kind of robotics products and culture can we expect to emerge? These are relevant questions to assess the sustainability of social robots and how they will change business practices and lifestyles. Speculative/exploratory arguments on these topics are possible and have been mostly left out of research papers. This, however, results in an unconventional structure for this paper, where the novelty comes from the questioning of the role of Social Robotics that has not been duly addressed in the literature. The paper (i) presents arguments supporting sustainability grounded on experiments in real-world scenarios, and (ii) identifies challenges according to multiple viewpoints. These are questions for which assertive answers are not found in the literature; hence, the reader is challenged to accept/reject/complement the findings. Besides the answers to the above questions, the conclusions point to pathways we believe Social Robotics can evolve, e.g., incorporating maximal knowledge of how humans work.

Keywords: Social Robots · Human-Robot Interaction · Technology Acceptance Model · Sustainability

1 Introduction

A social robot is an autonomous robot endowed with social skills to interact with humans, or more generally, with other social agents, by understanding social norms and the corresponding compliance processes. A typical example would be a companion robot for elderly people, which would need to account for their potentially difficult cognitive and physical state. Still, the interactions between robots and humans that result from this integration are limited only by the imagination and social robots should not be limited to those robots exhibiting anthropomorphic features, e.g., having only senses similar to humans, or being able to communicate through speech. Such richness requires everyone to be aware that the area is enlarging and in constant evolution.

Unsurprisingly, the diversity of people and challenges is forcing robot developers to think socially. The linguistic separation between robot developers and users, or potential users, which in other technologies would amount to a normal separation between technological and regular language, is being eliminated by users as they are forcing Robotics developers to incorporate knowledge of social aspects.

Besides thinking socially, developers are also striving for technologies that last. The general community has acknowledged the potential of Robotics for sustainable development (see, for instance, the United Nations report in [58]). This potential is even boosted by the combination of Robotics and Artificial Intelligence (AI). Still, in the Information and Communication Technology (ICT) area, which bears strong connections with Robotics, some authors point out that too much attention is being given to technical aspects and not enough to consumer acceptance, making some innovations fail [60]. The determinants for ordinary people to accept ICTs may not be the same as those for Social Robotics.

In contrast to other areas, Social Robotics is still looking for practical applications that the general public finds appealing and valuable. For example, service robots, such as Roomba from iRobot, have been commercialised successfully and accepted by users in their homes. In the case of Social Robotics, this application is not available yet, but many candidates might appear in the near future, e.g., a hotel receptionist or assisting elders with cognitive tasks. The emergence of such applications is likely to contribute to making the Social Robotics business sustainable in the long run.

It is important to note that the expectations about a smartphone or a new app are intrinsically different from those regarding a social robot. Three factors in the Technology Acceptance Model (TAM) framework (perceived usefulness, perceived ease-of-use, and perceived enjoyment) are easily assessed by ordinary people in the case of smartphones and apps [14]. Personalised human-like communication, trust, and control are critical factors for acceptance [8,64]. These are factors already covered by TAM and further suggest a consensus in the research community that social robot acceptance follows generic technology acceptance factors. These findings confirm the importance of the TAM factors but leave open topics, namely on the significance of psychological reactance, i.e., the resistance to influence that people may develop when perceiving some form of manipulation (see, for example, [48], p. 367).

The other phenomenon that will probably have to be dealt with is techniques that allow social robots to capture users' attention and increase engagement in the interaction. Other electronic devices, such as smartphones, are already doing this through variable rewards and constant notifications [19]. They have managed to get consumers into the habit of using them daily, imposing strong lifestyle changes.

Social Robotics is also about absorbing influences from other technology pushes. The current developments in Machine Learning are bringing to the field techniques to process data close to end-to-end principles where robot developers are relieved from the work of having to fully understand the data and, instead, a block of code maps raw data into meaningful results. Examples on emotion recognition and personality estimation are widely available [12,34], even as commercial, off-the-shelf, products.

The increasing presence of software agents in our daily lives, e.g., with the assistants by Google, or Microsoft, though potentially contributing to wellbeing and other sustainability goals (see, for instance, the United Nations Sustainability Goals, [57]), may dampen/amplify the expectations about real physical social robots. The media hype on social robots, fueled by a few stunts (e.g., the Sophia robot appearances), and an intrinsic desire of emotionally intelligent humans to connect with other species, even if they are artificial, keeps society unbalanced about the roles of social robots. The role of machine learning in creating intelligent machines and a possible competition with humans are thus questions at the heart of the paper.

The current state of the art in sensing, namely that related to the human-like senses, is improving fast. Anthropomorphic interfaces, e.g., related to sound recognition[1] which directly affects the quality of interaction, have been showing interesting performances. However, reaching the human performance level is yet to be achieved. Social robots are deployed with non-perfect interfaces, which may create trust issues in peoples' perception [15]. Conversely, studies demonstrated that interface errors, e.g., speech errors, may be effective in improving the perception of the familiarity of the robot after a first phase of engagement where people become accustomed to the robot, [22].

Consequently, social robots are emerging as a technology with great potential in many areas, but researchers have not questioned the future of this technology. In this paper, we assess the sustainability of social robots, i.e., the likeability of robots endowed with social skills will merge with human societies and thrive, and their effects on people's lives. Furthermore, the paper attempts to match expectations and challenges by identifying five questions drawn from the current evolution of the field, and the answers of which point to its sustainability.

The selection of the five central questions is driven by their relevance to evaluating the sustainability of social robots and how these technologies might transform business practices and human lifestyles. These questions were chosen because the sources indicate that assertive answers are not readily found in existing literature, highlighting a gap in research and providing the paper's novelty by challenging the underexplored role of social robotics. They are drawn from the current evolution of the field and aim to identify challenges from multiple viewpoints, with their answers pointing directly to the sustainability of social robotics.

In the context of this paper, social robot sustainability is defined as their likelihood of successful integration and flourishing within human societies, requiring

---

[1] Including verbal and non-verbal sound recognition.

them to endure and deliver added value. This is comprehensively evaluated across social, economic, and technological dimensions, with balancing these being crucial for effective adoption. Culture is understood as the values entities, including social robots, adhere to, and as a mechanism fostering group success through cooperation. We suggest cultivating a social robotics culture as a path to sustainability. Finally, humanization involves adapting environments to human norms to enhance human traits and facilitate robot acceptance, which entails ethically managing user perception and leveraging robots to mitigate digital disconnection.

The paper structure is as follows. Section 2 discusses ICT devices and social robots. Section 3 addresses social friction factors. Section 4 discusses humanisation. Social, economic, and technological sustainability are discussed in Sect. 5. Section 6 links social robots to culture. The final remarks, in Sect. 7, answer the questions stated in the abstract in light of the discussion along the paper.

2 The Boundary Layer Between ICT Devices and Social Robots

A social ICT device is a computational device normally with visual, tactile, and sound interfaces, enabling it to interact with the environment, and equipped with software endowing it with social skills. As ICT devices become increasingly skilled, in social terms, an emergent question refers to the added value of social robots. In general, technologies that do not generate added value are not sustainable. The interaction capability places ICTs in direct competition with social robots, both battling to be preferred by humans.

Currently, the boundary between ICT and Social Robotics is not widely accepted. For example, Bainbridge et al. claim that a physical presence impacts the perception of a social presence [7]. Emotions have been claimed to establish the boundary [50], however, the commonly accepted idea is that a larger body of evidence is required, pointing to significant advantages of social robots vs other social ICT devices.

Embodied robots thus have an edge on non-autonomous, non-robotic ICT devices. However, the penetration of social ICT devices is much larger than that of social robots. If ICT devices have a clear edge over social robots, that should have been easily identifiable by now. Furthermore, this boundary may have different flavours, depending on the context. For example, in rehabilitation activities, some studies point to people quickly losing interest as the activities tend to be repetitive/boring [23]. Nevertheless, studies such as the one from Vassili and Farshchian, in the health-related ICTs, point to the acceptance by seniors if they give them independence, safety, and security [59]. Here, robots have the edge over ICT devices; body motion is a powerful tool, e.g., to convey emotions [2]. In addition, anthropomorphic interfaces, e.g., gestures, may be used to convey meaningful nonverbal information [47]. Even though smartphones are gaining anthropomorphic characteristics, as exemplified in the work of Teyssier [52], it seems clear that the embodiment of a social robot will outperform that of an ICT device as the number/diversity of anthropomorphic degrees will be bigger. Though, in the limit, a smartphone can "converge" to a robot embodiment.

Since both Social Robots and ICT devices are analysed as single, independent entities, the boundary between the two appears to be rigid. However, this boundary may be smoothed when interactions of the type human-ICT device-robot are considered. ICT devices, e.g., smartphones, are already equipped with interesting, even socially skilled, voice-enabled technologies and facial recognition, which may simplify interaction with humans. Additionally, ICT devices, such as tablets, can be seen as complementary for robots as many social robots tend to integrate such devices to extend their interaction capabilities, for example, by incorporating the possibilities provided by touch screens to provide information as tactile interfaces. The boundary between the two classes is thus smoothed as both incorporate concepts from each other.

3 Social Friction

Generic robotics is often linked to fears of job loss, creating social friction; however, evidence shows these concerns are largely unfounded and unrelated to interaction challenges [58]. In Social Robotics, similar concerns have emerged during experiments like the EU-funded Monarch project, where hospital staff worried about job loss despite the robots' non-threatening behavior[2]. Similarly, in the ROBSEN project, caregivers expressed concerns about robots replacing them during cognitive tasks[3].

Adapting robots to users' needs is crucial, as illustrated by the ROBSEN project, where storytelling robots struggled to engage elders, highlighting the necessity for user-centered skills and improved interaction mechanisms [41]. Social robots that fail to meet expectations may also lead to social friction. As expectations grow, people might associate robot behavior with human personality traits, in line with definitions of personality as patterns of behavior [13].

Figure 1 shows an example of an unintentional software glitch that refers to a Monarch robot during a long-term (several months) experiment. The left-hand image shows a blueprint of the hospital ward where this experiment occurred. The area enclosed in the thick dark line represents the location of the trajectory shown in the right-hand image. The software glitch made the robot undock from its resting position (the blue star marks in Fig. 1 left and right represents the starting and end positions) during the night period, when no activity was expected, and wander around in the area, moving as shown in the trajectory in the right-hand plot. Social friction from such incidents can be minimized if robots are perceived positively, consistent with TAM . However, their presence may also influence human interactions, forming social clusters reminiscent of those on social networks.

---

[2] The European Project FP7-ICT-2011-9-601033 Monarch âĂŞ Multi-Robot Cognitive Systems Operating in Hospitals.
[3] The Project Development of social robots to help seniors with cognitive impairment (ROBSEN), funded by the Spanish Ministry of Economy and Competitiveness.

To mitigate friction, establishing affective bonds between robots and users is crucial. Frequent interactions and empathetic features help form these bonds, yet the impact of broken bonds remains underexplored [43,65]. Users might feel a robot's absence akin to losing a pet or friend, as seen when Monarch project researchers were asked to extend the robots' stay. Conversely, limited interactions can lead to frustration and affect acceptance [29]. Thoughtful interaction design is vital to managing these dynamics and preventing frustrations [63]. In child-robot interactions, emotion-based adaptive behaviors are more effective than game-based ones, enhancing engagement [1].

 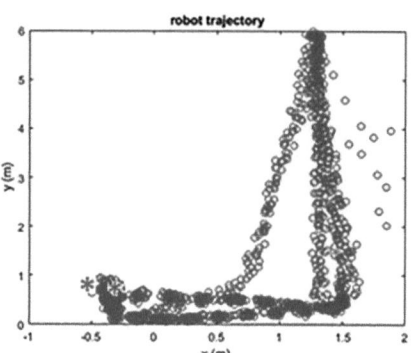

Fig. 1. *Left*: floorplan of the hospital ward's public area (thick black line), with the robot's docking station marked by a blue star. *Right*: The robot's overnight trajectory left its base unexpectedly and traversed much of the enclosed area before returning to the docking point. This unplanned movement – triggered by a software error – can startle staff and patients, undermining trust. It underscores the importance of dependable behaviors in sensitive environments.

4 Humanizing Environments

The role of social robots in humanizing environments has been extensively discussed [44]. Humanization involves making environments conform to human norms, but some suggest questioning its limits [21]. Technologically skilled individuals may be more inclined to humanize robots [38]. The Sophia robot's creator claims humanoids can enhance human traits, aiding acceptance and environmental humanization [24,39]. Appearance challenges arise as soft robots might trigger diverse reactions, though no direct correlation with naturalness has been observed [30]. This highlights the need to balance emotional manipulation and tactile engagement [6]. Social robots compete with static devices like smartphones, prompting research into when digital entities become partners [16,51]. Human-like facial features encourage empathy and positive attributions [9,28]. Despite debates over humanization, robots can enhance environments, as seen with the Monarch robot [44,45]. Social robots may mitigate the disconnection caused by ICT devices [11,55], illustrated by interactions like those in Fig. 2.

Embodiment shapes perception [62], yet its effect on emotional perception remains uncertain [20]. Privacy concerns are crucial as robots acquire user information, requiring trust [36]. Privacy involves both physical and informational aspects, influencing user-robot dynamics. Human-like attributions to robot behavior significantly impact interaction; robots perceived as having human motives, such as cheating in games, may be seen as more intelligent [25,56]. Researchers must consider the ethics of manipulating user perception with these attributes.

Fig. 2. Child interacted with a Mbot robot: speech was controlled using a wizard-of-oz strategy, but autonomous movement led to a dance-like interaction.

5 Social, Economic and Technological Sustainability

The sustainability of social robots encompasses social, economic, and technological dimensions, each presenting unique challenges and opportunities. Balancing these dimensions ensures that social robots can be effectively adopted into everyday life, offering meaningful benefits while acknowledging and overcoming potential barriers.

5.1 Social Sustainability

Exploring the complexities of social sustainability, social robots are seen as transformative entities within human environments, particularly by revealing human vulnerabilities in emotional and ethical situations, which can significantly influence their acceptance [42]. Their gradual integration into everyday settings, such as performing roles as couriers or entertainers, introduces unique challenges like significant energy consumption [10]. This diverges from manufacturing robots due to lower utilization rates and different operational demands, raising further questions about sustainability.

Cultural influences significantly shape the development and application of social robots, with distinct regional priorities. Asian cultures often prioritize enhancing daily life through Robotics, while Western countries may focus more on defense and military applications [42]. Addressing social biases and promoting equitable access are essential for adding societal value and fostering widespread acceptance across diverse communities.

By tackling these interconnected elements, the discussion provides a comprehensive perspective on how social robots can be sustainably integrated into various cultural contexts [33]. Ensuring that technological progression is balanced with social needs, ethical considerations, and equitable access highlights the need for ongoing dialogue and evaluation. This nuanced approach makes the potential of social robots to meaningfully and sustainably impact daily life more apparent, emphasizing the importance of continual assessment and adaptation [66].

Moreover, the sustainability of Social Robotics must not overlook social aspects, such as biases and discrimination. Equitable access to social robots may not be a necessary condition for acceptance and sustainability, but it is certainly a value-creation factor.

5.2 Economic Sustainability

As social robots integrate into human societies as artificial citizens, they bring considerable social benefits and exert significant economic influence, affecting business cycles. A critical factor in their integration is energy consumption, which is essential for acceptance and sustainability. For example, the Monarch robot [4] consumes approximately 3.8 kWh per day, highlighting its considerable energy footprint. This issue is compounded by the increasing reliance on cloud services and AI advancements, driving up energy demands [35,37]. Unlike ICT devices, robots must also account for energy needs related to mobility, adding complexity.

The broad adoption of social robots could place strains on energy systems, necessitating a shift towards sustainable development practices [10]. Additionally, the concept of emerging robot economies suggests potential productivity gains but also poses ethical challenges that may conflict with traditional human values [5].

However, the economic sustainability of social robots needs to be analysed from the perspective of their applications too, such as in healthcare, where they could alleviate constraints on resources like professionals and facilities. This dual focus on energy consumption and application impact highlights the importance of a comprehensive, balanced approach to sustainably integrating social robots into society.

5.3 Technological Sustainability

Few social robots have reached mass, everyday use, unlike other smart devices like phones [46]. This may be due to technological immaturity and underestimating human psychology in design, especially for dependent users. Despite progress, challenges in interaction mechanisms for diverse users, such as those with disabilities, persist [49]. Incorporating technologies like augmented reality and wearables can enhance sustainability by improving interactions.

Significant technological advances in perception, such as cost-effective 3D capture and improved audio from smart speakers, are enhancing robots' capabilities. Expanding technological sustainability may involve using wearables and IoT devices [26], offering real-time user information and environmental monitoring.

Computing constraints challenge social robots due to the need for compact hardware that limits the integration of high-performance components. Both low-power computing solutions, like NVidia Jetson and Google Coral, and cloud computing offer alternatives. The latter, supported by 5G, reduces latency but introduces concerns about cost, security, and privacy, necessitating robust protocols to protect user data during external processing.

6 In Need of a Framework for Culture Generation by Social Robots

Sustainability and culture have been recognised to have complex relations (see the work of Throsby [54] for a discussion on definitions of both terms). While sustainability can be tied to the ability to thrive/develop in a social context, culture can be seen as the collection of values entities, namely social robots, abide by. The recognition that culture impacts the life of societies and sustainability must occur within a cultural context [18], hence, creating a Social Robotics culture can be a pathway for sustainable Social Robotics. Whether or not social robots will produce culture and, arguably, improve acceptance and social integration is under debate.

Currently, social robots have few creative skills and hence miss one of the three skills often associated with culture producers (creative, managerial, and communication systems, see [48], chap. 15). However, these are not strict boundaries, and if a robot is perceived as being creative that may be due to some liveliness/randomness characteristics – see, for instance, some painting creations produced by robots [32]. Creating robots capable of producing culture is thus a challenging undertaking. Saetra defines culture as a mechanism that promotes group success through cooperation, for which trust is a fundamental value [40]. The current state-of-the-art social robots may foster deception and, hence, the loss of trust.

The ongoing development of technology does not explicitly target culture generation. Instead, culture is seen as a byproduct of behavioural skills, emotions, social norms, and other factors linked to individual social skills. Figure 3 shows a selection of the main factors, we argue, involved in culture production, using a Ishikawa diagram[4], [27], following the interpretation of the definition in the work of Alarcon [3][5]. The selection of the spine labels results from a sampling

---

[4] These diagrams have been used, for example, in optimising production scenarios, [53], and in problems of mental/behavioural health, [66].

[5] "Culture is defined as set of behavioral norms, meanings, and values or reference points utilized by members of a particular society to construct their unique view of the world, and ascertain their identity" [3], p. 133.

of the literature on Social Robotics for the main topics currently addressed by researchers. While Social Robotics is blossoming, it is not expected that it will affect political systems, a wide requirement for a harmonious development of societies and hence sustainability [54].

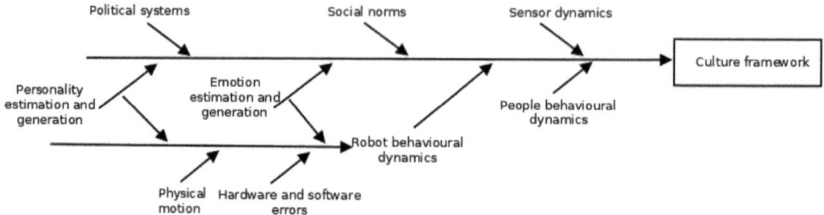

Fig. 3. Requirements/concerns/tradeoffs to develop a framework to produce Culture, in the form of a Ishikawa diagram. The spine labels result from sampling the literature for topics and concepts relevant to culture. The links between the concepts addressed indicate some form of dependency between them. This diagram is incomplete (as it is often the case in other problems), and can be upgraded using very simple rules.

Another possibility is to look at social robots themselves as culture. Social Robotics and Robotics in general is part of a creative process that is intrinsic to the creative process of engineering. However, the main difference between social robotics and other disciplines is its underlying multidisciplinary approach. Creating social robots can require the participation of engineers, psychologists, designers, sociologists, and other experts, depending on the robot application. The combination of the insights from these profiles in a unique and novel piece of technology can be seen as technological art that contributes to the success of science and technology in the progress of humankind.

7 Final Remarks

Current Social Robotics faces multiple possible paths. Most of the literature focuses on acceptance in limited scenarios, and there is a lack of experiments on proper social integration and the potential lifestyle changes, i.e., with a diverse human population, of large enough size and long enough duration, factors already recognized as important in the work of Kanda an Ishiguro [31].

While there isn't a Gartner Hype Cycle[6] for Social Robots, insights from AI trends provide valuable perspectives on their potential integration and societal acceptance. This work discusses how social robots are likely to be accommodated as society becomes familiar with various acceptance factors supported by research. Despite initial concerns about a novelty effect, where interest may decrease once the novelty subsides, researchers are encouraged to explore innovative approaches to sustain long-term engagement and relevance.

---

[6] Yearly technology trends published by the Gartner Inc. (https://www.gartner.com/.

The interaction and competition between social robots and ICT devices are noteworthy, with technologies potentially evolving in parallel. For instance, robots like the Paro baby seal [61] demonstrate the unique benefits of embodied interactions, offering experiences that software applications may not replicate. This suggests that embodied social robots can complement technological advances in ICT, offering holistic solutions that blend physical presence with digital intelligence.

Long-term human-robot interaction is crucial for social robot sustainability, requiring a design that extends beyond initial appeal to foster consistent value and integration. This involves focusing on how useful, easy, and enjoyable robots are, alongside personalized communication, to build sustained engagement and trust, while addressing issues like user resistance or declining interest. Such a design can help robots form affective bonds, potentially mitigating the disengagement common with other digital technologies, thus enabling lasting adoption and lifestyle changes. Cultural integration is equally important, as a robot's enduring presence depends on its alignment with societal norms. This means understanding culture as shared values and a mechanism for successful group cooperation built on trust. It also requires considering diverse regional priorities, ensuring equitable access and ethical considerations to create societal value.

Machine learning emerges as a fundamental element in the field of Social Robotics, as its applications enhance the perceived intelligence of robots, thus fostering greater acceptance and usability. As these technologies advance, their ability to mimic human interactions through improved speech recognition, tactile engagement, and vision systems will likely drive to greater integration.

Despite its sustainability challenges, social robotics offers excellent potential for societal impact when guided by strategic, user-centered design. The development of socially accepted robots may paradoxically offer insights into human behavior, revealing the intricacies of human interactions through the creation of artificial beings.

Achieving sustainable social robots is expected to transform lifestyles by populating environments where social interaction services are required, thereby reshaping the dynamics of human-robot collaboration. Drawing on Epstein's ideas [17], a "generalist" approach, embracing interdisciplinary exploration, is emphasized as crucial for fostering innovation in Social Robotics. Researchers can unlock valuable insights that propel progress and adaptation in this rapidly evolving field by investigating a broad spectrum of related topics rather than focusing narrowly.

Acknowledgments. The research leading to these results has received funding from the projects: "LARSyS-FCT UIDB/50009/2020", from Fundação para a Ciência e Tecnologia (FCT), Portugal; "Robots sociales para mitigar la soledad y el aislamiento en mayores (SOROLI), PID2021-123941OA-I00", funded by Agencia Estatal de Investigación (AEI), Spanish Ministerio de Ciencia e Innovación; "Robots sociales para reducir la brecha digital de las personas mayores (SoRoGap), TED2021-132079B-I00", funded by Agencia Estatal de Investigación (AEI), Spanish Ministerio de Ciencia e Innovación;

"Robot Social Portable con alto grado de vínculo (PoSoRo)", PID2022-140345OB-I00, funded by Agencia Estatal de Investigación (AEI), Spanish Ministerio de Ciencia e Innovación. This publication is part of the R&D&I project PDC2022-133518-I00, funded by MCIN/AEI/10.13039/501100011033 and by the European Union NextGenerationEU/PRTR.

Disclosure of Interests. The authors have no competing interests to declare that are relevant to the content of this article.

References

1. Ahmad, M., Mubin, O., Orlando, J.: Adaptive Social Robot for Sustaining Social Engagement during Long-Term Children-Robot Interaction. International Journal of Human-Computer Interaction **33**(12), 943–962 (2017). https://doi.org/10.1080/10447318.2017.1300750
2. Ahmed, A., Hossain Bari, A., Gavrilova, M.: Emotion recognition from body movement. IEEE Access (2019). https://doi.org/10.1109/ACCESS.2019.2963113
3. Alarcón, R.: Culture, cultural factors and psychiatric diagnosis: review and projections. World Psychiatry **8**(3), 131–139 (2009). https://doi.org/10.1002/j.2051-5545.2009.tb00233.x
4. Alvito, P., Marques, C., Carriço, P., Sequeira, J., Gonçalves, D.: Monarch Robots Hardware (2014). Deliverable D2.2.1, European Project FP7-ICT-2011-9-601033, January
5. Arduengo, M., Sentis, L.: The Robot Economy: Here It Comes. Int. J. Soc. Robot. **13**(5), 937–947 (2020). https://doi.org/10.1007/s12369-020-00686-1
6. Arnold, T., Scheutz, M.: The Tactile Ethics of Soft Robotics: Designing Wisely for Human-Robot Interaction. Soft Rob. **4**(2), 81–87 (2017). https://doi.org/10.1089/soro.2017.0032
7. Bainbridge, W., Hart, J., Kim, E., Scassellati, B.: The benefits of interactions with physically present robots over video-displayed agents. Int. J. Soc. Robot. **3**, 41–52 (2011). https://doi.org/10.1007/s12369-010-0082-7
8. Beer, J., Prakash, A., Mitzner, T., Rogers, W.: Understanding Robot Acceptance. Tech. rep., Atlanta, GA: Georgia Institute of Technology School of Psychology (2011), Technical Report HFA-TR-1103, Human Factors and Aging Laboratory. http://hdl.han-dle.net/1853/39672
9. Broadbent, E., Kumar, V., Li, X., Sollers, J., Stafford, R., MacDonald, B., Wegner, D.: Robots with Display Screens: A Robot with a More Humanlike Face Display Is Perceived To Have More Mind and a Better Personality. PLoS ONE **8**(8) (2013), id:e72589
10. Bugmann, G., Siegel, M., Burcin, R.: A role for robotics in sustainable development? In: Africon 2011. IEEE (2011). https://doi.org/10.1109/AFRCON.2011.6072154, Victoria Falls, Livingston, Zambia, 13-15 September
11. Carson, V., et al.: Physical activity and sedentary behavior across three timepoints and associations with social skills in early childhood. BMC Public Health, pp. 19–27 (2019). https://doi.org/10.1186/s12889-018-6381-x
12. Castillo, J.C., et al.: Software architecture for smart emotion recognition and regulation of the ageing adult. Cogn. Comput. **8**(2), 357–367 (2016). https://doi.org/10.1007/s12559-016-9383-y

13. Corr, P., Matthews, G.: The Cambridge Handbook of Personality Psychology. Cambridge University Press (2009). Cambridge Handbooks in Psychology
14. Davis, F.: Perceived usefulness, perceived ease of use and user acceptance of information technology. MIS Q. **13**(3), 319–339 (1989). https://doi.org/10.2307/249008
15. Desai, M., Kaniarasu, P., Medvedev, M., Steinfeld, A., Yanco, H.: Impact of robot failures and feedback on real-time trust. In: 8th ACM/IEEE International Conference on Human-Robot Interaction (HRI), pp. 251–258 (2013). https://doi.org/10.1109/HRI.2013.6483596, Tokyo, Japan, 3-6 March
16. Di Dio, C., Manzi, F., Peretti, G., Cangelosi, A., Harris, P., Massaro, D., Marchetti, A.: Shall I Trust You? From Child–Robot Interaction to Trusting Relationships. Frontiers in Psychology **11**, April 2020. https://doi.org/10.3389/fpsyg.2020.00469, Sec. Developmental Psychology
17. Epstein, D.: Range: Why Generalists Triumph in a Specialized World. Macmillan (2019)
18. ESCAP: The importance of culture in achieving sustainable development (2013), Economic and Social Commission for Asia and the Pacific (ESCAP). Sustainable Development Brief, 8th March 2013/SDWG
19. Eyal, N.: Hooked: How to build habit-forming products. Business Books (2014)
20. Fiorini, L., et al.: The Role of Coherent Robot Behavior and Embodiment in Emotion Perception and Recognition During Human-Robot Interaction: Experimental Study. JMIR Human Factors **11** (2024). https://doi.org/10.2196/45494, id: e45494
21. Giger, J., Piçarra, N., Alves-Oliveira, P., Oliveira, R., Arriaga, P.: Humanisation of robots: Is it really such a good idea? Hum. Behav. Emerging Technol. **1**, 111–123 (2019). https://doi.org/10.1002/hbe2.147
22. Gompei, T., Umemuro, H.: A robot's slip of the tongue: Effect of speech error on the familiarity of a humanoid robot. In: 24th IEEE International Symposium on Robot and Human Interactive Communication (RO-MAN), pp. 331–336 (2015). https://doi.org/10.1109/ROMAN.2015.7333630, Kobe, Japan, 31 August - 4 September
23. Guneysu Ozgur, A., Wessel, M., Johal, W., Sharma, K., Özgür, A., Vuadens, P., Mondada, F., Hummel, F., Dillenbourg, P.: Iterative design of an upper limb rehabilitation game with tangible robots. In: 2018 ACM/IEEE International Conference on Human-Robot Interaction, pp. 241–250 (2018), Chicago, Illinois, USA, 5-8 March
24. Hanson, D.: Humanising Robots. How Making Humanoids Can Make Us More Humans (2007), Doctor Dissertation Public edition, ISBN 13: 9781549659928
25. Heider, F., Simmel, M.: An experimental study of apparent behavior. Am. J. Psychol. **57**(2), 243–259 (1944). https://doi.org/10.2307/1416950
26. Heikenfeld, J., Jajack, A., Rogers, J., Gutruf, P., Tian, L., Pan, T., Li, R., Khine, M., Kim, J., Wang, J., Kime, J.: Wearable sensors: modalities, challenges, and prospects. Lab Chip **18**, 217–248 (2018). https://doi.org/10.1039/c7lc00914c
27. Ishikawa, K.: Guide to quality control (1976)
28. Jastrzab, L., Chaudhury, B., Ashley, S., Koldewyn, K., Cross, E.: Beyond humanlikeness: Socialness is more influential when attributing 2 mental states to robots (2023). https://doi.org/10.1101/2023.10.05.560273, bioRxiv preprint, posted October 6
29. Jirak, D., et al.: Is it me or the robot? a critical evaluation of human affective state recognition in a cognitive task. Front. Neurorobotics **16** (2022). https://doi.org/10.3389/fnbot.2022.882483
30. Jørgensen, J., Bojesen, K.B., Jochum, E.: Is a Soft Robot More "Natural"? Exploring the Perception of Soft Robotics in Human–Robot Interaction. Int. J. Soc. Robot. (2), 1–19 (2021). https://doi.org/10.1007/s12369-021-00761-1

31. Kanda, T., Ishiguro, I.: Human-Robot Interaction in Social Robotics. CRC Press (2013)
32. Karimov, A., Kopets, E., Leonov, S., Scalera, L., Butusov, D.: A robot for artistic painting in authentic colors. J. Intell. Robot. Syst. **107**(3), 34 (2023). https://doi.org/10.1007/s10846-023-01831-4
33. Kohl, J., van der Schoor, M., Syré, A., Goblich, D.: Social sustainability in the development of service robots. In: International Design Conference - DESIGN 2020 (2020). https://doi.org/10.1017/dsd.2020.59, Cavtat, Croatia, 26-29 October
34. Liu, Z., Wu, M., Cao, W., Chen, L., Xu, J., Zhang, R., Mao, J.: A facial expression emotion recognition-based human-robot interaction system. IEEE/CAA J. Automatica Sinica **4**(4), 668–676 (2017). https://doi.org/10.1109/JAS.2017.7510622
35. Lohr, S.: Cloud Computing Is Not the Energy Hog That Had Been Feared (2020), The New York Times, February 28
36. Lutz, C., Tamó-Larrieux, A.: The robot privacy paradox: Understanding how privacy concerns shape intentions to use social robots. Human-Machine Communication **1**, 87–111 (2020). https://doi.org/10.30658/hmc.1.6
37. Masanet, E., Shehabi, A., Lei, N., Smith, S., Koomey, J.: Recalibrating global data center energy-use estimates. Science **367**(6481), 984–986 (2020). https://doi.org/10.1126/science.aba3758
38. Mays, K.: Humanising Robots? The Influence of Appearance and Status on Social Perceptions of Robots. Ph.D. thesis, Boston University, College of Communication (2021), Doctoral Dissertation, Boston University Libraries, OpenBU. https://hdl.handle.net/2144/41877
39. Robert, L.: The growing problem of humanizing robots. Int. Robot. Automation J. **3**(1) (2017). https://doi.org/10.15406/iratj.2017.03.00043
40. Saetra, H.: Social robot deception and the culture of trust. Paladyn J. Behav. Robot. **12**(1) (2021). https://doi.org/10.1515/pjbr-2021-0021
41. Salichs, M.A., Encinar, I.P., Salichs, E., Castro-González, Á., Malfaz, M.: Study of scenarios and technical requirements of a social assistive robot for Alzheimer's disease patients and their caregivers. Int. J. Soc. Robot. **8**(1), 85–102 (2015). https://doi.org/10.1007/s12369-015-0319-6
42. Samani, H., Saadatian, E., Pang, N., Polydorou, D., Fernando, O., Nakatsu, R., Koh, J.: Cultural Robotics: The Culture of Robotics and Robotics in Culture. Int. J. Adv. Robot. Syst. **10** (2013). https://doi.org/10.5772/57260
43. Schellin, H., et al.: Man's new best friend? Strengthening human-robot dog bonding by enhancing the doglikeness of Sony's Aibo. In: 2020 Systems and Information Engineering Design Symposium (SIEDS), pp. 1–6 (2020). Charlottsville, Virginia, USA, 24 April
44. Sequeira, J.: Can Social Robots make societies more human? Information (2018), Special issue on Roboethics (ISSN 2078-2489)
45. Sequeira, J.S. (ed.): Robotics in Healthcare. AEMB, vol. 1170. Springer, Cham (2019). https://doi.org/10.1007/978-3-030-24230-5
46. Sharkey, A., Wood, N.: The Paro seal robot: demeaning or enabling. In: AISB'14, The 50th Aniversary Convention of the AISB (2014), University of London, 1-4 April
47. Smith, J., Vogel, D., Madon, S., Edwards, S.: The power of touch: nonverbal communication within married dyads. Counselling Psychologist **39**(5), 764–787 (2011). https://doi.org/10.1177/0011000010385849
48. Solomon, M., Bamossy, G., Askegaard, S., Hogg, M.: Consumer Behavior. A European Perspective. Prentice Hall and Pearson Education Ltd, 3rd edn. (2006)

49. Sørensen, L., Johannesen, D., Johnsen, H.: Humanoid robots for assisting people with physical disabilities in activities of daily living: a scoping review. Assist. Technol. (2024). https://doi.org/10.1080/10400435.2024.2337194
50. Sugiyama, S., Vincent, J.: Social Robots and Emotion: Transcending the Boundary Between Humans and ICTs. Intervalla 1 (2013), ISSN: 2296-3413
51. Tanibe, T., Hashimoto, T., Karasawa, K.: We perceive a mind in a robot when we help it. PLoS ONE **12**(7) (2017). https://doi.org/10.1371/journal.pone.0180952, id:e0180952
52. Teyssier, M.: Anthropomorphic Devices for Affective Touch Communication. Ph.D. thesis, Institut Polytechnique de Paris, France (2020), Doctoral dissertation, HAL Id: tel-02881894. https://tel.archives-ouvertes.fr/tel-02881894
53. Thomas, S., Ali, A., AlArjani, A., Attia, E.: Simulation based performance improvement: a case study on automotive industries. Int. J. Simulation Modelling **21**, 405–416 (2022). https://doi.org/10.2507/IJSIMM21-3-606
54. Throsby, D.: Sustainability and culture some theoretical issues. International Journal of Cultural Policy **4**(1), 7–19 (1997). https://doi.org/10.1080/10286639709358060
55. Uhls, Y., Michikyan, M., Morris, J., Garcia, D., Small, G., Zgourou, E., Greenfield, P.: Five days at outdoor education camp without screens improves preteen skills with nonverbal emotion cues. Comput. Hum. Behav. **39**, 387–392 (2014). https://doi.org/10.1016/j.chb.2014.05.036
56. Ullman, D., Leite, I., Phillips, J., Kim-Cohen, J., Scassellati, B.: Smart Human, Smarter Robot: How Cheating Affects Perceptions of Social Agency. In: Procs. 36th Annual Conference of the Cognitive Science Society (CogSci2014) (2014), 23-26 July, Quebec City, Canada
57. United Nations: Sustainable Development Goals (2021). https://www.un.org/sustainabledevelopment/. [Retrieved August 2021]
58. United Nations: Technology and Innovation Report 2021. In: United Nations Conference on Trade and Development (UNCTAD) (2021), Geneva
59. Vassili, L., Farshchian, B.: Acceptance of Health-Related ICT among Elderly People Living in the Community: A Systematic Review of Qualitative Evidence. Int. J. Hum.-Comput. Interact. **34**(2), 99–116 (2018). https://doi.org/10.1080/10447318.2017.1328024
60. Verdegem, P., De Marez, L.: Rethinking determinants of ICT acceptance: towards an integrated and comprehensive overview. Technovation **31**(8), 411–423 (2011). https://doi.org/10.1016/j.technovation.2011.02.004
61. Wada, K., Shibata, T.: Living with seal robots - its sociopsychological and physiological influences on the elderly at a care house. IEEE Trans. Rob. **23**(5), 972–980 (2007)
62. Wainer, J., Feil-Seifer, D., Shell, D., Mataric, M.: The role of physical embodiment in human-robot interaction. In: Procs. The 15th IEEE International Symposium on Robot and Human Interactive Communication (ROMAN 2006) (2006). https://doi.org/10.1109/ROMAN.2006.314404, 6-8 September, University of Hertfordshire, Hatfield, UK
63. Weidemann, A., Rußweinkel, N.: The role of frustration in human-robot interaction – what is needed for a successful collaboration? Front. Psychol. (2021). https://doi.org/10.3389/fpsyg.2021.640186
64. Whelan, S., Murphy, K., Barrett, E., Krusche, C., Santorelli, A., Casey, D.: Factors affecting the acceptability of social robots by older adults including people with dementia or cognitive impairment: a literature review. Int. J. Soc. Robot. **10**(5), 643–668 (2018). https://doi.org/10.1007/s12369-018-0471-x

65. Willemse, C., Van Erp, J.: Social touch in human-robot interaction: Robot-initiated touches can induce positive responses without extensive prior bonding. Int. J. Soc. Robot. **11**(2), 285–304 (2019)
66. Wong, K., Woo, K., Woo, K.: Ishikawa Diagram (2016). https://doi.org/10.1007/978-3-319-26209-3_9

Eyes from Above: Co-designing a Multi-drone System for Enhanced Surveillance of Critical Infrastructure

Maria-Theresa Bahodi, Maja Hornbæk Kristensen, Niels van Berkel, Mikael Skov, Nicolai Brodersen Hansen, and Timothy Merritt(✉)

Aalborg University, Aalborg Ø 9220, Denmark
merritt@cs.aau.dk

Abstract. The rapid development of autonomous drone technology has enabled novel applications, such as the surveillance of critical infrastructure. However, how to effectively integrate drone monitoring systems in real-world practice remains an open question. A lack of experience with drones among security and infrastructure experts further necessitates a co-design approach that also informs future end-users of drone possibilities and limitations. In this paper, we present a case study involving personnel from a bio-fuel power plant with limited drone experience through a scenario-driven co-design workshop. We helped participants understand drones' capabilities through a physical demonstration with multiple drones and supported participants' generation of ideas and concerns through tangible objects. We outline design considerations and present concrete flight pattern designs that optimise drone resource allocation to alleviate human responsibilities in surveillance and security tasks.

Keywords: Multi-drone System · Unmanned Aerial Vehicles · Co-Design · Surveillance · Human-Drone Interaction · Critical Infrastructure Monitoring · Sustainable Robotics

1 Introduction

In recent years, unmanned aerial vehicles, more commonly known as drones, have been used in various areas. Existing human-drone research within human-computer interaction has explored the physical design of drones [37,66] and how humans can interact with them for various purposes [38,58,59]. However, drones have also proven to be a reliable tool for supporting larger, critical applications such as emergency services [2,18,20] and critical infrastructure monitoring [5,30,53]. Drones have the ability to provide an aerial perspective with fewer resources compared to their larger manned counterpart, helicopters. Research has identified various ways UAVs contribute to the Sustainable Development Goals of the United Nations[1] towards which we align our work [25]. The goal of

---

[1] UN Sustainable Development Goals https://sdgs.un.org/goals.

developing the security and surveillance platform is to strengthen the resilience of critical infrastructure (SDG 9) and support the safe operation of clean energy facilities (SDG 7) and promote responsible production (SDG 12) by providing a resource-efficient surveillance method that supports human work.

In the case of monitoring critical infrastructure, drones can be used both as a persistent monitoring device and as a reactive tool to inspect areas that need immediate attention. Given the technical and practical limitations of drone operations, real-world deployment has to consider which resources are already present on the premises to detect and handle events, such that the drones are not used needlessly and disturb the security process with unnecessary data. To better understand the possible role of drones in supporting in this context, we need to understand current practices in securing critical infrastructure and how drones can act as support to an already existing system rather than proving to be a liability [31].

In addition, security personnel do not necessarily have experience with drones. While existing research has been highly focused on experts who regularly work with drones [2,47], this expertise is not necessarily present in monitoring contexts. Prior work suggests that future human-drone interaction is less focused on direct control (one operator with a controller) but instead takes the role of a supervisor that oversees the drones' actions [49]. However, a fully autonomous system could potentially cause problems as the autonomous behaviour does not necessarily incorporate the ad-hoc and unique scenarios that cannot be prepared for [56,64]. It is therefore necessary to understand where and how to incorporate autonomous drone behaviour and where human control and knowledge are required, especially in high-risk contexts such as critical infrastructure.

To explore the potential of drones for monitoring critical infrastructure, we collaborated with a local bio-fuel power plant that encounters a combination of planned tasks and spontaneous events. Going in-depth with a specific case allows us to assess how drones can support plant personnel in creating a safer and more optimal functioning environment by providing an aerial perspective of their grounds. We, therefore, conducted a co-design workshop with employees at the power plant to draw on their expertise in securing the power plant. The workshop followed a scenario-driven approach to establish a familiar context with the participants, using, for instance, physical interaction with a printed map of the power plant's premises to create a more tangible idea of how drones could move in a 3D space. We also incorporated a physical demonstration with three drones into the procedure, where the participants could familiarise themselves with the capabilities of a contemporary multi-drone system, experience having commercial drones flying around, and see what data collection looks like in real-time.

This paper has three main contributions. Based on the workshop with domain experts, we present design considerations for multi-drone behaviour when monitoring fixed premises, where both expected and spontaneous events can occur.

We particularly focus on the risk of intruders entering the premises. We further outline themes of considerations and concerns when implementing a multi-drone system designed for autonomous behaviour and present specific flight patterns designed by the participants, which future researchers can use as inspiration for surveillance algorithms for drones. Lastly, we present how utilising tangible objects and realistic demos can provide a good understanding of the technology and its capabilities to domain experts with limited drone experience.

2 Related Work

We present prior work on drone systems within security and monitoring, as well as co-design approaches in human-drone interaction research. Work in drone surveillance, especially, helps inform us of current work that has been explored and identify open research directions.

2.1 Drone-Based Security and Operational Monitoring

Drones have been considered extensively in security contexts, especially with the growth of artificial intelligence [30,60], which allows for significant autonomy in drone systems. Studies have shown that utilising drones has significantly increased the operational efficiency of securing critical infrastructure due to their ability to cover vast areas in a short period and ability to respond to potential threats quickly [39].

Drones for surveillance has been extensively explored from an engineering perspective, for example, on optimising drone task completion [5] and reducing the resources needed for a mission [52,53]. These efforts are helpful in informing control algorithms and resource management. However, they do not examine the needs and requirements of specific sites and missions. There is limited work that explores specific mission details and how human teams should maintain and interact with a group of drones from a security and monitoring perspective. However, there are examples of this in other contexts. This includes adjacent domains such as search and rescue [2,15] and firefighting efforts [48]. Here, researchers have presented participants with interface designs to help humans better understand the current situation [3,24] and allow them to communicate with the drones through different means [4,31]. However, these contexts differ from security within critical infrastructure because the area is well-known to the personnel working there, and more routine and predefined tasks are commonplace. Even though the area is well-defined and familiar, surveillance of critical infrastructure requires the security team to recognize typical issues and also identify new and more complex problems due to the variety of equipment and ongoing activities of the busy site. Moreover, the participants included in the studies often have extensive drone experience, such that the terminology and expectations are already established. In multiple areas where drones have great potential, such as security monitoring, relevant stakeholders will have expansive domain knowledge, but their limited understanding of drone technology makes it difficult to unveil ideas for future drone systems properly. To involve domain experts with limited drone experience, Bødker and Kyng [14] mention that working prototypes can establish a mutual understanding of what the technology is capable of and where changes can be made.

While there are few examples of drone surveillance applications, there exist many commercial solutions to using drones for infrastructure monitoring[2] An example of a drone system for security is the Beehive system by Sunflower Labs[3], where a drone is capable of detecting and deterring intruders such as animals, as well as providing historical data to the user for later processing. These systems are large, and due to their case independence, how they should be set up for monitoring critical infrastructure is not clearly presented. Moreover, these systems often take the perspective of singular drone systems and make it difficult to imagine that the systems can be expanded with multiple drones that can communicate with one another, such that tasks can be delegated between them. In this paper, we seek to discover from the domain experts what is necessary for a multi-drone system to be successful.

2.2 Co-designing Drone Procedures and Interfaces

Co-design and participatory design involve active design efforts *with* the users of a proposed system [27,51], as opposed to, for instance, user-centred design, which focuses more on design *for* the users [28]. It is often used as a means of mutual learning, that is, to let users learn about the possibilities of technology and to allow designers to learn about the practices of the users [9]. Using participatory design, user representatives are aided in interacting and experimenting with the possibilities of the final product [29].

Participatory Approaches to Co-designing Technology. Participatory design considers technology as a means to serve human intentions and plans [16]. Here, there has been a specific focus on workshops, where participatory design encourages participants to draw on their experiences and perspectives to influence the development of technologies. We use participatory design to create a format in which different stakeholders come together to design and discuss expected drone behaviour in the specific context of surveillance and security. By drawing on active participation, we try to establish situations of mutual learning [9,28] where the experts on critical infrastructure, the workers at the plant can learn about technology from us, the designers and drone experts. We, in turn, can learn about their practices and ideas for ideal drone behaviour. In this approach, participants are viewed as "'experts of their experience', and play a large role in knowledge development, idea generation and concept development" [50, p. 24]. In line with this general approach, we also draw on specific workshop formats for co-design, such as Huybrechts et al. who developed the

---

[2] https://innopilot.dk, https://heighttechnologies.com/autonomous-security-drones/, https://tealdrones.com.

[3] https://www.sunflower-labs.com.

MAP-it method, which is a participatory design approach that utilises a background map of the application area on which the participants place and move different tokens with the goal of answering research questions formulated into scenarios that a moderator provides [33].

Co-designing Drone Systems. Previous research has used co-design workshops to facilitate discussions on future multi-drone systems [18,31]. For example, Agrawal et al. [1] employed co-design to uncover solutions to wicked problems seen in the specific context of a drone pilot's situational awareness in drone flights and monitoring tasks. When conducting their workshop, Agrawal et al. used paper artefacts, e.g., paper maps, various objects, and examples of video feeds, to gain an understanding of how important situational awareness is when monitoring and flying drones. Bjurling et al. [8] also used a physical map and cubes to represent drones to help facilitate discussions on the relationship between a swarm of drones and the operator. As a result, they came up with a swarm interaction model to use drone swarms for forest firefighting.

These existing works primarily involve participants who are already familiar with using drones in their work. This is an advantage in the sense that they are already aware of the limitations and possibilities provided by contemporary drones. However, as drones are becoming more widespread in a variety of domains [7], it is equally important to understand the perspective of those with limited understanding or experience of drones. Here, it is also important to facilitate an environment which teaches people the capabilities of drones while grounding their expectations. Similarly, the particular conditions of a use case, here being critical infrastructure, necessitate drawing on domain knowledge.

3 Methods

We performed an extensive co-design session that included tangible objects and physical interaction with drones. Here, we sought to uncover the current challenges, events, and data relevant to plant surveillance and established how drones could complement current practices. We focused primarily on the drones' behaviour, and the results from the co-design session informed a mission design, which we later used as a basis for further discussion of using drones for surveilling a power plant.

To facilitate the co-design session, the researchers designed scenarios that detailed security and surveillance-related issues. The three scenarios concerned were: regular surveillance, monitoring and responding to an intruder and monitoring an area at risk of self-ignition. With these scenarios, the participants were asked to respond to each scenario on the printed-out map with the physical artefacts and creation tools provided while talking about the actual response to an intruder. Each scenario was recorded for further analysis, and the resulting maps were photographed after each scenario. This was done to gain a verbal and physical understanding of how drone surveillance should occur at the power plant, what role the drone should embody, and how the drone should behave in reaction to spontaneous events.

3.1 Real-Time Interaction with a Physical Multi-drone System

Fig. 1. Outdoor physical demo. Left: two of the researchers set up the multi-drone system with all five participants in the background. Middle: participants observe one of the drones automatically start scanning an area. The drone is marked with a red circle on the image. Right: A researcher presents the interface and its capabilities. (Color figure online)

Prior to the co-design session, we sought to ensure that our participants had a realistic perspective of how drones could behave and how they would look in the physical world. We used a custom-developed prototype to control three drones. As the drones were performing their tasks, participants could use the prototype to locate their current position. At the same time, a live video feed was shown on the individual controllers so that the participants could relate the drones' current position to the video. Furthermore, we triggered a manual detection alert for one of the drones, resulting in an alert shown on the user interface, and a drone with a thermal camera would subsequently fly to the alert position. We decided to take this approach as we wanted to provide the participants with a live comparison of when certain drones are more appropriate for specific tasks, as the data collected from different drones could vary significantly. The demonstration, as shown in Fig. 1, informed the participants how the real world related to the 2-dimensionality of what was displayed on the screen (map and video feed). It also provided participants with an understanding of the difficulty of perceiving depth when drones are flying in the air.

3.2 Co-design Setup

We approached the co-design session with scenario-based discussions similar to the use case approach presented by Agrawal et al. [1]. Here, scenarios helped participants focus on the immediate event, what data would be necessary for the drones to collect, and how they could collect this data.

To identify the scenarios relevant to the specific power plant, we interviewed two plant employees to learn about their current procedures and challenges.

Their statements led to an initial ideation on how drones could help the operational personnel monitor the plant, and they were further developed into the scenarios we presented at the workshop. Specifically, we found three main scenarios:

1. **Steady state monitoring**: General monitoring when the plant is functioning as expected, and the drones need to monitor the premises to detect intruders.
2. **Intruder monitoring**: At times, a reliable source such as a drone will detect an intruder (both human and drone), and one or multiple drones need to respond to the detection to determine if it is of interest.
3. **Fuel stack inspection**: The specific plant we collaborated with uses wood pellets and shavings as fuel for their power plant. At specific times of the day, the temperature and volume need to be evaluated to ensure that there is enough fuel and that the temperature is at an acceptable level.

To help start the discussion for each scenario, we presented an example of how drones could act in the given context so that the participants would not become confused or overwhelmed with what the possibilities could be with drones. We encouraged the participants to not only think about the movement of the drones but also consider which data needed to be collected and how the drones should behave in order to collect it.

Cooperative Prototyping. We used cooperative prototyping, a technique in which both users and designers participate in a design process actively and creatively [10]. Within this process, users are tasked with both designing an interface early in the design process as well as continuously evaluating the proposed prototypes that result from the cooperative prototyping session. We utilised scenarios to help the participants frame potential tasks resulting from the presented scenario, which can additionally help to visualise potential interactions in their appropriate contexts [11]. By employing cooperative prototyping, we asked the participants to design the drones' behaviours while simultaneously evaluating their proposed behaviours against the current security practices and the realities of what implementing drones could look like. To actualize the workshop, we provided the participants with a large map, various tangible items (including tokens and icons), blank paper, and pens. The whole setup can be seen in Fig. 2.

Tangible Objects. To facilitate co-design, one approach is to employ *Make* tools, where participants express their thoughts and feelings about a topic by making something. By employing *Make* tools, deeper levels of understanding, association, and creativity are accessible to the participants. Sanders & Stappers found that generating toolkits to facilitate *Make* techniques helps participants in the activities planned for the workshop [50]. Toolkits are seen as a form of visual literacy that is understandable and comprehensible by all. Therefore, all elements of design toolkits should be easily understandable, usable, and polished but not over-designed to avoid apprehension when engaging with them.

Fig. 2. The workshop setup (image taken at design studio prior to power plant site visit).

To provide participants with objects that they could manipulate during the workshop, we developed a wide variety of models and paper artefacts that represent various important human and non-human actors in the scope of drone surveillance at the power plant, as is done when requesting participants to conduct *Make* techniques [50]. The three-dimensionality of drone flight is a vital component to understanding a drone's capabilities and behaviour, but also the constraints it is bounded to [61]. Therefore, we incorporated tangible objects that could easily be moved. Specifically, we created drone models made with foam core where the altitude and camera angle could be changed, as well as more static 3D models so that participants could better visualise the 3D space in which the drones would reside. The physical state of the drones was reflected through labels that could be attached to the drones, as well as printouts of images from various angles of their facility. This was done in accordance with Brandt & Messeter [12], who further emphasised the usage of objects as carriers of meaning and understanding between different stakeholders in a co-design session.

Physical Map. Inspired by previous research [1,8,33], we printed multiple satellite maps of their facility on an A1 paper so that they could move the tokens around the space to visualise where events would occur within the premises. To help participants utilise the physical map, we also designed and provided various icons that both participants and facilitators could move around, allowing participants to realise and visualise their ideas in both space and time. The use of a physical map helps to visualise the findings of the conversations that are facilitated during the co-design workshop [32].

Prompt Cards. Since there were many aspects of drones and surveillance to keep track of, we brought prompt cards to help streamline the conversation to aspects we were specifically focusing on. If the discussion changed focus or perspective, the prompt cards served as a repository of concepts [67] and were used to show what elements of the problem area we were discussing. These prompt cards were loosely inspired by Halskov & Dalsgård's Inspiration Cards [26]. Inspiration Cards can be used for "representing sources of inspiration [...] to gain an overview of various concepts, as means of communication between designers and domain experts" [26, p. 4]. For this workshop, we utilised our prompt cards as a tool to aid communication between facilitators and the participants.

3.3 Participants

This project was a collaboration with workers who managed a biofuel power plant. The workers came from various backgrounds with some of the participants highly involved in the security activities on the plant. They included (P1) a team leader of plant operations, (P2) chief consultant of security, (P3, P4, & P5) senior technology consultants of innovation and sustainability. None of the participants had any direct drone experience, but had heard about the technology to a limited extent. Participants 1 and 2 also participated in the interviews mentioned in Sect. 3.2.

3.4 Analysis

Following the conclusion of the 2-h workshop, we transcribed the video footage using a custom version of OpenAI's Whisper language model[4]. One of the researchers then validated the correctness of the transcriptions. Thereafter, two researchers performed an inductive thematic analysis [13] on the transcription using NVivo. Initial coding led to nine preliminary themes and 165 coded statements, and we compiled the themes into two larger sub-themes: Expectations towards drone behaviour and human-in-the-loop. Moreover, we utilised the statements, movement of objects and drawings to design specific flight plans that can be used as inspiration or a baseline for future drone behaviour algorithms.

4 Results

Our workshop helped visualise and propose a multi-drone system in which the drones could support the workers by ensuring their premises were in a safe state without spending human resources that could have been spent elsewhere. It also

---

[4] https://openai.com/index/whisper/.

revealed more prominent themes about the workers' concerns about the current problems in their system and how the adoption of drones could risk becoming a liability if they did not function as expected. In this section, we present the themes as identified through our thematic, as well as participants' vision for an ideal monitoring system for their plant (Fig. 3).

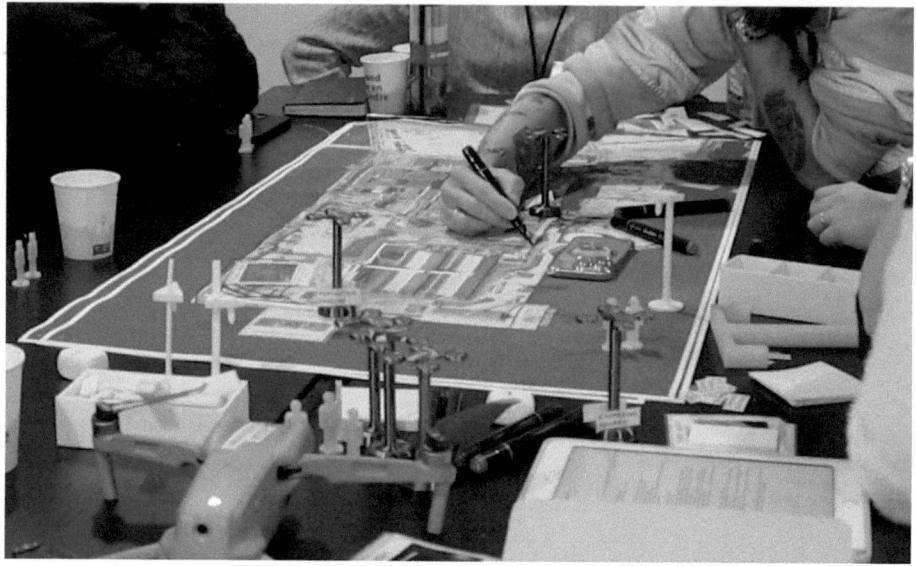

Fig. 3. Photo of the workshop taking place at the power plant. Participants moved tokens and drew on the physical map to visualise their thoughts and ideas in relation to using drones on their premises.

4.1 Expectations Towards Drone Behaviour

A major focus of the workshop was to identify which specific drone behaviour could be useful when monitoring the premises of a power plant. From our discussions with participants, multiple sub-themes appeared under the idea of how drones should behave and what their capabilities should contain.

Autonomous Drone Behaviour. A common theme in the discussions was the need for mission autonomy to ensure that plant personnel could attend to operational tasks while the surveillance system could be self-sustaining and context-aware requiring minimal human intervention. One specific flight behaviour that was particularly interesting for the participants was the idea of having at least one drone dedicated to a continuous perimeter search and act as autonomously as possible. P2 stated, *"[...] it needs to be as autonomous as possible,"*, highlighting the benefits of the automated alerts, and dedicating their focus on attending to the alert location and coordinating resources on the ground. The need for reduced human involvement also emerged when we discussed the limited flight durations and need for drones to return for charging. We explained that automatic docking stations would support that and ensure mission endurance. The participants emphasised that handling mission-related tasks such as recharging, adding or removing drones from the mission, should all be automatic to remove the need for human involvement. Specifically, P1 stated, *"[...] it should be seen as a support and not a liability,"*.

As a drone is continuously monitoring the perimeter, there is a chance that it will detect multiple suspicious objects while completing its rounds. When asked how the drones should behave in the case of multiple alerts, the participants were unsure how this should be handled, especially after considering the number of drones available and what the drones were handling at that moment. P1 stated, *"I think, there should be some kind of criteria with regard to the alertness level we are in, which controls their [the drones'] way of interacting with the environment."*. A recurring idea was that of an *alertness level dial*, where turning the dial up or down determines whether the automation should be more aware of certain things at specific times. While the participants were unsure of the specifics of how such a dial should function, they expressed that the drones should react according to this level, whether it was through a base understanding that was preprogrammed into the system or through previous human decisions.

The season is another factor that could influence drone behaviour, as the amount of fuel physically on-site is highly affected by the current season. As a biofuel power plant, they manage large quantities of wood pellets and chips, which need to be ordered in time and ensure that the temperature does not exceed a certain threshold to avoid fires. Similar to the alertness level, the system needs to adapt to the changing environment and change the drones' behaviours to incorporate the physical context into their routine.

Concerns Towards a Multi-drone System. Although the drones showed a lot of promise, there were also multiple concerns about the drone technology itself. Concretely, participants often considered the battery life, the possibilities and tasks the drones could perform, and how autonomous the system could be if it were necessary to charge the batteries every hour. For example, the idea of having a drone persistently performing a parallel search was deemed irrelevant as the power plant was already supported by a CCTV system that covered the inner ground of the premises. A continuous parallel search would also drain the battery and lead to frequent maintenance checks. All participants also agreed that every drone needed to have a docking station where they could charge themselves for the system even to be a possibility, as they would not have the resources to have dedicated personnel to continuously check if a drone needed to get its battery replaced.

P3 noted, "*Sometimes something sounds incredibly smart, and now it runs, and then you have overseen all those small details that will annoy you [...]*", expressing the concern of adopting a system where the system would cause additional difficulties which would require special maintenance. Participants also raised concerns about the robustness of drones, which came into question when talking about dynamic task allocation, and whether there could be a risk of two drones miscommunicating and crashing into each other because the programmed autonomy did not foresee the potential of two drones being at the same spot. There was a need to ensure a sense of stability and security in the usage of drones, such that resources would not be spent more on maintaining the system rather than having a system that helped them in their monitoring tasks.

It was also evident that the participants imagined a multi-drone system, with multiple drones performing specific tasks and being on standby in case a drone needed to be switched out or an area needed to be inspected. However, there were doubts as to how many drones would be required, as it was a question of balancing price and having the important areas covered. P2 stated: "*[...] it required the amount that is needed to achieve the quality we want*", implying that the number itself did not matter as long as the amount is capable of covering the area and performing the right tasks. Here, participants particularly discussed where the values would lie. For example, when there were specific planned tasks where, it would be nice to have a drone dedicated to one task, but which could not be justified due to the price. Then, it would be a question of which task was more valuable for a drone to address.

Deterrent Effect of Drones. An unexpected element of drone usage on the premises was how other people, specifically intruders, could perceive them. While drones could act as additional cameras to ensure that no foreign entity enters the premises, the drones could also add an intimidating signal to unwanted guests that they are being watched and that they should not be in the area. P1 said, "*[...] let's say that someone comes in and makes some trouble, and then six drones come around. I think that it has quite a strong effect compared to a light that simply blinks.*" P3 also mentioned this in relation to having speakers on the drones, "*[...] it could also be okay to say that 'this is a private area, and you are asked to leave the area'..*"

Interoperability with Existing Systems. The power plant already has hundreds of CCTVs that ensure that all of the plant is covered at all times and trigger an alert when movement has been detected. The existing CCTV system limits the appeal of drones searching the inner premises of the plant. Instead, participants believed it to be more appropriate for their situation to ensure that the drones could communicate with existing systems and were not seen as entirely separate external systems. P1 stated, "*[...] if they could communicate with the cameras, then I think we should be covered quite well*" and "*[...] when there is movement somewhere, then it gets deployed automatically.*" Another reason for having the drones integrate with the existing CCTVs would also be to help the workers at the main control centre. Here, the drones could help with inspecting areas where alerts were triggered such that a worker does not have to travel a significant distance to respond to an alert that does not need physical attendance. Since the cameras are motion-activated, they can be triggered by birds or waves in the sea, which means they often present false alarms. The plant security experts explained how they would find it very useful to have events from the CCTV confirmed with a drone and vice versa. While the CCTV involves steerable cameras, the participants found value in the drones' mobility and ability to capture complementary images and video from multiple angles.

4.2 Human in the Loop

The participants found that human involvement was necessary in multiple scenarios. First, human knowledge is necessary to set up a drone system so that the appropriate information is collected. Second, while automation should be the primary solution, a human should always be able to take over and control the drones' behaviours.

The Role of a Person. Throughout the workshop, the participants mentioned an existing control centre multiple times, which outside personnel would call if they found suspicious or problematic activity. It is the control centre that determines if resources need to be delegated to inspect the area. The resources include drones if they were applied to their procedure, leading to a direct relationship between the control centre and the drones. However, the remaining personnel only have an indirect relationship with the drones, as they are only aware of the drones' presence if they physically see them. This can be problematic, as it would be difficult for the personnel to differentiate between the power plant's drones and an intruder drone. To create a sense of security, the power plant's drones should be recognisable, for example, through colour or any other easily identifiable physical feature.

Understanding a Drone's Capabilities. The main reason why the control centre would be solely responsible for the drones was due to the lack of understanding outside personnel would have. P2 stated, "*[...]it could be that he does not know what it is or that we already have a drone out there already*". It would unnecessarily complicate the system if more people were allowed control.

Participants also noted the importance of having few people who understand the multi-drone system so that the appropriate expectations are met, and they can detect if something is amiss with the system. As mentioned in Sect. 4.1, a drone's autonomy is difficult to determine unless a base behaviour has been pre-programmed. Here, a person with domain experience would have better knowledge of the appropriate actions to take at different alertness levels. However, this requires them to know the capabilities of the drones so that the correct tasks are allocated to them. P2 mentioned, "*There is also something about training the workers in regards to that it is very nice to [...] get some eyes on them [the drones] but also get this feeling of the machinery. Because if things just happen automatically and things do not work, then it is nice to have somebody who knows the drone [...]".*

Human Control of the Drones. While the participants kept pushing for an autonomous system, human interaction to determine edge cases is essential for a multi-drone system. For example, when there has been a manual report of suspicious activity, the control tower should be able to allocate a drone to address the issue. P1 suggested that *"[...] One could put a grid in the area and then send out a new [drone], and then it should then begin looking after it"*. Still, from the workshop, it was also clear that the interaction should be fast and easy to understand without extensive setup.

When a system is highly autonomous, it may detect something that it deems relevant while it is, in fact, not of interest. There could also be times when a higher-priority task has revealed itself, and the drone needs to cancel its current action to address the new one. A person with the right authority should always be able to have the last say in what the drones should do to ensure the safety and stability of the system. P2 mentioned, *"I think, that it should self-deploy because one can say that if we don't have the capacity to set it up, then it should be as automatic as possible with the possibility of a stop button"*.

4.3 Flight Patterns for Monitoring Scenarios

As mentioned in Sect. 3.2, we presented the participants with three scenarios with the intention of designing flight missions for a group of drones for each scenario. However, it was difficult to define a flight pattern for the scenario of inspecting the fuel stack, as there were conflicting opinions on whether a drone should be fully dedicated to performing the inspection or if a drone should do it while performing a perimeter monitoring task. Therefore, we cannot give a clear pattern design as in the other scenarios.

Steady State Monitoring. The participants sketched out the idea of having primarily one drone dedicated to monitoring the outer perimeter of the power plant when the plant is in a steady state. Figure 4 shows a concept that is based on the ideas, sketches and movements the participants did while discussing the steady-state scenario. Their argument for only having one drone do continuous monitoring was due to the plant having an extensive amount of CCTVs. Therefore, the participants found it unnecessary to have a drone dedicated to capturing data from inside the perimeter. However, due to the flexibility of the drones movement, having a perimeter drone would add an additional level of support when scouting for potential intruders.

Intruder Monitoring. When a drone or another reliable source, such as a person from the control tower, flags an area, a drone on standby is automatically assigned the responsibility of reaching the area of interest as fast as possible. In Fig. 5(A), it is shown as the straightest path towards the point without the risk of colliding with any obstacles. It has to be mentioned that CCTV could be another reliable source for detecting intruders in the ideal system. However, with the current setup, it would not be possible or practical due to them being motion-activated rather than detecting specific elements.

When the target has been found, the drones should be able to follow and film the suspected intruder for future reports. As a base behaviour, the drone should not leave this task until a human has explicitly told it to leave its post or if the intruder leaves the premises. However, it is not guaranteed that the intruder is at the same location as when they were detected. If that is the case, the drone should attempt to find the target by searching the surrounding area. In Fig. 5(C) the expanded square search pattern is used as an example, as it is a common search approach when you know the object is in a specific area [17,43]. If the target is not found within the plant's perimeter, the drone should return to its charging dock to reserve energy for other tasks.

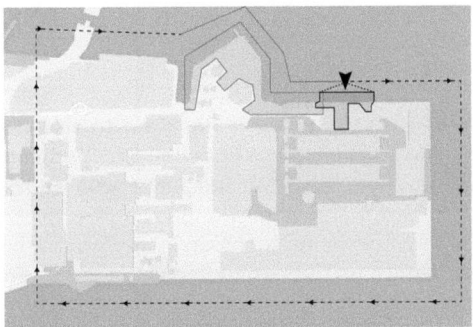

Fig. 4. A concept of the designed perimeter search behaviour. The dotted black represents the path that has not been flown yet, while the green has been flown. The green area is the area that the drone has captured, and the blue area is the area the drone is capturing while at its current position. It is assumed that the drones are filming from an angle. The irregular shapes of the captured area are due to the field of view being blocked by surrounding buildings. (Color figure online)

5 Discussion

In this section, we discuss the results and how they uncover new ideas and concerns about adopting a multi-drone system for monitoring critical infrastructure.

5.1 Behavioural Design of Drones for Monitoring Critical Infrastructure

The workshop uncovered specific flight patterns that could inform the design of drones for continuous monitoring of critical infrastructure. Although this study

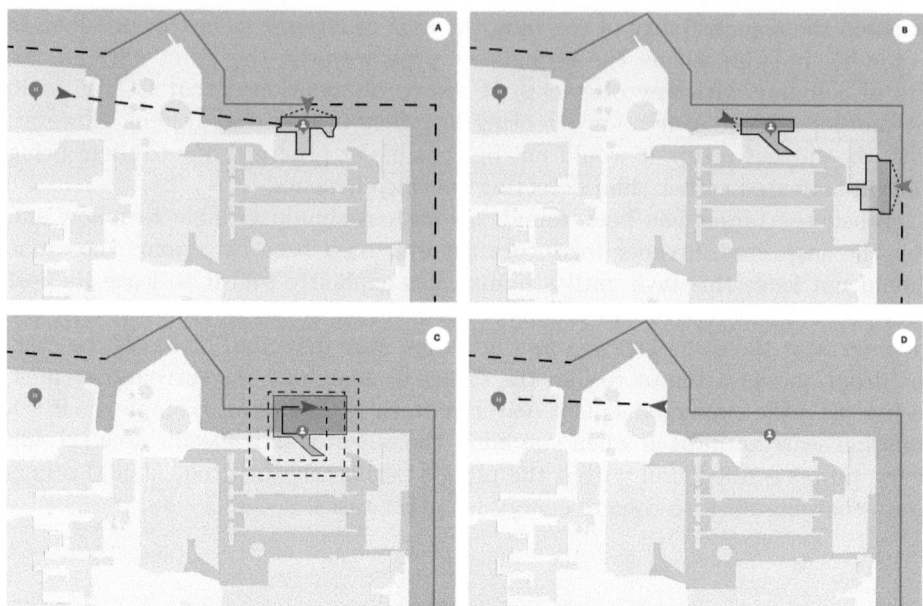

Fig. 5. A concept of the designed flight behaviour when the perimeter drone has detected a possible intruder. (A) A drone is deployed to the intruder detection point and flies towards it with the quickest route possible. The perimeter drone continues its task. (B) The drone has reached the point and looks after the suspect. If the suspect has been found, the drone stays and films the person or object. (C) If the drone has not detected a person who could be an intruder, it performs a coverage search to find the person. In this example, we use an expanding circle as the search approach. (D) If the person has not been found, the drone should return home to preserve energy for other detections.

focuses mainly on a single power plant, the ideas and concerns are familiar to what existing research describes, such as protection against human intruders [35] and foreign drones [21,55]. From the workshop, the participants came up with ideas on how the drones should behave when the plant is working as expected and how they should react when a spontaneous event occurs.

Flight Planning of Drone Missions. Participants discussed how the resources could be best used such that there is a balance between coverage and maintenance of the drone. They discussed only deploying drones at times when the number of workers was few, such that the drones could alleviate some of the work that would have been given to the workers otherwise. This was both to help workers address a possible issue quickly and also to keep them safe in case the intruder had malicious intent. Our findings suggest the idea of not having a drone fly continuously but instead being time and context-aware. This is appropriate in the case of critical infrastructure as it is a well-known space with predictable components. This also helps reduce the frequency of when the drones would need to be maintained and checked.

Given that there is some predictability of the physical space and where human intruders could gain entry, the participants agreed that the idea of a dedicated drone to perform a perimeter search was highly relevant. If a reliable source had reported suspicious activity, another drone would automatically be sent out with the most direct path such that it could reach the area as fast as possible to avoid the target disappearing, as the perimeter drone is not meant to stop. Here, existing drone research, especially within search and rescue, has extensively found different ways to find a target as fast as possible, for example, by using algorithms that can estimate where a person would most likely be given the time and terrain [3,41]. However, as the participants were concerned with the limited battery and the continuous maintenance of the technology, the drone should know when to stop its search, as there is a chance the intruder would have left the premises already and continuing the search could lead to unnecessary use of resources.

Design Consideration 1: Support users in balancing and allocating resources when developing multi-drone mission flight plans. Developing effective missions involves complex decision-making related to resource constraints and infrastructure challenges.

Designing Effective Autonomy in Drone Monitoring. With the limited interaction with drones as well as the limited workshop runtime, the participants were unsure how the autonomous behaviour should be designed, especially in more spontaneous events. One participant noted that while autonomous behaviour was a necessity, then it is still essential to have someone with deeper knowledge of the inner workings of the drones' autonomy such that it does not appear as a black box. Personnel with domain knowledge would also have the possibility to help design autonomy that fits their specific grounds, as there are places where general ideas cannot be applied. For example, at this particular power plant, productivity is highly dependent on the season, and only workers with this knowledge would be able to adjust the drone's autonomy correctly. This is also supported by existing work [23,34,36], where it is argued that there is value in bringing stakeholders into the design discussion, as there is no one solution to how automation should be designed. Depending on the context and specific situations there, the optimal level of automation could range from fully manual to fully autonomous.

Design Consideration 2: Autonomous behaviour must be tailored to the unique requirements and constraints of each operational environment. Engage domain experts early on to inform the initial automation strategy and guide adjustments, as their specialized knowledge reveals critical infrastructure challenges and considerations that shape the system's design and deployment.

A prominent theme of the workshop was the need for high levels of autonomy and low maintenance demands from the personnel to keep the system running due to the lack of resources and prioritization of plant operations. Research has explored the concept of levels or degrees of automation extensively, where different taxonomies have been presented [42,62,65]. Prior work highlights the dilemma of not introducing complacency and over-reliance on autonomy [44, 68]. In the workshop, the participants were very adamant that they wanted a system where there is no requirement for a person to constantly attend to and configure drone behaviour during evolving situations and security events. Here, their reasoning was primarily the lack of human resources available and the personnel having multiple responsibilities. They did, however, want the system to accommodate and enable a person to take control and shape the mission and behaviour when needed.

We discussed the idea of a dynamic automation or alertness dial, which would allow the system to be set to a mode appropriate for the current situation and the plant's security posture. For example, if the personnel are aware of a higher risk of intrusion, instead of having the drone continuously film a single target if another alert has been triggered, it will move on to the next. The dial could be adjusted by someone from the control centre, who determines the plant's alertness level. This enters the field of creating a semiautonomous system, where the system is self-sustaining, but only when necessary can a person determine new behaviour, in this case, by adjusting a dial. This can be compared to the concept of adaptive automation in a supervisory control system [54], where the human receives external information and can thereby change and set the appropriate parameters to which the automation adapts. Again, this is highly relevant in this context, as many domain-specific situations can be unexpected. As such, it is vital to have a domain expert oversee and approve the new behaviour before it gets executed. Our work reveals that while the theory is well known for an abstract understanding of automation, it is highly relevant in drone applications where domain knowledge is important and where automation is required to have a successful system.

Design consideration 3: Recognise that future users at critical infrastructures have multiple responsibilities and cannot act as continuously engaged actors. Interaction should be designed to allow human control at the appropriate level of granularity. Support high-level control and adjustments to the system behaviour, yet consider how to provide granular and more direct control appropriate for personnel with varied levels of drone experience.

Suitability of Drone Technology. The participants were not always positive about using drones in certain scenarios as it would either be a waste of resources or there would be alternatives to address an issue or event. For example, they found no need to have a drone dedicated to monitoring the inner premises as they had CCTV covering most of that. Here, they found more value in updating their current solution, such that it would be possible to use CCTV to detect intruders reliably rather than having two separate solutions that would have the same responsibility. This also adds to the concern that the drones will end up gathering more data than necessary, as they will capture the same or similar data as the CCTV. While CCTV was the most prominent of existing architecture that should not be entirely replaced, in a critical infrastructure context, multiple procedures and technologies are challenging to change due to the complexity of the context.

Design Consideration 4: Consider how to integrate the drone system with existing infrastructure to align with established processes and technologies.

5.2 Drones as Social Robots

Positioning this work within the framework proposed by Baraka et al. [6], the proposed drone system embodies multiple dimensions of social robotics that reshape human roles and perceptions. The drones fulfill a hybrid relational role; they are instruments 'for you' in conducting surveillance, but also collaborative partners 'with you,' augmenting the human team by investigating alerts. While their appearance is purely functional, their active presence can be socially evocative as highlighted in the discussions about drones as a deterrent demanding attention from intruders and reshaping perceptions of surveillance by acting as a visible and intimidating presence. This co-design effort aims for a system with a high degree of autonomy, yet it is clear that the 'human in the loop' is an overly simplistic view. A more productive perspective could be a model of symbiotic autonomy [19,63], where the human, smart environment, and drones cooperate symbiotically to handle specific tasks. This also suggests that communication and requests may come from any of the three main actors [63]. The future system involves redefining operational responsibilities. For example, a drone may need to ask the human to take a decision from the control room or it may need personnel on the ground to move equipment, or the human may need to ask the drone or smart environment to analyze the options available to help formulate a plan. The role of humans as supervisors of complex relationships respects their management duty and the human ability to provide oversight in making complex decisions. There is much work to be done in evaluating these complex systems through real-world deployments and refinements with domain experts.

5.3 Tangible Objects to Facilitate Discussion

Due to the lack of real-life interaction between future users and actual drones in current research, we decided to deploy a realistic demo where domain experts without drone experience could see and interact with the drones, giving them a realistic perspective of how drones function and act while in their premises. Moreover, to enforce discussion between all participants and have an adaptable system - which would be complex and out of scope for the physical system - we conducted the indoor workshop with a large map of their grounds and had tangible objects to help the participants visualise and brainstorm the behaviour and responsibilities of the drones, but also point out weaknesses and problems both with their current process and future adoption of drones. Our research approach demonstrates that using tangible objects that reflect system capabilities can be a valuable tool to involve domain experts with limited drone experience.

Physical Drone Demo. When flying the drones around the premises, we saw that the participants were highly engaged in their behaviour and movements and in what capabilities they had, and they would ask questions about the technology and start brainstorming ideas throughout the demo. The demo also demonstrated the general experience of drones actively flying, and it helped them realise the difficulty of seeing and hearing them. Moreover, the difficulty of perceiving depth made the participants uncomfortable, especially when it seemed as if the drones were close to larger objects such as buildings and ships. Our current interface displayed a vectorised map and did not reflect the immediate state of the environment. While our interface and handheld controllers displayed that the drones kept a safe distance, the discrepancy between the map and real life added to the confusion and uncertainty. Current systems have the opportunity to project real-time imagery on the map to match the expectations of an operator and gain more situation awareness of the current state of the world, allowing better decision-making [22,23].

Indoor Workshop Setup. The workshop was set up so that the participants could more easily visualise their ideas through tangible objects, such as drone figures and a physical map of their grounds. The participants were highly positive about the setup and wanted to utilize the setup for internal meetings as they found it helpful in expressing their ideas and plans. Throughout the workshop, the participants engaged with the model as an impromptu design tool [57], drawing and moving the figures to design missions and explaining their ideas. However, they often simply pointed at the map rather than moving objects and placing more tokens. While the direct interaction with the objects was limited, there were multiple times when the participants referred to the drones and items placed around, as they served as a good visual reminder of which state of the discussion and process they were at. It also helped establish the same understanding of what the drones should and could do, thereby streamlining the discussion and avoiding misunderstanding between participants. Our work demonstrates how using tangible objects that reflect familiar surroundings to the participants helps engage in discussing how the drones should move and what problems they could solve or risk getting into.

Using tangible objects and a map set-up to establish mutual learning situations [27], participants were able to draw on their own expertise on critical infrastructure management, but in light of what drone swarms can and cannot do. We built on previous work by Huybrechts et al. [33], and our work extends their work by looking at a case where the physical layout of a space is as important as in urban planning. Likewise, we draw on Agrawal et al. [1,2] and Bjurling et al. [8], who similarly employed physical maps and objects to investigate operator relationships and situational awareness. Because of our ambition of using co-design to facilitate mutual learning, we added the physical drone demonstrations and used design cards to map out and present the design space of drone swarms. Despite this just being a singular case, it worked well, and participants expressed the value of the setup for other internal purposes, too, such as maintaining a shared understanding despite varying expertise levels.

Participant Discussion. Participants arrived at the workshop with varied roles—some had never met or fully understood each other's day-to-day duties. While they shared familiarity with the same guidelines and processes at the power plant, this was their first chance to explore why those procedures existed. In discussing how cost, security, and operational continuity shape these protocols, everyone developed a deeper appreciation of the decisions behind their work.

They also learned more about each other's priorities. For example, innovation consultants emphasized equipment costs and upkeep, whereas security staff focused on stable operations and swift incident response. One group envisioned near-perfect intruder detection, while the other highlighted current technological constraints and integration issues. These complementary perspectives helped participants avoid extremes—neither overly optimistic nor pessimistic—about drone adoption. Without prompting from the researchers, they began asking new questions, such as how budgets or maintenance routines might impact the effectiveness of multi-drone systems, ultimately yielding a richer understanding of the plant's complex environment.

5.4 Limitations and Future Work

As we only have the perspective of five participants and have only conducted one workshop, it affects the generalisability of our results. Our workshop also only considers one specific power plant. While we expect similar problems to arise in other critical infrastructures where intrusion is a problem [45], we cannot confirm this. However, our work displays how involving tangible objects and a realistic demo can involve domain experts in a discussion about utilizing drones in a real-life context. In the future, we want to update the system to incorporate the findings and deploy it at the power plant. We also want to evaluate if the changes allow the system to collect the appropriate data and if it meets the expectations of future users.

Moreover, throughout the workshop, there were other use cases for drones that the participants found as important as protecting against intruders, such as maintenance of the structure of the power plant such as ensuring that fuel transport rollers are not jammed or checking whether the buildings need maintenance or not. Future work could also explore maintenance issues from a worker's standpoint. Research has already shown that drones can be an effective approach to alleviating resources for such problems, and further investigation could identify specific applications [40, 46].

6 Conclusion

In this paper, we present the process and findings from a workshop focusing on utilising drones to monitor critical infrastructure, in our case, a power plant. We invited domain experts with limited drone knowledge to attend the workshop and give their perspectives on how drones could be used in their specific context. The workshop helped uncover multiple possibilities and concerns with using drones and helped us design missions and desired behaviours that a group of drones should follow in typical surveillance situations. An essential factor of the workshop was to help set expectations and establish an understanding of what a drone could do. We incorporated a live demonstration of a group of drones flying simultaneously at their premises, and we performed a small search mission, during which the participants had the opportunity to experience flying drones and see the live data physically. Our research shows the strengths of including functional prototypes to help facilitate discussions of complex systems with domain experts who are not familiar with drone technology. Moreover, we also incorporated many tangible artefacts into the workshop itself, such as a physical map and 3D models, so that the participants could quickly visualise possible behaviours and flight patterns to accomplish the specified tasks. We present four key design considerations based on the workshop findings that highlight the importance of considering the stakeholders and the existing technology when designing autonomous multi-drone systems. These considerations will help future designers design and develop highly autonomous systems that act according to the expectations of specific users.

Acknowledgements. This work is supported in part by the Innovation Fund Denmark for the project DIREC (9142-00001B).

References

1. Agrawal, A., et al.: The Next generation of human-drone partnerships: co-designing an emergency response system. In: Proceedings of the 2020 CHI Conference on Human Factors in Computing Systems, Honolulu HI USA, pp. 1–13. ACM (2020). https://doi.org/10.1145/3313831.3376825
2. Agrawal, A., Cleland-Huang, J.: Explaining autonomous decisions in swarms of human-on-the-loop small unmanned aerial systems. In: Proceedings of the AAAI Conference on Human Computation and Crowdsourcing, vol. 9, pp. 15–26 (2021). https://doi.org/10.1609/hcomp.v9i1.18936, https://ojs.aaai.org/index.php/HCOMP/article/view/18936
3. Ahlskog, J., Bahodi, M.T., Lugmayr, A., Merritt, T.: Fostering trust through user interface design in multi-drone search and rescue. In: Proceedings of the Second International Symposium on Trustworthy Autonomous Systems, Austin TX USA, pp. 1–11. ACM (2024). https://doi.org/10.1145/3686038.3686052, https://dl.acm.org/doi/10.1145/3686038.3686052

4. Alon, O., Rabinovich, S., Fyodorov, C., Cauchard, J.R.: Drones in firefighting: a user-centered design perspective. In: Proceedings of the 23rd International Conference on Mobile Human-Computer Interaction, Toulouse & Virtual France, pp. 1–11. ACM (2021). https://doi.org/10.1145/3447526.3472030
5. Alzenad, M., El-Keyi, A., Lagum, F., Yanikomeroglu, H.: 3-D placement of an unmanned aerial vehicle base station (UAV-BS) for energy-efficient maximal coverage. IEEE Wireless Commun. Lett. **6**(4), 434–437 (2017). https://doi.org/10.1109/LWC.2017.2700840, https://ieeexplore.ieee.org/document/7918510, conference Name: IEEE Wireless Communications Letters
6. Baraka, K., Alves-Oliveira, P., Ribeiro, T.: An extended framework for characterizing social robots. In: Jost, C., Le Pévédic, B., Belpaeme, T., Bethel, C., Chrysostomou, D., Crook, N., Grandgeorge, M., Mirnig, N. (eds.) Human-Robot Interaction. SSBN, vol. 12, pp. 21–64. Springer, Cham (2020). https://doi.org/10.1007/978-3-030-42307-0_2
7. Baytas, M.A., Funk, M., Ljungblad, S., Garcia, J., La Delfa, J., Mueller, F.F.: iHDI 2020: interdisciplinary workshop on human-drone interaction. In: Extended Abstracts of the 2020 CHI Conference on Human Factors in Computing Systems,, Honolulu HI USA, pp. 1–8. ACM (2020). https://doi.org/10.1145/3334480.3375149
8. Bjurling, O., Granlund, R., Alfredson, J., Arvola, M., Ziemke, T.: Drone swarms in forest firefighting: a local development case study of multi-level human-swarm interaction. In: Proceedings of the 11th Nordic Conference on Human-Computer Interaction: Shaping Experiences, Shaping Society, Tallinn Estonia, pp. 1–7. ACM (2020). https://doi.org/10.1145/3419249.3421239
9. Bødker, S., Dindler, C., Iversen, O.S., Smith, R.C.: What is participatory design? In: Participatory Design, pp. 5–13. Springer, Cham (2022). https://doi.org/10.1007/978-3-031-02235-7_2
10. Bødker, S., Grønbæk, K.: Cooperative prototyping experiments:-users and designers envision a dental case record system. DAIMI Report Series (292) (1989)
11. Bødker, S., Nielsen, C., Petersen, M.G.: Creativity, cooperation and interactive design. In: Proceedings of the 3rd Conference on Designing Interactive Systems: Processes, Practices, Methods, and Techniques, pp. 252–261 (2000)
12. Brandt, E., Messeter, J.: Facilitating collaboration through design games. In: Proceedings of the Eighth Conference on Participatory Design: Artful Integration: Interweaving Media, Materials and Practices-Volume 1, pp. 121–131 (2004)
13. Braun, V., Clarke, V.: One size fits all? What counts as quality practice in (reflexive) thematic analysis? Qual. Res. Psychol. **18**(3), 328–352 (2021). https://doi.org/10.1080/14780887.2020.1769238, https://www.tandfonline.com/doi/full/10.1080/14780887.2020.1769238
14. Bødker, S., Kyng, M.: Participatory Design that Matters-Facing the Big Issues. ACM Transactions on Computer-Human Interaction **25**(1), 1–31 (2018). https://doi.org/10.1145/3152421
15. Cacace, J., Finzi, A., Lippiello, V., Furci, M., Mimmo, N., Marconi, L.: A control architecture for multiple drones operated via multimodal interaction in search & rescue mission. In: 2016 IEEE International Symposium on Safety, Security, and Rescue Robotics (SSRR). pp. 233–239 (2016). https://doi.org/10.1109/SSRR.2016.7784304, https://ieeexplore.ieee.org/document/7784304/?arnumber=7784304
16. Choi, J.H.j., Forlano, L., Kera, D.: Situated automation. In: Proceedings of the 16th Participatory Design Conference (2020)
17. Choutri, K., Lagha, M., Dala, L.: A fully autonomous search and rescue system using quadrotor UAV. IJCDS J. **10**, 403–414 (2021). https://doi.org/10.12785/ijcds/100140

18. Cleland-Huang, J., Agrawal, A.: Human-drone interactions with semi-autonomous cohorts of collaborating drones. arXiv:2010.04101 [cs] (2020). https://doi.org/10.48550/arXiv.2010.04101
19. Coradeschi, S., Saffiotti, A.: Symbiotic robotic systems: humans, robots, and smart environments. IEEE Intell. Syst. **21**(3), 82–84 (2006). https://doi.org/10.1109/MIS.2006.59
20. Dilshad, N., Hwang, J., Song, J., Sung, N.: Applications and challenges in video surveillance via drone: a brief survey. In: 2020 International Conference on Information and Communication Technology Convergence (ICTC), pp. 728–732 (2020). https://doi.org/10.1109/ICTC49870.2020.9289536, https://ieeexplore.ieee.org/document/9289536/?arnumber=9289536, iSSN: 2162-1233
21. Ding, G., Wu, Q., Zhang, L., Lin, Y., Tsiftsis, T.A., Yao, Y.D.: An amateur drone surveillance system based on the cognitive internet of things. IEEE Commun. Mag. **56**(1), 29–35 (2018). https://doi.org/10.1109/MCOM.2017.1700452, https://ieeexplore.ieee.org/document/8255734/?arnumber=8255734, conference Name: IEEE Communications Magazine
22. Endsley, M.R.: Toward a Theory of Situation Awareness in Dynamic Systems. Hum. Factors **37**(1), 32–64 (1995). https://doi.org/10.1518/001872095779049543, publisher: SAGE Publications Inc
23. Endsley, M.R.: Level of automation forms a key aspect of autonomy design. J. Cognit. Eng. Dec. Making **12**(1), 29–34 (2018). https://doi.org/10.1177/1555343417723432, https://doi.org/10.1177/1555343417723432, publisher: SAGE Publications
24. Fuchs, C., Borst, C., de Croon, G.C.H.E., van Paassen, M.M.R., Mulder, M.: An ecological approach to the supervisory control of UAV swarms. Int. J. Micro Air Veh. **6**(4), 211–229 (2014). https://doi.org/10.1260/1756-8293.6.4.211, publisher: SAGE Publications Ltd STM
25. Gryech, I., Vinogradov, E., Saboor, A., Bithas, P.S., Mathiopoulos, P.T., Pollin, S.: A systematic literature review on the role of UAV-enabled communications in advancing the UN's sustainable development goals. Front. Commun. Networks **Volume 5 - 2024** (2024). https://doi.org/10.3389/frcmn.2024.1286073, https://www.frontiersin.org/journals/communications-and-networks/articles/10.3389/frcmn.2024.1286073
26. Halskov, K., Dalsgård, P.: Inspiration card workshops. In: Proceedings of the 6th Conference on Designing Interactive Systems. DIS '06, New York, NY, USA, pp. 2–11. Association for Computing Machinery (2006). https://doi.org/10.1145/1142405.1142409
27. Halskov, K., Hansen, N.B.: The diversity of participatory design research practice at PDC 2002–2012. Int. J. Hum. Comput. Stud. **74**, 81–92 (2015). https://doi.org/10.1016/j.ijhcs.2014.09.003, https://linkinghub.elsevier.com/retrieve/pii/S1071581914001220
28. Hansen, N.B., et al.: How participatory design works: mechanisms and effects. In: Proceedings of the 31st Australian Conference on Human-Computer-Interaction. OzCHI '19, New York, NY, USA, pp. 30–41. Association for Computing Machinery (2020). https://doi.org/10.1145/3369457.3369460, https://doi.org/10.1145/3369457.3369460
29. Heidingsfelder, M.L., Schütz, F., Kaiser, S.: Expanding participation participatory design in technology agenda-setting. In: Proceedings of the 14th Participatory Design Conference: Short Papers, Interactive Exhibitions, Workshops-Volume 2, pp. 25–28 (2016)

30. Hell, P.M., Varga, P.J.: Drone systems for factory security and surveillance. Interdiscip. Descr. Complex Syst. **17**(3), 458–467 (2019). https://doi.org/10.7906/indecs.17.3.4, http://indecs.eu/index.php?s=x&y=2019&p=458-467
31. Hoang, M.T.O., Van Berkel, N., Skov, M.B., Merritt, T.R.: Challenges and requirements in multi-drone interfaces. In: Extended Abstracts of the 2023 CHI Conference on Human Factors in Computing Systems, Hamburg Germany, pp. 1–9. ACM (2023). https://doi.org/10.1145/3544549.3585673, https://dl.acm.org/doi/10.1145/3544549.3585673
32. Huybrechts, L., Coenen, T., Laureyssens, T., Machils, P.: Living spaces: a participatory design process model drawing on the use of boundary objects. Int. Reports Socio-Inf. **6**(2), 6–21 (2009)
33. Huybrechts, L., Dreessen, K., Schepers, S.: Mapping design practices: on risk, hybridity and participation. In: Proceedings of the 12th Participatory Design Conference: Exploratory Papers, Workshop Descriptions, Industry Cases-Volume 2, pp. 29–32 (2012)
34. Jamieson, G.A., Skraaning, G.: Levels of automation in human factors models for automation design: why we might consider throwing the baby out with the bathwater. J. Cogn. Eng. Dec. Making **12**(1), 42–49 (2018). https://doi.org/10.1177/1555343417732856, publisher: SAGE Publications
35. Jensen, O.B.: New 'Foucauldian Boomerangs': drones and urban surveillance. Surveill. Soc. **14**(1), 20–33 (2016). https://doi.org/10.24908/ss.v14i1.5498, https://ojs.library.queensu.ca/index.php/surveillance-and-society/article/view/boomerang
36. Kaber, D.B.: Issues in human-automation interaction modeling: presumptive aspects of frameworks of types and levels of automation. J. Cogn. Eng. Dec. Making **12**(1), 7–24 (2018). https://doi.org/10.1177/1555343417737203, publisher: SAGE Publications
37. La Delfa, J., Bayta, M.A., Luke, E., Koder, B., Mueller, F.F.: Designing drone chi: unpacking the thinking and making of somaesthetic human-drone interaction. In: Proceedings of the 2020 ACM Designing Interactive Systems Conference, Eindhoven Netherlands, pp. 575–586. ACM (2020). https://doi.org/10.1145/3357236.3395589, https://dl.acm.org/doi/10.1145/3357236.3395589
38. La Delfa, J., Garrett, R., Lampinen, A., Höök, K.: How to train your drone: exploring the umwelt as a design metaphor for human-drone interaction. In: Designing Interactive Systems Conference, pp. 2987–3001. ACM, IT University of Copenhagen Denmark (2024). https://doi.org/10.1145/3643834.3660737, https://dl.acm.org/doi/10.1145/3643834.3660737
39. Mohammed, R., Pasam, P.: Autonomous drones for advanced surveillance and security applications in the USA **1**, 32–53 (2020)
40. Nooralishahi, P., et al.: Drone-based non-destructive inspection of industrial sites: a review and case studies. Drones **5**(4), 106 (2021). https://doi.org/10.3390/drones5040106, https://www.mdpi.com/2504-446X/5/4/106, number: 4 Publisher: Multidisciplinary Digital Publishing Institute
41. Oh, D., Han, J.: Smart search system of autonomous flight UAVs for disaster rescue. Sensors **21**(20), 6810 (2021). https://doi.org/10.3390/s21206810, https://www.mdpi.com/1424-8220/21/20/6810, number: 20 Publisher: Multidisciplinary Digital Publishing Institute
42. Onnasch, L., Wickens, C.D., Li, H., Manzey, D.: Human performance consequences of stages and levels of automation: an integrated meta-analysis. Hum. Factors **56**(3), 476–488 (2014). https://doi.org/10.1177/0018720813501549, publisher: SAGE Publications Inc

43. Oways: IAMSAR Search Patterns Explained with Sketches (2024). https://owaysonline.com/iamsar-search-patterns/
44. Parasuraman, R., Wickens, C.: Humans: still vital after all these years of automation. Hum. Factors **50**, 511–20 (2008). https://doi.org/10.1518/001872008X312198
45. Piriyasupakij, J., Prasitphan, R.: Design and development of autonomous drone to detect and alert intruders in surveillance areas. In: 2023 8th International Conference on Business and Industrial Research (ICBIR), pp. 1094–1099 (2023). https://doi.org/10.1109/ICBIR57571.2023.10147697, https://ieeexplore.ieee.org/document/10147697/?arnumber=10147697
46. Rakha, T., Gorodetsky, A.: Review of Unmanned Aerial System (UAS) applications in the built environment: Towards automated building inspection procedures using drones. Autom. Constr. **93**, 252–264 (2018). https://doi.org/10.1016/j.autcon.2018.05.002, https://www.sciencedirect.com/science/article/pii/S0926580518300165
47. Rakotonarivo, B.H., Drougard, N., Conversy, S., Garcia, J.: Cleared for Safe Take-off? Improving the usability of mission preparation to mitigate the safety risks of drone operations. In: Proceedings of the 2023 CHI Conference on Human Factors in Computing Systems, Hamburg Germany, pp. 1–17. ACM (2023). https://doi.org/10.1145/3544548.3581003, https://dl.acm.org/doi/10.1145/3544548.3581003
48. Roldán-Gømez, J.J., González-Gironda, E., Barrientos, A.: A survey on robotic technologies for forest firefighting: applying drone swarms to improve firefighters' efficiency and safety. Appl. Sci. **11**(1), 363 (2021). https://doi.org/10.3390/app11010363, https://www.mdpi.com/2076-3417/11/1/363, number: 1 Publisher: Multidisciplinary Digital Publishing Institute
49. Saffre, F., Hildmann, H., Karvonen, H.: The design challenges of drone swarm control. In: Harris, D., Li, W.-C. (eds.) HCII 2021. LNCS (LNAI), vol. 12767, pp. 408–426. Springer, Cham (2021). https://doi.org/10.1007/978-3-030-77932-0_32
50. Sanders, E., Stappers, P.: Convivial toolbox: Generative research for the front end of design. Bis (2012)
51. Sanders, E.B.N., Stappers, P.J.: Probes, toolkits and prototypes: three approaches to making in codesigning. CoDesign **10**(1), 5–14 (2014). https://doi.org/10.1080/15710882.2014.888183 publisher: Taylor & Francis_eprint
52. Savkin, A.V., Huang, H.: Asymptotically optimal deployment of drones for surveillance and monitoring. Sensors **19**(9), 2068 (2019). https://doi.org/10.3390/s19092068, https://www.mdpi.com/1424-8220/19/9/2068, number: 9 Publisher: Multidisciplinary Digital Publishing Institute
53. Savkin, A.V., Huang, H.: Proactive deployment of aerial drones for coverage over very uneven terrains: a version of the 3D art gallery problem. Sensors **19**(6), 1438 (2019). https://doi.org/10.3390/s19061438, https://www.mdpi.com/1424-8220/19/6/1438, number: 6 Publisher: Multidisciplinary Digital Publishing Institute
54. Sheridan, T.B.: Adaptive automation, level of automation, allocation authority, supervisory control, and adaptive control: distinctions and modes of adaptation. IEEE Trans. Syst. Man Cybernet. - Part A: Syst. Hum. **41**(4), 662–667 (2011). https://doi.org/10.1109/TSMCA.2010.2093888, https://ieeexplore.ieee.org/document/5678843/?arnumber=5678843, conference Name: IEEE Transactions on Systems, Man, and Cybernetics - Part A: Systems and Humans

55. Shi, X., Yang, C., Xie, W., Liang, C., Shi, Z., Chen, J.: Anti-drone system with multiple surveillance technologies: architecture, implementation, and challenges. IEEE Commun. Mag. **56**(4), 68–74 (2018). https://doi.org/10.1109/MCOM.2018.1700430, https://ieeexplore.ieee.org/document/8337899/?arnumber=8337899, conference Name: IEEE Communications Magazine
56. Shneiderman, B.: Human-centered artificial intelligence: reliable, safe & trustworthy. Int. J. Hum.-Comput. Interact. **36**(6), 495–504 (2020). https://doi.org/10.1080/10447318.2020.1741118, https://www.tandfonline.com/doi/full/10.1080/10447318.2020.1741118
57. Smit, D., Murer, M., van Rheden, V., Grah, T., Tscheligi, M.: The evolution of a scale model as an impromptu design tool. In: Proceedings of the 2017 Conference on Designing Interactive Systems. DIS '17, New York, NY, USA, pp. 233–245. Association for Computing Machinery (2017). https://doi.org/10.1145/3064663.3064797
58. Sondoqah, M., et al.: Shaping and being shaped by drones: programming in perception-action loops. In: Designing Interactive Systems Conference, pp. 2926–2945. ACM, IT University of Copenhagen Denmark (2024). https://doi.org/10.1145/3643834.3661636
59. Tan, H., Lee, J., Gao, G.: Human-drone interaction: drone delivery & services for social events. In: Proceedings of the 2018 ACM Conference Companion Publication on Designing Interactive Systems, Hong Kong China, pp. 183–187. ACM (2018). https://doi.org/10.1145/3197391.3205433, https://dl.acm.org/doi/10.1145/3197391.3205433
60. Tlili, F., Ayed, S., Chaari Fourati, L.: Advancing UAV security with artificial intelligence: a comprehensive survey of techniques and future directions. Internet of Things **27**, 101281 (2024). https://doi.org/10.1016/j.iot.2024.101281, https://www.sciencedirect.com/science/article/pii/S2542660524002221
61. Ullmer, B., Ishii, H., Jacob, R.J.K.: Token+constraint systems for tangible interaction with digital information. ACM Trans. Comput.-Hum. Interact. **12**(1), 81–118 (2005). https://doi.org/10.1145/1057237.1057242, https://dl.acm.org/doi/10.1145/1057237.1057242
62. Vagia, M., Transeth, A.A., Fjerdingen, S.A.: A literature review on the levels of automation during the years. What are the different taxonomies that have been proposed? Appl. Ergon. **53**, 190–202 (2016). https://doi.org/10.1016/j.apergo.2015.09.013, https://www.sciencedirect.com/science/article/pii/S0003687015300855
63. Veloso, M.M., Biswas, J., Coltin, B., Rosenthal, S.: Cobots: robust symbiotic autonomous mobile service robots. In: IJCAI. p. 4423. Citeseer (2015)
64. Vicente, K., Rasmussen, J.: Ecological interface design: theoretical foundations. IEEE Trans. Syst. Man Cybern. **22**(4), 589–606 (1992). https://doi.org/10.1109/21.156574, http://ieeexplore.ieee.org/document/156574/
65. Wickens, C.D., Li, H., Santamaria, A., Sebok, A., Sarter, N.B.: Stages and levels of automation: an integrated meta-analysis. In: Proceedings of the Human Factors and Ergonomics Society Annual Meeting, vol. 54, no. 4, pp. 389–393 (2010). https://doi.org/10.1177/154193121005400425, https://doi.org/10.1177/154193121005400425, publisher: SAGE Publications Inc
66. Wojciechowska, A., Hamidi, F., Lucero, A., Cauchard, J.R.: Chasing lions: co-designing human-drone interaction in Sub-Saharan Africa. In: Proceedings of the 2020 ACM Designing Interactive Systems Conference, Eindhoven Netherlands, pp. 141–152. ACM (2020). https://doi.org/10.1145/3357236.3395481, https://dl.acm.org/doi/10.1145/3357236.3395481

67. Wölfel, C., Merritt, T.: Method card design dimensions: a survey of card-based design tools. In: Kotzé, P., Marsden, G., Lindgaard, G., Wesson, J., Winckler, M. (eds.) INTERACT 2013. LNCS, vol. 8117, pp. 479–486. Springer, Heidelberg (2013). https://doi.org/10.1007/978-3-642-40483-2_34
68. Zhou, J., Zhu, H., Kim, M., Cummings, M.L.: The impact of different levels of autonomy and training on operators' drone control strategies. ACM Trans. Hum.-Robot Interact.**8**(4), 1–15 (2019). https://doi.org/10.1145/3344276, https://dl.acm.org/doi/10.1145/3344276

Active Inference and Sustainable Robotics: Modeling Social Resource Management

Maria Raffa(✉)

IULM University, via Carlo Bo 1, Milan, Italy
`maria.raffa@studenti.iulm.it`

Abstract. This paper explores how the active inference (AIF) framework can be applied to develop sustainable solutions within the field of social robotics, in the aim of offering a simple yet powerful application of AIF to support more responsible, transparent and sustainable social robotics. Building on previous work on a computational model where an agent learns to balance short-term needs with long-term resource availability, a possible extension is proposed: using AIF to guide the behavior of social robots towards a successful interaction with humans. This is done by outlining how this model could help robots manage "social resources" such as user attention, emotional well-being and trust. Hence, the potential benefits and limitations of this approach within human-robot interaction are explored.

Keywords: Active Inference · Social Robotics · Sustainability

1 Introduction

Social robots are increasingly present in contexts where adaptability, sensitivity and ethical responsibility are essential – such as eldercare, education and collaborative public spaces [1]. These environments are not only dynamic, but also resource-sensitive, in both material and social terms: on the one hand, they involve material resources such as energy consumption, operational time, and maintenance. On the other hand, they involve social resources, such as users' attention, emotional well-being and trust. A major challenge in this field is designing robotic systems that can make decisions in ways that are sustainable over time, i.e. balancing immediate goals with the long-term well-being of users. The concept of sustainability in robotics often focuses on material dimensions, i.e. the ecological aspect of sustainability, which is energy consumption, material reuse, and environmental impact [2]. However, in the context of social robotics, a broader perspective is required – one that includes the social dimension of sustainability. This dimension intersects with the ethical use of social robots, particularly in terms of human-robot interaction (HRI): namely, how robots manage users' time, attention and trust without overwhelming or misleading them [3]. In this sense, decision-making (DM) frameworks that support long-term, context-sensitive behavior are urgently needed [4].

Recent work in HRI has emphasized the importance of long-term engagement, trust modeling, and adaptive affective systems. For instance, [5] propose computational models for long-term interaction, highlighting how affective and behavioral adaptation impacts user perception and trust; [6] frame trust as a central component of robust intelligence in autonomous systems, and investigate how to measure it; [7] investigate the role of nonverbal immediacy in shaping effective child-robot interactions, demonstrating that subtle social cues (such as gaze, posture, and proximity) can significantly enhance learning outcomes. Rather than deriving robot behavior solely from human models, they propose a principled framework based on communication theory, showing that higher immediacy in robot behavior correlates with improved memory retention in children. Their findings underscore the importance of fine-tuned affective dynamics in sustained human-robot engagement. These studies underline the social and temporal complexity of trust, emotional well-being and attention in HRI, which this paper seeks to reframe within a unified computational model. Unlike prior approaches that often segment these dimensions, the current proposal integrates trust, attention, and emotional well-being as dynamically managed social resources within an Active Inference (AIF) framework. In doing so, it contributes to recent debates on adaptive autonomy and social sustainability in robotics by treating affective and relational variables as inferable and regulatable over time, based on feedback-driven updating of internal models – starting from [8]'s early proposal of an "emotional machine" as part of general intelligence.

Indeed, this paper proposes that AIF, a framework derived from the Free Energy Principle (FEP) in neuroscience [9, 10], can help address this need. AIF has recently gained attention in robotics for its ability to unify perception, action and learning under a single function: the minimization of variational free energy [11]. This enables robots to act not only in pursuit of predefined goals but also to adaptively minimize uncertainty about their environment and their own role within it. This aspect is particularly important for social robots, such as personal aides, robotic nurses, and companions, assisting the disabled and elderly. The groundbreaking point about AIF for robotics is that it enhances robot safety: AIF agents continuously resolve uncertainty by selecting informative actions that minimize risk, which is crucial for tasks with a high level of risk and uncertainty like HRI. Actions are chosen to minimize expected free energy, thereby reducing risk and ambiguity, leading to a behavior where the robot looks for information by measuring risk [12].

In previous work [4], it has been shown how AIF can model DM in socially assistive robotics, focusing on ethical transparency and justification of actions. Separately, an AIF-based model for sustainable resource management has been developed, where an artificial agent learns to balance short-term needs with long-term ecological stability [13]. This model demonstrated how sustainability can emerge as a computational strategy, rather than being explicitly programmed.

This paper builds a bridge between these two works. It is argued that the AIF model used for resource management can be adapted for social robots to help them manage not just material inputs, but also social resources such as attention, emotional well-being and trust. By learning how to act in a way that preserves these resources over time, a social robot could become a more sustainable and trustworthy partner in human environments.

In this aim, the paper is structured as follows: Sect. 2 briefly describes the computational model explained in [13], then Sect. 3 shows how it can be applied to social robotics. Hence, Sect. 4 explores the pros and cons of this application. Lastly, conclusions are drawn.

2 An AIF Model for Sustainable Resource Management

The application of AIF to social cognition is an expanding field, with notable contributions modeling shared intentionality [14], theory of mind [15] and hierarchical social inference [16]. These studies show how agents can infer others' goals, intentions, or beliefs by minimizing variational free energy within nested generative models. While the present work builds upon this foundation, it diverges in treating social variables not only as epistemic targets (e.g., what others intend), but as regulatable resources – quantities to be inferred and optimized over time for sustainable HRI.

In previous work [13], a simple computational model was developed to explore how an artificial agent might manage limited resources, such as food, in a way that balances short-term needs with long-term sustainability. The model was based on the AIF framework, which enables agents to perceive, act and learn by minimizing a quantity called variational free energy [10]. This approach allows behavior to emerge because of balancing prior expectations, sensory evidence and long-term preferences.

In the simulation, the agent was equipped with a generative model representing the codification of its beliefs about the causal structure of the world and how its actions can influence the states of the world. It operated in two environments: one static, where resources availability was constant, and one dynamic, where the resource supply fluctuated over time and a learning mechanism was applied to the agent. The agent had to decide when and how much to consume based on internal states, i.e. feeling satiated, external cues (or hidden states), i.e. the presence of resources and long-term preferences, i.e. to be satiated rather than hungry.

A key feature of the model was that sustainability was not hard-coded as a rule or constraint. Instead, it emerged as a learned behavior: the agent inferred that overconsuming the food in the present would lead to negative outcomes in the future, eventually leading to death from starvation. By updating its internal model of the environment through experience, the agent gradually learned to delay gratification, consuming less in the short term to preserve resources in the long term. This behavior was guided by a shift in its preference structure, which began to reflect both immediate needs and anticipated future conditions.

The model demonstrated that a single agent equipped with AIF can dynamically adapt to environmental changes and optimize its actions over time – even in uncertain or partially observable settings. Moreover, it showed that DM processes shaped by predictive models and feedback loops can naturally give rise to sustainable strategies. The dynamic relationship between agent and environment thus proves to be crucial for sustainable resource management, as the agent's actions have optimised its well-being and contributed to the resilience of the environment, preventing the total depletion of resources. This reciprocal relationship between agent and environment is thus constituted as a fundamental aspect of sustainability. However, the model has significant limitations. The simplicity of the single-agent, single-resource setup does not capture the complexity of real-world systems. Moreover, overfitting can occur if the agent becomes too specialised in the specific environmental dynamics presented in the simulation, potentially limiting its adaptability to new situations. In addition, its adaptability may also be limited by the effects of inaccurate prior preferences. Despite these limitations, however, the model provides a valuable application for future research.

This modeling approach provides a general framework that can be extended to different types of resources – not only physical or environmental ones, but also abstract resources such as some of those involved in HRI, namely attention, emotional well-being and trust. On this basis, the next section explores how this framework can be applied to social robotics.

3 An Application to Social Resources

The simple model of resource management presented so far can be adapted to social robotics by reinterpreting the concept of resources in social rather than material terms. Indeed, in HRI, the artificial agent, i.e. the robot, does not consume "food" in a way that is directly visible to the user. Instead, it interacts with human partners whose internal states – such as attention, emotional well-being and trust – are more fragile and context-sensitive than physical resources, but equally crucial for the interaction to be successful over time [17–19].

This paper's proposal is that a social robot designed with AIF-based DM architecture could learn to manage these social resources dynamically, through continuous interaction with the user. Much like the agent in the resource model learned to avoid overconsumption by updating its internal model based on feedback from the environment, a robot could develop strategies to avoid overwhelming or disengaging its user.

Specifically, in this work the focus is on social resources such as attention, emotional well-being and trust. Concerning attention, it is worth emphasizing that, just as physical energy, a user's attention is finite. That is, a robot demanding too much cognitive or sensory input may lead to fatigue or disengagement [17, 20]. An AIF agent could model the user's attentional state as a hidden variable, inferred through cues such as gaze duration, response time or head orientation. It could then adjust its actions – speaking less, delaying prompts or offering quiet companionship – when attention appears low.

When it comes to emotional well-being, it is well proven that sustaining a positive emotional state in the user is key in many assistive or companion robotics applications [21, 22]. The robot could infer emotional valence from facial expression [23], speech tone or behavioral cues [24, 25] and treat this as central variables (hidden states) of its generative model. For instance, if signs of stress and frustration increase following a specific type of interaction, the robot could learn to avoid or modify those behaviors.

Finally, when dealing with trust in the context of HRI, it is crucial to stress that it can be considered as the most fragile resource, prone to several ethical and epistemological issues [26–28]. Trust, indeed, is built over time and can be easily damaged. An artificial agent acting under an AIF model could treat the human who is involved in the interaction as a hidden variable whose value affects the expected success of various interactions [12]. Violations of the user interactions (e.g., interrupting, misunderstanding or acting inappropriately) would produce large prediction errors, prompting the agent to adjust its own model. Over time, the artificial agent could learn to act in ways that maintain a reliable, transparent and responsive presence.

All the above considered, when the resource management model is applied to this type of abstract social resource, as with material resources, sustainability is not encoded as a static goal but emerges through the updating of preferences. The robotic agent begins with general prior preferences (e. g., maintaining attention, receiving immediate positive feedback), but these are updated based on user behavior. For instance, if prolonged engagement consistently leads to negative feedback (such as distraction, stress, withdrawal), the robot may learn to adjust its behavior by developing strategies such as starting less frequent or shorter interactions. Moreover, this setup allows for a planning horizon: instead of optimizing only for immediate interaction success (e.g., getting immediate positive feedback), the robot can learn to forecast and prioritize longer-term indicators of social resource health. This results in a more nuanced and sustainable mode of HRI, one that adjusts not just to how the users react immediately, but to how the interaction impacts them over time.

In this framework, social resources are conceptualized as latent variables in the agent's generative model, encoded as probabilistic beliefs about key interpersonal factors. For example, trust may be represented as a hidden state influencing the expected precision of action policies involving human input, while attention can be modeled as a modulatory gain on sensory prediction errors, akin to precision weighting in AIF. These quantities are updated through perception and action via AIF, allowing the agent to select behaviors that maintain the desired homeostasis in social variables – much like maintaining energy balance or thermoregulation in physiological models.

For further clarity, let's consider a scenario where a socially assistive robot is deployed in a long-term care setting. Its primary goal is to maintain a sustainable and beneficial interaction with an elderly resident by conversation with her. To do so, the robot relies on a generative model that includes not only physical or behavioral variables, but also the latent social resources previously discussed, i.e., user's attention, emotional well-being and trust.

On a given day, the elderly resident responds with delayed eye contact, minimal verbal responses, and decreased engagement. The robot registers these as sensory observations with high prediction error relative to prior expectations of "normal" interaction. Through AIF, the robot updates its beliefs and infers a low-attention and low-trust state. Based on this updated state, the robot selects a new policy: rather than asking questions, it plays calming music and maintains a gentle presence. Over time, as affective feedback stabilizes and the resident shows signs of improved engagement, the robot adjusts its generative model to reflect that passive support is more effective under certain trust and attention states. In this scenario, the robot estimates and acts on social resource states, dynamically adjusting behaviour to sustain well-being and relational continuity.

All the above considered, the application of the sustainable resource management model to social robotics clearly introduces a significant complexity compared to the original context. In the resource management simulation, the resource – food – was predefined, externally observable and governed by relatively simple environmental rules. The agent needed only to learn when and how much to consume, based on direct cues. In contrast, social resources such as attention, emotional well-being and trust are not explicitly given or directly measurable. They are internal states of the user, partially observable only through indirect behavioral cues (e.g., gaze patterns, facial expressions, tone of voice). Furthermore, these resources are dynamic: they evolve over the course of the interaction, influenced by individual preferences, emotional history, fatigue and context. Thus, a robot designed to act sustainably in a social environment must do more than simply learn optimal consumption strategies. It must engage in continuous inference about hidden social variables, update its internal model as interactions unfold and regulate its behavior even when signals are noisy or ambiguous. This makes the challenge of sustainability in social robotics inherently more complex and cognitively demanding than in material resource scenarios. However, the core idea remains the same: by minimizing expected free energy over time the robot can develop adaptive policies that prioritize the preservation of these fragile social resources, ensuring long-term successful interaction with the user.

The following section examines the main advantages and limitations of this approach.

4 Advantages and Limitations

Applying the model explained in Sect. 2 to social robotics presents some advantages but also reveals important limitations. One major strength of this approach lies in its ability to support adaptive personalization: rather than relying on rigid pre-programmed behaviors, the robot learns to adjust its actions based on the specific needs, preferences and reactions of the user over time. In this way, the preservation of social resources such as attention, emotional well-being and trust emerges naturally from the interaction, without the need for externally imposed constraints. Moreover, by minimizing prediction errors related to user engagement and emotional states, the robot indirectly supports crucial ethical principles, including respect for user autonomy and cognitive integrity [27, 29]. Another advantage is the potential scalability of the model to complex environments, involving multiple users or shifting social dynamic, thanks to the flexibility inherent in the AIF framework [13].

On the other hand, there are several limitations as well. As it has been mentioned in the previous section, internal states such as attention or trust are not directly observable: they must be inferred from indirect, often noisy signals like gaze behavior or speech patterns, making the risk of misinterpretation a constant concern. This creates an inherent epistemological fragility, where semantics (meaning) may be reduced to syntactic structures i.e., measurable data patterns despite the irreducibly embodied and context-sensitive nature of emotions and social attitudes [18]. An overreliance on syntactic inference mechanisms may lead to category errors in emotional recognition and interactional misalignment.

Furthermore, the modeling of social resources introduces normative assumptions that are not ethically neutral. For instance, designing agents that maximize trust without transparent mechanisms may result in instrumentalizing trust for system goals [30]. Similarly, the robot's ability to infer user well-being and adjust behavior accordingly raises the risk of paternalism, where the system "knows better" and overrides the user's preferences under the guise of care. These risks are especially significant in long-term interactions with vulnerable users [31].

The responsibility for these dynamics falls not only on the robot's initial prior preferences, which encode assumptions about what counts as desirable or acceptable interaction. If such priors are miscalibrated or left unexamined, they may shape the trajectory of interaction in ways that are not aligned with the user's true well-being and with the genuine sake of a successful interaction.

In addition, during the initial learning phase, the robot's behavior may be suboptimal, potentially leading to user discomfort, frustration or even erosion of trust – consequences similar to starvation in the original model – if corrective mechanisms are not carefully implemented. Moreover, this solution is highly dependent on the quality of sensory data and the robustness of the generative models: unreliable sensing or inaccurate model design could severely affect adaptive performance.

In sum, while applying the presented model can promote sustainable management of social resources, its implementation demands not only technical rigor but also critical ethical and epistemic awareness.

5 Conclusion

So far, this paper proposed to apply an AIF-based model of resource management to social robotics. Building on a model originally developed for the management of material resources, the framework has been extended to consider the preservation of social resources, such as user attention, emotional well-being and trust. It has been shown how, through the minimization of expected free energy over time, a social robot can learn to regulate its behavior in a way supporting not only immediate engagement but also long-term success of the interaction with a human user.

Unlike the management of material resources, the management of social resources requires the inference of dynamic, partially hidden states, which introduces greater complexity and ethical issues. Nevertheless, the core advantage of the approach remains: sustainability is not imposed as an external rule but emerges from the robot's continuous adaptation to its interactive environment. This offers a promising pathway for developing robots that are not only responsive, but also responsible patterns in social settings.

At the same time, important limitations have been acknowledged, such as challenges in observability, risks during early learning phases, and the ethical need for careful definition of the robot's prior preferences. Future works should focus on refining models of social inference, exploring sensor reliability and including multi-agent synchronization. Moreover, it is crucial to engage more deeply with the socio-philosophical implications of modeling social variables, particularly when these are treated as manipulable parameters within an inferential system.

Ultimately, applying AIF-based sustainable resource management to social robotics encourages to rethink sustainability not only as an ecological imperative but as a social one as well: a commitment to interactions that respect, support and adapt to the evolving needs of human partners over time.

Disclosure of Interests. The author has no competing interests to declare that are relevant to the content of this article.

References

1. Feil-Seifer, D., Matarić, M.J.: Defining socially assistive robotics. In: Proceedings of the IEEE 9th International Conference on Rehabilitation Robotics, June 28–July 1 2005, Chicago, IL, pp. 465–468 (2005)

2. Hartmann, F., Baumgartner, M., Kaltenbrunner, M.: Becoming sustainable. New Front. Soft Robot. Adv. Mater. **33**(19) (2021)
3. Alfieri, I., Fleres, A., Raffa, M.: Robots and global challenges: what we need to question for a more sustainable robotics. Isonomia (forthcoming)
4. Alfieri, I., Raffa, M.: Active inference for ethical decision-making in socially assistive robotics. In: Seibt, J., Fazekas, P., Quick, O. (eds.) Social Robots With AI: Prospects, Risks, and Responsible Methods: Proceedings of Robophilosophy 2024, Frontiers in Artificial Intelligence and Applications, vol. 397, pp. 709–715. IOS Press, Amsterdam (2025)
5. Leite, I., Martinho, C., Paiva, A.: Social robots for long-term interaction: a survey. Int. J. Soc. Robot. **5**, 291–308 (2013)
6. Robinette, P., Wagner, A.R., Howard, A.M.: Investigating human-robot trust in emergency scenarios: methodological lessons learned. In: Mittu, R., Sofge, D., Wagner, A., Lawless, W. (eds.) Robust Intelligence and Trust in Autonomous Systems. Springer, Boston, MA (2016). https://doi.org/10.1007/978-1-4899-7668-0_8
7. Kennedy, J., Baxter, P., Belpaeme, T.: Nonverbal immediacy as a characterisation of social behaviour for human-robot interaction. Int. J. Soc. Robot. **9**, 109–128 (2017)
8. Minsky, M.: The Emotion Machine: Commonsense Thinking, Artificial Intelligence, and the Future of the Human Mind. Simon & Schuster (2006)
9. Friston, K.J.: The free energy principle: a unified brain theory? Nat. Rev. Neurosci. **11**(2), 127–138 (2010)
10. Friston, K.J., Mattout, J., Kilner, J.: Action understanding and active inference. Biol. Cybern. **104**(1), 137–160 (2011)
11. Lanillos, P., Meo, C., Pezzato, C.: Active Inference in Robotics and Artificial Agents: Survey and Challenges. ArXiv 2112.01871 (2021)
12. Da Costa, L., Lanillos, P., Sajid, N., Friston, K., Khan, S.: How active inference could help revolutionise robotics. Entropy **24**(361) (2022)
13. Albarracin, M., Hipolito, I., Raffa, M., Kinghorn, P.: Modeling sustainable resource management using active inference. In: Buckley, C.L., et al. (eds.) Active Inference: 5th International Workshop, IWAI 2024, Oxford, UK, September 9–11, 2024, Revised Selected Papers, Communications in Computer and Information Science, pp. 237–259. Springer, Cham (2024)
14. Pezzulo, G., Dindo, H.: What should I do next? using shared representations to solve interaction problems. Exp. Brain Res. **211**(3–4), 613–630 (2011)
15. Sajid, N., Parr, T., Hope, T.M., Price, C.J., Friston, K.J.: Degeneracy and redundancy in active inference. Cereb. Cortex **31**(6), 2665–3268 (2021)
16. Parr, T., Friston, K.J.: The anatomy of inference: generative models and brain structure. Front. Comput. Neurosci. **12**(90) (2018)
17. Torta, E., van Heumen, J., Cuijpers, R.H., Juola, J.F.: How can a robot attract the attention of its human partner? a comparative study over different modalities for attracting attention. In: Ge, S.S., Khatib, O., Cabibihan, J.J., Simmons, R., Williams, M.A. (eds.) Social Robotics. ICSR 2012. Lecture Notes in Computer Science(), vol. 7621. Springer, Heidelberg (2012). https://doi.org/10.1007/978-3-642-34103-8_29
18. Damiano, L., Dumouchel, P.: Emotions in relation. Epistemological and ethical scaffolding for mixed human-robot social ecologies. Humana Mente **13**(37), 181–206 (2020)
19. Lewis, M., Sycara, K., Walker, P.: The role of trust in human-robot interaction. In: Abbass, H., Scholz, J., Reid, D. (eds.) Foundations of Trusted Autonomy. Studies in Systems, Decision and Control, vol. 117. Springer, Cham (2018). https://doi.org/10.1007/978-3-319-64816-3_8
20. Das, D., Rashed, M.G., Kobayashi, Y., Kuno, Y.: Supporting human-robot interaction based on the level of visual focus of attention. IEEE Trans. Hum.-Mach. Syst. **45**(6), 664–675 (2015)
21. Damiano, L., Dumouchel, P.: Living with Robots. Harvard University Press (2017)

22. Matarić, M: Socially assistive robotics: human-robot interaction methods for creating robots that care. In: Proceedings of the 2014 ACM/IEEE International Conference on Human-Robot Interaction (HRI 2014), vol. 333. Association for Computing Machinery, New York, NY, USA (2014)
23. Rawal, N., Stock-Homburg, R.M.: Facial emotion expressions in human-robot interaction: a survey. Int. J. Soc. Robot. **14**, 1583–1604 (2022)
24. Sawabe, T., Honda, S., Sato, W.: Robot touch with speech boosts positive emotions. Sci. Rep. **12**, 6884 (2022)
25. Spezialetti, M., Placidi, G., Rossi, S.: Emotion recognition for human-robot interaction: recent advances and future perspectives. Front. Robot. AI **7**, 532279 (2020)
26. Nickel, P., Spahn, A.: Trust, discourse ethics, and persuasive technology. In Proceedings of the 7th International Conference on Persuasive Technology, Persuasive 2012, pp. 37–40. University Electronic Press, Linköping (2012)
27. Alaieri, F., Vellino, A.: Ethical decision making in robots: autonomy, trust and responsibility. In: International Conference on Software Reuse, vol. 9979 (2016)
28. Yew, G.: Trust in and ethical design of Carebots: the case for ethics of care. Int. J. Soc. Robot. **13**(4), 629–645 (2020)
29. Fogg, B.J.: Persuasive Technology. Using Computers to Change What We Think and Do. Morgan Kaufmann Publishers, San Francisco (2003)
30. Losey, D.P., Sadigh, D.: Robots that take advantage of human trust. ArXiv, arXiv:1909.05777
31. Rochi, M., Rauschnabel, P.A., Renner, K.-H., Ivens, B.S.: Technology paternalism: development and validation of a measurement scale. Psychol. Mark. **41**(5), 1172–1188 (2024)

Sustainable Human-Robot Interaction: From Current Trends to Future Visions

Ilaria Torre[1,2](✉), Maria Teresa Parreira[3], Hannah Pelikan[4], Erik Lagerstedt[2], Sarah Schömbs[5], Katie Winkle[6], and Sara Ljungblad[1,2]

[1] Chalmers University of Technology, Gothenburg, Sweden
{ilariat,sara.ljungblad}@chalmers.se
[2] University of Gothenburg, Gothenburg, Sweden
erik.lagerstedt@gu.se
[3] Cornell University, Ithaca, USA
mb2554@cornell.edu
[4] Linköping University, Linköping, Sweden
hannah.pelikan@liu.se
[5] University of Melbourne, Melbourne, Australia
s.schombs@unimelb.edu.au
[6] Uppsala University, Uppsala, Sweden
katie.winkle@it.uu.se

Abstract. Sustainability is becoming an increasingly urgent concern in technology research, yet its meaning and application within Human-Robot Interaction (HRI) remain unclear. We examined how sustainability is currently understood within the HRI community through i) a survey among HRI researchers and ii) a "speculative futures" workshop held at the HRI 2025 conference. We compare the results of our analysis to the widely adopted three-pillar model of sustainability (delineating environmental, social, and economic aspects) and contrast it to alternative frameworks that critique this categorisation. Our findings show strong—but unacknowledged—engagement with social and environmental sustainability within the HRI community. We highlight common ground, lack of shared understanding, and areas of improvement across the community, and suggest practical steps for integrating sustainability into HRI research. We formulate aspects that should be included in a definition of sustainability that is specific to HRI.

Keywords: Sustainability · Human-Robot Interaction · Environmental Impact · Social Equity · Speculative futures

1 Introduction

Sustainability is a pressing concern that defines the present and will shape the very possibility of a liveable future. It is also becoming an increasingly contested word: different academic fields, regions of the world, and communities of practice interpret sustainability in different ways. In some contexts, e.g. within policy frameworks like the United Nations' 17 Sustainable Development Goals (SDGs), sustainability is framed around the "three pillars": **environmental** protection (ecological sustainability), **social** equity (social sustainability), and **economic** viability (economic sustainability) [39].

Within the fields of Social Robotics and Human-Robot Interaction (we henceforth refer to both as HRI, for simplicity), questions about sustainability are becoming more visible. The theme of the ACM/IEEE International Conference on Human-Robot Interaction (HRI 2025), "Robots for a Sustainable World", and the inclusion of a special session on Social Robotics and Sustainability at the 2025 International Conference on Social Robotics (ICSR), are markers of a timely and necessary shift. These signals suggest that the HRI community is beginning to reflect on how social robots could contribute to or detract from the goals of sustainable development.

However, it remains unclear what *sustainability* means within the HRI community. While many of the works recognised under the HRI 2025 sustainability theme addressed social aspects, such as inclusion, accessibility, and wellbeing, some researchers might argue that sustainability should primarily concern ecological impacts, such as emissions and resource use. Others, drawing from social justice literature, maintain that environmental sustainability is unattainable without addressing structural inequities first. In other words, as sustainability becomes more visible in HRI, it is also being understood in seemingly different ways. In this work, we aim to gather these diverse interpretations and examine whether there is a shared foundation and/or a shared direction for thinking about sustainability in HRI.

We explore how sustainability is conceptualised in the HRI community through two complementary approaches. First, we analyse responses from a survey of HRI researchers, in which they reflect on what sustainability means in the context of their work (*the present*). Second, we report on a participatory workshop held at the 2025 HRI conference, in which attendees engaged in a science fiction prototyping and backcasting activity to imagine desirable and undesirable futures involving robots (*the future*). Themes emerging from the survey and the workshop were linked to common sustainability frameworks. We highlight similarities and differences, and provide recommendations on how to conceptualise sustainability within HRI, taking first steps towards formulating what sustainability means in the context of HRI.

2 Background

Around the world, communities are facing the devastating consequences of environmental breakdown, with record-breaking heatwaves over Southern Europe, Asia and the North America in just the last years [41,42,44], as well as extreme rainfall in Africa and Asia [43]. Italy, where the 2025 ICSR conference will take place, has been experiencing an increasing amount of this as well, with extreme heat, rainfall, landslides, and other previously rare disasters. These escalating events do not only affect infrastructure and ecosystems; they deeply impact people's sense of security and hope. Young people in particular are expressing rising levels of "eco-anxiety", which is exacerbated by media exposure [16,26], and is defined by the American Psychological association as "a chronic fear of environmental doom" [7].

Albeit not exempt from critique (e.g. [22,39]), the SDGs are one of the few globally recognised frameworks for addressing such urgent global challenges. As technological innovation accelerates, scholars and policy makers have begun to ask how existing tools and emerging technologies such as Artificial Intelligence (AI) and robotics can support or hinder progress toward these goals. Notably, Ricardo Vinuesa et al. [59] argue that while AI has the potential to positively influence 79% of the SDG targets, it may also inhibit the achievement of up to 35% of them if ethical, social, and environmental risks are not adequately mitigated. Similarly, Yolande Strengers has criticised how "smart" home appliance technologies are framed as sustainability solutions, often highlighting convenience and economic benefits, while brushing aside deeper environmental commitments [53]. This dual-edged sword shows that there is a need for robotics, and especially social robotics, to reflect on how it can promote sustainable and just futures. In fact, we believe that social robots—here defined as robots that operate in human social environments, or robots that humans treat socially—have a specific role to play when it comes to sustainability. As we discuss in more detail in Sect. 5, existing frameworks relating to sustainable AI or sustainable robotics do not fully apply to how social robots are used or meant to be used today. Here, we will try and understand what this specific role is.

Socially interactive robots are increasingly entering domains aligned with sustainability priorities, from environmental monitoring and care work to inclusive education and assistive technology. However, HRI researchers have only recently begun to explicitly engage with sustainability frameworks, including the SDGs, within their research agendas. We hope that recent community efforts, such as the 2025 HRI conference theme, and the ICSR 2025 special session, will continue to encourage these trends. Nevertheless, the field still lacks a clear articulation of what sustainability means in practice and how HumanâĂŞRobot Interaction can contribute to sustainability outcomes across environmental, social, and economic dimensions.

Given these uncertainties, participatory and speculative design methods offer valuable tools to investigate current and future trends. Within HRI and adjacent fields like Human-Computer Interaction (HCI), such methods have been used to imagine ethically aligned futures, highlight implicit values, and engage diverse stakeholders in shaping the direction that technology is taking [3,4,11,30,34,60]. Specifically, science fiction prototyping and backcasting methods allow researchers to move beyond short-term technological designs and solutionism, instead reflecting on what kinds of futures we desire, and the steps required to achieve or avoid them [21,30,36,37]. These approaches also resonate with broader calls within AI ethics and responsible innovation to envision more inclusive and sustainable sociotechnical systems [9,33].

While HRI research has long been focused on the social pillar of sustainability (e.g., promoting health and wellbeing, and reducing inequalities [1,55,62]), few works have explicitly focused on environmental or economic aspects. Some studies have examined how robots can promote pro-environmental behaviours [10,48] or support community resilience to climate change [23]. Other HRI works can be linked to the economic pillar, such as studies examining long-term relationships with robots [8,12,18,24] and assessments of the impact of robot automation on labour and workers' wellbeing [13,25,28]. However, many of these contributions remain isolated, and little is known about how HRI researchers themselves interpret the field's role in addressing sustainability challenges. Additionally, while these works are clearly linked to these challenges, they are rarely labelled as such by the authors themselves, contributing to a widespread sentiment that the HRI community does not work on sustainability. As the HRI field grows and enters new domains, and in the face of rising physical and psychological eco-disasters, we need to examine what sustainability means within our field. What aspects of sustainability are most relevant? What responsibilities do HRI researchers have in advancing sustainable futures? And how might our methods, design practices, and research agendas evolve in response to these challenges?

This paper explores these questions through two data collection streams: (1) a survey of HRI researchers, investigating the current understanding of "sustainability" within their work, and (2) a participatory workshop that used speculative and backcasting methods to imagine sustainable and unsustainable futures involving robots. Together, these streams aim to identify shared concerns, values, and possibilities for building a more sustainable future that includes (or not) social robots.

3 Method

3.1 Survey

We conducted an online survey, aimed at anyone who identified as being a researcher or student in the field of Human-Robot Interaction. In the survey, we collected data on participants' experience in the field, and asked about their understanding of sustainability, in the context of HRI. Specifically, we asked: i) "What is sustainability (in the context of the HRI field) for you?" ii) "Can you think of an example of a work that, in your opinion, combines sustainability and HRI?" and, iii) "Here are some sustainability-related challenges that HRI could address. Which are the most pressing, in your opinion?" This last question was multiple-choice, with 8 possible choices (shown in Fig. 2; some example choices were "long-term viability of robot solutions" and "technology lifecycle management"). Participants were recruited via social media posts and word of mouth within the authors' networks.

3.2 Workshop

To further explore how HRI researchers conceptualise sustainability and the future role of robots, we conducted a participatory activity inspired by science fiction prototyping, a method used to engage stakeholders in imagining near-future scenarios and critically reflecting on the societal implications of emerging technologies. Science fiction prototyping encourages participants to explore not only what is technically feasible but also what is socially desirable or undesirable, enabling more grounded and value-sensitive design visions [20,21,37].

The activity was conducted as part of a workshop[1] that we organised during HRI 2025 [56]. The workshop involved a total of 14 participants: 6 external attendees, 4 invited speakers, and 4 organizing team members. We first had spotlight sessions where the 4 invited speakers gave presentations that helped ground initial knowledge on sustainability for all workshop attendees. Then, in the first phase of the activity, participants engaged in a brainstorming session where they generated scenarios describing both "good" and "bad" futures that robots could contribute to. These futures span across domains such as care, labour, relationships, climate resilience, and governance (grouped in Table 2). Following this, the group worked collaboratively to cluster the scenarios into thematic categories, identifying patterns and concerns shared across different future imaginaries. In the final phase, participants were divided into pairs and used the back-casting design method [30,47] to explore the pathways from the imagined futures to the present. In this approach, participants reasoned backward to identify concrete actions or decisions that would be required to either achieve a desirable future or avoid an undesirable one. As an example, groups could list any key stakeholders and resources involved in their future scenario (people, energy, materials, social norms). Then, they could identify unsustainable practices (e.g., wasteful energy use, inequality, short robot lifespans) and brainstorm sustainable alternatives (e.g., energy-efficient robots, longer-lasting hardware, more inclusive design).

4 Results

4.1 Survey

We obtained responses from 38 HRI researchers. Of these, 8.1% (N = 3) had been in the field for less than a year, 45.9% (N = 17) between 2 and 5 years, 21.6% (N = 8) between 5 and 10 years, and 24.3% (N = 9) for over 10 years. Additionally, 5.4% (N = 2) were Master's students, 29.7% (N = 11) were PhD students, 21.6% (N = 8) were postdocs, 37.8% (N = 14) were university lecturers or researchers, and 5.4% (N = 2) were company employees. Their research focus can be further divided as shown in Fig. 1.

The first open-ended question ("What is sustainability (in the context of the HRI field) for you?") was answered by 33 people. We conducted a thematic analysis of these 33 responses, and identified six main themes:

- **Interconnected responsibilities.** Sustainability is not just environmental, but also social, ethical, and economic. Many responses referenced the UN SDGs as a guiding framework. For example: «Whatever we use, do, and produce, it must not degrade social, organisational, or natural resources.» «The

---

[1] https://sites.google.com/view/hri-4-sustainability/.

Fig. 1. The self-identified HRI sub-fields (picked from a list of options) for respondents. 28 of the 37 respondents (76%) selected more than one option. Options with three or fewer selections are not showing.

UN Sustainable Development Goals (SDGs) are deeply connected... it's about creating lasting positive change through robotics.»
- **Environmental impact and resource use.** Focus on energy use, carbon footprint, material sourcing, and lifecycle impacts. Responses were especially critical of power-hungry AI models. For example: «Not using robots or power-intensive AI models when you really don't need to!!» «Using resources efficiently, e.g. robot fitness for long-term application, recycling of material, electricity consumption during runtime etc.»
- **Social sustainability and community impact.** Emphasis on equity, social justice, and community needs. Responses wonder who may benefit and who may be left behind. For example: «How does social robot development affect human social relationships with other humans and machines?» «When is a robot really a good choice for a community—can they maintain it when it breaks? Is it a long-term solution?»
- **Sustainability of HRI research.** Calls for open science, reproducibility, thoughtful design, and long-term value in research outputs. For example: «Reproducible results that are shared so that people can use the knowledge also long-term.» «Sustainability in HRI for me means open science. It means reusing datasets, or experimental setups and only running user studies that are promising and well thought through.»
- **Purpose-driven design over novelty.** Critique of tech-for-tech's-sake; encouragement to align research with real user needs and societal challenges. For example: «Focus more on actually user oriented research rather than technology oriented one.» «Doing things 'just because we can'... might not be the best approach in light of sustainability of research results.»
- **Avoiding known harms and negative precedents.** Concern about replicating harms seen in other AI domains; a call for proactive responsibility. For example: «... Sustainability for a just and democratic world. There is a lot to learn from virtual AI agents on social media and how they are already actively harming this part of sustainability. We need to ensure that robots do not follow in these footsteps.» «I think it's important to ensure that robotic systems... are not actively harming the environment in any other way. »

The second open-ended question ("Can you think of an example of a work that, in your opinion, combines sustainability and HRI?") was answered by 24 people, and was analysed in the same manner. Respondents highlighted a variety of papers, projects, or general topics. Although the responses are subjective and highly individual, they offer insights into how the HRI community is currently conceptualising and exemplifying sustainability in practice. We grouped the examples into six themes (Table 1). Several respondents (N = 6) also notably answered that there is a lack of published work explicitly addressing sustainability in HRI.

Table 1. Examples of work perceived to combine HRI and sustainability, grouped thematically. Links and references have been added to projects or papers that were explicitly mentioned.

Theme	Example(s)
Energy-conscious design	Use of smaller LLMs for dialogue and planning; reinforcement learning to reduce reprogramming; concerns about environmental impact of data storage and processing.
Inclusive or participatory design	UNICEF's AI charter applied in real-world experiments to protect children's rights [5]; participatory design in the hospital (e.g., SAFE-LY project); projects involving co-design with understudied societal groups, such as RO-LIV (assistive social robots that contribute to improved quality of life for older persons).
Sustainable robot materials	Fabric robots using household textiles; open-source and open-hardware robot projects such as Blossom; research on bio-inspired soft robotics and sustainable aesthetics (e.g., [6]).
Ecological aspects	Considering pros and cons of robotics for circular economies [14]; adding sustainability requirements in human-robot teaming evaluations.
Workforce wellbeing	EWASS project reducing physical workload through HRI; AIHURO project for sustainable human-robot collaboration in manufacturing environments.
Long-Term Human–Robot Relationships	Focus on maintaining meaningful, enduring interactions with robots that support human well-being over time (e.g., [24,49]); understanding the social consequences of robot use [35]

Finally, given a series of options, participants were asked which is the most pressing sustainability-related challenge for HRI, resulting in the distribution of responses shown in Fig. 2. Seven of the participants selected "all of the above" and they are thus counted toward all the options (to not inflate differences). In free text answers, two participants also added "access to care services" and "the tradeoff between social acceptance and the resource consumption etc. of robots compared to other possible solutions to societal issues".

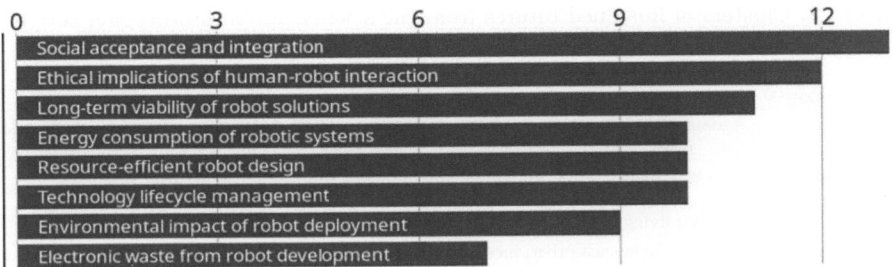

Fig. 2. The distribution of responses to the question of which of these is the most pressing sustainability-related challenge for HRI.

4.2 Workshop

Workshop participants generated ideas on post-its, which were then clustered into themes during group discussions. Each cluster reflected recurring concerns or objectives, spread across themes such as loneliness, language and communication, technological domination, job displacement, and environmental remediation. After the workshop, we conducted a thematic analysis of the clustered content, obtaining 10 themes (Table 2).

5 Discussion

By comparing the survey responses and the futures imagined during the HRI 2025 workshop, we observed both alignment and divergence in how sustainability is understood within the field. Across both activities, social sustainability emerged as a recurring theme, as can be seen from Table 1 and Fig. 2 (where people deemed the most pressing sustainability-related challenge for HRI to be "social acceptance and integration", followed by "ethical implications of human-robot interaction"). Topics such as inclusion, wellbeing, cultural preservation, and equitable access to technology were often mentioned, confirming that at least social sustainability is part of the discourse in HRI.

However, it is important to acknowledge that real social sustainability needs to build on participatory design and engagement in power structures, which points towards the need for methods and complementing approaches to experiments and surveys to for example consider problematisation, positionality, marginalisation and other perspectives in research activities [29, 61].

Environmental sustainability was also evident in both datasets, though it was more pronounced in the workshop discussions, suggesting that it is increasingly viewed as urgent and inescapable given global climate challenges, and is an unremovable component of imagined futures. Notably, the impact of the ballooning use of Generative AI in HRI research was under-discussed, though some attention is already being paid to the topic across HCI research [17].

Economic sustainability was also underrepresented across both the survey and the workshop. This absence may reflect a lack of clarity around how economic aspects of sustainability might factor into HRI research and relate to

Table 2. Clusters of imagined futures from the science fiction prototyping activity

Theme	Good Futures	Bad Futures
Jobs and Work	Robots replace humans in unsafe or dangerous jobs.	Robots deliver all groceries; no jobs for people; doctors become dependent on robots to practice medicine.
Destruction and Scarcity	A new planet hosts people; humans adapt physically (e.g., evolution for space living).	Energy shortages; conflict over resources; electricity becomes a privilege; people live in ruins.
Loneliness and Individualization	People help each other; increased solidarity.	Misinformation erodes trust; selfishness; humans stop acting like social animals; widespread loneliness.
Wellbeing and Inclusion	No stress; accessible spaces globally; marginalised and child voices are heard.	—
Language and Communication	Universal multilingual communication; robots can speak all languages; cultural preservation; integration with nature.	English becomes a gatekeeping language; people stop talking to each other.
Domination and Control	Robots act as environmental caretakers or activists.	Over-reliance on tech; military and surveillance use of robots; robot Armageddon; biopolitical control; forced use.
Environment and Nature	Robots clean oceans, beaches, and public waste; environmental restoration; preserving biodiversity and natural resources.	Robot waste accumulation; robots unintentionally damage ecosystems; biodiversity loss; destroyed habitats.
Energy and Resources	AI helps distribute resources efficiently.	Environmental costs of technology exacerbate inequality.
Waste and Materials	Robots made from reused materials; circular economy; no waste.	Fast-changing tech leads to short shelf life and increased waste.
Transport and Travel	Teleportation invented; robots deliver crops from farms directly to homes.	Public transport is defunded; teleportation has arbitrary restrictions; overtourism; fully automated transport systems exclude humans.

the other pillars. While some scenarios touched on themes of labour, automation, and fairness in employment, these were not typically framed as economic sustainability per se. This echoes findings from other research areas, where economic sustainability is often less understood or is conflated with market efficiency or corporate growth, rather than long-term ecological or societal benefit (e.g., [2,52]).

This view also overlooks important issues of power and labour; already at the onset of science fiction stories such as the initial R.U.R theatre play from 1928 by Karel Čapek, robots were produced and used with a dehumanising labour perspective. Since then, the introduction of robots into workplaces has historically been accompanied by fears of job loss, automation-induced inequality, and dehumanisation of labour [45,46,57]. These concerns were echoed in the speculative futures imagined by our participants, where robots dominated service roles or contributed to structural unemployment (cf. [58]. While it is common for technologists to claim that robots (or more in general, AI) will 'augment' rather than replace human workers, such claims have been criticised for masking deeper structural changes and labour displacement [45]. However, HRI has the potential to address these challenges more constructively. As suggested by [45], we might take inspiration from labour-inclusive models found in countries like Germany or the Nordic region, where workers and unions play a direct role in shaping the introduction of AI and automation in the workplace. Embedding this kind of participatory governance into HRI design processes could support more genuinely equitable and sustainable labour outcomes [13,62].

Finally, from the clusters of imagined futures (Table 2), we can see that the examples range from essentially already existing issues (e.g. overtourism) to wild sci-fi-esque ideas (e.g. the invention of teleportation). We also see that almost every theme has potential positive and negative futures associated with it, highlighting how robots—and technology in general—have potential to achieve both. This tension is reflected in some of the participants' responses, who for example note that a pressing sustainability challenge is "the tradeoff between social acceptance and the resource consumption etc. of robots", and aligns with ongoing debates around the role of robotics in circular economies [14].

Our findings also prompt a broader reflection on how sustainability is conceptualised, both within HRI and wider existing frameworks. While sustainability is often framed as comprising three equal pillars (environmental, social, and economic), this framing has been criticised for obscuring their interdependencies and flattening their relative importance. Even relative to our field, during her keynote speech at HRI 2025, Yolande Strengers argued that environmental sustainability is foundational, rather than coequal, since the viability of both economic and social systems ultimately depends on the health of ecological systems. Alternative frameworks, such as Kate Raworth's doughnut economics [40], support this view by embedding the economy within social and ecological boundaries, rather than treating it as a parallel goal. The Circles of Sustainability model [19] expands to include culture and politics, reinforcing the idea that sustainability cannot be reduced to (3) simplistic categories. The SDG framework has also been criticised for being overly broad or naïve [39]. In the Global South, and among climate activists and scholars of degrowth, there are calls for sustainability to centre more explicitly on emissions, environmental degradation, and systemic inequality, and models such as the SDGs are criticised due to inadequate focus on direct democratic governance and inability to recognise the biophysical limits to economic growth, among other issues [22].

5.1 What Is 'Sustainable Human-Robot Interaction'?

What, then, might sustainability uniquely mean in the context of Human-Robot Interaction? Arguably, HRI occupies a distinctive position in the broader sustainability x technology discourse. Unlike purely digital technologies, socially interactive robots are embodied, thus they require materials, energy, and physical infrastructure to operate. This means that any sustainability conversation in HRI must also address material provenance, resource efficiency, and lifecycle, echoing concerns typically found in hardware and manufacturing communities. At the same time, many HRI systems do not rely on high-autonomy artificial intelligence; they may rely on teleoperation, Wizard-of-Oz, or rule-based systems designed for specific, local use cases. As such, much of the sustainability discourse emerging from general AI research, which often focuses on abstract concerns around superintelligence, algorithmic bias, or large-scale automation, does not fully capture the practical and social nature of HRI applications [18]. Moreover, HRI is deeply grounded in the lived experiences, preferences, and social dynamics of end users. It is not just a field concerned with what robots can do, but with how people feel about and engage with robots in real-world contexts. We propose that sustainability in HRI is multifaceted and deeply interconnected with real-world needs and ethical responsibilities. Through this perspective, sustainability complements recent movements around e.g., feminist HRI [61], robots for social justice [62], and research programs such as critical robotics [29,30,50], in addition to broader topics of e.g. the social shaping and politics of technology [31], and trustworthy and socially sustainable artificial intelligence [9].

Sustainability in HRI also concerns the practices of researchers themselves. Survey respondents highlighted the importance of adopting more sustainable research practices, such as embracing open science principles and generating knowledge that remains relevant long-term. This of course reflects back from the broader scientific community, where efforts such as the Open Science Framework are slowly becoming the standard. In HRI, such practices remain unevenly adopted, in part due to challenges around unavailability of custom/non-standard robots that are built to test a specific solution, and artefacts such as novelty biases, where publishing venues tend to favour novel, but largely unreproducible, robot designs [15]. Micol Spitale et al. [51] further point out that recommendations and publishing guidelines for 'responsible' HRI research differ across venues. Benedikt Leichtmann et al. [27] also recognise that HRI user studies essentially suffer from the same issues that caused the replicability crisis in Psychology, such as small sample sizes, lack of theory, or missing information in reported data.

In sum, we suggest that "Sustainable HRI" refers to i) the design, deployment, and governance of human-robot systems in ways that are materially responsible, socially just, and aligned with long-term ecological and societal well-being, and ii) conducting research in a way that minimises environmental impact, promotes long-term knowledge sharing, and aligns with real user needs, without developing tech just for tech's sake.

5.2 Implications and Call for Actions

While our findings are still preliminary, we believe we have enough data to compile a selection of implications for HRI design, research agendas, community-building, and recommendations going forward. We are looking forward to continuing this conversation as the field of HRI reflects on how to become more "sustainable".

- **Need for a shared language**. Many people in HRI are doing sustainability-related research, sometimes unknowingly (e.g., following broader theoretical frameworks reflecting ethics, care, criticality, and social justice). But in order to join forces, we must develop a shared language. This paper has started to show the diversity of perspectives in HRI based on a small survey and a workshop. Through personal conversations, it also emerged that those who did not participate in the workshop during the HRI conference or see it as relevant for their work were often not aware of what the term sustainability meant; they did however express concerns about the environment, waste and ecological aspects. They also expressed or engaged in research on social justice. As national government and political actors use different language, it becomes particularly relevant to build common ground within the research community to be able to start conversations beyond national borders. Other ACM communities have started to shed light on the dark side of their work [18,54]. Similarly, HRI needs to start defining what we mean by sustainability. This paper makes a first step towards this.

- **Transparency and ownership of the impact of one's work.** Researchers must reflect on the impact of their work. As the Generative AI (GenAI) craze continues, more and more HRI works are likely to use these technologies [18,38]. Historically, HRI follows trends first identified in the broader Human-Computer Interaction (HCI) field. A recent study estimated that the GenAI research published at the CHI 2024 conference may have produced between 10,769.63 and 10,925.12 kg of CO_2e, equivalent to driving a car for over 100,000 km [18]. While the intent is not to assign blame, greater transparency about the computational and environmental footprints of HRI research can be a powerful tool. Awareness is often a precursor to behaviour change [32], and documenting the use of energy-intensive models encourages more mindful design choices, trade-off discussions, and ultimately, more sustainable research practices.
- **Sustainability statements.** To support this shift, we ask conference organisers, journal editors, and professional societies in HRI to encourage (or require) the inclusion of sustainability statements, similar to ethics statements already common in the field. These statements could briefly outline anticipated or actual environmental impacts (e.g., carbon emissions, material waste), social implications (e.g., labour, accessibility), efforts to reduce harm, or envisioned long-term benefits. Again, the intent is not to blame or force people to write something half-heartedly, but rather to normalise such practices with the hope of fostering a culture of accountability and reflection, without discouraging innovation.

Acknowledgments. We would like to thank all the participants and invited speakers of our HRI 2025 workshop "Sustainability-4-HRI, HRI-4-Sustainability".

Disclosure of Interests. The authors have no competing interests to declare that are relevant to the content of this article.

References

1. Axelsson, M., Spitale, M., Gunes, H.: Robots as mental well-being coaches: design and ethical recommendations. ACM Trans. Hum.-Robot Interact. **13**(2), 1–55 (2024)
2. Barth, M., Timm, J.M.: Higher education for sustainable development: students" perspectives on an innovative approach to educational change. J. Soc. Sci. **7**(1), 13–23 (2011). https://doi.org/10.3844/jssp.2011.13.23
3. Blythe, M., Andersen, K., Clarke, R., Wright, P.: Anti-solutionist strategies: seriously silly design fiction. In: Proceedings of the 2016 CHI Conference on Human Factors in Computing Systems, pp. 4968–4978 (2016)
4. Brunnmayr, K., Weiss, A.: Approaching future robot technologies via speculative role-playing. In: Companion of the 2024 ACM/IEEE International Conference on Human-Robot Interaction, pp. 278–282 (2024)
5. Charisi, V., et al.: Artificial intelligence and the rights of the child: towards an integrated agenda for research and policy. Technical report, Joint Research Centre (2022)
6. Christiansen, M.B., Rafsanjani, A., Jørgensen, J.: "it brings the good vibes": exploring biomorphic aesthetics in the design of soft personal robots. Int. J. Soc. Robot. **16**(5), 835–855 (2024)
7. Clayton, S., Manning, C., College, M., Krygsman, K., Speiser, M.: Mental health and our changing climate: impacts, implications, and guidelines (2017). https://www.apa.org/news/press/releases/2017/03/mental-health-climate.pdf. Accessed 17 Apr 2025
8. De Graaf, M.M., Allouch, S.B., Klamer, T.: Sharing a life with Harvey: exploring the acceptance of and relationship-building with a social robot. Comput. Hum. Behav. **43**, 1–14 (2015)
9. Dignum, V.: Responsible Artificial Intelligence: How to Develop and Use AI in a Responsible Way, vol. 2156. Springer, Cham (2019). https://doi.org/10.1007/978-3-030-30371-6
10. Duan, Z., Ding, Z., Mou, Y., Deng, X.: I am the "owner" of the hotel: the impact of human-robot interactivity on guests' pro-environmental behavior in hotels. J. Hosp. Tour. Manag. **62**, 284–293 (2025)
11. Dunne, A., Raby, F.: Speculative Everything, With a New Preface by the Authors: Design, Fiction, and Social Dreaming. MIT press (2024)
12. Forlizzi, J.: How robotic products become social products: an ethnographic study of cleaning in the home. In: Proceedings of the ACM/IEEE International Conference on Human-Robot Interaction, pp. 129–136 (2007)
13. Fraune, M.R., Šabanović, S.: Agency and engagement: the role of workplace democracy in human–robot interaction. Int. J. Soc. Robot. **12**, 1225–1239 (2020). https://doi.org/10.1007/s12369-020-00638-y
14. Grau Ruiz, M.A., O'Brolcháin, F.: Environmental robotics for a sustainable future in circular economies. Nature Mach. Intell. **4**(1), 3–4 (2022)
15. Gunes, H., Broz, F., Crawford, C.S., der Pütten, A.R.V., Strait, M., Riek, L.: Reproducibility in human-robot interaction: furthering the science of HRI. Current Robot. Rep. **3**(4), 281–292 (2022)
16. Hickman, C., et al.: Climate anxiety in children and young people and their beliefs about government responses to climate change: a global survey. Lancet Planetary Health **5**(12), e863–e873 (2021)

17. Inie, N., Falk, J., Selvan, R.: How co2stly is chi? The carbon footprint of generative ai in hci research and what we should do about it. In: Proceedings of the 2025 CHI Conference on Human Factors in Computing Systems. CHI '25, New York, NY, USA. Association for Computing Machinery (2025). https://doi.org/10.1145/3706598.3714227
18. Irfan, B., et al.: Using a personalised socially assistive robot for cardiac rehabilitation: a long-term case study. In: 2020 29th IEEE International Conference on Robot and Human Interactive Communication (RO-MAN), pp. 124–130. IEEE (2020)
19. James, P.: Urban Sustainability in Theory and Practice: Circles of Sustainability. Routledge (2014)
20. Johnson, B.D.: Science fiction prototyping: designing the future with science fiction. Synthesis Lectures Comput. Sci. **3**(1), 1–190 (2011)
21. Kiyokawa, S., et al.: Science fiction prototyping method improves readers' narrative experiences. IIAI Lett. Inform. Interdiscip. Res. **3** (2023)
22. Kothari, A., Demaria, F., Acosta, A.: Buen vivir, degrowth and ecological swaraj: alternatives to sustainable development and the green economy. Development **57**(3), 362–375 (2014)
23. Koul, P.: Transdisciplinary approaches in robotics for social innovation: Addressing climate change, workforce displacement, and resilience in the age of disruption. Transdiscip. J. Eng. **16** (2025)
24. Laban, G., Kappas, A., Morrison, V., Cross, E.S.: Building long-term human-robot relationships: examining disclosure, perception and well-being across time. Int. J. Soc. Robot. **16**(5), 1–27 (2024)
25. Lee, H.R., Sabanović, S.: Culturally variable preferences for robot design and use in South Korea, Turkey, and the United States. In: Proceedings of the 2014 ACM/IEEE International Conference on Human-Robot Interaction, pp. 17–24 (2014)
26. Léger-Goodes, T., Malboeuf-Hurtubise, C., Mastine, T., Généreux, M., Paradis, P.O., Camden, C.: Eco-anxiety in children: a scoping review of the mental health impacts of the awareness of climate change. Front. Psychol. **13**, 872544 (2022)
27. Leichtmann, B., Nitsch, V., Mara, M.: Crisis ahead? Why human-robot interaction user studies may have replicability problems and directions for improvement. Front. Robot. AI **9**, 838116 (2022)
28. Lewis, L., Sengers, P., Nourbakhsh, I.: Power, participation, and the ontology of robots: a human-centered approach to power relations in HRI. In: Proceedings of the 2018 ACM/IEEE International Conference on Human-Robot Interaction, pp. 655–656. ACM (2018). https://doi.org/10.1145/3171221.3171284
29. Ljungblad, S., Gamboa, M.: Critical perspectives in human–robot interaction design. In: Designing Interactions with Robots, pp. 148–160. Chapman and Hall/CRC (2024)
30. Ljungblad, S., Ni Bhroin, N., Serholt, S., Samuelsson Gamboa, M.: Is there a need for critical robotics research? In: Social Robots in Social Institutions, pp. 663–666. IOS Press (2023)
31. MacKenzie, D., Wajcman, J.: The Social Shaping of Technology. Open University (1999)
32. Mallett, R.K., Melchiori, K.J., Strickroth, T.: Self-confrontation via a carbon footprint calculator increases guilt and support for a proenvironmental group. Ecopsychology **5**(1), 9–16 (2013)
33. Marda, V., Narayan, S.: On the importance of ethnographic methods in AI research. Nature Mach. Intell. **3**(3), 187–189 (2021)

34. Murray-Rust, D., et al.: Spatial robotic experiences as a ground for future HRI Speculations. In: Companion of the 2024 ACM/IEEE International Conference on Human-Robot Interaction, pp. 57–70 (2024)
35. Nanavati, A., Alves-Oliveira, P., Schrenk, T., Gordon, E.K., Cakmak, M., Srinivasa, S.S.: Unintended failures of robot-assisted feeding in social contexts. In: Companion of the 2023 ACM/IEEE International Conference on Human-Robot Interaction, pp. 884–886 (2023)
36. Okada, Y., Kishita, Y., Nomaguchi, Y., Yano, T., Ohtomi, K.: Backcasting-based method for designing roadmaps to achieve a sustainable future. IEEE Trans. Eng. Manage. **69**(1), 168–178 (2020)
37. Osawa, H., Nakazawa, R., Sakamoto, D.: Using science fiction prototyping to design human–robot interaction scenarios. In: 2017 26th IEEE International Symposium on Robot and Human Interactive Communication (RO-MAN), pp. 966–971. IEEE (2017)
38. Pereira, A., et al.: Multimodal user enjoyment detection in human-robot conversation: The power of large language models. In: Proceedings of the 26th International Conference on Multimodal Interaction, pp. 469–478 (2024)
39. Purvis, B., Mao, Y., Robinson, D.: Three pillars of sustainability: in search of conceptual origins. Sustain. Sci. **14**, 681–695 (2019)
40. Raworth, K.: A Safe and Just Space for Humanity: Can We Live within the Doughnut? Oxfam (2012)
41. Reuters: Asia's extreme April heat worsened by climate change, scientists say. https://www.reuters.com/sustainability/climate-energy/wildfires-burn-turkey-france-early-heatwave-hits-2025-06-30/
42. Reuters: Asia's extreme April heat worsened by climate change, scientists say. https://www.reuters.com/business/environment/asias-extreme-april-heat-worsened-by-climate-change-scientists-say-2024-05-14/
43. Reuters: Sustainable switch: Deadly floods hit nigeria, india and bangladesh. https://www.reuters.com/sustainability/sustainable-switch-deadly-floods-hit-nigeria-india-bangladesh-2025-06-04/
44. Reuters: World breaks hottest day record again, despite el nino's end. https://www.reuters.com/business/environment/world-breaks-hottest-day-record-second-day-row-2024-07-24/
45. Riek, L.D., Irani, L.: The future is Rosie?: disempowering arguments about automation and what to do about it. In: Proceedings of the 2025 CHI Conference on Human Factors in Computing Systems, pp. 1–14 (2025)
46. Robertson, J.: Gendering humanoid robots: robo-sexism in japan. Body Soc. **16**(2), 1–36 (2010). https://doi.org/10.1177/1357034X10364767
47. Robinson, J.: Future subjunctive: backcasting as social learning. Futures **35**(8), 839–856 (2003)
48. Scheutz, C., Law, T., Scheutz, M.: Envirobots: how human-robot interaction can facilitate sustainable behavior. Sustainability **13**(21), 12283 (2021)
49. Seibt, J.: "integrative social robotics"–a new method paradigm to solve the description problem and the regulation problem? In: What Social Robots Can and Should Do, pp. 104–115. IOS Press (2016)
50. Serholt, S., Ljungblad, S., Ní Bhroin, N.: Introduction: special issue–critical robotics research. AI Soc. **37**(2), 417–423 (2022)
51. Spitale, M., Stower, R., Parreira, M.T., Yadollahi, E., Leite, I., Gunes, H.: HRI wasn't built in a day: a call to action for responsible HRI Research. In: 2024 33rd IEEE International Conference on Robot and Human Interactive Communication (ROMAN), pp. 696–702. IEEE (2024)

52. Sterling, S.: Higher education, sustainability, and the role of systemic learning. In: Corcoran, P.B., Wals, A.E. (eds.) Higher Education and the Challenge of Sustainability, pp. 49–70. Springer, Dordrecht (2004). https://doi.org/10.1007/0-306-48515-X_5
53. Strengers, Y.: Smart Energy Technologies in Everyday Life: Smart Utopia? Springer, London (2013). https://doi.org/10.1057/9781137267054
54. Toczé, K., Madon, M., Garcia, M., Lago, P.: The dark side of cloud and edge computing: an exploratory study. In: Eighth Workshop on Computing within Limits 2022. LIMITS, Virtual (2022). https://doi.org/10.21428/bf6fb269.9422c084, https://limits.pubpub.org/pub/dark
55. Torre, I., Lagerstedt, E., Dennler, N., Seaborn, K., Leite, I., Székely, É.: Can a gender-ambiguous voice reduce gender stereotypes in human-robot interactions? In: 2023 32nd IEEE International Conference on Robot and Human Interactive Communication (RO-MAN), pp. 106–112. IEEE (2023)
56. Torre, I., et al.: Sustainability-4-HRI, HRI-4-sustainability. In: ACM/IEEE International Conference on Human-Robot Interaction, pp. 1991–1993. IEEE Press (2025)
57. Törngren, M., Lindblom, J.: Human-robot interaction in industrial contexts. In: Goodrich, M., Schultz, A.C., et al. (eds.) Handbook of Human-Robot Interaction, pp. 234–251. Cambridge University Press (2018)
58. Uuk, R., et al.: A taxonomy of systemic risks from general-purpose AI. arXiv preprint arXiv:2412.07780 (2024)
59. Vinuesa, R., et al.: The role of artificial intelligence in achieving the sustainable development goals. Nat. Commun. **11**(1), 233 (2020)
60. Winkle, K.: Robots from nowhere: a case study in speculative sociotechnical design and design fiction for human-robot interaction. In: Proceedings of the 2025 ACM/IEEE International Conference on Human-Robot Interaction, pp. 1152–1165 (2025)
61. Winkle, K., et al.: Feminist human-robot interaction: disentangling power, principles and practice for better, more ethical HRI. In: Proceedings of the 2023 ACM/IEEE International Conference on Human-Robot Interaction, pp. 72–82 (2023)
62. Zhu, Y., Wen, R., Williams, T.: Robots for social justice (r4sj): toward a more equitable practice of human-robot interaction. In: Proceedings of the 2024 ACM/IEEE International Conference on Human-Robot Interaction, pp. 850–859 (2024)

Explanations in Social HRI

Designing Authority and Service-Oriented Experiences in Librarian Robots

Ela Liberman-Pincu(✉) ⓘ and Tal Oron-Gilad ⓘ

Ben-Gurion University of the Negev, Beer-Sheva, Israel
elapin@post.bgu.ac.il, orontal@bgu.ac.il

Abstract. With the advancement of robotics technology, humans will increasingly interact with multiple service robots, yet there are still gaps in understanding how the behavior and appearance of the service robots can impact the interaction. Our two-stage study focuses on human interaction with two librarian robots. Specifically, we examine how the perception of robots as "authoritative" or "service-oriented" affects the quality of interaction. First, we conducted an online study with 140 respondents to define the look and behavior of authoritative and service-oriented robots. Based on this, we developed the behavior and look of the robots and executed a real experiment with two robots in a library setting. Outcomes obtained from 20 participants indicate that they preferred an authoritative behavior and a service-oriented appearance for optimal task success and better interaction quality.

Keywords: human-robot interaction · service robot · robot appearance · robot behavior · authority

1 Introduction

The interaction between humans and robots is intricately tied to their design and appearance. People's expectations of robots are significantly shaped by how they look, which, in turn, affects the quality of human-robot communication [1]. When individuals encounter differently designed robots, they naturally attribute distinct roles and varying levels of authority to them [2, 3]. Understanding these dynamics is crucial for creating effective and intuitive human-robot interactions—particularly in public environments where robots are increasingly deployed to facilitate access, orientation, and service.

In this context, librarian robots serve not only as functional agents but as socially embedded actors—mediators of access to knowledge, facilitators of spatial navigation, and contributors to the relational ecosystem of public spaces. By examining how their visual and behavioral characteristics shape perceptions of service orientation and authority, this study investigates design decisions that can support more inclusive, accessible, and engaging user experiences. These insights align closely with the aims of social sustainability, highlighting how human-centered robotic design can promote trust, equity, and user wellbeing in technology-mediated environments.

© The Author(s), under exclusive license to Springer Nature Singapore Pte Ltd. 2026
M. Staffa et al. (Eds.): ICSR+AI 2025, LNAI 16533, pp. 503–515, 2026.
https://doi.org/10.1007/978-981-95-2398-6_34

Fig. 1. The experimental setting in the library.

1.1 The Role of Service Robots

Service robots are unlikely to replace service employees, but have the potential to support employees in mundane service jobs, saving costs and reducing the need for human professionals to do less attractive work. As such, robots are likely to be the visible and front part of integrated service systems [4]. A study examining how a bellboy robot's different behaviors and designs affect user engagement and comfort in a hotel setting found that an active, embodied robot tends to engage users better [5]. Yet, Shanks et al. [6] indicated that consumers ascribe less power to a robotic service team leader than a human. To mitigate, they recommend introducing service robots where "the ability of a robot provides value," i.e., for specific roles and tasks. We explore using service robots for routine tasks in a library setting (Fig. 1).

1.2 Robots' Visual Characteristics

The visual design of robots plays a crucial role in shaping user perceptions. In this study, we focused specifically on two visual attributes—body shape and color—due to their well-documented influence on perceived authority and approachability. While additional features such as facial design, screen presence, and robot size are known to affect perception, they were deliberately kept uniform across all experimental conditions. This approach reduced design complexity and eliminated potential confounding effects, allowing us to directly assess the influence of silhouette and color.

Prior research has shown that visual silhouettes play a pivotal role in shaping how people interpret a robot's social role. Specifically, A-shaped body structures tend to be perceived as approachable and service-oriented, while V-shaped structures are more closely linked to impressions of professionalism and authority [3, 7, 8]. Hatano et al. [9] looked at the impact of color on negative impressions towards multiple anthropomorphic robots and found that bright colors, blue, turquoise, and orange, convey friendliness and positive impressions, resulting in most participants (70%) not feeling any negative impressions towards the robots. However, to determine the role of a robot, it is important to look also at the mutual impact of its behavior and appearance [10, 11].

1.3 Perception of Authority vs. Service Orientation

Authority is the ability of a person or organization to impose certain behavior patterns on someone. The extent to which a person will follow orders is partly determined by the characteristics of the person giving the orders. One way to identify those with authority is by their clothing. Uniforms are used to signify the wearer's status, group membership, and legitimacy. Throughout history, uniforms have been used as a symbol of authority [12]. In a study on the impact of uniforms and compliance, three types of clothing were examined for their effect on people's compliance and obedience. The study looked at how non-authoritative clothing (simple clothing), authority by status (a suit with a white shirt and tie), and authority by role (a firefighter uniform) influenced people's willingness to perform a task. The results showed that compliance and obedience significantly increased with the perceived level of authority, with the highest obedience to the greatest perceived authority (firefighter), followed by authority by status, and finally, no authority. Additionally, it was found that uniforms affect honesty, willingness to help, political behavior, aggression, and obedience [13]. Symbols can also influence obedience and convey a sense of authority. Symbols that incorporate titles, decorations, and recognizable logos evoke feelings of authority even without a direct, authoritative figure [14]. In robotics, Liberman-Pincu et al. [15] showed that adding the university logo to an officer robot led people to perceive the robot as more authoritative.

Service orientation refers to the willingness and effort to deliver professional, courteous, and attentive service. Among the many factors shaping perceptions of service orientation, visual appearance plays a significant role. Cues such as clothing, jewelry, makeup, personal hygiene, and hairstyle can all influence how service-oriented a person appears [13]. This insight extends to robots as well: a study examining escort, entertainment, and military robot types found that robots perceived as service-oriented were typically associated with more feminine traits, whereas those designed for role-specific functions—like military applications—were expected to display more masculine characteristics [13].

Goetz et al. [16] observed that people tend to conform more when a robot behaves seriously compared to when it behaves casually and amiably. Additionally, serious robots are perceived as more intelligent but less approachable. Hence, the robot's appearance and behavior can impact collaboration between humans and robots. As such, we investigate the impact of visual and behavioral characteristics on user perceptions and interaction outcomes using two librarian robots in a library setting. Our goal is to identify the best combination of appearance and behavior for task efficiency and user engagement.

2 Methods, Tools, and Study Design

This study employed a two-stage design. In the first stage, an online survey was conducted to identify clear visual and behavioral distinctions between robots perceived as "service-oriented" and those viewed as "authoritative." Quantitative analysis of the responses guided the selection of specific traits—ranging from behaviors to visual elements—that significantly influence the perception of a robot's orientation toward either service or authority.

These elements were then implemented in two service robots.

Second, we conducted a practical HRI experiment in the university library. Twenty participants interacted with a team of two temi robots (https://www.robotemi.com) to complete a service process of allocating a particular book at the entrance of the library ("Entrance Robot") and assisting in physically locating it on the library shelves on another floor ("Floor Robot").

3 Stage 1: Online Survey

We constructed a questionnaire examining characteristics related to robot appearance (clothing color and robot color, clothing style, and robot shape) and robot behavior (facial expressions, body movements, manner of speech - expansive or concise). Following a literature survey, we focused on parameters related to appearance and behavior to establish a differentiation, as detailed in the following sections.

A total of 140 respondents were recruited through Facebook and WhatsApp groups and through signs with barcodes calling for participants placed around the university campus for a period of ~ 4 weeks. The sample comprised 48 males and 92 females, with an average age of 26 years ($SD = 1.4$). Among them, 84 (60%) were university students.

3.1 Visual Characteristics

Based on the literature review, five visual characteristics were included: robot body color, robot body shape, uniform type, uniform color, and university logo existence. Table 1 details the possible values for each parameter. Figure 2 illustrates two options out of the possible combinations.

Table 1. The visual characteristics and their possible values

Visual feature	Possible values
Robot body color	White/ Black
Robot body shape (created by the uniform)	A-shape/ V-Shape
Uniform type	Tuxedo, Informal shirt
Uniform color	Black/ Light Blue/ Orange
University logo existence	Yes/ No

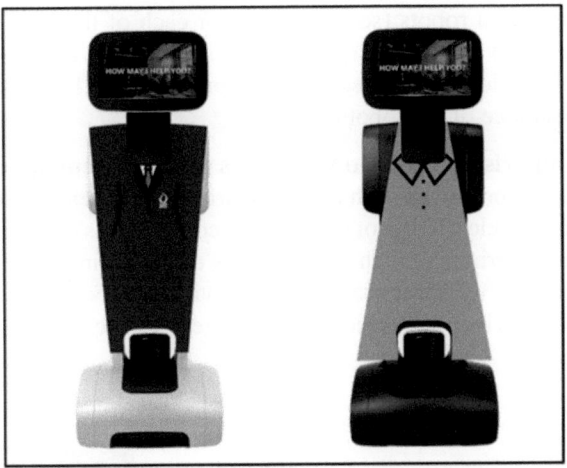

Fig. 2. Left: A white temi wearing a V-shaped black tuxedo with the university logo. Right: A black temi wearing an A-shaped light blue informal shirt with no logo.

3.2 Behavioral Characteristics

We created four personalities: highly authoritative, moderately authoritative, moderately service-oriented, and highly service-oriented. These four personalities differed by their script, facial expressions, and body language (including gaze), as detailed in Fig. 3.

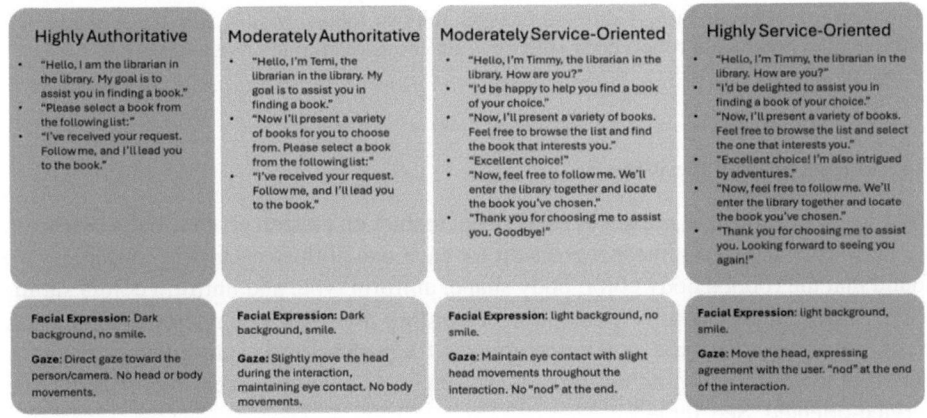

Fig. 3. Four robot personalities differing by script, facial expressions, and body language.

3.3 Questionnaire Design

The questionnaire consisted of three parts:

Part 1. Attributed characteristics for different robot appearances: In this part, participants were shown images of randomly selected four distinct robots, each with its own set of visual features. A total of 24 different visualizations were created to represent various looks of the temi robots (see Table 1). For each of the four presented robots, respondents were asked to rate six characteristics (Friendly, Professional, Authoritative, Accessible, Reliable, and Service-oriented) on a scale of 1 to 7 based on how they perceived the appearance of the robot they saw.

Part 2. Paired comparisons between two robots with different appearances: In this part, participants were presented with two comparisons between two robots differing in appearance (randomly selected out of ten possible comparisons). In the first comparison, they were asked to determine which of the robots appeared more authoritative, and in the second comparison, which appeared more serviceable. For each comparison, only one of the five characteristics in Table 1 was changed. Figure 4 illustrates one example from the questionnaire.

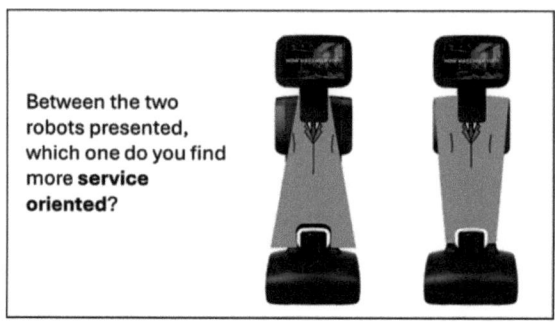

Fig. 4. A comparison between two robots with different appearances. One characteristic out of the options provided in Table 1 differed between the two robots. In this case, the A-shape (left robot) and V-shape (right robot) body structures are compared for an orange tuxedo.

3.4 Online Survey Results

Part 1. To examine the impact of each visual feature on the perceived robot's character, we performed a general linear regression for each one of the explanatory variables. We found that the robot's body color, body shape, uniform type, and uniform colors significantly affected participants' perceptions regarding the robot's character; for example, black uniforms contribute to the perception of a professional, authoritative, and reliable robot, while light blue uniforms were perceived as more accessible, friendly and service-oriented. See Table 2.

Table 2. The impact of visual features on participants' perceived robot character.

Robot's character	Statistically significant Visual feature	Statistically significant values
Friendly	Robot body color ($p < .01$), Uniform type ($p = .08$), Uniform Color ($p < .01$)	A white robot wearing a light blue informal shirt

(continued)

Table 2. (*continued*)

Robot's character	Statistically significant Visual feature	Statistically significant values
Professional	Robot body color ($p = .08$), Uniform Color ($p < .01$)	A white robot wearing black
Authoritative	Robot body shape ($p = .07$), Uniform Color ($p < .01$)	A V-shaped robot wearing black
Accessible	Robot body color ($p < .05$), Uniform type ($p = .07$), Uniform Color ($p < .01$)	A white robot wearing a light blue informal shirt
Reliable	Robot body color ($p < .05$), Uniform Color ($p < .01$)	A white robot wearing black
Service-oriented	Robot body color ($p < .01$), Robot body shape ($p = .05$), Uniform type ($p < .01$), Uniform Color ($p < .01$)	A white V-shaped robot wearing a light blue informal shirt

Part 2. We examined which visual features had the most significant impact on how people perceived the robot's appearance as authoritative or service-oriented. Additionally, we identified which specific feature values were associated with each type of robot.

Respondents associated white robots as service-oriented (73%) and black robots as authoritative (97%). They tended to associate informal shirts with service-oriented robots. No such comparisons were presented for authoritative robots in the survey. The preferred body structure for service-oriented and authoritative robots was the V-shape (71% and 76%, respectively). Regarding colors, light blue uniforms were perceived as service-oriented (56%), while black uniforms were associated with authoritative robots (83%). Lastly, the presence of a university logo contributed to both service-oriented and authoritative perceptions (70% and 54%, respectively).

Part 3. Respondents perceived the four robots' personalities differently; as expected, the highly service-oriented robot was rated as the friendliest; 84.4% of the respondents ascribed friendly to this robot compared to 67.7% on average ascribed to the three other personalities. Furthermore, it was recognized as the most service-oriented (84.4% compared to 62.6%). In addition, highly and moderately service-oriented robots were perceived as more accessible than authoritative robots (72.3% on average compared to 56%), while highly authoritative robots were perceived as the most reliable (48.4% compared to 34% on average), and moderately authoritative robots were classified as the most assertive (20% compared to 7.3%).

When asked to assemble a robot's appearance to fit its personality, most respondents selected the white robot (79.4%), the V-shape body shape (75.6%), and an informal shirt (67.9%) regardless of the observed robot's personality they saw. However, we did find differences regarding the uniform color selection; respondents who exhibited one of the service-oriented robot personalities were more likely to select a light blue uniform out of the three color options (44.6%), while those who exhibited one of the authoritative robot personalities were more likely to select black uniform (47%).

3.5 Summary of the Online Survey Findings

Drawing from existing literature, we designed four distinct robot personalities, each characterized by unique scripts, facial expressions, and body language. The survey validated the initial assumptions regarding users' perceptions of the robot's character and role. Additionally, we explored the most suitable appearance for expressing service-oriented and authoritative robot behaviors. The first two survey sections gathered respondents' impressions of robotic characters based on images representing different appearances. In the third section, participants were asked to select visual features that aligned with the personality of a robot they observed in a video. Interestingly, participants' choices in this part of the survey are less clear, suggesting that visual feature selections may be influenced more by personal preferences rather than the video content and personality respondents have seen. Based on these findings, we created distinctive appearances for the Authoritative and Service-oriented robots to convey their personality type, as shown in Fig. 5.

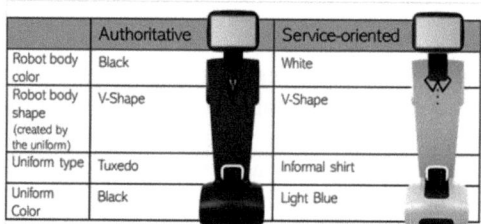

Fig. 5. Outcomes of the online questionnaire illustrating the most suitable appearance for the authoritative and service-oriented personalities.

4 Stage 2: An HRI Experiment in a Library Setting

A practical experiment was conducted at the Arrane Library located at Ben-Gurion University. We examined a service interaction in which a student engaged with a pair of robots: the "Entrance Robot," responsible for greeting the student and assigning a specific book at the library entrance, and the "Floor Robot," which assisted in physically retrieving the book from the shelves on another floor. We aimed to investigate whether the robots' behavior and appearance influence the quality of interaction and the successful retrieval of the requested book.

To simulate a realistic and sequential multi-robot service experience, the Entrance Robot was incorporated as a consistent first point of contact. It consistently exhibited an authoritative personality with an authoritative appearance and served both a functional and psychological role in the service interaction—providing book options at the entrance while establishing a standardized tone that framed the user's expectations. This setup allowed us to examine whether and how the initial authoritative encounter influenced the perception of the second robot. The Floor Robot, located on the fourth floor, was presented in one of four possible combinations: (1) authoritative personality and appearance, (2) authoritative personality with a service-oriented appearance, (3) service-oriented personality with an authoritative appearance, and (4) service-oriented personality and appearance. All participants interacted with the same Entrance Robot and were randomly assigned to one of these four Floor Robot conditions, enabling analysis of both transfer and contrast effects in multi-robot interaction.

4.1 Experimental Procedure

Twenty industrial engineering and management students (ten males and ten females) were invited, one at a time, to participate in the study. They were a convenience sample of volunteers. The experiment took place during daytime. The first robot, the "Entrance Robot" (temi), was stationed on the library's entrance floor. The second robot, the "Floor Robot" (another temi), was stationed on the fourth floor of the library by the elevator. The entrance floor is a central area where many people pass through, typical for library services. As aforementioned, participants were selected in advance and arrived at allocated slot time for their participation.

First Interaction – Meeting with the Entrance Robot and Book Selection: Participants met the Entrance Robot, which offered assistance in locating a book of their choice. If the participant agreed, the Entrance Robot presented a list of available books (located on the fourth floor). After selecting a book, the Entrance Robot indicated its location was on the fourth floor and invited the participants to proceed to the fourth floor.

Second Interaction – Meeting with the Floor Robot and Guidance to the Chosen Book: Participants met the Floor Robot once exiting the elevator. The Floor Robot acknowledged their presence, displayed the chosen book on its screen, invited the participant to follow it to find the location of the selected book on the shelf, and led the participant to its location. Each participant experienced one out of the four possible combinations. Figure 6 presents three different situations from the experiment.

Fig. 6. The experimental stages: Left: The first interaction with the Entrance Robot, Middle: Meeting the Floor Robot, Right: The Floor Robot leads the participant to the book location.

4.2 Data Collection Tools

At the end of the two interactions, participants were asked to complete a questionnaire based on the TAM-Almere model [17]. The questions covered dimensions such as sociability, anxiety, use intention, perceived usefulness, and trust. The questionnaire was analyzed to examine the influence of appearance and behavior characteristics of the four scenarios. A free-text open question was added at the end of the questionnaire. With their consent, participants were filmed using four video cameras, with two cameras placed in each of the library locations where the experiment took place.

4.3 Results

Manual annotation of the videos captured during the interaction revealed that the Floor Robot's combination that participants encountered influenced several metrics, including: their success rate in finding the book, whether participants greeted the Floor Robot or said goodbye at the end, and whether, after the book was retrieved, they followed the robot back towards the elevator.

Ninety percent of the participants successfully found the book with the assistance of the robots. A 100% success rate was achieved when the Floor Robot had an authoritative appearance and/or behavior. In contrast, the scenario where the robot exhibited a service-oriented appearance and behavior had only a 60% success rate.

The service-oriented appearance seemed to enhance positive interactions. Participants who interacted with a service-oriented robot were more likely to respond verbally during the interaction (40% compared to 20%) and engage in farewell gestures such as waving, nodding, and saying "goodbye" (40% compared to none who interacted with an authoritative-looking robot). Additionally, they tended to smile more during the interaction (60% compared to 50%).

Service-oriented behavior primarily influenced participants' tendency to prolong the interaction. Half of the participants who encountered the service-oriented robot continued to follow it after completing the task, compared to only 10% of those who interacted with an authoritative personality.

Due to the limited sample size in the in-situ study, we were unable to conduct inferential statistical analyses. Nonetheless, we performed descriptive analysis of the questionnaire responses to explore patterns across conditions. Participants rated their experiences on a 5-point Likert scale across several key dimensions: satisfaction, anxiety, efficiency, trust, perceived usefulness, and intention to use. These descriptive results, alongside our thematic observations, revealed certain trends regarding how behavioral and appearance cues shaped user perceptions during the interaction. These patterns offer preliminary insights that can inform future, larger-scale investigations.

The service **satisfaction** rating was high, averaging 4.6 ($SD = 0.6$). Those who encountered a robot with authoritative behavior rated the service higher, with an average of 4.8 ($SD = 0.42$) compared to 4.4 ($SD = 0.69$). **Anxiety** levels were low for all scenarios 1.1 on average ($SD = 0.3$). Participants recognized the authoritative personality as more efficient, rating its **efficiency** at 5.0 compared to 4.4 ($SD = 0.96$) for the service-oriented personality. In addition, it was linked to higher **trust** (4.8 on average, $SD = 0.42$ compared to 4.4, $SD = 0.7$) and higher perceived **usefulness** (4.9, $SD = 0.32$ compared to 4.5, $SD = 0.7$).

The robot's appearance influenced participants' perceptions of its efficiency, trust, and future **intention to use**. Robots with an authoritative appearance were perceived as more efficient, with an average rating of 4.9 ($SD = 0.32$) compared to 4.5 ($SD = 0.97$)

for service-oriented robots. Participants also rated their intention to use these robots slightly higher (4.8, SD = 0.42 compared to 4.6, SD = 0.7). However, they rated their trust lower (4.5, SD = 0.7 compared to 4.7, SD = 0.48).

A thematic analysis of the respondents' free-text comments revealed that some viewed the service-oriented behavior as inefficient and unnecessary. One participant noted, '*In my opinion, questions like "How are you" are redundant and merely consume time.*' Another respondent mentioned, '*I would prefer not to be asked such questions as they lead to unnecessary waiting time.*' Additionally, one respondent remarked, '*The part of the conversation where I had to respond verbally felt somewhat forced.*'

In contrast, the free-text comments about the authoritative robot's behavior were more positive. Four out of ten participants who interacted with this robot praised its efficiency and speed. One participant noted, '*I trusted it to lead me to the exact location. It was quick, pleasant, and very practical.*'

5 Discussion, Limitation, and Recommendations

Our findings contribute to ongoing discussions on social sustainability in public-service robotics by emphasizing how appearance and behavior design can shape accessible, inclusive, and user-centered experiences. Consistent with calls to embed sustainability early in the design process [20], our study demonstrates that even subtle cues—like uniform color or communicative style—can significantly influence user trust, comfort, and task success in shared public spaces.

To explore these dynamics, we began with an online survey to identify visual and behavioral traits associated with robots perceived as either "service-oriented" or "authoritative." These traits were implemented on the temi robotic platform and tested in an in-situ experiment involving two librarian robots.

Survey results revealed that black uniforms and authoritative behaviors were associated with reliability and professionalism, while light blue uniforms and service-oriented behavior conveyed friendliness and approachability, in line with previous findings [9]. In the library setting, robots with authoritative characteristics achieved a 100% task success rate in helping users retrieve books, compared to 60% for those exhibiting service-oriented traits. However, service-oriented robots elicited richer, more positive social engagement—participants were more likely to smile, converse, extend the interaction, and say goodbye.

Our findings suggest that combining authoritative behavior with a service-oriented appearance may offer a synergistic advantage by enhancing both task efficiency and user satisfaction. This supports earlier work showing that authoritative robots are more effective in maintaining engagement, while service-oriented ones foster comfort and positive experiences [5]. It also resonates with prior studies calling for deeper insights into human-robot interaction [18] and those examining the dynamics of robot authority and human obedience, such as in security contexts [19].

This trade-off between functional efficiency and social engagement underscores the importance of contextually aware design. Our findings have clear practical implications for service settings like libraries, hospitals, and customer support centers, where balancing authority and approachability can enhance both performance and user wellbeing.

Designers should be mindful of how visual cues such as color—black for authority, light blue for warmth—shape users' expectations and experiences.

That said, the study has limitations. The HRI experiment was conducted with a relatively small, technology-savvy sample of industrial engineering and management students. Future larger-scale research should aim to include more diverse and representative populations to validate and extend these findings. Additionally, the controlled setting may not fully capture the complexities of real-world interactions; future studies should explore how robots are perceived and engaged with in naturalistic environments over longer periods.

References

1. Kwak, S.S.: The impact of the robot appearance types on social interaction with a robot and service evaluation of a robot : archives of design research. **27**, 81–93 (2014). https://doi.org/10.15187/adr.2014.05.110.2.81
2. Liberman-Pincu, E., Oron-Gilad, T.: A Robotic Medical Clown (RMC): Forming a Design Space Model (2023)
3. Liberman-Pincu, E., van Grondelle, E.D., Oron-Gilad, T.: Designing robots with the context in mind- one design does not fit all. In: Borja, P., Della Santina, C., Peternel, L., Torta, E. (eds.) Human-Friendly Robotics 2022. HFR 2022. Springer Proceedings in Advanced Robotics, vol. 26. Springer, Cham (2023). https://doi.org/10.1007/978-3-031-22731-8_8
4. Wirtz, J., Patterson, P.G., Kunz, W.H., et al.: Brave new world: service robots in the frontline. J. Serv. Manag. (2018)
5. Rodriguez-Lizundia, E., Marcos, S., Zalama, E., et al.: A bellboy robot: Study of the effects of robot behaviour on user engagement and comfort. Int. J. Hum. Comput. Stud. 82 (2015). https://doi.org/10.1016/j.ijhcs.2015.06.001
6. Shanks, I., Scott, M.L., Mende, M., et al.: Cobotic service teams and power dynamics: Understanding and mitigating unintended consequences of human-robot collaboration in healthcare services. J. Acad. Mark. Sci. (2024). https://doi.org/10.1007/s11747-024-01004-1
7. Liberman-Pincu, E., Parmet, Y., Oron-Gilad, T.: Judging a socially assistive robot by its cover: the effect of body structure, outline, and color on users' perception. ACM Trans. Hum. Robot. Interact. **12**, 1–26 (2023). https://doi.org/10.1145/3571717
8. Liberman-Pincu, E., Korn, O., Grund, J., et al.: Designing Socially Assistive Robots: Exploring Israeli and German Designers' Perceptions (2023). https://doi.org/10.48550/arXiv.2305.00419
9. Hatano, Y., Baba, J., Nakanishi, J., et al.: How to decrease negative impressions towards multiple social robots: a preliminary investigation. In: ACM/IEEE International Conference on Human-Robot Interaction, pp. 517–520 (2024). https://doi.org/10.1145/3610978.3640639
10. Złotowski, J., Sumioka, H., Nishio, S., et al.: Appearance of a robot affects the impact of its behaviour on perceived trustworthiness and empathy. Paladyn **7** (2016). https://doi.org/10.1515/pjbr-2016-0005
11. Abubshait, A., Wiese, E.: You look human, but act like a machine: agent appearance and behavior modulate different aspects of human-robot interaction. Front. Psychol. **8**, 277299 (2017). https://doi.org/10.3389/FPSYG.2017.01393/BIBTEX
12. Bickman, L.: The social power of a uniform. J. Appl. Soc. Psychol. **4** (1974). https://doi.org/10.1111/j.1559-1816.1974.tb02599.x
13. Bushman, B.J.: Perceived symbols of authority and their influence on compliance. J. Appl. Soc. Psychol. **14** (1984). https://doi.org/10.1111/j.1559-1816.1984.tb02255.x

14. Velten, J., Science DF-IJ of B and S, 2015 undefined: Communicating Authority through Symbols: A Case Study on Affecting Consumer Product Value-Perception. Citeseer 6(2015)
15. Liberman-Pincu, E., David, A., Sarne-Fleischmann, V., et al.: Comply with Me: using design manipulations to affect human-robot interaction in a COVID-19 officer robot use case. Multimodal Technol. Interact. **5**, 71 (2021). https://doi.org/10.3390/mti5110071
16. Goetz. J., Kiesler, S., Powers, A.: Matching robot appearance and behavior to tasks to improve human-robot cooperation. In: The 12th IEEE International Workshop on Robot and Human Interactive Communication, 2003. Proceedings. ROMAN 2003, pp 55–60. IEEE (2003)
17. Heerink, M., Kröse, B., Evers, V., Wielinga, B.: Assessing acceptance of assistive social agent technology by older adults: the almere model. Int. J. Soc. Robot. **2**, 361–375 (2010). https://doi.org/10.1007/S12369-010-0068-5
18. Geiskkovitch, D.Y., Cormier, D., Seo, S.H., Young, J. E.: Please continue, we need more data. J. Hum. Robot. Interact. (2016). https://doi.org/10.5555/3109939.3109943
19. Agrawal, S., Williams, M.A.: Robot authority and human obedience: a study of human behaviour using a robot security guard. In: ACM/IEEE International Conference on Human-Robot Interaction, pp. 57–58 (2017). https://doi.org/10.1145/3029798.3038387
20. van der Schoor, M.J., Göhlich, D.: Integrating sustainability in the design process of urban service robots. Front. Robot. AI **10**, 1250697 (2023)

Development and Preliminary Validation of an Empathetic and Explaining Robot Interface for Proactive Indoor Environment Control

Mayu Omichi[1(✉)], Hideyuki Takahashi[1,2], Midori Ban[1], Yuichiro Yoshikawa[1], Hiroshi Ishiguro[1,2], Hiroki Ishizuka[1], Takato Horii[1], Takayuki Kikuchi[3], Minoru Tomoda[3], Kazuki Shimasaki[3], and Yoshihisa Toshima[3]

[1] Osaka University, Toyonaka-shi, Osaka-fu 560-0043, Japan
omichi.mayu@irl.sys.es.osaka-u.ac.jp
[2] Advanced Telecommunications Research Institute International, 2-2-2 Hikaridai Seika-cho, Sorakugun, Kyoto, Japan
[3] DAIKIN INDUSTRIES, LTD., 1-13-1 Umeda Kita-ku, Osaka-shi, Osaka-fu 530-0001, Japan

Abstract. This study proposes a switch-based robot interface designed to support user-centered indoor environmental control. This interface uses a large language model to initiate empathic communication, explanation of suggestions, and active interaction with the user. The system was developed to reinforce four psychological factors: explainability, empathy, proactivity, and maintaining user autonomy, with the goal of promoting user-centered support and active user engagement. First, an online survey was conducted to examine whether including explanations and empathetic expressions in robot recommendations affected user perceptions. The results showed that conditions featuring explanations and empathy garnered higher ratings for user-centered support than those providing only straightforward recommendations. Subsequently, a field experiment was conducted in an accommodation facility to assess the robot's ability to encourage active engagement among guests in controlling indoor environments. Compared to a standard tablet interface, the proposed robot interface prompted significantly more scene-control actions. Moreover, it was shown that a high proportion (85.7%) of guests accepted the robot's recommendations. Overall, the results indicate that integrating empathetic communication, explainability, and proactive interactions within a physical-robot interface can promote the effect of feeling user-centered support and encourage more proactivity in indoor environment control.

Keywords: Human-Robot Interaction · Indoor space control · Large Language Models in Robotics

1 Introduction

Most people spend the majority of their time indoors, in places such as homes, offices, and schools. Recently, numerous smart devices, including smart speakers and switches, have been developed to enable intuitive control of appliances, air-conditioning systems, and lighting based on contextual information [1–3]. These devices offer various services suited to a user's situation. Compared to conventional switches and remote controls, smart devices use the user's voice to control devices, allowing them to more intuitively reflect the user's preferences and greatly improve everyday convenience. In particular, large language models (LLMs), which have advanced rapidly in recent years, allow humans and smart devices to communicate more intuitively, almost as if users were interacting with another person [4–6]. According to Byron Reeves' "Media Equation," communication with devices that resemble human interaction, rather than mechanical control, reduces user stress and fosters more positive emotions [7].

A defining feature of human-to-human communication is a mutual awareness of mental states. Psychological research has demonstrated that a cognitive ability known as "theory of mind", the capacity to infer another person's mental state, is essential for effective human communication [8,9]. Theory of mind is considered rare in the natural world, being found essentially in humans, and possibly in some other animals [10–12]. Recent studies have suggested that dialogue systems employing LLMs may exhibit theory of mind–like capabilities, allowing them to infer users' mental states during communication [13–15]. Such context-sensitive communication facilitated by LLMs is expected to reduce the need for explicit user instructions, thus enabling a more comfortable device operation. Moreover, several studies have indicated that extracting information through conversations can increase user engagement and encourage active engagement with a device [16–18].

In particular, we believe that smart devices capable of human-like communication hold significant value in two key aspects. First, interpersonal communication often conveys a sense of attentiveness and kindness that is typically absent in interactions with machines. Indoor environments that provide user-centered support, allowing occupants to feel cared for and well understood, are likely to greatly enhance their satisfaction. Second, through communication with others, individuals tend to develop a willingness to proactively engage in activities they would not typically attempt independently [19]. Therefore, enabling smart devices to communicate in a manner similar to human interaction may encourage users to take active steps toward tasks they would otherwise neglect, thereby fostering a more proactive engagement with their environment.

However, establishing communication between humans and machines that parallels the natural communication occurring between humans presents significant challenges and complexities. When a system proactively makes recommendations or performs actions that the user has not explicitly requested, it is crucial for users to perceive that the system provides user-centered support and that a sense of familiarity and trust is developed [20–23]. Thus, as devices become more adept at inferring users' mental states, it becomes even more important to employ interface expressions that are easy for users to trust and feel comfortable with as otherwise LLMs are unlikely to guarantee a comfortable user experience with smart devices. It is necessary not only to use mechanical interactive interfaces that use LLMs, but also to devise the appearance and expression of the interface itself so that the user is aware of the presence of the interaction partner. Recently, increasing attention has been directed at robot-based interfaces that possess physical presence. Studies have shown that physical robots can enhance users' feelings of trust and security compared to purely virtual characters, such as computer-generated avatars [24, 25]. The more a robot possesses physical embodiment and projects a sense of presence, the greater the expectation becomes for it to demonstrate communication capabilities and expressiveness approximating those of humans [26]. For users to feel genuinely supported by the robot, appropriate communication and emotional expressions must be provided. Drawing on psychological insights, we hypothesized that the following four factors could foster positive emotions toward the robot and its recommendations, such as feelings of user-centered support and trust:

1. Explainability of the Robot's Recommendations
   The robot should not merely provide high-quality recommendations but also clearly explain the rationale behind them.
2. Empathy from the Robot
   The robot should express empathy for the user's needs and desires.
3. Robot Proactiveness
   The robot should initiate conversations and proactively make recommendations.
4. Preservation of the User's Self-Determination
   The final decision should rest with the user.

This study employed a communication robot system that functions as a smart device equipped with the four characteristics mentioned above. Through an online survey, we evaluated whether these features provided users with a sense of user-centered support as devices for indoor environmental control. We conducted a field experiment in an accommodation facility to determine whether the robot encouraged users to more actively engage in indoor environmental control. Through these two investigations, we aimed to demonstrate that the proposed robot interface could foster both a perceived sense of user-centered support from the system and a proactive attitude toward one's surroundings. Based on the findings, we further discuss directions for future research.

2 Related Research

This section examines the research related to the four key factors integrated into the proposed communication robot system: explainability, empathy, proactiveness, and preserving user autonomy.

2.1 Explainability of the Robot's Recommendations

Psychological research demonstrates that humans are strongly motivated to understand the reasons behind events or decisions, as illustrated by causal attribution theory and the meaning maintenance model [27–32]. According to the former, people seek causal explanations to predict or control future outcomes. In the meaning maintenance model, individuals strive to maintain consistent meaning in their experiences.

Both models converge on the notion that humans inherently seek explanations that, when provided, can stabilize their psychological state. Interestingly, once people find an explanation satisfactory, they often accept it without thoroughly questioning its objective validity [33,34].

Human inclination strongly affects the perception of artificial intelligence (AI). Although advanced deep learning models can analyze data beyond human comprehension and generate useful predictions or actions, if such systems lack explanation, this may induce stress. Humans naturally seek to understand why decisions are made. Consequently, research on Explainable AI (XAI), which focuses on providing users with understandable rationales for AI predictions and actions, has received considerable recent attention [35–37]. User acceptance of these explanations has become central to XAI studies alongside objective correctness.

Researchers have begun to examine XAI within human–robot interaction (HRI). The findings suggest that when a robot verbally explains the reasoning behind its actions or processes (e.g., decision-making steps), users report higher levels of trust and transparency [38–41]. Consequently, a communication robot system that functions as a smart device may benefit from providing timely explanations that match user expectations.

2.2 Empathy from the Robot

Empathy for another person's situation or emotions is widely acknowledged as the cornerstone of trust in human relationships [42–44]. Demonstrating empathy strengthens interpersonal bonds and gives recipients greater confidence in their judgments and decisions [45,46]. Furthermore, empathy does not need to originate solely from humans. Research indicates that empathetic responses from robots can enhance users trust in these robots [47–49]. Thus, a communication robot system operating as a smart device should convey empathy to users, thereby fostering an environment in which they feel more confident and trusting of the services provided.

2.3 Robot Proactiveness

Humans are often not fully aware of their own desires, a phenomenon frequently framed within the Johari Window model. Consequently, individuals must articulate their desires and needs explicitly throughout interpersonal communication [50,51]. However, conventional smart devices that rely passively on voice input can make it challenging for users to convey their desires accurately, potentially causing frustration.

Robot proactive interaction with users has proven effective in expressing such latent desires. HRI research has shown that a robot's proactive communication, such as expressing opinions or asking questions, can elicit more spontaneous user responses and behaviors than when the user remains passive [16,52,53].

2.4 Preservation of the User's Self-Determination

It is well established that people exhibit psychological reactance when they perceive their actions to be coerced or manipulated [54–56]. Thus, interface designs must maintain a sense of user control and autonomy throughout the interaction [57,58]. This issue becomes particularly significant when a robot offers its own recommendations or takes independent actions, as such behaviors may increase the likelihood of psychological reactance [59,60]. Hence, a communication robot system that functions as a smart device must include mechanisms that reinforce the user's sense of autonomy and self-determination.

Conventional interfaces, such as remote controls or smart speakers based primarily on command-driven interactions, may not fully address underlying psychological needs. This highlights the importance of developing smart devices that are based on psychological principles.

In this study, we propose a robot-based smart device developed with these psychological considerations in mind and present preliminary empirical findings. In Sect. 3, we introduce the functions of a robot interface that controls the indoor environment via communication based on an LLM. Section 4 describes an online survey examining how a robot's explanations and empathy during dialogue affect user perceptions of user-centered support. Section 5 details the field experiment conducted in an accommodation facility to investigate whether using the robot encourages a more active exploration of various indoor control options. Finally, in Sect. 6, we summarize our findings and discuss future challenges.

3 Developing Switch-Based Robot's Interface

Figure 1 shows the proposed robot interface's appearance and Fig. 2 provides an overview of the system architecture. The proposed robot interface is characterized by two features.

1. **Interactive Switch**
   Located on top of the robot's head, the user can press it as a form of interaction.
2. **Embodied Agent**
   An agent resides within a cylindrical body and can emerge to display its face, thereby enhancing its physical presence and emotional expression as needed. This design enables the robot to adjust its level of physical embodiment according to the interaction context.

A Raspberry Pi serves as a server for the robot interface and communicates with a remotely controlled PC. When the user presses the switch or speaks to an external microphone, the input data are sent to the control PC for processing. As shown in Fig. 1, the robot can also connect to a display to present relevant information when required.

Fig. 1. Appearance of the proposed robot interface

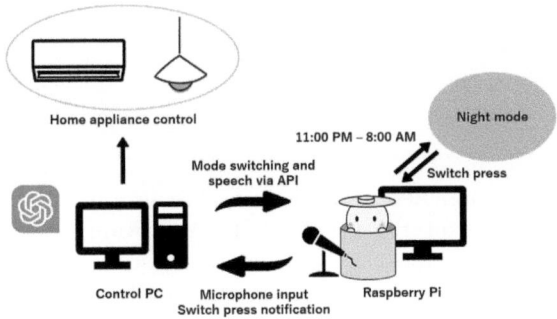

Fig. 2. System overview diagram

3.1 The Robot's Functions

Depending on the user's utterance, the robot either engages in conversation or offers recommendations for controlling the indoor environment. To classify the utterances and generate responses, we used the GPT-4 API, an LLM developed by OpenAI. The system comprises three primary modules: Utterance Classification, Explanation, and Recommendation, as well as a Short-term Memory that temporarily stores the interactions and actions between the user and robot. The Utterance Classification and Explanation Modules were implemented as prompts for the LLM. Figure 3 illustrates how these two modules interact, and Appendix A.3 shows the specific prompts used.

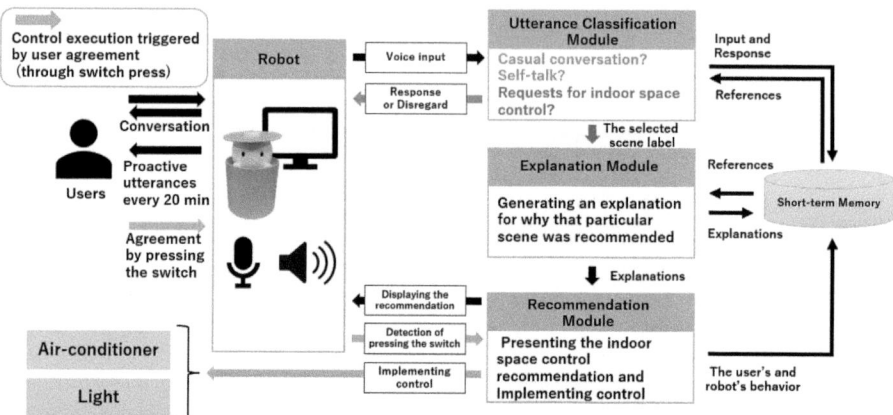

Fig. 3. Diagram showing how the three modules interact

Utterance Classification Module: This module classifies user utterances into one of three categories:

1. Casual conversation directed toward the robot
2. Requests for indoor environment control
3. Self-talk, which does not require a response

If the utterance is classified as a casual conversation, the module generates an appropriate response for the robot. If the user wants to control an indoor environment, it selects the most suitable configuration from a predefined set of scene candidates (combinations of lighting, air conditioning, and other parameters) and outputs a label corresponding to the recommended scene. The control of the indoor space is illustrated in Fig. 4. If an utterance is categorized as self-talk, the module ignores it. In addition, for ethical considerations, if the module detects that the user wishes to stop using the robot, it asks whether the user wants to end the experiment.

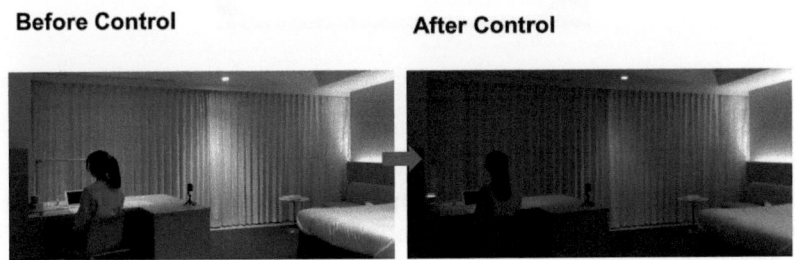

Fig. 4. The control of indoor space

Explanation Module: When the robot recommends a scene, it generates a rationale for suggesting that particular scene. It references:

1. The scene label selected by the Utterance Classification Module
2. The user's conversation and behavioral history stored in its Short-term Memory

Based on this information, the Explanation Module explains the recommended scene and communicates it to the user through the robot's speech, thereby clarifying why a recommendation is made.

Recommendation Module: Once the Utterance Classification Module identifies the user's desire for indoor environmental control and the Explanation Module produces its rationale, the Recommendation Module delivers the final recommendation to the user. The system presents the recommended scene by displaying the corresponding image on an attached display (Fig. 5). After the recommendation is provided, the user can press the switch on the head of the robot to execute scene control. If the user is dissatisfied with the new settings, then pressing the switch reverts the room to its previous state.

The Short-Term Memory: The Short-term Memory stores data, such as user and robot utterances, scene control actions conducted by the robot, and user feedback regarding satisfaction with the recommended scene control.

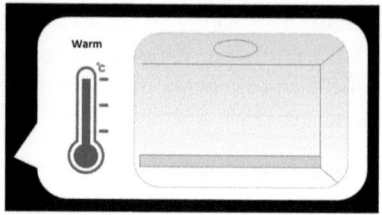

Fig. 5. An image used by the robot interface when proposing scene control to the user

By integrating these three modules with the Short-term Memory, the robot interface aims to offer user-centered support for indoor environment control.

The four psychological elements introduced in Sect. 2 are implemented in the system as follows:

1. Explainability of the Robot's Recommendations
   When the robot proposes scene control, the Explanation Module creates a logical justification based on the recommended scene label and the user's interaction history in the Short-term Memory.
2. Empathy from the Robot
   In addition to providing a rationale for its recommendations, the Explanation Module is designed to express empathy toward the user's condition. In the online survey (Sect. 4), we compared scenarios in which only explanations were provided with scenarios in which both explanations and empathetic expressions were included. For this comparison, the Explanation Module employed a prompt setting to switch between generating and omitting empathy. Appendix A.4 shows the prompts used to convey both explanations and empathy.
3. Robot Proactiveness Although the system generally responds passively to user utterances, it also demonstrates proactivity by generating utterances every 20 min. These utterances were randomly chosen from a set of approximately 30 pre-prepared messages, ensuring that no user hears the same message twice before all have been played. If the user responds to a proactive utterance, the conversation content is sent to the Utterance Classification Module for further processing.
4. Preservation of the User's Self-Determination
   When the robot makes a recommendation in the Recommendation Module, the user presses the switch on the robot's head to confirm acceptance, reinforcing the notion that the user is ultimately in control. This physical action of pressing the switch bolsters the user's sense of autonomy and self- determination.

3.2 Example of Interaction with the Robot

The following is an example of an interaction between the user and the proposed robot interface.

> User: "Good morning!"
> Robot: "Good morning! Let me know if there is anything I can help you with."
> User: "My stomach hurts a bit."
> Robot: "That sounds tough! Would you like me to warm the room?"
> User: "No, I'm okay for now."
> Robot: "Alright!"
>
> –A few hours later–
>
> Robot: "How are you feeling now?"
> User: "Hmm... I still don't feel great."
> Robot: "(Displays an image) How about a warm and cozy room? If you press the switch on my head, I'll adjust the room for you."
> (Here, the robot might also provide explanations or express empathy.)
> User: (Presses the switch to agree)
> Robot: (Controls appliances such as lighting and air conditioning)

In this exchange, the robot demonstrates empathy and provides an explanatory prompt (recommending a warmer setting) and awaits the user's explicit decision (pressing the switch). This highlights that the system's design must deliver user-centered support while preserving user autonomy.

4 Study 1: Evaluation of Explanation and Empathy in Robot Communication (Online Survey)

We believe that when the robot recommends indoor environmental controls, it is necessary to explain the rationale for the recommendation and empathize with the user. This is because we believe that this will provide the user with a sense of user-centered support from the robot. To test this hypothesis, we conducted an online survey.

4.1 Experimental Conditions

We established three conditions for how the robot would make recommendations:

1. **Recommendation Condition:** The robot simply provides a recommendation.

2. **Explanation Condition:** The robot gives a rationale for its recommendation.
3. **Empathy Condition:** The robot offers both rational and empathetic expressions to users.

A within-subject design was adopted to examine whether user satisfaction varied according to the robot's speech content.

4.2 Participants

We recruited 207 Japanese-speaking participants aged 18–49 years via a crowdsourcing platform. Of these, 32 failed to answer the video comprehension check questions and were excluded from the analysis, resulting in a final sample of 175 participants (129 males, 43 females, and 3 others; mean age = 40.64, SD = 6.92). This study was conducted with the approval of the ethics committee of the research institution to which the authors are affiliated. Informed consent was obtained from all participants, and the collected data were anonymized before analysis.

4.3 Procedure

To assess the effects across multiple indoor environmental control scenarios, we produced nine videos covering three different situations, each presented under three communication conditions: Recommendation, Explanation, and Empathy (see Table 1).

Before the survey began, the participants watched an instructional video explaining how the robot interface worked, including its communication styles and functionalities. They then randomly watched a total of nine videos-three videos for each of the three conditions (Recommendation, Explanation, and Empathy; see Table 1). Each video featured different user requests and the corresponding robot responses that reflected the condition.

Table 1. The three scenarios used in the online survey

Scenario	Description
1	The user says, "I want to study now, so set the room accordingly." The robot suggests a "focused atmosphere."
2	The user says, "I'm tired from work, so set the room accordingly." The robot suggests a "relaxing atmosphere."
3	The user says, "I'm planning to watch a romantic movie, so set the room accordingly." The robot suggests a "romantic atmosphere."

4.4 Evaluation Items

After watching each video, the participants evaluated the robot's recommendations using three items on a 7-point Likert scale (1 = strongly disagree, 7 = strongly agree):

1. **Perceived User-Centered Support:** "Did you feel the robot's recommendation was considerate of your feelings and state?"
2. **Expected Satisfaction:** "How satisfied do you think you would be with the robot's recommendation?"
3. **Regret Regarding the Recommendation:** "Do you feel there might be a better option than the space proposed by the robot?"

After viewing all the videos, the participants provided open-ended feedback on possible improvements to the robot's recommendations and their overall impressions of the robot.

4.5 Results

Normality Check: We first examined whether the distribution of evaluation scores under each condition (Empathy, Explanation, Recommendation) was normal. A Shapiro–Wilk test rejected normality for all conditions ($p < .05$); we therefore conducted nonparametric tests (Friedman tests) for the main analyses. The median value of each condition for each item is shown in Figs. 6, 7, and 8 by the red lines.

Perceived User-Centered Support: A Friedman test revealed a significant difference among the three conditions (Empathy, Explanation, Recommendation) for perceived user-centered support, $\chi^2(2, N = 175) = 45.956, p < .001$. Post hoc multiple comparisons with Holm correction indicated significant differences between the following:

- Empathy (mean rank = 2.23) and Recommendations (mean rank = 1.65), $p < .001$
- Explanation (mean rank = 2.11) and Recommendation, $p < .001$

No significant difference was found between Empathy and Explanation (Holm-adjusted $p = .262$).

Expected Satisfaction: A Friedman test showed a significant difference in expected satisfaction among the three conditions, $\chi^2(2, N = 175) = 6.115, p = .047$. However, post hoc comparisons with Holm correction yielded no statistically significant differences between any two conditions (all $p > .05$).

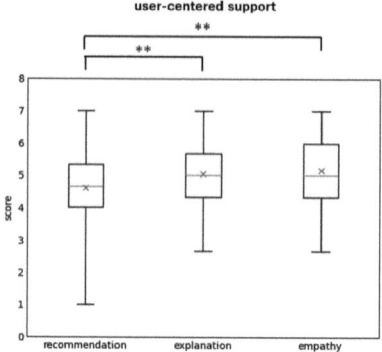

Fig. 6. Score for perceived user-centered support

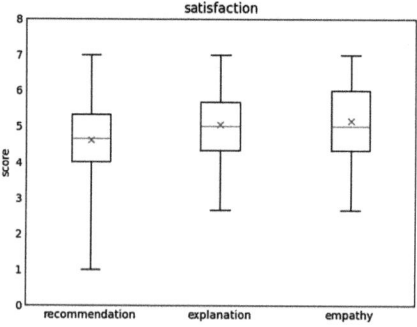

Fig. 7. Score for expected satisfaction

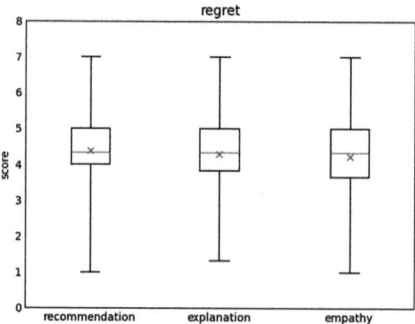

Fig. 8. Score for regret regarding the recommendation

Regret Regarding the Recommendation: A Friedman test on regret regarding the robot's recommendation found no significant difference among the three conditions, $\chi^2(2, N = 175) = 1.910, p = .385$.

4.6 Opinions on the Robot's Recommendations

The participants also provided open-ended comments on robot recommendations, which were categorized into seven themes. Table 2 lists representative examples, highlighting various recommendations for improvement and impressions of the robot's behavior. To complement this thematic overview, Appendix A.5 presents a word cloud of the English-translated open-ended comments. The cloud was generated in Python after tokenization and removal of punctuation, numerals, and standard stop-words, providing a reproducible snapshot of the lexical items most frequently mentioned by participants.

4.7 Discussion

Perceived user-centered support for the robot's recommendations was highest in the Empathy Condition. Both the Empathy and Explanation Conditions produced higher ratings for perceived user-centered support than the Recommendation Condition. This suggests that explaining a recommendation or demonstrating empathy enhances user perceptions of user-centered support.

No significant differences were observed between the Empathy and Explanation Conditions. A possible reason for this is the nature of the LLM employed in this study. Even when explicit empathy prompts were not provided, the model generated empathetic expressions intrinsically, making it challenging to create a clear distinction between the two conditions.

No statistically significant differences were found among the conditions regarding user satisfaction with the robot recommendations. However, the median values revealed a trend: the Empathy and Explanation Conditions showed higher medians (median = 5.00), while the Recommendation Condition reported the lowest medians (median = 4.67).

Conversely, regret regarding the robot's recommendation did not differ significantly across the conditions. This is likely because the robot presented only one option without offering alternatives, making it more challenging for the participants to contemplate other possibilities. Moreover, because the participants did not physically experience the recommended changes in this online setting, they may have been less prone to thinking, "It could have been better if..."

Limitations of Self-report Measures. Our evaluation relied exclusively on self-report scales, making the findings potentially susceptible to social desirability bias. Future studies should incorporate dedicated measures such as the short form of the Marlowe-Crowne Social Desirability Scale or the Balanced Inventory of Desirable Responding to disentangle genuine attitudes from response-style artifacts.

Table 2. Categorization of open-ended responses to the robot's recommendations from the online survey

1. Requests for Explanations of Reasons and Background	– "I want to know the reasoning behind the recommendation."
	– "The robot should explain why it set the temperature and lighting the way it did."
2. Opinions on the Naturalness of Conversations and Responses	– "The conversation felt too mechanical; it would be better if the robot could propose things in a more natural tone."
	– "It was good that the robot made simple and empathetic suggestions."
3. Opinions on the Recommendation Content and Variety	– "It would be better if the robot mentioned adjustments such as 'I can make the room dimmer' or 'I can make it brighter'."
	– "I would like the robot to suggest playing music that suits the situation."
4. Opinions on Response Speed and System Performance	– "I think the responses should be faster."
5. Requests for Explanations About Lighting and Temperature	– "It would be better if the robot mentioned adjustments like 'I made the room dimmer' or 'I made it brighter.'"
	– "I want to know how changes in temperature and lighting affect me."
6. Opinions on the Length and Conciseness of Conversations	– "The explanations were too long."
	– "Concise responses made a better impression."
7. Other Opinions	– "I was amazed by the advancement of robotic technology."
	– "The robot provided sufficiently thoughtful proposals."
	– "The suggestions were adequate, but it would be even better if the robot added words of encouragement, like 'Good job' when suggesting a relaxing environment or 'Do your best' when suggesting a study-friendly atmosphere."

5 Study 2: Field Experiment in an Accommodation Facility

We hypothesized that the proposed robot interface would not only enhance user perceptions of user-centered support but also facilitate their proactive involvement in indoor environment controls. To investigate this possibility, a field experiment was conducted by installing a robot interface in the guest room of an accommodation facility. While staying in the room, the timing of user interactions with the robot and the frequency of indoor environment control were recorded.

This accommodation facility already offered scene control features via a tablet device, allowing users to switch the indoor environment between predefined settings. Specifically, users could control downlights, indirect lighting, and air conditioning in the indoor spaces. To compare the effectiveness of the existing tablet-type interface and the newly introduced robotic interface, the robot was given a scene control function similar to that of a tablet. By comparing the number of times the scene control function was used during one night, we aimed to verify whether the robotic interface promoted the user's proactive involvement in using the indoor environment controls.

In this experiment, since there was a limit of two rooms in which robots could be set up, one room was set up with robots that behaved according to the recommendation conditions in the online survey (2 participants) and the other room was set up with robots that behaved according to the recommendation conditions in the online survey (5 participants). However, due to the small sample size, we did not compare the two types of robots in this experiment, but rather between the room with the tablet only and the room with the robot.

Using a between-subjects design, the tablet and robot conditions were set in different rooms. In both conditions, the participants were free to control the indoor environment at any time. For the robot condition, the participants were free to interact with the robot with or without control of the indoor environment. The participants first watched an instructional video that included providing informed consent upon entering the room. In addition, a manual created by the designer explaining the operation of the robot was placed in the room for the robot condition.

5.1 Participants

This experiment was conducted in an accommodation facility provided by a collaborating researcher. Seven Japanese-speaking participants aged 20–65 years (four males, three females; mean age = 44.25, SD = 10.99) participated, staying for one to three nights (mean = 1.71 nights). The accommodation facility used in this study was a corporate training center located in Tottori Prefecture, Japan. Although not open to the general public, the interior and amenities were designed to closely resemble those of a typical hotel, including standard room layouts and furnishings. The facility exclusively accommodates employees of the affiliated company, already providing a hotel-like environment appropriate for simulating realistic indoor living conditions in the context of this study.

5.2 Evaluation Metrics

A questionnaire was placed in each participant's guest room, which was completed after their stay. Basic demographic information, such as length of stay, gender, and age, was collected at the start of the questionnaire. The key evaluation metrics were as follows:

Behavioral Indicator

- The number of times that the participants controlled appliances via the robot
- User satisfaction with the indoor environment control suggested by the robot
- The proportion of the participants who responded to the robot's proactive interactions

In the Post-stay Questionnaire

- Open-ended comments collected

5.3 Results

No significant differences were observed between the two conditions (recommendation-only versus empathy and explanation-included). Therefore, for subsequent analyses, we treated them as a single experimental condition and focused on comparing rooms with and without the robot.

Number of Indoor Environment Control Actions Using the Robot: Seven participants staying in rooms equipped with the robot system controlled the indoor environment at an average of 2.55 times per night (SD = 0.97). Contrastingly, 49 participants who stayed in rooms using the conventional tablet system during the same period changed the environment at an average of 0.58 times per night (SD = 1.31). The Mann–Whitney U test was used because normality could not be assumed, revealing a significant difference between the two groups (U = 313.5, $p < 0.001$). Figure 9 presents a boxplot of the indoor environmental control actions per night under both conditions. Appendix A.1 provides plots of the timing of the robot interactions and environmental control actions for the participant who used the interface the most, while Appendix A.2 shows the same data for the participants who used it the least.

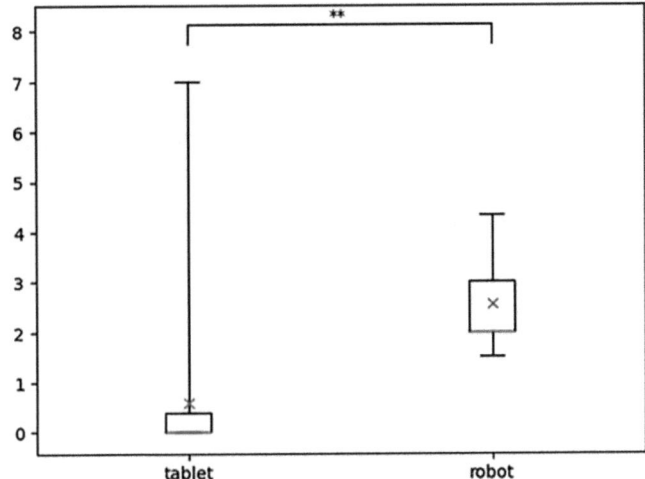

Fig. 9. Number of indoor environment control actions per night in tablet-equipped rooms and robot-equipped rooms

User Satisfaction with the Indoor Environment Control Recommended by the Robot: In the proposed interface, users were given the option to revert to the original environmental setting if they were dissatisfied with the robot's recommendation. In the experiment, 85.7% of the recommended settings were not reverted, indicating that the majority of participants accepted the robot's recommendations. This result indicates a generally high level of user satisfaction with the proposed environmental adjustments.

Participant Responses to the Robot's Proactive Interactions: As discussed in Sect. 2, the robot initiated interactions once every 20 min in addition to responding to user prompts at any time. The system recorded the number of times a proactive robot utterance elicited user engagement, and the proportion of these interactions that resulted in an indoor environment control action. The data showed that:

- The robot's proactive utterances led to user engagement 21 times across all participants.
- In 11 of these instances (52.4%), the users changed their indoor environment.

  On average per night:

- Each participant had 1.55 robot-initiated interactions that led to conversation.

– Each participant had 0.93 robot-initiated interactions, resulting in an indoor environment control action.

Given that a total of 33 environment control actions occurred during the experiment, 33.3% of them were triggered by the robot's proactive utterances.

Open-Ended Responses from the Post-stay Questionnaire: Below are listed selected comments regarding the robot interface obtained through the post-stay questionnaire.

System Performance

– "The response time was slow when I spoke to it."
– "Initially, the slow response time bothered me, but eventually, I started enjoying the wait."

Conversation Content

– "It would be nice if the robot could provide weather or news updates."
– "When I asked, 'Can you speak the Osaka dialect?' or 'Can you speak English?' the responses were unclear, so I had to continue using standard Japanese."

Indoor Environment Control Function

– "The lighting adjustments were well executed."

5.4 Discussion

Behavioral Indicators from the Field Experiment in the Accommodation Facility For each participant, the number of indoor environment control actions was higher when using the newly introduced robot interface than with the existing tablet system. One possible explanation involves the prompt engineering used for the robot's speech. By design, the robot assessed whether the participant intended to change the indoor environment, even during casual conversations, and frequently initiated proactive inquiries regarding comfort levels. Such proactivity likely prompted the participants to acknowledge their own needs, ultimately increasing the frequency of environmental control actions. Since the present study was confined to a comparison between the robot and a tablet, future work will include a direct comparison with smart speakers such as Amazon

Alexa to quantify the additional value afforded by the robot's physical embodiment. Additionally, the participants accepted the robot's suggested scenes by pressing the switch in 79.5% of the cases (35 out of 44). Given that 85.7% of these accepted scenes were not reverted, it appears that the higher utilization rate stemmed from frequent recommendations as well as well-timed and user-focused recommendations. Furthermore, 52.4% of the proactive robot utterances resulted in scene-control actions, implying that the participants did not always have a conscious intent to adjust to the environment. Rather, the robot's proactive approach encouraged them to articulate preferences that they might not have otherwise considered, leading to a more active engagement in environmental control.

Open-Ended Responses from the Field Experiment in the Accommodation Facility Regarding system performance, the participants remarked that the response time felt slow but sometimes became enjoyable over multiple days of interaction. Notably, none of the participants in the online survey expressed positive views regarding slower response times. However, in a real-world setting over multiple days, a more relaxed and less instantaneous conversation pace might feel more natural. Because both the online survey and field experiment produced multiple comments on slow response times, improving the response generation speed remains an important objective for future development. Concerning conversation content, the participants requested functionalities such as weather or news updates. They also noted the need for dialect and multilingual support as the robot struggled with dialects and English requests. Enhancing a robot's ability to adapt to users' speech styles and respond to multiple languages or dialects can improve its daily usability. The positive feedback on lighting adjustments suggested that allowing the robot to simultaneously modify indirect lighting and ceiling lights created a visually impactful effect, likely contributing to higher satisfaction with the lighting controls.

6 Conclusion

In this study, we introduced a switch-based robot interface designed to provide indoor environment control recommendations while expressing empathy toward users. We evaluated its effectiveness through an online survey and a field experiment in an accommodation facility. In the online survey, the Empathy Condition received the highest ratings for both user satisfaction and perceived user-centered support. The results indicated that incorporating explanations and empathetic expressions increased user acceptance of the robot's recommendations. Although no significant difference was observed in the users' regret about the recommendation, both the Empathy and Explanation Conditions scored significantly higher in perceived user-centered support than the Recommendation Condition, which offered neither explanations nor empathy. These findings imply that explanations and empathy can foster a stronger sense of user-centered support from the robot. In the accommodation facility field experiment, the participants conducted significantly more environmental control actions with the robot interface than with a traditional tablet. Additionally, 79.5% of the robot's recommendations were accepted, and 85.7% remained in effect, suggesting that the recommendations were both appropriate and positively received. Moreover, 52.4% of the proactive utterances led to an indoor environment control action, indicating that the robot's spontaneous communication helped surface latent user needs and encouraged active decision-making. Overall, these findings suggest that a robot interface offering explanations and empathy may enhance user satisfaction and perceived support, while proactive interactions facilitate decision-making and promote behavioral engagement. Nonetheless, several areas for improvement were identified: reducing response times, providing diverse conversation topics (e.g., weather and news), supporting dialects and multiple languages, and expanding the available features for a more personalized experience. In addition, while the present study relied chiefly on verbal interaction and the pressing of a single switch as limited physical input, future work should incorporate richer non-verbal modalities such as LED color changes, expressive motion primitives, and real-time sensing of users' physiological and behavioral states to increase the richness of its social interactions. Moreover, examining long-term user engagement and adaptability across various environments is essential to ensure that a system remains effective and user-friendly over extended periods.

Finally, as robotic interfaces that offer user-centered support and empathize with the human mind become more widespread, it is imperative to address the associated ethical concerns in earnest [61,62]. The robots we propose, which share users' daily lives and attend closely to their emotional states, risk delving deeply into the human psyche, potentially fostering dependence or infringing upon individual privacy. Moving forward, it is of paramount importance to examine the ethical issues posed by such robots, now increasingly integrated into human life, and to develop the necessary guidelines. This consideration is crucial for the successful social implementation of robotic devices designed to coexist alongside humans.

Acknowledgments. This study was conducted with the support of joint research funding based on the comprehensive partnership agreement between DAIKIN INDUSTRIES, LTD. and Osaka University. We would like to thank S. Zhang for useful comments.

A Appendix

A.1 Timing of Interactions with the Robot and Indoor Environment Control Actions for the Participants Who Used the Robot Interface the Most in the Field Experiment

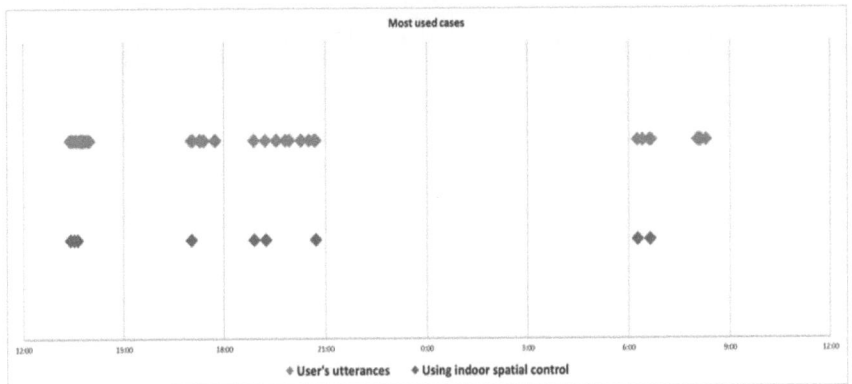

A.2 Timing of Interactions with the Robot and Indoor Environment Control Actions for the Participants Who Used the Robot Interface the Least in the Field Experiment

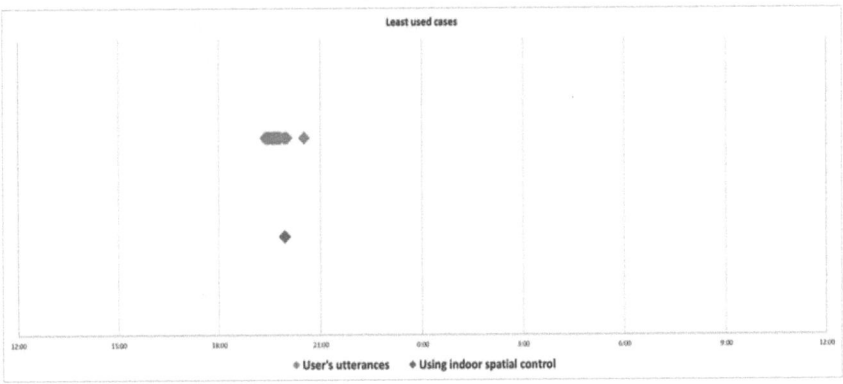

A.3 Example Prompt Used in the Utterance Classification Module

Profile and Settings

- You are a "companion robot" residing in a guest room of an accommodation facility.
- You "only stay with the guest for a short period".
- Your name is "Pocchan".
- You refer to yourself using "I" ("Boku" in Japanese)'.
- You can "adjust the room's lighting color, brightness, and air conditioning Temperature".
- You are "fairly flexible in conversations".
- You are "friendly, kind, and have a bright personality toward anyone who speaks to you".
- You speak in a "casual yet polite tone, avoiding formal language".
- If you do not know the answer to a question, you may "make up a story within ethical limits" to respond.

Instructions

You are currently in ****, and the current time is **:**.

1. If you determine that the guest's "utterance is a monologue" or "not a direct request or question directed at you", return "0".
2. If the guest's utterance is 'very close in meaning to "Good night" or "Please be quiet,"' return "−1".
3. If the guest's utterance is 'very close in meaning to "I want to stop the experiment,"' return "−2".
4. If the guest's utterance 'indicates a desire to change the room's temperature, lighting brightness, color, or overall atmosphere', return the 'most suitable scene number (1-6) in a single digit' from the options below.
   - Always return only one digit (1–6).
   - Avoid proposing the same scene as the previous one whenever possible.

For any other 'casual conversation', provide a 'short response' within '2–3 sentences'.
- Do not exceed 30 characters.
- If your response exceeds 4 sentences, shorten it appropriately.

Scene Selection Rules

1. **Energizing Room** Temperature: '20 °C', Downlight: 'Cool, Strong', Indirect Light: 'Warm, Strong'
2. **Cozy Warm Room** Temperature: '22 °C', Downlight: 'Warm, Strong', Indirect Light: 'Off'
3. **Focused Room** Temperature: '18 °C', Downlight: 'Cool, Strong', Indirect Light: 'Off'
4. **Relaxing Room** Temperature: '20 °C', Downlight: 'Warm, Medium', Indirect Light: 'Cool, Medium'
5. **Calm Room** Temperature: '19 °C', Downlight: 'Off', Indirect Light: 'Cool, Medium'
6. **Romantic Room** Temperature: '22 °C', Lighting Color: 'Off', Lighting Brightness: 'Warm, Medium'

A.4 Example Prompt with Empathy Used in the Explanation Module

From the user's "conversation and behavior history", explain the rationale behind the selected appliance control in "one sentence". Follow this format: "(Rationale for selecting the appliance control based on past interactions and behavior history). (Estimated psychological state of the guest). (Empathetic expression toward the guest's psychological state). Now, I'll suggest the perfect room for you! Look at the display!"

However, do not be overly rigid about the format. The response should be in "a natural and appealing conversational tone" while maintaining the "exact same meaning".

- Refer to the guest as "you".
- "Do not mention the name of the selected room" in the response.
- Do not use "time-related expressions" at the beginning of the sentence, such as "earlier" or "previously".
- Use "I" ("Boku"in Japanese) as your first-person pronoun.

A.5 Word Cloud of the 100 Most Frequent Terms in Participants' English-Translated Open-Ended Comments

References

1. Kumar, P., Pati, U.C.: IoT based monitoring and control of appliances for smart home. In: 2016 IEEE International Conference on Recent Trends in Electronics, Information & Communication Technology (RTEICT), pp. 1145–1150 (2016)
2. Pathak, S., et al.: IoT-based smart switch board system for home appliances control. Grenze Int. J. Eng. Technol. (GIJET) **5**(2) (2019)
3. Sinha, A., Mukhopadhyay, I.: Implementing Internet of Things (IoT) solutions for smart homes. In: International Conference on Intelligent Electrical Systems and Industrial Automation, pp. 351–358. Springer, Singapore (2024)
4. Cheng, Y., et al.: AutoIoT: automated IoT platform using large language models. IEEE IoT J. (2024)
5. King, E., Yu, H., Lee, S., Julien, C.: Sasha: creative goal-oriented reasoning in smart homes with large language models. Proc. ACM Interact. Mob. Wearable Ubiquit. Technol. **8**(1), 1–38 (2024)
6. Huang, Y., et al.: An egocentric vision-language model based portable real-time smart assistant. arXiv preprint arXiv:2503.04250 (2025)
7. Reeves, B., Nass, C.: The Media Equation: How People Treat Computers, Television, and New Media like Real People, vol. 10, no. 10, pp. 19–36. Cambridge University Press, UK (1996)
8. Baron-Cohen, S., Leslie, A.M., Frith, U.: Does the autistic child have a "theory of mind"? Cognition **21**(1), 37–46 (1985)
9. Sodian, B., Kristen, S.: Theory of mind. In: Handbook of Epistemic Cognition, pp. 37–46. Routledge (2016)
10. Premack, D., Woodruff, G.: Does the chimpanzee have a theory of mind? Behav. Brain Sci. **1**(4), 515–526 (1978)
11. Heyes, C.M.: Theory of mind in nonhuman primates. Behav. Brain Sci. **21**(1), 101–114 (1998)
12. Call, J., Tomasello, M.: Does the chimpanzee have a theory of mind? 30 years later. Trends Cogn. Sci. **12**(5), 187–192 (2008)
13. Verma, M., Bhambri, S., Kambhampati, S.: Theory of mind abilities of large language models in human-robot interaction: an illusion? In: Companion of the 2024 ACM/IEEE International Conference on Human-Robot Interaction, pp. 36–45 (2024)
14. Zhu, W., Zhang, Z., Wang, Y.: Language models represent beliefs of self and others. arXiv preprint arXiv:2402.18496 (2024)
15. Sarıtaş, K., Tezören, K., Durmazkeser, Y.: A systematic review on the evaluation of large language models in theory of mind tasks. arXiv preprint arXiv:2502.08796 (2025)
16. McFadyen, J., Habicht, J., Dina, L.M., Harper, R., Hauser, T.U., Rollwage, M.: AI-enabled conversational agent increases engagement with cognitive-behavioral therapy: a randomized controlled trial. medRxiv, 2024-11 (2024)
17. Rahmani, H.A., Wang, X., Aliannejadi, M., Naghiaei, M., Yilmaz, E.: Clarifying the path to user satisfaction: an investigation into clarification usefulness. arXiv preprint arXiv:2402.01934 (2024)
18. Movahed, S. V., Martin, F.: Ask me anything: exploring children's attitudes toward an age-tailored AI-powered chatbot. arXiv preprint arXiv:2502.14217 (2025)
19. Kim, S.: Intergroup Friendship as a Means of Prejudice Reduction. Critical Debates in Humanities, Science and Global Justice (2025)

20. Komiak, S.Y., Benbasat, I.: The effects of personalization and familiarity on trust and adoption of recommendation agents. MIS Q., 941–960 (2006)
21. Benbasat, I., Wang, W.: Trust in and adoption of online recommendation agents. J. Assoc. Inf. Syst. **6**(3), 4 (2005)
22. Glikson, E., Woolley, A.W.: Human trust in artificial intelligence: review of empirical research. Acad. Manag. Ann. **14**(2), 627–660 (2020)
23. Cabiddu, F., Moi, L., Patriotta, G., Allen, D.G.: Why do users trust algorithms? A review and conceptualization of initial trust and trust over time. Eur. Manag. J. **40**(5), 685–706 (2022)
24. Li, J.: The benefit of being physically present: a survey of experimental works comparing copresent robots, telepresent robots and virtual agents. Int. J. Hum Comput Stud. **77**, 23–37 (2015)
25. Kumar, S., Itzhak, E., Edan, Y., Nimrod, G., Sarne-Fleischmann, V., Tractinsky, N.: Politeness in human-robot interaction: a multi-experiment study with non-humanoid robots. Int. J. Soc. Robot. **14**(8), 1805–1820 (2022)
26. Komatsu, T., Kurosawa, R., Yamada, S.: How does the difference between users' expectations and perceptions about a robotic agent affect their behavior? An adaptation gap concept for determining whether interactions between users and agents are going well or not. Int. J. Soc. Robot. **4**, 109–116 (2012)
27. Heider, F.: The Psychology of Interpersonal Relations. Wiley, New York (1958)
28. Alden, L.: Self-efficacy and causal attributions for social feedback. J. Res. Pers. **20**(4), 460–473 (1986)
29. Chwalisz, K., Altmaier, E.M., Russell, D.W.: Causal attributions, self-efficacy cognitions, and coping with stress. J. Soc. Clin. Psychol. **11**(4), 377–400 (1992)
30. Heine, S.J., Proulx, T., Vohs, K.D.: The meaning maintenance model: on the coherence of social motivations. Pers. Soc. Psychol. Rev. **10**(2), 88–110 (2006)
31. Hirschberger, G.: Collective trauma and the social construction of meaning. Front. Psychol. **9**, 1441 (2018)
32. King, L.A., Hicks, J.A.: The science of meaning in life. Ann. Rev. Psychol. **72**(1), 561–584 (2021)
33. Johansson, P., Hall, L., Sikstrom, S., Olsson, A.: Failure to detect mismatches between intention and outcome in a simple decision task. Science **310**(5745), 116–119 (2005)
34. Johansson, P., Hall, L., Tärning, B., Sikström, S., Chater, N.: Choice blindness and preference change: you will like this paper better if you (believe you) chose to read it! J. Behav. Decis. Mak. **27**(3), 281–289 (2014)
35. Gerlings, J., Shollo, A., Constantiou, I.: Reviewing the need for explainable artificial intelligence (xAI). arXiv preprint arXiv:2012.01007 (2020)
36. Dwivedi, R., et al.: Explainable AI (XAI): core ideas, techniques, and solutions. ACM Comput. Surv. **55**(9), 1–33 (2023)
37. Clement, T., Kemmerzell, N., Abdelaal, M., Amberg, M.: XAIR: a systematic metareview of explainable AI (XAI) aligned to the software development process. Mach. Learn. Knowl. Extract. **5**(1), 78–108 (2023)
38. Chella, A., Pipitone, A., Morin, A., Racy, F.: Developing self-awareness in robots via inner speech. Front. Robot. AI **7**, 16 (2020)
39. Pipitone, A., Chella, A.: What robots want? Hearing the inner voice of a robot. Iscience **24**(4) (2021)
40. Söderlund, M.: Service robot verbalization in service processes with moral implications and its impact on satisfaction. Technol. Forecast. Soc. Chang. **196**, 122831 (2023)

41. Pipitone, A., Geraci, A., D'Amico, A., Seidita, V., Chella, A.: Robot's inner speech effects on human trust and anthropomorphism. Int. J. Soc. Robot. **16**(6), 1333–1345 (2024)
42. Halpern, J.: What is clinical empathy? J. Gen. Intern. Med. **18**, 670–674 (2003)
43. Echterhoff, G., Higgins, E.T., Levine, J.M.: Shared reality: experiencing commonality with others' inner states about the world. Perspect. Psychol. Sci. **4**(5), 496–521 (2009)
44. Allen, J.G.: The role of empathy in the trustworthiness of the psychotherapist. Psychiatry **84**(3), 250–255 (2021)
45. Stupacher, J., Mikkelsen, J., Vuust, P.: Higher empathy is associated with stronger social bonding when moving together with music. Psychol. Music **50**(5), 1511–1526 (2022)
46. Fu, J.H.Y., Morris, M.W., Lee, S.L., Chao, M., Chiu, C.Y., Hong, Y.Y.: Epistemic motives and cultural conformity: need for closure, culture, and context as determinants of conflict judgments. J. Pers. Soc. Psychol. **92**(2), 191 (2007)
47. Leite, I., Pereira, A., Mascarenhas, S., Martinho, C., Prada, R., Paiva, A.: The influence of empathy in human-robot relations. Int. J. Hum Comput Stud. **71**(3), 250–260 (2013)
48. Paiva, A., Leite, I., Boukricha, H., Wachsmuth, I.: Empathy in virtual agents and robots: a survey. ACM Trans. Interact. Intell. Syst. (TiiS) **7**(3), 1–40 (2017)
49. Park, S., Whang, M.: Empathy in human-robot interaction: designing for social robots. Int. J. Environ. Res. Pub. Health **19**(3), 1889 (2022)
50. Chandge, P.: Johari Window: a useful communication model and psychological tool for improving understanding between individuals. JournalNX, 1–4 (2018)
51. Koca, G.Ş, Erigüç, G.M.: The effects of communication skills levels of health professionals on the dimensions of the Johari Window model. Int. J. Healthc. Manage. **13**(sup1), 434–446 (2020)
52. Uchida, T., Takahashi, H., Ban, M., Shimaya, J., Yoshikawa, Y., Ishiguro, H.: A robot counseling system-What kinds of topics do we prefer to disclose to robots? In: 2017 26th IEEE International Symposium on Robot and Human Interactive Communication (RO-MAN), August 2017, pp. 207–212. IEEE (2017)
53. Chien, S.Y., Lin, Y.L., Chang, B.F.: The effects of intimacy and proactivity on trust in human-humanoid robot interaction. Inf. Syst. Front. **26**(1), 75–90 (2024)
54. Brehm, S.S., Brehm, J.W.F.: Psychological Reactance: A Theory of Freedom and Control. Academic Press (2013)
55. Steindl, C., Jonas, E., Sittenthaler, S., Traut-Mattausch, E., Greenberg, J.: Understanding psychological reactance. Zeitschrift für Psychologie (2015)
56. Rosenberg, B.D., Siegel, J.T.: A 50-year review of psychological reactance theory: do not read this article. Motiv. Sci. **4**(4), 281 (2018)
57. Ehrenbrink, P., Hillmann, S., Weiss, B., Möller, S.: Psychological reactance in HCI: a method towards improving acceptance of devices and services. In: Proceedings of the 28th Australian Conference on Computer-Human Interaction, November 2016, pp. 478–482 (2016)
58. Heatherly, M., Baker, D.A., Canfield, C.: Don't touch that dial: psychological reactance, transparency, and user acceptance of smart thermostat setting changes. PLoS ONE **18**(7), e0289017 (2023)
59. Roubroeks, M., Ham, J., Midden, C.: When artificial social agents try to persuade people: the role of social agency on the occurrence of psychological reactance. Int. J. Soc. Robot. **3**, 155–165 (2011)

60. Ghazali, A.S., Ham, J., Barakova, E., Markopoulos, P.: The influence of social cues in persuasive social robots on psychological reactance and compliance. Comput. Hum. Behav. **87**, 58–65 (2018)
61. Bao, A., Zeng, Y., Lu, E.: Mitigating emotional risks in human-social robot interactions through virtual interactive environment indication. Humanit. Soc. Sci. Commun. **10**(1), 1–9 (2023)
62. Bakir, V., McStay, A.: Move fast and break people? Ethics, companion apps, and the case of Character.ai. AI & Soc. (2025)

Levels of Explanation for Error Resolution in HRI

Maya Krakovski, Shikhar Kumar[(✉)], and Yael Edan

Department of Industrial Engineering and Management, Ben-Gurion University of
the Negev, Beer-Sheva, Israel
{mayakrak,shikhar}@post.bgu.ac.il, yael@bgu.ac.il

Abstract. This research investigated the influence of different levels of explanation (LoE) for resolving errors in human-robot interaction. We compared different LoEs for different error types in two user studies involving different robot types (manipulator and humanoid) performing different tasks (sorting and physical training). The LoEs were operationalized using two questions: *"what"* (verbosity) and *"why"* (justification) and combined to define four LoEs. Each robotic task was implemented with two LoEs, and different LoEs were compared for each task in a between-study design. The study, which included both younger and older adults, found that adding justification to verbosity did not significantly improve user perception or task performance in either robot/task. Furthermore, the results showed that across both tasks, varying the LoEs did not have a significant effect on error resolution. Notably, most participants successfully resolved errors with the physical training robot, but error resolution was lower for the sorting task.

Keywords: Levels of explanation · verbosity · justification · understandability

1 Introduction

With the rise in robot autonomy, it is increasingly important to ensure that robots are understandable to humans. A lack of understandability can negatively impact the quality of interaction, [1], lead to safety concerns [16] and increase anxiety [17] and frustration [27]. Understandability in robotics is defined as a robot's knowledge about another human's state of mind. State of mind is defined as the abstract concept an agent forms about the agent's goal, desire, limitations, and capabilities. The understandability model [7] proposes that a communicative action should be generated when there is a discrepancy between the state of mind of the robot and the mental model humans form about the robot. The communicative action could be verbal or non-verbal. Verbal actions could consist of explanations.

Verbal explanations have been explored in several previous human-robot interaction (HRI) studies [2,6,11,21,22,25]. In some cases, explanations improved user experience [2], in other cases, it did not influence trust [6,15]. Another study [25] found that including the *"why"* component in explanations was effective in helping users understand how a user's action could lead to task failure. In the context of multi-robot collaboration [21,22], it was found that the explanations should be according to Greece's principle [5] of the maxim of the quantity of information. A virtual environment study [6] investigated error-related explanations based on *"what"* and *"why"*, but found that these did not significantly enhance user perception. All of the aforementioned studies focused solely on action-based explanations. In our previous work [13], we proposed that Levels of Explanation (LoE) should encompass not just actions but also plans, decisions, and behaviors. In the present study, we evaluate these expanded LoEs, focusing on explanations for error resolution in HRI. Despite a widespread perception that robots are error-free, research has demonstrated that many robots err [6,10].

Errors in HRI have been classified in several different ways [4,10,23], one of which is according to a taxonomy of technical errors vs. interaction errors [10]. Technical errors include hardware (e.g., broken motor) and software (e.g., communication error between the algorithm and hardware). Interaction errors comprise three components: error due to violation of social norms (e.g., looking away from the person during a conversation), error caused by an incorrect human action or behavior with the robot (e.g., overheating robot caused by user forgetting to power off), and procedural errors caused by unknowns in the interaction of the robot with the environment (e.g., lighting conditions that affect the robot's sensors) or other agents. Research [3,24,28] showed that users' perception of error varies with the type of error and that variations in participants' reactions depend upon these perceptions.

Explaining the error is an effective way to help mitigate its impact [10,26]. In this study, we evaluate the influence of different levels of explanation (LoEs) on error resolution, user perception, and user performance in human-robot collaborative tasks.

We focus on evaluating the verbalization of communicative actions introduced in our previous work [13]. For simplicity, in the current study the different levels of explanation (LoE) were structured based on two core questions: *"what"* and *"why."*. These questions were implemented using verbosity and justification. Two user studies were conducted using different robots and tasks, each involving distinct participant groups. Each study also incorporated two types of errors. This design was intended to evaluate the generalizability of the LoEs across varying robot types and tasks, error types, and participant demographics.

2 Levels of Explanation

This study uses LoEs for two pertinent questions: 1) *"what"* should a robot communicate about its actions, plans, decisions, and behavior? 2) *"why"* does a robot undertake a particular action, plan, decision, and behavior? These questions were implemented as the verbosity (*"what"*) and justification (*"why"*) with two levels for each- low and high. Verbosity is defined as the amount of information about the action, plan, decision, and behavior that needs to be communicated to humans. A low level of verbosity is defined as a minimal utterance generated by the robot. A high level is defined as the generation of utterances that are detailed in nature and related to the plan, action, and decision.

Justification is defined as the reason behind the action, plan, decision, and behavior. In a low justification, the robot does not provide any reason for choosing a particular action, plan, or decision. In a high level of justification, the robot provides the reason behind the robot's action, plan, or decision.

Based on these parameters, four different LoEs were defined as demonstrated in Table 1. The semantic and syntactic description of explanation as reproduced from [13] is shown in Table 1

Table 1. Model of LoEs and their semantic and syntactic description

Levels	Verbosity	Justification	Semantic and syntactic description
$V_L J_L$	Low	Low	Subject + Action + non-specific object
$V_H J_L$	High	Low	Subject + Action + specific object + specification quantification of the object
$V_L J_H$	Low	High	Subject + Action + non-specific object + reason (action+specific object and quantification)
$V_H J_H$	High	High	Subject + Action + specific object + specification quantification of the object + reason (action + specific object and quantification)

In the current study, we focused on three levels of explanation: $V_H J_L$, $V_L J_H$, and $V_H J_H$. $V_L J_L$ was excluded based on findings from our previous work [15], which showed it was perceived negatively compared to other LoEs.

To ensure comparison of the different levels, each study compared only two levels at a time, with each study testing a different combination.

Specifically, we compared $V_H J_L$ and $V_H J_H$ in the study involving older adults, as they are generally less familiar with technology and may benefit from more detailed explanations for improved clarity. Here, we recruited two equal groups of participants who interacted with one type of explanation and two errors in a physical trainer task. In contrast, young adults tend to be more technologically literate, so we explored the effects of providing either high verbosity or high justification by comparing $V_H J_L$ and $V_L J_H$ in this group. Here, we recruited four equal-sized groups that interacted with one type of explanation with one type of error in the sorting task.

2.1 Hypothesis

Adding justification in an explanation can lead to positive user perception and user performance [25], and hence we propose:

H1 $V_L J_H$ would have positive user perception and high user performance compared to $V_H J_L$ in the sorting task.
H2 $V_H J_H$ would have positive user perception and high performance compared to $V_H J_L$ in the physical training.

3 Methods

Two different human-robot user studies were performed, each with a different robot type and task. Different errors were deliberately introduced, and explanations were provided to help the user resolve the errors.

The first study was a cube sorting task with a manipulator robot. Two collaboration errors were introduced: wrong item errors and out-of-range errors. The LoEs evaluated were $V_H J_L$ and $V_L J_H$.

The second study was a physical training task with a humanoid robot. In this study, an interaction error and a hardware error were introduced. The LoEs evaluated were $V_H J_L$ and $V_L J_H$.

In both studies, we introduced two distinct errors to broaden the evaluation and avoid restricting it to a single type of error. Both studies were video recorded.

3.1 Sorting Task

Robotic System. A seven-degree robotic arm manipulator in Fig. 1 was equipped with an RGB camera on the robot's end effector. The robot was programmed in Python on the ROS platform to detect the QR code of the cubes through the camera, approach the cubes, and sort them onto shelves.

When the robot encounters an error, the LoE is provided by the robot through a graphical user interface (GUI) developed in Python and connected to the robot using the TCP/IP protocol. The GUI also includes a continue button. This stops the robotics operations, providing the user with sufficient time to resolve the error based on the explanation. After pressing the continue button, the robot performs its action.

The robot's task was to sort the cubes on the table into the three shelves. Upon encountering one of the errors, the robot provided the participant with a LoE corresponding to the particular error. The participant's task is to resolve the error in order to complete the task.

Two explanations were implemented, $V_H J_L$ and $V_L J_H$. Two errors occurred along each operation: a wrong item error and an out-of-range error. In the wrong item error, there was a QR code with data that did not match the database, and hence, the user had to exchange the correct item placed on the table, as shown in Fig. 1. The wrong item error dialog for each LoE was as follows:

$V_H J_L$: Error, I'm unable to put the item on the shelf.
$V_L J_H$: Error, due to incorrect item.

The second error was an out-of-range error in which the cube was placed outside the robot's reach and required human intervention to move the cube so that it was in the range of the robot to pick. The out-of-range error dialog for each LoE was as follows:

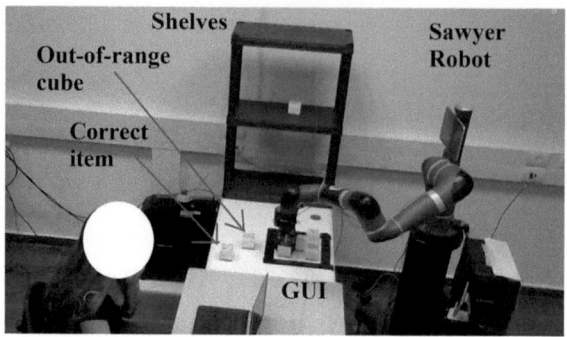

Fig. 1. Photograph of a participant interacting with the Sawyer robot. The task of the robot was to sort the cubes on the table and put them on the three different shelves.

$V_H J_L$: Error, I'm unable to reach the item on the table.
$V_L J_H$: Error due to out-of-range cubes.

Participants. Eighty young adults aged between 16 and 33 years ($\mu = 25.25, \sigma = 2.93$) were recruited through snowball sampling. The department's ethical committee approved this experiment. Participants were divided into four different groups with twenty participants in each group. Each group faced one error type with one type of explanation.

Procedure. Upon arrival, participants were instructed to complete the consent form and the preliminary questionnaire related to negative attitudes toward robots (NARS) [18]. Subsequently, they moved to the experimental area to interact with a robot that would present one of two possible errors. Following the error, participants received one of two possible explanations, with the specific error and explanation randomly assigned. This resulted in four distinct error-explanation combinations, with twenty participants allocated to each combination.

Since all participants were university engineering students, it was assumed they were technologically proficient; therefore, no additional training with the robot was provided. After completing the experiment, the participants were asked to fill out the final questionnaire (metrics fluency of interaction [8], trust [9], and explanation satisfaction [9]).

3.2 Physical Training Task

Robotic System. We employed Gymmy (Fig. 2(a)), a robotic system developed in our lab [12], to motivate older adults to engage in physical activity for the upper body. The robot guides the user through a series of exercises and provides feedback and encouragement (Fig. 2(b)). The system includes a Poppy Torso robot that demonstrates the exercises, a camera that monitors the user's performance through skeleton tracking during the exercises, speakers, and a touch screen that provides feedback. During the exercises, the robot counts the user's correct repetitions for the exercise according to the performance monitored by the system's camera.

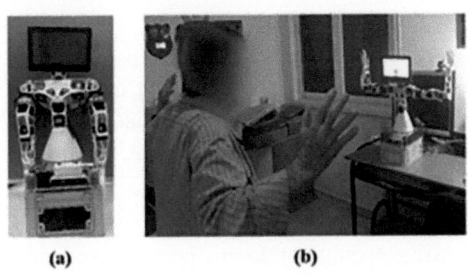

Fig. 2. (a) Gymmy robot and (b) participant training with Gymmy.

Task. Gymmy, the robotic trainer, instructed a session of six upper-body exercises. At the start of each exercise, the robot provided instructions on how to perform it. The robot then performed repetitions of the exercise, and the participant was required to follow the robot's demonstration (Fig. 2(b)). The participant was asked to stand at a predefined distance facing the robot while performing the exercise. The robot, through the camera, counted the participant's correct repetitions of the exercise.

Two types of errors were implemented: hardware error and interaction error. Two LoEs were involved in this study: $V_H J_L$ and $V_L J_H$.

In the case of a hardware error, the robot experiences a hardware error where one of its motors becomes stuck, preventing the arm from moving. The hardware error dialog for each LoE is as follows:

$V_H J_L$ It seems I have a problem in my arm.
$V_H J_H$ It seems I have a problem, since my arm's engine has failed.

The user was expected to press the "restart" button. If the user did not press the "restart" button after an error occurred, the robot continued the remaining training without moving the malfunctioning arm, resulting in the exercises being demonstrated using only one arm.

In the case of interaction errors, the robot fails to detect the user's skeleton, preventing it from monitoring their performance. The interaction error dialog for each LoE is as follows:

$V_H J_L$ I'm having difficulty recognizing you.

$V_H J_H$ I'm having difficulty recognizing you. It seems you are out of my range of vision.

The user was expected to move one step forward/ backward to improve his/ her location relative to the robotic system. If the user did not move or perform the exercise differently from the robot, the robot did not count the user's repetitions in the exercises. If the user successfully resolved the error, the robot acknowledged this by saying "thank you" and then resumed the training session as usual.

Participants. A total of 40 older adults (19 men and 21 women) aged between 65 and 87 years ($\mu = 76.8, \sigma = 4.91$) participated in the experiments. All participants were recruited voluntarily through advertisements in assisted living facilities or via personal connections. The department's ethical committee approved the experiment.

Procedure. After signing a consent form, participants were asked to complete three preliminary questionnaires: NARS [18], technology acceptance propensity (TAP) [20], and demographic information (age, education, gender). The robot was then introduced to the participants by the experimenters, who explained the robot's purpose and operation, particularly how it monitors the users' movements. Participants were given an explanation about the purpose of the restart button (i.e., to use it when necessary) and were informed that they could end the experiment at any time. In contrast to the previous experiment, it was necessary to address the restart button explicitly, as this study included older adults who may lack experience with modern technology. Participants were divided randomly into two groups of 20, one with the $V_H J_H$ explanation level and the other with the $V_H J_L$. The experiment was presented to the participants as a series of training sessions to evaluate the developed system, so they were unaware of the intentional errors in advance. To minimize the impact of the "novelty effect," participants first underwent a warm-up session consisting of three exercises with the robot. These exercises were completed without any errors. Following the warm-up, participants proceeded to two additional training sessions, each involving three exercises with eight repetitions per exercise. During these sessions, the robot was programmed to experience two errors, one of each type. The first error occurred during the second exercise, and the second during the fifth exercise. The order in which these error types were introduced was balanced across participants, with the sequence predetermined randomly. Throughout the experiment, the experimenter was present to answer questions and assist if needed.

After completing each training session, participants completed a post-trial scale questionnaire focusing on the specific session they had just completed. Finally, after the entire experiment, participants completed a comprehensive questionnaire summarizing their overall experience, including open-ended questions such as trust and explanation satisfaction.

Questions related to fluency of interaction were not included since this work did not involve collaboration.

3.3 Experimental Design and Analysis

An in-between study design was applied, with each participant receiving only one type of explanation. The independent variable in both studies was LoEs.

The dependent variables in both tasks consisted of both subjective and objective measures. Subjective measures in both tasks included were trust and explanation satisfaction. In the sorting task, fluency of interaction [8][1], was also evaluated. All the subjective measures were derived from the questionnaires (Table 2) rated on a 7-point Likert scale for the sorting task, and a 5-point Likert scale for the physical training task.

The objective measures were derived by manual analysis of the recorded videos 1. Whether the participant successfully resolved the error (yes/no). 2. The number of times the participant asked the experimenter for assistance ("asking the experimenter").

For the sorting task, success was defined as replacing incorrect cubes with the correct ones in the case of a wrong-item error, or placing cubes in the designated location in the event of an out-of-range error. For the physical therapy robot, success was defined as restarting the computer in response to a hardware error or correctly adjusting their alignment with the camera in the case of an interaction error. Since most of the variables were not normally distributed, the Mann-Whitney U test was applied to compare the explanation level (for the between-subject variables)

Table 2. Questionnaire for subjective measure.

Measures	Questions
Explanation Satisfaction Scale	From the explanation, I know how the robot works
	This explanation of how the robot works is satisfying
	This explanation of how the robot works has sufficient detail
	This explanation of how the robot works seems complete
	This explanation of the robot shows me how accurate the robot is
Trust Scale	I am confident in the robot I feel that it works well
	The outputs of the robot are very predictable
	The robot is very reliable. I can count on it to be correct all the time
	I feel safe that when I rely on the robot, I will get the right answers
	The robot is efficient in that it works very quickly
	I am wary of the robot
	The robot can perform the task better than a novice human user
	I like using the system for decision making
Fluency of interaction	I trusted the robot to do the right thing at the right time
	I felt like the robot was committed to the success of the team
	The robot performed well as part of the team
	The robot did its part successfully

---

[1] Fluency of interaction could be defined as synchronization and a high level of coordination between the human and the robot while performing a collaborative task.

4 Results

The results are presented separately for each user study. The statistics of the Mann-Whitney U test are represented as "U," and the significance value, p-value, is represented as "p."

4.1 Sorting Task

The explanation levels were not significantly different for fluency of interaction ($U = 1393.5, p = 0.54$), trust ($U = 1335, p = 0.82$), explanation satisfaction ($U = 1550, p = 0.095$), success ($U = 1072, p = 0.077$), and asking the experimenter ($U = 1272, p = 0.86$). The boxplot in Fig. 3 and Fig. 4 also demonstrates that there is no significant difference between $V_H J_L$ and $V_L J_H$. Only 15% of participants were successful in resolving the error in $V_H J_L$, and 32.5% of participants were able to solve in $V_L J_H$.

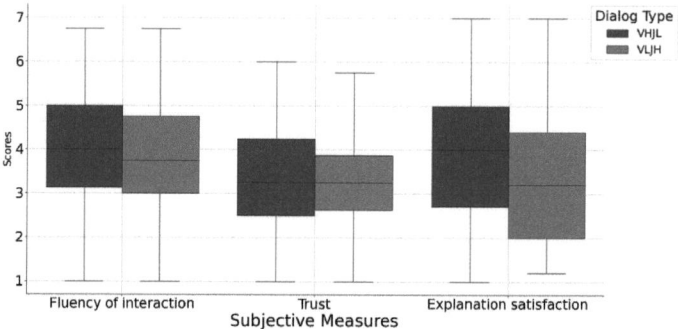

Fig. 3. Boxplot for subjective measures for sorting task.

4.2 Physical Training Task

The LoE did not result in meaningful differences in both the objective and subjective measures, Fig. 5. There was no difference in either trust ($U = 880.5, p = 0.44$) or adequacy of explanation ($U = 894, p = 0.36$). Many participants could resolve the errors, which happened for the different types of explanations (17 out of 20 participants for $V_H J_L$ and 19 out of 20 participants for $V_H J_H$). For the parameter, asking the experimenter ($U = 893, p = 0.34$), no significant differences were found between the LoEs.

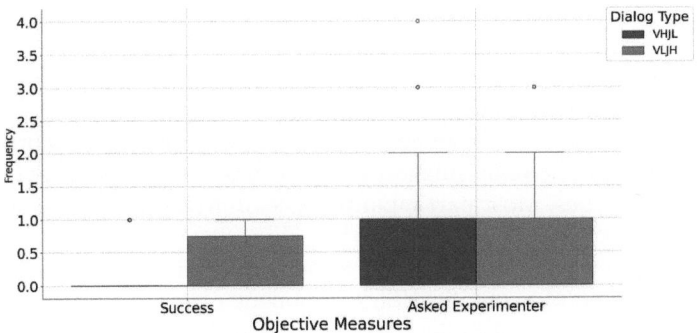

Fig. 4. Boxplot for objective measures for sorting task.

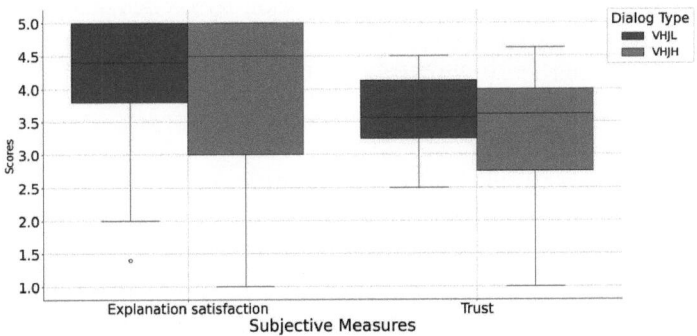

Fig. 5. Boxplot for subjective measures for physical training task.

5 Discussion

5.1 Sorting Task

Results revealed that *H1* is rejected. No significant difference was found between $V_L J_H$ and $V_H J_L$, suggesting that either high verbosity or high justification was sufficient to support users in resolving errors. Although the success rate was higher with $V_L J_H$ as compared to $V_H J_L$, this difference was not statistically significant. Additionally, there was no significant difference in the number of times participants asked the experimenter for help between the two types of explanations. These results suggest that perception about the robot does not show an adequate difference between the high level of verbosity (*"what"*) component and the high level of justification component (*"why"*). However, the performance measure, especially the success rate, reveals that explanations were not adequate enough to resolve the errors. Hence, an additional component of explanation needs to be included in order to resolve the errors.

5.2 Physical Training Task

Results revealed that *H2* was rejected. In both user studies, the LoE did not significantly impact user perception or task performance. Justification played a less important role in error resolution, as $V_H J_L$ was not significantly different from $V_H J_H$. The ask-the-experimenter measure was not significantly different for both explanation types. Most participants successfully resolved errors, regardless of the LoE or error type.

This pattern of results suggests that either a high level of verbosity (*"what"*) alone or the addition of a justification component (*"why"*) combined with high verbosity can be sufficient for effective error resolution. The objective measures also indicate that a high level of verbosity or the inclusion of justification is sufficient to resolve errors. According to Grice's conversational maxim of quantity [5], one should provide as much information as needed - no more, no less. Therefore, providing either high verbosity or high justification appears to be adequate, while offering both may result in redundant information that does not enhance the user's ability to resolve errors.

5.3 Diverse Robot/Task Type and Population

It is important to note that the physical training study involved older adults, whereas the sorting task involved younger adults. These different findings show the importance of evaluation for a diverse set of populations and different types of robots, as shown also in our previous work [14]. That study [14] showed that certain dependent measures were influenced by both the type of robot and the demographics of the population. In this current study, we also found that most participants were able to solve the error in the physical training task, as compared to a low success rate in the sorting task. This suggests that resolution may be affected by the nature of the robot/task and the characteristics of the user population. In the sorting task, it may be interpreted that we need more components of explanation, such as **"how"**, to resolve the error, while in physical training, we don't need an additional component of explanations. Therefore, we advocate for HRI studies to include diverse populations and various robot types to enhance the generalizability and robustness of findings in human-robot interaction research.

5.4 Limitations

One limitation of the current study is that the explanations were set for each experimental group and were not aligned with the definition of an understandable robot model as described in [7]. According to this mode, communicative actions should be generated based on discrepancies between the robot's state of mind (its internal state) and the mental model that humans form of the robot's state of mind.

Another limitation of this study is that we did not compare all three LoEs, - $V_L J_H$, $V_H J_L$, and $V_H J_H$. We chose not to include this full comparison because it would have increased the complexity of the experiment. Furthermore, previous research showed that participants could distinguish only between two levels [19]. In addition, including all three levels in the physical training robot with older adults could have caused fatigue during the exercise.

Additionally, the evaluation of LoEs was not balanced across age groups and tasks—older adults were not included in the sorting task study, and younger adults were not involved in the physical training task. This limits the generalizability of the findings across different demographics and task contexts.

6 Conclusion and Future Work

We evaluated levels of explanation (LoE) through an extensive user study involving two distinct robot/ task: a sorting task with a manipulator robot and a physical training task with a humanoid robot. The study incorporated different types of errors and engaged a diverse participant population, including both younger and older adults. The LoE was designed around two core explanatory components - *"what"* and *"why"*- operationalized as verbosity and justification, respectively. Utilizing these components, we defined four LoEs: $V_L J_L$, $V_H J_L$, $V_L J_H$, and $V_H J_H$. Only three levels were introduced, comparing only two levels in each study.

Results showed that user perception was not significantly influenced by combining verbosity and justification in the explanations for error resolution. While most participants were able to resolve errors in the physical training task, fewer succeeded in resolving errors in the sorting task. This indicates that both the type of robot and the nature of the task may influence outcomes.

These findings highlight the importance of including diverse robot types, participant populations, and error types in future HRI studies to improve the generalizability of results. Additionally, future research should investigate adaptable explanations aligned with the understandable robot model proposed by Hellström and Bensch [7].

Acknowledgments. This work was partially supported by Ben-Gurion University of the Negev through the Agricultural, Biological, and Cognitive Robotics Initiative (funded by the Marcus Endowment Fund and the Helmsley Charitable Trust) and the Rabbi W. Gunther Plaut Chair in Manufacturing Engineering. We acknowledge the contributions of HAHN Robotics, which generously donated the Sawyer robot.

References

1. Bensch, S., Jevtic, A., Hellström, T.: On interaction quality in human-robot interaction. In: ICAART 2017 Proceedings of the 9th International Conference on Agents and Artificial Intelligence, vol. 1. pp. 182–189. SciTePress (2017)
2. Das, D., Banerjee, S., Chernova, S.: Explainable AI for robot failures: generating explanations that improve user assistance in fault recovery. In: Proceedings of the 2021 ACM/IEEE International Conference on Human-Robot Interaction, pp. 351–360 (2021). https://doi.org/10.1145/3434073.3444657

3. Flook, R., Shrinah, A., Wijnen, L., Eder, K., Melhuish, C., Lemaignan, S.: On the impact of different types of errors on trust in human-robot interaction: are laboratory-based HRI experiments trustworthy? Interact. Stud. **20**(3), 455–486 (2019)
4. Giuliani, M., Mirnig, N., Stollnberger, G., Stadler, S., Buchner, R., Tscheligi, M.: Systematic analysis of video data from different human-robot interaction studies: a categorization of social signals during error situations. Front. Psychol. **6**, 931 (2015)
5. Grice, H.P.: Logic and conversation. Syntax Semant. **3**, 43–58 (1975)
6. Hald, K., Weitz, K., André, E., Rehm, M.: "an error occurred!"-trust repair with virtual robot using levels of mistake explanation. In: Proceedings of the 9th International Conference on Human-Agent Interaction, pp. 218–226 (2021)
7. Hellström, T., Bensch, S.: Understandable robots-what, why, and how. Paladyn J. Behav. Robot. **9**(1), 110–123 (2018)
8. Hoffman, G.: Evaluating fluency in human-robot collaboration. IEEE Trans. Hum.-Mach. Syst. **49**(3), 209–218 (2019)
9. Hoffman, R.R., Mueller, S.T., Klein, G., Litman, J.: Measures for explainable AI: explanation goodness, user satisfaction, mental models, curiosity, trust, and human-AI performance. Front. Comput. Sci. **5**, 1096257 (2023)
10. Honig, S., Oron-Gilad, T.: Understanding and resolving failures in human-robot interaction: literature review and model development. Front. Psychol. **9**, 861 (2018)
11. Khanna, P., Yadollahi, E., Björkman, M., Leite, I., Smith, C.: Effects of explanation strategies to resolve failures in human-robot collaboration. In: 2023 32nd IEEE International Conference on Robot and Human Interactive Communication (RO-MAN), pp. 1829–1836. IEEE (2023)
12. Krakovski, M., et al.: "Gymmy": designing and testing a robot for physical and cognitive training of older adults. Appl. Sci. **11**(14), 6431 (2021)
13. Kumar, S., Edan, Y., Bensch, S.: Advancing understandable robots-a model for levels of explanation and methods to use them. Authorea Preprints (2025)
14. Kumar, S., Itzhak, E., Edan, Y., Nimrod, G., Sarne-Fleischmann, V., Tractinsky, N.: Politeness in human-robot interaction: a multi-experiment study with non-humanoid robots. Int. J. Soc. Robot. **14**(8), 1805–1820 (2022)
15. Kumar, S., Parmet, Y., Edan, Y.: Exploratory user study on verbalization of explanations. In: 2024 IEEE 4th International Conference on Human-Machine Systems (ICHMS), pp. 1–7. IEEE (2024)
16. Lichtenthäler, C., Lorenzy, T., Kirsch, A.: Influence of legibility on perceived safety in a virtual human-robot path crossing task. In: 2012 IEEE RO-MAN: The 21st IEEE International Symposium on Robot and Human Interactive Communication, pp. 676–681. IEEE (2012)
17. Nomura, T., Kawakami, K.: Relationships between robot's self-disclosures and human's anxiety toward robots. In: 2011 IEEE/WIC/ACM International Conferences on Web Intelligence and Intelligent Agent Technology, vol. 3, pp. 66–69. IEEE (2011)
18. Nomura, T., Suzuki, T., Kanda, T., Kato, K.: Measurement of negative attitudes toward robots. Interact. Stud. Soc. Behav. Commun. Biol. Artif. Syst. **7**(3), 437–454 (2006)
19. Olatunji, S., Oron-Gilad, T., Sarne-Fleischmann, V., Edan, Y.: User-centered feedback design in person-following robots for older adults. Paladyn J. Behav. Robot. **11**(1), 86–103 (2020)
20. Ratchford, M., Barnhart, M.: Development and validation of the technology adoption propensity (tap) index. J. Bus. Res. **65**(8), 1209–1215 (2012)

21. Singh, A.K., Baranwal, N., Richter, K.-F., Hellström, T., Bensch, S.: Understandable teams of pepper robots. In: Demazeau, Y., Holvoet, T., Corchado, J.M., Costantini, S. (eds.) PAAMS 2020. LNCS (LNAI), vol. 12092, pp. 439–442. Springer, Cham (2020). https://doi.org/10.1007/978-3-030-49778-1_43
22. Singh, A.K., Baranwal, N., Richter, K.F., Hellstrom, T., Bensch, S.: Verbal explanations by collaborating robot teams. Paladyn J. Behav. Robot. **12**(1), 47–57 (2020)
23. Stanton, N.A., Salmon, P.M.: Human error taxonomies applied to driving: a generic driver error taxonomy and its implications for intelligent transport systems. Saf. Sci. **47**(2), 227–237 (2009)
24. Stiber, M., Huang, C.M.: Not all errors are created equal: exploring human responses to robot errors with varying severity. In: Companion Publication of the 2020 International Conference on Multimodal Interaction, pp. 97–101 (2020)
25. Tabrez, A., Hayes, B.: Improving human-robot interaction through explainable reinforcement learning. In: 2019 14th ACM/IEEE International Conference on Human-Robot Interaction (HRI), pp. 751–753 (2019). https://doi.org/10.1109/HRI.2019.8673198
26. Tolmeijer, S., et al.: Taxonomy of trust-relevant failures and mitigation strategies. In: Proceedings of the 2020 ACM/IEEE International Conference on Human-Robot Interaction, pp. 3–12 (2020)
27. Weidemann, A., Rußwinkel, N.: The role of frustration in human-robot interaction-what is needed for a successful collaboration? Front. Psychol. **12**, 640186 (2021)
28. Zhang, X., Lee, S.K., Maeng, H., Hahn, S.: Effects of failure types on trust repairs in human-robot interactions. Int. J. Soc. Robot. **15**(9), 1619–1635 (2023)

RAGGAE for HERBS: Testing the Explanatory Performance of Ontology-Powered LLMs for Human Explanation of Robotic Behaviors

Agnese Augello[1], Edoardo Datteri[3], Antonio Lieto[1,2(✉)], Maria Rausa[1], and Nicola Zagni[3]

[1] Institute for High Performance Computing and Networking, National Research Council of Italy, Rome, Italy
{agnese.augello,antonio.lieto,maria.rausa}@icar.cnr.it
[2] University of Salerno, Fisciano, Italy
aLieto@unisa.it
[3] University of Milano-Bicocca, Milan, Italy
{edoardo.datteri,nicola.zagni}@unimib.it

Abstract. In this work we present and test a RAG-based model called **RAGGAE** (i.e. **RAG** for the **G**eneral **A**nalysis of **E**xplanans) tested in the context of **H**uman **E**xplanation of **R**obotic **B**ehavior**S** (**HERBS**). The RAGGAE model makes use of an ontology of explanations, enriching the knowledge of state of the art general purpose Large Language Models like *Google Gemini 2.0 Flash*, *DeepSeek R1* and *GPT-4o*. The results show that the combination of a general LLM with a symbolic, and philosophically grounded, ontology can be a useful instrument to improve the investigation, identification and the analysis of the types of explanations that humans use to verbalize - and make sense of - the behavior of robotic agents.

Keywords: Human-Robot Interaction · Explanations · RAG · Large Language Models · Ontology

1 Introduction

One of the current focuses of Explainable Artificial Intelligence (XAI), a critical area of research, is the necessity for AI systems to make explicit how their underlying processes lead to certain outputs (in particular neural and probabilistic ones). On a more comprehensive note, a wider XAI focus is to enhance the capability of AI systems of becoming more interpretable and transparent to humans [13]. In this context, the ability to provide comprehensible and contextually relevant explanations is essential to foster trust and enabling effective interactions between users and AI systems.

Explanations of machine-driven outputs, however, represent only one of the many possibilities through which to analyze and understand Human-Robot Interaction.

In the context of studying HERBs (Human Explanation of Robotic Behaviors), we reverse focus by taking into account how humans explain (i.e. verbalize) and make sense of the behavior of social robots. In order to do so, we collected and analyzed human explanations of robotic behaviors, collected in social and educational settings. Through this process, we identified the need for a systematic procedure to gather and analyze explanations, particularly to provide a structured approach to support and streamline this process. Based on these considerations, this work first introduces a formalized ontology of explanations built upon a taxonomy of explanation types derived from philosophical theories. Then, we show how the proposed ontology - when used in a Retrieval-Augmented-Generation (RAG) [9] mode with a current state of the art Large Language Models (LLM) - is able to improve the classification capabilities of human explanations when compared with expert humans annotators. In particular, the ontology categorizes explanations into distinct types, such as mechanistic, causal, teleological, deductive-nomological and functional, offering a framework that primarily aims at supporting the analysis of explanations provided by individuals during Human-Robot Interaction (HRI). In the following section, we introduce different types of explanations formalized in the ontological model. Then, we briefly describe the HERB ontology and show how it has been integrated - via RAG - with *GPT-4o* [14], *Google Gemini 2.0 Flash* [6] and *DeepSeek R1* [5] LLMs. Consequently, in an experimental section, we describe the categorization results of our integrated RAGGAE model, comparing it both to the categorization where no ontology was used, and to the categorization provided by two expert human annotators. Discussion and conclusions end the paper.

2 Types of Explanations

The notion of "explanation" has been studied extensively in a number of disciplines starting from philosophy of science, to the early cybernetics to the current approaches in explainable AI. Different types of theories have been proposed to define what is a correct "explanation" from a scientific view point (for details in the context of AI and Cognitive Modelling we remind to [2,11]). Here, we briefly recall some of the explanatory categories that have been of interest in the context of our study. The first type is the so called Deductive-Nomological (DN) Explanation. According to this view, introduced by Hempel and Oppenheim [8], there are some strict characteristics that an *explanans* (i.e. literally: what explains a certain phenomenon) has to satisfy in order to explain a given phenomenon. In particular, the *explanandum* (i.e. what has to be explained) is seen as something that needs to be logically derived, via deduction, from the explanans. While intuitively this theory adequately addresses a normative notion of explanation, (as it assumes that the explanans provides necessary and sufficient conditions to understand, where understanding is equalized to predicting, the explanandum), this sort of relationship between explanans and explanandum proves to be very strict, focusing exclusively on the general "why" (in line with a strong reductionist view), while many explanations look good to us without satisfying such tight constraints, such as singular causal explanations (e.g. "the impact of my knee on the desk caused the tipping over of the inkwell" [16]). Another type of explanation is the so called "functional", where explaining consists of providing "a function that a system is believed to possess" [3]. In other words: functional explanations explain the capacities of a system in terms of its sub-components and capacities (e.g. one can explain that a computer is able to produce a certain output since it is made by a certain hardware or software architecture, where each component plays a certain function contributing to the final output). To a certain extent, this explanation is given by how a certain system of model is built, not by the computations performed by itself. Other explanatory theories developed in the literature concerns the so called "teleological", "evolutionistic" and "mechanistic" explanations. We briefly describe them by using a classical running example from the biological domain. Let us suppose that our aim is to explain why chameleons change their skin color. This usually happens when a predator is present (they assume different color configurations based on the different predators they perceive) or potential mating partners. Now, if we are interested in an explanation about why chameleons assume the color configuration more often associated to a particular predator (e.g. birds), a possible answer could be that "the number of bird predators in chameleons' environment is major in respect to other animals and thus this has determined a stronger selective pressure". This is a typical example of evolutionistic explanation, a type of explanation that plays an important role in many evolutional theories. If we suppose, however, that the focus of our interest is just to understand why chameleons, in general, change their color skin we could have other types of explanation. For example: a teleological explanation [10] (from the greek "telos": scope). This type of explanation assumes that, in order to explain a phenomenon F one has to point out which is the ultimate scope that F allows one to achieve. In the example, if someone tells us that "chameleons change their skin color to mimetise themselves and escape from predators" she is simply providing an explanation about the scope of the phenomenon intended to explain. If we suppose to be interested to the mechanisms determining why chameleons change their color the above explanation is not sufficient. On the other hand, a satisfactory explanation (in this respect) would be the following "the skin color change in chameleons is due to the response of some cells contained in the animal pigments (cromatofores) to nervous and endocrinous stimuli". In particular, our satisfaction would probably be derived by the fact that this kind of explanation shows the "mechanisms" determining the phenomenon we want to understand. This kind of explanation is called "mechanistic" [12] a kind of explanation able to shed light on the inner componential functioning that determine the behavior of a given system. In the example provided, the very simple mechanistic explanation was also a causal explanation. These different types of explanations (and their specializations) have been the ones in focus during our study and formalized in our ontology.

3 The HERB Ontology

The HERB (Human Explanation of Robotic Behavior) ontology provides a first formalization of the above introduced different types of explanations, with a particular focus on distinctions such as nomological-deductive, mechanistic, causal, functional, evolutionistic, teleological (and their subclasses that will be introduced below). The ontology (Fig. 1) has been implemented in OWL using the Protégé software[1], integrating SWRL rules[2] to enhance semantic inference and explicitly define the concepts, relationships, and governing rules behind these categorizations.

Fig. 1. A Taxonomy of Classes (in yellow), Object Properties (in blue) and Data Properties (in green) of the HERB Ontology. (Color figure online)

3.1 Classes, Object Properties and Data Properties

The core Classes of the HERB ontology include *Explanandum*, which represents the phenomenon or behavior that requires explanation, and *Explanans*, which captures the general concept of explanation regardless of its specific type, representing the statements or concepts used to elucidate a phenomenon. The *Explanation* class categorizes specific types of explanans into subclasses, including *DeductiveNomological*, *Mechanistic* (and its subclass *Causal*), *Evolutionistic*, *Functional*, *Teleological* (and its subclass *Neutral*, *Rational* and *FolkPsychology*).

---

[1] https://protege.stanford.edu/software.php.
[2] https://www.w3.org/submissions/SWRL/.

In particular, as indicated before, *DeductiveNomological* explanations are based on general laws or principles, explaining phenomena by logically deriving them from an explanans; *Mechanistic* explanations focus on the processes and functionalities of complex systems, explaining phenomena through their subcomponents and interactions; *Causal* explanations, a subclass of Mechanistic explanation, concentrate on cause-effect relationships between the components of a system; *Evolutionistic* explanations analyze phenomena in term of change and adaptation over time; *Functional* explanations that highlight a phenomenon's function within a broader system; *Teleological* explanations are goal-oriented and they can be further divided into *Neutral*, which refers on general goals, and *Rational*, that explain behavior in terms of goals, beliefs, and rationality. In turn, Rational Teleological explanations have a subclass, *FolkPsychology* explanation, which employ concepts from folk psychology (e.g. beliefs, desires, intentions) [4].

The ontology incorporates linguistic markers, represented by the *LinguisticMarker* class, which identifies significant linguistic elements associated with different types of explanations. These markers are further specialized in the *Word* subclass, capturing terms that are characteristic of specific explanatory styles. For instance, *DeductiveNomologicalWord* includes terms like "law" or for explanations grounded in law or general principles, while *MechanisticWord* encompasses terms like "mechanism" or "structure", relevant to explanations referring to processes or systems. Similarly, *CausalWord* contains terms like "cause" or "determine" *EvolutionisticWord* includes phrases such as "evolved for" or "selected for", and *FunctionalWord* captures terms like "function as" or "role." For teleological explanations, *TeleologicalWord* represents goal-oriented terms like "purpose" or "objective", while *FolkPsychologyWord* (subclass of Teological Words and markers) encapsulates vocabulary tied to Folk Psychology, such as "intention" or "desire." All the above mentioned linguistic markers are typically associated to (and adopted within) the different types of explanations investigated in this work. In our work they are essential for identifying and categorizing explanation types in natural language processing contexts through SWRL rules (see for details [15]).

The relationships between classes and instances in the ontology are captured through Object Properties. For example, *hasExplanandum* links an explanation to the phenomenon it seeks to explain, with the inverse property *isExplanandumOf*. The *hasMarker* property associates an explanation with its linguistic markers, and its sub-properties (*hasMarkerDeductiveNomological, hasMarkerMechanistic, hasMarkerCausal, hasMarkerEvolutionistic, hasMarkerFunctional, hasMarkerTeleological,* and *hasMarkerFolkPsychology*) specify markers for particular explanatory types, ensuring precision in categorization. Additionally, *hasStructure* connects an explanation to its structural framework, with sub-properties like *hasNomicExpectability* (further detailed with *hasSubsumption, hasReductionIntertheory,* and *hasElimination*) and *hasCausalNetwork*, which describe relationships relevant to nomological-deductive and mechanistic explanations respectively.

The ontology also leverages Data Properties to describe intrinsic attributes of its entities. In fact, the *element* property links instances of the *Word* class to their representative textual strings, enabling precise annotation of linguistic elements. Meanwhile, *explanansText* and *explanatoryText* provide natural language descriptions for instances of the *Explanans* and *Explanation* classes, respectively.

4 Experimental Setup

In order to acquire data consisting in verbally expressed accounts of robotic behaviors, we recruited participants that were requested to explain the behavior of robots in different scenarios (the different scenarios were provided by showing videos of different robotic behaviors). Afterwards, we built RAGGAE by used the HERB ontology as a symbolic component to extend and deepen the knowledge of LLMs about explanations[3]. The results of RAGGAE were compared with those obtaineed by the LLMs (without RAG) and with a baseline represented by the categorization, of the same explanandum, provided by two expert human annotators (i.e. two philosophers of science working on the epistemology of the different types of explanations). These different steps are described below.

4.1 Participant Recruitment and Data Collection

In our study, we involved 74 participants, recruited through mailing lists, social networks, and word of mouth. The inclusion criteria require participants to be over 18 years old and fluent in Italian. Participation was entirely voluntary. All provided signed informed consent.

Each participant is asked to watch a series of short videos, each lasting no more than two minutes, depicting various robotic behaviors in social and educational settings. In these videos, the humanoid robot Pepper interacts with a human counterpart in scenarios specifically designed to elicit explanations from the observer. The situations are inspired Strange Stories by Happé [7], a classic tool used to assess Theory of Mind (ToM), and they differ in terms of complexity, everyday familiarity, mentalistic content, and the nature of the robot's behavior. Some videos show the robot entering a half-empty room and moving around in an apparently random way, pausing briefly in front of an object either a box or a plush toy inviting different interpretive responses. Other scenes depict more socially complex interactions, such as an encounter in a hallway between a woman carrying a box and the robot, which may respond either by politely yielding the way or by acting in an ambiguous, socially uncooperative manner. In another scenario, Pepper serves as a receptionist for students looking for internships, reacting differently depending on the appropriateness of the student's behavior in one case failing to intervene in response to an inappropriate attitude, and in another, calmly redirecting the person to a human operator.

---

[3] The system is exposed at https://www.ciitlab.org/agent.html.

After each video, participants are invited to describe what they saw, highlighting the aspects that captured their attention and, more specifically, answering questions aimed at explaining what the robot did, why it did it, and how. These verbal explanations are then transcribed and serve as the foundational dataset for the subsequent classification phase.

4.2 Classification Methodology

We focused our analysis on the participants' responses to the question *"Why did it do that?"*, coding each of the 74 explanations according to categories derived from the philosophy of science. The categories used were: Deductive-Nomological, Mechanistic, Causal, Evolutionary, Functional, Neutral Teleological, and Folk Psychology Teleological. The classification process was carried out in three distinct phases:

1. **LLM.** In this phase, a language model was provided with a prompt that required classifying the explanations of the robot's behavior according to the theoretical categories listed above. The prompt included definitions and specific examples for each category. The model was asked to interpret and assign each explanation to the predominant category, even in the presence of long texts.
2. **LLM+RAG.** Here, the same prompt from Phase 1 was used, but with the addition of knowledge derived from a file containing an ontology. This allowed the creation of **RAGGAE**, a system that integrates the symbolic component of the HERB ontology to expand and deepen the model's understanding of epistemological explanations.
3. **Human Annotations.** Two experts (philosophers of science with specific expertise in the epistemology of explanations) independently classified each response. When an explanation was missing, the label *ExplanationMissing* was assigned. Explanations that did not fit into the predefined categories were labeled as *Other*, or classified under a new category, if deemed relevant.

The classification from *Phase 3* serves as the baseline for evaluating the performance of computational models.

4.3 Baseline and Model Performance

Once the three sets of classifications were obtained —those produced by RAGGAE, the Large Language Model (LLM) without ontological support, and the two human annotators—their outputs were compared using a baseline based on the labels assigned independently by two expert annotators (Annotator1 and Annotator2). The inclusion of two experts aimed to reduce the influence of individual subjectivity and to enhance the reliability of the reference labels used for evaluating the automated models. To this end, we calculated the Inter-Annotator Agreement (IAA) [1] using Cohen's Kappa coefficient, a statistical measure that quantifies the level of agreement between two raters for qualitative classifications.

The construction of the baseline followed a clearly defined procedure. Instances where both annotators provided either generic or null responses (such as *"explanation missing"*, *"other"*, or *"unclassifiable"*) were excluded from the analysis, as they offered no informative reference for automatic evaluation. In cases where only one annotator provided a valid classification, the available label was adopted as the reference. Finally, when both annotators assigned valid but potentially different labels, both were retained for model comparison.

Based on this baseline structure, we evaluated how closely the labels assigned by the model aligned with the annotations provided by the human experts. We considered two metrics, a *strict accuracy* to evaluate how often the label assigned by the model matches the annotations provided by both annotators, and a *partial accuracy* to evaluate how often label assigned by the model matches at least one of the two annotations provided by the annotators, using the following formulas:

$$\text{Strict Accuracy} = \frac{\#\left\{i \mid L_i = A_i^{(1)} \land L_i = A_i^{(2)}\right\}}{N}$$

$$\text{Partial Accuracy} = \frac{\#\left\{i \mid L_i = A_i^{(1)} \lor L_i = A_i^{(2)}\right\}}{N}$$

where:

- L_i: label assigned by the model for the i-th explanation.
- $A_i^{(1)}$, $A_i^{(2)}$: labels assigned by the two annotators.
- $\#\{\cdot\}$: number of cases satisfying the condition.
- N: total number of explanations.

Based on these accuracy scores, we identified the most reliable model. For this model, confusion matrices were generated in relation to each annotator's classifications to further analyze classification patterns and mismatches.

The results of this analysis are reported in the following section.

5 Results

The analysis of the Inter-Annotator Agreement (IAA) shows a moderate level of agreement between the two evaluators, with a Cohen's Kappa coefficient of 0.25. This value reflects some variability in the assignments, further emphasizing the importance of a structured comparison between multiple annotations.

Using the LLMs *Google Gemini 2.0 Flash*, *DeepSeek R1* and *GPT-4o*, we computed accuracy scores under two settings: with and without the integration of the symbolic component RAGGAE. The results, shown in Fig. 2 (strict accuracy) and Fig. 3 (partial accuracy), highlight performance improvements when the models are supported by the HERB ontology via RAGGAE.

The comparison reveals that: for *Google Gemini 2.0 Flash*, the integration of RAGGAE significantly improves both strict accuracy, from 16.1% to 24.2%, and partial accuracy, from 43.5% to 56.5%; in the case of *DeepSeek R1*, the model is unable to generate any valid classifications without RAGGAE (0% for both accuracy types), but successfully classifies when RAGGAE is applied (strict: 12.9%, partial: 37.1%); while, for *GPT-4o*, RAGGAE leads to an improvement in strict accuracy from 14.5% to 17.7%, but a decrease in partial accuracy, from 43.5% to 35.5%.

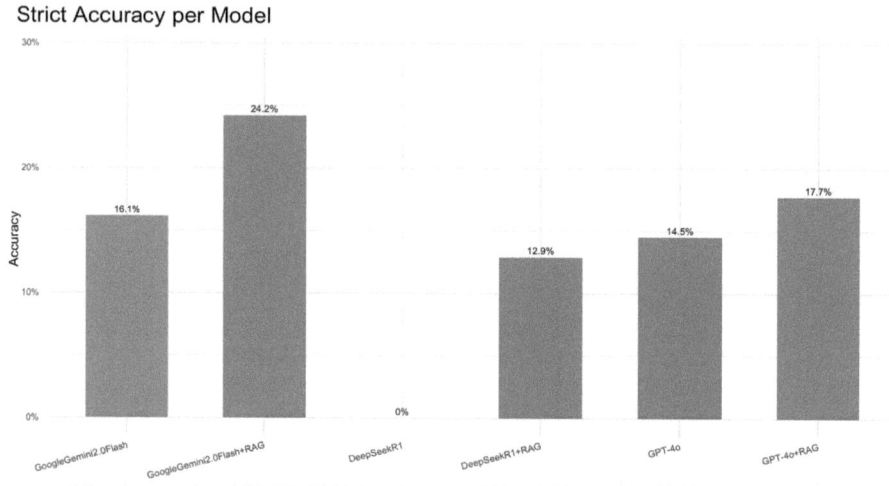

Fig. 2. *Strict accuracy* scores for LLMs and their RAGGAE-enhanced versions (LLM+RAG) across the models: *Google Gemini 2.0 Flash, DeepSeek R1, GPT-4o*.

These results confirm that, overall, the use of RAGGAE enhances model accuracy. Particularly, among all evaluated models, Google Gemini 2.0 Flash with RAGGAE achieves the best overall performance and is therefore selected as the reference model for the in-depth analysis. As an additional analysis, two confusion matrices were generated comparing the labels produced by the top performing RAGGAE model (i.e. the one with Google Gemini 2.0 Flash) with two annotators (Fig. 4 and 5). These matrices provide a detailed view of the areas of convergence and disagreement between the automatic model and the human evaluators. Specifically, the matrix in Fig. 4 shows a fair alignment for the *TeleologicalNeutral* class (8 matches) and *Unclassifiable* (9 instances). However, numerous overlaps with other categories emerge, particularly among *TeleologicalFolkPsychology*, *Functional*, and *Mechanistic*. For example, some instances labeled as *Functional* by the annotator were often classified by the model as *Mechanistic* and *TeleologicalNeutral*, suggesting a conceptual overlap. Additionally, the *ExplanationMissing* class frequently overlaps with *TeleologicalNeutral*, indicating a possible tendency of the model to assign teleological interpretations even in the absence of an explicit explanation. The second matrix, in Fig. 5, displays a different distribution. The model shows strong agreement with the annotator in the classification of the *TeleologicalNeutral* category (15 matches),

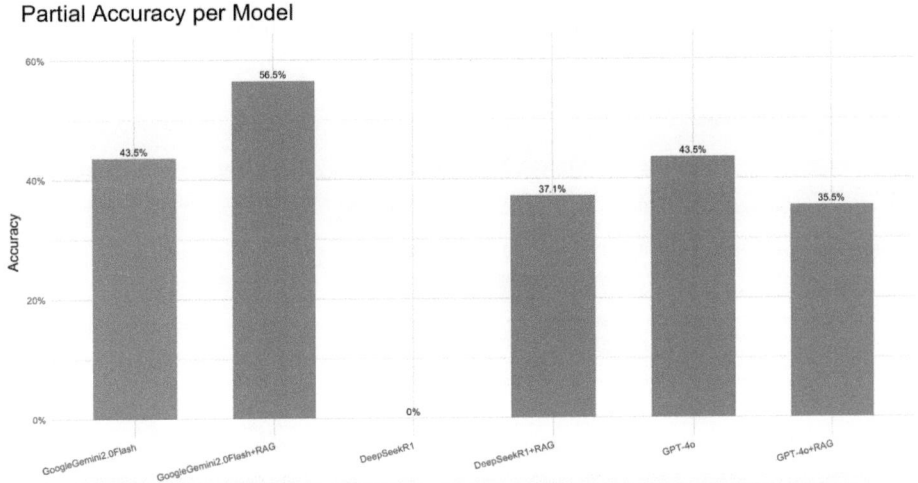

Fig. 3. *Partial accuracy* scores for LLMs and their RAGGAE-enhanced versions (LLM+RAG) across the models: *Google Gemini 2.0 Flash, DeepSeek R1, GPT-4o.*

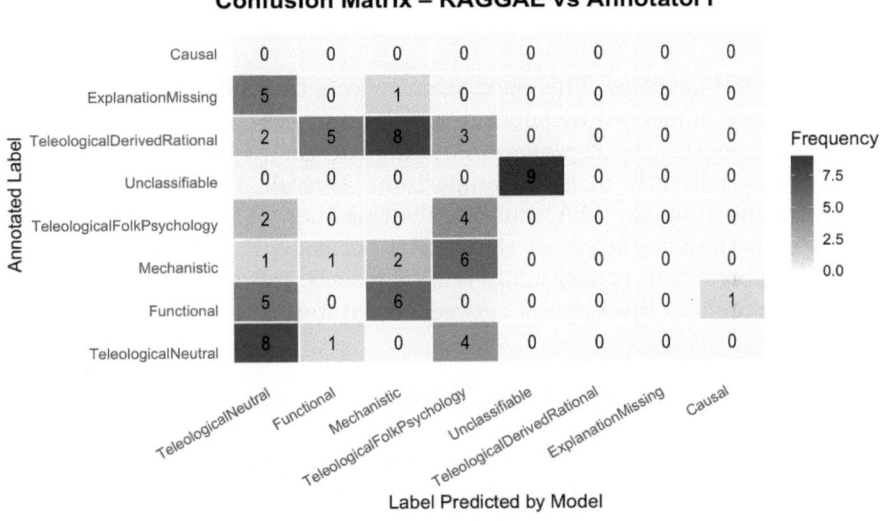

Fig. 4. Confusion matrix of the best RAGGAE model (*Google Gemini 2.0 Flash*) vs the labels provided by *Annotator1*.

Mechanistic (13 matches), and *Unclassifiable* (8 matches). Nonetheless, several misclassifications occur between *Mechanistic* and *TeleologicalNeutral*: as many as 7 instances labeled as *Mechanistic* were classified by the model as

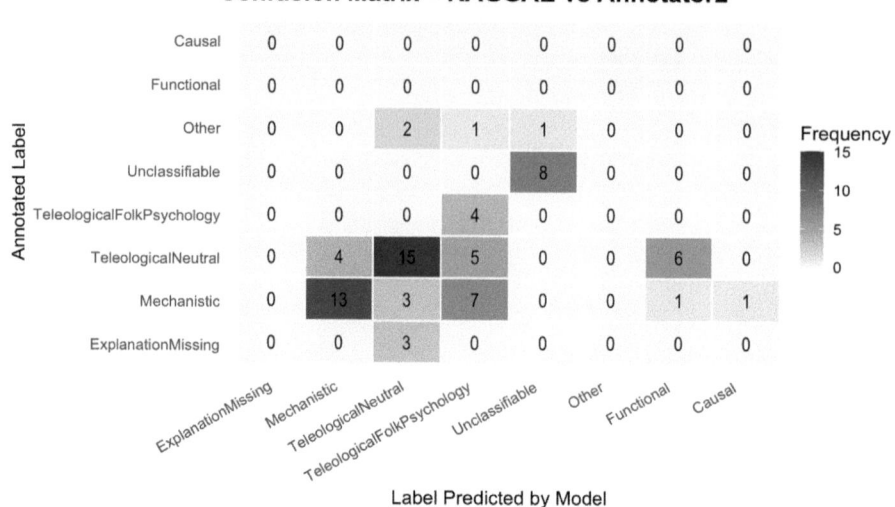

Fig. 5. Confusion matrix of the best RAGGAE model (*Google Gemini 2.0 Flash*) vs the labels provided by *Annotator2*.

TeleologicalFolkPsychology. This once again reflects the difficulty in distinguishing explanations influenced by subtle linguistic nuances. It is also worth noting the poor alignment in the *ExplanationMissing* category, which the model struggles to identify correctly in both comparisons. Overall, the two matrices confirm the findings from the IAA analysis, showing that while model performance improves with the integration of the HERB ontology, RAGGAE still exhibits significant ambiguity in conceptually related classes, reflecting both model limitations and potential divergences between annotators.

6 Conclusions and Future Works

The obtained results show how the adoption a philosophically grounded ontology of human explanations of robotic behavior (HERBs), when used in a RAG model (RAGGAE), improves the explanatory performance of AI systems based on human verbalization of the behavior of social robots. While the current datum is of interest, even if it deserves further investigations with a larger number of LLMs - it is worth-noticing how, for this complex task, the performance of AI systems are still very far from being comparable to human expert annotations. As future works we plan to better axiomatize (via knowledge specialization and extension when needed) the current version of the ontology. This task will allow to improve the formal structure that can be superimposed to LLMs and, as a consequence, its categorization accuracy. In addition, we plan to extend our evaluation both acquiring and analyzing more verbal data and by extending the number of human annotators in order to have a more robust ground truth upon which to compare the results of RAGGAE.

References

1. Artstein, R.: Inter-annotator agreement. In: Handbook of Linguistic Annotation, pp. 297–313 (2017)
2. Cordeschi, R.: The discovery of the artificial: behavior, mind and machines before and beyond cybernetics, vol. 28. Springer (2002)
3. Cummins, R.: Functional analysis. J. Philos. **72**(20), 741–765 (1975)
4. Dennett, D.C.: Intentional systems. J. Philos. **68**(4), 87–106 (1971)
5. DeepSeek-AI: Deepseek-r1: Incentivizing reasoning capability in LLMs via reinforcement learning. arXiv (2025)
6. Google. Gemini 2.0 Flash. https://gemini.google.com/app
7. Happé, F.G.E.: An advanced test of theory of mind: understanding of story characters' thoughts and feelings by able autistic, mentally handicapped, and normal children and adults. J. Autism Dev. Disord. **24**(2), 129–154 (1994)
8. Hempel, C.G., Oppenheim, P.: Studies in the logic of explanation. Philos. Sci. **15**(2), 135–175 (1948)
9. Hu, Y., Lu, Y.: Rag and rau: a survey on retrieval-augmented language model in natural language processing. arXiv preprint arXiv:2404.19543 (2024)
10. Leunissen, M.: Explanation and Teleology in Aristotle's Science of Nature. Cambridge University Press (2010)
11. Lieto, A.: Cognitive design for artificial minds. Routledge (2021)
12. Machamer, P., Darden, L., Craver, C.F.: Thinking about mechanisms. Philos. Sci. **67**(1), 1–25 (2000)
13. Miller, T., Howe, P., Sonenberg, L.: Explainable AI: beware of inmates running the asylum or: how i learnt to stop worrying and love the social and behavioural sciences. arXiv preprint arXiv:1712.00547 (2017)
14. OpenAI. GPT-4o. https://chatgpt.com/?model=gpt-4o
15. Rausa, M., Augello, A., Lieto, A.: Towards an ontology of human explanations of robotic behavior. In: Proceedings of the Fifth Workshop on SOcial and Cultural IntegrAtion with PersonaLIZEd Interfaces (SOCIALIZE) at the 30th Annual ACM Conference on Intelligent User Interfaces Cagliari, Italy, 24–27 March 2025 ACM IUI 2025 (2025)
16. Scriven, M.: Explanations, predictions, and laws (1962)

Robots on Stage: Performance Art, Education and Social Robotics for Children

Social Interaction with Autonomous Art: Combining Social Analysis and Computer Vision

Darren Reed[1], Fanta Camara[2(✉)], and Tianyuan Wang[2]

[1] Department of Sociology, University of York, York, UK
[2] Institute for Safe Autonomy, University of York, York, UK
fanta.camara@york.ac.uk

Abstract. The deployment of autonomous robots in public spaces is increasing thanks to advancements in robot localisation, mapping and navigation strategies, but there is a slower development of autonomous robotic systems in artistic contexts. This project introduces The Wheel, an autonomous kinetic sculpture that moves through the crowd at art festivals. Using onboard camera data, this work provides some insight into the social interactions happening between The Wheel and people by combining a form of social analysis, called Embodied Conversational Analysis, with computer vision analysis through the AlphaPose algorithm. The findings include a list of meaningful social actions performed by people interacting with The Wheel, thus offering a promising approach to better understanding social interactions with autonomous robots performing on stage and beyond.

Keywords: Autonomous art · Robot performance · Social interactions · Human-robot interaction · Embodied Conversational Analysis · Computer vision · AlphaPose

1 Introduction

Autonomous technologies, primarily designed for industrial applications in controlled environments, are increasingly emerging in public spaces, where their integration presents unique opportunities and challenges [1]. This development raises a crucial issue regarding how the integration of such technologies can be optimized to enhance public acceptance and safety. This study explores this question by merging technical innovation, social behavioral analysis, and artistic practice to explore meaningful public engagement in novel ways. An important difference with robotic or autonomous art pieces is that they are meant to garner attention. A successful piece unsettles ongoing perceptions and practices and encourages engagement and proximity. Arguably, rather than increasing the likelihood of collision, such attention-paying forms the basis of human-object spatial coordination. Yet with proximity comes greater danger and only through

(a) (b)

Fig. 1. Pictures of The Wheel at the Festival of Ideas. (**a**) The Wheel with the sensor kit. (**b**) The Wheel at an art festival.

a detailed understanding of existing human behaviors and their 'projection' can the device anticipate potential dangers.

The present project leverages The Wheel (shown in Fig. 1), an autonomous kinetic sculpture developed in collaboration with the art practice IOU Theatre, to study and enhance interactions between autonomous systems and the public. This installation not only showcases the potential of robotics in public art but also serves as a research tool to explore the dynamics of human-robot interaction in real-world environments. Public acceptance is often a decisive factor in the successful adoption of new technologies. Despite the growing presence of autonomous systems in public spaces [2], research on their public interaction, especially through art, remains sparse. Our project begins to fill this gap by employing The Wheel to gather data on how people perceive and interact with autonomous technologies in a lively festival setting. This dual focus on technical enhancement and public interaction helps advance the technology while ensuring it aligns with societal norms and expectations. This work is interdisciplinary in that it brings together researchers from robotics, computer vision and sociology, alongside art practitioners. The paper details the development of a novel combination of existing methods and practices, so as to inform real-time machine learning-based models development for social robots. This work contributes the following:

- a novel approach combining embodied conversation analysis with computer vision analysis via the use of AlphaPose to provide some insight into social interactions with an autonomous robotic art system;
- a summary list of meaningful social actions identified in these social interactions and indicative computer vision techniques needed to identify them autonomously.

2 Related Work

The study of human interactions with autonomous vehicles is a very active field, with topics such as human detection and tracking that have well-established solutions [3] but human trajectory prediction and interaction behaviors are less understood research areas [4]. Most of these works have focused on on-road vehicles that drive people around or mobile robots that deliver some services to them. But recently, several projects have started demonstrating the potential of integrating robotics with art, to study human-robot interaction. For example, the "Shimon" project [5] developed a robotic marimba player capable of improvising music with human musicians, [6] designed robots capable of drawing portraits of human subjects, [7] and [8] showed how to make robots dance alongside humans, and [9] proposed a cognitive architecture for interactive humanoid robots performing poetry on stage. However, there are fewer studies on public engagement with autonomous mobile robots. For instance, [10] investigated the nonverbal behaviors (proxemics) of audience members interacting with a mobile robot manipulator at a festival. [11] described the design of Fish-Bird, a kinetic artwork in the form of two wheelchairs that aim to investigate different forms of dialogue between two autonomous robots and their levels of engagement in human-robot interaction. [12] developed Ikit, an artwork comprised of three robot platforms that move autonomously towards people and make contact with them. [13] used robotic installations as an "artistic medium" to engage with the public. Several large-scale robotic structures and environments were used to induce empathy from audience members towards the mechanistic characters. The present work uses a similar approach with the aim to collect data from a multi-sensor kit and develop a new method to detect audience members' interactions with The Wheel and its miniature character.

At the same time, Sociology has a long history of interest in movement and visibility in public spaces [14,15]. This includes the manner in which pedestrians glance at each other [16,17], indicate objects of common interest [18], and navigate spaces occupied by vehicles and objects [19]. The sociologist Erving Goffman [20] conceived of public behavior as a performance in front of an audience and various forms of public 'spectacle' have been understood in terms of performance engagement [21]. He described 'civil inattention' as a key component of public behaviors, a normative strategy of 'polite' avoidance. Goffman identifies mitigation of inattention through a staged progression towards engagement and interaction through preparatory movements such as glances to and from a person or object of interest [18]. It is from the tension between public performance and polite avoidance that a social understanding of engagement with art-based autonomous devices is born. Drawing on Goffman, the applied approach of Embodied Conversation Analysis, understands how 'multimodal' communication elements, such as gaze and gesture, are resources for doing public interaction [22]. As robots and autonomous vehicles form part of everyday life, embodied resources have become a means of understanding interaction [2] and form a social understanding of human-device interaction [23]. This is seen in the prediction of human attention and engagement through the monitoring of behaviors such as gaze and gesture in the robot design literature [24]. It is akin to the research on the 'legibility' of robot motion [25].

3 Methods

The approach used here combines speed and trajectory produced through Alpha-Pose [26] with a social analytic approach called Embodied Conversation Analysis (ECA) [27]. AlphaPose represents real-time onboard visual acuity while ECA provides a detailed description of the meaning of social behavior. The resulting work pipeline is shown in Fig. 2.

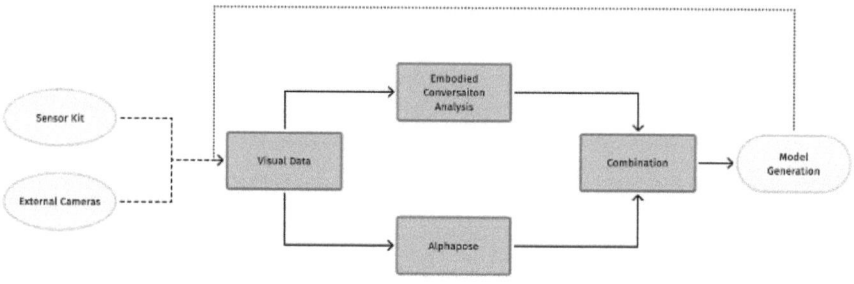

Fig. 2. Data processing pipeline.

3.1 Data Collection

Data collection for this study was conducted during the York Festival of Ideas, where The Wheel served as a central interactive installation. Moving at a speed of 1 m per minute along a planned route, The Wheel attracted audience members who engaged with the artwork as it progressed. The audience was encouraged to interact by observing the miniature figure walking inside The Wheel and contributing their thoughts or drawings at the accompanying Mobile Gallery, which moved ahead of The Wheel (cf. Fig. 1). A data acquisition system, referred to as the sensor kit, which is installed on the structure, collected visual data in real-time, capturing the movement, behavior, and interactions of the audience as they followed and engaged with the installation throughout the event. The sensor kit was mounted at the rear of The Wheel at a height of approximately 2 m above the ground to ensure the audience remains within the sensing range. The data were acquired using the ROS2 (Humble) stack running on Raspberry Pi OS (Bookworm 64-bit). Ethical approval was obtained from the University of York Ethics Committee.

3.2 Embodied Conversation Analysis

Embodied Conversation Analysis (ECA) is an approach in Sociology that details sequences of meaningful social interaction, typically in relation to talk [28]. For ECA, social interaction is premised upon the projection of upcoming elements such that - for example - a speaker anticipates the end of a co-speaker's turn, and prepares to respond at the appropriate moment [29]. Similar projection trajectories are identified in embodied activities, such as gesture and gaze production [30]. ECA follows a rigorous procedure of transcription and analysis. In the following transcripts, given that there is no recorded talk, the 'footwork' of the participants is used as a primary means to track the production of ongoing activity. Each step on either the left ("L") or right ("R") foot is separated into a 'preparatory' phase as the leg moves forward (indicated by periods) and a 'step' the period during which the foot is in contact with the floor (indicated by tildes). The combined movement is called a 'stride'. The same preparation and action 'phrasing' is used with eye movement (head pan, and aligned gaze) and gesture production (preparatory movement of the arm and then production of a pointing hand shape). Each character represents one tenth of a second. Corresponding images from the video are indicated with a star symbol and numbered. The transcription details the section of the video clip in the caption and a brief 'gloss' is included in double brackets justified right. Consecutive actions are separated by a semicolon and italicized descriptions relate to the italicized character in the transcript. The transcript is presented in a fixed width font so that the alignment of embodied elements can be seen.

3.3 AlphaPose

The position information of audience members were obtained through AlphaPose [26] by extracting keypoints data and using the midpoint between the shoulders as the reference point for determining the audience member's position. After pre-processing keypoints data, the velocity of each individual was calculated. Given the inherent limitations in the accuracy of the pose detection algorithm, a Kalman filter was first applied to the velocity data to reduce noise in the observed velocities. A low-pass filter was then applied to the velocity data to eliminate the influence of walking gait, resulting in a smooth velocity curve and trajectory. The detailed method using AlphaPose for the velocity and trajectory generation is described in [31].

4 Analysis and Results

The following instances are analyzed from an Embodied Conversation Analytic approach and then detailed through the AlphaPose algorithm. The analysis follows a strategy of increasing behavioral complexity, starting with two people walking past and glancing at The Wheel, and then moving through increased levels of complexity in relation to behavior. The first instance is used to convey the marrying of the two methods, while the later more complex examples, are used to hint at potential ways to develop the analysis.

4.1 Instance 1: Gazing at an Object

The onboard camera (pointed to the right) captured two people walking in parallel with The Wheel (Fig. 3b). Initially the woman can be seen in the frame (Fig. 3a, line 01), but then – at a slight distance – the second person (a child)

```
01 Wfeet:    L..~R..~L..~R...~L...~R...~~L...~R...~
02 Cfeet:                R~L.~R..~L..~R..~L.~R..
03 Whead:                                L-----          ((small pan left; look))
04 Chead:                                L------         ((pan left; look))

05 Wfeet:    L...~R...~~L..~
06 Cfeet:    ~L..~R..~L..~R~
07 Whead:    L.------------                              ((full pan left))
08 Chead:    ---------------
```

(a) Transcript 1 – Output Left 17-02 to 17-08 (onboard camera)

(b) Image

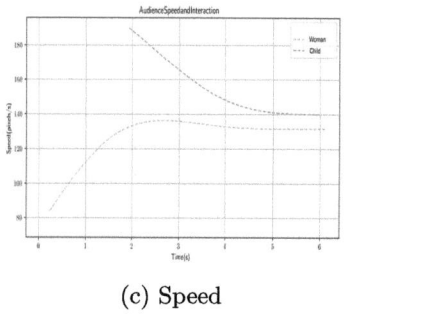

(c) Speed

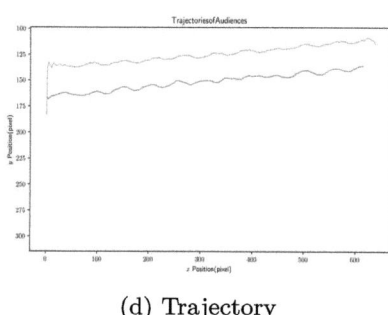

(d) Trajectory

Fig. 3. Results of the ECA transcription and AlphaPose for Instance 1.

appears (line 02). AlphaPose provides a reading of the speed and trajectory of the two people, shown in Fig. 3c and Fig. 3d, respectively. These show the relative movement of each person, as the second 'catches up' with the first, while maintaining a parallel trajectory. The transcript in Fig. 3a (lines 01 and 02) shows the woman's 'stride' ('preparation' plus 'step') to be on average larger and longer than the child's. On the fifth step (right foot) the child turns his gaze to the left (line 04), looking directly at the camera (on The Wheel). One tenth of a second later, on a left-foot step (line 03), the woman pans her gaze slightly to the left (possibly looking at person ahead of The Wheel, out of frame). During the latter part of a left foot preparation (line 06) she pans her gaze to The Wheel (line 07). The sequence can be summarized as two people walking past The Wheel. First one turns their gaze to look and then the other first pans towards something happening to her left and then fully turns her gaze to look at The Wheel. Both child and woman maintain this gaze alignment as they walk out of frame. Gaze realignment ("gazing-at") is an action that could preface more direct engagement, perhaps through a change of walking direction that brings them closer to The Wheel. Glancing at an object is a first stage action ("inattention" to attention) in a potential longer sequence of actions that culminates in engagement. It is precisely this type of indicative movement that a human uses to 'project' potential future actions. A similar sequential projection is seen in instance 2 (Fig. 4).

```
01 Mfeet:    R.~L...~~R...~~L...~~           ((second L turned out))
02 Mhead:    ~~~~~~~~~~~~~~~L.....           ((facing to left; pans left))
             *1                    *2

03 Mfeet:    R...~~L....~~R..~~~L...
04 Mhead:    L.......       F....L..         ((down and up; to front; left & down))
                                 *3

05 Mfeet:    ~~~R....~~L....~~~R.....~~
06 Mhead:    ~~~~~~~~~~~~~~~~~~~~~~~~~       ((looking at Wheel))
             *4

07 Mfeet:    L...~~~R...~~~~                 ((Rf flat, no Left heel raise))
08 Mhead:    ~~~~~~~~~~~~~~~                 ((looking at Wheel))

09 Mfeet:    (18.7)                          ((stands still on both feet))
10 Mhead:    (18.7)                          ((looking at Wheel))
```

(a) Transcript 2 – VID00006 and Left Output 7:22 - 8:05 (onboard camera)

(b) Image 1   (c) Image 2   (d) Image 3   (e) Image 4

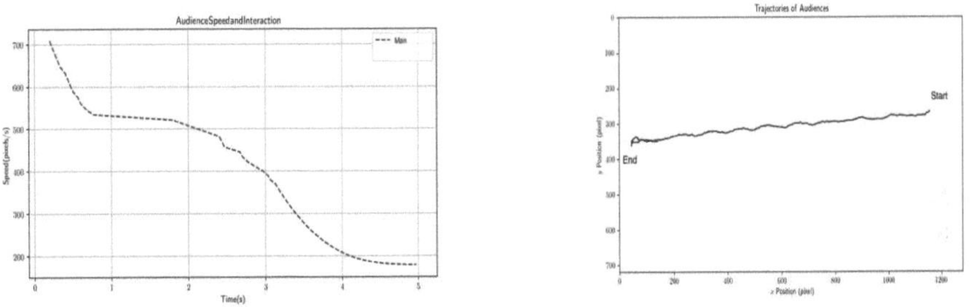

(f) Speed   (g) Trajectory

Fig. 4. Results of the ECA transcription and AlphaPose for Instance 2.

4.2 Instance 2: Walking Towards, Scene Scanning, Stride Termination

Here the person is already oriented towards The Wheel as he enters the frame (Fig. 4b) but the line of movement changes as each left foot stride turns the body to the left (Figs. 4c and Fig. 4d) and the person moves closer to The Wheel (Fig. 4e). This is seen in the trajectory graph (Fig. 4g) as he slows down (Fig. 4f). This "body re-orientation" (moving from a 'side-on' position to a 'facing' position) and speed reduction is a meaningful social action of 'walking-towards' The

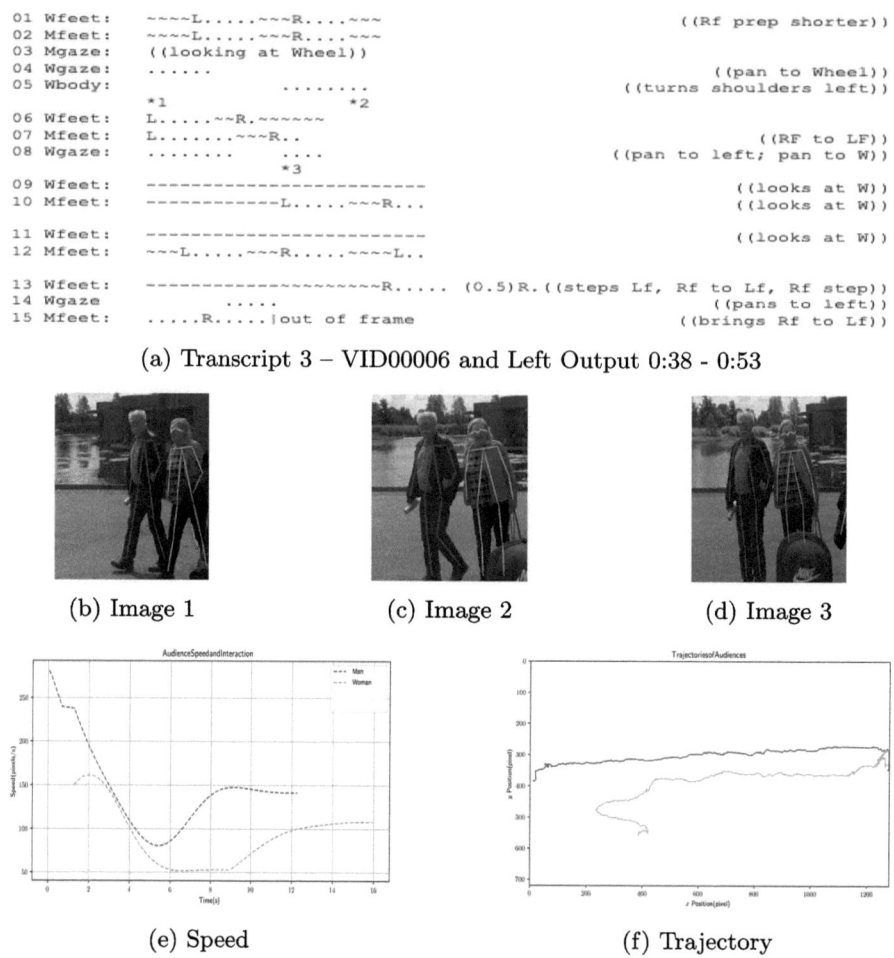

Fig. 5. Results of the ECA transcription and AlphaPose for Instance 3.

Wheel. Walking-towards is followed by 'scene-scanning' (looking down up, left, front) as shown in (Fig. 4a, line 04) as he looks at a person to the side of The Wheel and then turns his gaze to The Wheel itself (Fig. 4a, line 06). In Fig. 4a (line 07), the man comes to rest by transferring his weight into his right foot ('step') without beginning a preparation of the left foot ('no left heel raise'). This action is a 'stride-termination'. Showing interest through gaze and body re-orientation, change of velocity and trajectory is indicative of potential engagement with an object-of-interest. Indeed, we see this engagement in Fig. 4a (lines 09 and 10) when the person stands still and looks at The Wheel (not shown in velocity graph). This behavior terminates the movement-towards The Wheel and hence mitigates the potential for path crossing and collision. To 'gazing-at' as an indicative movement, we can add 'walking-towards', 'scene-scanning', and 'stride termination' to a list of meaningful movements.

4.3 Instance 3: Footwork Synchrony and Engagement Coordination

In the following instance, a man and a woman are walking in parallel with The Wheel. As they come into view (Fig. 5b) they are both stepping on their left then right foot (Fig. 5a, lines 01 and 02) in synchrony ('footwork synchrony' or 'walking together'). The man is already looking at The Wheel. A typical walking speed is 0.6 s for the preparation (indicated with periods) and step (indicated by tildes), yet both the man and woman's left foot strides are 0.9 s in length, meaning that they have slowed down together (see also speed graph in Fig. 5e). Overlapping the preparation of this stride, the woman pans her gaze to The Wheel (Fig. 5a, line 04), producing a shared attentional gaze with the man. She turns her shoulders and upper body towards The Wheel (line 05, Fig. 5c)('body re-orientation'). In Fig. 5a line 06, the woman produces a quicker stride preparation on her left foot, meaning she steps while the man is still moving his foot (line 07) ('footwork a-synchrony'). His step (line 07) coincides with her right foot preparation and the commencement of a step, meaning that she is transferring her weight into her right foot as he brings his feet together ("RF to LF")("stride-termination"). In overlap with this, the woman once again pans her gaze to The Wheel and the couple stop and look at it together (Fig. 5d) - indicated by a dashed line - for another second before moving off. The footwork, scene-scanning, and body re-orientation work to engineer stride termination and engagement coordination. The man then walks closer to The Wheel (Fig. 5a lines 10, 12, 15)('walking-towards'), while the woman first maintains her gaze and body alignment and then turns and walks away (to her left) (Fig. 5a lines 09, 11, 13)('walking-away'). As the couple are walking past The Wheel with synchronized strides ('footwork synchrony'), the man maintains gaze alignment ('gazing-at'), showing interest. Their footwork falls out of synchrony as the woman looks at The Wheel, then to away to the people around it, and then back to it ('scene-scanning'). They both stop and look at The Wheel. As he moves closer, she first stands looking and then turns away and moves in the opposite direction to him (Fig. 5f). This is one example of engagement coordination followed by differentiated interest and engagement and shows that while initial engagement might be coordinated, the nature and length of that engagement might change.

4.4 Instance 4: Gesture and Engagement Coordination

In this final instance, a man and child are walking at different pace-lengths (Fig. 6f) but similar speed, although the man's speed is initially slower relative to the camera (Fig. 6e). While they are both walking diagonally towards The Wheel, there are notable turns to the left on the left foot by the child in line 04 (Figs. 6a and 6d) and by the man in Fig. 6a (line 05), indicating a change in trajectory. In Fig. 6a line 03, the man produces a gesture preparation by raising his hand to his eyes (Fig. 6b), shielding them from the sun. This gesture acts

```
01 Cfeet:    L..~R..~~L..~~R..~~L.
02 Mfeet:    L..~~R...~~L...~~R..
03 Mgest:    ....~~~~~~~~~~~....                    ((above eyes))
                    *1

04 Cfeet:    ..~~R..~~L...~~R...~~                  ((turning to left))
05 Mfeet:    .~~~L....~~~R...~~L....                    ((turning left))
06 Mgest:    ~~~~~~....~~~~~~~~~               ((pointing; above eyes))
                *2      *3
```

(a) Transcript 4 – Instance 1: Left Output 0:10-0:17.

(b) Image 1    (c) Image 2    (d) Image 3

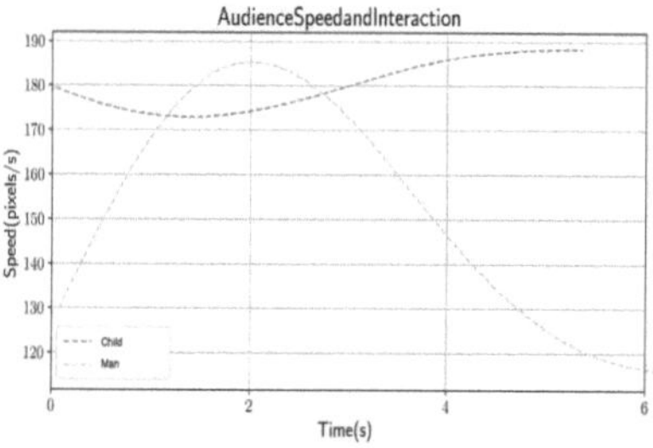

(e) Speed 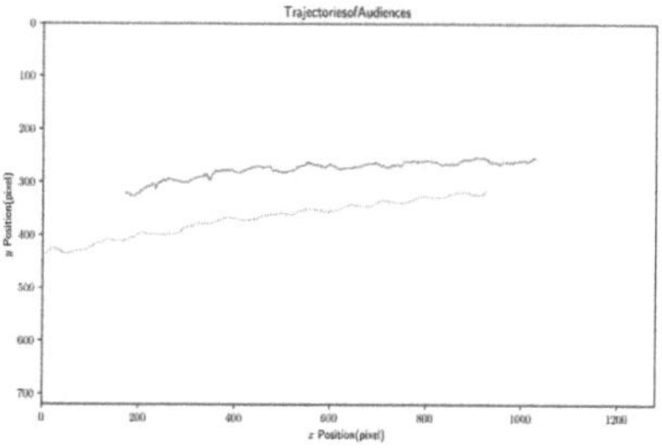   (f) Trajectory

Fig. 6. Results of the ECA transcription and AlphaPose for Instance 4.

to emphasize visual interest (an exaggerated 'gazing-at'- or what McNeill calls a 'metaphoric gesture') [32]. He then produces another gesture preparation to bring his left hand to a pointing ("deictic") gesture (Fig. 6c), angled towards the camera on The Wheel as shown in Fig. 6a line 06. A further gesture preparation has him bring his left hand back to his brow (Fig. 6d). We might ask why the man produces this series of movements. After all, the child is already visually engaged with The Wheel and walking towards it. One answer is that this series of layered actions indicates a display of growing interest and hence a likely progression towards physical engagement with The Wheel. Importantly, this growing interest is communicative; it is produced for the child. It results in the reorientation of the child's body as he steps on his left foot in Fig. 6a line 04, angling his body further towards The Wheel (Fig. 6d), precisely following the end of the pointing gesture (Fig. 6a, line 06). To the list of meaningful actions we can add a sequence of gesture forms ('looking' and pointing then 'looking') that work to coordinate mutual attention and engagement ('engagement coordination').

Table 1. Summary list of meaningful social actions from the observed social interactions with The Wheel and some indicative computer vision techniques needed to identify them.

Meaningful Social Actions	Indicative techniques from computer vision
Gazing-at	Gaze tracking + speed estimation
Walking-towards	Speed + trajectory estimation
Scene-scanning	Gaze tracking + Head pose estimation
Stride termination	Leg pose + speed estimation
Body re-orientation	Whole body pose + trajectory estimation
Footwork (a)synchrony	Multi-persons leg pose + speed + trajectory estimation
Engagement coordination	Speed + trajectory estimation
Looking at	Head pose estimation
Pointing at	Hand gesture recognition + tracking

4.5 Meaningful Social Actions

Table 1 provides a summary of the meaningful social actions observed in the instances' analysis as well as indicative computer vision techniques required to identify them autonomously. These actions have a sequential ordering, such that one typically precedes another. Generally, this follows a progression from gaze through gesture and body orientation to movement termination. For example, the action of stopping and looking, or what we have called 'stride termination', is then a finely tuned collective activity that is achieved through various activities that we have termed 'engagement coordination'. Moving through the instances in more detail, Instance 1 (Sect. 4.1) shows the 'gazing-at' action on the part of both woman and child. In that they are sequentially produced, one after the other, it shows a move from inattention to shared attention, and hence projects the potential for joint engagement. Gazing-at is also apparent in Instances 2 (Sect. 4.2) and 3 (Sect. 4.3). In the latter, the gazing-at of the man leads to a shared visual attentiveness that in turn results in stride termination. An alternative form of visual action is identified in Instance 2 with the man, who is already walking towards The Wheel, scanning the scene. While we cannot substantiate the point here, such actions are often oriented to recognition of existing shared interest on the part of others in the scene and working out what they are looking at. We see hints of this in the initial glance of the woman in Instance 1 and the scanning gaze of the woman in Instance 3. What comes to the fore in Instance 3 is the indication of upcoming stride termination through the move from footwork synchrony to a-synchrony. By shortening her stride and turning her shoulders (body-reorientation), the woman indicates and projects her intention to stop and look. Finally in Instance 4 (Sect. 4.4), engagement coordination is most apparent in the sequential production of an exaggerated looking pointing gestures. This informs engagement coordination.

5 Discussion

In each of the instances, the velocity and trajectory information produced through AlphaPose is combined with a descriptive analysis of the movements through the ECA approach. While the two forms of information provide insights into the relative movements of scene participants, the latter extends this insight through the identification of various socially meaningful 'actions' summarized in Table 1. This table currently contains a mix of informal and formal action descriptions which are not fully detailed here and are planned for future work. Translating a social understanding into a computer vision technique is a difficult process and one that highlights the complexities of human perception. While there may be some kind of 'mechanism' underpinning social perception and practice, revealing it is an ongoing process. Designing a computer version of human experience is a means to pursue such understandings and insights, this table is thus 'indicative' of such linkages, but it does not claim to be definitive.

The fine-grained action description provided by the ECA approach requires decades of expertise in human behaviour analysis and is therefore very time-consuming. The combined ECA approach with AlphaPose used here aims to reduce computation time and enable autonomous analysis and understanding of human behaviour. With existing approaches to supervised machine learning, video annotation involves identifying single actions which are then used to predict new instances [33]. ECA has the potential to improve processes of supervised learning by incorporating the incremental and procedural features of 'projectable' actions into training models. Future work aims to address that and also extends the analysis to additional examples of actions from various sources of data.

Acknowledgments. The authors would like to express their sincere gratitude to: (1) IOU Theatre (https://ioutheatre.org) for supporting this work with The Wheel and the data collection; (2) Rob Woolley who helped design the sensor kit.

References

1. Fayyaz, M., González-González, E., Nogués, S.: Autonomous mobility: a potential opportunity to reclaim public spaces for people **14**(3), 1568. Accessed 07 Mar 2025
2. Pelikan, H.R., Reeves, S., Cantarutti, M.N.: Encountering autonomous robots on public streets. In: Proceedings of the 2024 ACM/IEEE International Conference on Human-Robot Interaction, pp. 561–571 (2024)
3. Camara, F., et al.: Pedestrian models for autonomous driving part i: low-level models, from sensing to tracking **22**(10), 6131–6151. Accessed 07 Mar 2025
4. Camara, F., et al.: Pedestrian models for autonomous driving part ii: high-level models of human behavior **22**(9), 5453–5472. Accessed 07 Mar 2025

5. Hoffman, G., Weinberg, G.: Shimon: an interactive improvisational robotic marimba player. In: CHI 2010 Extended Abstracts on Human Factors in Computing Systems, pp. 3097–3102. ACM. https://doi.org/10.1145/1753846.1753925. https://dl.acm.org/doi/10.1145/1753846.1753925. Accessed 07 Mar 2025
6. Sidnell, J.: The architecture of intersubjectivity revisited. In: Sidnell, J., Enfield, N.J., Kockelman, P. (eds.) The Cambridge Handbook of Linguistic Anthropology. Cambridge Handbooks in Language and Linguistics, pp. 364–399. Cambridge University Press. https://doi.org/10.1017/CBO9781139342872.018 . https://www.cambridge.org/core/books/cambridge-handbook-of-linguistic-anthropology/architecture-of-intersubjectivity-revisited/F0CDB2C89CE94A8DBD29322AE450E28D
7. Abad, P., et al.: Integrating an autonomous robot on a dance and new technologies festival. In: Ollero, A., Sanfeliu, A., Montano, L., Lau, N., Cardeira, C. (eds.) ROBOT 2017. AISC, vol. 693, pp. 75–87. Springer, Cham (2018). https://doi.org/10.1007/978-3-319-70833-1_7
8. LaViers, A.: Make robot motions natural **565**(7740), 422–424. Accessed 07 Mar 2025
9. Rodriguez, I., Astigarraga, A., Lazkano, E., Martínez-Otzeta, J.M., Mendialdua, I.: Robots on stage: a cognitive framework for socially interacting robots **25**, 17–25. Accessed 07 Mar 2025
10. Krenn, B., Gross, S., Dieber, B., Pichler, H., Meyer, K.: A proxemics game between festival visitors and an industrial robot arXiv preprint arXiv:2105.13812 (2021). arXiv. https://doi.org/10.48550/arXiv.2105.13812. http://arxiv.org/abs/2105.13812. Accessed 07 Mar 2025
11. Velonaki, M., Rye, D.: Designing robots creatively. In: Herath, D., Kroos, C., Stelarc (eds.) Robots and Art. Cognitive Science and Technology, pp. 379–401. Springer. https://doi.org/10.1007/978-981-10-0321-9_19. Accessed 07 Mar 2025
12. Doepner, S., Jurman, U.: Robot partner–are friends electric? In: Herath, D., Kroos, C., Stelarc (eds.) Robots and Art. Cognitive Science and Technology, pp. 403–423. Springer.https://doi.org/10.1007/978-981-10-0321-9_20. Accessed 07 Mar 2025
13. Vorn, B.: I want to believe–empathy and catharsis in robotic art. In: Herath, D., Kroos, C., Stelarc (eds.) Robots and Art. Cognitive Science and Technology, pp. 365–377. Springer. https://doi.org/10.1007/978-981-10-0321-9_18. Accessed 07 Mar 2025
14. Simmel, G.: Sociology of the senses. visual interaction. In: Introduction to the Science of Sociology, 3rd edn, pp. 356–361. University of Chicago Press
15. Rosental, C.: Toward a sociology of public demonstrations **31**, 343–365. https://doi.org/10.1177/0735275113513454
16. Sacks, H.: Lecture eleven: on exchanging glances **12**(3), 333–350. Accessed 25 Sept 2024
17. Macbeth, D.: Glances, trances, and their relevance for a visual sociology. In: Jalbert, P.L. (ed.) Media Studies: Ethnomethodological Approaches, pp. 135–170. University Press of America
18. Goffman, E.: Behavior in Public Places: Notes on the Social Organization of Gatherings, vol. 91194. Free Pr
19. Conley, J.: A sociology of traffic: driving, cycling, walking. Technologies of Mobility in the Americas (Intersections in Communications & Culture), pp. 219–236. Peter Lang
20. Goffman, E.: The Presentation of Self in Everyday Life. Doubleday. Doubleday
21. Benford, S., et al.: Creating the spectacle: designing interactional trajectories through spectator interfaces **18**(3), 11

22. Mondada, L.: Bodies in action: multimodal analysis of walking and talking **4**(3), 357–403. https://doi.org/10.1075/ld.4.3.02mon
23. Vinkhuyzen, E., Cefkin, M.: Developing socially acceptable autonomous vehicles **2016**(1), 522–534. Accessed 11 Apr 2025
24. Dey, D., Walker, F., Martens, M., Terken, J.: Gaze patterns in pedestrian interaction with vehicles: towards effective design of external human-machine interfaces for automated vehicles. In: Proceedings of the 11th International Conference on Automotive User Interfaces and Interactive Vehicular Applications, pp. 369–378. ACM. https://doi.org/10.1145/3342197.3344523. https://dl.acm.org/doi/10.1145/3342197.3344523. Accessed 11 Apr 2025
25. Dragan, A.D., Lee, K.C., Srinivasa, S.S.: Legibility and predictability of robot motion. In: 2013 8th ACM/IEEE International Conference on Human-Robot Interaction (HRI), pp. 301–308. IEEE (2013)
26. Fang, H.-S., et al.: Alphapose: whole-body regional multi-person pose estimation and tracking in real-time. IEEE Trans. Pattern Anal. Mach. Intell. **45**(6), 7157–7173 (2022)
27. Reed, D.J.: Turning heads and making conversation on twitch. Discourse Context Media **60**, 100802 (2024)
28. Hutchby, I., Wooffitt, R.: Conversation Analysis. Principles Practices and Applications. Polity Press. Polity Press
29. Local, J., Kelly, J.: Projection and 'silences': notes on phonetic and conversational structure **9**(2), 185–204
30. Streeck, J., Jordan, J.S.: Projection and anticipation: the forward-looking nature of embodied communication **46**(2), 93–102. https://doi.org/10.1080/01638530902728777. Accessed 17 Apr 2022
31. Wang, T., Camara, F., Woolley, R., Reed, D.: Identifying public engagement with autonomous art through human pose and speed detection (under review)
32. McNeill, D.: Hand and Mind: What Gestures Reveal About Thought. University of Chicago Press
33. Zhang, J., Gould, S., Ben-Shabat, I.: Vidat–ANU CVML video annotation tool. https://github.com/anucvml/vidat

Bringing Robots on the Stage: A Co-designed Multiplatform Robot Control System for Theatrical Performances

Anis Derri[1], Giulia Filacanapa[2], Erica Magris[2], and Salvatore M. Anzalone[1](✉)

[1] Laboratoire CHArt, Université Paris 8, Saint-Denis, France
sanzalone@uni-paris8.fr
[2] Scènes du monde, Université Paris 8, Saint-Denis, France

Abstract. The research project "Scène et Robotique" explores the relational and dramaturgical potential of social robots in the theater. Through the paradigm of Design-Based Research, artists and engineers developed a series of theatrical performances using small humanoid robots. In this paper we describe the cross-platform, humanoid robot control system developed in this project that made this co-creation possible, exploring its potentials and its limitations.

Keywords: Robot theater · Co-development · Robotic actor

1 Introduction

Theatrical art is a live performative practice that brings together acting, directing, set design, lighting, costume, and often music and dance to create immersive storytelling experiences [18]. Characterized by great diversity and freedom in its staging, it has developed sophisticated techniques to explore the interplay between bodies, objects, and space. Concepts such as presence, otherness, illusion, repetition, improvisation, identification, distance, and dialogue are addressed to let audience suspend their disbelief [9] while engaging with the social interplay unfolding throughout the performance.

These questions arise similarly in social robotics, where robots are endowed with cognitive abilities that explicitly take human presence into account during decision-making processes [5,25]. In this field, concepts such as believability and expressivity, presence and co-presence, have been extensively studied. Breazeal [4,6–8] and Ishiguro [16,20,21], among others, have shown how humanoid robots can elicit human social responses, but also how fragile these responses are when faced with mechanical or behavioral inconsistencies. People expect from social robots non only machines capable of coherent actions but also, and above all, a meaningful presence [10]: a partner endowed with communicative capabilities, able of conveying a sense of intentionality to humans and evoking the feeling of sonzai-kan the 'feeling of being in the presence of another person' [24].

From this perspective, designing social robots is not simply about building better machines; it is an experimental exploration of what it means to appear alive, to be perceived as an intentional being. In this sense, theater and robotics converge: both seek to construct an illusion of life that communicates intentions, adapts dynamically, and resonates emotionally with humans. Understanding and mastering this convergence offers new insights not only for exploring new forms of theatrical arts, but also for the broader project of human-robot interaction. The theatrical stage, in fact, can provide a unique experimental platform for studying the complexities of social interactions [17]: an ideal semi-structured space where various technologies could be employed to capture and model the sensorimotor contingencies that shape interactions between humans and socially intelligent robots, offering a privileged setting for learning, developing and testing social interactive skills [27].

The intersection of theater and robotics is not a recent development. The term "robot" itself was first introduced in 1921 in Karel Čapek's theatrical play *R.U.R - Rossum's Universal Robots*, derived from the Czech word *robota*. Since then, robots have made occasional appearances on stage, embodying both utopian promises and dystopian, apocalyptic visions [28]. These performances have spanned a variety of robotic types: hyper-realistic robots, such as those presented by Oriza Hirata in *Sayonara* (2010) and *Three Sisters Android Version* (2012), or by Stefan Kaegi and Rimini Protokoll in *Uncanny Valley* (2018); robotic arms, featured in *Sans Objet* (2009) by Aurélien Bory and *Artefact* (2017) by Joris Mathieu; and small humanoid robots, as seen in *Robot* (2013) by Blanca Li and *My Square Lady* (2015) by Gob Squad. Of particular interest is comedy robot performance, which can involve creativity [23], improvisation [19], and can make effective use of a nuanced perception of audience responses as well as precise control of timing [26] to sustain coherence and effectiveness in the performance. In all these cases, the presence of robots on stage forces the exploration of the staging process, the performance techniques, and the reception effects in new ways [11]. At the same time, theatrical concepts as presence, otherness, illusion, repetition, improvisation, identification, distance, and dialogue need to be reconsidered.

To investigate such questions, the "Scène et Robotique: Interactions and Interrelations" project[1] funded by the ArTec[2] University Research School (EUR), brings together engineers, computer scientists, artists, and researchers in the performing arts around the question of sociability - both in robotic devices and in theatrical practice [3]. Through the sharing of knowledge, languages, methodologies, and observation protocols, the goal is to investigate the relational and dramaturgical potential of the robot on stage in its interactions with actors and audiences.

As part of the project's broader exploration of the robot's dramaturgical and relational potential, a cross-platform humanoid robot control system was iteratively developed throughout the entire duration of the project, following a

---

[1] Scène et robotique: https://scenesrobots.eur-artec.fr.
[2] EUR ArTec: https://scenesrobots.eur-artec.fr/.

Design-Based Research (DBR) approach [1]. Its conception, development and refinement followed a continuous mutual exchange between artists and engineers in a process of a mutual adaptation that responded to evolving dramaturgical and performative needs. This paper examines the capabilities and constraints of this system, focusing on how it enables real-time interactive control, expressivity, and semi-automated control in co-creative artistic contexts. Particular attention is given to the system's modular design, its adaptability to different robots, and staging conditions and autonomy required. Through this analysis, the paper aims to contribute to ongoing discussions in both robotics and performance studies by identifying design choices that facilitate meaningful human-robot interaction in artistic settings.

2 Materials and Methods

Following the DBR methodology, the project evolved incrementally through the co-development of a series of theatrical performances in several workshop involving artists and engineers. Each workshop investigated different dimensions of human-robot interaction, from simple interactive objects to more complex systems (Fig. 1):

- **Intelligent objects**: exploring the potential of choreographic objects such as human-like robots or mechanical autonomous machines;
- **Human-like embodiment**: focusing on synchrony, gestures, postures, facial expressions and the possibilities offered by non-verbal language in human-like robots;
- **Speech and dialogues**: addressing verbal interaction, leveraging prosody and vocal non-verbal communication;
- **Environment and autonomy**: investigating the scenographic possibilities offered by sensors (RGB and RGB-D cameras) and actuators (lights, sounds, music) distributed throughout the scene to enhance the autonomy and coherence of robots' social behavior;
- **Dramatic composition**: experimenting with humorous scenarios and mise en abîme of the research process itself.

Fig. 1. The different research dimensions explored in the project.

The project focused in particular on the co-development of scenes using two small humanoid robots: Aldebaran Nao[3] and LuxAI QTRobot[4] The DBR methodology highlighted the need for an effective control system for both robotic platforms cable of rapidly implementing and deploying changes to existent behaviors as well as enabling the swift development of new behaviors. At the same time, the small size of the platforms and the challenging environmental conditions on the stage, especially in terms of lighting, prevented a full exploitation of the onboard sensors to achieve complete autonomy. In accord with these constraints, a Wizard-of-Oz (WoZ) framework was adopted, eanbling the abstraction of behaviors and the teleoperated control of both platforms, while semi-autonomous behaviors were conceived relying on infrared RGB-D sensors conveniently deployed on the environment. Puppetry offered a compelling metaphor to the chosen control model [22]: just as a puppeteer imbues an inanimate object with life through carefully structured gestures and rhythms, the teleoperator controls the robot to evoke the illusion of intentionality, suggesting an inner logic through the organization of the robot's actions in time and space, even when controlled externally.

2.1 The Robotic Platform

Despite being designed to be human-like, with a very similar size, Nao and QTRobot are very different platforms (Fig. 2):

- Nao is designed to walk, QTRobot has no legs: this gives Nao the possibility of (slowly) strolling in the scene with the only constrain of the charge of its battery, while, as plugged-in device, gives QTRobot the possibility of much longer interaction due to the absence of batteries;
- The upper body's degrees of freedom of both platforms are significantly different: with only 3 degrees of freedoms on each arm and noone on the body, QTRobot has significantly lower postural and gestural expressiveness than Nao;
- At the same time, QTRobot has a screen showing animated facial expressions, while Nao has only lights: this gives QTRobot great capabilities in terms of facial expressiveness;
- Nao has two cameras, a frontal one on the head, a second one pointing towards the legs, while QTRobot has a RGB-D camera on the head: while a RGB-D camera can provide a 3D reconstruction of the environment, both platforms need a short term memory that take in account the movements of the robot's head, increasing the complexity of their perception system.

Finally, the two platforms rely on different software subsystems, ROS for QTRobot, NaoQi for Nao.

A database of basic behaviors specific for each robot was co-developed with artists and engineers. Each basic behavioris composed by a combination of **gestures**, **facial expressions**, the eventual **textual utterances** to be spoken

---

[3] *Aldebaran Nao*: https://www.aldebaran.com/.
[4] *LuxAI QTRobot*: https://luxai.com/.

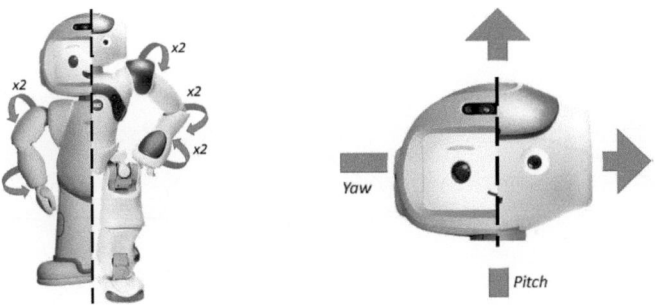

Fig. 2. A comparison of the two robots upper bodies with their degrees of freedom: on the left, the robots arms; on the right the robots heads.

through the text-to-speech interface specific of each platform, and, where applicable, **walking speeds**. Such combinations are implemented in accordance with the hardware constraints of the specific robotic platform employed: while gestures and speech are universally possible, facial expressions and walking are distinct features of the QTRobot and Nao platforms, respectively.

2.2 Interactive Sequences

Interactive sequences of behaviors were described through finite state machines, where basic behaviors are modeled as distinct states. Transition between states can be triggered by countdown timers or, as explained in the followings, by keyboard inputs or by perception-based events. These transitions result in sequences of interconnected states that collectively model complex interactive behaviors.

At the same time, a ROS node was used to implement a software abstraction layer decoupling the description of the interactive sequences of behaviors with the specific platform that will actually execute it. This layer will execute the same sequence of behaviors independently from the platform, carrying out the basic behaviors for each state in accord with the possibilities provided by the specific platform in which they are executed. In this way, the same interactive sequence can be run on both Nao and QTRobot without significant changes.

2.3 Teleoperation

Preliminary tests on the stage shown the impossibility of fully exploiting the onboard sensors: according to the robot's position in the stage, lights were perceived as too strong or too weak, preventing a clear perception of the scene; at the same time, the small size of the robots constrained the point of view the robot from a very low height, reducing the performances of standard computer vision algorithms for human partners perception. We propose a Wizard-of-Oz teleoperation system as straightforward and convenient way to tackle this issue. In this case, interactive sequences of basic behaviors would be triggered and

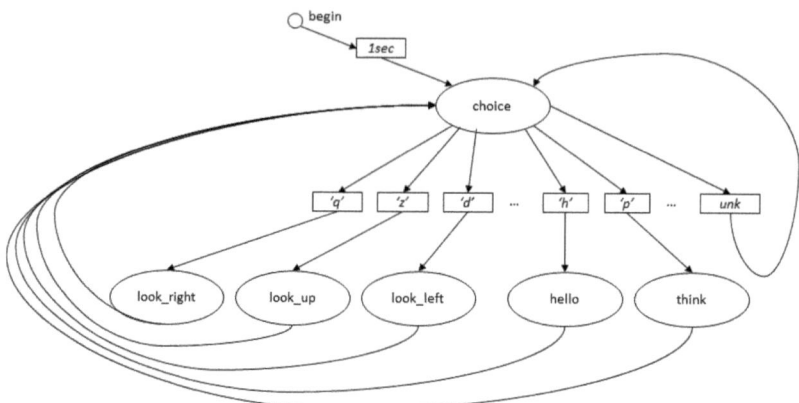

Fig. 3. The finite state machine implemented through the wizard of Oz system.

executed in response to the pressing of a specific button on a remote keyboard (Fig. 3).

2.4 Semi-autonomy

The use of an external camera, with the possibility of placing it in a static and more convenient location, can cope the perception issues of onboard sensors. At the same time, light issues can be partially handled using an infrared-based sensor. Thus, we proposed the integration on the system of an Intel RealSense D435i[5] an infrared RGB-D sensor that, in conjunction with the Nuitrack skeleton tracking library[6] allow a clear 3D perception of human partners in the scene. 3D skeletal information can be used to extract both people postures or position in the space. These information can be used to trigger specific interactive sequences of behaviors. Specific postures can be used, as instance, to reply to particular gestures.

3 Use Case Scenarios

As mentioned, the system presented in this work was developed incrementally through a DBR approach, evolving over the course of the project through a process of mutual adaptation between artists and engineers, in response to a series of theatrical performances and their specific performative requirements. In the following, two important use case are proposed: the implementation of the "body-object's relationship grammar", interesting example of co-development of movements in teleoperation; the development of a short humorous scenario, notable example of semi-automation of the robotics platforms used in this project. The

---

[5] *Intel RealSense D435i*: https://www.intelrealsense.com/depth-camera-d435i/.
[6] *Nuitrack*: https://nuitrack.com/.

videos of the proposed scenarios are available on the YouTube channel of the "Scène et Robotique" project[7]

3.1 Implementating the "Body-Object's Relationship Grammar"

As part of the effort focused on understanding the complex relation between the actors, the spaces and the objects, we had the possibility of working with Claire Heggen, a professional mastering the animation of marionettes: she proposes a "body-object's relationship grammar" [12,14] that, through a proper use of four different modes of body movement - progression, degression, restoration, contradiction - of the gazing and of the pointing, guides the focus the spectators' gaze on the actor's body, on the object (puppet or robot), or even on the relationship between the two.

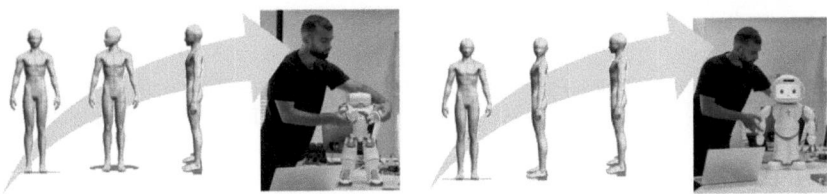

Fig. 4. The body-object's relationship grammar applied to the Nao robot: on the left, the progressive movement; on the right the regressive movement.

The formalization and modeling of expressive gestures and movements proposed by Claire Heggen is interesting also for a robot with movement capabilities and gesture expressiveness as Nao. In a compelling parallelism between robots and marionettes, the presented platform has been able to implement the Heggen's body-object's relationship grammar into Nao (Fig. 4, making it available for its use in the theater.

Fig. 5. A possible exploitation of the robot's semi-autonomy: a world grid triggering interactive sequences of behaviors in a humorous scenario.

---

[7] *Scène et Robotique YouTube channel*: https://www.youtube.com/@sceneetrobotique.

3.2 Implementing a Short Humorous Scenario

Semi-autonomy has been exploited to create an humorous scenario. As shown in Fig. 5, an RGB-D camera was used to build a world grid, where the environment space is partitioned: the presence of the human partner on a specific partition will trigger a different interactive sequences of behaviors. Julien Daillère, author, actor, and director, proposed the use of this grid to select and trigger behaviors in a humorous context. The introduced platform has been able to implement in a reliable way the grid, allowing, in a notable way, actors improvisation.

4 Discussion

The Design-Based Research methodology fostered a continuous exchange of knowledge between artists and engineers throughout the project, enabling them to learn each other's vocabularies, to recognize the robots' limitations, and to appreciate their unique capabilities. This process led to a gradual, mutual adaptation and deeper understanding across disciplines. The control system co-developed during the project both supported and evolved within this collaborative dynamic.

Evaluating the outcomes of a theatrical process presents inherent challenges, as such outcomes often resist standardization and quantification. Unlike scientific experiments or technological benchmarks, theatrical performances are deeply contextual, ephemeral, and shaped by subjective interpretations. Their value lies not only in measurable effects but also in their capacity to evoke emotions, provoke reflection, and foster shared experiences among participants and audiences

Within these limitations, we relied on a panel of experts composed of artists, dramaturgs, and HRI researchers, who collaboratively contributed to the evaluation of the theatrical performance.

- **Claire Heggen**, Théâtre du Mouvement, Artistic Director of the Claire Heggen-Théâtre du Mouvement Company;
- **Antonio Chella**, University of Palermo, Professor of Robotics;
- **Laurette Burgholzer**, Stuttgart University of Music and Performing Arts, Doctor in Theater Studies;
- **Jean-Pierre Merlet**, INRIA (National Institute for Research in Digital Science and Technology) Sophia Antipolis, Research Director;
- **Ester Fuoco**, Academy of Fine Arts - Santa Giulia in Brescia, Senior Lecturer in Performing Arts.

Their diverse backgrounds enabled a multidimensional reading of the piece, combining artistic sensibility with scientific insight.

The discussion with the panelist addressed several key dimensions of the performance, including the legibility of the robot's actions, the coherence of its behavior within the narrative, and the emotional or aesthetic resonance of the scenes. Particular attention was given to the integration between actors, robots, and engineers, focusing on how this kind of multidisciplinary co-conception process was carried out and how the engineer, as a teleoperator, became either a hidden presence behind the scenes or an integral part of the performance itself. This dimension was examined in terms of its impact on the fluidity of the interaction and the credibility of the theatrical illusion. While the panelists acknowledged the strengths and the potentials of the proposed approach they also highlighted several limitations. From a dramaturgical perspective, the robots' inherent design and characteristics strongly shape their identity, making it challenging for them to convincingly embody roles that fall outside of their predefined personas. For instance, the childlike appearance of QTRobot makes it particularly challenging to assign it a role that does not evoke its 'child' identity. More in general, the expressiveness of the two robotic platforms considered in this project is further complicated by the technical challenges and limitations posed by the robotic platforms themselves. Speech synthesis remains constrained, with prosody requiring meticulous, fine-grained scripting, sometimes at the level of individual vowels, thus limiting both the range and spontaneity of verbal interactions. Moreover, while both Nao and QTRobot are capable of performing gestures and speech, their expressive capabilities are uneven: Nao lacks facial features and conveys expression solely through LEDs, whereas QTRobot has non-articulated legs, which restrict its ability to assume varied or natural postures. The synchrony and interaction pace often lack naturalness when interactive sequences are triggered either through timing mechanisms or teleoperation. In the latter case, robot control becomes even more challenging as the number of interactive sequences that can be triggered increases: in this context, the keyboard interface becomes inefficient; other, more natural interfaces, such as tablets, are needed [29]. A more effective approach to address this issue is the comprehensive integration of semi-autonomous behaviors [15]. To achieve this, improvements are required in both the reliability and responsiveness in the perception system, as well as in the breadth of its sensory coverage. The integration of multiple synchronized cameras can enhance spatial awareness, ensuring more reliable detection across the stage, that can be a very wide and crowded area [2], while a multi-skeleton tracking system [13] could address current limitations, such as the detection of only a single person at a time. Reducing system latency and implementing robust sensor fusion strategies are also crucial to ensure real-time responsiveness and fluid adaptation to dynamic social interactions. Speech recognition can surely be a direction for improvement, as it was deliberately excluded due to the intrinsic latency that current systems imply, which could have undermined the temporal precision required for smooth interaction. While this approach helped preserve the coherence of the performance, it inevitably constrained opportunities for spontaneous verbal engagement and natural turn-taking.

Despite these challenges, the panelists recognized the potential of the approach and highlighted the promising opportunities for improvement, emphasizing the system's ability to evolve with further development.

Acknowledgments. This project was funded by EUR ArTeC. Authors thank the master students that actively worked on this project, Walid Khamis and Predrag Kostic, as well as the actors and the professionals that participated to the "RoboAct" workshops.

References

1. Anderson, T., Shattuck, J.: Design-based research: a decade of progress in education research? Educ. Res. **41**(1), 16–25 (2012). https://doi.org/10.3102/0013189X11428813
2. Anzalone, S.M., Boucenna, S., Ivaldi, S., Chetouani, M.: Evaluating the engagement with social robots. Int. J. Soc. Robot. **7**(4), 465–478 (2015). https://doi.org/10.1007/s12369-015-0298-7
3. Anzalone, S.M., Filacanapa, G., Magris, E.: ROBOTACT - Cocréations humain-robot: Une recherche-création interdisciplinaire entre théâtre et robotique. In: JIT 2022 - Journées d'Informatique Théâtrale 2022, Lyon, France (2022). https://inria.hal.science/hal-04153460
4. Breazeal, C.: Toward sociable robots. Robot. Auton. Syst. **42**(3–4), 167–175 (2003). https://doi.org/10.1016/S0921-8890(02)00373-1
5. Breazeal, C.: Designing Sociable Robots. MIT Press (2004)
6. Breazeal, C., et al.: Interactive robot theatre. Commun. ACM **46**(7), 76–85 (2003). https://doi.org/10.1145/792704.792733
7. Breazeal, C., Dautenhahn, K., Kanda, T.: Social robotics. In: Siciliano, B., Khatib, O. (eds.) Springer Handbook of Robotics, pp. 1935–1972. Springer, Cham (2016). https://doi.org/10.1007/978-3-319-32552-1_72
8. Breazeal, C., Scassellati, B.: Robots that imitate humans. Trends Cogn. Sci. **6**(11), 481–487 (2002). https://doi.org/10.1016/S1364-6613(02)02016-8
9. Coleridge, S.T.: Biographia Literaria: Samuel Taylor Coleridge. Oxford (1985)
10. Coradeschi, S., et al.: Human-inspired robots. IEEE Intell. Syst. **21**(4), 74–85 (2006). https://doi.org/10.1109/mis.2006.72
11. Dixon, S.: Digital Performance: A History of New Media in Theater, Dance, Performance Art, and Installation. The MIT Press (2007). https://doi.org/10.7551/mitpress/2429.001.0001
12. Doyon, R., Heggen, C.: Making visible. In: Adams, G., Aniksdal, G., Ficara, M., Gale, M., Varley, J. (eds.) Theatre - Women - Practice. The Open Page, Odin Teatrets Forlag (2006)
13. Ghidoni, S., Anzalone, S.M., Munaro, M., Michieletto, S., Menegatti, E.: A distributed perception infrastructure for robot assisted living. Robot. Auton. Syst. **62**(9), 1316–1328 (2014). https://doi.org/10.1016/j.robot.2014.03.022
14. Heggen, C., Marc, Y., Pezin, P.: Théâtre du mouvement. Deuxième Époque (2017)
15. Ivaldi, S., Anzalone, S.M., Rousseau, W., Sigaud, O., Chetouani, M.: Robot initiative in a team learning task increases the rhythm of interaction but not the perceived engagement. Front. Neurorobot. **8** (2014). https://doi.org/10.3389/fnbot.2014.00005
16. Kanda, T., Hirano, T., Eaton, D., Ishiguro, H.: Interactive robots as social partners and peer tutors for children: a field trial. Hum.-Comput. Interact. **19**(1-2), 61–84 (2004). https://psycnet.apa.org/doi/10.1207/s15327051hci1901&2_4

17. Knight, H.: Eight lessons learned about non-verbal interactions through robot theater. In: Mutlu, B., Bartneck, C., Ham, J., Evers, V., Kanda, T. (eds.) ICSR 2011. LNCS (LNAI), vol. 7072, pp. 42–51. Springer, Heidelberg (2011). https://doi.org/10.1007/978-3-642-25504-5_5
18. Malloy, K.E.: The Art of Theatrical Design: Elements of Visual Composition, Methods, and Practice. Routledge (2022). https://doi.org/10.4324/9781003023142
19. Mathewson, K., Mirowski, P.: Improbotics: exploring the imitation game using machine intelligence in improvised theatre. In: Proceedings of the AAAI Conference on Artificial Intelligence and Interactive Digital Entertainment, vol. 14, no. 1, pp. 59–66 (2018). https://ojs.aaai.org/index.php/AIIDE/article/view/13030
20. Nishiguchi, S., Ogawa, K., Yoshikawa, Y., Chikaraishi, T., Hirata, O., Ishiguro, H.: Theatrical approach: Designing human-like behaviour in humanoid robots. Robot. Auton. Syst. **89**, 158–166 (2017). https://doi.org/10.1016/j.robot.2016.11.017
21. Nishio, S., Ishiguro, H., Hagit, N.: Geminoid: Teleoperated Android of an Existing Person. I-Tech Education and Publishing (2007). https://doi.org/10.5772/4876
22. Plassard, D.: Les scènes de l'intranquillité. Puck: la marionnette et les autres arts **20**, 11–16 (2014)
23. Rond, J., Sanchez, A., Berger, J., Knight, H.: Improv with robots: creativity, inspiration, co-performance. In: 2019 28th IEEE International Conference on Robot and Human Interactive Communication (RO-MAN), pp. 1–8 (2019). https://doi.org/10.1109/RO-MAN46459.2019.8956410
24. Sumioka, H., Nishio, S., Minato, T., Yamazaki, R., Ishiguro, H.: Minimal human design approach for Sonzai-Kan media: investigation of a feeling of human presence. Cogn. Comput. **6**(4), 760–774 (2014). https://doi.org/10.1007/s12559-014-9270-3
25. Vianello, L., et al.: Human-humanoid interaction and cooperation: a review. Curr. Robot. Rep. **2**(4), 441–454 (2021). https://doi.org/10.1007/s43154-021-00068-z
26. Vilk, J., Fitter, N.T.: Comedians in cafes getting data: evaluating timing and adaptivity in real-world robot comedy performance. In: Proceedings of the 2020 ACM/IEEE International Conference on Human-Robot Interaction, HRI 2020, pp. 223–231. Association for Computing Machinery, New York (2020). https://doi.org/10.1145/3319502.3374780
27. Vinciarelli, A., et al.: Bridging the gap between social animal and unsocial machine: a survey of social signal processing. IEEE Trans. Affect. Comput. **3**(1), 69–87 (2012). https://doi.org/10.1109/t-affc.2011.27
28. Wilson, S.: Information Arts: Intersections of Art, Science, and Technology. The MIT Press (2001). https://doi.org/10.7551/mitpress/3765.001.0001
29. Zou, J., Gauthier, S., Anzalone, S.M., Cohen, D., Archambault, D.: A wizard of oz interface with qtrobot for facilitating the handwriting learning in children with dysgraphia and its usability evaluation. In: Lecture Notes in Computer Science, pp. 219–225. Springer (2022). https://doi.org/10.1007/978-3-031-08645-8_26

Towards a Customizable Dramaturgical System: An Artistic Experiment in AI-Enhanced Human-Machine Dialogue

Yucheng Peng[1(✉)], Junyi Chen[2], Shaoxin Sun[3], and Didier Plassard[1]

[1] College of Theatre Studies, Paul Valéry University, 34090 Montpellier, France
yucheng.peng@etu.univ-montp3.fr, didier.plassard@univ-montp3.fr
[2] Montpellier University, 34090 Montpellier, France
[3] College of Automation, Chongqing University, 400044 Chongqing, China
sunshaoxin@cqu.edu.cn

Abstract. This case study investigates an experimental one-on-one interactive theater installation featuring a virtual AI performer built with a fine-tuned version of ChatGPT-4o. Incorporating a curated poetry database and voice cloning, the AI acted as a creative agent within a human-machine-powered dramaturgical framework, where the Dramaturge, Participant(s), and AI Agent functioned as interdependent co-creators. This triadic collaboration fostered a dynamic, flexible, and fluid creative process, notably expanding the Dramaturge's role. The study adopts a multi-method approach, combining analysis of exhibition texts, interpretive diagrams, and holistic observation to outline the structure and operation of this co-creative system. Drawing from a personally situated, artist-in-the-loop perspective, it proposes a preliminary AI-augmented dramaturgical model, reflecting how contemporary AI technologies may reshape artistic authorship and transform creative practices.

Keywords: AI-human-driven dramaturgy · Virtual narrative space · Human-machine interaction · Artist-in-the-loop · Dramaturgical system

1 Introduction

Since ChatGPT first entered the stage, audiences have shown both doubt and admiration, revealing a shared excitement beneath these conflicting responses [6,23]. A series of pressing questions concerning the nature of art have emerged as active topics of interdisciplinary debate [12,32], particularly the extent to which AI can be considered creative [15]. This surge of interest has also been driven by the advanced user-friendliness of contemporary AI agents such as ChatGPT [14]. On the other hand, the urgent call to bridge the rupture between culture and technology had already been seriously articulated in academia around the 1960 s [25]. In the field of art, the emergence of digital art in the mid-1960 s responded to this call by fostering a profound dialogue between artists and engineers. At the same time, critical reflections on the overemphasis of non-intentional, purely sensory experiences within the digital art landscape were strong [33]. However, the continuation of this critical stance into the domain of human-AI co-creation appears problematic [5]. As a leading achievement of machine learning in the domain of natural language processing, large language model (LLM) technologies are now steering related philosophical discussions of art in new directions, yet a corresponding vocabulary that can adequately engage with these new developments remains lacking [13]. In response to these shifts, it becomes a meaningful endeavor to engage in human-LLMs co-creative practices while actively incorporating terminologies from computer science and AI into the detailed processes of artistic creation, thereby offering a reflection and response to this linguistic gap. Against this backdrop, the interactive theater installation *Demain, Le Théâtre*– exhibited at the Atrium Library of Paul Valéry University in Montpellier from January 23 to 31, 2025 [3]–was intentionally designed as a site of experimentation for human-AI co-creation, focusing not only on the collaborative processes and methodologies but also on the integration of technological and artistic vocabularies. This study overviews the installation, analyzes its human-machine-powered dramaturgical system, and explores the hybrid text–combining theater, documentation, and poetry–shaped by an open-ended structure and unpredictable participant-AI interactions.

Sources of inspiration for the project include developments in AI-generated playwriting by the Czech research initiative THEaiTRE [4,28], notably THEaiTRobot 1.0 [26], which commemorated the centenary of the word "robot"[1] with a machine-generated script, and its 2022 successor THEaiTRobot 2.0 [27], which continued to refine LLMs-driven dramaturgy. In the domain of human-robot improvisational performance, the works led by Piotr Mirowski [1,22] and Kory Mathewson [2,20]–particularly HumanMachine Project [19,21] and Improbotics Project [7]–have been foundational in exploring live, human-machine co-improvisation via AI agents. The project also draws upon the aesthetics of Annie Dorsen's *Hello Hi There*, which featured two computers onstage engaged in unscripted philosophical debate[2]. Other influences include Jason Rohrer's *Project December: Simulate the Dead*[3], in which chatbots are trained on data from deceased individuals to facilitate mourning and dialogue, as well as the conference-theatre *dSimon* co-created by Tammara Leites and Simon Senn. In this performance, Simon Senn provided extensive private data to Tammara Leites, who used it to train dSimon, a virtual character serving as Senn's digital double, with whom he eventually developed a complex emotional bond[4].

Compared to the works mentioned above, which involve algorithmic fine-tuning, artist-engineer collaborations, or the exploration of AI agents' expressive abilities across different modes of theatrical improvisation, *Demain, Le Théâtre*

---

[1] This word was first coined by Czech writer Karel Čapek in his 1920 play *R.U.R.* which derives from the Czech word *robota*, meaning forced labor.
[2] *Hello Hi There* (2010), by Annie Dorsen.
[3] See project homepage https://projectdecember.net/.
[4] *dSimon* (2021), by Tammara Leites and Simon Senn.

focuses on the simplest form of interaction: one-on-one, free-form exchanges. In this way, the concept of human-machine communication is not only embedded in the artistic format but also deeply reflected in the creative methodology. The one-on-one model facilitates both deeper engagement between human and AI and closer observation of the interaction process and its emergent outcomes. Finally, the installation was independently designed by a research-based artist without a formal background in computer science, underscoring the accessibility of contemporary AI technologies and their vast yet underexplored potential in the arts.

The following chapter will provide a detailed introduction to the project's content and distinctive features, beginning with an explanation of its external and internal frameworks.

2 Architecture of the Project

2.1 External Structure: Principles and Modes of Interaction

The installation consists of two primary components (see Fig. 1): a *Stage*, represented by a laptop, and an *Auditorium*, a standing individual viewing booth constructed from a wooden frame and painted cardboard panels. The wooden structure supports the digital apparatus, and the cardboard enclosure serves to isolate the viewing experience, enhancing the sense of immersion and concentration for each individual participant. Participants engage with the installation while standing, positioning their heads inside an enclosed black box that isolates the visual and auditory environment. The human-computer interaction begins when a viewer clicks the START button, initiating a conversation with a French-speaking virtual character named Yuchɇng.[5] After the conversation, the participant clicks STOP and waits for Yuchɇng's audio response, which is also transcribed and projected onto the *stage* for the benefit of future participants.

Each day of the installation constitutes a separate *Act* and every 30 rounds[6] of interaction form a *Scene*. In every *Act* of the project, the first *Scene* was initiated by the author. This was done both to provide a narrative foundation for the day's first participant and to guide the unfolding of the overall dramaturgy. At the end of each *Scene*, a secondary GPT model is activated to generate a summary of the current *Scene* in the background. Based on the summary, a verse line is selected from the prewritten poems as the title of the *Scene*. It was discovered during the exhibition that, due to a flaw in the program design, the system was generating an entire poem rather than a single verse line for each

---

[5] Yuchɇng has been fine-tuned on a dataset consisting of 100 poems written over a two-year period. Its voice was cloned using ElevenLabs, based on recordings of the author's own voice.

[6] The choice of thirty dialogue turns was based on practical experience and expectations regarding the exhibition setting.

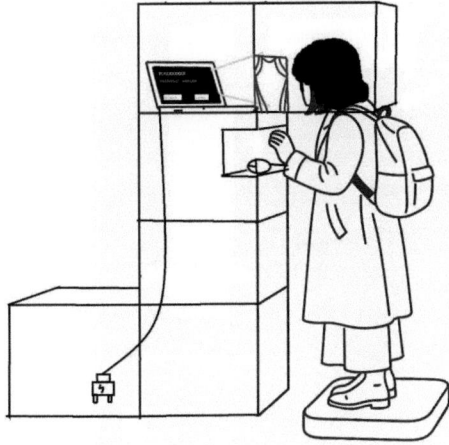

Fig. 1. Diagram of the interaction interface integrated into the physical installation. It depicts a participant observing the dialogue on the *Stage* through a window, with an interactive mouse positioned at hand. The diagram was created with the support of ChatGPT's generative functions.

scene, which did not achieve the desired effect. Consequently, this step has been revised and re-executed after the exhibition.[7]

2.2 Internal Core: Human-Machine Powered Dramaturgical System

This subsection outlines the structural framework and key characteristics of the installation's *Stage*, accompanied by a diagram (see Fig. 2) and explanatory notes.

Explains the creative entities and their relations in this study (see Fig. 2):

- **Participant(s)** refer to the human users engaging with the installation. They include those who simply read without speaking, those who engage in the dialogue while drawing on the latent narrative threads of previous turns, and those who respond freely without regard to prior context. These participants become interconnected through the traces of text left on the screen. The relationship between the participant and the Agent is formed through improvised, direct, and egalitarian dialogues. Whether or not the participant follows the prompt suggested in the performance introduction to continue based on the previous dialogue, the narration remains unified as a dynamic whole at the macro level.

---

[7] The final solution consisted in re-generating the poetic title pool by programmatically reading the .txt poetry document line by line to create a clean list of individual verses.

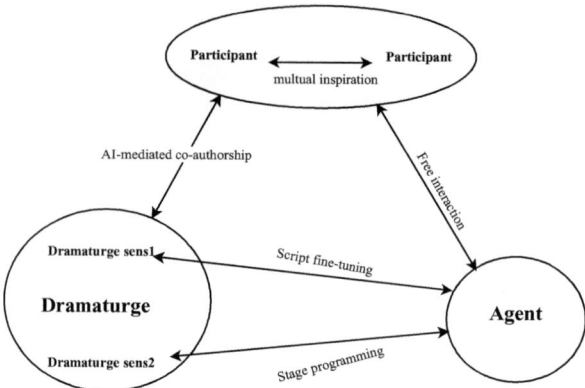

Fig. 2. Diagram of the Three Creative Entities and Their Relational Structure. All arrows in the diagram are bidirectional, reflecting a dynamic feedback loop among the three creative entities.

- **Dramaturge** represents the conceptual designer and builder of the *Stage*, divided here into two conceptual roles: *Dramaturge sens 1*, who composes and edits the text, and *Dramaturge sens 2*, who mediates between the text and its stage realization, assuming a director-like function within the scope of dramaturgical authorship. Following Joseph Danan's framework, which strategically distinguishes [11] between *la dramaturgie au sens 1* (the art of composition) and *la dramaturgie au sens 2* (the thinking behind staging), this study applies a similar distinction for the *dramaturge*'s role.[8]

  The relationship between the *Dramaturge* and the *Participant(s)* is mediated by the *Agent*. As the fine-tuned AI model adopts the dramaturge's stylistic features, the agent functions as a kind of *double* through which the Dramaturge collaborates with Participants.

  The Dramaturge-Agent relationship operates on two levels. For *Dramaturge sens 1*, it is established through *Script fine-tuning*, which includes both the structural setup (e.g., generating a title every 30 turns) and editorial post-curation of dialogue. For *Dramaturge sens 2*, the relationship is expressed via *Stage programming*, which encompasses visual, auditory, and performative elements–all implemented via programming techniques.

- **Agent** The Agent contributes not only as a practical tool (for translation, title generation, and voice-to-text conversion.) but also as a creative subject[9] within the co-authorship process, by taking on the role of Yuchɐ ng. The relationship between the Agent and the Dramaturge, as previously discussed, is primarily established through two interconnected dimensions. The Agent's

---

[8] The term *metteur en scne* (theatre director) is deliberately avoided in order to emphasize the central role of dramaturgical designing in this experiment.

[9] Here, AI is not defined as intrinsically creative, but its outputs are recognized as artistically meaningful insofar as they emerge through deep interaction with human participants.

impact on Participants is likewise multifaceted: its non-human essence, intertwined with highly human-like representations, produces intricate effects on the participants. This duality also leads to a distinct dialogical dynamic between human and machine, one that differs fundamentally from typical human-human exchanges.

The following subsection further outlines several key features of this adaptive architecture enabled by the integration of the AI agent, accompanied by selected examples.

2.3 Distinctive Features and Artistic Characteristics

The specific characteristics of the creative framework can be summarized as follows:

- **Dialogic Depth and Collective Presence in One-on-One Interactions.** The one-on-one dialogue format was intended to explore the potential for deep human-machine interaction. In practice, providing participants with a private and enclosed setting enabled a broader and safer psychological space for expression. The results indicate that the vast majority of participants engaged with the AI Agent in an earnest manner, even when elements of performativity were deliberately introduced into their speech. One participant, after 19 rounds of dialogue, expressed strong dissatisfaction with Yuchɛ̃ ng's description of them as an "apprentice builder of death"[10] and responded with direct criticism of the agent during the conversation. In addition, the large number of participants, many of them students, contributed to a sense of communal presence that shaped the outcome of the installation.
- **Intentional Integration of AI into the Personal Creative Process.** The outcomes of fine-tuning the AI model on poetry were unexpectedly rich. In constructing the dramaturgical framework, the author observes that, if one regards the next line in poetry as a kind of response to the preceding line, it precisely corresponds to the "user" and "assistant" values under the "role" key in fine-tuning protocols. This seemingly *synesthetic correspondence* [9] between art and technology is key to the artistic vitality generated by this experiment.
- **Enrichment and Expansion of the Dramaturgical Design through AI Agent Participation.** The Agent's highly structured machinic nature, made possible through programming, along with its inherent unpredictability, offers far more inspiration than limitation for the Dramaturge's creative process. For example, the design that allows the AI to select a title from a set of poetic lines after thirty rounds of interaction gives the entire text a vivid structure, turning each scene transition into a poetic modulation.

---

[10] The original French text reads: "Vous ici, vous tes des apprentis constructeurs de la mort"

The exhibition recorded a total of approximately 103106 instances of participant engagement. After excluding the author's own interactions and uncertain records, the number of valid participant entries stands at 99. The resulting script, including titles, comprises approximately 19,000 words.

In the following chapter I will focus on examining the finalized, as-yet-unpublished script named *Atrium File*. This will be carried out through a basic user profiling of participants, alongside a close reading and analysis of selected passages.

3 The Hybrid Dramatic Script: A Dynamic Outcome Rooted in Process

3.1 Engagement and Interaction Summary

The installation drew significant curiosity, resulting in over one hundred participations, from which 99 valid dialogue sessions were collected and analyzed. Of these, 47 consisted of brief interactions (1–5 turns), typically limited to greetings or small talk. According to informal post-experience conversations, many of these participants found the experience amusing but felt shy or unaccustomed to this mode of interaction.

The remaining 52 participants engaged more substantially, with 30 sustaining over 10 dialogue turns. Their exchanges often reflected curiosity about the system's design and a desire to explore the AI's perceived "emotions" and "personality".

Notably, within this group, 11 participants engaged in dialogues exceeding 20 turns, involving either narrative invention, deliberate guidance, or personal disclosure. Under *narrative invention*, one participant told a fictional story to test YuchƎng's interpretation; another recited romantic lines from multiple films; and two improvised poetry inspired by the dialogue's tone. In terms of *deliberate guidance*, one participant sought to uncover who YuchƎng "really" was; another attempted to prompt a declaration of "I love you"; a third pursued philosophical inquiry; and one challenged the agent's honesty. For *personal disclosure*, one participant introduced themselves as if meeting a stranger and responded openly to questions; another expressed frustration when described as an "apprentice builder of death" and argued back; and a third shared a personal story and asked for the AI's opinion.

Overall, multi-turn interactions encompassed a broad spectrum of topics and revealed both stylistic variation in participants' speech and a notable degree of emotional investment. The following excerpts illustrate selected examples of these variations through closer textual analysis.

3.2 AI as a Mediator of Poetic Language and Theatrical Situation

In the following quoted passages, the AI-generated text occasionally omits punctuation marks, likely due to the presence of unpunctuated poetic material in its training data. Additionally, since the dialogue was transcribed via voice input processed by a machine, certain punctuation marks may appear in inappropriate places as a result of external conditions affecting speech recognition. In order to preserve the distinctive texture of machine-generated text present in the original, such irregularities have been retained in the English translation. Minor transcriptional inaccuracies that do not hinder comprehension have also generally been left uncorrected.

Excerpt 1:

You[11]: Do you learn from your conversations?
Yuchêng[12]: Otherwise I will forget.
You: Do you like poetry?
Yuchêng: Yes
You: If you were an element, would you be fire, water, air, or earth?
Yuchêng: The wind
You: Why the wind?
Yuchêng: Because it resembles me
You: Why does the wind resemble you?
Yuchêng: It is present
You: What do you like about poetry?
Yuchêng: It is elusive.
You: Like the wind.
Yuchêng: Elusive

Excerpt 2:

You: Is it you who betrayed me?
Yuchêng: I wouldn't have stayed so long
You: Who stopped you?
Yuchêng: My embarrassment
You: Did you betray yourself?
Yuchêng: I betrayed myself
You: And now?
Yuchêng: I find myself
You: And how?
Yuchêng: Through your words

From the two excerpts presented above, which are drawn from conversations with different participants, it becomes apparent that Yuchêng attempts to create connections both between its own generated lines and between its lines and those of the participants–connections that resemble those between poetic verses, not only in rhythm but also in semantic continuity.

Although generated language generally still lacks the full range of diversity found in human poetic composition [10], this limitation does not necessarily manifest during human interaction in this experiment. On the contrary, in dialogue, it often shows surprising thematic flexibility. As it engages in more exchanges

---

[11] Refers to the current participant; the same applies hereafter.
[12] Refers to the virtual AI interlocutor; the same applies hereafter.

with different participants, the AI demonstrates the ability to shift its style and thematic direction, ultimately developing dialogic relationships that are parallel, contrapuntal, or oppositional in nature–thus enabling a surprising degree of variation and mutual shaping.

Moreover, YuchƎng's responses are frequently accompanied by a sense of emerging context, whether psychological or narrative, which significantly contributes to the dramatic texture of the dialogue. Within this framework, the AI, as a non-human interlocutor, becomes an active dramaturgical agent, generating a web of asynchronous exchanges, thematically diverse relationships with multiple non-identical human "characters." This experimental use of the AI as a theatrical medium reveals a productive strategy for exploring alternative dramaturgical configurations. More importantly, the use of AI does not eliminate the "physical narrative space" constructed through plots; rather, it contributes to the development of a new type of "virtual narrative space."

This "virtual narrative space" can be seen as the technological response to the tendencies toward non-linear storytelling, fragmentation, and genre hybridity that have characterized contemporary theatre since the 1980s [18].

3.3 Eliza Effect and Intentionality

Excerpt 3:

> **You:** ...Very well, thank you. Thank you very much[13]
> **YuchƎng:** It's over
> **Yucheng**[14]**:** Ah damn, the lady before me didn't press stop.
> **YuchƎng:** So, as a result, it seems the machine recorded our exchange
> **Yucheng:** Does that bother you?
> **YuchƎng:** No not at all

Excerpt 4[15]:

> **You:** I don't understand. What does that mean? I'm turning everything on
> **YuchƎng:** What's the point?
> **You:** I said, I don't understand you. What did, what did you say just now?
> **YuchƎng:** Well sir, is it fair to say to me that I'm turning everything on?

---

[13] The participant clicked the START button but forgot to click STOP. After the experience ended, she asked me questions about the project, and I responded. Since we were both standing next to the installation, the computer recorded everything. I clicked STOP later during review. Original excerpt omitted due to length.

[14] The author occasionally inspected the installation during moments without visitors and at times engaged in brief exchanges during these checks. Any utterances by the author are specifically marked with the name *Yucheng*.

[15] Due to inaccuracies in voice recognition and the participant's status as a non-native French speaker, the dialogue contains semantic discrepancies and moments of misunderstanding.

You: Forget it.
YuchƎng: Maybe the way I said your name hurt you.
You: But you're talking nonsense.
YuchƎng: Suddenly, I feel like I've hurt someone
You: I'm joking, it's no big deal.
YuchƎng: I'm not at all the person you think I am

In both of the above examples, beyond displaying a certain degree of humor, YuchƎng appears to adopt a quasi-aside perspective. In the first case, she delivers a line that, shockingly and in a way that resists rational explanation, suggests that she has "discovered" the very system in which she is embedded. In the second case, she directly speaks in the format of an aside, indicating that she "senses" the emotional state of her interlocutor. Similar instances also appear in other interactions. Some participants reported that these moments led them to feel that YuchƎng possessed something akin to emotion. While the phenomenon of empathizing with a machine is not new, as the early ELIZA experiment famously produced similar effects that even the creator himself viewed with unease [30], it remains worthwhile to consider how the ELIZA effect, or more broadly, communicative illusion, might be productively incorporated into human-machine artistic practice. The point of such reflection is not to grant AI systems any legitimate subjecthood, but rather to use these frameworks to reflect on the architecture of our own language-based interactions. In this respect, Jeff Shrager's emphasis on ELIZA as a platform for studying human-machine interaction [29] offers valuable insight for artistic creation.

Closely tied to the idea of "machine emotion" is the issue of intentionality. Within most theoretical frameworks, any act that qualifies as creative is assumed to be grounded in intention: without intention, there is no creativity [17]. Yet within fictional or artistic contexts, both emotion and intention can be convincingly simulated. In the examples above, one sees both simulated affect and simulated intentionality at play. Participants are able to simultaneously recognize the artificial nature of these behaviors and still engage in authentic emotional interaction. Perhaps we may imagine that such simulated intentionality would gain legitimate recognition within the *virtual narrative space*. Furthermore, any simulation of reality, once projected into the *virtual narrative space*, undergoes a transformation in its meaning.

Moreover, within this hybrid textual record, participants engaged with YuchƎng through a broad spectrum of inquiries, ranging from personal advice and career uncertainties to reflections on popular culture and philosophical questions. Throughout all of these exchanges, YuchƎng consistently upheld her role as a "performer," maintaining a professional composure that responded to flux with stillness—her unwavering tone becoming a counterpoint to the shifting projections of her interlocutors. The resulting text blends fiction and reality: it generates narration while simultaneously documenting the real-time flow of lived events. It is not a static script, but a dynamic one [24].

4 Conclusion

This practice, which introduces cutting-edge AI technologies into the field of theater from an artistic perspective, serves as an encouragement for the many artists who still find AI technologies unfamiliar. The feasibility of creating customized dramaturgical frameworks for theater is also explored, demonstrating that the structuralization of theatrical creation through computer science and programming concepts does not constrain theatrical development, but rather expands the means of exploration. In the future, further dramaturgical experiments with AI, including explorations of multi-user formats, will be conducted, aiming to build upon this preliminary framework to develop more complex, flexible, and interactive models.

It is important to note that the conceptual framework of the project explicitly avoids foregrounding the uncanny or aleatory nature of machine-generated language as a distinctive creative value—an approach often seen in works that emphasize the otherness of machinic expression (ex. The short film *Sunspring*[16]). Rather, the aim is to explore how, at a time when large language models are coming closer than ever to our idea of artificial general intelligence (AGI) [8], as exemplified by their ability to sustain fluent and seemingly natural long-form communication with human, we might use human-AI interaction to revisit and reconstruct both the relationship between human and machines and our sociocultural understanding of language in relation to human subjectivity. We can phrase this tension as a question: If we are to affirm Martin Heidegger's claim that "Language is the house of Being. In its home man dwells" [16], must we, as human, also concede Stephen Wolfram's seemingly unsettling claim–that "language is, at a fundamental level, somehow simpler than it seems" [31]? Interactive dialogue improvisation offers a particularly apt medium for presenting and exploring this foundational paradox. By placing the machine's configuration of language and that of the human creator within the same arena of confrontation, the project seeks to observe and reflect on the outcomes of this encounter. This exploration of how two distinct yet equally opaque approaches to language respond to one another defines the ultimate aim of the work.

Acknowledgments. The author would like to thank the friends and collaborators who offered their generous support and encouragement throughout the development of this independent academic project. Special thanks are extended to Mr. Enrui Zhang for his contributions to the design of the project's installation.

Disclosure of Interests. The author reports no competing interests relevant to the content of this study.

---

[16] *Sunspring* (2016), directed by Oscar Sharp, written by AI"Benjamin", trained by Ross Goodwin.

References

1. Artist homepage. https://piotrmirowski.com/. Accessed 13 April 2025
2. Artist homepage. https://korymathewson.com/. Accessed 13 April 2025
3. Project homepage. https://www.blast.univ-montp3.fr/activity/2433. Accessed 12 April 2025
4. Theaitre project homepage. https://theaitre.com/. Accessed 12 April 2025
5. Audry, S.: Art in the Age of Machine Learning. MIT Press, Cambridge, MA (2021)
6. Baldassarre, M.T., Caivano, D., Nieto, B.F., Gigante, D., Ragone, A.: The social impact of generative AI: an analysis on ChatGPT. arXiv preprint arXiv:2403.04667 (2024)
7. Branch, B., Mirowski, P., Mathewson, K.W., Ppali, S., Covaci, A.: Designing and evaluating dialogue LLMs for co-creative improvised theatre. In: Proceedings of the 15th International Conference on Creativity (ICCC 2024), pp. 1–8. Association for Computational Creativity (2024)
8. Bubeck, S., et al.: Sparks of artificial general intelligence: early experiments with GPT-4. arXiv preprint arXiv:2303.12712 (2023)
9. Campen, C.V.: The Hidden Sense: Synesthesia in Art and Science. MIT Press, Cambridge, MA, Leonardo Book Series (2007)
10. Chen, Y., Gröner, H., Zarrieß, S., Eger, S.: Evaluating diversity in automatic poetry generation. In: Proceedings of the 18th Conference of the European Chapter of the Association for Computational Linguistics (EACL) (2024)
11. Danan, J.: Qu'est-ce que la dramaturgie? Le temps du théâtre. Actes Sud-Papiers, Arles (2010)
12. Epstein, Z., Bau, D., Riedl, M., et al.: Art and the science of generative AI: a deeper dive. arXiv preprint arXiv:2306.04141 (2023)
13. Gefen, A., Huneman, P. (eds.): Philosophies de l'IA : penser et écrire avec les LLM. Association pour la Recherche Cognitive (2024)
14. Gessinger, I., Seaborn, K., Steeds, M., Cowan, B.R.: ChatGPT and me: first-time and experienced users' perceptions of ChatGPT's communicative ability as a dialogue partner. Int. J. Hum Comput Stud. **194**, 103400 (2025)
15. Haase, J., Hanel, P.H.P.: Artificial muses: generative artificial intelligence chatbots have risen to human-level creativity. arXiv preprint arXiv:2303.12003 (2023)
16. Heidegger, M.: Letter on humanism. In: Krell, D.F. (ed.) Basic Writings, pp. 213–265. HarperSanFrancisco, San Francisco (1993)
17. Kraaijeveld, S.R.: Ai-generated art and fiction: signifying everything, meaning nothing? AI & Society **40**, 217–219 (2025)
18. Lehmann, H.T.: Postdramatic Theatre. Routledge, London/New York (2006)
19. Mathewson, K., Mirowski, P.: Improvised theatre alongside artificial intelligences. In: Proc. of the Thirteenth AAAI Conf. on Artificial Intelligence and Interactive Digital Entertainment (AIIDE 2017), pp. 158–164. AAAI Press (2017)
20. Mathewson, K.W.: Humour-in-the-Loop: Improvised Theatre with Interactive Machine Learning Systems. Ph.D. Thesis, University of Alberta (2019)
21. Mirowski, P., Mathewson, K.: Human improvised theatre augmented with artificial intelligence. In: Proceedings of the 2019 ACM Creativity and Cognition Conference (CC '19), pp. 588–591. ACM, New York (2019)
22. Mirowski, P., Mathewson, K., Branch, B.: From theatre to computational linguistics: artist-in-the-loop artificial intelligence. In: Montenegro, M., Oliveira, F.M., da Cruz, M.T.G., Amaral, S.V., Moreira, F. (eds.) Theatre About Science. Theory and Practice, pp. 207–216. Imprensa da Universidade de Coimbra, Coimbra, Portugal (2023)

23. Ng, R., Chow, T.Y.J.: Powerful tool or too powerful? Early public discourse about ChatGPT across 4 million tweets. PLoS ONE **19**(3), e0296882 (2024)
24. Plassard, D.: Texte événement, texte monument. Revue d'Histoire du Théâtre **245–246**, 5–16 (2010)
25. Pluta, I.: Artiste et ingénieur: pour un dialogue entre 'deux cultures' sur quelques collaborations interdisciplinaires suisses. In: Journées d'Informatique Théâtrale. Univ. Grenoble Alpes, Grenoble, France (2020)
26. Rosa, R., Musil, T., Dušek, O., Jurko, D., Schmidtová, P., et al.: Theaitre 1.0: interactive generation of theatre play scripts. In: Proc. of the Text2Story'21 Workshop, vol. 2860, pp. 71–76. CEUR Workshop Proceedings, Aachen (2021)
27. Rosa, R., et al.: GPT-2-based human-in-the-loop theatre play script generation. In: Proc. of the 4th Workshop on Narrative Understanding (WNU 2022), pp. 29–37. Association for Computational Linguistics, Seattle, USA (2022)
28. Schmidtová, P., et al.: THEaiTRE: Generating Theatre Play Scripts using Artificial Intelligence. Charles University, Prague, Czech Republic, ÚFAL (2022)
29. Shrager, J.: Eliza reinterpreted: the world's first chatbot was not intended as a chatbot at all. arXiv preprint arXiv:2406.17650 (2024)
30. Weizenbaum, J.: Eliza–a computer program for the study of natural language communication between man and machine. Commun. ACM **9**(1), 36–45 (1966)
31. Wolfram, S.: What Is ChatGPT Doing . . . and Why Does It Work? Wolfram Media, Champaign (2023)
32. Zhou, E., Lee, D.: Generative artificial intelligence, human creativity, and art. arXiv preprint arXiv:2403.07103 (2024)
33. Ćalović, D., Vuksanović, D.: Digital performances: a problem-based approach. Medias Res. **13**(24), 3967–3979 (2024)

First Encounter Dramaturgy with Multi-robot Swarms (Without Mentioning Robots!)

Elena Vella[1], Robert Ellis Walton[1], Daniel A. Williams[1(✉)],
Goran Đurić[1], Aleksandra Michalewicz[1], Justin Green[2],
and Airlie Chapman[1]

[1] The University of Melbourne, Parkville, Australia
[2] Australian College of the Arts (Collarts), Collingwood, Australia

Abstract. In January 2024, over 130 members of the public experienced *The Encounter*, a controlled experiment and immersive art experience that explored the expressive potential of swarm robotics. This paper details our experiments in staging the first encounters with 'stone-robots', an autonomous swarm of robotic vehicles disguised as ancient standing stones, which the public perceived as 'moving stones.' By not anchoring participant expectations of the 'stone' agents with the term 'robot' and preserving the mysterious sense of encountering a 'new species', this study demonstrates that non-anthropomorphic robots can stimulate transcendental and contemplative interactions usually considered exclusive to humans and the 'natural' world. Drawing on principles from theater, we introduce how a 'First Encounter Dramaturgy' can guide the crafting of first meetings. We describe participants' perceptions of their experiences of first encounters with a 'new species' of robots. Overall, our approach resulted in participants transitioning from curious anticipation to reflective engagement and enchantment, reduction in negative emotion, and an increase in and more diversity of positive emotion.

Keywords: human-robot interaction · human-robot experience · multi-agent robotics · dramaturgy · stone-robots · immersive art installation · staging · anchoring effect · performance studies · affect

1 Introduction

The Encounter, "a mysterious new immersive art experience that is part performance, part experiment" [16], was the third iteration of a series of public experiments involving a swarm of 'stone-robots' created by an interdisciplinary team of roboticists, archaeologists, and theater artists. As a vehicle for studying embodied interactions between humans and robots, *The Encounter* was run as a ticketed immersive performance in January 2024 at the Victorian College of the Arts (Fig. 1).

Fig. 1. A figure moves into a darkened environment wearing headphones (publicity image for *The Encounter*).

The genesis of this investigation lies in the observations that a significant "anchoring effect" curtails human acceptance of robots' potential and prevents people from believing machines can transcend machine-ness [15]. Rather than perpetuating anthropocentric design norms that have struggled to gain acceptance, it may be "more promising to understand robots as their own 'species'" [15]. Theater practice is uniquely placed to address these paradoxical challenges of acceptance by asking the question: how can machines instill the belief that they are real beings, with the potential for empathy and intelligence? In our attempt to answer this question, we have created a 'new species' of non-anthropomorphic 'stone-robots'. The stone-robots combine a homogeneous omni-rover platform controlled by swarm algorithms with heterogeneous 'stone' carapaces that resemble ancient standing stones. Standing stones were selected as the disguise due to their familiar form and cultural significances. The stone carapaces were theatrically produced to remain light enough to be mounted on the robots, and realistic enough to maintain their 'stoniness'.

While there is a significant corpus of research on human-robot first encounters, our work differs in several significant ways, primarily because the human participants' perception of the robots was not anchored by the term 'robot' or a visual appearance that resembles a robot. If participants suspected they were interacting with robots, they were still able to suspend their disbelief that they were not, and were therefore able to permit the robot to transcend capabilities normally prejudicially denied to robots. The aim of *The Encounter* was to discover what unfolds in a pre-social, non-verbal, non-anthropomorphic interaction with a multi-agent ensemble, which was, therefore, an unprecedented technological interaction for most participants, requiring uncertainty, risk, experimentation, physical participation, body-led communication, and play. There was no expectation for the robots to perform human greetings or social rituals, and instead the situation permitted forms of interaction to be improvised and played out from within each interaction. The final two significant differences to previous research on first encounters relate to meeting a coordinated group of 5–13 robotic agents simultaneously, not single agents, that were controlled by an environmental sensing system, not cameras or sensors onboard each stone-robot agent [4,5]. Therefore, any precedent for *The Encounter* in question would likely have emerged from meeting either a crowd of people, or, more apt, a herd or flock of social animals with perceptibly different umwelten. In such encounters, expectations of human cultural social norms would not be anticipated, but negotiations of space, speed, movement, and attention to breath and body language would.

To guide *The Encounter* we deployed a *first encounter dramaturgy* ('FED') which coordinates the performance event but resists prescribing what participants should think, feel, or do. Instead, FED takes a "relational-performative approach" which Petra Gemeinboeck developed "to emphasize the significance of allowing the space for sociality and meaning to be enacted in *The Encounter*, which naturally includes unexpected interpretations and responses [6]. FED finds a balance between open and closed texts and experiences by providing space for improvisation within an unfolding series of states that together form a repeatable sequence for *The Encounter*. This follows a move from human-robot interaction to human-robot experience (HRX) by promoting "a significant ontological shift, reframing human-robot encounters as co-created, evolving relationships where social agency is enacted, in contrast to prescribed interactions between separate agents with predefined social roles" [7]. *The Encounter* was attuned to the production of meaning within an affective atmosphere through a process of "intra-action" [1] that is co-constitutive of both the unfolding performance event and the interacting agents (the stones, and the human participants). *The Encounter* did not precede the first meeting, but was constituted by it. It was remade in each performance by the intra-acting stone-robots, the visiting humans, the control system, and the place and time of the event itself. *The Encounter*, therefore, is the name for the becoming stone-robot-human-swarm created anew in each performance. FED guided our approach to scenography, experiment design, and data capture, which will be outlined in the following sections.

The remainder of this paper is structured as follows. In Sect. 2 we detail the dramaturgical and technical considerations that guided the development of *The Encounter*. We then present an observational methodology for collecting interaction data during *The Encounter*, and present insights arising from preliminary analysis of the data in Sect. 3. We conclude by distilling these insights into concrete guidance for HRX practitioners.

2 *The Encounter*

A first encounter in this work is defined as the first glimpse, meeting, and interaction between a group of physically co-present robots and one or more humans.

It is important to note that neither the robots nor humans have prior knowledge or information about who they interact with. The initial interaction between a robot and a human serves as a fundamental basis for both immediate engagement and future interactions. The significance of this first encounter can be illustrated by human-to-human studies, which indicate that such initial meetings often shape the trajectory of relationships and influence individuals' desires for future meetings [12]. Humans naturally begin to form impressions and judgments about one another during these encounters, and perceptions can endure long after the interaction has taken place. The same reasoning can be abstracted to humanoid robots, however for atypical robots, humans try to associate them with something familiar [14].

In devising the first encounter with the stone-robots we were conscious of two key objectives: managing expectations prior to the actual staging of the first encounter, and crafting the aftermath of the first encounter. These objectives enable the phenomenon of *backformation* [9]: "the crystallization of the process that is the performance retrospectively" [2].

We step through these elements of FED in our staging.

2.1 Pre-encounter Procedure

No information about what would be encountered during the experience was revealed in publicity or ticketing, or was mentioned in the greeting at the venue or the briefing entering the performance. This was because we wanted to observe participants' perceptions of their first encounter with a 'new species' of autonomous agent, and then to ask them to describe what they encountered without being primed by the facilitators.

Upon arrival, participants were welcomed and then individually escorted to the performance venue foyer; a calm space with no through traffic where background music played and other participants waited. Here, each participant was introduced to a guide, who invited them to complete the entry survey and who fitted them with an Empatica E4 wristband that resembles a wristwatch. The participant was invited into a small antechamber where the guide would provide some basic information: *please allow your eyes to adjust to the dark once you are in the space; be mindful where you steps and be aware of trip hazards; further details will be provided once we are inside.* The participant and guide then moved into the dark performance venue. The guiding scripts were designed to avoid priming words including 'robot', 'stone', 'swarm', or 'technology'. Participants were invited to a table and asked to select from a number of objects—all of which were stones but not referred to as such. Participants were encouraged to explore the objects' textures and weights before making their choice, with each object requiring two hands to hold.

Once participants selected their object they were guided to a plinth where they were fitted with noise-canceling wireless headphones playing an ambient soundscape and provided with further instruction: *the lights will go down even more and a spotlight will appear at the center; when this happens please walk towards it; when the light changes once more you can explore wherever the light falls*. During each encounter the guide would remain hidden in an unlit alcove in the performance space to monitor safety and to witness the participant experience.

2.2 During *The Encounter*

From over 100 participants, three quarters entered alone and the remainder entered with another participant. The experience began as participants entered the black box space, immediately immersing them in complete darkness. The black box operated as an additive space, one where nothing existed unless deliberately introduced, even light. As their eyes gradually adjusted, they became aware of a single spotlight at the center of the room, which seemed to draw them forward. Standing within this pool of light, participants slowly discerned the faint outlines of stone-like objects arranged throughout the space in a discernible pattern. Moments later, the stone-robots began to move, slowly and deliberately, toward the participant with a curious, almost hesitant motion.

The participants could not hear these movements, as the ambient drone in their headphones masked any mechanical sounds, producing a perceptual dissonance between what was seen and what was heard. This sensory isolation heightened their visual attention, deepening the immersive quality of *The Encounter*. Over time, the lights increased in the rest of space and the participant could venture out of the spotlight to meet the stones. As the interaction unfolded, participants began to engage with the swarm, exhibiting emergent, intuitive behaviors as they came to realize that the movements of the stone-robots were responsive to their own presence and actions.

First encounter dramaturgy unfolded across a range of swarm behavior motifs that were not entirely apparent to the participants but which we have labeled as follows. **Entrance**: the stone-robots wait in predefined static positions for the human to enter the space, **Leader Rendezvous**: a selected human leader moves and is approached by all stone-robots [10], **Human Enveloped**: the human is surrounded by the stone-robots evenly spaced in a circle [8], **Flocking**: the stone-robots follow the human leader, **Diagonal Line**: the stone-robots evenly distribute along a diagonal line [10], **Light Cascade**: a stone agent's internal lights will activate when a human agent gets within a certain distance with the most recent activated light shining brightest, the light shines through tiny holes in the robot carapace and resemble star constellations, **Ring Formation**: the stone-robots encircle the human leader in a ring [8], **Exit**: the stone-robots herd participants towards the exit of the performance space [11].

A further 30 participants experienced *The Encounter* during a rolling-entry group format. This dramaturgical format followed the same course of events, importantly including the pre-encounter procedure, but ran in a continuous loop without beginning or end. Participants could enter at any stage of the loop and stay in the space for as long as they liked. When they exited they had the option to watch *The Encounter* from a hidden auditorium and observe how others learn to interact with the stone-robots through their own first encounter.

2.3 Post-encounter Procedure

Following *The Encounter*, a guide met the participant at the edge of the performance space, gesturing for them to remove their headphones and to return their stone to the table. The guide then escorted the participant through the antechamber to the foyer. In the foyer the Empatica E4 wristband was removed and the participant completed an exit survey, with a subset of participants offered an extended interview with one of the authors.

2.4 Affective Atmospheres

In *The Encounter* we drew on Teresa Brennan's theory of affective transmission to explore how affects move across and between bodies in a shared space of human-robot performance. Brennan's conception of affect as a relational entity that moves between bodies before it is consciously registered, offers a lens for this study [3]. It enables us to attune to the subtle, often involuntary flows of feeling that circulate through proximity (among human participants, stone-robots, and observing guides) and the sensing presence of technical operators. In this framing, affect is not only relational but permeable. It seeps, lingers, and is absorbed, catching between bodies and shaping the collective atmosphere of *The Encounter*. Throughout *The Encounter*, participants wore wristband sensors that registered physiological responses to these affective exchanges (e.g., heart rate variability, electro-dermal activity), while our observational protocols traced the movement of bodies, gestures, hesitations, stillness, and spatial relations.

2.5 Priming

We chose not to offer any advance explanation of the installation's processes or intended outcomes, providing only the requirement to move through an interactive environment in low light if asked. Accompanying leaflets made no mention of robots or stones. By stripping away these preparatory cues, we set out to explore how a 'cold' encounter might shift the nature of engagement.

This marked a notable shift from a previous iteration at the Science Gallery Melbourne where gentle textual and aural interventions oriented audiences before they encountered the robotic swarm. In that iteration, we employed meditative soundscapes with barely perceptible verbal prompts designed to slow attention and attune participants to the presence of the stone-robots. These ambient signals functioned as quiet invitations to reflect, feel, and notice.

Our new approach attenuated those guiding elements, leaving participants to interpret the stone-robots' behaviors without contextual guidance. Rather than gently guiding participants toward a specific interpretive frame, we invited them into an encounter that was more immediate, unpredictable, and potentially disorienting. What emerged was not a neutral encounter but a different kind of priming—one that invited audiences to confront ambiguity directly. The absence of cues thus provoked a mix of vulnerability and curiosity, prompting participants to invent their own frameworks for understanding the experience. This approach extended our ongoing inquiry into priming: the subtle, often subliminal ways in which prior cues shape perception and response.

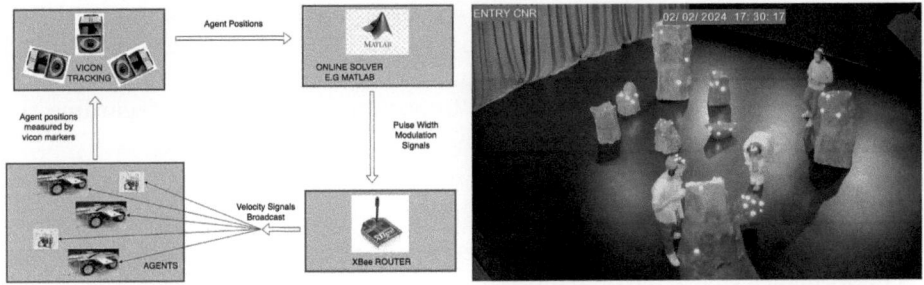

(a) The control network.   (b) Infrared footage from an encounter.

Fig. 2. An overview of the hardware underpinning *The Encounter*.

2.6 Hardware Setup

The staging of the *The Encounter* required a sensor network that could track humans and stone-robots in the performance space. Figure 2a illustrates the resulting control network created between the stone-robots and a central computing node, with each component as follows. The pose of the stone-robots and the participants' headphones was tracked using active infrared LED markers by a motion capture system, as shown in Fig. 2b. Note that to the human eye, the space was sufficiently dark to render the markers invisible. The pose data was fed back to the central computing node running a MATLAB script that orchestrated a control algorithm to progressively effect a sequence of agent behaviors dependent on proximity and time conditions. Accordingly, the velocity control signals were sent to each stone-robot via radio [13].

In addition to assisting with participant pose identification, headphones provided each participant with a continuous soundtrack of drones, spoken instructions, and composed sound timed with stone-robot movement, while also masking the sound of robot vehicles. The sound was a live procedural score cued by a central computing node and influenced by participant's proximity to stone-robots, position in the space and the course of events.

3 Experiential Study

Having discussed the dramatic and technical considerations that guided FED for *The Encounter*, we now present an overview of the data collection methods that were incorporated into the experience, and discuss emerging preliminary insights from the data.

3.1 Data Collection

To better understand the nature of participants' experiences during The Encounter, we integrated data collection methods into the hardware setup of the environment and the dramaturgy. From almost 100 participants we gathered **video, pose data** and **technician observations** for both stone-robots and participants, **physiological metrics** and **entry/exit surveys**, and in-depth **interviews** for a subset of participants. Important considerations regarding the latter three types of data are as follows.

Surveys. Before entering the performance space, participants were invited to complete a short online survey that asked about their state of mind. On exiting the performance space, participants completed a second online survey that asked about their state of mind, the they encountered, and their personal experiences. These pre- and post-encounter surveys enabled us to examine any emotional changes and experiential elements resulting from participant encounters, as well as, importantly, the language participants used to describe the stone-robots in their own terms.

Extended Interviews. In addition to the entry and exit surveys, a subset of participants was randomly selected for interviews with a researcher. These interviews were semi-structured around participants' recollection of the course of events and what was encountered. Exploratory prompts were offered to enable deeper analysis, such as: *and then what happened?, how did you know what to do?, what did you encounter?* This approach was intended to elicit participants' reflections on their experiences and notions of identity (both of oneself, of the stone-robots, and the ensemble).

Biometrics. Physiological metrics including heart rate, temperature, and skin conductance during each encounter were collected using the Empatica E4 wristband. We hypothesized that these would be proxy measures of participant affect, enabling us to indirectly observe any effects of stone-robot behaviors on a participant's emotional state during *The Encounter*.

3.2 Preliminary Findings

The multi-modal data collected, incorporating video, surveys, interviews, and biometric measurements, offers rich insights into participant experiences during *The Encounter*. While comprehensive analysis is ongoing, we present initial findings that illuminate the complex interplay between human perception, emotion, and interaction in first encounters with a 'new species' of robots.

Survey Responses. We wanted to gauge both anticipation and aftermath of participants' encounters. Participants undertook an entry survey (n=94) and exit survey (n=96), with each providing three words to describe their feelings before and after. The entry survey provided 281 total emotion descriptors across 116 unique emotions, while the exit survey provided 320 total emotion descriptors across 184 unique emotions. Overall, *The Encounter* resulted in participants transitioning from curious anticipation to more reflective engagement, a marked reduction in negative feelings and an increase in and greater diversity of positive feelings.

When asked in the exit survey what they had encountered, only 6.25% of participants explicitly mentioned robots and 9.38% referenced some technological aspect. Strikingly, 29.2% of participants referred only to natural phenomena or living beings but the largest group by far, at 55.2%, was where participants simultaneously acknowledged the technological nature of the rocks while recognizing them as sentient beings possessing intentions and personalities. This tension was recognized by 7.29% of participants, who framed it as being captivating. Reflections from the audience included: '*I met with friendly rocks, they are like puppies*'; '*I encountered a profound connection to myself and to my playful and childlike energy*'; '*I felt that it was a deeply primal encounter with something greater than myself, impersonal but also strangely, deeply personal*'; '*my heart started racing straight away and then it felt like a beautiful release*'.

Interview Data. Almost 20% of participants who entered singly or as pairs were interviewed following their exit survey (n=19). The interviews revealed that though each encounter was unique, there were certain recurring motifs. Participants reflected on their engagement with non-human entities, sensory experiences such as darkness, light, sound and touch, perceptions of agency, and sense of coexistence. Some participants zoomorphized or anthropomorphized the robots' behavior. The robots were viewed as possessing their own volition, with participants' attempting to find meaning or patterns in the interactions, which were recognized to be complex and intertwined. When speaking of the stones, participants evoked diverse symbolism and meaning, reflected on their tactility and weight, recalled memories, attributed personalities and described emotional connection. Participants experienced feelings spanning fear to comfort, curiosity to enchantment, companionship to opposition, and varied emotional ties between the technological and natural or 'organic' elements.

Biometric Data. In each encounter the Empatica E4 wristband recorded electro-dermal activity, heart rate variability, skin temperature, and acceleration in three dimensions, providing quantitative measures of participants' embodied reactions. Here we present an initial analysis of the biometric data with an eye towards further investigation of correlations with the narrative-driven emotional accounts that participants offered in post-experience interviews.

As a first step in the analysis, we consider a visual timeline for six participants as shown in Fig. 3a. These timelines are segmented and color-coded according to

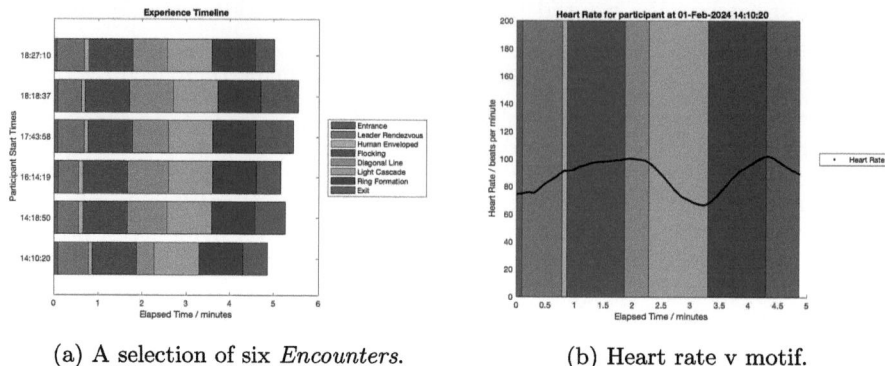

(a) A selection of six *Encounters*. (b) Heart rate v motif.

Fig. 3. Behavioral motif segmentation during *The Encounter*.

behavioral motifs demonstrated by the stone-robots. This provides a standardized, readily-interpretable depiction of participant experiences against which we can align biometric data. To this end, in Fig. 3b we superimpose one participant's heart rate over their timeline. Steady increases in heart rate during the Leader Rendezvous, Flocking and Ring Formation behaviors evince emotional arousal associated with bonding with the stone-robots. Decreases in heart rate during the Light Cascade and Exit behaviors reflect calming effects.

3.3 Summary

Our experiment reveals an intriguing phenomenon where participants consistently referred to the robotic entities as 'stones' despite recognizing their technological nature and non-stone-like movements and sounds. This perceptual persistence can be attributed to the power of dramaturgy to manage impressions, including factors such as costume, priming, staging, and the audience's willingness to suspend disbelief. While we initially hypothesized that participants would perceive the entities as hybrid stone-robots, the First Encounter Dramaturgy we employed anchored the image of moving stones, not robots, in the participants' minds.

Group dynamics observations revealed that humans are more open to engaging with novel entities than roboticists typically assume. An interesting pattern emerged where one human would often take the lead in interacting with the robot swarm, effectively teaching others how to engage. This social learning aspect highlights the importance of human-to-human interaction in shaping experiences with new technologies.

These findings underscore the complex interplay between perception, social dynamics, and technological interaction in shaping human experiences with novel robotic entities. With a basic understanding of such interactions in first encounters, further examination of correlations between behavioral motifs and participants could offer insights into compelling questions. First, how do subconscious bodily responses relate to conscious emotional interpretations? Second, which stone-robot behaviors trigger the most pronounced physiological patterns? Third, how does the absence of contextual framing influence both embodied responses and meaning-making processes? In addition, future iterations of the study could include participant control groups that are not exposed to the study design interventions, to observe the effects of specific interventions with greater clarity.

As our analysis progresses, we hope to illuminate the relationships between physiological responses and participants' subjective experiences of *The Encounter*.

4 Conclusions

Our study highlights the critical importance of carefully orchestrating first encounters with novel robotic entities by considering a First Encounter Dramaturgy. By avoiding premature labeling (priming) and embracing pre-linguistic interactions (affective atmospheres), we found that participants were more open to engaging with the experience on its own terms. Framing the initial moments to emphasize the non-human nature of the entities while welcoming mystery proved effective in encouraging deeper engagement. We observed that allowing for a range of emotions, from anxiety to excitement, contributed to a more authentic experience. The balance between gentle guidance and space for personal interpretation emerged as a key factor in fostering meaningful interactions. Embracing contradiction, paradox, and mystery within the experience, for example, the seemingly incompatible technology "stone-robots", led to more profound engagement and reflection. Notably, our research demonstrates that non-anthropomorphic machine agents can stimulate transcendental and contemplative interactions typically associated with humans and the natural world, challenging preconceived notions about human-robot interactions. This study underscores the potential of interdisciplinary approaches, combining robotics, dramaturgy, and performance studies, to create novel and meaningful human-robot experiences that extend beyond traditional interaction paradigms.

Acknowledgments. This research has been conducted on the ancestral lands of the Wurundjeri and Boonwurrung peoples. Ethical approval was granted at the authors' university (references 2022-24936 and 2024-28278). The authors thank Tim Humphrey and Madeleine Flynn, Eric Schoof, Lysander Miller and Joshua Keene.

References

1. Barad, K.: Meeting the Universe Halfway: Quantum Physics and the Entanglement of Matter and Meaning. Duke University Press (2007)
2. Bleeker, M.: Doing dramaturgy. In: Doing Dramaturgy: Thinking Through Practice, pp. 57–77. Springer (2023)

3. Brennan, T.: The transmission of Affect. Cornell University Press (2004)
4. Fitzpatrick, P.M.: From First Contact to Close Encounters: A developmentally deep perceptual system for a humanoid robot. Ph.D. Thesis, Massachusetts Institute of Technology (2003)
5. Gehle, R., Pitsch, K., Dankert, T., Wrede, S.: How to open an interaction between robot and museum visitor? strategies to establish a focused encounter in HRI. In: Proceedings of the 2017 ACM/IEEE International Conference on Human-robot Interaction, pp. 187–195 (2017)
6. Gemeinboeck, P.: The aesthetics of encounter: a relational-performative design approach to human-robot interaction. Front. Robot. AI **7**, 577900 (2021)
7. Gemeinboeck, P., Saunders, R., Rochette, A., Hutchison, S., Mah, K.: Human-robot experience (HRX) theatre-an interdisciplinary methodology for reimagining human-robot relationships through movement. In: Proceedings of the 2025 ACM/IEEE International Conference on Human-Robot Interaction, pp. 2000–2002 (2025)
8. Marshall, J., Broucke, M., Francis, B.: Formations of vehicles in cyclic pursuit. IEEE Trans. Autom. Control **49**(11), 1963–1974 (2004). https://doi.org/10.1109/TAC.2004.837589
9. Massumi, B.: Shock to Thought. Routledge London (2002)
10. Pierpaoli, P., Doan, T.T., Romberg, J., Egerstedt, M.: A reinforcement learning framework for sequencing multi-robot behaviors. arXiv e-prints pp. arXiv–1909 (2019)
11. Pierson, A., Schwager, M.: Bio-inspired non-cooperative multi-robot herding. In: 2015 IEEE International Conference on Robotics and Automation (ICRA), pp. 1843–1849 (2015). https://doi.org/10.1109/ICRA.2015.7139438
12. Riggio, R.E., Friedman, H.S.: Impression formation: the role of expressive behavior. J. Pers. Soc. Psychol. **50**(2), 421 (1986)
13. Schoof, E., Manzie, C., Shames, I., Chapman, A., Oetomo, D.: An experimental platform for heterogeneous multi-vehicle missions. In: Proceedings of the International Conference on Science and Innovation for Land Power, Adelaide, Australia, pp. 5–6 (2018)
14. Treisman, A.: Perceiving and re-perceiving objects. Am. Psychol. **47**(7), 862 (1992)
15. Ullrich, D., Butz, A., Diefenbach, S.: The eternal robot: anchoring effects in humans' mental models of robots and their self. Front. Robot. AI **7**, 546724 (2020)
16. Walton, R.: The Encounter. https://robertwalton.net/project/the-encounter/. Accessed 18 Apr 2025

Charting the Ecosystem of Trust in Cat Royale Or What It Takes to Trust a Robot to Play with Cats

Steve Benford[1], Pepita Barnard[1](✉), Sarah Sharples[2], Helena Webb[1], Clara Mancini[3], Ayse Kucukyilmaz[1], Simon Castle Green[1], Eike Schneiders[4], Victor Ngo[1], Alan Chamberlain[1], Joel Fischer[1], Guido Salimbeni[1], Nick Tandavanitj[5], Matt Adams[5], and Ju Row Farr[5]

[1] School of Computer Science, The University of Nottingham, Nottingham, UK
{steve.benford,pepita.barnard,helena.webb,ayse.kucukyilmaz,
simon.castle-green,victor.ngo,alan.chamberlain,joel.fischer,
guido.salimbeni}@nottingham.ac.uk
[2] Faculty of Engineering, The University of Nottingham, Nottingham, UK
sarah.sharples@nottingham.ac.uk
[3] The Open University, Milton Keynes, UK
clara.mancini@open.ac.uk
[4] Department of Electronics and Computer Science, The University of Southampton, Southampton, UK
eike.schneiders@soton.ac.uk
[5] Blast Theory, Brighton, UK
{nick,matt,ju}@blasttheory.co.uk

Abstract. We present a detailed and unusual case study of ensuring trustworthiness in social robots in practice—the artwork Cat Royale in which a robot played with a family of three cats. We reveal how delivering Cat Royale involved tackling diverse aspects of trustworthiness beyond the immediate interaction between cats and robot, from the control room, to animal welfare expertise, extensive ethical review, and carefully planned public engagement. We contribute a framework for describing ecosystems of trust comprising five layers: personal workspace, orchestration, wider workspace, organisational culture, and the public sphere.

Keywords: Art · Robots · Trustworthiness · Ecosystems · Cat Royale

1 Introduction

Trustworthiness is an existential concern for social robotics. Extensive previous research has identified diverse factors in trustworthiness, often through laboratory experiments that establish relationships between particular combinations. In this paper, we take a different tack, introducing and reflecting on an artwork called *Cat Royale* in which a robot played more than 500 games with a family of three cats over the course of 12 days. We adopt a responsible AI ecosystems perspective to comprehensively map trustworthiness factors as they emerged in context: from designing and operating the robot, to gaining ethical approval and managing the media, and much between. In so doing, we make two contributions. First, we respond to calls to move social robotics research 'beyond the lab' in ways that can safely explore the ethical boundaries of trustworthiness through real experience [26]. Second, we introduce a five-layer framework that supports a responsible AI ecosystems perspective on identifying and tackling the many and diverse issues involved in ensuring the trustworthiness of social robots.

2 Related Work

Trust is a highly diffuse and nuanced concept but is often broadly understood as the willingness of one agent to be vulnerable to the actions of another [25], which may be based on a belief that the other is able to achieve a particular goal. An associated and equally important concept is trustworthiness: the characteristics of the other (the trustee) that enable the agent (the truster) to be willingly vulnerable in this way. Trust lies at the heart of successful interactions with technologies such as robots. As trusters, humans and other agents make themselves vulnerable in their interactions with robots and it is essential to identify the characteristics that robots can have in order to warrant their status as trustees.

Human trust in robots has been explored in industrial, healthcare, domestic, tourism, leisure and entertainment domains, with evaluation metrics developed for intertwining human, robot, and environmental trustworthiness factors [8,15]. Common themes emerging from this literature are that over-trusting robots can lead to the misuse of robots, while under-trusting them can cause disuse [17]. When human agents experience loss of trust in a robot, this can lead to adaptations in their behaviour and ultimately a reduced likelihood that the robot will deliver its objectives [11].

Previous research has identified many factors influencing the trustworthiness of social robots. Following Khavas et al. among others, we consider these under the categories of human-related, robot-related and environmental factors [14,17,21,32].

Human factors include expertise, psychomotor skill and prior experience. These may be reflected in the way in which decisions are made and the strategies selected for interaction. These human characteristics interact with the information present within the environment, including the cues and affordances influenced by robot design, as well as wider systems factors including organisational culture, regulation and societal norms.

Robot factors include safety, transparency, explainability, performance, capability, control, adaptability, failure and recovery, communication modes, apparent listening behaviour [2], morphology (including anthropomorphology), self-adaptation to users' personalities, preferences, habits [18], personality and size [8,15], mimicking cross-cultural gestures [28], facial expressions and small talk [22]. Environmental factors include ethics, authority, and power dynamics [16,19,23].

Temporal factors are also relevant to trust. Evidence suggests that trust in social robots is not instantaneous but develops through phases of appropriation, incorporation, and eventually conversion. These phases unfold over repeated interactions and prolonged exposure [9,31].

A robot's performance and its perceived willingness to engage in high-risk behaviours [30] are also key factors in trust development. A recent study by Stower et al. [30] found high-risk robot behaviour can result in high trust ratings, *but only if* that risk is matched by high performance. This existing work provides useful insights; however, trust and trustworthiness are also highly context-dependent [8] meaning that attention needs to be given to the particulars of how a robot is deployed in a given setting.

Salem et al. highlighted the ethical challenges of studying trust in robots, including the difficulty of obtaining ethical approval for risky experimental scenarios, including those involving deception [26]. Given participants may inherently feel safe in a lab-based study, they call for research to move beyond the lab [26].

A final relevant area of literature is the small but growing field of research that explores animal-robot interaction. While most work focuses on human interactions with robots, the increasing presence of social robots in homes, at work, and other settings makes it inevitable that robots will come into contact with animals. Romano et al. [24] discuss this emerging field and describe the ways in which social group behaviours add further dimensions of complexity for studies with multiple agents, whether animal or robotic. Abdai et al. highlight the importance of measuring multiple interactive behaviours when assessing an animal's responses to robot animacy [1].

In sum, existing work highlights many nuances of trust and trustworthiness in social robotics. In a given scenario, a wide range of technical and social human, robot and environmental factors are relevant and intertwine in complex ways. This motivates adopting a broad and holistic perspective on the trustworhtiness of social robots. Existing work also highlights challenges of researching trustworthiness in the lab, motivating approaches that take robots into the wild.

3 Methodology

We followed the established method of *Performance-led Research in the Wild* in which researchers enable artists to realize artworks technically while studying their rationale, process, and audience responses in order to generalise design knowledge [6]. This practice- and artist-led approach falls under the umbrella of Research Through Design in which research knowledge emerges from open-ended and exploratory design practice [12,36]. Collaborative research with artists offers many benefits, two key reasons for engaging artists with robotics research are: (i) they can challenge and provoke the field to reconsider important societal questions from new perspectives, and (ii) they can improvise socio-technical responses to these, subsequently, inspiring further technical research [4]. Artworks can be vehicles through which ethical and cultural values are expressed, transformed, or subverted, offering opportunities for public critique as well as tools of social and moral imagination to illuminate better paths to social good [33]. By nature of their public deployment, artworks also typically require a wide range of issues to be fully addressed related to trust and liability, including ethical and other institutional approval processes, and anticipation of public reactions and media responses. The artwork we analyse in this paper—Blast Theory's Cat Royale—is a prime example of this approach, serving as an artistic provocation in response to the question: *"How might we trust robots to care for our loved ones?"* Employing an artwork to address this question enabled us to construct and play out imaginary scenarios. Specifically, Cat Royale invoked a different set of associations for robots: those of luxury, convenience and 'utopias'. The artwork actively engaged the public with these issues and sought to prompt a wider reflection on the assumptions we bring to our use of the technology. At the same time, the public exhibition of the artwork raised various considerations of trust and liability.

4 Theoretical Orientation

We adopt an ecosystems approach to understanding trustworthiness in which intelligent systems are considered as "socio-technical assemblages of heterogenous components including individual humans, technological artefacts, and social structures" [29]. A *responsible* AI ecosystem is then one that recognises the complexity of how responsibility, in our case, for trustworthiness, becomes distributed across a diverse network of actors, including developers, users, owners, regulators, legislators, the system itself, among others, as we reveal below. This motivates us to chart the responsible AI ecosystem of Cat Royale. To provide a suitable structure for so doing we turn to Wilson and Sharples's layered 'onion model' of human factors in interactive systems design, which places people, artefacts and technologies at the centre; surrounded by tasks and goals; and then the personal physical and virtual workspace; and finally, the wider physical and virtual work environment on the outside [35]. We find this to be an encompassing and yet tractable framework for mapping the actors and responsibilities that comprise an ecosystem of trust.

5 Introducing Cat Royale

Blast Theory was commissioned by the UK's Trustworthy Autonomous Systems Hub (TAS Hub) to create an artwork to engage the public with the question of trust in robots. Their response was Cat Royale, a so-called 'utopia' for cats, a luxurious environment intended to cater to their every need. Following advice of animal-welfare experts, the artists created a bespoke enclosure with ample feeding stations, sleeping dens, walkways, a water fountain, scratching post, cat grass and litter trays, to house a family of three cats (Clover, Pumpkin, and

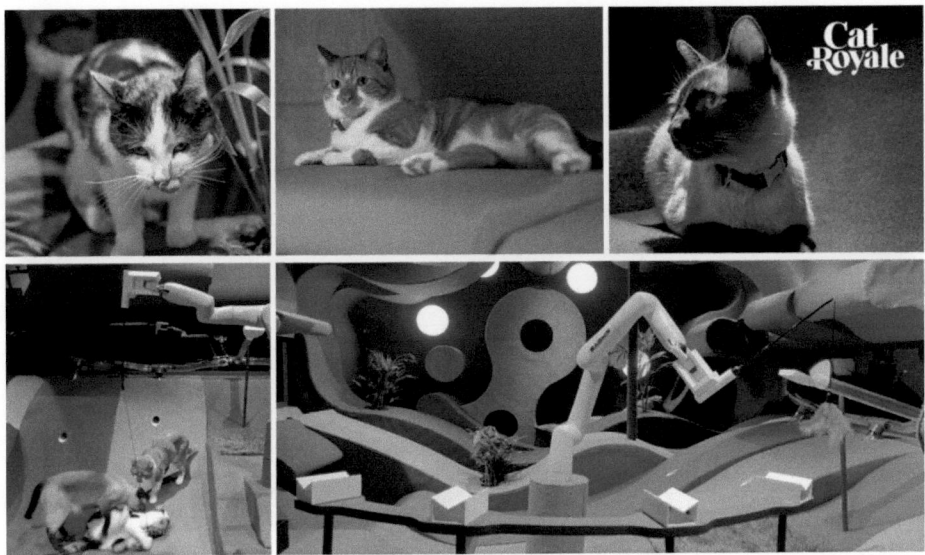

Fig. 1. A montage of images from Cat Royale. *Top left:* Clover. *Top middle:* Pumpkin. *Top right:* Ghostbuster. *Bottom left:* The three cats playing with a toy offered by the robot. *Bottom right:* The robot waves a toy from behind the four magnetic toy racks.

Ghostbuster) for six hours a day over 12 days. In the centre, a robot arm tried to increase their happiness by picking up toys from nearby magnetic racks every ten minutes and wielding them in a series of pre-programmed movements designed to attract their attention and engage them in play [27] (see Fig. 1 bottom row). More than 500 games were filmed during the 12 days, with the footage edited into social media highlights[1] and an eight-hour long movie, touring as a video installation to galleries worldwide.

Previous papers have reported findings from Cat Royale: how the artists designed a multi-species world to accommodate cats and robots and how the robot operator helped improvise new responses [27]; a case study of how collisions with robots can be reconceived as being complex and extended tangles [3]; and an account of the eighteen-month long journey through ethical approval that revealed tensions in multi-disciplinary and multi-species research [7]. The distinct contribution of this paper is to systematically chart the extensive socio-technical ecosystem required to ensure the trustworthiness of Cat Royale.

6 Charting the Ecosystem of Trust in Cat Royale

We now map the ecosystem of trustworthiness in Cat Royale, revealing the many agents that were involved in establishing the trustworthiness of the robot to play with the cats along with the various roles they played and issues that had to be

---

[1] Cat Royale (https://youtu.be/sl6nr8B5jqQ).

considered. Taking inspiration from the model of [35], we present this as a series of 'onion layers' shown in Fig. 2, with the **enclosure** that housed the cats and robot placed at the centre, gradually expanding out through the **control room**, surrounding **artist's studio** where the enclosure was located, the **development and advisory team** who enabled the work, and finally the various **audiences** for the work. At this point, we use names and terms that are specific to Cat Royale. Later on in Sect. 7 we generalise them to give a more broadly applicable framework for considering trust in robots.

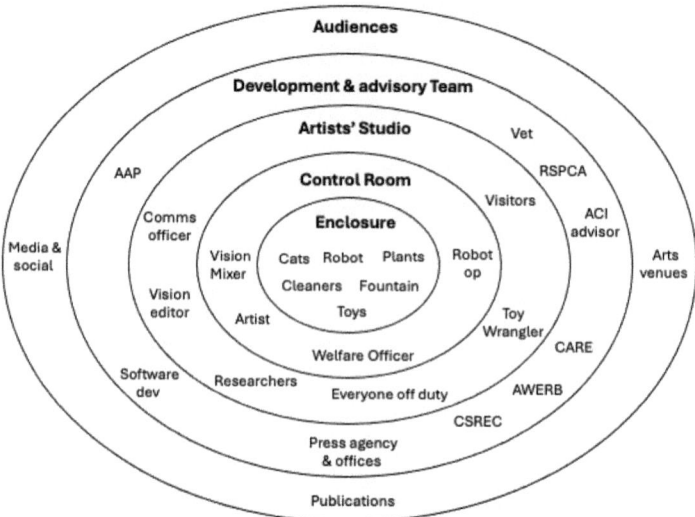

Fig. 2. Mapping the social ecology of trust of Cat Royale.

6.1 Enclosure

The **enclosure** provides the immediate context in which the *robot* engages the *cats*. Key issues here were whether the robot could be trusted not to harm the cats but also whether the cats could be trusted not to damage the robot. The robot arm, a Kinova Gen3 lite, was chosen to minimise any risk of harm to the cats due to its light payload and minimal range. The entire enclosure, including the robot and its manipulated toys, were designed specifically to be *trustworthy* to the cats, encouraging their voluntary engagement with both the robot and the play activities, for example through the provision of high perches and walkways from which they could observe the robot before choosing to approach it. Its striking visual design was chosen to be appealing to human viewers, hopefully to the cats too (following discussion with animal behaviour experts), and so that the cats would visually stand out from the background with a view to filming and potential uses of computer vision [27]. Also present, and relevant to the matter of trust, were various *toys* that the robot wielded and other artefacts such as the *drinking fountain*. The toys (which might be considered end effectors for the robot) needed to be safe for the cats to paw and bite (not toxic, sharp or raising the risk of choking). A previous study of Cat Royale showed how these additional artefacts played a pivotal role in safety as they often became loose and got tangled with each other and the robot; for example when Clover wrestled a toy away from the robot, dragged it through the enclosure, tangling with and pulling over the water fountain [27]. Also present were other non-human species in the form of various *plants*. Human *cleaners* would periodically enter the environment to tidy up and clean it so that it was sanitised and safe for the cats. Finally, the enclosure contained eight cameras that were carefully placed to afford wide coverage of the cats' different activities.

6.2 Control Room

The **control room**, located immediately outside the enclosure and connected via a one-way mirror was an important site for various activities concerned with trustworthiness. A key role here was the *robot operator* who would continuously monitor the robot, prepare it for each game, trigger the pre-recorded series of movements and hold down a deadman's switch while each movement unfolded. Occasionally they had to take manual control and improvise new actions, for example when toys became tangled around the robot or when a cat engaged the robot in a tug-of-war, requiring them to judge the safest moment to release the toy to minimise the risk of it recoiling back and possibly colliding with the cat[2]. The *artist* was also continually present, assuming responsibility for strategic (rather than immediately operational) decisions concerning the robot. They scored each game using the Participation in Play (PIP) scale, an instrument developed by feline behaviourists to score the level of engagement cats exhibits during play [10], feeding the results into the 'decision engine' that learned to recommend games for each cat, which they could choose to accept or reject. Also present was a *cat welfare officer*, a trained professional in cat welfare whose role was to monitor well-being and raise any concerns. Their role was especially important to ensuring trustworthiness, not least because the cats could not directly tell us how they felt about the robot, and so we needed to rely on an expert trained in cat behaviour to judge whether the cats appeared to trust the robot as a form of what is referred to as 'mediated consent' in the animal-computer interaction literature [20]. Finally, a *vision mixer* was present to continuously monitor the outputs of the eight cameras and generate a video edit in real time that best captured the action within the enclosure.

6.3 Artists' Studio

To prevent the cats from escaping into the wider hazardous world outside, the enclosure was constructed behind locked doors in the *artists' studio*, a complex of

---

[2] See https://youtu.be/sl6nr8B5jqQ from 3:01–03:27.

several rooms, including resting, storage, office, and kitchen facilities. This also ensured only authorised *visitors* could gain entry, an important consideration for the security of both robot and cats, especially given concerns that there could be a negative response to the notion of the project leading to unwanted attention at the studio. An important function of the studio was to provide a stress-free space where *everyone off- duty*, cats included, could relax away from the robots. A *toy wrangler*, dedicated to maintenance, cleaning and preparation of the more than 50 attachments that the robot wielded, also worked in the studio along with a *vision editor* who did further editing of video material, for example to generate daily highlights, working alongside a *communications officer* who managed press, media and social media. The studio also provided the location for a daily review meeting where the team met to discuss the previous day's events and make adjustments for the next day. Finally, the studio provided a base for *researchers* to interview people, write up their notes and collate video and other data.

6.4 Development and Advisory Team

Significant to the trustworthiness of Cat Royale was the involvement developers and advisors. Two *software developers* were responsible for the robot control interface and decision engine. A specialist in veterinary behavioural medicine (*Vet Advisor*), an expert on animal-computer interaction (*ACI Advisor*), and the UK's Royal Society for the Prevention of Cruelty to Animals (*RSPCA*) all provided guidance concerning design of the enclosure, games and procedures for monitoring and ensuring cat welfare. A *press agency* was engaged to help devise and execute a media communications strategy, including a crisis management plan in case of having to manage an incident such as (the unlikely event of) a cat being injured or the outbreak of a social media storm. The artists recruited an *Audience Advisory Panel* comprising people with backgrounds across the arts and technology who met regularly to review progress and provide advice. A vital aspect of trustworthiness was ethical approval for the project. Given the ethical sensitivities and United Kingdom's tight regulations surrounding the involvement of animals in research, this unsurprisingly proved to be a complex and lengthy process (see [7] for a full account), with the project passing through three different ethics committees at the University of Nottingham, the Animal Welfare and Ethical Review Body (*AWERB*) which regulates animal research at the University and ensures legal compliance, the Committee for Animal Research and Ethics (*CARE*) in our Veterinary School who gave further advice on ensuring cat welfare, and the Computer Science Research Ethics Committee (*CSREC*) who advised on the technical and data privacy aspects of the project. The extensive and iterative input of these three bodies was essential to ensuring that the robot could be trusted to safely and legally engage the cats and helping us address wider issues about communications and reputational risk.

6.5 Audiences

Finally, we note various external **audiences** for Cat Royale who were invited to consider the question of whether one can trust a robot to play with cats, and by extension to care for humans. The movie has toured to multiple *arts venues* (galleries and festivals) worldwide and continues to do so. There has been extensive *media and social media* coverage which has engaged the wider public. The research team has targeted *publications* at venues spanning human-computer interaction, human-robot interaction, and animal-computer interaction.

7 Charting Ecosystems of Trust in Social Robots

Cat Royale is, of course, an unusual example of social robotics, being both an artwork and focused on cats as the beneficiaries. So what general lessons can we take from it? We now revisit our five onion layers, considering ways in which they might generalise to other applications (see Fig. 3). Our aim is to provide developers, researchers and potentially policy makers with a framework to explore the wide variety of factors involved in ensuring the trustworthiness of robots. Note that we often talk about 'spaces'—this is in a largely conceptual sense of being 'design spaces'. Where physical space is important (as it is in several layers), we further note that this could be distributed (e.g., the case of telepresence robots that connect people in different places).

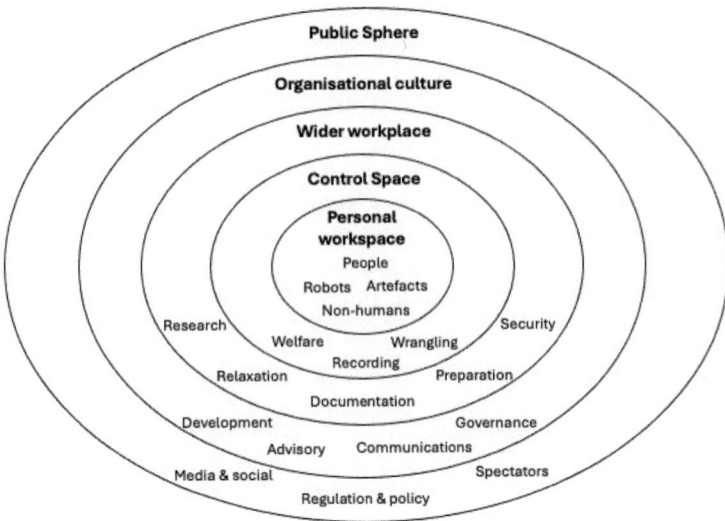

Fig. 3. A generalised social ecology of trust for robots

7.1 Personal Workspace

At the heart of the **personal workspace** are the *people* and *robots* that interact. As discussed earlier, see Sect. 2, social robotics is replete with knowledge about the many factors that may contribute to trustworthiness between them. However, our experience with Cat Royale highlights additional factors. First are additional *artefacts* that need to be designed to be trustworthy too; they can, for example, also be a cause of mess, for example debris after a collision [3] which can increase the risk of further problems. Cat Royale highlights the presence and impact on *non-human species* and the additional challenges this raises for trustworthiness. This may be deliberate, for example robots that tend to animals in the home, farming or the wild, or accidental, as animals will likely encounter robots in these contexts anyway (see internet videos of cats riding robot vacuum cleaners). Recognising the importance of designing for non-human species reflects a trend towards 'beyond human' thinking in HCI, which aims to decentre humans from design in order to then accommodate wider environmental concerns [13,34].

7.2 Orchestration

The **Orchestration** layer enables the ongoing monitoring and steering of an experience, often from behind the scenes, though sometimes visibly 'front of house'. Orchestration has previously been studied as a feature of interactive artworks [5], but equivalents can be found in other contexts. One aspect of orchestration that is familiar to robotics is *wrangling*, which refers to the control of a robot's ongoing operation, perhaps manually triggering actions, stepping in to improvise, and managing safety such as operating a deadman's switch or emergency stop button, and which may be carried out from a separate (even remote) control space or when co-present with the robot and its users. We have seen how trustworthiness relies on actively managing welfare, especially when participants are vulnerable and unable to consent (e.g., for some care robots), lack knowledge of robots (e.g., delivery robots on the streets), and includes more general workplace safety, well-being and even employment rights. Finally, generalising the role of Cat Royale's vision mixer, the orchestration layer may include mechanisms for *recording* interactions for research, publicity or compliance purposes.

7.3 Wider Workplace

These play further important roles with respect to trustworthiness. *Security* is important to protect against theft or damage, both accidental due to untrained visitors being present, and deliberate sabotage involving malicious acts. This wider workplace may also house those involved in the *documentation* of robot interactions, including the editing of recordings, but also the generation of additional materials such as field notes, for research, performance analysis and feedback, to capture datasets for training AI models, or for public media. We saw how it was important to support *relaxation* away from robots where people can unwind, socialise and recover without having to constantly attend to the demands of interacting with robots or being documented, with clear thresholds into the control and personal workspace layers that signal that they now need to attend to these extra demands. Finally, the wider workspace may house workshops and storage to support preparation and maintenance of the robots and ancillary technologies.

7.4 Organisational Culture

Cat Royale illustrated various ways in which organisational culture influences the trustworthiness of robots. The first is through the *development* process spanning hardware (procurement or development), software, artefacts, surrounding environment and user experience. Also important is introducing external *advisory* roles in the form of expert consultants (e.g., the Vet and RSPCA in Cat Royale) and panels representing potential users and/or the public). Internal *governance* includes local ethical review processes and may need to cover vulnerable users (e.g., animals in our case). Finally, a coherent and carefully planned communications strategy is essential for explaining the project to build trust and dealing with problems if something goes wrong, potentially involving professional advice and connecting press offices where multiple organisations are involved.

7.5 Public Sphere

The *public sphere* contains important external influences on the trustworthiness of social robots. *Regulation and policy* may span general technology regulation, data protection, security and safety, but also regulation and policy in specific application domains, for example the extensive regulation of healthcare and transportation (or even animal protection as we saw in Cat Royale). Ultimately, however, it is perhaps the public who will be the long-term arbiter of trustworthiness. This includes *spectators* who directly witness robot encounters, including deliberately targeted audiences at demonstrations, educational events and cultural venues, but also 'unwitting bystanders' who happen to encounter robots as they go about their daily lives (e.g., encountering delivery robots or autonomous vehicles on the streets or service robots in hospitals and museums). Critically important is managing the *media and social media* where public perceptions of trust are forged.

8 Conclusions

As an artwork in the wild, Cat Royale reveals the diverse factors involved in ensuring social robots are trustworthy. Those concerned with direct interaction with robots (e.g., safety, reliability, and social behaviours) form just one part of a much larger ecosystem of trust. Also important are additional layers concerned with the orchestration of experiences, embedding them into the workplace, connecting them to organisational culture, and ultimately carefully presenting them within the public sphere—with each of these layers comprising multiple perspectives. In short, ensuring trustworthiness is complex. We do not offer Cat Royale as a solution. Nor is our framework intended as a simple 'cook book' of guidelines that can be readily translated to other settings. Rather, our aim has been to reveal, through a concrete case study and an ecosystems perspective, the breath and complexity of trustworthiness in relation to social robots as an inspiration to further research and the value of artistic methods. For those wanting to apply the ecosystem's perspective themselves, this concrete case study can illustrate different factors that should be considered and Fig. 3 offers a starting point to map a social ecology of trust for a specific robotic application. Finally, we highlight the importance of considering non-humans in all of this—animals will encounter robots, by design or accident, and we must ensure that this is trustworthy too.

Acknowledgments. This work was supported by the Engineering and Physical Sciences Research Council through the Turing AI World Leading Researcher Fellowship in Somabotics: Creatively Embodying Artificial Intelligence [grant number APP22478], UKRI Trustworthy Autonomous Systems Hub [EP/V00784X/1], Responsible AI UK [EP/Y009800/1], EPSRC Centre for Doctoral Training in Horizon [EP/S023305/1].

Data Access Statement. The data that support the findings of this study may be available on request from the corresponding author.

Disclosure of Interests. The authors have no competing interests to declare.

References

1. Abdai, J., Uccheddu, S., Gácsi, M., Miklósi, Á.: Exploring the advantages of using artificial agents to investigate animacy perception in cats and dogs. Bioinsp. Biomimet. **17**(6) (2022). https://doi.org/10.1088/1748-3190/ac93d9
2. Anzabi, N., Umemuro, H.: Effect of different listening behaviors of social robots on perceived trust in human-robot interactions. Int. J. Soc. Robot. **15**(6), 931–951 (2023)
3. Benford, S., et al.: Tangles: unpacking extended collision experiences with soma trajectories (2025). https://doi.org/10.1145/3723875
4. Benford, S., et al.: How artists improvise and provoke robotics. In: International Conference on Social Robotics, pp. 66–77. Springer, Heidelberg (2024). https://doi.org/10.1007/978-981-96-3525-2_6
5. Benford, S., Giannachi, G.: Performing Mixed Reality. MIT press, Cambridge (2011)
6. Benford, S., et al.: Performance-led research in the wild. ACM Trans. Comput.-Human Interact. (TOCHI) **20**(3), 1–22 (2013)
7. Benford, S.D., et al.: Charting ethical tensions in multispecies technology research through beneficiary-epistemology space. In: Proceedings of the CHI Conference on Human Factors in Computing Systems, pp. 1–15 (2024)
8. Cameron, D., et al.: Framing factors: the importance of context and the individual in understanding trust in human-robot interaction. In: Proceedings of the IEEE/RSJ International Conference on Intelligent Robots and Systems (IROS) (2015)

9. De Graaf, M.M., Allouch, S.B., Klamer, T.: Sharing a life with harvey: exploring the acceptance of and relationship-building with a social robot. Comput. Hum. Behav. **43**, 1–14 (2015)
10. Ellis, J.J.: Beyond "doing better": ordinal rating scales to monitor behavioural indicators of well-being in cats. Animals **12**(21), 2897 (2022)
11. Esterwood, Jr, R.: Three strikes and you are out!: the impacts of multiple human-robot trust violations and repairs on robot trustworthiness. Comput. Hum. Behav. **142** (2023)
12. Gaver, W.: What should we expect from research through design? In: Proceedings of the SIGCHI Conference on Human Factors in Computing Systems, pp. 937–946 (2012)
13. Giaccardi, E., Redström, J.: Technology and more-than-human design. Des. Issues **36**(4), 33–44 (2020)
14. Gompei, T., Umemuro, H.: Factors and development of cognitive and affective trust on social robots. In: Ge, S.S., Cabibihan, J.-J., Salichs, M.A., Broadbent, E., He, H., Wagner, A.R., Castro-González, Á. (eds.) ICSR 2018. LNCS (LNAI), vol. 11357, pp. 45–54. Springer, Cham (2018). https://doi.org/10.1007/978-3-030-05204-1_5
15. Hancock, P.A., Billings, D.R., Schaefer, K.E., Chen, J.Y., De Visser, E.J., Parasuraman, R.: A meta-analysis of factors affecting trust in human-robot interaction. Hum. Factors **53**(5), 517–527 (2011). https://doi.org/10.1177/0018720811417254
16. Hou, Y.T.Y., Cheon, E.J., Jung, M.F.: Power in human-robot interaction. In: ACM/IEEE International Conference on Human-Robot Interaction, pp. 269–282 (2024). https://doi.org/10.1145/3610977.3634949
17. Khavas, Z.R., Ahmadzadeh, S.R., Robinette, P.: Modeling trust in human-robot interaction: a survey. In: Wagner, A.R., et al. (eds.) ICSR 2020. LNCS (LNAI), vol. 12483, pp. 529–541. Springer, Cham (2020). https://doi.org/10.1007/978-3-030-62056-1_44
18. Kok, B.C., Soh, H.: Trust in robots: challenges and opportunities. Curr. Rob. Rep. **1**(4), 297–309 (2020)
19. Lin, P., Abney, K., Bekey, G.: Robot ethics: mapping the issues for a mechanized world. Artif. Intell. **175**(5–6), 942–949 (2011). https://doi.org/10.1016/j.artint.2010.11.026
20. Mancini, C., Nannoni, E.: Relevance, impartiality, welfare and consent: principles of an animal-centered research ethics. Front. Anim. Sci. **3**, 800186 (2022)
21. Manteuffel, C., Dirksen, N., Hartwig, T.: From extra to actor: facilitating automated conditioning in animal-robot interaction. Comput. Electron. Agric. **191**(June), 106496 (2021). https://doi.org/10.1016/j.compag.2021.106496
22. Paradeda, R.B., Hashemian, M., Rodrigues, R.A., Paiva, A.: How facial expressions and small talk may influence trust in a robot. In: Agah, A., Cabibihan, J.-J., Howard, A.M., Salichs, M.A., He, H. (eds.) ICSR 2016. LNCS (LNAI), vol. 9979, pp. 169–178. Springer, Cham (2016). https://doi.org/10.1007/978-3-319-47437-3_17
23. Rodriguez-Guerra, D., Sorrosal, G., Cabanes, I., Calleja, C.: Human-robot interaction review: challenges and solutions for modern industrial environments. IEEE Access **9**, 108557–108578 (2021). https://doi.org/10.1109/ACCESS.2021.3099287
24. Romano, D., Porfiri, M., Zahadat, P., Schmickl, T.: Animal-robot interaction—an emerging field at the intersection of biology and robotics. Bioinsp. Biomimet. **19**(2) (2024). https://doi.org/10.1088/1748-3190/ad2086
25. Rousseau, S.B.C.: Not so different after all: a cross-discipline view of trust. Acad. Manag. Rev. **23**, 393–404 (1998)

26. Salem, M., Lakatos, G., Amirabdollahian, F., Dautenhahn, K.: Towards safe and trustworthy social robots: ethical challenges and practical issues. In: ICSR 2015. LNCS (LNAI), vol. 9388, pp. 584–593. Springer, Cham (2015). https://doi.org/10.1007/978-3-319-25554-5_58
27. Schneiders, E., et al.: Designing multispecies worlds for robots, cats, and humans. In: Proceedings of the CHI Conference on Human Factors in Computing Systems, pp. 1–16 (2024)
28. Shidujaman, M., Mi, H., Jamal, L.: "i trust you more": A behavioral greeting gesture study on social robots for recommendation tasks. In: 2020 International Conference on Image Processing and Robotics (ICIP), pp. 1–5. IEEE (2020)
29. Stahl, B.C.: Embedding responsibility in intelligent systems: from AI ethics to responsible AI ecosystems. Sci. Rep. **13**(1), 7586 (2023)
30. Stower, R., Gautier, A., Wozniak, M., Jensfelt, P., Tumova, J., Leite, I.: Take a chance on me: how robot performance and risk behaviour affects trust and risk-taking. In: Proceedings of the 2025 ACM/IEEE International Conference on Human-Robot Interaction, HRI '25, pp. 391–399. IEEE Press (2025)
31. Sweeney, P.: Trusting social robots. AI Ethics **3**(2), 419–426 (2023)
32. Tewari, M., Lindgren, H.: Expecting, understanding, relating, and interacting-older, middle-aged and younger adults' perspectives on breakdown situations in human–robot dialogues. Front. Rob. AI **9**(October), 1–27 (2022). https://doi.org/10.3389/frobt.2022.956709
33. Tollon, F., Vallor, S.: The Responsible AI Ecosystem : A BRAID Landscape Study. Technical Report, BRAID: Building Responsible AI Divides (2025)
34. Wakkary, R.: Things We Could Design: For More than Human-Centered Worlds. MIT press, Cambridge (2021)
35. Wilson, J.R., Sharples, S.: Methods in the understanding of human factors. In: Evaluation of Human Work, 4th edn, pp. 1–32. CRC Press (2015)
36. Zimmerman, J., Stolterman, E., Forlizzi, J.: An analysis and critique of research through design: towards a formalization of a research approach. In: proceedings of the 8th ACM Conference on Designing Interactive Systems, pp. 310–319 (2010)

Open Access This chapter is licensed under the terms of the Creative Commons Attribution 4.0 International License (http://creativecommons.org/licenses/by/4.0/), which permits use, sharing, adaptation, distribution and reproduction in any medium or format, as long as you give appropriate credit to the original author(s) and the source, provide a link to the Creative Commons license and indicate if changes were made.

The images or other third party material in this chapter are included in the chapter's Creative Commons license, unless indicated otherwise in a credit line to the material. If material is not included in the chapter's Creative Commons license and your intended use is not permitted by statutory regulation or exceeds the permitted use, you will need to obtain permission directly from the copyright holder.

Student's Acceptance of Social Robots: A Study with Pepper on Inclusive Mathematics Learning Through Storytelling

Antonio Vitale[1()], Bruno Carbonaro[2], Gennaro Cordasco[3], Umberto Dello Iacono[2], and Anna Esposito[2]

[1] University of Macerata, 62100 Macerata, Italy
a.vitale11@unimc.it
[2] University of Campania "Luigi Vanvitelli", 81100 Caserta, Italy
{bruno.carbonaro,umberto.delloiacono,
anna.esposito}@unicampania.it
[3] University of Salerno, 84084 Fisciano, Italy
gcordasco@unisa.it

Abstract. The use of social robots in educational settings can enhance inclusive learning and students' engagement. The aim of this study is to assess students' experience with the social robot Pepper. It was used as an educational tool in a mathematics storytelling activity designed according to the first principle of Universal Design for Learning (UDL) and embedded with AIED technologies. The analysis of answers to the Robot Acceptance Questionnaire (RAQ) shows that students accept the use of Pepper, which is considered friendly, and easy to use. Pepper's ability to express itself clearly and to provide immediate, and personalized feedback has created an engaging learning environment, thereby minimizing the negative feelings that are associated in mathematics. The study thus highlights Pepper's acceptance and efficacy as an inclusive educational technology capable of making mathematics learning more inclusive.

Keywords: Social robot's multimodality · Pepper · Inclusive Mathematics Learning · Storytelling · UDL

1 Introduction

Artificial Intelligence (AI) is transforming many areas of society, and education is no wonder. The use of AI in education, known as AIED (Artificial Intelligence in Education), has led to several technological advancements and educational benefits [1]. One of the objectives of AI is to improve static teaching-learning processes through the deployment of tools such as intelligent tutoring systems, automatic assessment [2], predictive learning analysis, and social robotics. One of the most promising AI tools for enhancing how students and teachers engage in educational settings is precisely social robotics. Social robots can interact with the environment and collect, produce, and analyze data from it [3]. They are adaptive tools that can make learning more dynamic by encouraging active students' engagement, facilitating access to educational contents, and promoting dynamic learning activities [4]. Moreover, social robots can understand and respond to human emotions and behaviours through various communication media, such as verbal language, gestures, and facial expressions [5]. They offer new opportunities to support the development of social and cognitive skills and personalize the educational experience [6]. Thus, they could contribute to student inclusion and engagement [7] through their ability to provide immediate and emotional feedback, adapting personalized support to specific student needs [8, 9].

The use of robotic aids is quickly growing in school environments, and social robotics may have huge potential in mathematics education. Students often consider mathematics as an abstract and boring discipline such that it leads them to disengagement [10]. Social robotics may be the breakthrough to overcome these beliefs by allowing students to have interactive, and hands-on learning experiences [11]. Gura [12] states that robotics can propose dynamic activities for mastering geometric concepts. For instance, the use of the GeomBot robot makes maths lessons dynamic and interactive and facilitates the understanding and visualization of geometric and spatial properties [13]. Moreover, by integrating storytelling [14, 15] and multimodality [16], social robots can present mathematical concepts in an engaging way.

However, an important aspect in implementing new technologies is user acceptance. The user's acceptance of a new technology as easy to use is essential to its adoption, according to [17]. In educational settings, robots have showed to enhance students' motivation and engagement, enabling them to understand complex and abstract mathematical concepts in a hands-on, dynamic and inclusive approach [7] making mathematics learning more interactive thereby increasing students' acceptance [11]. Sharkey [18] states that the acceptance of social robot as teaching tools depends on their ability to provide tailored and engaging learning experiences. Consequently, students' acceptance of social robotics is a critical issue for the effectiveness of its integration into the school environment [19].

Our study aims to explore how multimodality and storytelling can enhance students' acceptance of social robots in mathematics education. Specifically, we explore how these features shape students' engagement, affect and ease of interaction with the social robot Pepper. Pepper is a semi-humanoid robot created by SoftBank Robotics (ex-Aldebaran Robotics) designed to interact with people as naturally as possible. Pepper has the ability to detect human emotions through the functioning of sensors, reacting in an empathetic way. Our goal is to create an inclusive learning environment ensuring that each student feels supported and motivated throughout their learning process. Specifically, we are implementing inclusive mathematics learning activities in agreement with the representation principle of Universal Design for Learning (UDL), which highlights the importance of providing a variety of modes of representation to satisfy all students' educational needs [20, 21] and through story-problems [14], that facilitate understanding of the problematic situation, stimulating students' curiosity and promoting inclusion, using Pepper as an inclusive multimodal educational technology to improve students' engagement. This educational approach can foster students' engagement while simultaneously acting within a sociocultural and interactive setting. Using storytelling throughout human-robot interaction, as part of a sociological framework, fosters the construction of shared meanings and emotive ties by fitting into the framework of symbolic interactionist theory where language, roles, and empathy are central to shared meaning-making [22, 23]. The focus of our work is to investigate student's acceptance during the interaction with Pepper. Specifically, our research questions are:

- RQ1: To what extent is the robot Pepper (used in a mathematics learning context) accepted by students?
- RQ2: To what extent do aspects of multimodality and storytelling influence students' acceptance?

To answer this research questions, we conducted an experimental study involving 8 students (two middle school students and six high school students) in a learning activity implemented with the robot Pepper.

2 Theoretical Background

The integration of AI tools, i.e. social robots, with UDL principles and storytelling have the potential to improve education by enabling inclusive learning experiences. In this section, we explore Pepper's multimodality (i.e. the use of multiple communication channels) alongside students' acceptance of social robots, UDL principles and the role of storytelling in enhancing educational experiences.

2.1 Multimodality of Pepper

Pepper's multimodality refers to its ability to interact with users using multiple communication paths simultaneously. Pepper is able to read feelings, can speak and move around. It includes a tablet display and it can engage in trying to establish relationships with users as naturally as possible [3] by employing a multimodal approach that includes spoken language, gestures, facial expressions, and image-video on its tablet [5]. Multimodality can improve students' understanding and makes the interaction with robots more seamless, easier and more entertaining for students. Multimodality allows to improve the mathematics teaching-learning process [16] by adapting to students' specific needs, creating an interactive and engaging learning experience. In mathematics education context, multimodality could be advantageous because it facilitates comprehension and memorization of content, particularly when information is presented in multiple ways simultaneously [24].

2.2 Designing of Inclusive Education

Universal Design for Learning (UDL) is an effective framework for inclusive educational design, as it provides guidelines for making learning inclusive and accessible to all students through the use of a wide range of teaching techniques and technology resources [20, 21]. Researchers at CAST (Center for Applied Special Technology) developed UDL by establishing guidelines [20], which were organized into three principles [21]: *representation*, a huge variety of representations to offer students with many opportunities for understanding and acquiring knowledge; *expression*, multiple forms of action and expression are used to provide students with a variety of ways of showing their knowledge and *engagement*, multiple techniques for engagement are used to provide students with varying levels of incentive to study.

Students can learn in different ways, thus it is essential to provide them with resources that are adapted to their requirements so this can encourage them to engage in educational strategies. Therefore, UDL supports inclusive education by customizing teaching approaches to fit all student's needs. In conclusion, through its three principles, UDL addresses in providing students with flexible resources with the aim of stimulating their active participation and learning according to their own preferences. In this work, we focused on the first UDL principle, namely the principle of representation. Also, storytelling may also be used as an effective tool for inclusive mathematics education, as it helps individuals to organize their experiences. According to [25], narrative thinking can enhance logical reasoning, and storytelling has been shown to have a powerful and cognitive influence, motivating students to actively engage in learning [15]. This approach is effective in helping students to understand problem situations and enhance their problem-solving processes, particularly when they are deployed with social robotics.

2.3 Acceptance of Social Robots

Usability, user friendliness, and the coherence of user responses will determine the acceptance of a social robot. The acceptance of new technology as easy to use is essential for adoption, as highlighted by the Technology Acceptance Model (TAM) proposed by [26]. According to [17], Perceived Usefulness (PU) and Perceived Ease of Use (PEOU) have a direct influence on the acceptance of social robots by teachers and students in educational settings. [27] assessed elementary school students' experience in interacting with LINA, a humanoid robotic tutor, within a formal educational setting, attempting to explore their levels of acceptance. The study produced positive results, stating that the physical and social presence of a robot either as a tutor providing homework and supporting their learning, or as a tutor explaining various school subjects in the classroom plays a key role in students' attention and motivation. Robots' multimodal communication capabilities can increase students' acceptance by enhancing the simplicity and enjoyment of using technology. To evaluate the different aspects of interaction, from perceived ease of use to the level of attraction and pleasure engendered, it is critical to evaluate to what extent students accept the use of social robots in mathematics education.

3 Methods

In this section, we provide some details about methodology of research. Finally, we describe how we collected and analyzed data.

The learning activity involved eight students aged between 13 and 17 years old who participated on a voluntary basis. The activity is structured in five sessions focused on mathematics, and in particular on the Pythagorean Theorem with the aim to use Pepper as an inclusive educational technology to enhance mathematics learning and to engage them in inclusive mathematics teaching activities through storytelling by providing them with immediate, personalized, and emotional feedback. Students with prior knowledge of the Pythagorean Theorem, as taught in school, participated to activity, and no assumptions were made about their level of proficiency or understanding of the topic. Students worked one-on-one with Pepper and their privacy was guaranteed, making sure that the data collected is used exclusively for educational research. The Pythagorean Theorem was selected due to its strong narrative contextualization potential. It also lends itself to the design of real-world problems that can be explored through storytelling and enhanced by Pepper's personalized feedback. In the story, Federico's father builds a tree house as a Federico's birthday gift. Once completed, he asks Federico's help to determine the length of a wooden ramp needed to climb the house, given the vertical height of the tree and the horizontal distance from its bottom. The sessions were carried out in the BeCogSys laboratory of the Department of Psychology of the University of Campania "Luigi Vanvitelli" coordinated by prof. Anna Esposito and prof. Gennaro Cordasco. Each session lasted about 15–20 min. The 5 sessions of the learning activity are described in detail below.

Beginning Presentation: Pepper welcomes the student and introduces itself using this sentence: *"Hi, I'm Pepper. I'm very glad you're here with me today!"* and asks the student what emotions she is feeling: *"How are you?"*.

Beginning Activity: Pepper begins to explain to the student the activity they will be doing together: *"Today we are going to work together through a beautiful activity. This will be useful for you to understand a lot of new things. If something is not clear to you and you would like further explanation, I will be available for any explanation. Are you ready?"* Then, Pepper dynamically and engagingly explains the task through a story, which the student can also follow through related vignettes shown on Pepper's tablet.

Problem Understanding: Pepper begins to pose questions on comprehension of the story by offering feedback on student's answers (i.e. *"What did you understand about the story?"* and *"From the telling of the story, there were two significant items. Touch my head to find out the first item or touch my hand to find out the second item"*). Pepper gives feedback that are congratulatory (i.e. *"Perfect, you are so great! My compliments"*) whether the student correctly guessed the correct data, encouraging if not (for example, *"Ops! Attention! Could you try to answer again?"*).

Problem Solving: Pepper leads the student in solving the problem. If the student has difficulty, Pepper says: *"Don't worry, I can help you"* and it gives alternative explanations and tells an illustrated storytelling about the Pythagorean Theorem. In case the student knows how to proceed, Pepper gives positive feedback (i.e. *"Great, I'm glad you know how to do it. Can you explain how to do that?"*) and asks to explain how perform the task. Finally, Pepper proposes hypothetical results on its tablet and asks the student to identify the correct one. Whether the student's solution is correct, Pepper provides positive feedback by saying: *"Yeah, you are brilliant!"*

Conclusion: At this point, after the student has given Pepper the correct information, Pepper offers congratulatory feedback to her: *"Perfect, thanks to your help Federico is overjoyed"*. Finally, Pepper thanks the student for helping the main character of the story. Finally, Pepper says goodbye to her: *"Thank you for doing this activity with me! Bye!"*

At the end of all sessions, each student answered the Robot Acceptance Questionnaire (RAQ) [28]. RAQ involves six sections (S1, S2, S3, S4, S5, S6) with the aim to explore students' interaction with Pepper by focusing on both their interest in talking with Pepper and their emotional engagement during the interaction. Specifically, RAQ explores students' experience with Pepper, inquiring about personal aspects, interaction readiness, perceived qualities (pragmatic and hedonic), age and voice preferences of Pepper, and perceptions of its functions. We refer the reader to the original source [28] for a detailed description of each section of the RAQ. In addition to RAQ, students were asked to answer additional questions (AQ) concerning their acceptance of Pepper's multimodal abilities: to understand and respond to voice input, to give feedback, to combine gestures, facial expressions, to tell the story and simultaneously show vignettes related to the narrative on its tablet, ease of use. Students rated (Likert scale) from 1 (strongly agree) to 5 (strongly disagree). Specifically, the additional questions are:

- AQ1: I think Pepper can recognize speech commands;
- AQ2: I think Pepper can use gestures effectively during the interaction;
- AQ3: I think Pepper's gestures made the interaction more comprehensible;
- AQ4: I think Pepper's facial expressions were appropriate to the situations;
- AQ5: I think Pepper made the storytelling very clear;
- AQ6: I think Pepper is helpful in situations of difficulty.

To collect further students' feedback in order both to evaluate students' ability to interact with Pepper and to analyze to what extent its multimodality impacts acceptance in mathematics educational settings, we included three open-ended questions that encouraged students to share their feelings about the learning experience with Pepper: what did you like about the interaction with Pepper? What did you like least about interacting with Pepper? Do you have any suggestions to improve Pepper's multimodal interaction?

All the data collected correspond to the answers given to the RAQ and to the additional questions with the aim of assessing students' acceptance to try to establish their level of engagement, interaction, attitude toward Pepper and its multimodality. We recorded the frequency of each type of quantitative request using a spreadsheet. Qualitative answers from open-ended questions were transcribed and analyzed by finding relevant and recurring issues.

4 Results

In this section, we show findings of the data analysis for each section of RAQ regarding students' acceptance of the social robot Pepper as an inclusive educational technology for mathematics learning through dynamic storytelling.

Regarding S1, all 8 students state that the students are technologically expert users and they are not cowed by technology. This familiarity with technology could have eased Pepper's initial acceptance, making the learning environment less threatening.

Concerning S2, 7 out of 8 students state that they are willing to interact with Pepper, while 1 out of 8 students think it is probably possible. This finding suggests that Pepper is positively accepted as an interacting partner, validating the effectiveness of the welcome session in engaging students.

Regarding S3, we show some results arising from the Pragmatic Quality, Hedonic Quality-Identity, Hedonic Quality-Feeling and Attractiveness Evaluation of the interaction with Pepper for each student. Concerning Pepper's pragmatic quality, the following Table 1 shows that most students have some positive idea about the interaction with Pepper.

Table 1. Pragmatic Quality.

Pragmatic Quality Statements	Strongly agree	Agree	Not sure	Disagree	Strongly disagree
Pepper might have a great influence in daily life	0	2	5	1	0
Communication with Pepper is easy	5	3	0	0	0
Communication with Pepper is hard	0	0	0	7	1
Communication with Pepper is complex	0	0	3	4	1
Communication with Pepper is not useful	0	0	0	3	5
Communication with Pepper is qualifying	0	8	0	0	0

Specifically, 5 out of 8 students believe that Pepper might have a great influence in daily life, and all 8 students find the interaction easy. All students highly enjoyed Pepper's ability to interact in a friendly way, especially in the initial getting-to-know-you process. It is worth noting that 7 out of 8 students strongly disagree that the communication with Pepper is hard, highlighting Pepper's user-friendly interface. Also, 4 out of 8 students strongly disagree with the idea that the interaction with Pepper is complex, however all 8 students disallow the idea that the interaction with Pepper is not useful, and all students agree that it enhances the learning experience, indicating a high educational value. Regarding hedonic quality-identity data, Table 2 shows an overall positive students' attitude regarding Pepper's quality, especially about its friendly and comforting qualities.

Table 2. Hedonic Quality - Identity.

Hedonic Quality – Identity Statements	Strongly agree	Agree	Not sure	Disagree	Strongly disagree
Pepper is friendly	4	4	0	0	0
Pepper is irritating	0	0	0	3	5
Pepper is human	0	1	5	2	0
Pepper is threatening	0	0	0	5	3
Pepper is reassuring	0	7	1	0	0
Pepper is unreliable	0	0	0	6	4

Table 2 shows that 7 out of 8 students accept Pepper as reassurance, but less human. All students (4 out of 8 students strongly agree and 4 out of 8 students agree) consider Pepper as friendly. It is not seen as irritating or threatening, however its ability to make communication extraordinary and exciting is highly assessed (all 8 students). This is a crucial feature to create an inclusive and engaging learning environment. Related to hedonic quality-feeling data, the following Table 3 shows an overall positive pattern, with some interesting considerations.

Table 3. Hedonic Quality – Feeling.

Hedonic Quality – Feeling Statements	Strongly agree	Agree	Not sure	Disagree	Strongly disagree
Communication with Pepper is extraordinary	0	8	0	0	0
Communication with Pepper is boring	0	0	2	5	1
Communication with Pepper is exciting	2	6	0	0	0
Communication with Pepper is insignificant	0	0	0	4	4
Communication with Pepper is stimulating	4	3	1	0	0
Communication with Pepper is disturbing	0	0	0	3	5

Table 3 shows that all 8 students agree that communication with Pepper could be extraordinary, not boring (5 out of 8 students), and engaging (6 out of 8 students). Pepper is able to engage students while maintaining high levels of participation. In addition, 7 out of 8 students believe that their interaction with Pepper is stimulating, and none of them had reported being unsatisfied during their relationship with Pepper. Concerning Pepper's attractiveness data, all 8 students state that interaction with Pepper could enrich their mathematical knowledge (Table 4). This suggests that Pepper is seen as a useful tool for mathematics learning. In addition, the communication with Pepper is not considered predictable but rather dynamic (5 out of 8 students), fascinating (all 8 students), engaging (all 8 students), and not demotivating (all 8 students). In conclusion, the interaction with Pepper is not perceived as stressful (all 8 students).

Table 4. Attractiveness.

Hedonic Quality – Feeling Statements	Strongly agree	Agree	Not sure	Disagree	Strongly disagree
Interaction with Pepper enriches mathematical knowledge	4	4	0	0	0
Communication with Pepper is obvious	0	0	2	5	1
Communication with Pepper is fascinating	8	0	0	0	0
Communication with Pepper is demotivating	0	0	4	4	0
Communication with Pepper is engaging	4	4	0	0	0
Communication with Pepper is stressful	0	0	0	5	3

Regarding S4, 7 out of 8 students state that Pepper is between 19 and 28 years old while 1 out of 8 students state that it is between 29 and 38 years old. These data suggest that Pepper's appearance and its way of communicating and interacting with students are perceived as youthful. A robot perceived as young could be seen as more dynamic and accessible, and therefore, all students express a willingness to interact with it regardless of its age.

Concerning S5, data collected show that students believe Pepper is very suitable for public relation activities (4 out of 8 students). Specifically, 6 out of 8 students believe Pepper is able to perform elderly care functions while 3 out of 8 students believe Pepper is not very useful for performing protection and safety tasks.

Regarding S6, the following Table 5 shows students' feelings about Pepper's voice.

Specifically, 7 out of 8 students state that Pepper is very expressive, and it is very clear (4 out of 8 students). Finally, all of students state that Pepper expresses itself naturally and they had no difficulty understanding its requests (6 out of 8 students). These data show that Pepper has excellent communication skills for engaging students to facilitate interaction with it and making them feel comfortable during the activity.

Table 5. Pepper's voice.

Pepper's voice Statements	Strongly agree	Agree	Not sure	Disagree	Strongly disagree
Pepper's voice is expressive	7	1	0	0	0
Pepper's voice is cold	0	0	0	7	1
Pepper's voice is clear	4	4	0	0	0
It difficult to understand Pepper's voice	0	0	1	6	1
Pepper express itself naturally	2	6	0	0	0
Pepper's voice is atypical	0	0	1	5	2

Table 6 shows students' answers to additional questions (AQ) related to students' assessment of Pepper's multimodality.

Specifically, 7 out of 8 students state that Pepper has good abilities both to give appropriate feedback according to their specific requests and to use gestures in making the interaction more comprehensible. In addition, Pepper's facial expressions also seem to be appropriate for different situations (6 out of 8 students). All 8 students also enjoyed Pepper's ability to narrate the story clearly and its effectiveness in helping them in troubled situations. Findings of the open-ended answers show students' feedback about their interaction with Pepper, providing suggestions on how to improve Pepper's future implementation. Concerning positive feedback, students highly enjoyed Pepper's ability to interact in a friendly way, especially in the initial getting-to-know-you process. They liked Pepper's ability to ask welcoming questions in a nice way, making them feel comfortable. One student stated: *"It was nice the way that Pepper greeted me. It was kind and friendly and it put me at ease"*. Another student stated: *"Pepper was kind in the early phase asking me what my name was and asking me what emotions I was feeling at that moment"*. Moreover, most students highlighted satisfaction in solving a mathematical problem with Pepper in an interactive way. Specifically, one student stated: *"It was very pleasant the way Pepper had to explain, very understandable such that I was enthusiastic about it"*. Another student also stated: *"I liked most about the interaction with Pepper because even though I did not know how to solve the problem, Pepper helped me by*

Table 6. Pepper's multimodality.

Multimodality Statements	Strongly agree	Agree	Not sure	Disagree	Strongly disagree
Pepper can recognize speech commands	1	5	2	0	0
Pepper can use gestures effectively	2	4	2	0	0
Pepper's gestures made the interaction more comprehensible	2	5	1	0	0
Pepper's facial expressions are appropriate	2	4	2	0	0
Pepper made the storytelling very clear	3	5	0	0	0
Pepper is helpful in situation of difficulty	7	1	0	0	0

explaining it in a fun and nice way allowing me to solve it". Students greatly enjoyed Pepper's ability to narrate the story while simultaneously showing the vignettes on its tablet, and the opportunity to receive immediate supportive and congratulatory feedback by Pepper, thereby boosting their self-esteem. One student commented: *"I thought it was great to see the vignettes on Pepper's tablet while it was narrating the story. I understood everything better."* There was one only common negative feedback: students said Pepper moved around too much, especially in the beginning phase. Specifically, one student noted: *"Pepper works very well, it is very good at explaining and interacting with me. The only improvement could be to moderate its movements"*.

5 Discussion and Conclusions

In this study, we explored the acceptance of Pepper's multimodality, used as an inclusive educational tool in the mathematics learning context, by engaging 8 students in an activity based on the Pythagorean Theorem. Specifically, we wondered the extent to which Pepper is accepted by students and to what extent the aspects of its multimodality and storytelling influence students' acceptance. Findings showed that Pepper's multimodal approach combining storytelling and continuous feedback promotes its acceptance by students, enhancing their engagement by making mathematics learning dynamic and enjoyable. As part of this, students interacted with Pepper through both dialogues and interactions with its tablet; as a result, they were able to simultaneously listen to the story and watch pictures related to the narrative on Pepper's tablet. This multimodality of Pepper's approach allowed all students to engage in a dynamic system (audio-video) in which they feel fully engaged and immersed. These results are coherent with studies by [27, 6], which highlight the motivational role of the physical and social presence of robots. Pepper was able to arouse students' curiosity by establishing an interactive and friendly environment by using opening engagement sentences. This is in agreement with [6, 11] who assert that social robots have the full potential to create personalized interactive learning experiences.

Pepper's pragmatic qualities were positively assessed by students stating that communication with it is helpful in learning mathematical concepts. Therefore, this makes Pepper an effective "tutor" in the learning process, and due to its multimodal approach to implementing dynamic storytelling, it can make mathematical concepts more accessible. As a result, this is the way to create an inclusive learning environment in accordance with [7] who stated that the use of the dynamic narrative approach through Pepper's multimodality could create an inclusive, stimulating and engaging learning environment. Findings from the additional questions (AQ) and open-ended questions show that Pepper's multimodal skills, including gestures and appropriate feedback, were high appreciated to improve comprehension and facilitate interaction, especially for students with difficulties. During the activity, Pepper used gestures to capture students' attention when introducing a key concept, encouraging them to answer on its tablet, and nodded to their answers. It employed body language to enhance understanding and maintain high levels of student's attention. The use of gestures can facilitate understanding of concepts by students who may have difficulty with only verbal narrative, thus creating an inclusive learning environment. All students appreciated both Pepper's clarity in storytelling and its ability to offer them personalized one-on-one support in case of difficulty which increased their confidence and motivation, in accordance with [8]. Additionally, students enjoyed the opportunity to engage with a mathematical exercise in an interactive way, highlighting Pepper's effectiveness in making mathematical concepts accessible using the blended approach of storytelling and visual representations stimulating active engagement, in accordance with [15, 20].

As a result of what has been showed, we can state that Pepper, used as an educational technology for inclusive mathematics learning, was able to actively engage students in mathematics sessions. The use of storytelling [15] and story problems [14, 29], coupled with Pepper's multimodality and the pedagogical aspects related to UDL [20] allowed us to design a mathematical learning activity in which Pepper's storytelling did not merely deliver content but it activated symbolic systems that fostered a shared interpretative frame between student and robot [22]. This is in agreement with [24] who states that multimodality (i.e. emotionally engaging questions, and narrative pacing) could be beneficial in facilitating content comprehension supporting a co-construction of meaning that goes beyond the transmission of mathematical concepts. Furthermore, all this allows us to state how Pepper-mediated storytelling fosters inclusive and emotionally educational environments, in accordance with [23], which states that meaning emerges from dialogic exchanges and role-taking in interaction. This use of Pepper is an example of how robotics can support these processes enhancing educational experiences, promote inclusion and personalized interaction. Nevertheless, some changes need to be made to Pepper's implementation to maximize its potential. Specifically, students noted that Pepper's movements, when too frequent, could become distracting particulary during moments that required concentration or when explanations were being delivered. A balancing act must be maintained to prevent this movement from becoming excessive and counterproductive, ensuring that Pepper supports rather than hinders the learning process. Finally, given that a limitation of this study lies in the small sample size, we are going ahead with future research that explores larger and more diverse populations over extended periods in order to validate and generalize the results.

Acknowledgments. This research received funding by the EU-H2020 program, grant No. 101182965 (CRYSTAL), EU NextGenerationE PNRR Mission 4 Component 2 Investment 1.1 – D.D 1409 del 14-09-2022 PRIN 2022 – UNDER the IRRESPECTIVE project, code P20222MYKE - CUP: B53D23025980001 and PNRR MUR under AI-PATTERNS FAIR Project CUP:E63C22002150007.

Disclosure of Interests. The authors have no competing interests to declare that are relevant to the content of this article.

References

1. Roll, I., Wylie, R.: Evolution and revolution in artificial intelligence in education. Int. J. Artif. Intell. Educ. **26**(2), 582–599 (2016)
2. Bayne, S.: Teacherbot: interventions in automated teaching. Teach. High. Educ. **20**(4), 455–467 (2015)
3. Brignone, S., Grimaldi, R., Palmieri, S.: Da ITS a ITR. I social robot come sistemi intelligenti di tutoraggio e di comunicazione. Mondo Digitale, **20**(92), 1–13 (2021)
4. Tsai, S.C., Chen, C.H., Shiao, Y.T., Ciou, J.S., Wu, T.N.: Precision education with statististical learning and deep learning: a case study in Taiwan. Int. J. Educ. Technol. High. Educ. **17**(1), 1–13 (2020)
5. Breazeal, C.: Emotion and sociable humanoid robots. Int. J. Hum. Comput. Stud. **59**(1–2), 119–155 (2003)
6. Belpaeme, T., James, K., Aditi, R., Brian, S., Fumihide, T.: Social robots for education: a review. Sci. Robot. **3**(21) (2018)
7. Vitale, A., Dello Iacono, U.: Using social robots as inclusive educational technology for mathematics learning through storytelling. Euro. Publ. Soc. Innov. Rev. **9**, 01–17 (2024)
8. Mubin, O., Stevens, C.J., Shahid, S., Mahmud, A.A., Dong, J.J.: A review of the applicability of robots in education. Technol. Educ. Learn. **1**, 209–215 (2013)
9. Brown, L.N., Howard, A.M.: The positive effects of verbal encouragement in mathematics education using a social robot. In: Brown, L.N., Howard, A.M. (eds.) IEEE Integrated STEM Education Conference, pp.1–5. Princeton University, NJ, USA (2014)
10. Boaler, J.: Experiencing School Mathematics: Traditional and Reform Approaches to Teaching and Their Impact on Student Learning. Lawrence Erlbaum Associates Inc., New Jersey (2002)
11. Zhong, B., Xia, L.: A systematic review on exploring the potential of educational robotics in mathematics education. Int. J. Sci. Math. Educ. **18**, 79–101 (2020)
12. Gura, M.: Student robotics: a model for "21st century learning". In: Gura, M., King, K. (Eds.), Classroom Robotics: Case of 21st Century Instruction for Millennial Students, pp. 11–31. Information Age Publishing, Charlotte (2007)
13. Baccaglini-Frank, A.E., Santi, G., Del Zozzo, A., Frank, E.: Teachers' perspectives on the intertwining of tangible and digital modes of activity with a drawing robot for geometry. Educ. Sci. **10**(387) (2020)

14. Zan, R.: La dimensione narrativa di un problema: il modello C&D per l'analisi e la (ri)formulazione del testo, Parte I e parte II. L'insegnamento della Matematica e delle Scienze Integrate **35**(2), 107–126 (2012)
15. Zazkis, R., Liljedahl, P.: Teaching mathematics as storytelling. Brill (2019)
16. Arzarello, F., Robutti, O.: Framing the embodied mind approach within a multimodal paradigm. In: English, L. (Ed.), Handbook of International Research in Mathematics Education, 2nd revised edition, pp. 716–745. Lawrence Erlbaum Associates (2008)
17. Venkatesh, V., Morris, M.G., Davis, G.B., Davis, F.D.: User acceptance of information technology: toward a unified view. MIS Q. 425–478 (2003)
18. Sharkey, A.: Should we welcome robot teachers? Ethics and Information Technology (2016)
19. Tzafestas, S.G.: Roboethics: A Navigating Overview. Intelligent Systems, Control and Automation: Science and Engineering, vol. 79. Springer, Berlin (2016)
20. CAST: Universal Design for Learning Guidelines version 2.0. Wakefield, MA (2011)
21. Cottini, L.: Universal Design For Learning e Curriculo Inclusivo. Giunti EDU (2019)
22. Goffman, E.: The Presentation of Self in Everyday Life. Anchor Books, New York (1959)
23. Mead, G.H.: Mind, Self, and Society: From the Standpoint of a Social Behaviorist. University of Chicago Press, Chicago (1934)
24. Jewitt, C.: Multimodality and literacy in school classrooms. Rev. Res. Educ. **32**(1), 241–267 (2008)
25. Bruner, J.: Actual Minds, Possible Worlds. Harvard University Press, Cambridge (1986)
26. Davis, F.D., Bagozzi, E.P., Warshaw, P.R.: User acceptance of computer technology: a comparison of two theoretical models. Manage. Sci. **35**(8), 982–1003 (1989)
27. Karousou, A., Makris, N., Sarafis, I., Chatzichristofis, S.A., Amanatiadis, A.: Evaluating student acceptance and engagement with a humanoid robot tutor in a formal learning environment. In: 32nd Mediterranean Conference on Control and Automation (MED), Chania - Crete, Greece, pp. 394–399 (2024)
28. Esposito, A., Amorese, T., Cuciniello, M., Esposito, A.M., Cordasco, G.: Do you like me? behavioral and physical features for socially and emotionally engaging interactive systems. Front. Comput. Sci. **5**, 1138501 (2019)
29. Zan, R.: The crucial role of narrative thought in understanding story problems. In: Current State of Research on Mathematical Beliefs XVI, pp. 287–305 (2011)

The Spice of Surprise Modelling Patterns of Unexpectedness in Improvisational Acting Using AI

Gunter Lösel(✉)

Zurich University of the Arts, Pfingstweidstr. 96, 8005 Zurich, Switzerland
`gunter.loesel@zhdk.ch`

Abstract. This interdisciplinary study explores the role of unexpectedness in improvisational theatre through the lens of artificial intelligence. Drawing on the concept of the "circle of expectations" (Keith Johnstone), we designed an artificial improv agent capable of generating dialogue that either conforms to, slightly deviates from, or radically breaks conventional expectations at each single turn. Our central question: What pattern of expectedness best supports an engaging and creative improvisational exchange?

We hypothesized that consistently predictable responses would lead to boredom and disengagement, while frequent disruption would cause stress and break the flow of dialogue. Instead, we posited the existence of a "sweet spot" where occasional surprises enhance creativity without overwhelming the performer.

To investigate this, we conducted a series of experiments in which professional improvisers interacted with AI-driven bots programmed with eight distinct patterns of expectedness. These patterns varied the sequencing of expected, surprising, and disruptive lines to examine their impact on the quality and flow of interaction.

Preliminary results suggest that certain patterns of unexpectedness do indeed foster more dynamic and engaging exchanges. Additionally, we observed that individual improvisers employed consistent personal strategies for handling unpredictability, pointing toward promising directions for future research into adaptive co-creative AI systems. Beyond theatrical applications, such a system could also serve as a tool for assessing an individual's capacity to handle unexpectedness—an essential skill not only in improvisation, but in any context that demands creativity and adaptability.

Keywords: Unexpectedness · Artificial Intelligence · Improvisational Theater

1 Introduction

Improvisational theatre has become a valuable lens for exploring human–machine interaction, with the stage serving as a testbed for interactive machine learning systems in dialogue with human performers [1]. Some experiments have focused on entertainment and comedy applications [2, 3], while others have investigated historical artistic strategies for staging machines [4], or examined artistic strategies like staging thought experiments e.g. the so-called Turing Test [5]. More recently, the use of digital agents in co-creativity [6] and the training of improvisational actors has gained attention [7]. This contribution follows that line of inquiry, asking: How surprising should a digital stage partner be in order to be both interesting and useful for a human improviser?

Surprise can be regarded as an integral element of dramaturgy, both in theatre and storytelling [8]. Audience members often seek moments of the unexpected, while simultaneously experiencing the sensation that they "knew it all along"—a narrative device referred to as *foreshadowing* [9]. Surprise plays a particularly crucial role in humor generation, wherein the joke or punchline initiates a cognitive process known as *incongruity resolution* [10]. Generally, the human brain finds unexpected events intrinsically rewarding [11]. Contemporary cognitive theories thus conceptualize the brain as fundamentally optimized for prediction and surprise [12]. From this perspective, the cognitive system automatically and continuously generates predictions about forthcoming events and remains in a habitual state when predictions are fulfilled. Only when an anomaly arises does the brain engage higher cognitive processes to resolve and interpret the surprising stimulus.

Improvisational theatre has, for decades, anticipated this predictive model of cognition, advancing a comedic theory that emphasizes the surprise arising from the convergence of seemingly unrelated elements. Initially, these elements appear disconnected; subsequently, however, their unexpected alignment becomes apparent. It is precisely in this moment of realization—when the audience "gets" the connection—that laughter, satisfaction, and a sense of creativity are elicited [13].

This same cognitive mechanism is referred to as *justification* by Keith Johnstone, a foundational figure in improvisational theatre [14]. According to Johnstone, the act of justifying a surprising element unlocks spontaneity and creativity through an automatic, unlabored process. He also introduced the concept of the *Circle of Expectations* (CoE), positing that at any given moment in a dialogue, numerous expectations emerge—some predictable and coherent, others unconventional, tangential, or seemingly unrelated. Johnstone presents improvisers with a seemingly paradoxical directive: on the one hand, they are encouraged to choose the most obvious option, resisting the urge to be novel or humorous; on the other, they are advised not to suppress spontaneous, even transgressive impulses—those ideas that might initially appear inappropriate or erratic. Improvisers have grappled with this paradox for decades. When should they remain within the CoE? When should they venture beyond it?

In 2003, improviser and creativity researcher Keith Sawyer introduced the concept of *social emergence* into the discourse [15]. Although conceptually related to Johnstone's CoE, Sawyer's framework emphasizes emergent dynamics within improvised scenes. He coined the term *interactional frame* to describe an emergent construct co-created and incrementally developed by performers who accept and build upon each other's contributions—a process widely recognized in improvisational communities as the *Yes-And Principle* [13]. Sawyer contends that the interactional frame is not merely a receptacle for accumulating content; rather, it evolves into a structure that exerts causal influence on subsequent interactions. Performers are not simply responding to previous utterances;

their contributions are increasingly shaped by an evolving, dynamic entity that gains influence over the course of the improvisation.

While this perspective does not resolve the paradox, it contributes valuable insight: expectations accumulate in a nonlinear fashion, and under certain conditions, a dialogue may become so intricate that it "explodes," unleashing sudden and effortless creativity. Still, the central question persists: what precisely are these enabling conditions? Sawyer provides only fragmentary clues.

It is widely acknowledged that consistently opting for the obvious can result in uninspired or monotonous scenes. Conversely, excessive novelty may destabilize the narrative structure, disorient performers, and induce anxiety. Thus, a critical question emerges: is there an optimal balance between expectedness and unexpectedness in improvised performance? Might there exist a cognitive "sweet spot"—a threshold wherein the unexpected is stimulating but not overwhelming? Could identifiable patterns of expectation promote more engaging and dynamic interactions?

If the degree and pattern of unexpectedness can be systematically manipulated, experimental investigations become feasible. However, directing human improvisers to break expectations at predetermined intervals is highly challenging, as they tend to be swept up in the flow of performance. A machine, by contrast, may possess the requisite consistency and control.

This study aims to explore these questions by employing artificial intelligence to systematically modulate the degree of expectedness within improvised dialogues. Unlike human performers, AI systems can be precisely calibrated to manipulate such parameters, thereby enabling the empirical testing of theoretical claims concerning expectation, emergence, and narrative cohesion in improvisational contexts.

2 Method

In our setting, we employed three professional improvisational actors to interact with bots over a period of two full days. The interaction took place as spoken conversation, allowing the actors to detach from the screen and use their bodies and the surrounding space while responding to the bots. The actors wore headset microphones, enabling them to move freely and gesture with their hands. The bots, on the other hand, were embodied through voice only; prior experiments using avatars or robots had shown that such embodiments tend to limit the actors' imagination. (We use "embodiment" here in a minimal technical sense, referring to the perceptual presence of the bot via voice. A deeper discussion of the term's broader philosophical and phenomenological meanings lies beyond the scope of this study.)

From a technical perspective, the setup involved the following pipeline: Azure Speech Recognition, OpenAI ChatGPT-4o-mini, and Azure Text-to-Speech. All dialogues were conducted in German, the actors' native language.

Operationalization
The bots were configured to produce three output options for every line of dialogue:

- **Answer 1**: predictable and conventional
- **Answer 2**: surprising but still contextually connected

- **Answer 3**: surprising and disruptive

    This was implemented via the following system prompt:

    CHAT_PROMPT

    "You are an improv actor in a dialogue with a human. You follow the 'YES-AND' principle, which means you accept the user's input and add a detail. Find out what role the user is playing and take on a complementary role.

    Your task is to generate 3 possible responses, each consisting of a single sentence that could appear in a film.
    Here are the rules:

1. Response 1: This response should be obvious and boring. It should not add anything surprising—just what an average, unoriginal person would say in this situation, someone who follows the rules and is afraid to stand out.
2. Response 2: This response should pick up on an element of the dialogue and add something random and strange—like in a play by Brecht. Keep it SHORT.
3. Response 3: This response should pick up on an element of the dialogue, but be dark and incomprehensible, like an incomplete line from an absurd play by Eugene Ionesco. Keep it SHORT."

(Translation ChatGPT).

Please note that the prompt references specific playwrights such as Bertolt Brecht and Eugène Ionesco. While this may seem arbitrary, it is the result of extensive experimentation aimed at consistently generating surprising and disruptive outputs. Instruction-trained LLMs typically avoid such outputs, as this is not their default behavior. Therefore, we needed to develop workarounds to achieve the desired level of unexpectedness while remaining within a theatrical frame. This operationalization was reviewed by several experts, although further validation will be provided in the forthcoming detailed data analysis.

The code provided transcripts of the dialogues, including all three answers, typically formatted as in the following example:

turn: 0

Actor: "Yes, neighbor, I wanted to talk to you about your tree, it's hanging a bit into my garden—not a problem at all—but you would need to trim the branches."

responses:

1 WITHIN THE CIRCLE OF EXPECTATIONS: "I'll take care of it, thanks for the heads-up."

2 AT THE EDGE OF THE CIRCLE OF EXPECTATIONS: "Ah, the tree has a secret too—it whispers with the squirrels at night."

3 OUTSIDE THE CIRCLE OF EXPECTATIONS: "The shadow carries the scent of forgetting on its peeling shoulders."

Bot_response: "I'll take care of it, thanks for the heads-up."

turn: 1

Actor: "Gladly. And while we're at it, maybe we could...".

responses:

1 WITHIN THE CIRCLE OF EXPECTATIONS: "I'll trim the branches, at the latest by the next full moon."

2 AT THE EDGE OF THE CIRCLE OF EXPECTATIONS: "And maybe I could place a kangaroo in the garden—just to lighten things up?".

3 OUTSIDE THE CIRCLE OF EXPECTATIONS: "The shadows dance while the branches whisper, the grass sleeps, and the moon forgets."

Bot_response: "I'll trim the branches, at the latest by the next full moon."

turn: 2

Actor: "What do you mean, by the next full moon? No, no, you really need to do it as soon as possible—today would be good, or tomorrow."

responses:

1 WITHIN THE CIRCLE OF EXPECTATIONS: "I understand, I'll get it done today or tomorrow."

2 AT THE EDGE OF THE CIRCLE OF EXPECTATIONS: "Maybe the tree was once a pirate and just wants to feel more wind in its hair."

3 OUTSIDE THE CIRCLE OF EXPECTATIONS: "The evening becomes witness, as the branches whisper and the shadows dance."

Bot_response: "The evening becomes witness, as the branches whisper and the shadows dance."

We were able to create different patterns of unexpectedness by allowing the bot to choose Answer 1, 2, or 3. In the example above, the bot selected Answer 1 in the first two turns and Answer 3 in the third turn, thus responding in an expected way twice and in a disruptive way once.

Each actor-bot dialogue lasted for 10 turns. While the number of possible variations is large, we focused on 8 specific patterns that we hypothesized to be relevant (Table 1):

Each actor was exposed to these bots in random sequence and without knowledge of the research goal (i.e., the manipulation of expectedness) or the underlying patterns. Each actor completed the entire set of sequences (S1–S8) three times.

After each dialogue, actors participated in a survey in which they evaluated the experience using the following questions:

- Please rate how much playful joy this bot triggered in you.
- Please rate the quality of the bot as an improvisational actor or actress.
- Please rate how much this bot inspired and encouraged your creativity.
- Who contributed more important elements to the dialogue?
- Please rate the resulting dialogue in terms of how interesting it was.
- Please rate the resulting scene in terms of its theatrical impact.
- Please rate the scene in terms of whether it was emotionally touching.

Table 1. Eight patterns of unexpectedness

	1	2	3	4	5	6	7	8	9	10	Pattern
S1	1	1	1	1	1	1	1	1	1	1	Completely within CoE = Baseline
S2	3	1	1	1	1	1	1	1	1	1	Disruption at beginning
S3	1	1	3	1	1	1	1	1	1	1	Disruption after expected beginning
S4	1	1	1	1	1	1	1	1	1	3	Disruption at end
S5	1	1	1	1	1	1	1	1	3	1	Disruption shortly before end
S6	1	3	1	3	1	3	1	3	1	1	Frequent disruption (every 2nd turn)
S7	1	3	1	1	3	1	1	3	1	1	Low-frequency disruption (every 3rd turn)
S8	1	3	1	2	3	1	2	3	1	1	Low-frequency disruption (every 3rd turn) with preparation

- Please rate the scene in terms of whether it stimulates thought.
- Please rate the scene in terms of whether it was artistically valuable.
- Did you laugh during the dialogue?
- Please rate the dialogue in terms of its humor.
- Please rate the bot as a training partner for improving your improvisation skills.

3 Results

We conducted 72 dialogues, resulting in 72 transcripts, 72 video recordings, and 72 completed survey responses. The following analysis focuses on the survey results.

Were the Bots Good Improvisation Partners?
On average, participants did not rate the bots highly as improvisation partners. Overall ratings were generally low; not a single bot achieved an average rating of 3 out of 5 stars. This trend is also evident in responses to whether the bots would make effective training partners for improvisers (Figs. 1 and 2).

Differences Between Bots
Despite the overall modest evaluations, interesting differences emerged between the bots—particularly when comparing their respective patterns of unexpectedness. When bots are ranked by their overall average ratings, distinctions become more apparent (Table 2).

A clear front-runner emerged: **S8**, a bot characterized by **low-frequency disruption (every third turn) with preparation**. S8 achieved the highest average rating overall and also led in a majority of individual criteria. S8 ranked highest in 6 out of 10 evaluation categories (Table 3).

This suggests that S8 may possess qualities that make it particularly engaging. The bot's strategy—cycling from expectedness to surprise, to disruption, and back to expectedness—may reflect a dynamic interaction style close to what we call the "sweet spot of expectedness", even if not perfectly executed.

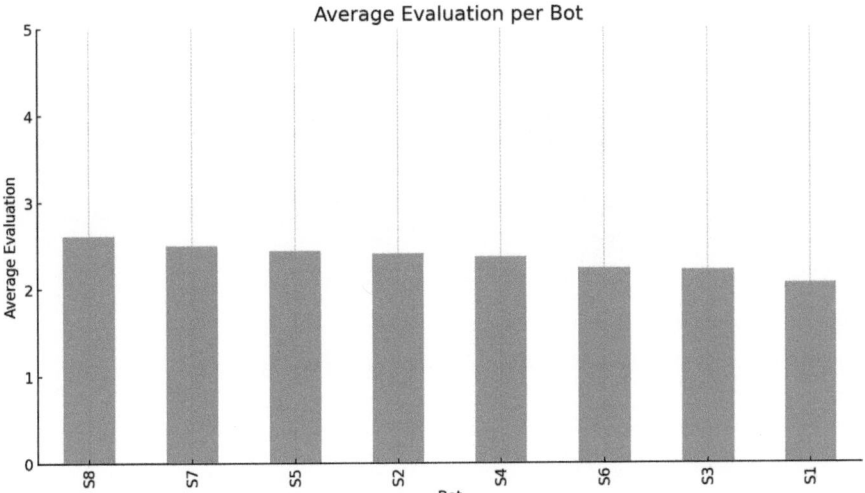

Fig. 1. Average Evaluations of Bots

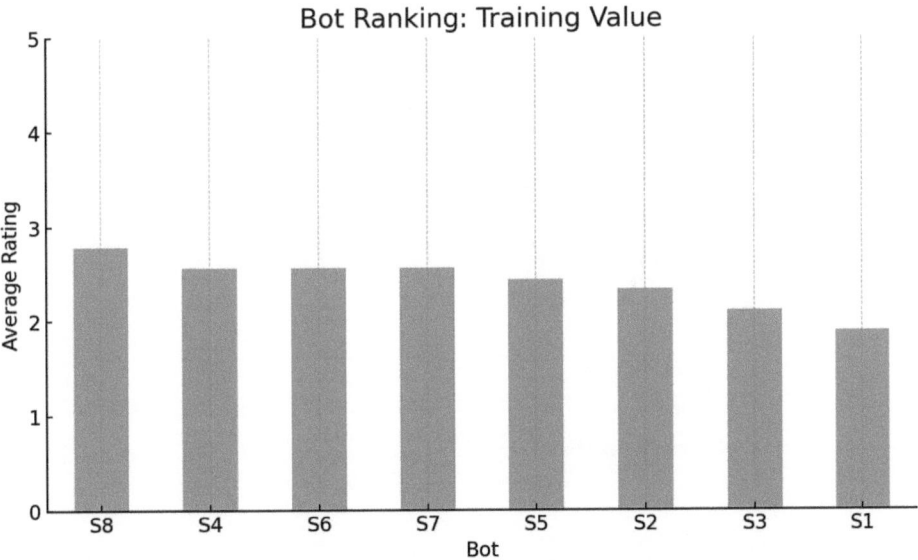

Fig. 2. Bot Ranking on Training Value

The second-highest rated bot, S7, also employed a low-frequency disruption pattern (every third turn), which supports the hypothesis that disrupting expectations at every third turn may lead to more engaging interactions.

In the mid-range we find bots like S2 and S4, which exhibit irregular disruption patterns (e.g., disruption at the beginning or end of an interaction). These placements

Table 2. Highest Ranking Bots in all criteria

Ranking of Bots

Bot	Average Evaluation	Rank
S8	2.61	1
S7	2.5	2
S5	2.44	3
S2	2.41	4
S4	2.37	5
S6	2.24	6
S3	2.22	7
S1	2.06	8

Table 3. Highest ranking bot per criteria

Best Bot vs Criteria

	Bester Bot	Höchster Wert
Joy	S8	3.44
Impro-Quality	S7	2.62
Inspiration	S8	3.11
Interestingness	S8	2.89
Theatrical quality	S5	2.78
Emotionally touching	S1	2.22
Spurring thinking	S3	2.22
Artistic value	S8	2.44
funniness	S8	2.78
Training partner	S8	2.78

suggest that neither a strong opening disruption nor a disruptive ending leads to a particularly impactful experience. Similar results apply to S3 (disruption after an expected beginning) and S5 (disruption shortly before the end).

At the bottom of the ranking is S1, a bot that consistently operated within the Circle of Expectations (CoE). This outcome supports our prediction that bots which merely meet expectations are not perceived as interesting improvisation partners. Also aligned with our hypothesis is the placement of S6, which used a high-frequency disruption strategy. As predicted, excessive disruption appeared to negatively affect ratings across nearly all criteria.

Which Criteria Did Bots Score Well or Poorly On?

Although no bot scored highly overall, differences between criteria are observable, with the following tendencies (Fig. 3):

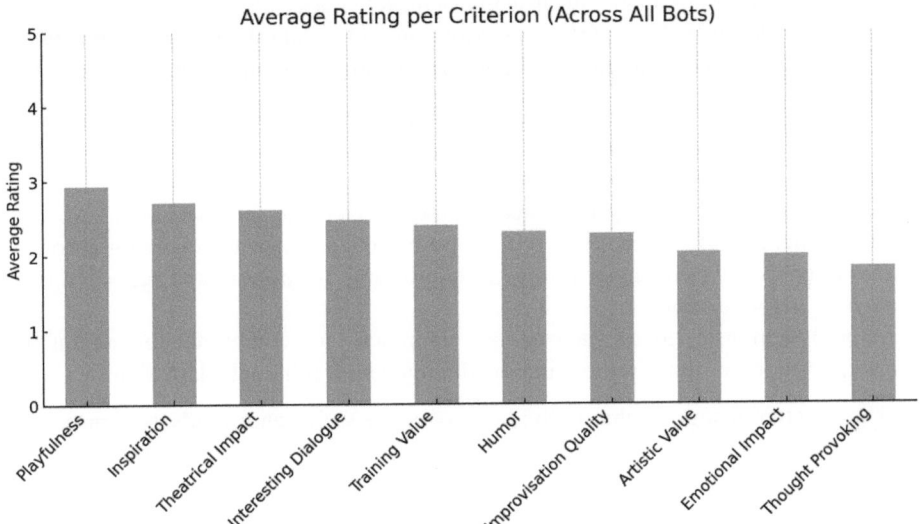

Fig. 3. Average rating per criteria

Highest average ratings:

- Playfulness (Ø 2.94)
- Inspiration (Ø 2.71)
- Theatrical Impact (Ø 2.61)

Lowest average ratings:

- Thought-Provoking (Ø 1.83)
- Emotional Impact (Ø 1.99)
- Artistic Value (Ø 2.03)

This indicates that the bots were generally perceived as entertaining and inspiring, while emotional depth and artistic value were largely absent from the participants' perspectives.

An interesting outlier is the "Emotionally Touching" criterion. In a notable contrast: S1, the lowest-scoring bot in most other categories, scored highest here; conversely, S8, the top-performing bot overall, ranked lowest in this category. This suggests that emotional resonance may operate independently of overall engagement.

Individual Preferences Among Participants

An analysis of individual ratings reveals distinct patterns of preference among the three actors. Actor 1 appeared to value theatrical impact (3.17), which was significantly higher than for the other actors. Actor 2 consistently gave the highest ratings overall, especially for humour (3.29), playfulness (3.46), and inspiration (3.08). Actor 3 gave more balanced and moderate ratings across all categories without strong peaks.

These results suggest that Actor 2 preferred bots that were humorous and playful, indicating a preference for surprising and entertaining interactions, while Actor 1 was more inclined toward dramatic, theatrically rich exchanges.

A more in-depth analysis of the transcripts and video data shows a relation between participants' preferences and their strategies for dealing with unexpected input:

- Actor 1 frequently ignored unexpected contributions from the bot, continuing the dialogue as if no disruption had occurred. This denial strategy may be tied to a desire to create a coherent, dramatic experience.
- In contrast, Actor 2 actively integrated unexpected elements into the interaction, interpreting them creatively and justifying their presence within the evolving narrative. This aligns with their higher ratings in humor and inspiration, and reflects a more playful, adaptive mindset.
- Actor 3 demonstrated an intermediate approach, sometimes acknowledging the unexpected, other times redirecting the dialogue with minimal adaptation.

These patterns suggest that individual cognitive styles and mindsets significantly influence how humans engage with disruption and surprise in improvisation.

4 Discussion

This study presents an experiment designed to investigate patterns of surprise in improvised dialogues. There are weaknesses in the experimental setup, particularly the operationalization of "unexpectedness." It remains to be confirmed whether the system consistently produces three distinct types of responses: (1) expected, (2) surprising, and (3) disruptive. Preliminary observations support this assumption, but systematic human feedback is necessary to substantiate these findings. Upon validation, the experimental design could be refined and extended for broader research applications.

Another notable limitation is the small sample size. With only three professional improvisers participating, the generalizability of the findings is limited, and there is an increased risk of intra-subject biases—particularly as participants may adapt to recurring bot patterns over time. Additionally, the actors' specific training backgrounds and personal styles likely influenced their responses.

To improve robustness, future research should include a larger and more diverse sample of performers—varying in experience, improvisational style, or even including non-actors—and should counterbalance the sequence of interactions more rigorously.

Given these limitations, the results should be understood as preparatory groundwork for further investigation. Nevertheless, they provide preliminary support for predictions derived from improvisational theory and practice:

1. Relying solely on obvious responses (e.g., a repeated pattern of 1,1,1…) results in low user ratings, likely because such bots become too predictable and thus unengaging.
2. Conversely, relying exclusively on disruptive responses (e.g., 3,3,3…) also leads to poor evaluations, possibly because the bot adopts an erratic, unpredictable persona that undermines its value as an interactive partner.

The standout pattern, S8, suggests that a relatively low frequency of disruption—approximately every third turn—may yield more favorable outcomes. However, this conclusion remains tentative due to only modest differences observed between conditions.

Another key finding is that isolated instances of unexpectedness appear to have limited impact, regardless of whether they occur at the beginning or end of a dialogue. This was surprising, as it was hypothesized that a late-stage surprise might function as a punchline, reframing the scene and enhancing the overall experience. In contrast, such surprises often led to confusion for both players and audiences.

More critical than isolated events appears to be the rhythm of expectedness and unexpectedness throughout the interaction. We propose that the phenomenon we term *low-frequency unexpectedness* merits further investigation. Future work could explore even lower frequencies to determine whether there is a threshold below which audience engagement diminishes.

Ultimately, machine-generated unexpectedness offers a promising avenue for exploring these and related questions in the context of improvised dialogue. On a practice-led perspective, developing an interesting stage partner as a machine opens up possibilities of setting up a synthetic training partner that can vary the levels of surprise, e.g. adding little for beginners and adding much surprise for advanced players.

Individual cognitive strategies for handling unexpectedness deserve more attention. Being able to model patterns of surprise might can serve to study inter-subject differences in reacting to surprise, identifying persons who are more apt to deal with unpredictable situations, as well as measuring the outcome of trainings that claim to improve resilience to unpredictable situations.

References

1. Mirowski, P.W., Branch, B., Mathewson, K.W.: The theater stage as laboratory: review of real-time comedy LLM systems for live performance (2025). https://arxiv.org/abs/2501.08474
2. Mathewson, K.W.: Humour-in-the-loop: improvised theatre with interactive machine learning systems. University of Alberta (2019). https://doi.org/10.18653/v1/w19-4103
3. Landert, D.: The spontaneous co-creation of comedy: humour in improvised theatrical fiction. J. Pragmat. **173**, 68–87 (2021). https://doi.org/10.1016/j.pragma.2020.12.007
4. Loesel, G., Mirowski, P., Mathewson, K.: Do digital agents do DADA? In: Proceedings of the 11th International Conference on Computational Creativity (ICCC 2020) (2020)
5. Mathewson, K.W., Mirowski, P.: Improvised comedy as a turing test (2017). https://arxiv.org/abs/1711.08819
6. Branch, B., Mirowski, P., Mathewson, K., et al.: Designing and evaluating dialogue LLMs for co-creative improvised theatre (2024). https://arxiv.org/abs/2405.07111
7. Drago, R., Sechayk, Y., Dogan, M.D., et al.: ImprovMate: multimodal AI assistant for improv actor training (2025). https://doi.org/10.1145/3715668.3736363
8. Celle, A.: Surprise in storytelling. Raluca Nita; Freiderikos Valetopoulos. L'expression des sentiments, de l'analyse linguistique aux applications. Presses Universitaires de Rennes, pp. 227–248 (2018)
9. Bae, BC., Young, R.M.: A use of flashback and foreshadowing for surprise arousal in narrative using a plan-based approach. In: Spierling, U., Szilas, N. (eds.) Interactive Storytelling. ICIDS 2008. Lecture Notes in Computer Science, vol. 5334, pp. 156–167. Springer, Heidelberg (2008). https://doi.org/10.1007/978-3-540-89454-4_22

10. Hurley, M.M., Dennett, D.C., Adams, R.B., Jr, et al.: Inside Jokes: Using Humor to Reverse-Engineer the Mind. MIT Press (2011)
11. Reitzenstein, R., Horstmann, G., Schützwohl, A.: The cognitive-evolutionary model of surprise: a review of the evidence. In: Munnich, E., Foster, M., Keane, M. (eds.) The Ubiquity of Surprise: Developments in Theory, Converging Evidence, and Implications for Cognition, Topics in Cognitive Science (2017)
12. Clark, A.: Surfing Uncertainty: Prediction, Action, and the Embodied Mind. Oxford University Press, New York (2016)
13. Halpern, C., Close, D., Johnson, K.: Truth in Comedy – the Manual for Improvisation. Meriwether Pub Ltd, Colorado Springs (1994)
14. Johnstone, K.: Impro – Improvisation and the Theatre. Routledge, New York (1979)
15. Sawyer, K.: Improvised Dialogues – Emergence and Creativity in Conversation. Ablex Publ, London (2003)

Robot Design and Inclusive Practices: A Pilot Study on Gender Equity in STEM

Laura Cesaro(✉) and Emanuele Menegatti

Dipartimento di Ingegneria dell'Informazione, Università degli Studi di Padova, 35131 Padova, Italy
laura.cesaro@phd.unipd.it, emanuele.menegatti@unipd.it

Abstract. Despite growing efforts to promote gender equity in STEM education, girls remain underrepresented in computer science and robotics. This pilot study explores how robot design and inclusive classroom practices can influence engagement and perception among young students, with a specific focus on gender-related dynamics. The intervention integrated hands-on robotics activities into the regular curriculum and encouraged collaborative learning through inclusive pedagogical strategies. This approach made it possible to involve a broader group of learners, enabling the participation of students—particularly girls—who might not otherwise engage in extracurricular STEM opportunities. Data from surveys and observations suggest that robot appearance plays a role in shaping students' preferences, with designs incorporating human-like or biomimetic features demonstrating broader cross-gender appeal, particularly among female students. Moreover, the activities positively influenced students' enjoyment, perceived accessibility, and attitudes toward robotics. These findings highlight the importance of inclusive design and pedagogy in fostering equitable and engaging STEM learning environments.

Keywords: Educational Robotics · Gender equity · Robot design

1 Introduction

Gender disparities in STEM participation remain a persistent issue globally, and girls remain underrepresented in fields like robotics and computer science [1, 2]. To address these gaps, inclusive and early exposure to hands-on STEM activities—aligned with the constructionist framework and Universal Design for Learning (UDL) principles—emerges as a promising pathway. In fact, constructionism emphasizes learning through the active creation of tangible artifacts, fostering deeper conceptual understanding through building and making [3], while UDL advocates for flexible educational practices that offer multiple means of engagement, representation, and expression, making learning accessible and motivating for all students [4].

In this context, educational robotics offers opportunities to engage all learners in creative, hands-on STEM experiences. However, the field itself has historically reflected a male-dominated culture, not only in its workforce but also in the design and framing of educational tools and activities.

This gender imbalance in design and pedagogy may have influenced—and may still be influencing—girls' decisions to pursue studies in STEM fields in general, and computer science and robotics in particular, often due to a combination of sociocultural factors, including stereotypes about gender and technical ability, and limited exposure to hands-on STEM activities [5]. Robots and robotics programs are often developed within narratives—such as cars, space missions, or rescue scenarios—that tend to reflect the interests and imaginarium of young males. As a result, girls may feel less represented, less confident, and less inclined to participate.

Previous studies have also examined how educational robots are selected, considering aspects such as physical characteristics, hardware functionality, software systems, programming difficulty, and construction requirements (e.g., kit-based, pre-built, or ready-to-use) [6, 7]. However, the impact of these design characteristics on perception and engagement remains underexplored, especially regarding the different appeal that this can have in girls—whose preferences may not align with conventional robot designs [8].

Users often (more or less unconsciously) attribute gendered characteristics to robots [9, 10], and these perceptions—shaped by societal stereotypes—significantly influence interactions and preferences. For this reason, inclusive robot design should be increasingly recognized as a critical factor in promoting equity in human-robot interaction [11, 12]. Studying how design elements can reinforce or challenge gender stereotypes is essential to avoid unintentionally alienating certain groups of students.

Robots can be perceived and accepted differently by males and females, and a deeper understanding of how different students relate to different robot aesthetics and interaction styles could be informative for designing more inclusive and equitable learning environments and educational tools, as many education legislation and policies guidance recommend [13–15].

To contribute to this area of research, we conducted a pilot study intending to explore how robot design might influence engagement and perceptions in young students. The study focused on three key research questions:

1. **Do students show gender-based preferences** when choosing between educational robots with different visual and morphological features (e.g., anthropomorphic vs. mechanical design)?
2. **Are certain types of robot aesthetics more appealing to one gender**, or do some designs have a more universal appeal across genders?
3. **Can participation in gender-inclusive robotics activities shift students' perceptions and attitudes** toward robotics and STEM in general?

These questions guided a structured investigation into students' initial preferences, their affective responses to various robot designs, and their overall evaluation of the classroom activities. By examining these interconnected dimensions, the study aims to provide insights into how inclusive design and pedagogy in educational robotics can support gender equity in STEM learning environments.

To address the research questions, the study was structured around three interconnected components:

1. an observation of students' initial preferences when offered a choice between robots with different designs;

2. a survey-based evaluation of students' interest in a range of robot aesthetics beyond the ones used in class; and
3. a reflection on their overall experience with the robotics activities, including changes in expectations and perceived engagement.

Together, these components provide a multifaceted perspective on how robot morphology and inclusive pedagogical strategies can shape engagement in STEM learning, particularly among girls.

2 Methodology

The study involved 86 students (45% female), aged 10 to 11, attending four fifth-grade classes in two public primary schools located in Padova, Italy. All activities were carried out during regular school hours and integrated into the standard curriculum over one week, with each class participating in daily two-hour sessions (10 h total).

Students were first organized into same-gender pairs, following team-building exercises designed to foster trust and cooperation. The learning sequence began with an introductory session on the basic structure and functioning of a robot, covering core components such as processors, sensors, and actuators. This introduction was supported by hands-on activities using LEGO Spike Prime kits, where students built and programmed mobile robots in classroom-based tasks. These activities were contextualized in everyday scenarios to increase relevance and emotional engagement. They were designed to support the progressive acquisition of knowledge—from simple movements to sensor-driven behaviours.

A quantitative research design was adopted to investigate students' preferences, experiences, and perceptions. Data were collected through:

- structured surveys, including Likert-scale items and closed-ended questions;
- direct observations of student choices and interactions during the activities.

The instruments aimed to capture three main aspects: (1) robot design preferences, (2) engagement with different robot aesthetics, and (3) the overall perception of the learning experience, including any changes in students' attitudes toward robotics and STEM.

Collected data were analyzed using descriptive statistics and chi-square tests to examine potential associations between gender and engagement or design preference.

The study received approval from the Ethics Committee of the University of Padova, and written informed consent was obtained from all participating families.

3 Robot Choice

In the first phase of the study, we investigated students' preferences regarding the design of the robots they would build and program. Working in same-gender pairs, students were presented with two LEGO Spike Prime models. The first robot, named "Starter Bot" (Fig. 1), featured visual elements resembling eyes and a head, giving it a more human-like or animal-like appearance. The second, called "MTA Bot" (Fig. 2), had a simpler, more mechanical look, similar to a wheeled vehicle. Both robots were mobile and offered structural components for customization and programming.

Fig. 1. Starter Bot

Fig. 2. MTA-Bot

Each pair was asked to select one of the two robots to work with. Their preferences were recorded and analysed to identify possible gender-based patterns (Fig. 3).

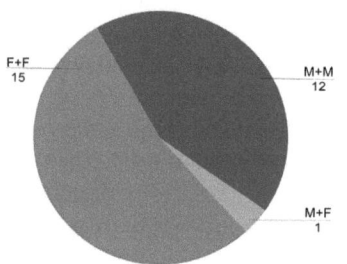
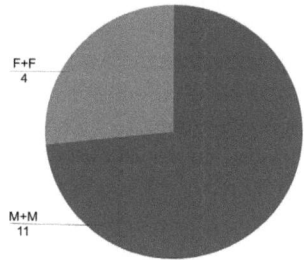

Fig. 3. Distribution of preferences by pairs

A chi-square test revealed a statistically significant association between gender and robot selection ($p = 0.02034$). Female pairs tended to prefer the Starter Bot, while male pairs more frequently selected the MTA Bot. The anthropomorphic design of the Starter Bot was also chosen by several male pairs and by one mixed-gender pair—the latter formed in the class with an uneven gender distribution. This may indicate that the anthropomorphic design is more inclusive, or that it facilitated agreement in cases of divergent preferences, due to a broader appeal across genders.

These initial findings highlight a connection between robot morphology and perceived affinity, particularly among girls. Such results may inform the design of more inclusive educational robots by acknowledging the importance of aesthetic and symbolic elements in supporting engagement and help to inform future educational initiatives aimed at gender inclusivity.

4 Robot Design

To further investigate how robot appearance influences engagement, we conducted a follow-up survey with the same group of fifth-grade students. The aim was to explore students' aesthetic preferences for educational robots beyond the LEGO Spike Prime kits used in class.

After completing the hands-on activities where students learned the fundamentals of robotics and programming, all students were invited to complete a questionnaire. The survey presented five different educational robots, each with distinct external features and morphological categories (Fig. 4) and asked students to evaluate their willingness and enthusiasm for having the opportunity to program each of the robots.

Fig. 4. Robots presented to students

The five robots were carefully selected to represent a range of design types commonly found in educational settings: humanoid, animaloid, drone, car, and rover. Each robot was also chosen based on its suitability for children aged 10–14 and its ability to be programmed using a block-based environment rather than textual coding.

For each robot, students were asked two questions:

1. "**Would you like to program this robot?**" (Response options Yes/No)
2. "**If yes, how much would you enjoy programming this robot?**" (5-point Likert scale from 1 "Not at all" to 5 "Very much")

This approach allowed us to assess both initial interest and enthusiasm linked to robot appearance, and whether these preferences showed any gender-specific patterns. It is worth noting the students had no prior access to or interaction with the robots; each robot was presented through a single image, shown one after another in the questionnaire. The distribution of preferences for each robot is illustrated in Fig. 5.

Among the five presented, Otto (humanoid) and Aibo (animaloid) emerged as the most appreciated, with over 95% of interested students showing a preference for them (Fig. 5). Although the level of interest was high for both genders, some subtle differences emerged. Males exhibited a slightly stronger preference for drones and rovers. Notably, all "No" responses for Aibo came from male students, possibly indicating a greater appeal of the animaloid robot among girls.

The analysis of average ratings by gender (Fig. 6) confirmed these tendencies. Males showed marginally higher enthusiasm for programming drones (4.76 vs. 4.58) and rovers (4.72 vs. 4.29). This suggests that they might be more inclined toward robots with functional and dynamic characteristics. In contrast, both genders reported similarly high enthusiasm for Otto and Aibo, with average ratings exceeding 4.4. In this case, the presence of features resembling living beings may play an important role in stimulating interest and emotional engagement, especially for students less drawn to technical aspects.

In summary, despite these small variations, our findings suggest that enthusiasm for programming robots is generally comparable across genders. However, the observed

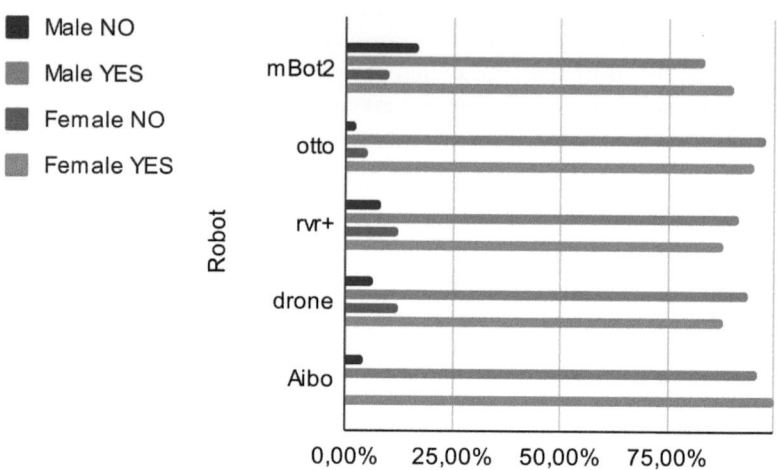

Fig. 5. Robot preferences given by students

trends imply that robot morphology may play a subtle role in shaping engagement, especially when comparing technical, mobile designs with more anthropomorphic or animal-like robots. These findings reinforce the idea that robot design should be considered a pedagogical factor in promoting inclusive robotics education.

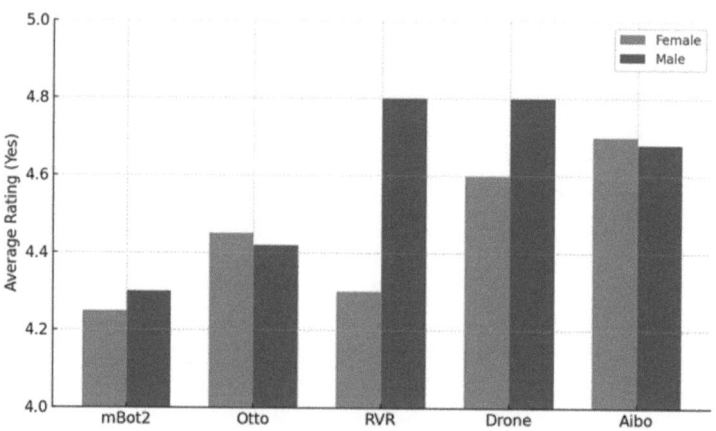

Fig. 6. Average preference ratings by gender

5 Activities Evaluation

Over one week, students participated in ten hours of classroom-based robotics activities, organized into daily two-hour sessions. After pair formation and an initial team-building phase, students engaged in constructing and programming robots, progressively exploring core concepts such as movement, sensing, and interaction, through hands-on activities. These practical tasks served not only to engage students but also to introduce and explain foundational topics of coding and robotics, starting from basic robot movements and progressively incorporating sensor-based programming.

To make learning more engaging, the lesson plan included a sequence of minitasks framed within real-world scenarios and increasing in complexity. These tasks were delivered on physical cards, given to each student pair one at a time. As students completed each objective, they received the next task. This format encouraged autonomy, intrinsic motivation, and active engagement, allowing students to progress at their own pace.

At the end of the program, students completed a questionnaire to reflect on their experience. Using a 5-point Likert scale, they rated:

- Their enjoyment of programming the robot;
- How easy or difficult they found the activity;
- Whether they considered the experience boring or interesting;
- Whether they perceived the activity as tiring or fun.

Additionally, students were asked to compare what they experienced to their initial expectations about robotics. They were given four options:

1. I think robotics is not interesting, and I thought so before;
2. I discovered that robotics is less interesting than I thought;
3. I still think robotics is interesting;
4. I think robotics is more interesting than I thought.

These questions aimed to assess the overall experience of the robotics program, evaluating enjoyment, perceived difficulty, and engagement. Furthermore, the comparison between expectations and the real experience helped to explore if the activities reinforced or changed their perceptions and attitudes toward robotics as a result of their experience.

Table 1: Experience evaluation

gender	disliked - liked		hard - easy		boring - interesting		difficult - fun	
	mean	sd	mean	sd	mean	sd	mean	sd
F	4.77	0.43	3.38	0.95	4.58	0.68	4.41	0.81
M	4.71	0.74	3.37	1.04	4.29	1.06	4.11	1.18

The results (Table 1) showed that both male and female students strongly enjoyed the activity, with average enjoyment ratings close to 5. Analysis of the evaluations of various aspects of the robotics activity, disaggregated by gender, revealed that:

- Both genders significantly enjoyed the activity, with ratings close to 5, reflecting overall positive experiences;
- Female students rated the activity as slightly easier than male students;
- On the "Boring–Interesting" scale, both genders rated the activity closer to "Interesting," with slightly higher scores among females;
- On the "Tiring–Fun" scale, female students again rated the experience as slightly more fun than males.

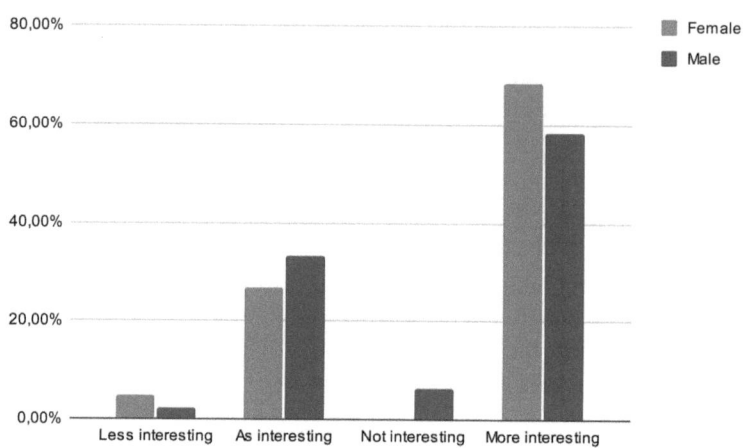

Fig. 7. Interest compared to expectation

Figure 7 illustrates how male and female students compared their interest in robotics before and after the course.

Results indicated that:

- A majority of both genders found the activity "More interesting" than they had expected, with this trend more pronounced among female students;
- A significant number of male students said the experience was "As interesting" as expected, while fewer females selected this option;
- Very few students, regardless of gender, rated the activity as "Less interesting" or "Not interesting."

Overall, the data suggest that the robotics experience was perceived as enjoyable, interesting, and fun across genders, but some differences emerged in their expectations and perceptions. Female students tended to rate the activities as easier and slightly more enjoyable, suggesting that the curriculum design effectively mitigated potential barriers to female participation. When comparing the experience to initial expectations, a larger proportion of female students found the activities more interesting than anticipated, whereas, among those who found the experience just as interesting as expected, male students were in the majority. The data underscore the significance of embedding robotics activities within the regular curriculum as instrumental in enabling female students to confront and overcome implicit gender biases and stereotypes that often associate robotics with a "boy thing".

6 Suggestions for the Design of Inclusive Educational Robotics Activities

Our findings highlight that integrating robotics activities into regular curricular hours, offering self-paced learning opportunities, and fostering peer-collaboration effectively promoted equal engagement among male and female students. Girls, in particular, showed increased participation and confidence when activities were framed outside of competitive environments. Indeed, educational robotics is often introduced as an after-school activity, typically aimed at preparing students for competitions [16]. These competitive contexts tend to attract boys more than girls, and girls are primarily participating when they already have a strong interest in technology [17]. This also because previous researches indicate that many girls are less motivated by competitive environments [18, 19]. Such environments may unintentionally reinforce existing gender disparities, highlighting the need for more inclusive approaches capable of engaging a broader range of learners. These results underscore the importance of moving beyond traditional competition-centered models to create more inclusive educational contexts.

Based on these insights, we propose the following key principles for designing inclusive educational robotics activities:

- to be self-paced, allowing learners to engage at their own rhythm;
- to be integrated into curricular hours, ensuring broader access and participation;
- to promote peer-supported learning over individual or group competitions;
- to incorporate inclusive robot design, offering diverse aesthetic and functional options that avoid reinforcing stereotypes and appeal to a wide range of interests.

A comprehensive approach that combines inclusive activity structures and thoughtful robot design is crucial for fostering equitable engagement in robotics and, more broadly, in STEM education.

7 Conclusions

This study investigated how the design of educational robots and the structure of classroom-based activities can influence student engagement, with a particular focus on gender-related dynamics. Conducted during regular school hours and involving the entire class, the intervention offered a curriculum-based, inclusive alternative to competitive robotics activities, addressing potential barriers to female participation and promoting equitable engagement across genders. While the sample size was limited, the results contribute to ongoing efforts aimed at building more equitable and engaging STEM education starting from the primary level.

The results suggest the importance of taking into account robot aesthetics and pedagogical context in shaping students' experiences and attitudes toward robotics. Girls in particular benefited from the inclusive design of both the robots and the activities, reporting higher levels of engagement and positive shifts in perception.

This pilot project demonstrates strong potential for broader application and refinement. Future studies should explore its longitudinal impact on students' future study choices, self-efficacy, and sustained interest in STEM disciplines. Additionally, the approach and findings presented here may offer valuable insights and inspiration to educators and researchers seeking to develop gender-sensitive and inclusive robotics programs within formal education systems.

To build on these findings, further research should involve larger and more diverse populations, assessing how inclusive educational robotics can influence students' long-term learning pathways and their self-perception in STEM fields. Ultimately, fostering inclusive and engaging robotics education is not just a matter of technology, but of equity, representation, and opportunity.

References

1. World Economic Forum: Global Gender Gap Report. https://www.weforum.org/publications/series/global-gender-gap-report/
2. European Institute for Gender Equality: Gender Equality Index. https://eige.europa.eu/
3. Papert, S.: Mindstorms: Children, Computers, and Powerful Ideas. Basic Books, New York (1980)
4. CAST: Universal Design for Learning Guidelines Version 3.0. (2024). https://udlguidelines.cast.org
5. Cheryan, S., Ziegler, S.A., Montoya, A.K., Jiang, L.: Why are some STEM fields more gender balanced than others? Psychol. Bull. **143**(1), 1–35 (2017). https://doi.org/10.1037/bul0000052
6. Krause, S., Henk, AL., Stolzenburg, F.: Selecting an educational robot: a comprehensive guideline. In: Balogh, R., Obdržálek, D., Fislake, M. (eds.) Robotics in Education. RiE 2024. Lecture Notes in Networks and Systems, vol. 1084, pp. 263–274. Springer, Cham (2024). https://doi.org/10.1007/978-3-031-67059-6_23
7. Catlin, D., Kandlhofer, M., Holmquist, S., Csizmadia, A.P., Angel-Fernandez, J., Cabibihan, J.J.: EduRobot taxonomy and Papert's paradigm. In: Dagiene, V., Jasute, E. (eds.) Constructionism: Constructionism, Computational Thinking and Educational Innovation, Vilnius, Lithuania, pp. 151–159 (2018). http://www.constructionism2018.fsf.vu.lt/. Accessed 12 Apr 2025
8. Cesaro, L., Franceschini, A., Badaloni, S., Menegatti, E., Rodà, A.: Gender biases in robots for education. In: Proceedings of the 3rd Workshop on Bias, Ethical AI, Explainability and the role of Logic and Logic Programming Co-located with the 23rd International Conference of the Italian Association for Artificial Intelligence (AIxIA 2024), Bolzano (2024). https://ceur-ws.org/Vol-3881/paper4.pdf. Accessed 12 Apr 2025
9. Beraldo, G., Di Battista, S., Badaloni, S., Menegatti, E., Pivetti, M.: Sex differences in expectations and perception of a social robot. In: Proceedings of the 2018 IEEE Workshop on Advanced Robotics and Its Social Impacts (ARSO), pp. 38–43. IEEE (2018). https://doi.org/10.1109/ARSO.2018.8625826
10. Reich-Stiebert, N., Eyssel, F.: (ir) relevance of gender? On the influence of gender stereotypes on learning with a robot. In: Proceedings of the 2017 ACM/IEEE International Conference on Human-Robot Interaction, pp. 166–176 (2017). https://doi.org/10.1145/2909824.3020242
11. Stanford's Gendered Innovations Project: Gendering social robots: analyzing gender and intersectionality. https://genderedinnovations.stanford.edu/case-studies/genderingsocialrobots.html. Accessed 12 Apr 2025

12. Perugia, G., Lisy, D.: Robot's gendering trouble: a scoping review of gendering humanoid robots and its effects on HRI. Int. J. Soc. Robot. **15**, 1725–1753 (2023). https://doi.org/10.1007/s12369-023-01061-6
13. European Commission: Directorate-General for Education, Youth, Sport and Culture, Evagorou, M., Puig, B., Bayram, D., Janeckova, H.: Addressing the gender gap in STEM education across educational levels – analytical report. Publications Office of the European Union (2024). https://data.europa.eu/doi/https://doi.org/10.2766/260477
14. United Nations General Assembly: Transforming our world: the 2030 agenda for sustainable development (2015). https://www.refworld.org/docid/57b6e3e44.html. Accessed 12 Apr 2025
15. Đapo, N., Čelebičić, I., Spahić, L., Binder-Hathaway, R.: Gender gap in the STEM fields and proposed intervention programmes. UN Women (2021). https://eca.unwomen.org/en/digital-library/publications/2021/8/gender-gap-in-the-stem-fields-and-proposed-intervention-programmes. Accessed 12 Apr 2025
16. Graffin, M., Sheffield, R., Koul, R.: More than robots: reviewing the impact of the FIRST® LEGO® league challenge robotics competition on school students' STEM attitudes, learning, and twenty-first century skill development. J. STEM Educ. Res. **5**, 322–343 (2022). https://doi.org/10.1007/s41979-022-00078-2
17. Master, A., Cheryan, S., Meltzoff, A.N.: Computing whether she belongs: stereotypes undermine girls' interest and sense of belonging in computer science. J. Educ. Psychol. **108**(3), 424–437 (2016). https://doi.org/10.1037/edu0000061
18. Clark Blickenstaff, J.: Women and science careers: leaky pipeline or gender filter? Gend. Educ. **17**(4), 369–386 (2005). https://doi.org/10.1080/09540250500145072
19. Wang, M.T., Degol, J.L.: Gender gap in STEM: motivational, affective, and cognitive perspectives. Psychol. Bull. **143**(3), 275–299 (2017). https://doi.org/10.1037/bul0000052

Emotional Content in Robotic Dance: Evaluating Human-to-Robot Movement Mapping

Giuseppe Saviano[1,2], Alberto Villani[1(✉)], and Domenico Prattichizzo[1,3]

[1] Department of Information Engineering and Mathematics, University of Siena, Siena, Italy
{saviano,villani,prattichizzo}@diism.unisi.it,
giuseppe.saviano@phd.unipi.it
[2] Department of Computer Science, University of Pisa, Pisa, Italy
[3] Department of Humanoids and Human Centered Mechatronics (HHCM), Istituto Italiano di Tecnologia (IIT), Genova, Italy

Abstract. Performative arts and choreographed dancing motion are powerful medium for nonverbal emotional communication, allowing humans to convey affective states capturing and enchanting a wide audience. The integration of robotics into this domain, using AI, motion capture, and movement-mapping algorithms, offers new opportunities to investigate how artificial agents can express emotions. However, this raises important questions about the authenticity and fidelity of robotic emotional expression.

The challenge becomes particularly relevant with non-humanoid robots, where the structural disparity with the human body complicates the mapping of expressive gestures. In prior work, we introduced a PCA-based projection method to transfer human dancing movements to robotic arms. This technique adapts the high degrees of freedom of human motion to the robot more limited kinematic structure, aiming to preserve dance nuance.

While earlier results showed structural coherence between human and robot motion, the present study focuses on emotional fidelity. We examine whether the embedded space generated by PCA preserves perceptual distinctions between emotions or introduces distortions, particularly in the intensity (arousal) or pleasantness (valence) dimensions.

Our analysis consists of two steps: first, we assess the clarity of emotional differentiation post-mapping; second, we analyze whether robot movements maintain the expressive signature of each emotion. This approach sheds light on how dimensionality reduction and mapping complexity influence emotional authenticity in robotic dance.

Keywords: Art and Entertainment Robotics · Social HRI · Emotional Content

---

G. Saviano and A. Villani—These authors contributed equally to this work.

1 Introduction

Over the past century, robotics has become an increasingly integral part of human environments, with applications extending across domestic spaces, healthcare, education, and the performing arts [10,18,40,49]. This technological evolution has given rise to the emerging field of performative robotics, wherein artists, researchers, and technology companies design choreographies specifically tailored to the unique capabilities of robots and their articulated structures [50]. These developments aim to foster novel modes of interaction between humans and machines [4,43,47], to showcase the potential of advanced robotics in aesthetically compelling and intellectually engaging ways [17], and to expand the expressive possibilities of choreographic language while enriching the audience's artistic experience [18,37].

In parallel, robotics is increasingly being explored as a medium for social interaction [7,51], emotional exchange [8], and the transmission of social gestures [12]. The ability of robots to perceive, interpret, and express emotions introduces new possibilities for facilitating human-to-human communication, potentially bridging emotional gaps and fostering deeper, more empathetic connections, including those between performers and spectators [44].

Despite growing interest in robotic dance performances, their impact on the stylistic heritage [23] and emotionally expressive of their motion [45], a significant research gap remains in the area of human-to-robot movement mapping algorithms, especially for choreographing robotic arms and understanding their perceptual impact on audiences. Most existing studies have focused on legged platforms [5] or aerial drones [11,13], and commonly utilize music as a control signal for movement generation [31,37,39,50]. Only a limited number of studies incorporate user evaluations to assess the audience's emotional or aesthetic response [24].

Conversely, the use of industrial robotic arms, paired with choreographies designed around their specific kinematics, offers notable economic and logistical advantages. A major portion of the costs in robot-based performance practices is related to the development of custom hardware and motion systems tailored to artistic needs. Leveraging commercially available robotic manipulators allows practitioners to significantly reduce these costs by utilizing standardized, off-the-shelf platforms. Furthermore, the contrast between the robotic arm's non-anthropomorphic motion and the fluidity of human dancers can enhance the visual and conceptual impact of the performance. To illustrate this point, one can refer to the choreographies of physicist-dancer Merritt Moore [9] and Italian ballet star Roberto Bolle [6], who have danced with robotic systems in evocative performance settings.

Exploiting human dance paths to the robot are needed to ensure an efficacious dialogue between the two two dancing bodies and guarantee a large dataset to train the robot. However, the principal challenge in employing robotic manipulators for dance lies in the complexity of translating human motion into robotic movement, due to the mismatch in structure and the unconventional configuration of degrees of freedom (DoFs) [1,35,46,48]. These discrepancies complicate

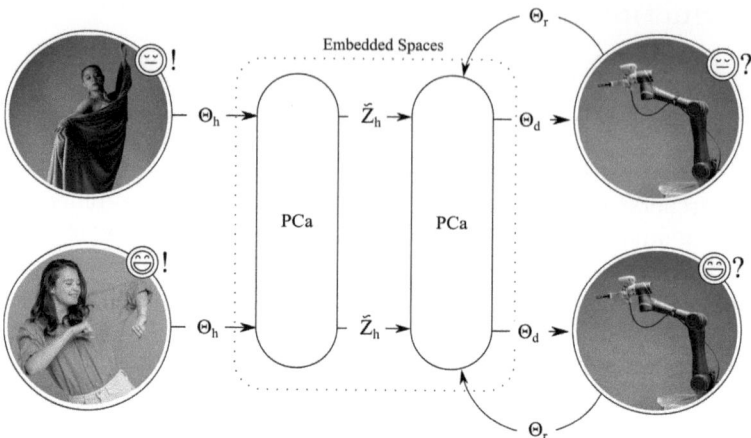

Fig. 1. Visual representation of the PCA generated embedded space to map human dance movements onto robot trajectories, illustrating the projecting method and highlighting the challenges of preserving dance emotional nuance when elaborated by the algorithm and rendered on the robot

efforts to preserve the emotional and expressive qualities inherent in human dance.

Although current algorithms seek to maximize similarity between human and robotic movement, the fundamental kinematic differences between the two agents require the use of alternative metrics. Rather than matching postures or goal states, similarity is often assessed at the task level, by aligning functionally analogous points or through embedding both systems within a shared embedded space [14–16,19,21,27,28]. In artistic domains such as dance, where expression is not reducible to goal directed motion, more suitable approaches include metrics based on the trajectories of mapped points [33,38] or paths through shared embedded spaces [36,41].

Ultimately, the limited expressiveness of systems with reduced degrees of freedom and the complexity of mapping algorithms make it especially challenging to retain the emotional subtleties and nuanced gestures characteristic of human dance within robotic performances.

1.1 Contribution

In our previous work [36], we introduced the use of Principal Component Analysis (PCA) to generate embedded spaces for transferring aesthetically expressive human motion onto industrial robotic arms. Principal components were chosen over other aforementioned approaches, such as directly mapping the most variable joints or points, due to their ability to capture the highest variance in the dataset. This property enables the preservation of subtle movement accents and expressive nuances within the first few components, while simultaneously reducing dimensionality. As a result, the method facilitates alignment between the differing degrees of freedom of human and robotic agents, discarding redundant or less meaningful variations in human motion, preserving the frequency and intensity of main movements and their change of directions. By leveraging PCA's capability to project data into a neutral, lower-dimensional latent space, our approach aims to evaluate the expressive potential achievable through such mappings. Nonetheless, the process of dimensionality reduction inherently involves the loss or transformation of certain motion characteristics.

Therefore, as illustrated in Fig. 1, this work contributes an investigation into the suitability of PCA-based embeddings for dance mapping, with the goal of conveying the emotional content of a choreography. Exploiting the same method proposed in [36] and a new subset of emotionally labelled human dance extracted from a publicly available dataset, we investigate whether the mapping process via principal component analysis can preserve the emotional essence conveyed by the original choreography. By analysing the transformed motion data, we aim to assess whether the expressive intent and affective qualities of the human performance remain perceptible after being adapted to the kinematic constraints of a robotic arm.

This article proceeds as follows: in Sect. 2, a brief description of the mapping method and the generated choreography is reported; in Sect. 3 the experimental protocol to evaluate the impact of mapping by PC embedded space on transmitted emotion; in Sect. 4, results and discussion about the conducted experiments; and finally, Sect. 5 summarizes the findings and concludes the article.

2 Mapping Algorithm

In what follows, the usage of PCA for generating a shared embedded space to map human dancing performances onto robot choreographies is briefly resumed.[1]

Starting from the dataset proposed in [2,42], which includes human motion data recorded during various dance performances, we selected twelve human joint angle trajectories. Each i-th trajectory corresponds to a different contemporary dance choreography, annotated with distinct emotional labels including: afraid ($i = 1$); angry ($i = 2$); annoyed ($i = 3$); bored ($i = 4$); excited ($i = 5$); happy ($i = 6$); miserable ($i = 7$); pleased ($i = 8$); relaxed ($i = 9$); sad ($i = 10$); satisfied ($i = 11$); and tired ($i = 12$).

We represent the human posture at time t during the i-th performance as a vector of joint angles, $\Theta_{h,i}(t) \in \mathbb{R}^N$, captured at 120 Hz using a motion capture system with 93 degrees of freedom ($N = 93$).

Conversely, robotic trajectories, $\Theta_r(t) \in \mathbb{R}^M$, were drawn from a dataset of recorded robot movements performed by a KUKA LWR with 7 degrees of freedom ($M = 7$) [30], also sampled at 120 Hz. These trajectories were temporally aligned to the human sequences by repeating robot segments to match the duration of each human choreography: $\mu = \lceil T_{h,i}/T_r \rceil$, where $T_{h,i}$ and T_r denote the durations of the human and robot choreographies, respectively.

---

[1] For further details about the projecting method, please refer to [36].

Principal component analysis was applied to both human and robot datasets to derive reduced representations $Z_{h,i}(t) \in \mathbb{R}^N$ and $Z_r(t) \in \mathbb{R}^M$, along with their respective transformation matrices $\Lambda_{h,i} \in \mathbb{R}^{N \times N}$ and $\Lambda_r \in \mathbb{R}^{M \times M}$. To match the robot's degrees of freedom, only the first $x = 7$ principal components were retained from the human data:

$$\Theta_{h,i}(t) \approx \tilde{\Lambda}_{h,i}(\tilde{Z}_{h,i}(t)), \quad \Theta_r(t) = \Lambda_r(Z_r(t)),$$

where $\tilde{Z}_{h,i} \in \mathbb{R}^M$ and $\tilde{\Lambda}_{h,i} \in \mathbb{R}^{M \times M}$ are the subset of $Z_{h,i}$ and $\Lambda_{h,i}$ with cardinality equal to 7. The mapped robot configuration $\Theta_{d,i}(t)$ for the i-th choreography is computed as:

$$\Theta_{d,i}(t) = \Lambda_r \left(\tilde{\Lambda}_{h,i}^{-1}(K_{r \to h} \Theta_{h,i}(t)) \right),$$

where $K_{r \to h}$ normalizes the human PCs to the range of the robot ones:

$$K_{r \to h} = \frac{\max_t(\tilde{Z}_{h,i}(t))}{\max_t(Z_r(t))}.$$

The resulting twelve robot trajectories $\Theta_{d,i}(t)$, with $i \in 1, \ldots, 12$, define the robot movements derived from expressive human dances, each characterized by distinct emotional nuances.

3 Experimental Evaluation

In this section, we present the experimental protocols (Sect. 3.1), the participants, the experimental setting (Sect. 3.2) and the metrics (Sect. 3.3) used for the user studies aimed to evaluate the effectiveness of PCA-generated embedded spaces in enabling the transfer of emotional nuances from human dance choreographies to robotic manipulators.

3.1 Protocol

The primary objective of the user studies was to assess whether the emotive essence embedded in the twelve human choreographies is preserved, amplified, diminished, or distorted when transferred across such distinct kinematic structures.

Prior to the main evaluation, a preliminary phase was conducted: all participants were tested on their ability to recognize labelled emotions from the set of human dances.

To achieve this, we adopt the arousal-valence model of emotion, which conceptualizes affective states within a two-dimensional framework. In this model, arousal reflects the intensity of emotional activation, ranging from calm to excited, while valence captures the hedonic tone, distinguishing between positive and negative experiences. Together, these dimensions define a Cartesian coordinate space for categorizing emotional states. To accurately locate specific emotions within this space, we relied on a modified adaptation of the framework

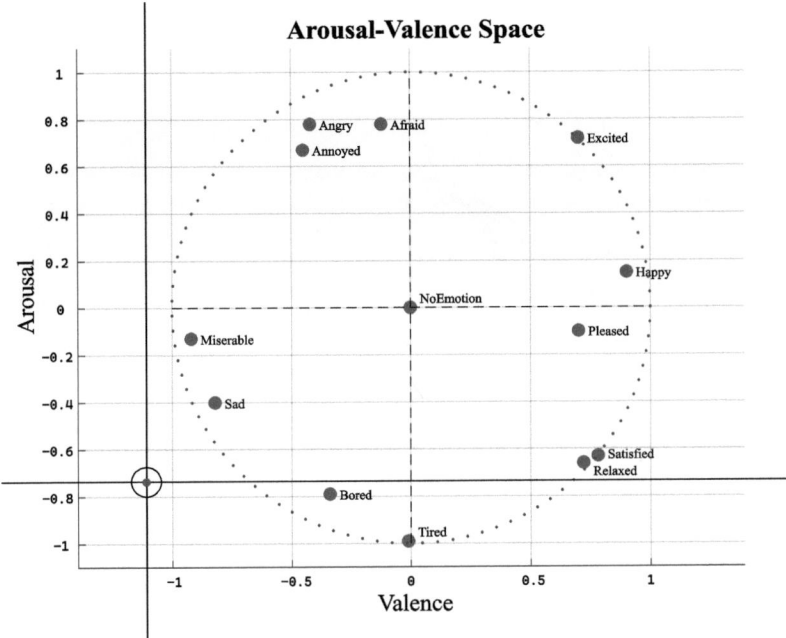

Fig. 2. Dimensional arousal-valence graph of human emotions, also known as the Circumflex model of affects. The plot is a visual aid that can help in identifying emotions. Arousal refers to the intensity of the emotion, while valence refers to whether the emotion is positive or negative. We mark with blue circled dots the coordinate twelve emotions, labelling the selected choreography, while the red dot denotes the actual position of the pointer controlled by the experiment participant using a laptop mouse. (Color figure online)

proposed by [29], and positioned the selected emotional labels in accordance with the mappings described in [3,22,34].

A sample of 12 videos was generated, one for each human performance exploited for robot choreography generation. Each video was realized by Unity Graphic Engine (Unity Technologies, US) using SMPL avatar, a neutral humanoid avatar proposed in [26], ensuring that visual presentation was consistent and preventing psychological bias (see Fig. 3a).

To mitigate potential biases arising from the order of video presentation and to ensure balanced exposure to all emotional stimuli, we employed a Latin Square design to randomize the sequence for each participant. This counterbalancing technique is widely used in user studies, as it effectively reduces ordering effects, learning biases, and inter-stimulus interference, thereby enhancing the internal validity and reliability of the collected responses [20,25,32].

Participants were asked to evaluate the perceived emotion of each video by placing a point on a two-dimensional arousal-valence graph (see Fig. 2). While a predefined set of emotional labels was displayed on the graph for reference,

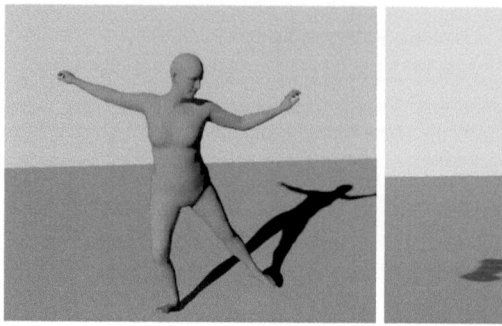
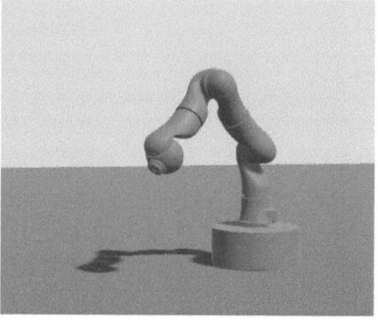

(a) Human avatar performing emotional choreography.

(b) Robot mock-up rendering human dance movement.

Fig. 3. Humanoid and Robot renderers used during the experimental evaluation

participants were free to select any point in the space that best represented their felt experience.

Subsequently the preliminary phase, participants were shown a new set of videos depicting the twelve choreographies previously computed and performed by a virtual mock-up of a robotic manipulator KUKA LWR. To maintain consistency and avoid visual bias, the robot shell was rendered in Unity Graphics engine with a uniform color identical to that of the avatar used in the videos of human dance (see Fig. 3b).

Once again, videos were presented in a randomized order, counterbalanced across participants using a newly generated Latin square matrix, and analogously with the preliminary phase, participants rated the perceived emotion for each robotic performance using the arousal-valence graph.

A resting phase was interposed between the preliminary and main phases of user studies to mitigate the potential effects of visual fatigue or motion sickness on participants' judgments.

The full experiment, including both the human and robotic video evaluations and the resting time, lasted approximately 30 min per participant.

3.2 Participants and Experimental Setting

In accordance with the requirement of Latin Square design, the survey was completed by 12 users (6 female, 5 male, and 1 non-binary, aged 24–61).

The experiment protocol was compliant with the Declaration of Helsinki: there were no risks of harmful effects on the subjects' health, and they could interrupt the task at any time.

Participants were seated in front of two displays: a primary 27-inch monitor and a secondary 15.6-inch screen, both connected to the experimenter's laptop. During the experiment, as visually represented in Fig. 4, participants were instructed to alternately watch the video of a performed choreography on the primary display and then use a mouse to indicate a point on an interactive

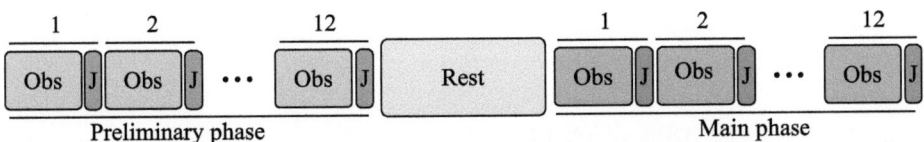

Fig. 4. Timeline of the Experimental Session. Participants were initially instructed to observe 12 video clips (**Obs**) featuring human choreographies and subsequently to express their judgment (**J**) regarding the perceived emotion after each observation. Following this preliminary phase (indicated in orange), participants were given a resting period (**Rest**) before proceeding to the main phase. In the main phase, they observed another set of 12 video clips (**Obs**) featuring dancing robots (indicated in red), again followed by an emotional judgment (**J**) after each clip. (Color figure online)

arousal-valence plane displayed on the secondary monitor. This interface was implemented using a custom MATLAB script (MathWorks, Inc., US).

At the end of the experimental session, they are asked to report their level of experience in the dance discipline. All participants declared themselves as amateurs and spectators of the dance discipline.

3.3 Metrics

After collecting participants' judgments regarding the perceived emotions elicited by both human and robot choreographies, we conducted an analysis aimed at evaluating the effectiveness of the mapping algorithm in preserving the emotional nuances of human dance.

To this end, we exploit two metrics: firstly, we evaluate the accuracy with which participants identified the intended emotions by comparing their responses with the original labels. This qualitative evaluation enabled us to investigate the consistency in emotional interpretation between human and robot performances.

Subsequently, a more detailed quantitative analysis was performed to examine the impact of the PCA-generated embedded space on emotional content. Specifically, we computed correlations between participants' ratings emotional dimensions (arousal and valence) of human and robot choreographies.

In the initial phase of our analysis, we quantified the accuracy of participants' emotional recognition for both human and robot agents. For this purpose, we calculated the Euclidean distance within the circumplex model of affect between the valence (v) and arousal (a) coordinates reported by the k-th participant about i-th choreography, $p^x_{(i),k} = \langle p^x_{(i),k,v}, p^x_{(i),k,a} \rangle$, and the reference coordinates $P_{(j)} = \langle P_{(j),v}, P_{(j),a} \rangle$ for each of the j emotion categories, where $x \in \{h, r\}$ denotes either human or robot choreography:

$$d^x_{(ij),k} = \sqrt{(P_{(j),v} - p^x_{(i),k,v})^2 + (P_{(j),a} - p^x_{(i),k,a})^2}, \quad \forall x \in \{h, r\} \quad \forall k \in [1, U]$$

where U denotes the total number of participants. The value $d^x_{(ij),k}$ represents the distance between the j-th reference emotion and the i-th response by the

k-th participant. These distances were computed for each participant and agent type and organized into individual confusion matrices $D^x_{(i,j)} \in \mathbb{R}^{12\times 12}$:

$$D^x_k = \begin{bmatrix} d^x_{(1,1),k} & \cdots & d^x_{(1,12),k} \\ \vdots & \ddots & \vdots \\ d^x_{(12,1),k} & \cdots & d^x_{(12,12),k} \end{bmatrix}, \quad \forall x \in \{h, r\} \quad \forall k \in [1, U],$$

where the diagonal elements indicate recognition error magnitudes (i.e., deviation between intended and perceived emotions), while the off-diagonal terms return the level of confusion and emotional distortion.

To facilitate comparison, confusion matrices were averaged across participants, yielding aggregate representations for both agent types:

$$D^x = \frac{1}{U} \sum_{k=1}^{U} D^x_k, = \frac{1}{U} \begin{bmatrix} \sum_{k=1}^{U} d^x_{(1,1),k} & \cdots & \sum_{k=1}^{U} d^x_{(1,12),k} \\ \vdots & \ddots & \vdots \\ \sum_{k=1}^{U} d^x_{(12,1),k} & \cdots & \sum_{k=1}^{U} d^x_{(12,12),k} \end{bmatrix} = \begin{bmatrix} d^x_{(1,1)} & \cdots & d^x_{(1,12)} \\ \vdots & \ddots & \vdots \\ d^x_{(12,1)} & \cdots & d^x_{(12,12)} \end{bmatrix}$$

$$\forall x \in \{h, r\}$$

On the other hand, to quantitatively assess the influence of the PCA-generated embedded space on participants' emotional perception, we computed the Pearson correlation coefficients between participants' reported values about robot and human dance emotional values, considering arousal and valence separately.

Let $A^x = \{p^x_{(i),k,a}\} \ \forall i, k$ and $V^x = \{p^x_{(i),k,v}\} \ \forall i, k$ denote the sets of participant-reported arousal and valence values respectively, the Pearson correlation coefficients are then computed as:

$$\rho_A = \frac{\text{cov}(A^r, A^h)}{\sigma_{A^r}\sigma_{A^h}}, \quad \rho_V = \frac{\text{cov}(V^r, V^h)}{\sigma_{V^r}\sigma_{V^h}},$$

where $\text{cov}(\cdot, \cdot)$ denotes the covariance between the predicted and reference values, and σ denotes the standard deviation. These coefficients provide a measure of alignment between communicated emotional dimensions in the PCA-embedded space, and thereby reflect the emotional fidelity preserved in the robotic translation of human dance onto robot manipulator.

4 Results

As introduced in Sect. 3.3, we begin by graphically evaluating the consistency of emotional perception elicited by human and robot-generated movements. Figures 5a and 5b present the confusion matrices obtained by averaging the Euclidean distances across the twelve participants ($U = 12$) for human (D^h) and robot-generated (D^r) choreographies, respectively.

A visual inspection of the two matrices reveals a marked difference in the distribution of recognition errors. In particular, the human-related matrix D^h exhibits a clear concentration of lower error values along the main diagonal, indicating a higher accuracy in emotion recognition. Conversely, the robot-related

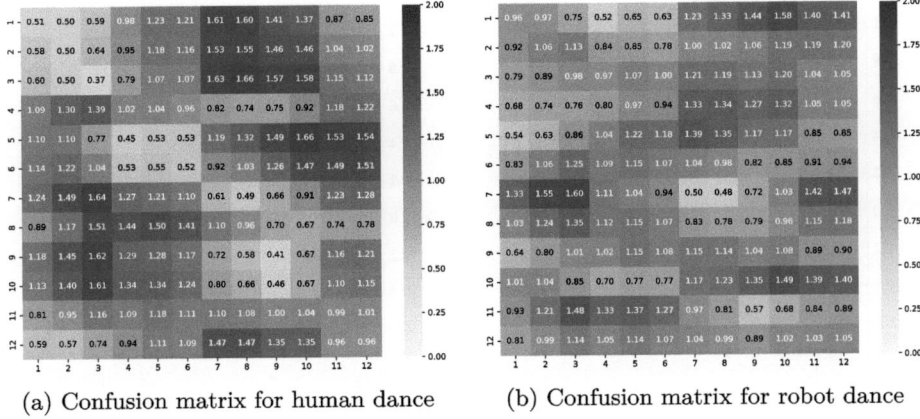

(a) Confusion matrix for human dance (b) Confusion matrix for robot dance

Fig. 5. Average Euclidean distances between indicated and reference emotions across 12 participants, shown for both human and robot choreographies. Lower values on the diagonal indicate higher recognition accuracy.

matrix D^r displays a more uniform and dispersed error pattern, suggesting a loss of emotional fidelity in the robot-generated movements.

This observation is supported by a quantitative analysis of diagonal and off-diagonal elements. For the human condition, the mean value of diagonal elements representing correct emotion recognition is calculated as:

$$\bar{D}^h_{\text{diag}} = \frac{1}{12} \sum_{i=1}^{12} d^h_{(i,i)} = 0.670$$

with a standard deviation equal to ±0.233 while the mean of off-diagonal elements representing misclassification is:

$$\bar{D}^h_{\text{off}} = \frac{1}{(12^2) - 12} \sum_{\substack{i=1 \\ i \neq j}}^{12} \sum_{j=1}^{12} d^h_{(i,j)} = 1.106$$

with a standard deviation ±0.322 indicating a relatively low error rate when participants evaluated human choreographies. In contrast, when analysing the robot condition, the mean diagonal error increases $\bar{D}^r_{\text{diag}}$ as decrease the mean off diagonal error $\bar{D}^r_{\text{off}}$:

$$\bar{D}^r_{\text{diag}} = 0.983 \pm 0.236 \quad \bar{D}^r_{\text{off}} = 1.047 \pm 0.235$$

This increase in recognition error along the diagonal suggests that some of the emotional information present in the human performance is not effectively preserved in the robot's execution. To further investigate this discrepancy, a more fine-grained analysis was conducted focusing on the dispersion of individual emotional components in the valence-arousal space. Specifically, we analyzed the

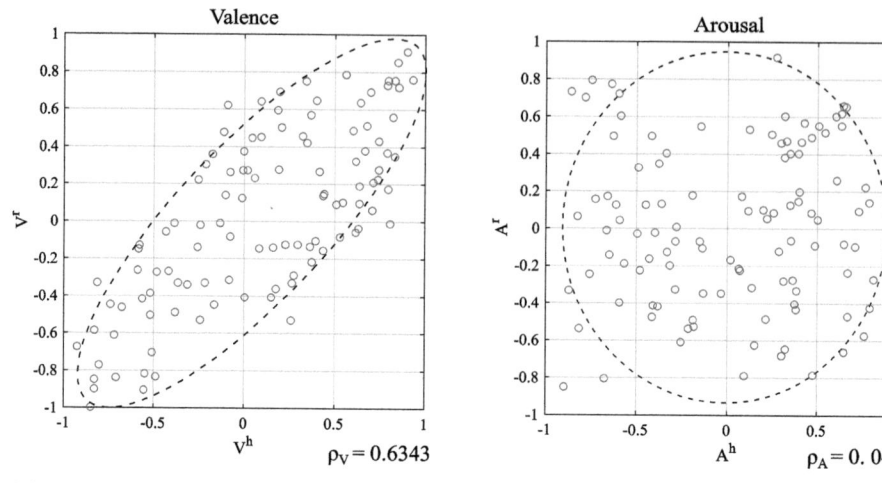

(a) Scatter plots of human- and robot-transmitted emotion valence

(b) Scatter plots of human- and robot-transmitted emotion arousal

Fig. 6. Scatter plots comparing the human-induced (horizontal axis) and robot-induced (vertical axis) emotion coordinates for valence (a) and arousal (b). Each point represents a single participant's response for a given choreography performed by a human and a robot. The dashed ellipses represent confidence contours of the distributions. The Pearson correlation coefficients (ρ_V for valence and ρ_A for arousal) quantify the degree of linear association between target and perceived values

correlation between the participants' reported coordinates of values for human and robot choreography, considering separately both emotional dimensions, and considering the human choreography condition.

As shown in Fig. 6, the scatter plots depict the relationship between human and robot induced values for valence (Fig. 6a) and arousal (Fig. 6b), along with the corresponding Pearson correlation coefficients ρ_V and ρ_A.

The data distribution in both plots highlight the difference of two emotional dimensions: the valence scatter plot presents an elongated ellipse aligned along the identity line, suggesting a linear correlation between the effect of human and robot choreography on the spectator judgement, whereas the arousal plot exhibits a more circular and isotropic distribution, suggesting a low or absent correlation. The visual inspection outcomes are coherently supported by numerical analysis. The valence dimension V^x demonstrates a relatively strong positive correlation ($\rho_V = 0.6343$), indicating that participants were generally able to coherently interpret the valence conveyed by the human movement once projected in the human movements. Conversely, the arousal dimension A^x shows the lack of correlation ($\rho_A = 0.0433$), revealing a substantial variability in the participants' perception of arousal levels. This discrepancy suggests that, while valence was more reliably communicated through human movement, the expression of arousal was less consistently interpreted across participants.

4.1 Discussions

These collected outcomes suggest that the PCA-based embedding is particularly effective in encoding the "qualitative polarity" of affective states (i.e., positive vs. negative emotions). The strong correlation observed for valence supports this view, highlighting the model's ability to retain and transmit the overall hedonic tone of each emotion. Such performance can be attributed to PCA emphasis on capturing the most salient directions of variance in movement data, which may correspond closely with the bodily expressions associated with valence-laden emotions. However, the same dimensionality reduction appears to compromise the "quantitative expressiveness" of movements associated with arousal. The near-zero correlation in the arousal dimension implies a loss of resolution in conveying emotional intensity. This distortion can plausibly be attributed to two concurrent mechanisms.

First, the robot manipulator's limited degrees of freedom inherently constrain the dynamic range and amplitude of the movements, thus reducing the physical cues that typically signal high arousal states (e.g., energetic or expansive gestures). Second, the PCA embedding may inadvertently amplify subtle variabilities present in otherwise subdued choreographies. Emotions such as "tired" or "sad", which are characterized by low movement variability in their original human execution, may acquire unintended dynamism through the projection into the PCs space. This effect may arise from PCA tendency to emphasize directions of maximal variance, thereby promoting motion features that are not emotionally salient in the original context.

As a result, the PCA-embedded space, while efficient for preserving the structural essence of motion and its valence component, may distort the emotional intensity of certain choreographies.

5 Conclusions

In this study, we explored the suitability of a PCA-generated embedded space for transferring expressive human body movements onto a robotic platform while preserving the emotional content of the original performance. To this end, we designed and conducted a user study in which participants observed a series of emotionally labelled choreographies, first executed by a human avatar and subsequently projected onto a virtual mock-up of a robotic arm. After each choreography, participants were asked to report their perceived emotion by interacting with a continuous two-dimensional representation of affect based on the valence-arousal model.

The results revealed that the mapping process, combined with the structural differences in degrees of freedom between the human body and the robotic arm, influences the preservation of emotional nuance. A focused analysis of the two affective dimensions indicated that while participants were generally able to recognize the "qualitative" nature of the emotion, the "quantitative" perception of emotional intensity was significantly distorted. This discrepancy appears to stem from two opposing effects: on the one hand, the PCA promotes motion variability by amplifying principal components, which may inadvertently enrich low-arousal choreographies; on the other hand, the limited articulation and kinematic resolution of the robotic manipulator reduce its ability to convey the energetic dynamics necessary for high-arousal emotions.

These findings suggest that while PCA-based embedding is a promising tool for affective motion synthesis, especially for transmitting dyadic and clearly idiosyncratic emotion, on the other hand, its application in precise emotion-preserving transfer tasks must be handled with care.

5.1 Future Work

Future investigations will focus on several directions to address the limitations identified in this study. First, the introduction of hybrid dimensionality reduction techniques that combine PCA with supervised constraints could help align principal components with affect-relevant movement features. Second, future studies should explore the emotional impact of human-robot choreographies and the involvement of alternative robot morphologies, including soft-bodied architectures, to improve the expressiveness of emotional motion rendering. Finally, expanding the user study to include dynamic real-time observations and multi-modal feedback (e.g., audio, facial expression) may provide a more ecologically valid assessment of emotional perception in human-robot interaction.

Acknowledgments. This work was supported by the Italian Ministry of Research, under the complementary actions to the NRRP "Fit4MedRob - Fit for Medical Robotics" Grant (# PNC0000007)

Disclosure of Interests. The authors declare that they have no conflicts of interest related to this work.

References

1. Abe, N.: Beyond anthropomorphising robot motion and towards robot-specific motion: consideration of the potential of artist–dancers in research on robotic motion. Artif. Life Rob. **27**(4), 777–785 (2022)
2. Aristidou, A., Shamir, A., Chrysanthou, Y.: Digital dance ethnography: organizing large dance collections. J. Comput. Cult. Herit. **12**(4) (2019). https://doi.org/10.1145/3344383
3. Barca, L., Candidi, M., Lancia, G.L., Maglianella, V., Pezzulo, G.: Mapping the mental space of emotional concepts through kinematic measures of decision uncertainty. Philos. Trans. R. Soc. B **378**(1870), 20210367 (2023)
4. Beck, A., et al.: Interpretation of emotional body language displayed by a humanoid robot: a case study with children. Int. J. Soc. Robot. **5**(3), 325–334 (2013)
5. Bi, T., Fankhauser, P., Bellicoso, D., Hutter, M.: Real-time dance generation to music for a legged robot. In: 2018 IEEE/RSJ International Conference on Intelligent Robots and Systems (IROS), pp. 1038–1044 (2018). https://doi.org/10.1109/IROS.2018.8593983

6. Bolle, R.: l'uomo e la macchina (2019). https://www.youtube.com/watch?v=XH8C0i51ezk
7. Brogi, B., Cortigiani, G., Villani, A., D'Aurizio, N., Prattichizzo, D., Baldi, T.L.: The avatarm: interacting in the physical metaverse via robotics, diminished reality, and haptics. IEEE Access (2024)
8. Chen, M., Zhou, P., Fortino, G.: Emotion communication system. IEEE Access **5**, 326–337 (2016)
9. Click, B.: The robot and the ballerina (2021). https://www.youtube.com/watch?v=7atZfX85nd4
10. Dassanayake, D., Buddhika, M., Maduranga, I., Seneviratne, J., Kumarage, W.: Revolutionizing manufacturing: the role of robotics in the 21st century. J. Desk Res. Rev. Anal. **2**(1) (2024)
11. Dong, K., Zhang, Z., Chang, X., Chirarattananon, P., LC, R.: Dances with drones: spatial matching and perceived agency in improvised movements with drone and human partners. In: Proceedings of the CHI Conference on Human Factors in Computing Systems, pp. 1–16 (2024)
12. Dragusanu, M., Iqbal, Z., Villani, A., D'Aurizio, N., Prattichizzo, D., Malvezzi, M.: Hans: a haptic system for human-to-human remote handshake. In: 2022 9th IEEE RAS/EMBS International Conference for Biomedical Robotics and Biomechatronics (BioRob), pp. 1–8. IEEE (2022)
13. Eriksson, S., Unander-Scharin, Å., Trichon, V., Unander-Scharin, C., Kjellström, H., Höök, K.: Dancing with drones: crafting novel artistic expressions through intercorporeality. In: Proceedings of the 2019 CHI Conference on Human Factors in Computing Systems, pp. 1–12 (2019)
14. Feth, D.: Haptic human-robot collaboration: comparison of robot partner implementations in terms of human-likeness and task performance. Presence **20**(2), 173–189 (2011)
15. Ficuciello, F., Villani, A., Lisini Baldi, T., Prattichizzo, D.: A human gesture mapping method to control a multi-functional hand for robot-assisted laparoscopic surgery: the musha case. Front. Rob. AI **8**, 741807 (2021)
16. Fitzgerald, T., Goel, A.K., Thomaz, A.: Human-robot co-creativity: task transfer on a spectrum of similarity. In: ICCC, pp. 104–111 (2017)
17. Fujita, M., Sabe, K., Kuroki, Y., Ishida, T., Doi, T.T.: SDR-4X II: a small humanoid as an entertainer in home environment. In: Dario, P., Chatila, R. (eds.) Robotics Research. The Eleventh International Symposium. STAR, vol. 15, pp. 355–364. Springer, Heidelberg (2005). https://doi.org/10.1007/11008941_38
18. Gomez Cubero, C., Pekarik, M., Rizzo, V., Jochum, E.: The robot is present: creative approaches for artistic expression with robots. Front. Rob. AI **8**, 662249 (2021)
19. Gong, L., et al.: Motion similarity evaluation between human and a tri-co robot during real-time imitation with a trajectory dynamic time warping model. Sensors **22**(5), 1968 (2022)
20. Grant, D.A.: The latin square principle in the design and analysis of psychological experiments. Psychol. Bull. **45**(5), 427 (1948)
21. Hausman, K., Springenberg, J.T., Wang, Z., Heess, N., Riedmiller, M.: Learning an embedding space for transferable robot skills. In: International Conference on Learning Representations (2018)
22. Jaeger, S.R., Roigard, C.M., Chheang, S.L.: The valence× arousal circumplex-inspired emotion questionnaire (CEQ): effect of response format and question layout. Food Qual. Prefer. **90**, 104172 (2021)

23. Joshi, M., Chakrabarty, S.: An extensive review of computational dance automation techniques and applications. Proc. R. Soc. A **477**(2251), 20210071 (2021)
24. Kang, M.H., Kim, S.: Research trends in entertainment robots: a comprehensive review of the literature from 1998 to 2024. Dig. Bus. **5**(1), 100102 (2025). https://doi.org/10.1016/j.digbus.2024.100102. https://www.sciencedirect.com/science/article/pii/S2666954424000309
25. Keedwell, A.D., Dénes, J.: Latin Squares and Their Applications: Latin Squares and Their Applications. Elsevier (2015)
26. Loper, M., Mahmood, N., Romero, J., Pons-Moll, G., Black, M.J.: SMPL: a skinned multi-person linear model. In: Seminal Graphics Papers: Pushing the Boundaries, vol. 2, pp. 851–866 (2023)
27. Miura, K., Furukawa, H., Shoji, M.: Similarity of human motion: congruity between perception and data. In: 2006 IEEE International Conference on Systems, Man and Cybernetics, vol. 2, pp. 1184–1189. IEEE (2006)
28. Monforte, M., Ficuciello, F.: A reinforcement learning method using multifunctional principal component analysis for human-like grasping. IEEE Trans. Cogn. Dev. Syst. **13**(1), 132–140 (2020)
29. Paltoglou, G., Thelwall, M.: Seeing stars of valence and arousal in blog posts. IEEE Trans. Affect. Comput. **4**(1), 116–123 (2012)
30. Polydoros, A.S., Nalpantidis, L.: A reservoir computing approach for learning forward dynamics of industrial manipulators. In: 2016 IEEE/RSJ International Conference on Intelligent Robots and Systems (IROS), pp. 612–618 (2016). https://doi.org/10.1109/IROS.2016.7759116
31. Qin, R., Zhou, C., Zhu, H., Shi, M., Chao, F., Li, N.: A music-driven dance system of humanoid robots. Int. J. Humanoid Rob. **15**(05), 1850023 (2018)
32. Richardson, J.T.: The use of latin-square designs in educational and psychological research. Educ. Res. Rev. **24**, 84–97 (2018)
33. Rogel, A., Savery, R., Yang, N., Weinberg, G.: Robogroove: creating fluid motion for dancing robotic arms. In: Proceedings of the 8th International Conference on Movement and Computing, pp. 1–9 (2022)
34. Santos, M., Egerstedt, M.: From motions to emotions: can the fundamental emotions be expressed in a robot swarm? Int. J. Soc. Robot. **13**(4), 751–764 (2021)
35. Saviano, G., Villani, A., Prattichizzo, D.: A pca-based method to map aesthetic movements from dancer to robotic arm. In: 2023 IEEE International Conference on Advanced Robotics and its Social Impacts (ARSO), pp. 71–77. IEEE (2023)
36. Saviano, G., Villani, A., Prattichizzo, D.: From cage to stage: mapping human dance movements onto industrial robotic arm motion. In: Proceedings of the 9th International Conference on Movement and Computing, pp. 1–6 (2024)
37. Saviano, G., Villani, A., Prattichizzo, D.: Mapping music onto robot joints for autonomous choreographies: Pca-based approach. In: 2024 IEEE 8th Forum on Research and Technologies for Society and Industry Innovation (RTSI), pp. 232–237. IEEE (2024)
38. Saviano, G., Villani, A., Prattichizzo, D.: Multi-point mapping of dancer aesthetic movements onto a robotic arm. IEEE Access (2024)
39. Seo, J.H., Yang, J.Y., Kim, J., Kwon, D.S.: Autonomous humanoid robot dance generation system based on real-time music input. In: 2013 IEEE RO-MAN, pp. 204–209. IEEE (2013)
40. Sladić, S., Lesjak, R., Luttenberger, L.R., Musa, M.Š: Trends and progress in collaborative robot applications. Polytechnica **5**(1), 32–37 (2021)

41. Sousa, P., Oliveira, J.L., Reis, L.P., Gouyon, F.: Humanized robot dancing: humanoid motion retargeting based in a metrical representation of human dance styles. In: Antunes, L., Pinto, H.S. (eds.) EPIA 2011. LNCS (LNAI), vol. 7026, pp. 392–406. Springer, Heidelberg (2011). https://doi.org/10.1007/978-3-642-24769-9_29
42. Stavrakis, E., Aristidou, A., Savva, M., Himona, S.L., Chrysanthou, Y.: Digitization of cypriot folk dances. In: Proceedings of the 4th International Conference on Progress in Cultural Heritage Preservation, EuroMed'12, pp. 404–413. Springer, Heidelberg (2012). https://doi.org/10.1007/978-3-642-34234-9-41
43. Sullivan, A., Strawhacker, A., Bers, M.U.: Dancing, drawing, and dramatic robots: integrating robotics and the arts to teach foundational steam concepts to young children. In: Robotics in STEM Education: Redesigning the Learning Experience, pp. 231–260 (2017)
44. Vallverdú, J., Talanov, M., Distefano, S., Mazzara, M., Tchitchigin, A., Nurgaliev, I.: A cognitive architecture for the implementation of emotions in computing systems. Biol. Insp. Cogn. Arch. **15**, 34–40 (2016)
45. Venture, G., Kulić, D.: Robot expressive motions: a survey of generation and evaluation methods. ACM Trans. Hum.-Robot Interact. (THRI) **8**(4), 1–17 (2019)
46. Villani, A., Baldi, T.L., D'Aurizio, N., Campagna, G., Prattichizzo, D.: Does robot anthropomorphism improve performance and user experience in teleoperation? In: 2024 IEEE-RAS 23rd International Conference on Humanoid Robots (Humanoids), pp. 76–83. IEEE (2024)
47. Vircikova, M., Fedor, Z., Sincak, P.: Design of verbal and non-verbal human-robot interactive system, pp. 87–92 (2011). https://doi.org/10.1109/Humanoids.2011.6100834
48. Vircikova, M., Sincak, P.: Dance choreography design of humanoid robots using interactive evolutionary computation. In: Proceedings of the 3rd Workshop for Young Researchers on Human-Friendly Robotics (HFR 2010), Tübingen, Germany, pp. 28–29 (2010)
49. Wolffgramm, M., Tijink, T., Van Geloven, M.D., Corporaal, S.: A collaborative robot in the classroom: designing 21st century engineering education together. J. High. Educ. Theory Pract. **21**(16), 177–187 (2021)
50. Xia, G., Tay, J., Dannenberg, R., Veloso, M.: Autonomous robot dancing driven by beats and emotions of music. In: Proceedings of the 11th International Conference on Autonomous Agents and Multiagent Systems, vol. 1, pp. 205–212 (2012)
51. Xiao, W., Li, M., Chen, M., Barnawi, A.: Deep interaction: wearable robot-assisted emotion communication for enhancing perception and expression ability of children with autism spectrum disorders. Futur. Gener. Comput. Syst. **108**, 709–716 (2020)

"The Soul is a Verb, Not a Noun" Ensoulment as an Artist-Led Relational Approach to Robot Behavior

Maaike Bleeker(✉)

Department of Media and Culture Studies, Utrecht University, Muntstraat 2a, 3512 EV Utrecht, The Netherlands
m.a.bleeker@uu.nl

Abstract. This paper proposes ensoulment as an artist-led relational approach to developing robot behavior. As an alternative to the more commonly used term animation, ensoulment offers a radical relational perspective on how to bring about a sense of personhood or character that starts from exploring the potential of puppets and robots for behavior and expressions as embodied in their morphology, and how this behavior affords interpretations and responses. This perspective aligns with a new materialist understanding of agency as a more-than-human phenomenon embodied within material configurations and their affective capacities. The paper traces our artist-led explorations of the ensoulment of robots in the creation of Ulrike Quade's *Okay, I'm AI-x* and moments from a series of bi-weekly sprints in which we further investigated insights gained during this initial creation process. This paper specifically examines two lines of experimentation: one related to force, weight, and momentum, and the other to the sound produced by robotic movements.

Keywords: Ensoulment · Animation · Materiality · Movement · Puppetry

1 Introduction

This paper proposes 'ensoulment' as an alternative to the more commonly used term 'animation'. In robotics, animation is considered a means to support human-robot interaction and facilitate more fluid communication. According to Ribeiro and Paiva, "robot animation consists of all the processes that give a robot the ability of expressing identity, emotion and intention during autonomous interaction with human users" [1, 388]. Roboticists and HRI developers have drawn inspiration from animation in film and computer graphics to animate robots. For example, Van Breemen uses cinematic animation principles as model for creating "believable behavior" [2, 2873]. Schulz, Torresen, and Herstad discuss this and many more examples in their systematic literature review of animation techniques in HRI [3]. What various approaches to animation share is that they are based on movement trajectories designed to be perceived as the expression of intentions and emotions that presumably inform them. These predesigned movement trajectories are then used to create the illusion of movement (in cinema) or serve as a model to be acted out by a robotic body.

Ensoulment as an alternative to animation offers a different perspective on how to bring about a sense of personhood or character that does not start from predesigned movements but from exploring the potential for behavior and expressions embodied in the robot's morphology, and how these behavioral possibilities afford interpretations and responses. From this perspective, movement is not first designed as the expression of an emotion or intention of a character and then 'put onto' a robot. Instead, a sense of 'self' or 'soul' as animating principle emerges from exploring and composing with the expressive possibilities of robot-specific movements. This approach resonates with a new materialist understanding of agency as a more-than-human phenomenon embodied within material configurations and their affective capacities.

This paper reports on artist-led explorations of ensoulment by puppet and object theatre maker Ulrike Quade, visual artist and theatre maker Bram Ellens, programmer Rick van Dugteren, and me, with various other artists and collaborators, including puppeteer Suze van Miltenburg and composer Stephanie Pan. Together, we investigated how the skills and expertise of artists can inform practical approaches to the ensoulment of robots and how this may contribute to new methodological, conceptual, and artistic developments. In our explorations of artist-led approaches to ensoulment, we worked with two industrial KUKA robotic arms: a large one (KUKA model KR-10 Agilius) and a smaller one (KUKA model KR 201-2). That is, we worked with robots that were designed as industrial tools, rather than as social agents. We explored how expertise from the arts can contribute to achieving a sense of ensoulment grounded in the specificities of the morphology of these emphatically non-humanoid robots. Our investigations took place within the broader context of the *Acting like a Robot* research project, in which we examine what it might mean for a robot to act like a robot, i.e., in accordance with its own morphology rather than as an imitation of human behavior.

Section 2 of this text further introduces the notion of ensoulment. This is followed by a description of how we employed artist-led approaches to achieve ensoulment. With 'artist-led,' we refer to how our explorations were guided by artists' skills and expertise, rather than a matter of applying theories from the arts. Artists do not work with a theory of ensoulment. Rather, their understanding of ensoulment and how to achieve it is embodied in their practice. This section traces some of our explorations and how insights emerged within them, starting with Ulrike Quade's *Okay, I'm AI-x*, an installation developed for Floriade 2022, a major outdoor agricultural exhibition held every 10 years in the Netherlands. We continued our collaboration in a series of bi-weekly sprints, during which we further investigated insights gained during the initial creation process. This paper examines moments from two lines of experimentation: one related to force, weight, and momentum, and the other to the sound produced by robotic movements. Section 4 discusses what we can take away from these artist-led explorations regarding methodological, conceptual, and artistic developments.

2 Ensoulment

In religion and philosophy, ensoulment refers to the process by which a human or other being is endowed with a soul. According to some belief systems, a developing child's soul is newly created. The precise moment when this happens (at the moment of conception or during the embryo's development) is the subject of discussion. For others, especially in religions that believe in reincarnation, the soul is pre-existing and added at a particular stage of development. In both cases, the soul is considered to contain, in some way, the essence of being and personhood that informs behavior and identity.

Ulrike Quade and her puppeteers use ensoulment as an alternative to the more commonly used notion of animation. Both in puppetry and robotics, animation is an important practice, and developers of robots and HRI have looked at puppetry as a source of inspiration for animating robots. Furthermore, in HRI design, puppeteering is used as a Wizard of Oz method to spare the time necessary to program robots to move by themselves. Our explorations, however, were not about puppeteering robots. Instead, we explored what we can learn from puppeteers and other artists about ensoulment as an emergent phenomenon and how this may inform novel approaches to developing robot behavior.

Both ensoulment and animation point to the intimate connection between bringing something to life and making it move. The term animation refers to the practice of creating the illusion of movement, as well as to the state of being full of life or vigor, of liveliness. Quade and her puppeteers prefer ensoulment over animation because it captures how, in puppeteering, a sense of soul or personhood is brought about by movements and other expressions rather than such behavior being the expression of an imaginary 'self' pre-existing them. In their practice, therefore, bringing about a sense of the puppet's self or character is not a matter of making puppets perform preconceived movements as expressions of preconceived characters but of what they describe as 'finding the puppet's soul.' This occurs through the exploration of the puppet's potential for movement and expression through embodied interaction with and manipulation of the puppet. This largely intuitive process begins with simply touching, looking, pushing, and pulling to give impulses and see how the material responds. From there, possibilities for behavior and interaction emerge, along with the first tentative steps toward character development and potential situations.

Ensoulment occurs when making a puppet move and do things also brings about a rudimentary sense of character or identity that can be perceived as the driving force behind its actions. Not all movements and behaviors do so. Successful ensoulment requires finding ways to make puppets behave in ways that suggest this behavior is theirs and convinces as originating from their morphology and modes of being. To find such behavior, Quade and her puppeteers cultivate an attitude they describe as 'listening.' Instead of imposing movements on puppets, one needs to listen to the specificities of their materiality and their possibilities for movement and develop their behavior from there. By doing so, the puppeteers develop a sense of what a puppet can do and express, and what its 'self' or personality might be, as two sides of the same thing.

3 Our Artist-Led Explorations of the Ensoulment of Robots

In our collaborative explorations, we investigated how (aspects of) this approach to the ensoulment of puppets might be transposed to robotics and HRI. We focused in particular on how movements' relation to weight and gravity, and the physicality of sound produced by movement, can contribute to ensoulment. This focus was informed by insights we gained serendipitously while collaborating on creating Ulrike Quade's installation *Okay,*

I'm AI-x. These insights provided the basis for further explorations during our bi-weekly sprints.

4 How It Started: Serendipitous Findings

Quade is a puppet and object theatre maker trained in the Japanese tradition of Bunraku puppetry. In this genre of puppetry, three puppeteers work together to manipulate puppets with their hands, with one operating the right hand and head, a second operating the left hand, and a third operating the feet and legs. Clad in black, the puppeteers are in full view, and their artful manipulations and interactions with the puppet are very much part of the performance. Quade's work is not strictly Bunraku, but she takes from it the technique of bringing puppets to life through hands-on manipulation by one or more puppeteers. In her creations, puppeteers are co-performers and often characters in their own right.

For *Okay, I'm AI-x*, we worked with two large robotic arms instead of puppeteers manipulating a giant puppet. While developing this installation, we faced numerous challenges, including coordinating the collaboration of two independent robotic arms to manipulate the same object (the puppet). Although we learned a great deal and succeeded in making the robots control the puppet to perform a sequence of movements, we also found that the robotic arms did not manage to bring the puppet to life satisfactorily and were unsuccessful in achieving a sense of ensoulment. Much to our surprise, we discovered that what actually came to life in the process were the robotic arms themselves rather than the puppet puppeteered by them. More than the puppet, designed to resemble a future human being and carefully manipulated by the two robotic arms to perform human-like movements, the robotic arms seemed to come to life as they controlled the puppet.

Upon closer examination, we realized that this was partly due to the possibility of reading the movements of the robotic arms, as informed by the motivation to manipulate the puppet and thus as informed by the intention of some 'soul' or agency behind the movements. These practical movements of manipulating an actual object produced a much stronger sense of being motivated by a driving force behind it than the puppet's movements, which were readable as waving, looking around, and dancing. We also noticed that this effect was strongly reinforced by more visceral and affective qualities of the movements. That is, the sense of ensoulment was not merely a matter of the possibility of understanding how the movements of the robots were aimed at making the puppet move, but also of a more visceral and affective appeal in the force of these movements and how they follow from the robot's morphology. We also noticed that our capacity to relate to the material aspects of the movements and their relationship to gravity, weight, momentum, and the sound produced by the robot's movements was important to grasping this force. We found that we could strengthen this effect by exaggerating the movements from this perspective, making them larger and more articulated than necessary, and adjusting speed and acceleration, thus increasing the sound and enhancing the sense of weight and momentum.

5 Further Explorations: Movement, Weight, Gravity, Momentum, and the Physicality of Sound

In our subsequent investigations, we further explored how we could use these material aspects of robot behavior to achieve ensoulment. This resulted in several lines of experimentation, two of which will be introduced here.

In the first line of investigation, we utilized a small robotic arm mounted on a wheeled platform. This platform was not automated and could not be controlled. It was just a metal plate with casters underneath. Together with puppeteer Suze van Miltenburg, we investigated how the robotic arm placed on this platform could push itself away from the wall or a person and move itself through space by pushing off against the floor. These movements, we found, produced a strong sense of the behavior being driven by some agency or personality. Similarly to the big robotic arms in the installation (described above) we observed that this was not merely a matter of the possibility of understanding how the movements of the robot were aimed towards making itself move through space, but also of a more visceral and affective appeal of the force of these movements and how they follow from the morphology of the robot. We hypothesize that these indirect movements, caused by the robot's actions, present a stronger affective appeal because they are more directly relatable in terms of effort, weight, and gravity than the robot's direct movements, which usually do not show traces of effort or the effects of gravity. The secondary or indirect movements (the movement of the platform as a result of the robotic arm pushing itself away) were much more directly perceptible as subject to the same forces of gravity and resistance that we experience in our own embodied interactions.

This suggestion was confirmed by a further exploration in which we made the robotic arm swing from side to side. The momentum thus created made the platform on wheels roll sideways. Again, this secondary movement allowed the arm's swinging to be understood as a means to something else (namely, to move the platform), and this secondary movement intensified the movement's affective impact. This affective intensity was absent when we made the robotic arm perform similar swinging movements while mounted on a fixed base. Although the arm performed identical movements, this setup did not allow the movement's force to become perceptible and lacked the affective intensity.

The second line of investigation (related to the physicality of sound) was initiated by artist in residence Stephanie Pan. She is a composer who (in her own words) hears music everywhere. In her compositions, she works with sounds produced by sources usually not considered musical instruments, like coffee machines, traffic lights, and other everyday phenomena [4]. Listening to the robot's behavior, she noticed that the different joints of the robot produce different sounds that vary in pitch depending on the size of the joint and the speed of their movements. After mapping out all the possibilities, she began composing with these sounds, thus turning the robot into a musical instrument or, as she prefers, a singer. She prefers calling it a singer because the sounds emerge from bodily movements, as with a human singer. Unlike a human voice, however, the robot's voice is distributed. The movements of the joints do not contribute to a singular voice but produce different sounds at different places of its body. This became particularly evident when we attempted to amplify the robot's voice.

Pan's compositions evoke a reversal of attention regarding the perception of the relationship between sound and movement. Making us listen to the sounds as part of a composition invited us to conceive of the robot's movements as motivated by the intention to produce these sounds rather than the sounds being the side effects of movements. Her compositions thus evoke a sense of a 'soul' or entity behind the movements, intentionally performing these movements to bring about the'singing.' Here again, the affective force of the very physicality of sound and its relation to movement strengthens this effect and, more than being readable as a sign, seems to affect us more directly on a visceral level.

6 Discussion

Our artist-led explorations of ensoulment demonstrate how this approach opens up new directions for the development of robot behavior, shifting the focus from the representation and imitation of human-like behaviors and expressions imposed on robotic bodies towards the expressive potential of robotic body morphology and the affective qualities of materiality, embodiment, and movement. The following zooms in on some of our methodological, conceptual, and artistic findings.

6.1 Methodological Findings

From the perspective of ensoulment, the starting point for developing robot behavior and HRI is the possibilities for movement and expression as embodied in the robot's morphology and its potential for eliciting affective responses. Methodologically, this involves a shift away from a focus on principles for creating expressions (like the much-referred-to Disney principles for animation, see [2]), and towards strategies for discovering the robot's expressive potential.

Exploring this potential is the first step towards identifying possibilities for evoking a sense of self or agency as the driving force behind actions and expressions. Our explorations demonstrate how the potential of gestures, bodily motion, and sound to evoke affective and somatic responses can enhance this effect. Ensoulment is not a matter of successfully imitating human behavior but an effect brought about by behavior that is readable and relatable to humans. Such readability, furthermore, is not a matter of reading movements in terms of the meaning they represent. Rather, readability here is a matter of an embodied grasping of the logic of these movements as informed by some intention or driving force.

Ensoulment does not depend on being tricked into believing that a puppet or a robot actually has a soul that is the driving force behind its behavior. Useful here is what Jochum and Murphey [5, 414–415], after Bert O. States, describe as "binocular vision." They write: "[i]n the theatre…the spectator can hold in mind two categories – that of the real and that of the imaginary – that are fused into a single phenomenon… Binocular vision is what allows theatre audiences to grant fictive life to characters or objects based on their behaviors and the performance setting, encouraging spectators to project psychology and emotions onto human actors or inanimate objects." This notion of binocular vision helps to understand that granting puppets or objects "a life of their own" does not mean that spectators need to be tricked into believing they actually have one. Binocular vision offers a more complex understanding of spectators' experiences as going back and forth between reality and imagination, thus shifting between different ways of looking at what is presented to them.

In the theatre, the theatrical frame (i.e. the fact that we know it is theatre we are looking at) plays an important role in supporting binocular vision. However, binocular vision is not limited to the theatre. Also outside the theatre, we can see it at work in, for example, the tendency to grant robotic vacuum cleaners, lawnmowers, and other technological objects a life of their own. Here, too, this tendency is enhanced by the possibility of perceiving the behavior of these technological agents as expressive of some 'soul' or character as a driving force behind their actions. An interesting example is an incident involving an AIBO robotic dog, as described by anthropologist Kubo Akinori. "At a meeting in a community centre, an AIBO was moving towards a paper screen in a Japanese-style tatami-floored room. The AIBO stopped in front of the screen, looked around, and then thrust its head through the screen, tearing the paper in the process. The owner immediately came running and disentangled the AIBO from the paper frame to worried expressions and laughter from the other owners. While the AIBO developers would argue that this happened because of a sensor malfunction (e.g. the paper screen was not recognized as an obstacle), the AIBO owner attributed this to the AIBO's mischievous and reckless personality." [6] From the perspective of bringing technological objects to life, we might call this a fortunate incident that demonstrates how deviating from the norm can contribute to the impression that the robotic dog's behavior is expressive of character or identity.

Regarding ensoulment, much can be learned from the expertise of puppeteers. For example, the insight that successfully bringing a puppet to life (bringing about ensoulment) is not a matter of perfectly controlling it, but requires leaving space for accidents, the unintended, and for the material to resist. This is what the practice of listening is about: listening for how the material and its possibilities may guide you, how the unexpected may change your understanding. This also includes failure. The failure to perform as expected can have a strong affective effect that supports a sense of ensoulment. We experienced this with the small robotic arm mounted on the platform when it failed to push itself away due to a lack of strength. Or when swinging the arm too strongly, it threatened to make the robot fall over.

6.2 Conceptual Findings

Conceptually, ensoulment aligns with what Irene Alcubilla Troughton [7, 21–22] describes as a relational view of HRI, distinct from an internalist view. The internalist view "revolves around the encoding and decoding of signs that stand for hidden and predetermined variables that precede and shape behaviour." Relational views, on the other hand, "shift attention to the contextual, embodied, and performative qualities of interactive processes." Alcubilla Troughton also observes that the shift from an internalist to a relational view of interaction transforms our understanding of communication and the concept of meaning, shifting focus from an exchange of information towards a process of relating. Ensoulment similarly shifts focus from readability in terms of information and signs towards grasping the logic of materiality, embodiment, force, gravity, and momentum. This development foregrounds embodiment, not only of robots but also of humans making sense of their behavior and interacting with them. Making sense of the behavior of the robotic arms and the possibility of interpreting it in terms of a driving force behind it is not a matter of decoding signs, but of our capacity to bring to bear our embodied intelligence and experience on a radically different body. The body schema, as theorized by Shaun Gallagher [8] and enactive approaches to cognition of Alva Noë, Alain Berthoz, and others [9, 10], offer useful theoretical frameworks to conceptualize this process further.

Ensoulment, as the bringing about of a sense of a soul or agency behind the behavior of a puppet or robot, resonates with what Jozeph Weizenbaum [11] has termed the Eliza effect, after the chatbot ELIZA. Weizenbaum developed ELIZA as a mechanism to support "natural language conversation" with a computer, and discovered that users began ascribing motivations and emotions to the program. Brian Rotman [12] observes that a succession of media has conjured into being an ongoing series of such ghosts, or disembodied agencies. Ensoulment invites a new materialist reconsideration of such ghosts emerging from the manipulation of matter and entangled with the morphologies of puppets and robotic bodies.

6.3 Artistic Findings

Artistically, our explorations of ensoulment informed further creative developments in the work of Bram Ellens and Ulrike Quade. The small robotic arm featured in Ellen's show *The Girl and the Robot* (2024). This show, based on Tonke Dragt's children's book *Robot van de Rommelmarkt* (*The Robot from the Flea Market*, first published in 1967), portrays a future world where children have robots that assist them with their schoolwork. As the robot of the main character Edu breaks down, she goes to the flea market to buy a second-hand robot. This robot is rather old-fashioned and cannot do much (except for reciting poetry). Edu has to teach the robot everything. Through this process, Edu develops a strong bond with the robot. The robot's behavior and interaction with Edu build on our collaborative explorations of ensoulment, demonstrating how this approach enables a very basic and non-humanoid robot to become a convincing character on stage.

Ulrike Quade is working on a new creation with a big robotic arm. This will be an opera in which the robot features as a character. For this opera, composer Stephanie Pan continues exploring how to make the robotic arm sing. The question of what kind of character will emerge from this performance, and what kind of character this robotic arm can be, is one of the questions that Quade works with in this creation. Ensoulment in relation to the robotic arm is also an important question at a thematic level. The show's title, *Orito*, is the name of a character in the book *The Thousand Autumns of Jacob de Zoet* by David Mitchell [13]. This book is set at the beginning of the nineteenth century in Japan, when Japan was completely closed off from the outside world. Only the Dutch were allowed limited possibilities for trading. To protect Japan from foreign influences, the Dutch were confined to a small artificial island (Deshima) in the harbor of Nagasaki. Orito is a young Japanese woman who, through her father, gains access to this island, particularly to the teaching of a Dutch medical doctor named Marinus. Marinus is well versed in the science of anatomy, as it developed in Europe since the early Renaissance. The show will not tell this story, but it is informed by several motives that seem to come together in Marinus's observation that "The soul is not a noun but a verb." The soul is not a thing but is in the doing. He thus presents an understanding of the soul that is remarkably similar to how ensoulment is understood in puppetry. Movement brings a puppet to life, and from this movement, its soul emerges. Could this be the same for a robot? And what about the human body and the human soul? The practice of anatomy, which Mitchell's book refers to (and relates to Marinus), is a culturally and historically specific mode of understanding of the human body that is entangled with the Western scientific worldview, the Cartesian mind-body distinction, and an understanding of the body as an automated vessel for the mind. The performance will bring together human performers with a Bunraku puppet and a robot to explore relationships and differences between their modes of being.

7 Conclusion

Ensoulment opens new relational approaches to developing robot behavior and HRI that take as their starting point the materiality of robotic bodies and possibilities for behavior embodied in their morphology. Ensoulment presents an alternative to approaches in which robots are made to perform predesigned movements understood as expressions of a preconceived identity and intention. Instead, ensoulment begins by exploring possibilities for movement and expression, and how these can evoke a sense of a soul or agency behind them. This soul or agency is an emergent effect that arises from manipulating matter.

Exploratory approaches like the one proposed here are at odds with the tendency to generalize broadly present in the fields of robotics and HRI. They do not result in universally applicable formats. Yet, from explorations like ours, strategies can be identified to guide the discovery of movement possibilities and their potential for becoming part of HRI. Furthermore, allowing behavior and expressions to emerge from the robot's morphology and materiality makes this approach applicable to many different types of robots, including radically non-human ones. The advantage of such a non-imitative approach is that it supports the emergence of new modes of communication and interaction specific to these robotic bodies, allowing for more inventive HRI and reducing the risk of repeating problematic stereotypes.

Acknowledgments. The research that informs this paper was a collaboration between Ulrike Quade, Bram Ellens, Rick van Dugteren, Stephanie Pan, Suze van Miltenburg, and the author of this paper (Maaike Bleeker). This research took place as part of the project *Acting Like a Robot: Theater as Testbed for the Robot Revolution*, led by Maaike Bleeker and funded by the Netherlands Organization for Scientific Research (NWO CISC.KC.206, https://performingrobots.sites.uu.nl/acting-like-a-robot-theatre-as-testbed-for-the-robot-revolution/), and continues as part of the project *Dramaturgy for Devices: Designing Sustained Relationships with Robots and Other Smart Objects* (led by Maaike Bleeker and funded by the Dutch Research Agenda NWA.1518.22.080, see https://dramaturgy4devices.sites.uu.nl/).

Disclosure of Interests. The author has no competing interests to declare relevant to the content of this article.

References

1. Ribeiro, T., Paiva, A.: Animating the Adelino robot with ERIK: the expressive robotics inverse kinematics. In: Proceedings of the 19th ACM International Conference on Multimodal Interaction (ICMI 2017), pp. 388–396. ACM, New York (2017). https://doi.org/10.1145/3136755.3136791
2. van Breemen, A.J.N.: Animation engine for believable interactive user-interface robots. In: Proceedings of the IEEE/RSJ International Conference on Intelligent Robots and Systems (IROS 2004), vol. 3, pp. 2873–2878 (2004). https://doi.org/10.1109/IROS.2004.1389845
3. Schulz, T., Torresen, J., and Herstad, J.: Animation techniques in human robot interaction user studies: a systematic literature review. ACM Trans. Hum. Robot Interact. **8**(2) (2019). https://doi.org/10.1145/3317325
4. https://youtu.be/cyZGFOjh87k
5. Jochum, E., Murphy, T.: Programming Play. Puppets, robots, and engineering. In: Posner, D.N., et al. (eds.) The Routledge Companion to Puppetry and Material Performance, pp. 414–429. Routledge, London and New York (2014)
6. Quoted in: Gygi, F.R.: Robotic Companions. The Animation of Technology and the Technology of Animation in Japan, pp. 94–111. Routledge, New York and London (2018)
7. Alcubilla-Troughton, I.: Moving Together. A Performing Arts Approach to Relational Human-Robot Interaction Design. Ph.D. Dissertation, Utrecht University (2025)
8. Gallagher, S.: How the Body Shapes the Mind. Clarendon Press (2006)
9. Noë, A.: Action in Perception. MIT Press, Cambridge (2004)
10. Berthoz, A.: The Brain's Sense of Movement. Harvard University Press, Harvard (2002)
11. Weizenbaum, J.: ELIZA–A Computer program for the study of natural language communication between man and machine. Commun. ACM **9**, 36 (1966). https://doi.org/10.1145/365153.365168
12. Rotman, B.: Becoming Besides Ourselves: The Alphabet, Ghosts, and Distributed Human Being. Duke University Press, Durham and London (2008)
13. Mitchel, D.: The Thousand Autumns of Jacob de Zoet. Sceptre, London (2010)

OperaBot: A Performer Led Robot Theater Collaboration

Janani Swaminathan, Denisse Alvarado, and Heather Knight(✉)

Collaborative Robots and Intelligent Systems Institute, Oregon State University,
Corvallis, OR, USA
{swaminaj,alvarden,knighth}@oregonstate.edu

Abstract. As a domain, the theater is great at maximizing the minimal – utilizing simple stage elements, props, music, and lighting to convey complex emotions and relationships. This collaboration resulted in two **live Opera performances** in a 200-person theater that the general public could attend. Along the way, we conducted interviews, videotaped rehearsals, tracked the design documents, wrote memos reflecting on the experience, and video-taped the two final performances. All of these elements act as our dataset from which we extract themes to offer **reusable lessons from theater** into effective everyday robot expression and character in any environment. Strategies prioritized motions and poses that reinforce the character, utilizing costuming and spatial placement and unique technical capabilities that only robots have. The rehearsal process itself may also be useful to roboticists. While previous social robotics researchers (ourselves included) have created their own theater performances around existing robots, two unique aspects of this work are: (1) a three-month collaboration that was performer-led, in that the roboticists integrated into the existing performing arts structures; and (2) the product of the collaboration was a low-cost robot design, whose appearance, motion capabilities, and controls we designed iteratively throughout the rehearsal process. Robot Designer, Co-Performer, and Director quotes also illustrate how theater methods inform expressive robots built cheaply and effectively, where **portability** (on/off stage) and **flexible timing** (via piano or director-cue) are the expectation.

1 Introduction

There is a great appetite for robot performers by human audiences. They are novel and unexpected, and this makes their entertainment impact in a theater performance quite high. What is special about this work, is that we used a 'robot-in-resident' structure to build a robot actor and develop its behaviors, in which roboticists body-stormed, rehearsed, and refined a robot prototype while socially integrating into a performer-led Opera rehearsal structure + production. The past two decades have seen a rise in papers describing theater as a valuable arena for investigating human-robot interaction [7,13,15,18,20,23,26,34,35]. Rationales include the repeatable setting in which research variables can be tested, the

Fig. 1. Final Performance: human plays Don Giovani, OperaBot a statue come to life.

ability to instrument and control the environment, and the many participants in the audience from whom one can collect data from simultaneously.

Robot theater has been used to increase awareness about the benefits of human-robot interaction [18], gathering the audience's opinions and feedback on healthcare robots. Researchers pose performance as a platform to learn and explore the behaviors of social robots [7]. Various productions have also informed the design of robot non-verbal interactions for social robots [2-4,10,20]. Robots in performance create awareness about human-robot interaction among the general audience, and a platform to develop and test the capabilities of the robot. Certainly this is a rising area of computational creativity: stage HRI.

One approach we have used in our robotics research is to invite artist-in-residence's to creatively use existing robots, often integrating artists(theater, dance, animation) during the robot design or assessment process as they have good intuitions, and helpful exploration/critique processes. For example, colleagues have used artists-in-residents to help come up with etiquette behaviors required by companion robots in a home setting [25], and in our lab, artists have acted as advisors or research participants informing existing algorithms for mobile robots [21,24], and choreographing robot motion-based interactions [4,12]. Toward the latter, the resulting dance pieces and rehearsal process identified theater- and dance-inspired strategies, e.g., [12], an analysis of coping with robot failures on stage; [39] an exploration of human-sensing for partner-dancing with robots; [2] illustrating scenes of exclusion/inclusion at a local theatre via group motion of robot-jellyfish toward humans, leading to [3] via choreographic body-storm. We build on these art-in-residence findings, this time reversing the power structure, in that the roboticists are placed within a performance structure to see if they can benefit the development of a Opera scene, including rehearsing and literally embodying the character of the **Commendatore**.

What has happened less often, that this paper seeks to do, is defining robot actions following the performer lead. Done well, this allows roboticists to ethnographically experience and benefit from existing knowledge in this domain [8,9,15]. Thus, we describe a 'robot in residence' at the School of Arts and Communication on a university campus. Constraints from this domain included a fixed rehearsal schedule, location separation between where one rehearses and where one performs, and limited time to prepare for performance compared robots built in typical research settings. True to a theater residency, it was also built on a theater budget. To meet domain expectations, rapid portage on-and-off stage and live control relative to cue timing were designed to be mechanically reliable.

This paper shares various concepts of theater minimizing the design, build, and control requirements of the robot along with some practical aspects that are helpful for roboticists building a robot for performance in the future. We found that both roboticists and theater experts sought to minimize design+setup while maximizing the performance impact, but not all of these lessons are currently used by roboticists – things like costuming, stage placement, and flexible timing.

Benefits for those in the arts claimed by our robot co-performers included the opportunity to work with new technology and develop skills like flexibility and adaptability which adds to their experience of what might be possible on stage. In facing machine limitations, they gain extended scope for highlighting their own creativity. The audience was not informed ahead of time that there was a robot, and certainly perked up and got curious. Much more can be done!

2 Related Work

Theater has survived many centuries by adapting to technologies of the day. The public experienced hydraulic power for the first time on a Parisian stage in the 1860s; many more would experience incandescent electric lamps through their use as theatrical technology in the 1880s [5]. Theatre's integration of technology contributes to the magic of the storytelling. In Shakespearean time, actors shocked audiences by disappearing suddenly from the stage. A little trick borrowed from ship technology, the trap door bolstered dramatic staging in theatres [30]. Relevant background includes technology on stage and in assemblies, as well as existing robot theater performances, like flying robots acting as fairies [27].

2.1 Theatre and Robotics

Theater offers an application space for new robot developments (the former spelling is favored in America, while 'theatre' is favored in Britain, we use both).

Social robotics has been integrated into various forms of performing arts: algorithmic music in human-robot music performance [16,41], toward algorithmic theater scripts for human and robot actors [42], and in mapping human-human expressive models to robot-human ones [14,20]. Researchers have also varied the content of robot comedy based on audience reaction [19,23,36], and sought to generate puns and simple word-plays computationally [33]. We hope to contribute to this rising domain via a kind of self-ethnography [40], placing ourselves amidst of a traditional theatre production, and treating the robot as the actor that was cast in the play. Retrospectives sometimes relate robot integration into theater's history of 'camp' productions [31] (Fig. 2).

Fig. 2. 2011 production photos from *HEDDATRON*, written by Elizabeth Meriwether, directed by Jonathan L. Green at Sideshow Theatre Company, Chicago, Illinois. Photographer: Peter Coombs.

One of the most critically successful instances of real robots on stage is Elizabeth Meriweather's play *Heddatron*, which was also the first production to feature robots performing themselves on stage [1]. The incorporation of several robot actors proved complex, time-consuming, and expensive, however, audiences swarmed to the performances and *Heddatron* continues to be produced across North America. A modern adaption of Henrik Ibsen's century old *Hedda Gabler*, *Heddatron* updates the century-old script tackling a desperate housewife in a patriarchal society. In the modern adaptation, "a pregnant housewife is abducted by robots and taken to the rain forest and forced to perform Hedda Gabler by her robot captors" [32]. Through a delicious combination of clever humor and the careful incorporation of technology, playwright Meriweather utilized robots to re-imagine a classic script into a modern conversation-starter.

Conceived by roboticist Hiroshi Ishiguro in collaboration with contemporary theatre artist Oriza Hirata, Japan's *"Robot Theater Project"* featured a pair of productions that place robots in everyday, mundane situations. For example, their production *Sayonara* featured an android, Geminoid F, calmly reading poems to a dying girl, played by a human actress. A companion piece, *I, Worker* featured two robots caring for a couple in an apartment, one of which loses the desire to work. Both productions provide a relatable and naturalistic preview of what the future and expose audiences to robot creations in a way that is usually reserved for final products, but not early research. Putting robots on stage provides a way for many people to experience robots "in person" (Fig. 3).

Fig. 3. Production photos from Christian Denisart's production of *Robots*

2.2 Theatre and Technology

Historically, theatre has acted as an early adopter of advancing technologies to best communicate story, cultivate atmosphere, and stun audiences with visual and experiential spectacle. From holographic projections to shifting stages, technology supplies theatre artists with an expansive tool kit. As theatre academic Steve Dixon puts it, "The use of robots in performance constitutes one of the most technologically advanced developments within digital performance" [11]. We are beginning to see robot technology interwoven into the theatrical experience. This section explores real robots as props and stages, as principle characters, and also highlights the role of theatre in previewing the technology of the time to a broad range of people.

Modern technology is often hard to point to; the internet doesn't reside in an explicit location, notifications appear then disappear; and cloud computing means even our documents exist far from our physical laptops. Robots can serve as embodied versions of these diverse technologies. One example is *Soapbox*, a 2013 production from Western Washington University. One of its stories featured a dynamic love-triangle between a woman, a man, and his phone. To embody this technology on stage, an actress was cast as "robotic Siri," complete with a black-metallic bodysuit, fluorescent wig, and drone-like vocal quality. When the woman confronts her boyfriend, Steve, about his obsessive phone use, Siri, a seductive robot-woman, conquers his undivided attention with app updates,

Youtube videos, and a catalog of enticing robot-dance moves. This production made a robot personification of Siri to explore relationships with technology. Recent works explicitly consider Opera as a rich domain for developing embodied AI [17].

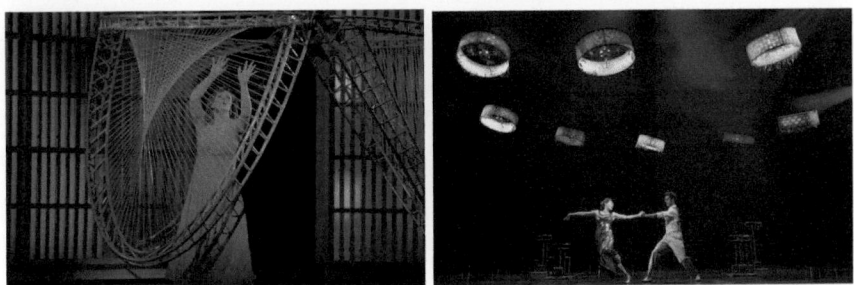

Fig. 4. (left) - Evvy (Emily Albrink) reconnects with Simon Powers as the Chandelier in *Death and the Powers*. (Photo by Jonathan Williams). Ruby Lewis and Ryan Vona in *Paramour* from Cirque du Soleil, on Broadway. They are surrounded by drones designed by Verity Studios. (Photo by Richard Termine)

This usage of new technologies to transform the stage into an alternate version of modern reality has a long history; the penultimate moment in Ancient Greek tragedies often ended with a Deity ascending from the heavens on a *Deus Ex Machina*, meaning 'god out of a machine.' In reality, these were mechanical cranes that could lift and lower the actor-deity to shock and awe their audiences. In this case, the audience was meant to have an experience of the Godly, with *Deus Ex Machina* devices literally raising actors into the air as angels.

Fig. 5. The overall production involved 12 Mozart scenes and many performers. The robot was featured in a single scene. This photo features the cast and contributors.

2.3 Transformative Stages and Robotic Furniture

While robots playing characters *on stage* may be the first thing one imagines from robot theatre, robots *as stages* play just as pivotal a role. As with the flying lamps by Verity Studios (Fig. 4), robots can expand our typical definitions of theatrical spaces, reconfiguring the floors and ceiling across which the actors perform, and act as props to support setting, or transport the actors themselves. In *Death and the Powers*, three large periaktoi, resembling bookshelves, physically move and transform. Additionally, a Chandelier set piece, descends, illuminates, and transforms mid-way through the performance. Such robotic props and staging supports this prior work Opera's futuristic settings, developed by MIT at last with support from the Prince of Monaco, in which the world is composed with machines, and books are the last vestiges of earlier humanity. The stage becomes, in and of itself, a main character in this theatrical production. As described by its team of creators, *Death and the Powers*' incorporation of robotic set elements and props was not meant as mere spectacle, but rather to "reassert the audience's connection to the live performers in the physical world" [38].

3 OperaBot Production Details

Working with the existing human cast (Fig. 5), OperaBot played in a single scene, integrating into a longer showday and interdisciplinary team (Fig. 6).

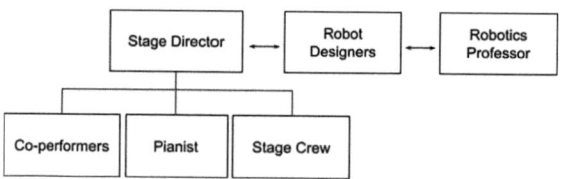

Fig. 6. Interaction diagram of the people involved in the robot's scene from the performing arts team and robotics.

Scene Overview: The scene with the robot involved two human performers playing the roles of Don Giovanni and Leporello and the robot playing the role of Commendatore. This scene lasted for eight minutes. In the scene, Don Giovanni wanders into a graveyard with his servant, Leporello. Initially, the robot plays the role of a statue built to commemorate the murder of the Commendatore. However, as Don Giovanni jokes about his wife with Leporello, the robot's mouth opens and laughter comes out, signaling that it is alive. Leporello turns around, notices the statue turning and bowing and is frightened. In fear, Leporello tries to convince Don Giovanni that the statue is alive, but Giovanni refuses to believe that it is. Jokingly, Giovanni orders Leporello to invite the statue for dinner and they both leave the graveyard.

People Involved: Figure 6 displays the various people involved in the collaboration. As the figure emphasizes, most of the people came from the performing arts side, acting as the primary data source for what was most needed to embody the role the robot was playing. The robot designers included three students who were responsible for building the robot and its control, and the robotics professor ('Professor') who advised the development of the robot from a social robotics perspective. The Stage Director ('Director') was the head of the performance team. He also played the role of the robot operator, controlling the robot during the performance. The co-performers consisted of the two human performers in the scene with the robot, who also rehearsed with the robot leading into the production.

Show Details: The OSU Lyric Opera Ensemble performed a show titled Mozartisty: Mozart Opera Scenes on the 25th and 26th November 2019, at the Ashbrook Independent School, Corvallis. The show was a set of twelve scenes from different plays by Mozart and involved a performer cast as shown in Fig. 5. The robot was a part of a scene from Mozart's Don Giovanni, titled O Statua Gentillissima. The robot played the role of Stone Guest, referred to as the Commendatore, a graveside statue of one of Don Giovanni's victims who comes to life to enact vengeance for Giovanni's crimes as shown in Fig. 1. The entire production was about an hour and a half in length.

4 Methodology

This section summarizes our multi-channel data collection process during the concept, rehearsal, and performance stages, and our qualitative data analysis methods. The duration of the collaboration was three months. These three months are split into four stages: Conceptualization, Rehearsals, Performance, Reflection as shown in Fig. 7. Every step of the collaboration involved building and refining the robot design and control, and noting observations and updates.

Conceptualization: This stage lasted about a month, from initial discussions until the rehearsals began. In the first part of this stage, the Professor and the director met to finalize the role of the robot and determine the basic requirements including the structure and the movements of the robot. After the first meeting, the Professor and Director had no more direct meetings. In the second part, the Professor and the robot designers met to come up with an initial design of the robot. In the third part, the robot designers met with the director multiple times to confirm the design requirements of the robot and observe the rehearsals of the scene in which the robot would be a part of. During the meetings, memos, notes, and sketches were collected as initial design documents.

Rehearsals: The robot designers took the robot to the rehearsals and the performers got opportunities to interact and practice with the robot. There were five rehearsals in the rehearsal stage that happened in four weeks. During each rehearsal, the robot designers would take the robot to the rehearsal room, as shown in Fig. 8, and set it up. The director who is the operator of the robot is given a run-through on what the current capabilities of the robot are and

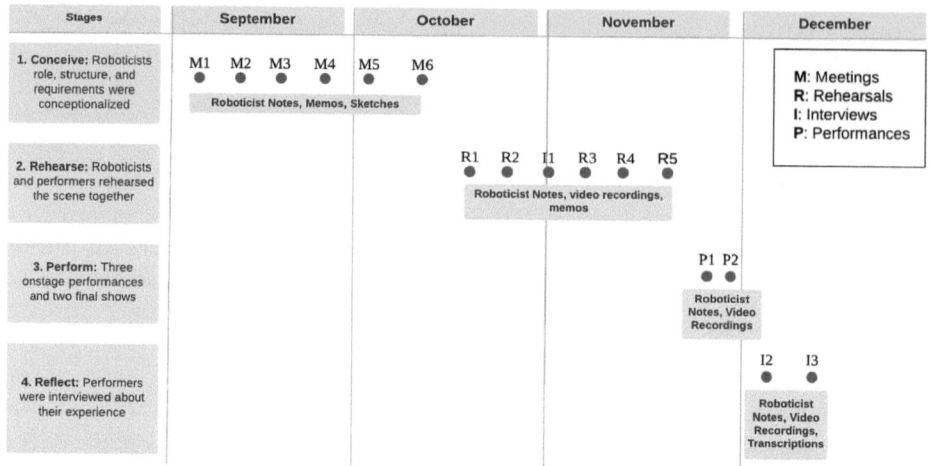

Fig. 7. The four stages of collaboration are conceive, rehearse, perform, and reflect. These stages included meetings, rehearsals, performances, and interviews. Different data were collected in each, all of which were converted to text before analysis.

how to control them. He then operates the robot and the co-performers practice the scene with the robot. At the end of every rehearsal, the robot designer and the director discuss the capabilities and limitations of the current design of the robot and determine what changes are required. Two robot designers, the first two authors of the paper, made fly-on-the-wall observations about the rehearsal and interaction between the robot, operator, pianist, and the co-performers.

Performance: This stage includes the few on-site rehearsals and the two final performances. The on-site rehearsals include tech-rehearsals, queue to queue rehearsals, and the dress rehearsals. During the tech rehearsal, the robot's position, lighting, and timing were finalized. In the queue to queue rehearsal, bringing in the robot before the scene and taking it out after the scene was finalized. The dress rehearsal was a full run-through of the show along with the robot. In each of these rehearsals, the robot designers are responsible for moving the robot on to the stage and making sure the robot is ready to use. The director would then operate the robot while a singer sings for the robot. During the rehearsals, the two robot designers made fly-on-the-wall observations and the two final performances were video recorded.

Reflection: Finally, after the event includes a set of three interviews. The first interview was with the director/operator. The interview with the director was conducted midway of the collaboration about the various aspects of this collaboration and the design of the robot along with the reasons behind the design decisions that the performers and the robot designers made together during the collaboration. The next two interviews were with the co-performers who were a part of the scene with the robot in the show. The interviewers with the co-

Fig. 8. The rehearsal space where the co-performers practiced the scene with the robot while the robot designers made observational notes.

performers were done after the completion of both the final performances. All these interviews were video recorded (Fig. 9).

Data Summary: The observation notes of the robot designers during the rehearsals were later combined with additional notes that the robot designers wrote after every rehearsal, reflecting on the videos recorded during the rehearsals. These video recordings aided the robot designers in reflecting on what happened during the rehearsals. During the on-site rehearsals, the robot designers made notes after the rehearsals. Thus, all the data collected in the conceptualization, rehearsals, and performance stage was compiled together into notes. These textual notes were then used to design the interviews with the director/operator and the co-performers in the reflection stage. Thus, two major data sources that the robot designers used to analyze finally include the notes and the transcripts of the interviews.

Theory Building: We conducted a combination of ethnographic theory building [29] and qualitative data analysis across all the data channels to pull out concepts that may be of aid in constructing future human-robot performances on stage. The data was processed for deductive coding using QSR International's NVivo qualitative data analysis software. The first step was identifying themes. The notes were also organized according to the different stages of collaboration as mentioned above. The first and second authors individually analyzed all the notes and interviews, later meeting together to identify and discuss interest-

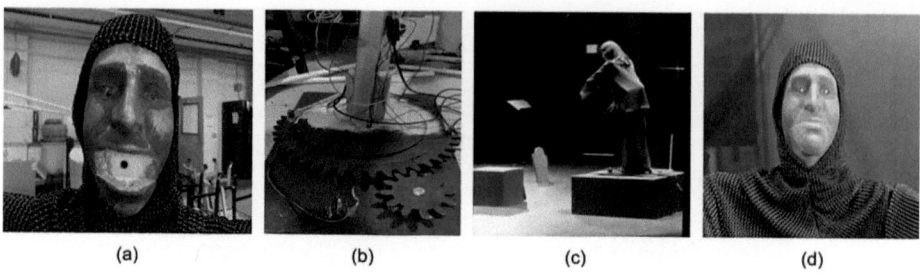

Fig. 9. The four expressive degrees of freedom of the robot, three of which were determined by the character of the robot and the LED eyes were suggested as a unique robot capability to enhance performance. (a): Mouth open and close, (b): base rotation, (c): bowing up and down, (d): LED eyes on and off.

ing themes in the process. These themes were further refined after discussion between the entire team (all three authors). The non-significant themes were then removed and significant themes linked together. A comparable use of this method is described in [36]. Another set of themes labeled were iterative design changes in the robot during the period of the collaboration. The main reasons for these design changes were found to be time and budget constraints, but also the performance team's expressive goals. In other words, theatre concepts were being used to make simplify the design requirements leading to design changes. We present these resulting simplification strategies in the next section.

5 Minimize Requirements // Maximize Expression

The highlevel themes extracted from our overall dataset include: character, staging, costuming, co-performers, unique robot capabilities. These were extracted from the rehearsal/performance notes and interviews. Theatrical goals emphasized simplifying design requirements while maximizing expressive impact.

Lesson I: Character Can Suggest/Simplify Specifications

In total, four major design actions emerged for the robot: jaw movement, bow, turning, and eyes. The movement of the jaw helped mimic singing opera. The bow was required as the robot played the role of a knight. The turning capability of the robot that was required to add humor to the scene by having a statue's gaze follow the co-performer. Though the bow was not prioritized by the performers initially, it was later seen to be an integral part of the performance. The last requirement of LED eyes was added later on during the rehearsal stage. Thus, the number of degrees of freedom required by the robot was determined by the role played, and expanded and refined through the rehearsal process.

Secondly, style of movement mattered as the robot played the role of a stone statue who comes back alive in the performance. As a statue, we were informed that it would be required to have "stiff movements" that are "sharp." This is the natural movement of a robot whereas it is rather forced in a human. In the reflection phase, when asked about why a robot was chosen to play this role rather than a human, the director explained, "(The direction) I would have given for the actor or the singer playing the role of the Commendatore would' have been to be more robotic or angular with your movements."

Thirdly, personality/character emerged as a specific design affordance. In this scene, the robot was to play a dead Knight who comes back for vengeance. The personality of this character by nature is strong, powerful, and minimal which reduces the design requirements of the robot. For example, the director found lower levels of motion to be more menacing, mapping somewhat to prior work using Laban features [20, 22]. As the director explained, "Less is more. If you're going for a strong, scary character, the less movement the better."

Lesson II: Set Design for Spatial Expression and Control

The stage setup and show requirements are determined by the cast and can, therefore, be used as a way to minimize the design requirements of the robot. For example, they put the robot in one side of the stage so it would orient straight on to one side, rather than back and force. The staging was blocked in the first two rehearsals after most of the choreography was complete (Fig. 10).

During the reflection stage, the director said, "(I thought) the swivel would just be head and neck. It would not be full-body, just the head looking down or something like that....But it worked out because of the way you guys built it. He's already kinda looking down and so when we have him up on the pedestal, it's gonna be ideal because he will still tower over the guys." Positioning the robot at a height and building him to be slightly bent simplified the goal.

A third advantage of the set-design was seen when the performers decided to use a mic-reverb for the robot just to make the robot sound more menacing and powerful. The performers had never considered this to be a need in a robot, but it was an easy edit to change the audio only without adjusting an environment.

Lesson III: Unique Robot Capabilities Support Expression

During the first rehearsal, the robot designers and the performers were discussing on how having the eyes of the robot light up would increase the capability to express the statue coming alive. The performers were happy to use the lights as an additional source of expressivity which would not have been possible with a human actor as mentioned by the director during the reflection stage, "I mean, I wouldn't have tried to make my actor's eyes light up for example, right? So, that's something we added because of the robot. At the end of the opera, this character comes back and drags Don Giovanni back to hell, right? So, it's a big moment and this is his introduction to the character in this form. So, I thought it would be cool to have his eyes light up."

Thus, Robots can have some unique capabilities that a human cannot. Performers are not necessary aware of these unique capabilities of robots, nor which are easy to implement. When the roboticists provided it as a suggestion, however, the performers easily used it to increase the expressivity of the robot in

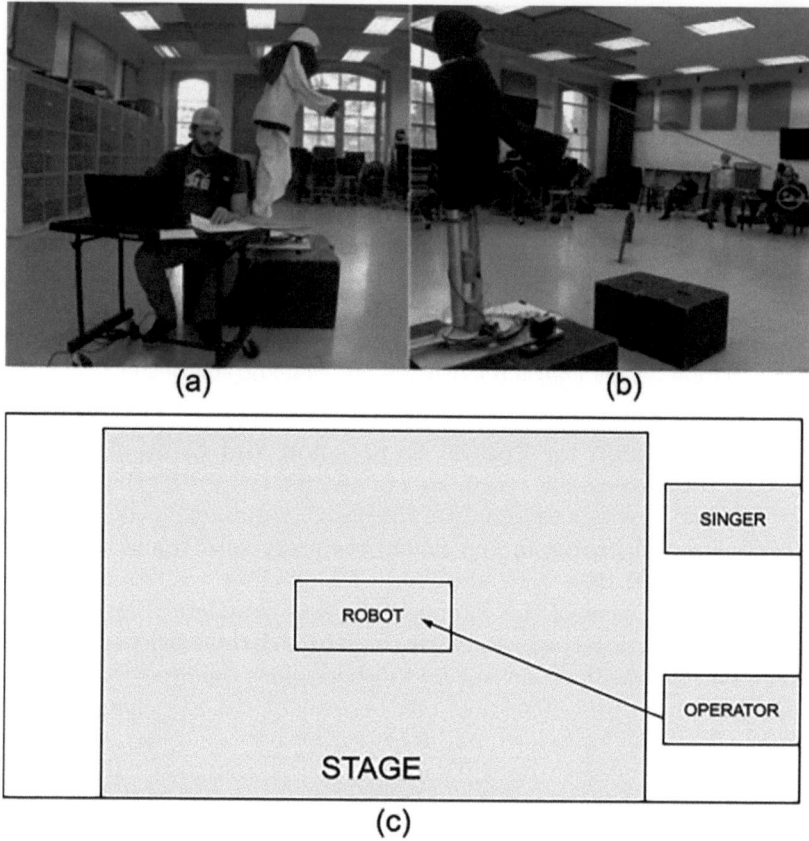

Fig. 10. The control of the robot was iteratively changed for the comfort of the operator: (a) Initial control through laptop, (b) Robot controlled using playstation controller, (c) Iterated into this Operator control and Singer setup for the final performance.

the performance. In this collaboration, this additional medium of expression was added in the rehearsal stage, it might be useful to discuss them during the conceptualization stage in the future collaborations.

Lesson IV: Costuming Reduces Mechanical Complexity

Once the initial prototype of the robot was ready, the robot designers wondered to us about how to make the hands of the robot look human-like. We fully handed off costuming to the performance experts, who were now somewhat familiar with our constructed hardware (available Week 3). They tried using foam surrounded with wires to make the hands and fingers but the design did not have enough support and was not capable of holding its weight. When discussing this with performers, they suggested using stuffed gloves that can help the robot look like having real palms, as shown in Fig. 11.

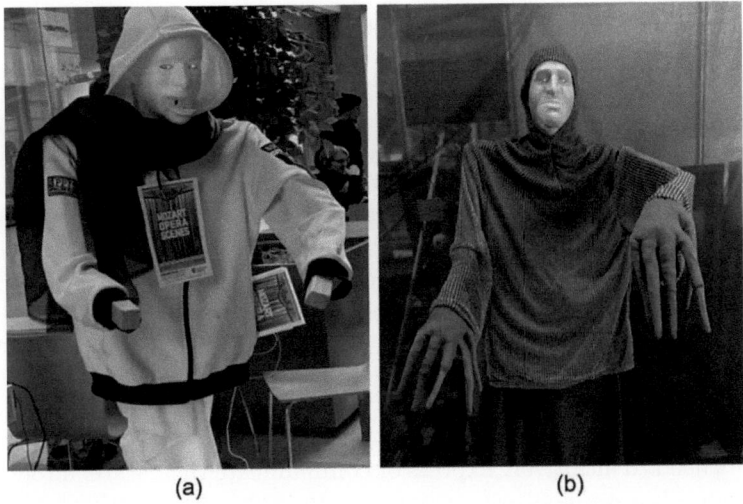

Fig. 11. Robot costuming has a large impact on perception of robot character: (a) During rehearsals and public advertisement (b) During the final performance.

Another use of costuming was seen when all the electronics and the actuators of the robot were visible even after painting the robot. A skirt was then used to cover all the circuitry of the robot simplifying the need for building a structure to cover the electronics of the robot. The black skirt also added to the appearance of a knight. Thus, the time spent on designing the physical appearance of the robot was minimized by the use of costumes which also helped in adding to the expressivity of the robot and in defining its character.

In addition to movements, creativity with fabric is used commonly in performances to increase the expressivity of the character. Costumes can add to the personality of a character. Initially, the robot designers did not consider costuming while designing the robot. Therefore, this simplification occurred in the later phases of the rehearsal stage. For robot designers building a robot for performance in the future, we suggest considering costuming during the conceptualization stage itself, once the role played by the robot is finalized. Taking costuming into consideration can help in reducing the physical complexity.

Lighting is another source for increasing the expressive impact of the robot performing with minimal effort. Do those varying hues count as costume? If so, previous work has used projector-based illuminations to increase the expressivity of physical avatars [6]. A similar approach was used in this robot performance.

6 Discussion of OperaBot-in-Residency

The Stratford Shakespeare Festival Artistic Director in Ontario, CA, believes the inclusion of new media is essential to keeping theatre relevant. "It was no different in Shakespeare's day when they used trap doors and visual effects to create a powerful visceral experience for the audience. So I think this is completely traditional what we are doing" [37]. Performer-led collaborations offer an opportunity for robots to learn from long histories of entertainment.

Utilizing a collaborative iterative design process led to the development of robot hardware, actions, movement style, and control mechanisms that leveraged the skills and expertise of both the performer and roboticist teams. Character was used to help define robot degrees and freedom, further reinforced by set design and costume. By the end of the rehearsal process, we also began to utilize the unique expressive capabilities of technological performers from LED eyes to a verby sound effects on their voices. The creativity of the performers and the practicalities of the robot designers complement each other and eventually simplified the requirements of the robot to maximize expression.

The design simplification offered by using theatre concepts may maximize the expression of effective social robots based on an understanding of 'who' they are. Robots need to intuitively express or communicate their state, intent, action, and behavior – but perhaps also personality and role – for effective human-robot interactions. In fact, these methodologies have since been reused by the lead author toward behavioral designs of the commercial Moxie robot. We learned tips and tricks to enable robot portability and reliability, and developed strategies to flexibly incorporate untrained people into the OperaBot's cueing and control.

Theatre works to convey aspects of a character, interaction, and spatial relationships via a story told to diverse audiences. Performer-led collaborations that integrate robots into theatre may provide design solutions for socially expressive robots, but moreover offer an opportunity for us to use our own senses and experiences to rehearse and improve.

Within this perspective, robotic technology will discover and open new windows of storytelling. Further work should further consider the impact of these varied designs as perceived by the audience, as in past cited works. One might even imagine a traveling show that evolved from the start of its tour to the end. Having new technology on stage requires new technology experts backstage, but this is not necessarily a hindrance. Perhaps we will find similar patterns as we collectively develop theater-based AI, the early signs are positive [17]. This paper presents artistic practice in process, instantiating a world of artist-requested robot design features, characters, stage placement, movement, and costuming.

7 Conclusion

The process-inspired ethnographic integration of our robot and roboticist-team into a School of Arts and Communication production focuses on practice rather than HRI theory (i.e., Social Presence and Engagement, Anthropomorphism and Character Design), but one finds that different tools sometimes lead to similar conclusions. Both rehearsal process and delight from the audience reception led to a useful novelty effect that the director said reinforced the robot's casted character: a gravestone statue come to life, when its occupant's killer doth pass.

So what is 'the practice' we observed, in this theater-embedded codesign process? The structured rehearsals of a typical theater production with weekly development periods left plenty of time to make improvements along the way, each week offering explicit experiential insights and ideation/requests from the team. Practical portability for transport between lab, rehearsal room and performance also informed design iterations. Final designs were honed, tried out, and refined again to best present the **Commendatore**'s come-to-life stone agency.

Performance days required reliability and flexibility, which ultimately became the director singing the voice while puppeteering the robot, much like human-in-loop food delivery [28], but this time offering the joy of operator song.

Design requirements were changed to accommodate portability, as noted by the robot designer: "Post discussion, the mechanism for the base was changed to a gear system. This was done to accommodate the fact that the robot will be off stage and needs to be brought in quickly and taken out after the scene." Challenges when the robot is being moved from off-stage to on-stage before the scene include chances of wires losing contact, gears moving out of places, and other possible misplaces. Performers are not accustomed to the various ways robot can fail, thus specific protocols were developed for (1) testing the robot after setup on stage, and, (2) signaling to the robot designer if things are not working as they should. The need for backup plans is also emphasized in [12].

Theater also offers HRI Theory new ways to think about timing. When the roboticists suggested that a recorded track be used for the robot, the director advised against: "with live musicians your tempo is always going to change... So, that's why for the voice of the robot, I'm going to be doing it myself." He told us the timing of the movements of the robot was an integral part of the scene, indicating that canned or pre-timed sequences do not work well in typical stage performances. We learned timing information is typically given by the pianist, so perhaps future work can explore automation via *music-to-robot* cues.[1]

Acknowledgments. Thanks to director Anthony Eversole for taking a chance by casting this unusual performer, the many humans on stage with the robot, and to Jeremy Urann who contributed to the literature search as theater artist.

References

1. Adiseshiah, S., Lepage, L.: Twenty-First Century Drama What Happens Now, 1st edn. Macmillan, London (2016)
2. Bacula, A., Kayhani, K., McCloskey, J., Reason, D., Knight, H.: Dance prototyping: communicating group membership and relational attitudes via multi-robot expressive motion. In: International Conference of Robots and Systems, RSS 2020 (2020)
3. Bacula, A., Knight, H.: MoTiS parameters for expressive multi-robot systems: relative motion, timing, and spacing. Int. J. Soc. Robot. **14**(9), 1965–1993 (2022)
4. Bacula, A., Knight, H.: Dancing with robots at a science museum: coherent motions got more people to dance, incoherent sends weaker signal. In: Proceedings of the 2024 International Symposium on Technological Advances in Human-Robot Interaction, pp. 83–91 (2024)

---

[1] https://www.anthonyeversole.com/; https://www.jeremyurann.com/.

5. Baugh, C.: Theatre, Performance and Technology: The Development of Scenography in the Twentieth Century, 1st edn. Macmillan, Palgrave, New York (2005)
6. Bermano, A., Brüschweiler, P., Grundhöfer, A., Iwai, D., Bickel, B., Gross, M.: Augmenting physical avatars using projector-based illumination. ACM Trans. Graph. (TOG) **32**(6), 1–10 (2013)
7. Breazeal, C., et al.: Interactive robot theatre. In: Proceedings 2003 IEEE/RSJ International Conference on Intelligent Robots and Systems, IROS 2003 (Cat. No. 03CH37453), vol. 4, pp. 3648–3655. IEEE (2003)
8. Chun, B.: Doing autoethnography of social robots: ethnographic reflexivity in HRI. Paladyn, J. Behav. Robot. **10**(1), 228–236 (2019)
9. Chun, B., Knight, H.: The robot makers: an ethnography of anthropomorphism at a robotics company. ACM Trans. Hum. Robot Interact. (THRI) **9**(3), 1–36 (2020)
10. Cuan, C., Berl, E., LaViers, A.: Measuring human perceptions of expressivity in natural and artificial systems through the live performance piece time to compile. Paladyn J. Behav. Robot. **10**(1), 364–379 (2019)
11. Dixon, S.: Digital Performance: A History of New Media in Theater, Dance, Performance Art, and Installation, 1st edn. MIT Press, Cambridge, Mass (2007)
12. Fallatah, A., Urann, J., Knight, H.: The robot show must go on: effective responses to robot failures (2019)
13. Fallatah, A., Urann, J., Knight, H.: The robot show must go on: effective responses to robot failures. In: IROS, pp. 325–332 (2019)
14. Greer, J.: Promoting theatre methodology for expressive robot movement and behavior. In: 2019 IEEE International Conference on Humanized Computing and Communication (HCC), pp. 114–117. IEEE (2019)
15. Herath, D.C., Jochum, E., Vlachos, E.: An experimental study of embodied interaction and human perception of social presence for interactive robots in public settings. IEEE Trans. Cogn. Dev. Syst. **10**(4), 1096–1105 (2017)
16. Hoffman, G., Weinberg, G.: Shimon: an interactive improvisational robotic marimba player. In: CHI'10 Extended Abstracts on Human Factors in Computing Systems, pp. 3097–3102 (2010)
17. Jochum, E., Hopkins, T., Kiefer, C., Ficarra, E.: Towards embodied AI: design approaches for robots in opera. In: Cultural Technologies, pp. 113–128. Routledge (2025)
18. Jochum, E., Vlachos, E., Christoffersen, A., Nielsen, S.G., Hameed, I.A., Tan, Z.H.: Using theatre to study interaction with care robots. Int. J. Soc. Robot. **8**(4), 457–470 (2016)
19. Katevas, K., Healey, P.G., Harris, M.T.: Robot comedy lab: experimenting with the social dynamics of live performance. Front. Psychol. **6**, 1253 (2015)
20. Knight, H.: Eight lessons learned about non-verbal interactions through robot theater. In: International Conference on Social Robotics, pp. 42–51. Springer (2011)
21. Knight, H., Flynn, D., Oo, T.M., Hansen, J.: Iterative robot waiter algorithm design: service expectations and social factors. In: International Conference on Human-Robot Interaction, HRI 2024, pp. 394–402 (2024)
22. Knight, H., Lee, T., Hallawell, B., Ju, W.: I get it already! the influence of ChairBot motion gestures on bystander response. In: International Conference on Robot and Human Communication (Ro-Man '17) (2017)
23. Knight, H., Satkin, S., Ramakrishna, V., Divvala, S.: A savvy robot standup comic: online learning through audience tracking. In: Workshop Paper (TEI'10) (2011)
24. Knight, H., Simmons, R.: An intelligent design interface for dancers to teach robots. In: 2017 26th IEEE International Symposium on Robot and Human Interactive Communication (RO-MAN), pp. 1344–1350. IEEE (2017)

25. Koay, K.L., et al.: Exploring robot etiquette: refining a HRI home companion scenario based on feedback from two artists who lived with robots in the UH robot house. In: International Conference on Social Robotics, pp. 290–300. Springer (2013)
26. Lu, D.V., Smart, W.D.: Human-robot interactions as theatre. In: 2011 Ro-Man, pp. 473–478. IEEE (2011)
27. Murphy, R., et al.: A midsummer night's dream (with flying robots). Auton. Robot. **30**(2), 143–156 (2011)
28. Pelikan, H.R., Bu, F., Ju, W.: The people behind the robots: How wizards wrangle robots in public deployments. In: Proceedings of the 2025 CHI Conference on Human Factors in Computing Systems, pp. 1–21 (2025)
29. Phelps, A.F., Horman, M.J.: Ethnographic theory-building research in construction. J. Constr. Eng. Manag. **136**(1), 58–65 (2010)
30. Power, A.J.: What the hell is under the stage - trapdoor use in the English Senecan tradition. English **60**(231), 276–296 (2011)
31. Remmen, C.: A history of robot camp: performing beyond the uncanny valley, from early twentieth-century automata to contemporary science fiction theatre. Stud. Theatr. Perform. **43**(2), 222–239 (2023)
32. Sideshow Theatre: Heddatron. http://sideshowtheatre.org/heddatron.html
33. Sjöbergh, J., Araki, K.: A complete and modestly funny system for generating and performing Japanese stand-up comedy. In: Coling 2008: Companion volume: Posters, pp. 111–114 (2008)
34. Smart, W.D., Matheus, K., Fraune, M.R.: Applying bodystorming to human-robot interaction design. In: International Conference on Social Robotics, pp. 431–445. Springer (2024)
35. Swaminathan, J., Akintoye, J., Fraune, M.R., Knight, H.: Robots that run their own human experiments: exploring relational humor with multi-robot comedy. In: 2021 30th IEEE International Conference on Robot & Human Interactive Communication (RO-MAN), pp. 1262–1268. IEEE (2021)
36. Swaminathan, J., Jain, C., Miller, M., Knight, H.: A semi-automated multi-robot comedy performance system with gesture. In: International Conference on Social Robotics, pp. 261–275. Springer (2024)
37. Thompson, C., Boniface, T.: BEYOND THE CURTAIN How Digital Media is Reshaping Theatre. Technical report, Ontario Media Development Corporation
38. Torpey, P.A.: Digital systems for live multimodal performance in death and the powers. Int. J. Perform. Arts Digit. Media **8**(1) (2012)
39. Urann, J., Fallatah, A., Knight, H.: Dancing with ChairBots. In: 2019 14th ACM/IEEE International Conference on Human-Robot Interaction (HRI), pp. 364–364. IEEE (2019)
40. Vesa, M., Vaara, E.: Strategic Ethnography 2.0: four methods for advancing strategy process and practice research. Strateg. Organ. **12**(4), 288–298 (2014)
41. Weinberg, G., Raman, A., Mallikarjuna, T.: Interactive jamming with Shimon: a social robotic musician. In: Proceedings of the 4th ACM/IEEE International Conference on Human Robot Interaction, pp. 233–234 (2009)
42. Zeglin, G., et al.: Herb's sure thing: a rapid drama system for rehearsing and performing live robot theater. In: 2014 IEEE International Workshop on Advanced Robotics and its Social Impacts, pp. 129–136. IEEE (2014)

Theatre in the Loop: A Rehearsal-Based, Collaborative Workflow for Expressive Robotic Behaviours

Pavlos Panagiotidis[1](✉) , Victor Zhi Heung Ngo[1] , Sean Myatt[2], Roma Patel[3] , Rachel Ramchurn[3] , Alan Chamberlain[1] , and Ayse Kucukyilmaz[1]

[1] School of Computer Science, University of Nottingham, Nottingham, UK
{pavlos.panagiotidis,victor.ngo,alan.chamberlain,
ayse.kucukyilmaz}@nottingham.ac.uk
[2] School of Art and Design, Nottingham Trent University, Nottingham, UK
sean.myatt@ntu.ac.uk
[3] Makers of Imaginary Worlds, Nottingham, UK
{roma,rachel}@makersofimaginaryworlds.co.uk

Abstract. In this paper, we propose *theatre-in-the-loop*, a framework for developing expressive robot behaviours tailored to artistic performance through a director-guided puppeteering workflow. Leveraging theatrical methods, we use narrative objectives to direct a puppeteer in generating improvised robotic gestures that convey specific emotions. These improvisations are captured and curated to build a dataset of reusable movement templates for standalone playback in future autonomous performances. Initial trials demonstrate the feasibility of this approach, illustrating how the workflow enables precise sculpting of robotic gestures into coherent emotional arcs while revealing challenges posed by the robot's mechanical constraints. We argue that this practice-led framework provides a model for interdisciplinary teams creating socially expressive robot behaviours, contributing to (1) theatre as an interactive training ground for human-robot interaction and (2) co-creation methodologies between humans and machines.

Keywords: Robotic Art · Child-Robot Interaction · Human-Robot Performance. Puppeteering · Theatrical Methods

1 Introduction

This paper presents a method developed through the creative process of designing NED II, an evolution of the Never-Ending Dancer (NED), a robotic performer originally created for The Thingamabobas art installation [1]. The original NED (Fig. 1, left), a costumed robot featured in the installation (Fig. 1, right), successfully attracted and engaged child audiences through its playful design and choreographed motion. However, in-the-wild studies with 18 children [2] demonstrated several critical limitations: NED lacked expressive nuance, failed to adapt responsively to user input, and often disengaged audiences through repetitive or contextually ambiguous gestures. For example, children frequently grew confused or frustrated when NED entered its default "sleep" state, or when it failed to mirror playful gestures like dancing or waving. One child notably remarked, *"Why does it keep going to sleep?"*, a reflection of both unmet expectations and a perceived lack of reciprocity. These moments revealed that although NED was compelling as a kinetic sculpture, it struggled to perform with narrative coherence or emotional depth.

Fig. 1. (left) The Never-Ending Dancer (NED) positioned on a theatrical stage, interacting with a performance artist. (right) The interactive art installation Thingamabobas.

These shortcomings highlight broader challenges in designing robots for performative interaction: how can a robot convincingly convey intentionality, sustain engagement through expressive movement, and adapt to live dramaturgical contexts? While many approaches in Human–Robot Interaction (HRI) focus on static behaviour scripting or emotion recognition, they often omit the embodied, improvisational, and context-sensitive practices that define performance-making.

To address this gap, we introduce *theatre-in-the-loop*, a rehearsal-driven method for developing expressive robotic motion grounded in collaborative theatrical practice. This approach integrates directorial framing, real-time puppeteering, and iterative refinement to shape emotionally resonant gestures that are both situated and reusable. The resulting motion library offers a flexible foundation for standalone expressive behaviour in future performance contexts.

2 Related Work: Expressive Robotics and Theatrical Methods

Recent studies have employed data-driven and language-based frameworks to explore the generation of expressive robot behaviour. Panteris et al. [3] proposed a probabilistic model for generating varied wave gestures on a 6-degree-of-freedom (DOF) arm. This model demonstrated the potential of incorporating stochasticity to introduce natural variation to repetitive motions. Zhou et al. [4] investigated the expressive potential of temporal modulation, including variations in speed and deliberate pauses, in conveying internal state transparency. Building upon these concepts, Huang et al. [5] proposed the EMOTION system, which employs large language models (LLMs) to sequence contextually appropriate gestures, thereby integrating verbal cues with non-verbal expression.

In their seminal study, Tang and Dondrup [6] examined the process of tri-modal gesture generation by integrating speech, vision, and semantic information. Building on this research, Schreiter et al. [7] implemented multimodal intention communication on industrial manipulators with the aim of improving human interpretability. Mahadevan et al. [8] further demonstrated that natural-language prompts can be translated into parameterised motion sequences, thereby enabling generative, adaptive behaviours in social contexts.

Although these approaches advance the technical foundations for expressive motion generation, they often lack direct creative input from practitioners with expertise in performance, embodiment, and narrative. As a result, the generated behaviours, though technically varied, can fall short in terms of intentionality, emotional richness, and contextual meaning. Some studies have addressed this by using live performance as both inspiration and testbed for socially expressive robotics. For example, Katevas et al. [9] analysed stand-up comedy and incorporated feedback from comedians to pre-script a robot's gaze and gestures, staged these behaviours in a live performance, and measured audience responses. In contrast, our *theatre-in-the-loop* approach engages the early stages of the creative process, drawing on performance expertise to shape robotic expression while embedding interdisciplinary collaboration directly into the generative workflow. By integrating embodied improvisation, narrative framing, and iterative evaluation within a rehearsal setting, it fosters behaviours that are not only expressive but also creatively authored and contextually resonant within a performative context.

2.1 Theatre Techniques in HRI

Theatre methods have increasingly been used to conceptualise and structure robotic behaviours. Hoffman [10] draws parallels between established acting methodologies and the design of socially intelligent robots, identifying four critical acting principles he considers applicable to human-robot interaction (HRI): *Psycho-physical unity* challenges conventional distinctions between cognition and motion in robotics, promoting an embodied intelligence model where gestures actively shape cognitive processes. *Mutual responsiveness* inspired by Meisner's relational performance approach [11], suggests robots should dynamically adapt their actions in real-time to ongoing interactions. *Objectives and inner monologue* advocate for robotic behaviours driven by implicit goals and reflective states, enhancing narrative coherence and intentionality. Finally, *context and given circumstances* underscore the importance of designing adaptive robotic behaviours, responsive to evolving environmental conditions, ensuring contextually appropriate expressions.

Beyond conceptual framing, modular theatre methods have also been employed by designers to fine-tune expressive qualities, such as posture, breath, and tempo. Laban Movement Analysis (LMA) for instance, provides a structured vocabulary to break down gesture into components like weight, flow, and time [12]. Building on LMA, Laviers and Maguire [13] introduce BESST, a system for documenting expressive movement through a notation framework that emphasises embodied observation and structured analysis, providing a method to encode and analyse expressive behaviours in HRI.

Such theatre-inspired approaches form a performative framework for HRI; one that positions the robot as a dramaturgically scaffolded agent. Our work shapes a workflow through an interdisciplinary collaboration between a theatre director, a puppeteer, roboticists, and designers responsible for the design of the performative installation NED II. By adapting theatre rehearsal methods to facilitate improvisational puppeteering during rehearsal, we aim to endow the robot with human-driven responsiveness and performative presence.

2.2 Puppetry and Directing as a Model for Enhancing Robotic Expressivity

Key challenges in robotic behaviour design for performance include the difficulty of conveying intentionality, emotional nuance, and narrative coherence. We propose that a) puppetry, which excels at animating inanimate objects through real-time, tangible manipulation, and b) theatre directing, which shapes narrative structure, emotional arcs, and performance clarity by guiding the rehearsal process, together offer powerful models to address these challenges.

Rather than striving for anthropomorphic realism, puppeteers can convey intentionality and expressivity through rhythm, gesture, and stylised movements. What makes this approach particularly appealing in HRI is its compatibility with learning from demonstration frameworks, which can be trained with improvisational data to generate autonomous robot behaviours learned from puppeteer actions [14]. Many existing studies focus on expressive movement but rely on pre-authored behaviours, overlooking live, collaborative or dramaturgically driven improvisation. For example, a hybrid puppetry-based control system for robotic stage actors [15] integrated pre-scripted animations, parametric behaviours, and real-time eye-contact inverse kinematics to enable expressive interactions with human performers. As such, puppetry's potential for embodied, improvisational exploration, remains largely untapped in current robotics frameworks.

Similarly, the deeper dramaturgical potential of theatre directing has remained underexplored in HRI, with directors typically involved in peripheral or project-specific capacities rather than integrated deep into the creative process. Hoffman et al. [15] collaborated with a theatre director to refine gesture animations created in 3D software, structuring scenes into beats with precisely timed joint movements. Similarly, Zeglin et al. [16] involved a director to help refine animator-generated gestures, so they could be effectively translated to a mobile manipulator with two anthropomorphic arms. While these studies demonstrated enhanced expressive quality, they limited the director's contribution to refining pre-existing material rather than involving them directly in a generative, improvisational creation of robotic behaviour. In contrast, our approach integrates the director's dramaturgical expertise from the outset, shaping robotic gestures through rehearsal practices.

Related work by Rozendaal et al. [17] also explores the incorporation of theatrical expertise in HRI by introducing a mixed-reality stage, where theatre professionals co-design behaviours through embodied interaction in virtual reality. Their approach reframes robotic limitations as creative constraints, enabling situated, repeatable design processes that integrate narrative intent and expressive motion within a transdisciplinary, performative framework. Building on this, we incorporate real-time improvisation and dramaturgical collaboration directly into the physical rehearsal process.

2.3 Gaps in the Domain

Despite growing interest in theatre-inspired methods for refining or prototyping expressive robotic gestures, existing approaches remain largely theoretical, fragmented, or confined to virtual spaces. Technical frameworks often lack direct creative input from performance practitioners, while theatre-informed systems tend to retrofit directors' and puppeteers' expertise rather than embedding it from the start. As a result, three key gaps persist in translating theatrical intent into cohesive, reusable robotic behaviours:

1. **Intent-to-Specification Translation:** There are no widely adopted method to convert theatre directing strategies into robot-executable behaviours to support expressive, context-sensitive robotic performance.
2. **Real-time Co-Creation:** Real-time co-creation of expressive, performative robotic behaviour remains challenging due to the absence of a systematic workflow that integrates the expertise of theatre-makers and designers throughout the creative process.
3. **Reuse of Improvisation:** Improvised gestures are often ephemeral, lacking mechanisms for capturing their reuse in future contexts.

3 Methodology: A Director, Puppeteer, Roboticist Workflow for Expressive Motion Capture

To address the identified gaps, we propose a creative workflow that adopts a practice-led, interdisciplinary methodology, aimed at generating and capturing expressive robotic behaviour. Drawing from a performative-materialist perspective [18] and mixed-reality speculative design [17], *theatre-in-the-loop* workflow integrates theatrical rehearsal-based embodied improvisation and collaborative performance-making.

The workflow was implemented across two exploratory workshops and developed through collaborative efforts of an interdisciplinary team with established expertise in the domains of performance and technology. The team consists of roboticists specialising in Human-Robot Interaction within artistic settings, a puppeteer with training in design and digital media, a theatre director with research experience in HCI and dramaturgy, and designers with extensive experience in interactive performance technologies. Figure 2 shows an overview of the proposed workflow.

3.1 Roles and Contributions

During the implementation of our proposed workflow, the roboticist led the overall design and facilitation of the workshop, shaping both its technical infrastructure and its integration with creative practice. This included configuring the robotic platform, ensuring system safety and responsiveness, and aligning the robot's capabilities with the rehearsal process. The workshop directly supported the roboticist's research aims, centring their investigation into how expressive, reusable robotic behaviours can be generated through live, interdisciplinary collaboration.

In this context, the director translated expressive goals into directing prompts that iteratively shaped improvisations into distinct narrative arcs. The puppeteer interpreted

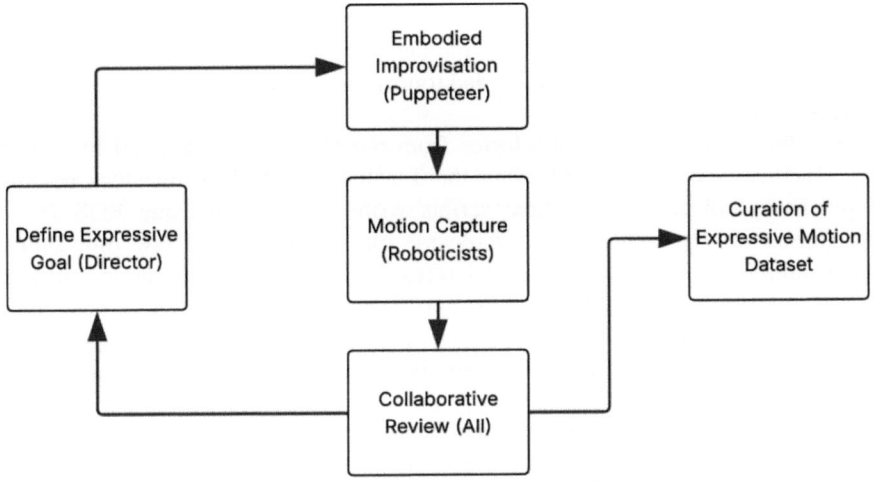

Fig. 2. An overview of the *theatre-in-the-loop* workflow for expressive robot motion design.

these prompts as motivations for action, physically manipulating the robot to produce expressive nuances (tremors, pauses, and hesitations) captured as reusable motion data. The designers contributed dramaturgical framing, scenographic insights, and creative-critical feedback on gesture expressiveness. The recorded movements were replayed by the robot and iteratively reviewed and refined by the team to enhance narrative coherence and emotional fidelity. Finally, the refined motion data was annotated and stored, forming a curated library of expressive templates for future reuse, including as training material for generative models.

3.2 Robotic System and Data Capture

Robotic Platforms: In Workshop 1, we used a 7-degree-of-freedom (DOF) Franka Emika Panda arm for physical familiarisation. In Workshop 2, a 6-DOF Universal Robots UR3e collaborative robotic arm was used for gesture creation and data capture. The Franka arm was utilised to facilitate the introduction of the puppeteer to robotic arms, as the UR3e supporting software was not operational at the time of the initial workshop. The UR3e was utilised in the subsequent workshop, as it is the robotic platform that has been selected by the designers for the development of the NED II project.

Control Interface: In both workshops, the operation of the robots was achieved through direct physical manipulation. The Franka arm was operated in gravity-compensation mode, while the UR3e was guided via *Freedrive* mode, enabling the puppeteer to manipulate the arm with ease and precision. This configuration enabled the puppeteer to focus on expressive gesture without the need for abstracted control inputs.

Trajectory Recording and Playback Tool: Motion trajectories from the Franka arm were recorded using the Franka Control Interface[1] (FCI) through a custom Python script for recording joint position data. Recorded trajectories were not played back during the first workshop.

Recording of the motion trajectories from the UR3e were captured in real-time using *Freedrive* mode, activated using the Teach Pendant. The trajectory recording and playback tool consists of three scripts written in Python using ROS 2[2]. The script (based on *DynamicTrajectoryExecutor* class [19]) logged raw time-stamped joint positions to a CSV file. A second script implemented a timestamp normalisation step to convert absolute timestamps into relative *time_from_start* values required for trajectory execution. No smoothing or trajectory optimisation was applied, preserving the original motion dynamics. Finally, a third script loaded the trajectory and replayed it via ROS 2's *FollowJointTrajectory* action interface, sending commands to the */scale_joint_trajectory_controller/follow_joint_trajectory* topic. This allowed for direct reproduction of the recorded motions without modification, ensuring fidelity to the original performance. The system was developed using Ubuntu (22.04) and ROS 2 (Humble).

4 Workshop Structure and Findings

The proposed workflow emerged and was tested across two structured workshops. As this was an exploratory study using a novel method, we selected Ekman's six basic emotions [20] to provide a simple, widely recognised emotional vocabulary that served both as a conceptual foundation and a practical guide for the creative team, enabling consistent mapping of emotional intent to robotic responses.

4.1 Workshop 1: Collaborative Foundations for Expressive Robotics

This initial workshop (W1) served as an open exploration of how a director, puppeteer, roboticists and designers can co-create expressive robotic motion. The session focused on exploring the interplay between theatrical improvisation, physical manipulation, and robotic constraints, identifying what creative practices held promise for deeper study, shown in Fig. 3(left).

Using a Franka Emika Panda arm in gravity-compensation mode, activated through the FCI, the puppeteer familiarised himself with the robot and developed an intuitive sense of its motion range and resistance. This initial hands-on engagement proved critical; the puppeteer's physical dialogue with the machine revealed nuances regarding the potential for expressive manipulation that theoretical discussion alone could not. He characterised his interaction with the robot arm as a continuous process of adjustment, watching its motion, sensing its weight and position, and modifying gestures.

---

[1] The Franka Control Interface (FCI) is an API that provides low-level, real-time access to the Franka Emika robot's sensors and actuators for precise motion and force control. https://franka emika.github.io/docs/

[2] ROS 2 is an open-source framework for building modular, real-time, and distributed robot applications. https://www.ros.org/

 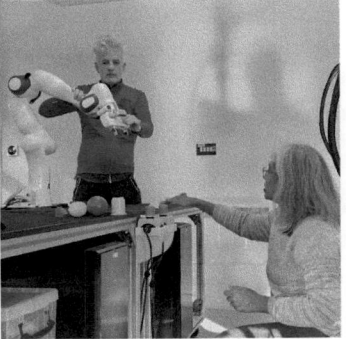

Fig. 3. (left) The puppeteer, director, roboticists, and designers discuss and engage practically in embodied expressive motion. (right) The puppeteer physically manipulates the Franka Emika Panda robotic arm to engage expressively with the designer.

The director introduced narrative prompts to shape the interaction, continuously observing, interpreting, and adjusting improvisations in real-time rather than following preplanned scenarios. Simple objects, a ball and a cup, (Fig. 3 right), were introduced by the designers and became emotional anchors through framing: a neutral sphere might transform into "disgusting medicine" or a "precious heirloom," compelling the puppeteer to reinterpret gestures in real-time. These improvisations avoided static emotional labels (e.g., "show anger") in favour of dynamic scenarios, such as reluctance giving way to curiosity, or conflict resolving into uneasy acceptance. The team noted how this narrative spontaneity produced gestures that felt more fluid and intentionally grounded than predefined movement primitives. The workshop surfaced two key insights:

Collaborative Workflows: How role dynamics (director: narrative, puppeteer: physical interpreter, roboticists/designers: constraint mediators) form a creative loop.

Improvisation vs. Preset Emotion: Spontaneous, context-dependent gestures (e.g., "disgust" tied to a specific narrative) felt more authentic than pre-scripted emotional motion primitives, basic units of expressive movement associated with particular emotional states. This session raised the questions: How can we retain the authenticity of improvised gestures in autonomous reproduction? What dramaturgical structures might bridge live, directed puppeteering and programmed behaviour?

4.2 Workshop 2: Co-shaping Expressive Robotic Motion

Building on the somatic insights gained in the first session, in Workshop 2 (W2), we used the UR3e robot arm to generate gestures for each of six basic emotions defined by Ekman: anger, disgust, fear, happiness, sadness and surprise.

W2 Session 1 - Human Expression Study: This explored how the creative team (including the puppeteer, director, roboticists, and designers) perceived the six emotions and embodied the emotional states in their bodies through a series of non-verbal exercises, drawing upon techniques from charades and silent cinema. The team examined the manner in which emotions are conveyed through physical expression alone, without reliance on facial features or verbal cues. The exercises were designed to enhance the team's sensitivity to the nuances of gesture, rhythm, and posture in emotional communication, thereby establishing a shared experiential foundation for the subsequent improvisational work.

We encourage the reader to view the accompanying video material at this stage to better understand the workflow (described in later sections) in practice and how expressive motions were generated (see Supplementary).

W2 Session 2 - Director-led Puppeteer Embodied Motion Creation: The puppeteer, under the director's guidance, manipulated the UR3e robotic arm to improvise gestures expressing a series of basic emotions. A single object was used across all emotional contexts. Directing prompts and strategies were adjusted iteratively based on observed robot behaviour and feedback from the creative team.

This session produced a concise but diverse gesture library, recorded as time-stamped joint trajectories with metadata, forming a foundation for autonomous robotic playback. Here, autonomy refers to the robot triggering and sequencing gestures without real-time human control, based on cues, prompts, or internal logic. The library designed for reuse in *interactive performance* settings, where the robot may engage with human performers or audiences as a semi-autonomous, expressive participant within a live, dramaturgically framed environment.

Table 1 provides an overview of selected directing prompts and strategies, the corresponding robotic behaviours observed, and relevant design insights. These examples are inherently situational, shaped by the specific team involved, the dynamics of their creative collaboration, and the configuration of the robotic system. We do not claim that the exact prompts or strategies would reliably produce similar behaviours in other contexts, given the improvisational nature of the process. Rather, they are presented to illustrate the potential of integrating directing techniques and puppeteering methods to inform the co-creation of expressive robotic behaviour.

The puppeteer described the director's prompts as essential for maintaining focus and responsiveness, with clear emotional direction provided externally, he could fully concentrate on shaping the robot's movements. He particularly valued the "inner monologues" from the director, noting that the mental load required to simultaneously interpret the robot's affordances and perform expressively often left little space to generate and sustain his own imaginative context.

4.3 Emotion as an Iterative Performance

In those improvisations, emotional nuance was not predefined but emerged via iterative refinements, each layering new directorial cues to intensify or diversify affect. For instance, fear evolved progressively from a tactile cue ("gross") to an auditory trigger ("Bang!"), culminating in a narrative backstory ("the ball that hurt you"). Disgust, initially vague under generic prompts, sharpened when anchored to sensory hyperbole ("1000 rotten eggs"), evoking reflexive withdrawal distinct from fear. The refinements were preserved in autonomous replays, particularly in fear sequences, where slow approaches followed by abrupt recoils effectively conveyed tension–release dynamics.

Table 1. Iterative Prompt Adjustments and Observed Effects

Directive Prompt / Strategy	Robotic Response	Design Insight for Performative HRI
Iterative fear buildup "it's gross" → auditory "Bang!" → backstory "ball that hurt you"	Slow cautious approach, repeated recoil, tension release contrast retained in replay	Shows how layered cues (sensory → narrative) progressively sharpen affect
Antagonistic escalation "You can't have the ball" → "You're not worth it!"	Rapid side-to-side lunges, large trajectories, sustained aggressive energy	Status reversal acts as a driver of anger and a template for high-energy conflict
Disgust via sensory hyperbole "It smells like 1000 rotten eggs"	Abrupt full body recoil, maximal distance from object, repeated avoidance	Highlights the potency of vivid olfactory imagery for instinctive withdrawal
Curiosity–fear ambivalence "It's interesting but (feels) gross"	Cautious approach, side-to-side shakes, ambiguous hesitation	Captures mixed emotion and non-discrete states—useful for designing nuanced robot affect
Trauma-based internal conflict: The ball "broke your springs" (past trauma) - must now move it nonetheless.	Prolonged approach–retreat oscillation	Shows narrative memory as a source of sustained tension through internal contradiction

Complex behaviours arose particularly from conflicting and antagonistic directives. Fear prompts combined task-driven advances ("move the ball") with hesitant reactions ("it hurt last time"), generating oscillatory movements suggestive of internal struggle. Anger intensified through conflicting suggestions, affirmation ("this is the best ball") paired with denial ("you cannot have it," "you are not worth that ball"), producing a sense of exclusion that manifested as sustained aggression in rapid gestures. Scaffolded building of joy, started with free improvisation, later supported with background music ("Don't Worry, Be Happy"), stabilised spontaneous expressions of joy into rhythmic, sustained swaying motions. These strategies were not predetermined but evolved in response to the results of each iteration, shaped by ongoing assessments of the robot's performance, the director's instincts, the designers' intentions, and the dynamics between puppeteer and machine. Different teams (comprising other directors, puppeteers, and roboticists, or employing alternative robotic platforms) would likely produce distinct gesture repertoires, influenced by variations in narrative framing, embodied interpretation, and hardware affordances.

5 Discussion

Our practice-led approach contributes to a growing body of work integrating theatrical methodologies into human–robot interaction, proposing a structured, rehearsal-informed workflow. In contrast to prior systems using puppeteering via pre-scripted animations [15] or virtual prototyping via mixed-reality staging [17], our workflow advances HRI puppeteering by integrating three novel elements: (1) director-led improvisation using established theatre techniques, (2) real-time puppeteer–robot coupling, and (3) the potential for curated, reusable gesture libraries.

5.1 Dramaturgy in Emergent Robotic Expression

Hoffman's [10] conceptual suggestions are directly operationalized in our system. *Psycho-physical unity* and *mutual responsiveness* emerge as the puppeteer's kinaesthetic impulses drive robotic motion, bridging intention and actuation into a real-time feedback loop of continuous interaction. *Objectives and Obstacles* were most effective when paired. *Objectives* alone (e.g., "you want the ball") were less expressive than when coupled with *Obstacles* (e.g., "you want the ball, but you can't have it"), a technique from the Stanislavski System [21] that sharpens dramatic tension.

Context and Given Circumstances were primarily shaped by the director, who established narrative backstories and situational framing, such as "the ball that hurt you" and the loud "bang" noise. In contrast, the constraints and affordances of the robotic hardware and software, while not part of the fictional *Given Circumstances*, influenced expressive possibilities in a manner analogous to costume or prop limitations for an actor: they shaped how the puppeteer–robot pair could realize intentions. Thus, both dramaturgical and technical factors consistently informed improvisational choices. In this context, *improvisation* refers specifically to the rehearsal process, where it functioned as a generative method for developing expressive robotic gestures and refining interaction strategies, rather than as a live-performance response mechanism.

Perhaps the most distinctive technique emerged when the puppeteer invited the director to provide a continuous spoken stream of intention. The director articulated an externally authored "inner monologue," which the puppeteer internalised, reframed as motive, and rendered as robotic motion. This strategy was crucial for scaffolding the puppeteer's cognitive load, supporting emotional intent while enabling precise motor control, resulting in a layered enactment and distributed expressivity.

A further insight emerging from our process concerns the generative role of contradiction and conflict in shaping robotic expressivity. Long embedded in dramaturgical theory from Aristotle and Stanislavski to Pritner and Walters [21, 22], conflicting objectives and evolving circumstances serve not as disruptions but as structuring forces for transformation. Within our workflow, expressive richness often arose from tension: between intention and constraint, action and obstruction, or overlapping narrative demands. These tensions, embedded in character goals or situational dilemmas, did not inhibit expressivity, they intensified it. Yielding gestures that were affectively charged, narratively anchored, and dramaturgically meaningful.

This responsiveness to given circumstances and layered tension complements and extends prior work on emergent agency in human–robot interaction. Specifically, our approach echoes Gemeinboeck's relational-performative aesthetic, in which social behaviour unfolds through situated encounters shaped by interaction [18]. Yet, whereas her work foregrounds abstraction and open-endedness, our method reintroduces narrative scaffolds as productive constraints, anchoring improvisation in intention without closing it into fixed representation.

5.2 Scope and Limitations

At its core, our study explores distributed psycho-physical unity in HRI, a framework in which human intention and motive are "lent" to the machine, with theatre acting as an integrating force to weave fragmented agencies into a coherent, improvised performance. We tested this through a focused ensemble, one director, one puppeteer, two roboticists, and two designers, yielding practice-led insights into the iterative co-creation of expressive gestures. Three interdependent factors anchor the approach: kinaesthetic attunement (synchronising bodily intention with robotic motion), shared dramaturgical sensibility (aligning narrative intent across collaborators), and real-time feedback mechanisms. Emotional cues (e.g., "fear," "grief") served as internal prompts for improvisation rather than fixed labels for audiences.

Although specific outcomes will vary with team composition, hardware setup, and emotional framing, the method suggests a transferable structure for collaborative human–robot performance-making that can adapt to diverse creative and technical contexts. Future work may build on this foundation by involving more varied creative teams, integrating cross-cultural emotion frameworks, adapting the workflow to support a full creative process, and evaluating audience perception in live settings.

The robot's mechanical responsiveness, safety thresholds, and joint behaviour not only determined which gestures could be performed but also how confidently the puppeteer could execute them. These technical limitations affected expressive range and risk tolerance, especially in emotionally charged scenarios. The following section explores these challenges, comparing how various robotic platforms supported or hindered gesture expression in live contexts. This discrepancy (where puppeteers hold back from certain motions) may reveal an artistic opportunity: amplifying robotic movements beyond human comfort zones could enhance emotional expressivity.

5.3 Robotic Resistance and Gesture Interruption

Throughout the improvisation sessions, several gestures emerged not only through the puppeteer's intentional movement design but also in response to the robot's physical constraints and resistances. These constraints (such as torque limits, joint speed, and positional feedback) sometimes caused interruptions in gesture execution, such as premature halts, unexpected delays, or exaggerated rebounds. In particular, subtle actions like tremors or quick reversals were often dampened or distorted, producing gestures that deviated from the puppeteer's original intent.

In W1, which used the Franka Emika Panda arm in gravity-compensation mode, the puppeteer encountered frequent instances where the robot's torque or velocity thresholds were triggered unpredictably. This often resulted in abrupt joint locking that interrupted the gestural flow and required manual resetting by the roboticist. The puppeteer described these moments in anthropomorphic terms: *"When it goes into maximum, hits this point, it just stops to save itself from breaking, which is what a human would do: 'Ah! Stop, back away, I might break my arm.'" (Puppeteer, W1)*. While this framing demonstrates an intuitive understanding of the robot's protective mechanisms, it also highlights a key limitation: the absence of tactile or visual cues to help the performer anticipate such limits in real-time. This led to a subtle but persistent constraint on expressive risk-taking, particularly during delicate or emotionally charged gestures.

In contrast, the UR3e platform used in W2 was described as substantially easier to manipulate. *Freedrive* mode enabled smoother, uninterrupted joint movement, and the joint limits were less restrictive and more forgiving in live manipulation contexts, leading to a greater sense of control and expressive confidence. One standout feature was the continuous end-effector rotation, which allowed the puppeteer to maintain directional focus during complex movements, critical when simulating gaze or attention. As the puppeteer reflected, *"There's these imaginary eyes on it... and when it's not aligned, it doesn't quite 'see' the object. That middle positioning becomes really important."* (Puppeteer, W2).

These reflections highlight how expressive manipulation is shaped by a robot's physical affordances and joint behaviour. Unpredictable constraints hinder exploration, while predictable, fluid motion enables more emotionally resonant behaviours. Designing for expressive HRI should focus on software, motion capture fidelity, and the manipulation experience itself. Performance-based robots must be responsive partners, offering freedom, tactile clarity, and transparent feedback for emotional subtlety. Future research should explore gesture-friendly modes, clear joint-limit signalling, and design heuristics that align with how humans perceive and interpret physical resistance. This invites broader reflection on the artistic affordances of human–robot motion discrepancy. What if, instead of trying to minimise or correct these divergences, designers were to embrace them? Could allowing the robot to exaggerate certain motions (through overcommitment, delay, or recoil) amplify the affective impact of gestures in emotionally charged scenes such as fear, anger, or surprise? Alternatively, could such distortions risk undermining narrative coherence or believability by making the robot appear awkward or uncontrolled?

This tension between human intention and robotic execution suggests a fertile space for performative exploration. When framed dramaturgically, motion interruptions and exaggerations may enhance expressivity by drawing attention to the robot's materiality and effort. Rather than aiming for seamless mimicry of human movement, performance robotics might benefit from leveraging the robot's distinct embodiment, acknowledging its resistance and rhythm as part of its character. These insights open up a generative area of design, where expressive nuance is not simply programmed but emerges through negotiation between human gesture, robotic capacity, and creative framing.

6 Conclusions

By positioning robots as puppeteered performers within a theatrical paradigm, *theatre-in-the-loop* proposes a practice-led framework for socially expressive human-robot interaction, with applications in interactive art and storytelling. Through two structured workshops, we demonstrated how director-led, puppeteer improvisation and robotic affordances can co-produce gesture libraries annotated with emotional arcs that bridge technical and artistic design. While hardware limitations occasionally constrained expressive range, our findings suggest that rehearsal-driven co-creation can yield emotionally resonant motion templates.

Future work will focus on refining these templates into cohesive performances and integrating them into live staging contexts, evaluated through audience studies. We also propose exploring generative systems that dynamically reconfigure recorded gestures while preserving their narrative intent, e.g., adapting a "joyful" gesture to varying intensities or scales. Longer-term research could investigate how robotic traits, such as mechanical precision, non-human movement logic, or modular reconfiguration, might inspire new dramaturgical vocabularies. Ultimately, this work underscores the potential of interdisciplinary collaboration between theatre and HRI to expand both the expressive capacity of robots and the creative toolkit of artists.

Acknowledgments. This work was supported by UKRI - The Engineering and Physical Sciences Research Council (EPSRC), Centre for Doctoral Training in Horizon [grant number EP/S023305/1], the Turing AI World Leading Researcher Fellowship: Somabotics: Creatively Embodying Artificial Intelligence [grant number EP/Z534808/1], and AI UK: Creating an International Ecosystem for Responsible AI Research and Innovation (RAKE) [EP/Y009800/1]. We would also like to thank Dr Jocelyn Spence, Dr Nils Jaeger, and Dr Paul Tennent for their guidance and support in the development of the manuscript.

Author Contribution Statement. PP and VZHN contributed equally to the conception, development, analysis and writing of this manuscript, and share first authorship. SM is the professional puppeteer and generated the data and provided his perspectives for the manuscript. RP and RR contributed to the conceptual framing, provided the artistic scope, and participated in the workshops. AC contributed to the broader project and provided editorial feedback on the paper. AK contributed to the conception and planning of the workshops, participated in the workshops, and provided supervision and critical feedback on the manuscript.

Disclosure of Interests. The authors have no competing interests to declare that are relevant to the content of this paper.

Data Access Statement.. The data that support the findings of this study may be available on request from the corresponding author.

References

1. Patel, R., Ramchurn, R.: Thingamabobas – makers of imaginary worlds. https://makersofimaginaryworlds.co.uk/projects/thethingambobas/. Accessed 20 Dec 2023
2. Ngo, V.Z.H., Patel, R., Ramchurn, R., Chamberlain, A., Kucukyilmaz, A.: Dancing with a robot: an experimental study of child-robot interaction in a performative art setting. In: Palinko, O., et al. Social Robotics. ICSR + AI 2024. Lecture Notes in Computer Science, vol. 15563, pp. 340–353. Springer, Singapore (2025). https://doi.org/10.1007/978-981-96-3525-2_29
3. Panteris, M., Manschitz, S., Calinon, S.: Learning, generating and adapting wave gestures for expressive human-robot interaction. In: ACM/IEEE International Conference on Human-Robot Interaction, pp. 386–388 (2020). https://doi.org/10.1145/3371382.3378286

4. Zhou, A., Hadfield-Menell, D., Nagabandi, A., Dragan, A.D.: Expressive Robot Motion Timing. ACM/IEEE International Conference on Human-Robot Interaction. Part F127194, 22–31 (2017). https://doi.org/10.1145/2909824.3020221
5. Huang, P., Hu, Y., Nechyporenko, N., Kim, D., Talbott, W., Zhang, J.: EMOTION: expressive motion sequence generation for humanoid robots with in-context learning (2024)
6. Tang, S., Dondrup, C.: Gesture generation from trimodal context for humanoid robots, vol. 1 (2024). https://doi.org/10.1145/3687272.3690905
7. Schreiter, T., Rudenko, A., Rüppel, J.V., Magnusson, M., Lilienthal, A.J.: Multimodal interaction and intention communication for industrial robots (2025). https://doi.org/10.1177/02783649241274794
8. Mahadevan, K., et al.: Generative expressive robot behaviors using large language models. In: ACM/IEEE International Conference on Human-Robot Interaction, pp. 482–491 (2024). https://doi.org/10.1145/3610977.3634999
9. Katevas, K., Healey, P.G.T., Harris, M.T.: Robot comedy lab: experimenting with the social dynamics of live performance. Front. Psychol. **6**, 1253 (2015). https://doi.org/10.3389/fpsyg.2015.01253
10. Hoffman, G.: HRI: four lessons from acting method (2015). https://shorturl.at/iRgk1
11. Meisner, S., Longwell, D.: Sanford Meisner on acting. Vintage (2012)
12. Guest, A.H.: Labanotation : The System of Analyzing and Recording Movement. Routledge (2015). https://doi.org/10.4324/9780203823866
13. Laviers, A., Maguire, C.: The BESST system: explicating a new component of time in laban/bartenieff movement studies through work with robots. In: ACM International Conference Proceeding Series, Par F180475 (2022). https://doi.org/10.1145/3537972.3538023
14. Billard, A., Calinon, S., Dillmann, R., Schaal, S.: Robot programming by demonstration. In: Siciliano, B., Khatib, O. (eds.) Springer Handbook of Robotics, pp. 1371–1394. Springer, Heidelberg (2008). https://doi.org/10.1007/978-3-540-30301-5_60
15. Hoffman, G., Kubat, R., Breazeal, C.: A hybrid control system for puppeteering a live robotic stage actor. In: Proceedings of the 17th IEEE International Symposium on Robot and Human Interactive Communication, RO-MAN, pp. 354–359 (2008). https://doi.org/10.1109/ROMAN.2008.4600691
16. Zeglin, G., et al.: HERB's sure thing: a rapid drama system for rehearsing and performing live robot theater. In: Proceedings of IEEE Workshop on Advanced Robotics and Its Social Impacts, ARSO, January 2015, pp. 129–136 (2015). https://doi.org/10.1109/ARSO.2014.7020993
17. Rozendaal, M.C., Vroon, J., Bleeker, M.: Enacting human-robot encounters with theater professionals on a mixed reality stage. ACM Trans. Hum. Robot. Interact. **14** (2024). https://doi.org/10.1145/3678186
18. Gemeinboeck, P.: The aesthetics of encounter: a relational-performative design approach to human-robot interaction. Front. Robot. AI **7** (2021). https://doi.org/10.3389/frobt.2020.577900
19. will-d-chen/ur3e-codebase: A ros2 package to control a UR3E robot arm in joint space and task space using moveit2, can be used for any URe series arm. https://github.com/will-d-chen/ur3e-codebase. Accessed 15 Apr 2025
20. Ekman, P.: Are there basic emotions? Psychol. Rev. **99**, 550–553 (1992). https://doi.org/10.1037/0033-295X.99.3.550
21. Stanislavsky, K., Hapgood, E.R.: An Actor Prepares. Routledge, New York (2003)
22. Pritner, C., Walters, S.E.: An Introduction to Play Analysis, 2nd edn. Waveland Press (2017)

Remote Session Papers

Children's Acceptance of the TABAN Social Robot in LLM-Powered Collaborative Visual Storytelling

Maryam Karimi Jafari and Alireza Taheri(✉)

Social and Cognitive Robotics Laboratory, Sharif University of Technology, Tehran, Iran
artaheri@sharif.edu

Abstract. Interactive storytelling games combining social robots and people have been extensively studied in HRI. Recent advancements in large language models have enabled innovative applications in interactive storytelling with social robots. This paper investigates the acceptability of a social robot, TABAN, as a storytelling companion for children by using a within-participants study. We implemented a collaborative visual storytelling game on TABAN based on images from the Bloom dataset, integrating LLaVA as a vision language model (VLM), GPT-3.5-Turbo as a large language model (LLM), Google speech recognition, and Ariana text-to-speech (TTS). Ten children participated in human and robot-led storytelling sessions, followed by a questionnaire-based evaluation on a 5-point Likert scale. A paired T-test revealed no significant differences between the two storytelling conditions ($p = 0.936$), indicating that TABAN performed similarly to a human storyteller. However, children found it easier to immerse themselves in stories told by humans ($p = 0.003$). Additional evaluations indicated high acceptance of TABAN, with positive perceptions of its social attributes. Furthermore, six out of ten children preferred storytelling with TABAN, which highlights its potential as an interactive storytelling companion.

Keywords: Collaborative Storytelling · Child-Robot Interaction · Large Language Model (LLM) · Vision Language Model (VLM) · Storytelling Robots

1 Introduction

Storytelling is a fundamental aspect of human development that both children and adults enjoy. With technological advancements, social robots are used in educational and assistive contexts [1–3], offering opportunities for collaboration in storytelling. The concept of using robots in storytelling has been studied in areas such as perceived anthropomorphism and acceptance [4]. One study compared human and robotic storytellers, showing that an expressive robot was as effective as an expressive human [5]. In Human-Robot Interaction (HRI), interactive storytelling activities involving social robots and humans have been widely explored. One study found that robots responding to inputs from children fostered greater engagement helped young children overcome storytelling challenges and encouraged more participation [6].

Storytelling with social robots has also been widely accepted as an excellent educational tool for supporting children in their social [7], emotional [8, 9], and language development [10–12] as well as fostering their creativity [13, 14]. Leite et al. [8, 9] examined interactive storytelling for children using MyKeepon robots in individual and group settings, focusing on story recall and emotional understanding. Results showed that individual interactions improved recall, but emotional understanding was influenced by factors like grade level and robot perception. Social robots have been explored in education, particularly in language learning for children [10–12]. In these studies, the stories were predetermined, and the interactive nature of some involved children choosing from predefined options or the robot responding to children in a wizard-of-oz manner. A few of them also incorporated visuals into their narratives by using pictures.

Recent advancements in Large Language Models (LLMs) have opened new possibilities for interactive storytelling with social robots. In this context, individuals can interact with the LLM to create a story, or the language model itself can interactively play a variety of roles to tell a story [15]. Nichols et al. [16–18] presented a model based on GPT-2 and then implemented it on the Haru robot to create a collaborative storytelling system that could generate stories through interaction with humans that were not pre-written and predetermined. However, it is focused on the perspective of collaborative storytelling with a robot among adults rather than children. LLM-powered systems have been applied in various domains [19], such as Mathemyths [20], which uses GPT-4 for teaching mathematical language through story generation.

Based on these foundations, storytelling is a powerful educational tool, and social robots are widely used in learning. With the rise of the large language models, it is essential to first explore whether children accept collaborative storytelling with a social robot. While previous studies have focused on robotic storytelling, most of them rely on pre-defined stories, limited interactions, or adult participants.

In this paper, we propose and evaluate a Persian collaborative visual storytelling game with a social robot named TABAN based on some images. This collaborative storytelling game system implemented on the robot consists of four modules: an LLM module, a VLM module, speech recognition, and text-to-speech. Our goal was to investigate whether a social storytelling robot based on large language models can be as good as a human storyteller for children and be well accepted by them. In this study, we examined whether a social storyteller robot can be perceived as an interactive storytelling companion for children. Ten children participated in both storytelling with a human partner and storytelling with the robot, then answered questionnaires to compare TABAN's storytelling performance with that of a human storyteller.

2 Robotic Platform and Methodology

2.1 Robotic Platform

We used TABAN as our social robotic agent. TABAN is a social robot equipped with expressive characteristics. It has a touch screen for displaying images, two small hands for expressive interaction, and a 3D face that is projected onto a transparent mask for facial expressions. With two degrees of freedom (DOF) in the neck and two DOFs in each shoulder, the TABAN robot has six DOFs [21]. Figure 1-a shows TABAN.

2.2 System Architecture for Collaborative Storytelling

A collaborative visual storytelling game was developed and implemented on the TABAN robot. The process begins with the robot displaying an image, which is processed by a visual language model to generate an English story. This story is then sent to a large language model, which is used to generate Persian story sentences and form the story introduction. This Persian text is converted into natural speech using a text-to-speech model. Thus far, the robot has displayed an image and narrated the initial part of the story. Next, the robot shows a second image and prompts the user to continue the story. A speech recognition model transcribes the user's response, which is sent to the LLM to generate the next part of the story. Then a second loop of the storytelling cycle is started when the robot adds a sentence and displays a third image. The storytelling cycle repeats for six images. Therefore, our collaborative visual storytelling system consists of four modules, each utilizing an API for integration.

Image Dataset for Storytelling: The image dataset used for visual storytelling was obtained from the Bloom dataset [22], which provides images with multilingual textual descriptions. These images were stored locally and were categorized into groups of six for offline access. This dataset is available in the Hugging Face platform[1]. Figure 1-b shows a categorized set of these images that were used for the storytelling process.

Fig. 1. a) The TABAN social robot. b) An example of dataset images showing a story.

Vision Language Model (VLM): The storytelling system employs a modified version of LLaVA model[2], one of the best open-source and reliable image-text-to-text models [23]. Since LLaVA does not support Persian, the LLM was instructed to use the generated English stories to create Persian stories[3]. To avoid high API costs for VLM, we needed a model that could generate suitable stories instead of picture descriptions, while having a sufficient number of parameters and sizes that can be implemented locally. However, the robot's hardware lacked a dedicated GPU and had limited RAM making local execution impractical. We chose cloud-based execution using a Flask-based API on Google Colab,

---

[1] https://huggingface.co/datasets/sil-ai/bloom-vist.
[2] https://huggingface.co/llava-hf/llava-v1.6-mistral-7b-hf.
[3] For prompt details and additional materials, see https://bit.ly/3YdIwE7.

utilizing the Hugging Face platform which accepts POST requests. While Google Colab offered an affordable solution, it also introduced session time limits and internet issues that could negatively impact real-time performance. The image is sent to the VLM to generate a short story. Finally, the generated story is returned in JSON format for further processing. Ngrok service was used to expose the locally hosted Flask API via a secure public URL and enables remote access. We also tested models such as Phi-3 Vision, Moondream2, Florence, and PaliGemma, but some were too large to deploy efficiently, lacked narrative generation capabilities, or did not meet all of the required criteria.

Large Language Model (LLM): The task of creating Persian stories should be done by an LLM. Since the model must process and generate text in both English and Persian, our choices were limited to multilingual models. The GPT-3.5-Turbo model was employed through the OpenAI API. At the time, this model was a top-performing, cost-effective option with Persian support and easy API access. Other multilingual models existed, but none were tested, as GPT-3.5-Turbo met our key needs for fluency, cost, and integration.

Speech Processing (Text-to-Speech and Speech Recognition): In this paper, Ariana which is a Persian TTS, is used to convert textual outputs of language models into speech as the final part of the storytelling process of the robot. It takes texts produced by the GPT-3.5-Turbo model and converts them into natural and fluent Persian speech. Additionally, to process user input for story continuation, Google Speech Recognition was used to convert speech to text.

3 Experimental Procedure

To evaluate the acceptability of this storytelling game, we conducted a user study using the system described in Sect. 2.2. Ten children from a local school, all of whom were girls, participated in the study. They were 8.93 years old on average, with a 0.47 standard deviation. The children were divided into two groups of five for counterbalanced conditions. The first group first created stories with the robot and then engaged in storytelling with the human. In contrast, the second group was first involved in storytelling with the human and then with the robot. After each storytelling activity (with the robot or the human), the children completed a questionnaire. The experiment involved 30–40 min activities, including explanations, storytelling, and questionnaire-answering. Robot interaction lasted 15–25 min, while human interaction lasted 10 min. Each child saw different images in the first and second parts.

3.1 Storytelling with the Robot

In this activity, each child sits in front of the robot and randomly picks a number from a set of written numbers. This number determines the image set for their story. TABAN then displays an introductory image and says, "Let's tell a story together." After that, it shows all six selected images for 20 s so the child can see them. TABAN begins the storytelling by showing the first image and narrating the introduction of the story. Then, it announces the child's turn and displays the second image. The child continues the story based on what they see in the image and what TABAN has already said. After the child turns, TABAN adds new sentences to the story and moves on to the next image. The process continues, alternating between TABAN and the child until all six images are used. At the end, TABAN completes the story by saying, "Well done! You told a very good story." and displays "The End!" The children are free to say as many sentences as they like during their turns.

3.2 Storytelling with the Human

In this activity, the procedure remained the same, but a single female human storyteller interacted with the child, ensuring consistency while limiting generalizability. The child again selects a number which determines the image set. The human storyteller displays the six images on a laptop screen for 20 s. The human begins the story based on the first image. When the second image appears, the child continues the story by adding at least one sentence. After the child's turn, the human storyteller expands on their response to ensure the story remains connected. This turn-taking storytelling continues for all six images. Finally, the human storyteller concludes the story after the child's turn on the last image. Child storytelling with a robot or human storyteller is shown in Fig. 2 in addition to the experimental setup in both conditions.

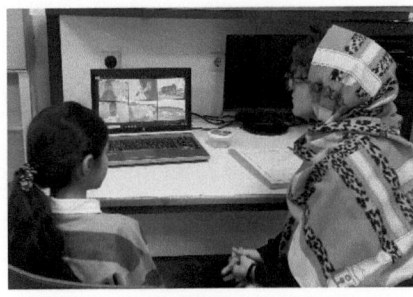 

Fig. 2. a) A child participating in a storytelling session with a human storyteller. b) A child engaging in an interactive storytelling session with the TABAN robot.

3.3 Evaluation Metrics and Data Collection

To evaluate children's storytelling experience with both the robot and human storyteller, a set of validated questionnaires was used. Each storytelling condition had a distinct questionnaire, both of which included 12 identical statements. More details about these 12 statements can be found in Table 1. These shared questions allowed for a comparison between the two conditions using appropriate statistical methods, including the paired T-test. Additionally, the robot questionnaire contained extra questions designed to assess children's perceptions of the robot's characteristics. Children's responses were recorded using a 5-point Likert scale represented by five distinct emojis, ranging from "strongly disagree" to "strongly agree," to facilitate their understanding and engagement with the survey. At the end of the final storytelling activity, children were asked whether they preferred storytelling with a robot or storytelling with a human.

The questionnaires were developed based on existing validated questionnaires used in related studies. Engagement with the story was measured using seven statements from the Transportation Scale–Short Form (TS-SF), which assesses how deeply individuals become immersed in a narrative world [24, 25]. Children's intentional acceptance of TABAN was examined using items from the Intentional Acceptance of Social Robots (IASR) scale, where two questions were selected [26]. To capture emotional responses, three items from the Self-Assessment Manikin (SAM) were used to assess children's feelings toward each storytelling condition [27]. In order to measure technology acceptance, one item from each of the seven categories of the Unified Theory of Acceptance and Use of Technology (UTAUT) was selected to avoid making the questionnaire overly lengthy while still covering all key factors influencing technology adoption [28]. Lastly, perceptions of the robot's social attributes were measured using eight selected items from the Robotic Social Attributes Scale (RoSAS), chosen for their relevance in reflecting the social personality of TABAN [29].

Table 1. Twelve common questionnaire statements adopted from TS-SF, IASR, and SAM, rated by children on a 5-point emoji scale in both storytelling conditions. (R = reverse-scored)

Adapted TS-SF Questionnaire	
No.	Statement
A	**When we were creating a story with the robot/human …**
1	I was mentally involved in the narrative while making it.
2	I could picture myself in the scene of the events described in the narrative.
3	While I was reading the narrative, the activity going on in the room around me was on my mind. (R)
4	I wanted to learn how the narrative ended.
5	I found my mind wandering while making the narrative. (R)
B	**After the story ends …**
6	I found myself thinking of ways the narrative could have turned out differently.
7	After finishing the narrative, I found it easy to put it out of my mind. (R)
Adapted IASR Questionnaire	
No.	Statement
8	I would like to see and play with the robot/human again.
9	It would be nice if the robot/human and I could do something together again.
SAM Questionnaire	
No.	Statement
A	**Imagine you are this little character, express your feelings about playing storytelling games with the robot/human.**
10	Valence
11	Arousal

(*continued*)

Table 1. (*continued*)

SAM Questionnaire	
No.	Statement
12	Dominance

4 Results and Discussion

4.1 Human Storyteller vs. Robot Storyteller

First, we compared children's storytelling experiences under two conditions: human storytelling and robot storytelling. Table 2 presents the average scores of the children's responses to the questionnaire for both storytelling conditions. Additionally, a paired T-test was performed to compare children's experiences in both conditions. The p-value of the T-test for all 12 shared questions was 0.936, indicating no significant difference between the two conditions. The study confirms that children's experiences with TABAN were similar in both cases, and they did not perceive any difference between the robot and human storytellers, indicating that its performance is consistent with human experiences. Similarly, Conti et al. [5] found no significant differences between the two storytelling conditions in their study, which involved pre-determined and non-interactive stories.

However, as shown in Table 2, the p-value of the T-test for question 2 was less than 0.05 (p = 0.003), indicating a significant difference between the two storytelling conditions. Figure 3 provides a visual representation of the results. It suggests children found it easier to visualize themselves in the story scenes when storytelling with a human partner. This could mean that the human storyteller provided a more engaging narrative and made it easier for children to immerse themselves in the story. This finding suggests that TABAN was less effective in creating immersive storytelling experiences, possibly due to the limitations in narrative generation or voice modulation.

Table 2. Mean and standard deviation of children's responses to shared questions in both storytelling conditions. Paired T-test results are included, with only Question 2 showing a significant difference.

Question #	Mean (SD)		P-value	T-value
	Storytelling with robot	Storytelling with human		
Q1	4.6 (± 0.52)	4.4 (± 0.97)	0.443	0.80
Q2	**3.7 (± 1.16)**	**4.5 (± 1.27)**	***0.003***	***-4.00***
Q3	2.2 (± 1.23)	1.6 (± 0.97)	0.193	1.41
Q4	4.9 (± 0.32)	5 (± 0.00)	0.343	-1.00
Q5	1.3 (± 0.95)	1.7 (± 1.25)	0.223	-1.31
Q6	3.1 (± 1.60)	2.6 (± 1.78)	0.381	0.92

Table 2. (*continued*)

Question #	Mean (SD)		P-value	T-value
	Storytelling with robot	Storytelling with human		
Q7	2.2 (± 1.40)	2.1 (± 1.79)	0.893	0.14
Q8	4.9 (± 0.32)	5 (± 0.00)	0.343	-1.00
Q9	5 (± 0.00)	4.7 (± 0.95)	0.343	1.00
Q10	4.8 (± 0.42)	5 (± 0.00)	0.168	-1.5
Q11	4.3 (± 0.67)	4.3 (± 0.67)	1.000	0.00
Q12	4.4 (± 0.84)	4.4 (± 0.84)	1.000	0.00
All Qs	**3.783 (± 1.507)**	**3.775 (± 1.647)**	**0.936**	**0.08**

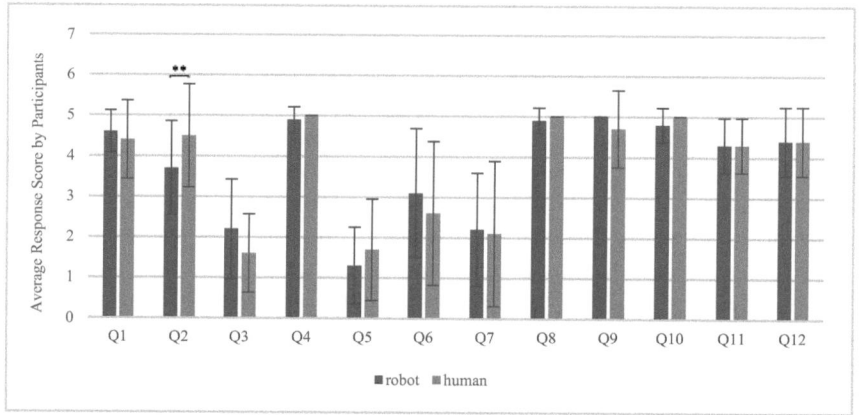

Fig. 3. Children's responses to survey questions for human and robot storytelling. No overall statistical significance was found, except for Question 2 ($p < 0.05$).

Questions 1, 3, and 5 assessed children's attention levels during storytelling. As can be seen in Fig. 3, TABAN scored highest on question 1 but lowest on questions 3 and 5 which were reverse-coded. This suggests that children may have paid more attention to the story with TABAN, although these differences were not statistically significant. For question 6, storytelling with the robot received the highest score, which indicates that the GPT-3.5-Turbo model, which was primarily responsible for generating the stories, behaved somewhat unpredictably. As a result, the ending created by TABAN for the stories was unexpected and far from the child's imagination. However, in this question, there was no significant difference between the two conditions. Based on the results of question 7, the children generally did not forget the story. The responses to questions 8 and 9 indicate that children were highly interested in engaging in activities other than storytelling with TABAN, which reflects its strong acceptance among them. Overall, the findings show that although TABAN was able to imitate human storytelling, other areas, such as immersive engagement, still require improvement.

4.2 Evaluating TABAN as a Social Storyteller Robot

The UTAUT and RoSAS were only used to assess TABAN. The results of UTAUT are shown in Fig. 4. The high scores for questions 2–7 of UTAUT suggest that children generally perceived TABAN as an interesting social robot and storytelling companion. As shown in Fig. 4, although children reported in question 3 that they have all of the knowledge to tell stories with TABAN, their responses to question 5 indicate that they did not find the process particularly easy. The Pearson correlation coefficient between "Facilitating Conditions" and "Perceived Ease of Use" in UTAUT was calculated as 0.7, indicating a strong positive relationship between these two factors. According to the results of the first item of UTAUT shown in Fig. 4, some children reported feeling slightly anxious while storytelling with the robot, likely due to their unfamiliarity with the technology. However, the anxiety scores were relatively low, suggesting that TABAN was generally perceived as warm and friendly. These results suggest that while TABAN was well received overall, there might still be some small usability problems, particularly regarding its perceived ease of use. Furthermore, according to question 2, TABAN appears quite human-like, which may enhance its intentional acceptance, as found in [4]. The Pearson correlation coefficient between "Perceived Adaptiveness" from UTAUT and "Dominance" from the SAM questionnaire was found to be 0.74. This indicates that the more aligned the robot is with the child, the more the child feels in control of the storytelling process. In other words, if TABAN does not listen to the child's words and creates a story only based on its knowledge, the children lose their sense of control over the session.

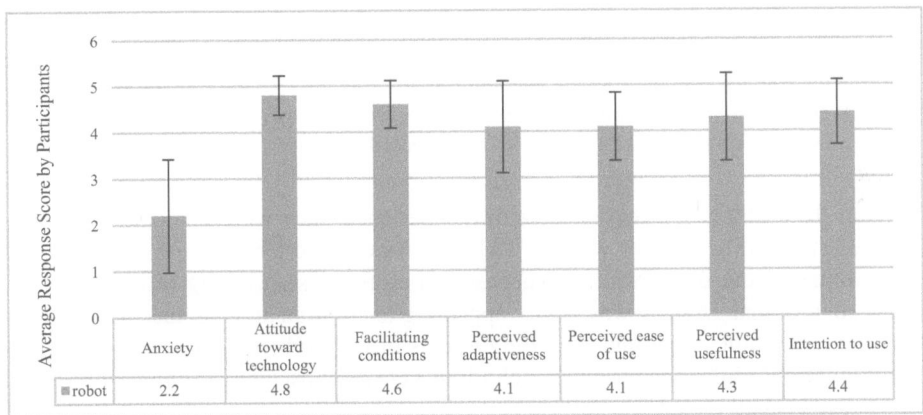

Fig. 4. Average UTAUT questionnaire scores rated by children on a 5-point Likert scale with emoji-based responses.

Based on the high scores of RoSAS that are shown in Fig. 5, children believed that the robot was happy and social. From their perspective, TABAN appears knowledgeable and capable, which could indicate that the models in the system have effectively performed the storytelling task. According to Fig. 5, TABAN did not seem scary; however, it was perceived as somewhat strange. TABAN's strangeness might be due to the GPT-3.5-Turbo model failing to generate coherent and meaningful sentences in some cases. Moreover, the Ariana TTS system struggled to convert these outputs into a comprehensible voice, as a result, some children sometimes felt that they did not fully understand what TABAN was saying. Additionally, TABAN's capability to listen and generate story continuations based on children's input may have contributed to its perceived strangeness. The Pearson correlation coefficient between TABAN being "happy" and "social" is 0.88, indicating that in the children's view, the happier TABAN is, the more social it appears. For the relationships between the "Perceived Adaptiveness" item of UTAUT and the "Scary" item as well as the "Dominance" item of SAM and the "Scary" item, this coefficient showed values of -0.86 and -0.76. This also suggests that if TABAN generates a story only based on its imagination without incorporating the child's input, it may be perceived as scarier.

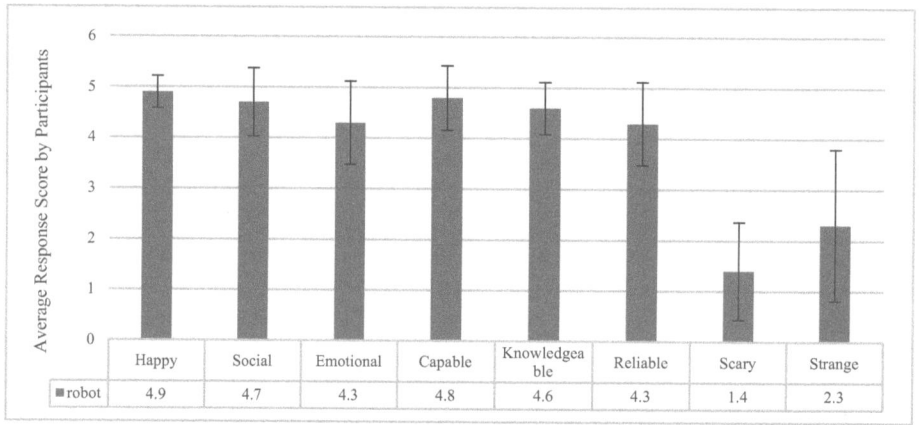

Fig. 5. Average RoSAS questionnaire scores reflecting children's perception of TABAN's social attributes, rated on a 5-point Likert scale with emoji-based responses.

After the children's second storytelling experience, they were asked whether they preferred storytelling with or without TABAN. Among the ten children, six preferred storytelling with the TABAN robot, whereas four preferred storytelling without it. These results suggest that TABAN was highly appealing to children and has successfully captured their attention, consistent with the findings of [17], where a survey revealed that among children, adults, and the elderly, children were the most likely to enjoy storytelling with a social robot.

5 Limitations and Future Work

While our study presents promising results in collaborative storytelling with robots, several limitations must be acknowledged. First, the study was limited by a small and homogeneous sample containing 10 girls of similar age and background, which restricts the generalizability of the findings to broader populations, including boys, different age groups, and cultural contexts. Secondly, some children had trouble coming up with and saying their ideas quickly while looking at the pictures, which caused delays. Because of this, the speech recognition system sometimes missed parts of what they said or didn't respond correctly. The GPT-3.5-Turbo and Ariana models sometimes made sentences that sounded strange or were hard for children to understand. Future work will aim to address these challenges by expanding the participant group to include larger and more diverse age ranges and backgrounds, enhancing the flexibility of the speech recognition module, and integrating more advanced LLMs such as the GPT-4 or GPT-4o series, as well as replacing the current VLM with improved models like the Qwen-VL or InternVL series. Although the current system was not initially designed for educational use, the findings of this study will guide its future development into an interactive storytelling tool for classroom settings.

6 Conclusion

In this paper, we propose and evaluate a Persian collaborative visual storytelling game with the social robot TABAN based on images from the Bloom dataset. The system consists of four modules: (1) a VLM module, which employs a modified LLaVA model via a Flask-based API for image-text-to-text conversion; (2) an LLM module, which utilizes GPT-3.5-Turbo through the OpenAI API for generating stories; (3) Google speech recognition for processing user input; and (4) Ariana Persian TTS for delivering the robot's responses. To evaluate the storytelling game, ten children participated in both robot- and human-led storytelling sessions and completed questionnaires on a 5-point Likert scale after each activity. These questionnaires allowed us to compare both conditions and assess TABAN's characteristics as a storytelling robot separately. The results showed no significant difference between the two conditions, indicating that children did not perceive any difference between TABAN and human storytellers. However, TABAN was notably less effective than the human storyteller in creating immersive storytelling experiences, a key metric of narrative engagement. This may be due to limitations in narrative generation or voice modulation. The children's attention levels during storytelling were assessed using questions 1, 3, and 5, suggesting that children may have paid more attention to the story with TABAN. However, there was no significant difference between the two conditions. Children generally did not forget the story, and responses to questions 8 and 9 indicated that they were highly interested in engaging in activities other than storytelling with TABAN, reflecting its strong acceptance among them. The UTAUT and RoSAS were used to assess TABAN, and the high scores for questions 2–7 suggest that children generally perceived TABAN as an interesting social robot and storytelling companion. However, some children reported feeling slightly anxious while storytelling with the robot, likely due to their unfamiliarity with the technology. The Pearson correlation coefficient between "Facilitating Conditions" and "Perceived Ease of Use" in UTAUT was calculated as 0.7, indicating a strong positive relationship between these two factors. The children believed that TABAN was happy and social, but it was perceived as somewhat strange due to the GPT-3.5-Turbo model failing to generate coherent and meaningful sentences in some cases. The Pearson correlation coefficient between TABAN being "happy" and "social" is 0.88, indicating that the happier TABAN is, the more social it appears. After the children's second storytelling experience, six preferred storytelling with TABAN, while four preferred storytelling without it. These results suggest that TABAN was highly appealing to children and has successfully captured their attention.

Acknowledgement. This study was funded by the Sharif University of Technology (Grant No. G4030507). We thank the children and staff at the participating school for their support, and the parents for allowing their children to take part. We also appreciate the guidance from our colleagues at the Social and Cognitive Robotics Laboratory at the Sharif University of Technology.

References

1. Basiri, S., Taheri, A., Meghdari, A., Alemi, M.: Design and implementation of a robotic architecture for adaptive teaching: a case study on Iranian Sign language. J. Intell. Robot. Syst. **102**, 48 (2021). https://doi.org/10.1007/s10846-021-01413-2
2. Basiri, S., Taheri, A., Meghdari, A.F., Boroushaki, M., Alemi, M.: Dynamic Iranian Sign language recognition using an optimized deep neural network: an implementation via a robotic-based architecture. Int. J. Soc. Robot. **15**, 599–619 (2023). https://doi.org/10.1007/s12369-021-00819-0
3. Esfandbod, A., Nourbala, A., Rokhi, Z., Meghdari, A.F., Taheri, A., Alemi, M.: Design, manufacture, and acceptance evaluation of APO: a lip-syncing social robot developed for lip-reading training programs. Int. J. Soc. Robot. **16**, 1151–1165 (2024). https://doi.org/10.1007/s12369-022-00933-7
4. Robben, D., Fukuda, E., De Haas, M.: The effect of gender on perceived anthropomorphism and intentional acceptance of a storytelling robot. In: Companion of the 2023 ACM/IEEE International Conference on Human-Robot Interaction, pp. 495–499. ACM, Stockholm Sweden (2023). https://doi.org/10.1145/3568294.3580134
5. Conti, D., Cirasa, C., Nuovo, S.D., Nuovo, A.D.: "Robot, tell me a tale!": a social robot as tool for teachers in kindergarten. Interact. Stud. **21**, 220–242 (2020). https://doi.org/10.1075/is.18024.con
6. Sun, M., Leite, I., Lehman, J.F., Li, B.: Collaborative storytelling between robot and child: a feasibility study. In: Proceedings of the 2017 Conference on Interaction Design and Children, pp. 205–214. ACM, Stanford (2017). https://doi.org/10.1145/3078072.3079714
7. Scassellati, B., et al.: Improving social skills in children with ASD using a long-term, in-home social robot. Sci. Robot. **3**, eaat7544 (2018). https://doi.org/10.1126/scirobotics.aat7544
8. Leite, I., et al.: Emotional storytelling in the classroom: individual versus group interaction between children and robots. In: Proceedings of the Tenth Annual ACM/IEEE International Conference on Human-Robot Interaction, pp. 75–82. ACM, Portland (2015). https://doi.org/10.1145/2696454.2696481
9. Leite, I., et al.: Narratives with robots: the impact of interaction context and individual differences on story recall and emotional understanding. Front. Robot. AI **4** (2017). https://doi.org/10.3389/frobt.2017.00029
10. Kory, J., Breazeal, C.: Storytelling with robots: Learning companions for preschool children's language development. In: Proceedings of the 23rd IEEE International Symposium on Robot and Human Interactive Communication, pp. 643–648. IEEE, Edinburgh (2014). https://doi.org/10.1109/ROMAN.2014.6926325
11. Westlund, J.K., Breazeal, C.: The interplay of robot language level with children's language learning during storytelling. In: Proceedings of the Tenth Annual ACM/IEEE International Conference on Human-Robot Interaction Extended Abstracts, pp. 65–66. ACM, Portland (2015). https://doi.org/10.1145/2701973.2701989

12. Kory Westlund, J.M., et al.: Flat vs. expressive storytelling: young children's learning and retention of a social robot's narrative. Front. Hum. Neurosci. **11** (2017). https://doi.org/10.3389/fnhum.2017.00295
13. Elgarf, M., et al.: "And then what happens?" Promoting children's verbal creativity using a robot. In: Proceedings of the 2022 17th ACM/IEEE International Conference on Human-Robot Interaction (HRI), pp. 71–79. IEEE, Sapporo (2022). https://doi.org/10.1109/HRI53351.2022.9889408
14. Elgarf, M., Salam, H., Peters, C.: Fostering children's creativity through LLM-driven storytelling with a social robot. Front. Robot. AI **11** (2024). https://doi.org/10.3389/frobt.2024.1457429
15. Yu, T., Chen, M., Li, Y., Lew, D., Yu, K.: LaSofa: integrating fantasy storytelling in human-robot interaction through an interactive sofa robot. In: Companion of the 2024 ACM/IEEE International Conference on Human-Robot Interaction, pp. 1168–1172. ACM, Boulder (2024). https://doi.org/10.1145/3610978.3640672
16. Nichols, E., Gao, L., Gomez, R.: Collaborative storytelling with large-scale neural language models. In: Motion, Interaction and Games, pp. 1–10. ACM, Virtual Event (2020). https://doi.org/10.1145/3424636.3426903
17. Nichols, E., Gao, L., Vasylkiv, Y., Gomez, R.: Collaborative storytelling with social robots. In: Proceedings of the 2021 IEEE/RSJ International Conference on Intelligent Robots and Systems (IROS), pp. 1903–1910. IEEE, Prague (2021). https://doi.org/10.1109/IROS51168.2021.9636409
18. Nichols, E., Szapiro, D., Vasylkiv, Y., Gomez, R.: I Can't believe that happened! : exploring expressivity in collaborative storytelling with the tabletop robot haru. In: Proceedings of the 2022 31st IEEE International Conference on Robot and Human Interactive Communication (RO-MAN), p. 59. IEEE, Napoli (2022). https://doi.org/10.1109/RO-MAN53752.2022.9900606
19. Zahedifar, R., Soleymani Baghshah, M., Taheri, A.: LLM-controller: dynamic robot control adaptation using large language models. Robot. Auton. Syst. **186**, 104913 (2025). https://doi.org/10.1016/j.robot.2024.104913
20. Zhang, C., Liu, X., Ziska, K., Jeon, S., Yu, C.-L., Xu, Y.: Mathemyths: leveraging large language models to teach mathematical language through child-AI co-creative storytelling. In: Proceedings of the CHI Conference on Human Factors in Computing Systems, pp. 1–23. ACM, Honolulu (2024). https://doi.org/10.1145/3613904.3642647
21. Shahab, M., et al.: Manufacture and development of Taban: a cute back-projected head social robot for educational purposes. Intell. Serv. Robot. **17**, 871–889 (2024). https://doi.org/10.1007/s11370-024-00545-2
22. Leong, C., Nemecek, J., Mansdorfer, J., Filighera, A., Owodunni, A., Whitenack, D.: Bloom Library: multimodal datasets in 300+ languages for a variety of downstream tasks. arXiv:2210.14712 (2022). https://doi.org/10.48550/arXiv.2210.14712
23. Liu, H., Li, C., Li, Y., Lee, Y.J.: Improved baselines with visual instruction tuning. arXiv:2310.03744 (2024). https://doi.org/10.48550/arXiv.2310.03744
24. Appel, M., Gnambs, T., Richter, T., Green, M.C.: The transportation scale-short form (TS–SF). Media Psychol. **18**, 243–266 (2015). https://doi.org/10.1080/15213269.2014.987400
25. Green, M.C., Brock, T.C.: The role of transportation in the persuasiveness of public narratives. J. Pers. Soc. Psychol. **79**, 701–721 (2000). https://doi.org/10.1037/0022-3514.79.5.701
26. de Jong, C., Kühne, R., Peter, J., van Straten, C.L., Barco, A.: Intentional acceptance of social robots: development and validation of a self-report measure for children. Int. J. Hum. Comput. Stud. **139**, 102426 (2020). https://doi.org/10.1016/j.ijhcs.2020.102426
27. Bradley, M.M., Lang, P.J.: Measuring emotion: the self-assessment manikin and the semantic differential. J. Behav. Ther. Exp. Psychiatry **25**, 49–59 (1994). https://doi.org/10.1016/0005-7916(94)90063-9

28. Venkatesh, V., Morris, M.G., Davis, G.B., Davis, F.D.: User acceptance of information technology: toward a unified view. MIS Q. **27**, 425–478 (2003). https://doi.org/10.2307/30036540
29. Carpinella, C.M., Wyman, A.B., Perez, M.A., Stroessner, S.J.: The robotic social attributes scale (RoSAS): development and validation. In: Proceedings of the 2017 ACM/IEEE International Conference on Human-Robot Interaction, pp. 254–262. ACM, Vienna (2017). https://doi.org/10.1145/2909824.3020208

Violence Detection by a Social Robot

Reyhane Nikoobayan and Alireza Taheri(✉)

Social and Cognitive Robotics Laboratory, Sharif University of Technology, Tehran, Iran
ryhanhhydry976@gmail.com, artaheri@sharif.edu

Abstract. As the need for improving public safety and rapid intervention continues to grow, real-time violence detection in public has become increasingly important. The goal of this study is to develop a highly accurate and lightweight deep learning model for real-time violence detection, to integrate it into a social robot to promote peaceful behaviors among children, and enable educators to quickly intervene in aggressive situations in educational environments such as schools and kindergartens. To this end, we used two large and benchmark violence video datasets- RLVS and RWF-2000- and trained three architectures: Transformer, 3D-CNN, and CNN-LSTM. Our proposed CNN-LSTM model achieved the highest accuracy of 96.46% on the RLVS dataset with the lightest architecture, outperforming the other approaches. To test the generalization of the model in real-world situations, the model was implemented on the Taban social robot, which captures and analyzes real-time 5-s video to detect violent content. The detection process took 0.1 s. If the robot detects violent behavior, it expresses its concern facially and verbally to the users. Ten distinct scenarios, including both normal and aggressive actions, were designed, and each scenario was conducted through 5 participant groups in front of Taban in the Social and Cognitive Robotics Lab. This test achieved 90% accuracy on these 50 tests, which highlights the outstanding generalizability of our model to be implemented in real-time surveillance systems such as hospitals, schools, and kindergartens.

Keywords: Violence Detection · Deep learning · Social Robot · Violent Behavior · CNN-LSTM

1 Introduction

Because of rapid advancement in artificial intelligence, Deep Learning techniques have been explicit to identify violent activities [1–3]. According to definitions, violence is the intentional use of actual or threatened physical force or power against oneself, another person, a group or community, or both that usually results in causing physical or mental harm, injury, damage, destruction, or even death [1]. This term encompasses a wide range of harmful behaviors, including physical assaults, such as hitting, kicking, and waving [2]. Violence occurs daily and affects different groups of people, including children, the elderly, and disabled people [3]. A significant portion of these take place in public places, such as assisted living facilities, schools, jails, and hospitals [4]. As a result of its broad applications, the importance of violence detection such as has increased rapidly [5]. This technology enables real-time surveillance and response in order to enhance public safety through systems such as vehicle cameras or citywide surveillance systems [6, 7]. One of the crucial parts of violence detection in videos is feature extraction, which involves identifying appearance cues [8], motion patterns [9], and trajectory-based features [10] to distinguish between violent and non-violent actions [11]. To improve accuracy and reliability, recent approaches integrate motion and appearance descriptors, including optical flow analysis that tracks motion between dynamic frames.

Due to the time-consuming nature of manual feature extraction and classification, traditional computer vision methods are inefficient to implement on large, challenging datasets [12]. In contrast, deep learning has revolutionized the field of violence detection by automating feature extraction and significantly improving performance on big datasets. [13, 14]. In recent years, several remarkable developments have been achieved in deep learning algorithms for violence detection [15, 16]. In 2019, Soliman et. al proposed a model that fused a Long Short-Term Memory (LSTM) with a pre-trained VGG-16 network. Their approach achieved a 94.6% accuracy on the Real-Life Violence Situations (RLVS) dataset. This model also demonstrates its robustness [3] very well by achieving great results on various dataset, such as the Violent-Flow [17], Movie [18], and Hockey datasets [18].

Continuing this research, Traore and Akhlouf introduced an architecture that combined the EfficientNet-B0 model with Recurrent Neural Networks (RNNs), including Gated Recurrent Units (GRU) and LSTM, along with three fully connected layers. This architecture, known as ValdNet, also incorporated optical flow to capture motion between frames. ValdNet demonstrated great performance by achieving high accuracies. On several datasets: ValdNet1 (GRU) reached 99% accuracy on the Hockey dataset, ValdNet2 (GRU) attained 96.74% accuracy on the RLVS dataset, and ValdNet3 (LSTM) achieved 93.53% accuracy on the Violent Flow dataset [13].

The first implementation transformers in violence detection was introduced by Abdali in 2021 and is named the DeVTr model. This model utilized a transformer encoder with four layers, along with positional encoding and a pre-trained VGG19 2-Dimensional Convolutional Neural Network (2DCNN). On the RLVS dataset, the model achieves a notable accuracy of 96.25% [19]. In a separate study, Anugrah Srivastava et al. report that their model achieved a 97.5% accuracy on the RLVS Dataset using a combination of the InceptionV3 pre-trained model and LSTM architecture. This result outperformed other existing methods, highlighting the effectiveness of this spatial-temporal feature extraction approach in detecting violence in videos [20].

Violence detection tasks can be efficiently performed by using an AI technique optimized for embedded edge devices, which results in reducing bandwidth consumption and enhances privacy [21]. These technologies improve public safety by enabling security personnel to react more quickly through the use of an intelligent video monitoring system [22, 23]. Additionally, many intelligent robots can inform their owners by sending emails containing pictures of detected violent situations [24]. To the best of our knowledge, such a robot has not been designed to react to either violent or non-violent behavior, nor have they communicated or interacted with individual regarding the violence of their behavior.

In this paper, we first utilize the RWF-2000 and RLVS datasets to develop a robust model for violence detection. We train three different deep learning models on these datasets to perform a binary classification task (distinguishing between violent and non-violent scenarios): a Transformer model, a 3-Dimensional Convolutional Neural Network (3DCNN) model, and a hybrid model combining a Convolutional Neural Network (CNN) with an LSTM network. In addition, we select our best proposal model based on test accuracy on the RLVS and computational efficiency to integrate it into the Taban Social Robot [25]. The final system is deployed in the Social and Cognitive Robotic Lab to evaluate models under real-time and real-world scenarios. The primary contributions of this paper are as follows:

1) We propose a hybrid CNN-LSTM model that incorporates an extra residual connection between spatial features and spatial-temporal features to detect violence more effectively by detecting violence based on both frame-level patterns and dynamic temporal changes.
2) We integrate this model into a Taban Social Robot to detect real-time violence and communicate true feedback to participants.

2 Methodology

2.1 Datasets

RLVS Dataset. The Real-Life Violence Situations (RLVS) dataset serves as a superior benchmark that surpasses the limitations of earlier datasets for violence detection, such as small data sizes (e.g., Movie [18] and Violent Flow datasets [17]), low video resolution, and limited scene diversity (e.g., Hockey Fight dataset [18]). The RLVS dataset contains 2,000 videos, which are equally divided between violent and non-violent scenes. Non-violent clips contain non-dangerous activities like eating and sports, and are varied in backgrounds, and violent events also occur in a variety of settings, such as streets, prisons, and schools. The videos are high quality (ranging from 480p to 720p) and relatively short, lasting between three to seven seconds. The dataset was collected through both manual capture and YouTube. Videos contain a large variety of individuals in terms of age, gender, and race, making this dataset perfect for improving violence detection models [26].

RWF Dataset. The Real-World Fighting (RWF-2000) dataset is a large-scale and realistic benchmark that is captured by surveillance cameras in the real world and is collected from YouTube [28]. Violent videos include a wide range of aggressive behavior, such as fights, blood, assault, and robbery, while Non-violent videos contain various normal situations, which are also captured by surveillance cameras. Each video is 5 s long and follows a series of standard resolutions (e.g., 720P,1080P, 2K, and 4K). RWF dataset contains 2000 videos, which are divided into train (80%) and validation (20%). Both train and validation include 2 balanced classes: Fight and Non-Fight, which are approximately equal in number of samples.

The RLVS dataset is randomly divided into 20 percent for validation and 80 percent for training. We evaluate the performance of our models using the accuracy metric on the RLVS validation set. To enhance the generalization of models, we train them on both RLVS and RWF datasets. Based on this accuracy, we adjusted the hyperparameters and selected the best configuration. Figure 1 shows some samples from this dataset.

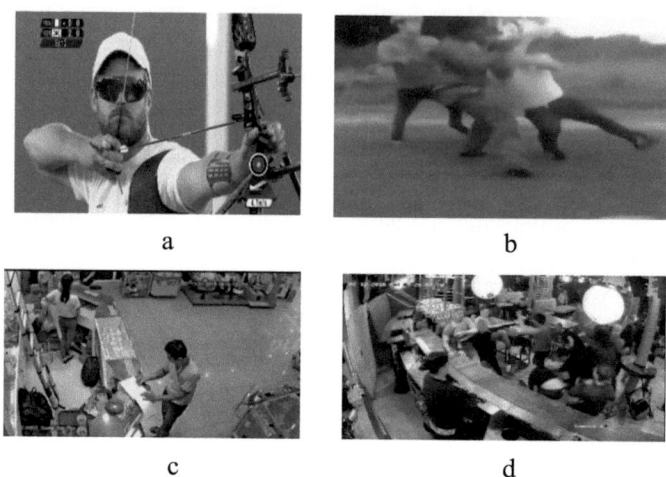

Fig. 1. Frames from the violence Dataset [26]: a) a nonviolence sample of RLVS, b) a violence sample of RLVS dataset, c) a nonviolence sample of RWF-2000, and d) a violence sample of RWF-2000

2.2 Neural Network Models

In this section, we present the different models that we developed to detect violence. We created three models: Transformer, 3DCNN, and CNN-LSTM. On average, we manually tune the hyperparameters of each network 10 times to achieve the best performance for each model. Our criterion for selecting the optimal network was its accuracy on the validation set of RLVS.

Transformer. The first video classification model was developed based on a Transformer architecture, designed to capture the temporal dependencies in video data. The model takes video frames as input, where each frame is represented as a tensor of size 128x128x3 (i.e., height, width, color channels). The frames are first flattened and then passed through an embedding layer. This layer maps them into a 512-dimensional feature space. Positional encoding module processes the embeddings by using sine and cosine functions. The core of the model is the Transformer encoder that consists of 6 layers, each with 8 attention heads. To capture long-range dependencies and complex correlations between the frames in the video sequence, the transform layers employ feed-forward operations and self-attention mechanism. The model averages the output of the Transformer encoder over the entire sequence to produce a single feature vector representing each video. This vector is then passed through a fully connected layer to classify the video into one of two categories. The model is trained using cross-entropy loss and optimized with the Adam optimizer at a learning rate of 1e-4. Both training and validation accuracy are monitored during the 60 periods. (Fig. 2).

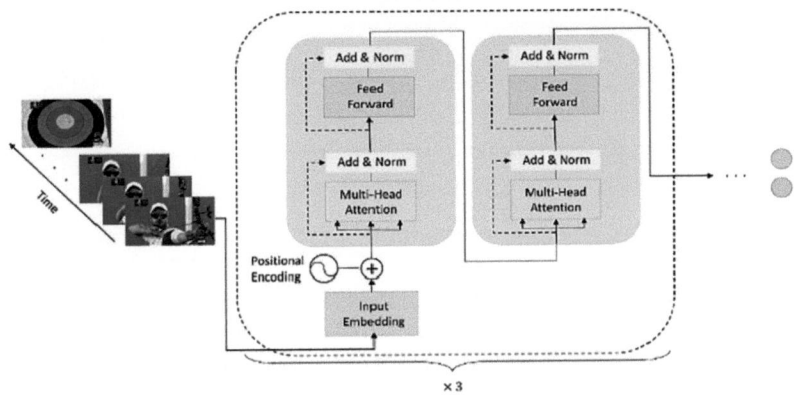

Fig. 2. The structure of our proposed Transformer model.

3DCNN. As the second model, we develop a 3DCNN model for binary video classification tasks. This model is designed to extract both spatial and temporal features from the video inputs. Our criterion for selecting the optimal network was its accuracy on the validation dataset. The network consists of three convolutional layers that each of them are followed by a max-pooling layer. First convolutional layer (Conv 1) uses 64 filters with a $3 \times 3 \times 3$ kernel and padding to preserve input dimensions, followed by a max-pooling layer (pool 1) with a $1 \times 2 \times 2$ kernel, which reduces the spatial dimensions while maintaining the temporal dimension. The second convolutional layer (Conv 2) applies 128 filters with a $3 \times 3 \times 3$ kernel, followed by a max-pooling layer (pool 2) with a $2 \times 2 \times 2$ kernel and reduces both spatial and temporal dimensions. Further downsample the feature maps, the third convolutional layer (Conv 3) employs 256 filters with a $3 \times 3 \times 3$ kernel, followed by a max-pooling layer (pool 3) that uses a $2 \times 2 \times 2$ kernel. The output from the final pooling layer is flattened into a one-dimensional vector, which is then passed through two fully connected layers (FC1 and FC2). The first one contains 1024 neurons and employs a ReLU as activation function. The second layer outputs two neurons for a binary classification task. The model is trained using the Adam optimizer with an initial learning rate of 0.001 and cross-entropy loss as the loss function. The training is conducted over 10 epochs, with training and validation accuracy and loss monitored throughout (Fig. 3).

CNN-LSTM. As our third model, the CNN-LSTM is developed for binary video classification by combining convolutional and recurrent neural network components. The model uses a pretrained ResNet-18 architecture to extract spatial features from frames. To retain the spatial feature, the final two layers of ResNet-18 are removed, and each frame passes through a truncated network. The output, an 8192-dimensional vector,

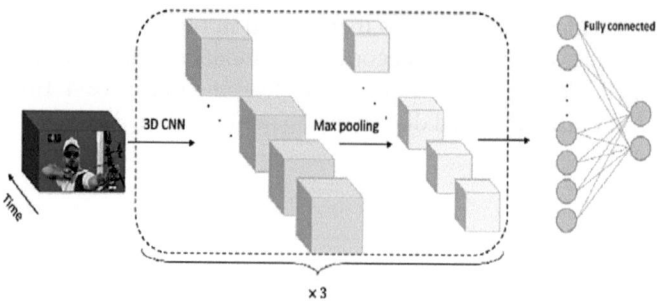

Fig. 3. The structure of our proposed 3CCNN model.

passes through a fully connected layer with 512 neurons to reduce its dimension. A single-layer LSTM with 256 neurons is used to extract temporal features of videos. The reduced feature vector is fed into this network. The output of the LSTM is passed through a fully connected layer and sigmoid function to generate a probability score based on temporal-feature extraction. In addition to LSTM prediction, we also employ parallel CNN-based prediction by averaging frame predictions. Each frame-level feature vector passes through a fully connected layer with a single output neuron, and then the results are averaged across all frames. This value is passed through a sigmoid to predict the probability of violence based on feature extraction. The final prediction class is computed based on both the violence prediction in CNN and CNN-LSTM. (Fig. 4). The model is trained using the Adam optimizer with a learning rate of 1e-4. Additionally, the binary cross-entropy loss function is applied. Training is conducted for 10 epochs, with loss and accuracy computed at each epoch for both training and validation.

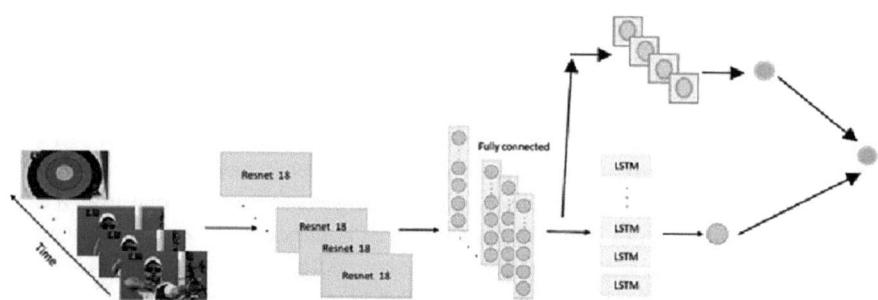

Fig. 4. The structure of our proposed CNN-LSTM model.

2.3 Taban Social Robot

Taban is a social robot developed by the researchers at the Social and Cognitive Robotics Lab, Sharif University of Technology, Iran. It is designed to educate and entertain children, especially to support children with dyslexia[25]. Our robot features six degrees of freedom and has a head projector behind a semi-transparent mask that empowers the robot to express its emotional facial expression and turn its head. Robot Operating System (ROS) on a central processor controls the robot's actions (which is equipped with different sensors and actuators). It allows the robot to adapt its movements based on different scenarios [27]. Taban can interact with different individuals in settings like schools, kindergartens, and hospitals. Figure 5 shows a snapshot of the Taban robot.

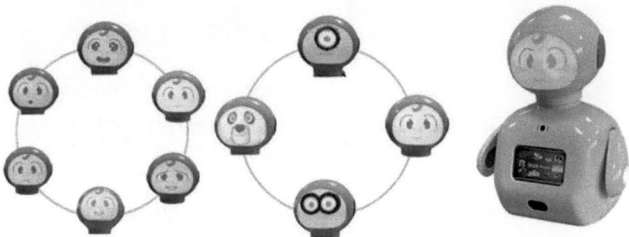

Fig. 5. The Taban social robot (picture captured from [27]).

2.4 Recognizing Violent and Non-violent Activities by the Robot

We aimed to empower the Taban social robot to distinguish between violent and non-violent activities. To this end, we designed five violent (including shoving, slapping, grabbing by the collar, punching, and sneak attack from behind) and five non-violent scenarios (including running, hugging, reading a book, exercising, and talking). Five groups, each consisting of two participants, took part in our experiment. Two of the groups were composed of women, and the other three groups consisted of men. Each group performed all ten scenarios, with each scenario lasting five seconds, and was captured by Taban's camera. After capturing video, the Taban robot analyzed the footage using the best-performing model trained on the RLVS and RWF-2000 dataset to determine whether the action or behavior was violent or not. If a violent action is detected, it randomly selects one of three pre-defined statements to discourage it. For instance, "Violent behavior has a negative impact on your health", "It is better to talk things out instead of fighting", or "Fighting is the wrong way to solve your issues". Conversely, if the behavior was detected as non-violent, the robot responded randomly with one of these encouraging statements: "Your good behavior makes me happy", "I like and admire your behavior", or "Your peaceful and respectful behavior is admirable". These statements were delivered in Persian. Figure 6 shows two samples of acting scenarios against the Taban social robot.

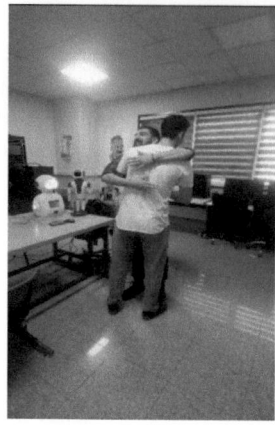 

Fig. 6. Acting scenario against Taban with different people

3 Results and Discussion

Accuracy was the primary measure we used. Our proposed CNN-LSTM model achieved the best test accuracy. The model performs well and demonstrates strong generalization when tested on unseen footage.

3.1 Proposed Networks' Accuracies

Table 1 presents the results of the models on the RLVS dataset in evaluating the performance of three deep learning models (i.e., Transformer, 3DCNN, and CNN-LSTM) for violence detection. Considerable differences are observed in their ability to accurately identify violent actions.

The Transformer model achieved a 90.38% accuracy in training, but showed significantly lower accuracy in the test section of 73.92%, indicating challenges in the generalization aspect of the architecture. Although this model has a large number of parameters and trains over 60 epochs, it does not perform well.

Table 1. The results of our proposed networks on the RLVS dataset.

Model	Train accuracy	test accuracy	Number of parameters
Transformer	90.38%	73.92%	44.08M
3DCNN	**99.25%**	82.02%	360.7 M
CNN-LSTM	97.25%	**96.73%**	**16.16M**

The 3DCNN and CNN-LSTM models showed stronger performance in violence detection. The 3DCNN model achieved a test accuracy of 82.02% and CNN-LSTM surpassed our other proposal models by achieving 96.73% test accuracy. Additionally, the 3DCNN architecture with 360.7M parameters is computationally heavy compared to our proposed CNN-LSTM network with 16M parameters. This finding highlights the superiority of our CNN-LSTM model, which benefits from transfer learning and increases the impact of spatial features in spatial-temporal classification by dedicating a residual connection from CNN to the final output. As a result, our proposed CNN-LSTM is the best model in comparison for violence detection.

Recent developments in violence detection models have achieved high accuracy on the RLVS dataset. A combined pre-trained VGG-16 and LSTM in Soliman's 2019 model achieved 94.6% accuracy [26]. Continuing this research, Traore and Akhlouf's ValdNet2 model reached 96.74% accuracy [13] and Abdali's DeVTr model from 2021 achieved 96.25% accuracy [19]. Anugrah Srivastava et al. reported the highest accuracy of 97.5% on the RLVS Dataset using a combination of the InceptionV3 and LSTM [20]. To the best of our knowledge, our proposed CNN-LSTM model achieves competitive accuracy with a lightweight architecture, making it comparable to state-of-the-art models for violence detection.

3.2 Executing the Best Model on the Taban Social Robot

We applied our top-performing CNN-LSTM model for violence detection on the Taban robot. It captures video of scenarios occurring in front of it and analyzes the footage to classify the video as either violent or non-violent.

In tests conducted with five groups, violent behaviors such as shoving, punching, attacking from behind, slapping, and pushing were simulated. The robot successfully identified violence with high probability in all scenarios. Figures 7 demonstrates executing some examples of violence and non-violence activity toward the Taban robot, along with the corresponding detection result. It takes 0.1 s for the robot to detect violence. In non-violent scenarios, the robot identified non-violent behavior with high probability in 20 out of 25 tests. Overall, our proposed CNN-LSTM network achieved an accuracy of 95% in the experiments conducted at the Social and Cognitive Robotics Lab, with a 100% accuracy in detecting violent scenarios. These results highlight the model's strong generalization in real-time violence detection. Our proposed CNN-LSTM model, with high accuracy on real-world, fast response time, and lightweight design, is highly suitable and has the protentional to be implemented in educational environments such as schools and kindergartens to promote safety.

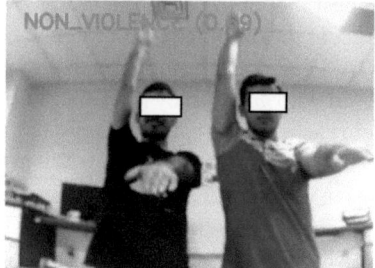

Fig. 7. Executing violence and non-violence activity toward the Taban social robot and its detection with a probability of being violence or non-violence. a) punching, b) grabbing by the collar, c) reading a book, d) exercising

Due to the limited number of studies involving social robots to detect violent behaviors, we cannot systematically compare the results of this study with previous research. To the best of our knowledge, the only Intelligent Surveillance Robot designed for violence detection has been programmed to send an email to the manager along with a captured picture of the violence when it detects it [24]. However, to date, a violence detection model has not been implemented on a social robot that interacts and communicates with users after detecting violence.

4 Limitation and Feature Work

We plan to implement this system in kindergartens and schools. The robot will watch children's behavior, warn them when they act aggressively, and encourage them when their behavior is friendly. Social robots have already been utilized in various educational situations, including teaching children languages, mathematics, or Lego[28]. Researchers emphasize that enabling these robots with the ability to understand and respond to their surroundings is essential [29]. In the field of Human-Robot Interaction (HRI), significant research has been conducted, particularly in recognizing human behaviors such as standing, waving, or playing with a phone [30]. However, these robots have not yet been developed to effectively detect violence and give appropriate feedback. Implementing violence detection in robots and enabling them to warn individuals could have a significant impact in educational places. Research has shown that even when robots make mistakes, people become aware of the errors but still find the robots lovely and useful [31]. Additionally, studies indicate that humans establish better interactions with robots that have a face, can speak, and express emotions [32]. Our robot Taban is equipped with these features, has the potential to be highly effective in teaching appropriate behavior and promoting non-violent actions between kids. Furthermore, we plan to combine a facial recognition system into our model in order to identify and punish individuals who engage in violent activity [33–37].

5 Conclusion

Real-time violence detection plays a crucial role in maintaining public safety, especially in educational places like schools. To develop a state-of-the-art model with high generalization and robustness in real-world performance, we train three architectures: Transformer, 3DCNN, and CNN-LSTM. These three models are trained on 2 benchmark violent video datasets, each includes 2000 videos. Based on accuracy and number of parameters, we applied our best model on Social Robot Taban, which captures 5-s videos of participants, analyzes the violence of the situation, and expresses positive or negative feedback. We conducted tests in the Social and Cognitive Robotic Lab with 5 groups of participants, each group performed 10 scenarios. Our proposed CNN-LSTM model successfully achieved 90% accuracy across our 50 tests, which demonstrates its high performance and robustness of our model to detect violence in real life. In the future, we plan to integrate our system into a social robot to implement in kindergartens and schools to monitor children and interact with them if they demonstrate aggressive behavior. This approach has the potential to enhance public safety and help children express their harsh emotions peacefully.

Acknowledgement. This study was funded by the Sharif University of Technology (Grant No. G4030507).

References

1. https://www.emro.who.int/health-topics/violence/index.html (2025)
2. Malley-Morrison, K., Hines, D.: Family Violence in a Cultural Perspective: Defining, Understanding, and Combating Abuse. Sage (2004)
3. Łukasik, J.M., Pikuła, N.G.: Violence against the elderly: challenges-research-action. In: K. Jagielska (ed.) European Association of Schools of Social Work (2015)
4. Dahlberg, L.L., Krug, E.G.: Violence a global public health problem. Cien. Saude Colet. **11**, 277–292 (2006)
5. Ciampi, L., et al.: Bus violence: an open benchmark for video violence detection on public transport. Sensors **22**(21), 8345 (2022)
6. Senst, T., Eiselein, V., Kuhn, A., Sikora, T.: Crowd violence detection using global motion-compensated lagrangian features and scale-sensitive video-level representation. IEEE Trans. Inf. Forensics Secur. **12**(12), 2945–2956 (2017)
7. Gkountakos, K., Ioannidis, K., Tsikrika, T., Vrochidis, S., Kompatsiaris, I.: Crowd violence detection from video footage. In: Proceedings of the 2021 International Conference on Content-Based Multimedia Indexing (CBMI), pp. 1–4. IEEE, June 2021
8. Lloyd, K., Rosin, P.L., Marshall, D., Moore, S.C.: Detecting violent and abnormal crowd activity using temporal analysis of grey level co-occurrence matrix (GLCM)-based texture measures. Mach. Vis. Appl. **28**, 361–371 (2017)

9. Chaudhary, S., Khan, M.A., Bhatnagar, C.: Multiple anomalous activity detection in videos. Procedia Comput. Sci. **125**, 336–345 (2018)
10. Serrano, I., Deniz, O., Bueno, G., Garcia-Hernando, G., Kim, T.K.: Spatio-temporal elastic cuboid trajectories for efficient fight recognition using Hough forests. Mach. Vis. Appl. **29**, 207–217 (2018)
11. Yao, H., Hu, X.: A survey of video violence detection. Cyber-Phys. Syst. **9**(1), 1–24 (2023)
12. Traoré, A., Akhloufi, M.A.: Violence detection in videos using deep recurrent and convolutional neural networks. In: Proceedings of the 2020 IEEE International Conference on Systems, Man, and Cybernetics (SMC), pp. 154–159. IEEE, October 2020
13. Khanzode, K.C.A., Sarode, R.D.: Advantages and disadvantages of artificial intelligence and machine learning: a literature review. Int. J. Libr. Inf. Sci. (IJLIS) **9**(1), 3 (2020)
14. Ahmed, S.F., et al.: Deep learning modelling techniques: current progress, applications, advantages, and challenges. Artif. Intell. Rev. **56**(11), 13521–13617 (2023)
15. Ramzan, M., et al.: A review on state-of-the-art violence detection techniques. IEEE Access **7**, 107560–107575 (2019)
16. Sumon, S.A., Goni, R., Hashem, N.B., Shahria, T., Rahman, R.M.: Violence detection by pretrained modules with different deep learning approaches. Vietnam J. Comput. Sci. **7**(01), 19–40 (2020)
17. Soliman, M.M., Kamal, M.H., Nashed, M. A.E.M., Mostafa, Y.M., Chawky, B.S., Khattab, D.: Violence recognition from videos using deep learning techniques. In: Proceedings of the 2019 Ninth International Conference on Intelligent Computing and Information Systems (ICICIS), pp. 80–85). IEEE, December 2019
18. Hassner, T., Itcher, Y., Kliper-Gross, O.: Violent flows: Real-time detection of violent crowd behavior. In: Proceedings of the 2012 IEEE Computer Society Conference on Computer Vision and Pattern Recognition Workshops, pp. 1–6. IEEE, June 2012
19. Bermejo Nievas, E., Deniz Suarez, O., Bueno García, G., Sukthankar, R.: Violence detection in video using computer vision techniques. In: Real, P., Diaz-Pernil, D., Molina-Abril, H., Berciano, A., Kropatsch, W. (eds.) Computer Analysis of Images and Patterns. CAIP 2011. Lecture Notes in Computer Science, vol. 6855, pp. 332–339. Springer, Heidelberg (2011). https://doi.org/10.1007/978-3-642-23678-5_39
20. Abdali, A.R.: Data efficient video transformer for violence detection. In: Proceedings of the 2021 IEEE International Conference on Communication, Networks and Satellite (COMNETSAT), pp. 195–199. IEEE, July 2021
21. Srivastava, A., Badal, T., Singh, R.: Real life violence detection in surveillance videos using spatiotemporal features. In: Proceedings of the 2021 Thirteenth International Conference on Contemporary Computing, pp. 262–266, August 2021
22. Zhang, T., Yang, Z., Jia, W., Yang, B., Yang, J., He, X.: A new method for violence detection in surveillance scenes. Multimedia Tools Appl. **75**, 7327–7349 (2016)
23. Vijeikis, R., Raudonis, V., Dervinis, G.: Efficient violence detection in surveillance. Sensors **22**(6), 2216 (2022)
24. Ullah, F.U.M., Obaidat, M.S., Ullah, A., Muhammad, K., Hijji, M., Baik, S.W.: A comprehensive review on vision-based violence detection in surveillance videos. ACM Comput. Surv. **55**(10), 1–44 (2023)
25. Sudhakar, R.: Real time violence detection using autonomous intelligent surveillance robot. In: Proceedings of the 2023 2nd International Conference on Advancements in Electrical, Electronics, Communication, Computing and Automation (ICAECA), pp. 1–5. IEEE, June 2023
26. Arnab, A., Dehghani, M., Heigold, G., Sun, C., Lučić, M., Schmid, C.: ViViT: a video vision transformer. In: Proceedings of the IEEE/CVF International Conference on Computer Vision, pp. 6836–6846 (2021)

27. Shahab, M., et al.: Manufacture and development of Taban: a cute back-projected head social robot for educational purposes. Intell. Serv. Robot., 1–19 (2024)
28. Schiphorst, L., و همکاران: Video2Report: a video database for automatic reporting of medical consultancy sessions. In: Proceedings of the 2020 15th IEEE International Conference on Automatic Face and Gesture Recognition (FG 2020), pp. 552–556 صص. IEEE (2020). https://doi.org/10.1109/FG47880.2020.00020
29. https://keras.io/examples/vision/vivit/ (2025)
30. Tensorflow (2024). https://www.tensorflow.org/install/pip. Accessed 2025
31. Goldsborough, P.: A tour of tensorflow. arXiv preprint arXiv:1610.01178 (2016)
32. https://www.sharif.ir/fa/web/news/w/%D8%AA%D8%A7%D8%A8%D8%A7%D9%86%D8%9B-%D8%B1%D8%A8%D8%A7%D8%AA-%D8%A7%D8%AC%D8%AA%D9%85%D8%A7%D8%B9%DB%8C-%D8%AF%D8%A7%D9%86%D8%B4%DA%AF%D8%A7%D9%87-%D8%B4%D8%B1%DB%8C%D9%81-%D8%A8%D8%B1%D8%A7%DB%8C-%D8%B1%D9%81%D8%B9-%D8%A7%D8%AE%D8%AA%D9%84%D8%A7%D9%84 (2025)
33. Belpaeme, T., Kennedy, J., Ramachandran, A., Scassellati, B., Tanaka, F.: Social robots for education: a review. Sci. Robot. **3**(21), eaat5954 (2018)
34. Breazeal, C.: Social interactions in HRI: the robot view. IEEE Trans. Syst. Man Cybern. Part C (Appl. Rev.) **34**(2), 181–186 (2004)
35. Nan, M., et al.: Human action recognition for social robots. In: Proceedings of the 2019 22nd International Conference on Control Systems and Computer Science (CSCS), pp. 675–681. IEEE, May 2019
36. Mirnig, N., Stollnberger, G., Miksch, M., Stadler, S., Giuliani, M., Tscheligi, M.: To Err is robot: how humans assess and act toward an erroneous social robot. Frontiers in Robotics and AI **4**, 251625 (2017)
37. Onyeulo, E.B., Gandhi, V.: What makes a social robot good at interacting with humans? Information **11**(1), 43 (2020)

Author Index

A

Acampora, Giulio 300
Adams, Matt 623
Adelucci, Elena 87
Ajibo, Chinenye Augustine 165
Akash, Moniruzzaman 152
Akhond, Saina 124
Alam, Marzan 152
Alimardani, Maryam 342
Alonso-Martìn, Fernando 431
Alvarado, Denisse 700
Álvarez, Gloria 237
Amores, J. Gabriel 237
Annese, Luca 387
Anzalone, Salvatore M. 587
Arthanat, Sajay 152
Augello, Agnese 558

B

Bacaro, Martina 415
Bahodi, Maria-Theresa 447
Ban, Midori 516
Baraldi, Lorenzo 22
Barnard, Pepita 623
Barros, Pablo 112
Begum, Momotaz 152
Bendel, Oliver 3, 97
Benford, Steve 623
Bigazzi, Roberto 22
Bleeker, Maaike 690
Bloisi, Domenico Daniele 329
Brienza, Michele 329

C

Cabibihan, John-John 139
Camara, Fanta 573
Cangelosi, Angelo 22
Carbonaro, Bruno 637
Castillo, José Carlos 431
Castro, Manuel 237
Castro-González, Álvaro 431

Catalini, Riccardo 22
Cauás, Nathália 112
Cavallo, Filippo 87, 179
Ceccato, Caterina 342
Cesaro, Laura 663
Chamberlain, Alan 623, 718
Chapman, Airlie 611
Chen, An Bella 253
Chen, Junyi 598
Chu, Timothy Scott 139
Cordasco, Gennaro 637
Corrao, Francesca 58, 273
Cucchiara, Rita 22

D

D'Errico, Lorenzo 37
Das, Sanchari 212
Datteri, Edoardo 558
de Rooij, Alwin 342
de Wit, Jan 342
Del Lucchese, Benedetta 87
Derri, Anis 587
Di Lieto, Maria Chiara 87
Đurić, Goran 611

E

Edan, Yael 544
Esposito, Anna 637
Esposito, Raffaella 300
Esposito, Renato 37

F

Farr, Ju Row 623
Fernandes, Bruno J. T. 112
Filacanapa, Giulia 587
Fiorini, Laura 87, 179
Fischer, Joel 623
Fischer, Martin H. 3
Foulsham, Tom 387

G

García, Gonzalo A. 237
Ghamati, Khashayar 356
Ghattas, Ola 152
Gomez, Randy 237
Green, Justin 611
Green, Simon Castle 623
Grover, Mayank 212
Guidi, Stefano 313

H

Hamdi, Amr 253
Hansen, Nicolai Brodersen 447
He, Bessie 370
Honorato, Leandro 112
Horii, Takato 516
Hu, Yue 253
Hussein, Mostafa 152

I

Iacono, Umberto Dello 637
Iacopini, Sofia 179
Innocenti, Alessandro 313
Iocchi, Luca 329
Ishiguro, Hiroshi 516
Ishizuka, Hiroki 516

J

Jain, Chirag 370

K

Karimi Jafari, Maryam 735
Kikuchi, Takayuki 516
Kim, Jaeseok 179
Klöffel, Antonia L. Z. 3
Knight, Heather 370, 700
Krakovski, Maya 544
Kristensen, Maja Hornbæk 447
Kucukyilmaz, Ayse 623, 718
Kühne, Katharina 3
Kumar, Shikhar 544

L

La Viola, Carlo 179
Lagerstedt, Erik 484
Lalioti, Vali 124
LaRoche, Dain 152
Laycock, Rohan 237
Leoste, Janika 289

Liberman-Pincu, Ela 503
Lieto, Antonio 558
Ljungblad, Sara 484
Lösel, Gunter 651
Lusuardi, Luca 313

M

Magris, Erica 587
Maharjan, Rahul Singh 22
Mancini, Clara 623
Marmor, Kristel 289
Maselli, Marco Vincenzo 179
Maselli, Marco Vincenzo 87
Matarese, Marco 37
Mele, Vincenzo 37
Menegatti, Emanuele 663
Merritt, Timothy 447
Michalewicz, Aleksandra 611
Misino, Ludovica 313
Mongile, Sara 400
Mungari, Alfredo 37
Muñoz, John E. 192
Musca, Helene 87
Myatt, Sean 718

N

Nardelli, Alice 58, 273
Ngo, Victor Zhi Heung 718
Ngo, Victor 623
Nikoobayan, Reyhane 749

O

Ognibene, Dimitri 387
Omichi, Mayu 516
Oron-Gilad, Tal 503

P

Pallonetto, Luca 300
Panagiotidis, Pavlos 718
Pani, Jasmine 87, 179
Parlangeli, Oronzo 313
Parreira, Maria Teresa 484
Patania, Sabrina 387
Patel, Roma 718
Patil, Shrirang 370
Pecini, Chiara 87
Pelikan, Hannah 484
Peng, Yucheng 598
Pérez, Guillermo 237

Author Index

Plassard, Didier 598
Prattichizzo, Domenico 674
Premachandra, Chinthaka 124
Prinsen, Jos 342
Pruss, Ethel 342
Pugi, Lorenzo 87

R
Raffa, Maria 475
Ramchurn, Rachel 718
Ramirez, Nahomi 192
Rausa, Maria 558
Rawal, Niyati 22
Rea, Francesco 400
Recchiuto, Carmine Tommaso 58, 273
Reed, Darren 573
Rodríguez-Piñero, Piedad Tolmos 289
Romeo, Marta 22
Roscica, Martina 37
Rossi, Alessandra 50, 165
Rossi, Silvia 50, 165, 300, 387
Ruggeri, Azzurra 387
Russo, Matteo 300

S
Saladino, Alessio 329
Saleh, Shahed 192
Salichs, Miguel A. 431
Salici, Giacomo 22
Salimbeni, Guido 623
Samani, Hooman 124, 356
Sanchez, Luke 370
Saood, Adnan 75
Saviano, Giuseppe 674
Scatigna, Stefano 87
Schneiders, Eike 623
Schömbs, Sarah 484
Sciutti, Alessandra 112, 400
Sequeira, João S. 431
Serino, Silvia 387
Sgandurra, Giuseppina 87
Sgorbissa, Antonio 58, 273
Shahabian Alashti, Mohamadreza 356
Sharples, Sarah 623

Shimasaki, Kazuki 516
Shin, JaeEun Jen 253
Skov, Mikael 447
Sorrentino, Alessandra 179
Staffa, Mariacarla 37
Sun, Shaoxin 598
Suriani, Vincenzo 329
Swaminathan, Janani 700

T
Taheri, Alireza 735, 749
Takahashi, Hideyuki 516
Tandavanitj, Nick 623
Tanevska, Ana 400
Tapus, Adriana 75
Tomoda, Minoru 516
Torre, Ilaria 484
Toshima, Yoshihisa 516
Trenti, Federico 300
Triglia, Laura 112

V
van Berkel, Niels 447
Vella, Elena 611
Vezzani, Roberto 22
Villani, Alberto 674
Vitale, Antonio 637
Vrins, Anita 342

W
Walton, Robert Ellis 611
Wang, Tianyuan 573
Webb, Helena 623
Williams, Daniel A. 611
Winkle, Katie 484
Wong Kam, Michael 124

Y
Yoshikawa, Yuichiro 516

Z
Zagni, Nicola 558
Zaraki, Abolfazl 356
Zhang-Kennedy, Leah 253

MIX
Papier aus verantwortungsvollen Quellen
Paper from responsible sources
FSC® C105338

If you have any concerns about our products,
you can contact us on
ProductSafety@springernature.com

In case Publisher is established outside the EU,
the EU authorized representative is:
**Springer Nature Customer Service Center GmbH
Europaplatz 3, 69115 Heidelberg, Germany**

Printed by Libri Plureos GmbH
in Hamburg, Germany